Russian Women Writers

Volume 2

Women Writers of the World
Volume 3
Garland Reference Library of the Humanities
Volume 1866

Women Writers of the World

Katharina M. Wilson, *Series Editor*

Women Writing in Dutch
edited by Kristiaan Aercke

Russian Women Writers, Vols. 1 and 2
edited by Christine D. Tomei

Women Writers in Pre-Revolutionary France
Strategies of Emancipation
edited by Colette H. Winn
and Donna Kuizenga

RUSSIAN WOMEN WRITERS

Volume 2

CHRISTINE D. TOMEI
Editor

GARLAND PUBLISHING, INC.
A member of the Taylor and Francis Group
New York and London
1999

Library of Congress Cataloging-in-Publication Data

Russian women writers / edited by Christine D. Tomei.
p. cm. — (Garland reference library of the humanities ; vol. 1866. Women writers of the world ; vol. 3)
Includes bibliographical references.
ISBN 0-8153-1797-2
1. Russian literature—Women authors—Translations into English. 2. Russian literature—Women authors—Biography. 3. Women authors, Russian. I. Tomei, Christine D. II. Series: Garland reference library of the humanities ; vol. 1866. III. Series: Garland reference library of the humanities. Women writers of the world ; vol. 3.
PG3203.W64R868 1998
891.708'09287-dc21 98-48028
CIP

Printed on acid-free, 250-year-life paper
Manufactured in the United States of America

Contents

Volume II

Section VI: The Trial Begins

Series Editor's Preface

The Garland series Women Writers of the World presents writers from diverse languages in modern English translations. Each volume in the series focuses on a particular language, country or distinct culture and offers a chronologically and generically representative selection of texts from its women writers. Each anthology commences with a general introduction, and the text selections are preceded by precise bio-critical introductions followed by bibliographies.

Given the broad range of the anthologies, the individual methodologies differ from volume to volume; still, throughout the series our efforts were aimed at making texts accessible to the English-speaking reader that in the past have been the domain of a few specialists in their respective linguistic fields.

Russian Women Writers, by its complexity and richness, necessitated much coordination of effort as a consequence of which the volume has been in production since late 1995.

KATHARINA M. WILSON
UNIVERSITY OF GEORGIA

Contributors

Harold D. Baker
University of California, Irvine

Adele Barker
University of Arizona

Luc Beaudoin
University of Denver

Elizabeth Beaujour
Hunter College, NY

Justyna Beinek
Harvard University

Christine Borowec
Bryn Mawr College

Rebecca Bowman
University of Virginia

Diana Lewis Burgin
University of Massachusetts, Boston

Maria Carlson
University of Kansas

Catherine V. Chvany
Massachusetts Institute of Technology

Olga Muller Cooke
Texas A&M

Nancy Lynn Cooper
Independent Scholar, Munich

Jane Costlow
Bates College

Mildred Davies
University of Waterloo, Ontario

Kathleen Dillon
Polytechnic School, Pasadena, CA

Leslie J. Dorfman
University of Michigan

Sibelan Forrester
Swarthmore College

Jehanne M. Gheith
Duke University

Laura Goering
Carleton College

Diana Greene
New York University Library

George Gutsche
University of Arizona

Jane Gary Harris
University of Pittsburgh

Martha Hickey
Portland State University

Beth Holmgren
University of North Carolina

Gerald J. Janecek
University of Kentucky

Catriona Kelly
New College, Oxford

Sonia I. Ketchian
Harvard Russian Research Center

Natasha Kolchevska
University of New Mexico

Ruth Kreuzer
St. Lawrence University

Martha Kuchar
Roanoke College

Andrea Lanoux
University of California,
Los Angeles

Marcus Levitt
University of Southern California

Trina Mamoon
University of Illinois

Lawrence Mansour
United States Military Academy,
NY

Bonnie Marshall
Independent Scholar,
Meredith, ME

Laura Jo McCullough
Independent Scholar,
Minneapolis, MN

Ronald Meyer
The Harriman Institute,
Columbia University

Nyusya Milman
Indiana University

Grace Anne Morseberger
University of California,
Berkeley

Rosina Neginsky
Kenyon College

Mary Nicholas
Lehigh University

Norma Corigliano Noonan
Augsburg College

Tatiana Osipovich
Lewis and Clark College

Temira Pachmuss
University of Illinois

Solomea Pavlychko
Institute of Literature, Ukrainian
Academy of Sciences

Valentina Polukhina
University of Keele

Teresa Polowy
University of Arizona

HELEN REEVE
Connecticut College

NATALIE REPIN
University of Illinois

MAUREEN RILEY
USIA Fulbright Office, Moscow

NATALIE ROKLINA
Skidmore College

PETER ROLLBERG
George Washington University

KAREN ROSNECK
University of Wisconsin, Madison

CHRISTINE A. RYDEL
Grand Valley State University

STEPHANIE SANDLER
Amherst College

BARRY P. SCHERR
Dartmouth College

VERONICA SHAPOVALOV
San Diego State University

RIMVYDAS ŠILBAJORIS
Ohio State University

GRETA SLOBIN
Stevenson College,
U.C. Santa Cruz

MELISSA T. SMITH
Youngstown State University

RUTH SOBEL
Beaconsfield, UK

KARLA THOMAS SOLOMON
University of Kansas

JULIETTE STAPANIAN-APKARIAN
Emory University

JANE A. TAUBMAN
Amherst College

ANNA TAVIS
Fairfield University

LISA TAYLOR
Indiana University

KLAWA THRESHER
Randolph-Macon Women's College

CHRISTINE D. TOMEI
The Harriman Institute,
Columbia University

RIMMA VOLYNSKA
University of Toronto

SOPHIE T. WISNIEWSKA
Pennsylvania State University

ALEXANDER WORONZOFF-DASHKOFF
Smith College

MARY ZIRIN
Independent Scholar,
Altadena, CA

Introduction

The work in *Russian Women Writers* really needs no introduction; its importance is manifest on each page, in the works of all the seventy-one authors and equally so in the corresponding seventy-one critical biographies. However, other important aspects related to this work benefit from explanation.

While the two present volumes span the centuries between Catherine the Great and the present and offer a point of departure for a new understanding and appreciation of women's work as well as a solid foundation for further research, there is no claim for being exhaustive of the study of women's writing in Russia. Recent research has identified over four hundred Russian women writers,[1] clearly indicating the limitations of even an ambitious work like this one.

As the third title in the series Women Writers of the World, *Russian Women Writers* is defined within European literary history. The first book in this series, *Women Writing in Dutch,* exploits the commonality of language as the basis for neutralizing differences in writers' ethnicity and geographic location. While our title does not indicate it as explicitly, women of likewise complex and cosmopolitan backgrounds are represented here, and the leveling by language is sometimes even more dramatic. Some of the "Russians," for example, are as Germanic as some of the "Dutch." Some are of French extraction, some of Jewish descent, some of central Asian parentage, and so on. They all shared a place in Russian culture and literary life, whether at home or in emigration, and this extended focus pervades the present anthology.

An interesting study of gender as a function of time could emerge from a serious study of the works represented in *Russian Women Writers*. Certain facts of these women's lives, of their ambience and working conditions, reflect the incremental changes and phases of women's writing. For example, in the early chapters, three women, Catherine the Great, Princess Dashkova and Nadezhda Durova, all took part in military actions while dressed in men's uniform. Durova, as a cavalry "man," was promoted and distinguished with the St. George Cross for valor. These women participated in historic battles and common military life, indicating that the rigid barriers between the sexes exhibited significant flashpoints. In the subsequent chapters, female revolutionaries conducted their work as women, although sometimes writing under male pseudonyms. The attendant confusion over the importance of their gender, the diffidence and even derision in social arenas, are signs more suggestive of a backlash than of an attestation of women's cultural relevance. Such attitudes revolve around issues first articulated in the second half of the nineteenth century under the rubric of the "women's question": What should women be allowed to do?

The issues subsumed in this problem find representation, both direct and indirect, in the essays and anthological pieces offered here. While the terms enabling availability of women's education and prosperity were not symmetrical with men's, the results were quite similar: better education replaces the characteristic of increased wealth as the gateway to greater opportunity. Not too surprisingly, since women in general commanded the disposition of considerably less education and wealth, the number of women who succeeded in literary life remained relatively small. However, it should not be assumed that this quantitative dearth would reflect a narrowness in contribution or a qualitative deficiency. Women contributed significantly in all literary modes and genres—lyric, polemic, novel, short story, memoir, drama, historical fiction—there is not one important gap. Neither should it be inferred that since no female Dostoevsky or Tolstoy emerged from the relative scarcity of female writers that this confirms an inferiority of women. Many female writers were vastly superior to, and greatly more successful than, many men writing at the same time—a fact still true today.

The editor of *Women Writing in Dutch,* Kristiaan Aercke, was fortunate to say that the writers represented had all been fairly well established in the literary canon. As editor of *Russian Women Writers*, I feel no less richly endowed by the power and significance of the contributions in my book, yet incomparably less able to claim canonic acceptance of the writers. Among the group of contemporary women writers, there is every hope that each one, and many more, will be allowed to break through the resistance and be fully accepted. Otherwise, three or possibly four women have, to date, achieved lasting eminence. I will, however, reiterate the thought of my predecessor in this series that "the anthology is a two-edged sword, capable both of preserving the existing canon and defending it, *and* of carving out a new canon."[2] I believe that providing a comprehensive treatment for such a number of women supplies a substantial basis for reevaluating the value of this writing vis-à-vis the canon.

The Conceptual Apparatus

In response to the unconscious manipulations of periodization, categorization and other aspects of historification that have caused women writers to be compartmentalized or otherwise marginalized, the apparatus of the present volumes is designed to circumnavigate such conceptual barriers. The women are grouped into periods roughly around the dates of their death. This rather unorthodox, but not unprecedented, approach was chosen to affirm the lives of these women in their entirety and to represent better their creative work in this context. Akhmatova, for example, was always disconcerted when her readers persisted in assigning value only to her early works, even as she was still writing. The presentation offered here acts to address this issue and thus places her, not in the teens and twenties, but the sixties, where, after achieving international acclaim and awards, her works actually ceased to be written.

Rather than use a simple chronological presentation or involve some numeration for the writers, which might have been subliminally presumed to be a ranking system, emblematic titles have been chosen to represent the time with the purpose of directing the reader to the dialectic between literature in its traditional understanding and literature expanded to include the female-authored contributions offered here. Except for during two periods, Catherine's and the present, it is posited that men writers dominated literature. Thus the titles chosen for all but those two periods issue from works of male-authored literature.

All the titles represent peaks in the zeitgeist of Russian literature and can be identified with well-established movements and ages in Russian literary history. The thematic occupations of the anthology works offered here can be counterposed with the emblematic attribute to reveal a tension as well as a resonance between male- and female-authored literature. The dominant themes are well known in works by men, yet women are writing about the same things at the same time, albeit using a different voice. Sometimes the difference in women's writing is overlooked or dismissed due to qualities associated with the female gender. However, such overgeneralization is undoubtedly poorly founded: women's perspective on historical and literary life is quite diverse and revelatory.

Consider the difference between Lermontov's *A Hero of Our Time*, published between 1837 and 1840, and the works in our section falling under this title. In Lermontov's story, "Bela," a woman is ruthlessly kidnapped, abandoned and betrayed, functioning as a fairly typical foil for the romantic exploits of one of the coldest heroes in Russian literature, Pechorin. Romanticism, in the eyes of men, presupposes that women should be this one-dimensional objectified personification of male ambition, perhaps owing to the logic that describes the nature of men as Napoleonic. Rather illogically, Tatiana Larina, a female character created by Pushkin during the same period, is typically considered the epitome of dignity and sacrifice as she negates her personal feelings for the sake of her marriage. However, such empty vessels of literary origin seem precisely that to real women. The real women writing in this volume, a much more energetic group, examine such sacrifice and offer creative artistic solutions and insight into the helplessness of women in that society. At the same time, they provide a valid counterpoint to the male version of romance.

Similarly, consider the section called "What Is To Be Done?" based on the positivist premise created by Chernyshevsky in a novel by that name, published in 1863. Chernyshevsky, a radical, constructed his vision of utopia in a society where women are not dominated by but are still subordinated to men. In the works offered here, many of the general tendencies of Russian program literature are evident either as the defining model or through its denial. However, regardless of its relation to the paradigm, women's literature does not assign the significance to the sewing machine as a means of attaining freedom as Chernyshevsky did; women move into the public world as individuals, as would be expected, to achieve equality. Chernyshevsky, even preaching a more equitable sexual freedom for women, could not envision women rising as diverse individuals and intellectuals, but instead he saw them only as a group of laborers not dominated by men—something represented altogether differently in the work of the writers in this volume.

The biographies included here also illuminate the movement of women into the public realm. This was the time when women first acquired access to the universities, albeit in very limited numbers. The world's first female professor, Sofiia Kovalevskaia, finished her doctoral degree in mathematics and took her position in Stockholm during this time. If the contemporary male writers—Turgenev, Tolstoy and others—would comment only negatively on women in "masculine" behavior, the women writers experienced an entire array of opportunities, deceptions and traps in the changing political winds. Perhaps the biographical material is more convincing than the characteristics of fiction. Even though the fictional Anna Karenina was punished for asserting her choice of a partner, the real Vovchok denied the real Turgenev his satisfaction by choosing hers.

Some of this sexual independence resonates with the social change described by Chernyshevsky who was still very influential in the next period commonly referred to as the Silver Age, titled here as "My Sister, Life," after the autobiographical poetic cycle written by Boris Pasternak at about the end of that period in 1917. Many factors naturally unite the writing of this time to this title, including the renewed emphasis on autobiography that marks this period and a preference for other intimate genres such as lyric poetry for artistic expression. A most compelling uniting feature is the explosion of energy that Pasternak considered life, which could be called feminine, and the similar burst in creativity and variety in works by women writers of the time. While many of the same problems persisted, for example, unequal pay for equal work or the prohibition against women in literary society meetings—women were not allowed to attend unless they were actually members of the society—the elemental forces of life itself seem to burst forth, bringing the tradition of women in literary salons to a new level of importance and allowing women writers unprecedented representation in literature.

The next section is named "I Have Forgotten the Word I Wanted to Say," the first line of a poem by Mandel'shtam published early in the Soviet period. This line has elemental resonance for literature of all writers. The forces of history essentially closed the door to free creativity to men and women alike. In the Soviet Union after the end of the Women's Department, marking the fall of Aleksandra Kollontai, a chorus of voices clamoring to vie for a spot on the socialist realist bandwagon arises, as among the many men of like minds. This movement, insofar as it is a corruption of the right to free expression, is not well represented in the present volume. The writers who did run that gauntlet deserve our lasting admiration if only because they were risking their lives. Many of the writers in the present work suffered overt repression, political coercion and imprisonment. Others fell silent, yet remained under surveillance and pressure.

The next section is named for the Siniavsky novella, *The Trial Begins*, published abroad in 1948. The title responds to multiple developments in literature. While Siniavsky's realistic portrayal of society depicts a profound moral corruption of all Soviet individuals, its publication abroad likewise signals the changing venue of Russian thought. Many women, Teffi and Gippius in particular, prevailed in their literary ambitions in emigration. Others are recognized abroad as well. The final chapter in the Stalinist period in Russian literature where the most radical extremes of literary activity and biography appear is especially curious.

Kataev's novel, *The Grass of Oblivion* (1967), heads the final section named for male-authored works and alludes to both the ineffable survival of things even through the greatest disasters; and the backward glance, the reversion to the past, a preoccupation with bridging the gap between the society lost in the twenties and the orphaned culture of the seventies. Most of the writers from this period focus both on a present and a distant past for their concept of self, with a blur and a war separating the two points of their lives. Thus in literature there is an emphasis on the experience of the present with a reassertion of a former self, even if only through a theoretical postulate.

Male-authored literature does not lend titles for the first and last periods in this book for the reason that literature is not especially male-dominated during these times. The first, "The Age of an Empress," sounds more like a chapter in a history book, as well it should since it reflects the time of Russia's last ruling empress; after her demise, it was written into law that women could not accede to the Russian throne. This era in Russia, marked by the principles of the Enlightenment, relied heavily on Catherine's presence. As the reknowned Russian literary critic Belinsky recognized: "In the reign of Catherine literature existed only at the court; people engaged in it only because the empress engaged in it."[3] The age of Catherine is most remarkable for the "masculinity" of the female principals, both in terms of action and rank. Nowhere in the following sixty-nine chapters will women rise again to such heights as Princess Dashkova, head of two academies of science, or Catherine herself. However, this period languishes compared to others in terms of scholarly attention, especially true for the women writers.

The final chapter, devoted to living authors, reverberates anew with legitimacy and eminence among women writers. The title for this section, from a poem by Gorbanevskaia, "She is not concerned over the fate of her children," serves as the basis for many different levels of examination. Critics who long travailed attempting to dismiss women by virtue of their childbearing nature, confront women who, for the most part, had real children yet describe their literary works as creative offspring, placing the latter in the more prominent position. Thus the writers themselves seek to determine the value of reproduction and establish their reputations by virtue of the intrinsic value of their work, instead of allowing themselves to be defined by narrow, external parameters. It is hoped, as the final line in the poem expresses, that "it will never happen again," that the history of subordinated Russian women writers will not have to be repeated.

About Russian Writers

As with any book on Russia, the names will present some difficulty and for good reason: most of them have not penetrated into English usage, and they tend to be long and consonant-rich; moreover, they seem to change in context. Those that have been successfully integrated and anglicized only produce the next problem, that they look different in the bibliographies where Russian language works use direct transliteration of names and titles. To address this problem, the index of names has been cross-referenced. As to the changing in context, the matter is associated with crossing cultures.

The individual bibliographies also present a challenge in that much information is not actually attributed, but garnered from other published bibliographies. Thus the names of publishers or page numbers may be missing, as they presumably were in the other bibliographies. Some contributors, though, have personally handled all the works listed and are publishing absolutely new material for the benefit of this publication, a welcome contribution to the field.

In *Russian Women Writers* the writer is presented by her first and last names, a form of address common in the West, but only recently considered acceptable in Russia. Formerly, the patronymic (father's) name always appeared with the given name except among close friends. Since this form of address is still used in Russia, after the title of the chapter, in the first lines of the text the writer's name will change to include the patronymic. Alternative spellings (e.g., Hahn for Gan), other names used, such as pseudonyms or married/maiden names, and the writer's dates will follow as well. In the bibliography, Russian titles bear the Library of Congress transliterated version of the names, facilitating future research for speakers of Russian. However, English language research will be cited using the spelling of the title, whatever form that might take. First names will be anglicized only for the most prominent historical figures where they are conventional: Belinsky, Herzen, Catherine and so forth.

The subsections described essentially follow the major movements in Russian literature. For further reference, Catriona Kelly's *History of Russian Women's Writing* is recommended. Also, the invaluable *Encyclopedia of Russian Women Writers* by Marina Ledkovsky, Charlotte Rosenthal and Mary Zirin is recommended. For general questions about movements, genres and specific authors, Victor Terras's *Handbook of Russian Literature* stands out, as well as his *History of Russian Literature*. Many of the writers in this volume are represented in the Terras *History* as well.

The inclusion of these writers and not others of their gender does not reflect a position statement on the value of any woman's writing. Many articles on other writers were solicited, but not delivered, including Voznesenskaia, Sadur, Makarova and E. Ginzburg, among others. Ratushinskaia was excluded by the offices of her agent, who declined to respond on her behalf. Still others were declined due to other constraints. By and large, the authors represented here are currently the subject of someone's research that which was tapped to produce this volume, a high recommendation for the present level of involvement in studies of women writers, indeed.

Russian Women Writers is first to offer these English translations, with exceptions only for Tolstaia and Bashkirtseva. Akhmatova's complete works have been translated previously; however, the selections offered here are original to this work. Two of the authors have graciously contributed previously unpublished works especially for inclusion in *Russian Women Writers* , Lisnianskaia and Gorbanevskaia. Thus, the anthology works in *Russian Women Writers* present an unknown or unseen facet of literature. It is hoped that the reader will benefit as greatly as I, the first reader, have.

CHRISTINE D. TOMEI
THE HARRIMAN INSTITUTE,
COLUMBIA UNIVERSITY
1998

Notes

1. See *The Encyclopedia of Russian Women Writers*, eds. M. Ledkovsky, C. Rosenthal and M. Zirin (Westport, CT: Greenwood Press, 1994). 440 women writers were identified.

2. K. Aercke, "Introduction," *Women Writing in Dutch* (NY: Garland Publishing, 1994), p. 3.

3. C. Rydel, *The Ardis Anthology of Russian Romanticism*, ed. Christine D. Tomei (Ann Arbor: Ardis, 1984), p. 454.

Acknowledgments

I would like to thank all those who contributed and otherwise participated in the successful preparation of *Russian Women Writers* for this publication. The compiling, writing and editing of this book took place during a time that was for many wracked by personal struggles—including death or the onset of disability—alongside complex professional challenges. I feel that this work is a monument to human dedication and perseverance.

With respect to copyright, I have made every effort to contact the proper agents representing works previously published. Most of our works and photographs are not covered by previous copyright; the U.S.S.R. did not participate in international copyright laws before May 1963, and our translations and photos come primarily from works in editions produced previous to that date.

I was honored to have contacted Lidiia Chukovskaia prior to her death to receive permission to translate from the specified edition (Moscow, 1990) of *Protsess iskliucheniia*. I assume personal responsibility for conforming to her requests that the translator remain true to the original and not "shorten arbitarily the text and not eliminate names (*otchestva*) from the personae, as sometimes happens." I would like to express my gratitude to Alfred Knopf Publishers in New York and Virago Press in the United Kingdom for allowing the reprint of Antonina Bouis's translation of Tat'iana Tolstaia's "On the Golden Porch" (1989) to appear in this book.

Gratitude is also due to the publishers Lenizdat for not objecting to the translation of Ol'ga Berggol'ts's piece; to the press of the Czech Academy of Sciences for letters of Marina Tsvetaeva to A. Teskova; to the publisher Lepta for Peter Tempest's translation of a poem by Larisa Vasilieva; to Sovremennyi Pisatel' for the use of Natal'ia Baranskaia's *Day of Remembrance,* Irina Grekova's "Rothschild's Violin" and Natal'ia Il'ina's "My Unknown Homeland"; and to the publisher of the journal Oktiabr' for translations of Vera Merkur'eva's poems. Many thanks especially to the writers themselves who allowed these translations: Bella Akhmadulina,

Natal'ia Gorbanevskaia, Inna Lisnianskaia, Elizaveta Mnatsakanova, Marina Palei, Liudmila Petrushevskaia, Ol'ga Sedakova, Larisa Vasilieva and Ruf' Zernova.

This project would never have been undertaken without the prompting of Katharina M. Wilson, editor of the Garland series Women Writers of the World. Her continued support significantly contributed to the successful publication of the book, and I would like to add, her personal integrity and professional dedication provided the keystone supporting the entire work. The editorial staff at Garland also deserve special mention for their transforming this massive manuscript into a real work of art. Especially important were the ideas of Phyllis Korper, senior editor, the special design work of Anne Vinnicombe and the production expertise of Christine Murphy.

Research for the chapter on Lokhvitskaia was supported by a grant from the International Research and Exchanges Board with funds provided by the U.S. Department of State (Title VIII) and the National Endowment for the Humanities. None of these organizations is responsible for the views expressed.

Research for the chapter on Lisnianskaia was made possible, in part, by a PepsiCo Fellowship awarded to The Harriman Institute, Columbia University.

Many people responded to my requests for assistance throughout various stages of this work. I would like to take this opportunity especially to thank Adele Barker, Carole Emerson, Helena Goscilo, Barbara Heldt, Marina Ledkovsky, Temira Pachmuss, Charlotte Rosenthal, Stephanie Sandler and Mary Zirin, all of whom contributed at various stages to the organization of this work. Dierdre Keegan offered important comment on some of the earliest drafts of these articles. Others responded by translating additional works. For this special service I would like to thank Sibelan Forrester, Catriona Kelly, Maureen Riley, Lisa Taylor and Carole Ueland.

Harold Leich, the Slavic Specialist at the Library of Congress, has earned special mention for his assistance in many of the most arcane aspects associated with this project. Other people whose legal advice and services I would like to acknowledge are Peter Maggs and Howard Protter.

Most of all, I gratefully acknowledge Natal'ia Gorbanevskaia and Inna Lisnianskaia for providing original artistic material for this volume.

Finally, I would like to express my gratitude to the Harriman Institute of International Studies, Columbia University, for their unfailing support of this project.

Christine D. Tomei, Ph.D.
The Harriman Institute
Columbia University
1998

RUSSIAN WOMEN WRITERS

Valentina Dmitrieva

Valentina Dmitrieva (1859-1947).
Courtesy of Mildred Davies.

Valentina Dmitrieva (1859–1947) is unique in Russian literature because she came from a peasant family and depicted this milieu from personal experience.[1] She also portrayed the struggles and doubts of Russia's radical intelligentsia in the last decades of the tsarist regime, basing her work on her experiences as a village schoolteacher, physician and revolutionary activist. Publishing nearly seventy works of realistic fiction in various leading journals, including *Russian Wealth, The Herald of Europe, Russian Thought* and *The Northern Herald,* Dmitrieva enjoyed considerable popularity in the 1880s, 1890s and early 1900s. In the Soviet period she wrote memoirs but was largely forgotten except as the author of "Malysh and Zhuchka," a children's story that became a classic.

Dmitrieva's difficult journey from serf's daughter to physician and writer is well documented in her lively memoirs, *The Way It Was* (*Tak bylo*).[2] They show a precocious girl engaged in reading and writing that was unusual for her class and gender. She owed her early love of Pushkin, Zhukovskii, Nekrasov and other Russian writers to her mother, Anna Gavrilovna, who came from a family of educated serfs. Her maternal grandfather had been trained as a doctor's assistant (*fel'dsher*). Her father, Iov Filippovich Dmitriev, who had been sent to an agricultural school by his master, E.D. Naryshkin, was overseer of the latter's estate in the village of Voronino in the Balashov district of Saratov province, where Dmitrieva was born 28 April 1859. Not long after the emancipation of the serfs the family was reduced to poverty and a transient existence. Even in these circumstances Dmitrieva managed to read everything she could, from rented books to old, torn copies of journals. During her family's three-year stay in the overcrowded hut of a kindly peasant woman, the inhabitants filled their long, hungry winter days and evenings telling stories. To make up for the lack of reading material, Dmitrieva kept a diary, often writing on bits of paper or envelopes turned inside out. She maintained the diary from age ten to twenty-three, when it was confiscated by the police during the first of many searches she was subjected to in her long career as a revolutionary sympathizer.

Eventually the family returned to her maternal grandfather's household, where the young teenager felt confined by the traditional role prescribed for girls. It seemed unfair to her that she was made to knit stockings while her brother was given the chance to study with the son of a wealthy family. Relying on textbooks sent by her brother's tutor, she studied secretly in the attic for entrance exams to the Tambov Girls' Secondary School (*gimnaziia*). She was admitted to the Fourth Class in 1873 and managed to stay in school thanks to the support of a sympathetic teacher and earnings from tutoring jobs. By the time she graduated in 1877 she had become thoroughly radicalized and was writing reviews of works by leading critical thinkers, including Mikhailovskii, Dobroliubov, Gleb Uspenskii, Zlatovratskii among others for her Tambov discussion and reading group. She tried to publish a satirical work about her school written in the manner of Saltykov-Shchedrin. Signing the name of her brother's friend (with his permission), she sent it to *Alarm Clock* (*Budil'nik*), a humorous magazine. The editor rejected it for political reasons but asked her to send something else. She describes herself as being "in seventh heaven; even though under someone else's name I had received recognition of my writing talent."[3] Her reason for using a male name may have been due more to her fear of being expelled from school for writing something critical than to the feeling of reluctance most women had about revealing their gender. Later, as a professional writer, she signed her works V.I. Dmitrieva. (The final vowel of her name in Russian marks her as a female.)

Dmitrieva's decision to become a village teacher is hardly surprising since teaching was one of the few professions available to educated women and was an obvious choice for radical students. At her first teaching job she encountered instant hostility when she refused to substitute for the drunk village priest in leading school prayers. Suspicion that she was spreading revolutionary ideas among the people eventually led to her dismissal and posting to a school far worse than the dirty, cramped building with broken windows where she had come to love the eighty children in her charge. Unable to teach, she decided that medical practice would be an ideal outlet for her ambition and political convictions; it was also a promising field for Russian women in the 1870s. Entering the Women's Medical Courses in St. Petersburg in 1878, she found herself in a program whose precarious existence was dependent on the influence of the minister of war, D.A. Miliutin, an advocate of medical education for women. Women medical students were constantly reminded that the courses could be terminated at any time, and indeed they were closed to new students in 1882 in the reactionary aftermath to the assassination of Tsar Alexander II. While most female medical students in St. Petersburg reined in their revolutionary sympathies,[4] Dmitrieva spent almost as much time aiding revolutionary activists as she did on her courses, letting her room be used as a storage place for illegal literature and a safe house for revolutionaries hiding from the police. Her connections led to her arrest and a short stay in the prison of Peter-Paul Fortress in 1880. In the early 1880s, with the arrest or disappearance of most of her friends who were members of the People's Will terrorist group and finding herself in dire financial straits, she turned increasingly to writing. She also had to deal with an accusation, which she claims was false, that she was a spy for the tsarist police. (The accusation would come back to haunt her ten years later; a secret inquiry she instigated to clear her name ended inconclusively.)

After graduation from medical school in 1886, Dmitrieva studied gynecology and obstetrics in Moscow but was arrested again in 1887 and exiled to Tver' with her sister for four years. In 1892 she and her husband, Ershov, a revolutionary who was arrested in 1891 and served a six-month sentence in St. Petersburg's Krestyi prison, moved to Voronezh. Like many Russian women physicians who had trouble establishing themselves, Dmitrieva found work as an "epidemic doctor" during outbreaks of cholera in 1892–1893 and diphtheria, scarlet fever and typhus in 1894. Out in the field in remote villages, Dmitrieva and other women physicians found an outlet for their burning desire to help the less fortunate and effect social change.[5] During the cholera epidemic she forcefully stood up to local authorities, demanding a decent salary, equipment and sober staff, all of which were being denied her.

Dmitrieva turned to writing full time in 1895. Although she and her husband lived until 1917 in Voronezh, where they maintained close connections with the radical community, she also made trips to Europe and to Moscow and St. Petersburg. During the civil war[6] she fled to Sochi after losing three brothers and her mother to cold and starvation. She very nearly starved to death herself and did lose her husband, who died as a result of being imprisoned by the Bolsheviks. Dmitrieva's fiction was less appreciated in the Soviet period; as a result, she devoted her time to the cause of literacy and to writing memoirs and children's stories. She died in Sochi on 18 February 1947.

Dmitrieva made her literary debut in 1877 as a writer of peasant stories at a time when educated Russians were eager to read accounts of the village to find an answer to the question "Who is the peasant?" The reading public's fascination with rural Russia had started more than a decade earlier when the peasant question became a burning issue in the new social and economic circumstances of post-emancipation Russia.[7] The vast majority of writers, among whom Gleb Uspenskii, Zlatovratskii and Engel'gardt were especially prominent, came from nonpeasant backgrounds and described the village as outside observers. Dmitrieva's intimate knowledge of peasant ways and language based on her own background as one of the *narod* contributed to the ring of authenticity that critics and readers discerned in her writing. A.P. Dobryv found her background "clearly evident in all her fine works which are notable for their thorough knowledge of peasant life, masterful psychological analysis and deep social significance. . . . "[8]

Her first story, "To Seek Justice" ("Suda prosit'," 1877), appeared in a newspaper in Saratov, where Dmitrieva lived briefly and was acquainted with radical members of the Saratov circle. She continued writing peasant stories in St. Petersburg as her means of support in medical school. "According to the Heart, Not the Mind" ("Po dushe, da ne po razumu," 1880) was published in *Thought,* followed by "Akhmetka's Wife" ("Akhmetkina zhena," 1881) in *Russian Wealth*. The latter work attracted favorable attention from critics and from Nadezhda Khvoshchinskaia, a well-established woman prose writer who wrote Dmitrieva a letter praising the story and expressing a desire to meet her. "She was surprised at my youth," Dmitrieva wrote, "[for] reading my story she had imagined that it was written not by a woman, or at the very least if by a woman then not a young one. . . . I remember that Iakubovich was also very surprised at this and many critics noted my masculine pen."[9] "Akhmetka's Wife" follows the emotional turmoil of Spiridonikha, a *soldatka* (soldier's wife) who discovers she has two husbands. Dmitrieva turns the image of peasant woman as victim around, depicting her struggles as a kept woman in the city and then her new life when she returns to her village to become a successful farmer. Believing her husband dead, she marries a poor widower with children and provides them with a home only to learn that her first husband is returning after a twenty-year absence. She welcomes him, now a broken man, to her hut too. Spiridonikha is the first of a number of strong female characters in Dmitrieva's writing. She wrote mainly on peasant themes throughout the 1880s,[10] combining crime plots with depictions of economic and social conditions. Critics praised the content of her stories with their focus on the peasant milieu but criticized them for being too "bloody" and melodramatic.[11]

A new type of hero appeared in her fiction in the 1890s—the literate peasant who will lead the *narod* out of dark ignorance. "Mitiukha the Teacher" ("Mitiukha—uchitel'," 1896), about a sensitive young married peasant who defies his father to become a teacher, presents such a type. Dmitrieva looks critically at husband/wife and parent/child relations in a typical patriarchal peasant family. By the end of the story Mitiukha has established a much better relationship with his wife and even interested her in learning to read. The story brings out one of Dmitrieva's recurring themes: the superiority of the country over the city.[12] One reviewer praised the story's "true simple Russian speech, and not the imitation of it that often occurs in works of this kind" but found totally false Mitiukha's lack of religious piety.[13] One of Dmitrieva's most interesting depictions of peasant life is a series of sketches, "In the Villages" ("Po derevniam," 1896), about her experiences as an "epidemic doctor" combating diphtheria, scarlet fever and typhus in the Zadonsk region. An exacting eye for detail and a masterful use of peasant dialogue capture scenes of tragedy and humor as she describes her travels from village to village, hut to hut, painting throats and dispensing candy as well as disinfectants. In this and other works she slightly idealizes but never sentimentalizes her peasant subjects.

She also turned her attention to urban workers, poor peasants who had been forced off the land and felt alienated in the city. While investigative journalism was not typical for Russian women writers at this time—it was not until the 1920s that Soviet women writers such as Marietta Shaginian left their desks to travel extensively gathering information firsthand—Dmitrieva went to the Crimea in 1896, where she obtained permission to visit a coal mine. Two works critical of the miners' working conditions resulted: "White Wings" ("Belye kryl'ia") and "The Woman Ivan and Her Godson" ("Baba Ivan i ee krestnik"). She also became acquainted with an Odessa dockworker who became the subject of one of her best portraits—Vaska Dukachev, an irreverent, larger-than-life figure who recounts his adventures as a ship's stoker in "Childhood Friends" ("Druz'ia detstva," 1904).

Dmitrieva treated a wide variety of settings and characters convincingly. Her settings include not only central, rural Russia, where most of her peasant stories take place, but also Ukraine, the Crimea and the Caucasus. One of her best stories, "Bandits" ("Razboiniki," 1909), follows the journey of a group of Russian tourists through a wild, mountainous region in Georgia. Among her characters, peasant children, especially the tiny boy depicted in her most popular story, "Malysh and Zhuchka" ("Malysh i Zhuchka," 1899), stand out. Malysh, an eager pupil at the village school where he has been sent by his poor widowed mother to get him out of their crowded hut and away from his seven sisters, almost perishes in a snowstorm but is saved by his dog. His right to attend school while his sisters stay home reflects the prevailing attitude in rural Russia at the time. "Khves'ka the Orderly" ("Bol'nichnyi storozh Khves'ka," 1900), written a year later, depicts a bright thirteen-year-old peasant girl whose industriousness, knowledge of medicines and burning desire to learn suggest hope for Russia's future and an important role for women. "Dimka" (1900), about a ten-year-old boy who works in a Moscow glass factory, presents another memorable portrait and a devastating picture of child labor, drinking, violence and the degradation of women. Dmitrieva's story about a rural priest's daughter who dies as a result of being raped in prison by a tsarist officer is both an endearing portrait and an inflammatory political pamphlet against the tsarist regime. *Lipochka the Priest's Daughter* (*Lipochka-popovna,* 1902), written abroad under a pseudonym and published in Geneva in 1902, was later smuggled into Russia along with another illegal story by Dmitrieva "For the Faith, Tsar and Fatherland" ("Za veru, tsaria, i otechestvo," 1902). These works circulated among Russia's revolutionary-minded students and workers.

Dmitrieva's major fictional works, which dealt with the intelligentsia, appealed especially to Russia's radical youth, who sympathized with her populist ideals and saw reflections of themselves in the young students, teachers and medical students populating her fictional world. *The Volunteer* (*Dobrovolets*, 1889), about radicals of the 1870s, based on her association in 1877 with Saratov revolutionaries including I.I. Mainov, P.S. Polivanov and others, sounded an unusually optimistic note at a time of general gloom, when the radical populist movement had been weakened for a decade. Soviet critics called attention to its final uplifting graveyard scene—a model "socialist realist" ending. (Dmitrieva did write a more elegiac ending, which was never published.)[14] Although often discouraged herself by the repression most of her friends had suffered, Dmitrieva wrote the novella to raise the consciousness of Russia's younger generation. Her optimism reflects the life-affirming quality that characterizes most of her work.[15] Her next novel, *Gomochka* (1894), follows the life of a young woman medical student falsely accused of embezzling funds raised to help needy students. A selfless, loving person who lives only for others, she dies in the end having changed all who knew her.

Later novels reflect increasing doubt about the future of Russia and the possibility for change. *Under the Southern Sun* (*Pod solntsem iuga*, 1899), set in Balaklava in the Crimea, brings together a group of young vacationers, all grappling with the question of what to do with their lives. The breathtaking scenery stands in sharp contrast to their increasing, gnawing awareness of the poverty and terrible conditions in which most of Russia's population lives. Dmitrieva's major novel, *Chervonnyi Manor* (*Chervonnyi khutor*, 1900), reflects the peasant unrest leading up to the 1905 revolution. Set on a farm in Ukraine, it portrays the social milieu of the region's landowners (whom Dmitrieva depicts in her characteristic way with barbed satire) and the blighted love of two young radicals who part over their disagreement about the use of force to build a better society. The action culminates in a dramatic night of rampage as transient unemployed peasants set fire to the area's estates. *Clouds* (*Tuchki*, 1904) paints a vivid picture of life in a provincial town where the leading socialite, a talented singer, feels trapped in a meaningless marriage. The main women characters, Nadezhda, a teacher, and Dora, a doctor's assistant, whose corrupt *zemstvo* bosses mouth platitudes about service to the people, have no chance for personal happiness. Dora, ever selfless in her service, dies of typhus, and Nadezhda loses both her teaching job and the student revolutionary she loves when he leaves her for the uncertain task of carrying on the revolutionary cause. One of Dmitrieva's most mature works, it attracted the attention of Lunacharskii[16] and others. Ignatov, writing in 1901, found Dmitrieva's "view of the fate of the Russian intelligentsia" . . . "permeated with deep pessimism,"[17] a view that runs counter to the way she has been portrayed by Soviet literary historians.

Russian critics, both prerevolutionary and Soviet, noted Dmitrieva's "masculine pen," that is, her concern with social and political issues as opposed to the intimate emotions of love relationships and family life. Most critics found it admirable that a woman would write about these issues, but the prerevolutionary woman critic, E.A. Koltonovskaia, whose perceptive criticism has shed much light on Russian women writers, found Dmitrieva's writing deficient because of the seemingly unimportant role love plays in the lives of her characters.[18] Dmitrieva's neglect of love-driven plots followed naturally from her childhood reading preferences: articles on international and domestic politics; crime and adventure novels; and most important, works by Chernyshevsky (especially *What Is to Be Done*, which she claims changed her life), Dobroliubov and Pisarev. Like Masha, the ascetic heroine of *Under the Southern Sun*, Dmitrieva skipped the love scenes in novels, and as a writer she kept love in the background, only occasionally allowing her heroines and heroes to wrestle with the dilemma of personal happiness versus service to a higher ideal. Her overwhelming concern with social problems set her apart from the flood of Russian women writers at the turn of the century who were writing so-called ladies' literature (*damskaia literatura*), treating matters of the heart and the "woman question." Dmitrieva saw women's emancipation as part of the larger battle for social justice, although she was sharply critical of the patriarchal nature of Russian family life, the hurdles women faced in obtaining an education and the condescending, hypocritical way women professionals were treated by men in authority. A few of her resourceful heroines offer models of strong females who will lead Russia to a better day.

Dmitrieva belongs to the tradition of nineteenth-century Russian realism as practiced by Turgenev, Goncharov and Tolstoy. Her prose seemed slightly old-fashioned, tendentious and overdone to critics of her time although colorful, lively and rich in its variety and use of language. Koltonovskaia found Dmitrieva extremely talented but, in the end, superficial.[19] Others complained of her need to explain everything to readers as if they were incapable of grasping the difference between good and evil on their own. Her characters were too black and white instead of shades of light and dark as in real life, according to another reviewer.[20] For today's reader Dmitrieva's writing retains its narrative and human interest and is notable for its ease. That she did not sympathize with new trends in Silver Age culture seems clear from her satirical treatment of a symbolist painter and poet dilettante in *Under the Southern Sun*, where she makes the point that art must serve the people.

Although Dmitrieva was acquainted with a number of male writers, including Garshin, Gleb Uspenskii, Zlatovratskii, Gorky and Andreev, she was initially shy about speaking to them, especially at the beginning of her literary career. As a student she felt extreme embarrassment in asking Saltykov-Shchedrin for a small favor on behalf of her medical school class. She felt nervous in approaching L.O. Kotelianskii, the author of a work about Ukraine: "I was a terrible coward: to talk to a real writer, especially about my own work—that was much more frightening than hiding dynamite or illegal literature." She does not mention, however, any shyness communicating with women writers. Her connection with Nadezhda Khvoshchinskaia has already been mentioned, but in fact it began much earlier when Dmitrieva was a child. On hearing about the unusual peasant girl who was studying all on her own, the writer sent Dmitrieva a box of books. Referring to this incident, Dmitrieva wrote: "In general, I consider myself very lucky: in my life I have met so many wonderfully good people that simply the remembrance of them in the most difficult minutes of my life sustained my courage of spirit, and no misfortunes or setbacks could shake my faith in the human being."[21] Dmitrieva mentions that she "maintained the most friendly relations with Khvoshchinskaia until her death [in 1889] and retained the fondest memories of her."[22] She was encouraged as well in the early years of her literary career by Kapitolina Nazar'eva. Both wrote crime novels,[23] an unusual genre for women writers at the time. Dmitrieva's awareness of the importance of women's support of one another is illustrated in her medical school novel, *Gomochka*. It seems clear that she felt close to the women writers mentioned and that they had some influence on her development as a writer. Whether she felt herself to be part of a Russian female literary tradition is unclear since she makes no reference to such a tradition.

Blok had the impression in 1907 that Dmitrieva had been "adorning the pages of *Russian Wealth* with her works since time immemorial."[24] Her popularity did not last much longer, however. A decline in the quality of her fiction after 1910 coupled with her adherence to outdated populist themes contributed to her fading popularity. As a provincial author, living in such places as Tver', Voronezh and Sochi, she had fewer literary connections than if she had lived in the capitals and therefore a much greater chance of being forgotten.[25] For her, though, the provinces remained her source of inspiration. As she wrote in 1916:

> I settled definitively in Voronezh although I received permission to live in the capitals. I was no longer attracted by either Piter [St. Petersburg] or Moscow; I decided to remain in the provinces where people are needed more and up to the present, I have no regrets. Here such a huge wave of people and events has swept in front of me, such a wide field for all kinds of activities and interesting observations has unfolded that one can probably say that life in the capital[s] in some kind of closed literary circle would not have given me even a hundredth part of what I received from the dear and funny, sometimes wild and preposterous but completely distinctive and fundamentally healthy provinces.[26]

In the mid-1920s *Red Virgin Soil* and *Young Guard* rejected her stories on Komsomol themes. Her writing, nevertheless, impressed at least two Soviet writers: Nikolai Ostrovsky, a fellow writer in Sochi and author of the socialist realist classic *How the Steel Was Tempered*[27] and Gorky, who so admired her memoirs that he suggested her name along with several other prominent women of Russia and the world for the popular biography series *The Lives of Remarkable People*.[28] Gorky's wish was never fulfilled, and Dmitrieva's considerable literary legacy, which Koltonovskaia compared to that of Khvoshchinskaia and Eliza Orzeszkowa,[29] Poland's first professional woman writer, largely disappeared from Russian literature until 1976, when a children's story and the first of three collections of her stories were published in the U.S.S.R. One of her stories, "The Bees Are Buzzing" ("Pchely zhuzhzhat"), about a peasant revolt in which women play a decisive role, also appeared in *Only an Hour* (*Tol'ko chas,* 1988), a Soviet anthology of prose by late-nineteenth and early-twentieth-century Russian women writers.

Mildred Davies

From Notes of a Rural Doctor

Khves'ka the Orderly

I arrived in the village of Steben'ki on one of the gloomiest days of a gloomy November by way of an abominable road and in a foul mood. The clinic I had been assigned to as a doctor was still under the direction of a *fel'dsher,*[1] and at the *zemstvo*[2] board I had been warned that things were rather badly run there and that the board would not be opposed to my firing the *fel'dsher* if I found it necessary. Thus I wasn't expecting anything pleasant and was convinced beforehand that I would find a most depressing situation in Steben'ki. I didn't even know if I would find lodging for the night or a glass of hot tea, and meanwhile I was chilled, hungry, jolted from the journey and soaked to the skin because the sky had poured the bitterest tears on me, as if mourning my fate.

I drove up to the hut where the *fel'dsher* lived and the pharmacy and clinic were housed. The hut was large, divided by a small entry into two halves with a porch, over which hung a faded sign with the inscription "Zemstvo Clinic." Because of the bad weather, there wasn't a soul in sight, and nobody met me on the porch, but since the door was wide open, I had no trouble going into the entry where, next to a trough, a piglet with a turned-up nose busied himself and grunted with displeasure. Doors stood to the right and left, but not knowing which one I should take, I stood in the middle of the passage and, like a knight of the Russian folk epic in an open field, I exclaimed in a loud voice, "Is anybody alive here?"

In answer to my call the door on the left opened noisily, and out jumped a barefoot girl of thirteen or fourteen in a torn coat with sleeves far too long for her, a dirty rag on her head and a baby in her arms.

"I am the new doctor," I announced. "Where is the *fel'dsher?* Where is the orderly? Can't someone be called here?"

The girl gave me a quick glance with her eyes, blue as cornflowers, and darting back through the same door she had come from, shouted piercingly, "Uncle,[3] come, Uncle, the doctor has arrived!"

The door slammed behind her; in the hut anxious voices could be heard, and I was left alone again with the snub-nosed piglet, who obviously was not pleased with my arrival and tried in every way to express to me his hostile feelings.

The girl soon returned and, with the hem of her threadbare coat trailing across the dirty floor, led me to the right.

"This way, Uncle. Uncle will be here in a minute."

"Is this your clinic?" I asked, entering the large hut divided in half by a plank partition.

"It's the clinic, Uncle; and Uncle lives in the other part," the girl explained glibly, standing in front of me with her baby, like a soldier with a rifle in front of his commander.

I looked around. The first section of the hut undoubtedly served as a waiting room because long benches stretched along the walls, and in the corner on a stool stood a bucket with water, and on a nail a rusty mug was hanging. In the next section, which served as a pharmacy and examining room, a large cupboard filled with jars and bottles stood behind a counter, and closer to the door were two rickety chairs, a dilapidated sofa and a wobbly table where a bulging book for registering the patients lay. The disorder everywhere was appalling: on the floor layers of dirt were accumulating; the walls, which had not been whitewashed for a long time, were covered with yellow stains; one window was broken and stuffed with some kind of rag; piled about on the counter were a copper scales turning green with age, unwashed mortars which stank of mold, vials, tablets and all kinds of rubbish. While I was surveying all this, the girl continued to stare at me and only occasionally turned aside in order to wipe the baby's nose with two fingers.

"Well, really, there's not much to see here!" I said. "Who is looking after things? Where is the orderly?"

"Oh, I am the orderly," answered the girl.

I looked at her in astonishment.

"You? Some orderly! What kind of an orderly are you, performing your duties poorly, eh!"

The girl's eyes blinked, startled.

"But, Uncle, I do everything that Uncle orders," she uttered quickly. "Ask Uncle, he will tell you!"

"Well, all right, little Auntie, a bit later; for now go and tell the driver to carry my things in here."

In a minute all my soaked belongings were brought into the clinic, the girl energetically helping the driver. Not putting down the baby, she dashed back and forth like a whirlwind while the poor infant kept finding himself in the most impossibly awkward positions, sometimes even practically upside down. I dismissed the driver and took off my wet outer garments, but the *fel'dsher* still had not appeared. I was beginning to lose hope of seeing him at all, when suddenly the door quietly creaked and in front of me appeared a short, rather plump gentleman of about thirty, with narrow gray eyes in which hostility and fear were clearly visible. It was obvious he had changed his clothes: he was wearing a rather respectable frock coat, buttoned up all the way; his hair was greased.

"Allow me to introduce myself—Fel'dsher Kudakin," he introduced himself.

"Very pleased to meet you. Please, sit down!"

"Never mind, sir. I will stand," the *fel'dsher* said quickly, and in his eyes fear and hostility appeared even more distinctly. Such a beginning clearly boded ill.

I asked him if it would be possible to fetch a samovar and heat up the stove in the clinic and, having received his gracious agreement, I sent the girl orderly after wood and a samovar. We were left alone.

"Tell me, please, do you always have such dirt and disorder?" I asked.

Mr. Kudakin looked around uneasily, and his mustache quivered.

"The premises are bad, sir."

"Premises are premises, but what's all this dirt? Is this girl working as the orderly of your hospital?"

"S . . . so it is, sir," the *fel'dsher* said hesitantly. "It's hard to find anybody suitable. The people here are loafers, Mr. Doctor, they don't want to work."

"Maybe the wages aren't high enough. How much are you paying her?"

Kudakin turned red, and his eyes darted like mice.

"T . . . two and fifty kopecks," he mumbled, as if he didn't believe his own words.

"That's very little. It should be raised."

After this time, the girl, freed of the infant, brought the samovar, and the *fel'dsher*, having wished me bon appetit, left. While I was unpacking my suitcases and boiling tea, my barefoot orderly proved to be a marvel of efficiency and quick-wittedness. In an instant she cleared the book and ink off the table, fetched a tablecloth and dishes from the *fel'dsher*, lit the stove, swept the floor, helped me trim and light the lamp and stood in the doorway, not taking her lively eyes off me.

"Maybe you'd like me to get you some eggs, Uncle?" she asked.

"Yes, where can you get them?"

"From the landlord. Just a minute, I'll run and get them. Maybe you'd like some milk?"

"Yes, let's have some milk too."

The girl flew off somewhere and brought back a dozen eggs and a large earthenware pot of milk. The hut became cozier: the wood crackled gaily in the stove; the samovar boiled and bubbled as hard as it could. I grew warm and cheered up.

"Well, orderly!" I addressed the girl. "What is your name, anyway?"

"Khves'ka!"

"That's short for Fedos'ia! Well, Brother Fedos'ia, thank you: you have warmed me up, given me food and drink! Thank you."

"Don't mention it!" the girl said gravely.

"Why not? Without you I would have been done for. Tell me, now, how was it you came to be an orderly?"

"Why, like this. We've got five kids at home, and all little. I'm the biggest, but Ma's ailing and Pa's a hard drinker. So Uncle says, 'Let the girl, he says, hire herself out in the clinic as an orderly; why should she loaf around at home, she'll get fifty kopecks a month and board.' So I took the job."

"What do you mean fifty kopecks? The *fel'dsher* told me two rubles fifty."

Khves'ka's eyes lit up with indignation.

"What! He's lying!" she exclaimed. "What two fifty? Not on your life two fifty. Fifty kopecks a month and board."

"Well, you won't be continuing any longer because you are performing your duties poorly. Look at these dirty floors!"

"Well, you see, good heavens, you see, if they would order me . . . I clean at Uncle's place every day, and here only sometimes, because Uncle says, 'It makes no difference; it'll get tracked up again all the same with dirty footmarks.'"

"So what do you do here?"

"What, indeed? Everything! I scrub Uncle's floor, wash the linen, carry water, put on the samovar, milk the cow, and whatever I'm told. . . ." She gasped for breath, enumerating all her duties.

"And whose child was that?"

"Why, Uncle's, of course."

"So, you are also a nanny?"

"Why, of course. The agreement was that I take care of the baby. I do everything I'm told."

"You don't see patients, do you?" I asked jokingly.

But, to my surprise, my joke didn't appear to be a joke at all.

"But, of course, I see patients sometimes!" Khves'ka answered seriously. "If somebody comes after dinner and Uncle is resting, I know who needs what and I dispense it. Just the other day, Auntie Lupandikha needed some quinine—I dispensed it, and yesterday Van'ka Pakhomov was screaming for all he was worth with a toothache—I gave him some drops."

"Well, you're really a clever girl, Fedos'ia," I exclaimed, laughing. "You're a jack of all trades, and for only fifty kopecks."

"May lightning strike me dead, if I'm not telling the truth—I get just fifty kopecks and board! And what's this two fifty—I haven't laid eyes on it, I swear on the cross and the Holy Trinity!"

After tea I decided to go to bed right away and to get up early because I was already convinced that things were on the verge of disaster. The *fel'dsher* didn't appear, and a sepulchral silence reigned, as in the enemy camp before battle. Again, it was Khves'ka who made up a bed for me. With that same catlike agility, she brought in hay and spread it on the floor next to the stove—I didn't dare sleep on the sofa. Then she put everything in order, even hung sheets over the windows, and went out only when I absolutely didn't need anything else.

The next day just as it was getting light, I was awakened by the steps of bare feet carefully moving back and forth, some kind of scraping and the splash of water.

"Who's there?" I asked.

"It's me, Uncle, you're sleeping!" a little voice answered. "I'm washing the floors!"

I couldn't sleep anymore and, having dressed, I lit the lamp. The floor in the examining room was already washed, and kindling burned brightly in the stove.

"When did you find time for all this?" I asked Khves'ka.

"Look! It's not that early anymore, is it? I've already milked the cow. Should I bring the samovar?"

"Yes, is it possible it's ready?"

"A long time ago! You said yourself, you were getting up early. Well, I got it ready."

"Bring it!" I said gaily. I liked the little lass more and more.

I was having tea when the *fel'dsher* appeared and, coldly greeting me, started to poke about in the medicine cupboard. He already felt the precariousness of his situation but just in case was trying all the same to demonstrate his love of his work and diligence. I asked him for his account book and, on the very first page, my eyes caught the entry: "to the orderly—five rubles."

"Mr. Kudakin!" I said. "Why did you tell me yesterday that you are paying Fedos'ia two rubles fifty, when here it says five rubles?"

"That's exactly right, five," Kudakin answered sullenly. "But since my wife took on several duties, for example, washing the floors and the pharmaceutical utensils, I divided it in half."

"A strange division! But there's more to the story: Fedos'ia told me that you pay her only fifty kopecks and meanwhile make her milk your cow and take care of your baby in addition. What kind of a division is that?"

Now the *fel'dsher* actually snapped at me. "As you wish! If you believe a peasant girl more than me, that's up to you. And as far as the baby goes: is it some kind of a sin to provide care for an infant? I find it truly amazing. . . ."

He retreated behind the counter grumbling, and in a minute the crash and clatter of broken crockery announced to me that he was totally upset.

Meanwhile daylight arrived, and patients began to gather in the clinic. The first patient, having received her prescription, suddenly reached into her bosom somewhere and without a word laid a five kopeck coin in front me.

"What is this?" I asked with surprise, knowing that the dispensing of medicine is free of charge.

"Why, for the tablet?" the peasant woman answered, also with surprise.

[As other patients try to pay, it becomes clear that Kudakin has been charging them for prescriptions, which the clinic is supposed to provide free of charge. The doctor is amazed at Khves'ka's knowledge of the various medications and their location, which she knows better than the *fel'dsher*.]

By two o'clock the clinic had emptied. I was left alone with Khves'ka.

"Well, really, Fedos'ia," I said. "Now I'm satisfied with you and you can stay on as orderly." (Her face beamed.) "Only look sharp that everything is in order—I like cleanliness. I'm going to establish a new regime. No more work as a nanny; you won't be milking the cow either, but make sure there is order and cleanliness in the clinic. Your wages will be five rubles a month plus board. I'll be very exacting about disorder: the minute something displeases me—out you go. Well, there you are: do you want the job or not?"

Khves'ka, turning red and then pale, looked at me with big eyes as if not believing her own ears. Then she clasped her hands, sighed, burst out laughing and was about to run off somewhere when I stopped her.

"Stop, what's the matter? My, you are overjoyed! You'd better work first; maybe we won't get along."

The girl shook her head negatively. "I'm going to try, Uncle—so hard!"

[After agreeing to find another post, Kudakin and his wife create a commotion outside the clinic, demanding that Khves'ka remove her clothes, which they claim they gave her. A peasant woman in the crowd and the landlord lend her some other clothes.]

In two weeks' time our clinic was unrecognizable. The walls had been whitewashed, the windows repaired and the floors shone like a mirror because Khves'ka rubbed them everyday with a brick and then washed them. The cupboard was a model of order, again thanks to Khves'ka, who made sure that everything was in its place and even sometimes scolded me when I would put some medicine in the wrong place. The Kudakins had already moved, and I now lived in their premises. A *fel'dsher*-midwife, Maria Frantsova, whom Khves'ka called "Frantovna," had taken the *fel'dsher*'s position. The three of us hit it off, living in peace and quiet. Khves'ka grew to be our favorite and delighted Frantovna and me with her quickness and unusual brightness. For her it seemed nothing was impossible; whatever you asked she did immediately, never getting anything mixed up and doing everything with pleasure, with a beaming face and without any urging, which was especially nice to see. It was clear that she liked the work, and often one even had to stop her when she was overzealous.

"Fedos'ia, you should sit for a bit," one of us would say to her.

Immediately she would smile from ear to ear, and enthusiasm would light up in her eyes. "Oh, come on!" she would object. "It's boring to sit still—my legs get a cramp!"

She knew our patients better than we ourselves—by name, who came from where and even the name of their illness.

On the twentieth I made a trip into town to collect the monthly pay, and having returned in the evening, I called Khves'ka.

"Well, here you are, Fedos'ia, your wages for the month," I said, handing her the money. "Tomorrow Frantovna is going into town, so talk to her about what to buy you. You already have shoes, and you have a jacket [all of this Frantovna had given her], but, well, you don't have a dress, or a blouse. Everything you're wearing, you know, belongs to somebody else, so you'd better think about what you need."

I glanced at her, expecting to see her shining face (I loved it when her face lit up: everything about her seemed to smile then—her eyes, her dimples and even the tip of her nose), but to my surprise, she stood in front of me hanging her head and indecisively fidgeting with the coins in her hand.

"What's the matter with you?" I asked. "Aren't you happy?"

"No, I'm happy," Khves'ka said, sighing. "But, you know, Pa will drink it all up in any case."

"How, drink it up?"

"Just like that—he'll come and take it all."

"Aha! Very well then, give the money back to me. I'll buy everything you need myself, and when Pa comes send him to me."

The next day after we had finished seeing patients, Fedos'ia announced to me, "Uncle, Pa's here. He's waiting in the entry."

"Call him in."

In a minute cautious coughing and a secretive whisper announced to me the arrival of "Pa." I went out into the anteroom and by the door saw a shabby-looking man in worn birch bark shoes, a hat full of holes with wisps of straw sticking out of it and with a long stick in his hands. Everything about him was somehow straggling: his hands hung loose as if good for nothing, his knees stuck out from his skinny legs as if he didn't have the strength to hold up his clumsy torso. His good-natured face was covered with many fine wrinkles out of which gazed untroubled, clear blue eyes, amazingly resembling Khves'ka's, but the main adornment of this face was the nose—large and crimson, it blossomed and shone like a blossoming poppy. Khves'ka stood to one side and with pity and sadness, as mothers look at their unsuccessful children, looked at her parent.

"What do you say, good man?" I asked.

"I came for the wages," answered the peasant and smiled happily.

"What wages? You don't work here."

[Pa argues and finally threatens to take his daughter home if he isn't paid the five rubles. When the doctor says that Khves'ka will have to remove the clothes that don't belong to her, Pa leaves. Part of her wages, it is decided, will be used to buy flour and other necessities for her family so that Pa can't spend it on drink.]

Khves'ka gained weight with us, dressed more smartly and became even more agile and merry. She and Frantovna became fast friends and were always whispering among themselves either about some kind of unusual woman's jacket with a flounce in the back, seen on the priest's wife in church, or about the village patients and their affairs, which Khves'ka knew down to the last detail, or finally about what a person really is, how the mind works and where one's soul is. Khves'ka was very interested in all of this, and Frantovna taught her this and that, so that Khves'ka now could not only "dispense" drops, as she would say, but also knew how to boil various medicines, prepare complicated ointments and even apply bandages for "blood poisoning," as she used to say.

"You should be a doctor, Fedos'ia," I joked sometimes.

"What are you saying!" she said. "A doctor . . . if I could read!"

"And why not? Let's buy a reader and start studying."

"But isn't that embarrassing? Girls don't study. People will laugh."

"Let them laugh. Fools laugh, but the wise are proud."

The girl became thoughtful. Soon I started noticing that she would suddenly look intently at books and newspapers, and once I was very surprised when Khves'ka suddenly pointed her finger at a book that was lying in front of me and, smiling, announced in a loud voice, "Why, you know, that's an *a*!"

"How do you know?" I asked.

"The landlord's Mishan'ka showed me. He goes to the school and knows all his letters. And now I know. I can pick out the big ones easily, but the little are still hard."

"Clever girl!" I commended her. "Well, just wait, I'll go into town and bring you a reader. We'll study."

But Khves'ka became embarrassed and shook her head. "No, Uncle, don't do it. People will laugh at me, for heaven's sake. I won't do it for anything. It's not possible, is it?" And, laughing, she ran out.

But Khves'ka was crafty, and I suspected that she was continuing to quietly memorize the ABC book because suddenly we began to run out of kerosene, and a light burned in the clinic until almost midnight. Before, she would go to bed right after she tidied up, but now whenever one looked out the window bands of light were still coming from the clinic, signifying that our orderly was awake. I tried to question her.

"What's going on, Fedos'ia? So much kerosene is being used up."

"What?" the girl asked, frightened. "Am I not allowed?"

"Why not? Burn as much as you like, only what are you doing there? Practicing witchcraft or something?"

"What are you saying? Practicing witchcraft . . . you shouldn't say those words lightly . . . then, I won't light the lamp at all!"

"Oh, really! Stay up the whole night if you wish, do me a favor, I don't regret the kerosene. But I am curious, what are you sweating over?"

Khves'ka kept her mouth shut, but despite her cunning, she got caught anyway.

Once after dinner I went out into the entryway. I had just opened the door when under my very feet some kind of a chubby little boy made straight for the door. I only managed to see his large, shaggy cap and the cunning eyes flashing from under it. I looked and Khves'ka was standing close by pressed into a corner, her eyes frightened, hiding something behind her back. I had scared the pair and obviously the chubby boy in the huge cap was a criminal accomplice.

"What are you doing here?" I asked sternly. "Who is this?"

"This is . . . this is the landlord's Mishan'ka . . . " stammered Khves'ka.

"So that's who it is. And what do you have in your hands? Well, show me!" From behind her back, she handed me a soiled, torn book, all impregnated with a peasant smell. It was *Our Folk*.

"You rascals!" I said, laughingly. "So this is why so much of our kerosene is disappearing. Well, how is it going? Do you still know just the big letters, or something else?"

"No, now I can read the little ones too," whispered Khves'ka.

"Well, read!"

Khves'ka took the book and, stumbling slightly, particularly on words with two vowels in a row, but all the same rather intelligibly, read a few lines.

"Clever!" I said. "Only why hide? This is good, there's nothing to hide—study openly and if you don't understand something, ask me or Frantovna; we'll help you with pleasure."

"And you won't laugh?" asked Khves'ka, beaming in her usual way.

From that day on she didn't hide anymore, and in every free moment one could see her curled up someplace by a window with a book from which she recited in a singsong voice: "Baldheaded Grandpa sits with his white beard. . . ."

Now Khves'ka reads and writes fairly well, is interested as before in where a person's soul is and, when returning late from patients, I see in the midst of the mute nighttime blackness a lonely little light glimmering in the clinic window, and over the light the bent head of Khves'ka, who is attaining knowledge with such labor and effort, and I think to myself: how many such lights are scattered across Russia!

1900

Translated by Mildred Davies

Notes to the Essay

1. A.P. Dobryv lists Dmitrieva as "the first woman writer in Rus' who comes straight from the *narod*. . . . " A.P. Dobryv, ed., *Biografii russkikh pisatelei srednego i novogo perioda* (St. Petersburg, 1900), 140. In fact, the prose writer Anna Kirpishchikova (1838–1927), who was of proletarian origins, is probably the first. Other Russian women writers who wrote on peasant themes in the late nineteenth century include S. Karaskevich, A. Kovalenskaia, A. Lukanina, E. Militsyna, M. Myshkina, L. Nelidova, N. Sokhanskaia, A. Shabel'skaia and S. Zakrevskaia. See *Dictionary of Women Writers*, ed. M. Ledkovsky et al. (Westport, CT: Greenwood Press, 1994). I am grateful to Mary Zirin for letting me use her bibliography and other materials on Dmitrieva.

2. V.I. Dmitrieva, *Tak bylo* (Moscow: Molodaia gvardiia, 1930). All quotations and biographical information are taken from this edition unless otherwise indicated. This 438-page book covers her life up to 1907 and includes numerous portraits of Russian radicals from the 1870s and 1880s. Other shorter autobiographical works by the author repeat essentially the same facts about her life.

3. Ibid., 98.

4. For discussion and the backgrounds and concerns of Russian women medical students in both Zurich and St. Petersburg, see Barbara Alpern Engel, *Mothers and Daughters: Women of the Intelligentsia in Nineteenth-Century Russia* (Cambridge: Cambridge University Press, 1983), Chapter 8. It includes a summary of Dmitrieva's biography.

5. Another Russian woman physician fiction writer, Adelaida Lukanina, wrote a memoir about her experiences in the 1892 cholera epidemic that is strikingly similar to Dmitrieva's account. See Mildred Davies, "Lukanina, Adelaida Nikolaevna," in *Dictionary of Russian Women Writers*, 385–88. For an acccount of the experiences of several women physicians see Toby W. Clyman, "Women Physicians' Autobiography in the Nineteenth Century," in *Women Writers in Russian Literature*, ed. T. Clyman and D. Greene (Westport, CT: Greenwood Press, 1994), 111–26.

6. Information about Dmitrieva's life after 1907 is included at the end of *Tak bylo* in a separate short autobiography.

7. On educated Russians' obsession with the peasantry, see Cathy A. Frierson, *Peasant Icons: Representations of Rural People in Late Nineteenth-Century Russia* (Oxford: Oxford University Press, 1993), 3–20; see also Richard Wortman, *The Crisis of Russian Populism* (Cambridge: Cambridge University Press, 1967), 27–34. For a summary of the depiction of the peasant in Russian literature see Donald Fanger, "The Peasant in Literature," in *The Peasant in Nineteenth Century Russia*, ed. W. Vucinich (Palo Alto, CA: Stanford University Press, 1968), 231–62.

8. A.P. Dobryv, "V.I. Dmitrieva," in *Biografii russkikh pisatelei srednego i novogo perioda* (St. Petersburg, 1900), 140.

9. Ibid., 210.

10. Her stories of the 1880s include "Out of Conscience" ("Ot sovesti," 1882), "Still Waters" ("V tikhom omute," 1882), "In Different Directions" ("V raznye storony," 1883) and "One's Own Justice" ("Svoim sudom," 1888).

11. "Novye knigi," *Russkoe bogatstvo* 3 (1893): 18–21.

12. Themes of the importance of literacy and the superiority of the country also occur in the work of Stefaniia Karaskevich, another gifted prose writer of the period. See Mildred Davies, "Karaskevich, Stefaniia Stepanova," in *Dictionary of Russian Women Writers*, 271–74.

13. N.a., *Russkoe obozrenie* 10 (1896): 914.

14. O.G. Lasunskii, "Nado idti . . . i zhit'," in V.I. Dmitrieva, *Povesti. Rasskazy* (Voronezh, 1983), 13.

15. See E.A. Koltonovskaia, *Zhenskie siluèty* (St. Petersburg, 1912), 145–50.

16. A.V. Lunacharskii, "Zhurnal'nye zametki," *Obrazovanie* 5, 3 (1904): 151–55.

17. I. Ignatov, *Gallereia russkikh pisatelei* (Moscow, 1901), 573.

18. E.A. Koltonovskaia, "Tvorchestvo, utverzhdaiushchee zhizn'," *Obrazovanie* 9 (1907): 74–88.

19. Koltonovskaia, *Zhenskie siluèty*, 146–47.

20. Review of V.I. Dmitrieva, *Rasskazy* (St. Petersburg, 1913), in *Russkoe bogatstvo* 5 (1913): 325–26.

21. Kolotonovskaia, *Zhenskie siluèty*, 149–50.

22. Ibid., 210.

23. Mary Zirin, "Nazar'eva, Kapitolina Valer'ianovna," in *Dictionary of Russian Women Writers*, 453–54.

24. Aleksandr Blok, "O realistakh," *Sobranie sochinenii v shesti tomakh,* Vol. 5 (Moscow, 1971), 101.

25. Lasunskii cites provincialism as a major factor of her decline. Lasunskii, "Nado idti," 7. On the negative effects that living in the provinces had on women's literary careers, see Mary Zirin, "Women's Prose Fiction in the Age of Realism," in *Women Writers in Russian Literature*, 78.

26. V.I. Dmitrieva, "Avtobiografia," in *Povesti i rasskazy,* Vol. 1 (Petrograd, 1916), 50.

27. Lasunskii, "Nado idti," 26–27.

28. A.V. Priamkov, "Valentina Iovovna Dmitrieva i ee knigi," in V.I. Dmitrieva, *Povesti i rasskazy* (Moscow, 1976), 6.

29. Koltonovskaia, "Tvorchestvo . . .," 76.

Translator's Notes to the Selected Work

1. *fel'dsher*—medical assistant or paramedic; from the German *Feldscher*. Because of the shortage of physicians, *fel'dshers* were indispensable in prerevolutionary Russia and often had to practice medicine on their own even though only trained to serve as assistants.

2. *zemstvo*—The *zemstvo* system of local self-government, introduced in Russia in 1864, was responsible for public health and provided free rural clinics to peasants.

3. Uncle—Russian children call all adults (even those unrelated to them) "Aunt" and "Uncle." In this story Khves'ka calls both the narrator and the *fel'dsher* "Uncle."

Bibliography

Primary Works

"Suda prosit'." 1877.

"Po dushe, da ne po razumu." *Russkaia mysl'* 4 (1880).

"Akhmetkina zhena." *Russkoe bogatstvo* 1 (1881): 1–59.

"Ot sovesti." *Russkaia mysl'* 3 (1882): 60–92. [Rpt. St. Petersburg, 1898.]

"V tikhom omute." *Delo* 6 (1882): 1610–12.

"V raznye storony." *Russkaia mysl'* 3 (1883): 182–219; 4 (1883): 120–51.

"Zlaia volia." *Delo* 4 (1883): 1696–97; 5 (1883): 1702–03; 6 (1883): 1712–13; 7 (1883): 1718–19; 8 (1883): 1726–27.

"Tiur'ma." *Vestnik Evropy* 8 (1887): 543–96; 9 (1887): 5–67; 10 (1887): 502–63.

"Svoim sudom. Iz vospominanii sel'skoi uchitel'nitsy." *Severnyi vestnik* 1 (1888): 93–134.

Derevenskie rasskazy. Moscow, 1892.

Gomochka. Severnyi vestnik 8 (1894): 260–80; 9 (1894): 1–44; 10 (1894): 65–98.

"Mitiukha—uchitel'." 1896.

"Po derevniam. Iz zametok vracha." *Vestnik Evropy* 10 (1896): 521–65.

Rasskazy. St. Petersburg, 1896.

Pod solntsem iuga. Vestnik Evropy 8 (1899): 582–633; 9 (1899): 5–56; 10 (1899): 437–90.

Chervonnyi khutor. Vestnik Evropy 3 (1900): 3–6; 4 (1900): 186–566; 5 (1900): 5–92; 6 (1900): 421–96. [Rpt. St. Petersburg, 1912 and Kharkov, 1925.]

"Ee vse znaiut. Iz zametok zemskogo vracha." *Vestnik Evropy* 12 (1900): 707–20.

[Novokreshchenskii, o. Ioann.] *Lipochka-popovna.* Paris, 1902. [Rpt. Berlin, 1904 and Rostov-on-Don, 1905.]

[Vol'nyi, Ivan.] "Za veru, tsaria i otechestva." London: 1902. [Rpt. Berlin, 1904 and Moscow, 1906.]

"Tuchki." *Russkoe bogatstvo* 1 (1904): 59–113; 2 (1904): 1–61.

Rasskazy. St. Petersburg, 1906.

Povesti i rasskazy. St. Petersburg, 1909.

"Razboiniki." *Russkoe bogatstvo* 10 (1909): 80–114; 11 (1909): 13–44.

Goriun i drugie rasskazy dlia detei. Moscow, 1910. [Rpt. 1913 and 1915.]

Veshnii tsvet. St. Petersburg, 1911.

Rasskazy. St. Petersburg, 1913.

Povesti i rasskazy. 3 vols. Petrograd, 1916.

Gorit Rossiia. Moscow, 1924. [Rpt. Moscow, 1930.]

"Teni proshlogo." *Katorga i ssylka* 2 (1924): 28–45; 4 (1924): 111–23.

Tak bylo. Put' moei zhizni. Moscow: Molodaia gvardiia, 1930.

Povesti i rasskazy. Moscow, 1976.

Povesti. Rasskazy. Voronezh, 1983.

Povesti i rasskazy. Krasnodar, 1986.

"Pchely zhuzhzhat." *Tol'ko chas: Proza russkikh pisatel'nits kontsa XIX-nachala XX veka*. Ed. V.V. Uchenova. Moscow, 1988. 259–316.

In Translation

Le terroriste. Trans. G. Savitch and E. Jaubert. Paris, 1912 [a translation of *Chervonnyi khutor*].

Love's Anvil: A Romance of Northern Russia. Trans. Douglas Ashby. London, 1921 [a translation of *Gomochka*].

Secondary Works

Azarova, N.I., and P.I. Ovcharova. "Dmitrieva Valentina Iovovna." *Russkie pisateli 1800–1917*. Ed. P.A. Nikolaev. Vol. 2. Moscow, 1990. 129–31.

Clyman, Toby W. "Women Physicians' Autobiography in the Nineteenth Century." *Women Writers in Russian Literature.* Ed. Toby Clyman and Diana Greene. Westport, CT: Greenwood Press, 1994. 111–25.

Davies, Mildred. "Dmitrieva, Valentina Iovovna." *Dictionary of Russian Women Writers*. Ed. Marina Ledkovsky, Charlotte Rosenthal and Mary Zirin. Westport, CT: Greenwood Press, 1994. 151–54.

———. "Elizabet Smit i Valentina Dmitrieva: zhizn' i deiatel'nost' kanadskoi i russkoi zhenshchin-vrachei v kontse XIX veka." *Otechestvennaia istoriia* 6 (November–December 1994): 209–15.

Dobryv, A.P. "V.I. Dmitrieva." *Biografii russkikh pisatelei srednego i novogo perioda*. Ed. A.P. Dobryv. St. Petersburg, 1900. 140.

Engel, Barbara Alpern. *Mothers and Daughters: Women of the Intelligentsia in Nineteenth-Century Russia*. Cambridge: Cambridge University Press, 1983. 156–72.

Ignatov, I. *Gallereia russkikh pisatelei*. Moscow, 1901. 573.

Kelly, Catriona. *A History of Russian Women's Writing 1820–1992*. Oxford: Clarendon Press, 1994. 121–152.

Koltonovskaia, E.A. "Tvorchestvo, utverzhdaiushchee zhizn'." *Obrazovanie* 9 (1907): 74–88.

———. *Zhenskie siluèty*. St. Petersburg, 1912.

Lasunskii, O.G. "Dva psevdonima pisatel'nitsy V.I. Dmitrievoi." *Vlast' knigi: Rasskazy o knigakh i knizhnikakh*. 2d ed. Moscow, 1980. 34–46.

———. "'Nado idti . . . i zhit'." *Povesti. Rasskazy*. By V.I. Dmitrieva. Voronezh, 1983. 5–27.

Ledkovsky, Martha, Charlotte Rosenthal and Mary Zirin, eds. *Dictionary of Russian Women Writers*. Westport, CT: Greenwood Press, 1994.

Priamkov, A.V. "Valentina Iovovna Dmitrieva i ee knigi." *Povesti i rasskazy*. By V.I. Dmitrieva. Moscow, 1976. 5–22.

Sotrudniki russkikh vedomostei 1863–1913. Moscow, 1913. 62 [bibliography].

Uchenova, V.V. *Tol'ko chas: Proza russkikh pisatel'nits kontsa XIX-nachala XX veka*. Moscow, 1988. 8–9, 586.

"V.I. Dmitrieva." *Istoriia russkoi literatury XIX v. Bibliograficheskii ukazatel'*. Ed. K.D. Muratova. Moscow, 1962. 290–91 [bibliography].

"V.I. Dmitrieva." *Slovar' chlenov obshchestva liubitelei russkoi slovesnosti pri Moskovskom universitete, 1811–1911*. Moscow, 1911. 99–100 [bibliography].

Vladislavlev'-Gul'binskii, I.V. *Russkie pisateli. Opyt bibliograficheskogo posobiia po russkoi literature XIX-XX stoletii*. 4th ed. Moscow, 1924. 48 [bibliography].

Zirin, Mary. "Dmitrieva, Valentina Iovovna." *Modern Encyclopedia of Russian and Soviet Literature*. Ed. Harry B. Weber. Vol. 5. Gulf Breeze, FL: Academie International, 1977. 79–180.

———. "Women's Prose Fiction in the Age of Realism." *Women Writers in Russian Literature*. Ed. Toby Clyman and Diana Greene. Westport, CT: Greenwood Press, 1994. 77–94.

Ol'ga Forsh

A benevolent heretic and no stranger to self-parody, Ol'ga Dmitrievna Forsh (1873–1961) would have appreciated the irony that her reputation as a writer was preserved by the Soviet literary establishment in the canon of social-realist historical narrative. Although considered a difficult and demanding stylist, her assimilation was made easy by the acceptable surface of her major novels—revolutionary themes with dramatic characters in conflict with the oppressive institutions of imperial Russia. She was forgiven "errors" of idealism and fictional melodrama that distracted from history's epic progress toward the proletarian state.

The official stamp of approval has, unfortunately, obscured some of the interesting and more original aspects of her fiction. Her choice of heroes, for example, was more problematic than easy familiarity would suggest—Aleksandr Radishchev and the Decembrists, Russia's first revolutionaries. They were writers and poets, artists and architects—men of culture and intellect who did not readily submit to institutionally propagated truths. Her works were also thematically at variance with official positivism. In Forsh's universe, uncritical dedication to a guiding principle or idea could cripple talent and the human soul as readily as uncertainty as to "in what name" one acted. Other, more radical readings of universal and modern Russian history and the nature of authority lay at the core of Forsh's mature work in the 1920s and early 1930s. In the face of mounting pressure for artistic and political conformity, she boldly asserted her right to a creative vision "unalarmed by logic" and seeking "to explode the border posts of time" and difference. These were crucial tenets of Forsh's "expansive realism," her answer to calls from the Left for a version of realism commensurate with the new order.[1] Among the first of her contemporaries to recognize the contingent nature of the artistic text, she challenged her readers to become collaborators in the act of creation, and to find in art a vehicle for personal and communal transformation.

Forsh's personal philosophy of history had roots in the cultural and philosophical "revolution of the spirit" that motivated the artistic and spiritual probings of her own and a succeeding generation of Russians—even inspiring "God-seeking" on the political left.[2] Nevertheless, it was probably domestic concerns supplying conflict in her early novels—the search for a partner who would amplify and liberate, rather than impede progress toward self-realization—that account for the popularity of her work in the Stalin era. Soviet literature was increasingly dominated by cardboard model workers and party activists. Even when the tendency to proselytize intruded on her later fiction, and lively dialogue gave way to discursive tableaux, the human motivations and conflicts of her idealized revolutionaries still rang true. Few of Forsh's narratives were directly anchored in a woman's point of view and the position of women in Russian society was usually an ancillary issue. Yet the concerns raised by the "woman question," the struggle for women's emancipation and the need to temper reason with feminine "emotional sense" are omnipresent and critical to a reading of Forsh.

Forsh chose writing as her profession when she was in her late thirties. Her career embraced fifty years of Russian literature, including nearly four decades of the Soviet period—years during which her contributions were both celebrated and reviled. Accounts of Forsh's childhood engender pathos—a tendency that she fiercely resisted with sometimes caustic humor. Ol'ga's father, General Dmitrii Vissarionovich Komarov, was Military Governor in Central Daghestan in the Caucasus at the time of her birth. Her mother (née Shakheddionova), an Armenian woman about whom little is known, died in 1873 when Ol'ga was only a few months old. The Petersburg woman hired by her father to care for his three children was apparently only perfunctory in her affection, and that for only as long as it took to persuade their father to marry her. After their father's death in 1881, the stepchildren were parceled off to boarding schools. There are signs in a reflective youthful diary of a painfully lonely childhood, as in her fiction there is an often unspoken empathy for those estranged from love, life and family. When suicide became a persistent motif in her work, it was more than just an echo of public discussion at the turn of the century of a contemporary "epidemic" of suicides in Russia. It was not the act of will evoked by Dostoevsky, but an inarticulate expression of despair and a radical defiance of logic.[3]

Forsh wrested from that sorry childhood an independence of spirit and expansive inner life spurred by hours of reading in her school's library. Perhaps Forsh's teachers modeled a more autonomous life, but the primary goal of women's educational institutions in the 1880s was still to inculcate the prevailing values of court society—an essential orthodoxy that is unmasked in her first novel *Clad in Stone* (*Odety Kamnem*, 1925). There was no one with any authority she recognized to say "no" to her unconventional aspiration to become an artist.[4] When she received her diploma at eighteen, she became eligible for her father's military pension. For five years she used the income to study and travel on her own. She went first to Kiev to enroll in a school of drawing, then Warsaw, then Odessa. In 1895 she enrolled in the St. Petersburg studio of P.P. Chistakov, a teacher whose influence would extend far beyond the few months she studied with him. Chistakov taught his students that only through mastery of the techniques of their predecessors would they learn to see in their own way. The repercussions of his advice are evident both in the role that literary stylization plays in the composition of her narratives and in her sense of responsibility as an artist.[5]

After her marriage to Boris Eduardovich Forsh in September 1895, Ol'ga had to surrender her pension. Although she was publicly reticent about her years of domesticity, clearly the diverse impressions of those years helped to shape the literary consciousness and preoccupations of the artist who had yet to find her enabling medium. There were nine difficult years as a military wife, first in the countryside of Poland and then later outside Kiev.[6] In 1904 Forsh's husband resigned from the army to protest its wanton administration of the death penalty—a gesture that she, no doubt, applauded. A shared enthusiasm for populist ideas and a search for Tolstoyan simplicity led Forsh, her husband and two children to seek out a more self-sufficient life in the countryside. When the family venture proved unsustainable, they returned to Kiev and the exhilarating currents of modernism, political radicalism and social idealism that had impelled Russia toward its first popular revolution in late 1905. Forsh's concern that so little of this cultural renaissance was reflected in children's literature was addressed when the Forshes found a creative and unconventional solution to their domestic difficulties. From 1906 to 1910 they joined their household with that of another struggling young professional couple, Evgenii and Elizaveta Kuzmin. Their alliance was also fused by common interests in theosophy and a commitment to explore the educative possibilities of art. An unexpected display of generosity from her stepmother gave Forsh the means to undertake her first trip to Europe in 1907. She traveled alone to Paris, Venice, Rome and Munich, most probably arriving there on the eve of the Second Conference of the International Theosophical Society held in May 1907. After her return, Forsh became an active member of the Kiev branch of the newly formed Russian Theosophical Society.[7] The organizers of the society believed that "a great synthesis embracing religion and science," translatable through art, would restore eternal beauty and harmony to human society.

Two "philosophical" fairy tales by Forsh were published in the society's journal in 1908. She also wrote several tales and a review of the life and teachings of Buddha for *Morning of Life*, a short-lived magazine for young people to which she and Kuzmin jointly contributed.

A restless intellect soon propelled Forsh in other directions. Her earliest stories bear the trace of efforts to work through a naive apprenticeship to Dostoevsky, theosophy and Russian Symbolism. Her impassioned but ineptly realized first novella, *The Knight of Nurenburg* (*Rytsar' iz Niurenberga*, 1908), was written under the impression of the mystical dualisms of Dmitrii Merezhkovskii's philosophical novels and a romantic interpretation of vampirism. A puzzled critical reception heightened her own realization of the narrative's weaknesses. Her use of a popular folk image in "Pursuing the Firebird" ("Za zhar-ptitsei," 1910) to evoke the tragic gap between the creative urges of the peasantry and their ability to express them won her first favorable professional notice. Forsh thought it flawed because the execution was not as persuasive as the concept—a difficulty that would continue to haunt her writing over the years. She preferred an earlier story, "He Was a General" ("Byl general,"1908). This story reveals a self-consciously modernist fascination with madness but is anchored in realistic detail and speech. It was one of the first expressions of her evolving view that the path to self-discovery lay in deviation from "normal" and conventional truth.[8]

By 1913, at a time when many women of her generation were moving into the background of public and private life, Forsh was beginning to find her voice: "It was as if turning forty was the beginning of a new era, the arrival of my second birth—in literature," she later wrote.[9] The Forsh family moved to St. Petersburg. Ol'ga renewed her acquaintance with Chistakov and sought out teaching opportunities in innovative private schools in Tsarskoe Selo—work that would lead to her first employment after the revolution in the Division of School Reform. She elaborated activities and skits that were intended to develop the children's imaginative faculties. These experiences practically grounded her theoretical embrace of a notion of art as a collaborative relationship between author and audience.[10] Critical writing became another vehicle for self-examination. Review articles she published in 1914 challenged the fashionable abstractions of Russia's apostles of symbolism. Forsh's answer to the generally acknowledged "crisis" was to recommend that universal visions be grounded once again in "real human feeling," in prosaic or sensual detail that could awaken a "reciprocity" of experience among readers.[11]

The October Revolution of 1917 brought its measure of personal tragedy to Forsh, but with it also came recognition as a writer and a fertile shift toward more historical concerns.[12] Forsh's husband died shortly after his release from a Red Army unit in December 1919. Her work on plans for a People's Academy of the Arts required a move first to Moscow in mid–1918, and then to Kiev in May 1919. Repeated occupation of the city cut short her professional ambitions. All through the years of war and revolution (1914–1917), Forsh worked on the novel *Oglasshennye* (*Filled with the Resounding Word*). Although the novel remained unpublished, as one informed reader observed, it had many "daughters."[13] One of these was a story drawn from the novel's central characters that appeared in 1925 as "Comrade Pful'" ("Tovarishch Pful'"). The conflicts the novel described between dedication to an artistic ideal and personal ambition and happiness were extended in the story to encompass the choices prompted by war and the Russian revolution. The story illustrates, in somewhat schematic form, key elements of Forsh's artistic vision. Forsh pushed the boundaries of a popular genre, the historical romance, to incorporate the demands of the novel of ideas. Narrative point of view is shared by the two protagonists: Valia, a young woman of privilege, determined to assert women's right to contribute to the world; and Melovoi, a working-class man whose artistic talent has given him an opportunity to escape his background. Their first meeting in a Kiev art studio was thwarted by their own prejudice and unyielding principles; their second, by Comrade Pful's dogmatic vision of the goals of the revolution. The logical links of Melovoi's anguished reconstruction of the events are deliberately suppressed when Valia's account is introduced. Her story emerges in feverish, hallucinatory recollections of events that led her to join a band of rebel partisans and, finally, to surrender to Melovoi. Her dramatic monologue draws in the temperamentally unsusceptible Comrade Pful'. Seduced by the affective power of her narrative, Pful' becomes a collaborator in the fiction that the past can become present once again. The melodramatic conclusion is a tragic one—Pful', reflexively suspecting her of complicity in the escape attempt of a fellow partisan, shoots her, but only as she is taking her own life by throwing herself out the window of Melovoi's room.

Although Forsh's later fiction seldom gave such immediate access to the woman's point of view, she was at pains in all of her work to demonstrate that ethical concerns were central to the actions of her exemplary characters, male and female alike. Valia's determination "to overcome nature" and "spread feelings by virtue of will" challenged contemporary ideas about the nature of woman recently propagated by Austrian psychologist Otto Weininger. Weininger, whose name is invoked in the text, had confessed that the entire structure of his argument would crumble "if only one single female creature [. . .] could be shown to have a real relationship to the idea of personal moral worth."[14] In "Comrade

Pful'," Valia's choice to become an artist is an act of self-definition and of disinterested sacrifice: "The time has come," she writes, "for woman to contribute all her tenderness and unselfish feelings to the treasury of the world."

If Valia's determination to speak was interrupted, Forsh's was not. In mid-1920 Forsh made the hazardous trip to St. Petersburg, then called Petrograd. She visited a city and a society that was uncertain whether it was witnessing the end of life and art or the birth of its new forms.[15] In lectures that she offered in Petrograd from 1920 to 1922, she began to elaborate her views of the tasks of the artist in a collectively organized, socialist society. She believed that a true community could emerge only from the growth of its individual members. Forsh embarked on a campaign to educate and empower the individual reader that would put her at increasing odds with proponents of proletarian art and Marxist orthodoxy in the 1920s. Like many members of the prewar intelligentsia, Forsh was indebted to the postrevolutionary literary enterprises of Maxim Gorky.[16] She was given her own room in Petrograd's House of Arts. In spite of illness, hunger and paralyzing cold, she began to write furiously—short stories, a play and a movie scenario that became the germ of Soviet literature's first historical novel, *Clad in Stone,* published in 1923. The following years, to 1933, were similarly productive, yielding four novels, three dramas, four collections of stories and a number of critical essays. Although she was chided for forays into idealism, the critics in party-sponsored journals and publishing houses of the middle 1920s were relatively tolerant of work that constructively reflected the birth pangs of the new order and a revolutionary look at the past. Her stories offered perceptive descriptions of the lives and everyday trials of her contemporaries. Otherwise grim tales are leavened by her appreciation of the human comedy in a self-consciously epic era.[17]

The title of the widely celebrated novel *Clad in Stone* alludes to the real fate of the imprisoned revolutionary Mikhail Beideman and to the burden of complicity in Beideman's arrest that robs the fictional narrator Rusanin of his sanity. The novel was Forsh's first attempt to enact her innovative ideas for an "expansive realism"—to trace the broadening ripple of an event or idea through time and individual consciousness. Rusanin survives to witness the realization of Beideman's dream, sixty years after his arrest. Problematic anachronisms arise when Forsh tries to bridge the gaps in Rusanin's biography by weaving into the events of the 1860s Rusanin's meeting with a willful courtesan and an out-of-body experience resonant of the decadent 1890s.[18] Forsh intended not only to evoke the ethical problem faced by her central characters—how to act in the face of tyranny—but to confront the reader with the ambiguities that bedevil moral choices. *Clad in Stone* also contains an intriguing portrait of a fictional noblewoman, Katia, who joins

Beideman's cause. Katia remains a half-realized figure in the shadows of Rusanin's devoted but uncomprehending account of her life. Her character initiated a line of principally male figures in Forsh's fiction who illustrate the belief that class or social background are not inescapable constraints on personal, ethical growth. Her example is provocatively cast against that of Rusanin, who has suppressed the feminine and artistic side of his nature and fails to realize his human potential.

Forsh's efforts to popularize historical fiction also signaled the beginning of an ambitious, if more covert, dialogue with the symbolist Andrei Belyi, whose views on the universal compass of art she in large part approved.[19] In *Petersburg*, Belyi, she believed, had brilliantly but tragically "summed up" nineteenth-century Russian literature and the fate of the Russian intellectual. Will and reason were undone by their own emptiness. So, too, was the central character of her next novel, *Contemporaries* (*Sovremmeniki,* 1926). *Contemporaries* eschewed overt links to Russia of the 1920s. Forsh relied on her reader's acumen and the title to suggest the relevance of her themes to postrevolutionary Russia. The inner struggles of two friends, writer Nikolai Gogol and painter Aleksandr Ivanov, provide the symbolic, historical background against which the individual destiny of the central fictional character Bagretsov is played out. Most of the events of the novel take place in Italy. Ivanov's struggles to put the dictums of the academy aside and pursue his own vision of a universal art are paralleled by Italy's struggle for national self-realization, leading to the revolution of 1848. Bagretsov's life is intertwined with Ivanov's through common calling and with Gogol's as an impressionable reader of Gogol's fiction. As befitting the literary authorities against whom the work is pitched, tragic fugue ultimately shades into operetta. Bagretsov discovers that the crime that has distorted his life and killed his talent was not, in fact, committed by him. Unable to bear this humiliation, Bagretsov spurns another's love, impelling her to suicide—and his own mirrored, phantom image then mocks his hopes for redemption.

A failed uprising was the setting of a second novel, *Hot Shop* (*Goriachii tsekh*), also published in 1926. The exemplary lives and inner struggles of the idealistic young heroes who are drawn into the events of 1905 in Russia play out a vision of what that revolution might have been. The knowledge of likely failure in the present is ennobled by a communal spirit that links strangers in certain movement toward the future. Appeals to historical optimism only partly blunted growing critical dissatisfaction on the Left with Forsh's writing. Demands for more direct subservience to the program and goals of the Communist party became sharper after the revolution's tenth anniversary and the onset of a new era of "cultural revolution."

Nowhere did Forsh more forcefully demonstrate her own "real relationship to the idea of personal moral worth" than in *Crazy Ship* (*Sumasshedshii korbabl',* 1930). It is the work in which she gave fullest rein to her own creative personality and her vision of "expansive realism." It is both a work of autobiographical fiction and an audacious summing up of her generation that the label *roman à clef* hardly does justice. The narrative's nine complex chapters tease out the complicated relationship of what she saw as the source of her own and her readers' authority—a personal and creative relationship to everyday events from whose rhythms universal truths arise. Although set in the House of Arts in Petrograd of 1920–1921, Forsh interweaves a poet's funeral in 1926, observations from a trip to France and Italy in 1927 and the work of Communist party iconographers upon Gorky's return to Russia in 1928. Forsh writes herself into the novel as the struggling woman writer, Doliva. Although Doliva's "feminism" and earnest purpose are humorously parodied, her creative voyages are not. Subsequent "restoration" in the Soviet era had already begun to "deface" the promising legacy of the House of Arts, where Doliva and other Soviet artists were once fortunate to have resided. The visible and foreseeable signs of these changes motivate discussions in the central chapters between an older and younger writer about the meaning of art for Soviet Russia. In the final chapter (or "wave"), enumerating the four cornerstones of prewar culture, the author names the peasant poet Kliuev as the fourth (after Blok, Belyi and Gorky). This unusual choice was, in part, a programmatic one: Kliuev's verse represented the self-creative, radical and feminine spirit in Russian literature.[20] History, Forsh believed, would come to recognize the necessity of that choice. She had the same confidence in her readers: "We write without regard to the 'readiness' or 'unreadiness' of the reader. This is a sign of our genuine respect for him. Not ready today, he will be ready tomorrow."[21] Critics on the left were skeptical and heavy-handed, although surprisingly astute in their assessment of her intentions. Publicists allied with the Russian Association of Proletarian Writers (RAPP) used the publication of *Crazy Ship* as an occasion to attack all writers who had failed to recognize the "great dawn of construction" of the new proletarian world. "Bourgeois" views of art and culture were to be unmasked so that "all theories and views harmful to the working class could be utterly routed."[22]

Hostilities abated briefly after the banning of RAPP and the creation of a single, "harmonious" Union of Soviet Writers in 1932. Forsh was allowed to publish two new novels she had been working on since the end of the 1920s. *The Symbolists* (*Voron. Simvolisty,* 1934) was her final application to "expansive realism"—a story within a story, juxtaposing the lives of pre- and postrevolutionary Russians. Forsh extended the traditional Russian motif of conflict between fathers and children to include mothers and daughters. The consequences of the ideas of symbolism for a generation of "trusting readers" that perceived symbolism not as a literary school but as a form of conduct, an attempt to blow up reality, were set against the accomplishments of the ideologically inspired rationalism of their children whose certainty in their "new faith" was beset with ethical blind spots. Critics rejected the latter hypothesis. In contrast, *Jacobin Ferment* (*Iakobinskii zakvas,* 1934) was greeted with enthusiasm for the new "historicism" of a narrative that focused on real rather than fictional events and characters. It and two succeeding novels, *Landed Lady of Kazan'* (*Kazanskaia pomeshchitsa*, 1936) and *The Fateful Book* (*Pagubnaia kniga,* 1939), traced the development of social and political thought in eighteenth-century Russia. (The three were subsequently christened the *Radishchev Trilogy* [*Radishchev*, 1939].) As in most of Forsh's novels, there was no single hero. The conflict emerged in the differing personal choices—for self or for others—made by Radishchev and his distinguished contemporaries. Her pedagogical intention tended to turn Radishchev, in particular, into just a mouthpiece for Forsh's favorite ideas about the interdependent development of culture and personality. Her supporters noted with dismay that the more interesting and vital portraits of Radishchev's antagonists, Catherine the Great and General Potemkin, were in danger of eclipsing those of its exemplary figures.

After 1938 and thirty years of literary activity, the range and tempo of Forsh's work diminished. This might be explained by her age (she was sixty-five); but Forsh had a well-deserved reputation for perpetual, combative youthfulness. Her interests trespassed on forbidden territory. In 1936 her play on the Georgian revolutionary Kamo was abruptly withdrawn from the program of the Leningrad State Theater, in all likelihood at Stalin's insistence.[23] In 1937 she published a play called *One Hundred Twenty-Second* (*Stodvadtsat' vtoraia*) after the article of a new constitution guaranteeing equal rights for women. Forsh had become more adept at cloaking her message in ostensible orthodoxy, but the play's theme—women's struggle for liberation—was at odds with the regime's decision to reassert traditional family values and the warrior ethos of high Stalinism.[24] The acceleration of Stalin's terror in 1937 and the arrest and disappearance of prominent writers and literary figures muted Forsh, as it had chastened or silenced others.

The novel *Mikhailovskii Castle* (*Mikhailovskii zamok*, 1946), a play based on the life of Maxim Gorky, and the autobiographical stories published from 1941 to 1946 were the offspring of the brief literary thaw that accompanied Russia's participation in World War Two. Forsh once again found the energy to work under extremely difficult conditions and poor health, evacuated from her beloved

St. Petersburg to makeshift housing in Sverdlovsk. *Mikhailovskii Castle* (named after the St. Petersburg landmark) is a partial return to Forsh's earlier pattern of historical novel. However, the lives of her historical personalities and fictional characters, men and women, are rendered with less palatable sentimental and didactic overtones. The novel begins in the reign of the reactionary tsar Paul I and celebrates the influence of the artistic vision of the architect Carlo Rossi. His life and the legacy of his Russian colleagues Bazhenov and Voronikhin and their students embody the novel's central idea—that creative and original ideas of value, even when they do not find adequate artistic expression or a receptive audience, are not lost to history or the cultural life of a nation.[25]

The first part of Forsh's final novel, *First Born of Freedom* (*Perventsy svobody*), was published in 1950, on the heels of a new round of purges and political witch-hunts. The full text was released only in 1953, the year of her eightieth birthday. Although her overview of the political discussions and personal choices faced by the noblemen who joined in secret societies and participated in Russia's first abortive revolt against imperial authority is convincing, her figures resemble mere static bas-relief. Only the concluding chapters describing the Decembrist uprising, including the imprisonment and sentencing of the Decembrists, have real dramatic qualities. The portraits of the duplicitous and vengeful Nicholas and his predecessor Alexander I invite comparison to the tyrant who had held Russia in his grasp until 1953. Forsh struggled to remain true to her belief, voiced by Ivanov in *Contemporaries*, that it is the artist's calling to "preserve the face of mankind" from the systematic and individual cruelties that threaten to erase it. The warmth and apparent universality of the public greetings that accompanied the celebration of her birthday in the month following the death of Joseph Stalin in April 1953 were, perhaps, an expression of hope for renewal of the legacy that she represented to her contemporaries.[26]

Forsh's final collection of largely autobiographical stories, *Yesterday and Today* (*Vchera i segodnia*), appeared in 1959. In 1958 she had affirmed a wish to address a theme she believed she had too long deferred: "I would still like to speak about women, to say what I have long and deeply considered [. . .] about questions of motherhood and the unique traits of women that are evoked not only by the conditions of their lives, but by the very nature of woman, her role on earth."[27] In her own way she had been pursuing that conversation for over three decades. The histories written during Forsh's lifetime had few pages for women's lives and seldom even recognized their actions as historical. Writing women back into history required an act of imagination. Forsh followed her intuition, her "own way of seeing," and proceeded against the current and critics who censured her for populating her historical novels with "fictional" characters. For Ol'ga Forsh, the necessities of compromise in choice of subject and style during the years of Soviet Russian literature were mitigated by her affinity for revolutionary themes. While the leveling hand of Stalinist institutions and the limits of her own talent frustrated her creative ambitions, they did not mute her "creative optimism." Forsh's work has not received much attention since the 1960s, and her readership has probably been limited by the unavailability of some of her more provocative narratives. However, with the republication of *Crazy Ship* and other stories that were once proscribed, critics are beginning to acknowledge her unique contributions to modern Russian literature.[28]

Martha Hickey

The Suitcase

I.

From north to south, like the sudden fall of snow on a passerby's head, Maria Ivanovna and her son Kolia collapsed onto her godfather's last unoccupied couch. For two days they ate and ate, saying all the while:

"This is not your seed cake, not roach, not horse-head. . . . "

"The professors are fine ones, too. You know they've discovered 'edible wild plants.' . . . Go ahead, Kolia dear, recite!"

"Blowweed, puffweed, milkweed, lion's tooth, dandelion and so on. . . ."[1]

"If it were just the hunger," said Maria Ivanovna, weeping quietly, as if astonished at what they had endured. "But the c-o-old! A degree below freezing is not a degree above. Above, at least you can sleep in a fur coat, and your nose is out of danger. . . . "

"Well, you just stay a while, lap up our home brew. It's not honey either!"

Godfather was as black as the devil, his arching brows not brows at all but the extension of a mustache that traveled, without much ado, from under his nose up over his eyes, while below the nose, where the razor had its way, was clean shaven and blue. Suddenly Godfather got angry; those Moscow rascals were bad, but there was disorder here, too.

"Yes, we've got pancakes now—because we sold our gramophone for a song. The little machine '*that plays itself and sings*'[2] is all the rage in the village. They won't even look at anything else anymore; they've each got two samovars—one for tea, one for coffee. They've made out well. . . . "

"My lordy, how they line up before the carts," the child's nurse chimed in. "Teachers 'n' ladies tramp around in the mud, while *herself* sits on her sacks like a peahen. Single file, they go, like they're on their way to heaven, worldly goods up over their heads, and she—that's not wanted, not wanted! How about somethin' *more interestin'*? Fixes her eye on people, whips through them: '*That one!*' A sorry sight. The next in line—pale as ash, glasses, a scholar type—bolts like a rabbit cornered in its burrow over to the sacks, scatters his crosses and his prize medal, too—for a measly little potato."

"If they're lining up, it means they trust the money." Her godfather pulled out his wallet. "The new government's got itself settled, no shooting for three months—or maybe it didn't suit them before? The devil knows how many different currencies we've got, but not a one's in use." And with a magician's sleight of hand he displayed a deck of bank notes before Maria Ivanovna—the Petliura white one, the Rada State "caterpillar," *srulik*, paper change *butterflies*, Denikin's boyar lady, and big-nosed Kostiushka.[3] "We've had sis'teen governments in three years' time," for some reason the nurse explained proudly. It's all the same to some what the occasion is, so long as there's something to boast about.

"The guns have taught our little Vania how to talk. Go on, Vania, tell your godmother about government turnovers."

The toddler, Vania, perched on his nurse's lap, threw back his large head and put his finger in his cheek: "Zh-zh-zh-poo!" Opening his eyes wide, he let out with all his might, "Tra-ta-ta . . . ta-ta."

"Machine guns!" declared his father with approval.

But suddenly it dawned on Maria Ivanovna—there were no ration cards here. How would they live? Sell their things? That miserable suitcase was all they had. And it still had to be fetched.

"They wouldn't check my suitcase all the way through when we changed trains," she said aloud. "They gave me a receipt only as far as this outlying town, and then some man there with the rebel forces ordered it off the train. I don't want to go myself. Couldn't you hire someone?"

Maria Ivanovna felt for the hidden place where she had sewn the receipt and her money, blanched and dashed into the other room. She threw off her dress and undergarments, shook them and ran her fingers over every inch—good as lost. Everything had been cut out; all that was left were a few dangling threads.

Her godfather consoled her as best he could. "Only the foolhardy are adherents of travel by rail. The notion of pockets, mine and yours, is a relic of the past, and there's the devil's own crush of people. Like it or not—you stew. According to logic, the suitcase should be left to rest in peace."

But Maria Ivanovna suddenly drew herself up, like an eagle over its nestling: "And Kolia should freeze again this winter? I will find the suitcase!"

"Don't you see, logically. . . . "

"Nothing's logical now!"

"That may be so. A professor of mathematics 'bakes bread for the surplus weight.'[4] Another poor fool in your Petersburg or Moscow swells up without a scholar's ration, yet goes on writing. The chairman of the Poor Peasant's Committee finagles a ration for guess who—a tapeworm! One way or another, my worm eats up everything, he reports. Give me two rations. No one questions it. He gets one for himself and one for the worm. So a vile invertebrate feeds like any other citizen."

"Nothing's logical now," laments Maria Ivanovna, and there is no more anger or bluster in her words. Just a trickle of tears. She's a little woman with a small face, the kind you glance at and then instantly forget. A face like any other. On her head sits a lace cap, yellowed with age, covering her topknot of hair.

"Nothing's logical. Our dear old granny, may she rest in peace, was an angel. All her life she did for others, even got ready for her own death, so as not to be a bother. She bought a plot, air from the Holy Sepulchre, a wreath, and put everything by. She had only one final wish—that white horses, not black, draw her to the funeral. A first-class funeral. Whose business was it? Granny never hurt a fly, people could have humored her. But how did it turn out, according to this, this logic? Granny died up on the stove. We used to heat the kitchen now and then. She climbed up, just to get warm once in a blue moon, and passed away. Little Kolia and I scurried from line to line for three days to get the coffin and the grave dug. Who could think of horses? No sooner did we get the papers than we lost them. When your head's spinning from hunger, you can't concentrate like you used to. We went back to the last official: 'You probably remember us, you just gave us permission.' 'Oh sure,' he says. 'You're burying your grandmother.' 'Well, just this minute, our paper and money were stolen,' I lied for the sake of appearances. 'No paperwork—start over!' says he. This late in the day, the lines are out into the street. Hundreds were dying from typhus. We tried to cut in, but no one let us. Their own dearly departed had gone stale. Get in line, get in line, they shouted. . . . Three more days we traipsed around and out in the cold granny's frozen solid. Even at the cemetery she was out of luck—had to get in line there, too. They kept her waiting outside a whole week. Coffin after coffin, all in a row, and the dogs come by sniffing. There's your first class!"

"So, spit logic in the eye and take yourself off to that town. I'll get you a paper with all the right seals," Godfather decided. "Make a list of your things."

No bluster, no anger. Maria Ivanovna drew herself into a tight, little lump and—just imagine—hoped. She made her list and set off for her favorite cathedral to pray for strength. She glanced up—a new signboard hung from the gate:

"Holy Sofia of Ukraine." And under the sign were two men—a Ukrainian and a Russian. What were they arguing about? About that same logic.

"You know, this is not the mother of countless namesakes, not the 17th of September, but *Pistis Sophia*—an abstract ideal, divine wisdom. It's not logical to Ukrainianize this; it's impossible."[5]

"If that's not possible, how then?"

"So we will write: Moscow Logos."

"Suit yourself."

"Where's the logic?"

"And what's that got to do with it?"

Maria Ivanovna was overjoyed: "This is my sign, a direction. I must go, and as for this logic—phooey."

II.

And her godfather did not dally. He got a document with the necessary and the unnecessary seals, and on a rainy day that boded well for the harvest, as they say, but not for the average citizen, Maria Ivanovna's godfather jostled her through to a railway carriage: "An old woman, Marinchikha, an acquaintance in the town—pay her a visit if you think of it. Find out about her sons. She has two of them."

The train was engulfed by swarms of people—buffer-riders and rooftop jockeys. Ordinary passengers hung artlessly out of its windows. Godfather managed to seize the weightless, tiny Maria Ivanovna and toss her, like a bomb, into a window that someone had lowered just for a minute.

Maria Ivanovna had scarcely vanished into the darkness when the window was pulled up and behind it rose a pile of angry, seemingly lopped-off heads, densely planted one on top of another, that slowly floated away from the station into the distance.

Toward morning they lumbered into the town. Maria Ivanovna went immediately to the baggage clerk. He poked his sleepy head through the little window. "Your receipt?" he asked.

"Can you imagine? It was stolen, but here's a paper. See the seals, Che-ka. . . . "[6]

The man did not even look. He extended his brawny fingers to the next in line. "Seals from Che-ka," Maria Ivanovna squeaked again.

The long mustache merely gave a twitch: "Take your seals and go home!"

"But all our winter clothes are in the suitcase, Kolia's and mine. . . . "

"Go home!" The line moved forward and Maria Ivanovna was crowded out.

It was now completely light. The poplars stirred in the breeze where she passed behind the station. A tidy little white house stood nearby, and people were drinking tea under the linden trees. The samovar had been polished to golden perfection. Catching sight of it, a large speckled hen with her downy brood rushed to the table to peck at the crumbs.

Maria Ivanovna calmed down and considered her situation: God gives even the chicken a way to get by. She should seek out the old woman Marinchikha, catch her breath at her place, and then things would look clearer.

An alley of lindens led into the town; to each side, a green meadow; and lining the road, *cottages* with vegetable gardens and cherry trees. A old man and his grandchildren were sitting on a broad bench by a wattle fence. The church bells were ringing for morning service. The old man unhurriedly removed his cap and, unhurriedly, made the sign of the cross.

Some girl drove out the geese; Maria Ivanovna counted ten. Up north a goose cost what a good trotter once brought. Should she tell her? Or else the silly girl would herd them around as if they were still worth only a few rubles: she stands there gawking, eyes on the lookout for berries. . . .

But it's so cheerful to see the geese and that girl; and, it's really true, there are pigs in that meadow—two mother pigs with their piglets.

"You've a real paradise here," Maria Ivanovna said to the stout *lass*. "Geese and piglets, too."

"The sow farrowed."

"Didn't ya' know sows farrow?" chuckled the old man.

"Yes, that's how it used to be; now everything is different."

"The sow always farrows in the spring," said the old man. "So it was, and so it will be!"

Maria Ivanovna sat down next to him on the bench.

"It's paradise here, Grandfather. Would be nice not to leave."

"*Where* can you go, when *every which way* people are fightin', everybody's plagued with the wait for their own death. . . . Why are they fightin'?"

"And what do you think, truly, Grandpa, why are people fightin'?"

"What should I think, I'm an o-old man." Avoiding her question, he looked again at the pig, drooping under the weight of her rosy piglets; and he said, as if to reproach someone, "So it was, and so it will be!"

"Where is Marinchikha's, not so far?" asked Maria Ivanovna, recalling her godfather's old woman.

"Not so far." The old man pointed beyond the lake. "She's planting radishes, she's got *handsome* radishes. . . ."

And he told her the way.

III.

The small lake is so clear that it looks as if the bottom has been swept and sprinkled with sand and someone has playfully filled it up with sky-blue water. There is a fisherman in a boat and green sweet flag growing along the bank. Not far off, clinging together in a half-circle, stand the houses of the town, each one like the next—white with blue shutters with a little garden of double hollyhocks.

The flowers are as big as a child's head—yellow, rose-colored, and some like flame, well, like the pure-gold necklaces worn by the young *lasses* going to church. There's a market here, too. The stalls sit on bricks assembled in a row, set down to last for a long time. Here they trade and there's a club and a live-performance newspaper.[7] There's no curiosity about things abroad, just their own local doings. One neighbor lady queries another: what's in the garden, how's the crop, how much did it bear, what did the worms eat, what did *those boys* carry off? The local people amaze Maria Ivanovna. "Maybe they don't even know what's going on in the world?" But then she remembers that the old man just as surely sits on his bench and looks at the pig and thinks. . . . Who on earth knows what he thinks?

Shop signs appear: "Soviet's Tailor"; under "*Barbershop,*" a postscript in chalk—"No haircuts for the bourgeois!" There is a big star in the market next to the cinema, and under it, "Rest for the Red Proletariat."

"So, is it always this quiet here? No one's been through here, no shooting?" Maria Ivanovna couldn't help asking the old women in the market.

"Course they've come," the women huffed, one after the other. "They've all come. . . . "

"Who's to say *who's next*!"

"*But what's it to us.* No matter. *Bang, bang, they shoot each other up at the station, you can hear them all over,* and then off they go."

"They kill the ones whose time has come."

"We had an engineer, thanks a lot; he got mad the town didn't pay up, so he up and moved the station two versts away, turned his back on the town. They cursed him good. Still, that station's time came, too."

"Were many people killed?" asked Maria Ivanovna.

"There were, all right. There's some killed in the war, and some killed now we're free of it. We live like people everywhere."

"How do you get to Marinchikha's?"

"Go on there 'round the bend, you turn and there's Marinchikha. She goes on plantin' radishes and waits for her sons. She's got good radishes, but she'll go on waitin' for her sons."

"One's with the Whites, the other with the Reds; maybe one's gone and killed the other."

"A mother'll go on waitin' 'til she dies."

"That's a mother for you."

IV.

Maria Ivanovna went through a gate hidden by fragrant honeysuckle and jasmine into old Marinchikha's front garden. On the porch was a *lass* in an embroidered shirt cracking sunflower seeds. "She's drinking tea in the back garden, *go on through*."

The balcony opening was enclosed by thick twine woven like a Japanese curtain; bindweed vines twisted up the screen's length from the ground to the roof. Dew sparkled in the deep chalices of its delicate flowers—white, rose and violet.

"Sit down, have some tea, maybe, some milk, too?" asked Marinchikha, pleased with the greeting from the city and the unknown guest. In passing, as she entered the storehouse, she pointed to branches heavily laden with plums. "They're so low to the ground; there'll be a bumper crop this summer!" On her return, she put out butter, jam in a bulbous pot and her famous radishes, "the pearl of her garden."

"I've already heard about your radishes," said Maria Ivanovna.

"It was probably old Grandpa. I've given him some for seed. One crop's finished, I plant another. I'm waiting for my sons. They both fancy my radishes."

Such great sadness appeared in the old face, like the light behind a transparent painting that summons the colors to life. Wrinkles were severely outlined, lips trembled.

"They were twins, you know," Marinchikha said very quietly. "It came out so wrong! Old folks say God gives twins the same soul, but brother went after brother. When the White Army takes our town, I look for mine among the Red Army dead; when the Reds take us, I search among the Whites. I still haven't gone after the last; they're lying five versts off. You catch a whiff, when there's a wind. They say there's a lot of ones unclaimed, though it's a week it's been quiet. My legs swell like logs, that's my affliction. 'It's your heart,' the doctor says; says I shouldn't walk so many versts. Tomorrow, I'm going. I'll take my shovel and be off, even if I end up burying a stranger. It still helps. . . . " They sat for a while, silent.

Maria Ivanovna told her tale, too, although, of course, it was not like Marinchikha's. All the same, it was the last of what they had. And where could you get winter things for Kolia, if you couldn't turn up the suitcase?

"But why should it disappear? You say it's in the baggage claim?"

"Yes, it's there."

"Well, there's Mikola and Stepan Petrovich. They only go home for dinner. The cottage is nearby, and Mikola's woman's the housekeeper. . . . "

"But, they won't give it to me without the receipt!"

"Well, how should that be? The suitcase is yours. How important could a receipt be? Whoever knows how, can write one himself."

Suddenly glancing through a gap in the bindweed, Marinchikha clapped her hands, just like the director of an orchestra; and making her way with difficulty down the step into the garden, she cried out, "*Khros'ka, you lazy girl, chase those boys away from the plums*!" Khros'ka rushed past like a windstorm, the crimson ribbon of her necklace beating at her white shirt like a fiery serpent: "*Scat, scat. . . .* " Boys dropped to the ground like heavy sacks and were gone in a flash over the wattle fence. The mild-mannered Marinchikha reappeared, sagely foretelling the outcome of events:

"*It may be* a banner crop, but the plums won't last. *Those boys* will cart them off still green. As for the suitcase, dear, don't fret. Since it's yours, no one here needs it. What rules are there now? No rules at all: what a person wants, he does. You get yourself acquainted with the baggage clerk, drink a little tea with him. . . . "

V.

Night was falling when Maria Ivanovna went again to the station. There was the clear lake again; only the market was no more—just the assembled pile of bricks in the trampled circle. They would come again tomorrow with their milk and greens to sit once more in accustomed places, lazily exchange a few words and quietly carry on their trade until midday.

Everything is so lasting here, someone's arranged things so well, so harmoniously: the grass is bright green, the lake doesn't muddy even toward evening. The sun sets into its mirror a distinct red-orange disk. The geese float sedately along some established line, and children, almost as well fed as they once were, go slowly step by step into the water, without splashing, thrilled by the clean, soft bottom.

Suddenly the wind came up and brought . . . a sweet, stifling smell. A lot of unclaimed ones—that's what Marinchikha says. Maria Ivanovna remembered the sow and her piglets, and the morning market, and the lake so clean and clear—and just five versts away, maybe both of Marinchikha's sons, maybe one brother by the other. . . . So how could all this be together?

Maria Ivanovna's head is a little one, and she is altogether such a small woman, nothing remarkable—just the lace cap on her thinning hair. Thinking torments her.

And yet above the road leading off to the fields where the last retreating soldiers had fought—what a sunset! Not golden, transparent air, but a kind of continuous, brightly polished bronze basin. An impenetrable yellow wall rises upwards—and cut and pasted onto it the nearly black contours of three disheveled dogs. They had assumed an uncharacteristic pose—hunched down on their hind legs with forepaws tearing into something large and swollen.

Maria Ivanovna shuddered but moved on without turning aside. A dead horse with protruding muzzle and un-doglike dogs. They were digging without pause into the carcass, poised like tigers on their hind legs, growling in a greedy, predatory way. Two women were approaching along the road—one taller than the other. From a distance it seemed they were quarreling and a fight might break out: one would jerk her arms up, scream; the other would grab them, and the first would suddenly began to cry—a restrained and plaintive sobbing. The road was white, the women black against the bright yellow, glossy sky. It was painful to look. They stopped suddenly, almost opposite Maria Ivanovna. She drew even, stopped and also stood, transfixed. A repellent pool of blood lay across the width of the road. The tall woman suddenly collapsed somehow onto the ground alongside it and cried out in such a penetrating, deliberate voice: "They killed him here! Ah-a-a. . . . "

"Get up, Son'ka, shut your trap," her friend admonished with a hoarse bark. "You can't turn back; let's go, we'll have a drink. We have to forget."

"You can forget, yours is whole; you buried him, put up a cross and there he is again. *But my one, my one, oh my God, people, please. . . .* "

She kneeled down and bowed, and reaching out through the air made a kind of delicate, circular motion with her arms, as if making some conventional figure; then she began to wail in a thin, unbearable voice: "*Ma-a-ma, my God, my one, mine*—the dogs gnawed at him. I tried to gather him up—I couldn't. I knew him by his little hand, by his little knee. Oh my head aches, oy, I want to hide myself away!" And taking her scarf from her shoulders, she wrapped her head with it and lay down in the white dust before the pool of blood.

VI.

They were having supper in the baggage department, just as Marinchikha had foretold.

"Eat well," Maria Ivanovna wished them. "Is Stepan Petrovich here?"

"That's me, what do you need?"

It was the same clerk who hadn't even looked when Maria Ivanovna had asked for the suitcase without a receipt.

"Greetings from Marinchikha!"

"She's produced a handsome crop of radishes—'the pearl of her garden.'"

Even here they all knew of Marinchikha's radishes. Emboldened, Maria Ivanovna said, "My suitcase is here. It's been held up here for three days."

"Ah, you're the one without a receipt? Nothing'll happen without it. They've jammed so many suitcases into the shed there, that a person with a receipt could go goggle-eyed and still not find his own; without a receipt, it's *hopeless*."

"Everything's so extraordinary now; it's true, I might just find my suitcase," stated Maria Ivanovna. "Let me take a look in the storeroom!"

Stepan Petrovich frowned and all of a sudden acting like the boss, said emphatically in strict Russian, "The baggage department storeroom is an official establishment and unauthorized persons are strictly prohibited."

"Lord, help me remember King David and all his meekness . . . " Maria Ivanovna thought to herself. Grief-stricken and plunging on heavens knows where, she marveled to hear herself say aloud, "I'm unauthorized? Didn't I bring you greetings from Marinchikha? I even like your town, and I all but went for a swim in your lake."

"The water's first class, and the carp in it . . . " Stepan Petrovich said suddenly, grinning. "*Mikola, what do say we go fishing 'fore sundown?*"

"Who needs your carp now?" Mikola responded scornfully. "*You gotta have* sour cream with carp—not just on top, but so's the tail's drowning in it, too. . . . And not just *everyday rye bread 'll do*. You have to eat carp with *flat cake*."

"Look at you here! Still choosy about what bread to eat it with!" And little Maria Ivanovna got mad and forgot all about her strategy. "How'd you like to eat it with seed cake, and no bread at all? And not just any old seed—hemp seed that even a wild boar couldn't swallow unless it were milled. But we ate it and said thank you very much to the cooperative, because without it, there would've been just greens day after day. Have you heard about edible wild plants? How about blowweed, puffweed, milkweed, lion's tooth—there's a wonderful borsch!"

"*Oh, my lordy, what those people go through*!" said the *lass* seated there, leaning on her fist. And sturdy, broad-shouldered Mikola, with beet-red cheeks, put in, "Hey, nobody here would eat that kind of weed soup, not if you killed us. We know one: *wild sorrel, some onion, garlic, dill, beans . . . , and something else they've thought up*—cauliflower. Well, doesn't sound tasty to me."

"Well, hunger wasn't the half of it," said Maria Ivanovna, now boldly cranking away at her barrel organ. "What cold! We chopped the wardrobes and chairs up for firewood, had to crouch shivering on our heels, like Tatars. Thought we'd warm up down here, but you won't give up the suitcase, and so now we're lost. Everything we own is in the suitcase. . . . "

"Mikola . . . no, I'll do it myself!" And for some reason touched by Maria Ivanovna's misfortunes, Stepan Petrovich stood up from the table and, jangling a bunch of huge keys, invited her to follow. "Come to the shed; you might be lucky and the suitcase will turn up."

"But they're up to the devil's . . . " Mikola began to say.

"We don't need your review, Mikola." Stepan Petrovich cut him off and led Maria Ivanovna on across the rails to the huge doors of a barn. When Maria Ivanovna entered the storehouse, she was assaulted by so many trunks and baskets, how could she think to liberate her own miserable suitcase? All was lost. But wound up as she was, she could only keep repeating, without any hope or sense, "Find it, lord, well, find it. . . . "

Stepan Petrovich presses: "*Hurry up about it*!" Maria Ivanovna spins round and round, the lace cap quivering on her thinning hair. And what do you think! That miserable suitcase! There it is to the side, nothing on top of it, distinguishing features in plain sight: its plaid color, the lock on its rings, the darned tear in its side.

"That's it!"

"If that's it, take it."

She grabbed for the handle and Stepan Petrovich's gaze suddenly darkened: something not to his liking had occurred, whether it was Maria Ivanovna's haste, or something else. He pushed her hand away. "Go for a stroll; come back tonight—you'll get it then."

Maria Ivanovna crossed her arms. "Give it to me now!"

"What?" Stepan Petrovich flushed and out came the boss again: "As if you didn't know it's impossible to release baggage without a receipt. Even a storeroom's an official establishment; unauthorized persons are not permitted. Why am I wastin' time with you? I have work to do." And when he and Maria Ivanovna had gone out through the barn doors, he rattled the key in its enormous lock and went back across the tracks.

Maria Ivanovna did not go for a stroll. She sat down under the poplars, resigned to submit patiently. She would sit there until morning, she would hatch that suitcase yet.

The moon coursed across the sky, entwined in a gossamer wedding veil of translucent clouds. Young *lasses,* high heels and necklaces clattering, rushed off somewhere with *those boys*. Maria Ivanovna leaned against a poplar and dozed; someone sat down heavily next to her, paused, spat, and suddenly touched her arm lightly: "Why haven't you taken that suitcase?" Stepan Petrovich.

"But you wouldn't give it to me."

"Wouldn't give it to you?" he grinned. "It's your suitcase, so take it. Mi-kola," he hooted over toward a thicket of uniforms. "Mikola, give out the suitcase; it's been claimed." Maria Ivanovna raced off after Mikola—where did she get the strength? Together they trudged over to the baggage shed.

"Stepan Petrovich, check the contents—everything's as I've indicated, all signed and sealed."

"We don't need your seals," he said without a glance, and his short, brawny fingers pushed the paper aside. "You say yourself what you've got there that's *interestin'*, what you'd call 'valuable.'"

"Well, there's a black fur with a collar."

"Mikola, take a look. What sort of lining?"

"A ragged one, you'll never mend it."

"*The lining's bad torn*," Mikola confirmed.

"So it's yours, take it away . . . and the stamp?"

"?"

"We need an official stamp."

Maria Ivanovna gasped. It was midnight; where could you get a stamp? The train was on its way—miss it, and there's another day in this station, or else a week, or even a month, the way things were. But Stepan Petrovich doggedly pursued his own course: this paper's official, you're supposed to sign official papers on a stamp. The stamp's not even expensive, fifty kopecks in all.

"And just where's it to be found this time of night?" cried Maria Ivanovna. "Here's two hundred, three hundred for the one who'll buy it tomorrow and stick it on for me. Let me leave on this train."

Stepan Petrovich glanced scornfully at the Kerensky notes[8] in Maria Ivanovna's trembling hand, clapped his brawny palm down on the table, and pronounced: "An official paper always requires a fifty-kopeck stamp." And without a backwards glance, that sturdy, robust fellow built to last forever stomped off in his fine cobbled boots to his hut.

"A *monolit*," declared Mikola, proud of his boss and his own erudition. "*What he says—goes*."

Scarcely alive, Maria Ivanovna went out onto the station porch. The moon was bright now and just as round as the sun during the day. And the night sky here was a soft green and cloudless, like the day. Under the cloak of that still, greenish light, the poplars and the *lads and lasses*—everything looked as if it were in some underwater kingdom. The stars appeared large and prominent; some hung down low, bending toward the earth, others flared overhead. Well, in depths like that you look and you drown, you want to remember nothing. Maria Ivanovna looked her fill; she forgot her own grief and the woes of others, and that hapless suitcase. . . . Those starry depths drew her, small, weightless, entire. There is rest for every person.

Then suddenly, commandingly, in her ear: "*Ask him*. He's a *tradesman* I know." Maria Ivanovna gave a start, jumped. Him again, the "*monolit,*" Stepan Petrovich. Twirling his mustache, all benevolence, he looks at Maria Ivanovna—what can you get from her? Be as nice as you please, if you want, or grind her to dust: she's resigned, submissive. "Say there, you've likely got an official stamp?"

The tradesman is a good-natured fellow. "And why not, if it's so?" he replies. And then and there under the moon, he offers a selection of all kinds and types.

Maria Ivanovna had no time to ponder before, once again, she found herself in the baggage department seated across the table from the monolith. He set that unforgettable, short, brawny finger of his down on the page of an account book and directed her where to stick the stamp, what to write.

"Sign on the stamp. What's your last name?"

"Fedorova."

"*Khve or Khva*?"

"*Khva*?" asked Maria Ivanovna, perplexed. "Oh, you're talking about the theta. But after all, they've abolished that letter from the alphabet since the reforms."[9]

"Depends who you are."

The two of them, Mikola and Maria Ivanovna together, hauled the suitcase into line with the departing passengers.

She no longer wanted to surrender it to the baggage car.

Translated by Martha Hickey

Notes to the Essay

1. See O.D. Forsh, *Sumasshedshii korabl'. Roman. Rasskazy (Crazy Ship. A Novel. Stories)* (Leningrad: Khudozhestvennaia literatura, 1988), 30, 127, 164. Forsh tried to capture her vision of "spatial" or "expansive realism" (*prostranstvennyi realizm*) by analogy to the temporal snapshot in a cross-section of a tree trunk: one must not look at the rings as discrete entities; a truer image of life was captured in the wedge between the cracks that radiated out from the center. See "O sebe, o Petrove-Vodkine i chitatele" ("About Oneself, Petrov-Vodkin and the Reader"), an unpublished essay cited in Anna Tamarchenko's wide-ranging and provocative study of Forsh's work, *Ol'ga Forsh: Zhizn', lichnost', tvorchestvo,* 2d ed. (Leningrad: Sovetskii pisatel', 1974), 274–81.

2. See Bernice Rosenthal and Martha Bohachevsky-Chomiak, eds., *A Revolution of the Spirit: Crisis of Value in Russia, 1890–1924,* trans. Martha Schwartz, 2d ed. (New York: Fordham University Press, 1990). The God-Seekers (roundly criticized by Lenin) included writers Maxim Gorky, Aleksandr Bogdanov and Anatolii Lunacharskii (Soviet Russia's first Commissar of Culture).

3. Biographical detail is drawn from A. Tamarchenko, *Ol'ga Forsh: Zhizn', lichnost', tvorchestvo*. As an adolescent Forsh had considered taking her own life; she determined, instead, to choose a life of action. A diary entry for July 1890 contains a remarkable declaration of that self-discovery: "All of my efforts have been going into analysis and self-destruction; now all that is confining. I want to live, that is to act; yes, I will live, because there is a force in me, there is reason and will, because I am a human being" (quoted in Tamarchenko, 15).

4. Forsh's experience also put her at a certain remove from peers whose lives were shaped by their mothers' and caretakers' examples of propriety, religious devotion and self-sacrifice. See Barbara Alpern Engel, *Mothers and Daughters: Women of the Intelligentsia in Nineteenth Century Russia* (Cambridge: Cambridge University Press, 1983).

5. Forsh campaigned at the end of the 1920s to preserve the memory of Chistakov, who had taught many of the important painters at the turn of the century. See Forsh, "Artist-Wise Man" ("Khudozhnik-mudrets") in *Pavel Petrovich Chistakov*, 1928, and *Bokovaia funktsiia*, 1934. Chistakov had encouraged Forsh's literary efforts. Her drawings evidently showed some talent, but success in oil eluded her.

6. This dismal life is evoked in Elena Gan's story "Ideal" (1837). (See also Engel's account, *Mothers*, 28–33.)

7. Forsh did not wait for institutional confirmation of her interest in theosophy and Eastern religions. The Russian Theosophical Society (formed in late 1907) subsequently identified the two public lectures Forsh gave in early 1907 in Kiev, "On Buddhism and Pythagoras," as "the first theosophical public readings in Russia" (see Tamarchenko, 38). Forsh's contact with the teachings of anthroposophist Rudolph Steiner also gave her an advantage when Andrei Belyi (who became a Steiner disciple in 1912) published the novel *Petersburg*—a novel that puzzled and dismayed many of his contemporaries.

8. "Pursuing the Firebird" echoes concerns raised by Symbolist poet Aleksandr Blok at the end of 1908 and early 1909 in lectures and essays that provoked heated and extensive debate about the divisions between Russia's educated and lower classes. "He Was a General," "Pursuing the Fire-Bird" and several other stories were published by one of Russia's leading "thick" journals, *Russkaia mysl'* (1908–1910) (see Tamarchenko 70 and 62).

9. Tamarchenko, 12.

10. Forsh could have found other advocates of this view in the innovative director Vsevolod Meyerhold and Symbolist Andrei Belyi. Meyerhold's exploration of the conventions of the "The Stylized Theater" (1907–1908) may have been of particular interest to Forsh.

11. See Shakh-Eddin (Forsh), "O novoi p'ese L. Andreeva" and "Ignatsio Zuloaga," reviews published in *Sovremennik* in 1914. Examples of a similar resolve can be found in the verse of a brilliant, younger contemporary, Anna Akhmatova.

12. At this time Forsh also abandoned her pseudonyms, A. Terek and Shakh-Eddin, and began to publish under the name of Ol'ga Forsh.

13. Tamarchenko, 133. There was an earlier, unfinished attempt at a novel entitled *Children of the Earth (Deti zemli)*. The first part was published in *Russkaia mysl'* in 1910 (see Tamarchenko, 71–75).

14. Otto Weininger, *Sex and Character,* translation of the sixth German edition (London: William Heinemann and G. P. Putnam, 1906), 261. Weininger's evocative description of character and genius was clouded by racist misogyny. According to Weininger, the ideal woman ("W") was an empty vessel of desire waiting to be filled by the ideas of her mate—diffuse, hysterical, amoral, incapable of reflecting the universe, without logic, will, genius, connected memory or particular destiny. Weininger's text was translated and published in Russia (*Pol i kharakter*, A.L. Volynskii, ed. [St. Petersburg: Posev, 1909]).

Given contemporary rhetoric supportive of women's emancipation, the question arises as to why Forsh so seldom spoke through a woman's voice. Her frequent recourse to masculine narrative authority was a strategy not unfamiliar to marginalized writers. The story "Live-Fish Tank" (1922) suggests Forsh did not adopt this tactic naively. A soldier on a crowded troop train pronounces God's curse on womankind to a nurse accompanying them: "You got a bird's voice, and the silly mind to go with it." Forsh's message is coded in the actions of the tale: her nurses act humanely in the face of intolerance and win the respect of their fellow passengers. The benighted (male) citizen through whom the tale is told flees from the train.

15. Forsh had been asked to help organize the Petrograd activities of the Free Philosophical Society (Vol'fil), founded by a group of writers and philosophers who wanted to lead a nonpartisan discussion of critical cultural issues through lecture, debate and study circles. Forsh was already acquainted with some members through her participation in 1917–1918 in the prominent literary circle, the Scythians. They included prose writers Aleksei Remizov and Evgenii Zamiatin, poets Sergei Esenin and Nikolai Kliuev, artist Petrov-Vodkin, critics Ivanov-Razumnik and E. Lundberg, publicist A. Shteinberg and philosopher Konstantin Sonnerberg. The latter five formed the nucleus of the Petrograd Free Philosophical Society branch that Andrei Belyi helped to establish in 1920 (thus establishing Forsh's personal acquaintance with Belyi).

16. See M. Hickey, "Gor'kii in the House of Arts: Gor'kii and the Petrograd Intelligentsiia," *Soviet and Post-Soviet Review* 20, 1 (Spring 1995): 40–64.

17. Like many of her contemporaries, Forsh was responsive to the example of popular speech and *skaz* narration, but she was generally less fascinated by the kind of extravagant primitivism attractive to younger writers with whom she shared quarters in the House of Arts. These writers, who would become significant figures in Soviet Russian literature, were first known collectively as the Serapion Brothers. The group included one woman poet, Elizaveta Polonskaia. Several (N.S. Tikhonov, K. A. Fedin, M.L. Slonimskii) carried on an affectionate correspondence with Forsh over the years. (*Skaz* means a literary stylization of oral "folk" narrative or idiosyncratic personal speech and worldview.)

18. There are deliberate stylistic echoes of a much-admired Dostoevsky in the narrative's nervous intensity, the play of voices and the elevation of scandal. Dostoevsky himself appears in two central scenes in the novel. Forsh was well informed about critical discussions of Dostoevsky's work among Petrograd's formalist critics and Iurii Tynianov's original analysis of the role that stylization had played in Dostoevsky's own development as an author. (See Tynianov's 1921 article, "Gogol and Dostoevsky," in *Twentieth-Century Russian Literary Criticism,* ed. V. Erlich. New Haven, CT: Yale University Press, 1975, 102–116.)

19. The major points of Forsh's "deconstructive" reading of Belyi's parodic novel *Petersburg* are illustrated in an article published in *Sovremennaia literatura,* 1925, "The Played Out Herbarium" ("Propetyi gerbarii"). (See Tamarchenko's extensive consideration of Belyi's significance for Forsh, 114–17, 209–32.) In this essay, Forsh also elaborates on her ideas about the changing relationship between authors and their readers.

20. Kliuev is also invoked as a spirit of "cosmos, unenlightened by Logos." There are other suggestive correspondences with the hypothetical "women's writing" of French feminist authors: Doliva's name, like those of all the characters in the book, is a telling one. It means "that which is added to fill up," or, one could say, the necessary supplement.

21. O.D. Forsh, *Sumasshedshii korabl'. Povest'*, ed. B. Filippov (Washington: Inter-Language Literary Associates, 1964), 207.

22. T. Ermilov, "Za boevuiu tvorcheskuiu perestroiku," *Na literaturnom postu* 2 (1933): 13; B. Riurikov, "Kuda idet korabl'," *Na literaturnom postu* 2 (1933): 19.

23. Stalin was sensitive about his historically insignificant role as a revolutionary in Georgia. In 1937 he ordered a purge of old Bolsheviks in Georgia that swept up everyone once connected with Kamo. Mosfilm's preparations for a movie based on Forsh's play were also canceled. (See Tamarchenko, 459–60.) Forsh "got the message." In 1936 she abruptly suspended work on a novel on the Georgian revolutionary underground based on material collected there in 1933. However, she was able to publish a brief article, on Georgian women poets, in 1931. "Pisatel'nitsy Gruzii," *Zvezda* 2 (1931): 147–55.

24. See Katerina Clark, *The Soviet Novel: History as Ritual* (Chicago: Chicago University Press, 1981). In the play, the egalitarian rhetoric of a "little Napoleon" is punctured with a reminder (from his wife) that he had also declared that "the best woman is the one with the most children." Another character chimes in with the opinion that "we women can do a better job remaking the world than men." That the play was published at all may also be due to the official neglect of the domain of women that Beth Holmgren identifies as opening creative opportunities for women in unofficial culture. See Holmgren, *Women's Works in Stalin's Time: On Lidiia Chukovskaia and Nadezhda Mandelstam* (Bloomington: Indiana University Press, 1993).

25. Forsh's act of faith in the transcendence of art was a difficult one in the Stalin years. Just a few years earlier Mikhail Bulgakov had been forced to conceal his novel *Master and Margarita*, a work that gives powerful expression to a similar theme.

26. The laudatory critics included such authoritative scholars as Boris Èikhenbaum, who had once readily declared his bias against novels that did not faithfully reconstruct the past. Èikhenbaum had justly observed that stylization was a significant compositional feature of Forsh's texts, although he thought her use of detail "decorative" rather than evocative. (See his review "Dekoratsiia èpokhi" in *Moi vremennik*.) Forsh was also invited, shortly afterwards, to give the keynote address at the Second Congress of the Union of Soviet Writers in 1954. No All-Union Congress had been held since 1934—the congress that had ushered in the era of socialist realism in literature.

27. O.D. Forsh, "Avtobiografiia," in *Sovetskie pisateli: Avtobiografii*, Vol. 2 (Moscow: Khudozhestvennaia literatura, 1959), 585.

28. See, for example, the introductory essay by S. Timina in Forsh's *Sumasshedshii korabl'. Roman. Rasskazy* (Leningrad: Khudozhestvennaia literatura, 1988).

Translator's Notes to the Selected Work

1. Kolia recites what is, apparently, a list of variant popular names for "dandelion" (*kulibaba, popovo gumentse*). Blowweed, puffweed and milkweed are suggested as equivalents for "*oduplesh', pustodui, molochainik.*" This translation uses the text of "Suitcase" ("Chemodan") published in O. Forsh, *Rasskazy. Skazki (1907–1923), Sobranii sochinenie v vos'mi tomakh*, Vol. 6

(Moscow: Khudozhestvennaia literatura, 1964), 520–39.

2. Godfather lives in Kiev, where Forsh had returned to work in 1919. Here, he quotes the speech of the local Ukrainian villagers, as does the nurse below. Russia's failure to acknowledge Ukraine's independent history, culture and language, as well as its right to self-determination, provided fodder for a rising nationalist movement in Ukraine at the turn of the century. Forsh deliberately marked these first Ukrainianisms with quotation marks and italics. This translation will italicize subsequent instances where Ukrainian words and speech are introduced.

3. These bank notes were designed by the various forces competing to rule Ukraine from 1917 to 1920. The Central Rada declared an independent Ukrainian Republic in November 1917 only to be challenged in February 1918 by the Red Army. Soviet rule was abrogated by the treaty of Brest-Litovsk, and the German army gave its support to a new government—Skoropadskii's Hetmanate. The Hetmanate lost its support when the German army retreated in late 1918 and was challenged by a coalition of nationalists, including Petliura, who established rule under the Directory. In 1919 General Denikin's Russian anti-Bolshevik forces—the Whites—gave token support to Ukrainian nationalists while waging a campaign against forces advancing from Moscow—the Reds—who ultimately installed a pro-Bolshevik government in early 1920.

4. The Russian phrase—*za pripek, khleb pechet* (to make a surplus, bake some bread)—suggests a punning intent, as well as a comment on the value of labor. *Pripek* refers to the difference in weight between the flour measured for the bread and the baked loaf—a seemingly "illogical" surplus.

5. 17 September is St. Sophia's day in the Julian religious calendar. Traditionally, children born into families of the Orthodox faith received the name of one of the church's saints. Each day of the yearly calendar was dedicated to a particular saint, and this day—the name day—was celebrated by the bearer of the saint's name. *Pistis Sophia,* or "Faith-Wisdom," refers here both to the Coptic Gnostic text and a vision of the role of divine wisdom in the world that was much debated in religious and philosophical circles and important to adherents of Russian Symbolism at the turn of the century.

6. Che-ka (ChK), the acronym for the Extraordinary Commission set up by Lenin to oversee internal security, and the forerunner of the NKVD and KGB.

7. When paper was in short supply during the civil war, "living newspapers"—gatherings where the news was read aloud and sometimes accompanied by skits—became popular substitutes.

8. Notes issued under the Russian provisional government established in February 1917, headed by Kerensky and overthrown by the Bolsheviks in November 1917.

9. Stepan Petrovich is asking which of two spelling variants Maria Ivanovna uses to write the first letter of her last name. In 1917 the new Bolshevik administration enacted reforms in the Russian alphabet that had been approved in 1914. Several letters of Greek origin were dropped, including the theta, which was converted to an *f.*

Bibliography

Primary Works

"Chereshnia." *Kievskii vestnik* 1 (1907).

[O.F.] "Aleksei Remizov. *Posolon*'" [review]. *Utro zhizni* (Kiev) 1 (1908): 57–58.

[Terek, A.] "Pered vratami." *Voprosy teosofii* 2 (1908): 61–68.

[Terek, A.] *Rytsar' iz Niurenberga.* Kiev: Petr Barskii, 1908.

[Terek, A.] "Zhizn' i uchenie Buddy" [essay]. *Utro zhizni* (Kiev) 3 (1908): 37–43; 4 (1908): 48–54.

[Terek, A.] "Passiflora." *Voprosy teosofii* 1 (1909): 91–95.

"Deti zemli" [later title: "Bogdan Sukhovskii"]. *Russkaia mysl'* 8 (1910).

"Figury iz bumagi i spichek. Risunki avtora." *Tropinka* 6 (1912): 515–16.

[Shakh-Eddin.] "*Moi malenkii Trot* Andre Likhtenberzhe" [review]. *Zavety* 6, 2 (1913): 240–42.

[Shakh-Eddin.] "O. D. Durnovo. *Tak govoril Khristos*" [review]. *Zavety* 1, 2 (1913): 172–74.

[Shakh-Eddin.] "Demon u Lermontova" [essay]. *Sovremennik* 17–20 (October 1914): 139–43.

[Shakh-Eddin.] "Ignatsio Zuloaga" [review]. *Sovremennik* 7 (1914): 117–19.

[Shakh-Eddin.] "O novoi p'ese L. Andreeva" [review]. *Sovremennik* (December 1914): 255–58.

[Shakk-Eddin.] "V.A. Serov" [review of exhibit]. *Zavety* 1, 2 (1914): 14–17.

[Terek, A.] *Chto komu nravitsia. Skazki i rasskazy.* Moscow: Tovarishchestvo I. Sytina, 1914. [Contents: "Chto komu nravitsia," "Medved' Panfamil," "Ivanov den'," "Rusalochka Rotozeechka," "Chereshnia," "Dukhovnik," "Na chernom dvore," "Pumpin sad," "Faraonovy zmei," "V Neapole."]

[Shakh-Eddin.] "Novyi Gamlet" [essay]. *Nash put'* 2 (1918): 177–81.

[Terek, A.] "Kupel'." *Znamia truda* (Moscow) 26 (13 April 1918).

[Shakh-Eddin.] "Khudozhniki dukha" [essay]. *Znamia* 2 (1919): 20–21.

[Shakh-Eddin.] "Pod znakom Leonardo (K probleme khudozhestvennogo masterstva)." *Zapiski* (Peredvizhnoi teatr P. Gaideburova i N. Skarskoi) 21 (1919): 1–2.

[Terek, A.] *Smert' Kopernika. Sovremennyi dramaticheskii ètiud.* Moscow: Revoliutsionnyi sotsialism, 1919.

[Terek, A.] "Attestat zrelosti." *Put'* 3 (1919): 3–8.

[O.F.] "O detskom teatre" [review]. *Zhizn' iskusstva* (August 1921): 2–7.

"Kum-kumu. Pis'mo pervoe." *Rossiia* 2 (1922): 13–15.

Indrigin skaz. Peterburg: Èpokha, 1922. [Contents: "Shelusheia," "Bezglazikha."]

[A. Terek.] *Ravvi. P'esa v 3–kh d.* Berlin: Izdatel'stvo "Skify," 1922.

Obyvateli. Petrograd: Byloe, 1923; Moscow-Petrograd: Krug, 1923. [Contents: "Shelusheia," "Zastrel'shchik," "Afrikanskii brat," "Idilliia," "Katastrofa," "Negolodaiushchii indus," "Bezglazikha," "Marsel'eza," "Chemodan," "Iz Smol'nogo," "Geroi," "Zhivorybnyi sadok," "Korrektiv," "Khiruroid," "Sinekura," "Klimov kulak."]

"Shimka i Stepa." *Kryl'ia. Detskii al'manakh.* Vol. 1. Moscow-Petrograd, 1923. 7–15.

Derevnia (with G. Vereiskii.) Leningrad: Leningradskii komitet popularizatsii khudozhestvennykh izdanii pri Rossiikoi akademii istorii material'noi kul'tury, 1924.

Dvorets i krepost' (with P. Shcheglov) [film script]. Director A. Ivanovskii. Sevzapkino, 1924.

Odety kamnem. Rossiia 1 (1924), 2 (1924), 4 (1925).

"Petropavlovskaia krepost'" [essay]. *Krasnaia niva* 44 (1924): 336–38.

"Pushkin v institute," "V Smol'nom institute." *Rossiia* 2 (1924): 174–76.

Odety kamnen. Moscow: Rossiia, 1925.

Letoshnii sneg. Sbornik rasskazov. Moscow: Zemlia i fabrika, 1925. [Contents: "Primus," "Tovarishch Pful'," "Dlia bazy," "Bez sigary," "Zhivtsy," "Lisogor'e."]

"Propetyi gerbarii" [essay on A. Belyi]. *Sovremennaia literatura.* Leningrad, 1925. 31–47.

Moskovskie rasskazy. Leningrad: Priboi, 1926. [Contents: "Bashnia," "Viktoria Regia," "Vsemirnaia bania," "Piatyi zver'," "Saltychikhin grot," "Vo dvortse truda," "Rozarnum," "Sovmestitel'," "Babii vagon."]

Sovremenniki. Moscow: Gosudarstvennoe izdatel'stvo, 1926.

"Tovarishch Pful'." *Rasskazy*. Moscow: Gosudarstvennoe izdatel'stvo, 1926.

Goriachii tsekh. Moscow: Gosudarstvennoe izdatel'stvo, 1926.

Tata i Allochka, Khiruroid. Paris: Izdatel'stvo "Ocharovannyi strannik," 1927.

"[O svoikh tvorcheskikh planakh']." *Chitatel' i pisatel'* (18 February 1928): 22–23.

Pavel Petrovich Chistakov (with S.P. Iaremich). Leningrad: Gosudarstvenaia akademiia istorii material'noi kul'tury, Leninskii komitet popularizatsii khudozhestvenykh izdanii, 1928.

"Portrety" [M. Gor'kogo]. *Gor'kii. Sbornik statei i vospominanii o M. Gor'kom*. Moscow, 1928. 443–50.

Sobranie sochinenii v 7 t-kh. Moscow, 1928–1932.

Pod kupolom. Leningrad: Priboi, 1929. [Contents: "Pod kupolom," "Kukly Parizha," "Parizh s ptich'ego 'duazo'," "Kladbishche Per-Lashez," "Sobach'e zasedanie," "Tetka Borodkina," "Lebed' Neoptolem," "L'vitsa Liusi," "V avtomobile," "Posledniaia roza," "Kukiny deti," "Lurdskie chudesa."]

"[Kak ia pishu]." *Kak my pishem*. Leningrad: Izdatel'stvo pisatelei v Leningrade, 1930. 182–85.

"Pisatel'nitsy Gruzii." *Zvezda* 2 (1931): 147–55.

Sumasshedshii korabl'. Leningrad: Izdatel'stvo pisatelei v Leningrade, 1931.

"Za kachestvo sovetskoi literatury" [essay]. *Smena,* 12 May 1932.

"Pisatel', kritik, chitatel'" [essay]. *Leningradskaia pravda,* 23 April 1933.

Vcherashnii den'. Rasskazy. Leningrad: Izdatel'stvo pisatelei v Leningrade, 1933. [Contents: "Zastrel'shchik," "Bogdan Sukhovskii," "Idilliia," "Katastrofa," "Afrikanskii brat," "Byl general," "Za zhar-ptisei," "V monastyre," "Nochnaia dama," "Negolodaiushchii indus," "Gnezdyshko," "Zhena Khama."]

Bokovaia funktsiia. Leningrad: Izdatel'stvo pisatelei v Leningrade, 1934. [Contents: "Bokovaia funktsiia," "Medved' Panfamil," "Dukhovnik," "Rusalochka Rotozeechka," "Na chernom dvore," "Pumpin sad," "Faraonovy zmei," "V Neapole," "Khudozhnik mudrets" (essay), "Khamovnoe delo" (essay), "O stengazete" (essay).]

Iakobinskii zakvas. Moscow: Izdatel'stvo russkikh pisatelei, 1934.

"O kaprize i novatorstve" [essay]. *Literaturnyi Leningrad,* 8 April 1934.

Voron. [*Simvolisty*.] Leningrad: Gosizdat, 1934.

Kazanskaia pomeshchitsa. Moscow: Sovetskii pisatel', 1936.

"O nashei zhenshchine" [essay]. *Zvezda* 2 (1937): 254–57.

Sto dvadtsat' vtoraia. P'esa v 4–kh d. Leningrad: Khudozhesvennaia literatura, 1937.

Pagubnaia kniga. Leningrad: Gosizdat, 1939.

Radishchev. Leningrad: Goslitizdat, 1939.

"Ernesto Rossi" [from the unpublished novel *Mikhailovskii zamok*]. *Zvezda* 10 (1940): 140–42.

Nachalo puti. P'esa v 4–kh d (with I. Gruzdev). Moscow: Iskusstvo, 1941.

Novye rasskazy. Sverdlovsk: Sverdlgiz, 1942. [Contents: "Shapoliak," "Plombir," "Pervaia liubov'," "Viev krug," "Filaretki," "V starom Tiflise," "Novyi pamiatnik," "V Parizhe," "Dva strafa."]

Rozhdenie Rusi. P'esa v 3–kh d (with G. Boiadzhiev). Moscow: VUOAP, 1943.

Kniaz' Vladimir. Istoricheskaia-geroicheskaia p'esa v 5–i d., 8–mi kart. Moscow: Iskusstvo, 1943.

Alesha Peshkov. P'esa v 4–kh deistviiakh. Moscow: Vsesoiuznoe upravlenie po avtorskim pravam, 1944.

Mikhailovskii zamok. Leningrad: Sovetskii pisatel', 1946.

Perventsy svobody. Part 1. Moscow: Molodaia gvardiia, 1950.

Perventsy svobody. Parts 1–2. Moscow: Molodaia gvardiia, 1953.

"S glubokoi otvetstvennost'iu pered narodom" [About the Second All-Union Congress of Soviet Writers]. *Leningradskaia pravda,* 25 December 1954.

"Sila khudozhestvennogo slova" [essay]. *Literaturnaia gazeta,* 16 September 1954.

Vchera i segodnia. Moscow: Pravda, 1959. [Contents: "Dni moei zhizni (Avtobiografiia)," "Vchera i segodnia," "Rovesniki," "Mednyi vsadnik," "Inzhenernyi zamok," "Belaia noch'," "Pamiatnik istorii," "Vernyi sputnik."]

Sobranie sochinenii. v 8 t-kh. Moscow: Goslitizdat, 1962–64.

"Gor'kii-O. D. Forsh" [letters]. *Gor'kii i sovetskie pisateli. Neizdannaia perepiska.* Moscow: Literaturnoe nasledstvo, 1963. 580–613.

Sumasshedshii korabl'. Povest' [with an introductory article, commentary and excerpts from various authors]. Ed. Boris Filippov. Washington: Inter-Language Literary Association, 1964.

Sumasshedshii korabl'. Rasskazy. Ed. S. Timina. Leningrad: Khudozhestvennaia literatura, 1988.

Radishchev: Trilogiia. Moscow: Izdatel'stvo "Pravda," 1987.

Perventsy svobody i rasskazy. Moscow: Izdatel'stvo "Pravda," 199[0].

In Translation

Pioneers of Freedom. Moscow: Foreign Language Publishing House, 1953.

Palace and Prison. Trans. F. Solasko. Westport, CT: Hyperion Press, 1978. [First published in Moscow: Foreign Language Publishing House, 1958.]

"The Little Mermaid Rotozeechka" and "Ham's Wife." *Russian and Polish Women's Fiction.* Ed. and trans. Helena Goscilo. Knoxville: University of Tennessee Press, 1985. 90–107.

"The Substitute Lecturer" [one-act play]. *An Anthology of Russian Women's Writing, 1777–1992.* Ed. Catriona Kelly. Oxford: Oxford University Press, 1994. 243-55.

Secondary Works

Barta, Peter I. "Ol'ga Forsh." *An Encyclopedia of Continental Women Writers.* Vol. 1. Ed. Katharina M. Wilson. New York: Garland Publishing, 1991. 419–20.

Èikhenbaum, B. "Dekoratsiia èpokhi." *Moi vremennik.* Leningrad: Izdatel'stvo pisatelei v Leningrade, 1929. 126–27.

Galmanova, M.A. "Chelovek umnoi dushi." *Russkaia rech'* 3 (1983): 23–34.

Goscilo, Helena. Introduction. *Russian and Polish Women's Fiction.* Ed. and trans. Helena Goscilo. Knoxville: University of Tennessee Press, 1985. 85–90.

Gromov, P. "Tvorcheskii put' O. D. Forsh." *Geroi i vremia.* Leningrad: 1961. 212–60.

Lewis, Kathleen B. "Ol'ga Dmitrievna Forsh." *Modern Encyclopedia of Russian and Soviet Literature.* Vol. 8. Ed. G. Gutsche. Gulf Breeze, FL: Academie International, 1987. 15–18.

Lugovtsov, N. *Tvorchestvo Ol'gi Forsh.* Leningrad: Lenizdat, 1964.

Messer, R. *Ol'ga Forsh.* Leningrad: Lenizdat, 1965.

Muratov, L.G. "Peterburgskaia tema O. Forsh i Iu. Tynianova." *Russkaia literatura* 4 (1982): 196–208.

"O.D. Forsh" [bibliography.] *Russkie-sovetskie pisateli prozaiki.* Vol. 5. Leningrad: Biblioteka, 1959–1972, 467–90.

Shaginian, Marietta. "Ol'ga Forsh." *Literaturnyi dnevnik. Stat'i.* Moscow: Krug, 1923. 160–67.

Skaldina, R.A. *O.D. Forsh. Ocherk tvorchestva 20–30–kh godov.* Riga: Izdatel'stvo "Zvaigzne," 1974.

Tamarchenko, Anna V. *Ol'ga Forsh: Zhizn', lichnost', tvorchestvo.* 2d ed. Leningrad: Sovetskii pisatel', 1974.

Timina, S. "Ol'ga Forsh i sovremennost'." *Sumasshedshii korabl'. Rasskazy.* Leningrad, 1988. 3–22.

Zinaida Gippius (Hippius)

Zinaida Gippius (1869–1945).
Courtesy of Christine D. Tomei.

Zinaida Nikolaevna Gippius (also Hippius, 1869–1945) was a major Russian modernist writer and religious thinker who played a central role in the promotion of Russian culture for more than fifty years, both inside Russia and in emigration.

An author of novels, short stories, plays, literary criticism, memoirs, diaries, a biography and essays on politics, philosophy and religion, she is most famous as a lyric poet whom Andrei Belyi, a fellow poet and philosopher, described in the early years of the twentieth century as "the most talented woman writer" in Russia.[1] Even though Gippius's overall poetic output was modest, consisting of five small volumes published between 1904 and 1938, she made significant contributions to the development of Russian poetry and to the tradition of Russian women's writing. Her poetry is highly intellectual, focusing on spiritual and metaphysical questions, and at the same time highly concrete, presenting these questions in concise forms and precise, memorable images. Gippius's poems challenge readers to participate in her quest to understand the large issues of life—the nature of humanity, God and the devil, the meaning of death and the difficulties of achieving faith and love. These poems possess a disturbing emotional intensity, reflecting internal conflicts Gippius was never able to resolve and making them unforgettable. Alternating between expressions of hope and cries of despair, between belief in the value of love and fear of its physical dimension, between a desire to communicate and a stubborn delight in isolation, Gippius's poetry reveals her own psychological and spiritual struggles, her attempts to come to terms with what she took to be deeply divided elements in herself and in human nature and to understand mankind's place in the universe.

In addition to these personal concerns, Gippius's poetry mirrors the development of Russian literature during the Silver Age from its decadent beginnings to high Symbolism. Gippius began writing verse at the age of eleven, when she was attracted to poetry of the Nadson school popular in the 1870s and 1880s, with its civic themes and pessimistic tone, but by the time critics began to recognize her works, she had moved beyond Nadsonist verse to explore the decadent current entering Russian literature in the 1890s. Decadence was a widespread phenomenon in European fin-de-siècle culture, an artistic expression of the idea that the century was coming to an end and that the present generation was doomed to be the last of a historical line. Decadent literature is characterized by a preoccupation with death and decay, a yearning for the unattainable and a desire to justify self-indulgence, often resulting in extreme aestheticism and sensationalism, manifested by elaborate depictions of sensuality and cruelty, along with unsettling images of the grotesque, the morbid, the bizarre. Gippius's first lyric poems to receive critical acclaim and notoriety appeared in 1893 in *The Northern Herald* (*Severnyi vestnik*)—a journal known for its sympathy with any new literary trends. In Gippius's poetry of the 1890s images of death and decay abound, although they are counterbalanced by expressions of longing for the otherworldly, the mysterious and the ineffable. Avowals of faith in the existence of a heavenly realm alternate with portrayals of a horribly oppressive earthbound life, the latter embodied in memorable images of fat, indefatigable spiders, clinging leeches, malevolent flowers and malicious pine trees that plague Gippius's lyric persona. Conservative critics were quick to reproach Gippius for her decadent imagination, which no doubt seemed doubly shocking in a woman, who was expected to write on more decorous subjects.

Gippius liberated women's writing in Russia from these narrow expectations of female devotion to themes of domestic life and amorous encounters as she turned to serious cultural and philosophical ideas. Her works revealed a sharpness of intellect that was both highly praised by her contemporaries and characterized as a nonfeminine virtue. D.S. Mirsky, for example, writes that "the most salient feature in all her writing is intellectual power and wit, things rare in a woman. In fact there is very little that is feminine in Mme. Hippius."[2] Gippius's keen mind became simultaneously her greatest literary asset and a complicated aspect of her gender identity as manifested in both her life and her writings.

Gippius was born on 8 November 1869 in the town of Belev of the Tula province, the eldest of four daughters of a chief prosecutor in the Senate. Gippius's childhood was unsettled: the family moved frequently due to her father's tubercular condition and, after his death in 1881, resided for short times with various relatives. She and her sisters nonetheless received a solid education from a series of governesses and tutors, and all four of them displayed marked artistic or scientific abilities, Gippius's three sisters subsequently choosing painting, sculpting and medicine as their respective careers.

In 1889 Gippius married Dmitrii Merezhkovskii, who was soon to become a prominent Russian writer and philosopher. The couple settled in St. Petersburg and immediately began to play a major role in the cultural life of the capital. They became acquainted with the group of writers and artists involved in the publication of the avant-garde journal *World of Art* (*Mir iskusstva*), including Lev Bakst and Sergei Diaghilev, and began to write for it, as well as for other journals. Gippius soon became "the uncrowned queen of the literary life of the capital,"[3] socializing with prominent writers and philosophers such as Lev Tolstoy, Maxim Gorky, Anton Chekhov, Nikolai Leskov, Konstantin Bal'mont, Valerii Briusov and Nikolai Berdiaev. For years Gippius and Merezhkovskii gathered the Petersburg cultural community around them at their weekly Sunday salons, where they promoted the discussion of literary, philosophical and religious issues.

Around the turn of the century Gippius and Merezhkovskii became particularly active in efforts to reorganize and revitalize Christianity in Russia. In order to encourage renewed interest in spirituality in modern Russian culture, in 1901 Gippius initiated a public series of what she called religious-philosophical meetings, at which she brought members of the Russian Orthodox clergy together with members of the intelligentsia who were interested in religious issues. In a manner unprecedented for a woman, Gippius took full part in these public discussions, occupying a place on the platform and expressing her views forcefully, thereby earning herself the nickname "white she-devil" from the conservative clergy.[4] In opposing the Russian Orthodox church, Gippius and Merezhkovskii did not reject all its teachings, but rather its focus solely on the sanctity of the spirit with the consequent devaluation of the flesh. They sought to affirm the equality of spirit and flesh, both to corporealize the spirit and to spiritualize the flesh, thereby figuratively uniting the two. As a means to demonstrate and promote this unity, Gippius and Merezhkovskii devised a new, apocalyptic form of Christianity that they named the Church of the Third Testament, which was based on a belief in the future merging of heavenly and earthly realms as symbolized by the second coming of Christ and the resultant transformation of humanity into one harmonious entity. Gippius and Merezhkovskii actually tried to effect their brand of neo-Christianity, creating their own liturgy and secret rites and recruiting other believers. Gippius also aggressively promoted their religious cause in print, establishing a journal, *The New Path* (*Novyi put'*), to publicize the meetings and disseminate the group's ideas.

After the revolution of 1905 Gippius began to take an interest in politics as well, writing polemical articles and cultivating the acquaintance of political activists. Her increasing political involvement is also reflected in a shift in her philosophy during this period, as she emphasizes the individual's need to participate in a community in order to find a transcendent type of love for other people. In the name of such a community Gippius supported Russia's efforts to defend itself against outside invaders during World War I, even though she was a vehement opponent of war in general on both intellectual and religious grounds. When the world war yielded to revolution in 1917, Gippius at first welcomed the upheaval, believing it would bring true freedom to Russia. Her optimism soon faded, however, as she realized that the Bolsheviks were eradicating individual freedom. In her diaries about the years immediately following the revolution she contends that "even in an earthquake there is more life and more sense than in . . . what is happening now"[5] in Russia, a conviction that would only strengthen as time went on; she was ultimately to conclude that the Bolsheviks had inaugurated the kingdom of the Antichrist.

Perceiving that there was no longer a place for their religious endeavors in Russia, in late 1919 Gippius and Merezhkovskii left for Poland, where they tried to organize opposition to the Bolsheviks. They initially found support there among Russian émigrés and Polish government leaders, but discontinued their efforts when Poland and Russia signed an armistice in October 1920 and anti-Bolshevik activities became illegal. They subsequently left Warsaw in December 1920 to settle in Paris, where they promoted Russian culture among members of the émigré community. Gippius and Merezhkovskii's home became a center of Russian cultural life in the French capital as they reinstituted their Sunday salons, which continued until the outbreak of World War II. During these years Gippius took a special interest in new émigré literary journals and in the encouragement of young Russian writers, while she herself contributed political and philosophical essays to many publications. She continued to write poetry and prose fiction as well, publishing short stories and two volumes of verse along with some of her diaries and memoirs.

In Paris Gippius and Merezhkovskii also renewed their religiously oriented activities, founding a philosophical society, the Green Lamp (Zelenaia lampa)—named after the Decembrists' secret society—to discuss the spiritual regeneration of humanity, a goal that took on added urgency for Gippius as she perceived the Russian people losing physical and psychological freedom in the process of becoming virtually enslaved by the Soviet government. Gippius expressed fiercely anti-Soviet views throughout her life in emigration, refusing to acknowledge the achievements of Soviet writers and cutting off relations with former friends who cooperated with the new government. She even welcomed the Nazi invasion of Russia as the potential liberation of her homeland, a stance that alienated many Russian émigré friends and contributed to her isolation in her last years, a very difficult period of her life. Merezhkovskii died in 1941, and Gippius's ensuing loneliness and despair were compounded by financial hardships caused by the war. Gippius died in Paris on 9 September 1945, at the age of seventy-five, having spent her final days writing a biography of Merezhkovskii, which was published posthumously in 1951.

Gippius lived through a period of Russian history characterized by turmoil and instability when, alongside changing political and economic structures, social, cultural and sexual relations between men and women were also changing. While not outspoken about women's rights per se, Gippius advocated equality between men and women in what she considered to be the most important elements of life—sexuality and spirituality. Her desire for such equality manifested itself in her personal relationships and social activities, as well as in her writings on these topics. Gippius refused to occupy a subordinate position to men, whether in religious, literary or amorous affairs. She often disregarded conventional ideas about gender, reversing traditional male and female roles in her private relationships and combining feminine and masculine elements in the public persona she projected. Contemporaries of Gippius frequently commented on her androgynous appearance; for instance, her deliberate combination of explicit femininity with a masculine quality. Akim Volynskii, an influential literary critic and editor of *The Northern Herald,* who was in love with Gippius during her early years in St. Petersburg, described her as a sylph, "a woman-girl, slender and tall, lithe and delicate as a straw, with a cascade of golden hair [and] an almost boyish chest" who nonetheless gave "an overall impression of complete femininity."[6]

Gippius used clothing to emphasize alternately her feminine and masculine traits. She sometimes appeared in revealing dresses that drew attention to her femininity, and at other times wore men's clothing, as shown in a well-known portrait by Lev Bakst. Although many avant-garde writers enjoyed shocking people by dressing in unusual ways, Gippius found that varying her apparel had the added potential of reflecting her belief that she possessed both a male and a female essence. In "Contes d'amour," Gippius's diary about her intimate relationships between 1893 and 1904, she explicitly describes this blend of genders within herself. "I do not desire exclusive femininity, just as I do not desire exclusive masculinity," she writes. "In my thoughts, my desires, in my spirit—I am more a man; in my body I am more a woman."[7]

Gippius found herself attracted to homosexual men, a feeling she explains by her perception in them of a "tinge of bisexuality" similar to that which she senses to be at the core of her own identity: "This [bisexuality] is terribly akin to me . . . one *seems* to be both man and woman."[8] It should be stressed that Gippius used the term "bisexuality" not in its modern sense of dual sexual orientation but in the sense of being bigendered—combining physical and behavioral characteristics conventionally assigned to opposite, polarized genders. Gippius's notion that one individual could possess two genders informed the literary personae she developed as well as her own sexual activities.

During the first three decades of her career, when Gippius was deeply involved in her religious cause, she also was intellectually preoccupied with the role of sexuality in relation to human spiritual life. As a result of this preoccupation, Gippius wanted to understand her physical attraction to others in spiritual terms. In her writings about her love affairs she reveals a deep ambivalence toward physical intimacy. She observes in her diaries that she finds the act of sex insulting, because it creates physical inequality between people. Although she does not elaborate on this idea, it seems that Gippius finds unacceptable the different male and female roles—active and passive—traditionally present in sexual relations, and that she was unwilling to play such a passive female part.[9] Her marriage to Merezhkovskii apparently remained unconsummated, although the couple shared numerous intellectual interests and a deep spiritual bond. Even in her diaries and letters Gippius remains reticent about her actual sexual experiences, which, combined with the bigendered persona she projected in public, have fostered much speculation, but no definite conclusions, about her sexuality.[10] In "Contes d'amour" she confesses distaste for heterosexual intimacy and hints at her love for a woman,[11] suggesting that, had Gippius lived in our time, she might have identified herself as a lesbian. Since in Gippius's day, however, people often associated lesbianism with prostitution, radical feminist activity or the lack of fully fledged sexuality[12]—none of which applies to Gippius—she understandably avoided this term, even when admitting that she considered same-sex affairs a possible solution to her difficulties with physical intimacy.[13] Gippius herself apparently never fully determined the nature of her sexuality or its relation to her strivings for spiritual enlightenment.

Gippius's grappling with the import of her sexuality can best be understood in the context of her ideas about the dichotomous nature of the universe. Gippius shared with other Russian symbolists a view of the world as fundamentally dual: the physical, earthly realm is merely a pale and perhaps corrupt imitation of a spiritual, otherworldly one. For Gippius this Platonic weltanschauung was not merely a theoretical stance but a conception of the universe rooted deeply in her psyche and sense of gender identity. The division of physical and spiritual realms of existence pervades Gippius's self-image, as implied in her description of herself as bigendered—physically feminine, spiritually and intellectually masculine. Gippius constantly sought ways to transcend these divisions between the physical and metaphysical, the feminine and the masculine, and to reconcile these seemingly opposed aspects not only in herself, but in all of humanity.

As ways to achieve a reconciliation of these dichotomies Gippius sets forth two ideals in her theoretical writings: consecrated flesh and androgynous love.[14] The first of these, consecrated flesh, she conceives of as human corporeality infused with spirituality by means of continual, active pursuit of divine love. While Gippius remains vague about how this process occurs, she believes love to be a key to its accomplishment, for, according to her, love is the one element of human life on earth that partakes of the divine and therefore provides access to understanding of the metaphysical realm. Gippius' second ideal, androgynous love, is a pure, incorporeal bond that unites male and female sexes into a single human entity. When human beings are no longer divided into polarized genders, sexual activity will become obsolete, Gippius maintains, and mankind can then pursue love without the complication of earthbound physical desire. Androgyny thus represents for Gippius an emblematic, unified physical and spiritual state.

Gippius was not the only Russian writer to advocate androgyny as a sexual ideal,[15] but she was the only major woman writer in Russia to make this concept a cornerstone of her philosophy, influencing not only the themes but also the formal features of her poems. In her diaries she declares that she wants to write "not just as a woman, but as a human being,"[16] implying both the existence of a category of humanness that transcends gender and her desire to write about questions that confront all people. Gippius most often chooses not to specify the gender of the lyric voice in her poems,[17] supporting the idea that she was seeking to portray a universal human voice. When Gippius does choose to identify the gender of her lyric persona, it is almost always masculine, a choice that had several motivations. Russian lyric poetry at the end of the nineteenth century was grounded in a tradition in which the lyric voice was usually male and in which masculine grammatical forms were presumed to represent an unmarked, universal human essence.[18] Because a female lyric persona was strongly associated at this time with a limited number of themes, especially those drawn from domestic and social spheres, using a male persona gave Gippius a greater range of possible topics,[19] as well as ensuring that her poems would be read seriously. By using a male persona Gippius also indirectly expanded the thematic scope of women's poetry to include expressions of love for women. In her love lyrics Gippius often uses a male ego and female addressee, masking her own gender as a woman poet and presenting her feelings in a form that society would find acceptable at this time.[20]

In view of Gippius's conception of androgyny as a sexual ideal, her use of a male voice can also be read as a way of creating an androgynous literary persona. In her critical essays Gippius similarly adopts a male pseudonym, Anton Krainii, which both disguises her gender as author of this traditionally unfeminine mode of discourse and creates an androgynous authorial figure for those readers who know, as did most of Gippius's contemporaries, that Anton is masculine verbal garb for Zinaida. Only in Gippius's literary works themselves, however, is she able to create an explicitly bigendered persona, a lyric ego specified as androgynous by combining masculine and feminine grammatical forms—the quintessential expression of her androgynous ideal.

The poems in this volume include an excellent example of Gippius's androgynous lyric persona. "The Eternal Feminine" presents a bigendered persona who longs for a new kind of love, a pure love worthy of the three women invoked in the poem—the Virgin Mary, St. Theresa of Lisieux, and Solveig, a character in Henryk Ibsen's play *Peer Gynt*. All three figures personify Gippius's image of the principle of divine wisdom as a woman whose love is selfless, eternally faithful and nonsexual. This poem from Gippius's last book of verse conveys her vision of ideal love as transcending gender and transforming sexuality into spirituality. "The Kiss" also treats the themes of sexuality and love, but in this poem a male lyric persona addresses a specific female lover, proclaiming love's unrealized potential as its most compelling aspect by depicting the happiness of a moment when love is still uncomplicated by physical intimacy.

"Stone" portrays in a more detached, philosophical manner the consequences of human physicality, the fettering of both spirit and sacred flesh by the physical body that isolates people from each other and chains mankind to the earth. The oppressiveness of earthly existence, which is keenly felt in "A Cry" and "Earth," gives way to profound despair in "Monotony," where the lyric persona expresses one of Gippius's greatest fears—that in the heavenly world life will be no better than on earth. More hopeful images conclude "Ballad," which contrasts the beauty of God's earthly creation with dusty trappings of religion, "Snowflakes," which ends with a vision of death as eternal love, and "Ticking," which expresses the faith that light of God's word will issue from the darkness of the present, no matter how long the darkness may last. In "Gentle Flame" and "I (in someone else's name)," the lyric personae reveal intense feelings of profound isolation and defensiveness vis-à-vis the outside world. Each tries to preserve something, a candle's flame or a modicum of self-love, against what seem to be hostile, intrusive forces. Earthly reality becomes even more alarming in "Yellow Window," where the wildly horrific apocalyptic imagery constitutes a response to the destruction caused by revolution and civil war. These poems thus display both the chronological range and major themes of Gippius's verse.

Although Gippius always considered the ideas expressed in her poetry to be of paramount importance, she did not neglect lyric form. The aphoristic quality of her verse—her combination of conciseness with precision of imagery—has been compared with the classical style of Pushkin.[21] At the same time, Gippius broke with nineteenth-century traditions by using several new or unusual verse forms in her poetry, including nontraditional rhyme patterns, unrhymed free verse and tonic meter *(dol'niki),*[22] the latter becoming famous during subsequent decades in the works of Aleksandr Blok and Anna Akhmatova. Gippius skillfully uses sound patterns and rhythms in her poetry to accentuate particular themes, especially the monotonous, oppressive nature of earthly existence and human physicality, to which she contrasts the lightness and freedom of the soul, often portrayed in flight imagery. Her sound effects are, unfortunately, almost impossible to reproduce in translation.

Gippius's poetry imparts overall the image of a deeply divided individual struggling to understand her place in the universe and to justify the less than ideal nature of human existence. A feeling of profound despair at the bleakness and oppressiveness of earthly life overwhelms the lyric persona in some poems, while faith in the possibility of harmony, love or life after death dominates others. Attachment to the physical world and appreciation of its beauties alternate in her poetry with yearning to reach and comprehend a metaphysical realm. Faith in God is juxtaposed to anger at His seeming abandonment of humanity; the desire for human love contrasts with fear of intimacy. Gippius's poems encapsulate these disparate emotions in gems of lyric form, which Aleksandr Blok, the most famous Russian Symbolist poet, described as "exhausting and works of genius!"[23] They remain so to this day, an intellectual and emotional challenge for readers willing to encounter them, their metaphysical speculations and profound psychological insights rewarding modern readers with moments of genuine inspiration about the timeless mysteries of the human condition.

Christine Borowec

Ballad

Dank passageways
Beneath the bright Dniepr.
Old-fashioned arches
Overgrown with moss.

In a deep cave
Burns a small flame,
A heavy lock hangs
On a wrought-iron door.

And drops, like tears,
Tremble on the archways,
As nocturnal reveries
Torment an anchorite.

Long unable to sleep . . .

He lit the icon lamp.
He wanted to pray,
And could not pray.

"As you see, Savior,
I'm worn out, exhausted,
Reveal to me, Teacher,
Where is Your truth!

Fasting and fetters
Are not God's bidding.
Christ, in your book
Are forgiveness and light.

I remember: once at a window
I glanced into a garden;
There was a kind sun,
And I was glad of the sun.

There in the dark thickets
No one would notice me.
There homeless birdlings
Find a green refuge.

There lilacs weep
With the morning dew,
And shadows tremble
From transparent birches.

There seagulls flicker
Along the willful river
And children play games
On the dampened sand.

I am happy like the children,
And understand once more
That in God's bidding
Is pure and simple love.

It's dark in my cell . . .
I'm worn out, exhausted,
But life—and happiness
And your truth . . .

Are found not on dusty pages,
Not in somber candles,
But in the sky, and birds,
And bright stars' rays.

With love, O Lord,
I gazed at everything:
This is more precious,
For this is truly Yours!

1890

Snowflakes

Along a remote untrodden path
In the pale decline of day
I walk in a snowy forest,
Sadness leads me on.

The strange road is silent,
Silent too the obscure forest . . .
It is not misty darkness
That leaks from lifeless heavens,

But . . . snowflakes circle round
And like a gentle shroud
Noiselessly, endlessly,
Lie down in front of me.

The white flakes are fluffy,
Like swarms of cheerful bees,
The bold flakes gambol
And rush along behind me.

And they fall and fall . . .
The sky comes nearer to earth . . .
My heart is strangely gladdened
By the quietness and death.

Reality and dream
Mingle, flow together,
While ever lower descends
The sinister horizon.

I walk along and fall,
Submitting to my fate
With mysterious delight
And musings—about you.

I love the unattainable,
That which may not exist . . .
My dear beloved child,
My one and only light!

I can feel in my dreams
Your gentle, quiet breathing.
And this snowy coverlet
Seems light and sweet to me.

I know, eternity is near,
I hear my blood freezing . . .
The silence is interminable
Like this twilight . . . And love.

1894

Monotony

In the evening hour of solitude,
Despondency and weariness,
  Alone, on unsteady steps,
I search in vain for consolation,
Alleviation of my anxiety
  In the stagnant, freezing waters.

Reflections of the last glimmering rays,
Like visions which have never been,
  Lounge on the drowsy clouds.
From the silence of this iciness,
My soul fills with confusion . . .
Oh, were there only a shadow of movement,
  If only a sound from these dense reeds!

But I know, there is no absolution for this world,
No oblivion for the sadness of the heart,
And no resolution of this silence—
Everything is forever without alteration,
  Both on earth and in the heavens.

1895

A Cry

I grow numb from exhaustion,
  My soul is wounded and bloody . . .
Is there really no pity for us,
  Really, for us, no love?

We fulfill an implacable will,
  Like shadows, noiseless, without a trace,
We walk an unforgiving road
  And don't even know where we're bound.

And the burden of life, a sacred burden,

The further we go, the heavier it grows . . .
While an unknown demise awaits us
At an eternally locked door.

Without a murmur, without surprise
We do what God desires.
He created us without inspiration,
And, after that, could not love us.

We fall down, an impotent lot,
Weakly believing in miracles,
While from above, like a tombstone slab,
The blind heavens press down.

1896

Ticking

Midnight shadow. Silence.
Heart thumping, clock ticking.
Incomprehensibly black night!
How heavy is its shroud!

And I know, more immovable still
Is the gloom of weak hearts.
I pray to you, O Father!
Give me a sound or a sign.

I love my soul within me
More than myself or people.
And yet with my own will
I'll break my soul in two.

The silence has grown more lively.
In it, darkly, I hear an answer:
Let the night be endlessly long,
From the darkness will come light!

1900

Gentle Flame

I will find my own comfort.
Here all is mine; I alone exist.
I'll light my gentle icon lamp.
I love it. It is wholly mine.

How dear to me its timid flame!
It does not blind, does not burn.
What need have I for a crude luminary
Shining from unattainable heights?

Alas! The dawn disturbs me
Through the silk of closed curtains,
This flickering little fire cannot
Struggle against the heavenly flame.

My timid lamp blanches . . .
The first sunbeam—a scarlet blade . . .
And my heart weeps . . . unable
To save the lamp's small fire!

1901

I (in someone else's name)

I am offended by God forever.
Because of this I don't believe in Him.
I am the most pitiful person,
I dissemble before everyone.

In me—toward me—there's a sick passion:
I gaze into myself, judge, and analyze . . .
Oh, if only I had strength! If only—power!
For although I love, I don't believe in myself.

I constantly tremble and fear everyone,
The eyes of people frighten me . . .

But I don't give in, I stand to the side—
They will not guess I am here.

And all the while I can't escape;
In company I dream, become indignant . . .
Trying to hide from them that I am lying,
I ramble on about God's truth.

And in this way I play my game,
Though prevaricating becomes a bore . . .
Only I exist . . . And I will die!
What good is any truth to me?

But I will not leave, I am too weak,
I warm myself in the rays of another's love;
I'm forever a slave of people and falsehood
And have no hope of liberation.

Sometimes I want to curse everyone—
But I can only insult them timidly . . .
In me, towards me, there is a sick passion.
This self of mine I love . . . and despise.

1901

Earth

A moment of weakness . . .
  A moment of hesitation . . .
And broken are the wings
  Of sacred madness.

I stand above a grave
  Where boldness slumbers.
Alas, all that has passed away,
  The merriment and agitation,

And delight in a passing glance
    Lightning quick and pure,
Dawns in early springtime,
    And sprigs of eight-leaved lilac . . .

Were they ever really here?
    It all seems so deceitful.
Now I stand above the grave
    With only an uncertain hope.

Beneath the dust and ashes
    I search for any movement,
With a prayer and with horror
    I await a resurrection . . .

But waiting becomes more terrible
    As I stand here quite defenseless . . .
And laughing, showing blackly
    Is the open, uncovered grave.

With my all-powerful soul
    I demand something miraculous . . .
While from below wafts only
    The odor of graveyard earth.

1902

The Kiss

Agnes, when I bring my smile
Closer to your lips,
Don't run away, timid fish,
What will happen—I don't know.

I know the joy of coming nearer,
The happiness of restless thoughts,
But can I link these moments in a chain
And will I touch your tender lips?

Don't be afraid. Look, my gaze is honest,
My heart is anxious and alive,
So splendid is this moment of promise!
Please don't be impatient, Agnes . . .

Distance and closeness are similar.
In both there is an uncertainty.
Agnes, I love the unknown,
Not fulfillment, but possibility.

Your lips tremble, not knowing
What fire I might hold for them.
Agnes, Agnes, I'll only barely
Touch the surface with a nimble kiss.

1903

Stone

The body-stone oppresses the spirit,
  White wings, rustling,
  Thoughts light and creative . . .
The body-stone oppresses the spirit.

The body-stone stifles the sacred flesh,
  Joy of childhood, joined with mystery,
  A caress, quick and honest . . .
The body-stone stifles the sacred flesh.

There is no path from one stone to another.
  Entombed in a single earth,
  We are divided within ourselves . . .
No path for us from one to another.

1907

Yellow Window

Come over here and look
Through the yellow pane.
Look, how wild the sky is,
Subterranean, aglow.

A smoky, swirling, worm-eaten
Mass of clouds crawls by.
The willows turn deathly red
Above the yellow of hot slopes.

At the ravine bottom
The brook looks like black wine.
And from my window the grass
Appears to be burnt paper.

How senselessly bloody are
The bodies of April glades.
A rusty, dry, and bitter rain
Drips and drizzles down.

Outward onto everything face
These panes, infernal window.
My poor land has faded,
The earth has been scorched.

April 1918

The Eternal Feminine

With what word can I touch
  Her white garments?
With what new revelation
  Pour out Her essence?
Oh, all your earthly names
  Are known to me:

Solveig, Theresa, Maria . . .
    They all are One, are you.
I love and pray . . . Yet insufficient
    Are my love and prayers to you.
Yours, male and female from inmost depths,
    I want to abide in myself,
So that my heart might answer you—
    My heart—in itself alone,
So that the Gentle One might see
    Her own pure image in it . . .
There will be other paths,
    It's time for a new kind of love.
Solveig, Theresa, Maria,
    Bride-Mother-Sister!

1927

To Her in the Mountains

I.

I saved my little lilac flower,
Not halfheartedly or idly.
I brought it, with its longish stem,
And laid it down at her dear feet.

But you don't want it, you're not pleased . . .
In vain I try to catch your eye.
So be it! You don't want it—leave it;
But I still love you all the same.

II.

I will find a new flower in the forest.
    I do not believe your non-reply!
I'll bring the new one, lilac-colored,
    To your glassy house with the narrow door.

But I grew frightened there at the stream:
A cold mist rose up from the ravine,
Quietly hissing, a snake slithered past . . .
And I did not find a flower for my dear.

1928

Éternité Fremissante

—to V.S. Varshavskii

My love is whole, it's whole,∫
But even so I cry, indignant:
It's whole, and yet also divided,
Because I love dividedness.

O, Time! I love your movement,
Impulsiveness and measuredness.
I love the trajectory of your romp,
Your fluctuating faithfulness.

But how can I not also love
The other joyous miracle:
The lively flow of timelessness,
The fire, the faint breath from "up there."

A pity, that they are divided—
Timelessness and humanness.
But a day will come: days will intertwine
Into a whole—a Tremulous Eternity.

Mountain Light

The last pine tree is illumined,
Beneath it the dark ridge swells.
Now it too will be extinguished.
The day is done—it won't return.

The day has ended. What did it hold?
I don't know, it sailed by like a bird.
It was an ordinary day,
And even so—it won't return.

Translated by Christine Borowec

Notes to the Essay

I am grateful to Elizabeth Cheresh Allen for her many helpful comments on this essay.

1. Andrei Belyi, *Arabeski* (Moscow, 1911), 445 [rpt. Munich: Wilhelm Fink Verlag, 1969].

2. D.S. Mirsky, *A History of Russian Literature* (New York: Knopf, 1955), 440.

3. Renato Poggioli, *The Poets of Russia, 1890–1930* (Cambridge, MA: Harvard University Press, 1960), 111.

4. Olga Matich, *Paradox in the Religious Poetry of Zinaida Gippius* (Munich: Wilhelm Fink Verlag, 1972), 9. Matich documents several other colorful nicknames applied to Gippius, including Russian Messalina, Circe of the Merezhkovskii menage, and the Petersburg Hedda Gabler.

5. *Peterburgskie dnevniki, 1914–1919* (New York: Orfel, 1982), 283; quoted in *Stikhotvoreniia. Zhivye litsa* (Moscow: Khudozhestvennaia literatura, 1991), 6.

6. A. Volynskii, "Sil'fida," quoted in Stanley J. Rabinowitz, "A 'Fairy Tale of Love'?: The Relationship of Zinaida Gippius and Akim Volynsky (Unpublished Materials)," *Oxford Slavonic Papers* 24 (1991): 133.

7. Z. Gippius, "Contes d'amour," in *Between Paris and St. Petersburg: Selected Diaries of Zinaida Hippius*, trans. and ed. Temira Pachmuss (Urbana: University of Illinois Press 1975), 77.

8. Ibid., 74.

9. Simon Karlinsky similarly concludes that Gippius wanted the upper hand in her relationships with men and would not take on a traditional, submissive female role. See Karlinsky, "Who Was Zinaida Gippius?" in Vladimir Zlobin, *A Difficult Soul: Zinaida Gippius*, ed., annotated and with an introductory essay by Simon Karlinsky (Berkeley: University of California Press, 1980), 7.

10. Gippius has been characterized variously as a hermaphroditic, androgynous, lesbian, bisexual and frigid.

11. Z. Gippius, "Contes d'amour," 71–78.

12. Several recent studies analyze conflicting depictions of lesbianism during this period. See Diana Lewis Burgin, "Laid Out in Lavender: Perceptions of Lesbian Love in Russian Literature and Criticism of the Silver Age, 1893–1917," in *Sexuality and the Body in Russian Culture*, ed. Jane T. Costlow, Stephanie Sandler and Judith Vowles (Stanford: Stanford University Press, 1993), 181–82; Laura Engelstein, *The Keys to Happiness: Sex and the Search for Modernity in Fin-de-Siècle Russia* (Ithaca, NY: Cornell University Press, 1992), 128–64; Elaine Showalter, *Sexual Anarchy: Gender and Culture at the Fin de Siècle* (New York: Viking Penguin, 1990), 23–27.

13. Z. Gippius, "Contes d'amour," 73.

14. See especially Gippius's article "Vliublennost'," in Anton Krainii, *Literaturnyi*

dnevnik 1899–1907 (Petersburg, 1908), 187–212. Detailed studies of these concepts can be found in Temira Pachmuss, *Zinaida Hippius: An Intellectual Profile* (Carbondale: Southern Illinois University Press, 1971), and Olga Matich, *Paradox in the Religious Poetry of Zinaida Gippius.*

15. Androgyny appears as a theme in the works of several Russian Symbolist writers, including Dmitrii Merezhkovskii, Andrei Belyi, Fedor Sologub and Konstantin Bal'mont. For a discussion of several of these authors see Olga Matich, "Androgyny and the Russian Silver Age," *Pacific Coast Philology* 16 (1979): 42–49.

16. Temira Pachmuss cites this statement from Gippius's remarks to Georgii Adamovich in *Zinaida Hippius: An Intellectual Profile*, 17.

17. Antonina Filonov Gove calculates that the gender of the lyric persona is unspecified in 51.2 percent of Gippius's poems, masculine in 45.2 percent, and feminine in 3.6 percent. "Gender as a Poetic Feature in the Verse of Zinaida Gippius," in *American Contributions to the Eighth International Congress of Slavists* (Columbus, OH: Slavica), 381.

18. Sibelan Forrester discusses this assumption in her essay "Wooing the Other Woman: Gender in Women's Love Poetry in the Silver Age," in *Engendering Slavic Literatures,* ed. Pamela Chester and Sibelan Forrester (Bloomington: Indiana University Press, 1996), 107.

19. Charlotte Rosenthal makes a similar observation in "The Silver Age: Highpoint for Women?" in *Women and Society in Russia and the Soviet Union,* ed. Linda Edmondson (Cambridge: Cambridge University Press, 1992), 39.

20. Burgin discusses Gippius's use of a male persona to disguise lesbian desire in "Laid Out in Lavender," 185.

21. Sergei Makovskii, *Na Parnase 'Serebrianogo veka'* (Munich, 1962), 95–99.

22. For a detailed description of Gippius's innovative verse forms see Oleg A. Maslenikov, "Disruption of Canonical Verse Norms in the Poetry of Zinaida Hippius," in *Studies in Slavic Linguistics and Poetics in Honour of Boris O. Unbegaun* (New York: New York University Press, 1968), 89–96.

23. Aleksandr Blok, letter of 12 December 1903 to Andrei Belyi, quoted in Avril Pyman, "Aleksandr Blok and the Merezhkovskijs," in *Alexandr Blok: Centennial Conference,* ed. Walter N. Vickery (Columbus, OH: Slavica, 1982), 249.

Bibliography

Primary Works

Novye liudi: Rasskazy, pervaia kniga [*New People: Stories, First Book*]. St. Petersburg, 1896.

Zerkala: Vtoraia kniga rasskazov [*Mirrors: Second Book of Stories*]. St. Petersburg, 1898.

Pobediteli. Roman [*The Victors. A Novel*]. St. Petersburg, 1898. [Rpt. Munich: Wilhelm Fink Verlag, 1972.]

Tret'ia kniga rasskazov [*Third Book of Stories*]. St. Petersburg, 1902.

Alyi mech: Rasskazy, chetvertaia kniga [*A Scarlet Sword: Stories, Fourth Book*]. St. Petersburg, 1904.

Chernoe po belomu: Piataia kniga rasskazov [*Black on White: Fifth Book of Stories]. St. Petersburg, 1908.*

[Krainii, Anton.] *Literaturnyi dnevnik: 1899–1907* [*Literary Diary*]. St. Petersburg, 1908. [Rpt. Munich: Wilhelm Fink Verlag, 1970.]

Chortova kukla [*The Devil's Doll*]. Moscow, 1911. [Rpt. Munich, 1972.]

Lunnye murav'i. Shestaia kniga rasskazov [*The Moon Ants. Sixth book of stories*]. Moscow, 1912.

Roman-Tsarevich. Moscow, 1913. [Rpt. Munich: Wilhelm Fink Verlag, 1972.]

Nebesnye slova i drugie rasskazy [*Heavenly Words and Other Stories*]. Paris, 1921.

Zhivye litsa [*Living Faces*]. Prague, 1925. [Rpt. Munich: Wilhelm Fink Verlag, 1971.]

Siniaia kniga. Peterburgskii dnevnik, 1914–1918 [*Blue Book. Petersburg Diaries*]. Belgrade, 1929. [Rpt. Tel Aviv: Arkhivy, 1980.]

Dmitrii Merezhkovskii. Paris, 1951.

P'esy. Ed. Temira Pachmuss. Munich: Wilhelm Fink Verlag, 1972.

Stikhotvoreniia i poèmy. Ed. Temira Pachmuss. Munich: Wilhelm Fink Verlag, 1972.

Pis'ma k Berberovoi i Khodasevichu [*Letters to Berberova and Khodasevich*]. Ed. Erika Freiberger Sheikholeslami. Ann Arbor, MI: Ardis, 1978.

Stikhotvoreniia. Zhivye litsa. Moscow: Khudozhestvennaia literatura, 1991.

In Translation

["Song" and twenty-one more poems]. *Modern Russian Poetry*. Ed. Vladimir Markov and Merrill Sparks. Indianapolis: Bobbs-Merrill, 1967. 56–89.

["Heavenly Words" and twelve stories]. *Selected Works of Zinaida Hippius*. Ed. and trans. Temira Pachmuss. Urbana: University of Illinois Press, 1972.

"He Has Descended" [a story]. Trans. Samuel Cioran. *Russian Literary Triquarterly* 4 (1972): 117–23.

Intellect and Ideas in Action: Selected Correspondence of Zinaida Hippius. Ed. Temira Pachmuss. Munich: Wilhelm Fink Verlag, 1972.

Between Paris and St. Petersburg: Selected Diaries of Zinaida Hippius. Ed. Temira Pachmuss. Urbana: University of Illinois Press, 1975.

"He Has Descended." Trans. Samuel Cioran. *The Silver Age of Russian Culture*. Ed. Carl and Ellendea Proffer. Ann Arbor, MI: Ardis, 1975. 313–19.

["Autumn" and nine more poems, three stories]. *Women Writers in Russian Modernism: An Anthology*. Ed. and trans. Temira Pachmuss. Urbana, IL: University of Chicago Press, 1978. 26–84.

["L'Imprévisibilité" and "A Greek Frock," poems]. *Penguin Book of Women Poets*. Ed. Carol Cosman et al. New York: Viking, 1978. 187–89.

["Rain" and five more poems, two stories]. *A Russian Cultural Revival: An Anthology of Russian Emigre Writing Before 1939*. Ed. and trans. Temira Pachmuss. Knoxville: University of Tennessee Press, 1981. 26–54.

["Radiances" and nineteen more poems]. *The Burden of Sufferance: Women Writers in Russia*. Trans. Pamela Perkins and Albert Cook. Garland Publishing, 1993. 77–98.

["The Seamstress" and two poems]. *Anthology of Women's Writing in Russia, 1777–1994*. Ed. Catriona Kelly. Oxford: Oxford University Press, 1994. 166–69.

Secondary Works

Berberova, Nina. *The Italics Are Mine*. Trans. Phillipe Radley. New York: Harcourt, Brace and World, 1969.

Burgin, Diana Lewis. "Laid Out in Lavender: Perceptions of Lesbian Love in Russian Literature and Criticism of the Silver Age, 1893–1917." *Sexuality and the Body in Russian Culture*. Ed. Jane T. Costlow, Stephanie Sandler and Judith Vowles. Stanford: Stanford University Press, 1993. 177–203.

Forrester, Sibelan. "Wooing the Other Woman: Gender in Women's Love Poetry in the Silver Age." *Engendering Slavic Literatures*. Ed. Pamela Chester and Sibelan Forrester. Bloomington: Indiana University Press, 1996. 107–34.

Gove, Antonina Filonov. "Gender as a Poetic Feature in the Verse of Zinaida Gippius." *American Contributions to the Eighth International Congress of Slavists.* Columbus, OH: Slavica, 1978. 379–407.

———. "Disruption of Canonical Verse Norms in the Poetry of Zinaida Hippius." *Studies in Slavic Linguistics and Poetics in Honour of Boris O. Unbegaun.* New York: New York University Press, 1968. 89–96.

Maslenikov, Oleg A. "The Spectre of Nothingness: The Privative Element in the Poetry of Zinaida Gippius." *Slavic and East European Journal* 4 (1960): 299–311.

———."Androgyny and the Russian Religious Renaissance." *Western Philosophical Systems in Russian Literature.* Ed. Anthony M. Mlikotin. Los Angeles: University of Southern California Press, 1979. 165–75.

———. "Androgyny and the Russian Silver Age." *Pacific Coast Philology* 14 (1979): 42–50.

———. "Dialectics of Cultural Return: Zinaida Gippius's Personal Myth." *Cultural Mythologies of Russian Modernism*.Berkeley: University of California Press, 1992. 52–72.

Matich, Olga. *Paradox in the Religious Poetry of Zinaida Gippius.* Munich: Wilhelm Fink Verlag, 1972.

——— "Zinaida Gippius and the Unisex of Heavenly Experience." *Die Welt der Slaven* [single volume] 19–20 (1974–1975): 98–104.

Mirsky, D.S. *A History of Russian Literature.* New York: Knopf, 1955.

Pachmuss, Temira. *Zinaida Hippius: An Intellectual Profile.* Urbana: University of Illinois Press, 1971.

Poggioli, Renato. *The Poets of Russia, 1890–1930.* Cambridge, MA: Harvard University Press, 1960.

Pyman, Avril. "Aleksandr Blok and the Merezhkovskijs." *Alexandr Blok: Centennial Conference.* Ed. Walter N. Vickery. Columbus, OH: Slavica, 1982. 237–70.

Rabinowitz, Stanley J. "A 'Fairy Tale of Love'?: The Relationship of Zinaida Gippius and Akim Volynsky (Unpublished Materials)." *Oxford Slavonic Papers* 24 (1991): 121–44.

Rosenthal, Charlotte. "The Silver Age: Highpoint for Women?" *Women and Society in Russia and the Soviet Union.* Ed. Linda Edmondson. Cambridge: Cambridge University Press, 1992. 32–47.

Zlobin, Vladimir. *A Difficult Soul: Zinaida Gippius.* Ed., annotated and with an introductory essay by Simon Karlinsky. Berkeley: University of California Press, 1980.

Aleksandra Kollontai

Aleksandra Kollontai (1872–1952).
Courtesy of Rimma Volynska.

Aleksandra Mikhailovna Kollontai (1872–1952) was a prime feminist mover in the great social revolutions of the early and mid-twentieth century and an original believer in and propagator of communism. In the 1920s and 1930s she became a household name far beyond her native Russia. Through her fearless and brilliant political activism, she was a passionate, inspired advocate of free love and women's rights whose tongue and intellect took flight in her writing and public speeches. She was a staunch individualist whose socially committed work and lifestyle brought her both extreme admiration and harsh censure.

Kollontai was fascinated by literature, a facet of her work that is rarely treated. She was dedicated to bringing the art of the word to the great, culturally deprived mass of society. Zealous in her efforts to make literature relevant to the vital issues of human life, she necessarily engaged in creative writing, and the conviction with which she wrote made what she produced fiction with a vengeance.

Kollontai stands alone as the preeminent Soviet feminist. Her views regarding problems of sexual morality, issues related to labor unions and the status of women in post-Tsarist Russia were so extremely controversial that they were grossly distorted, discredited and branded heretical by her enemies even as she formulated them. By the early 1920s, her writing was already banned from publication in Soviet Russia. Fortunately, her works were not destroyed but only locked away in secret vaults until our time. For her unorthodox views, Kollontai was ridiculed in the Soviet Union as a proponent of the "glass of water theory," the idea that sex should be as easy and uncomplicated as drinking a glass of water.

During the early 1960s the women's movement in the West acknowledged Kollontai as an important figure in feminist history, thereby rescuing her from virtual oblivion. Germaine Greer wrote: "In this era of the New Left in the Western World . . . we particularly needed to discover the despised and rejected political credo of Alexandra Kollontai."[1]

The conceptual and literary importance of Kollontai's work may be best framed by a recounting of her life and formal achievements. She was born in 1872 as Aleksandra Mikhailovna Domontovich to a wealthy former general in the tsar's army, a fairly liberal and erudite man. Her mother, from whom Aleksandra undoubtedly inherited an assertive and independent nature, was herself a rebel of sorts. Six years before Aleksandra's birth she left her first husband, and from her passionate love with Mikhail Domontovich she bore a son and two daughters. Aleksandra was the first born of this second marriage. At the age of eighteen she left home, rebelling against parental authority—not by joining a socialist circle, but by marrying a distant cousin, Vladimir Kollontai, an impoverished but elegant army officer. The idyll of this marriage lasted for five years, during which she was devoted to bringing up their son Misha. In 1896, while her husband was working as an engineer on a ventilation system at the Krengolmskaya Factory near the Baltic industrial port of Narva, Kollontai saw firsthand the terrible working conditions at the plant. This face-to-face confrontation with the harsh reality of human labor marks the emergence of her social conscience and her turn toward the revolutionary cause. She first sought progressive ideas through illegal literature, which was difficult to obtain in the politcally reactionary and censured atmosphere of late-nineteenth-century Russia. Her intellectual maturation began in earnest in 1899, when she left St. Petersburg to study political economy at the university in Zurich.

By 1915 Kollontai had joined the Bolshevik party, and until 1917 she was busy agitating for the leftist cause during lecture tours in Germany, Denmark, Sweden and the United States. From the very beginning, her involvement in radical political circles was inseparable from her preoccupation with the emancipation of women. At first, she believed that the cause of women's liberation was possible within the framework of social democracy. However, the Social Democratic party opposed her ideas about the rights of women very early on in her activity. Had it not been for her high status within the Bolshevik party ranks at the time of the victory of the First Revolution in February 1917—a status that was due primarily to Lenin's personal respect for Kollontai—her first initiative on behalf of women's rights might have been stifled. Her vision took shape in presenting a proposal for setting up a Women's Bureau that would be staffed by women to the forthcoming Party Conference. This office would document the changes in women's issues brought about by the revolution. Somewhat reluctantly, Lenin consented to let her present this plan. However, the conference rejected it outright as impractical and politically improper. The official position of the Bolsheviks was that setting up "women's organizations" would introduce "sexual divisions into the grand ideal of the united Party." As the period of civil war began in postrevolutionary Russia, a time of social collapse and extreme famine, with marriages failing and revolutionary zeal slackening under the strain of everyday hardships, Kollontai strove to clarify her radical position on the status of women in Russia. Her efforts at this time received the moral support of Inessa Armand, the French-born Russian revolutionary, close assistant and mistress of Lenin, who together with Kollontai brought women's issues to the forefront of the revolution.

In November 1918, Kollontai achieved her first political success by organizing the first Women's Congress in Moscow. Over a thousand red-kerchiefed activists crossed the war zone to participate in this event. The women were hungry and exhausted; their mood, angry and desperate. They demanded that the authorities set up more cafeterias and nurseries. At the same time, they expressed concern that the government not take away their children. Kollontai responded with her famous speech on "Communism and the Family." She assured her listeners that the communists had no intention of separating women from their children, and she outlined the measures by which the government should help the lot of women. The impact of this First Women's Congress is evident in the chief resolution it adopted: every party organization should set up its own Women's Commission under the supervision of Kollontai and Armand. Even though by December 1918 Kollontai was suffering from a heart condition and was confined to bed, she nevertheless oversaw the opening of a Women's Commission in virtually every province of European Russia. In September 1919, the commission was upgraded to an official Women's Bureau. Until it was disbanded in 1930, this bureau, known as Zhenotdel, dealt with the most vexing issues then affecting the lives of women: abortion, alimony, prostitution and venereal disease.

Kollontai was the only woman to hold a prominent position in Lenin's government and had his special respect and support. As long as the party leader was alive and well, she was politically successful. She was soon appointed Commissar of Social Welfare, then People's Commissar of Propaganda and Agitation. She was elected Deputy to the International Women's Secretariat and became a spokesperson for the Worker's Opposition—a movement within the party that pressed for the democratization of industry through the introduction of trade unions. But by 1921, all of this—her party position and prestige, and her personal life, as well—began to fall apart. Eventually, she withdrew from active political life.

The conservative elements within the party, which gradually gained power as Lenin's health failed in the early 1920s, harboured animosity toward Kollontai. For the most part, these were cautious men radical only in their political ideology. In practice, they were social reactionaries who could not stomach her "female" reforms, her ideas about sexual morality, her staunch opposition to the New Economic Policy of the 1920s and her support for the Workers' Opposition that was so antagonistic to the idea of party solidarity. In particular, her views on free relationships between men and women—and her individualistic flair for filtering her avid readings of Havelock Ellis and Sigmund Freud into her ideas about human sexuality and the new morality—were considered "decadent." Clearly, Kollontai's notion of universal social liberation was much more than the conservative, male-dominated party—and mainstream Soviet society, in general—could tolerate.

Soon, she was relieved of the directorship of Zhenotdel and appointed advisor to the Soviet delegation in Norway. This was, of course, a graceful but nonetheless effective way of removing her from the sphere of real influence in the government. She became, in effect, an exile from policy-making. The state of political impotence in which she found herself was complicated by a serious reversal in her personal life—the end of her relationship with the greatest love of her life. Pavel Dybenko was twenty-two years her junior, of peasant origin and little education, a revolutionary leader of sailors in the Baltic Fleet and the man with whom Kollontai had registered in marriage under the New Marriage Law of 1918. Her break with him mirrors the political trauma she experienced at this time. It was in 1922, then, when she was in diplomatic exile in Oslo, that she turned inward, away from politics and public affairs and toward the words and writing of pure thought and feeling. She would cleanse her soul and transform into fiction all the ideas that had previously made up the essence of her struggle.

Kollontai's entire body of writing, be it political, social or belletristic, dealt with the problems of women. With a frankness that addressed mundane life issues in a way unprecedented among the socially committed writers of her time, she went beyond writing only about exploitation and oppression under capitalism. More vital for her was the contemporary abyss that existed between Soviet reality and the socialist ideal. She focused on the extent and manner in which the Soviet government had distorted the early revolutionary, humanistic ideas about sexuality, family and gender equality. By highlighting the disparity between social ideology and everyday social practice, she raised the kinds of questions that—in the view of party dogmatists—were not supposed to be asked, questions about the nature of Soviet society and the direction of its transformation.

Kollontai's fictional writing, the subject of relatively little critical attention, when surveyed in the light of her spiritual work is something of a revelation. During her Nordic "exile" she wrote two trilogies. The first, with the title *Love of the Worker Bees* (*Liubov' pchel trudovykh*), was written soon after she arrived in Oslo, in 1922. It was published in the following year in a small edition as part of the series "Revolution in Feelings and Morality." It consists of a long novel bearing a title after its heroine, *Vasilisa Malygina* (sometimes translated as *Red Love* or *Free Love)*, and two short stories: "Love of Three Generations" and "Sisters." The second trilogy bears the title *Woman at the Threshhold: Psychological Sketches.* It echoes the format of the first trilogy, consisting of a long novel, *A Great Love,* and two short stories: "Thirty-Two Pages" and "A Conversation Piece." In her fiction Kollontai translated into accessible, realistic narrative the ideas that she had constantly lectured on and written articles about: changes in the emotional life of women, especially in their sexual feelings, as played out against the years of the Bolshevik revolution and the New Economic Policy (NEP) period. Her fiction presents a vivid picture of the history-making years around the revolution. In addition, it brings out into the open the private passions of Soviet citizens, as well as the general nature of human sexuality.

Kollontai wrote her fiction not for a select few but for a large audience of women. Her aim was to appeal to all women, but foremost to those who might otherwise not pick up a book unless it were simple and accessible and reflected in story form their own lives and experiences. Through their candid relations, the characters of Kollontai's fictional *oeuvre* authenticate in the most poignant way the lives and struggles of Soviet women at the time. Yet beneath their expository directness, the reader senses a drive to appeal to and persuade an audience, a mission to which the author all too willingly subjugates them. This overpronounced engagement diminishes considerably the artistic level of Kollontai's works. Classical in the rationalist, didactic sense, she is an author who writes with the need to overwhelm and convince readers, rather than leave them with the freedom to interpret or doubt.

In the short story "Sisters" ("Sestry"), literary intricacies take second place to the direct message. Kollontai lashes out at both government indifference and the regressive effect of the official New Economic Policy on the relations between the sexes. Written in 1923, it is the story of a young couple, both party members, whose lives are disrupted by NEP. The wife loses her job during the decline in employment in the early 1920s, because government policies ensured that within a marriage when anyone lost a job, the woman would always precede the man and become his dependent. Her husband, demoralized and corrupted by his new circle of bourgeois friends, brings home a prostitute one night. While he falls asleep in a drunken stupor, the women begin to talk and find a common "women's language." At dawn, some time after the prostitute leaves, the wife decides to go out and find her, convinced that they are "sisters"—both unemployed, both working-class women, each with only one means of earning her living.

This curious, didactic tale causes us to pause and reflect. Its message of solidarity with a fallen woman, reminiscent of some of Dostoevsky's characters, is shaded with expressionist tones of gloom and hopelessness. Coming from the pen of a leader in Russia's women's movement, it immediately provoked vitriolic reaction from her Bolshevik compatriots for its so-called feminist espousal, the advocacy of the particular economic condition of women. The story dwells on the ill effects of women's economic dependence on men, and it condemns the way in which the government's economic plan intensifies the sexual oppression of women. Indeed, Kollontai hated NEP. She saw it as betraying the goals of the revolution by suppressing the communist spirit. And in the true spirit of communism as she understood it, she insisted on protesting, now at least through the art of her plume, against the policies of the Red bureaucracy. Ironically, this erstwhile pillar of the Russian Communist party—one of its founders—became one of the party members most hazardous to its health! Similarly, this most outspoken leader of the socialist women's movement became the member most disliked by that movement, which labeled her a "feminist" for her views.

The novel *Vasilisa Malygina* is a case in point. It is a fictional exploration of the nature of changing female-male relations within a transforming socioecocomic system. The novel's treatment of this theme was distasteful to the Bolshevik leadership for its insistence that personal life must change in response to the revolution. Earlier, before the revolution of 1917, Kollontai had been careful to use the term "feminism" as an undesirable epithet. Now that she was herself indicted by her former party fellows as a bourgeois feminist, feminism became her goal. The novel brilliantly articulates the plight of women after the revolution. It insists that NEP was a setback for women in both economic and social terms. As such it made more urgent the need for women to join together on feminist grounds. As Kollontai clearly saw, the party was not, afterall, dealing adequately with the "woman question."

Vasilisa, a young working-class communist, falls in love with Volodia, a fellow party member with anarchist leanings. While their relationship is successful during the civil war, it begins to lose cohesiveness as Volodia's financial success grows during the NEP period. He succumbs to the pleasures of bourgeois life and falls in love with Nina, a pampered bourgeois woman (*burzhuika*), who is the diametrical opposite of the modest and dedicated Vasia. Step by step, the novel traces the disintegration of Vasia and Volodia's five-year relationship.

The power of the novel lies in its candid, psychologically valid account of the couple's breakup. It addresses very sensitively the emotional dimensions of the two communist lovers, with their mutual, although very different, expressions of despair over a relationship that is at an end. Yet the novel's strong personal theme provides grounds for the work's stylistic weakness. Kollontai undercuts the potentially artful use of image and metaphor in favor of a tendentious objective—to present plain and drab life. All of the *Worker Bees* trilogy was written with this purpose in mind: to aid simple, uneducated women who needed insights into the relevant dilemmas of life.

Through the example of Vasilisa Malygina's choice, Kollontai wanted other women to recognize and begin to examine their own complicated sexual feelings, the strength as well as the sense of confusion felt by their gender, during the very disorienting NEP period. And she wanted to empower them by showing them how to make a choice with their lives as Vasia did—a choice of their own. Eventually, Vasia decides to live with her child, an infant newly born from her old love, in a collective. She chooses such a life over the confines and humiliations of a marriage that has become loveless on her husband's side.

Kollontai sounds convincing here, more convincing than in her numerous appeals. Writing fiction gave her a more pliable and open-ended forum than political writing. It allowed her to explore the personal, human connections between the economic pressures of female unemployment, the lack of social services such as child care, and ever-increasing prostitution—a cycle of social dislocation that was driving women back into the confines of loveless, monogamous marriages.

Vasilisa Malygina is not a stilted novel with a stereotypical female protagonist, the kind that would become the norm in Soviet literature within a few years. Rather, it is a genuinely feminist book in the sense that it emphasizes the dual aspirations of female self-realization and sisterhood. The book also contains a stance that is a remarkable departure from Kollontai's earlier writings. For at some point, Vasilisa begins to feel compassion for Nina, the very woman who takes away her husband and whose concern for humanity goes no further than the care and attention she gives to the length of her nails. Thus the heroine forgives the very woman whose venality embodies NEP. This, of course, suggests that now Kollontai has accepted a doctrine she had always fought against before and during the revolution: that there exist bonds between women that transcend class difference.

Yet regarding her endeavor, one ought not interpret her brand of activism in the name of women narrowly, as revisionist or individualistic. What she sought to do was to synthesize communism and feminism. In her two novels, *Vasilisa Malygina* and *A Great Love* (a roman à clef dealing with the Lenin-Krupskaya-Inessa Armand relationship), both heroines reject their basically patronizing and humiliating love relationships in favor of communist camaraderie.

At the core of *Vasilisa Malygina* and the rest of this fiction are the female characters' "silent psychological dramas born from the transformation taking place in sexual relations."[2] In these words of self-interpretation Kollontai supports what she had asserted earlier in her publicistic writing: as long as women had no duties to the state and society, civilized nations demanded nothing else of a woman but to display "good morals" in sexual and family life. But as the social situation changed, as women began to labor and struggle as individual identities, society put new demands on them. *Vasilisa Malygina* is an examination of these new demands put upon woman not only by society, but by herself. What Kollontai examines is a new feminine difference: that once a woman accepts the social duties of a citizen, in addition to the roles of a mother and a wife, she is also judged differently—in response to her larger civil obligations to society. In sum, the traditional "untarnished image" of woman fades as a measure of her value to society.

The focus in Kollontai's fiction is precisely on the new criteria used to evaluate a woman, criteria quite incompatible with the old bourgeois morality. Much of her writing, both publicistic and fictional, was devoted to the issue of the changing sexual morality. "Only half a century ago," she wrote, "Dumas-fils wrote of a divorcee as a 'fallen' creature, while today France openly discusses the question of equalizing the rights of unwed mothers with those legally married."[3] Further, she reasoned that the changes in society's perception of the morality of sex have gone so far that, given the choice between an "unsullied" family woman and a woman who is "not so spotless" (from the point of view of bourgeois morality) but yet is an outstanding figure in politics, arts or science and benefits her country or humanity, the choice will be obvious. Moreover, out of respect for her position and accomplishments, no one will whisper behind her back.

By far the most controversial piece in the trilogy of the *Worker Bees* is the short story "Love of Three Generations." It is a diaristic account of the feelings of an aged middle-class party worker, Ol'ga Sergeevna, who for far too long has kept the question of her own liberation separate from her commitment to the theoretical liberation of women. She is deeply shocked when she discovers that her daughter, Zhenia, has a sexual relationship with her own lover. The daughter does not do this out of malice. She simply believes that there is no crossover of loyalties, no mixing of moral standards, between what she calls "sex for the sake of sex" and her interests in working for the party. What Kollontai explores here is not, as her critics charged, the license of sexual promiscuity, but rather the issue of sexual revolution. We ask: Is Zhenia's sexual amorality the aberrant result of the chaos of war and revolution? Or is it simply a novelty of the politically oriented times, when life is lived expediently, without the chance to learn the value of a lasting relationship? Kollontai's contemporaries attacked her vehemently for propagating a model of social irresponsibility and the idea of free love, charging that Zhenia's promiscuity was a moral disease, not a class idea.

Kollontai's second trilogy, *Woman at the Threshhold: Psychological Sketches,* consists of the novel *A Great Love* and two short stories, "Thirty-Two Pages" and "A Conversation Piece." This novel was written with the same passion and purpose as *Vasilisa Malygina*—to unravel and plumb the psyche and everyday spiritual reality of a revolutionary woman. It differs from the earlier novel insofar as it deals with highly placed revolutionary activists. Nevertheless, these are characters who have to come to grips with the same essential issue as the "lesser citizens" of *Vasilisa Malygina*—the conflicting demands of sexual passion and revolutionary zeal.

The story here draws its inspiration from the pantheon of the revolution: Lenin, Nadezhda Krupskaya and Inessa Armand. Here we find Lenin disguised as Senia (Senichka), identifiably if ironically presented as a pedantic bore who is constantly preoccupied with his "latest article." He is a man who intentionally lets his intellect dominate his emotions, a person plagued by financial failure, marital problems and minor illnesses. In drawing her characters, Kollontai retains a certain truthfulness with respect to her objects of inspiration simply by not depriving them of their recognizably human nature. Senichka, for example, displays certain features of male attractiveness, such as his sense of humor, buoyant élan and commanding authority. And, of course, there is his cap and pointed beard. Krupskaya, Lenin's legal wife, is presented here as Aniuta. On the whole, she is a gentle and intelligent creature, but with all the tediousness and tendencies toward ailments of her real-life prototype. (Krupskaya did in fact have a bad heart and weak nerves, which Lenin was always anxious not to excite.)

The third character of this famous *ménage à trois*, Natasha, is modeled after Inessa Armand, a radical and dedicated revolutionary agitator. It was thanks to the ideological fervor of people like her that the Bolshevik revolution of 1917 was successful. Armand, a contemporary of Kollontai, was her equal in every sense of the word. She was wholeheartedly dedicated to the improvement of the lot of women and was a founding member of the Women's Committee of the party. In her private life she instinctively defied all bourgeois conventions. Born of a French father and English mother who had settled in Russia as actors, she was well educated and, like many women radicals of the 1880s and 1890s, a Tolstoyan. By the age of maturity, she had qualified as a governess, but instead of putting her teaching certificate to work, she married a wealthy businessman, Alexander Armand, known for his generosity and liberal inclinations. She bore him four children, and then with his consent, left them to join his brother Vladimir, a dedicated revolutionary, with whom she had fallen passionately in love. She joined Vladimir in his Siberian exile, where he died shortly afterwards. It was not until 1910, after a period of exile and personal disappointments, that Armand met Lenin and Krupskaya in Paris. The trio became inseparable for a decade.

In *A Great Love*, Natasha, the "new woman," comes to know herself as she realizes that her support for Senia and her loyalty in performing the secretarial tasks he assigns her means burying her own talents. As her personal enthusiasm and passion are subordinated to the male dominating her life, her "great love" for him is smothered. Senia, however, takes her devotion to him for granted. He belittles the importance of her political work and is jealous of her and her relationships with others in the party. Painfully, she is forced to admit how insensitive he is to her need for work, sexual fulfillment, political activity and financial independence. She feels imprisoned by the secrecy of their relationship and the boredom and isolation it brings. The story concludes as Natasha boards the train that will take her away from Senichka forever. She prepares to face solitude and danger in her new life in the revolutionary underground. By then the "great love" for the "great man," which she was certain would never fade, was gone forever and "nothing, no tenderness, no prayers, not even understanding could reawaken it."

There are many interesting similarities between Natasha, ergo Armand, and Kollontai herself. Both are preeminently "new women," both are full-time women revolutionaries, both are products of the old liberal tsarist culture. They are vital and generous women, attractive (Armand was considered to have been strikingly beautiful), sexually liberated and ambitious. Both wanted to integrate the new sexual politics into the new political life and thinking about social class.

Kollontai's descriptions of the Senia-Natasha relationship sensitize and inform us as to the mood and essence of the times and the tensions experienced by women revolutionaries, particularly around 1910, for by then the Bolsheviks were at a turning point and were, at last, gaining real strength. At the same time, new attitudes toward the place of women in political society emerged that would eventually set the tone and deeply impact the ideological discussions after the Bolshevik revolution. Conservative voices such as Krupskaya stood for conventional marriage and a puritanical attitude toward sex; they were more concerned with literacy programs and the sharing of housework. Kollontai and Armand, the leading radical voices, advocated sexual freedom and communal child care. Their progressive views linking gender and political liberation were quite unacceptable to traditionalists among the Bolsheviks.

A Great Love is Kollontai's attempt to reconcile herself to the fact that in the process of defining themselves and helping to make a better society, women must, like her protagonist Natasha, make work—not love—the ethical center of their lives. And as she came to realize during her isolation in Scandinavia after the tragic debacle of her own affair with Dybenko, the choice of work over love is often prompted by despair. For the new woman, breaking free is a desperate act; the price women must pay for being strong may be to endure solitude, uncertainty and ridicule.

The short story "Thirty-Two Pages" from the second trilogy is a logical continuation of Kollontai's lifelong preoccupation with the issue of sexual morality. Expressed in fictional form, however, her views complement and deepen her sociopolitical writings on the same theme, in particular her essays "Love and the New Morality" and "Sexual Relations and the Class Struggle." In "Thirty-Two

Pages," an ingenious but largely forgotten short story, Kollontai elaborated a pioneering line of inquiry into the connection between the psychological and the sociological aspects of one's personal life. She illustrates the failure and, perhaps, the inherent inability of official political institutions to address the question of distinct male and female identities and attitudes.

The story deals with the mutually dependent nature of female and male psyche and sexuality vis-à-vis the kind of social consciousness that spawns professionalism and creativity. The theme here involves the classic theoretical conflict between the interpersonal and suprapersonal, between every person as both *homo eroticus* and *homo politicus*, between the ego-oriented and other-oriented in each of us.

Written in a style alternating between third-person narration and internal monologue, the story follows the self-accusing thoughts of a female protagonist as she travels for the hundredth time from her research job in the city to her lover in the remote suburbs. The internal monologue uncovers all her sheepish feelings of guilt over her sexual subjugation. She mulls over the mindless passion that motivates her to travel back and forth, barely allowing her to manage her daily life and causing her to delay and finally abandon her unfinished research thesis, the "thirty-two pages." On the way to her lover's apartment, she resolves to end the deadening relationship and return to her beloved work. But her decision is contradicted as the two reunite in the bedroom. The heroine's betrayal of her self-worth and ethical work is final: her manuscript will remain unfinished.

Kollontai posits the woman's dilemma straightforwardly as a contradiction between personal and social identity. The female character is torn between her devotion to research and her need for a lover. Her psychological dependency makes his stroking of her ego at once a denial of her free self. The tension between these strivings blunts her ability to discriminate between her professional conscience and her sexual habit. She vacilliates schizophrenically between commitment to one and addiction to the other. In the end, she is sure of only one thing—that love and work are mutually exclusive.

A core issue of this story revolves around the main character's attempt to hold on to what Anna Akhmatova has called "the white bird" (*belaia ptitsa*)—the voice of inspiration and creativity in woman. Kollontai deeply admired and defended Akhmatova. Her explicit praise of the poetess in her article "Make Way for the Winged Eros" ("Dorogu krylatomu èrosu") antagonized the party conservatives even further.[4] In their view, praising Akhmatova meant refusing to operate along Marxist lines; concentrating on the "battle of the sexes" had nothing to do with communist notions of reality.

"Thirty-Two Pages" is compelling fiction, and Kollontai was apparently aware that it was an exceptional piece. Later she repudiated her trilogy *Love of the Worker Bees* for its lack of aesthetic merit, but she never rejected this model story, which became an inspiration for later women writers. Approximately half a century after Kollontai's story appeared, Natal'ia Baranskaia wrote a novella, *A Week As Any Other* (1968). Written during the heyday of communist achievements in the Soviet Union, Baranskaia's story is a testimonial to the failure of the working woman to resolve the imbalance between work and love. Through diaristic format and internal monologue we learn that *this* plight of woman has only worsened. Baranskaia's novella may be read both as a fictional elaboration of "Thirty-Two Pages" and a refutation of the theoretical vision Kollontai set forth in her article "Communism and the Family."[5]

In evaluating Kollontai's fiction it is worth noting that she gave in prose form what her contemporary Akhmatova conveyed in poetry: the voice of a woman from a woman's point of view. Writing allowed Kollontai the possibility of creative commitment, of giving flight to her "white bird." At a time when she experienced both ideological and emotional rejection, when her two greatest loves—the Communist party and Pavel (Dybenko)—abandoned her, she found it possible to purge her feelings and separate herself from her losses, political and personal.

Through her literary *oeuvre*, Kollontai should be studied from the perspective of our time, as a progenitor of the themes, protagonists and styles predominant in Russian women's fiction today. In view of the works produced by contemporary Russian women writers, it remains to be seen whether Kollontai's vision of women's progress within the social fabric of Soviet society, her idea of reshaping the relations between men and women, her assessment of the Russian woman's self-image, her insistence on the need to achieve both feminine self-fulfillment and independence have been attained, at least partially, or remain only figments of a woman's utopia.

Rimma Volynska

Thirty-Two Pages

A short story from the trilogy Woman at the Threshold
published under her maiden name A. Domontovich

Part 1

Bright stains of factory windows, workers' quarters, houses and barracks flashed by, one looking like another. The bridge shook and rumbled. Street lights cast bright spots onto the autumn darkness. The train finally came to a stop. Footsteps rustled along the gray stone surface of the platform. The wind played a moment with the station lights and then vanished into the pitch dark of the fields behind the factory wall.

She looked back at the train car. Had she forgotten anything? She buttoned up her sweater and walked toward the exit.

In front of her stretched a street without an end. Without people, without speech. On both sides of the street were barrack buildings, each one like the other . . . twenty or thirty houses . . . one like another, one like another . . . in the windows—only darkness. The factory settlement was sleeping. The lights in the sparcely placed lampposts flicked dimly and limply. Soundlessly. Darkly.

Muffled by distance, an incessant and familiar crush and rumble reached her ears. The night shift was at work. As she walked, she was startled by the shrieking, nervous bark of a dog. "What's the matter with you, silly? Stop that barking! It's me who is scared."

She smiled at the dog in the darkness and quickened her pace. Somehow it was easier now, brighter. Perhaps, she thought, all her decision-making is forced and unnecessary. Not necessary whatsoever. It's hard enough just to live, to take it as it comes, as everyone else does. But what about the deadline for her research work? What about her "great" scientific project? To hell with it all. Cross it all off. Live by love itself. And if she does, if she does go off into the provinces, she'll never fulfill her project, will never work out her scientific theory. She sighed and shook her head. Impertinent, unbearable thoughts. . . .

She passed the last house in the factory settlement. The tea shop at the corner was closed. The shutters were closed, and the lights turned off in the lantern over the doorway.

Could it really be so late? She stopped near the last streetlight and took out her watch. A quarter past two. The night shift ends at three. There was still a long time to wait. She turned off the road, cutting across an empty lot, walking past the gray, windowless walls of an unfinished building, stepping with difficulty over the crushed stone and boggy sand. She was beginning to feel tired.

She turned the corner of the unfinished building, and for a moment she was blinded by the flood of bright light from the massive factory building, which was panting and clanking and clamoring. The factory gates were shut tight. All around it was deserted and empty. Yet inside, behind the dazzling wall of windows, there was a different, endless and creative life . . . where hundreds of figures in their blue work shirts were going about their business steadily, rhythmically, with concentration in their eyes; where the conveyor belts were rolling, wheels turning, heavy hammers falling, sharpened steel hissing and throwing hot sparks into the air.

And there, inside, was he . . . he, among hundreds of look-alike figures all dressed in blue . . . where was he now? In exactly what position? Was he between the fifth and the sixth windows? One, two, three . . . would she recognize him if she stepped right into the factory? Of course she would recognize him. She would recognize him anywhere just from the movement of his head, from the way he turns his head. Everything in him is so familiar, so much a part of her. What was the expression of his face at this very moment? Was it strained and concentrated like the faces of the others? Or was it sad?

The wall of light disappeared before her eyes, and suddenly she saw everything clearly, as clearly as if she had walked right through the door of the workshop. The figures in blue were all moving as if to the same beat. So were the wheels, the drive belts and the hammers.

And there he was. His face, his eyes were troubled by something . . . what was the matter with him? Perhaps he was suffering? Perhaps he knew what decision she was bringing to him today. And her decision was indeed irreversible, well thought-out and definite, yet tormenting. He is suffering, perhaps not less than she. . . . Why then is she experiencing this sudden, piercing pain, this sign of the longing and suffering awaiting her? And this overwhelming feeling of tenderness toward him . . . hopefully, this feeling will not squash and drown out her decision, hopefully, it will not weaken her will. She must stop looking at the factory window. Let them keep on clamoring. Let him have sadness in his eyes. She still has to go her own way, she will not let the chains of love bind her. She will only make sure not to keep thinking about him, not to turn around. She'll go straight ahead, toward her goal. She'll go alone, not be diverted to the side . . . she'll head just the way she is now, through the darkness, but knowing that there is a flame ahead of her, and that that flame is her very goal—her scientific research.

It would be difficult, she knew. But the difficulty of her path would not deflect her. It was difficult enough now with her feet sinking into the sand, with the heaviness of the books that she was carrying, the heavy grocery bags, and the annoying hem of her skirt flapping around her ankles. It was hard to be alone, she knew. But there was a reward—her freedom; her wholehearted belonging to one thing and one thing only—her research work. Just she and her work. Everything else vanishes—the insults, the differences, his lack of appreciation of her beloved work. Could it really be that one could live without suffering, without the feeling of desperation? Without being misunderstood? He'll go on not understanding her, he'll go on not hearing her . . . it doesn't matter that much if they are together, as long as she sees him, as long as she reassures herself again and again that he still loves her . . . but what about her work? Her beloved project, so well thought-out and planned? It had been at a standstill all these months. She clearly recollected her mornings, when she would wake up with the painful awareness that in the past five months she had written only thirty-two pages . . . that she had done absolutely nothing more on her research; that she had stopped concentrating on the words of her old advisor, who used to inspire her in her work. Instead of steady work habits, as the old mentor used to teach her, she was in a perpetual state of anxiety and worry. The eternal waiting from one meeting to another. The everlasting exhaustion and the hollow feeling in her head. And all this in the middle of that feeling of grief over another day lost, and the thirty-two pages . . . untouched.

And yet, what if it's he who is right, not she? What if she is incapable of achieving anything? Other women somehow manage to reconcile the irreconcilable. Why can't she? And yet, maybe all of them are facing the same discord between work and love. Such doubts are accumulating and growing, consuming her soul and tormenting her. It's terrifying to be left alone. She must be closer, closer to him. When she is next to him her fears and torment somehow disappear. And she already sees herself dialing his factory office number: "Hello, has the lunch break begun yet? . . . It has? . . . Would you be so good as to ask Petr Mikhailovich to come to the phone? . . . Is that you, my dear? When can we meet? Can we see each other today? You can't? You're too busy? Well, I'll come to you, then. I can't bear it here without you any longer."

And off she would go. At the sight of him her heart would leap for joy. She would throw herself into his arms the moment she saw him. And then she would start her tale of woe about how her work had come to a halt. Yet she knew that the longer she talked, the heavier and the more impenetrable the walls between them would become. He would listen to her, but he wouldn't hear her. Your work isn't moving along? he'd say. Why make such a fuss about it? Why not bring your work with you? Better yet, why not move in with him and put an end to all this going back and forth? She'd stop wasting time constantly commuting. She could visit the library, if she needed to, but the bulk of her "woman's fuss" would be gone. And he'd go on and on like this.

Sometimes, when they were lying in bed together, she would snuggle into his arms as closely as she could, and yet there was something gnawing at her. They were close together . . . yet separate. The chill in her heart could not be explained in words. The words would only wound him, and be wasted. He would not understand, and once more she would be overwhelmed with the feeling of pity toward him. It's safer to be silent and forget about her work.

Forget about her work? No! She has definitely got to do something about it. She's got to save herself, save her strength, her precious time, her work . . . the days are running away, disappearing. She's got to put an end to her suffering, her agony, and all the insults. She's got to stop wasting herself with him, stop killing hour after hour waiting for him to appear. She's got to live alone, live the way she knows how to. And she surely knows how—how to listen to her mentor, how to collect her material. She's got to work, work, work . . . it's still not too late. Her whole life is ahead of her. She still has a chance to make a contribution, a contribution to science and to the life of her country. She's got to force herself to carry out her decision, and it will be over! Her troubles with love were at an end. It was easier to walk now. She could almost experience joy.

She quickened her step and soon she was outside the area lit by the factory lights. She was plunged into total darkness, and a chilly feeling came over her. The wind tugged sharply at the ends of her scarf. There was nothing but the endless darkness of the field . . . it was deathly silent and empty. The feeling of dread came over her.

She looked behind herself longingly. Perhaps she should return, return to the brightly lit windows of the factory. Perhaps she should wait by the gate until the night shift ended. Such cowardice, such childishness to be afraid of the dark. Suddenly her eye caught sight of the slope on her right, and she saw something running down it and rustling the bushes at the bottom. It couldn't be anything but the wind, and yet it was terrifying. What if something was hiding in those bushes? Then she would scream, call for help. It would be pointless, no one could hear her. Even he wouldn't hear her cries, surrounded as he was by blinding lights and the clamor of the factory. Even he . . . so close, yet so far away. There was no way of getting through to him . . . she must keep on walking. She can't just keep waiting here on the slope. It's freezing and she is all surrounded by darkness. "Hey there, little coward," he'll say. "Are you afraid of the dark? But aren't you supposed to struggle with life by yourself? That's the way you reason, miss 'independent woman.' What sort of independence is this? You're just like the rest of the womenfolk." That's what he'll say for sure, and then he'll laugh with his contagious laughter. But this time he'll surely be right.

She quickened her pace and walked on more decisively. She should think of something else, other than the darkness. She must think how she was going to tell him. When should she approach him with this subject? Today. As soon as he comes back from work. Then again, he'll be so tired and happy to see her again. "Aha," he'll say, "my housewife decided to visit me today. Okay, tell the truth. What brings you here today? But just before you do that. . . ."

And again she'd press herself close to him, and with her eyes closed she'd feel the needles going up her spine and her heart submitting to him in delight. No, today would be the wrong time to tell him. Tomorrow would be much better, tomorrow morning.

As she walked along the hillside the wind lashed her in the face, painfully tearing off her hat and stirring the fallen leaves. What a dark and desolate place she was in. She turned again in the direction of the factory where the illuminated windows looked like bright patches of light now. From the distance she could barely hear the hum of the machinery. She was alone, alone in the middle of the darkness. Somewhere up ahead she could make out the blinking lights of the workers' quarters in the settlement. That was where his apartment was, his single room and kitchen. She could barely drag her legs anymore, and there was still quite a way to go. Her arms ached from the weight of the packages and shopping bags. She shivered from the cold. Why was the wind rustling the leaves so ominously, making the bushes stretch their gnarled branches out toward her? Suddenly she was struck with fright. What if it weren't the wind? She was overcome by the feeling she so often had when she was left alone in her room as a child, and it seemed to her that some unknown evil forces would crawl out at her from all the corners.

On the narrow trail cocklebursl were scratching her legs and clinging to her skirt. She wished so much to be in the city, in the midst of lights and people. She had only herself to blame for being here in the middle of the night. Whatever had possessed her to come here now, now, and confess the whole thing to him at this point? Was it that necessary to put the dot over the *i* at this very moment, to have the feeling that she was finally alone, alone in her very own room with her manuscripts and books and her desk lamp, where the only thing she would hear would be. . . .

What was that, what was that she heard? A muffled, silvery bell? It sounded like a church bell, but she couldn't make out whether it was coming from under the ground or from above. Oh, it's just a railroad signal carried on the wind from far away. How stupid of her to be scared again. She quickened her pace again, but her skirt was flapping and hampering her every step. She picked it up around her knees so she could step freely. But she couldn't free herself from the unsettling sensation that someone was following her . . . and that someone would grab her from behind. Who . . . who was it?

She turned around. Again no one. Complete quiet . . . the air so thin and raw. She sensed the smell of the earth, and she filled her lungs with the pungent dampness. She raised her face up toward the sky only to meet the same impenetrable darkness again. By now the factory lights had disappeared completely. Only the nighttime wind was swirling, whipping, rustling everything. A mysterious wind, as if it alone had power over everything at night. It was chasing long phantom-like shadows. She could not see the eyes of these phantoms, but she could hear them as they brushed past, spinning, swishing, surging. She was beginning to feel sick now, sick from the fright that had come over her. By now the darkness felt like a thick, stifling trap. Her legs had become too heavy and no longer obeyed her. She wanted to shout out, but her own voice frightened her. She thought of running but was stifled by fear again . . . her only thought was just to see someone, anyone, to pull herself out of this darkness, to be where there was light. . . .

The darkness flapped its invisible and murky wings around her head. It breathed its ice-cold breath in her face. The long phantoms stretched out all around her and began to take control. They whirled and reached out to touch her. The wind was laughing at her now, pulling her hat off and untying her white scarf. She felt she could not stand it any longer. She needed air . . . red and blue circles of fire spun in front of her eyes. A dull bell rang in her ears. She darted forward but stumbled and fell to the ground unconscious.

Part 2

"I still can't figure out what happened to you, my brave woman. Did someone frighten you? Did you stumble and fall? Why are you crying again? Are you hurt? Calm down, now; calm down, my dove."

"I'll come to myself in a moment. I'm just so happy that it's you, and that you are close to me again."

"What silliness. You're happy that it's me. What's so unusual about that? What's strange is finding you in the field. You still have to explain that to me. I was walking home after work and suddenly I hear someone squealing or sobbing, the sound of someone being strangled or robbed, or of someone committing suicide. I run as fast as I can to the spot the sound is coming from and what I find is a person on the road all curled up in a bundle, and lying all around this person are parcels. What could have happened? Who frightened you? I can't understand it."

"Nothing really happened. I just stupidly became afraid of the dark. I tried to run, my heart started racing, my head began to spin, and so I collapsed. But I'm all right now, now that you are with me. You are so very good to me . . . and I love you, love you . . . much more than you think . . . and I'll never leave you, never, for anything in the world."

"Why are you talking such gibberish? Who is chasing you away? Why are you crying again? Come closer, put your head right here, let me calm you down. Look at your hands, they're cold as ice. Let me warm them. You see, you're calming down. Now, tell me everything in order. What actually happened in the field? Who insulted you? Shouldn't I know?" His voice expressed impatience; his eyes were filled with disbelief.

"The whole thing is that no one, no one insulted me. It was just nothing. . . ."

"Why do you say it was nothing, when I found you lying all alone in the field, with all those packages scattered around, your dress all messed up?"

"Well, what happened was that I made up my mind to come to you immediately, in the middle of the night, without waiting until morning. I decided to come and tell you that I can't go on like this anymore. I can no longer stand the fact that you love me not as your friend or comrade, but as your woman . . . and you don't grasp the fact that I need to work, to work . . . no, I can't go on with you like this."

"You can't go on with me like this? Why can't you?" He pulled himself away from her.

"Because of our life, the way we've lived it up till now. Quarreling over stupid things, not trying to understand each other. Wasting time and energy. Coming home exhausted without a thought in our heads. Please try to understand; it's been five months since I've touched my work, with only thirty-two pages written. Vera Samsonova sent me a note the other day telling me that her work is being typeset right now, and I . . . why can't you understand that if I don't finish my work, I won't get my degree, and if I don't get it, I might as well say goodbye to all my dreams and to continuing my research?"

"What I can't understand is who is standing in your way," he said in a dry and withdrawn manner.

"Who? Our relationship . . . the fact that I am constantly torn between you and my work. How come you don't understand that? It would all be much easier to handle if . . . I weren't so attached to you, if I didn't love you. . . ."

"Oh, come now! You say you love me. What kind of love is this? When people love each other they strive to be close together. That's how 'unlearned' folk understand the word love. I don't understand your problem. Most of the time you're by yourself, in your city, while I'm alone. And you know only too well how much work I have, as well. I could also use *your* support. But *I'm* not asking for it, *I'm* not complaining. I understand that you've made up your mind to become an educated woman, and I'm not one to distract you from your course."

"Please, dear, try to understand that if I'm not living here with you, it's solely because of my work. . . ."

"Because of your work, huh? You mean to tell me that you can't work at my place? Is it my constant presence that's bothering you? Aren't I away for ten hours a day slaving at the factory? Why, why is it that you can't work at my place here?"

"Haven't I told you that I must be where my lectures, my lab, my books and my library are? I can't always be camping out. . . ."

"Well, settle in at my place and you won't be camping out."

"You know I've tried that, too, and it didn't work out. I got all bogged down with the rotten housework, the washing and the cooking. . . ."

"Yes, of course, why should an 'educated person' be bogged down with the cooking."

"Oh, please stop it! You're making me really angry now. I'm fed up with the whole thing."

"*You're* fed up? What about *me*? Don't you think it's no longer bearable for me too to constantly have to put up and adjust to you? You think I have it easy with you?"

"Then why, why are we continuing this affair?" she suddenly exploded. "This is precisely what I came to tell you. That this relationship is destroying my will, my whole ability to be on my own. It's taking all my joy away from me, it's pure torture. And I see it's the same for you. We must put an end to it. *The* end. I must leave."

"Then leave, go on and leave. What I don't get is why you came in the first place. Did you think that I would get on my knees and beg you to stay? Don't count on it! That's not the sort I am!"

"Why are talking like this? You're turning this into a revolting conversation."

"Revolting, you say? Well, I suppose it *is* revolting for a person on a pedestal such as youself, don't you think so?"

"No, I don't think so. In fact, I can't think anymore at all . . . leave me alone."

"Who's not leaving you alone?"

The two of them fell silent, both with their own thoughts. The oil lamp was burning faintly. Dawn was beginning to glimmer through the window.

"I still say that something strange happened to you out there in the field. You were alone. It was night. And that decision of yours. Something happened. It couldn't be anything else." He looked suspiciously at her again.

"You're at it again. Didn't I tell you? Perhaps it's my nerves. I've been sleeping poorly lately. And on these sleepless nights I've been thinking, searching for a way out."

"Ahuh."

"You have such a look on your face, like you just don't believe me."

"Well, it's hardly believable. Those packages scattered all over, the desperate look on your face, tears pouring down your cheeks. Now that it's all over, why don't you tell what really happened. Didn't something happen to you out there in the field? I'm not going to blame you, only just tell the truth. There are so many strange tramps wandering around. . . . Tell me exactly what happened to you, talk to me like a companion."

"I really don't believe what I'm hearing! How can you even have such shameful thoughts? You're insulting me, on purpose!" She became more and more agitated as she guessed what he was talking about. "What kind of companion and comrade are you, if you don't respect me? If you suspect me of . . . this is exactly what I was talking about, now you've proven it yourself. Here is the very reason why I want to leave you. I want to get away from these kinds of insults, run away, just like I was running away from those phantoms last night. If it only weren't for the fact that I . . . am still in love with you."

"You mean it? You mean what you just said to me?"

"It's my downfall that I *do* still mean it. What I went through the past few days was pure agony. I made up my mind differently about twenty times. One time it seemed to me that I really couldn't make it without you. Another time it seemed to me that I couldn't make it with you. And then again I started thinking about your attitude. . . ."

"My attitude?"

"Yes, your attitude. I mean, you love me, but it's not the way I understand love."

"I don't know how you understand love, but one thing I do know," he said, lightly confident, "is that despite all your learnedness and all your ambitions you do seem to lack common sense. On the one hand, you love me. On the other, you want to run away from me. What nonsense! Well, my lady," he took her head into his arms, "do give me a smile. Let me see if you in fact still do love me. How can a tale like this happen to an intelligent and independent woman, my lady? You look more like a coward to me, and yet you're all set to do without me. However, the worst thing is that you know yourself that you can't manage without me. Come on, then, snuggle up a little closer to me and stop all this fuss. Where did you get all this desire to torment me? Yes, I'll be treating you differently from now on. I'll be holding you by the bridle, the way a woman should be kept, and I absolutely, positively won't let you out of my sight. No later than tomorrow we're going to the city and bringing all your books and clothes back to my place. We're done fooling around. We'll live differently now. Happily. You'll see. Why, why are you pretending to be scared now?"

"Scared?"

"Yes. Scared."

"I'm just absorbed in my own thoughts."

"What thoughts?"

"It's not worth talking about."

"You know, you are strange, after all. Here the sun is almost up and we haven't slept a wink yet. Aren't you tired? Or are you thinking your thoughts again?"

"No, it's nothing. You *are* good."

She caressed his head tenderly and began thinking of a way to manage her life without pain, without hurting him. He was so good to her, after all. Sometimes he acted infantile, yet he loved, loved in his own way. She convinced herself to stop her torturous efforts to make a decision, to give time a chance. . . .

"So, it's decided. Tomorrow after lunch we're leaving to get your books . . . we'll put up some shelves here . . . and you'll be my homemaker. Do you hear me?"

"I hear you," she said limply. "My books. . . ." So I'm coming here for good this time. But what about my old mentor, what about my library? It's my complete end, and the end of my research. It will never be done by January. No, I must run away from here, run . . . I'll come up with an excuse that I have to go to the city alone. I must run, run away from here. Without delay. Tomorrow. Tomorrow.

"What is it now with you again? Why such a wretched look on your face, and tears in your eyes?"

"It's because I love you after all. I love you, love you, love you. . . ."

1923

Translated by Rimma Volynska

Notes to the Essay

1. Foreword by Germaine Greer in Alexandra Kollontai, *An Autobiography of a Sexually Emancipated Communist Woman* (New York: Herder and Herder, 1971), ix.
2. A. Kollontai, Foreword to the English edition, *Red Love* (Westport, CT: Hyperion Press, 1975), 5.
3. Ibid., 6–7.
4. A. Kollontai, "Dorogu krylatomu èrosu," *Molodaia gvardiia* 3 (May 1923): 111–24.
5. A. Kollontai, "Communism and the Family," in *Selected Writings of Aleksandra Kollontai,* trans. Alix Holt (Westport, CT: Lawrence Hill, 1977), 250–60.

Bibliography

Primary Works

Liubov' pchel trudovykh. (Moscow, 1923). [Contains *Vasilisa Malygina,* "Liubov' trekh pokolenii" and "Sestry."]

Zhenshchiny na perelome: Psikhologicheskie Ètiudy. Moscow, 1923. [Contents: *Bol'shaia liubov',* "Tridtsat' dve stranitsy," "Podslushannyi razgovor."]

Ziel und Wert Meines Lebens. Munich, 1926.
Bol'shaia liubov'. Moscow, 1927.

In Translation

A Great Love. Trans. Lily Lore. New York, 1929.
The Autobiography of a Sexually Emancipated Woman. Trans. Salvador Attanasio. New York, 1971.
Love of the Worker-Bees. Trans. Cathy Porter. London, 1977. [Includes *Vasilisa Malygina*, "Sisters" and "Three Generations."]
Selected Writings. Trans. with an introduction by Alix Holt. London, 1977. [Contains mostly political writings.]
A Great Love. Trans. Cathy Porter. New York, 1981. [Includes "Thirty-Two Pages" and "A Conversation Piece."]

Secondary Works

Clemens, Barbara. *Bolshevik Feminist: The Life of Aleksandra Kollontai*. Bloomington: Indiana University Press, 1979.
Farnsworth, Beatrice. *Aleksandra Kollontai: Socialism, Feminism and the Bolshevik Revolution*. Stanford: Stanford University Press, 1980.
Greer, Germaine. Foreword. *The Autobiography of a Sexually Emancipated Woman*. New York: Herder and Herder, 1971.
Mullaney, Marie Marmo. *Revolutionary Women: Gender and Socialist Revolutionary Role*. New York: Praeger, 1983.
Noonan, Norma C. "Kollontai, Aleksandra Mikhailovna." *Dictionary of Russian Women Writers*. Ed. M. Ledkovsky, C. Rosenthal and M. Zirin. Westport, CT: Greenwood Press, 1994. 305–08.
Porter, Cathy. *Alexandra Kollontai: The Lonely Struggle of the Woman Who Defied Lenin*. New York: Dial Press, 1980.

Vera Merkur'eva

Vera Aleksandrovna Merkur'eva (1876–1943) was almost completely unknown in her lifetime and has remained so to the present.[1] Clearly this is due to the limited publication of her works. Her poems appeared in print only twice during her life, in almanacs published in 1918 in Moscow: *The Poets' Spring Salon* (*Vesennii salon poètov*) and in 1926 in Vladikavkaz: *The Golden Zurna* (*Zolotaia zurna*). A volume of selected poems by Shelley in Merkur'eva's translation was published in Moscow in 1937 (*Selected Verse* [*Izbrannye stikhi*]), along with assorted other shorter translations, also in the 1930s. This dearth of publications is striking, for it seems she wrote in quantity: there are elegant chapbooks of her verse bound by her friend E.Ia. Arkhipov, cycles, collections and even an autobiography, all still to be found only in her archive. More importantly, her poetry is vigorous and sophisticated, compelling both in intellect and feeling. She should have earned her place in the contentious but broad poetic culture of her time.

At the same time she was known and recognized by many contemporary poets. She received recommendations in 1933 for an official poets' reception in Moscow not only from the then-influential M.N. Rozanov, V. Veresaev and G. Chulkov, but also from Osip Mandel'shtam, Boris Pasternak and Boris Pil'niak. Viacheslav Ivanov, with whom her ties were the closest, saw in her "unusual gifts, extraordinary strength and daring." After moving to Moscow from her native Vladikavkaz in 1917 she lived for a month or so in the Ivanovs' apartment on Zubovskii Bul'var; during the four highly productive years she spent in Moscow she was a regular in Ivanov's salon, and in 1920 they both moved out of Moscow to the northern Caucasus (Ivanov's wife had died by this time). Ivanov continued to Baku, but his letters to her in Vladikavkaz testify to the intense, if short-lived, friendship that had developed between them.

Far from the capital and center of Russian literary life, Merkur'eva created around herself a microclimate of cultural activity and exchange. At first there was a literary circle named "Puppet Theater" ("Vertep"),[2] then "Vineta," supposedly referring to a legendary undersea city. Among her closest friends in these groups were A.S. Kochetov and E.Ia. Arkhipov, both writers of modest note; in the latter's archives is a biography of Merkur'eva entitled *A Book About Vera Merkur'eva: The Empress of Ashes* (*Kniga o Vere Merkur'evoi: Pepel'noi tsaritse*). It describes her as follows: "Her eyes are deep amber and shadowy, questioning and wanting her question not to be heard. A smile that caresses and blesses with subtle derision. . . . Her speech is somewhat long-winded, and it sings as in a fairy tale. She has a sliding walk, but her steps are small and anxious. In her touch there is more coolness than warmth. . . ."[3] Through all her years in Vladikavkaz she lived with her sister; when the latter died by the early 1930s, she returned to Moscow, seriously ill herself, following her friends the Kochetovs. With their help and that of others she was able to eke out a living by translating even after she had been confined to her bed.

Starting in 1935 Merkur'eva spent her summers in the Kochetovs' hut (*izba*) in Starki, outside Moscow near Kolomna. Here she was visited by Anna Akhmatova, who recoiled from the quantity of stray and invalid animals in the house—Merkur'eva's lifelong weakness—but apparently was not deterred from returning. Merkur'eva's acquaintance with her fellow poet utterly captivated her. Closer to the war years Marina Tsvetaeva returned to Russia, and Merkur'eva, who had known her slightly before the move to Vladikavkaz, initiated a brief correspondence. Tsvetaeva and her son lived two weeks with Merkur'eva in Starki in the summer of 1941, just before the outbreak of war. Merkur'eva was evacuated to Tashkent, where she died in 1943.

M.A. Gasparov offers the following introduction to Merkur'eva's poetry:

> Voloshin, as we know, told young Tsvetaeva that there was enough of her for several poets; one of those poets could have been Merkur'eva. Let's perform an experiment in psychological arithmetic: let's subtract from Tsvetaeva's verse its most glaring feature—her pathos of self-affirmation; let's imagine that her most programmatic poem is this—"And perhaps, the best victory over time and gravity is to pass through and not to leave a trace, to pass and not to leave a shadow. . . ." What remains from such a psychological subtraction is Vera Merkur'eva.[4]

Gasparov seems to mean that Merkur'eva lacks the aggressive, expansive *persona* or poetic self that is so distinctive in Tsvetaeva, but has something else in common with her—the insistent, rhythmic incantation of woman's fate and woman's suffering, what Julia Kristeva saw in Tsvetaeva as the cataclysmic subconscious *pulsion* of feminine identity.[5] Indeed, it was the sense of incantation (*zaklinanie*) that Tsvetaeva noted and remembered in Merkur'eva's poetry. It is apparent in one of Merkur'eva's most finished and acrid poems, "A Tale About Sorrow":

> There were two winters without a summer,
> Two fogs, two darknesses—
> Two years of prison camp,
> Two years of slavish silence.
> I bore it all. Did you?
>
> I do not yield. I laugh, I joke
> In the claws of penury,
> I write my verse, I want it all,
> Beauty as though it were bread.
> I do not mourn. Do you?
>
> In a two years' dance of two shadows—
> Deceit and vanity—
> I see only the dream of a dream
> Of a final emptiness.
> And I am my dream—like you.

Despite Merkur'eva's admiration for Akhmatova, the latter's complex archaism is clearly foreign to her, Tsvetaeva's visceral modernist textures far closer. When Merkur'eva pays tribute to Akhmatova she depicts her as a poet of incantation, a voice that calls a beating heart into existence, a conjurer's hands fluttering upward ("A drawn-out voice sang from the dark fold," "For What Is in Her"). Merkur'eva's ideal of the poet is a figure of shamanistic power, able to command both human and external nature:

> And he will become of a rank
> To tell fortunes in the hollow night,
> And to charm sorrow,
> And to dry the heart out with drowsing.
>
> And early in the morning he will go out into the field;

Like me, to bow to the mountains—
And the song of his powerful will
Surges forth on the four wild winds.

Her successor-poet in the cycle "With a Song-Hook" is depicted as a man, the only equal she can find; this doesn't prevent her, in another place, from representing Russian poetry as a smoking grandmother with "unneeded, fruitless asexuality."[6]

The comparisons and contrasts with other Russian poets can be multiplied. As with Shkapskaia, her relentless thematic focus is on the suffering of women, their physical and spiritual exhaustion, their self-depleting generosity and deep loneliness. Yet where Shkapskaia finds some kind of cosmic recompense for women's suffering, however late and irrational ("The Cunning Sower"), Merkur'eva sees only sadistic torment, embodied in her recurrent image of the wheel on which she is stretched (or tossed helplessly in the air). Her suffering has neither the grinding physicality of Bunina's nor the aching emotional directness of Guro's; rather, it is reflected, taken up into an abstract system whose expression in some poems attains Mandel'shtam-like tonalities of refined ratiocination. A characteristic turn of argument is to resolve the contradiction between social surface and inner sorrow by denying the apparent solidity of the real, as in the poem cited above ("And I am my dream—like you"). One consequence of this is that experience becomes climactic, acquires the texture of existential discontinuity, as she says in "The Sabbath of Remembrance":

There is no repetition
Either of a leaf, or of love, or of a tale,
And all that happens with us
Is being accomplished for the first time.

And if the sun has faded
In the light of those eyes there—
We will smash life like a mirror
For the last and first time.

This is particularly true, one infers, for the woman poet whose reality is inherently double, toiling the day and "howling her verses" the night. On the other hand, the poet's vision imparts a superiority to time or immunity to time, a true view of the world transcending the change of generations and of "idols," a superiority even to God, who, in the "Rabbi" poem, is merely the product of a generation's contingent framework of awareness:

The death of a generation is God's death too.
Each new tribe has a new idol.
But ours is a road in eternity;
God is not eternal, but the world is.

And ever we will fuss in vain
To blindly drive off of that road,
Both in horror and in wonder
At the world's boisterous loveliness.

And we, by our drowsy coasts,
Cannot taste the peace of death,
Praying to that Time on which
We must wear our Eternity out.

Reversing Mandel'shtam's formulation, it is eternity here that is the burden, not time; time offers the escape of finitude and relief from the pitiless clarity of the poet's consciousness.

This is a remarkable vision, and a remarkable poet. Her complexities cannot be fully addressed in this short compass. What, then, is the reason for her almost complete lack of published work? Obviously her gender played the key role. Hers was not the unmistakable talent of an Akhmatova or a Tsvetaeva, and there was room for only these two on a scene that tolerated much lesser gifts in men. Women poets could succeed only as superstars, and Merkur'eva was not that kind of superstar. Also, she lived her critical years in the 1920s far from the center of literary life in Russia, far from those contacts who could have (and seemingly would have) helped her get her work into print. In the 1930s not only was she physically weakened, but the politics of literary life had been altered radically, and Merkur'eva could probably never have written the Stalinist civic poetry that was published then. Akhmatova was also refused publication in the 1930s (as through most of the 1920s); many other writers with integrity similarly dropped out of view in this period or failed to survive it. Merkur'eva was not clearly opposed to the Soviet state, but like many others she saw culture as a martyr of the revolution (as in "Stanzas"). Her reaction to the history of her times is profoundly characteristic of the modern Russian intelligentsia: she withdrew from public view to a highly restricted audience on which she could count for security and a reasonable level of comprehension. The important point to be made about her, one that bespeaks both her personal dignity and the dignity of her tradition, is that she did not require the success that publication represents; she created her work laboriously and conscientiously with no hope of recognition. And hers was not a self-conscious sacrifice with one eye on posterity; her attitude was natural, fostered and supported by the cultural milieu in which she lived. It was normal for such "public" figures as Akhmatova and Tsvetaeva (and Viacheslav Ivanov, and Il'ia Ehrenburg) to seek her out as interlocutor and friend: she was their equal in culture and in the values culture imposes, and for them this was paramount. As for her status as a poet, the duty and privilege of deciding that has fallen to a later generation.

Harold D. Baker

From the cycle Souls of Non-Living Things

A Jolly Soul

She's curtained the window in black,
And lit two white lamps.
It's scary for some reason, and fun—
Nothing good will come of her fun.

You get so pooped from the long, long day,
Going from one strange house to another.
When it's the little ones they wear you down,
You get twice as worn down from the big ones.

So let me get dressed up a bit more attractively,
I'm going visiting to see myself!
It will be more marvelous and more engaging
To converse with one's own self.

—My dear, you're very frivolous.
—My dear, I'm on the wheel.
—Poor thing, there are things you can take, they're painless . . .
—Poor thing, I've tried them all.

—Tender one, where is your heartsick friend?
—Tender one, he is cast aside and forgotten.
—Songstress, where is your crystal voice?
—Songstress, my crystal is smashed.

—Ruined one, you need a sorcerer.
—Ruined one, that sorcerer is me.
—Prideful, there are chasms in hell.
—Prideful, they know me there too.

—Sinful, what about God, the Loving?
—Sinful. I know. It's not in the cards.
—Oh, destitute, the rotting and the rags?
—Oh, destitute, it's certain and ridiculous.

What's the point of big names,
Pathetic, agonizing words.
It's simpler to stagger about without aim;
It's righter, one thing and not two.

The heart, when broken, turns out
To be the hoop of a tossing-catching game.
It loops up merrily and spins;
It leaps with me—the wheel.

Like Everyone

To Evgenii Arkhipov

—Live like everyone!—That's nice,
But I did live like everyone:
Stretched out, I joked
On the torturer's wheel.

When I had gone a single step
Of poverty mute as the crypt,
Like everyone, I threw money,
Hungry as I was, for flowers.

All day long, at manual labor
I prayed away my sins;

Like everyone, in a delirious half-sleep
I howled my verses all night.

Like everyone, I came to my lover
In a weary, calamitous dream.
I gave away sweetness for anger,
Love for enmity, like everyone.

Stepping past my life,
I faced the scythe of death—
For I have long lived an imagined life
And only appear like everyone.

A Tale About Sorrow[1]

1.

I wander round about
The entryway steps,
I've been waiting for my Fenist,
My bright falcon, for many, many days.
I lived like a white turtle-dove
Behind a stone wall,
Like one vowed to silence, one locked up,
In my sixteenth spring.
Will I forget how in the early dawn
My Fenist flew in to me,
In my bright little chamber
Radiant, feathered, fiery?
Will I forget, until
I am pierced by an arrow,
His falcon's eyes,
The wing of his arm?

2.

Like drizzle, my tears dropped,
Like the dews on the meadows;
Can you catch up to the wind in the field,
Or a bird in the clouds?
I set off by roads and byways
To seek my little falcon;
With my pampered foot
I stepped in thorns.
I found squirrels' and rabbits'
Paths to lead my way;
I bowed to all and asked,
Where might I find the Bright one?
They did not know—neither the rush,
Nor the fern, nor the fir-tree.
But my heart led me
Over twenty-seven lands.

3.

My Falcon is in a tower strong
A captive to fierce sorrow,
Behind ten doors
With twenty locks.
"You tiresome one, parter of lovers,
Open up the doors,
Let me see the bright beam of his face
And then take all that is mine."
The evil, greedy one let me in
To spend three nights,
Three nights of deepest darkness
Caressing Fenist.
I bought those three little nights
For a dear price:
We changed places, tit for tat—
I became the witch, the witch me.

4.

Out from under my kerchief I
Gave her my braid,
And the witch became light-haired,
I—white like the ring-tail.
Without fuss we changed
My rosy cheeks and lips;
She burns now like a cherry,
And I am a twisted bush.
I took from under my necklace
My young voice;
Now she is a trilling song-bird,
And I whistle like a snake.
For until then I did not know,
So easily did I change,
That it is merriment to be sorrow,
And sorrow to be merriment.

5.

With my sweet winged one
I spent two nights;
Whether drunken or enchanted,
He would not be waked by anything.
In vain I sorted through
Each feather on his wing,
In vain I kissed him
On the eyes and forehead.
Ah, can an oak, a high one,
Care for the grass that's scythed?
Can Fenist, bright falcon, care
For abandoned beauty?
On the third night I
Cried myself out in a single tear,
And his falcon's heart
Was burned through by it.

6.

He looked, I also looked,
I could not gasp or sigh.
And my heart sank in a trice
Like a pebble to the bottom.
I took a step hopelessly,
As though to the edge of a pond:
I am the true one, I am the former one,
I am your beloved.
And I hear, as though from a tower,
Through the fire and convulsion:
—You are old, you are ugly,
I am young and comely—
I went back to skulk,
Alone, all by myself.
And now the falcon consoles himself
With his young wife!

There were two winters without a summer,
Two fogs, two darknesses—
Two years of prison camp,
Two years of slavish silence.
I bore it all. Did you?

I do not yield. I laugh, I joke
In the claws of penury,
I write my verse, I want it all,
Beauty as though it were bread.
I do not mourn. Do you?

In a two years' dance of two shadows—
Deceit and vanity—
I see only the dream of a dream
Of a final emptiness.
And I am my dream—like you.

Stanzas

There are stone guests at the door—
Death and Fear have come for the end.
And the shadow-people, the stick-people
Are on excessive city squares.

The kids' arms are only spokes,
A hungry bird's knock on the window.
Soon we will say: children, birds—
Yes, there was all that, but long ago!

Poor woman, get up, wave your arms—
You did not give the children bread.
But above a buried woman there is only stone,
On a burned woman there is only ash.

For the truth was dearer to us
Than you and your house.
Is not truth God's affair,
And nature man's?

Not ready, we were ripened
By thunders that had spoken out.
Our shelter is stone crevices,
Our homes are heavy-layered.

We wait in silence, we've dug our graves,
Our necks bared to the blow—
As a slave on the chopping-block waits for the axe,
As an ox at the slaughter waits for the knife.

Like an ox at the slaughter, a slave on the block—
We've been tied and gagged,
And in bitter dust, in fatal fear
Is the poet silent and the people mute?

It will not be so. I swear by the graves

Which have already been opened for us:
Enslaved by slaves,
We will sing to them for the last time.

We will sing that the sovereign peasant shoe is right
To cast down crowns today,
But tomorrow tears will drop
On the creases of Pushkin's pages.

We will sing that the colors of parties are ancient,
And through the faded sheets
Will show the signs of everlasting charters—
All the same stars and blossoms.

We will sing that the word of truth is with us,
That the anger of life's word is fearsome,
That the one who cast a stone at the word
Will turn to stone and not revive.

On the place of execution, to redeem
The wicked age's crying sins,
We faithfully will keep our word,
Without betrayal or retreat.

We will weave lyrical ravings
Into a whirl of free accords—
And finish our iamb, our final iamb,
On a parting rhyme with the word: death.

The evening was equal to the sun's morning—
Each moment was shot though with light,
And in the old shop the old Rabbi
Leafed through the pages of books.

"God finds His losses
On the floors of seas, in the sands of the desert

And pays them back sevenfold
To the defilers of sanctuaries.

But if we fall on our faces
At God's fearsome feet—
He will not revenge himself, but be reconciled:
Anger is not eternal, but God is."

The dark tatters of rags,
The rustle of paper, the loud trading—
And the magnificence of the stern hands,
The delight of the ecstatic's eyes.

And nearby is the city: in the lava of sound
A motor hums, a streetcar rings.
Oh old rabbi, wise rabbi,
Do not cause me useless dreams.

The death of a generation is God's death too.
Each new tribe has a new idol.
But ours is a road in eternity;
God is not eternal, but the world is.

And ever we will fuss in vain
To blindly drive off of that road,
Both in horror and in wonder
At the world's boisterous loveliness.

And we, by our drowsy coasts,
Cannot taste the peace of death,
Praying to that Time on which
We must wear our Eternity out.

From the cycle She Remained

On My Sister's Death

Meeting

She sat down next to me, not taking off her coat,
Drawing her kerchief snug.
She said, "I've come to get you,
We're going to live at my place."

I ask: "What should I take along,
What should I lay out?"
She answered: "Don't take your dress,
We won't be able to wear it out."

I ask: "What should I take for the house,
What do you have?"
She answered: "We don't need anything,
We're not going to be drinking or eating."

And then she stopped to think and sighed:
"No, you can't."
And then the white fog
Swallowed the Milky Way.

The breathing of our stove is hot,
Its fire is even,
And in my eyes is spread out in the fog
A grayish kerchief.

Without you I cannot wear anything flowery
Or eat anything sweet.
Come quickly back for me again,
And take me away with you.

She Came

—Are you ready? So we then can leave the yard,
Someone else's, and go home.
—Wait a minute, there's a headstrong tot,
Restless and dear.

—One's own mother has a child here,
And yours is waiting for you with me.
—Are you ready?—without mourning
To wake up from the dream of earth?

—Wait a minute, those who wandered with me,
Their tears will be salt.
—Yours have their own left,
While I have only you.

—Are you ready—to leave these petty sinful ones
With me and not look back?
—Wait just till spring begins to thaw,
And let the snowdrops start to bloom.

—What do you want the snowdrops for?
So I can put one on your grave?
—Are you ready? Wake up, arise.
The night is ending, light is near.

—Wait a minute, in captivity and sickness
My last verse has not been sung.
—There you'll compose such songs
As here they have no words to sing.

—Are you ready?—What about our cat,
The beast crippled by torture?
Without us her road leads to the earth,
To death by starvation.

She'll never really understand, legless one,

Why the door does not open.
And she stopped to think and said,
Stopping her bosom in a light sigh:

—Anyone who could forget a little creature,
I would forget about them too.
Remain—she said
And left without a sound.

The Sabbath of Remembrance

What if—afraid to forget about us,
Recalling us is the concern of the deceased?
Our Sabbath *here* is that of the parents,
There that of the children, perhaps?

And we for them are long since dead,
Although they recall us today,
And on heavenly church porches they read
The woeful memory-lists of the living?

A summons from us to them, or from them to us,
This mutual whispering of double recollection.
Both eternal memory, and eternal life
The dead ask for the dead—have they forgotten?

A captain pouring gold
Into the green trembling of a pond—
His memory has been jealously pricked—
Is the same as that one, then.

The silence of clenched lips
Is tortuously delivered,
And a song bubbles up like tar
Just like then.

He hides his eyes under his eyelashes.
The star, in rising, is eclipsed—
And the heart is seized by the clamp
Of sorrow, the same as then.

Untrue. There is no repetition
Either of a leaf, or of love, or of a tale,
And all that happens with us
Is being accomplished for the first time.

And if the sun has faded
In the light of those eyes there—
We will smash life like a mirror
For the last and first time.

From the cycle With a Song-Hook

For a long time I have dragged my sorceress's mask about
With a song-hook,
It has long been time
To put these tired bones to a coffin's rest.

Yet you cannot leave until you pass
Your cursed gift to someone else—
The horrific languor of that song,
That impenetrable darkness of enchantment.

And with entreaty and with sorrow
I dream along in others' yards:
Whom shall I give my witch's word,
Whom shall I give my strength?

It does not suit one person's taste,
For others it is beyond their strength.
Who will give up happiness, like an amusement,
For a cursed dream?

There is no answer from the less-than-equal,
Such a burden is too much for them.
But the time will come—a blood-relation will emerge
And take my spirit, lips to lips.

And he will become of a rank
To tell fortunes in the hollow night,
And to charm sorrow,
And to dry the heart out with drowsing.

And early in the morning he will go out into the field;
Like me, to bow to the mountains—
And the song of his powerful will
Surges forth on the four wild winds.

To Anna Akhmatova

A drawn-out voice sang from the dark fold,
Like the speech of waves in a damp seashell.
And in it there were fused harmonies,
Like clouds rising up over the water.

It sorrowed in the anticipation of parting,
It scolded for a tryst not kept,
It conjured by an inviolable vow,
It tempted with an impossible answer.

And to that conjuration beat the heart.
Clenching the throat, clouding sight,
It called forth a soundless, bodiless
Song, like an unheard echo or sigh,

Swearing by the sorrow of nighttime parting
Not to know oblivion on the ways of wandering
Until the perfection of another morning
Illuminates its sleepless bliss.

For What Is in Her

To Anna Akhmatova

For the fact that she swings there in the cage of rooms,
Clings to the grate of walls—
And it seems that our frail house stands above
The surf of ringing foams.

For the fact that all transparency, all bottomlessness,
All the blue of the firmament—
Is in her, through all the unfaithfulness, all the infatuation
Of the high tide's wave surging in.

For the fact that in her are pitilessness and tenderness
In a diamond prism, and
Fused in an inhuman contiguity
Are doves and snakes.

For the fact that above her, risen from the wounds
Of the times, the storm has passed, and
Has not blinded nor mortally wounded
Her transparent eyes.

For the fact that again—and ceaselessly again—
In the upflight of those hands
We hear in the beating of our own blood
The knock of another heart.

And with a new heart, one prophetic and submissive,
We will understand that with us is the one
By whom are captured in a bondage without term
Both song and beauty.

For the singing glow of beauty,
For the lightfall of song
How can one not give up one's last breath
And one's last look

To those pinkish little seashells
On their shaky rings,
Cast up—by the wash of what seas?—
Onto our coastal dust.

I came to the poets with my verses,
But they themselves were making verse.
They had no time for me, of course,
And hurriedly they said, "Eternal."

I went to my friends, they were reading me,
But my friends were buying groceries,
And it was so expensive and difficult to buy them,
So sadly they said, "Wonderful."

I went to strangers: take it and read it through,
And believe me, and love me.
But strangers are fatefully polite,
And sighing they said, "A genius."

Where should you be, where should you most fitly be,
Poor things, you homeless songs?
Can it be, throughout the whole wide world
You haven't your own sweet home?

Hide yourselves in the earth, become a magnet there—
But the earth is covered over with granite.
Disappear into the sky in riots of thunder—
But the sky is closed with the stories of houses.

I will throw you out the window, to the wind,
To your father and lord.
Stribog's grandson is wafting, carrying songs,
And he will cast them on someone's heart.

Someone's heart will answer with an echo,
Laughter will flow out to someone's song—
And that someone will not know with whom they laugh together,
Just as I too cannot hope for news of them.

Translated by Harold D. Baker

Notes to the Essay

1. M.A. Gasparov begins his essay with this point. He comments: "There are famous poets, forgotten poets, and unknown [*bezvestnye*] poets. Vera Aleksandrovna Merkur'eva . . . was unknown." I follow throughout Gasparov's biographical information on Merkur'eva.

2. Originating in Ukrainian folk culture, this word also means "den of thieves."

3. Quoted in Gasparov, 150.

4. Ibid., 151.

5. J. Kristeva, "About Chinese Women," in *The Kristeva Reader*, ed. Toril Moi, trans. Séan Hand (New York: Columbia University Press, 1986), 157–58.

6. C. Kelly, ed. and trans., "The Grandmother of Russian Poetry: A Self-Portrait," in *An Anthology of Russian Women's Writing* (New York: Oxford University Press, 1994), 235–36.

Note to the Selected Works

The poems translated here are all the poems published by Gasparov except for "The Grandmother of Russian Poetry: A Self-Portrait," which is translated in Kelly. The translations, by Harold D. Baker, are judiciously literal.

1. Variant title: "A Little Tale About Me."

Bibliography

Primary Works

[Poems.] *Vesennii salon poètov*. Moscow, 1918.

[Poems.] *Zolotaia zurna*. Vladikavkaz, 1926.

Translations by Merkur'eva

Merkur'eva Archive F. 2209 TsGALI.

Shelley, Percy Bysshe. *Izbrannye stikhi*. Trans. V.A. Merkur'eva. Moscow, 1937.

In Translation

"The Grandmother of Russian Poetry: A Self-Portrait." *An Anthology of Russian Women's Writing, 1777–1992*. Ed. Catriona Kelly, trans. Catriona Kelly et al. New York: Oxford University

Press, 1994. 235–36. [With brief biographical essay and translator's notes. Russian original, "Babushka russkoi poèzii: Avtoportret," 436.]

Secondary Work

Gasparov, M.A. "Vera Merkur'eva. Iz literaturnogo naslediia. 'Kassandra'." *Oktiabr'* 5 (1989): 149–59. [Introductory essay, selection of poems.]

Anna Radlova

The name of Anna Dmitrievna Radlova (1891–1949) has recently started reappearing in the press, with selected poems included in Russian anthologies and other collections. While many writers from her generation enjoyed rehabilitation after Stalin's death, the fate of Anna Radlova and her husband, Sergei Radlov, took another thirty years to be redressed. As a result, very little of her poetic legacy survived.

Anna Radlova (née Darmolatova) was one of three sisters who married famous men: one married the brother of Osip Mandel'shtam, while the other sister, Sarra Darmolatova, herself a respected sculptor, was married to Vladimir Lebedev. Radlova's own husband, Sergei Radlov (1892–1958), in addition to being a protégé of Meyerhold, was a leading Soviet theatrical producer of the 1920s. During the 1930s he directed original productions of Shakespeare, using Radlova's translations. Although Kornei Chukovskii criticized Radlova's translating style, there is no question that her translations ranked in fame with those of Mikhail Lozinskii. Indeed, her translations of *Romeo and Juliet, Othello, Hamlet, King Richard III* and *Macbeth* formed the cornerstone of Sergei Radlov's theatrical repertoire.

Radlova's life was marked by a series of turbulent events, the most significant of which was the October Revolution, emerging as the principal theme of her poetry. Like Voloshin and Tsvetaeva, Radlova's abhorrence for Bolshevism could not have endeared her to the powers that be. However, two advocates singled out her growing stature as a poet in the early 1920s, namely Mikhail Kuzmin, whose circle she joined, and D.S. Mirsky. According to Mirsky, Anna Radlova was part of the so-called Petersburg school of poetry, the school whose best-known poets were Gumilev, Akhmatova and Osip Mandel'shtam. At the same time, Mirsky calls her one of its more "independent" members, whose poetry "takes the form of exceedingly strained and unrelieved rhetoric." Radlova took a particular beating from critics of her day, whether the criticism was aimed at her religious intensity, her penchant for elaborate metaphors or her alleged competition with the "other Anna" (Nadezhda Mandel'shtam's term). In "Literary Moscow," a vitriolic attack on all women poets, Osip Mandel'shtam killed two birds with one stone, if you will, by declaring the following: "as far as Moscow is concerned, the saddest symptom is the pious needlework of Marina Tsvetaeva, who seems to echo the dubious solemnity of the Petersburg poetess, Anna Radlova."[1] Lev Trotsky's attack on women poets in his *Literature and Revolution* paved the way for Radlova's abandoning poetry in favor of translating. Trotsky grouped Radlova along with Akhmatova and Tsvetaeva as "poetesses" who possessed a "narrow" lyrical world, which "encompasses the poetess herself, a certain gentleman in a derby hat or military spurs, and, inevitably, God, shown rather indistinctly."[2] But no criticism matches Nadezhda Mandel'shtam's in harshness. Focusing on the loyalties that Radlova demanded from her circle of acquaintances, Mandel'shtam goes to great lengths in describing Radlova's obsessive jealousy toward Akhmatova.

Anna Radlova began her literary career as a poet publishing in *Apollon* as early as 1915. Radlova's output spanned almost a decade; she produced three volumes of poetry: *Honeycomb* (*Soty*) in 1918, *Ships* (*Korabli*) in 1920 and *The Winged Guest* (*Krylatyi gost'*) in 1922. Her only play, *The Ship of the Virgin Mother* (*Bogoroditsyn korabl'*), appeared in 1923. Distinct in mood and tone, Radlova's poetry reveals an adherence to classical and biblical motifs and the principles of precision and harmony. *Honeycomb* consists predominantly of love poems, with numerous religious echoes, that resound in powerful intensity and with rhetorical devices. Based on the dates of the individual poems, one discerns that those poems written before the fall of 1917 are more replete with themes of personal loss, the sadness of parting and the inability to communicate from a distance. However, after the autumn of 1917 Radlova introduces the theme of ships, not unlike Homer's, all of which stand as metaphors for the revolution. Whereas *Honeycomb* is punctuated by an obviously personal feminine voice, the second and third volumes read as universal denunciations of the Bolshevik revolution. According to Kuzmin, her most avid fan in the 1920s, Radlova's second collection of poetry had earned her a place with the greats of the twentieth century, such as Akhmatova, Blok and Mandel'shtam. Replete with heavy and archaic diction, Radlova's *Ships* is strewn with images of violence and wholesale bloodshed. Superimposed upon classical motifs are themes of carnage, war and eschatological tempests, clearly drawn from the Revelation of St. John.

The Winged Guest represents her lengthiest collection and her most mature poetry, showing extensive growth over her earlier work. Fueled by the bloody aftermath of the civil war, her poetry reveals abhorrence of all violence, on national and cosmic levels. Angels pervade her verse, whether warning of the apocalypse ahead, or bearing the burdens of mortals. A maternal concern for the fate of all children orphaned by war is juxtaposed with catastrophic, barren landscapes. By the time Radlova's third volume of poetry appeared, and Trotsky's denunciation soon followed, it was clear that Radlova's demise as a poet was imminent.

Radlova's poetic drama, *The Ship of the Virgin Mother*, incorporates historical and religious elements, entailing false empresses, sectarian Khlyst rituals and miracles. The apocryphal story line opens with Elizabeth, daughter of Peter the Great, abandoning the throne and handing it to her maidservant. Razumovskii, based on the historical personage, discovers that Peter's daughter, having adopted the name Akulina Ivanovna, leads a heretical sect. Surrounded by her followers who take on the guise of a Greek chorus, Akulina transforms into the Virgin Mother and accepts punishment for her betrayal: decapitation. Resembling Paul Claudel's mystical drama, Radlova's play has no equal in Russia.

When it was politically inadvisable, Radlova courageously depicted her moral credo in her poetry. In one of her earliest poems, disguised as the Greek prophetess Cassandra, she prophesied her own fate in prophesying the doom of Russia (see translation). Soon after the blockade of Leningrad, the Radlovs and their theatrical company were evacuated to Piatigorsk, which also fell into Nazi occupation. Their troupe performed in Ukrainian, German and French prisoner of war camps. Because of his German ancestry Radlov was offered German citizenship, but he resolutely refused at every turn, knowing that he belonged in the Soviet Union. Through secondhand sources gossip began spreading that the Radlovs were collaborators with the enemy. But any person of Soviet origins, caught behind enemy lines, was officially considered a traitor; in that sense the Radlovs were not alone. With the close of the war, they willingly chose to repatriate to Russia, where a son still resided. Upon arrival the Radlovs were promptly arrested and taken to the Lubyanka prison. A long trial ensued, and they were each sentenced to nine years in a labor camp in Shcherbakov in Iaroslavskaia oblast'. They were not permitted to see their son. Anna Radlova died there in 1949, while her husband was rehabilitated after Stalin's death and died in 1958 in Riga. Although Radlova herself devoted several decades to translating, none of her poetry has been translated before.

Olga Muller Cooke

From Honeycomb

From the dead shores of Troy flies
Your violent voice, sister mine,
And your involuntary sin,
Your most heavy sin
Is with me always. I see ships
Upon the full northern river
Like a flock of evil, tethered beasts,
Thronging in a trap,
They feel the close pursuit,
The hunter's victorious horn.
And you prophesy grief,

Death, death, fire and fierce wars.
They neither listen nor believe, they say
That an ill-disposed deity touched you,
Calling you a foolish prophetess.

I see the ships and yellow torch . . .
Fire, fire . . .
How sad is your voice
Lost in the incessant din . . .
And only through amazing centuries
Through amazing lands you extend
Your very arms toward me with love.

Spring 1918

I used to envy every God-made creature
With profound hurt and longing:
The little sparrows, resembling children
Prancing about on the hot pavement,
The fluffy cat, the dear horses
And even the gray stones in the street.
I wanted to be a smooth stone,

So as not to remember my recent
Parting with you, my silent friend.
Barely feeling pain at that moment,
Getting up, you said: enough,
Let's not drag out this pitiful illness.
And after, only after a spare moment—
Spare moments are unkind to me—
My heavy heart raged in fear
And the night seemed like the light of day.

From Ships

Ablaze in copper lonely October
Bloomed under the sign of Sagittarius
A huge ship emerged
And covered the century in a shadow
The taking of the Bastille was merely a plaything
With wolverine's milk, Rome,
Your stones poured
Wolf's love into the victors' veins.
And in my bloodied Russia,
Be she victorious or captive,
Beats the heart of the universe.

Spring 1920

Petersburg

The streets are desolate, like the fields,
Under the burning asphalt the land has grown silent
Houses, destroyed by people and flames—
How the goldenwinged, goldenfaced Angel of Rebellion,
Flew over the city, breathing universal alarm,
How he blinded the eyes of the wounded and frightened
How they conquered, how they fell under the winged banner
The land does not recall when enveloped in death,

Only the more pungent poplars have turned up in spring
And the goldenhorned solar bull,
Sensing the smell of blood,
Left his Aravic, his Sicilian sultry dens
And given over to Pasiphae's new love,
He rises above the capital and pierces her day and night,
The memory of the past burns and prophesies the sun.

Spring 1920

Spare us millennial peace,
The marble of Athens,
The words of Dante.
Children play in the squares,
Covered with blood,
And the crying grass grows.
The flame has devoured books, pain and joy
Whirl and sing, you joyful storm!
We drink the sweetness of oblivion from your hands,
Thoughtless peace alone.

Spring 1920

The years dragged on like an insane herd—
God will count them as centuries—
Naked death shamelessly caroused,
And the children have stopped smiling.
And we learned to measure all things,
And death became the sole arbiter
Of love winged or wingless
And about love of vain speech.

But the heart is a troubled new Titanic
It sleeps in the Atlantic depths,

And ships sail overhead in chains,
In heavy armor and heavy dreams.

The earth is the Lord's tenderest star,
Without oblivion in your mute seas,
Without peace in your thick gardens,
In crimson dawns—but in the sterile night
A verse ascends, like a cold razor blade.

Summer 1920

From The Winged Guest

The earth screamed in a black voice,
The sword-bearing angel spoke to the poet about a miracle,
Killing and falling, the people fought and were beaten,
And not a single stalk remained on the ground.
Stars spun round from hunger and winds,
As did people, beasts, birds, trees and torches,
And there was neither a morning nor an evening dawn,
Only a black, whistling and cutting wind.
My heart whirled like a spinning top,
The star broke away and flew toward me,
It grazed my heart with its sharp diamond edge,
Blood spurted and the thousand-dayed die was cast
Dizziness makes my legs tremble,
Once again I am on a dusty white road,
Milestones, shepherds and sheep,
And the eastern star is nailed to the heavens.

May 1921

You were a nation like all nations
With her factories, tramways and cripples,
With sinful towns and clean rivers,
In the winter frost, and in the summer intense heat.

And there were expansive fields, wild winds and schismatic songs
—Your Highness, white dove, arise—
And Europe, listening to Chaliapin, would ooh and aah
—What genius did the turtle give birth to—
You were the turtle and became the lyre from the Black to the White Seas,
The dove pecked at your flesh and the wind scattered it over the fields,
When sad I dream of an empty world—
No tramways, no factories, no Chaliapin, save the song—
Your Highness, white dove, arise.

* * *

The city is like a nailed-up house,
The sky in tatters,
And the wind around
Whirling, wafting, flying, flying,
Making the forgotten shutter pound
This is not a city, nor a house, but a ship,
Rotten wind, lethal September.
Like a river flows your anguish,
How can the granite take such anguish.
An inconceivable cyclone wails,
The unbearable ring of your resonant heart.
The yellow leafy tornado spins and spins
Like torn rustling silk,
Water and land on the assault,
Impossible, impossible to save the ship
And a gentle mouth smiles—
Hear the wreck on board.

October 1921

Translated by Olga Muller Cooke

Notes to the Essay

1. O. Mandel'shtam, "Literary Moscow," in *Osip Mandel'shtam: Selected Essays* (Austin: University of Texas Press, 1977).
2. L. Trotsky, *Literature and Revolution* (Ann Arbor: University of Michigan Press, 1960).

Bibliography

Primary Works

Soty [Honeycomb]. Petrograd: Fiametta, 1918.

Korabli [Ships]. Petrograd: Alkonost', 1920.

Krylatyi gost' [The Winged Guest]. Petrograd: Petropolis, 1922.

Bogoroditsyn korabl' [The Ship of the Virgin Mary]. Berlin, 1923.

Secondary Works

Cheron, G. "Soobshcheniia i zametki." *Novyi zhurnal* 183 (1991): 358–64.

Chukovskii, K. *Vysokoe iskusstvo*. Moscow: Iskusstvo, 1941.

Gaidabura, V. "'Tak rasskazhi pravdivo . . . '." *Sovetskaia kul'tura,* 22 August 1989.

Gasparov, M.L. *Russkii stikh*. Daugavpils, 1989.

———. *Russkie stikhi 1890–1925 godov v kommentariiakh*. Moscow: Nauka, 1993.

Gusman, V. *Sto poètov*. Tver': Oktiabr', 1923.

Karlinsky, S. *Marina Tsvetaeva: The Woman, Her World, and Her Poetry*. Cambridge: Cambridge University Press, 1986.

Kuzmin, M. "Krylatyi gost', gerbarii, i èkzameny." *Uslovnosti*. Moscow: Poliarnaia zvezda, 1923.

———. "Golos poèta." *Uslovnosti*. Moscow: Poliarnaia zvezda, 1923.

Mandel'shtam, N. *Hope Abandoned*. Trans. M. Hayward. New York: Atheneum, 1974.

Mandel'shtam, O. "Literary Moscow." *Osip Mandel'shtam: Selected Essays*. Austin: University of Texas Press, 1977.

Mirsky, D.S. *Contemporary Russian Literature, 1881–1925*. New York: Alfred Knopf, 1926.

———. "O sovremennom sostoianii russkoi poèzii." *Novyi zhurnal* 131 (1978). [Rpt. D.S. Mirsky. *Uncollected Writings on Russian Literature*. Ed. with introduction and bibliography by G.S. Smith. Berkeley, CA: Berkeley Slavic Specialties, 1989.]

Nikol'skaia, T.L. "Tema misticheskogo sektsanstva v russkoi poèzii 20–kh godov XX-veka." *Trudy po russkoi i slavianskoi filologii Tartuskogo universiteta. Literaturovedenie* 883 (1990).

Pasternak, E. *Boris Pasternak: The Tragic Years. 1930–1960*. London: Collins Harvill, 1990.

Presman, N. "Radlova, Anna D." *Literaturnaia èntsiklopediia*. Ed. A. Lunacharskii. Moscow, 1935.

Trotsky, L. *Literature and Revolution*. Ann Arbor: University of Michigan, 1960.

Uchenova, V.V., ed. *Tsaritsy muz. Russkie poètessy XIX-nachala XX veka*. Moscow: Sovremennik, 1989.

Lidiia Seifullina

It is not surprising that the name of Lidiia Nikolaevna Seifullina (1889–1954) is unknown to the Western reader since only two of her short stories were ever translated into English.[1] In Russia, however, Seifullina has been considered one of the founders of Soviet literature. Her first publications in the early 1920s won the acclaim of Soviet critics and enjoyed great popularity among the Russian reading public. Her short novel *Virineia* (1924) was a tremendous success, and in collaboration with her husband, V.P. Pravdukhin (1892–1939),[2] Seifullina adapted it for the stage. The play premiered at Vakhtangov's theater in 1925 and was later performed throughout Soviet Russia. In the late 1960s, *Virineia* made a successful comeback as an opera and a popular film.[3] Together with Seifullina's other creations, *Virineia* became a Soviet literary classic and was included in many anthologies. The writer published her six-volume *Collected Works* (*Sobranie sochinenii,* 1929–1931) after less than a decade of her creative career, and from then on devoted herself mostly to administrative and educational activities in the Soviet literary establishment.

Seifullina's career as a successful Soviet author and one of the leaders of the Union of Soviet Writers (established in 1932) required not only talent and hard work but also "working class consciousness" and "revolutionary enthusiasm." Although the writer's social origins and early education were not "ideal" for the proletarian state, they were nevertheless acceptable.[4] Seifullina's mother, a peasant, died when she was only five. She and her younger sister were raised by their maternal grandmother and father, an Orthodox village priest of Tatar extraction. She began her formal education at the parish elementary school in the village of Aleksandrovsk in the Orenburg region, and later continued at the Orenburg Diocesan School. Upon her graduation from the Omsk Gymnasium in 1906, she went to work as a teacher and librarian in Omsk and Orenburg for a few years.

After her success in a local amateur theater, Seifullina decided to become a professional actress. She performed with a provincial theater troupe in such towns as Orenburg, Vilno, Tashkent and others for several years, but in 1912 she left the stage, later giving the following explanation: "I haven't felt satisfied with either my performance or my position in the theater."[5] It is possible that Seifullina's failed attempt to get a contract with the Moscow Art Theater contributed to this decision.

The years 1912–1917 were very important in shaping the future writer. Seifullina returned to working as a teacher and librarian in Siberian and Mordvinian villages. Not only did she teach peasant children and adults, but she organized reading rooms, gave talks, wrote letters for villagers to their relatives at the war front and helped everyone who needed her, especially peasant women. According to Seifullina's sister, Zoia, the villagers respected their "tiny" but "brainy" Tatar teacher and called her *bab'ia zastupnitsa* ("the women's defender").[6] Seifullina's populist convictions and her extensive experience in working with village people in rural communities brought her to the Socialist Revolutionary party, of which she was a member for two years (1917–1919). In May 1917, at a seminar organized by the Moscow People's University for provincial librarians, she discussed the limitations of such populist activities. She reported: "I began my work among peasants as a schoolteacher in the most remote regions of the Orenburg province. The last three years I spent there showed me the enormous difficulties in overcoming peasants' ignorance and superstition, and, most importantly, their deeply rooted mistrust for the intelligentsia. These three years opened my eyes to my own ignorance and demonstrated to me the poverty of ideas which I brought to the countryside. . . . I left the village with deep dissatisfaction and a depressing understanding of how microscopic my contribution was, especially when compared with the energy and hopes I had invested in it. But, besides this bitter feeling, I left the village with a significant plus: better knowledge about peasant folk and my experience in their environment."[7]

This experience enabled Seifullina to become a very sensitive reporter for a number of Siberian periodicals and a highly valued employee for the local government. She contributed to and edited such Socialist Revolutionary party newspapers as *People's Thought* (*Duma narodnaia*) and *Struggle* (*Bor'ba*) and was the only woman elected to the Omsk Zemstvo Council, which she chaired just before it was disbanded by the Bolsheviks and replaced by their new Soviet. Seifullina's decision to join the new government was not easy. In her 1921 autobiography she declared: "I cannot be a Marxist due to a certain populist inclination in my previous experience and in my beliefs."[8] However, the painful choice had to be made, and years later she wrote: "I am a person born and raised under the old way of life, with a different set of moral and other values. I was twenty-eight when the October Revolution took place. I was consciously and willingly making the choice whether to leave for the old life or to stay here as a citizen of the new Russia."[9]

In the years following her resignation from the Socialist Revolutionary party, Seifullina served as chief librarian in Cheliabinsk, was an instructor of literacy for the Red Army soldiers, contributed to local newspapers, performed for amateur theaters and helped with *besprizorniki* (homeless and neglected children). "Life itself made me a writer." She wrote later:

> In 1920 some Cheliabinsk intelligentsia committed sabotage, as we used to say then. And the intelligentsia which collaborated with Soviet authorities did everything that needed to be done: if schoolteachers refused to work, we went to the schools and taught; if preschool employees committed sabotage, if the nursery lacked educators, we substituted for them; if in the newly organized sanatorium for miners there was a lack of managers or receptionists, we went there. We participated in the campaign for abolishing illiteracy and we lectured on Russian literature or simply taught Russian to the Red Army soldiers. In exactly the same fashion, I became a writer.[10]

Seifullina's first fiction appeared in the local press: a sketch entitled "Unhappy Shrovetide" (1917) in the *Orenburg Country Cause* (*Orenburgskoe zemskoe delo*), the short stories "Young Communist" (1920) in *Soviet Truth* (*Sovetskaia pravda*) and "Pavlushka's Career" (1921) in *Soviet Siberia* (*Sovetskaia Sibir'*). In 1919 Seifullina and her husband Pravdukhin authored a three-act play, *Egorka's Life*, about the life and death of a peasant boy, Egorka. The play was performed by the Cheliabinsk children's theater, which Seifullina herself had established. The author starred in this production and was awarded a first prize for her play by the city council committee. (She received a gift that was very valuable in those days—some meat and cigarettes!) In 1921 Seifullina and Pravdukhin were assigned to Nikolaevsk (now Novosibirsk) to work at a publishing house. It is in this central Siberian town that Seifullina's literary career really began. A newly created journal, *Siberian Lights* (*Sibirskie ogni*), needed contributions for its first issue, and Seifullina was asked to submit something. In three weeks, she completed a short novel entitled *Four Chapters: A Tale in Fragments* (*Chetyre glavy,* 1922). A brief preface to the novel explained: "Life is vast. One must write volumes on it. But everything is in turmoil. No time for writing and telling stories. Better—just fragments."[11] The extremely busy readers of this turbulent time appreciated Seifullina's brevity and her quick, telegraphic style, but most importantly, they liked Anna, the central character in the novel.

Anna was one of the first Soviet "New Women," a very popular theme in Russian literature of the 1920s. Seifullina asserted that the life of a woman Bolshevik she had met in a Siberian town had given her the idea for this character, but certain autobiographical traits were obvious. Like the author herself, Anna, a peasant by origin, received an education thanks to her benefactors and became a provincial actress. Unlike Seifullina, Anna left the stage for her rich lover, the owner of a gold-mining business. After his death, she moved to the village and became a schoolteacher. Here, back to her roots, Anna underwent drastic changes in her life. She became involved in political activities and joined the Bolsheviks. However, due to the fragmentary nature of *Four Chapters*, the protagonist's conversion to Bolshevism was not convincingly presented.

In her first serious attempt at fiction writing, Seifullina demonstrated her mastery not so much in character development as in the depiction of the Siberian countryside during the revolution. She portrayed the Russian village as starving, confused and struggling to make a leap from the old familiar way of life to the new and unknown future. Unlike many nineteenth-century writers, Seifullina was not one to idealize the Russian peasant community. While she admired their great skill at survival and plain spoken wisdom, she candidly presented Russian peasants as superstitious, mistrusting and sometimes very violent. *Four Chapters* shocked readers with a naturalistic bloody massacre in which angry villagers brutally killed seven gypsies, including some women and a child, for a crime they may not have committed. Seifullina gave a very realistic account of the life of peasant women as well. Overworked and severely abused by their husbands, rural women suffered even more during World War One and the revolution, when they became the only providers for their large families. It should be noted that, in spite of this grim portrayal of the Russian countryside, Seifullina's novel was not pessimistic. The writer strongly believed that the revolution would bring a new social order to the Russian village and would transform backward peasants into conscientious citizens.

Four Chapters was well received by the provincial Russian reading public. One of the founders of *Siberian Lights*, G. Pushkarev, later recalled the success of the novel in his little town of Barnaul: "The novel made a great impression on everybody. It was read in libraries and in army units and passionately discussed by its readers. The three hundred issues of the journal received in Barnaul immediately sold out."[12] The new journal and Seifullina's novel attracted the attention of many Russian periodicals, including the well-known *News* (*Izvestia*) and *Red Virgin Soil* (*Krasnaia nov'*). A. Lunacharskii and E. Iaroslavskii, both prominent Bolsheviks, gave favorable reviews, and a few months later, the novel appeared in a separate book edition.

Encouraged by her first success, Seifullina wrote several stories for the next issues of *Siberian Lights*. One of the best and most popular of these publications was a short story entitled "The Lawbreakers" (1922). Written in just four days and placed in the second issue of *Siberian Lights,* the story reappeared in other periodicals and book editions many times and became recommended reading for schools and juvenile delinquent reformatories. In this story, Seifullina addressed an urgent issue facing the new Soviet state, *besprizornichestvo:* the problem of thousands of homeless and neglected children driven to the streets by revolution, war and hunger. For many of these children, crime was the only means of survival, and the state desperately needed money and ideas to combat this social disaster.

In "The Lawbreakers," Seifullina not only painted a very realistic picture of the life of abandoned children in postrevolutionary Russia but also proposed some constructive ideas to turn young people who were wasting their lives into useful citizens. The main character of the story, a fourteen-year-old boy, Grishka Peskov, runs away from the orphanages and reformatories repeatedly, because he considers them bureaucratic and boring. "It's O.K. there, but too boring," he tries to explain, "they fed us in the morning and brought us to a big room. They read sometimes. But always about something boring. Good boy and bad boy. . . . I always feel an urge to smack this good boy! . . . I got sick of listening, singing songs and dancing their silly dances."[13] However, after one of the street round-ups, Grishka is offered something unusual—work in a self-governed children's colony with no sentry or policing. It was this particular new kind of reformatory that made Seifullina's story required reading for many Soviet educators.

As in most of Seifullina's writing, "The Lawbreakers" was based on personal experience and observations. The founder of the colony in the story, Martynov, had a real-life prototype in Mikhailov, the director of the Turgoiak children's colony. Seifullina knew Mikhailov and had visited his institution in 1921, living with the children, helping and observing them for several weeks. In the story, she presented Turgoiak's reform school as a place where troubled children were offered trust, respect and a strong conviction in their ability to transform themselves. The educators of the commune emphasized personal responsibility and camaraderie in their treatment of the young colonists, and they engaged them in cooperative management and self-sufficiency. The Mikhailov team considered collective labor and communal living in a natural setting absolutely essential for the children's reformation, as well as for their basic survival in a country stricken with hunger and devastation.

In addition to its contribution to the development of Soviet pedagogy, "The Lawbreakers" was also a well-written story on a topical theme. Seifullina impressed her reader with believable and likable characters, lively language and an optimistic view of the educational process. She avoided the literary clichés of her time, giving neither romanticized nor sentimentalized portrayals of the young "lawbreakers" and presenting the life of city riffraff through the eyes of her main character, Grishka Peskov. Colored with the immediacy of Grishka's experience, this portrayal lent the reader direct access to the boy's curious mind and his ingenuity. Grishka appeared to the reader as a bold, carefree and optimistic person, sometimes rough and impudent, but never "a hopeless case." His discourse, as well as the story's witty and colorful dialogues, manifested Seifullina's matured mastery in the technique of storytelling. The characterization of the teacher, Martynov, also turned out well; while not without faults, he proved both admirable and believable.

After the tremendous success of "The Lawbreakers" and the publication of several other well-received stories, Seifullina became a celebrity and was invited by A. Voronskii, the editor of *Red Virgin Soil* to work for his journal. She moved with her husband to Moscow in 1923, to a little apartment on Basmannaia Street, which became a sort of literary salon frequented by such well-known or promising authors as S. Esenin, I. Babel', M. Sholokhov, V. Ivanov and others. One of these visitors, the writer V. Lidin, recalled later:

> In the 1920s, a little Tatar woman with very black bangs on her forehead appeared in Moscow and she immediately won our hearts. She came to Moscow as a provincial teacher and librarian who had already had her first short novel published in Siberia. The novel, witty and lively, attracted attention to this young talented author. At once, Seifullina became a part of the Moscow circle of writers. . . . We appreciated her straightforward character with no compromise for special friends. She always spoke sincerely, passionately, without trying to please; she had a distinctive way of speaking. Her words were impressive and to the point; and even when Seifullina did not like something, she could express this in such a way that no one was offended.[14]

One day, as Seifullina would later recall, the telephone in her apartment rang, and *Red Virgin Soil* asked her to submit a story to the journal's International Women's Day issue; naturally, they wanted something about women. Always inspired by these "social demands," Seifullina agreed to take on the assignment.[15] Unable to write about the life of urban women due to her lack of knowledge, she began a story about a peasant woman. As in her previous works, Seifullina turned to her personal experience. As a teacher in the Mordvinian village of Karaigyr, she had known a woman named Arisha, a custodian in her school. A beautiful and hardworking individual, Arisha lost her parents at age eight and since then supported herself by taking various jobs in her village or in the nearest town. Many young and wealthy male peasants sought Arisha's hand, but she chose to live with a poor railroad worker infected with tuberculosis. When her sick mate became too weak to hold a job, Arisha took care of him and supported his whole family of his old mother and two sisters. The other person whom Seifullina claimed inspired her to write the story was a woman Bolshevik she had met in Siberia right after the October Revolution. In her new novel Seifullina combined the images of these two real-life women and gave her protagonist an unusual Old Believer's name, Virineia.

Virineia first appeared in the June 1924 issue of *Red Virgin Soil* and later in other periodicals and single book editions. The novel won the immediate acclaim of both critics and readers and made Seifullina's name known all over Soviet Russia. The major reason for the novel's success lay in the portrayal of the new type of a simple, ordinary woman who, under the influence of the revolution, became an active and conscious supporter of the Bolsheviks and gave her life for their revolutionary cause. Such a character was new for Russia, and in the following issue Voronskii emphasized the novelty of Seifullina's work:

> The protoganist of *Virineia* is new, unique and generously portrayed; she wins our hearts with the fullness of life she contains within herself, and the novel is very contemporary. . . . Virineia is full to the rim with powerful and mighty instincts; they provide her with strength and soundness, and they restrain neither her will nor her individuality. On the contrary, the richness and complexity of her nature is nourished by the presence of this great life energy. She is able to defend herself. She is stubborn, self-willed, capricious; frank to the point of being rude, and at the same time feminine for she needs to love, bear the child and do her work. She is a drunk and good-for-nothing, but sober-minded and prudent when it is necessary. She is a mother, lover, sister, friend, comrade, worker. And most importantly, she does not have even a trace of the widely portrayed and exaggerated peasant's passivity. . . . [16]

In his statement, Voronskii was right in emphasizing the traditional female qualities in this nontraditional Russian peasant woman, for otherwise Virineia would be less believable. Later, Seifullina explained her decision to portray the protagonist the way she did, writing: "I wanted to conclude my novel with Virineia being a real revolutionary, a political instructor of the Red Army. But when I thought my character through, I realized that she could not be a political instructor. The only possible end for this rebellious woman would be to die honestly and be remembered well because, if placed in the organized social environment, she would bring anarchy and discord to it. . . . In order not to ruin my favorite protagonist this way, I had to kill her; there was no other choice."[17] At the end of the novel, the rebellious Virineia becomes a mother and dies in a trap set up for her by the Cossacks during a visit to feed her infant.

Some critics (including Voronskii) considered the novel's final episode too weak. Others blamed the protagonist for being too spontaneous and personally motivated in her attitude toward the revolution. They stated that Virineia helped the Bolsheviks because of her involvement with a village communist, Pavel Suslov, and not as a result of her own understanding of revolutionary goals.[18] Regardless of the critics' dispute, Seifullina's character proved to be more credible and full-blooded than her literary counterparts of later creations, such as Dasha Chumalova in Gladkov's *Cement* (1925), who allows her daughter to die so that she may better serve the revolution. One of the reasons for Virineia's verisimilitude lay in Seifullina's portrayal of the complexity of her personality. The author presented her protagonist both as a part of the traditional peasant culture, where family life, children, work and community were deeply valued, and as an outcast and rebel against the cruelty of this tradition toward women. "Why is it that in the books everybody is so nice to each other?" Virineia asked an engineer who was interested in her.

> They talk about love and so forth. But it is not like that for our village lads. They seldom speak to their sweethearts and never to their women. To the cow or horse a man sometimes says "dear," but no tender word does he find for his old lady. She is in the house for work and children, not for his affection. And at work, he pities his cattle, not his wife.[19]

In her own way, Virineia protested against such mistreatment of peasant women. She lived with an ailing and poor peasant man, Vasilii, out of wedlock, because he was good to her, and she left his house when her affection for the man ended. A strong and independent woman, Virineia learned to defend and support herself from her earliest years, after she had lost both parents and had begun working. Sometimes Virineia could misuse her freedom in mischievous and seductive behavior, but never did she lose her sense of dignity or display any disrespect for others. Even when Vasilii's mother cursed her for her promiscuity, Virineia held her sharp tongue, for she did not want to hurt the old woman's feelings.

Most critics of the 1920s failed to see that Virineia's association with the Bolsheviks resulted not only from her common-law marriage with village communist Pavel but from her whole life experience. Always rebellious and straightforward, she disobeyed traditional peasant morality and stood against social injustice. As a woman of "loose morals," she was nevertheless respected by the countrymen for her bravery and bold spirit. A mighty blacksmith did nothing to her when she publicly broke up with him, threatening to kill him if he would not leave her alone: "Her reckless boldness disarmed men, leaving them with mixed feelings of fear and admiration."[20] She ridiculed her unfortunate admirers of higher social stature by openly revealing their true lecherous intentions. Virineia made fun of "new" urban sexual morals as well. She left a family she worked for in annoyance because, after noticing her husband's interest in beautiful Virineia, the landlady insisted on "talking it over." The only simple and honest relationship Virineia had was with Pavel. A widowed peasant who just had returned from the war, Pavel needed help with his household and he made Virineia an offer. On her inquiry "about night service," he replied, "About not pestering you at night, I cannot promise. We are both young and we'll live together. How can we avoid it? But I'll promise you one thing, nothing happens if you don't want it."[21] Next morning upon Virineia's arrival, he questioned, "Well, did you come only to work or to be my woman?" and she answered in the same disarmingly simple manner: "Well, let's try to live and sleep together."[22]

Seifullina acquired a reputation of an author who realistically described the brutality and cruelty of everyday life in the Russian countryside, who would not avoid a naturalistic episode or a strong word in her writing, whose own basic life values were very simple. She perceived sex as a natural instinct, justified by procreation and family, and she considered peasants more fit for healthy and honest relationships than their masters. Although she advocated the urgent need to improve the life of Russian peasant women, she expressed no interest in the women's emancipation movement, which was popular during her time. On the contrary, Seifullina saw a woman's destiny primarily in traditional terms, insisting that a woman's real fulfillment rests in motherhood. Almost all of her positive characters yearned to become mothers. Even free-spirited Virineia admitted that, had she had a child with Vasilii, she would not be able to leave him: "Many town women look with envy at my flat stomach, but I as a native peasant woman (*korennaia muzhichka*) know that even a dog feels happy when she licks and takes care of her puppy."[23]

Neither her belated love for Pavel, nor her peaceful family life with him, brought Virineia real happiness, since she failed to have a child by him. Only at the end of the novel was Seifullina's favorite character redeemed for her sufferings by giving birth to a long-awaited son. However, violent times made motherhood itself vulnerable, and Virineia's joy was short-lived. Her death in the Cossacks' trap, when "like a wolf for its cub, she made her way to feed her infant,"[24] could not be perceived as heroic, but it certainly had a point. According to Seifullina, only hostile and violent forces were able to destroy the otherwise inviolable bond of mother and child. "Twice I have read *Virineia*, and twice an acute pain pierced my heart when Virka [Virineia] was killed," wrote Soviet author D. Furmanov. "One can feel such pain only at the death of a very close and dear person. . . . And when she was gone, it became especially clear that there was no more of this significant and strong person; that less than a tenth of her inner energy awakened by the Revolution found its realization; that she really belonged to the future."[25]

The personal drama of this simple but memorable woman not only formed the core of the novel but also demonstrated the author's creative maturity. Seifullina portrayed her character in a series of dramatic episodes, showing her both in action and through the medium of her speech. The technique of avoiding authoritative description helped create the illusion that the novel's events were presented as seen by Virineia herself. This intimate look at the life of the Russian village, as well as Seifullina's authentic use of folk language, contributed to the novel's tremendous success. A few months after its publication, *Virineia* was adapted for the stage and became a Soviet theatrical hit. Later, the play was chosen for an international theater tour and appeared in Prague (1927) and Paris (1928).

Seifullina's successful fiction writing came to a prolonged halt at the end of the 1920s. Now and then, she would publish something, but she never reached the level of her early creations. In 1934 she tried to explain why she hadn't written any fiction since 1929 and why she didn't have any works about socialist construction:

> Here and there, people ask these questions and they reproach me, saying that I don't want to see our success, don't want to participate in our country's socialist reconstruction. No, comrades, I do, but my experience as a writer, as well as my sense of responsibility, don't allow me to produce low-quality work. I could write about Magnitogorsk, where I spent a few days; I could write about Sverdlovsk, where I spent a month, or about the factory "Krasnii Treugol'nik," where I was for a year . . . I could do this, but it is here that my responsibility for the social order begins. I don't feel comfortable with this material, I don't feel the way I felt when I was writing about life in the countryside or "The Lawbreakers." I need to know this new life better. Don't forget that I came here from another world. . . . The greater part of my work

> and my life were spent in the country, and it is not easy for me to turn to the new topic of industrial urban life.[26]

However, by this time Seifullina was unable to write about peasant life either, for she was out of touch with the Soviet countryside as well. She continued her active involvement in Soviet literary life as an educator and a journalist until her death in 1954 but remained primarily known for her early writing about life in the Russian countryside during revolutionary times.

Tatiana Osipovich

From The Lawbreakers

II.

Spring soaked up the snow still more greedily. The church doors opened. The sun-filled air refreshed the gloomy vaults. It burst in, intoxicated and unfettered. But it rushed out of the church with the sorrowful Lenten howl of the people, with their lament about the kingdom they couldn't enter. Shadowlike nuns floated toward the church more frequently. In an ecstasy of repentance, people went on screaming to God. Grishka was completely confused by the noiseless black shadows on the face of spring, the Lenten psalms and the agitated hubbub of the springtime streets. He'd satisfied his teachers. He studied anything. He'd sit quietly for hours. It was just that his eyes would become empty. But Grishka lived inside himself. At night he'd wake up and think about freedom. It was hard to run away. Six of his older fellow reform school captives had robbed the convent and escaped. But they got caught. As if they could really revolt. They were already young men, sprouting mustaches. They got sent to a work camp. And those who remained were watched more closely. They added a sentry, a secret police agent and more teachers. But then something helped.

As the war between the children and the nuns got more intense, their clashes became their most vivid moments in the dreary succession of days. They lived for them in their monotonous incarceration. Then the jail sent another fifty people. The nuns had to be evicted. A big two-story house on the other side of the river was cleared for them, close to the outskirts of town. They were ordered to move. The nuns obediently accepted the authorities' decision. All they asked was permission to use the nunnery's church. But little by little each one gave voice to her grief.

In the mornings peasant carts would halt a little way from the high nunnery walls. Some days there would be two or three. The guilty-looking men and women who huddled there would work their way up to the nunnery gates. Entreating and coaxing the sentries, they would sneak up to the gate. The courtyard would greet them with the echoes of a new, alien life. The words "comrade," "orphanage" and "delinquent" hung in the air. The ancient cloistered life had hidden itself fearfully deep inside. They'd pass the noisy children and the silent ones whose eyes asked the inevitable question, and go into the little houses in the rear. Icons of the saints and stirring, thin voices greeted them there. The nuns poured their souls out to those who donated in secret. The Mother Superior would sign papers as the humble Evstoliia, Mother Superior of the monastic labor collective. At meetings in the nunnery church, she would claim: "All power is from God." But she couldn't keep everything inside herself either. She complained to an acquaintance, Astaf'ev, a layman who had once had two movie theaters and had donated generously to the nunnery, but now worked in the provincial union. However, he still hadn't forgotten about God. She told him, "They're tearing us away from God's house."

And messengers went to the houses where God had not been forgotten.

"They're evicting the nuns!"

"There'll be theaters in the nunnery!"

"They're taking the frames off the icons!"

"They took everything from the church altar to the provincial secret police chief's apartment."

"They tortured the Mother Superior at the secret police office."

The news flew from the houses to the bazaar located next to the nunnery. On the day the move was scheduled, women in the wagons crossed themselves. One was upset—she hadn't gotten the entire three thousand for some cabbage. Sighing, she mixed bits of prayers with women's curses, shrill and incoherent.

"Mother, Queen of Heaven, Blessed Virgin of the Three Hands.[1] They don't stop at nothin' . . . they shove money at you, an' run off! Communist devil! Kike! Merciful Nikolai. . . . The prayers, y' see, got answered. . . . They're devils, afraid of the incense. The sisters, the brides of Christ . . . where're they goin'? May they be crushed by a mountain, the monsters, seeds of the Antichrist! Well, take this . . . I looked, someone was there, and then there wasn't nobody. Well, I remember your bug-eyed face! Come back, why don't you . . . you canker!"

The men didn't wag their tongues, but even though they'd finished bartering, they didn't leave the bazaar. They moved their nags closer to the nunnery.

Wagons were brought for the nuns. The big gates opened. The sentries stood near them. The news traveled as if by some secret wire. Like a wave, the motley-colored crowd immediately rushed forward. Mother Evstoliia watched attentively from underneath her black headdress. And she halted at the gates, tall and officious. She unhurriedly turned toward the icon nailed above the gates. She bowed down to the ground. Women in the crowd started babbling. And at her wagon, the Mother Superior bowed at the waist in all four directions. Her face was like that of an old icon. Stern. Behind her, the nuns moved like black shadows. Whatever the Mother Superior did, everyone copied. The black figures, distinct against the blue summer air, made everyone sad. One woman ran toward the nuns with a ringing howl: "Sisters who pray for us! Forgive us, for Christ's sake!"

Another followed her. She cried even louder: "Where're they chasing you, away from God's house?"

A third fell right at the hooves of the Mother Superior's horse and let go a rooster from her hand. "Don't find fault with us! Don't complain to God about us!"

A heartrending wail arose. Dozens of piercing women's voices responded. Pedestrians turned off the street toward the wailing. A mounted soldier carrying a packet reined in his horse in mid-gallop. He froze in curiosity. The vendor Filatova abandoned her pie cart. She ran toward him.

"How come you're blasphemin' the Christian faith? You'll get yours! Leave us in peace, you'll get yours!"

The crowd began to move. The women's wails inflamed everyone. The men started shouting.

"We won't let the nunnery be destroyed!"

"The nuns didn't bother anybody!"

A graying, bustling teacher at the former seminary school, a church elder, was near the wagons. The old man's exclamation rattled out, inciting the crowd, "Where's our freedom of religion? The freedom of religion allowed by the government—where is it?"

"There's no rights!"

"We oughta send a complaint to Lenin!"

"It's government coercion!"

"Apostates! They didn't put anybody in the kike synagogue. The kikes, the Christ-sellers!"

"Aha! Right! They didn't go into the mosque or the Catholic church! They put orphans in the Orthodox nunnery. In the Orthodox one . . . not in those. . . ."

But the "orphans" had already spilled out of the courtyard in a noisy bunch. Wide-eyed, they looked around at everyone. They were intoxicated by the merriment of a scandal. Like mindless puppies, they got under everybody's feet. Grishka forgot about longing and escape. His gray eyes sparkled, and his little head turned from side to side in delight.

It was wonderful! The women howled, the men's mugs were red. And the nuns were like black dolls on springs. They bowed here and there. Their lips were compressed.

"Hey! Their feelings are really hurt!"

And, filling his lungs with air, brimming with rebellion, Grishka shrieked near the Mother Superior, "Blacktailed scum!"

The women replied in a frenzied concerto:

"That nasty kid cursed the Mother Superior!"

"He cursed the sisters who pray for us!"

They would have crushed Grishka. But a sentry grabbed him by the scruff of his neck. He was shoved toward the nunnery walls. But he just collected his wits to start watching the scene. Someone else straightened himself up and shouted into the courtyard, "Get on the phone! We need a detail!"

But the noise had already traveled throughout the town. Mounted soldiers bolted in from everywhere.

"Disperse . . . disperse. . . ."

"Citizens who don't belong to the nunnery, get back . . . back!"

A nun whimpered and collapsed on the ground. A mounted soldier charged toward her.

"Put the sister in the wagon . . . hold her by the legs . . . set her down . . . citizen Mother Superior, get in the wagon, please. Help her! Give her a hand!"

The humorous glazier, stuck in the crowd, chortled, "Looky here! The military ladies' man's doing some sweet-talking."

It caught on like wildfire:

"Hee-hee . . . Ha-ha . . . he wants to be one of the nuns' fancy men."

"He wants to be a ladies' man . . . ha, ha, ha."

"You damned devils. Running your yaps. Our poor sisters!"

"Hee-hee-hee . . . if that's what she does for a kopeck, I wonder what she'd do for ten Soviet rubles. . . ."

"Mischief makers! Damned dogs!"

"Oh, don't curse, please. Let's go, Mania."

"Hee-hee-hee . . . 'Let's go, Mania.' You, you, you got bow legs . . . wide skirts, side pockets . . . young ladies!"

"Look, look, the nuns are packing their stuff."

"They found a pot full of gold in the Mother Superior's basement."

"A hundred arshins of fabric!"

"What martyrs, just imagine! They're not being kicked out into the street. They can pray and fast there too. Isn't that right, Vasia?"

"As a communist, I approve of the provincial executive committee."

"And I'm not a communist, but I understand them on this. There's no place for the kids to go. I un-der-stand."

"So are the kids supposed to die off, or what? They get their peace and quiet and their novices, and the kids get locked up."

"They're orphans . . . do they just get lost, or what?"

"All right, all right, disperse. . . . Citizens, citizens! Get back!"

The nuns gathered their skirts. They busily packed their things. They had lost their iconic demeanor. The crowd buzzed. Sympathy toward the nuns evaporated. Grishka quietly moved away from the wall and plunged into the crowd.

III.

At the station, a man was talking about himself and how many different towns he'd wandered through. And he said, "I'm not meant to have an easy life." Grishka laughed too, along with everyone else, but he didn't understand. But now he remembered, and thought about himself, "I'm not meant to have an easy life."

It so happened that right then the kids were getting sandwiches and tea, and Grishka was walking down the street and listening to his stomach growl. He sure didn't want to go back there. But he just couldn't convince his stomach. You'd make it through a day, and then another, but a fellow gets tired. And their supplies—ai! Everything was wiped out. Six of them were hiding in the graveyard. Grishka found the other five. They'd robbed the school warehouse along with a driver and had run away from the reception center at the orphanage. And so they would spend the nights in the graveyard. They had some money, and Grishka sold the shirt off his back and his pants. He swapped his issue overcoat for a shabby one. They gave more money. Everything got eaten up. During the day they could beg around town without fear. Who would look for them? New fellows came every day. If you ran into someone bad, they would badger you.

"Who are you? Where're you from?"

And the good ones would just go on about their business, wherever they were supposed to go. And they wouldn't look!

A bad one turned up today. Grishka was standing by the council cafeteria, but no one would give him a ticket. At the children's cafeteria, if you didn't have a card, they'd let you eat the food left on the plates, but today they chased him off. They were expecting some "workers' and peasants' inspection team." He stuck his head into one building:

"Give, for Christ's sake . . . my father got killed in the war, and my mom died from typhus."

They threw him out. "Go," they said, "and ask your commissars. They brought you into the world, so they can feed you."

Grishka was bewildered. "Whaddya mean, the commissars brought us into the world? Our mothers and fathers did that. But I got sent to them already. Well, hey, that's what y'get for talking to fools! But I wanna eat. The cafeterias are closing already. What rotten luck!"

Dejected, he smacked a Bashkir, who was also standing by the cafeteria, in the ear. But the fellow was quick. He punched him in the stomach. He groaned, caught his breath, and went on his way.

"Comrade . . . give me some money for food. . . ."

"Get out of the way. They multiply like flies!"

"Hey, get lost, swinging your briefcase around! Fat-ass tightwad!"

There was a kid selling cigarettes, and he went up to him. "How much are a dozen?"

"Get lost, jailbird! These cigarettes ain't for you to smoke."

Grishka squinted his eyes. "Ain't we stuck up! And maybe I got ten thousand."

"You got ten thousand, you go fool someone else. Well, show 'em to me!"

"Like I'm gonna show 'em to everybody. Maybe I had even more."

"Yeah, you had it and now it's gone. Scram before I bust you in the mug!"

"Do it!"

"I will!"

"Try it!"

"I will!"

They stood in the middle of the sidewalk and jumped at each other. Then some lady showed up: "What's this? Are you selling something, boy?"

And that fellow still had the box with some cigarettes in his hand. Stupidly, he blurted out, "The best kind. How many? A dozen?"

But she grabbed him by the sleeve. "We're going to the police station. Have you seen the decree about children speculating? Can't read? We'll stop by your parents'."

He resisted, but she dragged him. Grishka got scared, naturally; he'd almost gotten caught. O.K., she was weak, but she could have grabbed both of them. What a day!

And the day was almost over. The sky turned gray, gloomy. There was just one cheery pink strip left. But it wasn't warm. People were hurrying home. A nasty wind began blowing.

He shambled along, but there was nothing he could do. He trudged toward the graveyard. It was in a bare expanse between the town and the train station. It was surrounded by stone walls, but the gate wasn't locked. The trees there were creaking in the wind now. And the snow hadn't melted completely. The nights were chilly. But it was warmer in their hole in the corner of two walls. Twice they dared to light a fire. But they couldn't do that often. They'd get caught.

Grishka came in with a sigh, but happiness awaited him. The fellows had swiped some food and saved some for him. Full, two girls started softly singing a song. And the four boys told each other about their days. They sat close together in the hole. It was crowded, but better that way. Warmer, and at night it was less scary. At night it got scary in the graveyard. When the wind was blowing and it was dark, it was better. But when the moon loomed in the sky and it was quiet all around, then it was scarier. Dogs howled far away. There, where people were alive. But here it was quiet. It was really a grave. You'd imagine something, hide, and clamp your jaw so as not to breathe, but then you'd look. You'd peep out of the hole and the moon would light up the crosses. All the crosses and headstones stood straight, unmoving. It was like they were hiding, but they were threatening. Tonight it was dark and windy. They told about real life in the town. Freckle-faced Vas'ka, as the rich fellow, always told stories. And he started today. The girls got quiet and started listening.

The story was about living people sometimes getting buried. Vas'ka began the story:

"So I'll tell you guys about this one time. In this town . . . well, there was this girl . . . she didn't really go to the modern school or the high school . . . she comes home and 'Ah, ah . . .' and 'Ah, Daddy, ah, Mommy, I'm dying.' Bing-bang, and she falls on the floor. Her mom and dad run to her, and she says, 'I'm dying, I'm dying.' 'Course they get the doctor right away. They bring the doctor. 'Bla-bla-bla, Mr. Doctor, I wanna die.' The doctor tries to help her. And of course they give her kvass and chocolate, but she says, 'No, no, I'm dying.' Bing-bang, and she stops breathing. 'Course the doctor leaves. Her mom wails and wails, and they have a funeral. And they bury her. In the graveyard. 'Course she lays there and lays there and then this rustling starts. The watchman hears the rustling!

"And he listens and listens and then goes to the girl's parents. They get some people and dig up the grave, and of course she'd died again. But suddenly there's rustling. She'd tucked one leg under herself, like this. And then the doctor says, 'She's in a coma.' And that's what was in the newspapers. And that's when I told my parents: 'Don't bury me till I start to go sour and rotten.'"

The kids listened, holding their breath. And when he finished, dumb Pol'ka whined, "I'm scared."

Grishka reasoned with her. "Stupid, what're you blubbering for? Vas'ka made all that up."

But Vas'ka swore: "I swear, may my eyes burst, it was in the paper. She didn't really go to the modern school or the high school."

Pet'ka, the leader, was Grishka's age, but strict. He was the commander. He barked, "Just keep on howling, bitch. The guard'll hear and you'll get something scarier than Vas'ka's story. And you, you dirty liar, shut up!"

Vas'ka got really mad. "Hey! 'Shut up!' What'd I do, print it in the papers myself? When I give you a good smack, then you'll believe me."

Right then there was a "bang-bang" in the woods, which started right behind the graveyard fence. The children got quiet.

"They're shooting," Anet'ka whispered.

She said it softly, but there wasn't any fear in her voice anymore. It wasn't the first time they'd heard shooting.

Grishka scowled matter-of-factly. "They executed them. The counterrevolutionaries."

"Why?" Pol'ka whimpered.

"What a dummy. How many times have we told you: they're the ones who're against Soviet power."

Quiet Antropka joined in. "I get scared when they shoot people. It hurts."

And there was another "bang-bang" in the woods. They hushed again, listening in curiosity. They were afraid of dead people, but they still didn't know death. And those who'd been shot weren't afraid of suffering. Antropka just shook. He'd seen the war in his own village. His heart shrank into a lump. Anguished, swallowing his tears, he said softly, "It woulda been better to put 'em in jail."

Pet'ka spit disdainfully. "And how about the one who's truly scum, who's killed who knows how many? What about him?"

"He can go to jail too. . . ."

"And he escapes, and kills again."

"If soldiers guard him, he won't escape."

"But he kills the soldiers."

"But he doesn't have a revolver; he can't kill. . . ."

That shut Pet'ka up. He thought—and simply said, "You're an idiot, Antropka!"

And Grishka didn't say anything, but he was thinking.

"When they shoot them, do they shut their eyes?"

And suddenly, it was as if he could see them: they shut them. His heart ached, like Antropka's.

The shots died down. The children waited: would there be any more? They didn't wait it out. Sleep came, closed their eyes, and took away all their thoughts. Only Antropka whimpered softly in his sleep.

In the morning, when the sun warmed them, everyone was lively and happy. The darkness hid itself and took the anguish away with it. Behind the graveyard wall, they played "secret police" and "execution." Pet'ka was the chief of the provincial secret police. He pretended to hold a revolver in one hand and shoot a machine gun with the other. They brought Pol'ka and Aniutka to be shot. Antropka and Grishka did the shooting. Grishka exuberantly commanded, "Shut your eyes! Shut them!"

There was neither blasphemy, nor fear, nor anger in the children's shrill cries. In their innocence, they were pretending to be grownups. The sun warmed them through and through. It was as if with its caress it promised: they'll think up still another game and forget this one.

It was a fun day. They were celebrating the Paris commune. You could eat in the children's cafeteria without a card. The graveyard residents got in the nearest line and got fed. And then they went around the streets with the crowd, following the red flags. They sang the "International." The square had been covered with red boxes. On top of them, communists waved their hands around and shouted something about the Paris commune. Grishka watched one of them more than the others. He was big, shaggy-headed and loud. You could hear him from far away! He ran around the box tossing his greasy locks, and then it was like he hit the side of the box with his fist: "Hats off! I'm going to speak about the martyrs of the commune!"

He bellowed loudly and clearly. Grishka remembered the words, and then shouted them into the crowd himself: "Hats off, I'm going to speak about the martyrs of the commune!"

He'd shouted near some woman, and she punched him in the ear. "Piglet, howling like an idiot! He doesn't know what the commune is, yet he's screaming!"

Grishka rubbed his head where he'd been hit and dashed ahead, happy. How couldn't he know? He knew. Communes were what the communists had, and Paris . . . that was a town. Somewhere beyond Moscow. When he was still at the orphanage, he'd heard: "If to Paris you should go, you'll go crazy, you know." No, pal, Grishka knew. And again, in rebellious excitement he shouted: "By my own hand!"

The crowd stopped again. Not quite a lady, not quite a peasant woman was screeching from atop one of the boxes. What she said you couldn't understand, but she was funny to look at. She ran out of steam. Grishka mimicked her with his thin voice, too: eee-tee-tee-tee! And he went on. But some little drunkard jumped out of the crowd.

His coat was clean, and his hat had long earflaps on the sides, and he had a red bow stuck on his shirtfront. He was kind of skinny, was missing some teeth, and was cockeyed. And he was waving his arms, too, and bellowing, "Comrades, I raaquest that you caantribute money!"

A woman, doubtless his wife, grabbed him by the coat, and he bolted toward a box. "I sincerely raaquest that you caantribute money!"

Two mounted soldiers flew toward him and seized him by the arms. There was laughter in the crowd:

"There's your donation!"

"And what was he drunk on?" a hoarse bass asked enviously.

This was a new delight for Grishka. With a shrill shriek he ran toward the graveyard. "Comrades, I request that you donate money!"

One night they cordoned off the graveyard. They were looking for someone important but found Grishka's commune. And in the clear predawn hours, stumbling, half-awake, the young delinquents trudged down the familiar path. The tired Red Army soldiers cursed but didn't beat them.

Translated by Lisa Taylor

Notes to the Essay

1. "The Old Woman," in *Azure Cities: Stories of New Russia*, ed. Joshua Kunits, 1929, and the first chapter of "The Lawbreakers" in *Soviet Literature*, ed. and trans. George Reavey and Marc Slonim, 1934.

2. Valerian Pavlovich Pravdukhin (1892–1939) was a writer, playwright and critic. His fiction, however, never received the same level of popularity and acclaim as his wife's. In addition to the play *Virineia*, he collaborated with Seifullina in writing such dramatic works as *Egorka's Life* (1919) and *Chernyi iar* (1931). Like many of his compatriots, Pravdukhin fell victim to the Great Purge and was posthumously rehabilitated.

3. The first opera performance (music by S. Slonimsky) took place in the Leningrad Malyi Opera and Ballet Theater and the Stanislavsky Moscow Music Theater (1967). The film was directed by V. Fetin and starred L. Chursina (1969).

4. In the 1920s, Seifullina was sometimes referred to as one of the so-called fellow travelers (*poputchiki*), Soviet writers of nonproletarian and/or nonrevolutionary background who were nevertheless willing to accept the ideals of the revolution and to work constructively within and for the socialist order.

5. Lidiia Seifullina, *Khudozhestvennye proizvedeniia, vospominaniia, stat'i* (Orenburg, 1959), 157.

6. Zoia Seifullina, "Moia sestra," in *Seifullina v vospominaniiakh sovremennikov* (Moscow: Sovetskii pisatel', 1961), 27.

7. Lidiia Seifullina, *Sobranie sochinenii v 4–kh tomakh*, vol. 4, Moscow, 1968, 7–8.

8. Lidiia Seifullina, "Avtobiografiia ot 9. XI. 1921," quoted in N. Ianovsky, *Lidiia Seifullina: Kritiko-biograficheskii ocherk* (Moscow: Sovetskii pisatel', 1972), 16.

9. Lidiia Seifullina, *Sobranie sochinenii v 4–kh tomakh*, 1: 44.

10. Ibid., 4: 316.

11. Ibid., 1: 53.

12. G. Pushkarev, "Zachinatel'nitsa nashego zhurnala," *Sibirskie ogni* 3 (1954): 155.

13. Lidiia Seifullina, *Sobranie sochinenii v 4–kh tomakh*, Vol. 1 (Moscow, 1968), 102.

14. V. Lidin, "L.N. Seifullina," in *Seifullina v vospominaniiakh sovremennikov,* ed. A. Koptelov (Moscow: Sovetskii pisatel', 1961), 285.

15. Lidiia Seifullina, "Kritika moei praktiki," in *Sobranie sochinenii v 4–kh tomakh*, Vol. 4 (1968), 270–71.

16. A. Voronskii, "Literaturnye siluèty," *Krasnaia nov'* 5, 22 (1924): 297.

17. Lidiia Seifullina, *O literature: Stat'i, zametki, vospominaniia* (Moscow: Sovetskii pisatel', 1958), 90.

18. See, for example, Iu. Pukhov, "Gor'kii i Gladkov (20–e gody)," in *Voprosy sovetskoi literatury*, Vol. 3 (Moscow, 1956), 410–411, or Iu. Golovashenko, *Geroika grazhdanskoi voiny* (Leningrad, 1957), 55.

19. Lidiia Seifullina, *Sobranie sochinenii v 4–kh tomakh*, Vol. 2: (1968), 34.

20. Ibid., 72.

21. Ibid., 74.

22. Ibid., 78.

23. Ibid., 21.

24. Ibid., 99.

25. D. Furmanov, "*Virineia* L. Seifullinoi," in L. Seifullina, *Sobranie sochinenii v 4–kh tomakh*, Vol. 3 (Moscow, 1968), 309.

26. Lidiia Seifullina, "Kritika moei praktiki," in *Sobranie sochinenii v 4–kh tomakh*, 4: 273.

Translator's Note to the Selected Work

1. This is an ancient icon, in which the Virgin is depicted with three hands.

Bibliography

Primary Works

Chetyre glavy [*Four Chapters*]. Barnaul: Altaisky Gubizdat, 1922.

Pravonarushiteli [*The Lawbreakers*]. Novonikolaevsk: Sibgosizdat, 1922.

Peregnoi [*Black Soil*]. Moscow: Izdatelstvo "Krug," 1923.

Virineia. Krasnaia nov' 4 (1924).

Sobranie sochinenii v chetyrekh tomakh [*Collected Works in Four Volumes*]. Leningrad: GIZ, 1924–1926.

Muzhitskii skaz o Lenine [*A Muzhik Story of Lenin*]. Leningrad: GIZ, 1925.

V strane ukhodiashchego islama [*In a Land of Disappearing Islam*]. Leningrad: GIZ, 1925.

Kain-kabak. [*Cain's Tavern*]. Moscow: Gosizdat, 1926.

Sobranie sochinenii v shesti tomakh [*Collected Works in Six Volumes*]. Leningrad: GIZ, 1929–1931.

Tania. Moscow: Gosizdat, 1936.

O literature: Stat'i, zametki, vospominaniia [*About Literature: Articles, Notes, Memoirs*]. Moscow: Sovetskii pisatel', 1958.

In Translation

"The Old Woman." *Azure Cities: Stories of New Russia*. Ed. Joshua Kunits. New York, 1929.

"The Lawbreakers." *Soviet Literature: An Anthology*. Ed. and trans. George Reavey and Marc Slonim. New York: Friede, 1934. 129–36.

Secondary Works

Aseev, N. "Po moriu bumazhnomu." *Krasnaia nov'* 4 (1922).

Ianovskii, N. *Lidiia Seifullina: Kritiko-biograficheskii ocherk*. Moscow: Sovetskii pisatel', 1959.

Kardin, V. *Dve sudby: Lidiia Seifullina i ee povest' "Virineia."* Moscow: Khudozhestvennaia literatura, 1976.

———. "Sluzhitel' sovetskogo suda." *Novyi mir* 11 (1968).

Kerzhentsev, V. "*Peregnoi* Seifullinoi." *Prozhektor* 7 (1923).

Koptelov, A., ed. *Seifullina v vospominaniiakh sovremennikov*. Moscow: Sovetskii pisatel', 1961.

Kutlina, L. *L.N. Seifullina i iuzny Ural: Ukazatel' literatury*. Cheliabinsk, 1975.

Lezhnev, A. "Russkaia literatura v istekshom godu." *Pechat' i revolutsiia* 1 (1926).

Mass, V. "Virineia na stsene." *30 dnei* 4 (1925).

Nikitina, E. *V masterskoi sovremennoi khudozhestvennoi prozy*. Moscow: Izdatelstvo Nikitskie subbotniki, 1931.

Ovcharenko, A. *Ot Gor'kogo do Shukshina*. Moscow: Sovetskaia Rossiia, 1984.

Palei, A. *Literaturnye portrety*. Moscow: Izdatel'stvo "Ogonek," 1928.

Poreba, S. *Twórczość Lidii Seifulliny lat dwudziestych*. Wroclaw, 1974.

Pravdukhin, V. "Molodaia literatura v Sibiri." *Pravda*, 22 October 1922.

Rozanov, I. "Deti v proizvedeniiakh Seifullinoi." *Narodnyi uchitel'* 5 (1924).

Seifullina, Zoia. *Moia starshaia sestra.Vospominaniia*. Moscow: Sovetskii pisatel', 1970.

Voronskii, A. "Literaturnye siluèty." *Krasnaia nov'* 5 (1924).

———. *Literaturnye tipy*. Moscow: Izdatel'stvo "Krug," 1927.

Mariia Shkapskaia

Mariia Mikhailovna Shkapskaia (1891–1952) is one of those Russian writers whose work reflects the transition from prerevolutionary, highly individualistic culture to the propagandistic art of the Soviet state. Author of lyrical and intensely religious poetry glorifying the woman—wife, lover and mother—in 1925 Shkapskaia devoted herself almost completely to journalism. She traveled throughout the Soviet Union, and in her essays, within the ingenious patchwork of *skaz*, humor, fairy tales, historical data and statistics, we come upon the grim facts about things such as the devastation of the country through the untrammeled export of grain, fish and lumber, about the appropriation of patented foreign inventions, and about crime, dismal housing conditions, correctional institutions and the high price in human life paid for the unveiling of the Uzbek woman. In 1934 Shkapskaia renounced her own earlier poetry as "socially uninformed." The theme of motherhood, which had allowed her to create some of the most powerful and insightful poetic identifications of Mother Russia, was repressed by the author herself in her new role as a propagandist, in her political environment. Pushed underground, this theme reappeared in her prose in tiny, quick strokes: in brief interviews with women or as a stylistic device in metaphors and similes.

The poetry of Mariia Shkapskaia, published in the early 1920s, was greeted as one of the highest achievements of contemporary Russian culture by Maxim Gorky, Aleksandr Blok and Father Pavel Florenskii. Boris Filippov called her "Vasilissa Rozanova of the woman's theme" and described her poetry as "an attempt at a resurrection of the flesh and even its idolization, hitherto unknown in Russian literature."[1] Her later essays, on the other hand, reflect a steadily growing conformity to the dictates of Soviet propaganda. This transition can be traced through the changing implications of the pronouns "we" and "our" in her work over an eighteen-year period: in the poem "To Louis XVII" (1921) Shkapskaia speaks for all mothers who oppose war, violence and bloodshed:

> I remember clearly in my sorrow—
> I am a mother, and our law is simple:
> We have no part in this blood,
> As we had no part in that other one.

"We" and "our" in this poem pertain to women, to mothers; they are above the battle, because they bear sons for life, not for massacre. In an essay of 1916, the pronoun "our" also defines a party that maintains neutrality, a nonparticipant in the bloodshed: "The ship is ours, Norwegian, neutral. . . ."[2]

In contrast to the above examples, in her speech at the All-Union Congress of Writers in 1934 Shkapskaia uses the pronoun "our" to define the class-oriented, proletarian worldview: "The images in Larissa Reisner's essays are not ours—they are too sophisticated, too intellectual."[3]

Threatened by unemployment, loneliness and poverty, rescued by Maxim Gorky's project to compile the history of all major Russian factories, Shkapskaia abandoned her lyrical theme, violated it, then rejected and finally denounced it. However, in spite of her dedication to the Soviet propaganda machine and the excellent literary quality of her work in the 1920s, she remains to this day practically unknown in her native country. Only one edition of her collected poetry has appeared since its original publication, a volume prefaced by Boris Filippov and Evgeniia Zhiglevich called *Poems—Stikhi*, which appeared in Russian in London, in 1979.

Mariia Mikhailovna Shkapskaia (née Andreevskaia) was born in St. Petersburg in 1891. Her parents were educated and cultured, but the family had to struggle on the father's small pension, which was barely sufficient to pay for Shkapskaia's tuition at the gymnasium on Vasilievskii Island.

Shkapskaia wrote her first essay at the age of nine. After three revisions, in the course of which she introduced romanticized sociology in the style of Victor Hugo and Vladimir Korolenko, the essay had a successful debut and brought tears to the eyes of her listeners. Shkapskaia recalled her childhood as that "of a ragamuffin of St. Petersburg streets, a rag-picker growing up in a dump where we collected bones and rags."[4] She began to work at the age of eleven, doing laundry, writing addresses at the post office, tutoring and acting with a Ukranian company. Her political education began at the gymnasium, in a student self-educational reading group. The group published a journal, and Shkapskaia contributed poetry to it.

She married young. Between 1909 and 1911 Shkapskaia lived with her husband in Pskov, where she participated in an expedition for the study of the lake region, organized by her husband's uncle, the well-known economist O.A. Shkapskii. She conducted interviews and polls, collected statistical data and, as a hobby, compiled a list of 200 dialectisms not included in Dahl's *Dictionary of the Russian Language*. This experience later became quite valuable for her work as a reporter. Shkapskaia and her husband participated in a Marxist circle organized by the workers of a local print shop.

A fairy tale in prose by Mariia Shkapskaia appeared in the newspaper *Narva Leaflet* in the summer of 1910, and her poem "Weep!" ("Plach'te!"), on the death of Leo Tolstoy, was published in *Pskovian Life* the same year.

In 1911 Shkapskaia enrolled in the department of general medicine at the St. Petersburg Psycho-Neurological Institute, but she stayed on as a student only for one year. Two arrests followed, one after another, in 1912. First, Shkapskaia was arrested for demonstrating in protest against the shooting down of the striking mine workers on the Siberian river Lena, for which she spent ten days in prison. In December of the same year, she was arrested together with her husband for their connection to the political student organization of the O.K. Whitmer gymnasium. The trial of thirty-four students attracted the attention of the Duma, which ruled, after discussing the case in five consecutive sessions, that politics were harmful to school students. The case and the trial stirred up strong emotions and to a large degree shaped the ideas of a whole generation. Like many others, Shkapskaia and her husband were sentenced to three years of exile. A merchant philanthropist offered scholarships to all the defendants in the "Whitmer case," which allowed them to continue their education outside Russia.

Shkapskaia and her husband spent three years in France. She completed the course of study at the department of belles lettres at the University of Toulouse and attended lectures at the School of Oriental Languages in Paris. During this time, her poetry appeared in St. Petersburg journals, forwarded and recommended by Vladimir Korolenko, whom she had met in France.

With the outbreak of World War I the scholarship money ran out. Shkapskaia went to work in organizations for the relocation of French and Belgian refugees, which allowed her to live in a number of urban and rural communities around France and to observe how the network of support for the civilian population, refugees and French prisoners of war was put in place by private organizations, communities and the government. These observations provided material for her four essays published all under one title, "Over Here and Over There" ("U nas i u nikh") upon her return to Russia in the spring of 1916.

The publication of this series was preceded by the essay "From Paris to Petrograd," which appeared in the Sunday, 26 June 1916 issue of the Petrograd newspaper *Day*. It describes a fifteen-day journey ("Alas, an almost round-the-world trip these days!") via England, Norway and Finland, by train and by boat, the only remaining route between Paris and Russia during the war. Apart from a precise record of the strict passport and customs control at every border, the selection of episodes and their rendition are informed by a certain fairy-tale quality that seems to dismiss the reality of war: Russian prisoners simply walk away from their jobs in Germany because "there was no one to guard them," an Estonian captain and his crew are rescued by a German submarine because "one sailor will never harm another, such is the naval ethic." Russia is seen as a nostalgic safe haven, a yearned for home where "everything stays as it was. . . ."

In reality, however, Shkapskaia was shocked by the indifference, corruption and greed that she found in Russia. The unfavorable comparison between Russia and France at the time of war is the subject of her four essays published during the summer of 1916 in the newspaper *Rostov Speech*.[5] Shkapskaia lists the measures taken by the French government, communities and private organizations to ease the burden of war on the civilian population, to involve refugees in agricultural and industrial work and to assist the rehabilitation of war veterans: "Like a caring mother, France makes sure to find a place for all her children who have been returned to her disfigured or crippled."[6] She contrasts the diplomatic steps taken by the French government to ensure decent conditions for the French prisoners of war with the obliviousness of the tsarist government. Shkapskaia also analyzes the high rate of draft dodging in Russia upon the Russian society and economy, which resulted in increased social stratification and left the countryside stripped of male manpower for years. Shkapskaia portrays Mother Russia as betrayed and abandoned by her sons "when she was scourged and crucified."

A powerful naturalistic image of motherhood is also applied to Europe, combined with the revolutionary promise of the "Internationale" and the symbolist hope for a rebirth:

> In these trying days Europe writhes in painful labor, but these pains are a guarantee of the new beautiful future for the rebirth of humankind that will live after this bloody but inevitable war, the humankind that will create a new world on the ruins of the old one . . . we wish to believe that the birth will go well and the results achieved after the war will at least partially justify all this uncounted sacrifice.[7]

In counterdistinction to the Slavophile nationalistic belief in Russia's special historical mission, Shkapskaia expresses doubts about Russia's future because of the lack of systematic support on the part of the Tsarist government and community leaders for the civilian population and economy: "The general organization and proper planning guarantee not only the victory but also our future social well-being which otherwise we may have to buy after the war at a very, very high price."[8] Young essayist and lyrical poet Mariia Shkapskaia did not know at the time that the price would be the Bolshevik revolution, three years of civil war and four decades of Stalinism.

The revolutionary years of 1917–1919 saw Shkapskaia in many politically controversial situations. She continued her association with the Petrograd newspaper *Day,* which dispatched her to Rostov to replace a reporter who had fled the country. Under White Army fire taking up the railroad tracks behind them and laying them down ahead of the train, Shkapskaia joined a group of reporters from Rostov, arriving in Novocherkassk in December 1917 to attend a general meeting of the united Cossack forces, "The Circle" ("Krug"), which sanctioned the civil war. Shkapskaia observed the sessions from a box of the Winter Theater; they were held literally on stage. Shkapskaia perceived the whole event as a dramatic stage production and wrote a play about it. The play remained unpublished. Shkapskaia refers to it in her memoir but does not indicate its title.[9] Stationed in Rostov, which was controlled by the Red Army, Shkapskaia worked as a nurse in the hospital.

In 1919 she returned to Petrograd, where she met Aleksandr Blok and was introduced to Maxim Gorky. In 1920 she became a member of the Petrograd division of the All-Russian Union of Poets, of which Blok was chairman. She later recalled that Blok had warned her against all contacts with Nikolai Gumilev and had "simply forbidden" her to participate in the Poets' Guild, which Gumilev had founded.[10] In 1920–1921, Shkapskaia and Blok participated together in poetry readings which he organized in the House of the Arts, in the former Tenishev school and on board ships of the Baltic fleet.

Her first collection of poetry, *The Evening Hour* (*Chas vechernii*), was published in 1920. It includes poems written in 1913–1916, mostly in France, and describes the author's nostalgia for St. Petersburg and the Russian countryside veiled in Christian imagery. The typically Symbolist emphasis on the grayness of the fallen world is common in the earlier poems. The use of Christian imagery describes the expectation of a miracle that never takes place. Poetic seascapes and meditations on the theme of art, reminiscent of Maksimilian Voloshin's early poetry,[11] introduce color and vivid metaphors into her work. Many of her poems are written in paragraphs, like prose. The love theme involves the triumph of the individual's willpower over the grayness of the world, the protagonist's identification with Mary Magdalene seeking communion with Christ and the anthropomorphism of the earth, which culminates in metaphorically establishing the identity of the earth as a woman.

Shkapskaia dedicated her second collection of poetry, *Mater Dolorosa* (1921), to her sons. This book describes the tragic pain of mothers who lose their children through miscarriage, abortion and early death. The inaccessible and the impossible attains a spiritual value; the corporeal and material is redeemed through compassion and the Word. The reevaluation of the religious theme involves a debate between the mother and God; the woman accepts the divine right to measure the duration of each person's lifetime but declares her prerogative as mother to grant God this right. Conforming to a modernist sensibility, Shkapskaia questions God and her own faith. She boldly develops a new literary expression until then nonexistent in Russian literature, the language of the flesh revealed by the sensations of the woman's body. Three thematic components of the book are compassion, the physical sensation of pregnancy or miscarriage and prayer for protection.

Shkapskaia seeks spirituality in pregnancy. The power of her poetry, her bold declaration of woman's self-realization through motherhood, is rooted in the tight link of the emotional, physical and spiritual. She sees motherhood as a sign of chosenness, links it to the Neoplatonic tradition and challenges the biblical story of Hagar, who was expelled from the house of Abraham. The lyrical female protagonist in Shkapskaia's poetry desires motherhood with the same intensity as she desires Christ. Pregnancy renders the woman's physical experience into a union with her spiritual quest.

The later part of *Mater Dolorosa* was written in a Russia ravaged by the civil war. This adds a new tragic dimension to woman's experience. Fear of losing the husband or lover in the war without preserving the memory of their love through a child pushes the protagonist to transgress the borderline imposed by religion, to embrace dark forces, to seek a deal with the Devil in order to be assured pregnancy. Personal tragedy reaches historical and political proportions in the mother's prayer to spare her the sight of her son's death or execution. The resonance of the political theme increases as both the earth torn by the war and Russia, whose "suntanned hands" are covered with her "sons' sticky blood," join the ranks of mournful mothers. The ultimate image of Russia as Mater Dolorosa seals the book with a most powerful poetic statement of Russia's identity in this century.

Mariia Shkapskaia's next collection, *The Drum of the Stern Master* (*Baraban strogogo gospodina,* 1922), can be divided into two parts. The first one develops earlier themes: faith, motherhood, loss of the beloved. She does not concede death as a real end but sees it as a beginning of life elsewhere, in "the blooming fields of God." This offers little comfort to the grieving mother: she chastises God for violating the order of the line while digging with her bare hands in order to exhume her son.

Two poems in this collection can be considered as the turning point in Shkapskaia's aesthetics and worldview: for the first time, she employs a cliché of the party propaganda. The first of these is a dull, prosaic poem, "Under the Heavy Step," which parodies egalitarian slogans and proclaims the alienation of mothers and children and mothers' obliviousness to children as a norm. The other poem (untitled) stands out as an outright record of the Communist party demands imposed on writers:

No, in my paths I was not destined
To delight in sparkling Chios wine.
In my paths I was told to remember
Nothing else but the stern sorrows of October
And, perhaps, the little grievances of April.
And since then my every week is Passion Week
And my every single dawn is darkened.

The second part of the book consists of five longer poems: "Russia" and "Peter-and-Paul Fortress" establish Russia's identity as a woman; "To Louis XVII" declares the solidarity of women and mothers throughout the centuries in their denunciation of bloodshed; "Saratov Calvary" and "Being" ("Iav'") describe the horrors of the civil war. The two latter poems are characterized by the use of *skaz* (colloquial and nongrammatical speech) and polyglossia (reproduction of several voices speaking simultaneously) as a background for Christian miracles. Shkapskaia did not ally with any class position at this point, but the closing poem of the book, "These Days Are Not for Creativity," expresses her lack of faith in the promise of postwar reconstruction. On the whole, this collection of excellent, albeit disparate, poems gives the impression of having been hurriedly lumped together in order to be published before prohibition of individualistic lyrical poetry would completely rule out such a possibility.

Blood-Ore (*Krov'-ruda*, published in 1923) is a collection of mystical poetry in which the protagonist's identity is established as an intermediate link in the continuous flow of blood from cavemen's primal days to the ideal Eternal Feminine.

Through the bold use of sexual metaphor Shkapskaia creates a fusion of paganistic and Christian imagery. By making her female protagonist the center of such fusion, Shkapskaia reconciles the physical, earthbound aspirations with a spiritual quest, and by doing so resolves the conflict personified by Leo Tolstoy, for whom the two aspects of human psyche, pagan hedonism and Christianity, were forever in conflict.[12] To this day *Blood-Ore* remains the only attempt in all of Russian literature to produce a feminist myth of creation.

Blood-Ore received several very outspoken reviews both in the press and private letters. Valerii Briusov was clearly disappointed.[13] Soviet critic Innokentii Oksenov found it necessary to support his judgment with the authority of Leon Trotsky, who had labeled the book as "genuinely organistic, biological and gynecological."[14] Maxim Gorky, on the contrary, praised the book and its author for giving the woman's experience a new voice:

> You are the elemental force yourself and, above all, the force of nature in whose depth the awareness originates of the complexity of being and of your own biological significance. . . . You are already on a new and broad path, before you woman has not yet spoken of her significance so assertively and so truly.[15]

However, Gorky was dissatisfied with the longer poem "Being," which depicts the execution of a revolutionary and concludes with a vision of religious miracles. Gorky characterized Shkapskaia's position of political indifference in the face of bloodshed, which she maintained throughout her work, as a weakness that prevented her "from taking the first—and rightfully deserved—place among all contemporary women-poetesses."[16]

The little book of stylized rhythmical prose, entitled *Tsa-Tsa-Tsa*, appeared in 1923. It is a coded work both in title and content. Allegedly a Russian language rendition of Chinese poetry that a Russian émigré woman living in France heard from her Chinese husband, it is in fact the story of the author's own fear and alienation. The title is a threefold repetition of the feminine suffix for Russian nouns denoting women's professions, such as a woman worker (*rabotnitsa*), a woman writer (*pisatel'nitsa*), a female tool adjuster (*naladchitsa*) or a saleslady (*prodavshchitsa*). The Chinese-sounding title allows Shkapskaia to re-create with subtle irony the insistent hammering of these alleged proofs of the Soviet woman's equality into the readers' minds, although in the piece entitled "Liu-lin" the sound "tsa-tsa-tsa" evokes the monotonous murmur of a spinning wheel. The heroine's fear of being kicked out by her husband after many years of "building a life with him" is a metaphor of a more general sense of insecurity. Shkapskaia, who had been a political émigré in France, returned to Russia in order "to build a new life." Threatened by the ideological pressure that ruled out lyrical poetry, personal themes and all philosophies except the Marxist theory of class struggle, a Neoplatonic and Christian visionary such as Mariia Shkapskaia had to change her theme and style in order to find employment.

In 1925 she published a small collection of nursery rhymes, entitled *Alesha's Galoshes* (*Aleshiny galoshi*), and her last book of poetry, *The Earthly Crafts* (*Zemnye remesla*, 1925). In lyrical and philosophical poems, richly presented in the latter collection, Shkapskaia remains loyal to her theme, declaring that motherhood is "almost the only warrant of realized immortality." She does not appear to be a convinced believer in the promise of a bright future: the poem "Insidious Sower" mixes the typically propagandistic, revolutionary image of rebellious raging streams with praise of the divine wisdom, which "tricks the bad blood to collapse in an avalanche onto the desert for the sake of an appearance of happiness and glory, where it will be slowly dried up under the burning rays of the sun."

The long poem "Man Goes to the Pamir" is equally ambiguous. Although dedicated to the Siemens-Schuckert factory in Berlin, it fails to glorify factory work. The poem is a history of human civilization presented as a step-by-step perfection of tools of destruction. Thematically close to Maksimilian Voloshin's poem "In the Paths of Cain,"[17] the poem by Shkapskaia maintains a woman's perspective on history and distinguishes archetypal male behavior as a pursuit of distant goals, which in the end turns out to be the path to destruction. The poem's innovative feature is its choppy meter, which resembles the rhythms of Mayakovsky and N. Tikhonov. Together with another poem in this book, "The Heirs of the Best and First Nation," which declares international brotherhood of all workers:

> Next to all machines and levers—
> All are brothers among themselves,

"Man Goes to the Pamir" is an attempt at ideological mimicry, the ultimate suicidal blow to her original theme as well as her aesthetic and philosophical perception of the significance of woman's existence. It earned Shkapskaia a pass into Soviet journalism.

Mariia Shkapskaia's last poem, "Stone Music" ("Kammenaia muzyka"), was published in January 1925 in the Leningrad journal *Star* (*Zvezda*), in the same issue as Innokentii Oksenov's review of her collections *Blood-Ore* and *The Earthly*

Crafts. Oksenov's positive remark on the poem "Man Goes to the Pamir," which he characterized as "the turning point away from her old theme, already exhausted to the end and a continuation of which could be clearly risky," qualified her as a capable writer of "proletarian," that is, simplistic literature, and granted her admission to the Soviet press. In December 1925 Shkapskaia joined the staff of the evening edition of the *Red Newspaper* as an itinerant reporter and remained in that capacity for eight years.

Soviet scholar K. Nakoriakova observes that "Shkapskaia was one of the first Fellow-Travelers to switch to newspaper reporting," and explains this decision by the 18 June 1925 Resolution of the Central Committee of the All-Russian Communist (Bolshevik) Party "On the Party's Policy in the Area of Literature (Fiction)," which stated the need "for a tactful and careful approach to Fellow-Travelers, the approach which would guarantee all the conditions for their fastest possible transition to the side of the communist ideology."[18] The year 1925 thus became "the borderline which marks the beginning of a new period of creative life for many writers."[19]

In 1926 the *Red Newspaper* published forty-seven essays by Shkapskaia. A prolific writer and erudite researcher, Shkapskaia spent weeks in the Leningrad Saltykov-Shchedrin Public Library in preparation for each assignment. Her essays are a patchwork of statistics, historical backgrounds, manufacturers' lists, interviews, humorous comments, dialectal idioms, entertaining episodes and frightening revelations. On her first assignment to Belorussia she described a correctional colony as a model society whose well-being is threatened by the criminal local population. In the essay about Murmansk she gives a detailed account of the devastation of Soviet natural resources through uncontrollable export policies. Outrageous crime scenes in the Pskov region are interspersed with episodes from the 1864 novel by Vsevolod Krestovskii, *The Slums of Petersburg*.[20] The essay about Soviet patent procedure explains why it is legal to adopt foreign patented inventions for free instead of paying Soviet inventors.[21] And all this is presented in lively narrative style, mixed with exuberant erudition and humor.

Shkapskaia was praised for the dynamic, "cinematographic" technique of her writing style.[22] She achieves the effect of visual presence by introducing the reader into each scene and by vivid descriptions of people whom she interviews. Her articles appeared in *Truth* (*Pravda*), *Red Virgin Soil, Red Panorama, The Flame* (*Ogonek*), *The Building* (*Stroika*), *The Projector* (*Prozhektor*), *Star* and *Literary Contemporary*. Most of her essays were later collected in three books: *All by Myself* (*Sama po sebe,* 1930), a record of her travels throughout the Soviet Union in 1926–1927; *Fifteen and One* (*Piatnadtsat' i odin,* 1931), about the fifteen Soviet republics and Leningrad; and

Water and Wind (*Voda i veter,* 1931), about fishermen's collective farms in the Far East. In 1927 Vera Inber praised Shkapskaia as one of the four best women journalists, next to such committed party ideologues as Larissa Reisner and Marietta Shaginian:

> Shkapskaia's literary past, where "in literature she was a woman and nothing but a woman," seemed to be the least conducive to this kind of work. . . . At present she tirelessly travels to all ends of our Union, observes how bridges are erected, how fish is salted, how roads are laid. . . . Her past "eternal femininity" found a new river bed: she stands face to face with the everyday life of women workers, their needs, joys and sorrows. . . . Indeed our revolution is a great destroyer of petty hearths and a creator of one common source of light and warmth for all, if M. Shkapskaia, a natural woman and mother, was transformed into a woman activist. [23]

From 1931 to 1936 Shkapskaia participated in the gigantic project launched by Gorky, the creation of *The History of Factories and Plants*. The project involved several thousand writers all across the country. Shkapskaia worked on the history of the Karl Marx factory in Leningrad, founded in 1832 by Gustav Lessner. Her book, entitled *Lessner's Workers* (unpublished), consisted of three parts: historical background, from the 1850s to 1909; the growing revolutionary movement, 1909–1914; and the war, 1914–1917. Only separate chapters of the book appeared in journals and almanacs in 1933–1936. The manuscript has never been published in its entirety.

And yet it was Shkapskaia's favorite project. She discussed it in her letters to Gorky, in workshops and in her speeches at the All-Russian Writers' Conferences. This work allowed her to play an active role in the discussions of the artistic method of Soviet literature. In a letter to Gorky dated May 1934, she complained about editors who "insert rattling phrases if you don't do it yourself. You struggle against that one year, then two, then three, but finally you lose your hearing. . . ." She agreed with Gorky that the legacy of lyrical poetry enveloped her writing in a style "reminiscent of Fedor Sologub, which is in disharmony with our epoch."[24]

Gorky's goal was to create a new genre, scholarly artistic history. Historians from the ComAcademy, L. Averbakh[25] and other theoreticians from RAPP (the Russian Association of Proletarian Writers), who supervised the project, insisted on a schematic, consequent narrative and total adherence to documentation. Against their accusations of "creeping empiricism," Shkapskaia defended the author's right to experiment with literary form and imagery. She traced the history of the revolutionary movement following individual characters and enriching the raw material of archival documents with her artistic vision. She even produced a fictitious diary to enhance the emotional verisimilitude of the story. The theme of motherhood received a new treatment, too: women workers are no longer indifferent to political struggle. Wives of revolutionaries follow their husbands into Siberian exile, bringing small children with them, worried about the children but convinced that the hardship in the present is a warranty of a forthcoming bright future for all. Two chapters about revolutionary women were published in the collection *Tales of the Past* (*Povesti bylogo*) in 1937.

Shkapskaia declared "a unified political perspective" as a structural principle of her book.[26] In her speech at the First Congress of Soviet Writers in 1934 she defined her earlier position of political outsider as "liberal objectivity which amounted to indifference," "social ignorance" and "class illiteracy," and praised the party for giving writers a "political quota":

> In our perfectly planned country the factor of social evaluation is made easy. Essay writing is more affected by planning than any other kind of literature. . . . In the Far East, five years ago the focus was on economics. Three years ago—on collective farms. If you go now, the focus will be on the defence. There is no need to mention the fact that the Far East will be suggested to you only if its theme is crucial at this point. The work of an essayist begins long before him—in the Central Committee of our party, in planning organizations. All you need to do is plug yourself into this circuit at a certain moment.[27]

In 1936, following repeated invitations from Aleksandr Fadeev, Shkapskaia went on her third trip to the Far East. The resulting collection of essays, *Man Is Working Well* (*Chelovek rabotaet khorosho*, 1938), turned out to be didactic and trite. The characters do not act but mostly philosophize. Their "unified political perspective" obliges them to come to the same conclusions reiterated in every story. An essay published in 1935 in the collection *Motherland* (a year before the trip to the Far East), based on the same earlier observed episodes, does not include dogmatic repetitions and is more dynamic.[28]

During World War Two Shkapskaia wrote over 100 propagandistic newspaper articles and a collection of essays for children about the atrocities of the Nazis in occupied territories. This book was published in Moscow in 1942 both in Russian and English.[29] After the war she continued writing for the radio and for the

Antifascist Committee of Soviet Women. These later works exist in handwritten copies only. In 1949, on assignment from the Central Committee of the Communist party, Shkapskaia joined the organizational board of the journal *The Soviet Woman*.

Mariia Shkapskaia died in 1952. She left three manuscripts unfinished: a book about children, one about the Dnieper hydroelectric power station and *Essays of Our Days* (unpublished). These three genres represent the three facets of her work: the woman's theme, the Soviet construction and mosaic-type essays woven from actual interviews, facts and fiction, of which she was a superb master. This outstanding lyrical poet who lived on the watershed between the prerevolutionary Russian and Soviet cultures, whose work of unparalleled expressivity is the true culmination of the woman's theme in Russian literature, was known to the postwar generation in Russia primarily, if not exclusively, as the inspiring source of cultural expertise behind some of the best educational radio programs.

Natalie Roklina

From The Evening Hour

I remember a lovely wanderer
Whose name was Tristan.
I still keep my doleful fingers
Inside the scars of my healing wounds.
He was—and he left—like the clouds
That rise from the mountain slopes at dawn,
Like a big river leaving its bed
Every spring at the time of the flood.
But the rocks still remember the clouds
(This memory is light and alive),
So do the crystals in mountain ravines,
So does the foliage in mountain vales.
Let the rivers take to the ocean
Their transparent waters—
Those riverbeds are the open wounds
In the bosom of the weary earth.

1920

From Mater Dolorosa

I love my dark earth
SOLOGUB

My Earth, from Chile to Brittany,
And from the Pleiades to the Southern Cross,
O ancient, for your living touch
Cracked lips are yearning everywhere.

Dismembered by hostility's piercing sword,
Devoured by the raging graves,
You offer all the same life-giving
Drink from your life-oozing veins.

Never enraged, into your silent bosom
You accept human sacrifice together with the priest.
You won't hide your stolid face
From anyone who bends toward you in death.

O, to cling to you, to enter in communion!
We shall all descend into the infinite fields
To become inseparably part of you,
My ruler and my mother, earth.

How shall I prove that I was loved and that a child was given me for love? And that my face is scorched at night by flames of fire, not by black smoke?

Who equated the rights of a wife with those of a concubine? What angry Hebrew God could have allowed them, even for a moment, to be equal in their sons—Hagar roaming through the desert, and Sarah, lying between her husband's legs?

Allow to conceive without love and not be marked with a terrible Sign of God? Allow half-brothers to share the father's same glance and measured step?

* * *

O Lord, did I not rise when Thou summoned me? Am I not a tiny loop in Thy tight lace?

All of us, we are just ripe berries in Thy bast-box, Thy white flowers on the edge of the woods Thou protecteth.

We rise from the damp earth as Thine ears-of-rye in the fields of our meager motherland, in her roadside dust.

But give us time to ripen under warm rays, let flowers gather into stooks, let the grain ripen.

Do not touch us with Thy slender fingers before it's time, do not pick green berries, do not rip barren stalks, do not remove the tight unwoven tissue when it is bleeding at night.

—Give time to my children that Thou bestowed upon me to grow up.

* * *

Yes, they said it was necessary. . . . So, there was plenty of frightening food for carnivorous Harpies, and my body was slowly losing its strength, rocked to sleep by the comforting chloroform.

And my blood gushed, unabated—not in joy like it did that last, other time, and afterwards our embarrassed gaze found no comfort in the sight of the empty cradle.

Again, like pagans, for the life of our children we make human sacrifice. And You, O Lord, You don't rise from the dead at the crunching of babies' bones!

Russia

Rejoice, because drops of your blood were sweeter
than honey for our most beloved Jesus.

LIFE OF SAINT BARBARA

Dogs' yelp from wilted cabins
And crows' unending shriek—
And above all raised high and immobile
Your icon-like face, untouched by a brush.

As you walk through the steppe and the meadow,
It's unbearable to meet your wild gaze.
Under your restless foot
The scorched grass is ablaze.

A nun of defeated apostate churches,
You leave your face unveiled,
While your sons' blood, sticky like melted ore,
Cools on your suntanned hands.

Shaking your forged iron fetters,
In the halo of the evening censers,
You drag your widow's robes
Over the rows of their silent graves.

But Jesus Christ of Never-Darkening Glory,
In communion with your most honored pain,
Bows to you, and He presses His lips
To the hem of your robes soaked with blood.

Sweeter than any sweetest offering
And irresistible for His nostrils
Is the astringent smell and bitter smoke
Of your villages set ablaze in honor of the wake.

1921

From The Drum of the Stern Master

Russia (2)

In labor now for eight straight days
The Russian autumn soil has been spread,
Her worn-out quilted jacket sparsely mended
With green patches of winter crop.

From year to year she bears harvests,
Our daily bread, iron ore, poppy seeds,
Her mighty breasts pumping nourishment
To succulent wheat and other grains.

My Russia, dressed in hempen cloth,
A woman and my sister,
To a Messiah you'll give birth
Late at night, in the fall, by a smoky fire.

Yet, all you bring forth is barley and oats,

And pitch-black nights for your riots,
While deep in the woods a goat-legged goblin
Celebrates the baptism of his child and the wind, gone wild,
  Brushes through strands of straw.

Russia (3)

When the silver horn is hung
Over the sleepy Neva,
The twilight stretches on the cooling rocks
To rest his smoky head.

And the tower clock chimes through the night,
Forever mindful of the horns on Mount Sinai—
Russia awaits her husband Peter
On the gray old fortress' bulwark.

With his usual firm gait he abandons
The Tsars' burial place in the cathedral,
His gaze as stubborn as ever
After two hundred years of peace.

He comes in, her imperious husband.
He removes her wifely covers with his hand,
And for a long long time thereafter
Their amorous whisper disturbs the fortress' sleep.

She conceives every night
And bears children till morning.
Then, moaning, at dawn she delivers
New kids with the Emperor's features and gait.

Russia (5)

Above the ruts, the pits and bumps,
In the fields, in the swamps, in the moss,
She stood, like a numb stone peasant,
When the Lord our God summoned her.

And in response to Him, you, Russia,
The European scriptures' erroneous blot,
You smiled so meekly the smile of a martyr,
That it softened your Scythian traits.

These days are not for creativity, they are for dying.
And nothing is more saddening about them
Than the unfinished buildings
That will remain like this for many years.

Creative work which elevates high structures
Is not to flow through these empty beams,
And regular bookkeeping cannot quench
The avid thirst for an avalanche.

There's no happy painter singing
As he moves along the white walls in the flames of sunset
And there's no stern mason who would carry
His stone burden up to the shiny peaks.

Access to the scaffolding from the street is closed,
The empty cage keeps swinging,
And the naked jaws of wall frames
Will not be dressed in flesh of bricks.

* * *

Under the heavy important step, like blades of grass, they have entangled themselves in our stern, many-storied, urban days.

We forget about them for weeks on end, after taking them to day care in the morning, them—never painted by Rafael or exalted by Tagore.

Here no one is wonderful or special, and they are just like us—children of the same meager motherland, prisoners of the same jail.

There's no way we could have made them in any other image but our own since there was no one to make their mothers happy at the hour when they were conceived.

1922

From Blood-Ore

The fair maiden walked on yellow sand and planted a fiery-red rose.
O you, fiery-red rose, do not take root; and you, the river
of blood, abate; and you, blood-ore, clot—the composite ore,
the ore of the veins, the ore of the flesh, the ore of the bones. . . .

FROM OLD INCANTIONS ON HEALING OPEN WOUNDS

Pushing through the veins like waves, blocking within itself the darkest springs, our blood avoids the daytime sun. We raise our swords at night and love our wives in the dark of the night.

God of all blood, dark blood and fiery-red, prepare your most terrible vengeance: violators of the ancient law, we ruthlessly conquered at every step and unlocked a great flow of blood in this world.

* * *

A playful Shepherd, Thou watcheth over us laughing, when, blinded, one body is drawn to another. Caring for the prosperity of Thy farm, Thou coupleth us with Thine own laborious hands.

Carried along by passionate winds, we are weightless in front of Thee—pleased with the destiny we choose for ourselves, we call it love.

* * *

Forever flowing—from our foremother Eve into these days overburdened with things, through every new womb, making a communion with each new one of us.

We spill it in love and in battle, when conceiving, giving birth, creating anew. Our blood has made rivers scarlet, and it blossoms in the seas of the earth.

It flows as one, morose and red, since the beginning of time. It is part of all days, of all ages.

It makes us akin to all.

* * *

Only my dress, my language and my hair, also my dwelling may be slightly different, with Darwin and Losskij on the shelves—but my body is so ancient.

What ancient mysteries abound in my unchanging blood—since the first days of Creation they've been preserved until our time.

* * *

The passionate sting was shearing, burning within me. Amidst the turbulent fire of chaos I bore ancient cubs in a pit. For them I squeezed to the last drop the brim of this chalice, full of my golden-red, frothing blood.

It was dark-red and endlessly in stock. On the nights of the full moon and on dark days it boiled up, wild and unrestrained—then new children were born through me.

But gradually, thinning with each century, it slowly flowed into this flesh, and now, desperately, I keep trying to divide its last pale drops among our small cups.

* * *

Elle était toujours enceinte. . . .

PARISIAN SONG

O this Golgotha of women! Give all your resilient strength once again to your child, carry within, feed with your strength—there will be no rest for you, no breath.

Until you fall on your path, all withered—those willing to be born gnaw you from within.

The rules of the earth are simple and strict: give birth, then die.

* * *

In the fields of the earth I blossom as a woman, unacquiesced, soft-spoken, common-looking. My lot is simple and ungratifying (there may be no other lots for us): we blossom in the morning, bear a juicy fruit at noon and droop at night when dew descends from the fading heights turning dark and merging with the night.

1922

From Tsa-Tsa-Tsa

Lonely Like a Crane

Since times immemorial and unto these days it has been customary to send away the wife, if she becomes old and unattractive.

But in the past at least a place was found for her, and if You chase me out today, I don't even know where I'll go.

I don't know where my family is because I was making a family with You.

I shall return to the place where my house used to be, and I shall cry under someone else's gates. . . .

So little life is left in me, but even this little, where should I take it to? How could I remain beautiful? Even yellow blossoms fall into the dark pond when autumn comes because wind swings the trees and carries off their withered leaves.

A woman gets all from her man: if he desires, she will remain forever young like a pine tree sustained by fresh water.

Ponds shield themselves from the sun with yellow water lilies, but if water leaves the pond, water lilies fall on the bottom, into the sleazy slime.

The husband is like water, the wife is like a water lily. How can I go on living, if my husband has abandoned me?

1923

From The Earthly Crafts

Insidious Sower, solicitous for Your harvest, preparing fields for love, You plow them on time and put in seeds and always know when to deroute the heavy frothing blood into a proper river bed.

The healthy blood—onto the fertile soil which gives us succulent grass. As for the weak, You shall lure its flooded brook skillfully to fall into the desert, for the appearance of happiness and glory—and there You shall dry it up under the burning ray of the sun.

1925

Stone Music

Architecture is very appropriately called stone music.

FROM THE BROCKHAUS-EFRON ENCYCLOPEDIA

This is how one begins to live by poetry.

B. PASTERNAK

I.

Hammering again on all intersections.
After such intermissions—
The glitter of brick dust
On broad shoulders means that
We are alive.
Floors cling to floors and climb higher,
Steel sings and screeches—
As if blood rushing to a fresh cut
In a healthy body.
Proud and drunk
Thrust after thrust—
The city's wounds are healing,
The city's fever is gone.
This is how countries recover.

II.

From downtown get on number twenty-two,
Then walk on foot from People's station.
There, to confirm the newspaper report,
A new building is coming up!
Not built by a crane—this is not Germany,
Germany has nothing to do with it—
Just a mason walking all by himself
Along the scaffold, carrying bricks.
And he sings as he walks, about his Verka,
About the summer and the heather clump—
A happy hangman in a cage—
A leaf on the branch made of rock.

III.

Bodies are built from cells, honeycombs from wax,
Universes—from stardust.
Could we resist
These laws, so simple and sharp?
The most persistent of earthly temptations—

Known in numerous forms—
To conceal within a warm construction
A certain portion of space.
And we are so rejoiced with this eternal impulse
To oppose our warm need
To settle, again and again,
To the nomadism of the planets and the wind.

IV.

Boards and planks were torn apart,
Chopped and taken for firewood.
Tin and iron—to build the "bourgeois"
Stoves—take all you want!
And while we carried the breakage—
Through the bald pedestrian streets—
They desired to sprout houses
And to buzz once again like beehives.
Tormented by the sorrowful passion
For life, for the living life, for warmth,
Windowpanes in the abandoned buildings
Popped every winter.

V.

The pentagonal building
Is resolved geometrically
And in the sky beams the electric
Lamp executed in Belgium.
I have been accounted for by this chart
And I'm neither too proud nor quick to take offense.
I am included by the zealous draft
Into one of the floor grids.
And in this many times verified structure
I am placed on the fifth stairway landing,
Which assigns me a certain exertion
Of the lungs and a certain number of minutes to reach.

1925

Translated by Natalie Roklina

Notes to the Essay

1. Boris Filippov, "O zamolchannoi," in Mariia Shkapskaia, *Poems—Stikhi* (London: Overseas Publications Interchange, 1979), 16.

2. M. Shkapskaia, "Iz Parizha v Petrograd," *Den'*, 26 June 1916.

3. Excerpts from this speech were published in a newspaper article: M. Shkapskaia, "Puti i poiski," *Literaturnyi Leningrad,* 14 June 1934, 3.

4. Ibid.

5. M. Shkapskaia, "U nas i u nikh," *Rostovskaia rech',* 26 July 1916, 2–3; 6 August 1916, 5; 23 August 1916, 2; 25 September 1916, 5.

6. Ibid., 23 August 1916, 2.

7. Ibid., 6 August 1916, 5.

8. Ibid., 25 September 1916, 5.

9. Shkapskaia mentions this episode in her speech at the All-Union Congress of Artistic Essays in June 1934 but does not indicate the title of the play. See M. Shkapskaia, *Puti i poiski* (Moscow: Sovetskii pisatel', 1968), 27.

10. K. Nakoriakova, *Ocherki Shkapskoi. K voprosu o metodike analiza khudozhestvennogo ocherka* (Moscow: Avtoreferat dissertatsii, 1968), 10.

Blok's warning probably saved Mariia Shkapskaia's life: N. Gumilev was executed in 1921 for an alleged plot and conspiracy against the Bolshevik government; his associates at the Poets' Guild, Osip Mandel'shtam and Anna Akhmatova, were banned from publication in 1923.

11. Besides this artistic kinship, Shkapskaia's analysis of French society, published in *Rostovskaia rech'*, presented her to the Russian public as a follower of Maksimilian Voloshin, whose reviews of the art scene in France appeared in Russian journals in 1904–1909.

12. D. Merezhkovskii, *L. Tolstoi i F. Dostoevskii*, Vol. 2 (Moscow: Izdatel'stvo "Respublika," 1995), 147–50, 155.

13. V. Briusov, "Sredi stikhov," *Pechat' i revoliutsiia* 1 (1923): 148.

14. I. Oksenov, "Bibliografiia," *Zvezda* 4, 10 (1925): 300–01.

15. M. Gorky's letter to Shkapskaia of January 1923, in "Dva pis'ma, Publikatsiia Arkhiva A. M. Gor'kogo," *Rabotnitsa* 3 (1968): 1.

16. M. Gorky's letter to Shkapskaia of May 1924, ibid.

17. M. Voloshin's long poem, "In the Paths of Cain," includes pieces written between 1915 and 1926 and traces the history of human culture in terms of the anthroposophical Christian teaching of Rudolf Steiner, whose lectures Voloshin attended before World War I.

18. *O partiinoi i sovetskoi pechati. Sbornik dokumentov* (Moscow, 1956), 345.

19. K. Nakoriakova, *Ocherki Shkapskoi. K voprosu o metodike analiza khudozhestvennogo ocherka* (Moscow: Avtoreferat dissertatsii, 1968), 5.

20. M. Shkapskaia, "Belarus'," "Pod znakom dikobraza," "Po Pskovshchine," in *Sama po sebe* (Leningrad, 1930).

21. M. Shkapskaia, "Za pestroi ptitsei," *Piatnadtsat' i odin* (Moscow, 1931), 185–215.

22. K. Nakoriakova, "M.M. Shkapskaia," in M. Shkapskaia, *Puti i poiski* (Moscow: Sovetskii pisatel', 1968), 12–15.

23. Vera Inber, "Chetyre zhenshchiny," *Zhurnalist* 11 (1927): 23–25.

24. M. Shkapskaia's letter to A.M. Gorky of 2 June 1934, *A.M. Gor'kii i sozdanie istorii fabrik i zavodov* (Moscow: Sotsekgiz, 1959), 126–27.

25. Leopold Averbakh, a literary critic and theoretician, one of the founders of the Russian Association of Proletarian Writers (RAPP) in 1925. Another ideological hardliner, Grigorii Lelevich (Laborii G. Kalmonson), who had published a review of Shkapskaia's poetry in 1925, was expelled from RAPP in 1926 for his unbending line on Fellow Travelers. After the liquidation of RAPP in 1932, both tried to maintain ideological control in literature but failed to obtain privileged positions with the Writers' Union, organized in 1934. They were both arrested in 1937 as "enemies of the people." Averbakh was executed. Lelevich perished in the gulag.

Sensing the need to walk the tightrope of ideological polemic and the impending purges must have had a tremendous impact on Shkapskaia's moral condition when she spoke at the First Congress of Soviet Writers in 1934. The published excerpts from that speech read as frightened delirium. She paints her childhood memories black in order to pass for a descendant of an impoverished social class. Her praise of the Communist party's role in choosing the topic and location of the writer's assignment must have been provoked by terror. Under these circumstances it is hard not to see her departure to the Far East in 1935 in response to Aleksandr Fadeev's insistent invitations as a flight to salvation (see below). Aleksandr Fadeev may have saved her life—for at least the second time.

26. K. Nakoriakova, *Ocherki Shkapskoi. K voprosu o metodike analiza khudozhestvennogo ocherka,* 11.

27. M. Shkapskaia, "Puti i poiski," *Literaturnyi Leningrad*, 14 June 1934, 3.

28. M. Shkapskaia, *Chelovek rabotaet khorosho* (Leningrad: Gosudarstvennoe izdatel'stvo khudozhestvennoi literatury, 1938). Cf. her essay in *Rodina* (Moscow: Izdatel'stvo "Molodaia gvardiia," 1939).

29. M. Shkapskaia, *Èto bylo na samom dele. Kniga faktov* (Moscow: Detgiz, 1942). (M. Shkapskaia, *It Actually Happened. A Book of Facts* [Moscow: Foreign Languages Publishing House, 1942].)

Bibliography

Primary Works

"Iz Parizha v Petrograd." *Den'* (Petrograd), 26 June 1916.
"U nas i u nikh." *Rostovskaia rech'*, 26 July 1916, 2–3; 6 August 1916, 5; 23 August 1916, 2; 25 September 1916, 5.
Chas vechernii. 1913–1916. Petersburg, 1920.
Mater Dolorosa. Petersburg, 1920 [2d ed., Berlin, 1921].
Baraban strogogo gospodina. Berlin, 1922.
Krov'-ruda. Berlin, 1923.
Kniga o lukavom seiatele. Moscow, 1923.
Tsa-Tsa-Tsa. Berlin, 1923.
Iav': Poèma. Moscow, 1923.
Aleshiny galoshi. Leningrad, 1925.
"Kamennaia muzyka." *Zvezda* 4, 10 (1925): 123–24.
Zemnye remesla. Moscow, 1925.
Sama po sebe. Leningrad, 1930. [Book of essays.]
Piatnadtsat' i odin. Moscow, 1931. [Book of essays.]

Voda i veter. Moscow, 1931. [Book of essays.]

"Puti i poiski." *Literaturnyi Leningrad*, 14 June 1934, 3. [Excerpts from the speech at the First Congress of Soviet Writers.]

A.M. Gor'kii i sozdanie istorii fabrik i zavodov. Moscow: Sotsekgiz, 1959. 123–27. [M. Shkapskaia's letter to A.M. Gorky of 2 June 1934.]

Al'manakh god XVIII. Moscow, 1935. 6: 215–64. [Two chapters from the unpublished *History of the Lessner Factory*, "Dispozitsiia boia" and "Pravdisty."]

Povesti bylogo. Moscow, 1937. [Two chapters about women, from the unpublished *History of the Lessner Factory*.]

Chelovek rabotaet khorosho. Leningrad: Gosudarstvennoe izdatel'stvo khudozhestvennoi literatury, 1938. [Book of essays about the Far East.]

"Rodina." Moscow: Izdatel'stvo "Molodaia gvardiia," 1939. [Collection of essays by various authors.]

Èto bylo na samom dele. Kniga faktov. Moscow: Detgiz, 1942.

Puti i poiski. Moscow: Sovetskii pisatel', 1968. [Book of essays.]

Poems—Stikhi. London: Overseas Publications Interchange, 1979.

In Translation

It Actually Happened. A Book of Facts. Moscow: Foreign Languages Publishing House, 1942.

Secondary Works

Bakhrakh, A. "Vspominaia Shkapskuiu." *Novoe russkoe slovo*, 9 December 1979.

Briusov, Valerii. "Sredi stikhov." *Pechat' i revoliutsiia* 1 (1923): 148.

Fedin, K.A. "Pis'ma A.M. Gor'komu." *Gor'kii i sovetskie pisateli. Neizdannaia perepiska.* Vol. 70. Moscow: Akademiia nauk, Literaturnoe nasledstvo, 1963. 545, 549.

Filippov, Boris. "O zamolchannoi." *Poems—Stikhi.* By Mariia Shkapskaia. London: Overseas Publications Interchange, 1979.

———. "Zadushennyi talant." *Novoe russkoe slovo*, 1 May 1973.

Gor'kii, Maxim. "Dva pis'ma, Publikatsiia arkhiva A. M. Gor'kogo." *Rabotnitsa* 3 (1968): 1.

Heldt, Barbara. *Terrible Perfection: Women and Russian Literature.* Bloomington: Indiana University Press, 1987.

Inber, Vera. "Chetyre zhenshchiny." *Zhurnalist* 11 (1927): 23–25.

Lelevich, G. "Krov'-ruda"—"Zemnye Remesla" [review]. *Krasnaia nov'* 1 (1925).

Nakoriakova, K.M. "Mariia Shkapskaia." *Puti i poiski.* By M. Shkapskaia. Moscow: Sovetskii pisatel', 1968. 12–15.

———. "Neizdannaia kniga." *Vestnik moskovskogo universiteta* 5 (1966): 13–21.

———. *Ocherki Shkapskoi. K voprosu o metodike analiza khudozhestvennogo ocherka.* Moscow: Avtoreferat dissertatsii, 1968.

———. "Po stranitsam zabytoi rukopisi (Pravka A. M. Gor'kim rukopisi M. Shkapskoi)." *Kniga. Issledovaniia i materialy*, sb. XVII [n.p., n.d.].

Oksenov, Innokentii. "Bibliografiia." *Zvezda* 4, 10 (1925): 300–01.

Sinkevich, Valentina. "Dvoinaia sud'ba: o stikhakh M. Shkapskoi." *Novoe russkoe slovo*, 27 January 1980.

Zhiglevich, Evgeniia. "Dve bespredel'nosti byli vo mne. . . ." *Mariia Shkapskaia. Poems—Stikhi.* London: Overseas Publications Interchange, 1979.

Nadezhda Teffi

Nadezhda Teffi (1872–1952).
Courtesy of Christine D. Tomei.

Nadezhda Aleksandrovna Teffi (pseudonym for N.A. Buchinskaia, née Lokhvitskaia, 1872–1952) was a prolific professional writer, whose remarkable popularity reached celebrity status in Russia before the revolution and followed her into emigration in Paris, where she lived from 1920 until her death. Her witticisms were widely quoted, she was often recognized in crowds, and chocolate and perfume were named after her. While her writing was admired by both Tsar Nicholas II and V.I. Lenin, she remained politically independent and a liberal to the end of her life. Teffi wrote feuilletons in the periodical press and was on the staff of a major Petersburg weekly, *The Satyricon*, the Moscow newspaper *The New Word* and others. Her first volume of *Humorous Stories* (*Iumoristicheskie rasskazy*), published in 1910 with three editions that year, was an instant best-seller, setting the pace for future work. During her successful fifty-year career, Teffi published several collections of poetry, plays, critical and publicist prose, and many collections of stories, both humorous and serious.

Nadezhda Teffi was born in 1872 in to an old gentry family. Her great grandfather wrote mystical verse during the reign of Alexander I. Her father, a lawyer and scholar, was a prominent public figure in St. Petersburg. Teffi's mother was of French descent, loved poetry and knew Russian and European literature. Her older sister, Mirra Lokhvitskaia, was a well-known poet called the "Russian Sappho," who died in 1905 at the age of thirty-five. Nadezhda's literary interests began early. She remembers her old-fashioned upbringing and "reading everything, constantly."[1] Tolstoy looms large in her childhood reading and in the story titled "The Book," she tells of her first unmediated encounters with books, of reading *War and Peace* at the age of fourteen, of falling in love with Prince Andrei while feeling jealous of Natasha.[2] Elsewhere, she remembers being taken to visit Leo Tolstoy at the age of thirteen and intending to ask him to make changes in *War and Peace*, so that Prince Andrei would not have to die, but being too embarrassed to do anything but ask for an autograph.[3]

Teffi married a Polish lawyer and judge, Vladislav Buchinskii, but they separated in 1900 after the birth of their second daughter and a son. Teffi returned to St. Petersburg and launched her literary career at a time when a great number of women writers were active in literature as serious critics, translators and popular fiction writers, exploring new possibilities offered by the expanding commercial market.[4] Teffi's position, however, was unique in this context—unlike her contemporaries, the best-selling authors Verbitskaia, Nagrodskaia, Charskaia and others, she was not primarily a writer of "middlebrow" women's fiction. She worked as a journalist in the traditionally male field of humor, satire and parody.

The provenance of her literary pseudonym, a foreign-sounding name without a gender ending, remains somewhat mysterious. She began to use it with her one-act play, *The Woman's Question* (1907, on gender roles and code switching). The author herself provided two explanations: one was the shortened version of a friend's name, whom his servant called Steffi; or it may have come from Rudyard Kipling's song: "Taffy was a Walesman / Taffy was a thief."[5] Teffi dated her first appearance in print in 1901 with a short poem in the journal *North* (*Seves*), signed N. Lokhvitskaia. Her first short story, "The Day Has Passed" ("Den' proshel"), was returned by the journal *God's World* (*Mir Bozhii*) in 1904, but appeared in the *Grainfield* (*Niva*) supplement (no. 8) in 1905.

In the answer to a questionnaire distributed to writers, published in 1911, Teffi remembers that in her early creative work "the element of observation dominated my fantasy. I liked drawing caricatures and writing satirical verses. My first published work was written under Chekhov's influence."[6] Her early direction toward humor and satire led her to writing feuilletons in major Petersburg papers of the time, *Stock Exchange News* (*Birzhevye vedomosti*), *Russian Speech* (*Russkaia rech'*) and others. She was very much a part of the Petersburg elite literary life, attending gatherings at Viacheslav Ivanov's Tower and at Fedor Sologub's salon, where she read her verse and met the major poets of the time, Aleksandr Blok, Mikhail Kuzmin, Viacheslav Ivanov and N. Gumilev.

Teffi greeted the 1905 revolution and new freedom of the press with excitement as she attended political meetings and listened to the speeches of Bogdanov, Kamenev and Kollontai.[7] Her poem "The Little Bee" ("Pchelka"), written in the spring of 1905, proclaimed: "We have sown a bloody standard of freedom, / we will guard for years, / And we will never part with it!" It was sent to Lenin in Geneva and published, without attribution, under the title "The Standard of Freedom" in the newspaper *Forward*.[8] In the same year she started working for the leftist newspaper *New Life* (*Novaia zhizn'*), published jointly by the Social Democrats, who were in charge of the cultural section, and the Bolsheviks, who were responsible for the political section. But when the Bolsheviks took full control of the paper, Teffi and some of her colleagues resigned. Teffi also wrote for satirical papers, such as *Signal*, *Red Laughter* and *Summer Lightning* (*Zarnitsy*), as well as *Russian Speech* and the Sunday supplements to *Stock Exchange News*. Her plays were performed in several theaters, including The Crooked Mirror, the most popular comic theater of St. Petersburg from its opening in 1908.

In the same year Teffi joined the major weekly journal of the period, *The Satyricon*, which continued publication as *The New Satyricon* in 1913, edited by Arkadii Averchenko. The journal's contributors included a few established writers,

L. Andreev and A. Kuprin, and some of the foremost young male humorists of Teffi's generation, such as Sasha Chernyi, Don Aminado, P. Potemkin and others, joined by talented caricaturists. Continuing the nineteenth-century tradition of great satirists, Saltykov-Shchedrin and others, the editorial statement in the first issue of the journal announced the intention "to satirize the lawlessness, lies and vulgarity that reign in our political and public life. . . ."[9] The journal's hard satirical edge sought to provide opposition to the numerous reactionary, chauvinistic and anti-Semitic cheap humor publications. Satire and "the resistance of evil by humor" were the journal's slogan, its importance underscored by a reviewer: "the appearance of the *Satyricon* signaled the birth of laughter."[10] Teffi's broad range of professional experience, her work on the *Satyricon* and, later, as a regular feuilleton writer for the major newspaper *The Russian Word* were invaluable for her literary career.

The year 1910 was a turning point in Teffi's literary life. Her first published collection of verse, titled *Seven Fires* (*Sem' ognei*), received a favorable review from Nikolai Gumilev (*Apollon,* no. 7, 1910), who thought her poetry to be "literary in the best sense of the word," while a critical one from Valerii Briusov (*Russkaia mysl'*, no. 8, 1910) found it to be derivative. She was among the major writers who contributed to the two collections devoted to Tolstoy's memory, published soon after his death.[11] The publication of the first volume of *Humorous Stories* in 1910 by a serious publisher, Shipovnik, established Teffi's enormous popularity as a talented writer with an ironic view of repressive society and a sharp eye for the petty and vulgar in human relations. All reviews commented on her language and her brilliant dialogue. Writing in *Apollon*, the prominent poet and writer M. Kuzmin complimented her "gift of observation, gaiety and the literary language," expressed certainty of her potential to make a contribution to humorous literature and wondered whether she would try her pen at other genres.[12] Another critic, V. Kr. (V. Kranikhfeld), remarked that "the lively and fiery humor of the gifted young storyteller," her "excellent and graceful Russian," together with her skill "to portray a character's inner world in a few words," distinguished her humorous stories from most others in the marketplace.[13]

Teffi's acknowledged indebtedness to Chekhov was underscored by the similarity in their beginnings as feuilleton writers for the press. Her humor revealed the pettiness, hypocrisy, banality and kitsch in daily life, presenting a striking range of social types—functionaries, office clerks, maids, ladies, patres familias, students, peasants and eccentrics. Teffi emphasized the economy of means in her short prose: "Every word, every movement is weighed in miniature, leaving only what's most necessary."[14] She had a Gogolian ear for capturing dialect and funny names—

Zhuravlikhin, Shchupak, Rubashkin, Kulich, Elvel' Khasin (a country Jew). Although some critics lauded her comedy in characterizing and depicting small details of daily life, it was still remarked that her work seemed distant from problems and politics of contemporary society. This was not entirely true, since Teffi was a sharp social observer and her satire was directed at the social confusion and tension of the years before the revolution: tsarist bureaucracy ("The New Circular"); the proliferating acronyms of various political parties recited ad absurdum ("Politics and Study"); police training of a dumb double agent, who had to memorize radical political slogans without understanding them ("The Corsican"); the failure of the justice system ("The Fashionable Lawyer").

A pointedly long title for her story about a session at the cinematograph, "In Stereo-Photo-Mato-Scopo-Bio-Phono Etc.-Chart," emphasizes the confusion created by new technology with its false promise of "developing intellectual capacity and emotional nature" in an audience that can see the world pass before it on the screen "while sitting in comfortable chairs." The opening of "Two Willies: An American Story" is reminiscent of Zoshchenko: "Do you think, gentlemen, that American millionaires have an easy life?" Teffi's celebrated "humor instead of tears," forged through language play, was often couched in a first-person *skaz* narrative, whose witty puns and expressions entered the readers' vocabularies.

The public perception of Teffi's work was that humor overshadowed the serious side of her writing even in the stories that expressed pessimism and a sense of life's emptiness. The second volume of her *Humorous Stories*, published in 1911, opens with an extended philosophical meditation on Genesis, titled "Humanlike" ("Chelovekoobraznye"), a statement of the writer's worldview that would inform her entire corpus. Written in the *Satyricon* tradition of humorous revisions of history, her version of human evolution begins with the divine creation of man "in God's image" and continues through the stages of creation in which the human species becomes distanced from divine origin and comes to resemble creatures from the animal world. In this parable, "people are mixed with the humanlike" through marriage and family. As a result, the "humanlike are divided into two categories": the higher ones, who imitate spiritual life and the life of reason "but are not capable of creativity," though they admire genius; and the lower ones, who are fertile, acquisitive and adaptable. These species understand neither laughter nor love, but possess an undifferentiated sexual drive: "They have recently multiplied. There are indisputable signs of this. Their books have appeared in great numbers as have their circles. They are excellent at pretending and have assimilated the habits of real people." "They," who live anywhere between Petersburg and Paris, remain the main target of her satire for the next forty years.

Teffi's skepticism of received ideas and mindless conformity marks a collection published in 1915, titled *Nothing Like It* (*Nichego podobnogo*), which opens and closes with several tales about the vagaries of Russians abroad, a preview of what would become Teffi's main theme in emigration. In the main body of the collection, the familiar satire of contemporary mores gives way to an explicit literary and cultural critique. The metaliterary Petersburg cycle, composed of stories about different times of year in the city, whose climate had become a topos of the Petersburg myth in Russian literature from Pushkin to Gogol and Dostoevsky to the present, revealed Teffi's acknowledgment of the canon.

The confidence of a mature writer was apparent in her self-conscious parody of its conventions in such stories as "Life and Themes," "Accursed Questions" and "The Auteur and the Staging." Other stories made light of modern artistic movements, such as the notoriously serious Petersburg symbolists and their influence on contemporary culture. "The Sun's Wife" ("Zhena Solntsa") is a takeoff on Bal'mont's famous poem "Handsome as the Sun" ("Krasivyi kak solntse"). The hero of "The Pink Student," who plays a cynical game of seducing an older spinster chemistry professor, concludes "I fulfilled my Symbolist mission. . . . I awakened in her the eternal feminine, I took the peel off her Eros." In the story "The Language of Roots" ("Pochvennyi iazyk"), Teffi mocks the Symbolist quest for an authentic Russian language and the reiterated complaint that "when one lives in Petrograd for a long time, one longs for the real Russian of roots." As in the story "Stereo-Photo-Mato-Scopo-Bio-Phono Etc.-Chart" from a previous collection (see above), Teffi is skeptical about the advent of the newest technological trends coming from America in "More About Taylor," a satire on Taylorism and efficiency theories in Russia long before Zamiatin's postrevolutionary dystopian novel *We*.

As the range of Teffi's literary interests becomes broader, she wants to forestall the misapprehension of her craft as "light fiction" only. In the preface to another 1916 collection, titled *A Lifeless Beast* (*Nezhivoi zver'*), reprinted in Paris in 1921 under the title *Quiet Backwater* (*Tikhaia zavod'*), she states: "I warn those who while looking for laughter find tears here—the pearls of my soul—would not turn and tear me apart." The stories in this volume reveal the tragic in everyday life and empathy for the downtrodden and the marginal, especially for children. In the representative title story, a little girl's natural emotions of love and pity, repressed by controlling, heedless adults, turn into a nightmare and affect her vulnerable personality: "She will live quietly, so quietly that no one will know."

The metaliterary interest is combined with pathos in "The Fairytale of Life: To the Memory of Iambo," which addresses the commonplace misperception of the nature of literary realism, understood as art imitating life, that has dominated the Russian literary tradition. The opening, "I have been saying for a long time that life is bad fiction," turns the commonplace notion on its head and is followed by the narrator's acerbic comment on the artless and tasteless creations of life that would "ruin the reputation of any self-respecting author." The narrator then proceeds to illustrate her point with an "exception"—a parable of a circus elephant, who performs for a paying public that does not perceive his suffering in capitivity because of the commonplace notion that "art ennobles the soul." However, when the desire for freedom overtakes the elephant, he rebels against his bondage. At the end, he is killed by the very same people who love sentimental verses about prisoners and freedom. In this parody of realism as in that of the Petersburg myth, discussed earlier, Teffi points to new trends in literary modernism.

One of the most poignant stories in the collection is Teffi's response to World War I, titled "Vania Shchegolek," in which a handsome wounded young soldier desperately wants to defy the inevitable—he is not ready to die and wants to return to his Siberian home to see the wild swans drinking water and watch the bear in the moonlight. But when the nurse arrives the next morning, his bed is made up and empty. The pathos of this elliptical narrative is achieved through interpolated poems in prose—lyrical outbursts of the soldier, whose keen sense of the beauty of life becomes all the more urgent in the face of a senseless death.

Teffi joined other writers in response to the war, which she abhorred. She wrote for the first issue of the journal *The Fatherland* (*Otechestvo*), with L. Andreev, A. Remizov, K. Chukovskii and others.[15] She participated in a poetry reading at Fedor Sologub's, along with Akhmatova, Severianin and Mandel'shtam, where "everything in this numerous gathering of poets was about the war, or associated with it, or because of it! There were no other topics of discussion."[16] Teffi became active in numerous fund-raising collections for causes, ranging from the sick to the poor, children, striking students and victims of the war, an activity she would continue in emigration. She also joined writers' protests against anti-Semitism and signed the proclamation "To the Russian People" in *The Morning of Russia* on 1 March 1915, demanding equal rights for the Jewish people. She contributed to the collection *The Shield*, edited by L. Andreev, M. Gorky and F. Sologub, intended to combat anti-Semitism.[17] In the words of longtime friend G. Aleksinskii, who wrote her obituary, Teffi was "outside any practical or active politics, she was not a party member . . . but she was a democrat by nature."[18]

The anxiety dominating the country in the period between the two revolutions affected Teffi, and her anarchic irreverence for power, imperial or ecclesiastical, found a brilliant outlet in the expressionist story titled "Protective Coloring" ("Zashchitnyi tsvet"), first published in Paris in 1920. As described in the story, the craze for the tango and attempts at its prohibition, begun in Russia in 1912–1913 and followed by the Austrian emperor and the Vatican, rendered its spread across borders only more irrepressible, making it both a symbol of impotent power and a harbinger of war and revolution in Europe: "The political atmosphere was condensed. International intrigues were created, secret plans hatched. . . . Revolutionary seismographs showed distant shocks and the earth's tremors. . . . Clouds were gathering. The thick air, saturated with electricity, pressed on the lungs."[19]

The expressionist montage and staccato images of revolutionary Petrograd in Teffi's story recall revolutionary Blok's poem "The Twelve," as she depicts how "suffering and death, in a bitter embrace, falter, swirl, sweep across the land . . . follow the footprints of the tango. . . . The sailor with the bared chest . . . embraces the street walker. A speculator, a *noveau riche,* and just a simple little thief, follow him in a wild dance."[20] Beginning in 1912 Teffi became a regular contributor to the major Moscow paper, *The Russian Word*, headed by the "king of the feuilleton" Vlas Doroshevich, who valued her literary talent. After the newspaper was closed down in 1918, Teffi and many of her colleagues decided to leave Russia. Her wanderings began in 1919. Like many Russians at the time, she did not plan to emigrate but was caught in the exodus.

Her *Reminiscences* (*Vospominaniia*), begun in 1928 and published in Paris in 1932, described her last days in Russia, her travels south to Kiev and Odessa, and then to Paris via Constantinople. Once again, Teffi wrote a preface in which she attempted to clarify her position to the reader and, most of all, to distinguish her work from the common émigré memoirs. She warned readers that they "will not find here either the celebrated heroic figures of the epoch, with their deeply significant statements, or the unmasking of one or another political line, nor any 'enlightenment or conclusions.'" She promised instead "a true and simple story about the author's involuntary travel across Russia. . . ."[21] Written with acerbic wit and remarkable presence of critical faculties, *Reminiscences* depicted the terror and confusion of the first postrevolutionary years when, along with many of her compatriots, she believed her painful parting with her homeland to be temporary. The exile's longing, nostalgia and the painful confusion of displacement would become the central theme in her tales of émigré life.

Teffi settled in Paris in 1920 and, despite the difficulties of émigré existence, she resumed an active social and literary life, attempting to re-create her Petersburg apartment, and opening a salon.[22] Don Aminado, one of the several *Satyricon* authors now in Paris, described the reconfigured Russian literary community: "the chief role belonged, of course, to Teffi, both because of her definite talent and because of the table of ranks set once and for all."[23] Indeed, as a prominent Russian writer of the older generation in Paris, Teffi became one of the major literary figures in the émigré literary scene, along with I. Bunin, Z. Gippius, D. Merezhkovskii, A. Remizov, B. Zaitsev and M. Tsvetaeva. She wrote regularly for Russian journals and newspapers and was active in émigré cultural life as a member of "The Real Russian Club" and the "Green Lamp" literary societies.

Teffi participated in readings and festivals of Russian culture and contributed her name and talent to many fund-raising projects, including the creation of the Herzen library in Nice. The Union of Russian Theatre and Cinematography elected her and Merezhkovskii as their representatives. She took part in dialogues between Russian writers and their French colleagues. When the Russian Theater opened in Paris in 1936, her sketches entered the permanent repertoire. Her four-act drama, *A Moment of Fate* (*Moment sud'by*), premiered in Paris to general acclaim, touring in Russian theaters all over Europe and even Shanghai. The production of her play *Nothing Like It* (*Nichego podobnogo*), directed by Nikolai Evreinov, followed two years later. In her literary memoirs, *On the Shores of the Seine*, Irina Odoevtseva remembered Teffi as being full of joie de vivre, as someone whose appearance would immediately enliven a gathering, such as a Sunday at the Gippius-Merezhkovskii salon.[24]

As Teffi strove to re-create her Petersburg life in Paris, her keen view on the banality in everyday life remained in her writing, but now combined with a sense of tragic loss as in her adopted habitat. Her tales, called by one critic "the monuments of émigré life," created the cultural and social ethnography of the Russian diaspora. They explored the universe of exile: longing for a return, nostalgia for the motherland, loss of identity and the painful confusion of dislocation. These themes, presented without sentimentality but with a sharp irony of Russians abroad, connected her stories with the work of a younger émigré writer, Vladimir Nabokov. Both were masters in the use of language as the perfect medium for representing a clash of cultures through interlingual punning, pidgin Russian and russified French.

Some of the best-known émigré tales appeared in the collection *The Lynx* (*Rys'*), published in Berlin in 1923 and reprinted in the Russian collection *Nostalgia*.[25] The narrator in the stories often addressed readers directly and let them speak about themselves. The general opinion among émigrés was that "the confusion" at home would not last longer than another two months. Painful, unrelieved nostalgia followed the exiles in a story of the same title into the foreign land. As soon as they were settled, the refugees changed: "Their eyes are dull, limp hands drop and the soul wilts. . . . We believe in nothing, await nothing, want nothing. Dead." They were aware of their impossible choices: "afraid of the Bolshevik death—we died passing away here [*umerli smert'iu zdes'*]." They attempted to go on living with the challenge of how to "translate the Russian soul into French. . . ." The story "About Eternal Love" from a later collection, *All About Love* (*Vse o liubvi,* Paris, 1930), showed aging émigrés living in a time warp, where the present recedes before the nostalgia for a distant youth, remembered to the faint sounds of Tchaikovsky's "The Dying Swan" coming from the radio. In the story "Two Affairs with Foreigners" French insouciance and social code clash with Russian seriousness in matters of the heart, exposing social differences in attitudes toward love.

In the story "Raw Material" Teffi showed that although the familiar trappings of Russian culture, opera and ballet, were transported to Paris, something new was ever-present: "A Great Sadness" (*Velikaia pechal'*). The exile's life was compared to "life after death" (*zagrobnaia zhizn'*), and the exiles themselves were "like a poor relative who finds herself at a birthday party in a rich house." At night the "Great Sadness" took the soul back to the devastated native land. In "Two Encounters" the émigré voice intoned, "All is over. Russia is dead. Sold. Drunk. Finished." The fear of losing memory of Russian culture and literature led to the question "How can one write? Our life is dead." In a warning against the misrepresentation of the immediate past, the narrator pointedly recalled the forgotten courage of both the Reds and the Whites in the revolution and the civil war. Teffi juxtaposed her story to the émigré penchant for memoirs as a creation of "false memory."

Rumors of terrible sufferings in the new Russia saturate the exile's consciousness in the story "Cosmic Space" ("Mirovoe prostranstvo"). The émigrés fall into two categories: those who are selling Russia and those who are saving her ("Ke fer"). One problem that divides people in this small community is general paranoia, and in the story "Kontr" it reaches absurdity, when everyone is suspect: "Some are simply in intelligence, some are in counter-intelligence . . ." and one fellow reports on himself and gets money from both sides. Humor locates the bright side in the descriptions of bleak existence where the émigré condition is also seen as a great leveler: "Ah, we're all equal before the borscht."

The exile's shattered sense of identity was subject to conflicting emotions. Cut off from the homeland, Russians suffered from a false sense of cultural superiority: "Of course, we, who gave the world Tolstoy and Dostoevsky, don't have much in common with them." Émigré prejudice against everything French provides "an aesthetic directive: not to like the Eiffel Tower." Instead, the Russians continued to look for the familiar constellation, the Big Dipper, in the Paris sky so as not to feel "so foreign and alone." At the same time, they internalized a sense of inferiority about their country and its past. In denigrating Russian culture, the émigré finds satisfaction in taking great figures off the pedestal to reveal their human weaknesses, pointing out with glee that Dostoevsky was a gambler and Tolstoy a man of the flesh, and all the émigrés are "thieves."

In a later collection, *A Small Town* (*Gorodok*, 1927), subtitled *A Chronicle*, the writer took on the role of a chronicler sketching the town, where "women sewed each other's dresses and made hats. Men made debts with one another. Besides men and women, the population of the small town consisted of ministers and generals." The cultural impoverishment and vulgarity of émigré life was most evident in the dissolution of language, a mixture of Russian, German and French. Teffi ridiculed the new pidgin of the émigrés, which she ironically calls "neologisms." In one of her most famous stories with a bilingual pun, the French interrogative "Ke fer?" is russified by a general with a Russian particle to "fer-*to* ke?" which expresses the existential dilemma of "so-called le Russy" who live "a most strange life, unlike any other" abroad. Exiles, bound by mutual dislike, invented a "neologism," the three-letter word "thief" (*vor*), attached to every name like a particle. In her attention to language as the endangered part of Russian culture Teffi joined the efforts of the Paris literary community in the belief that "language was an instrument that had to be maintained and kept in good working order."[26]

The metaliterary concerns of the earlier, prerevolutionary stories returned as Teffi acknowledged the difficulty of her position as a chronicler, as well as her continued predicament of being typecast as a humorist. She countered the readers' complaints in the story "How to Be?" where a banker she knew gave her his honest opinion, asking, "How can you laugh when our country is suffering?" Someone else criticized her craftsmanship, another suggested that "simplicity is true art," while a charming lady reported that her feuilletons no longer pleased the public, and someone else said that "this was no Beecher Stowe." In conversations with Irina Odoevtseva, Teffi complained: "I am pained, because my serious things are not recognized, especially my verse."[27] She was aware of the "temporality" of her work as a satirist and of being forgotten "like a white moth with a day-long lifespan." On another occasion, she revealed the common predicament of humorists: "every one of my funny stories is, in essence, a little tragedy turned humorous."[28]

Although Teffi was one of the most popular and prolific writers in emigration, writing for the press and publishing about twenty collections of stories between 1920 and 1940, her work has not received appropriate attention. Teffi's creative life and literary legacy continue to be marked by paradox. Her early career was part of the history of Russian modernism, when women entered literature and arts in considerable numbers and achieved unprecedented stature. As a woman humorist, she was unique in a traditionally male-dominated field. Despite her thematic range and repeated pleas to the reading public to see her as a serious writer, she remained primarily known and loved as a humorist both in Russia and abroad.

One of the prominent members of the Paris literary community, Mikhail Aldanov, compared Teffi to Griboedov, and her stories to his classic play *Woe from Wit* as a source of witticisms and puns: "Your *bons mots* and expressions have entered the émigré language and enriched it." He thought her stories "probably the most valuable creation of émigré literature. They are our annals, chronicle of the times, material for future historians. They are simply a monument of emigration."[29] In a more recent survey of Russian émigré culture, P.E. Kovalevskii referred to her as "the ethnographer" of Russian émigré life.[30] Contemporary American scholars note an affinity between her depiction of the alienated Russian exile and the image of the maladjusted new Soviet citizen in the satires of Mikhail Zoshchenko.[31] Zoshchenko himself understood her popularity and appreciated her craft: "She is considered a most amusing and 'funny' writer and a volume of her stories usually comes along on a lengthy journey."[32]

In the chapter devoted to her work in *Russian Literature in Exile*, Gleb Struve understood Teffi's predicament and demonstrated how difficult it was to categorize her work as serious literature. He noted the paradox in the fact that Teffi's Paris stories were published primarily in the Russian newspapers, but favorably reviewed in serious literary journals, such as *Sovremennye zapiski*.[33] He explained that, though it was possible that Teffi's feuilletons were perhaps considered to be below the journal standard, "in any case, one can say without hesitation that she belonged to real literature."[34] The divide between "serious"/high and "popular"/low literature, as well as verbal innovation, was problematic for the conservative émigré literary community that strove to preserve the national tradition threatened in the homeland.[35]

Some of the émigré critics, such as Mark Slonim and D.S. Mirsky, insisted that in the 1920s real literary life was going on in the Soviet Union, not in emigration.[36] It is probable that the formalist critics would have taken Teffi's work seriously. For example, in his 1924 essay, "The Literary Fact," Iurii Tynianov "argued against static, *a priori* definition of literary phenomena and insisted that, while at any given moment a clear distinction can be made between what is and what is not literature, 'the notion of literature changes all the time.'"[37] This was why Boris Èikhenbaum could undertake a serious analysis of O. Henry's novel, *Cabbages and*

Kings, considered "lightweight" by serious literary critics, making it a "touchstone of critical theory."[38] The formalists considered such popular hybrid genres as the feuilleton, memoir and reportage to be indispensable in literary evolution.

In the publication of his correspondence with Teffi ten years after her death in 1963, Russian-American writer Andrei Sedykh comments that "this is too short a time in order to define her place in contemporary Russian literature," but adds that not only has she not been forgotten, but she is emerging as a major writer in the Gogolian tradition.[39] More than forty years since Teffi's death in 1952 there is no monograph on the writer, nor an edition of her collected works, which would number ten volumes.[40] In the essay "Women's Prose in the Silver Age," Charlotte Rosenthal concludes: "Teffi still has not been given her rightful place in the serious canon of Russian literature."[41] Another scholar, Marina Ledkovsky, attributes this to "the general neglect of Russian émigré literature, not to speak of its women contributors, by American Slavists."[42] Teffi has not been published in Russia since the late 1920s, although she was offered Soviet citizenship after the war. Small collections appeared in 1967 and 1971, after which she was "forgotten" again.[43] A collection of Paris stories, titled *Nostalgia,* published in Moscow in 1989, and two volumes of *Humorous Stories* in 1990 attest to the considerable interest in the writer's work in her homeland. This confirms Aldanov's statement in a 1923 review of Teffi's poetry collection *Passiflora* that her work can be read "by both Russias."[44]

In a recent study of *Russia Abroad*, Marc Raeff wrote about the Russian humorists in Paris, Teffi, Don Aminado and Damanskaia: "To the extent that these prose writers had not participated in the innovative experimentation of the Silver Age . . . or in the early twenties, they did not contribute anything new esthetically, but their novels and stories were captivating and beautiful examples of the heights that Russian prose had attained in the past."[45] The literary historian Catriona Kelly, however, noted the historic importance of Teffi's language and in a discussion of her 1907 play *The Woman's Question*, wrote that "both neologistic and conventional, the language of Teffi's play reflects the limits of contemporary views on androgyny, but in her insistence that the 'woman question' has a linguistic dimension, she was a rare transitional figure between realism and modernism."[46] Indeed, Teffi's language continued to be innovative and irreverent as she sought to capture the cultural and linguistic confusion of the Russian diaspora. Its role as that of her entire *oeuvre* in Russian literary history awaits a proper appraisal now that the literary achievements of the diaspora and the motherland can be considered as part of one cultural tradition.

Greta Slobin

The Pipe

You never know exactly what will change your life or throw a curve into your otherwise straight trajectory. It just isn't given for us to know.

Sometimes something which we see as a total nonentity, a trifle we encountered a thousand-thousand times and passed by without any consequence—this very "something" suddenly takes on such a role that you don't forget it all your days.

It may not even be worth bringing up examples. It's like when someone sees a button lying on the ground:

"Hey, is this mine?"

At that moment, that is, during the few seconds he is bent over and can't see what's going on around him, the one person he's earnestly been trying to find for many years walks by.

Or the other way around—the man stops a minute to see if that's his button, and this momentary delay is just enough so that, raising his head, he meets face to face someone he's been trying everything possible to avoid for years.

However, the incident I would like to talk about is somewhat more complicated.

There once lived a certain Vasilii Vasilievich Zobov. He was rather a modest being. He came to Petersburg from someplace in the south and started working for a newspaper as a proofreader.

He made a lousy proofreader. Not because he let mistakes slip by, but because he was always correcting the writers.

An author would write a story about life on the farm:

"'Wa'al, whaddya'll need?' Jake asked."

Zobov would correct it:

"'What can I do for you?' Jake asked."

The author would write:

"'How dare you!' flared Ellen."

And Zobov would correct it:

"'How dare you!' having flared up, said Ellen."

"What are you adding words for?" the author would rage. "Who asked you to do that?"

"Well now," Zobov would answer with dignity. "You're writing that Ellen flared up, but who said the sentence, 'How dare you,' remains unclear. Finishing and correcting sentences is the duty of the proofreader."

They cursed him, almost beat him and, eventually, they sent him packing. Then he became a journalist.

He wrote sensational articles about "city kids," or "fathers of the city and the pie of society," or "the robbery and inferior goods of ice-cream vendors."

They didn't let him cover fires. His reports about fires acquired inflated, Nero-like nuances all too often:

"Labaz was in flames. It seemed like Mt. Etna itself was exploding into the heavens, burned to their innermost recesses, causing inestimable damage to the merchant Fertov and his sons."

They didn't let him cover fires.

He was always spinning around the office and the typesetters', taking all sorts of loans from whomever he came across and always making up some kind of scheme which, although it was elaborately thought up and executed with fanfare, rarely brought him more than a half-dollar.

On the exterior, Zobov was ugly with a little black, well-sucked mustache and a leaden-colored collar, worn out to gauze:

"Soft collars are now in fashion."

His family life was, like anyone's who doesn't have a family, extremely complicated.

He had a cohabitant, huge, puffy Susanna Robertovna, the daughter of the "late theatrical artist," or, stated frankly, a circus magician. Susanna had a mother and two children from two former liaisons previous to Zobov: a deaf-mute son and half-blind daughter.

Susanna rented out rooms, her mother prepared meals for the boarders, and Zobov lived like the husband: that is, he didn't pay either for the food or the room and often fought with Susanna, who was jealous of him. The mother also participated in these fights, but never entered the fray; she just stood at the threshold and directed with her advice.

Thus went the life of Vasily Vasilievich Zobov along its open path. It went on and on and then, suddenly, it came to a halt and turned.

You're thinking—some sort of unusual meeting, a new love, something vivid and irrevocable?

Nothing of the kind. It was simply—a pipe.

Here's how it happened. Zobov was walking down Nevsky Avenue. He glanced at the shop windows and rather indifferently stopped at a tobacco shop. It was a big store, nicely decorated, and it exhibited in its window a whole assortment of every kind of pipe imaginable. What wasn't there! There were old *chubuks* with amber tips and some sort of elbowed ones like wind instruments, ones with silken stems, Tyrolean ones, what have you. And there were perfectly straight ones, nice ones, thick ones, appetizingly bent to hang on one's lip and, lifted slightly, to draw out smoke. Nosewarmers.

Zobov looked over these pipes for a long while and finally stopped at one in particular—and couldn't tear his eyes off it.

This was a small, thick one for a smoker to grip lovingly, firmly in his fist, the pipe of an old sailor from English novels.

Zobov looked at it and the longer he looked, the stranger he felt. Just like hypnosis. What was this? Something sweet, something forgotten like a particular fact, but precise and clear like a sensation. Something like when a person is remembering the menu of a meal he has eaten:

"There was something else . . . really tasty, something farm-like . . . oh yes, fried sausage."

The taste, the impression—all of that stayed in the memory, only the form was forgotten, the appearance, the name that created this impression.

That's what it was like now. Zobov stood in front of that fat pipe and didn't know what it was all about, but he felt a sweet joy of the bygone past.

"A little English pipe . . . an old captain. . . ."

And suddenly the foggy curtains of his memory swayed and parted and Zobov caught sight of a page from a children's book; on the page was a little picture. A hefty man in a slicker, frowning slightly, pressed his shaved lip on a small fat pipe. And the caption:

"The captain was vigilant all night."

That was it!

Zobov had been ten at that time when the captain was vigilant all night. And out of excitement and great delight, Zobov read there, instead of "vigilant"—a word which in children's parlance was not only rare but even nonexistent—Zobov read "vigitant":

"The captain was vigitant all night."

And this "vigitant" didn't surprise him a bit. There were more than a few unusual words in such books: yardarms, spar decks, tacking, some sort of warping. Among these secret objects a wise person was entirely permitted to be vigitant.

Such a fabulous world of bravery, honesty and valor, where even pirates kept their promises and, without blinking, sacrificed their lives to save their friends.

Zobov entered the store lost in thought, bought the pipe, asked for English, absolutely English tobacco, and sniffed the thick, honeyed aroma for a long while. He filled his pipe right there, drew on it and cast an eye in the mirror.

"I have to get rid of this mustache."

Already shaved clean, he sat quietly at the office, ironically, like an American, lowering the corners of his mouth and puffing on his pipe. When two journalists began to argue in front of him, he suddenly stretched out his arm severely and said pedantically:

"Shh! Don't forget, the most important thing is to remain gentlemen."

"Wha-at?" the journalists said incredulously. "What is he joking about?"

Zobov moved his pipe over to the other side or his mouth, threw one leg over the other and thrust his fingers into the armholes of his vest. Composed and cool.

On this day he had not taken any loans from his coworkers.

At home they regarded his pipe with suspicion. Even more suspicious was his shaven face and imperturbable manner. But when he unexpectedly walked into the kitchen and, having kissed the mother's hands, asked whether he might be of any assistance, the suspicion was replaced by overt fear.

"Put him to bed as soon as you can," the mother whispered to Susanna. "Wherever was he gadding about all day? Where did he butt his head, I'm asking you?"

And that's how it went.

Zobov became a gentleman. A gentleman and an Englishman.

"Zobov," someone said to him at the office. "Your surname is ugly. Defective. It comes from a defect, from *zob,* the word for 'goiter.'"

"Well, yes," Zobov replied calmly. "The majority of English surnames seem strange to the Russian ear." And he drew on his pipe.

His interlocutor was not an expert in English surnames and thus preferred to remain silent.

He started wearing high starched collars and starched cuffs that were so huge that they slid into his sleeves only at the very edge. He was shaved, bathed and all the time was either expressing his gratitude or apologies. And completely drily, coolly and with dignity.

Puffy Susanna Robertovna stopped being jealous. Her envy was replaced by fear and respect and the combination of these two unpleasant feelings together extinguished the pleasant one—passion.

The mother also began to be afraid of him. Especially after he gave her money for her expenses and asked for a rare beefsteak and a half-bottle of port for dinner.

The children, when they saw him, chased him out of their rooms, bumping into each other in the doorway.

The change of his essence also was reflected in his writing. The superfluous pathos disappeared. A sober matter-of-factness appeared.

The burning fires of Etna were replaced by dry lines about a small fire quickly extinguished by the prompt firefighters.

Every excess fell aside.

"Everything on earth must be simple, clear and gentlemanly."

The only diversion he allowed himself and even encouraged was the love of the ocean. He had never in his life seen an ocean, but he was certain that this love was "his from the blood of his ancestors."

On rainy days he loved to put on his waterproof coat, raise the hood, stick his pipe in his mouth and, grunting in dissatisfaction, go wandering through the streets.

"This reminds me of something. Maybe it was summer in Iceland or winter on the shores of Northern Africa. I've never been there, but we have this in our blood."

"Vasil' Vasilich!" the mother groaned. "But you're a Russian!"

"Well, yes if you like," Zobov replied, sucking on his pipe. "That is, Russian in fact."

"There you go, playing the fool!"The mother couldn't suppress herself.

"I beg your pardon," said Zobov coolly, politely. "I'm not about to argue with you. For me, every woman is a lady and gentlemen don't argue with ladies."

Susanna Robertovna started having an affair with one of the boarders, an excise taxman. Zobov reacted to this with a demonstrable politeness toward his rival and remained attentive to Susanna.

The revolution separated them. Zobov turned up in Marseilles, Susanna and her mother and children and, according to rumor, the excise taxman, got stuck in Bulgaria.

Zobov, older and more feeble, at first worked as a stevedore at the port, then at the same place as a guard; and all his money, saving only the most necessary pittance for himself, he sent off to Susanna Robertovna. In reply, Susanna Robertovna sent him threatening letters in which she reproached him for his ingratitude, for his cruel heart and, completely confusing time and dates, she heaped shame on him for abandoning his unhappy, handicapped children, leaving her, a weak woman, to her own devices to care for them.

He shrugged his shoulders ironically and continued to send everything he could to his lady.

The epilogue arrived quickly.

Returning from work, he lost his pipe. He looked for it a long time in the rain. He got soaked, chilled to the bone, and caught pneumonia.

For three days he raved about helms, crew's quarters and warping.

A Russian workman from the wharf dropped in to visit. He witnessed his last breath.

"Stand up, old Bill!" muttered the dying man. "Stand up! Get upstairs as fast as you can. The great Captain is calling you."

Thus old Bill passed away, the Englishman, seafarer and gentleman, a tradesman from the Kursk district, Vasilii Vasilievich Zobov.

Translated by Christine D. Tomei

Notes to the Essay

1. F. Fidler, "Nadezhda Aleksandrovna Tèffi," in *Pervye literaturnye shagi. Avtobiografii sovremennykh pisatelei* (Moscow: Tipografiia I.D. Sytina, 1911), 202.

2. In *Nichego podobnogo* (St. Petersburg, 1915), 23–27.

3. "Moi pervyi Tolstoi," *Prezhde/Segodnia* [Riga], 18 May 1930.

4. "Introduction: Russian Women Writers: 1760–1992," in *Dictionary of Russian Women Writers*, ed. M. Ledkovsky, C. Rosenthal and M. Zirin (Westport, CT: Greenwood Press, 1994), xxxv.

5. "Psevdonim," *Vozrozhdenie* [Paris], 20 December 1931.

6. F. Fidler, 204–05.

7. "45 let," *Novoe russkoe slovo* [New York], 26 June 1950.

8. D.D. Nikolaev, "Zhemchuzhina russkogo iumora," in N.A. Tèffi, *Iumoristicheskie rasskazy*, edited with an introduction and commentary by D.D. Nikolaev (Moscow: Khudozhestvennaia literatura 1990), 5.

9. *Satirikon* 1 (1908): 2.

10. P. Ryss, "O smekhe," *Den'*, 22 February 1914. Quoted in *Poèty "Satirikona,"* ed. L.A. Evstigneeva (Leningrad: Sovetskii pisatel', 1966), 23.

11. B. Bialik, ed., *Russkaia literatura konca XIX-nachala XX v.: 1908–1917*, Vol. 3 (Moscow: Nauka, 1972), 473.

12. Ibid., 458.

13. *Sovremennyi mir* 9 (1910). Quoted in *N.A. Tèffi, Iumoristicheskie rasskazy*, 12.

14. "Ominiatiurennye," in *Dym bez ognia* (St. Petersburg, 1914), 172.

15. *Russkaia literatura kontsa XIX- nachala XX v.: 1908–1917*, 595.

16. Ibid., 600.

17. Ibid.

18. G. Aleksinskii, "Ee dobroi i svetloi pamiati (Vospominaniia o N.A. Tèffi)," *Grani* 16 (1952): 135–36.

19. N. Tèffi, "Zashchitnyi svet," *Poslednie novosti*, 23 May 1920. [Paris; rpt. in *Rys'* (Berlin, 1923), 156.]

20. Ibid., 156.

21. "Vospominaniia," *Nostalgiia. Rasskazy. Vospominaniia* (Leningrad, 1989), 268.

22. G. Aleksinskii, 135.

23. Don Aminado, "Vospominaniia," in *Nasha malen'kaia zhizn': stikhotvoreniia. Politicheskii pamflet. Proza. Vospominaniia* (Moscow: Terra, 1994), 673.

24. I. Odoevtseva, *Na beregakh Seny* (Paris: Presse Libre, 1983), 96.

25. References for the following stories come from *Nostalgiia* (Leningrad: Khudozhestvennaia literatura, 1989).

26. Marc Raeff, *Russia Abroad: A Cultural History of the Russian Emigration, 1919–1939* (New York: Oxford University Press, 1990), 110.

27. I. Odoevtseva, 102.

28. Ibid., 94, 114.

29. Ibid., 97–98.

30. P.E. Kovalevskii, *Zarubezhnaia Rossiia* (Paris: Librairie de cinq continents, 1971), 256.

31. T. Pachmuss, ed. and trans., *Women Writers in Russian Modernism* (Urbana: University of Illinois Press, 1978), 265. See also her article [signed T. A. P.] "Teffi," in *Handbook of Russian Literature*, ed. Victor Terras (New Haven, CT: Yale University Press, 1985), 465.

32. M. Zoshchenko, "N. Tèffi," in *Ezhegodnik rukopisnogo otdela Pushkinskogo doma 1972*, ed. K.D. Muratora (Leningrad: Nauka, 1974), 140.

33. See Boris Zaitsev, "N. A. Tèffi, *Avantiurnyi roman.* Paris, 1932," *Sovremennye zapiski* 49 (1932).

34. G. Struve, *Russkaia literatura v izgnanii* (New York: Chekhov, 1956), 111.

35. For specific problems in the study of émigré literature, see L. Fleishman, F. Bowlt, and D. Segal, "Problemy izucheniia literatury russkoi èmigratsii pervoi treti XX veka," in *Slavica Hierosolymitana*, Vol. 3 (Jerusalem: The Magnes Press, Hebrew University, 1978), 75–88.

36. See D.S. Mirsky, "O nyneshnem sostoianii russkoi literatury," *Blagonamerennyi* 1 (1926): 97.

37. V. Erlich, *Russian Formalism: History, Doctrine,* 3d ed. (The Hague: Mouton, 1969), 121.

38. Ibid., 248.

39. Andrei Sedykh, "Tèffi v pis'makh," in *Vozdushnye puti,* ed. R.N. Grinberg, Vol. 3 (New York: R.N. Grinberg, 1963), 192.

40. Elizabeth B. Neatrour, "'Zhizn' smeetsia i plachet . . .' O sud'be i tvorchestve Tèffi," introduction to *Nostal'giia. Rasskazy. Vospominaniia,* ed. B. Averina (Leningrad: Khudozhestvennaia literatura, 1989), 18.

41. C. Rosenthal, "Women's Prose in the Silver Age," in *Women Writers in Russian Literature*, ed. Toby W. Clyman and Diana Greene (Westport, CT: Greenwood Press, 1994), 162.

42. Marina Ledkovsky, "Women Writers in Émigré Literature," in *Women Writers in Russian Literature*, ed. T. Clyman and D. Greene (Westport, CT: Greenwood Press, 1994), 250.

43. Dmitrii Nikolaev, "Zhemchuzhina russkogo iumora," *Iumoristicheskie rasskazy* (1900): 18.

44. "Tèffi. *Passiflora*. Berlin: Izdatel'stvo zhurnala 'Teatr,' 1923," *Sovremennye zapiski* [Paris] 17 (1923): 485.

45. Raeff, 112.

46. Catriona Kelly, ed., *An Anthology of Russian Women's Writing* (Oxford: Oxford University Press, 1994), 205.

Bibliography

Primary Works

Iumoristicheskie rasskazy. 2 vols. St. Petersburg: Shipovnik, 1910–1911. [Rpt. Moscow: Khudozhestvennaia literatura, 1990.]

I stalo tak . . . . St. Petersburg: M.G. Kornfel'd, 1912.

Karusel'. St. Petersburg, 1913.

Vosem' miniatiur. St. Petersburg, 1913.

Dym bez ognia. St. Petersburg, 1914.

Miniatiury i monologi. St. Petersburg, 1915.

Nichego podobnogo. St. Petersburg, 1915.

Nezhivoi zver'. Petrograd, 1916.

Zhit'e-byt'e. Petrograd, 1916.

"Zashchitnyi svet." *Poslednie novosti,* [Paris]. 23 May 1920.

Chernyi iris. Stockholm: Severnye ogni, 1921.

Tikhaia zavod'. Paris: Russkaia zemlia, 1921. [Reprint of *Nezhivoi zver'*.]

Vostok i drugie rasskazy. Shanghai, 1921.

Passiflora. Berlin: Izdatel'stvo zhurnala "Teatr," 1923.

Rys'. Berlin: Otto Kirchner, 1923.

Vechernii den'. Prague: Plamia, 1924.

Provorstvo ruk. Moscow: Zemlia i fabrika, 1926.

Gorodok. Paris: Izdanie tovarishchestva N.P. Karabashnikov, 1927.

Parizhskie rasskazy. Moscow, 1927.

Tango smerti. Moscow. Leningrad, 1927.

"Lolo. Ustnaia gazeta." *Segodnia,* 20 January 1929.

"Moi pervyi Tolstoi." *Prezhde/Segodnia* [Riga], 18 May 1930.

Vse o liubvi. Paris, 1930.

Kniga-iun'. Belgrade: Izdatel'skaia komissia, Palata Akademije Nauka, 1931.

Avantiurnyi roman. Paris: Vozrozhdenie, 1932.

Vospominaniia. Paris: Vozrozhdenie, 1932.

Ved'ma. Berlin: Petropolis, 1936.

O nezhnosti. Paris: Russkie zapiski, 1938.

Zigzag. Paris: Russkie zapiski, 1939.

Vse o liubvi Paris: La Presse française et étrangère, 1946.

"45 let." *Novoe russkoe slovo* [New York]. 26 June 1950.

Zemnaia raduga. New York: Chekhov, 1952.

Predskazatel' proshlogo. Moscow, 1967.

Rasskazy. Introduction by O. Mikhailov. Moscow, 1971.

Nostalgiia. Rasskazy. Vospominaniia. Ed. B. Averina. Leningrad: Khudozhestvennaia literatura, 1989. [Introduction by E. Neatrour.]

Iumoristicheskie rasskazy. Edited with an introduction and commentary by D.D. Nikolaev. Moscow, 1990.

In Translation

[A selection of stories.] *Women Writers in Russian Modernism*. Ed. Temira Pachmuss. Urbana: University of Illinois Press, 1978. 261–313.

[Stories]. *A Russian Cultural Revival*. Ed. Temira Pachmuss. Knoxville: University of Tennessee Press, 1981. 106–31.

All About Love. Trans. Darra Goldstein. Ann Arbor, MI: Ardis, 1985.

"The Woman Question" and "Walled Up." *Anthology of Russian Women's Writing*. Ed. Catriona Kelly. Oxford: Oxford University Press, 1994. 261–313.

Secondary Works

Aleksinskii, G. "Ee dobroi i svetloi pamiati (Vospominaniia o N.A. Tèffi)." *Grani* 16 (1952): 131–37.

Amfiteatrov, A. "Iumor posle Chekhova." *Segodnia* 3 (31 January 1931): 2.

Don Aminado. *Nasha malen'kaia zhizn'. Stikhotvoreniia. Politicheskii pamflet. Proza.Vospominaniia.* Moscow: Terra, 1994.

———. *Poezd na tret'em puti*. New York: Chekhov, 1954. 256–67.

Bialik, B.A., et al. *Russkaia literatura konca XIX-nac. XX veka. 1908–1917.* Vol. 3. Moscow: Nauka, 1972. 203.

Bowlt, F., Fleishman, L., and Segal, D. "Problemy izucheniia literatury russkoi èmigratsii pervoi treti XX veka." *Slavica Hierosolymitana*. Vol. 3. Jerusalem: The Magnes Press, Hebrew University, 1978. 75–88.

Chebotarevskaia, A. "Tèffi. I stalo tak . . . *Iumoristicheskie rasskazy*." *Novaia zhizn'* 7 (1912): 255.

Erlich, Victor. *Russian Formalism: History, Doctrine*. The Hague: Mouton, 1969.

Evstigneeva, L.A. *Poèty "Satirikona."* Leningrad: Sovetskii pisatel', 1966.

Fidler, F. "Nadezhda Aleksandrovna Tèffi." *Pervye literaturnye shagi. Avtobiografii sovremennykh russkikh pisatelei*. Moscow: Tipografiia I.D. Sytina, 1911. 202–05.

Haber, Edith. "Nadezhda Teffi." *Russian Literary Triquarterly* 9 (Spring 1974): 454–72.

———. "A Note on Teffi." *Russian Literature and Culture in the West: 1922–1972. TriQuarterly* 28 (Fall 1973): 481–82.

Kelly, Catriona. *An Anthology of Russian Women's Writing*. Oxford: Oxford University Press, 1994.

———, ed. *A History of Russian Women's Writing*. Oxford: Clarendon Press, 1994.

Kovalevskii, P.E. *Zarubezhnaia Rossiia: Istoriia i kul'turno-prosvetitel'naia rabota russkogo zarubezh'ia za polveka 1920–1970*. Paris: Librairie de cinq continents, 1971. 256–57.

Ledkovsky, Marina. "Russian Women Writers in Émigré Literature." *Women Writers in Russian Literature*. Ed. Toby Clyman and Diana Greene. Westport, CT: Greenwood Press, 1994. 249–60.

Neatrour, Elizabeth, B. "Miniatures of Russian Life at Home and in Emigration: The Life and Works of N.A. Tèffi." Ph.D. dissertation, Indiana University, 1973.

———. "Teffi." *Dictionary of Russian Women Writers*. Ed. M. Ledkovsky, C. Rosenthal and M. Zirin. Westport, CT: Greenwood Press, 1994. 642–43.

———. "'Zhizn' smeetsia i plachet . . . ' O Sud'be i tvorchestve Tèffi." Introduction to *Nostal'giia. Rasskazy i vospominaniia*. Ed. B. Averina. Leningrad: Khudozhestvennaia literatura, 1989.

Nemirovich-Danchenko, V.I. *Na kladbishchakh: vospominaniia*. Revel, 1921.

Odoevtseva, Irina. *Na beregakh Seny*. Paris: Presse Libre, 1983.

Pachmuss Temira, ed. and trans. "Nadezhda Teffi (1872–1952)." *A Russian Cultural Revival: A Critical Anthology of Émigré Literature Before 1939*. Knoxville: University of Tennessee Press, 1981. 106–08.

———. "Teffi" and "Émigré Literature." *Handbook of Russian Literature*. Ed. Victor Terrras. New Haven, CT: Yale University Press, 1985. 119-124, 465.

———, ed. and trans. *Women Writers in Russian Modernism*. Urbana: University of Illinois Press, 1978.

Raeff, Marc. *Russia Abroad: A Cultural History of Russian Emigration. 1910–1939*. New York: Oxford University Press, 1990.

Rosenthal, Charlotte. "Achievement and Obscurity: Women's Prose in the Silver Age." *Women Writers in Russian Literature*. Ed. Toby Clyman and Diana Greene. Westport, CT: Greenwood Press, 1994. 160–61.

Sedykh, Andrei. "Tèffi v pis'makh." *Vozdushnye puti, al'manakh.* Vol. 3. Ed. R.N. Grinberg. New York: R.N. Grinberg, 1963. 191–213.

Struve, Gleb. *Russkaia literatura v izgnanii*. New York: Chekhov, 1956.

Zaitsev, B.K. "N.A. Tèffi, *Avantiurnyi roman*. Paris, 1932." *Sovremennye zapiski* 49 (1932): 453.

Zoshchenko, Mikhail. "N. Tèffi. Publikatsiia V.V. Zoshchenko." *Ezhegodnik rukopisnogo otdela Pushkinskogo doma 1972*. Ed. K.D. Muratova. Leningrad: Nauka, 1974. 140.

Marina Tsvetaeva

Marina Tsvetaeva (1892–1941).
Backplate from Pis'ma k A. Teskovoi, Prague, *1969.*

Marina Ivanova Tsvetaeva (1892–1941) is now acknowledged as one of the giants of twentieth-century poetry. But full access to her writings for readers in Russia, along with wide recognition in the West, finally came only as her 1992 centennial approached and the Soviet regime disintegrated. Tsvetaeva herself did nothing to speed that recognition. Never a member of any literary school or movement, she was a prickly, difficult personality, often on the "wrong side" politically, always a defender of underdogs and losing causes. A brilliant innovator in the language and rhythm of Russian poetry, she made giant creative leaps from volume to volume, leaving most of her readers behind. In 1922 she left Russia and lived in exile for seventeen years among a conservative émigré public largely hostile to her revolutionary artistic achievements. In Prague and Paris, as earlier in Russia, she preferred contact with a few understanding readers, usually fellow poets, to the mass reader. She returned to purge-torn Soviet Russia on the eve of World War II to find herself a pariah and her work unpublishable. When she committed suicide in August 1941, her husband, sister and daughter were all imprisoned; her teenaged son died three years later at the front. For fifteen years after her death, hardly a word was published anywhere in the world by or about her.

The Khrushchev thaw allowed Tsvetaeva's daughter Ariadna Efron to return from Siberian exile and begin the preservation and publication of her mother's literary legacy. Tsvetaeva's friends Boris Pasternak and Ilia Ehrenburg wrote of her in their memoirs,[1] bringing her to the attention of a new generation of Russian readers and to the West. Western Slavists began to collect and study the tiny émigré editions of Tsvetaeva's poetry and her many publications scattered among rare, and largely defunct, émigré journals.[2] In 1965 Ariadna Efron published a large collection of her mother's poetry in the prestigious *Biblioteka poèta* (*Poet's Library*) series, including many previously unpublished poems from the poet's archive. Soviet editions of Tsvetaeva's works, at least of those deemed politically acceptable, began to appear with increasing frequency. Letters, memoirs, and other biographical materials emerged. By the 1980s Tsvetaeva's high-energy poetry and tragic biography had made her practically a cult figure among poetry lovers in Russia, some of whom dubbed themselves "Marinisty." The central Moscow tourist bureau introduced bus excursions to "Tsvetaeva places" around Moscow, and work began to save the house where she lived before her emigration and turn it into a Tsvetaeva museum.[3] Tsvetaeva's 1992 centennial was commemorated by scholarly conferences in Moscow, the United States,[4] Paris and Prague. In Moscow, a large exhibition about her life and work was mounted in the central hall of the Pushkin Museum of Fine Arts, the museum her father had founded,[5] and the Tsvetaeva museum on Pisemskii Street was opened with great ceremony. There are now smaller Tsvetaeva museums in Tarusa, where the Tsvetaev family spent summers and where Ariadna Efron is buried; in Alexandrov, where Tsvetaeva and her sister lived in the summer of 1916; in the Bolshevo dacha where Sergei and Ariadna Efron were arrested in 1939; and in Tsvetaeva's father's native town of Talitsy, Ivanovo province. The English-language publication of Viktoria Schweitzer's biography[6] finally made Tsvetaeva's name familiar to the nonspecialist Western reader; a lengthy article about her life and poetry even appeared in the *New Yorker.*[7] Tsvetaeva has attracted the attention of such major Western critics as Hélène Cixous and Susan Sontag.[8] A new generation of Western Slavists has used feminist approaches to ask fresh questions about her work; Russian scholars have so far concentrated largely on textual and biographical issues. Tsvetaeva's work has entered the canon of undergraduate courses in Russian literature, but much remains to be done. When Ariadna Efron died in 1975, she left her mother's archive to the Central State Archive of Literature and Art (TsGALI, now RGALI), but closed it to researchers for twenty-five years. As the year 2000 approaches, the opening of the archive and projected publication of Tsvetaeva's working notebooks and letters promises a third wave of Tsvetaeva scholarship and new glimpses into the poet's creative workshop.

Marina Ivanovna Tsvetaeva was born in Moscow in September 1892. Her father, the son of a poor priest from central Russia, had risen to become a professor of classics at Moscow University. His life's greatest accomplishment was the founding and construction of the Alexander III Museum (now the Pushkin Museum of Fine Arts), Moscow's major museum of West European art. As a widower in his forties with two small children, Tsvetaev married Maria Mein, who gave him two more children, Marina and Anastasia (Asia, 1894–1993). Mein agreed to marry the aging professor and give up a promising career as a pianist to please her father, who disapproved of the man she really loved. Tsvetaeva's writing gives multifaceted and sometimes contradictory views of her complicated family heritage, first in the "happy childhood" that fills her first two books of poetry, then in the psychological investigations of her own genesis as a poet in her pathbreaking autobiographical prose of the 1930s.[9]

Maria Mein devoted her energy, talent and passion to her daughters' artistic and moral education. She poured her soul into Marina's piano lessons, hoping her daughter would have the musical career she herself gave up. This was not to be, but her mother's musical gift lived on in the melodies, complex rhythms and passion of Tsvetaeva's poetry. Tsvetaeva thanked her father for her dedication to her craft and her dogged determination to write nearly every day, sometimes under appalling conditions: she ultimately produced a huge body of poetry, prose and letters.[10] From 1903 to 1905 Marina and Asia lived and studied in Italy, Switzerland and Germany as their mother vainly sought a cure from tuberculosis. At her death in 1906, she left her daughters a considerable inheritance that, until it was lost in the Bolshevik revolution, gave them a degree of independence unusual for young girls of the time. The teenaged Marina and Asia were largely unsupervised: the grandfatherly Tsvetaev drowned his grief in the work of his museum. Marina was expelled from two high schools and gave up the piano for poetry.

When she was eighteen, Tsvetaeva had a collection of her early poems, titled *Evening Album* (1910), privately printed. A second collection, *Magic Lantern*, appeared in 1912. Many of the poems in these first two books describe the world of Tsvetaeva's lost childhood, and attempt to recapture and fix the memory of her mother. The debut volume unexpectedly attracted favorable reviews by major poets, including Briusov and Gumilev and introduced Tsvetaeva to the poet, critic and painter Maksimilian Voloshin. Voloshin became her literary godfather, introducing her to his unconventional circle in Koktebel', in the Crimea, where he and his formidable mother ran an informal boardinghouse for writers and artists. There, in May 1911, Tsvetaeva met seventeen-year-old Sergei Efron, whom she married in January 1912. Their daughter Ariadna was born later that year, and motherhood and domesticity temporarily eclipsed poetry in Tsvetaeva's life. In 1913 the young family went back to live in the Crimea as Efron sought a cure for the tuberculosis that had claimed Tsvetaeva's mother. Tsvetaeva returned to poetry in a new key, highly romantic, glorifying her delicate, beautiful young husband, their precocious child and herself.

The Koktebel' circle, however, brought Tsvetaeva other lovers: in 1914, she began an intense and open affair with the lesbian poet Sofiia Parnok that lasted for more than a year. Efron volunteered as a medic on a hospital train and late in the war became a junior officer in the Russian army. Tsvetaeva's poems to Parnok, collected in the cycle "The Girlfriend" ("Podruga"), are the bridge from Tsvetaeva's early verse to the mature poetic voice that emerged in her lyric diary of the year 1916, *Mileposts I* (*Versty,* published 1922). This collection, with its brilliant cycles addressed to Osip Mandel'shtam, Anna Akhmatova and Aleksandr Blok, is Tsvetaeva's self-proclamation that she has taken her rightful place among her generation's great chorus of poetic voices. Mandel'shtam met her in Koktebel' in the summer of 1915 and courted her unsuccessfully in the early months of 1916. The infatuation of poet for poet left a legacy of magnificent lyrics by both and introduced the theme of Moscow's history and architecture to the quintessential Petersburg poet Mandel'shtam. In 1915–1916 Tsvetaeva published some new work in a St. Petersburg literary journal, but the reading public was largely unaware she had grown into a major poet. She never published the poems of 1913–1915 (known as "Juvenilia") as a separate book, at first because of the intimate nature of the Parnok poems, later because of the war and revolution which changed her life, and Russia, almost beyond recognition.

In April 1917 Tsvetaeva gave birth to her second daughter, Irina. Sickly from birth and born into a world of chaos, the child did not live to her third birthday. She died of starvation in an orphanage where Tsvetaeva had placed her because she had no means to feed her; Ariadna nearly died of malaria. After the Bolshevik seizure of power, Sergei Efron fled to the Crimea, where he joined the White Army and fought through the civil war. Tsvetaeva planned to join him but was trapped in Moscow with the two children. She lived by selling off the possessions in their large apartment and by the charity of friends. She refused to accept the Bolshevik seizure of power and was incapable of adapting to the new Soviet reality. Publicly, and defiantly, she read her poems in praise of the White Army. Yet these first years after the revolution were a time of intense creativity and artistic growth, of new friendships with a circle of young acting students. She began to write plays in verse, while her numerous lyrics, characteristically brief in these years, continued to record the intensity of her emotional life and her many infatuations. She selected poems from 1917–1920 for her slim volume *Mileposts,* but many others remained unpublished in her notebooks. Her poems about the revolution and civil war were unpublishable in Soviet Russia; she published some after her emigration, but the entire collection (*The Swans' Encampment* or *Demesne of the Swans* [*Lebedinyi Stan*]) was first published in Munich in 1957. A series of aphoristic diary observations ("October on the Train," "Attic Life," "On Gratitude") were her first works in prose; she published them after her emigration, as she did the plays she had written for her young actor friends.[11] Her daughter Ariadna (Alia) was her constant companion and confidante. At six, she could recite many of her mother's poems by heart, and she was writing poems herself: Tsvetaeva included a selection of them in her collection *Psyche. Romanticism* (*Psikheia. Romantika,* 1923).

"On a Red Steed" ("Na krasnom kone,"1920) is a complex allegory of the poet's sacrifice of life for her art. This was Tsvetaeva's first mature *poèma* (long poem), a genre that became increasingly important for her in the 1920s. Many critics feel her *poèmy* are her best and most important works. Several of those from the early 1920s (*Tsar-Maiden*, "The Swain," "Sidestreets") are based on folklore motifs. In them, Tsvetaeva continued to explore the folk diction first heard in her 1916 poems. In the poems of *Craft* (*Remeslo,* written 1920–1921 and published 1923), she broadened her focus to the fate of Russia as a whole, drawing parallels between the civil war and earlier calamities in Russia's past. Her language became increasingly dense and compressed. In the eloquent cycle

"Separation" ("Razluka," 1921) she cries out to her absent husband, not knowing whether he is still alive. As she was writing the cycle, she learned that Efron had been evacuated to Constantinople with the remnants of the White Army and was headed for Prague, where Russian émigrés received scholarships to finish educations interrupted by war and revolution.

In May 1922, Tsvetaeva and Alia left to join Sergei in Berlin. The Berlin summer of 1922 was an intense period of publication, creativity and new literary friendships. Two small books, *Poems to Blok* (*Stikhi k Bloku,* 1922) and *Separation* (published in 1922) had appeared there even before she arrived. *Craft* and *Psyche. Romanticism* were published in 1923. In revolutionary Moscow, she had a nodding acquaintance with Boris Pasternak and his poems but had not paid him much attention. A few days after her arrival in Berlin, she read his newly published *My Sister, Life* and was intoxicated by these poems of 1917. At roughly the same time, in Moscow, Pasternak discovered her slim volume *Mileposts I* and was "immediately overcome by the immense lyrical power of her poetic form."[12] Tsvetaeva wrote her first literary essay, "A Downpour of Light," in ecstatic response, beginning a conversation with Pasternak in poetry and letters that would be the major emotional involvement of her emigration. There was a brief romance with her Berlin publisher, Abraham Vishniak, which resulted in letters she later tried to publish in French (*Florentine Nights*).

From September 1922 through the spring of 1925, Tsvetaeva lived with her family in a series of villages around Prague, and briefly in the city itself. She kept house, took long walks in the forested hills and wrote the poems of *After Russia* (*Posle Rossii,* 1928), the last collection published during her lifetime. The lyrics and *poèmy* of this Prague period are her most difficult, elliptical and allusive, yet in many ways most accomplished, verse. Life was materially only a bit easier than in Moscow, and she lived largely in isolation, even from the Czechs around her, although the Czech government provided her a modest stipend as a Russian writer. She began an epistolary romance with her "poetic brother" Pasternak, dedicating to him the long poem *The Swain* (*Molodets*, 1924), the cycle "Wires" ("Provoda," 1923) and several other lyrics. There was a brief flood of letters and poems to Aleksandr Bachrach, a young critic who had praised her books. A passionate and very real love affair with Efron's fellow student Konstantin Rodzevich was transmuted into the "Poem of the Mountain" and the "Poem of the End"—here Tsvetaeva's poetry broke new ground in its emotional intensity and rhythmic power. In February 1925 she gave birth to her third child, a son whom she named Georgii but always called "Mur."

Later that year, she moved to Paris, the new center of Russian émigré life, to try to reenter the literary world and find publishers for her work, which had now become the family's main support. Although she was at first welcomed and even lionized, attendance at her benefit readings soon grew thin. We can follow her life in France, in the low-rent outskirts of Paris, through her letters to the women who supported her both emotionally and financially: Anna Teskova, a Czech translator from Russian; Vera Bunina, wife of the wealthy émigré writer Ivan Bunin; Salomea Andronikova-Halpern, the Petersburg beauty who had inspired a famous poem of Mandel'shtam's; Raissa Lomonosova, wife of a Russian railroad engineer; and Ariadna Berg. Along with her letters from Czechoslovakia to her former neighbor Ol'ga Kolbasina-Chernova, these letters to women friends give us a unique view of a proud woman of genius trying to sustain both her writing and her family under increasingly difficult conditions.

During the summer of 1926, which she spent at the French seacoast with her two children, Tsvetaeva entered into an emotionally intense exchange of letters and poems with the great German poet Rainer Maria Rilke, to whom Pasternak had provided an introduction.[13] The relationship temporarily eclipsed that with Pasternak; together and separately, Pasternak and Rilke became the addressees of several of Tsvetaeva's *poèmy* ("From the Sea," "An Attempt at a Room," "A New-Year's Letter"). But during the years in France, prose gradually became Tsvetaeva's primary genre: émigré journals paid more for it, and it provided material for her benefit readings. The deaths of her poetic contemporaries inspired retrospectives of Briusov ("A Hero of Labor"), Belyi ("A Captive Spirit"), Voloshin ("A Living Thing About a Living Man") and Mayakovsky ("Epic and Lyric of Contemporary Russia"). There were also philosophical essays on the poet and her craft ("The Poet on Criticism," "Art in the Light of Conscience," "The Poet and Time"). The death of her half-brother Andrei in Moscow triggered a series of autobiographical investigations that truly opened a new path for Russian prose ("Mother and Music," "The Devil," "Father and His Museum," "The House at Old Pimen," "Mother's Tale," "My Pushkin").

But she continued to write poetry, and occasionally to publish it. The poems she wrote after 1925 form a final book of eloquent simplicity, moving beyond the hermetic concentration of *Craft* and *After Russia*. There are cycles of poems to the young poets Nikolai Gronskii and Anatolii Shteiger, and much-anthologized poems about the loneliness and isolation of emigration. Life in France grew increasingly difficult, especially in the depression of the 1930s. Sergei, without Tsvetaeva's knowledge (it was perhaps a willed ignorance) had become a Soviet agent. In March 1937 Ariadna, full of pro-Soviet optimism, returned to Moscow. Later that year Sergei, implicated in a political murder in Switzerland, fled there, too. Much of Tsvetaeva's time in 1937 and 1938 was spent sorting her archive and copying over her notebooks in preparation for the return to the Soviet Union she knew was inevitable. The Nazi takeover of her beloved Czechoslovakia inspired the magnificent rhetoric of the "Poems to Bohemia," testimony that her poetic gift, despite her own fears, was undiminished.

In June 1939, isolated and forgotten by the émigré community, with her teenage son urging return and with the clouds of war gathering, but with a clear knowledge of the fateful step she was taking, Tsvetaeva returned to the Soviet Union. Most of the literary community, traumatized by the purges of 1937–1939, dared have nothing to do with this returned émigré, the wife of a failed Soviet agent. For the first few months, the reunited family lived in isolation in Bolshevo, outside Moscow, in a KGB-owned dacha. The atmosphere of impending doom was palpable. In August 1939 Ariadna was arrested; in October, Sergei. Tsvetaeva and Mur found refuge with Sergei's sisters, sharing cramped space in their Moscow apartment. With Pasternak's help, she got some translation work and was able to rent a room near the writer's sanatorium in Golitsino, outside Moscow. In 1940 she finally met Akhmatova; she went to ask her advice about intervening with the authorities on behalf of Sergei and Alia. Tsvetaeva even wrote a few new poems, some addressed to the poet Arsenii Tarkovsky, father of the filmmaker Andrei Tarkovsky. When the war with Germany began in June 1941, she managed to get a place on a boat evacuating writers from Moscow. She found herself in the small town of Elabuga, near Chistopol, where the Writers' Union members were evacuated. She tried to find work in Chistopol but was promised only a possible job as a dishwasher in the writers' cafeteria. In despair, she returned to Elabuga, where she hanged herself at the end of August 1941. The story of Tsvetaeva's last days has been told by Viktoria Schweitzer and by Lidiia Chukovskaia,[14] who met her in Chistopol days before her suicide. Sergei was executed in prison as Russian forces retreated from Oreol in October 1941; Georgii perished at the front in 1944.

Tsvetaeva once told Voloshin that "there are at least seven poets in me." It is Tsvetaeva's genius that she did indeed possess a whole chorus of voices—a result, perhaps, of her impeccable musical ear—but that all of them are recognizably her own. The most important thing about Tsvetaeva's writing is its origin in the speaking voice, and its intense relationship to her reader/addressee, real or imagined. That addressee was vital to Tsvetaeva's poetics—an unusual number of her poems are openly or privately addressed or dedicated to a specific individual. Poems often served as letters, whether delivered or not, much as they did for

Emily Dickinson. Read chronologically, as Tsvetaeva wanted them to be, her poems constitute a lyric diary, the record of an emotional life sometimes more imagined than real.

The language in which she wrote posed a particular problem for Tsvetaeva. Russian, like most Slavic languages, forces the speaker to identify his or her gender in past tense verb forms and often in adjectival and pronominal endings. When Tsvetaeva began writing at the beginning of the twentieth century, the Russian poetic voice, at least as she knew it, was overwhelmingly male. Gippius and other women poets of the symbolist movement often disguised their gender by using the masculine persona. Tsvetaeva never denied her gender—but she sought to make the gender of her voice irrelevant. In her earliest books, Tsvetaeva used several strategies to avoid grammatical forms that would mark her voice as female.[15] She described the world of the nursery in a third-person narration; she linked herself with her sister Asia as the plural and nongendered "we"; she addressed her poems to a "you" or clothed her lyric voice in a series of literary masks. While Akhmatova, whose poems are often mininarratives, frequently uses a past tense feminine verb early in a poem to underline the femininity of the lyric "I," Tsvetaeva prefers the more dynamic present and future tenses, or the imperative, which allow her to leave her gender unspecified.

Akhmatova and Tsvetaeva made their debut in print in the same year, 1910, a year that saw the emergence of a new wave of women poets writing in Russian. But Akhmatova's fame came more easily, particularly after the publication of *Rosary* (1914). Tsvetaeva admired Akhmatova the poet and idolized Akhmatova the woman, but she always remained for Tsvetaeva a rival and a touchstone for comparison, although it is hard to imagine two poetic voices more different. While Akhmatova's poems are characterized by their emotional detachment, Tsvetaeva's, on the contrary, are always emotionally intimate, sometimes too much so for some readers. "Marina often begins a poem on high C," Akhmatova once remarked.[16] The Symbolist poet and critic Valerii Briusov noted this "eerie intimacy" in reviewing *Evening Album*: "At moments you feel awkward, as if you have indiscreetly gazed through a half-open window into someone else's apartment and seen a scene not for the eyes of outsiders."[17] This relentless intimacy in the exploration of her own emotions reaches its apogee in the "Poem of the End." She proudly proclaimed her infatuations in her lyrics, be they for her young husband, for Sofiia Parnok, or, at a distance, for Akhmatova, Blok, Mandel'shtam or Pasternak.

Even in her first two collections, Tsvetaeva mastered the resources of traditional Russian versification and soon began to explore new possibilities. Her most original contribution was the development of the *logaed*, a line composed of a regular combination of binary and ternary feet, which, in effect, makes the line, rather than the foot, the basic metrical unit of the poem. She explored the possibilities of masculine rhyme, of elliptical, sometimes verbless syntax and of the dash. The dash is particularly characteristic of Tsvetaeva's syntax (as it was, again, for Dickinson's).[18] This "pause in the middle of the line" often seems to anticipate a response from her addressee. It also leaves freedom (sometimes almost too much) for the reader to interpret the juxtapositions she presents in her increasingly elliptical and compact verse.[19]

Jane A. Taubman

A good deal of Tsvetaeva's poetry, and most of her prose, has been translated into English, with varying degrees of success (see bibliography of translations below). Three important verse collections have been translated in full: The Swans' Encampment *(1917–1920) as* The Demesne of the Swans, *by Robin Kemball,* Mileposts *(1917–1920) as* Miles *by Mary Jane White, and* After Russia *(1922–1925) by Michael Naydan. The selections below concentrate on previously untranslated poems, largely from the earlier and later periods. References to the original texts are to the five-volume Slavica edition (see bibliography below). It also includes examples of Tsvetaeva's letters to women friends. With the exception of Tsvetaeva's correspondence with Pasternak and Rilke, very few of her letters are as yet available in English. Translations of Tsvetaeva's poetry are by Sibelan Forrester (SF) and Jane Taubman (JT); the letters were translated by Catherine Ciepiela.*

Mama Reading a Book

A muffled whisper . . . the flash of a dagger . . .
—"Mama, build me a house out of blocks!"
Mama, agitated, clasped to her heart
The little volume.

The count's eyes blazed with anger:
"I am here, princess, by the grace of fate!"
—"Mama, can a giraffe drown in the ocean?"
Mama's soul is far away!

—"Mama, look: there's a cobweb in the cutlet!"
In the childish voice there's reproach and a threat.
Mama's awakened from her fantasies: children—
Are bitter prose!

1909/1910 (I, 67) JT

To V. Ia. Briusov

I forgot that your heart is only a night light—
Not a star! I forgot
That your poetry comes from books
And your criticism from envy. Old prematurely,
For a moment you again seemed to me
A great poet. . . .

1912 (I, 252) JT

To S[ergei] E[fron]

I wear his ring defiantly!
—Yes, his wife in Eternity, not on paper.
His too-narrow face
Is like a rapier.

His mouth is silent, corners drawn,
His brows excruciatingly magnificent.
In his face the tragic confluence
Of two ancient bloods.

He's slender with the first slenderness of branches.
His eyes are marvelously useless!—
Beneath the wings of wide-open brows—
Two abysses.

In his person, I am faithful to chivalry.
—To all of you who lived and died without fear!
It is such as you—in fateful times—
Who write stanzas—and go to the block!

Koktebel', 3 June 1914 (I, 166) JT

To Alia

You will be innocent, slim,
Charming—and a stranger to all.
A captivating amazon,
An impetuous miss.

And you'll wear your braids, perhaps,
Like a helmet.
You'll be the queen of the ball—
And of all youthful poems.

And many, my queen,
Will be pierced by your mocking blade,
And all that I only dream about,
Will be at your feet.

Everything will obey you,
Everyone hushed in your presence.
You'll be like me—indisputably—
And you'll write better poems. . . .

But will you—Who knows?—
Clutch your temples in mortal despair,
As your young mother
Clutches them right now.

5 June 1913 (I, 166–167) JT

To Grandmother

An oblong and firm oval,
The dark dress's bell-shapes . . .
Youthful grandmother! Who kissed
Your arrogant lips?

Hands that in the halls of a palace
Played Chopin waltzes . . .

Along the sides of the icy face—
Locks in the form of a spiral.

A dark, direct and demanding gaze.
A gaze ready for defense.
Youthful women don't gaze like that.
Youthful grandmother—who are you?

How many possibilities did you carry away—
And how many—impossibilities?—
To the insatiable glutton, the earth,
Twenty-year-old Polish woman!

The day was innocent, the wind was fresh.
Dark stars were extinguished.
Grandmother! This cruel rebellion in my heart—
Is it not from you? . . .

4 September 1914 (I, 176) SF

The Girl Friend (To Sofiia Parnok)

You're happy? You don't say! Hardly!
But better—why not?
It seems you've kissed too many,
That's why you're sad.

In you I see all the heroines
Of Shakespeare's tragedies.
No one has saved you,
Young tragic lady!

You're so tired of repeating
The recitative of love!
The iron rim on your bloodless hand—
Is eloquent!

I love you.—Sin hangs over you
Like a storm cloud—
Because you're sarcastic and sharp
And better than the others,

Because we—our lives—diverge
In the dusk of roads,
For your inspired temptations
And dark fate,

Because to you, my steep-browed demon,
I'll say "Forgive!"
Because, even bursting a gut above your grave!—
You can't be saved.

For this frisson, because—is it really
All a dream?—
For that ironic fascination
That you're—not *he*.

16 October 1914 (I, 176–77) JT

To Anna Akhmatova

A slender, un-Russian waist—
Above the folios.
A shawl from Turkish lands
Fell, like a mantle.

You could be drawn
With one broken black line.
Coldness in gaiety, heat—
In your despondency.

All of your life is a fever,
And how will it culminate?
The clouded—dark—brow
Of a young demon.

To lure astray every earthly creature
Is a trifle for you!
And an unarmed verse
Aims at our heart.

At a drowsy morning hour,
—Quarter past four, I think—
I fell in love with you,
Anna Akhmatova.

11 February 1915 (I, 191) JT

Like burning, sharp-whetted flattery
Under the Roman sky, on a night veranda,
Like a fatal goblet within a garland of roses
—There are two such magic words.

And the dead arise as if by command,
And God is silent—it's the airy news
Of a pagan—the pagan revenge:
Ars amandi that I have not read!

Blue of the sky and blue of beloved eyes
Blind my eyes. Poet, don't be offended
That I have no time for Latin!

Do female lovers read, Ovid?
—Did yours read you?—Don't reject
The heiress of your own heroines!

19 September 1915 (1988, I, 54–55) SF

They lie here, written in haste,
Heavy with bitterness and languor.
Between love and love are crucified
My moment, my hour, my day, my year, my age.

And I hear that somewhere in the world there's thunder.
That Amazons' spears shine anew.
—But I won't restrain my pen!—Two roses
Have sucked the blood out of my heart.

20 December 1915 (I, 197) SF

From Don Juan

After so many roses, cities and toasts—
Ah, are you really not too tired
To love me? You're all but a shell,
I'm all but a shade.

And why should I know that you had
To cry out to the heavenly powers?
And why would I want to know that my hair
Smelled of the Nile?

No, better *I'll* tell you a fairy tale:
It was January then.
Someone threw a rose. A masked monk
Carried a lantern.

Someone's drunken voice begged and raged
By the cathedral walls.
At that very hour Don Juan of Castile
Would meet with—Carmen.

22 February 1917 (II, 194) SF

"Marina" you inscribed on your dagger—
As you stood to defend your homeland.
I was the first and only one
In your magnificent life.

I remember the night and the radiant visage
In the hell of a transport wagon.
I loose my hair to the wind
And keep your shoulder-straps in my casket.

18 January 1918 (II, 59) JT

God—is just
In the rotting of grass,
The drying of rivers,
The howling of cripples,

In thief and serpent,
Slaughter and hunger,
Shame and stench,
Thunder and hail.

In the trampled Word.
The cursed year.
The captive tsar.
The people uprisen.
(NB! Obviously, it should be read: God is *nonetheless* just, *just—despite*).

29 April 1918 (II, 72) JT

From The Play-Actor

Am I kissing hair—or air?
Eyelids—or wafting wind above them?
Lips—or a sigh beneath my own lips?
I won't find out and I won't break the spell.

I know only: this brief little cloud
Of a sigh will pause like a whole blessed epoch—
Like a kingly epos
Stringed and strange.

Friend! On the earth all passes—alleluia!
You and love—and nothing will be resurrected.
But my dark song will preserve—
Voice and hair: strings and streams.

9 November 1918 (II, 247) SF

From The Play-Actor

Perishable lips and perishable hands
Have blindly ruined my eternity.
In separation from my eternal Soul—
I sing of perishable lips and hands.

The roar of divine eternity—dulls.
Only sometimes, in the hour before dawn—
From the dark sky—a mysterious voice:
"Woman! Remember your immortal soul!"

End of December, 1918 (II, 245) SF

My attic palace, my palace attic!
Come on up. A mountain of manuscripts . . .
So. "Give me your hand! Keep right,"

There's a puddle from the leaky roof.

Now—seat yourself on a trunk,
And admire the Flanders a spider has woven for me.
Don't heed those idle rumors,
That woman can do without lace!

Well, then, a catalogue of our attic wonders:
Here we are visited by angel and demon,
And by him who is higher than both.
It's not far, after all, from heaven—to our roof!

My children—two attic princelings,
With my jolly muse, will show you my empyrean—
While I cook you up
A phantom dinner.

"And what will happen when you run out of wood?"
"Wood? But a poet always has
A stock of—flaming—words!
This year is no danger to us. . . ."

For centuries poets have eaten stale crusts,
And what is Red Moscow to us?
Just look—from one end to the other—
Our Moscow is noble sky-blue!

And if even a poet is too tired out
By this plague-stricken Moscow '19,
So what—we'll live without bread!
It's not far, after all, from our roof—to heaven.

1919 (II, 263) JT

Do I love you?
I fall into thought.
My eyes get very big.

In the woods—a river,
In curls—a hand
—A stubborn one—gets tangled.

Love—It's old hat.
I bite my pen.
It's dark, and I'm too lazy to light the candle.

A tale must exist!
That's why, after all,
You're born into the world as a poet!

I gave for an hour,
Took it right back.
(The pen already flies in the darkness!)

So. We'll cope.
An equal sign
Between love—and God be with you.

What's passion?—Old hat.
There's passion!—My pen!
—Suddenly—a rose grove—
Comes into the house!

There are aromas—
Like commandments . . .
I drop my brow onto my hands.

22 March (Palm Sunday) 1920 (II, 275) SF

To S[ergei] E[fron]

I've grown no prettier in years of separation!
You won't be angry at my coarse hands,
Grasping for bread and salt?
—The hard-earned callous of comradeship!

Oh, love can't be spruced up for reunion.
Don't be angry at my common speech—
I'd advise you not to scorn it:
Otherwise—the chronicle's firearm speech.

Disillusioned? Don't be afraid to admit it!
Otherwise—a spirit purged of friendships and good will.
Into the muddle of anchors and hopes
The incorrigible breach of *insight*!

10 January 1922 (II, 152) JT

To Boris Pasternak

Give my regards to the Russian rye,
To the wheat fields where a peasant woman could hide.
Friend! There are rains beyond my window,
Troubles and caprices on my heart. . . .

You—as free in the melody of rains and troubles
As was Homer in hexameter,
Give me your hand—to all *that* world!
Here—mine are both occupied.

7 May 1925 (III, 126) JT

Quiet, praise!
Don't slam the door,
Glory!
    The corner
Of a table—and an elbow.

Commotion, stop!
Heart, calm down!
Elbow—and brow.
Elbow—and thought.

Youth—is for loving,
Old age—to warm yourself:
No time—to *be,*
Nowhere—to go.

Even a pigsty—
Only—alone!
Faucets—drip,
Chairs—scrape,

Mouths speak:
Mumble-mouthed
They thank me
"For beauty."

If only you knew,
Those close and far,
How sorry I am
For my own head—

As for God in the Tatar horde!
The steppe—a jail cell—
Paradise—that's where
They *don't* talk!

Skirt-chaser—pig—
Or shopkeeper—details!
He'll be my god—
Who gives me

—Don't waste time!
My days are numbered!—
For silence—
Four walls.

26 January 1926 (III, 135) JT

Conversation with Genius

The laurels of praise
Are like clods—to the brow.
"I can't sing!"
"You will!"

"The sound has vanished,
Like milk from my breast!
(Switch the baby over
To oat-flour gruel!)

It's empty. I'm dry.
In full springtime—
I sense the noose!"
"An old song!

Quit it, stop fooling!"
"Better for me—
To break stone from now on!"
"So sing right now!"

"What am I, a bullfinch
To sing all the livelong
day?"
"Don't be *able,*
birdie, but sing!

To spite the enemy!"
"And if I can't put
Two lines together?"
"Who ever—could?!"

"It's torture!" "Endure!"
"My throat's a mown meadow!"
"Wheeze:
That too is a sound!"

"This is lions' business,
Not women's." "*Child's play*:
Even disembowelled—
Orpheus sang!"

"And so to the grave?"
"And from the grave, too."
"I can't *sing*!"
"Sing of *that*!"

Medon, 4 June 1928 (III, 138) SF/JT

He's gone—I don't eat:
Empty—the taste of bread
All—is chalk
Wherever I reach

. . . He was my bread,
And my snow.
Now snow's not white,
And bread's not sweet.

23 January 1940 (III, 211) JT

—"Enough! You're too old—
For *this* fire!"
    —"Love is older than I!"
—"A mountain of fifty
Januaries!"
    —"Love's older still:
Old as a horsetail, old as a dragon,
Older than Livonian ambers,
Older than all the ghost
Ships!—than stones, older than seas. . . ."

But the pain that's in my breast
Is older than love, older than love.

23 January 1940 (III, 212) SF

To Arsenii Tarkovsky

"I set the table for six . . ."
I keep repeating the first line
And keep correcting a word:
—"I set the table for six. . . ."
You forgot one—the seventh.

It's somber for the six of you.
Rivulets rain down your faces . . .
How could you, at such a table,
Forget her—the seventh. . . .

It's somber for your guests,
The crystal decanter sits idle.
It's sad for them, you're sad yourself.
Saddest of all—is the uninvited.

It's somber and gloomy.
Ah! You're not eating or drinking.
—How could you forget the number?
How could you miscount the guests?

How could you, dare you, not understand
That six (two brothers, you yourself—
Your wife, your parents both)
Is seven—since I'm on the earth!

You set the table for six,
But the world doesn't end with six.
Rather than a scarecrow among the living—
I want to be a ghost—among your kin,

(My kin) . . .
Timid, as a thief,
Oh—not touching a *soul*!
I'll sit at the unset place
The uninvited seventh.

There!—I've tipped over a glass!
And all that was thirsting to spill out—
All the salt from my eyes, all the blood from my wounds—
From the tablecloth—onto the floorboards.

And—there is no grave! No—separation!
The table's freed of its spell, the house awakened.
Like death—to a wedding feast,
I'm life—come to sit at your supper.

. . . I'm no one: not brother, nor son, nor husband,
Nor friend—and still I reproach you:
—Setting the table for six—*souls*
You didn't put me at the corner.

6 March 1941 (III, 212–213) JT

A Letter to America

Several of Tsvetaeva's correspondents were also her benefactors. Raisa Lomonosova, the wife of a prominent engineer, was a patron of the arts who emigrated from Russia in 1927. She discovered Tsvetaeva through Boris Pasternak, who, knowing Tsvetaeva's straitened circumstances, often pleaded for aid on her behalf. Tsvetaeva and Lomonosova developed an epistolary friendship that lasted for three years (1928–1931). In the following letter, she writes from Paris to Lomonosova in California.

Meudon (S. et O.)
2, Avenue Jeanne d'Arc
Feb. 1, 1930

Dear Raisa Nikolaevna!

You live in a country I have always feared. Two terrors: on the horizontal plane—terror of its distance from all other countries; and on the vertical plane—terror of its skyscrapers. My letter will cross the ocean for an eternity and then climb—for a second eternity—to the one-hundred-and-fortieth floor. It will not make it; or, it will be out of date by the time it does. And will no longer be mine.

That's the reason for it, that is, for my ugly silence after your marvelous letter, strong as a voice, along with your gift. There's a friend I have in Kharbin. I think about him all the time and write to him never. It's a feeling that from, or at, such a distance everything is already heard, seen, known—as it is in the afterworld—and that therefore it's impossible to write, that it's unnecessary. For such distances there is only verse. Or dreams.

You don't see it that way because you live there and *there* for you is "here," but if you were to spend just *one hour* with me, at will, alone, then you'd immediately understand me, since I consist entirely of such feelings, fears, behavior. Also, I know I'll never go to America. Never mind the visas (visas are nonsense!)—the sturdier, better-built and more dependable the steamship, the more terrified I am. My conviction, i.e., the conviction of my fear (of WATER) would cause a crash—or whatever it's called at sea. For the sake of one unbeliever (Sodom in reverse!) the entire ship would go down.

I don't know a more continental person. I like rivers: they're on the same continent as I am. At the beach—the most harmless, even domestic beach ("plage de famille," as they say in the guidebooks)—I pine away; I don't know what to do with myself. I've been to the shore in France twice so far, and each time by evening of the first day: "This isn't it!" No—this is it, that very sea, that first childhood sea of Genoa after Pushkin's "Farewell, free element!": *disenchantment*. After the first time, it's ordinary. How many times I've tried to love it. Like love.

But my whole family adores it: Mur for the sand, Alia for the freedom (from housework and, perhaps, a little, from me), Serezha (my "husband," which sounds just as strange as it would sound applied to Pasternak, an alien word, but I use it to avoid confusion) for his early youth: Crimea, the Caucasus and a second Crimea, in 1919–1920. I alone, like a white wolf—though browned by a suntan—don't know what to do on that sand, with that sand, in that sand. I *cannot* lie out and I'm afraid to swim. I like smooth water and rugged land, *not* the other way around.

Those who travel to America—for a set, limited time—and who *come back* seem to me wondrous beings, creatures from Mars or even farther. . . .

From Tsvetaeva's Letters to Anna Teskova

No. 18

Paris, 7 December 1925

Dear Anna Antonovna,

I found out from S. Ia.'s letter that you still haven't gotten anything from us. Alia and I wrote as soon as we arrived, i.e., the next day, with details about our trip—sights, emotions, fellow passengers, conversations. About our last Czechoslovakia, our brief Germany, our first France. Everything.

While waiting for your answer we got settled in and then, without a break, I finished the last two cantos of "The Pied Piper" by the deadline (for *Russia's Will*). I haven't made you a copy, not for lack of desire but for *total* lack of time: I've been in Paris for five weeks and still haven't seen Notre Dame!

Until the 4th (today's the 7th) I was writing and rewriting the poem. Everything else is the same as it was in Vshenory[1]: cooking Mur's kasha, dressing and undressing him, taking him for walks, giving him baths; seeing people, most of whom I could do without; and making *fruitless* efforts to arrange my reading. (To rent a hall it's 600 francs and a third of the ticket sales. There are some for free, private ones, but they can't be had. So three refusals already.) Time flies.

The neighborhood we're living in is horrible, straight out of a trashy novel like *London Slums*. An abandoned canal, the sky blocked out by chimneys, all soot and rumbling (heavy trucks). There's nowhere to walk and not a tree in sight. There's a park, but it's a forty-minute walk, which you can't do in the cold. So we stroll—along a rotting canal.

Gas (for the stove) costs 200 francs a month.

As you see, there are few joys . . .

Perhaps it would be possible to get from Mrs. Iurchinova some sort of *dark* dress for me, *for the reading*. I don't go out because I have nothing to wear and no money to buy anything. Perhaps since she's wealthy she can spare a dress, one she doesn't wear anymore. We could have it altered here. If you find it possible to ask—please do. I've been invited to a number of places, but I can't make an appearance without a silk dress, stockings and patent leather shoes (the local "uniforme"). So I sit at home, accused by all of being a snob. Don't tell S. Ia. that I'm asking this favor—tell him I have everything I need. Give him the dress, if you can get one, and just say "So-and-so sends this to Marina." . . .

No. 31

Meudon (S. et O)
2, Avenue Jeanne d'Arc
Third day of Easter, 1927
Happy Easter, dear Anna Antonovna!

My last letter to you must have disappeared, I wrote as soon as we moved into a new apartment, about a month ago.

The apartment is comfortable and not too expensive: three rooms (two are a decent size, one—mine—is small), a shower, a tiny kitchen (like a gorilla cage—I'm being exact), our own central heating, all for 350 francs a month. (We're paying for the heat, of course.) But it's unfurnished. We had to accumulate—rather: quickly acquire—some possessions. Some were donated, others bought on installment. It's a three-year lease. For you, a separate room—mine—if you were to come. I sleep with the children and could work happily in your presence. I haven't at all given up hope that you'll come, I believe in it like I believe in all impulses that come naturally, from within.

I read your letter and smile: little Prague, yet so many names and episodes. I have a big Paris—and *rien*, maybe because I don't look. I'm surrounded by Eurasians, who are interesting and worthy and right in their convictions—but there are things more precious than a country's future, even when that country is Russia. More precious than a future or a country.

In their beliefs and actions, the Eurasians express values of the highest order. But my order is even higher, *au dessus de la mêlée*. I cannot seriously contemplate how the map will change tomorrow, because today it has one face, in a week it will have another, and someday it won't have any at all. When there's fighting in the streets, I'll take one side or the other, instantly and firmly. But when it's a battle of ideas, I (honestly) feel nothing, except: it was, it is and it shall be.

With rare exceptions, émigré Paris hates me; they write all kinds of trash about me, find ways to avoid me, etc. They hate me for being here but not being present, since I *never* appear in public and *don't* respond to *any* attacks. The press has done its job. My involvement in *Milestones*,[2] my Eurasian husband—and they conclude that I write Komsomol poetry and take money from the Bolsheviks.

Schwamm (und Schlamm!) drüber! . . .

But—a sudden stroke of luck. A publisher has been found for my latest (1922–1925) collection of lyrics, most of which I wrote in Prague. (Prague minus my two first months in Berlin.) This publisher loves my poetry and wants to see it appear. The book (this is for you alone!) is called *After Russia*—good, no? I hear a lot in that title. First—and there's nothing to be "heard" here—it's a simple attestation: all of them—I'm talking about the poems—were written after Russia. Second, man does not live by Russia alone. Third, Russia is in me, not I in Russia (these are Serezha's words to himself, while fighting on the Don with the White Army. NB! Russia for us is Moscow). Fourth: the next stage after Russia is—where?—almost the Heavenly Kingdom.

Also, the title is plain and exact.

Don't say a word to anyone about this (it's coming out in the fall!) or they'll jinx it. I'm not telling anyone here.

We live not far from a large forest in Meudon; our Avenue Jeanne d'Arc leads right into it. Unfortunately, families and couples have settled around the edge, and further on it's too steep to push Mur. You have to walk at least a half-hour to find some real woods. My half-hour becomes an hour-and-a-half with Mur. It was better in Czechoslovakia. . . .

I have too much housework and too many people. That's my frustration. All my mornings disappear. Four times a week I go to the market, that's an absolute. The other three go to suddenly necessary and necessarily sudden demands. Besides breakfast for everyone and preparations for lunch, now there's the wash, now ironing, now an urgent sewing job—there are many "nows." Alia helps a lot . . . she's a good, healthy, beautiful girl—very beautiful, more so every day. She's already almost as tall as I am and she'll be taller. . . .

This winter I wrote just less than half of "Phaedra," my letter to Rilke (a long poem), an essay about Rilke: "Your Death" (about two printer's sheets), which I'm proposing that you translate.[3] The subject: it's about neighboring graves—the story of Mlle. Jeanne Robert's death—of a young Russian boy, Vania—and an effort to interpret Rilke's death. A lyrical prose piece. It will be translated into French and German. I would be *very happy* if you would translate it into Czech. It's beyond nationalities, *supra*-national. It's coming out in the next number of *Russia's Will*; I'll send you the proofs. I think it's a good piece. After all, Russia has made no answer to Rilke's death: it was my duty. (He loved Russia the way I love Germany, impartially and with the unforced passion of the soul.) In his penultimate letter to me he wanted to know the word for "Nest—in deiner Sprache, die so nah ist, alle zu sein."[4] . . .

Both our lives, dear Anna Antonovna, are works in progress. And they're like the lives of those others in the beyond. More simply: we live the same lives, but ours are rough drafts and theirs are clean copies. Prague or Paris, then, makes no difference. However, I *clearly* prefer Prague. In Paris one must live and breathe Paris, or neither you nor the city has any meaning. Besides, Paris is diffuse, an archipelago of hearts, while Prague has one center—the knight.[5] (How illustrative of today's Prague that he stands *under* the bridge! You and I are also *under* the bridge!) My dream (still unfulfilled) of coming to visit you for a while: to be myself. We would wander around Prague and doubtless arrive at the very heart of the country, the wildest part.

Oh yes! In my book there will be only two dedications: one to Pasternak and the other (an entire cycle) to you. It's already copied out and will be typeset in a few days. When, exactly, I still can't say. It's my very favorite cycle and entirely bound up with you.

No. 33

Meudon
20 October 1927
Dear Anna Antonovna,

Heartfelt thanks for the letter and the gift, which both got here. I've been out of bed for a week. I'm all better, except for the pain in my hands, which has stayed behind—I'll leave it behind on some summer walk.

I'm very happy that a trip to Prague seems relatively possible. March is very good; my hair will be grown out by then. By the way, I'm shaving for the seventh and last time; it's difficult to stop—I like it so much—but S. Ia. is embarrassed and refuses to let it continue.

Yesterday I handed in the galleys for my book of poems *After Russia*. Out of 153 pages of text, 133 belong to Prague. The Czechs should be persuaded that all those years of stipends were not in vain. In Czechoslovakia I wrote *After Russia*, "The Swain," "Theseus," "The Pied Piper," "Poem of the Hill," "Poem of the End," and a series of essays. The greatest help was *nature*, which doesn't exist here, since a forest with hoodlums on workdays and couples promenading on the weekends is less a forest than an annoyance.

You know something strange? Do you remember my friendship with the *Russia's Will* crowd—with Marc Slonim?[6] I've seen him only once this whole time, i.e., since he moved to France. Lebedev,[7] with whom I was the least friendly, has turned out to be the most faithful. He is truly well disposed toward us, the only one who has helped us in our troubles. . . .

Have you read the vicious attacks on the Eurasians in *Renaissance*, *Russia*, *Days*? "Confirmed reports" that the Eurasians have been receiving *huge sums* from the Bolsheviks. They have no proof, naturally, since there is none!—but they know their émigré audience! In a few days it will be necessary to make rebuttals—

however disgusting it is to acknowledge known liars. I stay away from it all, but even my indifference to politics has been shaken. It's as much as accusing *me* of taking Bolshevik money! It's that plausible.

S. Ia., of course, is very upset and losing his health over it. His income: from 5:30 a.m. to 7 or 8 in the evening he works as a film extra for forty francs a day, out of which five francs go for transportation and seven for lunch—in sum, twenty-eight francs a day. And it's a lot if there are two such days in a week. There they are, your Bolshevik sums! . . .

No. 41

Meudon
11 March 1928
. . . Many thanks for arranging the subscriptions; you accomplished a miracle.[8] Teffi[9], for example, who has excellent connections (the Grand Princes, generals, actresses, French nobility) couldn't manage a single one. B. Pasternak's father, Leonid Pasternak the artist[10] (he lives in Berlin), got three more. Generally speaking, I do well wherever I'm not—that's where I reign supreme. The book will soon be out. Unfortunately, my editor is like an author: everything in its own good time. "Somewhere, sometime." We used to have cab drivers like that in Russia: they would sleep while the horse went. And sometimes the horse slept, too.

A few days ago I had another of my regular encounters with death (remember my essay "Your Death"—who's next?). My brother's friend, Volodia—twenty-eight years old, though you'd take him for eighteen—died of tuberculosis. He was with the White Army, then became a bank clerk in London. . . . Not for a minute through the whole illness did they suspect any danger. "I'll get better." But he didn't need his life for himself, others needed it. He lived to work and worked so that others could live. He died quietly, dreamed all night long. "Mama, what a funny dream I had: a red bull was chasing me through a green field." . . . And in the morning he fell asleep for good. That was on the eighth—yesterday, the tenth, they buried him. The French don't fill the grave in the presence of relatives, who take leave of a gaping hole. We forced the undertaker to do it for us and it took one hour and twenty minutes. For one hour and twenty minutes his mother stood and watched them bury her son. Miniature spades, grudging workers, snow and wet clay underfoot. But the next day it was like summer and all the trees were flowering. As though nature, pitying the poor exile, had wanted to give him Russian sky and earth at his final hour. I took his mother and sister home, and when I entered the apartment: an aunt setting the table, someone borrowing three eggs from a neighbor, everyone talking about yesterday's meat.—Life.—That same night his mother took up sewing beaded handbags; that's what they're living on now. And so she'll mix tears with beads. . . .

No. 76

Meudon
1 January 1932

Happy New Year, dear Anna Antonovna! I'm writing on a page of the manuscript with which I ended last year and began this one.

This spring it will be exactly ten years since I left Russia—this summer, exactly ten years since I arrived in Czechoslovakia—this fall (1 November), exactly seven years since I left Czechoslovakia and came to France. But it's strange: I feel as though I spent more time in Czechoslovakia than in France, as though I were there for seven years and in Paris for three. Despite everything that's happened here (and I know the value of that everything), I've never come to like France, perhaps because there's been nothing—spiritually—to remember it by. I haven't made any real friends here, though I've had brief relationships that didn't survive. The only person I've really loved here, and who really loved me, was Elena Aleksandrovna Izvolskaia, who's gone—she got married and moved to Japan, I told you about that farewell. In France—during the seven years of my France—Alia has grown up and left me behind. After seven years in France I've grown terribly cold. Sometimes I feel like saying, like that French princess on her deathbed: *Rien ne m'est plus. Plus ne m'est rien.*

I still have Mur: he's very difficult and demanding, but he still (for another seven years or so) needs me. After these seven—or ten—years, I will no longer be needed by anyone. Perhaps I will begin my real life then, the solitary life that ended *seventeen years ago*. Perhaps I can write a few more good things, or maybe just one: *mine*. I'm still living off old capital, some left over from Russia, some from Prague (that sounds ridiculous coming from me, especially this winter!). Paris has given me nothing to work with. Do you know how people talk to each other here? In crowded dining rooms or with the next-door neighbor, in conversations that are always accidental, occasionally amusing—then it's goodbye forever. That happened to me many times before I stopped going to visit people (I'm talking about the French). It's a feeling that everyone knows and understands what's going on, but they're completely preoccupied with themselves—and, in literary circles (which I'm talking about), with their next book. A feeling that there's no place for you. I just spent an entire evening with a famous travel writer

(*A la poursuite du soleil*). And? It turns out that the most engaging, the most apparently soulful conversation with a Frenchman leads to nothing. No consequences, no strings attached. They talk to me like they would talk to anyone, I'm just an audience. The French care only about themselves. That's what they call the art of conversation.

No. 82

Clamart
24 November 1933
Dear Anna Antonovna,

At last—a letter!

I'm writing to you during a break between two manuscripts: "The House at Old Pimen"—a family chronicle of the Ilovaiskiis (the historian Ilovaiskii—perhaps you know his name? My father's first wife was his daughter, I am *not her* daughter). It's a grim and truthful story: a house where everyone except the old man died—it may come out in *Contemporary Notes*. I'm between that and "The Erlking" (a go at interpreting Goethe). There's little hope of placing it: who in the emigration is interested in the Erlking (Erlkönig) or even Goethe these days! I, who have been so long maligned for the "modernity" of my verse, now am continually reproached for the outdated *themes* of my prose. (But don't you think that "modernity" and that "outdated" are the same thing—i.e., myself?!)

I'm writing almost no verse and here's why: I can't confine myself to a single poem. They come to me in families, in cycles, like a whirlpool into which I *fall*—and it's a question of *time*. I can't write regular essays and poetry at the same time and couldn't even if I had the time. I work concentrically. Also, forgetting that I'm a poet, no one is accepting my poems, not anywhere, not a line. "Anywhere" means *The Latest News* and *Contemporary Notes*—there's no place else.[11] The excuse is that I'm incomprehensible to the reader, which is to say, to the editor, who is Miliukov at the *News* and Rudnev at *Notes*—by profession a doctor, by avocation a political commentator and by mistake an editor (NB! of the literary section). "It would be funny if it weren't so sad. . . ."

Emigration has made me into a prose writer. Of course, the prose is *mine*, and the next best thing after poems, lyrical prose—but still just next best.

Of course, I occasionally write poems—rather, I write down lines that come to me. But more often I don't write them down—I just let them go back *ins Blaue* (never *Graue*, even in November in Paris!).

So much for my literary affairs. When I receive the Nobel Prize (*never*), I will write poems. Like others take off to sail around the world.

The Nobel Prize. On the 26th I will sit on the stage and honor Bunin.[12] Declining would be interpreted as a protest. I don't protest, I just don't agree, because Gorky[13] is so much greater than Bunin: greater and more humane and original and essential. Gorky is a whole epoch, while Bunin is the end of an epoch. But since there are politics involved, since the King of Sweden can't pin a medal on the communist Gorky. . . . However, the third candidate was Merezhkovskii and he, too, clearly deserved the Nobel more than Bunin, because if Gorky is an epoch and Bunin is the end of an epoch, then Merezhkovskii is an epoch at the end of an epoch, and his influence in Russia and abroad is incomparably greater than Bunin's, who has had *no* genuine influence either here or there. But the *News*, comparing his style with Tolstoy's (as if it were a question of "style," i.e., the *pen* you're writing with!), concluded that Tolstoy wasn't as good—just shameless. Of course, I can't actually say these things.

Merezhkovskii and Gippius are furious.[14] Perhaps the first time in their lives that complicated pair has experienced a simple emotion.

They are both very old: he's around seventy-five and she's sixty-eight. They are both *hideous*. He's completely twisted, like ancient old root, a *Wurzelmännchen* (only without the coziness and the forest!); she's a painted *skeleton*—no, worse than a skeleton: a cross between a husk and a waxen doll.

Everyone fears them now because they're both malevolent. Malevolent as demons.

I haven't seen Bunin yet. I *don't like* him: he's a cold, cruel, arrogant *baron*. I don't like *him*, but I very much like his wife. She has helped me a lot with my manuscript, since she was a friend of my older sister (Ilovaiskii's granddaughter) and remembers that world well. We've been corresponding for about six months. They live in Grasse (Côte d'Azur), a big horticultural region (where they manufacture perfume), in the villa "Belvedere" on a high cliff. Now they'll probably move onto a higher one.

Things at home are so-so. First of all, though no one is sick (seriously), neither is anyone healthy. Mur's liver, his diet, bothers him and he's lost a lot of weight—from the liver and from that idiotic French school: from their "system": of sitting and cramming . . . Alia is getting thinner all the time, transparent, listless—clearly a bad case of anemia. Six years of art school so far have been in vain, since she doesn't get any work drawing, just occasional jobs like stuffing toy animals; or now, maybe, she'll become a dental assistant, because we have *nothing* to live on. She has changed *very much* spiritually, as well. . . . It's dirty and cold where we live (from coal and the lack thereof). It was dirty in Vshenory, too, but there was also a big warm stove and the forest through the windows; there were the *comforts of poverty* and the emotional release of *real* natural surroundings. I remember all those places, all the walks, all the little paths. I always remember Czechoslovakia kindly.

Enormous thanks for the monthly package, it always comes at the *last* possible moment.

You are the only one I have left.

No. 103

Vanves
15 February 1936

. . . Do you, dear Anna Antonovna, know a good fortune-teller in Prague? Because it seems I can't manage without one. Everything comes down to this: stay or go. (If I go, then it's forever.)

In short: S. Ia., Alia and Mur are desperate to go back. Everywhere there are threats of war and revolution, of general catastrophe. There's nothing for me to live on if I stay here alone. The emigration *hates* me (the only job that pays: I could, as a lark, write one *feuilleton* a week for 1,800 francs a month) and *The Latest News* (*Miliukov*) has driven me out: I won't be published anymore. And the grand Parisian patronesses can't stand my habit of independence.

Finally, Mur has no prospects here. I've seen these twenty-year-olds, trapped in a dead end.

In Moscow there's my sister Asia, who loves me, perhaps more than her own son. There's also a circle of genuine writers instead of this wreckage. (The writers here hate me, don't consider me one of their own.)

Finally, there's the landscape: the expanse.

Those are the pros.

The cons: Moscow has turned into New York, an ideological New York, without open spaces or hills, just asphalt lakes with banks of loudspeakers and colossal billboards. No, I didn't start off with the main reason: Mur, whose imagination has been totally seized by that Moscow. And the second main reason: myself—with my *Furchtlosigkeit*, who am *incapable of not answering back*, who could not sign a welcoming address to the great Stalin because *I* didn't call him great—and even if he is great, it's not my sort of greatness—and because I hate any kind of victorious official church.

And—I'll be leaving you: *with the hope* of meeting again—and A.I. Andreeva and the Lebedev family (I don't have anyone else).

There you have it.

I'll be alone there, with no Mur. They won't leave *any* of him for me. For one thing, he'll have no time: now after school he's mine, but there he'll belong to them, to everyone: pioneering, brigades, mock trials, summer camps, with all the enticements: drums, physical culture, clubs, banners, etc., etc. . . .

Maybe I should go. Maybe it's the final (final?) *Kraftsprobe*? But then why did I raise children for eighteen years?? Because it's the law of nature?—Small comfort. . . .

No. 126

Hôtel Innova
24 November 1938
Dear Anna Antonovna!

Here are the poems.[15] A note to the third poem (if it's not clear): there is an ache in the breast of all peoples: one among us is felled! That is, the nations are mourning your disaster as if it were their own: peoples could never rejoice in it, only individuals. And they are mourning their own future disaster, unless. . . . But the inability to draw consequences is an attribute not just of nations or the common people but of the so-called "cultural elite." "How horrible—they've taken another sixty villages. . . ." "How horrible, what's happening to the Jews!" . . . "How horrible—sixty-cent stamps now cost ninety-five!" Everything's "horrible," but *why* all these things are horrible and how they are related, no one (from my milieu: cultured, writers) wishes to contemplate—they don't even ask these questions because they're too afraid to hear the *answers*. It's the same shallowness and inertia and bestiality (or attraction to it!) that made happen what has happened. I, in the perfection and clarity of my anger, am utterly alone. I don't want them to pity the victims: you mustn't pity someone who's been buried alive: you must dig him out and bury the perpetrator. Such pity is worthy of the name. "How horrible!" No, you tell me exactly *how* it is horrible, and having grasped that, renounce whoever does or approves horrible things. Otherwise: "Yes, it's horrible, poor Prague," and then it turns out she's having an affair with a member of the Black Hundreds,[16] who dreams only of carting home someone else's gold—or the lady of the house powders her nose while the master of the house keeps on reading *Renaissance*, and you don't know whom to shake your fist at. At best, it's feeble-mindedness, but seeing how marvelously they conduct their *own* affairs, how cleverly they manage that, I fail to believe that "best." It's simply *lâcheté*: the force that moves the world (today).

No. 135

12 June 1939
in the train car before departure
Dear Anna Antonovna!

(I'm writing on my palm, that's why the childish handwriting.) We're in an immense train station with green panes: a terrifying green garden—and what isn't growing in it!—Before leaving the house, Mur and I observed a moment of silence according to the old custom and crossed ourselves at the empty spot where the icon used to hang (left in good hands, it's lived and traveled with me since 1918—well, there comes a time when you'll leave everything behind: *completely*! This is a lesson, so that death won't seem so frightening—or even strange. . . .) My life of seventeen years is ending. How happy I was then! And the happiest period of my life—remember this!—was Czechoslovakia, and my native hill. Strange—yesterday on the street I met him, the hero of that hill,[17] whom I hadn't seen in years. He flew up from behind and without warning thrust his hands into ours—he walked between Mur and me—as though it were nothing unusual. And I also saw—by the same miracle—that crazy old poet and his wife at a home they had not visited *for a year*. As though everybody sensed I was leaving. I kept running into everyone. (I just heard, resonant and ominous: Express de Vienne . . . and thought of the towers and bridges I'll never see.) They're shouting "En voiture, Madame" right at me, snatching me out of all the places I've ever lived. There's no need to shout—I already know. Mur is saving (the train just started to move) today's newspapers.

—We're approaching Rouen, where human gratitude once burned Joan of Arc. (And five hundred years later an Englishwoman set up a monument on the spot.) We've passed Rouen—full steam ahead!—I'll expect news of all of you. Give my warmest greetings to the whole family; I wish them all health, courage and long life. I dream about our meeting in Mur's birthplace, which is more native to me than my own. I turn around when I hear "Prague," as though someone called my name. Remember that I had a friend named Sonechka,[18] and everyone said "Your Sonechka"?—Well, I'm leaving in *your* necklace and in a coat with *your* buttons, and around my waist is *your* belt. All of them humble and insanely beloved, I'll take them to the grave or burn with them. Goodbye! It doesn't feel agonizing anymore, now it's just fate. I embrace you and yours, each individually and all together. I love and cherish you. I believe in you as I believe in myself.

Notes on the Essay

1. Boris Pasternak, *I Remember. Sketch for An Essay in Autobiography* (New York: Pantheon, 1959), 104–10; Ilya Ehrenburg, *People and Life,* Vol. 1 (New York: Knopf, 1962), 252–259.

2. The pathbreaking work was done by Simon Karlinsky. See his *Marina Cvetaeva: Her Life and Art* (Berkeley: University of California Press, 1966), and *Marina Tsvetaeva: The Woman, Her World, and Her Poetry* (Cambridge: Cambridge University Press, 1985).

3. The museum in fact opened in time for Tsvetaeva's 1992 centennial, although it has been plagued since by financial problems and dissension among the staff.

4. For papers from the centennial symposia at the Norwich Russian School and at Amherst College, see *Marina Tsvetaeva 1892–1992,* ed. Svetlana Elnitsky and Efim Etkind (Northfield, VT: Russian School of Norwich University, 1992), and *Marina Tsvetaeva: One Hundred Years*, ed. Viktoria Schweitzer, Jane A. Taubman, Peter Scotto and Tatyana Babyonyshev (Berkeley, CA: Berkeley Slavic Specialties, 1994).

5. The exhibition was called *Marina Tsvetaeva. Poèt i vremia. Vystavka k 100–letiiu so dnia rozhdeniia*, and took place in Moscow, 1992.

6. *Tsvetaeva* (London: Collins, 1992; New York: Harvill, 1993).

7. Claudia Roth Pierpont, "The Rage of Aphrodite," 7 February 1994, 90–98.

8. See bibliography.

9. A third version, not always accurate, is provided by the memoirs of her younger sister Anastasiia (*Vospominaniia,* 3d ed., Moscow, 1983) translated in *Soviet Studies in Literature*, 18, 2 (1982): 3–90; 18, 3 (1982): 3–8; 18, 4 (1982): 3–93.

10. The most complete Russica editions (see bibliography) contain three volumes of lyric poems, one volume each of long poems and verse dramas, and two volumes of prose. Her voluminous correspondence, a major part of her *oeuvre*, will surely fill at least three volumes when it is finally collected.

11. The plays, largely untranslated, are seldom staged, although the iconoclastic Moscow theater director Roman Viktiuk did stage an adaptation of *Phaedra* in the late 1980s.

12. Pasternak, 106.

13. Boris Pasternak, Marina Tsvetaeva and Rainer Maria Rilke, *Letters: Summer 1926* (New York: Harcourt Brace Jovanovich, 1983).

14. "Predsmertie," in *Stikhotvoreniia i poèmy v piati tomakh*, Vol. 3 (New York: Russica, 1983), 394–416.

15. See Jane Taubman, "Tsvetaeva and the Feminine Tradition in Russian Poetry," in Schweitzer et al., *Marina Tsvetaeva: One Hundred Years*, 77–90.

16. Joseph Brodsky, *Less Than One* (New York: Farrar, Straus and Giroux, 1986), 182.

17. *Russkaia mysl'* [Moscow] 2 (1911): 233.

18. See Jane Taubman, "Tire u Emili Dikinson i Mariny Tsvetaevoi (Pauza vnutri stikhotvoreniia)," in Elnitsky and Etkind (1992), 206–18.

19. See, for example, the poems "God—is just" (1918) or "Quiet, praise!" (1926) in the selected works.

Translator's Notes to the Selected Works

1. Small town outside of Prague where Tsvetaeva lived for a time. She gave birth to her son Mur there in February 1925.

2. *Milestones*, a literary journal coedited by Efron, was attacked by émigré critics for including the works of authors living in the Soviet Union such as Boris Pasternak and Isaac Babel.

3. "Phaedra" is one of Tsvetaeva's two verse tragedies, part of an uncompleted trilogy based on the story of Theseus. The "letter to Rilke" is a long poem entitled "New Year Letter" (1926), translated by David McDuff in *Selected Poems* (Newcastle upon Tyne: Bloodaxe, 1991).

4. Tsvetaeva was introduced to Rilke by Pasternak, who was a close friend and passionate admirer of her work. Their three-way correspondence during the last year of Rilke's life has been translated as *Letters, Summer 1926: Pasternak, Tsvetayeva, Rilke* (New York: Harcourt Brace Jovanovich, 1985).

5. The statue of Bruncvik that stands beneath the Charles Bridge in Prague.

6. The literary editor of *Russia's Will*, the organ of the Socialist Revolutionary party in Prague. Slonim, a friend and admirer of Tsvetaeva, frequently published her work.

7. A prominent socialist revolutionary and former minister in the provisional government who emigrated in 1919. The Efrons and the Lebedevs met in Czechoslovakia.

8. The cost of publishing *After Russia* was offset by subscriptions.

9. Nadezhda Teffi (1872–1952) was a popular writer of humorous fiction who emigrated to Paris in 1919.

10. Leonid Pasternak (1862–1945) was an outstanding Russian impressionist. The Pasternak family emigrated to Berlin in 1921; Boris and his brother Alexander remained in Soviet Russia.

11. The two most influential publications of the Russian emigration in Paris. *The Latest News* was a daily newspaper and *Contemporary Notes*, a monthly journal.

12. Ivan Bunin (1870–1953) wrote short stories, most famously "The Gentleman from San Francisco," and was the first Russian writer to receive the Nobel Prize. Tsvetaeva was a close friend of his wife, Vera Muromtseva.

13. Maxim Gorky (1868–1936) was a writer, playwright and critic who, although he emigrated in 1921, maintained ties with the Bolsheviks. He returned to Russia in 1931 to play a prominent role in establishing the doctrine of "socialist realism," of which his novel *Mother* was considered a model.

14. Dmitrii Merezhkovskii (1865–1941) and Zinaida Gippius (1869–1945) were the elder statesmen of Russian émigré literature, having been leading figures in the Symbolist movement. Merezhkovskii's major achievements were an influential book on Tolstoy and Dostoevsky and several historical novels, while Gippius was a controversial poet and essayist. They were virulent foes of Bolshevism.

15. Tsvetaeva wrote a cycle of poems to Czechoslovakia in response to the Nazi invasion. These poems appear among Elaine Feinstein's translations of Tsvetaeva in *Selected Poems of Marina Tsvetayeva* (New York: Dutton, 1981).

16. The Black Hundreds were reactionary supporters of the monarchy who engaged in lynchings and street violence during the 1905 revolution.

17. Petrin Hill in central Prague, where she lived in 1925. The "hero" was Konstantin Rodzevich, with whom Tsvetaeva had a passionate affair. She recorded the end of their relationship

in two of her most famous poems, "Poem of the Hill" and "Poem of the End" (translated by Elaine Feinstein in *Selected Poems*).

18. Sofiia Gollidey (1894–1934) was an actress with the famous Vakhtangov Studio whom Tsvetaeva knew in Moscow during 1918–1919. Tsvetaeva described their friendship in a lengthy autobiographical essay ("The Story of Sonechka," 1937) after learning of her death.

Bibliography

Primary Works

Vechernii al'bom. Stikhi [Evening Album. Poems]. Moscow, 1910.

Volshebnyi fonar'. Vtoraia kniga stikhov [The Magic Lantern. Second Book of Poems]. Moscow: Ole Lukoie, 1912.

Iz dvukh knig [From Two Books. (Selections from two earlier books)]. Moscow: Ole Lukoie, 1913.

Versty. Stikhi [Mileposts. Poems]. Moscow: Kostry, 1921 and 1922.

Konets Kazanovy. Dramaticheskii ètiud [The End of Casanova. A Dramatic Étude]. Moscow: Sozvedzdie, 1922.

Razluka. Kniga stikhov [Separation. A Book of Poems]. Moscow: Gelikon, 1922. [Includes the long poem "Na krasnom kone'" (On a Red Steed).]

Stikhi k Bloku [Poems to Blok]. Berlin: Ogon'ki, 1922.

Tsar'-Devitsa. Poèma-skazka [The Tsar-Maiden. A Tale in Verse]. Moscow: Gosizdat, 1922 and Berlin: Èpokha, 1922.

Versty. Stikhi. Vypusk I [Mileposts. Poems. Part I]. Moscow: Gosizdat, 1922.

Psikheia. Romantika [Psyche. Romanticism]. Berlin: Grzhebin, 1923.

Remeslo. Kniga stikhov. [Craft. A Book of Poems]. Berlin: Gelikon, 1923. [Includes the long poem "Pereulochki" (Sidestreets).]

Molodets. Skazka [The Swain. A Tale]. Prague: Plamia, 1924.

Posle Rossii. 1922–1925 [After Russia. 1922–1925]. Paris: Imp-Union, 1928.

"Pis'ma M.I. Tsvetaevoi Iu.P. Ivasku (1933–1937)" [12 letters to Iu.P. Ivask]. Iu.P. Ivask, *Russkii literaturnii arkhiv.* Ed. Dmitry Chizhevsky and Michael Karpovich. New York: Chekhov, 1956. 207–37.

Lebedinyi stan. Stikhi 1917–1921 [The Swans' Encampment. Poems 1917–1921, posthumous]. Ed. G.P. Struve. Munich: n.p., 1957.

Izbrannye proizvedeniia [Selected Works]. Ed. Ariadna Efron and Anna Saakiants. Moscow: Biblioteka poèta, 1965.

Pis'ma k A. Teskovoi. [123 of 135 Letters to Anna Teskova]. Ed. Vadim Morkovin. Prague: 1969. [Rpt. with preface and new annotations by Irma Kudrova, St. Petersburg: 1991].

"Pis'ma Mariny Tsvetaevoi" [24 letters to various addressees]. Ed. A. Efron and A. Saakiants. *Novyi mir* 4 (1969): 185–214.

Perekop [Perekop]. New York: 1967. [Corrected text in *Lebedinyi stan. Perekop*, posthumous. Ed. G. Struve. Paris: YMCA Press, 1971.]

Neizdannye pis'ma [unpublished letters, 176 in all, 1910–1941, including important letters to Anna Akhmatova, Ol'ga Chernova-Kolbasina, Boris Pasternak, Vera Bunina and others, and supplementary materials]. Ed. G. and N. Struve. Paris: YMCA Press, 1972.

Neizdannoe. Stikhi, Teatr, Proza [Unpublished Works. Poems, Theater, Prose]. Paris: YMCA Press, 1976.

"Pis'ma Mariny Tsvetaevoi Maksimilianu Voloshinu" [13 letters to Maksimilian Voloshin, 1910–1912. Ed. Irma Kudrova]. *Novyi mir* 2 (1977): 231–46.

Mon Frère Feminin: Lettre à l'Amazone [note by Ghislaine Limont, posthumous]. Paris: 1979.

Izbrannaia proza v dvukh tomakh 1917–1937 [Selected Prose in Two Volumes 1917–1937]. Ed. Alexander Sumerkin [preface by Joseph Brodsky]. New York: Russica, 1979.

Stikhotvoreniia i poèmy v piati tomakh [Lyric and Narrative Poems in Five Volumes]. Ed. and comp. Alexander Sumerkin [preface by Joseph Brodsky; biographical essay by Viktoria Schweitzer]. New York: Russica, 1980–1990.

Le Notti Fiorentine. Lettera all'Amazone [Neuf lettres avec une dixième retenue et une onzième récue et postface. Lettre a l'Amazone. French originals with Italian]. Trans., intro. and commentary by Serena Vitale. Milan: Mondatori, 1983.

"Iz pisem Mariny Tsvetaevoi k Salomee Andronikovoi-Gal'pern [20 letters to S. Andronikova-Gal'pern 1926–1934, 2 letters to D.G. Reznikov, 1926]. Ed. G.P.Struve. *Vestnik (Le Messager)* 138 (1983): 164–94.

[9 letters to A.G. Vishniak 1922, translated from the French original by R. Rodina]. *Novyi mir* 8 (1985): 156–70. [For the original text, see *Le Notti Fiorentine* above.]

Sochineniia v dvukh tomakh [Works in Two Volumes]. Ed. A. Saakiants. Moscow: Khudozhestvennaia literatura, 1988.

Teatr [Theater]. Ed. A. Saakiants. Moscow: 1988.

Proza [Prose]. Ed. A. Saakiants. Moscow: 1989.

"Pis'ma Mariny Tsvetaevoi k R.N. Lomonosovoi" [Letters to R.N. Lomonosova]. *Minuvshee. Istoricheskii al'manakh 8* (1989).

Pis'ma 1926 goda. Rainer Maria Ril'ke, Boris Pasternak, Marina Tsvetaeva [20 letters to Rainer Marina Rilke, Boris Pasternak 1926]. Ed. K.M. Azadovsky, E.B. Pasternak, E.V. Pasternak. Moscow, 1990.

Pis'ma k Ariadne Berg 1934–1939. [Letters to Ariadna Berg]. Ed. N. Struve. Paris: YMCA Press, 1990.

Stikhotvoreniia i poèmy. [Lyric and narrative poems] Ed. E.B. Korkina. Leningrad: Biblioteka poèta, 1990.

"Tsvetaeva v pis'makh" [Tsvetaeva in letters. From the Bakhmeteff Archive of Columbia University]. Ed. John Malmstad. *Literaturnoe obozrenie* 7 (1990): 102–12.

"Perepiska M.I. Tsvetaevoi s A.V. Bakhrakhom" [M.I. Tsvetaeva's correspondence with A.V. Bachrach]. Ed. John Malmstad. *Literaturnoe obozrenie* 8 (1991): 97–109; 9 (1991): 102–12.

"Alia (Zapisi o moei docheri)" [Alia (Notes about My Daughter). Ed. E.I. Liubiannikova]. *Zvezda* 10 (1992): 5–11.

"'Da, v vechnosti—zhena, ne na bumage.' Neizvestnye pis'ma iz arkhivov NKVD" ['Yes, his wife in eternity, not on paper . . . ' Unknown Letters from the Archives of the NKVD. Ed. Mael Feinberg and Iurii Kliukin]. *Literaturnaia gazeta* 36 (1992): 6.

"Zapisi iz rabochikh tetradei' [Notes from Tsvetaeva's working notebooks. Ed. E. Korkina]. *Znamia* 9 (1992): 180–89.

"Khotite ko mne v synov'ia?" Dvadtsat' piat' pisem k Anatoliiu Shteigeru ["Do You Want to Become My Son?" Twenty-five Letters to Anatolii Shteiger]. Ed. A. Saakiants. Moscow, 1994.

In Translation

[4 poems trans. by Denise Levertov, 1 poem trans. by Andrew Field]. *Pages from Tarusa*. Ed. Andrew Field. Boston: Little, Brown, 1964. 288–91.

"The Kirillovnas." *Pages from Tarusa.* Trans. Collyer Bowen. Ed. Andrew Field Boston: Little, Brown 1964. 292–300.

[18 poems adapted by Rose Styron, Olga Carlisle and Denise Levertov]. *Poets on Street Corners.* Ed. Olga Carlisle. New York: Random House, 1968. 165–93.

[4 poems trans. by Jamie Fuller, 5 poems trans. by George L. Kline]. *Russian Literature Triquarterly* 2 (1972): 214–19.

[5 poems trans. Lydia Pasternak Slater, 3 poems, trans. by Angela Livingstone]. *Russian Literature Triquarterly* 9 (1974): 21–24.

[4 poems, plain prose translation]. *The Heritage of Russian Verse.* Ed. Dimitri Obolensky. Bloomington: Indiana University Press, 1976.

[2 poems and an excerpt from "Poem of the End"]. *The Penguin Book of Women Poets.* Ed. Carol Cosman, Joan Keefe and Kathleen Weaver. Trans. Elaine Feinstein and Angela Livingstone. New York: Viking Press, 1978. 192–94.

[10 poems, including the cycle "To Mayakovsky]." Trans. by Paul Schmidt. *Sun* 4, 3 (Winter 1979–1980): 103–10.

[Poems 1917–1920]. *The Demesne of the Swans.* Trans. Robin Kemball. Ann Arbor: Ardis, 1980.

A Captive Spirit: Selected Prose. Trans. J. Marin King, with an introduction by Susan Sontag. Ann Arbor, MI: Ardis, 1980 and London: Virago, 1983.

[3 poems and an excerpt from "My Pushkin"]. *A Russian Cultural Revival: A Critical Anthology of Émigré Literature Before 1939.* Ed. and trans. Temira Pachmuss. Knoxville: University of Tennessee Press, 1981. 96–105.

[Poems]. *Three Russian Women Poets: Anna Akhmatova, Marina Tsvetayeva, Bella Akhmadulina.* Trans. Mary Maddock. Trumansburg, NY: Crossing Press, 1983.

"Two Poems from 1916." Trans. Joseph Brodsky. *The New Yorker,* 17 October 1983, 48.

Letters, Summer 1926: Boris Pasternak, Marina Tsvetaeva, Rainer Maria Rilke. Trans. Margaret Wettlin and Walter Arndt. San Diego: Harcourt Brace Jovanovich, 1985.

"Attic Life." Trans. Jamey Gambrell. *Partisan Review* 53, 4 (1986): 499–508.

"A Few of Rainer Maria Rilke's Letters." Trans. Jamey Gambrell. *Antaeus* 58 (Spring 1987): 248–55.

Selected Poems of Marina Tsvetayeva. Trans. Elaine Feinstein with Angela Livingstone. 2d ed. New York: Dutton, 1987.

[11 poems]. *Russian Literature of the Twenties.* Ed. Carl Proffer et al. Trans. Robin Kemball, Lydia Pasternak Slater, Jamie Fuller, Margaret Troupin, Robert Dessaix and J. Marin King. Ann Arbor, MI: Ardis, 1987. 407–13.

"Your Death (To Rilke)." Trans. Jamey Gambrell. *Partisan Review* 2 (1987): 190–211.

"October on the Train (Notes from those Days)." Trans. Jamey Gambrell. *Partisan Review* 54, 4 (1987): 517–26.

"October in a Railway Car (Diary Entries from Those Days)." Trans. and annotated by Laura Weeks. *Russian Literature Triquarterly* 22 (1988): 55–66.

"On Gratitude." Trans. Jamey Gambrell. *Formations* 5, 1 (1988): 24–28.

Starry Sky to Starry Sky: Poems by Mary Jane White with Translations of Marina Tsvetaeva. Stevens Point, WI: Holy Cow! Press, 1988. [A complete translation of the collection *Versty* (1921), here translated *Miles,* with a preface, chronology and late reply by Anna Akhmatova, 51–92.]

In the Innermost Hour of the Soul: Selected Poems. Trans. Nina Kosman. Clifton, NJ: Humara Press, 1989.

"Mother's Tale." Trans. Jamey Gambrell. *Formations* 5, 2 (1989): 24–28.

Selected Poems. Trans. David McDuff. 2d ed. Newcastle upon Tyne: Bloodaxe Books, 1991.

[Poems: 1 poem trans. by William Tjalsma, 2 poems trans. by John Glad, 7 poems trans. by Bob Perelman, Shirley Rihner and Alexander Petrov]. *Twentieth-Century Russian Poetry*. Ed. John Glad and Daniel Weissbort. Iowa City: University of Iowa Press, 1992. 140–48.

Art in the Light of Conscience: Eight Essays on Poetry. Trans. Angela Livingstone. Cambridge, MA: Harvard University Press, 1992.

[8 poems]. *Twentieth Century Russian Poetry: Silver and Steel*. Selected by Yevgeny Yevtushenko. Ed. Albert C. Todd and Max Hayward, with Daniel Weissbort. Trans. Elaine Feinstein. New York: Doubleday, 1993. 225–38.

[14 lyrics and Tsvetaeva's response to a questionnaire]. *The Burden of Sufferance: Women Poets of Russia*. Ed. Pamela Perkins and Albert Cook. New York: Garland Publishing, 1993. 99–136.

"Staircase" [long poem]. *An Anthology of Russian Women's Writing, 1777–1992*. Ed. Catriona Kelly. Oxford: Oxford University Press, 1994. 260–75.

"An Insistence of Memory" [from a 1925 questionnaire]; and "A Hero of Labor" [excerpts from Tsvetaeva's working notebooks]. *Altogether Elsewhere: Writers on Exile*. Ed. Marc Robinson. Trans. Catherine Ciepiela. Boston: Faber and Faber, 1994. 99, 269–70.

"Life Insurance." *Lives in Transit*. Ed. Helena Goscilo. Trans. Jane Taubman. Ann Arbor, MI: Ardis, 1995. 186–90.

[Poems 1922–1925]. *After Russia*. Trans. Michael Naydan with Slava Yastremski. Ann Arbor, MI: Ardis, 1992.

Poem of the End: Selected Lyrical and Narrative Poetry. Trans. Nina Kossman. Ann Arbor, MI: Ardis, 1995.

Secondary Works

Altschuller, Gregory I. "Marina Tsvetayeva: A Physician's Memoir." Trans. Paul Schmidt. *Sun* 4,3 (Winter 1979–1980): 103–10. [No known Russian original. This may be a work of creative writing by Schmidt.]

Baer, Joachim T. "Three Variations on the Theme 'Moi Pushkin': Briusov, Akhmatova, Tsvetaeva." *Transactions of the Association of Russian-American Scholars in the USA* 20 (1987): 163–83.

Bayley, John. "A Poet's Tragedy." *The New York Review of Books*, 23 October 1980, 3–4, 6, 7.

Beaujour, Elizabeth Klosty. *Alien Tongues: Bilingual Russian Writers of the "First" Emigration*. Ithaca, NY: Cornell University Press, 1989.

Bethea, David M. "Mother(hood) and Poetry: On Tsveteva and the Feminists." *For SK: In Celebration of the Life and Career of Simon Karlinsky*. Ed. Michael S. Flier and Robert P. Hughes. Berkeley, CA: Berkeley Slavic Studies, 1994. 51–70.

———. "'This Sex Which Is Not One' versus This Poet Which Is 'Less Than One': Tsvetaeva, Brodsky, and Exilic Desire." *Joseph Brodsky and the Creation of Exile*. Princeton, NJ: Princeton University Press, 1994. 174–213.

Boym, Svetlana. "The Death of the Poetess." *Death in Quotation Marks: Cultural Myths of the Modern Poet*. Cambridge, MA: Harvard University Press, 1991.

Burgin, Diana Lewis. "Mother Nature versus the Amazons: Marina Tsvetaeva and Female Same-Sex Love." *Journal of the History of Sexuality* (forthcoming).

———. "After the Ball Is Over: Sophia Parnok's Creative Relationship with Marina Tsvetaeva." *Russian Review* 47 (1988): 425–44.

———. "Signs of a Response: Two Possible Parnok Replies to Her 'Podruga'." *Slavic and East European Journal* 35 (1991): 214–27.

———. *Sofia Parnok. The Life and Work of Russia's Sappho*. New York: New York University Press, 1994.

Brodsky, Joseph. "A Poet and Prose" and "Footnote to a Poem." *Less Than One.* New York: Farrar, Straus and Giroux, 1986. 176–94, 195–267.

Brodsky, Patricia Pollock. "On Daring to Be a Poet: Rilke and Marina Cvetaeva." *Germano-Slavica* 3 (1980): 261–69.

———. "The Russians' Rilke: Reception as a Mirror of Literary Reality." *Germano-Slavica* 4 (1983): 143–50.

Brumfield, William C. "*Exegi Monumentum:* Ivan Tsvetaev and the Creation of the Alexander III Museum." *For SK: In Celebration of the Life and Career of Simon Karlinsky*. Ed. Michael S. Flier and Robert P. Hughes. Berkeley, CA: Berkeley Slavic Specialties, 1994. 80–87.

Chester, Pamela. "Engaging Sexual Demons in Marina Tsvetaeva's 'Devil': The Body and the Genesis of the Woman Poet." *Slavic Review* 53, 4 (1994): 1025–45.

Chvany, Catherine V. "Translating One Poem from a Cycle: Cvetaeva's 'Your Name Is a Bird in My Hand' from 'Poems to Blok.'" *New Studies in Russian Literature.* Ed. Anna Lisa Crone and Catherine Chvany. Columbus, OH: Slavica, 1986. 49–58.

Ciepiela, Catherine. "Leading the Revolution: Tsvetaeva's *The Pied Piper* and Blok's *The Twelve.*" Schweitzer et al., 111–30.

Cixous, Hélène. "Poetry, Passion, and History: Marina Tsvetayeva." *Readings: The Poetics of Blanchot, Joyce, Kafka, Kleist, Lispector, and Tsvetayeva.* Minneapolis: University of Minnesota Press, 1991. Chapter 4.

Demidova, Alla. "The Theatre Must Heal Souls." *Soviet Literature* 3 (1989): 178–81.

Dykman, Amindav. "Poetical Poppies: Some Thoughts on Classical Elements in the Poetry of Marina Tsvetaeva." *Literary Tradition and Practice in Russian Culture.* Ed. Valentina Polukhina, Joe Andrew and Robert Reid. Atlanta: Radophi, 1993. 163–76.

Ehrenburg, Ilya. *People and Life.* Vol. 1. New York: Knopf: 1962.

Elnitsky, Svetlana, and Efim Etkind, eds. *Marina Tsvetaeva 1892–1992.* Norwich Symposia on Russian Literature and Culture. Northfield, VT: Russian School of Norwich University, 1992. [Articles in Russian and English.]

Feiler, Lily. "Marina Cvetaeva's Childhood." Kemball (1991), 37–45.

———. *Marina Tsvetaeva: The Double Beat of Heaven and Hell.* Durham, NC: Duke University Press, 1994.

———. "Tsvetaeva's God/Devil." Elnitsky and Etkind, 34–42.

Feinstein, Elaine. *A Captive Lion: The Life of Marina Tsvetaeva*. New York: Dutton, 1987.

———. "Poetry and Conscience: Russian Women Poets of the Twentieth Century." *Women Writing and Writing about Women.* New York: Barnes and Noble, 1979. 133–58.

Forrester, Sibelan. "Bells and Cupolas: The Formative Role of the Female Body in Marina Tsvetaeva's Poetry." *Slavic Review* 51, 2 (1992): 232–46.

———. "Marina Tsvetaeva as Literary Critic and Critic of Literary Critics." *Russian Writers on Russian Writers*. Ed. Faith Wigzell. Providence, RI: Berg, 1994. 81–98.

Gifford, Henry. "Joseph Brodsky on Marina Tsvetaeva." *Russian Writers on Russian Writers*. Ed. Faith Wigzell. Providence, RI: Berg, 1994. 117–30.

Gladkova, Tatiana and Lev. Mnukhine, *Bibliographie des oeuvres de Marina Tsvetaeva.* 2d ed., revised and updated. Paris: Institute d'Études Slaves, 1993. [An exhaustive bibliography of the publication and republication of Tsvetaeva's works in the original and in translation.]

Gove, Antonina Filonov. "The Feminine Stereotype and Beyond: Role Conflict and Resolution in the Poetics of Marina Tsvetaeva." *Slavic Review* 36 (1977): 231–56.

———. "Marina Cvetaeva's Evolving Poetics of Love and Friendship, Moscow, 1921–1922." Kemball (1991), 170–78.

———. "The Modernist Poetics of Grief in the Wartime Works of Tsvetaeva, Filonov, and Kollwitz." *Russian Narrative and Visual Art*. Ed. R. Anderson and Paul Debreczeny. Gainesville: University of Florida Press, 1994.

———. "Parallelism in the Poetry of Marina Cvetaeva." *Slavic Poetics: Essays in Honor of Kiril Taranovsky*. Ed. Roman Jakobson, C.N. Van Schooneveld and Dean S. Worth. The Hague: Mouton, 1973. 171–92.

Hasty, Olga Peters. "Marina Tsvetaeva's Cycle *Poèty*." Schweitzer et al., 131–46.

———. "*Poema* vs. Cycle in Cvetaeva's Definition of Lyric Verse." *Slavic and East European Journal* 32, 3 (1988): 390–98.

———. "Reading Suicide: Tsvetaeva on Esenin and Maiakovskii." *Slavic Review* 50, 4 (1991): 836–46.

———. "Tsvetaeva's Onomastic Verse." *Slavic Review* 45, 2 (1986): 245–56.

———. "Tsvetaeva's Sibylline Lyrics." *Russian Literature* 19, 4 (1986): 323–40.

———. "'Your Death': The Living Water of Cvetaeva's Art." *Russian Literature* 13, 1 (1983): 41–64.

Heldt, Barbara. "Marina Cvetaeva and the Three Women of the Pushkin Myth." Kemball (1991), 142–45.

———. *Terrible Perfection: Women and Russian Literature*. Bloomington: Indiana University Press, 1987.

———. "Two Poems by Marina Tsvetayeva from 'Posle Rossii'." *The Modern Language Review* 77 (1982): 679–87.

Hingley, Ronald. *Nightingale Fever: Russian Poets in Revolution*. New York: Knopf, 1981.

Hughes, Olga R. *The Poetic World of Boris Pasternak*. Princeton, NJ: Princeton University Press, 1974. 105–06, 109–10.

Hughes, Robert. "Poets Without '-isms'—Cvetaeva and Chodasevich." Kemball (1991), 207–20.

Iswolsky, Helene. *No Time to Grieve: An Autobiographical Journey from Russia to Paris to New York*. Philadelphia, 1985. 173–74, 196–203.

Ivanov, Vsevolod. "The Poetry of Marina Tsvetaeva." *Pages from Tarusa: New Voices in Russian Writing*. Trans. Phillipe Radley. Boston: Little, Brown, 1964. 285–87.

Ivina, Zhanna. "With the Grandeur of Homer and the Purity of Sappho. . . ." *Women and Russia: Feminist Writings from the Soviet Union*. Ed. Tatyana Mamonova. Boston: Beacon Press, 1984. 155–63.

Kahn, Andrew. "Chorus and Monologue in Marina Tsvetaeva's *Ariadna*: An Analysis of Their Structure, Versification, and Themes." Schweitzer et al., 162–93.

Karlinsky, Simon. "Cvetaeva in English: A Review Article." *Slavic and East European Journal* 10 (1966): 191–96.

———. "Kuzmin, Gumilev and Cvetaeva as Neo-Romantic Playwrights." *Russian Theater in the Age of Modernism*. Ed. Robert Russell. New York: St. Martin's Press, 1990. 106–22.

———. *Marina Cvetaeva: Her Life and Art*. Berkeley: University of California Press, 1966.

———. *Marina Tsvetaeva: The Woman, Her World, and Her Poetry*. Cambridge: Cambridge University Press, 1985.

Kelly, Catriona. "Marina Tsvetaeva (1892–1941)." *A History of Russian Women's Writing (1820–1992)*. Oxford: Clarendon, 1994. 301–17.

———. "Missing Links: Russian Women Writers as Critics of Women Writers." *Russian Writers on Russian Writers*. Ed. Faith Wigzell. Providence, RI: Berg, 1994. 67–79.

Kemball, Robin. "Innovatory Features of Tsvetaeva's Lyrical Verse." *Russian Literature and Criticism.* Ed. Evelyn Bristol. Berkeley, CA: Berkeley Slavic Specialties, 1982. 79–100.

———, ed. *Marina Tsvetaeva: Actes du 1er colloque international, Lausanne, 1982.* Berne: Peter Lang, 1991. [Articles in Russian and English.]

Knapp, Liza. "Tsvetaeva and the Two Natal'ia Goncharovas: Dual Life." *Cultural Mythologies of Russian Modernism.* Ed. Irina Paperno. Berkeley: University of California Press, 1992. 88–108.

Kroth, Anya. "Androgyny as an Exemplary Feature of Marina Tsvetaeva's Dichotomous Poetic Vision." *Slavic Review* 38, 4 (1979): 563–82.

———. "The Poet and Time in Marina Tsvetaeva's Philosophical Essays." *Russian Literature and American Critics: In Honor of Deming Brown.* Ed. Kenneth Brostrom. Ann Arbor: University of Michigan Press, 1984. 139–47.

———. "Toward a New Perspective on Marina Tsvetaeva's Poetic World." *Wiener Slawistischer Almanach, Sonderband* 3 (1981): 5–28.

Livingstone, Angela. "Marina Tsvetaeva and Russian Poetry." *Melbourne Slavonic Studies* 5–6 (1971): 178–93.

Makin, Michael. *Marina Tsvetaeva: Poetics of Appropriation.* Oxford: Oxford University Press, 1993.

———. "Marina Tsvetaeva's 'Nayada.'" *Essays in Poetics* 11, 2 (1986): 1–17.

———. "Text and Violence in Tsvetaeva's *Molodets.*" *Discontinuous Discourses in Modern Russian Literature.* Ed. Catriona Kelly et al. New York: St. Martin's Press, 1989.

Malmstad, John. "The Bachmet'ev Archive of Columbia University—The Cvetaeva and Emigre Holdings." Kemball (1991), 411–16.

Marreo, Mara Negron. "Crossing the Mirror to the Forbidden Land: Lewis Carroll's *Alice in Wonderland* and Marina Tsvetaeva's 'The Devil.'" *Writing Differences: Readings from the Seminar of Hélène Cixous.* Ed. Susan Sellers. New York: St. Martin's Press, 1988. 66–70.

McDuff, David. "A Note on Translating Tsvetaeva." *Parnassus: Poetry in Review* 12–13, 2–1 (1985): 103–15.

Mirsky, D.S. "Marina Tsvetaeva." *Tri-Quarterly* 28 (1973): 88–93.

Mnukhin, Lev. *Marina Tsvetaeva: Bibliograficheskii ukazatel' literatury o zhizni i deiatel'nosti: 1910–1941 gg. i 1942–1962gg.* Vienna: Wiener Slawistischer Almanach 23, 1989. [A bibliography of secondary works in Russian from 1910 through 1962.]

Motailo-Kroth, Ania. "Marina Tsvetaeva i o nei: Bibliograficheskii ukazatel' sovetskikh publikatsii (1985–1990)." 267–278. [A useful bibliography of primary and secondary Tsvetaeva materials published in the Soviet Union during the glasnost years.]

Naiman, Anatoly. "Air. Suffocation. Muteness: Akhmatova, Mandelshtam, Pasternak, and Tsvetaeva." *Russian Writers on Russian Writers.* Ed. Faith Wigzell. Providence, RI: Berg, 1994. 99–116.

Naydan, Michael, "Tsvetaeva, Marina Ivanovna." *Dictionary of Russian Women Writers.* Ed. M. Ledkovsky et al. Westport, CT: Greenwood Press, 1994. 664–67.

Pasternak, Boris. *I Remember. Sketch for Autobiography.* New York: Pantheon, 1959.

Pierpont, Claudia Roth. "The Rage of Aphrodite." *The New Yorker*, 7 February 1994, 90–98.

Proffer, Elendea. *Tsvetaeva: A Pictorial Biography.* Ann Arbor, MI: Ardis, 1980.

Raevsky-Hughes, Olga. "Marina Tsvetaeva on Wealth and Gratitude." *For SK: In Celebration of the Life and Career of Simon Karlinsky.* Ed. Michael S. Flier and Robert P. Hughes. Berkeley, CA: Berkeley Slavic Specialties, 1994. 247–54.

Razumovsky, Maria. *Marina Tsvetayeva.* Chester Springs, PA: Bloodaxe Books, 1995. [Translation of her *Marina Zwetajewa: Mythos und Wahrheit.* Vienna, 1981.]

Sandler, Stephanie. "Embodied Words: Gender in Cvetaeva's Readings of Pushkin." *Slavic and East European Journal* 34, 2 (1990): 139–157.

Schweitzer, Viktoria. "Journey to Elabuga." *Russian Literature Triquarterly* 16 (1979): 269–77.

———. *Tsvetaeva*. New York: Harvill, 1993. [A slightly abridged translation of her *Byt i bytie Mariny Tsvetaevoi*, Paris, 1988.]

———, Jane Taubman, Peter Scotto and Tatyana Babyonysheva, eds. *Marina Tsvetaeva: One Hundred Years: Papers from the Tsvetaeva Centenary Symposium, Amherst College*. Berkeley, CA: Berkeley Slavic Specialties, 1994.

Scotto, Peter. "Toward a Reading of Tsvetaeva's *Feniks*." Schweitzer et al., 194–201.

Sloane, David A. "'Stikhi k Bloku: Cvetaeva's Poetic Dialogue with Blok." *New Studies in Russian Language and Literature*. Ed. Anna-Lisa Crone. Columbus, OH: Slavica, 1986. 258–70.

Slobin, Greta N. "Marina Tsvetaeva: Story of an Inscription." *For SK: In Celebration of the Life and Career of Simon Karlinsky*. Ed. Michael S. Flier and Robert P. Hughes. Berkeley, CA: Berkeley Slavic Specialties, 1994. 281–96.

Slonim, Marc. "Notes on Tsvetaeva." *Russian Review* 31 (1972): 117–25.

Smith, Alexandra. "The Cnidus Myth and Tsvetaeva's Interpretation of Pushkin's Love for N. Goncharova." *Essays in Poetics* 14, 2 (1989): 83–102.

———. "Tsvetaeva and Pasternak: Depicting People in Poetry." *Essays in Poetics* 15, 2 (1990): 94–101.

Smith, G. "Characters and Narrative Modes in Marina Tsvetaeva's *Tsar-Devitsa*." *Oxford Slavonic Papers NS* (1979): 117–34.

———. "Compound Meters in the Poetry of Marina Cvetaeva." *Russian Literature* 8 (1980): 103–23.

———. "Logaoedic Meters in the Lyric Poetry of Marina Tsvetayeva." *Slavonic and Eastern European Review* 53, 132 (1975): 330–54.

———. "Marina Cvetaeva's *Poèma gory: An Analysis*." *Russian Literature* 6 (1978): 365–88.

———. "Marina Tsvetayeva: Additions to the Canon." *Slavonic and East European Review* 56 (1978): 287–91.

———. "Versification and Composition in Marina Cvetaeva's *Pereulochki*." *International Journal of Slavic Linguistics and Poetics* 20 (1975): 61–92.

———. "The Versification of Marina Tsvetayeva's Lyric Poetry 1922–1923." *Essays in Poetics* 1 (1976): 21–50.

———. "The Versification of Russian Emigre Poetry 1920–1940." *Slavonic and East European Review* 16 (1978): 32–46.

Sontag, Susan. "A Poet's Prose." Introduction to M. Tsvetaeva, *A Captive Spirit*. London: Virago, 1983.

Taubman, Jane. *A Life Through Poetry: Marina Tsvetaeva's Lyric Diary*. Columbus, OH: Slavica, 1989.

———. "Marina Tsvetaeva and Boris Pasternak: Toward the History of a Friendship." *Russian Literature Triquarterly* 2 (1972): 304–21.

———. "Tsvetaeva and Akhmatova: Two Female Voices in a Poetic Quartet." *Russian Literature Triquarterly* 9 (1974): 335–69.

———. "Tsvetaeva and the Feminine Tradition in Russian Poetry." Schweitzer et al., 77–90.

———. "Women Poets of the Silver Age." *Women Writers in Russian Literature*. Ed. Toby Clyman and Diana Greene. Westport, CT: Greenwood Press, 1994. 171–88.

Tavis, Anna. "Lives and Myths of Marina Tsvetaeva." *Slavic Review* 47 (1988): 518–21.

———. "Marina Tsvetaeva Through Rainer Maria Rilke's Eyes." Elnitsky and Etkind, 219–29.

———. "Russia in Rilke: Rainer Maria Rilke's Correspondence with Marina Tsvetaeva." *Slavic Review* 52, 3 (1993): 494–511.

Thomson, R.D.B. "Cvetaeva and Pasternak 1922–1924." *Boris Pasternak and His Times*. Ed. L. Fleishman. Berkeley, CA: Berkeley Slavic Specialties, 1989. 58–90.

———. "The Metrical and Strophic Inventiveness of Tsvetaeva's First Two Books." *Canadian Slavonic Papers* 30 (1988), 220–44.

———. "Modulating Meters in the Plays of Marina Cvetaeva." *Russian Literature* 25 (1989): 525–49.

———. "Towards a Theory of Enjambment: With Special Reference to the Lyric Poetry of Marina Cvetaeva." *Russian Literature* 27, 4 (1990): 503–32.

———. "Tsvetaeva's Play *Fedra*: An Interpretation." *Slavonic and East European Review* 67 (1989): 337–352.

Toker, Leona. "Tsvetaeva's 'Novogodnee.'" *Explicator* 47, 1 (1988): 31–33.

Tsvetaeva, Anastasia. "Reminiscences." *Soviet Studies in Literature* 18, 2 (1982): 3–90; 3 (1982): 3–89; 4 (1982): 3–93.

———. *Vospominaniia*. Moscow: 1971, 1974, 1983.

Venclova, Tomas. "On Russian Mythological Tragedy: Vjaceslav Ivanov and Marina Cvetaeva." *Myth in Literature*. Ed. Andrej Kodjak et al. Columbus, OH: Slavica, 1985.

Vitins, Ieva. "Escape from Earth: A Study of Tsvetaeva's Elsewheres." *Slavic Review* 36, 4 (1977): 644–57.

———. "Mandel'shtam's Farewell to Marina Tsvetaeva: 'Ne veria voskresen'ia chudu.'" *Slavic Review* 46, 2 (1987): 266–80.

———. "Marina Cvetaeva's Poema 'S moria.'" Kemball (1991), 250–61.

Weeks, Laura. "'I Named Her Ariadna . . . ': The Demeter-Persephone Myth in Tsvetaeva's Poems to Her Daughter." *Slavic Review* 49, 4 (1990): 568–84.

Zekulin, Gleb. "Marina Tsvetaeva's Cycle: Poems for Bohemia." *Melbourne Slavonic Studies* 9–10 (1975): 31–38.

———. "Marina Tsvetaeva's Cycle 'Stikhi k Chekhii' and Its Translation into Czech." *Canadian Slavonic Papers* 34, 3 (1992): 301–09.

Zinaida Vengerova

Zinaida Vengerova (1867–1941).
Courtesy of Rosina Neginsky.

At the end of the nineteenth century the name of Zinaida Afanas'evna Vengerova (1867–1941) was well known to the Russian reader. Her works appeared in many leading Russian journals and newspapers—*The Herald of Europe* (*Vestnik Evropy*), *Education* (*Obrazovanie*), *God's World* (*Mir Bozhii*), *The Northern Herald* (*Severnyi vestnik*), *The Sun Rising* (*Voskhod*), *Theater News* (*Teatral'nye novosti*), *News* (*Novosti*), *Northern Courier* (*Severnyi Kur'er*), among others. Her works and four books were widely known, not only among the Russian intelligentsia, but among the general Russian reading public. Her articles, written in foreign languages about Russian literature and about events of Russian cultural life, were published and widely read in France, England and Germany.

After the revolution, however, Vengerova's name disappeared from the pages of Russian literary journals and newspapers and was quickly forgotten. Her association with the Russian Symbolist movement, considered by the Soviets as "conservative and bourgeois," and her emigration made her unfashionable in Soviet Russia.

At the present time, Vengerova's name is often associated with a critical analysis of Western literature, especially modernist literature, and with the promulgation of that literature in Russia. Vengerova, however, was more than a literary critic who supported and promoted western European modernism in Russia; she was herself a modernist writer and especially a representative of Russian Symbolism, in itself a part of Russian modernism. All Vengerova's articles were based on the principles of Russian Symbolism. In her "Autobiographical Essay" ("Avtobiograficheskaia spravka," 1914), she writes:

> I perceived Symbolism and continue to perceive it as an essence of Modernism, and that is how I endeavored to interpret it in all my works. . . . Under the sign of Symbolism I perceive the best that art created in the past and continues to create in the present. That view I consider to be the basis of everything I wrote.[1]

Vengerova did not choose fiction or poetry as a main vehicle for the expression of the philosophy of Russian Symbolism, but remained faithful to literary criticism, the area with which she was most familiar. Through writing about western European literature and art, little known in Russia, Vengerova professed her own version of the Symbolist views and ideas at the basis of all Symbolist writings. In writing about literature and art, Vengerova endeavored to show how, at best, they are dedicated to the embodiment of the disembodied. Literature and art do not the describe visible social reality, but the world of the invisible that surrounds us, influences us and is sensed by us. Vengerova perceives as Symbolist any kind of literature or art that describes the world of the invisible, independently of its "official" title. In her "Autobiographical Essay" she writes: "Symbolism is everything that is related to the essential *incarnation* of the *unincarnated.* A Symbolist is one who is not driven into the present moment and does not fade from it, but who centers his existence in it as a search for life's aim, as a path."[2]

Vengerova was born on 19 April 1867 in Sveborg.[3] Her mother, Paulina Iul'evna Vengerova (1833–1916), was the daughter of a rich and cultured merchant and achieved modest fame with her well-received book, *Memoirs of a Grandmother* (*Memoiren einer Grossmutter*), written and published in German in Berlin in 1908–1910. Vengerova's maternal grandfather, Ieguda Epstein, was known for his famous commentaries written about the Talmud. Zinaida's father was a director of a bank in Minsk and played an important role in the life of the city. Zinaida had two brothers, Semen and Vladimir, and four sisters—Elizaveta, Fanny, Mania and Isabella. The family was very learned and the children very talented.

Semen Afanas'evich Vengerov, the older of the brothers, was a literary critic and literary historian. He taught at the University of St. Petersburg, in the Institute of Higher Studies for Women (Vysshie zhenskie bestuzhevskie kursy) and at the Psychoneurological Institute. He was also the author of many books about the history of literature and of historical biographies of Russian writers. Zinaida's sister Fanny was married to Ludwig Zinov'evich Slonimskii, a man of letters and a journalist, who in 1882 became one of the editors of *The Herald of Europe* and was responsible for the Foreign Survey of that journal. Zinaida's dearest sister, Isabella, became a well-known music teacher and pianist, both in Russia and in America, to which she emigrated in 1923.

Zinaida studied literature and foreign languages from childhood. She spent her early years in St. Petersburg, then in Minsk, where she graduated from the gymnasium in 1881. Then for two years she lived in Vienna, where she studied western European literature. From 1884 to 1887 she was a student at the Institute of Higher Studies for Women in St. Petersburg. When she graduated she moved to Paris, taking classes in literature at the Sorbonne, and then to London, where she worked at the library of the British Museum. She also traveled in Italy and Switzerland during 1892–1893.

In Paris Vengerova met and became close friends with Sofiia Grigor'evna Balakhovskaia (1870–1966), the first woman in Europe who had graduated from a law school and was accepted at the lawyers' bar (*s'inscrire au barreau*). Balakhovskaia also became known because of the help that she, together with her husband, Eugene Petit (1871–1938), an influential politician, gave to the representatives of Russian culture who needed visas to emigrate to France. The beneficiaries of their help included the Merezhkovskiis, Shestov and his family, Bunin and Berdiaev. In Paris, Vengerova also became close to Petr Lavrovich Lavrov, a Russian revolutionary, philosopher and literary critic. At his house she met the middle daughter of Karl Marx, Laura, and her husband, Paul Lafargue.

In London Vengerova met and subsequently became close friends with Sergei Mikhailovich Stepniak-Kravchinsky, a Russian revolutionary and writer, and his wife, Fanny. Stepniak introduced Vengerova to a group of English liberal intelligentsia including Constance Garnett, a translator of Russian literature, and her husband, Edward Garnett, a literary critic; the Moscheles family of English painters, Felix and Marguerite; and the youngest daughter of Karl Marx, Eleanora Aveling, who was very absorbed in Shakespearean studies. Although Vengerova shared some of the political views of these people, they attracted her mainly for their literary interests.

The essence of Vengerova's literary creativity was established already in the late 1880s. In her first article, "John Keats and His Poetry" ("John Keats i ego poèziia), which appeared in *The Herald of Europe* for 1889, Vengerova emphasizes that the characteristic creativity of Keats' art is his glorification of those aspects of the universe that allow the individual to detach himself from the surrounding physical reality and to immerse himself in the world of dreams and beauty, a world of more complete and more perfect reality. The same theme continues throughout her articles of the early 1890s, especially in "Symbolist Poets in France" (Poètysimvolisty vo Frantsii),[4] "R. Browning and His Poetry" (R. Browning i ego poèziia"),[5] "George Meredith"[6] and others, and is predominant in the chronicles "News of Foreign Literature" ("Novosti inostrannoi literatury"), which she prepared for *The Herald of Europe* from 1893 to 1909.

All of Vengerova's articles, regardless of their philosophical essence, had an educational character. They were dedicated to western European writers who were little known or unknown in Russia and, written in a clear and accessible manner, were very popular with readers, despite the generally negative attitute toward Symbolism among the general public.

Boris Glinskii, in his derisive article "Illness or Advertisement" ("Bolezn' ili reklama")[7] about Russian Symbolists, in which he calls them "literary psychopaths," writes about Vengerova: "Her sketches are written with a great knowledge of her subject, in a quite literary manner and surprisingly, in an accessible and clear language, without any eccentricity and garish symbolisms. . . . Maybe the respectable editorial committee of *The Herald of Europe*, that freely publishes these articles about literary psychopathy, corrects the style of their colleague, but the most probable thing is to suppose that Mme. Vengerova is only in the first stages of her illness."[8]

In 1893, when Vengerova returned to Russia, she developed friendships within a group of Symbolists—Gippius, Merezhkovskii, Minskii, Sologub, Bal'mont, Fofanov—whose public center was the journal *The Northern Herald*, published by Liubov' Iakovlevna Gurevich and Akim L'vovich Flekser-Volynskii. She worked for that journal, wrote many articles and completed a number of translations until the journal closed in 1899. All of Vengerova's articles written for *The Northern Herald* were dedicated to the representatives of western Symbolism or to those whom she classified as Symbolists. In 1893 she wrote an article about William Morris, "The New Utopia" ("Novaia utopia"); in 1895, "Letter from Italy. The Painting Exhibit in Venice" ("Pis'mo iz Italii. Khudozhestvennaia vystavka v Venetsii"), about the spiritual novelty of Italian painting at the turn of the century. In 1896 she published articles on Paul Verlaine, Huysmans and an excellent article, "The Founder of English Symbolism" ("Osnovatel' angliiskogo simvolizma"),[9] about the eighteenth-century English painter, printer and poet William Blake.

In 1896 Vengerova joined the journal *Education* (*Obrazovanie*) as a literary critic and completed, among others, articles about Thomas Carlyle (1896), Henrik Ibsen (1896), "Literary Criticism in Modern France" (1897), Alphonse Dodé (1898), "Modern English Painting" (1898) and "Individualism in Modern Literature" (1898).

In 1897 Vengerova published the first volume of her first book, *Literary Characteristics* (*Literaturnye kharakteristiki*), which included the most interesting of her earlier published articles, such as articles on Dante Gabriel Rossetti, William Morris, Oscar Wilde, Dante Alighieri, George Meredith, Francis of Assisi, Sandro Botticelli and others. In her letters to S.G. Balakhovskaia-Petit, Vengerova states that, at first, she called her book *Book on Symbolism* (*Kniga po simvolizmu*). In the introduction to the first volume, Vengerova explains that the goal of her book is to identify typical characteristics of modern literature and art in western Europe, and to show the common philosophical basis of the creativity of modern poets, writers and painters of different western European countries. This approach was not understood by the majority of literary critics who reviewed her book, mainly because they could not see any similarities between Huysmans and Dante and could not accept that Vengerova put such writers as Ibsen and Hauptmann together in the same category with Oscar Wilde and the French Symbolists.

Vengerova's second and third books of *Literary Characteristics* appeared in 1905 and 1912 and contained articles on Émile Zola, Anatole France, Gabriele d'Annunzio, Guy de Maupassant and other "unconventional" Symbolists. Book reviewers treated these two volumes more charitably than the first, because they were learning more about her criteria for symbolism and were beginning to understand better the essence of that movement. In 1913, Vengerova published the first volume of a projected ten-volume work, *English Writers of the Nineteenth Century* (*Sobranie sochinenii. Angliiskie pisateli 19–ogo veka*). World War I interrupted that project, however. During the war, Vengerova lived in Great Britain, where she became acquainted with Ezra Pound and Wyndham Lewis, English imagists, and was the first to introduce them to the Russian audience.

In 1899 Vengerova began working for the new journal *The World of Art* (*Mir iskusstva*), published by Diaghilev and his cousin Filosofov. From 1901 she collaborated with Zinaida Gippius's journal *The New Path* (*Novyi put'*) and wrote two articles, "The Singer of the Time. Henri de Renier" ("Pevets vremeni. Anri de Renier")[10] and "The Mystics of Godlessness. Emile Verhaeren" ("Mistiki bezbozhiia. Emile Verhaeren").[11]

In addition to articles about the spirit of modernism in western European literature, Vengerova also wrote about the spirit of Russian modernism in Russian literature. The majority of articles on that subject were written in French, English and German. In France, Vengerova worked from 1897 to 1899 for *Mercure de France* and was responsible for the chronicle about Russian literature, "Lettres russes." She wrote articles about Zinaida Gippius, Fedor Sologub, Anton Chekhov, Fedor Dostoevsky and other Russian writers. In England, she worked for the *Saturday Review* during 1902–1903, where she also conducted a rubric about new trends in Russian literature. In *Saturday Review*, in addition to articles about previously mentioned Russian writers and poets, she published articles about Maxim Gorky and Leonid Andreev. In 1911 Vengerova published in *Fortnightly Review* "The Life and Death of Tolstoy." In this article she endeavors to describe the spirit and philosophy of modernism in Tolstoy's works. Vengerova also worked for the German journal *Magazin für die Letter. des Auslands*. Vengerova wrote only one article in Russian about Russian literature, "The Russian Novel in France" ("Russkii roman vo Frantsii," 1899).[12]

Vengerova was also very active in the theater. She translated for Russian theaters, often from manuscripts, the works of many Western playwrights, such as Hauptmann, Schnitzler, Wedekind, Ibsen and Shaw; she also wrote about Russian and western European theater in general and about theater news in particular. Her most philosophical article about theater, emphasizing the importance of its symbolistic essence, is "About the Abstract in Theater" ("Ob otvlechennom v teatre," 1914). In this article Vengerova claims that the only great theater is that which does not imitate or describe life, but which succeeds in conveying the condition of the protagonists' souls, spirits and essences.

In the world of the theater Vengerova was very well acquainted with an actress, Lidiia Borisovna Iavorskaia-Bariatinskaia, who frequently lived in England and was instrumental in arranging for Vengerova to give lectures on Russian literature and culture to her aristocratic connections. Vengerova was also well acquainted with Konstantin Stanislavsky, with whom she often worked and about whom she wrote an article in 1897 for Brokhaus and Efron's Encyclopedia.

Vengerova was greatly interested in a very fashionable theme of the modernist period—woman and her role in society. She wrote two articles on that subject, one in French, "La femme russe," and one in Russian, "Feminism and Woman's Freedom" ("Feminism i zhenskaia svoboda"). In both articles Vengerova remains faithful to her views of the Symbolist writer and places strong emphasis on the importance of inner freedom, which she sees as the critical element enabling Russian women to be strong-willed individuals, who make important contributions to the improvement and perfection of society. Vengerova suggests that a lack of inner freedom causes French women to be nothing more than the appendages of French men, making no contribution to the perfection of the human society, but rather eroding it. In "Feminism and Woman's Freedom," Vengerova also suggests that economical and political law about women's rights can be effective only when a woman perceives herself not merely as an object or appendage but as independent and entire.

These articles reflect very important issues in the perception of women in Russian modernism: women are similar to men; they need variety in life; and have many different talents and capacities that should be explored. Although they play a more important role in procreation than men, this should not mean that everything else they are endowed with should be ignored and suppressed. Their relationships with men, like men's relationships with them, should be and can be complementary to their other activities.

Vengerova spent many years of her life abroad. Ironically, the longest period abroad before her own emigration was related to Minskii's emigration to Paris in 1905. He was her lifelong friend and in 1925 became her husband. She left Russia in 1906 and stayed abroad, in Paris and London, until 1913, occasionally returning to Russia for short visits.

In 1921 Vengerova left Russia permanently. Originally, Vengerova chose as her final destination England or France, but she had to pass through Germany—the only western European country that maintained diplomatic relations with Soviet Russia. Although she had hoped to stay in Germany not longer than a few weeks, she remained there for two years. She lived in Berlin, the center of émigré Russian culture of the early twentieth century, and was extremely active in the life of Russian literary Berlin. She worked for a number of publishing houses, some of which, like

The Argonauts (Argonavty) and Scythians (Skify), were funded by the émigré community, and others, such as Universal Literature (Vsemirnaia literatura), by Soviets. She was also one of the main editors of the Russian newspaper in Berlin, *Voice of Russia* (*Golos Rossii*), and with Andrei Belyi, Nikolai Minskii and some other writers, was a founder of the apolitical Berlin Center for Russian culture, House of Arts (Dom Iskusstv), the role of which was to receive any Russian poet, writer, literary critic or philosopher independent of his or her political views and affiliations. Among people who performed and lectured at the House of Arts were representatives of Soviet Russia, such as Mayakovsky and Ehrenburg, and also an important number of literary émigrés, including Remizov, Minskii and Shestov.

In 1923 Vengerova, with the help of her friend the English writer Hugh Walpole, obtained a visa to England, where she lived until the late 1920s, after which she moved to Paris. In England she worked mainly as a translator and editor in different publishing houses, but was able to devote time to work on other subjects that interested her. She gave lectures on Russian literature in England and Scotland, wrote an article, "Paris Archive of Prince Urusov" ("Parizhkii arkhiv kniazia Urusova"), and kept memoirs of her meeting with Eleanora Aveling that she sent to the Institute of Marx and Engels in Moscow.

In 1937, after the death of Minskii, Vengerova moved to New York City to be with her sister Isabella. She died on 30 June 1941 of Parkinson's disease.

Although Vengerova's writings are mainly critical and journalistic, she is an important writer for studying and understanding the period of Russian modernism and particularly its philosophy and complexity. Her writings show her great interest in western European literature and made her one of the first cultural ambassadors between Russia and the West. Furthermore, she is of great significance for the study and understanding of universal questions of women's issues.

Rosina Neginsky

Feminism and Woman's Freedom

"Feminism" is a social phenomenon under a French name. It came to us from France. One should listen carefully to everything that comes from there because of the particular quality of the French culture. In the area of thought, the French are not as much creators as they are bearers and promulgators of ideas. When a philosophical or social idea born in a country where people lead more solitary and profound lives comes to France, it becomes the property of the entire world. The French dress it in such brilliant shapes, surround it with such noise and embody it in such a way that it seems entirely original and created to be accepted everywhere.

There are many movements in the history of Europe that became the property of the entire cultural world only after they passed through French thought and the creative will of French activity. It is sufficient to refer to the great French Revolution, founded in the influences of English philosophy, to be convinced of how much the cultural role of France is concentrated on propaganda and not on creativity. Now we have a new example of France's cultural mission. In all European countries, especially northern countries such as England, Scandinavia and Russia, the women's emancipation movement has been taking place for a dozen years. This movement consists of the struggle against different external obstacles that prevent morally free women from leading lives that participate in all aspects of their culture. But this external liberation, demanding law reform, is possible only where woman has been from time immemorial an internally free and equal human being and where she does not have to struggle to attain a right to moral freedom and recognition of her rights. In order to make the feminine question nonexistent, it is necessary to enable woman to gain those essential external conditions that she is not currently granted in some countries as a result of stagnant customs. This is the case in the northern European countries.

In Russia, the feminine question in its proper sense does not exist. Russian women had an inner freedom even in the time of the tower-chamber (*terem*), when the wife of the *boyar* was enchained by the steel customs of the state, and peasant women, although they suffered under the burden of patriarchal life and subordinated themselves to the whim of their fathers-in-law and to the lash of their husbands, remained spiritually free and were able to create for themselves their own special interior world. They knew the ecstasy of liberation through God and were free to be mistresses of their own hearts and to love whom they wanted. Through their interior freedom they were able to accept their exterior slavery. All popular literature of the old Russia witnesses the contrast of inner freedom and exterior slavery, proving that the Russian woman was not a spiritual slave even when she lived the physical life of one.

Between the woman of ancient Russia and the modern Russian woman, who is occupied by a free work and social life, the difference is only in the exterior conditions; and in the future, when, as we should believe, all obstacles for a woman wishing to study, live and work on an equal basis with other citizens will disappear, women's status will be comparable with our times again only by the difference of external conditions. In essence, the Russian woman has never considered herself to be without moral freedom; she has never been in a situation where she has had to defend her moral rights to spiritual equality. Woman has been one of the social groups oppressed by law, and it is only against the law, not against social opinion, that she has had to fight in our century. If the struggle for freedom goes successfully, it is only because there are no inner obstacles to feminine freedom, because the Russian woman lives now the same way as she lived before, for herself and within herself, and because the feminine question as a question about a woman's right to freedom and equality does not exist in Russian society. The same thing is applicable to other northern countries. In the same way as does a Russian woman, a Scandinavian woman perceives herself first as a human being. Her awareness of her dependence on the good will of men and on social prejudices does not make her psychology more complicated.

Ibsen's heroines brilliantly prove the presence of inner freedom in the Scandinavian woman. The conveyors of Ibsen's ideas about the freedom of the individual have always been women.

How far they should be from the struggle for their feminine independence if they went further than the commonly accepted notions about social and family relationships. They do go further, and, on the contrary, wish to replace the suffering caused by seriously obsolete outdated morals with a new aesthetic world perception free of prejudice. It is not feminine equality that represents the center of all these aspirations, and it is not feminine rights that preoccupy all these Noras, Hedda Gablers and others (in their rights they are sufficiently confident), but the abstract search for truth, human freedom and perhaps inhuman beauty. It is obvious that the breaking of all social and moral beliefs is incarnated in ideal images of women who are free and strong, stronger than their modern men who are ready to compromise with traditions; it is then obvious that there is no feminine question in countries where this is true, and that one cannot exist there. And in Scandinavia, as in Russia, the spiritually liberated woman, who now leads an independent life completely unrelated to the way men perceive her and allow her to lead her life, fought for social and human rights and obtained them to a great extent.

England is another example of the fact that feminine equality in the face of the law depends on the inner consciousness of the woman herself. The English woman became free despite a multitude of social prejudices existing in the English middle class. Her interests, inclinations and circumstances of life drive her to live a family-oriented life among empty responsibilities imposed on her by worldly existence, or to lead the lonely existence of the working person, or to actively participate in the interests of society, or, finally, to lead the epicurean life of a cultured person who knows and enjoys as a spectator the general development of human strengths in life and art. In all these conditions of life the English woman is equally free and calm without being disturbed by loneliness and overwhelmed with family and world responsibilities. She always feels herself to be herself, without perceiving any kind of occupation as beyond her feminine capabilities, and, as a woman, she is universally trusted. To her, in the same way as to the Russian woman, though to a considerably lesser degree, remains the struggle for her as-yet-ungranted rights in the social structure—that is the reason for a strong and organized emancipation movement in England in the same way as there is a movement for the self-government of Ireland. But this movement, to re-emphasize the point, does not represent the feminine question, and in the absence of the feminine question, in the complete and general recognition of the moral and legal capacity of the woman, is contained the security for the indubitable victory of the English woman.

But there is a country—the most central and the most cultured—where the feminine question exists, and where its situation is so unhealthy and so desperate that to cure it one has to use the most accidental and ineffective measures. That country is France. It has lived and flourished for a long time immersed in a purely masculine culture that has succeeded in making out of woman a very necessary, very valuable and very enjoyable servant. Woman has played an important role in the French culture—she has left an indelible impression on it. But this role is active only in its results, in its general domination of *blagueu* that has created in France the cult of woman as idol (an idol is different from divinity because it is created by human hands). The French woman has been created by the demands of French men and as such is, by her nature, an absolutely passive creature. She does not have any life of her own and exists exclusively in relation to man, her master and her slave, which two roles are essentially the same because the power of the French woman, however great it is in social life, in art and in the ideals of French men, is in reality spiritual slavery.

And that dual role, very luminous in appearance, has been very satisfying to the French woman. She knows that deprived of essential rights, she uses something that is more important than any rights—privileges: in her hands are threats that control the actions of her apparent masters, and life behind the curtain of social and political existence depends to a very large degree on her desires, goals and sometimes simply her caprice. But in using this tawdry, fictional power, the French woman does not feel that she lacks her own life or that she exists only in relation to male life, only according to her attitude toward those men among whom she exists or how they treat her. Typically (we are certainly not talking about exceptional women), the French woman does not lead a life of abstract interests; she does not participate in the common structure of human life. She is always aware of the fact that she is a woman, always thinks about her feminine victories and pursues her feminine goals. And that is why on the soil of this centuries-old feminine slavery, unconscious and for this reason even more hopeless, the question of feminine emancipation, the feminine question—worn out in other European countries and searching for the right place to take root—was destined to break out with a particular force.

A French woman is happy with her situation if life smiles on her, if she is beautiful, rich and surrounded by admiration, if her life is filled with vanity, which gladdens the heart of any French man and even more so that of a French woman. But there are unfortunate women in France: those who have to work. It is hard to imagine beings more unhappy than they. The working woman is a subject of both general contempt and offensive commiseration. If she is not beautiful, she does not exist for the people among whom she lives—French people know how to be cruel and insensitive, just as they know how to let themselves be transported with generosity if something touches their delicate nerves. But the worst effect not being beautiful has on the working woman is her continual inner suffering. Nobody understands that she would have liked to not work and to be joyful.

Intellectual feminine work is restricted to teaching. Contrary to the Russian woman, who often understands pedagogical activity to be a service to society and performs it with joy and passion, the French woman is far from any such kind of idealization. She studies with all her might (all governmental tests in France are extremely difficult, and in this there are no exceptions for women) to obtain a diploma and becomes a schoolteacher or a tutor, accepting her occupation as a necessary evil with the greatest boredom. She is angry with fate for not giving her a dowry and therefore not giving her an opportunity to get married, because the unmarried French woman is a lost being to whom social life is almost entirely closed. Obliged to work, reduced to misery, the French woman feels a double yoke: the dullness of work as well as the contempt of society.

Therefore, when news came to France about the ability of women in other countries to work, participate in social life, occupy professions that had up to that point been considered the exceptional privilege of men and simultaneously become equal members of society independent of traditional societal and family roles, the idea of outward freedom seduced the French women-slaves, who found in emancipation the solution to their situation. French women did not begin to think about the internal aspect of the feminine question. The notion of woman's spiritual freedom, of the fact that women are human beings with individual goals independent of the attitudes of men, is entirely foreign to a French woman. She accepts the order of things, exists in society, exercises her privileges, and thinks nothing of her rights. But the concept of external freedom as promised by emancipation caused working women to struggle to obtain it from their Motherland,

and thus the question about feminine freedom in France transformed itself into an aspiration to improve the conditions of the working woman. That this is the spirit of French feminism is a strange thing. From France, where there is no feminine freedom, feminism spread to other countries where the feminine question had not previously existed.

"Feminism" (such a barbaric word) became the universally accepted term to describe political agitation for the good of the woman. It is peculiar that in Russia, a country foreign to the feminine question, feminism manifested itself precisely in the form of an interest in congresses, the feminine question, the organization of exclusively feminine societies, feminine work, and so on. France, as always, exercised its habitual cultural pressure and created the external image of feminism (the essence of which it gleaned from other nations), simply remaking it in its own manner by supplying it with a purely exterior and practical image. And, as always, the influence of the French culture appeared to be useful. In those countries where women do possess inner freedom, feminism as an organized movement for the conquest of certain external advantages forms a very useful and important phenomenon. In Russia, where, in general, woman does not have any need of insulation because no one has ever thought of her as being separate, the recent feminist movement has been significant in improving the situation of individual social groups, perhaps, contributing to the removal of different obstacles that have been placed in the way of women's freedom to work. But what little effect it has had on the modification of women's social condition in the absence of inner freedom can be seen in the example of France.

Feminism in France is directed mainly toward the improvement of a woman's economic life and toward giving her an opportunity to survive as an independent worker when fate fails to realize her life-ideals of security and social status through marriage. The feminine question in France closely concerns only young women who are not married, widowed women busy seeking a salary, and charitable ladies who run committees, congresses and societies representing the variety of social Christian obligations that make up part of the spiritual attire of the Catholic French woman. Let us quickly amend that statement: among French feminists there are extremely serious and talented female writers and orators, but they also think to resolve the feminine question through social and economic reforms without giving a thought to the idea that one should begin not with outward conditions but with feminine psychology itself. They think that if they populate France with woman doctors, woman lawyers, and, maybe, in the distant future, woman members of Parliament, they will modify the paradigm of the French woman. But there is a profound mistake inherent in that idea.

The surface history of French feminism is venerable and quite uncomplicated. Protests against the enslavement of the French woman through law and social prejudices began to reverberate in 1848. But those protests were isolated and quickly smothered. The opinion of Prudhon, who saw woman as "the courtesan or the housewife" (*la courtisane ou la menaghre*), was too prevalent. The feminine question began to occupy the attention of society again at the beginning of the 1860s, when a famous defender of feminine rights, Marie Deraim, the first literary French feminist, appeared in print. She was a famous writer, the author of a few pert comedies, who drew attention to herself through her articles, which were printed in the most prominent newspapers of her time. In 1866 she gave a lecture, well known in her time, in defense of women's rights. She continued to read lectures and to write on that question for several years, and she tried to instill in French society a more correct understanding of a woman's fate and convince it of the necessity of equalizing women's rights with those of other French citizens. In her demands and her defenses of woman, Maria Deraim was guided by purely revolutionary principles: abstract notions about political equality and freedom for all of a country's citizens. She was too absorbed in political ideals to be able to scrutinize French feminine psychology. She directed her entire homily toward achieving the broadening of republican legislation in its relation to women. A talented and staunch republican, Deraim thought least about the personality of the French woman—whether she felt a need for reforms and whether it was important to begin a reform from inside by changing the common understanding of the notion of freedom itself and the goals of contemporary women's lives. Deraim revolted against some French writers who supposedly slandered the French woman; for example, she wrote a very well-aimed and impassioned booklet that criticized a famous pamphlet written by Dumas, "Homme Femme." In her other books and articles, the same aspiration to resolve the feminine question through legislation is present. Her works are essentially deprived of any understanding of French women and their psychology. In 1878 Maria Deraim was the representative of the congress of feminine rights. At the same time, she stood at the head of different social unions occupied with the dogma of atheism and the struggle against the clergy. She was instrumental in getting women accepted as members of the Freemasons. The influence of this talented revolutionary was so great that others offered to present her candidacy for the chairmanship of the Chamber a number of times, though she did not accept because she understood the inopportuneness of such an attempt. Maria Deraim died only few years ago, in 1894. All her life she was closely concerned with the future of the development of the feminine question in France.

During the last few years, the younger activists of the feminine question have begun to come forward, and again the feminine question is understood in France as a demand for economic rights for women who are compelled to work. Few of these feminists perceive the defense of rights as the conclusion of their extreme republican ideas, which treat freedom in an exclusively political context. This form of political propaganda for women's rights is the province of the famous Louise Michel and the well-known Pauline Mink. Pauline Mink is a socialist, Louise Michel, an anarchist, and feminine freedom is part of their political program. Clemence Rouillet, a woman writer famous for her consideration of economic questions, has also come forward as a defender of women's rights by using history and developing the idea of the matriarch in her work. There are a few more activists who are directly concerned with the feminine question and who are presently busy organizing women's work by arranging associations among French workers, founding societies in which women of all classes are infused with the idea of the necessity of fighting against the exploitation of women's work and securing the improvement of women's everyday economic and social life. One high-ranking activist is Mme. Potognier Pierre, who created the whole range of societies and leagues.

As well or even better known is the famous Jeanne Chmaal, English by birth and French by education, the founder of *Avant Courrière*, the most extreme feminist in France, busy with the propaganda of women's rights as long as their demands do not contradict traditions and, often, prejudices of the French society. The cornerstone of Jeanne Chmaal's propaganda lies in her demands for moderate, though purely practical, measures that would lead toward the improvement of women's everyday economic life. Thanks to the moderateness of her demands, she has succeeded in gathering much sympathy and in promoting some partial reforms in the condition of the French woman. She often emphasizes that her purpose is to defend and provide the possibility of existence for a woman who has been offended by fate and cannot take advantage of the protection of her husband and family. Thus, the labor of this outstanding defender of women's rights in France has a philanthropic nature. . . .

From this extremely brief survey of the feminist movement one may see its exclusively practical nature. In order to make all these measures and all the struggle against legislation have a true effect on women's freedom, it is necessary that feminine freedom be based on psychological foundations; that in the kind of woman created by French life the inner inclination toward freedom that is present in the northern woman be expressed.

However, if we pass from what has been done for woman's external liberation, that is, from the history of French feminism, to French reality, if we look at feminine paradigms created through centuries of French culture, we will have to admit that the French woman is not ready for and is not in need of real freedom. The feminism that became a completely European and to some degree Russian phenomenon after it had been so extensively and so beautifully discussed in French congresses and the French press is in France itself a purely superficial phenomenon; in defending women and women's rights, French men and women writers and public figures satisfy only their passion for beautiful words and actions. At the same time, life follows its own trend and the psychology of the French woman takes it own shape, which is completely different from the way supposed by the defenders of women's rights. They think, mistakenly, that it is necessary to defend a woman, to give her rights, to grant her something and make something out of her. Only when she becomes herself and is fully aware that she is not only a woman but also a human being, only then, perhaps, will the feminine question disappear, defense become superfluous and something that cannot be created either by law or by articles and congresses—the inner awareness of freedom—be born.

In the meantime, the psychology of the modern French woman can be reduced to a few main stereotypes, reflected in the works of the century's best writers of French literature, both those who are considered to be enemies of woman, and those who, on the contrary, raise woman up onto a pedestal. The entire novelistic tradition of the nineteenth century is preoccupied with the study of women, but that study is only concerned with the significance of woman with regard to man, to whom she represents the source of joy or suffering. Each novelist and dramatist considers it his own duty to judge woman and to pass sentence on her. All representations of woman are either accusations or defenses of her from the male point of view. The majority of writers, independent in their differences on everything else, similarly prescribe woman a subservient role and divide her psychology into several main types. For them, the entire question comes down to the degree to which each of those types is useful and desirable to those whom the French woman is doomed to serve even when it seems that she rules. Since the time of the above-mentioned Prudhon, all writers have reduced their feminine character-studies to two categories: the housewife (*la menaghre*)—that is, a woman with bourgeois tendencies and virtues—and the courtesan. The defenders of woman glorify her in the name of the family; her enemies attack her for the suffering she causes in the name of love—and in almost all French literature there is no attempt made to see woman as a creature living outside of her meaning for man.

In the present century, there were two women among the major French novelists—Mme. de Staël and George Sand. Freedom-loving and passionate, they were the first to rebel against feminine slavery and were up in arms against the social fetters that presented obstacles to the free development of the feminine soul. Mme. de Staël pronounced a woman's right to genius and a free lifestyle; George Sand revolted against marriage in the name of free love. Sand's heroine Fernanda represents the paradigm of "woman-flower." All her psychology, like the beauty of her soul, is in ignorance and in readiness to love the one who is destined to become her husband. From the young woman-flower she is later transformed to a passionate woman searching for pleasure, who easily sacrifices her not-very-young husband for the first youth she meets. Of course, in love the human soul is expressed in the most colorful way, but only when it is free and is not in all its feelings the resigned instrument of masculine will. Fernanda lives and acts, feels herself happy or unhappy, in conformity with how her husband and her beloved behave. Initiative is entirely absent from her feelings. She tries to bring herself to love Jacques because he is meant to be her husband. She manages to convince herself that she loves him, that she is happy and her life is therefore fulfilled. She is either ecstatic because of her husband's soulful qualities or sad if it seems to her that he does not love her enough. Her family life is happy because Jacques seems to her to be strong and she finds support in him.

In order to awaken in her soul the more powerful feelings of love and passion rather than calm friendship, she needs a foreign source of initiative. Octave, her beloved, has to conquer her, to awaken in her a true love, to rouse her toward the new life of her heart. When she is confronted with a dramatic moment in her life, when love conflicts with the feeling of family duty, Fernanda remains passive as always. She is unable to decide for herself, and besides writing complaining letters to a girlfriend, is incapable of undertaking anything. In order to heighten the drama of her life, it is necessary for Jacques to perform a deed of generosity by arranging the happiness of his wife and her beloved, without hiding from them that their union will be accomplished at the price of his own life. Fernanda understands that Jacques will kill himself and she accepts that sacrifice in the same passive way as she has accepted everything else that destiny has brought her. . . .

If we compare Fernanda . . . with any heroine of Russian literature—with Pushkin's Tatiana, Tolstoy's Natasha or Turgenev's Elena—we will understand the abyss that separates the free soul of a Russian woman, who solves the problems of her feelings by and for herself, from the soul of a French woman, who follows somebody else's initiative even in the most intimate feelings.

George Sand was a defender of women; that is why she idealized the "woman-flower." However, a whole range of minor novelists, such as Octave Fellillier, André Tainignier, Cherbullier, and, to some extent, Alfonse Dodé, continued the further development of that type of French ingenue (or, as she is less respectfully called, the *petite blanche*) as the most uninteresting type of French woman. And more and more in French life that type of young lady, created by monastic education and secular prejudices, tends to disappear. Works of literature, where such a woman still thrives, has long observed the absence of any kind of individuality in these artificial flowers, for whom empty cutouts of life fulfill their entire existence.

In the literature of other countries, especially in Russia, which is at the forefront of the European novelistic tradition of our century, the central feminine figures are mainly young women, young creatures who bring to their first emotional experiences the entire richness of the conscious and full lives of their open souls, whereas in French fiction the life of the young woman's soul is entirely absent. It is one of the most telling proofs of the dependent role of the French woman. A French man sees woman as a creature who has been created for his pleasure and convenience, and he is brought up in the conditions that most reinforce this belief.

The greatest pleasure a French man receives in marrying a young woman is her innocence. He wishes to be her teacher in all points of view, and with this purpose he kills in her any active attitude toward life. Her girlish life has been artificially transformed into a blank white page. It is not surprising that in the middle class, in which such an attitude toward young women is strongest, a young woman dreams of marriage as liberation. Before marriage she is not allowed to get acquainted with literature, so literature—novels, poetry and drama—does not really interest her. In order to fully develop the psychology of the French woman, it is first necessary that the chains imposed on her ignorance fall. She must have the right and opportunity to manifest herself and to show what is hidden behind the apparent naivete and ardent imagination of a young lady who writes diaries, exchanges letters with girlfriends from boarding houses and is busy with only one thought: marriage.

When a French woman gets married and this period of preparation is over, she is resurrected to the life of the soul, and she undergoes an astonishing metamorphosis. The "woman-flower" is replaced by something very evil; what Alexandre Dumas perhaps justly called *la femme-animal*. Balzac had already studied this type of woman, who either concentrates on playing a game of passion and uses her charm to attain her worldly goals, or who is just the opposite, perishing as a victim of an exclusively emotional life. The most profound representation of the latter kind of French woman is certainly Madame Bovary by Flaubert, who brilliantly represented the nostalgia and emptiness of a feminine soul condemned to inaction and the search for the likeness of life in accidental meetings and relationships, in other people, and not in herself. Madame Bovary is the most cheerless tale of feminine slavery in France. No women's rights will find adherents in France, no feminism will free women, as long as France is populated with such attractive, enthusiastic, but at the same time impersonal, creatures as Flaubert's famous heroine.

The great pessimist Flaubert is always busy with representing fatal contradictions between the unconscious ideals of the human soul and harsh reality. In his works, two truths are always illustrated: the high truth of the soul with its ideal demands of life and the triumphant, plain truth of life itself. By choosing a typical, average woman who is rather pleasant and has inclinations toward high aspirations as the heroine of his best novel, Flaubert gives himself the opportunity to depict a French woman's entire mind-set and to present the ideal world of her dreams as well as the collapse of these ideals in the fatal current of everyday life. Flaubert marks the ideals of his heroine at different stages in her life. Before marriage, she dreams about the monastery; she loves the church service and novels by Walter Scott. When she dreams about her marriage, she mainly imagines the environment in which she will spend her honeymoon. "To be able to experience its entire delight, it will be important," she thinks, "to go to places with sonorous names, where it will be gratifying to abandon oneself to the sweet bliss of love and idleness. . . ."

This is what Emma Bovary dreamed about and, as if to reject the romantic environment of her dreams, her ideals did not stray far from the possible in life; she would have been able to achieve them if the circumstances of her life had taken a different shape. But since the conditions of her life were against her, and the achieved goals became illusory, then, faithful to her desires and instinctive aspirations, she looked to attain happiness by roundabout ways, and paid for it later with the price of her own life. The suicide of Emma Bovary is a symbol of the feebleness of the soul of a French woman, who perishes when she loses masculine support because she is unable to face the difficulties of life by herself. Life cruelly deceived Emma: she dreamed of a husband-hero, who would transform her existence into constant exhilaration, but the graceless and businesslike Bovary turned out to be incapable of playing the role of a hero and immediately filled her heart with boredom.

The main characteristics of Emma's soul are vanity, love of luxury, sensuality and sentimentality, and she passes all her life in search of those aspects of existence that would be able to satisfy these instinctive aspirations of her soul. If in place of her husband had been her future lover—the graceful, strong Robert, or the narrow-minded but sentimental clerk Leon—then her life would not have become a tragedy. But since she herself contributes nothing to life except her responses and an instinctive desire to fill her emptiness, her life turns into a series of collapses throughout her whole net of lies, of which Emma herself, by already being the first victim of her instincts, is not guilty. All Emma's life is a struggle with that inner enemy whom she always feels within herself without realizing it: boredom, the great boredom of an empty soul that has not discovered active feelings and is the subject of outer influences. She tries everything to fill the emptiness. She tries to believe in the heroism of her husband; she pushes him to perform useless and risky operations to become famous. She hopes that the celebrity of Bovary will cure her of her attraction to Robert. Bovary's inner life and his deep love are unknown to her. She only responds to those things that please her vanity or her sentimental sensitivity. It is the psychology of a miserable creature, weak, always looking around for support and shelter. Tender, charming Emma is ennobled by her suffering, but her suffering occurs in a vacuum; its source is her lack of will and especially her lack of individuality. Emma is loved by a number of people—by her husband and two lovers—but each of them loves her by reflecting in her the characteristics of his own soul. One loves her deeply and reverentially, another one thoughtlessly and lewdly, but each of them in one way or another experiences this feeling himself and acts accordingly; whereas, in each of Emma's love stories she is turned into the reflection of the incidental hero of her adventures. Even her suicide is not the conscious action of an insulted soul that dies from the impossibility of asserting itself. It is simply a coward's escape from life's difficulties.

In his depiction of the character of a desperately weak and internally enslaved woman, Flaubert treats his heroine with a great deal of sympathy. In contrast, sharp judge and accuser of women in his dramas is Alexandre Dumas. Nobody in French literature denounced French women as did the moralist Dumas—but neither was anybody such a worshiper of French women as was the same Dumas; nobody was capable of showing the charm of a woman with the same subtlety as he. In the name of moral, family principles and even the good of the state, Dumas stigmatizes the same *femme-animal* that he praises in the name of beauty and earthly pleasure. But even when praising or worshiping a woman, Dumas remains faithful to himself in one respect: "Woman outside her relationship to man is nothing," he says, adding, "a woman will never be able to be equal to a man." In this conviction Dumas is a deeply national writer and meets with support from French social opinion. The women Dumas depicts are quite real and support his view. He is really *ami des femmes*, as he presents himself and his views in a play of the same name. But it is in exactly this quality of being a friend of woman that he is able to recognize her power rather than her equality. He raises woman up onto a pedestal, but as a threatening enemy of the society, as an apocalyptical seven-horned monster, devouring everything around her. In "Femme de Claude," the woman is an enemy of the state; in "Étrangère," the heroine embodies dark forces whose source nobody knows; she uses the weakness of men taken by her feminine charm to her own advantage. In "Demi-monde," a semi-mercenary woman has at her disposal the destiny of people who have given her their confidence and love. All these Dumas heroines are variations on the general theme of *femme-animal*, who sees man as an enemy and strives to conquer him through humiliations. Dumas explains the vocation of these women's lives: their influence is destructive, but it destroys the most pernicious element of society—idle people. The woman who uses her beauty and natural perfidy as a means in the struggle to conquer a man is successful in tangling in her nets only superfluous people, people who live solely for entertainment. "Look carefully," says Dumas in the introduction to "Ami des femmes,"

> and you will see that woman chooses to exert her force only on people who do not have a serious purpose in life; she finds them instinctively, like an animal choosing food only useful to itself. Taking that into consideration, it is necessary to give woman complete freedom; it is even necessary to assist her. She helps social elements condemned to perish die in joy. She delivers serious, hard-working people from the last onerous burden—the extermination of parasites. She swallows inheritances—and thereby helps the reestablishment of property through work. She destroys a family and helps its revival in the name of love. Through her victims she creates fruitful soil that society needs for future crops.

Such a view on the supremacy of women leads Dumas to preaching about man's liberation from women: man should give his soul only to the aspects of life that are infinite and imperishable. If, having the ability to become Socrates, Caesar or Columbus, he becomes Werther or Othello, he is turned from a whole person into a partial one by humiliating himself and by becoming merely a literary hero, the immortal instrument of poets and the source of immoral thoughts and dreams for common people and little girls.

Man should live for abstract interests; a woman, for a man: from these relationships Dumas—a striking representative of views on women in France—never escapes. From them follows his defense of the family and demands for legislative reforms of divorce, laws regarding illegitimate children, and so on. All these laws are warranties that provide a man's peace and honor in the home. By examining woman as a submissive creature, Dumas makes all her psychology dependent on the social rules necessary for a man. He never analyzes a woman's individual, active emotion, but instead reduces her feelings to two categories: legitimate love or adulterous; honest love for a husband or criminal for a lover; open motherhood or secret. If the social conditions glorified by Dumas, or those outside prejudices that he attacks, did not exist, then Dumas's plays would not exist, since he suggests that women do not have an inner attitude toward their feelings and lack the drama of the soul. All his heroines love in the same way—they are always the same idle admirers of their beauty—and the drama of their feelings does not depend on the quality of love, but on laws and customs that divide feelings and attachments into the respectable and the criminal.

The woman obedient to instincts, the *femme-animal*, moved from Dumas's plays into the so-called psychological novel. Goncourt warns against her in *Charles Demailly, la Faustin, Manette Salamon* and other novels in which the woman is represented as ruinous to the creativity of painters, a graceful and beautiful vampire who leaves her victim only when the last drop of blood has been drunk. Uncountable authors make her the subject of novels that portray her as reigning in France. Maupassant's, Bourger's, Lotti's and their followers' novels and stories exclusively represent (with the aim of criticism or elevation, or simply psychological analysis) the struggle of the *femme-animal* and her accomplice, the idle, worldly fop. Often these novels differ only in the number of the heroine's lovers, and every time one reads a new French novel, one has to wonder about the conditional character of the plot: if the laws about the indissolubility of marriage did not exist, if the heroine's love was not for one person moral and for another criminal, the novel would not exist. Outside of social etiquette there are no inner differences in the feelings of different heroines, and in a wide range of contemporary French novels there is a succession of women resembling puppets; preoccupied with the details of their superficial, empty lives, clever and intricate, miserable and proud, nervous, tired and, especially, useless in life, slaves of their instincts and their external demands from life, they are incapable of living and feeling freedom. They do not even demand it. Their slavery is crowned with victories and filled with triumph, and they prefer it to equality with their masters, who now bend down before their own slaves.

That is how French novelists have represented and continue to represent women. Feminism, with all its aspirations to equalize women's rights with those of men, has clearly not yet created new paradigms either in life or in literature. The reason why is quite obvious. I am endeavoring to show that feminism concerns only one part of the feminine population of France—women working in different professional areas—whereas literature is mainly preoccupied with feminine types created by the idleness of the rich bourgeoisie. As long as French feminism pursues exclusively practical goals, as long as it does not elevate woman from a spiritual perspective (that is, as long as it is not based on the self-consciousness of an internally free woman), any measures providing woman with social and political equality will not make her a free person. In French feminism's present condition, the feminine question is more urgent than ever. Women have judges and defenders, but their defense consists of panegyrics about women from the male point of view. One of the latest examples of such criticism is Jules Bois's book, *Eve nouvelle.* The author of the book claims to be a feminist, and to elevate woman he takes as his duty the humiliation of man. He represents the entire history of the French culture as barbarous, consisting exclusively of the constant violation and mockery of women at the hands of men. Jules Bois depicts woman as an angel—and of course, man as a demon—and his exaggeration reaches such heights that he claims woman to be a miracle. He says that if the fathers of children were not men, who are profoundly fallen creatures, women would give birth to gods. He ascribes the weakness of the female character to the crudeness of men.

Bois's chapter about the first *coup de poing* that influenced all future generations of women is very typical as an example of an all-too-zealous defense. Women who study seem to Bois to be celestial creatures, and all women's regular work and practical activities are great deeds in the eyes of this over-enthusiastic feminist.

This kind of defense, of course, is not very a desirable phenomenon—it is one of the symptoms of the feminine question that is so hostile to feminine freedom. As long as the "woman-angel" is glorified, *la femme-animal* will be convicted, and woman will not be a human being. It is on this problem first of all that both French men and women feminists—who forget that the psychology of French women is so far away from freedom—should concentrate their attention. The Russian woman, who cannot imagine how far the French woman is from freedom, might be envious that the universities are open to the French woman and that she can take advantages of different rights than those that Russian women possess. Of course, rights are very important things, but only when the soul is prepared, when there is no feminine question and when a woman does not need defenders ready to rescue a weak angel from a demon who overwhelms her with his fists.

1898

Translated by Rosina Neginsky

Notes to the Essay

1. "Avtobiograficheskaia spravka," in *Russkaia literatura XX veka. 1890–1910* [Russian literature of the twentieth century. 1890–1910], ed. S.A. Vengerov (Moscow, 1914), 136.

2. Ibid., 137.

3. However, according to Vengerova's correspondence (see Neginsky, 1995), her place of birth is Helsingfors.

4. *Vestnik Evropy*, 1892.

5. *Vestnik Evropy*, 1893.

6. *Vestnik Evropy*, 1895.

7. *Istoricheskii vestnik* 2 (1896).

8. Ibid., 632–33.

9. *Severnyi vzestnik* 9 (1896): 81–99.

10. *Novyi put'* 4 (April 1904) [St. Petersburg].

11. *Novyi put'* 2 (February 1904) [St.Petersburg].

12. *Vestnik Evropy*, 1899.

Bibliography

Primary Works

"John Keats i ego poèziia." *Vestnik Evropy* 10 (1889); 11 (1889).
"Pis'mo iz Italii." *Severnyi vestnik* 9 (1895).
"Sochineniia Shelly." *Severnyi vestnik* 5 (1896).
"La femme russe." *Revue Mondiale* 9 (1897): 489–99.
"Stanislavskii." *Èntsiklopediia Brokgausa i Èfrona.* St. Petersburg, 1897.
"Literaturnaia kritika v sovremennoi Frantsii." *Obrazovanie* 11 (1897).
Literaturnye kharakteristiki. 3 vols. St. Petersburg, 1897, 1905, 1912.
"Feminism i zhenskaia svoboda." *Obrazovanie* 4 (1898): 73–90.
"Individualizm v sovremennoi literature." *Obrazovanie* 12 (1898).
"Sovremennaia angliiskaia zhivopis'." *Obrazovanie* 2 (1898).
"Na zapade. Gorod vneshnei kul'tury." *Obrazovanie* 11 (1899).
"Russkii roman vo Frantsii." *Vestnik Evropy* 2 (1899).
"Teatr v sovremennoi Frantsii." *Obrazovanie* 3 (1899).
"Lev Shestov. Shekspir i ego kritik Brandes." *Obrazovanie* (1900): 73.
"A. Bocklin." *Obrazovanie* 2 (1901).
"Mistiki bezbozhiia. Emile Verhaeren." *Novyi put'* 2 (1904).
"Pevets vremeni. Anri de Renier." *Novyi put'* 4 (1904).
"Tolstoy's Last Days: His Life and Death." *Fortnightly Review* 95 (1911).
"Molière." *Niva* 12 (1912).
"Moskovskie teatry." *Novaia zhizn'* 12 (1912).
Angliiskie pisateli XIX veka. St. Petersburg, 1913.
"Novaia teoriia o lichnosti Shekspira." *Vestnik Evropy* 6 (1913).
"Novyi idealism vo Frantsii. Roman Rollan." *Zavety* 8 (1913).
"Ob otvlechennom v teatre." *Zavety* 8 (1913).

"Avtobiograficheskaia spravka." *Russkaia literatura XX veka. 1890–1910.* Ed. S.A. Vengerov. Vol. 1. Moscow, 1914.

"Simvolizm v sovremennom ego ponimanii." *Dnevniki pisatelei* 2 (1914).

"Angliiskie futuristy." *Strelets* 1 (1915).

"Parizhskii arkhiv kniazia Urusova." *Literaturnoe nasledstvo* 3 (1939): 33–34.

"Otryvki iz vospominanii ob Eleonore Marks." *Voprosy literatury* 9 (1963).

Secondary Works

Baranova-Shestova, Natal'ia. *Zhizn' L'va Shestova.* Paris: La Presse Libre, 1983.

Baskov, B. "Vengerov, Semen Afanas'evich." *Russkie pisateli 1800–1917. Biographicheskii slovar'.* Vol. 1. Moscow: Sovetskaia èntsiklopediia, 1989.

Bayer, Thomas R. "The House of the Arts and the Writers' Club. Berlin 1921–1923." *Russian Berlin Publishers and Writers.* Ed. Gottfried Kratz and Zenia Verner. Berlin: Berlin Verlag Arno Apitz, 1987.

Belyi, Andrei. *Nachalo veka.* Chicago: Russian Language Specialities, 1966.

Benoit, Aleksandre. *Moi vospominaniia.* Moscow: Nauka, 1980.

Berberova, Nina. *The Italics Are Mine.* New York: Russica, 1969.

Bogdanovich, A. "Kriticheskie zametki." *Mir Bozhii* 3 (1897).

Donchin, Georgette. *The Influence of French Symbolism on Russian Poetry.* 'S-Gravenhage: Mouton, 1958.

Gizetti, A. "Z.A. Vengerova. Sobranie sochinenii, t.1, Angliiskie pisateli XIX veka." *Sovremennik* 3 (1913).

Glinskii, B. "Bolezn' ili reklama." *Istoricheskii vestnik* 2 (1896).

Ivanova, E. "Vengerova, Zinaida Afanas'evna." *Russkie pisateli 1800–1917. Biograficheskii slovar'.* Vol. 1. Moscow: Sovetskaia èntsiklopediia, 1989.

Koltonovskaia, E. "Zin. Vengerova. Literaturnye kharakteristiki. Kniga vtoraia. St. Petersburg, 1905." *Obrazovanie* 11–12, 14 (1905).

Levinson, A. "Z.A. Vengerova. Sobranie sochinenii." *Sovremennyi mir* 2 (1913).

Minskii, N. "S.A. Vengerov." *Poslednie novosti*, 9 October 1920.

Neginsky, Rosina. "Zinaida Vengerova." *Kogo poteriala Rossiia.* Moscow: Èntsiklopediia pisatelei èmigrantov, 1994.

———. "Zinaida Vengrova and Her Unpublished Correspondence." *Revue des Études Slaves* 67, 1 (1995); 2 (1995); 3 (1995); 4 (1995).

———. *Zinaida Vengerova: The Aesthetic of the Incarnation of the Unincarnated.* Doctoral dissertation, University of Michigan, Ann Arbor, 1991.

Rosenthal, Charlotte. "Modernism and Women's Liberation." *Slavonic Studies* 8 (1987).

———. "Vengerova, Zinaida Afanas'evna." *Dictionary of Russian Women Writers.* Ed. M. Ledkovsky, C. Rosenthal and M. Zirin. Westport, CT: Greenwood Press, 1994.

Anna Akhmatova

Anna Akhmatova (1889–1966).
Frontispiece from Beg vremeni, *Leningrad, 1965.*

"I am happy to have lived in these years and to have witnessed unparalleled events," wrote Anna Andreevna Akhmatova (1889–1966), who had witnessed two world wars, the October Revolution and the Russian civil war.[1] While both circumstances and timing were propitious for her and Tsvetaeva to bridge the gap to greatness that predecessors like Pavlova and Lokhvitskaia had narrowed, and Akhmatova ably molded her image and persona to match her talent, it was Russia's tumultuous destiny and vigorous cultural heritage that determined her fate.

She was born Anna Gorenko in Bol'shoi Fontan, a suburb of Odessa, to progressive-minded parents. Her father, Andrei Antonovich Gorenko (1848–1915), of Russian, Ukrainian and Greek ancestry, was a maritime engineer in the Black Sea fleet. His sisters, Anna and Evgeniia, attended Women's Medical courses and were staunch supporters of the radical political group People's Will. Her father was dismissed from his teaching position at the Petersburg Naval Academy in 1881 for an incriminating letter and ties to a terrorist. He then contributed articles, reviews and stories to newspapers until he obtained a position on a commercial vessel. A tall, charming, flamboyant womanizer and a cultural enthusiast, he introduced his daughter to the opera and theater.

Akhmatova's mother, Inna Erazmovna (née Stogova, 1856–1930), traced her paternal lineage to Novgorod nobility and her maternal lineage to Genghis Khan. Sympathetic to the People's Will, she was a student of the Bestuzhev courses and attended readings by Dostoevsky. She knew the poetry of Derzhavin and Nekrasov by heart.

The spirited third of six children, Akhmatova favored her handsome, engaging father in character and appearance. Very tall (about five feet, eleven inches), slender and agile with fair skin, thick straight dark hair, gray-green eyes, a chiseled mouth, a determined chin and an aquiline nose resembling Dante's (in her estimation), Akhmatova exuded charm and beauty that matured into regal bearing.

About her childhood Akhmatova wrote, "In our family, as far as the eye could see, no one wrote poems, although the first Russian poetess Anna Bunina was my grandfather Erazm Ivanovich Stogov's aunt."[2] She wrote to Alexis Rannit, "At home no one encouraged my first attempts; on the contrary, they were all perplexed at why this was necessary."[3] Yet initially, her older sister Inna was the family poet. Indeed, the sisters were proud of writing "new-style" poems. Akhmatova's early female models were Sappho, Anna Bunina, Karolina Pavlova and Mirra Lokhvitskaia. The last seems to have served as a starting point for articulating amorous love from a contemporary woman's perspective.[4] Akhmatova subdued and refined Lokhvitskaia's "torrid" exclamations. For example, where Lokhvitskaia is descriptive with a focus on her speaker, Akhmatova is dramatic and manages to highlight the subtle emotions of the beloved.

In August 1890 the family moved to Pavlovsk and soon settled in Tsarskoe Selo; their dark green house became imprinted in Akhmatova's memory as her archetypal residence. Here she bonded to Pushkin's vision of the town with its palace and splendid parks. As he wrote in the poem "October 19": "All the world is alien to us / Our Fatherland is Tsarskoe Selo." Her first awareness of love is linked to this locus: "There was a fountain here. . . . And the first kiss" ("To Pushkin's Town").

Akhmatova's tomboyish, unconventional youth, which included summers in the Crimea and swimming far out to sea, was aestheticized in her ballad in blank verse "By the Edge of the Sea" (1914). This poem already showed a salient feature of her artistry: actual circumstances are distanced, aestheticized and yet remain uncannily true to life, so much so that people strove to discuss her biography on the basis of the poems. The ballad treats an adolescent girl's search for her destiny by the sea, where she swims and communes with the working-class populace—the fishermen, the inhabitants, the gypsy woman—in an attempt to escape the confining circumstances of her home with no mention of parents, only a bedridden beatific twin sister whose piety finds expression in embroidering a shroud for the church. The twin sisters symbolize Akhmatova's birth sign of Gemini, divided into the positive and negative—the pious sister versus the bold pagan one. Expecting a prince to claim her as queen, the speaker spurns a youth's marriage proposal and gives away her Christian belongings: her Bible to her sister and her gold cross to the fortune-telling gypsy. The essence of Akhmatova's early love lyrics becomes evident when the intrepid girl composes a love song to attract her prince. Help arrives from the Muse who began visiting her while she was dreaming by the sea. With the death of the young prince, ostensibly the youth in love with the girl in the boat race, the song remains as proof of art's endurance over life's sorrows.

At ten Akhmatova began attending the women's gymnasium in Tsarskoe Selo. She already knew Russian and French poets by heart. Her meeting with Nikolai Gumilev (1886–1921), a daring, tall, well-built young man whose arrogant demeanor disguised his shyness, took place at Christmastime in 1903. Akhmatova claims to have hardly noticed him; he spent seven years seeking her love. Literature drew them together and she must have learned much from Gumilev, who was well read, interested especially in the French Symbolists and already being published as a poet.

Following her parents' separation in 1905, Akhmatova completed her schooling at the Fundukleevskaia Gymnasium in Kiev. In 1907 she prepared for a profession at the Faculty of Law at the Kiev College for Women. Akhmatova lost interest once the courses in Latin ended and the history of law was followed by its legal aspects. Later she studied literature at the Raev Institute of Advanced History and Literature Courses for Women in St. Petersburg.

At the Sorbonne, Gumilev published one of Akhmatova's 200 poems, "On his hand are many shining rings," in his literary magazine *Sirius* (1907). She signed her name Anna G. Akhmatova and began publishing solely under this pen name after her marriage to Gumilev on 25 April 1910. The practical reason could be that her maiden and married names matched those of a relative—paternal aunt Anna Gorenko and mother-in-law Anna Gumileva. Moreover, she sought the most dramatic possibility for sound, impact and family lore and linked herself to Pushkin in bringing to the fore her non-Caucasian Tatar maternal great-grandmother Akhmatova, as Pushkin did his Ethiopian maternal great-grandfather Gannibal. Like Shakespeare and others before her, Akhmatova practiced a subtle play on the sounds and meanings of her names within her verse. The felicitous full *a* sounds blend advantageously with those in her first name to connote through the conjunction *akh* both admiration and a declaration of grief prevalent in her poetry. The much-repeated story of her father teasing her as a decadent poet and admonishing her against shaming his name is undoubtedly also true.

The pen name Anna Akhmatova was launched in 1911 with the publication in *Apollon* of "Four Poems," among them "The Gray-Eyed King." Fifteen poems were to appear in journals before their publication (at the author's expense) in 300 copies of her first collection of poems, *Evening* (*Vecher*, 1912). Many of the poems were crafted during the adventurous Gumilev's expedition to Africa in 1910–1911. Amanda Haight attributes the poems' tight construction to Akhmatova reaching "the end of the process of distillation Pushkin had begun with his 'Little Tragedies.'"[5] Although perfect in form and content, to this day these popular miniature poems are trivialized by critics as lightweight love lyrics of disenchantment and keening (forgetting that history has been kinder to Petrarch, who wrote exclusively on love, albeit from a man's perspective). Criticism aside, the sophisticated miniature love lyrics were her principal innovation in Russian poetry. Moreover, scholars have abundantly demonstrated additional levels of intricate profundity and allusive wealth hidden within the "simple" perfection of the early poems that culminated in the later overtly complex poems.

The leitmotif of most of Akhmatova's early poems is love gone wrong or unfulfilled aspirations. The poems often contain the nucleus of a plot, offered in hints, concrete details, dialogue and references to nature. The outcome is the denouement of the romantic relationship between the couple. The short, terse lyrics usually convey images in a first-person narrative through questions, oxymoron and other tropes and figures. The female speaker represents different individuals, often strongly divergent from the poet herself but always a general representative of many young women. The presence of biographical details has encouraged some investigators (e.g., Viktor Vinogradov) to view the poems as the fragments of a lyrical diary, "intimate" letters, brief novellas.[6] This intimate effect is enhanced by the time setting. Evening is the logical time for daily diary entries and stocktaking, as well as symbolically the time for the young Romantic heroine's awakening to and anticipation of love. Her expression remains simple and apt, the rhythm flows slowly. Most devices, other than the pervasive anaphoric "and" and "but" in the monumental style of Old Russian, are unobtrusive, so much so that Akhmatova's complexity and finesse were long overlooked.

Her early period is marked by both iambic and trochaic meters, used almost equally; in the late period the use of iambic meter triples. Mikhail Gasparov explains the change as movement from the "intimate" to the "elevated." *Dol'niki* are used equally with binary meters only in the very early period when Akhmatova gave the final touches to Blok's initial shaping of *dol'nik.*[7]

With the Symbolist movement in "crisis," Gumilev and Sergei Gorodetskii organized the Poets' Guild in 1911. Among its fifteen members were Osip Mandel'shtam (1891–1938) and Gumilev's relative by marriage, the poet Elizaveta Kuzmina-Karavaeva (Mat' Mariia), whose excessive mysticism Akhmatova deplored. Akhmatova's poetry served as the ideal for the emerging Acmeists, who formally established their movement in 1913 to espouse clarity and concreteness in verse.

From the outset Akhmatova aligned herself with the great poets of Russia and the world, and in doing so she distanced herself from contemporary women writers. Akhmatova disliked being put on a par with Anna Radlova early in her career. Her review of Nadezhda L'vova's posthumous poetry lacks kindness and acceptance, but it explains several of Akhmatova's own tenets. While Lokhvitskaia's theme of the beloved's gaze ("Zachem tvoi vzgliad—i barkhatnyi i shguchii" ["Why does your glance, velvety and burning"]) found resonance in Akhmatova's "Confusion," and Akhmatova's *Rosary* (*Chetki*, 1914) posits eye imagery in poems advancing togetherness, Akhmatova never acknowledges Lokhvitskaia anywhere. Neither did she acknowledge Tsvetaeva, who had dedicated a cycle to her in 1916, until their meeting in 1940. The impressions of those meetings generated the haunting poem of desolation and loss to a snowstorm symbolizing political and personal upheaval, "A Belated Reply." It connects with Akhmatova's "Stanzas," through the unspecified images of False Dmitrii and Stalin, and with "Requiem." The poem "There Are Four of Us" (1961) evokes Mandel'shtam, Pasternak, Tsvetaeva and herself as a quartet.

Although she had many women friends, Akhmatova did not act as mentor to any women poets, with the possible exception of Mariia Petrovykh, whom the regime denied publication. She praised Petrovykh's "Make Me a Date" as one of the century's best love lyrics. Akhmatova was not accepting of Bella Akhmadulina, who is half-Tatar and whose name begins with four of the same sounds as her own. Tacit rivalry with Tsvetaeva occasioned veiled literary responses, such as "If Only You Knew Out of What Trash Poems Grow" to the latter's "Poems Grow from Roses."

Gumilev's expedition to Africa in 1913 and military service in World War I effectively ended their floundering marriage. On leaving Gumilev's home, Akhmatova became "homeless" forever. From 1918 to 1921 she lived with the Assyrologist Vladimir Shileiko (1891–1930), who isolated her and, like Nikolai Punin (1887–1953), with whom she later lived until 1938, made her read and translate for him.

Her dissociation from Gumilev took a strange turn when at Blok's funeral early in August 1921 Akhmatova learned of Gumilev's arrest with the Tagantsev group and later in the month in Tsarskoe Selo read of his execution. Her pain was coded in the images of several poems in the collection *Anno Domini* (1923), discussed below. Thus began in earnest Akhmatova's artistic dialogue with Gumilev. Concerned that his life and works could be lost for posterity, in 1924 she enlisted the help of an enthusiastic young traveler and litterateur, Pavel Luknitskii (1900–1973), to collect the legacy and to interview his friends. Akhmatova oversaw the work. Luknitskii kept a diary of their conversations that he read to Akhmatova for factual corrections, for her recall was phenomenal as she strove to propagate Gumilev's memory: "No, I do not forget. . . . How can I forget? I am simply terrified lest I forget something. A kind of mystical fear . . . I remember everything."[8] Luknitskii's entries represent a fine early complement to Lidiia Chukovskaia's celebrated Akhmatova diary, which opens in 1938 and continues with the poet's, with a ten-year hiatus for the years 1942–1952.

Book-length studies were written on Akhmatova's work by Boris Èikhenbaum (1923) and Viktor Vinogradov (1925), whereas none appeared for Mandel'shtam, Tsvetaeva or Pasternak. In 1925 E. Gollerbakh's anthology, *Akhmatova's Image,* included poems to her by Blok, Kuzmin, Mandel'shtam and Tsvetaeva. She continued to be photographed and painted, but the tacit ban of 1925 on her works precluded the publication of new poems. Akhmatova now avoided writing letters and became circumspect on the phone. Her circle of friends changed: Boris Anrep emigrated to England, and Ol'ga Glebova-Sudeikina and Artur Lur'e invited her to join them in leaving, but Akhmatova, whose brother

Andrei had committed suicide in Greece in 1920, would not be tempted, for she believed that poets must live their own country's life. She responded in verse with powerful invectives: "I Am Not with Those Who Abandoned the Land" ("Ia ne s temi, kto brosil zemliu") and "A Voice Came to Me."

Akhmatova's poetic legacy falls into three main periods: the early period (1909–1922), the period of forced relative silence (1922–1940) and the late period (1940–1966). Her *oeuvre* consists of seven collections of verse, two of which, *The Reed* (*Trostnik*) and *The Seventh Book* (*Sed'maia kniga*), were never published; narrative poems; reminiscences of famous friends (Blok, Mandel'shtam, Modigliani); unfinished biographical memoirs; and literary criticism on the life and works of Pushkin. She also participated in the first volume of the Jubilee Edition of Pushkin's *Complete Works*. The remarkable feature of her *oeuvre* is the unifying elements within the poetry and even the prose. For example, while the "lyric diary" is a continuation of *Evening* (*Vecher*), it also links up with other connections to form an amorphous design across her *oeuvre*.

Russian and European echoes (Shakespeare, Keats) reverberate even in her early works. This interior communication with the literary world, "a nostalgia for world culture" as Mandel'shtam defined Acmeism, would culminate in Akhmatova's device of extending the parameters of her compressed poetry through intertextuality, what she described as "the box has a triple bottom" in her *Poem without a Hero* (*Poèma bez geroia,* 1940–1962). Some of Akhmatova's personae explore an intimate knowledge of culture and history through metempsychosis. She echoed W.B. Yeats in believing that reincarnation represents a symbolic means of affirming the truth of poetic creation and renewal.[9] In fact, these two devices complement each other in that multiple subtexts extend the boundaries of the poet's verse ("But perhaps poetry itself / Is one magnificent quotation"), whereas metempsychosis extends the persona's experiences ("But I Warn You").

The Muse of poetry is offered special favors through the imagery of fire and grief embedded in her inherited surname Gorenko—with *gore* meaning grief and *goret'* meaning to burn. Indeed, in many poems (*White Flock* [*Belaia stada*], 1917) the speaker lives, loves and grieves in the ongoing cycles of life to create song, which will be transmuted into finished verse at the altar of the Muses.

Each collection of verse represents a seminal chapter in the speaker's life and works. Where *Evening* symbolizes the precocious teenager's Romantic awakening to premature love and abandonment, in *Rosary,* as Amanda Haight shows, the women begin to learn survival.[10] Akhmatova plays on the dual meaning of *chetki*—beads with sexual overtones and the religious rosary. She develops a distinct image of doleful poems strung together to form a bead necklace. One of the personae connected with the beads is a femme fatale: "The boy said to me: 'How painful it is.' " *Rosary,* reprinted nine times before 1923 despite war, revolution and civil war, made Akhmatova one of the most popular and imitated poets in Russia.

Several poems in *White Flock* are dedicated to Boris Anrep ("I do not know whether you are dead or alive"). The motif of a bird denoting song to be transformed into a poem with the help of the Muse pervades the poems, whose arrangement is likened to a flock. Other poems reflect Akhmatova's bouts with tuberculosis, such as "Dying, I yearn for immortality."

Plantain (*Podorozhnik,* 1921), with thirty-eight poems in the first edition, is the smallest collection of verse, made compact as if to take on a journey. Its Russian root denotes a road, from *doroga.* As in *Romeo and Juliet*, the plantain fruit is mentioned for its healing powers. The sufferers to be healed include the ravaged country and the speaker bereft of friends, who have left Russia. Among other definitions for *podorozhnik* are pies or patties taken on a long journey, a bird and an absolution prayer for the dead. Because the main addressee, Boris Anrep, abandoned his native land and beloved woman, Akhmatova, for England, the speaker sends poems and prayers in the wake of this formerly dear man. At least seventeen poems in *White Flock* and fourteen in *Plantain* are dedicated to Anrep. The collection concludes with an addendum "To Zara" ("Zare"), a translation from Anthero de Quental on the death of a teenage girl signifying the figurative meaning of the road as death. The poem was written following the suicide of Akhmatova's brother Andrei in 1920.

In its first printing in 1922, *Anno Domini MCMXXI* contained predominantly poems of that vintage, but the date was dropped from the second edition, possibly for political reasons. The collection opens with "Petrograd, 1919," about preserving the city through the fire of revolution. The poem "Bezhetsk" is named after the town where the Gumilev estate of Slepnevo was located. The name is formed from the root *beg* ("to run, flee"), which underscores flight, in this case to the countryside away from the evil city where Gumilev was executed. A number of poems immediately allude to Gumilev's tragic fate both in somewhat veiled form, "You cannot be among the living" and through the long tradition of autumnal poems in "Tearful autumn like a widow."

A new facet of the poetic persona is that the formerly often submissive female speaker not being dominated by someone or something but instead begins dominating over fate and the circumstances of life: "Obedient to you? You have lost your mind." "Lot's Wife" from the cycle "Biblical Poems" vindicates a woman whose fond memories compel her to look back at the only place she had ever lived, despite God's admonishment. It evokes Akhmatova's loss of Gumilev and of her familiar Russia, burning in civil war.

Another new motif is introduced in the form of the reed, in a collection by that same name. The reed as a maker of musical sounds and an instrument of anamnesis is evoked in poems dealing with "repressed" poets (including Mandel'shtam) and her jailed son Lev. Other elements already present in her previous works reappear. The Muse figures prominently in poems such as "Muse" ("Muza"), and the collection features poems dedicated to other writers, such as Pasternak, Mandel'shtam, Mayakovsky and Dante.

Like Gumilev, Akhmatova has seven collections. Unlike Gumilev, seven is the number of her choice, possibly done to parallel him. She included many poems in her largest collection, *The Seventh Book*, for she intended to have no more, and seven denotes completion. Her affinity to number symbolism begins with the title and continues in titles of cycles (*Cinque*), sections (*Odd*) and subtitles (*Midnight Poems: Seven Poems*). Odd numbers predominate in the symbolism of numerology, lending strength (for the war poems) to the entire collection. Other aspects of seven can be easily attested. Thus each collection depicts a new stage in her artistic development while representing a continuum with the others, particularly the contiguous ones.

Akhmatova's anguish over the arrests and deaths of friends and family during the Stalinist Terror found artistic expression in a work of exceptional brilliance—"Requiem" (1935–1940). Her son Lev's and companion Punin's arrests in 1935, mitigated by Akhmatov's letters of appeal, precipitated the first pieces. However, when nothing helped in 1938 after Lev was rearrested and eventually sent to a Siberian hard labor prison camp, Akhmatova crafted a requiem that she wisely did not commit to paper for fear of discovery by the secret police. She entrusted the poem as it was being created to the memories of several devoted friends, including Lidiia Chukovskaia. In part, the situation could explain the fragmentary nature of "Requiem" that Akhmatova herself alternately labeled a cycle or narrative poem and alternately titled in Cyrillic and Roman script.

The innovative "Requiem" consists of seventeen disparate parts symbolizing the time Akhmatova spent in prison lines, seventeen months. Maria Luisa Dodero interprets its structure as following the Calvary scheme.[11] It also reveals links to Akhmatova's original family, consisting of the three Gumilevs, by opening with the coda of Gumilev's "From Iambic Pentameter." Each poem of "Requiem" has a different form and focus, as the grief-stricken mother's reeling head remains fixed on her loss. Akhmatova's subtlety in "Requiem" is easily misunderstood, as by Aleksandr Solzhenitsyn, who remarked that the entire country was suffering but Akhmatova concentrates on one mother and her son.[12] She presents suffering, universalized as dehumanized women stand hopelessly in the queue.

The function exactly mirrors the crucifixion theme, with the Mother's loss of her only Son and the inherent concept of death and resurrection. The Virgin Mary's silence is eloquently compelling, and Akhmatova's deft interweaving of the personal aspect with the universal and the religious is correctly explained in Anna Lisa Crone's assertion, "In no work does Akhmatova merge with the nation and set herself apart from it so many times."[13] Encoded are also Mandel'shtam's imprisonment and death and other atrocities committed elsewhere in the world. Akhmatova's voice reaches beyond the 100 million Soviets in this powerful denunciation of evil and affirmation of good.

When persecution and personal problems led to the decrease of her poetic output in the late 1920s and 1930s, Akhmatova studied the architecture of Leningrad, Pushkin's life and works, and translated the letters of Rubens, the poems of Daniel Varouzhan (1884–1915) and Eghishe Charents (1897–1937), a victim of the Stalinist Terror whom she had met. Her longstanding friendship with Osip and Nadezhda Mandel'shtam remained mutually supportive.

Upon ending her relationship with Punin, Akhmatova began a remarkably fruitful period at the threshold of 1940. Kees Verheul finds that "the larger and more encompassing forms of poetic expression which Akhmatova took up and developed to suit her personal artistic needs in and about 1940 may generally be said to have provided her with adequate and sufficiently pliable tools for the literary expression of her themes throughout the later phase of her career."[14] She wrote poems in pain over Lev's imprisonment and the loss of friends to the Terror, as earlier she had transformed her sorrow over Gumilev's execution. The year 1940 was the most productive in her life, a veritable annus mirabilis.

In 1940 Akhmatova began "Poem without a Hero: A Triptych" ("Poèma bez geroia"), a unique, complex, infinitely allusive masterpiece that she continued refining until her death. Sam Driver calls it "a private poem, a laying to rest of old ghosts, an exorcism of present terrors, a catharsis."[15] Creating her own mesmerizing strophe (based on Tsvetaeva's) for part 1, "1913: A Petersburg Tale," as Pushkin did for *Eugene Onegin*, she mythologizes the poet Vsevolod Kniazev's suicide allegedly for love of Ol'ga Sudeikina, the lovely actress who preferred Blok. The trio, along with other costumed shades from 1913, visit the narrator at Fontannyi Dom on New Year's Eve. In this ingenious work, Akhmatova has radically transformed the genre of the Romantic narrative poem. The second part, "Tails," treating a writer's artistic freedom in the face of editorial (and censorship) constraints, parallels Pushkin's "Conversation of a Bookseller with a Poet." It addresses an argumentative editor unable to comprehend the love triangle. Part 3, "Epilogue," returns the speaker from evacuation in central Asia to postwar Leningrad.

The poem constitutes a descent into the recesses of memory and art to immortalize former experience in verse. The poem's prevalent device of intertextual allusion is brought to the fore and even flaunted: "I write on your drafts." Dates carry allusive significance. More pronounced than in "Requiem" are the parts describing the poem's core: "In Lieu of a Foreword," three "Dedications," "Introduction," "Intermedia," "Lyrical Digression," even letters to fictional persons. The concept of doubles for the author assumes unusual characters, such as the Heroine City, although the absent hero of the poem cannot be pinpointed. Instead, as Tat'iana Tsiv'ian states, "The text instructs the reader, assumes an investigator in the reader, makes him work and at the same time puts limits before him in such a way as to make him strive to overcome them."[16] Ultimately, as Sam Driver notes on the coda to part 3: "The sense is not of history past, but of time in an unending continuum."[17] The poem's brilliant accessible form opens avenues to its dense content.

Although a volume of collected works, *From Six Books. Poems,* was recalled after publication in 1940, Communist party controls loosened during World War II. Akhmatova even addressed Leningrad residents on the radio. Her poem "Valor" from the cycle "Wind of War" was published, and she was allowed to publish other works also. Her patriotic war poems won her the award "For the Defense of Leningrad." When she was evacuated with other writers to Tashkent in 1942–1944, her son Lev volunteered for the army from Siberia. As a former political prisoner, he was placed in the most dangerous positions. He went as far as Berlin. Akhmatova remained in Tashkent and met her old friends, Nadezhda Mandel'shtam and Elena Bulgakova. She also met with her first friend from abroad in decades—the Polish artist Joseph Czapski, who was attached to General Ander's army. For him she wrote "That night we went crazy from each other." However, the Soviet government pressed its restraint on her and her work. Her Kafkaesque play written in those years, *Enuma Elish*, was burned following Lev's final arrest in 1949, as was most of her archive. Akhmatova later tried to re-create it as "Prologue, Or a Dream within a Dream."

The wartime lifting of the ban on her publications returned some recognition to Akhmatova. A volume of her poems appeared in Tashkent. She was invited to join the Writers' Union. Her presence at the Writers' Congress in August 1946 created a sensation. Her last meeting with Sir Isaiah Berlin generated the superb cycles "Cinque" and "The Rosebrier Blooms" ("Shipovnik tsvetet," 1946–1964). Her opportunities faded entirely, however, when in August 1946 the party hatchetman Andrei Zhdanov assailed the journals *Zvezda* and *Leningrad*, singling out Akhmatova (and Mikhail Zoshchenko [1895–1958]) for anti-party publications. Akhmatova was expelled from the Writers' Union, so she earned her living by translating poetry. Most of her translations relied on sublinear prose translations of the originals by native speakers. She translated about 150 poets from thirty languages, although she believed that translations sapped a poet's creative energy and originality. A number of translations were collaborative efforts with Nikolai Kharddzhiev or Lev. After the war Lev returned home and attended classes but was rearrested in 1949. To save his life, Akhmatova was advised to write the laudatory poems that horrified her to the end of her days: the cycle "Glory to Peace." Punin, arrested earlier in 1949, died in Siberia.

In her later period Akhmatova united poems into cycles, such as the seven "Northern Elegies," with seminal biographical and historical moments. Among them are "Midnight Poems," which Nikita Struve interprets as the completion of and the conclusion to her lyrics.[18] Infused with quiet reflections—the past, the present and the future in death—the cycle is narrated in the present with some future forms. Quiet equals poetry. In the early collections the addressee fused with the concepts of husband, friend and concrete images; in "Midnight Poems" concreteness cedes to reflected images and the addressee becomes imagined; he is betrothed to silence and no meeting will take place.

Recognition at this time came mainly from outside Russia. In 1956, for significant contributions in translating twentieth-century Armenian poetry and for participation in the preparation of the Festival of Armenian Art and Literature in Moscow, Akhmatova was presented the Distinguished Merit Award from the government of the Armenian Soviet Socialist Republic. In 1962 the American Slavist F.D. Reeve arranged a momentous meeting with the poet Robert Frost at the dacha of Academician Mikhail Alekseev. Another literary award followed—the Etna Taormina Award in Literature in 1964, boosted by Akhmatova's translations with Anatolii Naiman of the Italian poet Giacomo Leopardi (1798–1837). She traveled to Sicily to accept the award, abroad for the first time in fifty years. At the celebration she recited poems from "Prologue." Oxford University conferred an honorary doctorate on Akhmatova in 1965. In England she met Sir Isaiah Berlin, her old friend, and Andrei, the son of her brother Andrei.

Back at home many friends cared for Akhmatova. Young poets came to meet her. Four young poets brightened her last years—Joseph Brodsky, Anatolii Naiman, Dmitrii Bobyshev and Evgenii Rein. Naiman replaced Nika Glen as Akhmatova's secretary. Lev had become a noted historian despite the horrors of his life but was not reconciled with his mother. Misunderstandings between mother and son were fanned by those eager to ally themselves with Akhmatova's reknown. A volume of selected works, *The Course of Time*, appeared under Akhmatova's supervision in 1965. The regime begrudgingly had to accept Akhmatova's accomplishments, but the prolonged battles with terror, persecution and deprivation took their toll on the poet's health. Recovering from a severe heart attack, Akhmatova went with her friend Nina Ol'shevskaia to a sanatorium at Domodevodo, where she died on 5 March 1966.

Publications have proliferated since the centennial conferences. A research museum has opened in Fontannyi Dom, and asteroid 3067 was named "Anna Akhmatova" by the Soviet regime that never stopped persecuting the Gumilev family, three remarkably talented individuals.

Sonia I. Ketchian

Deception

To M.A. Gorenko

I.

Spring sunlight made this morning drunk,
And on the terrace roses smelling stronger,
And the sky is brighter than blue faience.
A notebook bound in soft morocco leather;
I read inside it elegies and stanzas
Written to my own grandmother.

I see the road up to the gate, and posts
Show clear white in the emerald turf.
Oh, the heart loves sweetly and blindly!
And the gaudy flowerbeds delight it,
And a crow's sharp cry in the black sky,
And far down the walk the arching crypt.

II.

Hotly blows the stifling wind,
Sun has scorched my arms,
Over me the airy vault
Just like dark blue glass;

The immortelles smell drily
In my tousled braid.
On the gnarled fir tree trunk
Ants have made a highway.

The pond shows a lazy silver,
Life's easy in a new way. . . .
Who will I dream of today
In the hammock's bright net?

III.

Dark-blue evening. The winds fall meekly silent,
Bright light calls me to the house.
I wonder: who's there?—isn't it my suitor,
Could it be my suitor there? . . .

On the terrace a familiar outline,
The quiet conversation barely audible.
Oh, until now I had never known
Such a fascinating languor.

In the poplars an uneasy rustle,
Tender dreams have come to visit them.
The sky is burnished steel in color,
The stars are dully pale.

I bring a bunch of white gillyflowers.
Secret fire hides in them for the one
Who, as he takes the flowers from timid hands,
Touches the warm palm.

IV.

I wrote down the words
That I long didn't dare to say.
My head hurts dully.
My body is oddly numb.

The distant bugle is silent,
In my heart all the riddles the same,
A light snow of early autumn
Lies on the croquet ground.

Time for the last leaves to rustle!
Time for the last thoughts to pine!
I didn't want to bother the one
Who's used to having a good time.

I forgave the dear lips
For their harsh joke. . . .
Oh, you will drive to our place
Tomorrow on the first snow.

They'll light the drawing-room candles,
The flickering by day is more tender,
They'll bring in a whole bouquet
Of roses from the greenhouse.

1910

I am not begging for your love.
It is now in a safe place. . . .
Believe me, I'm not writing
Jealous letters to your fiancée.
But you take this wise advice:
Let her read my verses,
Let her keep my portraits—
For bridegrooms are so obliging!
But these little fools need
The consciousness of total victory
More than the bright talks of friendship
And memory of the first tender days. . . .
When you have spent the pennies
Of happiness with your sweet girlfriend
And for your satiated soul

Everything gets so repellent—
Into my triumphant night
Don't come. I don't know you.
And how could I help you?
I can't cure happiness.

1914

Insomnia

Somewhere cats meow piteously,
I catch the sound of distant steps . . .
Your words lull me wondrous well:
For two months I haven't slept.

You're with me again, again, insomnia!
I recognize your unmoving face.
What, my beauty, what, my lawless one,
Do I sing so badly to you, then?

The windows are curtained in white cloth,
A blue half-darkness streams . . .
Or are we consoled by distant tidings?
Why am I beside you so at ease?

1912

The Muse went away along a steep,
Autumnal, narrow road,
And her dark-skinned legs
Were spattered with big drops of dew.

For a long time I begged her
To wait for winter with me,
But she said, "Why, this is a grave,
How can you still breathe?"

I wanted to give her a dove,
The whitest of all in the dovecote,
But the bird itself flew off
After my slender guest.

Looking after her, I was silent,
I loved only her alone,
And the dawn stood in the sky,
Like the gate into her land.

1915

And here I am, I stay alone
To count the empty days.
Oh my free friends,
Oh my swans!

And I won't call you with a song,
I won't return you with tears,
But in the evening at a doleful time
I'll mention you in prayer.

Caught by a deadly arrow,
One of you has fallen,
And another, kissing me,
Turned to a black raven.

But so it happens once a year,
When ice starts to thaw,
In Empress Catherine's garden
I stand by the pure waters

And hear the splash of wide wings
Above the blue smooth mass.
I don't know who flung the window wide
In the dungeon of the grave.

1917

Bezhetsk

There are white churches and ringing, glittering ice,
There bloom the cornflower eyes of my darling son.
Over the ancient city are diamond Russian nights
And the sickle under the sky, yellower than linden honey.

There strict memory, who is so miserly these days,
Opened her chambers to me with a deep, deep bow;
But I didn't go in, I slammed the frightful door . . .
And the city was full of merry Christmas ringing.

26 December 1921

Ah, you thought I too was the kind
That's easy to forget,
And that I would fling myself, pleading and sobbing,
Under the bay horse's hooves.

Or I would start asking witches
For a root in charmed water?
And I would send you a frightful gift—
My intimate, perfumed kerchief.

Damn you then. With no moan, with no glance
Will I touch the cursèd soul.
But I swear to you by the angels' garden,
I swear by the wonder-working icon
And the fumes of our fiery nights—
I will never go back to you.

1921

You cannot be among the living,
Cannot rise from the snow.
Twenty-eight from a bayonet,
Five wounds from a gun.

I sewed a bitter new garment
For my dear friend.
The Russian ground loves, loves
A little sip of blood.

1921

If the moon's eeriness splashes,
The city all dissolves in poison.
Without the least hope of dozing
I see through the green sediment
Not my childhood, and not the sea,
And not the butterflies' wedding flight
Above the bed of snow-white narcissus
In that year nineteen-sixteen or so . . .
But the round dance, eternally frozen,
Of your grave's cypresses.

1928

I hid my heart away from you,
As if I threw it into the Neva . . .
Tamed and wingless
I live in your house.
Only . . . at night I hear squeaks.

What's there—in the strangers' twilight?
The lindens of Prince Sheremetyev . . .
House spirits calling back and forth . . .
The little black whisper of disaster
Cautiously draws near,
Like the murmur of water,
And hotly presses to my ear—
And mutters, as if it means
To mess around here all night:
"You wanted comfort then,
Do you know where it is—your comfort?"

1936

It is your lynx eyes, Asia,
That spied something out in me,
Teased out something hidden,
And born of the silence,
And tedious, and difficult,
Like the great noon heat in Termez.
Just as if forememory all flowed
Into consciousness like scorching lava,
Just as if I drank my own sobs
From someone else's palms.

1945

The Burnt Notebook

Your more fortunate sister is already
Standing lovely on the bookshelf,
While above you are shards of star-flocks
And under you the coals of a bonfire.
How you pleaded, how you wished to live!
How afraid you were of the caustic fire!

But all at once your body trembled,
And the voice cursed me, fleeting away.
And all at once the pines began to rustle
And were reflected in the moon water depths.
And round the bonfire, the most sacred springs
Already were dancing their funeral dance.

1961

From Tashkent Pages

That night we went crazy from each other,
Only the ill-omened darkness glowed for us,
The canals muttered something their own,
And the carnations smelled of Asia.

And we made our way through an alien city,
Through the smoky song and the midnight heat—
Alone in the sign of the Serpent,
Not daring to look at each other.

It could have been Istanbul or even Baghdad,
But alas! not Warsaw, and not Leningrad,
And that bitter lack of resemblance
Smothered like orphanhood's vapors.

And it seemed that the ages were pacing beside,
And an unseen hand beat a tambourine,
And the sounds, like secret signs,
Spun before us in the darkness.

You and I were together in mysterious haze.
As if we walked over land that was no one's,
But the moon like a diamond felucca
Brusquely sailed out on our meeting-parting . . .

And if that night should come back to you as well

In your fate that to me is incomprehensible,
Know that someone has dreamed
Of that sanctified minute.

1959

Requiem

No, not beneath an alien horizon,
Nor under the protection of alien wings—
I was then together with my nation,
There where my nation, unfortunately, was.

1961

In Place of a Preface

In the horrible years of the Yezhov terror I spent seventeen months in prison lines in Leningrad. It happened once that someone "identified" me. Then a woman with blue lips standing behind me, who of course had never heard my name in her life, woke out of the numbness that marked all of us and spoke softly in my ear (there everyone spoke in a whisper):

"And can you describe this?"

And I said:

"I can."

Then something like a smile slipped across what had once been her face.

1 April 1957

Leningrad

Dedication

Faced with such grief the mountains bow,
The great river does not flow,
But the prison bolts are firm,
And behind them are the "convict holes"
And deathly anguish.

For someone a fresh breeze blows,
For someone a sunset ravishes—
We don't know, we're everywhere the same,
We hear only the vile gnashing of keys
And the heavy tread of soldiers.
We would rise, as if for early service,
We would go through the feral capital,
There we'd meet, more breathless than the dead,
The sun was lower, the river Neva foggier,
While hope kept on singing in the distance.
The sentence . . . and at once tears in a torrent,
Already set apart from everyone,
As if her life pulls painfully from her heart,
As if they rudely knocked her to the ground,
But she walks . . . she staggers . . . all alone . . .
Where now are the involuntary women friends
Of my two diabolical years?
What do they seem to see in Siberian blizzards?
What do they dimly glimpse in the moon's circle?
To them I send my farewell greeting.

March 1940

Prelude

It happened when only a dead man
Would smile, glad of the quiet.
And like an unneeded appendage
Leningrad swung alongside its prisons.
And when there came, witless from torment,
The regiments of the condemned,
And the brief music of parting
Was sung by the whistling trains.
The stars of death stood above us,
And guiltless Russia was twisted
Under bloody boots, and under
The tires of Black Marias.

I.

They took you away just at sunrise,
After you, like a mourner, I came,
In the dark parlor children were weeping,
The icon-case candle guttered.
On your lips the chill of an icon,
Deathly sweat on your brow. . . . Can't forget!
Like the wives of the Streltsy, I will
Howl under the towers of the Kremlin.

Autumn 1935
Moscow

II.

Quiet flows the quiet Don,
A yellow moon comes in the house.
Comes in with its hat askew.
The yellow moon sees a shadow.
This woman here is sick,
This woman here is alone,
Husband buried, son in prison,
People, say a prayer for me.

III.

No, it's not I, it is someone else who suffers.
I couldn't that way, and what has happened,
Let it be covered in coarse black cloths,
And let them carry out the lamps . . .
Night.

IV.

If I could show you, scoffing girl
And darling of all your friends,
Merry sinner of Tsarskoe Selo,
What would become of your life—
How three hundredth in line, with a parcel,

You would stand under the Crosses
And with your burning teardrop
Burn through the New Year's ice.
There the prison poplar sways,
And no sound—and there how many
Innocent lives are ending. . . .

V.

For seventeen months I shriek,
I call you to come home,
I threw myself at the hangman's feet,
You are my son and my horror.
Everything is mixed up forever,
And it's not for me to make out
Now, who's a beast, who is a person,
And is the execution soon.
And only the luxuriant flowers,
And the ring of the censer, and tracks
Leading somewhere into nowhere.
And a monstrously big star
Looks right into my eyes
And threatens speedy death.

VI.

Light fly the weeks,
What happened, I can't get it.
How the white nights, dear son,
Looked in at you in prison,
How they are looking again
With a hot hawk eye,
They speak about your lofty cross
And about death.

VII.

The Sentence

And the stone word fell

Onto my living breast.
It's nothing, I was ready,
Somehow I'll manage this.

Today I have so many tasks:
Have to kill all memory,
Have to petrify the soul,
Have to relearn how to live.

Or else . . . The hot rustle of summer
Like a holiday outside my window.
For so long I anticipated this
Radiant day and deserted house.

Summer 1939

VIII.

To Death

You're bound to come—so why don't you come now?
I'm waiting for you—things are hard for me.
The light's put out, the door is open wide
To you, who are so simple and wonderful.
Take on for this whatever form you like,
Burst in as a poisoned shell
Or sneak up with a pipe, like a seasoned bandit,
Or poison me with typhoid vapors.
Or as the fairy tale that you invented,
The one we all know sickeningly well—
So I will see the peak of a blue hat
And the apartment manager pale with fear.
It's all the same to me now. The Enisei
Swirls, the Polar Star shines.
And the ultimate horror spreads
Over the blue gleam of beloved eyes.

19 August 1939

IX.

Already madness with its wing
Has covered half my soul
And plies me with a fiery wine
And points to the black vale.

And I have understood that I
Must grant it the victory,
Eavesdropping on my own words—
Like someone else's ravings.

And it will not allow me to
Take anything along with me
(No matter how I beg it
And pester it with pleading):

Neither the horrible eyes of my son—
That petrified suffering,
Nor the day when the storm arrived,
Nor the hour of the prison meeting,

Nor the dear chill of his hands,
Nor the quaking aspens' shadows,
Nor the remote and weightless sound—
The words of final comfort.

4 May 1940

X.

Crucifixion

Weep not for Me, Mother,
Who am in the grave.

1.

A choir of angels hymned the lofty hour,
And all the heavens melted into fire.

He said to the Father, "Why hast thou forsaken!"
And to His mother, "Oh, weep not for me. . . ."

2.

Magdalena flailed her arms and sobbed,
The best-loved disciple turned to stone,
But there, where the Mother stood unspeaking,
No one even dared to cast a glance.

Epilogue

1.

I found out how it is that faces fall,
How fear can glance out from beneath the eyelids,
How the harsh pages of cuneiform
Write out one's suffering on the cheeks,
How locks turn to silver suddenly
From ash-blond and from black,
The smile wilts on submissive lips,
And fright shakes in a dry little laugh.
And I pray not for myself alone,
But for all those who stood with me
There in the fierce cold and in July heat
Beneath the red blinded wall.

2.

Again the memorial hour approaches.
I see you, I hear, I feel you again:
The one that they barely led up to the window,
And the one who does not walk her own native land,
And the one who, tossing her lovely head,
Said, "I come here as if it were home!"
I'd like to give everyone's name, but the list
Was taken away, and there's nowhere to ask.
For them I have woven a wide shielding cloak
Of poor words, overheard from themselves.

I remember them always and everywhere,
I won't forget them even in new misfortune,
And if they stop up my tormented mouth,
Through which a hundred million people cry,
Then let them remember me just the same way
On the eve of my own burial day.
And if some day in this country they get
The notion of raising a statue to me,
I give my consent to this solemnity,
But with the condition—they must not put it
There by the sea, where I was born:
The last link with the sea is broken,
Nor in the Tsar's garden by the cherished stump
Where a shadow unceasingly searches for me,
But here, where I stood for three hundred hours
And they never did open the bolt of the door.
Because even in blessed death I'm afraid
Of forgetting the rumble of the Black Marias,
To forget how the vile door sounded, slamming,
And an old woman wailed like a wounded animal.
And let the snow flow like tears as it thaws
From the motionless and bronze lids of the eyes,
And let the prison dove coo in the distance,
And the ships go softly along the Neva.

March 1940
Fountain House (*Fontanyi Dom*)

Translated by Sibelan Forrester

Notes to the Essay

1. A. Akhmatova, *Sochineniia v dvukh tomakh*, ed. V.A. Chernykh, Vol. 2. 2d ed., corr. and enlarged (Moscow: Khudozhestvennia literatura, 1990), 269.

2. Ibid., 270.

3. A. Akhmatova, *Sochineniia*, Vol. 2, ed. G.P. Struve and B.A. Filippov (Munich: Inter-Language Literary Associates, 1968), 305.

4. C. Tomei, "Mirra Loxvickaja and Anna Axmatova: Influence in the Evolution of the Modern Female Lyric Voice," in *Critical Essays on the Prose and Poetry of Modern Slavic Women*, ed. N. Efimov, C. Tomei and R. Chapple (Lewiston, NY: Edwin Mellen Press, 1998), 135–60.

5. A. Haight, *Anna Akhmatova: A Poetic Pilgrimage* (New York: Oxford University Press, 1976), 21.

6. V.V. Vinogradov, *O poèzii Anny Akhmatovoi: Stilisticheskie nabroski,* in *Izbrannye trudy. Poètika russkoi literatury* (Moscow: Nauka, 1976), 373.

7. M.L. Gasparov, "The Evolution of Akhmatova's Verse," in *Anna Akhmatova, 1889–1989. Papers from the Akhmatova Centennial Conference, Bellagio Study and Conference Center, June 1989*, ed. S.I. Ketchian (Oakland, CA: Berkeley Slavic Specialties, 1993), 68, 70.

8. P.N. Luknitskii, *Vstrechi s Annoi Akhmatovoi,* Vol. 1 (Paris: YMCA Press), 19.

9. H.H. Vendler, *Yeats's Vision and the Later Plays* (Cambridge: Harvard University Press, 1963), 97; D.A. Harris, *Yeats, Coole Park and Ballylee* (Baltimore: Johns Hopkins University Press, 1974), 112; S. Ketchian, "Anna Akhmatova and W.B. Yeats: Points of Juncture," in *Anna Akhmatova, 1889–1989*, 88–89, 107.

10. A. Haight, 30.

11. M.L. Dodero, *A.A. Achmatova—La memoria e il tempo* (Genoa, 1980), 86–87.

12. Quoted in Raisa Orlova and Lev Kopelev, "Anna vseia Rusi," *Literaturnoe obozrenie* 5 (1989): 103.

13. A.L. Crone, "Antimetabole in 'Rekviem': The Structural Disposition of Themes and Motifs," in *The Speech of Unknown Eyes: Akhmatova's Readers on Her Poetry*, Vol. 1, ed. Wendy Rosslyn (Nottingham: Astra, 1990), 28.

14. K. Verheul, *The Theme of Time in the Poetry of Anna Akhmatova* (The Hague: Mouton, 1971), 95.

15. S. Driver, *Anna Akhmatova* (Boston: Twayne, 1976), 119.

16. T. Tsiv'ian, "Anna Akhmatova's 'Poem without a Hero': Some Conclusions in Studying the Question of the Text-Reader," in *Anna Akhmatova, 1889–1989*, 248.

17. S. Driver, 125.

18. Nikita Struve, "O 'Polunochnykh stikhakh'," in *Anna Akhmatova, 1889–1989*, 186–93.

Bibliography

Primary Works

Belaia staia. Stikhotvoreniia. St. Petersburg: Prometei, 1917.

Anno Domini MCXXI. St. Petersburg: Petropolis, 1923.

Iz shesti knig. Stikhotvoreniia. Leningrad: Sovetskii pisatel', 1940.

Izbrannoe. Stikhi. Tashkent, 1943.

Izbrannye stikhotvoreniia. New York, 1952.

Stikhotvoreniia. Moscow, 1958.

Stikhotvoreniia, 1909–1960. Moscow, 1961.

Beg vremeni. Stikhotvoreniia, 1909–1965. Moscow: Sovetskii pisatel', 1965.

Sochineniia. 3 vols. Vols. 1–2 ed. G.P. Struve and B.A. Filippov. Munich: Inter-Language Literary Associates, 1967–68. Vol. 3 ed. N.A. Struve. 2d ed. corr. and enlarged. Paris: YMCA Press, 1983.

Izbrannoe. Moscow: Khudozhestvennaia literatura, 1974.

Stikhotvoreniia i poèmy. Ed. V.M. Zhirmunskii. Biblioteka poèta. Bol'shaia seriia. Leningrad: Sovetskii pisatel', 1976.

Stikhi, perepiska, vospominaniia, ikonografiia Anny Akhmatovoi. Comp. Carl Proffer. Ann Arbor, MI: Ardis, 1977.

O Pushkine: Stat'i i zametki. Ed. E.G. Gershtein. Leningrad: Sovetskii pisatel', 1977.

Stikhi i proza. Leningrad, 1977.

Ia golos vash. Ed. V.A. Chernykh. Moscow: Knizhnaia palata, 1989.

Sochineniia v dvukh tomakh. Ed. V.A. Chernykh. 2d ed. corr. and enlarged. Moscow: Khudozestvennaia literatura, 1990.

Sochineniia v dvukh tomakh. Ed. N.N. Skatov. Comp. M.M. Kralin. Moscow: Pravda, 1990.

In Translation

Forty-seven Love Poems. Trans. Natalie Duddinton. London: J. Cape, 1927.

Selected Poems. Trans. Richard McKane. London: Oxford University Press, 1969.

A Poem without a Hero. Trans. Carl Proffer. Ann Arbor, MI: Ardis, 1973.

Requiem; and, Poem without a Hero. Trans. D.M. Thomas. London: Elek, 1976.

Selected Poems. Trans. Walter Arndt. *Requiem*. Trans. Robin Kemball. *A Poem without a Hero*. Trans. Carl Proffer. Ann Arbor, MI: Ardis, 1976.

Way of All Earth. Trans. D.M. Thomas. London: Secker and Warburg, 1979.

Poems: Selected and Translated from the Russian. Trans. Lyn Coffin. New York: W.W. Norton, 1983.

Three Russian Women Poets: Anna Akhmatova, Marina Tsvetaeva, Bella Akhmadulina. Trans. Mary Maddock. Trumansburg, NY: Crossing Press, 1983.

Twenty Poems. Trans. Jane Kenyon. Saint Paul, MN: Eighties Press and Ally Press, 1985.

You Will Hear Thunder: Poems. Trans. D.M. Thomas. London: Secker and Warburg, 1985.

Poems. Moscow: Raduga, 1988.

Poem without a Hero and Selected Poems. Trans. Lenore Mayhew and William McNaughton. Oberlin: Oberlin College Press, 1989.

Selected Early Love Lyrics. Trans. Jessie Davies. Liverpool: Lincoln Davies, 1989.

Selected Poems. Trans. Richard McKane. Newcastle upon Tyne: Bloodaxe, 1989.

The Complete Poems of Anna Akhmatova. Trans. Judith Hemschemeyer. Ed. and introduction Roberta Reeder. Somerville, MA: Zephyr Press, 1990.

Evening: Poems 1912 in Parallel Text. Trans. Jessie Davies. Liverpool: Lincoln Davies, 1990.

The Complete Poems of Anna Akhmatova. Trans. Judith Hemschemeyer. Ed. Roberta Reeder. Expanded ed. Somerville, MA: Zephyr Press, 1992.

A Stranger to Heaven and Earth: Poems. Trans. Judith Hemschemeyer. Boston: Shambhala, 1993.

Translations by Akhmatova

Koreiskaia klassicheskaia poèziia. Moscow, 1956.

Golosa poetov. Stikhi zarubezhnykh poètov. Moscow: Progress, 1965.

Dzhokomo Leopardi. Lirika. Perevod s ital'ianskogo. Trans. A. Akhmatova and Anatolii Naiman. Moscow: Khudozhestvennaia literatura, 1967.

Liricheskaia poèziia Vostoka: Perevody. Moscow: Khudozhestvennaia literatura, 1969.

Iz armianskoi poèzii. Ed. K.N. Grigor'ian. Erevan: Sovetakan grokh, 1976.

Liricheskaia poèziia Drevnego Vostoka. Trans. Anna Akhmatova et al. Moscow: Nauka, 1984.

Dykhanie pesni: kniga perevodov. Moscow: Sovetskaia Rossiia, 1988.

Secondary Works

Amert, Susan. *In a Shattered Mirror: The Later Poetry of Anna Akhmatova*. Palo Alto, CA: Stanford University Press, 1992.

Chukovskaia, Lidiia. *The Akhmatova Journals.* Trans. Milena Michalski and Sylva Rubashova. New York: Farrar, Straus and Giroux, 1994.

———. *Zapiski ob Anne Akhmatovoi.* 3 vols. 2d ed. corr. and enlarged. Paris: YMCA Press, 1984.

Driver, Sam. *Anna Akhmatova.* Boston: Twayne, 1976.

Haight, Amanda. *Anna Akhmatova: A Poetic Pilgrimage.* New York: Oxford University Press, 1976.

Kats, Boris, and Roman Timenchik. *Anna Akhmatova i muzyka. Issledovatel'skie ocherki.* Leningrad: Sovetskii kompozitor, 1989.

———. *The Poetry of Anna Akhmatova: A Conquest of Time and Space.* Munich: Otto Sagner, 1986.

Ketchian, Sonia, ed. *Anna Akhmatova, 1889–1989. Papers from the Akhmatova Centennial Conference, Bellagio Study and Conference Center, June 1989.* Oakland, CA: Berkeley Slavic Specialties, 1993.

Leiter, Sharon. *Akhmatova's Petersburg.* Philadelphia: University of Pennsylvania Press, 1983.

Loseff, Lev, and Barry Scherr, eds. *A Sense of Place: Tsarskoe Selo and Its Poets.* Columbus, OH: Slavica, 1993.

Naiman, Anatolii. *Remembering Anna Akhmatova.* Trans. Wendy Rosslyn. New York: Henry Holt, 1991.

Reeder, Roberta. *Anna Akhmatova: Poet and Prophet.* New York: St. Martin's Press, 1994.

Rosslyn, Wendy. *The Prince, the Fool and the Nunnery: The Religious Theme in the Early Poetry of Anna Akhmatova.* Amersham, Bucks: Avebury, 1984.

———, ed. *The Speech of Unknown Eyes: Akhmatova's Readers on Her Poetry.* 2 vols. Nottingham: Astra, 1990.

Rude, Jeanne. *Anna Akhmatova: une étude.* Paris: P. Seghers, 1968.

Timenchik, R.D., ed. *Desiatye gody.* Moscow: Izdatel'stvo MPI, 1989.

———, ed. *Poèma bez geroia.* Moscow: Izdatel'stvo MPI, 1989.

———, ed. *Posle vsego.* Moscow: Izdatel'stvo MPI, 1989.

———, ed. *Requiem.* Moscow: Izdatel'stvo MPI, 1989.

van der Eng-Liedmeier, Jeanne, and Kees Verheul, eds. *Tale without a Hero and Twenty-two Poems by Anna Akhmatova: Essays.* The Hague: Mouton, 1973.

Verheul, Kees. *The Theme of Time in the Poetry of Anna Akhmatova.* The Hague: Mouton, 1971.

Wells, David. *Akhmatova and Pushkin.* Birmingham: University of Birmingham Press, 1994.

Anna Barkova

Anna Aleksandrovna Barkova (1901–1976) approached death in a manner entirely suitable, in its contradictoriness, to the character of her life. Though a staunch atheist, she asked her friends to arrange a church funeral; during her last months, a family Bible was constantly on her night table. This division in Barkova between skepticism, even cynicism, and a wary sense of respect for morality and spirituality was only one of the fissures shooting through the life and work of one of the most interesting Russian women poets of the twentieth century. With some justification in her late poem "Joke" ("Shutka"), she described herself as "the grandmother of proletarian poetry,"[1] but her poetry was in no sense a vehicle for the schematism of the official "class war." Instead, it was defiantly individualistic in terms of its opinions, and idiosyncratic in terms of its intonation, and also expressed a uniquely honest acknowledgment of the Soviet intelligentsia's complicity in its own destruction, and in the destruction of the country as a whole.

Barkova was in many senses a typical representative of the "Soviet intelligentsia." Born into the family of a private *gimnaziia* janitor, whose position gave her the opportunity—most unusual for working-class girls before 1917—to acquire a secondary education, she owed her entire career as a writer to Bolshevism. In 1918 she enrolled as a member of the Circle of Genuine Proletarian Poets, a writers' group based in Ivanovo, the textile town where she was brought up; soon afterwards, she began writing short pieces for the group's newspaper, *Land of the Workers* (*Rabochii krai*). She also published poetry in the paper, using the pseudonym "Kalika perekhozhaia ("Wandering Cripple"), a name given to blind or maimed singers who wandered from village to village singing *dukhovnye stikhi,* ballads of devotional content, in order to earn small gifts of alms. In 1931, Barkova was to invoke this persona again in one of her late poems, "I wander like a pathetic beggar / Accompanied by Russian beggar songs,"[2] and the tradition of the ugly, unloved social outsider who is also a maker of art forms the background to many other late poems in which the "wandering cripple" does not put in such an obvious appearance.

Barkova's early poetry soon attracted the attention of influential figures in the Bolshevik literary establishment, the leading critic Aleksandr Voronskii, and the Commissar of Enlightenment, Anatolii Lunacharskii. The latter became an important patron, and in 1922 Barkova moved to Moscow to work as his secretary. Also in 1922, her first collection, *Woman* (*Zhenshchina*), appeared, with a flattering foreword written by Lunacharskii himself; a year later, in 1923, her play, *Nastas'ia Bonfire* (*Nastas'ia Koster*), was published. For a while, Barkova also attended the writers' school in Moscow directed by Valerii Briusov, for whose journal, *Print and Revolution* (*Pechat' i revoliutsiia*), she was to compose a spiteful review of Sofiia Parnok's collection *The Vine* (*Loza*), which she dismissed as "of no interest to working-class young people."[3] Later, Lenin's sister, Mar'ia Ul'ianova, was to find Barkova employment at *Pravda*; Ul'ianova also helped her put together a second collection of poems, which was not destined, however, to see the light of day.

Despite enjoying the favor of the Soviet establishment, and apparently sharing many of its ideological perspectives, Barkova seems to have become increasingly disillusioned with Soviet life in the late 1920s; and in a poem of 1931, "I keep seeing that gloomy, stifling / And interminable corridor,"[4] she visualizes her death at the hands of a firing squad. Although this prophecy was, fortunately, to prove unduly pessimistic, Barkova was directly to suffer some of the lesser consequences of the Stalin purges. In 1934 she was denounced and arrested; a number of her poems were seized and used as evidence at her interrogation. Although Barkova received what was by the standards of the time a light sentence (five years' imprisonment), she was to endure repeat arrests (in 1947 and 1956, leading to stretches in the camps of nine years in each case); she also suffered two long periods of exile (in 1939–1947, and again in 1965–1967). Only in 1967, at the instigation of a group of prominent writers including Aleksandr Tvardovskii, the editor of *New World (Novyi mir)*, was she allowed to return to Moscow. Here she lived out the remainder of her life in considerable poverty and deprivation, quartered in a run-down communal flat on the Garden Ring, but with an unabated appetite for books, friendship and conversation.

Such is the skeleton of Barkova's life, which can be fleshed out a little from the memoirs composed by her friends, several of whom have left moving descriptions of her caustic wit, stoicism and kindness. (These friends have also repudiated the description of Barkova left in her memoirs by Pasternak's mistress, Ol'ga Ivinskaia, who portrayed Barkova as a dangerously malicious and morally none-too-trustworthy individual.) Despite the efforts of such chroniclers, however, many details of Barkova's life still await clarification. For example, the customary Russian reticence about such matters means that Barkova's relationship with Valentina Mikhailovna Makotinskaia has been mentioned only in embarrassed hints,[5] as indeed has Barkova's lesbianism in general. Barkova's literary legacy is equally rich in problems. Many poems have apparently been lost, the dating of those that survive does not always seem to rest on firm foundations and variants of the same poem have been published as independent texts.[6] Furthermore, some versions of Barkova's poems that have appeared so far are not free of obvious misprints and misreadings. Well might Barkova, in her bitingly humorous late poem "A Few Autobiographical Facts," have compared herself to a poet of whose work, like Sappho's, only a few fragments survive, which are then used by self-serving, obtuse critics in order to construct a mythic biography (here of the poet as political martyr, a role that Barkova insisted she did not deserve).

None of this uncertainty should, however, obscure the remarkable energy and clarity of Barkova's best work, which cannot in any sense be described as cryptic. Her early poetry is rather inclined, it is true, to favor self-dramatization. For example, in *Woman* (*Zhenshchina,* 1922) she poses as Bolshevik activist, as peasant woman and as various historical heroines. A hint of this remained in her late poetry too: she sometimes portrays herself as a "Tatar princess," a figure owing something to the early poetry of Elizaveta Kuz'mina-Karavaeva; and the poem about death by firing squad cited earlier reflects the romanticism of literary tradition rather than the squalid realities of Soviet capital punishment, which, notoriously, was administered by a revolver bullet in the back of the neck. Barkova could draw strength from linking her own destiny with that of heroines from the past, seeing herself, perhaps, as a religious heretic (her dramatic alter ego Nastas'ia Bonfire is a Russian Old Believer); and in "Once, in the days of Savonarola," published in *The Flame of Snows* (*Plamia snegov*), she sees herself as the famous Italian religious rebel. She was also capable of demythologizing history, as in her magnificent portrait of Robespierre, also from *The Flame of Snows,* which transforms the paragon of rational revolutionary politics into a demented dictator with messianic delusions. Furthermore, in many poems she directly confronted the dilemmas of her own generation in robust, embittered and graphic phrases. Her poems of imprisonment, such as "In the Camp Barracks,"[7] make historical grandeur seem illusionary in comparison with the reality of the camp itself. In other poems, such as "The Heroes of Our Time,"[8] she traces the fate of her contemporaries whose youthful enthusiasm for Tolstoy and Gorky was succeeded by political activism, then by imprisonment and suffering. In "What's the use of 'faith to the fatherland,'" she confronts the disillusionment of a generation whose ideals seem in retrospect not only ridiculous, but pernicious. The sardonically entitled "Patriotic Cycle" (1946) discusses Soviet ideology, and especially rhetoric, in the aftermath of the Second World War. Taking violent issue with official images of the Red Army as the saviors of Europe, it presents the returning soldiery as crippled beggars sitting in dusty marketplaces and wheedling passersby for money. Rather than preserving European culture, the war has made it seem futile. Pushkin and Shakespeare would have been "torn to shreds of meat" had they lived in these times, and a key couplet from the first part of the cycle invokes Pushkin's famous lines, "To the fog of low truths / I prefer a falsehood that elevates," putting them in the mouth of the reincarnated poet as he flees, mouselike, into the wainscot to avoid an air raid.[9]

All this illustrates how much Barkova's work departs from the lamentatory manner customary for Russian women poets when treating historical themes. Her poems of the Terror are radically different from those of Anna Akhmatova, or for that matter, Ol'ga Berggol'ts, both of whom invoked the sufferings of the Mother of God over the dead Christ as parallels for their personal anguish. Mary is absent from Barkova's poetry, except as the "Handmaid of the Lord" gazed upon to no good effect by the sinful protagonist of "Once, in the days of Savonarola." Barkova sees herself, and by extension other women of her generation, as actors in history; they are vicious aggressors rather than noble victims, persecutors as well as persecuted. The comforting sense of moral epiphany so often expected from Russian literature (by Westerners as well as Russian's) is absent; among the key words of this poetry are "angry," "vicious," "stupid," "corrupt" / "sold out," "hacking," "tearing" (*zloi, zlobnyi, glupyi, prodannyi, istiazat', razorvat'*). The shock effects of such language bypass the need for sophisticated patterns of imagery; although "Robespierre," for example, unforgettably brands the French revolutionary as having "ringlets like the most fastidious waiter's," it is the harsh intonation of Barkova's verse, rather than any specific phrases, which generally stay in the memory.

The fierceness of Barkova's voice means that her poetry can most certainly not be described as "feminine" in the sense in which that term is generally applied by Russian critics to mean poetry that is well crafted, plangent and decorative, if also lacking in power and significance. Yet Barkova herself insisted on the importance of her gender; one of the most important errors into which the idiot critic excoriated by "A Few Autobiographical Facts" falls is to assume that the caustic character of Barkova's verse is "masculine." "All my life, each hour, I was a *she*,"[10] the poet declares, which might come across as a simple statement of the obvious were it not for the ingrained Russian assumption that writing of such energy is beyond the capacity of anyone wearing a skirt. Barkova's defiance and the deliberate unmusicality of her verse (she preferred balladic stanzas of accentual verse, and on occasion the characteristically folkloric *raeshnyi stikh*—doggerel couplets—to the more easily melodious iambic, trochaic or ternary meters) have made the reactions of some Russian commentators rather guarded. Lev Anninskii has implied, for example, in "Krestnyi put' Anny Barkovoi," that Barkova would have written better poetry had she come under the influence of the acmeists,[11] a highly questionable assumption, for one has only to compare Barkova's genuine originality with the well-turned banality of Irina Odoevsteva to realize that the former may well have been fortunate in her escape. Barkova's strident anti-nationalism struck a chord with many readers when her work was first published in the late 1980s, yet this very feature of her poetry may mean that, with nationalist mythologies exercising an increasingly powerful grip on Russian culture, she will in the near future again revert to being "a voice crying in the wilderness." But if Barkova is unlikely ever to be "popular" in the sense of appealing to mass audiences, the stridency of her work makes it "popular" in another, and more lasting sense. Hers is a voice whose intonations constantly recall the biting cynicism of Russian working-class speech. Like Marina Tsvetaeva or the 1990s poet Mariia Avvakumova, Barkova speaks for all the women of peasant or working-class Russia ordinarily disenfranchised by Russian literature, employing the storehouse of popular invective to articulate the thoughts of those who, as she put it in one of her own poems, are "merciless" and "strong," yet also "indigent."[12]

Catriona Kelly

Sappho

On time's steppe, that stretches wider
Than eyesight, you bloom, passion's star;
Oh, the nets you cast are dangerous,
Just as you, with your sweetness, are.

Why, then, should you embrace me
With your languorous, secretive gaze?
I am hard, I am warlike, soldierly,
And strange to love's sickly ways.

I shall never drink, I swear it,
Your sapping, seductive draft:
I want to tear these dove-wings
That throb so, free from my heart.

But you smile when you hear my singing,
And now your eyes are sad;
So will you never vanish,
Am I to be always trapped?

The hollow, stinging mournfulness
Of your own insidious songs
Strikes to my heart's deep caverns,
Making them all resound. Sappho,

I fling my gauntlet
On your kingdom's fragrant earth!
I tear free from the nets that bind me,
You ringletted empress of love.

1922

Woman

I keep my distance from contemporary literature,
I have no truck with VAPP,[1] those righteous bores,
And all that gives my grieving spirit solace
Is Anatole France,[2] who described all this before.

The gods want blood . . . well, I shall wait in patience
Till they have had enough to make them drunk.
Just see how mercilessly they trample
Our times, making them ooze like trodden plums.

It'll all pass, no doubt: the broken basin
Will be made whole before our very eyes.
Perhaps we'll have the chance to fill our bellies;
We may be doomed to starve, not to survive.

They made a banquet for us out of nutshells,
We were victims in a cause that made no sense:
You can read it in those haughty, smirking features,
And in the gaze that nothing seems to shame.

I'll never gorge myself, blinkered, unthinking,
On the censored swill they dole us out
The Gods Are Athirst[3] is my only consolation,
Giving me the strength to sit it out.

1931

From Flame of Snows
Robespierre

A sky-blue jacket, a rose in his buttonhole:
An icing of powder smeared thickly over his hair;
When Robespierre got dolled up to worship
At the Supreme Being's festival, that's what he wore.

Striding neatly as any automaton,
His back elegant, stiff, unbending as wood;
Ringlets tidier than the most fastidious waiter's,
A pedant in his ways, but with a tyrant's power;

Thin-lipped, unkind, but dripping with sensibility,
Tightly he grips the capstan wheel,
Nursing inside his heart the image
Of fraternity's prophet, Jean-Jacques Rousseau.

His eyes are fogged by a mist of radiance,
The frills of his jabot ripple harmonious sighs;
"In the name of the Sacred General Good
The dead, I declare, are no better than flies

"It cannot be that the severed head of Desmoulins,
Or Danton, Lavoisier or Chenier

Has a greater value than our Republic,
Than the Republic now entrusted to me.

"Espionage, corruption and speculation—
I shall wash them away on a tide of blood,"
And his sky-blue gaze, tender and icy
Smiled at the heavens, and on the crowd.

And incorruptible as he, the Widow
Stood silent, on guard in the noisy square,
Whilst the thud of her knife-blade worked as an echo
And proof of his words.

November 1953

Patriotic Cycle

Blessed is he who visited this world
In its fatal moments.

TIUTCHEV

I.

. . . Shreds of meat, smeared in dirt
Were trampled in pits filled with the living dead.
What did you amount to? Beauty? Horror?
The feelings of a friend's, of an enemy's heart?
Scythed down, consumed by flames, and raging,
Heaven implodes into our darkened world.
Nothing you had to see was like this,
Radiant Pushkin, luminous Shakespeare.
Yes, you too would have been shredded
Like meat, and trampled in the dirt;
Over your heads, too, flocks of vicious crows
Would have wheeled, beating their metal wings,
While you darted, terrified and trembling,
Like mice, into closets, behind the wainscot,
Babbling helplessly, "Dearer to me than vulgar truths
Is a falsehood that elevates us."[4]

II.

We've dreamt it all, and we've lived it:
Prison, wickedness, war,
Blood, dung, and squealing fire-bombs,
(The future's seeds, you might say,)
And 1942's bitter winter,
Sickness, destitution, decay.
Our words are faded, threadbare
Our thoughts are worn away.
  "Nobility.
    Heroism.
      Courage."
What are they, something to eat?
But still, in tones hushed and obsequious
Of "honor," of "honesty" some prate.
For God's sake, leave off your lying!
Curiosity is all we have left,
So make the best, while you're able
Of the bones that do come your way.
Fill your bellies full on curiosity,
It'll kill the time until you go,
And when you die, be sure to die quickly,
Keeping your noise to yourself.

Victory Song

III.

Can you spare some change for us,
For the crippled soldiers who fought fit to bust?
Hey there you, you old cow,
Don't you feel sorry for us now?
Find a crust ye can spare
For your dead husband's comrades sitting here.
We don't look a picture, I know,
But we're the conquerors of Prague, Berlin and Warsaw.
We marched on victorious,
In every city they trembled before us.

We lost our eyes for our country,
We lost our limbs for our country,
And with the strange illnesses we caught abroad,
And with the strange sadnesses we brought from abroad,
We sat in the dust at markets,
Singing, "Harken, good people, harken!
Will ye spare some change for me, I promise to pray for ye."

1946

From Heroes of Our Time

What's bred in the bone never leaves you,
So I'm rough even when I'm in love;
I was raised in a hut in the provinces,
With three filthy small windows in front,

This was no cottage, you realize,
Smelling of hay and flowers,
But a town hut stinking of spirits,
Of the want and distress that we suffered.

Only books brought anything different,
They shone through the gray Russian dust
In the midst of that sickening existence
They gave me visions of life to come,

Arrogant, criminal, golden,
Though I might suffer torture, be burned;
But tsar Peter gave the order,
And our hair and our beards were cut;

They flogged Russian serfs in the stables,
They still flog, although somewhere else,
We curse our life of forced labor,
And burn slowly to death in this hell.

I'm no better, no worse than others,
Though my mind is sharper, more strong;

I live by submitting to circumstance,
The violations these times of ours bring;

And that's why I'm coarse and clumsy
As a chained-up bear might be:
I haven't learned how to be human,
And my paws are awkward, untrained.

1971

From Verses of Various Years

Smiling, you scatter
Caustic salt on my wounds;
No, my feelings are numbed by pain,
They have not cooled.

The green grass is dying,
Smothered by whitening frost
You smile still more sadly,
So innocent.

Gradually, tenderly, lovingly,
You poison our love,
As the chill eternity of winter
Follows summer's brief warmth.

1971

Translated by Catriona Kelly

Notes to the Essay

1. *Izbrannoe: iz gulagskogo arkhiva,* ed. L.N. Taganov and Z. Ia. Kholodova (Ivanovo, 1992), 178.

2. "Plamia snegov," *Literaturnoe obozrenie* 8 (1991): 12.

3. "Sofiia Parnok: *Rozy Pierii*," *Pechat' i revoliutsiia* 3 (1992).

4. "Plamia snegov," 11.

5. See M.A. Utevskii's preface to "Stikhi raznykh let," *Lazur'* 1 (1989), and Taganov's *Prosti moiu nochnuiu dushu* (Ivanovo, 1993).

6. Part III of "Patriotic Cycle," from *Stikhi raznykh let,* bears more than a passing resemblance to "What are you selling there, you stupid cow," published independently in *Plamia snegov,* while Part I of the cycle appears separately as "On Falsehood that Elevates," in *Geroi nashego vremeni.*

7. In *Geroi nashego vremeni*, 7–8.

8. In *Dodnes' tiagoteet*, 352.

9. In *Geroi nashego vremeni*, 7.

10. In *Stikhi raznykh let*, 340.

11. "A Few Autobiographical Facts."

12. "Krestnyi put' Barkovoi, " *Literaturnoe obozrenie* 8 (1991): 9.

Translator's Notes to the Selected Works

1. VAPP was a proletarian writer's association.

2. Anatole France (real name Jacques-Anatole-François Thibault, 1844–1924): his *Les Dieux ont soif* (1912) was a blistering indictment of corruption and fanaticism during the French Revolution.

3. *The Gods Are Athirst*, title for a political tract of 1920s.

4. "Dearer to me . . . elevates us": lines from Pushkin's 1830 dialogue "The Hero," in which The Poet, to the incredulity of his Friend, commends the heroism of Nicholas I in visiting a plague hospital.

Bibliography

Primary Works

Zhenshchina [Woman]. Petrograd, 1922.

"Kak delaetsia luna"; "Vosem' glav bezumiia"; "Schast'e statistika Plaksiutkina." *Izbrannoe: iz gulagskogo arkhiva*. Ivanovo, 1922. 89–222.

"Obretaemoe vremia" [essay]. *Izbrannoe: iz gulagskogo arkhiva.* Ivanovo, 1922. 225–66.

Natas'ia Koster [play]. Moscow, 1923.

[Poems]. *Dodnes' tiagoteet*. Ed. S.S. Vilenskii. Moscow, 1989. 335–55.

"Stikhi raznykh let" [Verses of Various Years]. *Lazur'* 1 (1989): 31–48.

"Rovesnitsa veka." *Volga* 5 (1989): 165–68.

Vozvrashchenie. Ivanovo, 1990.

Plamia snegov. [The Flame of Time]. *Literaturnoe obozrenie* 8 (1991): 10–12.

Geroi nashego vremeni. Moscow, 1992.

"Sofiia Parnok: *Rozy Pierii.* Stikhi" [review]. *Pechat' i revoliutskiia* 3 (1992).

Izbrannoe: iz gulagskogo arkhiva. Ed. L.N. Taganov and Z.Ia. Kholodova. Ivanovo, 1992.

In Translation

[Three poems (in Russian and translated into English)]. *An Anthology of Russian Women's Writing, 1777–1992.* Ed. Catriona Kelly. Oxford: Oxford University Press, 1994.

[Six poems]. *Russian Women's Prison Camp Memoirs.* Ed. J. Crowfoot and S. Vilensky. London: Virago, 1995.

Secondary Works

Anninskii, Lev. "Krestnyi put' Anny Barkovoi" [introduction to the selection of poems *Plamia snegov*]. *Literaturnoe obozrenie* 8 (1991): 8–10.

Kelly, C., and C. Ueland. "Anna Barkova." *Dictionary of Russian Women Writers.* Ed. M. Ledkovsky, C. Rosenthal and M. Zirin. Westport, CT: Greenwood Press, 1994. 57–60.

Lunau, S. "Anna Barkova: Untergrunde und Wandlungen." Beiträge zur Baltistik und Slavistik: Wissenschaftliche Beitrag der EMA-Universität. Griefswald, 1992. 63–70.

———. "Anna Barkova: verhinderte Weiblichkeit." *Russie aus der Feder seiner Frauen: zum femininen Diskurs in der russichen Literatur.* Ed. F. Gopfert. Munich: Verlag Otto Sagner, 1992. 142–57.

Taganov, L.N. Predislovie. *Vozvrashchenie.* Ivanovo, 1990. 1–12.

———. *Prosti moiu nochnuiu dushu.* Ivanovo, 1993.

Ol'ga Berggol'ts

Ol'ga Fedorovna Berggol'ts (1910–1975) was born into an educated family in St. Petersburg. Her father was a doctor and her mother, a homemaker. Berggol'ts writes in the preface to her book of poems, *Verses* (*Stikhi*), published in 1962, that her mother, who was an avid reader, desired her two daughters to grow up to be like the heroines in the novels of Turgenev. However, Berggol'ts attended School #117, which was located in a working-class district, and consequently, most of her schoolmates were from working-class families. Contrary to her mother's hopes, Berggol'ts grew up to be a product of the Soviet culture of the 1930s. She dreamed of donning a cap and a leather jacket, since like so many of the young people of her generation she was captivated by the romanticism of the civil war that had recently shaken the nation.

Berggol'ts's *oeuvre* can be divided into three stages of development: the early period, encompassing her years as a student, a member of the literary circle Smena (Change); her life as a journalist in Kazakstan; and her work as a journalist and archivist for the factory Elektrosila after her return to Leningrad. The early stage of her career ended roughly around 1940. Her second literary period covered the war years, the blockade of Leningrad and the victory of the Soviet Army over Nazi Germany, that is, basically the years 1941 to 1946. The last period is the post–World War II stage, when she moved on to other interests and topics, away from the heroism and patriotism of the Soviet people.

The themes and the style vary considerably in each of these three periods of Berggol'ts's life. The early period is marked by a naivete and ardor, typical of inexperienced people; her language and style still were not fully developed and lacked a mature style. The war had a great effect upon her as a person and as a writer. Berggol'ts abandoned her naive and enthusiastic style and rose to the occasion. As a radio broadcaster, she matured from a lively young poet to a woman of purpose and courage. The devastation of war left a noticeable imprint on her writings. In her third period, Berggol'ts experimented with different genres. She wrote memoirs, plays, critical articles on contemporary Soviet art, essays on current affairs and literature for children.

According to her own account of her early life, as portrayed in her autobiographical book, *Daytime Stars* (*Dnevnye zvezdy*, 1954–1958), Berggol'ts went through the typical stages of a Soviet youth's life. She became a member of the Pioneer League and in 1926, the year of her high school graduation, was accepted in the Komsomol organization. Her first poems and sketches were published as early as 1924, in the newspapers *Sparks of Lenin* (*Leninskie iskry*), *Change* (*Smena*) and *The Cutter* (*Rezets*) and the journal *Young Proletariat* (*Iunyi proletarii*).

In 1925 Berggol'ts became actively involved in the youth literary group Change. The members of this group experimented in writing, following the examples of the Acmeists and the Futurists. They imitated the styles of the then-fashionable writers and poets such as Esenin, Gorky, and Mayakovsky. The critic N. Bank notes that Mayakovsky's influence could be discerned particularly in the poems of Berggol'ts's early period, but the critic further remarked that the imitation of Mayakovsky's style was only on the level of "the assonance of the rhythm."[1] As far as the content was concerned, not much similarity could be found there.

The youthful writers of Change lacked formal training and professionalism, even though Marshak, Tikhonov and other notable literary figures of that period came to lecture to them and helped them to progress in their writing careers. Berggol'ts proudly recalls that she had such famous teachers as Akhmatova, Gorky and Marshak. These writers commented on and criticized her early attempts at writing, helping her to develop a style uniquely her own.

Berggol'ts, along with the members of Change, published their writings in various youth newspapers and journals, despite the fact that their works were rather weak and mostly imitative of more famous writers. It was in this circle that Berggol'ts met her first husband, the poet Boris Kornilov.

G.M. Tsurikova, in the preface to the book *Remembering Ol'ga Berggol'ts* (*Vspominaia Ol'gu Berggol'ts*), writes that at the time when Berggol'ts was a member of Change and composing poems of a lyrical nature, the word *lirika* or lyrical poetry was considered subversive in the Soviet Union. Berggol'ts emerges as a woman full of life and passion, inviting love and friendship; one of the poems of the early period is "You will have a good time with me" (1932). The poems of the prewar years are carefree and full of love of life, which was a characteristic trait of Berggol'ts as a person. Even in the most difficult moments of her life, which were numerous, Berggol'ts did not lack courage or lose sight of humor.

In connection with these carefree, energetic years, Berggol'ts, in a 1957 article dedicated to her ex-husband, Kornilov, writes about the literary and creative atmosphere reigning in Change and gives an insight into the activities of its members. Berggol'ts reminisces about their discussions and arguments on art and literature. The young writers frequented literary events and heard Mayakovsky recite, for the first time, the poem "Good" ("Khorosho"); they also attended an exhibition of his artworks. Berggol'ts portrays these youngsters as people in a hurry to get involved with the literary scene and to acquaint themselves with poetry, music and art—culture, in general.

After her graduation from Leningrad State University in 1930, where she received a degree in Russian philology, she was sent to Kazakstan to work for the local newspaper *The Soviet Steppe* (*Sovetskaia step'*). In 1932 Berggol'ts published her essays and sketches that had appeared in *The Soviet Steppe* in the anthology *The Backwater* (*Glubinka*).

In many different short stories, poems and sketches Berggol'ts wrote about Kazakstan and her life there. Particularly in "The Journalists" ("Zhurnalisty," 1933), she recorded her life experiences as a young journalist in a remote land. This short prose narrative describes the joys, disappointments, love and work experiences of a young, vivacious, naive girl, Tania, who closely resembles Berggol'ts herself. This work did not receive a very positive review from critics and was dismissed as a "raw" and "naive" piece of writing. "The Journalists" idealizes the heroine Tania and her work as a young communist. However, the portrayal of her supervisor and her colleagues lacks idealism and sentimentalism. The communist supervisor is an unbending bureaucrat who demands that Tania report false facts and figures about the agricultural and livestock industries in Kazakstan in order to pacify the chiefs back in Moscow. Berggol'ts describes her confrontations with the bureaucrat and writes honestly about the practical difficulties and hardships in a provincial Soviet town. She writes without embellishing the harsh life in Kazakstan, but there is much humor in this work.

In "The Journalists," the theme of love finds an important place and is treated from different perspectives. From Tania's point of view, love is rosy, optimistic and idealized; in her staunch communist boyfriend Pavel's view, love occupies a subordinate place after country and duty. The language of this work, as is true with the majority of Berggol'ts' *oeuvre*, is simple and devoid of all attempts at acheiving a high aesthetic standard. In spite of this weakness, "The Journalists" is humorous and full of naive charm.

Berggol'ts's often-repeated theme in different works—the experience in Kazakstan—was again portrayed in the collection of short stories *Night in the "New*

World" (*Noch' v "Novom mire,"* 1935). Berggol'ts's life and work were entirely encompassed by the upheaval in every aspect of life in the new Soviet Union; the preoccupation with her own work and with the building of the new state is, in this collection, easily discernible. Sometimes it seems in these earlier works that she was more interested in the life of her country than in her own private life. In fact, Berggol'ts writes in an autobiographical sketch that her biography is inseparable from the history of the nation. She further adds that all the important dates of the nation's history coincide with the important dates of her own life. Thus the private woman and the public citizen/writer in the early works of Berggol'ts are divided by a very fine line. This observation is validated by her cycle of poems "Poems about Spanish Children" ("Stikhi ob ispanskikh detiakh," 1937). The Soviet Union was bringing in children from Spain who had been orphaned or lost during the Spanish Civil War. Berggol'ts was one of the many Soviet women who adopted a Spanish child—a boy. In this cycle the voice of a loving mother can be heard; she also dedicates a poem to Spanish women who had taken up arms. Berggol'ts' humaneness and feelings of solidarity for women who are suffering finds a strong and clear expression in this cycle.

After finishing her assignment in Kazakstan, she returned to her native Leningrad, where she continued to work as a journalist at the newspaper of the factory Elektrosila. Following Gorky's advice to young writers to record the history of individual factories, Berggol'ts started to collect historical material from archives and from interviews with the old workers of Elektrosila; she subsequently became the official historian of the factory. Berggol'ts completed and published the first part of her project before World War II; however, the manuscript was not fully preserved.

The prewar works of Berggol'ts frequently dealt with the common Soviet themes of workers and labor. *The Heart of the Factory* (*Serdtse zavoda,* 1958) was written in connection with the event of the expansion of the plant Elektrosila. Here, the author depicts the zeal and enthusiasm of communist workers in a typically Soviet style. The workers are diligent and conscientious and dedicate themselves to the expansion of their factory with fervor, and Berggol'ts, as a citizen and writer, rejoices in their success. Berggol'ts not only wrote essays, articles and short stories on the theme of workers and factories, she also penned numerous poems on this topic. "Pervorosiisk" (1949) is a long poem in which the poet describes the endeavors and achievements of the first workers' commune in Russia. Berggol'ts devoted a large number of pages to the "heroic" struggle of the Soviet worker to build a commune. In works of this nature Berggol'ts is revealed as a communist writer. Nevertheless, a large amount of her prose and poetry deals with themes of a personal nature. In connection with such poems, Gorky criticized her for having "too many scenes of separation and railway stations"[2] in her poetry, which did not meet the official standards of the literary milieu.

In 1937 Berggol'ts was arrested on the charge of treason, or as she writes in one of her books, charged with being an enemy of the people. She is reticent and vague on this issue and writes that she was "released" (it is not clear from where) in mid-1939. Reference to this misfortune in her life is not documented in any of the biographical works published on her. In Berggol'ts's own words, she returned to an empty apartment, as both of her daughters had died before this "catastrophe" took place. Berggol'ts's reluctance to elaborate on this incident, one that had robbed her of her freedom and two years of her life, is understandable. Not only did she not want to incur the wrath of party officials, but being optimistic by nature, she probably wanted to put this terrible episode behind her and concentrate on the brighter side of life. Much later, in 1954 after Stalin's death, she makes a brief remark about Stalin having died and also about the "accursed Beria." This was the extent of her expression of her misfortune at the hands of the tyrants. After 1953 she started to write more on the themes of memory and her childhood and delved into other genres like children's literature. Her poems of the period immediately preceding the war were of a nostalgic tone, speaking of lost love, loss, separation and death.

War broke out in the Soviet Union in June 1941, and this monumentally tragic event had a major impact on Berggol'ts's life. Her writing style changed dramatically; she was no longer a *komsomol'ka* enraptured by the achievements of the Soviet workers, nor was she any longer a woman for whom life was a wonderful challenge.

Berggol'ts responded to the Nazi onslaught with the sense of purpose and courage typical of her. The delicate blonde girl was transformed overnight into a fighter. Three days after the war had broken out in the Soviet Union, Berggol'ts was appointed to carry out the antifascist propaganda for Radio Leningrad. During the entire length of the war and the blockade of Leningrad, Berggol'ts's ringing voice could be heard over the radio, updating the people on the news from the front, giving moral support to the bereaved and the stricken, and raising the morale both of the population and the people at the firing line. She also collaborated in the compilation of antiwar radio propaganda directed toward German soldiers occupying Soviet territory.

During the calamitous war years Berggol'ts developed a new personality and identity. She came to be identified as a poet of Leningrad. Her daily broadcasts on the radio dealt with the heroism and courage of the citizens of Leningrad.

Under the pseudonym "Krylov-vnuk" ("Krylov's grandson"), she created the humorous personality of Dar'ia Vlas'evna. She had to assume a pseudonym in order to preserve her stern and serious fighting image on the radio as the creator and reciter of the broadcast "Leningrad Speaking" ("Govorit Leningrad"). The image of Dar'ia Vlas'evna, a simple homemaker, was used by officials to instruct citizens on how to economize staples and other necessities, and what to do in case of an enemy air attack. Like Ivan Chonkin, Tetia Dasha became a popular wartime character who brought comic relief to thousands of people under siege; the image of Tetia Dasha was even used as the illustration of posters and fliers circulated to instruct the public on the questions of evacuation and other emergency measures.

Berggol'ts, along with Anna Akhmatova, Ol'ga Forsh and other women poets and writers, wrote an address on behalf of Soviet women to all the women around the globe, talking about the need for solidarity among women all over the world.

Many of Berggol'ts's poems recited on "Leningrad Speaking" became very popular; one such poem is "Letter to Kama" ("Pis'mo na Kamu," 1941). In this poem, Berggol'ts, as was common with her, emerges as a spirited woman. She persuades all those fighting at the front not to write to their mothers about their deprivations and hardships. She urges them to write home the truth of what will take place in the future, and not what is taking place now. In other words, she asks her fellow citizens to look forward to the moment of victory and reunion, and ignore the present state of affairs—a nation under enemy attack. It must be noted here that when people were fleeing Leningrad during the time of blockade, Berggol'ts refused to abandon her native city, even in the face of death. She, along with several of her colleagues, continued their work at the radio station, fighting to keep up the morale of the Soviet army.

"Leningrad Speaking," a collection of the wartime poems and addresses broadcast on Radio Leningrad, appeared much later in a printed version, compiled between 1947 and1959. Here and elsewhere, she describes the heroism of her fellow citizens and her colleagues who continue with daily, normal activities, and their jobs, despite the starvation, death and destruction all around. She writes that three of her close associates perish from starvation during the war. What Berggol'ts does not write about in her wartime or postwar works is of her own heroism and loss. In 1942 her second husband, Nikolai, died of starvation during the blockade of Leningrad.

Soon after the war was over, Berggol'ts wrote what she considered a tragedy, the play *Loyalty* (*Vernost',* 1954). However, critics have expressed other opinions regarding its genre. It is considered a tragic poem, rather than a tragedy, because of the poetic license of the author. In 1961 this piece was broadcast on the radio, as Berggol'ts had intended it to be, as a play.

After the war, when the entire nation was recuperating from the terrible ravages of war, Berggol'ts directed her attention and creative impulses away from the horrors of the war and concentrated her artistic energy on other issues closer to her heart. She returned to her favorite themes of memory and childhood. Most of the poems of the postwar period are nostalgic, and a strain of lament can be heard in them. She revisits the places and the happy moments spent with her *drug* (friend), her late husband, Nikolai. Unlike in her earlier works, these poems reminisce about a "paradise lost," with lyricism and romanticism. These poems abound in descriptions of nature, at times with idealized images of sunlit valleys, swaying pine trees and lush green countryside; at other times, the imagery is full of fog, sleet, rain and gloomy twilight. Berggol'ts at this point does not write for country and sisterhood, she writes for herself, for her "soul," as some critics put it; she expresses and shares her innermost thoughts and concerns.

At the beginning of her career she was a social poet and a writer, then she became a war poet, and finally the majority of her works assumed a personal nature. The sad, nostalgic style in these poems of the latter period reveal her as a woman of depth, possessing very strong loyalties and emotions. However, these poems also show her as a woman capable of coping with everyday reality and continuing with life despite its trials and blows. Even though she turned to personal poetry and prose at this time, her versatility and sense of responsibility as a journalist did not wane, as is seen by her many articles and essays on current issues and affairs, such as the progress of the construction of hydroelectrical stations in remote Siberia and critical essays on contemporary literature and art.

Her journey into memory, into her happy childhood, which was used as material for the prose narrative *Uglich* (which did not receive much positive criticism), was redeveloped and rewritten in the autobiographical narrative *Daytime Stars*. Marshak and especially Gorky had criticized her for having created the impression of being in a hurry to tell her story in *Uglich,* and of therefore having dispensed with choice of words and stylistic refinement. *Daytime Stars,* on the other hand, is a charming, lyrical reworking of an old theme. Berggol'ts moves away from her earlier prosaic, dry style to an animated, personal manner of writing.

This autobiographical narrative is about the childhood of Lelia, a childhood full of magic and charm. Lelia, like the rest of the unstable country, undergoes the hardships of the revolution and the civil war, but her childhood remains the beautiful land of happy memories.

Lelia's doctor father, like Berggol'ts's own, had gone away to care for the soldiers of the Red Army, and she, along with her mother and younger sister Musia, were evacuated from Leningrad. They went to their country home in Uglich for some time. The appeal of this book lies in the weaving of an interesting story from the difficult times while showing the wonder and mystery of life through the eyes of a young, curious girl. While describing the protagonist's life in Uglich, Berggol'ts digresses into the past, the history of the local countryside and of Russia. She uses many symbols to depict Russia as a land replete with beauty, virtue and spiritual qualities. The imagery of church cupolas, bells and icons bespeak the spiritual past of Russia, while the portrayal of the simple countryfolk, their customs and the beautiful countryside sheds light on people and the vast terrain of the land. This work, among her most important, reveals Berggol'ts as a skillful writer and shows the core of the Russian people without any official or political propagandist aim. This is the narrative of a writer who wants to journey back into time to rediscover her own essence and the essence of her native people. Through lyricism, the warm feelings toward her own land and countrymen, and the symbolism of glittering domes and bells, she evokes a picture of Russia, not unlike those in the prose of the *dereven'shchiki,* the writers of Village Prose. Whereas the Village Prose writers were critical of Soviet authorities for devastating their rich cultural heritage, Berggol'ts marvels at the glorious past of Russia and writes highly of its people, while at the same time praising the Soviet government for having built a new way of life in this immense and ancient land. This contradiction, or conflict of views, can be seen in her collection of essays and letters that she names "On the Enisei: Letters after the Journey" ("Na Enisei: Pis'ma posle dorogi," 1959). In "Letters" Berggol'ts paints a romantic picture of the Siberian wilderness, its mighty rivers, rugged and beautiful landscape and hardy people portrayed with love and awe. Berggol'ts, on the one hand, appreciates the wild allure of Siberia, regretting that its villages, its history, its past have to be literally erased, flooded, in order to give way to a new way of life, to build powerful hydroelectric stations; on the other hand, she accepts this destruction of Russia's history and culture as a necessary evil. It seems that the sensitive poet, aware of the robbing of the identity of her people, paradoxically condones this act on the grounds of progress and modernization. The "Letters" have a bittersweet mixture of praise for the old, for nature, for the past, and at the same time admiration for modern science and development. Perhaps this contradiction, the confrontation of the public with the private, the old with the new, the present with the past, joy with sorrow, makes Berggol'ts's works good reading; these features reveal her as a thinking writer, groping to find truth. It will not be an oversimplification to state that the dichotomy inherent in Berggol'ts's worldview, which finds expression in her voluminous works, makes her writings valuable, since she appears to have struck a balance between the pragmatic and harsh Soviet reality and the lyricism of life and love. True to Berggol'ts's own evaluation of her works, it should be pointed out that Berggol'ts's writings can serve as a chronicle of Soviet social history. Berggol'ts's works span fifty-some years, and those were fifty years crucial to the development of the Soviet ideology and society. Berggol'ts, with her dualistic, questioning weltanschauung, oscillating between conflicting yet overlapping identities, between that of a loving wife and mother and that of a conscientious citizen, and between the role of a sensitive writer and a "responsible" journalist, has contributed to a deep understanding of the Soviet mind and the complex communist society. What Berggol'ts's works lack in refinement and style is compensated for by her understanding of the human condition and her desire to record in the form of prose and poetry the life and times of her world.

Trina Mamoon

From On the Enisei: Letters after the Journey

The First Meeting

It took me a long time to recognize it, the river, gazing at the landscape that lay outside the windows of the the Peking-bound Moscow train; and frankly speaking, the first time that my heart missed a beat and shuddered was only at Krasnoiarsk, at the riverside railway station, on the banks of the Enisei, during the trip on the icebreaker.

The Enisei—it was sailing . . . it was . . . it was so very unlike all the rivers that I had so far seen, the dear Oka; the Volga, my beloved from early childhood; our stately Neva—the Enisei was one of a kind, unparalleled in its beauty. And this dissimilarity was not only accounted for by its width, its span, the power of its flow, but also by the fact that the Enisei realized, understood, how mighty, beautiful, and wide it was, how delightful were the ridges of the Saianian range, which in the vicinity of Krasnoiarsk, skirts its right bank, retreating here and there, like a lilac-blue border—he, the Enisei, wished them to be exactly like this. He also wished to be quieter this spring; he did not forge up the ice-laden riverside station, he did not flood the town, he only drew and tossed the huge, quietly resounding slabs of ice along himself, enjoying his down-pouring, his strength, his spring, his stormy clouds which gathered in the expansive, cold, blue sky.

The feeling that the sternly majestic Enisei is not at all a "blind force," but a living, thinking, creative force, which does not need to be vanquished, defeated, reconciled, but a force with which the generation of the seventh five-year plan can come to an agreement on the basis of mutual benefit (oh! how often we start a "struggle" when there ought to be agreement with Nature!)—this feeling was aroused in me even before I sailed aboard the ship *Nekrasov* from Krasnoiarsk down to Minusinsk. And we had to leave Krasnoiarsk only six days earlier than the *St. Nicholas* had left from this very spot sixty-two years ago, bearing Vladimir Ilych Lenin to a three-year-long exile.

How I longed to see on everything our route that Ilych had once seen! Fully aware that my question sounded somewhat absurd, all the same I asked Captain M.O. Likhanskii a few days prior to our departure: "Captain, has the Enisei changed very much since the days that Ilych sailed on it?"

We were having our conversation in the empty meeting room of the river station. The captain shot a quick glance out the window, looked to his right, looked to his left, looked back, and once again he fixed his eyes straight ahead—it seemed as if that his gaze traveled over all of the Enisei in that one second. He kept glancing at the Enisei throughout our lengthy conversation. And at that moment a thought occurred to me, that this probably was some sort of a special "captain's gaze," and would you believe it? I was not wrong.

"No, it has not changed," the captain answered me. "The Enisei is not a river of the plains; it has a steady course, it laid its trail in firm ground, it is not like the Amu-Dar'ia . . . and that is why the landscape is also unchanging. . . . Naturally, it is now different in the vicinity of Krasnoiarsk than it was then. Now it is an industrial center, a large port. But the course itself has remained unchanged since the days of Ilych." (I must say here that the river folk, instead of saying "Enisei," often call it the "course.") "It is true that toward the end of the seventh five-year plan, the entire course will change a lot, especially after the construction of the Krasnoiarsk hydroelectric power station—more than it has changed over the past sixty-two years. . . ."

Journey into the Unknown

"Poetry is a journey into the unknown," Mayakovsky once said. The route of the steamship *Nekrasov* up to Minusinsk was just such a "journey into the unknown"—journey into the poetry of life and its history.

Whether it was because of the Enisei, because of its beauty and its creative ambience (everything and everybody worked here, the river, the spring, the people!), or whether it was because the course had been charted out long ago, and prepared with feeling, or because of all these reasons, never before did what I saw and heard have such an impact on me; it aroused in me the thought that my, our, writers' vocation should be more perfect, more responsible, and more fearless.

I was introduced to the captain of the steamship, Ivan Vasil'evich Trofimov, and immediately after that I climbed onto the deck by way of a steep, narrow ladder. I examined the equipment of the deck house reverentially. There was a lot of equipment: two nickel-plated levers and the control panel, which glittered impressively, looking like a large writing table with huge buttons, multicolored lights, and circular instruments. Only the colorful yellow, romantic steering wheel in front of the control panel seemed like an old acquaintance. . . . But suddenly the door of the deck house was flung open, and two children rowdily clambered up the stairs: a pale, skinny little girl and a stout little boy, short, round-eyed, and pug-nosed, so that if one looked at him directly, one saw the round holes of his nostrils.

The children, after politely uttering, "Hello, Auntie," immediately jumped onto the revolving chair in front of the control panel, perilously close to the instruments, and began to whirl in a self-confident manner.

"Hey, kids!" I shouted without having wanted to do so. "Calm down, or you might break something." The revolving of the chair ceased. "You must be teasing, Auntie," the pale girl said with unhappiness in her voice. "We know our way around here. We are mechanic Ivan Dmitr'evich Chervikov's kids. I am Galia, and this is Vova. We came to see Daddy off."

Evidently the children discerned at once that I was not one of the locals, and Vova, looking at me with his round eyes and open nostrils, began to tell me: "There goes *Mayakovsky*; it ferries people to the inlet and back. Auntie, look, and there is *Pushkin,* the one who wrote the story of the fisherman and the golden fish." I felt invigorated and more confident in the company of these knowledgeable children; I understood then that I would be finding out about a lot of things from them, and would even learn a few things.

The stairs creaked and Captain Trofimov and the chief mechanic of the steamship, Chervikov, came up to the deck house. I recognized Chervikov immediately because he looked uncannily like Vova! The brave, copper-red, frank face, which looked as if it had been chiseled out with hasty strokes, had a straightforward, cheerful look. Beside the pug-nosed, strong, broad-shouldered chief mechanic with his broad cheekbones and arching bushy eyebrows, the captain looked almost fragile; he was of medium height, lanky, youthful, pale, with straight features. His face was very calm, almost immobile, and the gray-blue eyes were somewhat remote.

We were supposed to set sail in a short while. I was afraid that the children would not be able to get off the motorboat in time, but they managed. The journey into the unknown began—upwards along the Enisei. . . . The unknown immediately took control of me from my head to foot, took control of my vision, hearing, heart and brain—of my entire being—and this feeling did not slacken throughout the trip. No, I did not start to question the captain about the new method of the work of the Siberian people, I only asked when I would see the spot where the dam of the power station was going to be.

"Unfortunately," he answered, "you will not be able to see it; we will go by it late at night." I was very disappointed. I did not know then that I would see it—in Moscow.

The Captain's Gaze

The captain was speaking to the young helmsman, from time to time steadying his hands, and sometimes even taking over the steering wheel himself. "Aleksandr Vasil'evich, steer to the left. More. Watch out, don't go over the buoy! Look, Sasha, how the wave towered and died down. This means that there is a sandbank here. Steer to the right. Look, there is a 'silver braid' on the wave. Don't let the pretty name fool you. It means that below that wave there is a sandbank."

The captain spoke in a soft, even, and somewhat dry voice. Sometimes he coughed, and looking at him, I noted once again that like Captain Likhanskii, he continually kept glancing all around: he looked ahead, to his left, to his right, behind, again ahead of him, at the "course." I asked him whether I imagined it or not, or whether there was such a thing as the "captain's gaze." "Of course there is," replied the captain. "If I don't look around and look back, then I can't go forward."

"Well, just now when you looked back, what did you see?"

"Well, I saw that a wave from underneath was coming from the direction of the stern, which meant we went over a sandbank. And that means there can be another one ahead. Sasha, steer left, go left. And then go straight ahead."

"I thought that all the sandbanks were charted."

"There are about a hundred and sixteen sandbanks and shoals on the way from Krasnoiarsk to Minusinsk. But there are some like the one we just saw which are formed in the deep ice. The water from the depths has not come up yet, and the level of the water varies on the surface and shoals are formed temporarily. One has to keep them in mind for the future. Don't go too near the bank, Sasha!"

He fell silent, and then smiling a little from the corners of his mouth, he added: "Actually, I have known about this shoal from the first trip. I just looked back to make sure and sail on more steadily."

At that moment I thought that there are a lot of people in our literary milieu who continually proclaim, trying to teach writers: "Look only ahead," or "Aim for the future first," and imagine themselves to be the most progressive of people, believing that they are orienting literature in the correct direction. Some of them even assign to the writer the exclusive role of a prognosticator. Of course, it is a beautiful thought, but it is not quite correct, and therefore it is not true. It is true that on big ships there is a person who only looks ahead, for his job is only to look ahead, but the vessel is directed by the captain. In order to go ahead without accidents or delays, into the future, the captain has to not only look ahead but also back at the course left behind; he cannot let either of the banks out of his sight. The vision of the "prognosticator" is only a part of the vision of the captain. Our literature in general, and each individual writer according to his or her ability, should cultivate and perfect the glance of the captain, the vision of the captain, and the responsibility of the captain. And if writers are seriously concerned about the fact that our unparalleled march ahead be successful, they must write about that dangerous shoal or the treacherous sandbank, write about the deceptive ghosts and false friends with beautiful names. Writing about all this will help detect the yet unforeseen shoal that lies ahead, so that the ships that set sail after us will be forewarned. To practice the captain's gaze in literature will not let us down; it will prove to be timely, and will make note of the most current events, which is absolutely necessary for forward motion.

A Harsh Spring

The things that were visible this morning were, once again, the mountains and the sun. Here and there the mountains retreated from the river, and sometimes they loomed closer, painted in soft and harsh outlines. The sun, like a huge opaque-gold crown, rose again over the great expanse of the Enisei.

Maria Afanas'evna, the cashier who also acted as the stewardess occasionally, came in. She was a plump, humorous and friendly woman.

"How beautiful it is!" I exclaimed. In a singsong voice she answered with regret: "What a pity that you are traveling at such a time of the year. What a poor season! The weather is gray and the spring is still harsh."

The kindly dear, she did not know that this was the kind of spring I had been looking forward to.

Harsh spring, harsh spring, my first Siberian spring . . . harsh season . . . no, it is not harsh. There are a hundred times more colors in this harsh spring than there are in the height of green spring. The huge palette of the harsh spring has the most tender, the most delicate of all the watercolor hues. Over there the hills are all covered by a birch forest; in the backdrop of a lilac-pink glow there are innumerable silver-white tree trunks, and among the white and lilac tones, the pine needles are painted a dark green, and above all this, a net of black leafless branches reaches out to the pale blue sky.

I asked Chervikov whether the nearest stop was soon approaching. "Soon. Near the village of Ubei" [Murder].

"What a name for a village!"

Chervikov broke out in a broad smile. "In these parts we have many such names. On the Angara the rapids have names like Hangover, Drunkard, The Fallen One, Champagne, and so on."

The village of Ubei stands at the edge of a steep cliff cut by an even path, on the side of which are the nests of swifts, scattered about the whole place. Ubei, with its dreary cottages with log walls and rickety fences, has its back turned on the Enisei. The fences are tilted on one side in such a way that it looks as if strong winds had toppled them.

Trofimov entered the deck house. "The name suits the village," I told him, "it has such a gloomy look."

"This village also will be flooded," the captain replied calmly. "As soon as the Krasnoiarsk power station is built."

From the village of Ubei a crowd of people were running down the dirt path of the precipice. Three people were going to board the motorboat and a whole crowd came to see them off. For some reason there were a lot of children, even very small ones. Two girls, holding a bucket by the rims, were hauling it toward the gangplank. The bucket was full of bright pink geraniums. Behind them a lively old woman was tripping along briskly—she was going to return to her home with her present. She had been visiting the village. The people were cheerfully rushing toward the motorboat. It seemed as if the village was going to be immediately flooded and its inhabitants were hurrying to leave the place in order to escape the disaster.

"Will the water rise so high when it is flooded?"

"Oh, yes. It will be great sailing on those waters."

The captain had spoken about it several times. He had already begun to sail on the river of tomorrow, the Enisei of the future, which would be flowing over these ancient villages with their horrible names once the power station was built. It will flow over that old woman with the geraniums, over the little boy in a huge old border guard's coat. Not only will the crooked walls and fences sink down to the bottom, but so, too, the biographies, the fates, the foundations of entire generations. Someone's early childhood will be sunk, and the landscape of his native soil, the piece of land from where the world was for the very first time opened to him, will remain in his memory alone, untouched. . . .

"Now we will see the City Wall," Trofimov said softly. "Legend says that there was once a large city here, surrounded by such a wall."

Evening at City Wall

From the bridge, I looked ahead to where City Wall loomed. The apparition aroused thoughts about both the past and the future. I could see from a distance that it was not simply a cliff; it was a fortification, a piece of architecture. The nearer we came to it, and as we walked in front of it, it appeared that City Wall had been built carefully, layer by layer. Its very top, which reached up to the cloudy heights, had an even, flat surface; there were no jagged edges.

The wall was impressive because of its tranquility and its inaccessibility. It had no vegetation and was of a rusty green-gold color. And the Enisei, darkened by its reflection, meandered unhurriedly beneath.

Oh, what an enormous city was once surrounded by this wall! Perhaps this was the City of the Sun—the City of the Sun itself, which at this moment was slowly and majestically setting, columns of its rays shining through the ominous storm clouds.

City Wall was exactly like this when Lenin was here. Yes, he traveled almost on the same day as we now are, on the first or the second trip of the *St. Nicholas.* And the spring was as fierce then as now. He had spent his childhood and boyhood on the great and the most beautiful Russian river, the Volga. He must have been moved by the novelty and the strength of the Enisei.

He was young then; he had turned twenty-seven only three weeks before. As he peered up at the sky, at the setting of the sun, at the river that rushed between the cliffs, at City Wall, thoughts—great, courageous, and illuminating ones, like these clouds before the sunset—arose in his bosom, and just like the clouds, they were as close to the whole of nature. Those were thoughts about his people—fighters, creators, artists, and thoughts about the freedom and glory of his nation. . . .

And City Wall, which we walked past, did not leave our sight, shining with a dark copper hue. Instead it turned its back, towering over the Enisei with the blue mountains in the distance.

"I have not seen anything more beautiful," I told Trofimov.

"Beautiful! But it is only a small part of the Enisei," he answered and his sculptured pale face softened. "There are actually three Eniseis! The upper Enisei is one; apples and watermelons can be seen there. . . . The middle part, where the rapids are, is quite another sight, and the lower Enisei, where it is night half the year round and the sun shines the rest of the time, is unique. And people are very different on these three Eniseis, and so is life. I would like such a book written, one that would attract the reader to the Enisei and to Siberia. It is so beautiful and rich here. . . ."

I felt like telling him: "The most important resource of Siberia, it is you, comrades. The people who are building the bravest and the most intelligent of lifestyles. Life, about which Chekhov dreamed, and to which Lenin led us, creating a new way of life here, on the mighty Enisei, near City Wall. The main theme of Siberia is the fate of the people, of humanity, laden with labor and beauty."

Trofimov, coughed, smiled and left. "I see he has caught a cold," I told Chervikov. A light shadow passed over Ivan Dmitr'evich's broad, tanned face, a face alive with strength. "He did not catch a cold. He has one lung and nine ribs missing. He was wounded badly in the war."

Evening at City Wall slowly dwindled; the journey into the unknown, into poetry, continued. . . . The next morning we were supposed to be in Minusinsk.

1959

You will have a good time with me,
If you wish to live with me:
I will sing songs to you, and tell funny stories,
Here, I am holding out my hands to you, take them.

I will take you to meet my girl friends,
(How long have I waited for this moment!)
"Look!" I will tell them. "I have found you all
A friend, he is the best!"

Take pity on him, don't be shy, love him.
He is stubborn, but gentle and simple.
But I beg of you, my friends,
Don't take him away from me,
As I have done so from another.

This is what I would have told my friends.
This is how we would have lived, so happily—

Without regrets, sorrow or complaints,
Without farewells at railway stations at midnight.

1935

Lullaby for My Spanish Son

My new son, relax!
A calm wind is blowing outside.
Get used to your new mother,
And to the unfamiliar Russian tongue.

When you hear planes overhead,
Do not fear; it is our own, a plane of peace,
Bearing the Red Star banner.

My new son, learn to share our joys with us,
But do not forget your own,
Your native Spanish mother.
Your mom and her sisters are fighting this evening.

Your mom is liberating your land for you.
And when you return to your victorious native country,
Don't forget me, who loves you so dearly.
My migratory little bird,
Write a long letter in broken,
Half-Russian words to your Soviet mom.

1937

A Song

I wander about the city and lament,
Humming an unfamiliar tune.
This is where we took leave of one another.
This is where we parted and looked back at each other.

Now the city is full of pollen dust,
Tender green leaves, and puddles.

Let them laugh, I will give anything,
Even if the price is going to be dear,
Just to have another look at my beloved,
Fading far away from sight.

1939

A Meeting

The air is filled with the smell of pines.
Look! The little spring is gushing by . . .
This is the smell of liberation,
The sign of our eternal love.

Let's not count the days, the minutes,
Let's not make guesses about what the future holds
Oh! Sober, wrathful, cruel midday of happiness,
Don't go away!

1939

The Falling of Leaves

In the fall there are notices on the
streets of Moscow with the warning
"Careful: Leaves Falling!"

Autumn, oh autumn! Fog, smoke, and cranes
Flying over Moscow.
The gardens glow with their deep-gold foliage.
At street corners signs warn the passers-by,
Couples and loners alike: "Careful: Leaves Falling!"

Oh! How lonely it feels in an unfamiliar alley.
Evening envelops the windows which shudder
Under the falling rain.

Who am I waiting for here?

Who is dear to me, and by whom am I needed?
Why do I keep remembering: "Careful: Leaves Falling!"

All this was unnecessary,
That means, there is nothing left to lose.
I can't even say "beloved" to people dear to me.
Why am I sad that we are saying adieu,
My morose, sad, lonely friend?

Why the cynical smile, the indifference?
You will hang on there, you will survive. . . .

No, tenderness, like rain, is a thing most alien
When you are saying goodbye.
Dark rain, warm rain!
All shimmers and shudders.
Be cheerful, be happy, like the rain,
At the time of parting.

. . . I will go alone to the station,
I will say no to the people
Who come to take leave of us.

I did not tell you everything then,
But it is too late now.

The alley is pregnant with darkness,
And the notices tell the lonely passers-by:
"Careful: Leaves Falling!"

1938

Translated by Trina Mamoon

Notes to the Essay

1. Bank, *Ol'ga Berggol'ts. Kritiko-biograficheskii ocherk* (Moscow: Sovetskii pisatel', 1962), 7.
2. A.M. Gor'kii, "Dva pis'ma A.M. Gor'kogo," *Literaturnaia gazeta*, 29 March 1958.

Bibliography

Primary Works

"15 minut nad Leningradom." *Iunyi proletarii* 14 (1926): 21.

"Iskateli mozolei. [Kn.I. Griaznova]." *Smena,* 21 October 1928.

"Kak Vania possorilsia s baranami." *Krasnaia gazeta,* 1929.

"Zakoldovannaia tropinka." *Krasnyi galstuk* 3 (1929): 19–21.

Pyzhik. Moscow: Gosudarstvennoe izdatel'stvo, 1930.

Stasia vo dvortse. Moscow: Gosudarstvennoe izdatel'stvo, 1930.

Turman. Leningrad: Gosudarstvennoe izdatel'stvo, 1930.

Zapruda. Moscow: Gosudarstvennoe izdatel'stvo, 1930.

Zima-leto-popugai. Leningrad: Gosudarstvennoe izdatel'stvo, 1930.

"Imeni Furmana." *Zvezda* 10 (1931): 98–109.

Man'ka-nian'ka. Leningrad: Gosudarstvennoe izdatel'stvo, 1931.

Pionerskaia lagernaia. Leningrad: Molodaia gvardiia, 1931.

Poedem za moria. Leningrad: Molodaia gvardiia, 1931.

Glubinka. Leningrad: Lengikhl, 1932.

Gornaia zhvachka. Moscow: Molodaia gvardiia, 1932.

"Napishem istoriiu zavodskogo komsomola." *Elektrosila,* 9 March 1932.

"Taina Kara-Tau." *Chik* 1 (1932): 6–8; 2 (1932): 5–7; 4/5 (1932): 7–9; 6 (1932): 5–7.

Uglich. Moscow: Molodaia gvardiia, 1933.

Zima-leto-popugai. 2d ed. Moscow: Molodaia gvardiia, 1933.

Pimokaty s Altaiskikh. Moscow: Detgiz, 1934.

"Riadom s Marksom stoiali Pushkin i Nekrasov." *Elektrosila,* 21 June 1934.

Stikhotvoreniia. Leningrad: Izdatel'stvo pisatelei v Leningrade, 1934.

"Zhurnalisty." *Zvezda* 4 (1934): 3–29; 5 (1934): 3–29.

"Iz istorii zavodov 'Elektrosila' i im. Kazitskogo." *Zvezda* 1 (1935): 193–200.

Noch' v "Novom mire." Leningrad: Khudozhestvennaia literatura, 1935.

"Shkola." *Literaturnyi sovremennik* 7 (1935): 126–141.

"Syn." *Literaturnyi sovremennik* 12 (1935): 85–101.

"Zerna." Zvezda 3 (1935): 3–40.

"Doverie k sebe" [O zadachakh liriki]. *Literaturnyi Leningrad,* 8 January 1936.

Kniga pesen. Leningrad: Khudozhestvennaia literatura, 1936.

"Na vsiu zhizn'" [Pamiati M. Gor'kogo]. *Literaturnyi Leningrad,* 3 March 1936.

"Dva rasskaza'" [M. Zoshchenko "Netaktichno postupili" i "Ogni bol'shogo goroda"]. *Literaturnyi Leningrad,* 5 February 1937.

"Obraz Pushkina u sovetskikh pisatelei." *Literaturnyi Leningrad,* 17 January 1937.

Mechta. Moscow: Detskoe izdatel'stvo, 1939.

"Luchshii drug." *Koster* 11 (1940): 41–47.

"Baltiiskoe serdtse." *Smena,* 16 October 1942.

Leningradskaia poèma. Leningrad: Goslitizdat, 1942.

"Leningradskaia simfoniia [1–oe ispolnenie 7–moi simfonii Shostakovicha v Leningrade]." *Komsomol'skaia pravda,* 19 August 1942.

Leningradskaia tetrad'. Moscow: Sovremennyi pisatel', 1942.

Leningrad. Moscow: Sovremennyi pisatel', 1944.
Leningradskii dnevnik. Leningrad: Goslitizdat, 1944.
"Pervye chasy." *Literatura i iskusstvo,* 5 February 1944.
"Pis'ma druzei." *Literatura i iskusstvo,* 23 February 1944.
"Russkaia zhenshchina." *Izvestiia,* 19 August 1944.
Oni zhili v Leningrade. Moscow: Iskusstvo, 1945.
Tvoi put'. Leningrad: Molodaia gvardiia, 1945.
U nas na zemle. Moscow: Vsesoiuznoe upravlenie po okhrane avtorskogo prava. Otdel rasprostraneniia, 1947.
Izbrannoe. Moscow: Sovremennyi pisatel', 1948.
"Don prishel k Volge." *Literaturnaia gazeta,* 3 June 1952.
Pervorossiisk. Moscow: Goslitizdat, 1952.
"Zelenyi poias Volgo-Dona." *Literaturnaia gazeta,* 26 July 1952.
"Razgovor o lirike." *Literaturnaia gazeta,* 16 April 1953.
"S novym schast'em!" *Pravda,* 31 December 1953.
Izbrannoe. Moscow: Molodaia gvardiia, 1954.
"O nashikh detiakh." *Literaturnaia gazeta,* 25 March 1954.
"Protiv likvidatsii liriki." *Literaturnaia gazeta,* 28 October 1954.
Vernost'. Leningrad: Sovremennyi pisatel', 1954.
Lirika. Moscow: Goslitizdat, 1955.
Poèmy. Leningrad: Sovremennyi pisatel', 1955.
"Chelovecheskoe iskusstvo." *Teatr* 7 (1956): 182–84.
"Prodolzhenie zhizni." *Stikhotvoreniia i poèmy*. Ed. B. Kornilov. Leningrad: 1957. 3–12.
Dnevnye zvezdy. Leningrad: Sovremennyi pisatel', 1958.
Sochineniia v dvuch tomax. Moscow: Goslitizdat, 1958.
"Ne rekviem, a gimn muzhestvu." *Smena,* 5 April 1963.
"Kinopoema 'Pervorossiisk.'" *Sovetskii èkran* 17 (1964): 8–9.
"Slovo proshchaniia Pamiati A. Akhmatovoi." *Literaturnaia Rossiia,* 11 March 1966, 21.
"Moia zhizn'." *Russkie poèty*. Leningrad: 1968. 681–84.
"Avtobiografiia." *Pesnia, mechta i liubov'. Poètessy sovetskogo soiuza*. Moscow, 1969. 99–101.
"O sebe." *Rabotnitsa* 10 (1969): 16.
"Domik za Nevskoi zastavoi." *Izvestiia,* 14 April 1970.
"Popytka avtobiografii." *Sovetskie pisateli. Avtobiografii*. Vol. 4. Moscow, 1972. 72–83.
Sobranie sochenenii v 3–kh t. Leningrad: Khudozhestvennaia literatura, 1972–1973.

Secondary Works

Azarov, V. "Stikhi Ol'gi Berggol'ts." *Vechernii Leningrad,* 19 January 1946.
Bakinskii, N. "Noch' v 'Novom mire'." *Literaturnyi Leningrad,* 8 December 1935.
Bank, N. "Liricheskie poèmy O. Berggol'ts voennykh let." *Filolologicheskii sbornik studencheskogo nauchnogo obshchestva Leningradskogo universiteta,* Vol. 1. Leningrad, 1957. 63–86.
———. *Ol'ga Berggol'ts. Kritiko-biograficheskii ocherk*. Moscow: Sovetskii pisatel', 1962.
———, and Kofman, G. "O proze O. Berggol'ts dlia detei." *Sem'ia i shkola* 6 (1971): 39.
Danilin, Iu. "Ol'ga Berggol'ts." *Oktiabr'* 2 (1943): 109–11.

Èrenburg, I. "Liudi, gody, zhizn'." *Novyi mir* 1 (1965): 105.

Gor'kii, A.M. "Dva pis'ma A.M. Gor'kogo (Dec. 1931–Nov. 1934)." *Literaturnaia gazeta,* 29 March 1958.

Grinberg, N. "Svoi put'. O stikhakh O. Berggol'ts." *Iunyi proletarii* 18 (1933): 12–13.

Ketlinskaia, V. "Ispytanie dushi [Berggol'ts vo vremia blokady Leningrada]." *Neva* 3 (1965): 191–92.

Khrenkov, D. *Ot serdtse k serdtsu. O zhizni i tvorchestve Ol'gi Berggol'ts.* Leningrad: Sovetskii pisatel', 1982.

Pavlovskii, A. *Stikh i serdtse. Ocherk tvorchestva O. Berggol'ts.* Leningrad: Lenizdat, 1962.

Tarskii. M. "Pervorossiisk." *Bol'shevik Altaia,* 10 January 1951.

Tsurikova, G.M. *Ol'ga Berggol'ts.* Leningrad: Znanie, 1961.

———, and I.S. Kuz'michev, eds. *Vspominaia Ol'gu Berggol'ts.* Leningrad: Lenizdat, 1979.

Vera Inber

Vera Inber (1890–1972).
Courtesy of Mary Nicholas.

Vera Mikhailovna Inber's (1890–1972) long and prolific career as poet, journalist, short story writer, essayist, playwright and memoirist offers fascinating insight into the tumultuous history of Soviet Russian literature. Well known in her time and still considered one of the "classics of Soviet literature,"[1] Inber is now read relatively little. Only one full-length study of her work exists, and Iosif Grinberg's somewhat dated book, *Vera Inber: A Critical-Biographical Sketch* (*Vera Inber: Kritiko-biograficheskii ocherk*), reflects an expected bias toward her more orthodox socialist realist writings. In general discussions of the period, Inber usually elicits somewhat qualified admiration for her facility with words, cultured outlook and apparently heartfelt emotions. Evelyn Bristol, for example, is subdued in her praise, noting that Inber was one of a "number of deserving poets" in the socialist camp and arguing that the "modesty of her voice is everywhere at odds with her real sophistication and wide experience as a European correspondent." A. Markov, the editor of Inber's collected works, is similarly restrained in his evaluation. He offers a conditional endorsement, intimating that Inber is significant primarily as a historical figure important to an older generation of readers.[2]

Yet Inber's example is instructive nonetheless. Her personal history, like that of many of her contemporaries, is extraordinarily varied, punctuated throughout by the enormous social upheavals that rocked the twentieth century. She witnessed and documented some of the most cataclysmic events of the time, and her point of view—unassuming, at times even apologetic, enthusiastic yet intimate—is often a useful antidote to more grandiose accounts of the same period. Her long career can be seen as a geological cross section of the development of Russian literature and literary politics from just before the October Revolution to the now infamous "period of stagnation" under Brezhnev. Her creative works—from decadent lyric poetry through committed socialist realism and into the Thaw—reflect the most important stages in the evolution of Soviet literature and provide a useful point of departure for discussion of that complex period.

Inber was born on 10 July 1890[3] in the southern seaport of Odessa. The city was a colorful mix of nationalities and creative traditions, and it was home to a number of writers contemporary to Inber, including Eduard Bagritskii, Ilia Selvinskii, Iurii Olesha, Valentin Kataev and Isaac Babel'. Like Babel', Inber was Jewish, although her russified patronymic suggests a considerable though not unusual degree of assimilation. Her mother taught Russian at a school for young women, where she was later headmistress, and Inber's father ran Mathesis, one of the largest academic publishing houses in the city. This cultural background provided Inber with a level of worldliness and sophistication that was important from the very beginning of her creative life. She mentions, for example, that she began writing poetry as early as age nine, and the critic Leonard Gendlin notes that she published her first poem at age eleven.[4]

Inber's "petty bourgeois" background was to weigh heavily against her after the revolution when a working-class pedigree became de rigueur. But it was initially an advantage that included higher education at the prestigious women's institution in Odessa (Vysshie zhenskie kursy). As a young woman of twenty, Inber moved abroad in 1910 and lived in France and Switzerland until a month before the outbreak of World War I.[5] Her first book of poems was published privately in Paris under the suitably decadent title of *Melancholy Wine* (*Pechal'noe vino*) in 1914. Her second volume of poetry, *Bitter Delight* (*Gor'kaia uslada*), appeared in 1917, the year of the revolution, but it, like its predecessor, was influenced more by the Symbolists, whom Inber admired, than by the momentous political events of the time. A third collection, *Fleeting Words* (*Brennye slova*), was published in Odessa in 1922, and it, too, while somewhat less ornate, seemed largely untouched either by the political firestorms that surrounded Inber or by the avant-garde innovations that intrigued many other writers of the time.

Inber's youthful poetry varies widely in theme and quality, and as might be expected, much of the early verse involves timid experimentation with rhyme scheme and meter as well as a colorful variety of lyric personae whose voices often directly contradict one another. Thus in the poem "Snow" ("Sneg") from Paris in 1912, Inber imagines herself as a northerner whose tempestuous temperament seeks the extremes of the northern winter: "In January I don't want anything like the month of May. / I need snow. Snowdrifts among old, Yuletide pines. / Here, I'm nearly perishing from the spring that's not a spring, / And in the middle of these manicured gardens—I'm afraid, I'm afraid I shall die."[6] But in a poem from 1915 that begins "Wave without foam. Sun without fire" (*Volna bez peny. Solntse bez ognia*), the narrator describes herself as a southerner (*iuzhanka*), pining away in the frigid north for the delights of the south.[7] Her third volume opens with a programmatic statement, calculated at establishing her bohemian artistic credentials: "It's not the fact that I'm a wife and mother that nourishes the dry fields of my soul: I need to anguish a great deal in order to be peaceful and happy."[8]

Inber came to view these early volumes as a "pre-biography" in the history of the real beginning of her creative life.[9] That judgment reflects both the relative immaturity of her youthful poetry and the changing political atmosphere in which she and other bourgeois writers found themselves after the revolution. Her early lyrics and the comfortable social background that engendered them to an extent were to become liabilities in the years that followed 1917. Inber took to minimizing both whenever possible, claiming that she was "unlucky" in her biography (*mne ne povezlo s biografiei*) and noting ruefully that she "could have written a decent autobiographical piece" if only she "had had a different childhood and youth." Her comment in the autobiographical piece that she did produce suggests her disheartening self-awareness that her experience is not valued. "From time to time," she notes in "These Fifteen Years" ("Èti piatnadtsat' let," 1932), written for the anniversary of the revolution, "I take out of the memory stores one or another of my carefully packed memories, sprinkled with mothballs. I bring it out into the light, test its durability: the thing is well preserved; it's fresh; there aren't any defects in it. But it's not what's needed, not needed."[10]

This humble and self-dismissive attitude, familiar in many other women authors, marks much of Inber's autobiographical writing and stems from her uneasy position as a bourgeois writer in the new "classless" society.[11] As a "fellow traveler" in the struggle, Inber was sympathetic to but not wholeheartedly supportive of the communist regime. Her need to prove herself sufficiently orthodox occasionally lends her writing, particularly her poetry, a note of self-abnegation that seems cloying.[12] The self-consciousness her insecure social position created is apparent in her description of life during the civil war years. Separated from her first husband, Inber was alone with her young daughter[13] and the child's nanny in Odessa from May 1918 until April 1922, and she describes her experiences in the city in her memoir *A Place in the Sun* (*Mesto pod solntsem*), from 1928. One of her most interesting pieces, *A Place in the Sun* is artistically superior to most of her poetry.

Part of that appeal is the fascinating material with which Inber had to work. The society she inhabited was a chaotic one in which long familiar patterns of life coexisted uneasily with the new ways that threatened to replace them. The chaos surrounding Inber in *A Place in the Sun* inspires her to record this momentous but fleeting stage in the history of her country. As she describes her encounters with bandits, convinced revolutionaries, disillusioned intellectuals and petty merchants from the beginning of the New Economic Policy, or NEP, she is clearly aware that what she sees is ephemeral. "They lived, these people," she comments in the afterword to the piece. "Many of them passed by and disappeared, as if their feet had never touched the light, gray grass of the road. Their prints are left only on these pages."[14]

Her conviction that she is telling the story of a time that no longer exists helps Inber maintain a semblance of objectivity. Behind her terse and seemingly detached account stands a staunch defender of the "traditional notions of high culture and proper social conduct."[15] But Inber's willingness to avoid trite conclusions saves the work from a facile moral certitude that might otherwise have marred it. Her account is enhanced as well by her firm belief in the value of brevity and precision.[16] Her description in *A Place in the Sun* of an acquaintance who was planning to emigrate to western Europe to avoid the "barbarians" at the helm of the country is typical in its laconicism. "He disappeared," she remarks tersely. "But I stayed."[17]

Inber's experience as a poet stood her in good stead as a chronicler of the new era, giving her an awareness of the emotional power of language and making her sensitive to the single, telling detail. She describes her own behavior on New Year's Eve at the end of 1918, for example, in a passage typical both in its casually self-deprecating tone and its attention to everyday detail. Surrounded by acquaintances who bemoan the year that has deprived them of stability, tradition, comfort, even of some of the letters of the alphabet, Inber lets herself be lulled into a state of semi-oblivion. "Let's forget the past months," suggests one of the intellectuals present, "as though nothing happened." Musing over his words, Inber tries to comfort herself with the epicurean thought that life is too short to be taken seriously. "Nothing happened," she repeats as a mantra, as she leans back in an attempt to forget herself. *"Something happened,"* insists a louse, whose bite rouses her back into reality.[18]

This sort of prosaic detail is typical of Inber's writing. Her attention to everyday life, or *byt,* sets her apart from many of her contemporaries, particularly from writers in the Russian avant-garde of the time. As Catriona Kelly has pointed out, the attention to *byt* is a special concern of many Russian women writers, and this fact may have helped exclude them from the higher echelons of avant-garde literary circles, where quotidian existence was treated as somehow uniquely bourgeois and unworthy of attention.[19] Inber's writings include many of the topics often relegated as secondary to what is still sometimes disdainfully known as "women's literature," topics such as child rearing, housing and other domestic difficulties.

In *A Place in the Sun,* Inber is successful in weaving a tale of personal trial and tribulation into a larger story of general import. Particularly significant is her ability to describe an entire historical period in some detail, following her own idiosyncratic train of thought without seeming regard to the overall organization of her material. Her connections seem to be associative, and the epithet she somewhat disapprovingly assigns to the work—"lyrical chronicle" (*liricheskaia khronika*)[20]—is apt. The slight distaste with which she applies the term is undoubtedly a reaction to pressure she and other writers received from more radical literary groups in the 1920s.[21] Inber is successful in pieces in which she describes events she has witnessed because of her willingness to let the material stand on its own. One of her favorite genres, the sketch, or *ocherk,* was ideally suited to her chaotic times, as a number of her contemporaries discovered. Inber was perhaps most at home with this form of expression, and she continued to develop it throughout the 1930s and 1940s, in part, it is true, out of necessity.[22]

A Place in the Sun describes Inber's departure from Odessa on an overloaded freight train headed to Moscow in 1922, and she picks up this thread of her story in an essay written in 1932 for the commemoration of the fifteenth anniversary of the revolution. Her description of her arrival in the "new" capital city still evokes the heady excitement many felt in the early days of the Soviet Union. If Odessa was the meeting place for everyone who thought Bolshevism was a temporary phenomenon,[23] Moscow was the magnet for those who had decided that the new regime was here to stay. As a writer, Inber naturally turned her attention to the arts first, and she was amazed at what she saw. Boris Pil'niak's experimental novel *Naked Year* (*Golyi god*) had just appeared on the scene, and Inber was overwhelmed with the results of Pil'niak's innovative approach. She notes that she had almost given up writing before her arrival in the city and had lost nearly everything one needs to write: her themes, her skill, her feeling for the language, her nerve and "most important," her "feeling for her era." In this fragile condition, the "terrible blast" she received from Pil'niak's book caused her to "slam it shut just as people slam windows shut." The experience reminded her of how sheltered she had been from the world around her. "You understand," she recalled a friend's comment, "it's warm and comfortable inside, but on the street, it's raining and there's a revolution. . . ."[24]

Inber, like so many others at the time, was almost immediately swept up in the competition for power and influence that characterized the Moscow literary scene. She met the critics Kornelii Zelinskii and Ilia Selvinskii soon after her arrival in the capital, and with them and a small number of other poets, she formed a group of constructivist writers, who were set on adopting a technological and organizational approach to literature. Their stated goal was to bring the proletariat closer to the cutting edge of modern technology through their artistic creations. Their manifesto from 1924 is full of ambitious plans for the rationalization of literary production and its subjugation to the goal of advancing the proletariat. The writers organized themselves into the Literary Center of Constructivists (Literaturnyi Tsentr Konstruktivistov, or LTsK). The group produced two volumes before disbanding in 1930 under pressure—the *State Plan of Literature (Gosplan literatury)* in 1925 and *Business (Biznes)* in 1929—and Inber contributed to them both.[25]

In some ways, Inber's presence there was an anomaly. As Catriona Kelly and others have noted, there were few women writers associated with the Russian literary avant-garde in the 1920s,[26] and Inber was somewhat of an exception. Her inclusion in the group was not entirely convincing, as constructivist polemicist Zelinskii acknowledges in his discussion of her work. Zelinskii notes that Inber's relationship to constructivism was viewed skeptically at first, since her first three books had been filled with "lyricism." But, according to him, when Inber realized that her former approach had no future, she took the riskiest step a poet could take: "to rewrite herself from the beginning" (*perepisat' sebia nanovo*).[27]

Inber's constructivist volume *Goal and Path* (*Tsel' i put'*) from 1924 indeed offers a contrast to the salon-inspired stylizations that had marked her early writing, although the poetry in *Goal and Path,* far from shocking, is certainly less innovative than any number of avant-garde works by Inber's contemporaries.

Zelinskii notes that the collection is a record of Inber's search for a new artistic approach and includes poems on both neutral and revolutionary themes in which the influence of constructivism can be seen. Perhaps most famous of these is the short poem "Five nights and days" ("Piat' nochei i dnei"), written in a flush of revolutionary fervor after Lenin's death in January 1924.

The poem, an immediate success that found its way into countless subsequent anthologies, is typical of much of Inber's political verse. The studied naivete in the rhymes (*v mogile—polozhili; usnul—karaul*) and the warmth of sentimental feeling are characteristic of Inber's poetry, as is the note of human intimacy she adds to historic events. Describing the crowds that flowed past Lenin's body in state, she comments: "They flowed. But the frost over the land was so fierce that it was as if he had carried away a part of our warmth with him" (*Tekli. A stuzha nad zemleiu / Takaia liutaia byla, / Kak budto on unes s soboiu / Chastitsu nashego tepla*).[28] Typical, too, are both the strong narrative features of the work and Inber's heightened sense of revolutionary morality. Inber's writing is often didactic, a trait it shares with the work of a number of Russian women prosaicists.[29] According to Zelinskii, it is this strong moral sense, which he calls the "will to order" (*volia k uporiadochennosti*),[30] that characterizes Inber's approach to the revolution and her writing. Inber emphasizes this same impulse toward rationalization and order when she later describes her fascination with constructivism as "technicism of the soul" (*tekhnitsizm dushi*).[31]

Inber's contribution to the first constructivist collection, the *State Plan of Literature* (*Gosplan literatury*), is an experimental work that Inber perceived as a further evolution of her aesthetics. Billed as the first chapter of an eventual four-part poem (*poèma*), the work "Coal" ("Ugol' ") is Inber's attempt to construct a self-contained artistic entity (*konstruktivno-zamknutoe tseloe*) in poetry. She uses a variety of constructivist vocabulary to describe her methods there, most obvious of which is the attempt to localize (*lokalizovat'*) the images, figures of speech, rhythmic structure and other elements of the poem in accord with the thematics of the poem. As the first two stanzas suggest, "Coal" is an awkward but reasonably successful work; its frequent alliterations, vivid and raw imagery, and regular rhyme scheme with a heavy masculine ending and shortened third and sixth lines help evoke the subject Inber has chosen:

In rays and thunder, above the cooled earth,
From the chaos of rings of steam,
The rains rolled down in a flood.
And the first roots, loop by loop,
Sucked the swollen breasts of the hills
And the flora fed on the moisture.

And the day, not yet divided into hours,
Was slow, like a lizard inhaling and exhaling;
The rustle and crackle was just audible.
Then sweaty from the paleozoic dew,
Pushing through the moss, a bush,
Bent and feathery, rustled and hissed.

But although Inber included "Coal" in a number of subsequent collections, she speaks with irony of the work in her memoir "These Fifteen Years," noting that the piece, no longer part of an intended epic, included her "last socially undifferentiated hero with an unknown biography."[32] Inber's move away from the group she had identified as her first literary circle[33] was by no means unexpected. Along with her "avant-garde" poetry, she had continued to develop a number of different aspects to her writing throughout the early 1920s. Works for children, like the delightful "Fortylegs" ("Sorokonozhki") from 1924, and folk stylizations, like the popular "To the Son I Don't Have" ("Synu, kotorogo net")[34] from 1926, continued to interest her. She had been working as a correspondent for much of the time she was associated with the constructivist poets, and her journalism was an important part of her literary activity during the mid-1920s and beyond. In *America in Paris*, for example, she describes her experiences in Paris, Berlin and Brussels. Her journalistic pieces included "slice-of-life" reporting from within the new Soviet Union as well. In a variety of short essays, she describes, for example, the Moscow tram system, a training school for police dogs, visits to the city zoo, her historic participation in a "propaganda flight" (*agitoblet*) in 1925 and so on.[35]

Inber's writing from this period, like that of so many of her contemporaries, often tends to blur the lines between fiction and reporting, and it is easy to read biographical details into much of both her fiction and her journalism. Her love of her native south is obvious in works such as "The Time of the Apricots" ("Vremia abrikosov"); her admiration tempered with the necessary skepticism for western Europe emerges in short stories such as "Chimney of the World" ("Trubka mira") and "The Rape of Europe" ("Pokhishchenie Evropy"). In some of the short stories, a fictionalized Inber serves as narrator, as she does in "Apartment 32" ("Kvartira No. 32"). In a number of Inber's most successful stories, the narrator is a child, as in "Without Kid Gloves" ("Ezhovy rukavitsy").

Often Inber's tone is morally instructive, even openly pedantic, as in the short story from 1928 "Don't Cry, Ninel" ("Ne plach', Ninel'"). There, the authenticity of the child's point of view vies for space alongside an unidentified third-person narrator who interrupts the story to convey a strong social message. The child heroine of the tale, Ninel, has been informed by her young male companion that the earth's axis shifts during the night, causing the land to list and the seas to overflow. This offends Ninel's sense of order, and she takes matters into her own hands by writing to the leader of an upcoming Arctic expedition, offering her services on the trip during which, she imagines, it will be necessary to "straighten" the axis. "I will help them put up tents," she comments optimistically. "Nowadays, women are like men. They can do everything."[36]

Inber's cheerful championing of the female character is quite typical of both her poetry and prose from the late 1920s and 1930s. She appears genuinely impressed by the strides made by women in her lifetime, and her tone is often that of the sturdy Soviet girl-next-door, a faithful comrade who can be counted on in difficult times. The 1931 poem "Foremother" ("Rodonachal'nitsa"), for example, begins with a description of a little girl, whose portrait the poet is about to draw. The portrait soon becomes a self-portrait, however, as the poet remembers the first time she saw a woman working on a tram crew. She is amazed by the sight, which offers her a metaphoric escape from the dead-end street (*tupichok, tupik*) on which she has been walking: "So, it's a lie, that only men are born for *everything*." She notes how far women have traveled: from the kitchen all the way to representation on political delegations (*Kak ètot put' velik—Ot striapni . . . Do delegatki vo VTsIK*). And she ends the poem with the firm conviction that women's new role in society is assured. "I smile at you," she comments to her tram conductor muse, "but you don't see me because it's so crowded."[37]

Inber herself entered the 1930s still concerned about her place in society and intent on refashioning herself as a writer. She and other "fellow travelers" had been under attack for several years for their alleged lack of revolutionary fervor and lukewarm commitment to the cause, and the literary politics of the period exacerbated her tendency to self-abnegation. Her narrative poem from 1932, "Sotto Voce" ("Vpolgolosa"),[38] reflects her mood at the beginning of the 1930s in its evocation of her life before the revolution and her description of her changed circumstances since then. Written, like the memoir "These Fifteen Years," on the fifteenth anniversary of the revolution, "Sotto Voce" expresses both a sense of regret at having missed the opportunity to participate directly in the revolution and a subdued conviction that she can still make a contribution to society.

The poem has Inber's mildly apologetic tone, and it, like many of her other works, is so much a product of its times that it occasionally seems dated and clumsy. The statement of her activities during the revolution is typical: "But in the days of October, I was wallowing in verbal lace and embroidery. / Well, what can be done! It wasn't my fault alone, but also that of my social stratum." Although she argues in "Sotto Voce" that great feeling is foreign to her nature (*pafos mne nesvoistven po prirode*), her emotions clearly run high, particularly in the second section of the poem in which she defends the contributions of a poet who lacks the proper revolutionary credentials—"With revolutions he was on formal terms" (*S revoliutsiiami byl na "vy"*),[39] but who may nevertheless give his best to the cause.

The question of Inber's own "revolutionary" contribution is a complex one. She played a secondary but nevertheless significant role in the literary politics of the 1930s, and it is unclear to what extent she was compromised by those activities. She attended the first congress of the newly created Writers' Union, where she addressed the gathering and was chosen to serve on the editorial committee for the congress. Her address at the evening session on 29 August 1934 is characteristic of her public statements at the time in its enthusiastic boosterism and somewhat pedantic approach. "A new literature is being born . . ." she notes breathlessly, "an optimistic literature." She objects to the comments of Nikolai Bukharin, who, in his remarks at the morning session, had implied that Soviet literature still failed to measure up to world standards. Such an approach, according to Inber, ignores the fact that progressive Soviet literature is fundamentally different from the bourgeois literature it replaces. Soviet writers are writing against the grain (*protiv shersti*) of established literature, which is pessimistic in outlook: "Our main tonality is joy," Inber insists.[40] She acknowledges some problems, citing, in particular, the tendencies to be too wordy, abstract and schematic. The positive heroes of today are unsuccessful, she claims, because they are too perfect: the "writers of the past weren't afraid of the shortcomings of their heroes." She concludes her address with a Soviet bon mot: "How sad it becomes when we don't write sufficiently well about joy."[41]

Inber apparently played an even larger role in the other, major, staged literary event of that year: the production of a volume in honor of Joseph Stalin devoted to the construction of the White Sea Canal. Along with such illustrious writers as Maxim Gorky, Viktor Shklovskii, Mikhail Zoshchenko and others, Inber traveled to the canal, visiting the forced labor penal colonies there involved in its construction. The record of the writers' responses to the project—and its ostensible success in making the criminals who were building the canal into viable Soviet citizens—was published in a limited press run of 4,000 copies in 1934.[42] Inber's name appears as one of several writers on five of the collectively authored chapters in the book. The construction project, which was intended to connect the Baltic Sea with the White Sea, eventually failed, a testament to the hubris of

Stalin's elaborate plans for remaking the world. The book it produced remains as evidence of Stalin's greater success in compelling some of the best-known writers of the time to toe an ideological line.

The chapters in the volume are written from the expected point of view of a true believer. Many contain testimonies ostensibly from the prisoners themselves, and these *skaz* sections are provided with a commentary that suggests the proper interpretation and context for the prisoners' words. The canal work details included a wide cross section of society, ranging from nuns, who were put in charge of delousing the bedding, to thieves and prostitutes, who had turned to crime to escape neglect and abusive step families. Fragments of these women's stories, usually with a conclusion attesting to the benefits they have derived from work on the canal, make up part of the material Inber helped to create. Also included in the volume are copies of orders from the camp administration supposedly aimed at ameliorating the position of women in the camps.[43] The issues raised in the official documents—concerns over the women's inadequate housing, limited cooking and bathing facilities, lack of elementary medical care, high rate of illiteracy, mistreatment at the hands of the men in the camps and underutilization in positions of skilled labor—indicate the particularly intolerable conditions in which the women prisoners lived.

Inber's personal attitude toward the canal and her contribution to the volume is difficult to determine. Her published diaries are ambiguous regarding the canal project itself. The entry from 24 August 1933, for example, describes largely in neutral terms her participation in the five-day trip from which she has just returned. She notes that the criminals at work on the project prefer the destructive aspects of the job and suggests that this destructive power is being harnessed for good: "The thirst for destruction is a turn toward creation" (*zhazhda razrusheniia, obrashchennaia na sozidanie*).[44] But if she is somewhat reticent as to whether the canal would help "reforge" (*perekovat'*) the prisoners working on it, she is considerably more enthusiastic about the way in which the writers who participated in the project will make themselves over.

Not long after returning from the trip, Inber notes her intention to continue her memoir *A Place in the Sun*, which she now envisions as the story of the remaking of a writer. She contemplates beginning with the death of Esenin and ending with the trip to the canal. Esenin is important as an example of what Inber, drawing on Heine, calls the "pearl disease" (*zhemchuzhnaia bolezn'*), an illness to which writers of earlier eras were supposedly susceptible.[45] Alienated from bourgeois society, the artist became a rebellious recluse, and loneliness became the primary focus of creative endeavor. This separation of the artist from the masses is a thing of the past, argues Inber. "Our writer is tied to life as never before," she notes. "In our work it is necessary to work in step with the whole country and to breathe with it. That is very important."[46]

Inber never realized her plan to write a sequel to *A Place in the Sun*, but she did produce another memoir of import. Published in diary form, *Almost Three Years* (*Pochti tri goda*) is a record of her time in Leningrad during the siege.[47] She was there with her third husband, a physician with the unenviable task of watching his patients die from "the illness of starvation" for most of the blockade. In descriptions that range from the mundane to the heroic, Inber records her personal view of the events of the war from 22 June 1941 to 12 June 1944. For much of that period, she, along with Ol'ga Savich, Lidiia Seifullina and a number of male writers, was also a member of the literature section of the Soviet Information Bureau (Sovetskoe Informbiuro), established just after the beginning of World War II to help disseminate information about the war effort.[48] Inber also produced a long poem (*poèma*) during that time: *The Pulkovo Meridian* (*Pulkovskii meridian*), like most of her verse during the war years, alternates between quiet humility and fierce optimism engendered by her patriotic spirit. She became a Communist party member in 1943 and was awarded a State Prize for *The Pulkovo Meridian* in 1946.

After the war, Inber continued to work in a variety of genres, including translation, theater, film, memoirs and international journalism.[49] She was apparently hampered to an extent by her health: the traumas of both Stalinism and Nazism obviously must have taken their toll.[50] She continued to play her usual important, though secondary, role in literary politics until late in her life. Like a number of other writers, she was pulled into the controversy concerning the publication of *Doctor Zhivago*, and, like others, she apparently found the situation compromising but unavoidable.[51] Inber was always a follower of the prevailing winds, and she rallied herself during the Thaw to produce an essay in support of a degree of liberalization in literature.[52] She died in Moscow on 11 November 1972, having remained true to the sentiment with which she had ended her memoir nearly fifty years before: "Our time is not a time of cold objectivity," she stated, contrasting her own engaged approach to writing to that of Flaubert. "Everything that we write, whether it is good or bad, small or great, is colored by the participation of the author in the events described, touched by his breath. The author exists; he can't be hidden. . . ."[53]

Mary Nicholas

In this excerpt from her memoir, A Place in the Sun, *Vera Inber describes life during the early years of Soviet power. Alone in Odessa with her daughter Kitten and the child's nanny,*

Julia Martinovna, from 1918 to 1922, Inber describes the travails of existence in the city during this period of civil war. Her point of view is that of an intellectual who is sympathetic to but not part of the new regime. By the time she relates events in Moscow several years later in the second part of the excerpt, Inber's perspective has changed, along with her circumstances. She is now an inhabitant in the capital city of a country no longer at war, and her straitened circumstances—life in communal apartments, part-time employment as a cabaret actress—cannot dim her enthusiasm for her new life. In the second part of this excerpt, Inber describes her first successes as a writer and a journalist in the new era.

From A Place in the Sun

Everything was unusual that year in the south. At the end of the fall, when there were supposed to be annoying but essentially mild rains, suddenly it was 20 degrees below zero with a frightening, cloudless, pitiless blue sky with cutting winds. The sea was a violent shade of amethyst, with frothy waves like snow banks; tearing and swearing, it rained down on the pier and tried to destroy the lighthouse. And then the populace of the town, stung by the cold, began to sweep the streets in search of pipe.

No one had any fuel. The central heating had died. The radiators were fatally cold. Even the dutch and cast iron stoves didn't count: they ate up too much fuel. In place of all of them, the "bourgeois" appeared. They were uncomplicated sheet-metal creations with thin legs, a square belly and a long neck. They looked just like the horses that Kitten drew. On the very first cold day, these stoves began to appear all over town. People carried them on their shoulders, hired horse cabs to move them, hauled them in wheelbarrows and strollers. They bought them with their last money, traded things for them, exchanged them for bread. The tinsmith shops were instantly flooded with people blue from the cold, hungry for pipe. Pipe was sold by the length; joints and dampers went separately. Even the most wretched stove, like the most wretched person, needed at least two joints. And joints took time. As did dampers. As did pipe.

Julia Martinovna and I, like everyone else, went to the tinsmith, stood in line, cried to the important gray-bearded Jew there. He raised a gray eyebrow and set his time and price. We asked him to sell it for less and make it faster, but he didn't agree. It was his day, and he was right.

Having carried home the cold, sharp stove and the thundering pipes, we began to get organized for winter hibernation. Our house was located in the part of town near the sea, near where the summer homes started. That year the house—with its broken elevator, extinguished lights, dead heating system and waterless faucets—was frightening and pathetic.

The bottom floor was occupied by a warehouse for flowers and seeds. Cheerful herbs had normally grown in low boxes there. The seeds lay in cupboards, and on top of the cupboards lay plaster models of various root crops: carrots, beets, turnips and pumpkins. Everything was big, new and bright as a child's dream. Future flower beds, lawns and vegetable gardens lay sleeping in flat boxes.

Fourteen changes of government had nipped all that growth in the very bud: the bottom of the house was deserted. The other floors were just as deserted. And only on one of them lived the three of us, in the small nursery with a southern exposure to which we'd escaped from the big northern rooms. But of course the bit of warm air that the three of us exhaled wasn't enough to give even the impression of life to so much glass and cement.

The sea was near. At night it behaved like a fifteenth government, the most powerful, which was advancing on the city in order to swallow it. The wind of uninhabited open spaces shook our windows. An oil lamp twenty times dimmer than a candle trembled from these blows.

Water had to be carried from other, lower parts of the city. A line to the faucet would form in strangers' courtyards, in strangers' basements, in the dark. It took ten minutes to fill a bucket. From time to time someone would strike a match to check the level of water. But that rarely happened: matches were sold individually, and each one was expensive.

We fed our "bourgeois" wonderfully—mostly the classics and an oak sideboard. We began with the Brokhaus and Efron edition of Shakespeare. That edition was lavish and extremely useful as fuel. We began with it. The creations of the great Englishman were filled, just as they were meant to be, with the heat and light of passion, the ash of remorse and the crimson of crime. Lady Macbeth appeared in flames, King Lear wept in the chimney. The burning piece of the sideboard raged like a Moor in a fiery cloak, while overhead simple hot cakes were frying.

On one of those nights, when the unlit frozen town was so quiet that in the dark it seemed possible to trip over it, our door suddenly shook from pounding.

"Open up," said a sonorous male voice. "Search."

Into our room walked three people in military overcoats and one in a torn sheepskin coat cinched with a belt. One stood near the door. Another, completely bloated, sat down at the table and played with a hand grenade. And two of them conducted the search.

"We know you're hiding foreign currency," said the man with the beautiful voice. "Diamonds, grain and other valuables. So now. . . ."

"Otherwise—to hell with you!" croaked the one with the grenade at the table. "The revolution has no pity."

Just then Kitten woke up and began to howl. "That's mine," she said, grabbing [her stuffed animal] Jerry by his broken ear. "It's mine because it's a rabbit."

Everyone stirred uneasily, and the leader of them suddenly turned rude. "Hey, now, shut the little girl up," he said. "Otherwise I guarantee trouble."

"Neutralize the bastards," confirmed the man with the grenade, who was shivering with a chill. At that minute I became really scared: I realized that the man with the grenade was sick and drunk.

They left, carrying away with them much of what we had been planning to live on for several months. In the morning we found out that we weren't the only ones in the area who had been robbed. The band of four, which had been robbing people, was soon caught and their gang leader shot. I suspect he was the one who guaranteed us trouble.

A few days later, after it had already snowed, two sailors came to us with the intention of requisitioning the apartment for a group of special forces. One of the sailors, in a black peacoat, was neat and clean as a whistle. On his cap, on the silk ribbon, the fearsome, well-known name [of the ship] *Diamond* shone in untarnished gold, just like the words "Li'l Rascal" or "Mommy loves me" on a child's cap.

The sailor from the *Diamond* was absolutely calm, except that his cheek muscles were clenched and his bright blue eyes were troubled, just like alcohol in a barometer, when it indicates a storm.

We walked through the icy and abandoned rooms, through the living room, where they saw the windows, thick and furry with frost, the pile of frozen potatoes under the piano and the piano itself covered with iridescent frost. In the study, the bookcase was open and the shelf for Shakespeare glinted emptily.

The sailor from the *Diamond* instantly understood what was going on. "You're burning books," he said. "Burning books. Plundering a national resource. You were burning which author?"

"Shakespeare," I answered. "William. Lived in the sixteenth century."

"Never heard of him." He bent his head, reading the spines of the books sideways. "Don't burn Aleksandr Pushkin. Don't burn Nikolai Gogol. Don't burn Mikhail Lermontov either. That understood?" he asked, turning his wide, roughly clad back to me.

"Understood," I answered.

He strode like a cold wind through the nursery where we lived, passed in one door and out the other, without taking his hands from his pockets, without stopping and without dropping his eyes, which seemed directed on some distant horizon. Since he wasn't watching his feet, he destroyed one of Kitten's wooden block constructions as he passed by. But the secrets of the female heart are truly myriad. Instead of getting angry, Kitten smiled. Her delicate eyebrows arched upwards. Dimples flitted across her cheeks. "You are the cutest of the raiders," she said. The blood rushed to my ears at her words. But the sailor from the *Diamond* didn't even glance at her.

The apartment wasn't suitable for the special forces. Before leaving, the sailor wrote down an order with a crumbling pencil on a crumpled piece of paper: not to burn Pushkin, or Gogol and Lermontov either. The piano—standing in the cold, "inappropriate for pianos"—was to be covered with a blanket or rug. It was further noted that the piano was a national resource and that I would answer to the revolution for every broken string, just as for all my property.

The order was written with painfully square letters; an official seal was affixed immediately. The seal had been pulled from the sailor's bellbottoms and left a wavy mark on the paper. In fact, it wasn't there at all. And yet the order had a force to which it was impossible not to submit.

However, in a short time I partially plundered that national resource for which I would answer to the revolution: I secretly sold three door curtains in order to buy some pressed sunflower seeds and soap.

Julia Martinovna found the buyer. It was a man with bluish-black hair and a conspiratorial manner. He beat around the bush, discussing the deal while ransacking the walls with his eyes.

"What wonderful weather," he began, "simply a delight to the soul! I buy rugs and furs for cash. What a remarkable, adorable little girl! Sweetie, come here. A sewing machine would be nice if there are spare bobbins. Your view from the window is endless. I buy faucets, doorbells and parquet floors by the lot. The view is heavenly."

He hauled the curtains out in a stroller, having wrapped up the material to look like a child's body. The stroller cover was lowered and the legs were covered with a colorful little blanket so as not to give the baby a chill.

* * *

With the arrival of warm weather, our house became filled with life. All of its winter shortcomings—its distance from the center of town, its proximity to the sea, the rooms facing north—all turned into virtues. Besides everything else, the proximity of [the secret police] the Cheka became obvious. . . .

Two girls in sandals and blue peasant blouses, bareheaded, just lightly tanned, checked out our big cool rooms. Not paying any attention to me, they measured the floor by pacing across it and opened all the windows. I wanted to warn them that one of the windows was weak and shouldn't be touched but wasn't quick enough. The window flew open at the decisive touch; the frame crashed down; the glass tinkled, and the unpolished parquet was covered with diamond dust.

One of the girls, having stepped across the broken glass just as she had probably stepped over all obstacles in the world, said:

"The beds will go here."

"And the table will go here," said Number Two.

"If there isn't water, we'll haul it up on a pulley from below. It'll be possible to rinse off in the kitchen and the bathroom," said Number One.

"The piano is useless there: we'll take it to the club," said Number Two.

"Not to the club, but to the main garage. The guys organize concerts there," said Number One.

"Yeah," said Number Two.

Number One and Number Two left in order to return the next day. Our apartment, with the exception of two rooms, was from that day forward turned into a dormitory for the female employees of the Cheka.

Comrade Claudia, the one who broke the window, was first and foremost among all the rest. Comrade Claudia was very pretty. I've never had the occasion to see such perfect facial features, such a delicate nose and such trembling nostrils. Her black eyebrows parted like high, neat arches. Her dark hair with bronze highlights was cut short. It wasn't the clever and complicated haircut of a later time. Comrade Claudia's was cut like a boy, with a part. On the back of her head she had a cowlick.

In the morning she would walk to the bathroom in just her underpants to rinse off with the cold water that they had hauled up with a pulley. She walked from the far living room, past the corridor and the other rooms. A wisp of sun followed her on her shoulders and chest. When she walked into a shadow, her body cooled off, died out. The blue underpants became almost black. On the way from the living room to the bathroom, she whistled [the popular song] "Apple, where are you rolling?" She directed the music with a Turkish towel as she whistled.

There were always streams and torrents in the bathroom after her. The carefully saved piece of soap would be swimming in water, the wet sponge hanging from the edge of the bathtub. Julia Martinovna, gloomy and full of hatred, gritting her teeth, wiped up the floor and wrung out the sponge.

From all of this unfamiliarly rough work and from her implacable Latvian tidiness, Julia Martinovna's hands started to crack and coarsen. She made a concoction for herself to soften the skin from sheep's tallow, glycerine, and something else and kept it on a little shelf in the bathroom. Once in the morning after a bath, the slim, bobbed, bronze-haired Amazon Comrade Claudia, whistling "Apple" with her beautiful lips, sat completely naked on the windowsill in the pose of a little boy pulling a splinter out of his foot. She was oiling the parts of her pistol with the lotion.

It seemed to me that Comrade Claudia was immune to any sort of tenderness, that she didn't notice nature, didn't feel spring. But on moonlit nights, which were glorious that spring, returning home late at night in a sputtering old car, tired, worn-out Comrade Claudia took moon baths. Once again in nothing but underpants, as though she had to breathe with her entire body, she would throw herself down on the bed, lying down right under a moonbeam. "What a bitch, goddamn her!" she would repeat with delight and the deepest tenderness. That was directed toward the moon.

* * *

Events occur for a reason in life. Meeting Claudia was useful for me: she showed me a kind of woman I hadn't known before. Claudia was harsh in her dealing with people, and her most ardent admirer wouldn't have called her a pleasant conversationalist. But I saw the expression on her face when [her horse] Voronchik was dying. And I observed her during her conversations on the telephone. If somewhere out there, on the other end of the telephone line, they were talking about an assignment well done, about success in some affair, then her severe eyes sparkled to their very bottoms. She was impetuous in life: bang! slam! crash! she pushed obstacles aside. She didn't know what exhaustion is, this woman of a difficult era. She didn't have a single book or a single needle. She had a horse and a revolver. And the revolution, which had given birth to her. . . .

Once Julia Martinovna came back from the bazaar pale, which rarely happened with her. She wanted to speak and couldn't. Finally she explained that she had traded my black silk dress for a chicken. The hen was scrawny and old; under its feathers, its body was pimply and tough. But it looked hearty, and Julia Martinovna believed that it might lay eggs.

Holding the chicken in her arms, Julia Martinovna was walking between the loads and the baskets. Suddenly a street urchin bobbed up. "Let go, lady!" he yelled. She pressed her prize closer to her heart. "I won't give it up," she said. The urchin went wild. He threw himself at Julia Martinovna, and right on the spot, right on her chest, he plunged his teeth into the trembling chicken. He gnawed off the wing of it alive. Choking and hurrying, he swallowed the blue chicken meat. When they tore him off and led him away, his face was bloody and feathers were stuck to his eyebrows and lashes.

Another time [my friend] Avel Evseevich and I were walking along the street. The city was very frightening—spat upon, filled with peelings and garbage, all the signs taken down. Dust storms moved along the cobblestones like in a desert. . . . Suddenly the people in front of us started to run. Near one of the buildings, a crowd was standing. Heads were turned upward and dust was filling their eyes.

"In the attic," someone said. "There, they brought the fire department ladder."

"Stealing underwear, what will be next? Everyone's walking around half dressed as it is."

"He'll get what's coming to him."

"Con artist," said a distinguished old woman. "What can his mother be thinking of? It's just awful."

Everyone looked at her with surprise. No one had thought of the mother of the thief, but she had.

The people below were slowly and frighteningly heating up: each person was preparing a curse and a blow. But the thief fooled them all. Seeing himself surrounded on all sides, he threw himself out of the attic window. He didn't tell anyone what he was hoping for. Whether he wanted to save himself or preferred to die from the fall rather than from a beating—it was all unclear. But he jumped and fell on the sidewalk. He was already dead. He lay terribly awkwardly: his hands were twisted back, and in one of them was clutched a towel and a pair of long johns. Just then, a woman from the crowd, not the same one who had spoken about the con artist, but a different one, sighed deeply and threw out her arms.

"Mama," she shouted, "oh, God in heaven!" And she went into convulsions.

"Cholera!" everyone shouted in one voice, and the street emptied. The escape was instantaneous. The choleraic woman fell next to the corpse.

"What is going to happen?" I asked finally. "A little bit more, and there won't be any people left in our country. Everyone will die. Just who is going to be left? How are we supposed to live?" At that instant it no longer seemed to me that life was hopelessly short ("a wisp of a snow-white cloud in a dark blue haze"). Just the opposite: life seemed to me to be an endless, retreating distance, without end, without end.

But Avel Evseevich, who, apparently, knew everything and knew how to put everything in its place, answered me: "Don't worry. There have been much more difficult times. In the fourteenth century in England during the plague, one-third of the population died off. The roads were deserted; the cities turned wild. It seemed that civilization was ending. And keep in mind that it was the plague, a terrible illness of the Middle Ages, which they didn't know how to fight and which threatened humanity with extinction. Now it's not like that at all."

"Then it was the plague. Now it's cholera. The difference isn't all that great."

Avel Evseevich, not listening to me, continued. "Now it's not like that at all. We're suffering in the name of the future. I'm not an advocate of revolutions: they make it difficult to work. It's well known that Immanuel Kant lost a day of work because of the French Revolution. But scholarly egotism aside, it's impossible not to admit that revolutions benefit society."

As we talked, we walked unhurriedly past one street after another. There was no place for us to hurry to, especially me. . . . We walked on and on. On the deserted street, near the gates, stood a couple, a young man and woman, talking about love. The evening quiet carried their words to us. The youth was talking about how he loved her, how her eyes were the most lovely in the world.

And it so happened, that all the sensations of that evening—the death of the thief, the cholera contortions, the conversations about the plague in England in the fourteenth century and now these last words about love—all came together into a sensation of life, which keeps moving, never stopping for a minute.

Spring was approaching.

* * *

[In Moscow] I went back to the editor who had once refused me with the explanation that my heroes were loners, that each lived for himself, that the idea of "community" was foreign to them. I came to him in the rainy twilight, after a rehearsal. The streetlights were burning through the fog and rain. The fog and rain were painted with an iridescent shine. Next to each streetlight, in the air, on the rain, the shadow of the light was floating.

The editor had laryngitis. He was hissing like a goose. His throat was wrapped many times in a warm muffler, but despite all that, he instantly recognized me. "It's you," he said hoarsely and unwound one of the rings of the muffler. "I knew that you would come back. Did you bring something along?"

"I brought something."

The sketch or short story (I don't know what to call it) wasn't very big. The editor read it right there; that was a rare piece of luck, the rarity of which I came to appreciate only later. I observed him as he was reading. The dim electric lamp illuminated his pale eyelashes. His eyes moved from line to line. In one place the editor frowned: I never found out to what that pertained—to my manuscript or to his sore throat. Another time he scratched his nose approvingly: without any doubt I attributed that to my own account. His eyes glowed. He didn't smile with his lips, but a smile was spread over his entire face. The phone on his desk rang: he picked up the receiver without looking and continued to read. He read while holding the receiver in his hand, and it sounded as though another person with laryngitis was wheezing and croaking into the telephone, as though he had taken up residence there.

The editor finished reading and glanced at me. "The piece will go in," he said in a whisper and unwound another one of the loops of the muffler from around his neck. "I told you that you can write. That was good about the little guy with freckles. . . . Hello!" he said hoarsely into the receiver, suddenly having remembered the call. But a regal silence reigned there. He hung up. "Write more. You know what about?"

"About what?"

"About your guy. Show him more clearly. Describe his whole day, from the morning bell at the factory to the evening lights at the workers' college. Describe the working day. It should turn out."

"I can't," I answered, sick at heart. "I can't do more. I don't know anything more like that. It has to be seen, and it needs inspiration."

The editor put his elbows on the table, settled his chin firmly on his palms. Having gotten himself settled that way, he squinted his eyes. "Inspiration!" he whispered the word and drew it out. "Hmm . . . inspiration. Inspiration is the skill of situating oneself ideally for work." (He opened his eyes a bit. There, in the depths, among his pale eyelashes, his pupils were sparkling brightly, tiny as kernels of corn but piercing.) "Yes, ideally for work. Remember that. If a machine possessed the ability to reason, then when it was working full force, it would no doubt believe that inspiration had descended on it from above. Remember that." And he unwrapped his muffler completely.

* * *

A heavy frost appeared on the ground at dawn. The city grew brighter, looked younger, became completely fresh. The car horn called out in a high, clear voice near our house: it was young too, new; the flash of an unspent coin concealed itself in its call. The track of the automobile's tire lay like a well-defined pine tree across the white bridge. It was the first trace of the day. It was early morning, Everyone was still asleep.

The automobile called me. I came out, and we set off. Nothing slowed us down; the streets were empty. The overturned moon was still in the sky. In the west it was as dark as night, but the east was already awash with light: day was beginning from there.

The gates to the airport opened up in front of us. The airport was enormous. The sun was visible here. The flaming ball rose quickly, and gradually the frost melted. But having melted, it left behind crystal and ice in the air.

At the airport, people were standing around, cordoned off by ropes. Despite the early hour, many people wanted to see how the airplane, headed for a long propaganda flight to the south, would take off. People standing on the ground kept scanning the sky, talking about wings, about the wind. They were amazed by their own shadows, which were unusually large in the morning. Take a step and you could step across the airport. Two steps and you'll touch the horizon.

The doors of the hangar swung open, and they brought out a small aerial horse. Its grooved wings glinted in the sun: it seemed to have plunged into the morning and emerged from there all silver.

By then I had abandoned [the cabaret] Karavai forever. I didn't feel animosity toward it. My thoughts about it were abstract and detached. In its place I had gained access to a number of editorial offices. I especially loved one of them, where there was a wall of glass high above the city, which always elicited the feeling of flight in me. Now I was about to fly for real. This flight was the first serious test for me: until then I had not been higher than the zoo, higher than Moscow streets, building sites, schools and young pioneer camps. Now I was about to fly high over the river beds, far to the south, to look down on the flat lands near the sea where I had been born, and to see even farther to the lands of our country where I had never been.

Pilot Rotov was astonished by the fact that the newspaper correspondent who had been sent to him for the propaganda flight turned out to be a woman. Women bring bad luck to machines, whether it is electric razors or steam turbines; that's the belief at every latitude on earth. Japanese divers, after a woman visits their place of work, sprinkle salt on the deck and steps, in order to overcome the evil influence with an ancient power of purification.

Pilot Rotov was a Soviet pilot: he was above that kind of prejudice. Every morning, no matter what the weather, he washed himself with icy cold water in the open air. But all that together couldn't completely wash off his convictions against female journalists.

"You are a woman," he said, spotting me before the flight. I didn't dare deny that, and our relationship was temporarily ruined.

So, I was about to fly. I was about to discover the springiness of the air, the dust-free expanses where life flows by differently than it does on land. About to meet a host of people, to ask questions, to get answers, to remember them for a long time. Pilot Rotov, with whom I soon made friends, made an impression on me with one of his answers. Some time on the trip (on the ground, of course, not in the air), I asked what sort of occupational hazards there were for pilots and their mechanics. And Pilot Rotov, having given it some thought, answered me: "Occupational hazards? Except for death, there don't seem to be any."

But about that later. Now, through the mica windows, the earth is visible, still near, and a cut-off piece of the sky. My traveling companion, Efim Semenovich

Kromarov, an instructor from Aeronautics and an experienced flying "ace" completely wrapped up in belts and straps just like at the front, is getting firmly seated. Across his chest are high-powered binoculars, in his hands a map of the area. On the trip Efim Semenovich will give speeches from the wing of the plane, explaining the meaning of "weight-bearing supports, stabilizer, tail," and so on. "Ask your questions, comrades," Efim Semenovich will say. "Let whoever doesn't understand something, step up and speak."

And an old gray grandfather, who's ninety years old, will wipe his old eyes with a rag and ask a "technical question" about why goats are more afraid of the machine than sheep when sheep are afraid of almost everything. And he will add that he, farmer Emelian Mochalo, wouldn't mind joining the "Friends' Club" since, he, farmer Emelian Mochalo, understands everything about the aerial flotilla completely and is ready to pay his club dues.

And then his great-grandson, Komsomol member Grisha, will speak out and, looking with reverence at Rotov, will announce thunderingly that all of the members of the Komsomol of the Ukrainian Socialist Republic will support to the best of their ability our glorious air force and our pilots who are the best in the world. And the farmer women and men, who have gathered for the airplane and for market day, will begin buzzing and will press up closer and closer to the airplane so that Rotov will shout heatedly: "Hey, you boys! Don't crawl under the wings or I'll tan your hides!" But that will all be later. Right now the plane is moving across the ground faster and faster. There's a wind behind it and a rumble in front. And now it's no longer on the ground but in the air. Your body seems unfamiliar and loses weight, and—oooh!—your unfamiliar heart sinks.

Moscow is moving away from us, like a pier from a ship. Below is smooth green vegetation and a small blue stone; that's the round pond in the zoo over which we're flying. That very same zoo . . . who said that people feel like reorganizing their lives in the autumn? Life is already organized; the path is clear. We're taking it higher and higher. Pilot Rotov, turning his helmeted face toward me, smiles. He smiles and points with his head down toward Moscow. "Moscow," he says, and we guess the word by the movement of his lips: o-ow.

And below lies Moscow and the earth, illuminated by the sun. The propeller is roaring with the voice of the heights. The engine is breathing magnificently. And the whole airplane, its bright, strong wings, its chest, all of it, flying to meet the dawn, goes farther and farther into the expanse with every turn of the air, gets absorbed in movement, situates itself ideally for work. And if the airplane possessed the ability to think, it would think that inspiration had descended upon it from above.

Translated by Mary Nicholas

Notes to the Essay

1. That is how she is described in the *Dictionary of Russian Women Writers*, ed. Marina Ledkovsky, Charlotte Rosenthal and Mary Zirin (Westport, CT: Greenwood Press, 1994). Irina Corten's essay on Inber there is thoughtful and informative.

2. See Iosif Grinberg, *Vera Inber: Kritiko-biograficheskii ocherk* (Moscow: 1961); Evelyn Bristol, *A History of Russian Poetry* (New York: Oxford University Press, 1991), 257, 258; and A. Markov, "Vera Inber," in Inber, *Sobranie sochinenii*, Vol. 1 (Moscow: 1965–1966), 5, 42. Subsequent citations from Inber's works are from this collection, cited hereafter as *SS*.

3. Leonard Gendlin cites the year 1891, but most other sources list 1890 (see Gendlin, *Perebiraia starye bloknoty* [Amsterdam: Helikon, 1986], 188). Gendlin's essay on Inber contains some interesting biographical detail, but it lacks scholarly objectivity, and the information there must be used with a great deal of care.

4. For Inber's comment, see "Èti piatnadtsat' let," *SS*, 4: 27. She also describes her early upbringing in the short essay "O moem ottse," *SS,* 2: 293–311, where she recalls the reaction of her mother's cousin, a committed Social Democrat, to her childhood confession that she was a budding poet. "That's o.k.," remarked the woman. "It'll pass" (*SS*, 2: 300). For Gendlin, see *Perebiraia starye bloknoty,* 188.

5. Inber notes that her stay in Switzerland was occasioned by health problems; see her "Kratkaia avtobiografiia" in Inber, *Stikhi i poèmy* (Moscow, 1957), 7. See also M.N. Sorokina, "U istokov tvorchestva Very Inber," *Voprosy russkoi literatury* [Lvov] 38, 2 (1981): 14–21.

6. *S. SS* 1: 48. The gender of the narrative voice here is unspecified, opposed only to an unspecified "you" (*ty*), who prefers the warmth of the south.

7. *Ibid.*, 1: 59.

8. *Brennye slova: Treti'a kniga stikhov* (Odessa, 1922), 5.

9. See "Kratkaia avtobiografiia," in *Stikhi i poèmy,* 8.

10. "Èti piatnadtsat let" in *Stikhi i poèmy,* 4: 25, 26.

11. The extent of her unease is obvious in her comment from a diary entry in early 1932. She notes there that she is to partake in a poetry reading that evening with two other poets and expresses her apprehension. Yet her fears stem not from lack of self-confidence but from the falseness of her position as an alleged "petty bourgeois." See diary entry from 8 March 1932 in *Stikhi i poèmy,* 423. Her diaries provide an interesting though abbreviated account of the literary squabbles of the early 1930s.

12. See, for example, the last stanza of her poem "Travel Diary" ("Putevoi dnevnik"), in which she expresses her desire to do what she can "and even more" for her country and her era, in whose debt she remains (*Stikhi i poèmy,* 182). Inber describes "Travel Diary," a tribute to Georgia, as her favorite work (*liubimaia moia veshch'*) in *Stikhi i poèmy,* 9.

13. Her daughter, Zhanna Gauzer, became a writer as an adult. She was also an only child and preceded her mother in death, in 1962. See the entry for Inber in *Dictionary of Russian Women Writers*. Inber describes her complicated feelings toward her daughter in "O moei docheri," *SS,* 2: 312–23.

14. "Mesto pod solntsem," *SS,* 2: 531.

15. The phrase is Beth Holmgren's from "For the Good of the Cause: Russian Women's Autobiography in the Twentieth Century," *Women Writers in Russian Literature*, ed. Toby W. Clyman and Diana Greene (Westport, CT: Greenwood Press, 1994), 128. Holmgren comments

that many autobiographical accounts of early Russian women revolutionaries tend "to privilege the viewpoint of a Russian intelligentsia distinct from and somewhat dismissive of the peasants and the working class" (131). The same can be said of Inber's works, although her dismissive attitude is tempered by the note of humility required from a "bourgeois" writer in the 1920s and 1930s. See also Inber's comment that literature should not only be artistic but should "help and educate" as well ("Kratkaia avtobiografiia," *Stikhi i poèmy,* 11).

16. She mentions language, brevity and precision as the three elements most necessary for good writing in "Vdokhnovenie i masterstvo," *SS,* 4: 68.

17. Ibid., 4: 427.

18. Ibid., 4: 449, 452; emphasis in the original.

19. Catriona Kelly, *A History of Russian Women's Writing, 1820–1992* (Oxford: Clarendon Press, 1994), 345, 353. The topic of *byt* and the avant-garde deserves special attention in the work of both male and female writers from this period.

20. "Èti piatnadtsat let," *SS,* 4: 19.

21. Inber's background made her enormously sensitive to the kind of criticism RAPP and other groups meted out. She notes, for example, that RAPP writers had "forbidden" poets to write lyrics and adds that the "strongest laws are the unwritten ones" (*SS,* 4: 424). Her response to the party directive of 23 April 1925, which had been intended to reduce literary factionalism, was one of great relief (*SS,* 4: 426).

22. She admired the form in other writers as well; Amelia Earhart's journal made her list of best books of the year from 1938 (see *SS,* 4: 454). Her life in besieged Leningrad during World War II made the diary one of the only appropriate genres available to her.

23. "Èti piatnadtsat let," *SS,* 4: 22.

24. Ibid., 4: 19.

25. See Herman Ermolaev, *Soviet Literary Theories, 1917–1934, The Genesis of Socialist Realism* (New York, 1977) for a good general discussion of the constructivists in literature. Renato Poggoli's evaluation of the group is harsh; constructivism, he argues, disappeared with "fewer traces than Futurism and even Imaginism" (*The Poets of Russia, 1890–1930* [Cambridge: 1960], 240).

26. See Kelly, *A History,* 239, 276–83, 345.

27. Kornelii Zelinskii, "Gosplan literatury," *Gosplan literatury: Sbornik literaturnogo tsentra konstruktivistov* (Moscow: Krug, n.d.), 35–36.

28. *SS,* 1: 120.

29. See Kelly, *A History,* 444.

30. Zelinskii, "Gosplan literatury," 36.

31. Inber makes the comment in her diary from 1936, long after the constructivist movement had dissolved. In the same entry she describes "technicism" as a way to fight "spiritual disorder," which she suspects may be a "sign of petty-bourgeois consciousness" (diary entry from 13 March 1936, *SS,* 4: 437).

32. "Èti piatnadtsat let," *SS,* 4: 21.

33. Ibid.

34. This piece follows an imaginary son through the young Pioneers and the Komsomols into adulthood. Developmental milestones are marked by changes in the initial refrain *Mal'chik sozdan, chtoby plakat', / Mama—ctoby pet'* ("Boys are made to cry. / Mothers are made to sing"), which in the penultimate stanza sentimentally predicts the grown man's sorrow

at the death of the narrative mother (*Mal'chik budet gor'ko plakat', / Mama—budet spat'* ["The boy will cry bitter tears, / His mom will finally rest"]). The poem was set to music as a lullaby in the 1930s. See Oles Chishko, *Kolybel'naia* [for soprano and piano] (Leningrad, 1936.)

35. Her account of the flight in "From the Good Life" ("Ot khoroshei zhizni") (*SS,* 3 404–26) is interesting to compare to the fictionalized version offered by Boris Pil'niak, who also took part. Her adventures in the air are also described in *A Place in the Sun.* See the translation in the selected works.

36. "Ne plach', Ninel'," *SS,* 2: 163.

37. "Rodonachal'nitsa," *SS,* 1: 194–5.

38. I follow Evelyn Bristol's translation of the title here.

39. "Vpolgolosa," 1: 201–03.

40. *Pervyi vsesoiuznyi s"ezd sovetskikh pisatelei 1934: Stenograficheskii otchet* (Moscow, 1934), 546.

41. Ibid., 548.

42. See *Belomorsko-Baltiiskii kanal imeni Stalina: Istoriia stroitel'stvo*, ed. M. Gor'kii et al. (Moscow, 1934).

43. See, for example, the order (*prikaz*) for 8 February 1933, "O nedostatkakh kul'turno-vospitatel'noi raboty sredi zhenshchin," in ibid., 253.

44. *SS,* 4: 428.

45. Ibid., 4: 431. Her essay from 1930 by this title can be found in ibid., 4: 7–11.

46. Ibid., 4: 10.

47. *Pochti tri goda* includes a description of the death of Inber's only grandchild, who died in the evacuation as an infant in 1941.

48. For a brief discussion of the bureau, see S. Krasil'shchik, "Letopis' ognennykh let: Pisateli v Sovinformbiuro (1941–1945 gg.)," *Literaturnoe obozrenie* 5 (1981): 102–12.

49. Inber's collected works include her reminiscences about Ol'ga Forsh, Alexei Tolstoy, Larisa Reisner and others. Later journalism, including her reports from a trip to Iran after the war, can also be found there. See *SS*, vols. 3 and 4. *A Place in the Sun* contains a description of her early activities as both actor and playwright. Her 1938 rhymed play *Mothers' Union* is a curious example of her attempt to join her dual interests in drama and poetry; see Inber, *Soiuz materei: Komediia* (Moscow, 1938).

50. Gendlin, who describes Inber's failing health in later life, is rather severe in his criticism of her for compromises she made during the Stalin years. He suggests that Inber's relationship to Leon Trotsky, who was, according to Gendlin, a close relative of Inber's father, caused her moral acquiescence in the crimes of the Stalin period. See Gendlin, *Perebiraia starye bloknoty*. Inber's own comment from a diary entry in the purge year of 1937 indicates her incomplete understanding of the situation. Noting that it seems to her that she has been asleep and has just awakened in a "cold and stern hour," she wonders how she has arrived at this point. "I'm still trying to comprehend when, from what point my troubles began. Was it that unsuccessful performance in regard to the trial? Or the unsuccessful poem about Spain? Or was it all the result of my fascination with the construction of the house in [the writers' colony at] Peredelkino? . . . There's only one consolation," Inber concludes in her perhaps willfully blind way, "that I'm not the only one who just woke up" (*SS,* 4: 442).

51. Gendlin is sharply critical of her participation in the affair. See Gendlin, *Perebiraia starye bloknoty,* 190–91.

52. See Inber, "Vdokhnovenie i masterstvo," *Znamia* 9 (1956) 157–69 and 8 (1957) 168–78.

53. *SS,* 2: 532.

Bibliography

Primary Works

Pechal'noe vino. Paris: Privately published, 1914.

Gor'kaia uslada: Vtoraia kniga stikhov. Moscow, 1917.

Brennye slova: Tretia kniga stikhov. Odessa, 1922.

Tsel' i put'. Moscow, 1924.

Kroshki sorokonozhki. Leningrad: Raduga, 1925.

Uravnenie s odnym neizvestnym. Moscow, 1926.

Lovets komet. Moscow: Zemlia i fabrika, 1927.

Synu, kotorogo net. Stikhi 1924–1926. Moscow, 1927.

Amerika v Parizhe. Moscow: Ogiz, 1928.

Mesto pod solntsem. Berlin: Petropolis, 1928.

Solnechnyi zaiats. Moscow, 1928.

Solovei i Roza. Rasskazy. Kharkov: Proletarii, 1928.

Sochineniia. Kharkov, 1929.

Stikhi. Moscow: Federatsiia, 1932.

Izbrannye stikhi. Moscow, 1933.

Izbrannye stikhi. Moscow, 1935.

Pereulok moego imeni. Stikhi. Moscow, 1935.

Soiuz materei. Komediia. Moscow, 1938.

Putevoi dnevnik. Moscow, 1939.

Dusha Leningrada. Moscow, 1943.

O Leningrade. Poèma i stikhi. Leningrad, 1943.

Pulkovskii meridian. Poèma. Moscow: Khudozhestvennaia literatura, 1943.

Pulkovskii meridian. Poèma. Moscow: Ogiz, 1944.

Pulkovskii meridian. Poèma. Moscow: Pravda, 1946.

Izbrannoe. Moscow, 1947.

Pochti tri goda. Leningradskii dnevnik. Moscow, 1947.

Stikhi. Izbrannoe dlia detei. Moscow: Detskaia literatura, 1947.

Izbrannaia proza. Moscow, 1948.

Rasskazy o detiakh. Moscow, 1948.

Izbrannoe. Moscow, 1950.

Put' vody. Stikhi. Moscow, 1951.

Izbrannaia proza. Moscow, 1952.

Poèmy i stikhi. Moscow, 1952.

Povesti i rasskazy. Pochti tri goda. Ocherki. Moscow, 1954.

Izbrannye proizvedeniia. 2 vols. Moscow, 1955.

"Vdokhnovenie i masterstvo," *Znamia* 9 (1956): 157–69; 8 (1957): 168–78.

Stikhi i poèmy. Moscow, 1957.

Izbrannye proizvedeniia. 3 vols. Moscow, 1958.

Kniga i serdtse. Stikhi. Moscow: Detskaia literatura, 1961.

Vdokhnovenie i masterstvo. Moscow, 1961.

Za mnogo let. Moscow, 1964.

Sobranie sochinenii. 4 vols. Moscow, 1965–1966.

Stikhi. Moscow, 1967.

Pochti tri goda. Leningradskii dnevnik. Moscow, 1968.

Anketa vremeni. Izbrannye stikhi. Moscow: Detskaia literatura, 1971.

Izbrannaia proza. Moscow, 1971.

Sorokonozhki. Moscow: Malysh, 1976.

Stranitsy dnei perebiraia. Iz dnevnikov i zapisnykh knizhek. Moscow, 1977.

Stikhotvoreniia. Moscow, 1981.

O malchike s vesnushkami. Stikhi. Moscow: Malysh, 1991.

In Translation

"Maya." *Short Stories by Soviet Writers*. Moscow: Progress, n.d.

"Pulkovo Meridian." *Russian Literature since the Revolution*. Ed. Joshua Kunitz. New York: Boni and Gaer, 1948.

"Five Days and Nights (On the Death of Lenin)"; "Mayakovsky Memory" [from *Diary of a Journey*]; and "Dawn in Besieged Leningrad." *Russian Poetry, 1917–1955*. Ed. Jack Lindsay. London: Bodley Head, 1957. 72–73, 81, 114–15.

"Nor-Bibi's Crime" and "Spring Cleaning." *Loaf of Sugar and Other Soviet Stories*. Ed. Yvonne Kapp. London: Lawrence and Wishart, 1957.

"Razliv, or Water Meadow Halt" and "Two Lives in One." *Soviet Literature* 12 (1960).

"It Will Come to Pass." *Modern Russian Poetry*. Ed. Vladimir Markov and Merrill Sparks. London: Macgibbon and Kee, 1966. 730–31.

"Five Days and Nights." *Soviet Literature* 6 (1967).

Leningrad Diary. Trans. Serge M. Wolff and Rachael Grieve. New York: St. Martin's Press, 1971.

"To the Son I Never Had." *Three Centuries of Russian Poetry*. Ed. N. Bannikov and I. Zheleznova. Moscow, 1980.

"Nightingale and Rose." *North American Review* (March 1981).

"Pulkovo Meridian." *Land of the Soviets in Verse and Prose*. Ed. G. Dzyubenko. Moscow, 1982.

"Garlic in His Suitcase." Trans. M. Schwartz. *Literary Review* [Madison] 34 (Winter 1991): 259–66.

Related Works

Bristol, Evelyn. *A History of Russian Poetry*. New York: Oxford University Press, 1991.

Chishko, Oles. *Kolybelnaia* [for soprano and piano]. Leningrad, 1936.

Clyman, Toby W., and Diana Greene, eds. *Women Writers in Russian Literature*. Westport, CT: Greenwood Press, 1994.

Corten, Irina. "Inber, Vera." *Dictionary of Russian Women Writers*. Ed. Marina Ledkovsky, Charlotte Rosenthal and Mary Zirin. Westport, CT: Greenwood Press, 1994.

Gendlin, Leonard. *Perebiraia starye bloknoty*. Amsterdam: Helikon, 1986.

Gor'kii, M., et al., eds. *Belomorsko-Baltiiskii kanal imeni Stalina: Istoriia stroitelstvo*. Moscow, 1934.

Grinberg, Iosif. *Vera Inber: Kritiko-biograficheskii ocherk*. Moscow, 1961.

Kelly, Catriona. *A History of Russian Women's Writing, 1820–1992*. Oxford: Clarendon, 1994.

Krasilshchik, S. "Letopis' ognennykh let: Pisateli v Sovinformbiuro (1941–1945 gg.)." *Literaturnoe obozrenie* 5 (1981): 102–12.

Markov, A. "Vera Inber." *Sobranie sochinenii*. By Vera Inber. Vol. 1. Moscow, 1965–1966, 5–42.

Sorokina, M.N. "U istokov tvorchestva Very Inber." *Voprosy russkoi literatury* [Lvov] 38, 2 (1981): 14–21.

Zelinskii, Kornelii. "Konets konstruktivizma: K predstoiashchemu plenumu RAPP." *Na literaturnom postu* 20 (October 1930): 20–31.

———, and Ilia Selvinskii, eds. *Gosplan literatury: Sbornik literaturnogo tsentra konstruktivistov.* Moscow: Krug, n.d.

Vera Panova

Vera Panova (1905–1973).
Courtesy of Ruth Kreuzer.

Like many of her Russian contemporaries who survived two world wars, a revolution, famine, years of deprivation and the Stalin Terror, Vera Fedorovna Panova (1905–1973) learned to draw on her deepest human resources, strengths and ingenuity in order to cope with daily life. That she was able, under otherwise daunting conditions, to rise to fame as a writer is a credit to her strong will, her ability to adapt and her unwavering faith that she was ordained to be a writer.

Vera Panova was born in Rostov-on-Don on 20 March 1905 into a comfortable and cultured home. When Vera was only five, her father, an assistant bookkeeper in a bank, drowned in a boating accident. After that the family fell on hard times. Despite her impoverished life, young Vera developed a passion for reading, feeding her intellectual curiosity and imagination on books from her father's bookshelves. Vera's formal education, a brief span of two years at a girls' school in Rostov, was cut short because of the upheaval of the revolution of 1917 and the accompanying civil war. Despite her lack of formal education, Panova eventually became an exceptionally well-read, self-educated individual.

By age seventeen Vera was working full time at the newspaper *Laborer's Don* (*Trudovoi Don*). As she writes later, "Work at the editorial office was not a duty, but a marvelous life process, as natural as breathing."[1] Throughout the 1920s and 1930s Panova's byline (often the pseudonym "Vera Vel'tman") appeared in a number of Rostov papers and journals. She wrote numerous feuilletons, articles, stories and sketches (*ocherki*)—factual, but artistically embroidered, stories about real people. Her later prose style reflects the features of her sketches: lively dialogues, clear illustrations of human relationships, masses of details on daily life and a lyrical view of the world and ordinary people.[2] From 1930 to 1935 Panova wrote for *Campfire* (*Koster*), the Pioneer magazine for young people. Her interest in children—their relationships to others, their psychological development—became a large part of Panova's mature prose works. Panova's career as a journalist spanned the years 1922 to 1946.

Panova's personal life continued to be filled with hardships. In 1925, at age twenty, she married Arsenii Starosel'skii, a fellow journalist; their daughter Natal'ia was born in 1926. Unfortunately, Vera's marriage was not a happy one. In the fall of 1928 she divorced Arsenii and soon after married Boris Vakhtin, a journalist and an aspiring writer. Two sons were born to the couple—Boris (b. 1930) and Jurii (b. 1932). Tragically, in 1935, Vera's husband was falsely denounced and taken away in the night. The man about whom Panova had written that "[without him] home was not home to her and she was not herself, and life was not life"[3] died in one of Stalin's prison camps. After that Vera had difficulty finding work, and the family went through a period of being split apart and having to rely on others for survival.

Vera's dream of becoming a literary writer began early. When she was eleven one of her schoolgirl poems found its way into a student publication. In the early 1930s her first play, *Spring* (*Vesna*), enjoyed a brief run. Panova writes that this play "was completely crude and imitative, but the production was a whole storm of new experiences for me . . . it was like a first kiss."[4] A.J. Brushstein, a famous playwright and children's author, read Panova's next play, *Mercedes*, a tragedy in blank verse based on the current political events in Spain. Brushstein mercilessly criticized her play, but at the same time noted Panova's talent and predicted that she would succeed as a writer. Brushstein helped Panova get a contract for a children's holiday play, and for the first time Panova earned money as an author. In 1940 Panova's play *Il'ia Kosogor*, a four-act melodrama with a heavy social message, won a first-place prize in a contest. The following year her play *Old Moscow* (*Staraia Moskva*), ten scenes or "pictures" depicting the social disintegration of two old Moscow families, also received a first-place prize, and theaters in Moscow and Leningrad were clamoring to stage it. Panova felt herself a real playwright at last.

Panova's moment of success was short-lived, however, for on 22 June 1941, German troops rolled onto Soviet territory. That summer Panova and her daughter were living in Pushkin, near Leningrad. Panova awoke one morning to find herself a refugee behind German lines. She and her daughter trekked to the Estonian border town of Narva, where they were forced by the Germans to stay a while in a synagogue with other Russian refugees and prisoners of war. Exhausted and ill, Panova and her daughter eventually made their way to Shishaki in Ukraine, where they were reunited with Panova's two sons and her mother. In the fall of 1943 the Germans were finally driven from that area. With the help of Arsenii Starosel'skii, Panova resettled her family in the interior town of Perm'.

Life was difficult in Perm' too. Jobs on the local papers offered Panova only minimal compensation. Panova, her mother and the three children lived in one little barracks room; a bench served as Panova's writing table, a suitcase was her chair. In such conditions she wrote her play, *The Snowstorm* (*Metelitsa*), based on her experiences at the synagogue in Narva. Harsh wartime life in Perm' is reflected in another of her plays, *The Young Girls* (*Devochki*), written in 1945. Panova also wrote feature stories for a local radio station. In 1944 she published two stories about wartime life in Perm': "The Pirozhkov Family" ("Pirozhkovykh") and "The Evening of a Work Day" ("Vecher trudnogo dnia").

In December 1944, exhausted by overwork and the cold winter, Panova accepted an assignment to write a brochure about the work aboard a hospital train. In the process of listening to the stories of the train crew and the wounded, Panova also gathered material for her first novel, *The Traveling Companions* (*Sputniki*), called in its English version *The Train*. In May 1945, Panova presented the first pages of this new work, along with her early stories and plays, to the Writers' Union in Moscow for formal discussion. Her writing was greeted with enthusiasm. Soon after she signed a contract with the journal *The Banner* (*Znamia*) to publish *The Train*.

The Train is one of the classics of Russian literature about World War II. In the novel we learn of the war indirectly, through the tales of the wounded and the personnel on the hospital train. According to Panova, true heroism is found in the solidarity, vitality and endurance of the train crew, ordinary people who quietly fulfill their duty to their work. This approach to the theme of heroism makes Panova's novel a precursor of the later, more interpretive war literature published after Stalin's death.

The four main characters of *The Train* all suffer through loneliness, separation and other personal tribulations in their public and private lives; they all mature before our eyes. Danilov, the captain of the train, manifests the tempering aspect of war on people—his cold heart softens; Lena, an attractive young nurse, finds herself in her work and gains the courage to face the fact that her husband has abandoned her; Juliia Dmitrievna, a spinster nurse ardently pursuing her last chance for marital happiness, for all her external ugliness and awkwardness, grows in inner beauty; Dr. Belov, who begins as a comical character, emerges finally as an object of our deep respect and sympathy. Panova's method of characterization and its effect were explained by one critic this way: "Panova groups her characters in such a way that one individual biography interacts with another, independent human stories echo one another in motif, supplement each other, approach each other due to similarities or differ due to contrasts, yet all together they make up one tale about the fate of our contemporaries, about the variety and complexity of our historical being."[5]

In *The Train* we see the features of Panova's mature prose style: slice-of-life pictures; numerous contrasts and comparisons to build themes and characters; masses of details from daily life to create a backdrop of reality. Panova presents us with intimate portraits of ordinary individuals, delineating them through their daily activities, supplementing their present stories with ones from their pasts, letting their various points of view fully emerge, each in its own time and each rendered in an individual's own voice, which is blended with the narrator's.

In 1946 Panova's career as a journalist was largely behind her. With the publishing of *The Train*, she had arrived in full force on the literary scene. By the end of the year, the novel had been awarded a Stalin prize in literature, Panova had formally been accepted into the Writers' Union, she was living with her family again in Leningrad (this time comfortably), and she was now happily married to the writer David Ryvkin, best known by his pen name, David Dar. From 1946 to 1958 Panova wrote prose almost exclusively, publishing in this period the six major prose works that form the base of her reputation as a writer.

Panova's second novel, *The Factory* (*Kruzhilikha*, 1947), as it is called in one of its English translations, grew out of her experiences as a journalist in Perm' covering production in the local factories. As was the case for *The Train*, the characters and incidents in *The Factory* were largely taken from real life. The main theme of the novel is labor. Even the theme of love, especially when it centers on Nonna, an engineer and designer, and Listopad, the factory director, is subjugated to the theme of labor: this couple is destined to achieve a deep and abiding mutual love because they share a passion for work. The characters of the novel take control of their lives, and when they do, they dedicate their lives to the general cause of building socialism. The setting, characters and action of this novel largely fit the mold of a socialist realist "production novel." The huge postwar factory houses the standard cast of characters—shock workers, ambitious managers, dedicated Communist party men; we witness the race to production. However, what sets this novel apart from others of this type is that the main character in the novel, Listopad, is not the traditional "positive hero." In his personal life Listopad can be both compassionate and cruel; in his work life he is an autocratic industrial manager, unreformed by the party.

Panova's Listopad brought down the wrath of the conservatives. The press (literary critics, theorists and ordinary readers alike) debated Listopad to the point of absurdity: was he a "positive" or "negative" character? Was he a good director? Was he a good husband? Panova herself assumed her own defense, something she rarely did:

> I respect the red pencil, but I don't believe that it is conceivable to write a work where all the heroes are positive. I don't believe it and I don't understand why such a work would be needed, in what way it would help fulfill the general objective [of our society].
>
> If all the heroes firmly are the vehicles of the highest spiritual qualities, then, because of the unity of attitude and common life purpose, there couldn't be any kind of serious conflicts. In place of a workers' collective toiling in the sweat of their brows, overcoming the obstacles to communism, you would get some kind of an angel choir consisting of only the sweetest tenors![6]

Eventually Panova's supporters won out, and in the end *The Factory*, too, was given a Stalin prize.

That her fictional character could cause such a heated debate was a sure sign that Panova had touched upon a raw nerve in Soviet society. The sensation the novel caused put Panova in an uncomfortable position, and she retreated to a less risky course in her next novel, *Bright Shore* (*Iasnyi bereg*, 1949), also a winner of a Stalin prize.

At the official level her new novel was applauded for its more "correct" portrayal of socialism in action. The themes of social responsibility and labor dominate the work. Korostelev, the idealized dedicated director of the farm, is reformed by the party. His error in judgment, selling one of the prize calves, is forgiven.

Korostelev is so focused on his work that he has little time to put his personal life into order. It takes the singing of a nightingale to bring him and Mar'iana, the local schoolteacher, together. Panova herself admits her characters in *Bright Shore* are weak and are "inexpressively described," and thus they emerge "pale and anemic."[7] Only when Mar'iana is placed in her own sphere and we see her as a mother or as an inexperienced teacher with her young pupils does the novel become alive and interesting.

The best pages of the novel are those given to Serezha and his little friends. The children of *Bright Shore* stand out in bold relief. Serezha is the youngest and thus the most naive and vulnerable of the children. When he is at the center of a scene, Panova slows down the narrative tempo and assumes his point of view with tenderness and accuracy. For example, we fully experience Serezha's pleasure at watching an ant drag a crumb away. In the process of interpreting Serezha's world, Panova gives the reader an intimate understanding of his young mind. With her portrayal of Serezha, Panova achieves the rendering of life, at once accurate and poetic, that she tried to express in all her prose works.

Like most of the writers in the closing years of the Stalin era, Panova was compelled to gloss over real issues and problems. Soon after Stalin's death in 1953, the critic V. Pomerantsev wrote in his famous article "On Sincerity in Art" ("Ob iskrennosti v literature")[8] that writers should write about what they know and feel; they should cease "improving" reality in their works and leave out rhetorical clichés in favor of a more frank exposure of the real conflicts in life. Panova's *Seasons of the Year* (*Vremena goda*, 1954), or *Span of the Year* as it is known in its English translation, was among the first works to treat openly heretofore taboo themes and complex social problems.

Span of the Year took Panova over four years to create. The difficulties she had in composing the novel came from the complexity of the characters and subjects she chose to portray. Among other things, the novel discusses or touches upon bureaucracy, nepotism, bribery, speculation, hooliganism, suicide, attempted murder, parasitism, conflict between generations, blackmail, slander, housing shortages, class conflicts, personal greed for luxuries, embezzlement, vanity, drunkenness, abortion and sexual immorality. The novel explores the underworld of Soviet society.

The ordinary reading public greeted Panova's new novel with enthusiasm for its honest attempt to portray the real problems of the day. They were gripped by the story of the main hero, Gennadii Kupriianov, a young man who had grown up in a good communist family, but who chose for himself the life of a *stiliaga*—a rebellious youth who enjoys luxuries, dresses bizarrely, loves anything foreign, avoids work and indulges in outlandish behavior. The conservative literary critics of the establishment, on the other hand, were enraged by the novel. *Span of the Year* became the center of a heated controversy in the press, which culminated in a discussion of the novel at the Second Congress of Soviet Writers in 1954. Panova was accused of "naturalism" and "objectivism." She writes: "I really caught it from the critics because of my Gennadii, but I didn't renounce him and I will not. I saw him then much too clearly: his dirty, uncut hair, and jerky walk, his impudence and unwillingness to take into consideration anybody or anything and his disproportionate aspirations to personal comforts."[9]

The individuals in this novel are not united into some sort of collective effort, as was the case in Panova's first three longer prose works. Instead, *Span of the Year* takes as its focus Soviet citizens who are more concerned with themselves than they are with their responsibilities to others and their duty to build socialism for their country. These individuals seek their personal happiness in their private lives, rather than in their work. And unlike in the typical socialist realist novels, where the characters can be classified as "positive" or "negative," these characters are each imbued with good and bad traits, and their actions are much less predictable because of that. For example, Dorofeia, Gennadii's mother and the epitome of the new Soviet woman, misuses her power and position when she assumes the defense of her son; moreover, Stepan Bortashevich, who is a model father, carelessly leads his family to despair and ruin through his criminal behavior.

Despite all its innovative themes and characters, Panova's *Span of the Year* fails to plumb any great depths. This is the longest of Panova's published prose works, and the author often strains to hold together its many characters and situations. The good-hearted humor of the earlier novels is missing. Thus, overall, this novel is less pleasing aesthetically than the earlier ones.

On the other hand, Panova's *Serezha* (1956, spelled *Seryozha* in its first English translation), which appeared in print two years after *Span of the Year*, is a gem, both in showing real life up close and in providing aesthetic enjoyment for the reader. The author goes back to *Bright Shore* and transports her young hero, Serezha, along with his family and surroundings, to the pages of her new work. Serezha's character is rendered with almost flawless perfection. The charm of this simple tale is summed up by a reviewer of the English edition: "Panova has the rare perception which enables a writer to climb to the child's window, not stoop to it, and look from it without diminishing what she sees."[10] Where *Span of the Year* suffers because of its expansiveness, *Serezha* triumphs in its simplicity of theme, its limited number of characters and its compressed, precise, quiet style. Like *The Train*, *Serezha* brought the writer warm universal applause in the Soviet press. The famous critic Kornei Chukovskii said of the work: "You have written a classic book which sooner or later will make you a world name."[11] Indeed, this work has been translated into many languages and is known and loved around the world.

The theme of upbringing manifest in *Serezha* is a reflection of a feminine concern for nurturing the young. Panova clearly voices her views on the role and duty of society, as well as the family, to nurture the young. The workaholic director of *Bright Shore*, Korostelev, has been completely transformed into a loving, sensitive and wise stepfather in *Serezha*. He emerges a "positive hero," a caring parent truly worthy of emulation. Serezha's mother, Mar'iana, on the other hand, is much less sensitive and much more self-centered than she was in *Bright Shore*. Panova, thus, has created two strong opposing forces, and she puts Serezha squarely between them.

This novella, like Panova's other longer prose works, is mainly a study of character. The babyish Serezha from *Bright Shore* is transformed into a young boy who fully knows the differences between good and evil. This more mature Serezha has a deep respect and love for the world of Nature and the people around him, and he is willing to fight for justice. He must adapt to a new father, accept death, face his own and others' illnesses, cope with the presence of his new baby brother and deal with separation from his family. We see how these profound experiences, as well as the more simple ones, are assimilated into a young mind and heart. Panova helps us to penetrate deep into the child's inner world by using Serezha's voice indirectly, blending it with the narrator's own: "They made it up that he was like a little girl. That's really funny. Little girls wear dresses, and Serezha hasn't worn a dress in ever so long [*davnym-davno*]. Perhaps little girls have slingshots? Well, Serezha has a slingshot; one can shoot stones from it. Shurik made him the slingshot. . . . "[12]

By limiting the scope of her themes, characters and general elements of style in *Serezha*, Panova succeeds in creating a small masterpiece, permeated by insight, compassion and a gentle sense of humor. This work proves that Panova is at her best when she "speaks softly on some quiet theme."[13]

A Sentimental Romance (*Sentimental'nyi roman*, 1958) is the last of Panova's longer works of fiction published during her lifetime. The strongly autobiographical nature of this novel sets it apart from Panova's earlier works. The professional life of her hero, Sevast'ianov, the journalist, is given in all its details. We follow his feelings as he awaits and receives his first official reaction to his writing: anxiety, disbelief, pleasure, pride. Panova divulges her own experiences and feelings as a writer, as when she expounds on the independent life of the written word: "To convert life into the word . . . is more important and more fascinating than anything else there is. What is love in comparison to the word that sends forth shoots into eternity? Admit it: isn't perhaps the word that is printed in black color on white paper more real than the one you experienced? It has meaning. . . . It is an extract of the universe. . . ."[14] This autobiographical aspect of the novel is very satisfying for the reader who knows Panova's life and work.

Other features of *A Sentimental Romance*, however, are not as successful. For example, the narrative, as filtered through Sevast'ianov, shows that he obviously is deeply in love, but from our objective viewpoint we see how banal and sentimental his love affairs are, and we are not moved by them. In addition, Panova's overabundant use of details in this work fragments it into separate mosaic pieces that are never quite gathered up into one whole aesthetic picture.

The publication of the novel once again brought the writer both negative and positive criticism. The Academy of Sciences, in its history of the Soviet novel, concludes that Panova's attempt to "rehabilitate the individual personality of the ordinary man of the revolution suffers defeat" because the "theme of the Russian Revolution demands . . . bold colors, innovative artistic judgments, passionate philosophical thought, the deepest social analysis" and not Panova's "pastel tones, subtle mounting of details in the artistic fabric of the narrative, the even diffused light of [her] abstract humanistic view. . . ."[15] A Western critic was more kind, pointing out that the "1920s appear here [in Russian literature] for the first time freed of all ideological interpretation."[16] Panova's purpose in this work is consistent with that found in her other works: to write about the ordinary people. Historical forces do not motivate her main character Sevast'ianov. He is motivated by love and the joy of seeing his name in print, and by other aspects of his personal life that appeal directly to his emotions. By focusing on the individual and not on the era, Panova directs the reader's attention away from the romantic revolutionary themes found in socialist realist novels.

At the height of her career, Panova held a firm place in the top ranks of Soviet writers, one of the few Soviet women of literature to be so positioned. In 1954 and again in 1959 she was elected a member of the Presidium of the Union of Soviet Writers; she received the Order of the Red Banner of Labor in 1955 and again in 1965. As an established writer she was allowed special privileges, including travel to England, Scotland and Italy and, in 1960, to the United States.

In the 1950s and 1960s Panova also wrote a number of short stories, plays and film scenarios, along with a number of articles on her travels, her writing career, and her own literary works and the works of other writers—including an epilogue to the Russian version of *The Catcher in the Rye*. Two of Panova's short stories, "Valia" and "Volodia," became the subject of a film entitled *Entry into Life* (*Vstuplenie*, 1962), and her novella *Serezha* was adapted as a film by the same name in 1960 (in the West called *A Summer to Remember*). Both these films won international film awards. Other adaptations from her works followed. In addition, Panova wrote a number of original scenarios that became movies for the theater or for television. For the most part these films have been forgotten.

In the 1960s Panova at last rediscovered her voice as a Russian playwright when she wrote a cycle of plays on contemporary life. She addressed such problems as the rights and responsibilities of youth, in *Sending Off the White Nights* (*Provody belykh nochei*, 1960), and the housing crunch, in *How Are You Doing, Fellow?* (*Kak pozhivaesh' paren'?*, 1962). Features of Panova's prose style (for example, psychological portrayals and individualized speech patterns) find their way into her plays. The themes and character types found in her prose works also are realized in these plays. The main characters are not great heroes, but ordinary people in ordinary life situations. For example, people become stranded at an airport because of foul weather, and chance encounters lead to the renewal of an old love and the beginning of a new one in *It's Been Ages!* (*Skol'ko let, skol'ko zim!*, 1966). By the end of the 1960s Panova was experimenting with other dramatic forms such as melodrama and historical drama. Many of Panova's later plays were successfully staged during her lifetime, but they, like her films, are rarely seen in theaters today.

Panova's success as a playwright has always been overshadowed by her greater success as a prose writer. She herself preferred prose forms. She writes: "The dramatic form confined me. I couldn't put into its strict frame that which I wanted to relate to the reader. I thought that it would be more convenient and less constraining to narrate it all in a novel or a novella (*povest'*)."[17] Toward the end of her career, she experimented with a wide variety of prose forms: historical tales, published in the collection *Faces at Dawn* (*Liki na zare*, 1966); a novel in rough form, called in English *Synopsis of a Novel* (*Konspekt romana*, 1965); a collection of literary reminiscences, *Notes of a Writer* (*Zametki literatora*, 1972); and others. A book of personal reminiscences, *About My Life, Books and Readers* (*O moei zhizni, knigakh i chitateliakh*, 1975), and a fairy-tale novel, *What Time Is It?* (*Kotoryi chas?*, 1981), were published after her death.

Panova's last years, like her early years, were fraught with physical and emotional trials. In 1967 she suffered a stroke that left her partially paralyzed. Just before she died, she and her husband, David Dar, divorced after nearly twenty-five years of marriage. She died in Leningrad on 3 March 1973 and, at her request, had a Christian burial.

Panova cannot be labeled a feminist writer. Her career was roughly the same as that of many of her male counterparts. No doubt, however, being a woman excused her from having to answer for some of her more daring literary exploits because most men of her time, including Stalin himself, did not take women writers very seriously. Being a woman, especially one well entrenched in the literary establishment, meant that Panova was protected from some of the more crass abuse heaped upon the outcast female literary figures of her age—Anna Akhmatova, Nadezhda Mandel'shtam and others. Though not a feminist writer, Panova nonetheless was often very feminine in her writing, especially when it came to describing with sensitivity, perception and love the worlds of children and young people. These pages stand out and will be remembered as some of her best.

Panova does not move her readers to great philosophical depths or great aesthetic heights. Her themes and her characters are from everyday life, very recognizable and very comfortable; they do not stretch our imagination very far. Her works, which teem with details of a specific time and setting, seem very far removed from present-day realities. Set against the works of highly original Russian writers of the past such as Nabokov, Olesha, Akhmatova or later writers such as Solzhenitsyn and Tat'iana Tolstaia, Panova's writing appears pale. One wishes for more from her. The tragedies such as death, illness and family disintegration and the moving forces such as love, religion and ambition that shaped Panova as a person do not find a solid place in her work. The author stops short of revealing the depths of her own experiences. Where is the story, novel or play that gives voice to the loss of her second husband, Boris Vakhtin, to Stalin's Terror?

On the other hand Panova overcame much in her personal life, and she had a long and involved career. The scope of her writing is wide. She was continually experimenting with form, even though her literary taste stayed well within the range of "conservative." The general reading public greeted each new work of hers with enthusiasm because, overall, her writings were honest attempts to present real life. Her major prose works (except for *Bright Shore*) were always slightly out of step with the times, creating interest and often controversy in the press and literary circles and, as a consequence, helping move Russian literature forward. Panova can be admired, too, as a writer who did not wither away, a writer who believed fully in her talent and calling and was always ready with new ideas.

Panova's writings serve as witness and memory, rather than arousing the reader's conscience. They can be studied as parts of now-finished chapters in a book about the culture of a great people. Panova's literary gems (*The Train* and *Serezha*, and the short stories "Valia," "Volodia" and others) will live on in anthologies.

Ruth Kreuzer

From Bright Shore

There was in the house a being for whom the words *death, parting* and *sorrow* had no meaning. This being lived another, his own private, life.

This was Serezha.

On Aunt Pasha's shelf stood a big brass mortar with a heavy little pestle. Serezha was terribly fond of the mortar, and he would pester Aunt Pasha: "Let's crush something." Aunt Pasha would take the mortar from the shelf, glance into it, then with her short, hard fingernail scrape away the crumbs stuck to the bottom, and give Serezha a rusk or a little piece of sugar so that he could crush it down. Serezha would sit on the floor, place the mortar between his legs and crush away until he got tired. What music came from the mortar; what banging, thundering, ringing resounded through the house!

Serezha found many marvelous things in the world. There existed variously colored little stones; candy wrappers; empty match boxes; a mirror (for throwing off the reflected rays of the sun); nails (for pounding into walls and chairs); soap (which acquired meaning when it was a question of soap bubbles); not to mention little sleds; small boards on wheels on which it was possible to ride, pushing off with one foot; and Lukianych's dugout canoe in which Serezha was not permitted, no matter how much he cried.

But the most interesting were ants, birds, frogs, Buket the dog and Zaika the cat.

The ants lived under the yard and crawled out through the holes and cracks in the earth. They were very busy, always hurrying somewhere; Serezha never saw that any ant ever sat and rested. Mama said that their children are found there under the ground and that they bring food to their children. After dinner Serezha gathered up crumbs and leftover bits of bread from the table and scattered them around the ant holes. An ant would run by, coming across a crumb. For a time he would move his mustache, evidently trying to figure out what on earth it could be. Was it edible? Then he would seize the crumb and drag it to the entrance of his anthill. Often the crumb was five or six times bigger than the ant, but he was not afraid of straining himself. He dragged it off. And if he didn't succeed in moving the crumb from its place, then other ants would run up and help him, even though he hadn't called them. Serezha squatted down and looked at the ants.

In the neighbor's garden grew an old linden tree. In the linden tree there was a hollow. In the hollow lived hoopoes. They cried in a soft staccato: "U-du-du! U-du-du!" If you stole up quietly, then sometimes it was possible to see a little hoopoe, peeking out from the hollow: a little black-eyed head with a long beak and a brown crest. Waiting for his parents, the baby hoopoe breathed in the fresh air. At the smallest rustling sound, he disappeared in an instant into the hollow, as if he were popping into a trapdoor.

Once the neighbor boy, Vaska, brought over a nest that he had found in the grove to show off—a little woolen thing, in the form of a mitten, only with a hole in the thumb; a little mitten, ever so warm, woven from down, with hay and chips stuck into the down here and there. Mama laid it against her own hand and said: "My, just think, what a marvelous delight."

"And here is where they put their eggs," said Vaska in a bass voice, proud of his find.

"And where are the eggs?" asked Serezha.

"I made them into scrambled eggs and ate them up," said Vaska with a fierce expression on his face. That Vaska was a bad person; he caused a lot of grief for Serezha. He caught beetles and strung them on a piece of thread—twenty beetles on one thread. The beetles flew and buzzed as if they were groaning, but they couldn't tear themselves away. Serezha cried and tried to talk Vaska into untying them. At first Vaska refused, then he said, "OK. Pay a kopeck apiece for the beetles, and I will give them to you and you can do with them what you like."

"I don't have that many kopecks," answered Serezha.

"Ask your mother; she'll give them to you," said bad Vaska.

They counted the beetles, counted Serezha's money, and Serezha ran off to his mother and said excitedly: "Mommy, give me, if you can, fourteen kopecks. I don't have enough for the beetles!"

Frogs were most often found by the little river, especially in the damp places under the willow trees. Having plopped his big gray belly down onto the earth, a frog sat and looked at Serezha with bulging eyes. Serezha tried to catch it. The frog jumped into the water; its hind legs were so long that they made Serezha laugh loudly.

Zaika the cat was taken into the house before the war because the mice were breeding. With Zaika around they settled down a bit but didn't become extinct. Zaika was a lazybones. In the winter he slept for whole days while the mice became insolent and strolled around the rooms. Aunt Pasha woke up Zaika and whacked him, saying, "Go, go you loafer, go you scarecrow!" Then she seized him by the scruff of the neck, threw him into the storeroom and closed him in. After half an hour, she released him. He came out bored, with a mouse in his teeth, and walked unhurriedly through the house, as if showing everybody: "See, I don't refuse to serve you!" Finally he lazily ate the mouse in a dark little corner. Then for a long time he washed himself in disgust and again settled down to sleep.

In the summer Zaika came back to life a bit. He'd stand guard on the terrace for when Buket the dog would run into the yard. Then he'd dart out suddenly and give Buket a paw in his snout. Buket would run away with a whine. He was a flighty young smiley mutt; the thought never occurred to him that he could whip Zaika.

Serezha adored the cat, kissed and squeezed him, gave him his own food to eat. Everything enchanted him about Zaika: how Zaika sneezed, how he washed himself, the fine tail Zaika had. Getting into bed, he put Zaika in with him and tried to keep him there with his caresses and enticements, but Zaika couldn't be bribed. He didn't want to sleep with Serezha; he sat there haughtily, lashing with his tail, and finally he took off.

* * *

In the summertime life becomes simply radiant.

In the summertime a person swims in the little river, then he climbs out onto the shore and tumbles down onto the hot sand, like a cutlet into dried bread crumbs. And here he builds sand forts and sand towns, then he crawls again into the water. And long-legged frogs dive in after him from the shore, while on the very end of the branch, off in a dream, sits a golden dragonfly, drenched in the sun, hardly swaying with the branch.

In the summertime the grove, which in the winter is so far away, seems quite close to the house; Serezha goes there every day. This is the first summer that Mama lets him go to the grove with the boys, without the grown-ups. And how great it is without the grown-ups, if they only knew!

In the summertime you don't have to lace and unlace your boots (a useless occupation, thought up to make people suffer) and in general to waste time dressing and undressing. You can run around in your shorts, and only in the evening Mama shouts from the porch: "Serezha, where are you? Come put on your shirt. It's already cool!" And every day one finds a generous supply of unexpected discoveries and pleasures.

The biggest of Serezha's pleasures this summer is a jackdaw.

Vaska brought the jackdaw. She was a fledgling, couldn't fly, and walked with difficulty, limping and dragging her tail.

"Where did you find her?" asked Serezha.

"In the garden on the ground at our place," Vaska answered. "She fell out of the nest."

"Why didn't you put her back into the nest?"

"It's not written on her which nest she's from. There are jackdaw nests galore there. If you don't put her into the right nest, they'll beat her to death."

The jackdaw opened her beak and screamed: "Caw!"

"She wants to eat," said Vaska.

Serezha dug into the ground under the lilac bush with a knife, found several earthworms, and gave them to the jackdaw. She gobbled them up, choking from greed and screaming still louder: "Caw! Caw!"

"Give her to me," said Serezha.

"And what will you give for her?" asked Vaska.

"I don't know," said Serezha sadly, feeling that now Vaska would cheat him.

"OK, let's make a deal," said Vaska, not immediately making up the price to put on the jackdaw. "You feed her well, that's the most important thing, or else she'll die. Those crows never can get enough food."

He went away, and the black, disheveled, squawking bird with the twisting head remained at Serezha's.

Zaika the cat, awakened by the screeching, stretched himself and came out onto the terrace, sniffing gingerly.

"Don't you dare," Serezha shouted at him. "Don't you dare touch her! You'll get it if you do!"

"Oh, Serezha," said Mar'iana, "you've made trouble for yourself now."

Now from morning to evening Serezha was busy at work: he dug the ground and extracted worms for the jackdaw. The jackdaw lived in his room in a box made of blocks, lined inside with soft rags and cotton batting. All day her demanding shouts resounded through the house. From time to time it was necessary to give her something to drink. She stuck up her head and opened her beak up wide, and Serezha poured water into her mouth from a teaspoon. It was necessary to guard the door and window so that Zaika would not get into the room.

"Disgusting bird!" said Ikonnikov. "I am astonished, Mar'iana Fedorovna, that you allow it."

How could you not allow it, if Serezha was attached to the bird?

"Galia-Galia!" he shouted from the yard, bringing her worms in a little play bucket, and the jackdaw answered back from the room with a frantic: "Caw!"

He fed her and kept saying: "Poor thing! Hungry! Well, eat, eat, Galia-Galia-Galia!"

In this way he trained her to her name.

After about two weeks passed, the jackdaw refused to sit in the box. She demanded that they let her outside. Serezha opened the door. Turning her head and flashing her beady eyes, the jackdaw hopped over the threshold, crossed through the dining room, and went out onto the terrace. There under a chair, all sprawled out, slept Zaika. He opened his eye and looked at the jackdaw . . . the jackdaw, throwing out her chest, went up to him, cawed, and struck him smack in the eye with her beak—Zaika hardly had time to blink. He sat there for a little while observing the jackdaw. Then, apparently having decided that it was better not to get involved, he withdrew into the rooms sullenly, as if offended.

The jackdaw grew. She waddled and hopped her way through house and yard in a businesslike manner. By herself, she dug under the lilac bushes looking for worms. At dinnertime she flew onto the table and seized macaroni and cabbage from the plates. Zaika and the dog Buket were afraid of her; she flew up to their heads and painfully pecked them on the noggin. The chickens created an uproar when the jackdaw approached them.

She stole shiny things: teaspoons disappeared; Mar'iana's little scissors were lost. It took a while before they figured out to look for them in the jackdaw's box (as before, she slept in Serezha's room in the box made from blocks). Aunt Pasha was afraid to take off her glasses: she had only to lay them on the table or on the windowsill and see, the jackdaw already had sneaked up to them sidewise, skipping along, taking aim with her thievish eye.

"She needs to be put into a cage!" said Ikonnikov.

But nobody agreed with him. In that home they never kept birds in cages.

The boys on Dalniaia Street were out of their minds over the jackdaw.

For whole days shouts of "Galia-Galia!" rang out on the street.

The jackdaw answered with a "Caw!" but she didn't come out to anyone's call except Serezha's, which made him proud.

She went for walks with him. He walked along, surrounded by the boys, and she sat on his shoulder.

Once she disappeared from home. Serezha ran through the whole town calling: "Galia-Galia!" She did not respond. Serezha called again and again. In the evening Mar'iana led him back home by force and put him to bed. He looked at the empty box standing on the dresser and burst into tears. Suddenly the bushes beyond the window rustled, and the jackdaw flew into the room and came straight to Serezha!

"Galia-Galia!" he shouted, and jumped up.

On her leg was a scrap of a rag.

"Just think, Serezhenka," said Mar'iana, "she was tied up and she broke loose and flew to you!"

But then the jackdaw abandoned Serezha after all. Another jackdaw started to fly in to see her. For a long time they strolled together around the yard and conferred with each other about something.

"They will fly away," said Mar'iana. "They are thinking about building a nest.

You can't do anything about that, Serezhenka. A bird has to build a nest."

And the jackdaw did fly away. This was very sad, but there was nothing to be done—Serezha understood that there was nothing to be done.

Two times the jackdaw flew in for a call. She walked along the terrace, frightened Zaika, grabbed out macaroni from the soup, and the other jackdaw sat on a branch and watched how his friend carried on so disgracefully.

Then they stopped flying in. It had to be that they were very busy building their nest and had no time to go calling.

* * *

On the shore stands a new dugout canoe. Lukianych already has tried it out—it's a good dugout, stable, not heavy, a beauty of a dugout. With tender languor Lukianych dreams of taking it out. Today he is allowing himself to leave work earlier than usual, to use, as they say, a couple of compensatory hours of time off (he has thousands of such hours; he won't use them up in a century), and today he has promised to take the kiddies for a ride in the dugout.

There are a lot of those who wished to go. As a matter of fact, when things got better, in a year or two, why not buy a motorboat for the collective farm—a kind of river automobile—for taking the little kids for a ride, let them get a thrill . . . well, and for business needs. Everything, comrades, is before you and everything is in your hands. And meanwhile, kiddies, there are a lot of you, and only one dugout; I will take those whom I long ago promised a ride.

Serezha is like a grandson to me. How many years he has begged: "Give me a ride." Mariasha forbade it, but this year Sergei was given permission. Sergei is in seventh heaven; he can hardly wait. There's no way I can not take him . . . Vaska is a neighbor: he is promised a ride because with heroic strength he passed from third grade into fourth. His mom didn't expect it, shed a few tears of emotion; it's necessary to reward Vaska.

And I have a certain acquaintance, a red-haired beauty. I led her around by a towel when she was learning to walk—a certain Fimochka, the daughter of the assistant bookkeeper, Maria Vasilievna, and Mar'iana's pupil. Maria Vasilievna just the other day asked: "Pavel Lukianych, you will take my redhead? What kind of conversation can there be? My redhead, how could she not go?"

Not long ago I had the honor of becoming acquainted with the other young lady. She produced a strong impression on me. In the House of Culture there was a demonstration of school talent, and that young lady stood out as the epitome of technique, since she untiringly danced seven, or was it eight times, with scarves, without scarves, in high heels and in only little socks. Her name is Nadia. She had exceptional success. And it turned out she is the daughter of Tosia Almazova, a member of our collective. As a token of my admiration, I presented her with a chocolate and I promised to take her for a ride in the dugout.

An hour and a half before the appointed time Serezha, Vaska and Fima met near Lukianych's dugout.

"That girl," Serezha said confidentially to Vaska, "was at the Christmas party at the collective farm school. Her name's Fima."

"I spit on your girlies!" said Vaska rather loudly. Serezha didn't dare greet Fima in Vaska's presence; he squatted down and started playing with the wet sand. But he felt that he was behaving badly, and he was tormented by pangs of conscience. He thought up a ruse: he started digging a trench in the direction of the dugout, where on board Fima sat, defiantly having hung her strong, tanned little legs over the side. Serezha, energetically digging the sand, crawled toward her closer and closer; when the soles of her sandals were over his head he said:

"Hello."

"Hello," answered Fima from her height. "You haven't grown any at all; you were small and so you remained."

Serezha understood that she was offended by his meanness and was getting her revenge on him. He calmly crawled back along the trench, musing over the fact that it is not a good idea to be mean—everyone will despise you.

"All the same," said Vaska after ten minutes of waiting, "it looks like the old man blew us off."

Nadia came up in a white blouse with a Pioneer kerchief and a green hat with a red ribbon.

"He's out of his mind," said Vaska. "Sheer girlies. If I had known, I wouldn't have come."

When Lukianych appeared on the shore with an oar over his shoulder, the kids were sitting despondent, worn out from expectation, disillusioned with everything in the world. Serezha and Fima ran to meet Lukianych with a shout.

"We thought you weren't coming!"

Laughing a bit, Lukianych pulled his watch from his pocket and showed it.

"Five minutes to five. We agreed on five. You, in all probability, have been here since morning? Without dinner? OK, now we will sail off for a spell. I repeat, comrades, remember: a dugout is not a steamship. Jumping is not allowed; no leaning over the sides. If you can't sit quietly, I won't take you out again. Well then, hold onto the oar."

They took off the lock. The chain clanked, fatigued as never before, hearts pounding, eyes shining; how great, how happy that kid who was given the oar. . . .

Only Nadia conducted herself calmly and quietly. She was big, a ballerina; she was above all that.

"Heave to, lend a hand! Yo, heave ho, mateys. One, two and we're off!"

To each it seemed that just because he himself seized the side of the dugout with his hands, and then with a groan pushed with his chest, the dugout stirred, and with a quiet hiss moved across the wet sand and crawled toward the water.

"Give to, give to, my bogatyrs!" The boat was in the water.

"All aboard." Girls on one side, boys on the other.

"And don't forget the motto: sit ab-so-lutely still!" The quick silvery water snaked along the sides.

"Lovely water, lovely water!" said Fima in a patter, putting her hand into the water. Nadia also put her hand in, squealed and said: "Cold."

Vaska really wanted to put his hand into the water too, but he didn't do it; the girlies might think he was copying them.

Serezha sat quietly and looked at the magical shore swimming by.

The weather was bright but uneasy—the sun and heaps of thick round clouds in the sky, a wind swooping down in gusts; the sun baked, and the wind was cold. The whole time cold winds had been blowing. Up until now no swimming; only incorrigible kids like Vaska went swimming. The old folks say that the real summer will come only after a drenching rain that comes with a good thunderstorm.

They sailed against the current. The wind blew from the mouth of the river. It was not hard to sail upstream. Lukianych steered with careful strength.

"Here I will show you a certain little place I know," he said.

High above on the shore grew a clump of old aspen trees. When the wind dashed in, their silvery foliage poured like water, and their reflection streamed down below in the river. Jackdaws were shouting in the aspen trees.

"Is this the little place?" asked Fima.

"No," answered Lukianych, "the little place is beyond the bend. Possibly we can tie up and you young ladies can gather water lilies. I used to take Serezha's mama there when she was a little girl."

Serezha listened.

"What do you think?" he asked Vaska. "Isn't that Galia-Galia shouting?"

"Ah, come off it," said Vaska. "Don't you think there are other jackdaws besides yours?"

"What Galia-Galia?" asked Fima.

"He had a tame jackdaw," Vaska explained condescendingly. "I got it for him."

"Her name was Galia-Galia," said Serezha. "She flew away."

He continued to listen. His eyes became big and troubled. Suddenly he blushed all over—even his ears turned red—and with desperate hope he shouted with all the strength he could muster.

"Galia-Galia-Galia!"

"Caw!" loudly and distinctly resounded in answer, and something black flashed in the silver of the aspen trees.

"Galia-Galia!" shouted Serezha. Beside himself, he jumped up and rushed to the side of the boat where the girls were sitting. Vaska leaped up after him. The dugout rocked, took in a drink, and the little kids plopped into the water like peas.

All that happened in one second. Lukianych didn't have time to react to stop it. He sat alone in the empty dugout as it calmed down, rocking less and less; in the clump of aspens jackdaws were screeching.

"A-a-akh!" said Lukianych and began to tear off his boots. Feverishly taking off his boots he looked around: Fima was dog-paddling toward the dugout, her gaping little black eyes filled with terror.

"Not this way! Not this way!" shouted Lukianych. "Swim to the shore, there are shoals nearby! All the same, the dugout will drift away."

Fima, businesslike, turned and swam to the shore.

"Good girl!" shouted Lukianych to her, and he jumped into the water.

Vaska surfaced alongside, spitting, blowing his nose with his left hand, the right holding Serezha by the hair.

"To the shore!" shouted Lukianych. "Will you make it?"

"Need you ask!" Vaska panted, and he swam off, stroking with his left arm.

"Where's Nadia?" shouted Lukianych after him. Vaska didn't answer; evidently he was having trouble. Lukianych dived, surfaced about fifteen meters downstream, and looked around. Freely bobbing in front of him the dugout floated away, and after the dugout floated the hat, the current playing with the ends of the ribbons. "The hat couldn't have been torn off," Lukianych reasoned. "It was on a rubber band, a rubber band that went right under the chin. Where the hat is, there must be the head . . ."

He dragged Nadia out onto the shore. She was blue and unconscious. He began doing artificial respiration. She spit up and began to shake, and her eyes opened. The sand under her became soaked through and flowed away in liquid trickles. How was it she didn't go straight to the bottom, not knowing how to swim? Perhaps by habit she moved her legs unconsciously. Eh, they taught her to dance, but didn't teach her to swim. Some educators!

Wet Vaska walked up. Far down on the shore appeared two running little figures—Fima and Serezha.

"I sent them home," said Vaska. "I told them to run on the double. Or else they'd catch cold. The girlie swam out herself."

Lukianych followed the dugout with his eyes. The dugout was far off, spinning like a cork, floating off down the river. Lukianych stamped with his bare feet and started to wail.

Before they got to the town, people were already running out to meet them. They had seen the wet, frightened children, questioned them, and hurried off to help. They rushed Nadia to the hospital. They led Fima and Serezha off to Aunt Pasha's. Aunt Pasha met them at the corner. She herself was trembling, as if in a fever, but she was businesslike and spoke in a firm voice. Mar'iana was not at home. They put the children to bed, gave them hot milk to drink, surrounded them with hot water bottles. Lukianych refused medical help; he ordered Aunt Pasha to stoke up the bathhouse and buy a half liter of vodka.

"Vodka!" said Aunt Pasha. "It would be better to take some aspirin. You never drink, why on earth would you want a half liter? To hell with the dugout, let it perish! Pity though, your good boots are gone!"

But Lukianych did not want to listen to anything and did not want to carry on the conversation to the end. He shouted over to Vaska and ordered him to steam himself in the bathhouse and to drink vodka: "Drink, my eagle!" He came out of the bathhouse beet red, lay down on the bed, and groaned until night from shame and grief. . . .

Red-haired Fima sleeps in the dining room, covered with four blankets. Curled up beside her, Maria Vasilevna, Fima's mother, has fallen asleep. Out from under Lukianych's door drift long anguished "a-a-a's"—it is Lukianych reliving his shame and his loss.

Mar'iana returns from the hospital; in her stocking feet, having taken off her shoes at the entryway, she crosses over to her room.

Serezha sleeps, and the lamp on the table is shaded with a paper shield so that the light will not awaken him. Serezha is all sprawled out; the blankets have slipped off, and he's slipped off his pillow. Mar'iana adjusts the blankets, puts Serezha's head back on the pillow, kisses it on the top, all the while telling him what is happening:

"You silly-silly, you've pushed your blanket off, you've slipped down off your pillow. Pillow out of place, himself out of place; Mama will put you back on your pillow, Mama will cover you up, you silly-silly." She grows thoughtful, holding onto the headboard of the little bed and looking at her son; her face becomes stern. That separation which almost occurred would have been the worst of all separations. Serezha tosses in his sleep, whimpering thinly and humorously; he is dreaming about the recent events. "Sleep, my sweet darling, Mama is here, the light is burning, there is nothing to fear!"

* * *

After two days a thunderstorm passed through and the real summer began with its intensely hot days and warm evenings.

* * *

It is morning and everyone is off to work. . . . A little while later, amidst the fields that billow around the school, sails a blue frock with white polka-dots—that's the schoolteacher Mar'iana on her way to her charges.

And above the little river, along the high right shore far from town, Serezha is walking. He is in his sandals and shorts, with an uncovered head; the wind ruffles his soft fair hair. All around is a sea of yellow flowers: colza, chamomile, dandelions. Some dandelions are golden, just opened up; others stick up their transparent fluffy little balls. Serezha picks the dandelions and blows; the fluff flies.

Serezha goes to the old aspen trees. For their sake he has refused to go with Mama to the school flower beds. He has to call on the aspen trees and find out whether his jackdaw is there, his Galia-Galia. He is sure that it was her. What other bird would answer to his voice? Vaska can laugh as much as he likes. Everyone respects Vaska as a hero. Mama said that he was a marvelous lad, an excellent comrade and that Serezha owes him his life. Really, Vaska did a good thing by pulling Serezha immediately out of the water. Serezha was really scared when he fell into the water, and he was very grateful to Vaska, but all the same one shouldn't believe everything that Vaska says. Serezha is sure of that, based on the experience of many years. About the jackdaw Vaska is absolutely wrong. It was Galia-Galia.

A white butterfly flew in front of Serezha: it flew as if it were dancing. It would alight on a flower and fold its little wings. When Serezha would just about be ready to seize it, the butterfly would take fright and fly off farther to another flower. Again and again it would flutter up and fly away.

Thus Serezha walked along the high shore, the wind ruffled his soft hair and the white butterfly flew in front of him, from flower to flower.

1949

Translated by Ruth Kreuzer

Notes to the Essay

1. *Zametki literatora* (Leningrad: Sovetskii pisatel' 1972), 11.
2. S. Fradkina, *V mire geroev Very Panovoi: Tvorcheskii portret pisatel'nitsy* (Perm': Knizhnoe izdatel'stvo, 1961), 12–16.
3. *O moei zhizni, knigakh i chitateliakh* (Leningrad: Lenizdat, 1975), 127.
4. Ibid., 151.

5. A. Ninov, "Gody i knigi," *Druzhba narodov* 2 (1963): 265.

6. "Neskol'ko myslei o tekhnologii nashego remesla," *Literaturnaia gazeta*, 8 August 1950, 3.

7. Ibid., 3.

8. *Novyi mir* 12 (1953): 218–45.

9. *O moei zhizni*, 332.

10. D.B. Whitman, *Book World (Juv.)* 2 (1968): 33.

11. From a letter to Panova, quoted by A. Ninov in *Vera Panova. Zhizn'. Tvorchestvo. Sovremenniki* (Leningrad: Sovetskii pisatel', 1980), 205.

12. *Sobranie sochinenii v piati tomakh*, Vol. 2 (Leningrad: Khudozhestvennaia literatura, 1969), 201.

13. Anon., in a review of *Time Walked* by Vera Panova, *Time* 73 (1959): 109.

14. *Sobranie sochinenii*, Vol. 3, 485.

15. Akademiia nauk SSSR, Institut russkoi literatury (Pushkinskii dom), *Istoriia russkogo sovetskogo romana*, ed. A. Kovalev et al., Vol. 2 (Leningrad: Nauka, 1965), 225.

16. Johannes Holthusen, *Twentieth Century Russian Literature: A Critical Study* (New York: Ungar, 1972), 165.

17. *Zametki literatora*, 13.

Bibliography

Primary Works

Sputniki [novel]. *Znamia* 1 (1946): 3–95; 2/3 (1946): 3–64.

Devochki [play; completed 1945]. In the almanac *Prikam'e* 9 (1947).

Kruzhilikha [novel]. *Znamia* 11 (1947): 20–115; 12 (1947): 3–73.

Iasnyi bereg [novel]. *Zvezda* 9 (1949): 3–100.

Vremena goda [novel]. *Novyi mir* 9 (1953): 3–101; 12 (1953): 62–158.

Serezha [novella]. *Novyi mir* 9 (1955): 141–98.

V staroi Moskve [play; also called *Staraia Moskva*, completed 1940]. *Neva* 9 (1956): 13–51.

Metelitsa. Leningrad: Iskusstvo, 1957.

Il'ia Kosogor [play; completed 1939]. *Il'ia Kosogor. V staroi Moskve. Metelitsa. Devochki*. Leningrad: Sovetskii pisatel', 1958.

Sentimental'nyi roman [novel]. *Novyi mir* 10 (1958): 3–74; 11 (1958): 32–82.

Evdokiia [novella completed 1949, revised 1959]. *Leningradskii al'manakh* 16 (1959): 5–38.

"Valia." *Oktiabr'* 10 (1959): 28–51.

"Volodia." *Oktiabr'* 10 (1959): 51–73.

Provody belykh nochei. *Novyi mir* 2 (1961): 7–53.

"Troe mal'chishek u vorot." *Literatura i zhizn'*, 25 June 1961.

Kak pozhivaesh', paren'? [play]. *Teatr* 7 (1962): 3–67.

"Sestry." *Sestry. Rasskazy.* Moscow: Sovetskaia Rossiia, 1965.

Konspekt romana [abbreviated novel; excerpts]. *Literaturnaia Rossiia* 10 (1965): 17–19; 12 (1965): 5–7.

Liki na zare [historical tales]. Leningrad: Sovetskii pisatel', 1966.

Skol'ko let, skol'ko zim! [play]. *Novyi mir* 7 (1966): 3–38.

Nadezhda Milovanova [also called *Vernost'* and *Pogovorim o strannostiax liubvi*; play]. *Zvezda* 10 (1967): 13–51.

Eshche ne vecher. Zvezda vostoka [play]. 12 (1967): 61–97.

Tred'iakovskii i Volynskii [historical drama]. *Neva* 6 (1968): 3–34.

Sobranie sochinenii v piati tomakh. 5 vols. Leningrad: Khudozhestvennaia literatura, 1969–1970. [The revised and expanded edition in 1987 contains the most important of Panova's primary works.]

Zametki literatora [remarks on literature; reminiscences]. Leningrad: Sovetskii pisatel', 1972.

O moei zhizni knigakh i chitateliakh [reminiscences]. Leningrad: Lenizdat, 1975.

Kotoryi chas? [fairy-tale novel]. *Novyi mir* 9 (1981): 6–68.

P'esy [collection of plays]. Leningrad: Iskusstvo, 1985.

Zhizn' Mukhammeda [fictional biography with Iu.B. Vakhtin]. Moscow: Politizdat, 1991.

Film and TV Scenarios

Serezha. Mosfilm. Dirs. G. Daneliia and I. Talankin. 1960 [based on Panova's *Serezha*].

Evdokiia. Kinostudiia im. M. Gor'kogo. Dir. T. Lioznova. 1961. [Scenario: Iskusstvo kino 1 (1961): 7–50. Based on Panova's *Evdokiia.*]

Visokosnyi god. Mosfilm. Dir. A. Efros. 1962 [based on Panova's *Vremena goda*].

Vstuplenie. Mosfilm. Dir. I. Talankina. 1963 [based on Panova's "Valia" and "Volodia"].

Rano utrom. Tsentral'naia studiia detskiikh i iunosheskikh fil'mov im. M. Gor'kogo. Dir. T. Lioznova. 1964. [Scenario: Iskusstvo kino 11 (1964): 128–68.]

Poezd miiloserdiia. Lenfil'm Dir. I. Khamraevyi. 1964 [based on Panova's *Sputniki*].

Rabochii poselok. Lenfil'm. Dir. V. Vengerov. 1965. [Scenario: *Novyi mir* 9 (1964): 3–43.]

Mal'chik i devochka. Lenfil'm. Dir. Iu. Fait. 1966. [Scenario: *Iskusstvo kino* 7 (1962): 14–43.]

Chetyre stranitsy odnoi molodoi zhizni. Lenfil'm. Dir. P. Esadze. 1967. [Scenario: Iskusstvo kino 4 (1966) 138–73. Based on Panova's "Sasha".]

Svad'ba kak svad'ba. TV special. 1974. [Scenario: Teatr 1 (1973) 135–52. Adaption of Panova's *Svad'ba kak svad'ba.*]

In Translation

Sputniki [excerpts]. Trans. E. Manning. *Soviet Literature* 6 (1946): 13–50; 8 (1946): 2–26.

The Train. Trans. E. Manning and M. Budberg. London: Putnam, 1948.

The Train. Trans. Marie Budberg. New York: Knopf, 1949.

Kruzhilikha. Trans. H. Kazanina. *Soviet Literature* 2 (1948): 33–64; 3 (1948): 1–56.

The Factory. Trans. Moura Budberg. London: Putnam, 1949.

Bright Shore. Trans. B. Isaacs. *Soviet Literature* 3 (1950): 3–142.

A Year's Span [excerpts]. Trans. E. Manning. *Soviet Literature* 5 (1954): 9–162.

Seryozha. Trans. E. Manning. *Soviet Literature* 7 (1956): 3–72.

Span of the Year. Trans. Vera Traill. London: Harvill, 1957.

Time Walked. [Translator not listed.] London: Harvill, 1957. [Also published under this title at Cambridge: Arlington, 1959, and New York: Taplinger, 1959. Also published under the title *A Summer to Remember* at New York: Yoseloff, 1962, and Cranbury, NJ: Barnes, 1962. Reprinted as "Seryozha" in *Fifty Years of Russian Prose*. Ed. Krystyna Pomorska. Vol. 2. Cambridge: MIT Press, 1971. 245–326.]

Yevdokia. Trans. Julius Katzer. Moscow: Foreign Languages Publishing House, 1959.

Looking Ahead. Trans. David Skvirsky. London: Central Books, 1964.

"Notes for a Novel." Trans. Robert Daglish. *Soviet Literature* 1 (1966): 21–56.

"It's Been Ages!" Trans. F. Reeve. *Contemporary Russian Drama*. By F. Reeve. New York: Pegasus, 1968. 207–59.

On Faraway Street. Trans. Rya Gabel. Adapted by Anne Terry White. New York: Braziller, 1968.

"Sisters." Trans. Robert Daglish. *Soviet Literature* 4 (1971): 104–23.

Selected Works. Trans. Olga Shartse and Eve Manning. Moscow: Progress, 1976.

Secondary Works

Alexandrova, V. *A History of Soviet Literature, 1917–1962*. Westport, CT: Greenwood Press, 1963. 272–283.

Ar'ev, A. "Slovo dolzhno byt' chistym (K 80–letiiu so dnia rozhdeniia V.F. Panovoi)." *Zvezda* 3 (1985): 155–62.

Boguslavskaia, Z. *Vera Panova. Ocherk tvorchestva*. Moscow: Khudozhestvennaia literatura, 1963.

Brown, E.J. *Russian Literature Since the Revolution*. Cambridge: Harvard University Press, 1982.

Bushmann, I. "Panova, Vera Fyodorovna." *Portraits of Prominent USSR Personalities* 1, 3 (July 1968): 29–32.

Fradkina, S. "Chuvstvuiu k Permi samoe serdechnoe otnoshenie . . . (K 80–letiiu Very Panovoi)." *Ural* 3 (1985): 155–62.

———. *V mire geroev Very Panovoi: Tvorcheskii portret pisatel'nitsy*. Perm': Knizhnoe izdatel'stvo, 1961.

Gasiorowska, X. *Women in Soviet Fiction, 1917–1964*. Madison: University of Wisconsin Press, 1968.

Gornitskaia, N. *Kinodramaturgiia V.F. Panovoi*. Leningrad: Iskusstvo, 1970.

Isaev, B. "Tvorchestvo Very Panovoi." *Zvezda* 8 (1950): 166–78.

Iur'eva, S. *Vera Panova: stranitsy zhizni; k biografii pisatel'nitsy*. Tenafly, NJ: Hermitage, 1993.

Kreuzer, R.L. "A New Bright Shore for Serezha." *Slavic and East European Journal* 27, 3 (Fall 1983): 339–64.

Mihailovich, V.D., ed. "Panova, Vera (1905–)." *Modern Slavic Literature: A Library of Literary Criticism* 1 (1972): 228–31.

Moody, C. "Vera Panova" [introductory essay to Panova's "Serezha" and "Valya"]. New York: Macmillan, 1964. xi–xxvi.

Ninov, A. "Dramaturgiia Very Panovoi." *Siberskie ogni* 9 (1963): 162–74.

———. "Return to the Theater: On the Fate of Vera Panova's Plays." *Soviet Studies in Literature* 16, 1 (Winter 1979–1980): 47–87.

———. "The Novels of Vera Panova." *Soviet Literature* 3 (1965): 158–65.

———. *Vera Panova. Zhizn'. Tvorchestvo. Sovremenniki*. Leningrad: Sovetskii pisatel', 1980.

———, N.A. Ozernova-Panova, and V.D. Oskotskii, eds. *Vospominaniia o Vere Panovoi*. Moscow: Sovetskii pisatel', 1988.

Pankov, V. *Na strezhne zhizni*. Moscow: Sovetskii pisatel', 1962.

Plotkin, L. *Tvorchestvo Very Panovoi*. Leningrad: Sovetskii pisatel', 1962.

Segall, H. "Panova, Vera Fyodorovna (1905–73)." *Handbook of Russian Literature*. Ed. Victor Terras. New Haven, CT: Yale University Press, 1985. 329.

———. "You Describe Life As It Is." *Soviet Literature* 10 (1986): 141–46.

Starikova, E. "Chto my seem? Chto my pozhnem?" In *Poèziia prozy*. Moscow: Sovetskii pisatel', 1962. 205–71.

Tevekelian, D.V. "Everything Said Must Be True." *Soviet Literature* 3 (1981): 141–52.

———. *Vera Panova*. Moscow: Sovetskaia Rossiia, 1980.

Zolotnitskii, D. "Panova." *Ocherki istorii russkoi sovetskoi dramaturgii 1945–67*. Ed. S.V. Vladimirov. Leningrad: Iskusstvo, 1968. 240–78.

Mariia Petrovykh

In life I was so deeply forgotten
That posthumous oblivion does
not threaten me.

Mariia Sergeevna Petrovykh (1908–1979) belongs to a generation of Russian writers who began publishing in the literary excitement of the 1920s but were soon forced aside by the officially sanctioned, bureaucratic organization of literature. An exceptionally gifted poet, Petrovykh spent most of her creative energies translating, editing, teaching and supporting other poets; in a writing career that spanned over fifty years, she produced only about 150 completed extant poems. She was greatly esteemed in high culture and by unofficial poets, while readers outside those limited circles knew nothing about her original writing. Marina Palei located her entry in the card catalogue of Leningrad's Saltykov-Shchedrin library; it read "Mariia Petrovykh, translator." Next to this, someone in the know had added in pencil, "and poet!"[1] Recent interest among Russian scholars and readers in recovering the literary heritage that Soviet rule suppressed has produced new publications of Petrovykh's works, which are finally available to a wider readership. Her poetry and reputation can now assume their proper place in the history of twentieth-century Russian literature.

Petrovykh was born 13 March 1908 in Norskii posad, a settlement about nine miles from the city of Iaroslavl' on the upper Volga. Her father, Sergei Alekseevich Petrovykh, was director of a factory in Norskii posad; her mother, Faina Aleksandrovna (née Smirnova), was a native of the Iaroslavl' area. Her parents married in 1896. Mariia Sergeevna was the youngest of their five children and, according to her sister's memoirs, a favorite child who acquired confidence and a sense of her own special gifts early in life. She later recalled her happy and loving family as a crucial source of poetic power. The surroundings of the old house and garden were beautiful, with the Volga River a five-minute walk away. Petrovykh enjoyed strolling through fields and birch and fir woods with her sister Ekaterina. Petrovykh's nature poetry is always grounded in striking and concrete detail. Observing the beauty of her native region invested her with a lasting sense of nature as a supreme spiritual value and source of art, a neoromantic strand that continues through much twentieth-century Russian poetry, in defensive reaction to Soviet industrialization and collectivization.

Petrovykh remembered her first poetic experience: "At six years old I 'composed' my first poem (a four-line stanza), and this sent me into indescribable ecstasy. I perceived it as a miracle, and from then on everything began, and, it seems to me, my attitude towards the origin of verses has not changed since that time."[2] She learned to read at the age of four and to write soon afterwards. She lived at home until six and then attended school in Iaroslavl', preparing for study at the *gimnaziia* (high school with demanding classical curriculum) there. Iaroslavl' was a beautiful city with tree-lined avenues and a population of over 70,000; it had seventy-five Orthodox churches, three newspapers, ten book shops and six libraries or "people's reading rooms." This cultured provincial atmosphere also encouraged Petrovykh's creative talents.

After 1917, when his factory closed, Petrovykh's father moved to Moscow with the older children. Her mother stayed with the younger girls in Norskii posad while they completed school. At fifteen, Petrovykh began to attend meetings of the Iaroslavl' Poets' Union, where she shared the creative enthusiasm of the youthful Iaroslavl' poets and encountered a wider literary culture. In winter the group met in a library, between the rows of bookshelves; Petrovykh recalled that no one complained of the inconvenience. Summer meetings were held in a building on a wharf, where the soft sound of the Volga's waves accompanied readings and discussions. Before she finished high school, Petrovykh became one of the Iaroslavl' Union's youngest members.

In August 1925, Petrovykh moved to Moscow and enrolled in the year-old program of advanced literary courses at Moscow University. Fellow students included Arsenii Tarkovsky and Iulia Neiman; Tarkovsky later recalled that Petrovykh was highly regarded, the "first of the first" among the aspiring beginners. She started publishing poetry in 1926, and her work of the time tends to show the formal experimentation typical of the period. It was evidently a fruitful and productive time, as the young poet flourished in the student milieu and earned praise from her teachers and colleagues. The literary courses were closed in 1929, a year before she would have graduated, and so her group finished Moscow University as "externs."

Osip Mandel'shtam described Petrovykh's character and appearance as a young woman in "[Female] Master of Guilty Glances" ("Masteritsa vinovatykh vzorov"),[3] a poem of 1934, when he was briefly (and unrequitedly) infatuated with her. He recounts a tiny mouth, a frail and slender body ("in the warm body, little skinny ribs"), a shyness covering depths of almost "Oriental" passion, and a warm attractiveness that lasted for Petrovykh's whole life. The poem finally likens her to the Virgin Mary, an equivalence that may be determined by Petrovykh's first name and by Russian culture's expectation that all women be maternal, supportive and intuitive. For Mandel'shtam she is a support and intercessor, and she enjoys special access to the world of psychic and poetic truth.

In the early 1930s Petrovykh visited Max Voloshin, a surviving link with the great Symbolist poets and for decades a mentor and admirer of women poets. She met Boris Pasternak in 1928 and was a close friend by the early 1930s; she made the acquaintance of Anna Akhmatova in the fall of 1933. These poets had exerted a tremendous moral and creative influence on twentieth-century poetry, but by the early 1930s their writing and publishing careers had been suppressed or reshaped by the Soviet regime. Translating became unusually important in a society where writing nonsycophantic poetry was unprofitable and often horribly dangerous; even such fine Russian poets as Akhmatova and Pasternak had difficulty publishing original poetry and were compelled to work as translators for financial as well as political reasons. Tellingly, poets of Petrovykh's generation took up translation almost from the start. Petrovykh began working as a translator in 1934, with Yiddish poems by Peretz Markish. Poetic translation let her earn a living as a writer without having to extol new heroes like hydroelectric dams, and with less fear of costly political errors. In addition to Yiddish, Petrovykh translated poetry from Armenian, Bulgarian, Croatian, Czech, Lithuanian, Polish, Serbian and other languages, relying on sublinear literal translated versions when working from languages she did not know. Her translations preserve both the individual character of the authors and the high poetic refinement of the translator. They read well in Russian and are a worthy part of the era's outstanding translation culture.

Petrovykh was horrified at the changes she saw around her; she was a young adult as Russian society was changing drastically under collectivization and increasing Stalinist repression. Translation did absorb most of her writing energy through the rest of her life, but her poetic output, based on surviving publications, had already shrunk considerably by 1932–1933, even before she began working as a literary translator.

Petrovykh married Vitalii Dmitrievich Golovachev in 1934, after he returned from his first arrest and exile. He was arrested again in 1937 and reportedly died in a prison camp in 1942. Petrovykh remained alone with their young daughter Arina (affectionately nicknamed Arisha), who was, judging from the poems about her,[4] a crucial psychological anchor for her mother. Losing a husband to the Stalinist Gulag brought Petrovykh close to other widows and survivors like Akhmatova and Lidiia Chukovskaia; the threat of harm to her daughter was one more reason for her to handle the era's moral dilemmas with caution. Like Akhmatova and Chukovskaia, however, Petrovykh wrote works "for the drawer" that harshly criticized her society and all those who remained silent in the face of government crimes. Her poems form a small and bitter opus, condemning both Stalinist oppression and the cooperation of those who lived through it unharmed. For an author in this genre, as Osip Mandel'shtam's fate proves, obscurity was a definite advantage: writing about *that* was incredibly risky for anyone, but especially for a woman with a young daughter whose husband had died in a camp, who thus would be especially vulnerable to searches or denunciation. Such texts were too dangerous to keep in written form and could only be preserved through memorization. Several of these previously privately kept poems were finally published in the journal *Znamia* in January 1989, not long before the Soviet Union ceased to exist.

In July 1941, after the Soviet Union was drawn into World War II by the German invasion, Petrovykh and her daughter were evacuated with other writers south to the city of Chistopol' on the Kama River, in the Tatar Autonomous Republic. Since they could not make a living there, Petrovykh returned to Moscow as soon as possible, in September of 1942. Like many people who had survived the horrors of the 1930s, she experienced the war years as largely positive and affirming, and her poetic production in 1942 and 1943 swelled abruptly. The war inspired a new patriotic note in some poems, expressing the sense that this epochal and hard-fought struggle would change life in Russia for the better. She also took the fate of her own generation of writers and intellectuals as a poetic topic. By now Petrovykh's writing, perhaps influenced by her older, more famous friends, turned from youthful formal experimentation to more classical meters and forms. In 1942 she joined the Soviet Writers' Union.

In 1942 or 1943 Petrovykh submitted a manuscript of poems to the prestigious publishing house Sovetskii pisatel' (Soviet Writer). The manuscript was rejected in an internal review by Evgeniia Knipovich, formerly a close friend of Aleksandr Blok but now an influential Soviet critic. The rejection condemned Petrovykh's verses as pessimistic, not suited to contemporary Soviet reality. The fact that Petrovykh was the widow of a repressed "enemy of the people" cannot have helped her position. This failure both stung and threatened her; although she might shake off the insulting and tendentious description of her poetry, it suggested that even with the relatively free cultural climate of the war years her poetry would not find a place in the Soviet publishing establishment. Unlike the older poets she knew, she could not draw strength from past success, and being cut off from readers put a further block in her way. After she learned that the book had been rejected her writing production immediately dropped: eighteen poems survive from 1943, but there is only one extant poem dated 1945, and then a silence of about ten years punctuated by only four or five poems.

Given all her admiring friends and good connections in the literary establishment, the fact that Petrovykh did not publish more of her poetry has puzzled many of her readers. Several theories have been advanced to explain it: that she was shy, reticent and lacking in self-confidence; that she was too much of a perfectionist to publish anything but the very best poetry; that she was oriented toward the traditionally "female" roles of helping and nurturing other poets and the "feminine" literary professions of translating and editing; that she was too elevated and admirable a person to care about vulgar things like a publishing career. As Marina Ptushkina points out, these were indeed parts of Petrovykh's character, but the publisher's archival records place things in a different light.[5]

Another important experience during the war was Petrovykh's trip to Armenia in autumn of 1944, along with her friend, the poet and translator Vera Zviagintseva. There she met and worked on translations with talented young poets, and she fell in love with the splendid nature and culture of the southern republic. (The Armenians remembered her services too: the one small book including some of her original poems published in her lifetime was produced by her friends in Erevan.) She continued working hard as a translator, suffering chronic financial trouble. At the same time, she gave money to Akhmatova for her to send to her son in prison. The sacrifice Petrovykh made could not prevent her from preserving her own personality and human dignity. Even in her crowded communal apartment on Belovaia Street where she shared two rooms with her daughter, the larger room was often given over to guests such as Akhmatova.

Years of professional difficulty and personal suffering undoubtedly helped to forge Petrovykh's generous and self-sacrificing character, strengthening her mission to support and maintain what she could of her nation's culture; it did not encourage her to concentrate on her own creative career. Her triumph was personal: preserving her own personality, not abandoning friends who had fallen out of official favor and never writing a poem in praise of Stalin or the Soviet lie despite the hardships of her life. These accomplishments are described in her later poetry, as she evaluates her creative accomplishments.

After Stalin's death in 1953, Petrovykh slowly returned to writing original poetry. She lived in a small, tree-shaded apartment on Khoroshevskii Highway, and writers and friends would visit her there for professional and moral support. In the early 1960s she ran a translating seminar for young poets along with Zviagintseva and David Samoilov. She was a mentor to many young poets, especially those who found no support in the official system. Her characteristic word in addressing others, "Milyi" or "Milaia" (Dear),[6] shows that she chose to deal with the often troubled people who came to her on the basis of their essential *dearness*, providing them an unfailing emotional response and an almost familial connection. The gratitude that others owed her could presumably have influenced their high opinions of her poetry. Akhmatova, for example, informed Chukovskaia that she considered Petrovykh's poem "Grant me a meeting" ("Naznach' mne svidan'e")[7] a masterpiece of twentieth-century love poetry. Evgenii Evtushenko's comment that her poetry was underrated by official critics and overrated by her friends reflects a certain political as well as artistic stance,[8] but Petrovykh herself (who was critical of the prolific and often self-indulgent Thaw poets) might have agreed with it. She knew "her place" in a female poetic tradition dominated by the "meek" Akhmatova and the "furious" Marina Tsvetaeva, in the terms of one of her poems, and she also knew she would be compared to these two outstanding poets because of her gender. Petrovykh's poetry does relate to a female tradition of refined but unpretentious, often highly musical lyrics, recalling folk songs and lamentations; she combines ordinary words into extremely moving and subtle verse. Her poetry reveals a strong emotional variability, from deep depression to passionate infatuation, but often centers on the nature of poetry and the author's own fate as a poet, or poet manqué. Thus she maintains the concern with poetic personality and creation of a poetic "I" that so marked the first decades of the twentieth century. Her editing work was first-class; she saw Akhmatova's 1961 book *Stikhotvoreniia* as well as many others through the publishing process, receiving no credit in print. To shepherd someone else's poetry through the hurdles of the system, she could be a persistent and effective advocate.

Amid the many coerced compromises of the Soviet system, it is not surprising that even a strongly moral personality such as Petrovykh could wind up in a dubious position. "Grant me a meeting," the poem Akhmatova so admired, was addressed to Aleksandr Fadeev, who committed suicide in 1956 after stepping down as head of the Writers' Union, supposedly haunted by memories of his role in the official persecution of writers. For years after Petrovykh wrote poems mourning the anniversary of his death. This was a personal rather than political attraction, but the poet's own livelihood depended on her good standing in the union structures through which literary assignments and rewards were dispensed. Like everyone else concerned with publishing literature, she was coopted into the system. Petrovykh knew this and wrote about it, harshly criticizing her own lack of courage. Withdrawing from publishing her own work may also have served as one way to maintain her integrity.

In her later life, especially after Akhmatova's death in 1966, Petrovykh suffered a great deal from creative blocks and a sense of having buried her own talent. A few years before her death, she wrote in her notebook, "It's a misfortune when there is some talent and no sense of vocation" ("Beda, kogda est' kakie-to dannye i net prizvaniia").[9] She never forgot her own potential and the promise of her youth, but she judged her achievements severely against those of more productive or resilient writers. Her position after Akhmatova's death is comparable to that of late Romantic poets in the nineteenth century, especially women such as Karolina Pavlova and Evdokiia Rostopchina, who also emerged as artistic personalities just as the terms of literary valuation were about to change drastically. Petrovykh's creative personality, as her poems demonstrate, was an odd combination of blocks and gifts. In compensation, she maintained and advocated a moral vocation: "The point of life is not in bliss, but in development of the soul" ("Smysl zhizni ne v blazhenstvii, a v razvitii dushi").[10]

Since Petrovykh's death in 1979 interest in and publication of her poetry have gradually grown. Her original verses are no longer a well-kept secret, a mere pencil notation beside her achievements as a translator, and a far broader circle of readers can now judge their value. Her place on the "inside" of Russian poetry as friend, addressee, editor and mentor of poets means that her writing played a role in the development of Russian poetry in spite of meager and tardy publication. Now that her poetry is available to a wider audience, it may capitivate even readers who did not know the charming author personally.

Sibelan Forrester

The Sea

You, bisexual one, it's like this
I love you. How transparent your air is!
But long sleep is intolerable—
Your obstinacy demands: otherwise!

Dove-color has palled, and you give birth
To any color out of deep gloom—
Violet, lilac, or sky-blue,

Or a languishing green.

By day—the sun sails along the bottom,
Frightening the dolphin it meets.
Slit open the robust wave—
Inside it is a sunny heartwood!

But the dark green waves,
They retreat from the cliff,
Sensing the quiet of night,
And they press close together,

And the moon rises up
Above the strained horizon,
Through the sleeping sea it
Passes with a sleepless tremor.

No one can live alone in the world:
In the water a second moon shivers,
And the waves gleam, wailing,
Striking against the black shore . . .

One, a second, a millionth wave,
While a person is full of confusion:
He has recalled and started longing
For the unbegotten, the bisexual.

1929
Gurzuf

The Muse

When by some accident I dip my pen
Past the inkwell, next to it, into the moon—
Into a creeping lake of black nights,
A nightingale brook overgrown with daydream—
Different consonances race from the pen,
An astounded patina of silver is on them,

As if they are birds, I'm afraid to take them,
But the lines, crowding, fill up the notebook.
I encounter you, feral night,
Both our fate and our origin exactly the same:
We are both dark to untrusting eyes,
Our fatherland is single and immortal.
I recall how the day overcame you,
You remember how I was chipped off the cliffs,
You eternally wander from the milky paths,
You like to hide in the fissures of verse.
Offspring of a daydream, rough draft of a nightingale,
Single reader, my muse,
I see you out, not having thanked you,
But with the ecstatic foam that runs from rhymes.

1930

The Bottom of the Forest

Oh, thicket of flickering scales,
Milliongreened rustlingness,
Into my heart—your silvery breezes,
Into my face—your restless shadows.

I walk unsteadily below winged water,
Barely swaying with waves of coolness.
A young nightingale perches on my palm,
And roulades in the foliage answer with quivering.

And I see the motionless coral of the pine,
Crowned by a dark-needled storm-cloud . . .
Who has covered this stem with turbid fire?
Who dressed the branches in that prickly dusk?

I know, under the rude bark of the birches
Is hidden the most transparent heartwood.
Their branches are bowed by a richness of tears,
Green, like leaves, quivering innocently,

And the black scars of memory are fresh
On the white trunk . . . it's the forest's chronicle.
Read just the start—and an invisible ancient
Veil will slide from your soul.

And suddenly the whole forest is lit up
With instantaneous rain, shadowed by dense dreams . . .
How bitterly we thirst, how greedily we await
What is in front of us always and everywhere!

1932

Without looking around, don't take a single step.
Will there be enough bravery for bravery?
It's no wonder we aren't loud, aren't lively,
Tortures were lying in wait around us.
We dream of a raven with its ravenous cawing.
It's no wonder we won't breathe a single word,
It's no wonder a crust of ice forms on the heart
And we can no longer be saddened by anything.
And there's comfort only in the heavenly blue,
And in winter white hoarfrost on the branches,
And the green leaves in the spring . . .
Are *we* guilty in this pitiful disinterestedness!
We live without reasoning craftily,
And we aren't so very criminal, indeed. . . .

You are accursed, not only criminal!
Is it a great honor that you can't be bought,
However much you were frightened, trembled—
You lowered your eyelids, you tightened your lips
In a thunderous graveyard silence,
Age-long, helpless, all-powerful,
And neither there nor from us will come forgiveness,
Only an inherited call to vengeance.

1939

Don't cry, don't complain, you shouldn't,
You can't help grief with tears.
In the dawn a reward's concealed
For a night of martyrdom.

Cast off the fiery bedspread
And hastily put on your dress
And go away to anywhere
In the day, flushing with heat.

You are overcome by the sun.
Its irresistible ardor
Will flash in the very depths of your pupils,
Lie down in your heart, like a sunburn.

When the dominion of its rays
Pours together in your body,
Tell the truth—can it be
That you have been caressed more hotly?

Go to the river and throw yourself in the water
And, if you can—swim off,
What a freedom you will rouse,
What a love you'll entrust yourself to!

You'll hardly be able to recall your grief,
And you won't be able to name—when
You were kissed more tenderly
And more sweetly than by the water.

Again you're desirable and splendid,
And you won't come back to yourself at once
From these caressing and imperious
Hands flowing along your body.

And the air? It's with you to the grave,
Severe or blue as the sky,

You're both enviably fortunate—
You breathe it, and it breathes you.

And the rain will come to you over the roof,
Always varying the same rhythm.
In its heart straightest and highest of all,
All night it cries over you.

You see—there are many powers in love.
You must call them your own.
It's not true, you are not alone
In your repudiated love.

Don't cry, don't complain, you shouldn't,
You can't help grief with tears.
In the dawn a reward's concealed
For a night of martyrdom.

1942

What inspiration?—it's simply that
Anguish comes up and grabs you by the throat,
And the heart is burning out from quick growth
And the time of terrible minutes comes,
Deciding at once—a noose or a bullet,
A river or razor, but in defiance
An unclear something, guarding you,
Approaches to pronounce the verdict.
It reads—first wrathfully, then tenderly, muffled,
First distinctly, then leaving out words,
And only by a sheer effort of hearing
Can you barely make them out,
With a clumsy pen literally, word for word,
Barely keeping up, you keep a record,
Afraid to leave out or remember wrong . . .
(A noose or a bullet, a river or knife? . . .)

And you write further—not hearing, not seeing,
In a blissful fever not fearing nonsense,
Not remembering pain, not trusting offense—
And suddenly you realize that this is poetry.

1943

The Eve of August 6

In what a raging silence
You froze, grew quiet, night! . . .
You can't be estranged, nor overcome
By either days or nights.

In agitated silence
You are wrapped from end to end,
You perceive above the whole country
The beating of all its hearts.

Oh, how close you were to them
When along the sky and the earth
The first peals raced off
Over Belgorod and Orel.

More inspired, more triumphant than anyone
The thunders arose at full height,
Until the twelfth, the final one
Turned out to be the light of stars.

And it seemed that tears were pouring
From the most difficult depth—
They will draw, if only for a moment,
War's evil pain from the heart!

But that time has not arrived,
It has only come very very close.
You weren't gleaming, night, for nothing—
You make day bright there too.

In us a secret undarkenable ray
Is tensed now to the point of trembling.
You have become the most beloved,
I can't find any names fit for you.

1943

Universal

Even in my own dear residence
Beyond the walls live . . . other residents.
Softer, softer, my dear friends!
Not taking part in our conversation,
The most inquisitive of neighbors
Are listening, holding their breath . . .
Just one time to let slip a sharp word,
Just to know—am I timid or squeamish?
Is it frightening or disgusting to touch the mud?
But you walk around this sticky slush
With a wretched forgiving smile,
Drawing strength from your indignant heart.

(1950s?)

In a Minute of Despair

All your life you just search for a word,
One single word.
It will flash out of the darkness
And suddenly go out again.

You won't find the paths to it
And don't feel sorry about that:
It won't outpower the darkness,
It won't become a light.

So forget about it, understand
That searching is in vain,
That all the same it has no power
To connect people with people.

Why do you squander your strength
Your whole life in a fight with yourself,
When any sound will fall silent
Before the muteness of the grave.

7 August 1958

Armenia

There's only one Armenia in the world,
All people have—their own.
From timidity, from ineptitude
I haven't been celebrating her.

But how I have offended myself—
I haven't seen you for twenty years,
My faraway, my longed-for,
My promised land!

Believe me, my love under a bushel,
That you are my secret song treasure,
My love—mute and difficult,
It's not in tune with any old word.

Only the autumn days are with me
And that faraway mountain,
Which rises as the shield of Armenia
In snows of cast silver,

That magnificent two-headed
Dear distant mountain,
Which gleams with agelong glory,
As ancient as the universe.

And the secret of the island of Sevan,
Where, like tribute to gray-haired ages,
There are both the vaults of a Christian temple
And the smoke of sacrifices.

The eagles of Zvarnots are cut into the rock,
Their plumage is rusty moss. . . .
Oh distant land, beloved land,
My brief dream, my long sigh. . . .

1966

Fate looked after me with both eyes open,
So that no loss would suddenly pass me by.
I lost my friend, my husband, my brother,
I received letters from beyond the grave.

It was especially attentive to me
And generous with mute torments.
And happiness would disappear without return . . .
For what, I can't understand, such malice?

And all on the quiet, all in the dark.
And here on the edge of the threshold
Sits an old woman by a broken trough.

And so? you'd say. An old woman indeed.
No memory, no vision, no hearing.
She sits, mumbling about fate, about God. . . .

1967

Neither Akhmatovan meekness,
Nor Tsvetaevan fury—
In the start out of shyness,
And later on out of oldness.

Haven't so many years in this locale
Been lived through in futility?
Who, after all, who are you?
Call back out of obscurity! . . .

Oh, how the heart is poisoned
By the muteness of many years!
What on earth will be left
In that ultimate last minute?

Only the start of a melody,
Only the motif of a promise,
Only the torment of fruitlessness,
Only the scandal of beggary.

Only a reed will begin to sway
With that melody, hardly begun . . .
May someone catch the sound
Of how it sings, how it weeps.

1967

Translated by Sibelan Forrester

Notes on Biography

1. Marina Palei, "Tvoia nemyslimaia chistota," *Literaturnoe obozrenie* 6 (1987): 61.
2. *Izbrannoe* (Moscow: Khudozhestvennaia literatura, 1991), 346.
3. Osip Mandel'shtam, *Sobranie sochinenii,* Vol. 1 (Washington, DC: Interlanguage Literary Associates, 1964), 194–95.
4. One of these poems is very well translated in Stephanie Sandler, "Mother, Daughter, Self and Other: The Lyrics of Inna Lisnianskaia and Maria Petrovykh," in *Engendering Slavic Literature*, ed. P. Chester and S. Forrester (Bloomington: Indiana University Press, 1996), 203.
5. Marina Ptushkina, "Zhizn' kak tvorchestvo," introduction to *Koster v nochi* (Iaroslavi': Verkhne-Volzhskoe knizhnoe izdatel'stvo, 1991), 7.
6. Cited in Sandler, "Mother, Daughter, Self, and Other," 216.
7. Translated as "Give me a rendezvous" by Sharon Leiter in *Russian Language Triquarterly,* 105.
8. Sandler, in *Dictionary of Russian Women Writers*, ed. Ledkovsky et al., 503.
9. *Izbrannoe*, 370.
10. *Izbrannoe*, 366.

Bibliography

Primary Works

Dal'nee derevo. Stikhi. Iz armianskoi poèzii. Perevody. Erevan: Izdatel'stvo "Aiastan," 1968.

Prednaznachen'e. Stikhi raznykh let. Moscow: Sovetskii pisatel', 1983.

Cherta gorizonta. Stikhi i perevody.Vospominaniia o Marii Petrovykh. Erevan: Sovetakan grokh, 1986.

Izbrannoe. Stikhotvoreniia. Perevody. Iz pis'mennogo stola. Moscow: Khudozhestvennaia literatura, 1991.

Koster v nochi. Stikhi i perevody. Iaroslavl': Verkhne-Volzhskoe knizhnoe izdatel'stvo, 1991.

In Translation:

"The Line of the Horizon," "Give me a rendezvous in this world" and "The air is motionless with heat." Trans. Sharon Leiter. *Russian Language Triquarterly* 5 (Winter 1973): 103–06.

Secondary Works

Chukovskaia, Lidiia. *Zapiski ob Anne Akhmatovoi.* Vol. 2. Paris: YMCA Press, 1980. 183, 185, 270–71, 332, 446–7, 564 (n. 117).

Glen, Nika. "Introduction" [to Vol. 2. *Stikhi iz arkhiva* by Mariia Petrovykh]. *Znamia* 1 (January 1989): 90.

Lavrin, Aleksandr. "Polnoi meroi." Rev. of *Prednaznachen'e. Novyi mir* 8 (August 1984): 251–52.

Loiter, Sof'ia M. "I ia voskresnu ne dysha . . . " *Kareliia* 139 (1996): 286.

———. "'. . . I priniali Mar'iu Sergeevnu edinoglasno v angely': K 90-letiiu M. Petrovykh." *Litsej,* 3 March 1998.

———. "'. . . Sud'ba za mnoi prismatrivala v oba!': K 85-letiiu Marii Petrovykh" *Litsej,* 3 March 1993.

———. "Zametki o Marii Petrovykh." *Marii: Literaturnyi al'manakh,* Vol. 2 (Petrozavodsk: Izdatel'stvo Petrozavodskogo gosudarstvennogo universiteta, 1995), 226–40.

Mandel'shtam, Osip. "Masteritsa vinovatykh vzorov." *Sobranie sochinenii.* Vol. 1. Washington, DC: Inter-Language Literary Associates, 1964. 194–95 [variants 463, notes 519].

Palei, Marina. "Tvoia nemyslimaia chistota." Rev. of *Cherta gorizonta. Literaturnoe obozrenie* 6 (June 1987): 61–64.

Ptushkina, Marina. "Kak rasskazat' dushu." Rev. of *Prednaznachen'e. Druzhba narodov* 8 (August 1985): 263–65.

Sandler, Stephanie. "The Canon and the Backward Glance: Akhmatova, Nikolaeva, Lisnianskaia, Petrovykh." *Fruits of Her Plume.* Ed. Helena Goscilo. New York: M.E. Sharpe, 1993. 113–33.

———. "Mother, Daughter, Self and Other: The Lyrics of Inna Lisnianskaia and Mariia Petrovykh. *Engendering Slavic Literatures.* Ed. Pamela Chester and Sibelan Forrester. Bloomington: Indiana University Press, 1996. 201–22.

———. "Petrovykh, Mariia Sergeevna." *Dictionary of Russian Women Writers.* Ed. Marina Ledkovsky, Charlotte Rosenthal and Mary Zirin. Westport, CT: Greenwood Press, 1994. 502–04.

Sarnov, Benedikt. "Umeite domolchat'sia do stikhov." *Literaturnoe obozrenie* 8 (August 1985): 49–52.

Sergeeva, Emma. "'Vsegda—Rossiia. Vsegda—Armeniia.' Shtrikhi k portretu Marii Petrovykh." *Literaturnaia Armeniia* 8 (August 1985): 263–65.

Tarkovskii, Arsenii. "Taina Marii Petrovykh." Introduction to *Prednaznachen'e* by Mariia Petrovykh. Moscow: Sovetskii pisatel', 1983. 3–6.

Vinokurova, I. "Kak byt' neshchastlivym" [rev. of *Cherta gorizonta*]. *Znamia* 12 (December 1987): 231–33.

Elizaveta Polonskaia

Elizaveta Polonskaia (1890–1969).
Courtesy of Leslie Dorfman.

Elizaveta Grigor'evna Movshenson-Polonskaia (1890–1969), known to her readers as Elizaveta Polonskaia, was a poet, translator, children's writer, journalist and noted memoirist. Her career began before the revolution and spanned five decades of the Soviet period. In a 1921 review the formalist critic B. Èikhenbaum offered these words of praise: "Polonskaia's verse is distinguished by its expressiveness: in it one can feel a muscular tension, in it there are strong verbal gestures. . . . She does not sing, she speaks—with strength, with oratorical pathos."[1] As a member of the Serapion Brothers, a Petrograd literary circle of the 1920s, Polonskaia had personal ties to some of the most important writers and critics of her day. She was an active member of the Leningrad literary community, where she is still remembered with respect by the older generation and, at the same time, almost completely unknown to those too young to recall the publication of her last collection in 1966. There is no critical edition of Polonskaia's work. Aside from a few encyclopedia entries, a paragraph here and there in various memoirs, and a citation where the Serapions are listed by name, almost nothing has been written about Polonskaia, either in Russia or in the West, since her death in 1969.[2]

Polonskaia's poetry, like that of most of her female contemporaries, is not easily classified. Raised on Heine and the nineteenth-century Russian civic poets Nekrasov and Nadson, she was moved to write verse seriously only after discovering the Russian Symbolists. Forced to flee arrest for underground Bolshevik activity in 1908, she left St. Petersburg and went to Paris, where she studied medicine at the Sorbonne from 1908 to 1914. In Paris, Russian friends from the Communist party introduced her to the works of Bal'mont, Briusov and Blok, who became her idols. Her earliest poems are imitative, and most were never published; however, her awakening to the aesthetic and expressive possibilities in poetry was decisive. Having come to Paris as a political émigré, Polonskaia was soon drawn more to literary than to political activities. Her first published poems, a cycle of love lyrics, appeared in *Evenings (Vechera)*, a monthly published by her friend Il'ia Ehrenburg, in 1914. As she wrote later in a letter to the critic Pavel Medvedev, "I fell in love with Paris forever. Emigration alienated me from the Party."[3]

Polonskaia returned to Russia in 1915, serving as a doctor on the southwestern front and returning to Petrograd in the spring of 1917. The experiences of war and revolution are reflected in the emergence of a mature and decidedly public voice in her poetry. In addition to the change in content, Polonskaia's poetry acquired a formal restraint and expressive power, which she later attributed to her training at the Literary Studio established by Gorky for young writers and translators in 1919; in particular, she cites Gumilev, the founder of the Acmeist school, as having taught her to "give form to the lyric impulse."[4] Yet, although her poetic style has been compared by many critics with that of the Acmeists, in particular Mandel'shtam and Akhmatova, Polonskaia herself was never classified as an Acmeist. Having passed through Symbolism and Acmeism, she returned to her own particular brand of civic verse, written in a rhetorical, often biblical style sometimes described as masculine, yet with a distinctly feminine point of view.

From her first collection, *Omens* (*Znamen'ia,* 1921), Polonskaia's poetry expressed a deep, maternal concern for the fate of humanity. Revolution and civil war are treated metaphorically as birth pangs of Soviet Russia, the memory of which will eventually be overshadowed by love, as in "How strange that we shall forget everything" ("Ne stranno-li, chto my zabudem vse"): "Thus a woman, kissing the rounded forehead / Of her child, her own flesh, will not say, will not recall, / That she shuddered in terrible strain, / In the tormenting struggle of birth." Alongside the metaphor of revolution as birth, there is also a mother's drive to protect her young, to preserve fragile human life in a world turned treacherous and violent. "With a soft sponge, with warm water" ("Miagkoi gubkoi, teploi vodoi") is a mother's reproach to her country: "Is there, then, no longer in our land / Any proper place for our sons, / That we have given them to war / And given them death for a bride?" The mother in these poems is frequently compared to an animal; she is alternately the mama goat from Russian folklore, saving her kids from the belly of the wolf in "Fairytale" ("Skazka") or a wolf herself, hiding scraps to feed her young in "In memory of a harsh year" ("Na pamiat' o tiazhelom gode"). The stark imagery of Darwinian struggle for survival is cast in elevated, often archaic language and crafted into tight syllabotonic verse; the dominant meters are iambic tetrameter, pentameter and hexameter, with a few poems in the three-stressed *dol'niki* popularized by the symbolists.

As in *Omens*, the poet's attitude toward revolution in her second collection, *Under a Stone Rain* (*Pod kamennym dozhdem*, 1923), is ambiguous. She accepts its historical inevitability, even admires the courage of the "guileless host / Of those who labored with Her and grew heavy with weariness, / And can no longer rise from the fields of Mars" ("Triumphal days" ["Torzhestvennye dni," 1923]). The image of revolution takes on a bloody majesty, fascinates by virtue of sheer spectacle in "What are Thalia, Euterpe, Melpomene?" ("Chto Taliia, Evterpa, Mel'pomena?" 1923). The solemnity of events is heightened by the increasing frequency of stately Alexandrine verse. Yet Polonskaia retains misgivings about the violence and chaos that have been unleashed, even hinting that the actual event is a corruption of the ideal: "O, Revolution, O Book among books! / By blood and filth the lofty pages are stuck together / And, like an alarm your frenzied tongue sounds, / But there is no teacher, and no one to teach" ("O Revolution . . ."

["O Revoliutsiia, o kniga mezhdu knig," 1923]). Furthermore, she makes it clear that, in terms of social change, the revolution is far from complete. The gap between rich and poor still exists, and beggars, pickpockets and prostitutes still walk the streets of "the freest country in the world" ("So, then, you think it is over" ["Tak znachit ty dumaesh' èto konets," 1923]). Once again, freer forms are outnumbered by traditional syllabotonic verse, this time with an increase both in iambic hexameter and in ternary meters. However, the liveliest and most subversive piece in *Under a Stone Rain* is "Ballad of the Fugitive" ("Ballada o begletse," c. 1922); the alternation of free *dol'niki* with amphibrachs and the shifting rhyme patterns are a foretaste of Polonskaia's later formal experimentation.

Although Polonskaia had her champions, she also had to contend with political attacks by the more hard-line Marxist critics. Aside from the fact that she was openly critical of the regime in certain of her poems, not to mention her penchant for satire,[5] there was also the fact of her membership in the Serapions, who became embroiled in a fierce polemic with Marxist critics in 1922.[6] The Serapions maintained their right to be artists first and communists second, stressing the need for artistic freedom from any prescribed ideology; it was a position that was to haunt some of them in later decades. Polonskaia was attacked for her portrayal of Len'ka Pantaleev, a handsome bandit and murderer, in her popular narrative poem "In the Noose: A Lyric Film" ("V petle. Liricheskii fil'm," 1925). During a period of intensifying party concern about the morals of Soviet youth, one critic complained that young people were singing Polonskaia's refrain in the streets: "Len'ka Pantaleev, / The terror of detectives. / On his arm a bracelet, / Deep blue eyes."[7] Her portrait of a woman Bolshevik, "Carmen" (1924), also prompted some critics to include Polonskaia among writers considered a bad influence for "romanticizing criminals and prostitutes."[8]

This fascination with the more anarchic elements of Soviet society, reflected both in Polonskaia's heroes and in her frequent use of slang, reflects her twin rebellions. On the one hand, she resisted Lenin's New Economic Policy (NEP), which allowed a limited return to private enterprise and thus created conditions for a return to bourgeois values. Polonskaia's portrayal of the new class of "Nepmen" is consistently negative: for example, "human swine" watch the staged pursuit of a thief at the dog races in "Dogs" ("Sobaki," 1927), and a fur-clad passerby ignores a ragged beggar woman and her child in "The Bridge" ("Most," 1924).

On the other hand, Polonskaia's attitudes toward sexuality, marriage and the "woman question" also place her on the liberal side of public opinion in the 1920s, when the party was divided over these issues. Polonskaia was a living example of Kollontai's ideal of the modern single woman. She never married, although she did take her surname from Lev Polonskii, the father of her son. Her poetic persona encompasses both sacrificial motherhood and an assertive sexuality that subjugates both lover and son to a female will. In "Love" ("Liubov'," 1924), we read: "For I created you. You did not exist at all. / We all give birth to you, mothers, wives, lovers. . . . Therefore do not think, my darling, that you exist on this earth: / You are created only by my desire and will." Carmen, the "wanton factory girl" who takes up a rifle against Kolchak, is described emphatically as "no mother and no wife." Indeed, marriage is described as domestic slavery in "Carmen," as well as in another, "The Swan" ("Lebed'," 1924), in which the swan-maiden escapes captivity by a man who forces her to rear sons. Such attitudes could still be expressed in the 1920s, but once Stalin declared the "woman question" officially solved in 1930, they became taboo in art as in public policy.

Also problematic was Polonskaia's expression of her Jewish identity. She felt no allegiance to the religion, but she never lost her sense of kinship with the people. Certain critics, including her teacher, Gumilev, recoiled from the defiant and, some felt, tasteless assertions in such early poems as "Shylock" ("Sheilok," 1921) and "I cannot abide the infant Jesus" ("Ia ne mogu terpet' mladentsa Iisusa," 1921);[9] the reaction was so strong that it was not until 1929 that she published another "Jewish" poem, "Encounter" ("Vstrecha," 1929). Here kinship is affirmed, not with the proud Old Testament prophet or the vengeful Shylock, but with a hook-nosed beggar woman. Having once defiantly proclaimed herself a Jew, the lyric heroine now hesitantly acknowledges the connection, calling herself "a stranger," but the old woman recognizes in her the sad eyes, languid step and muted laugh of a true Jewess: "And though you have forgotten your faith and your kin, / A id iz immer a id." In 1930 the Jewish Section of the Communist party was shut down, as the Women's Section had been. A new campaign was launched against "all varieties of Jewish nationalism in a Communist guise,"[10] thus creating an environment hostile even to such ambivalent expressions of Jewish identity.

The increasing political and thematic complexity of Polonskaia's poetry in the late 1920s is accompanied by a corresponding growth in generic and metrical complexity. *A Stubborn Calendar* (*Upriamyi kalendar'*, 1929), which represents her output from 1924 to 1927, is a departure from the style of the first two collections. It includes lyrics, cycles and narrative pieces in various voices. Several are polymetric, mixing binary and ternary meters, syllabotonic and tonic verse, sometimes within a strophe. In addition, several types of logaeodic line appear. Polonskaia later described this collection as her poetic diary, chronicling "love, hate, contempt, and pride in the people of our epoch";[11] in it she ranges from sensual love lyrics, such as "You ask me why" (Ty sprashivaesh', pochemu") and

"Parting" ("Razluka," both undated), to the political invective of "Dogs" and "The Bridge." The unifying feature is rebellion, from Carmen and Len'ka Pantaleev to the elegy for Esenin, which ends with the lines: "Bon voyage to you from our most irreverent brotherhood! / For we are all madcaps. Someday / We too will grow tired of pretending" ("To Esenin" ["Eseninu," 1926]). In "Farewell Ode" ("Proshchal'naia oda," 1926), Polonskaia looks back fondly to her student days, a time of "iambs, love, and idleness." Chastened by the voice of "sober and humdrum years," she concludes with a resigned farewell to idleness: "My publisher is stern and my censor strict: / We part, dear friend, once and for all."

Throughout the 1920s Polonskaia practiced medicine, pursuing her literary activities in her scant free time. Besides publishing three collections of verse, she worked as a correspondent for *Leningrad Truth* (*Leningradskaia pravda*) and published translations and verse for children. In 1931 she quit her medical job and became a full-time writer. Ironically, the 1930s were to be her least productive years as a poet; she published only two collections, *Years* (*Goda*, 1935), a retrospective collection with only fourteen new poems, and *New Verse (Novye stikhi*, 1937). The bureaucratization of the literary profession in the early 1930s meant that, aside from her travels as a correspondent, much of Polonskaia's time was absorbed by congresses and meetings of the Writers' Union and with work in various "literary circles." One of these was a circle of young proletarian women writers associated with the journal *Worker Woman and Peasant Woman (Rabotnitsa i krest'ianka)*, for which she served as "literary consultant" throughout the 1930s.

Polonskaia's talent for civic verse served her well in the 1930s and 1940s, since practically no other type of verse was tolerated. However, she had to tailor her ideology carefully to the demands of socialist realism. She continued writing on the "woman question," but in a much more cautious vein. Although a few love poems appear in *New Verse* and *Times of Courage* (*Vremena muzhestva*, 1940), there is no hint of the bold sexuality of her earlier lyrics, and marriage is condemned only in Muslim or European contexts, as in "Sister from the East" ("Sestra iz vostoka," 1932) and "Margarita" (1936). In keeping with Stalinist rhetoric on the "new Soviet woman," Polonskaia's heroines in the 1930s and 1940s are agronomists ("Golden Rain" ["Zolotoi dozhd'," 1928]), parachutists ("Song of Youth" ["Pesnia iunosti," 1936], "The Young Falcon" ["Sokolenok," c. 1936]), war volunteers ("Three Gifts" ["Tri podarki," 1943]) and *komsomolki* ("Sister from the East" ["Sestra iz vostoka," 1932]; "Iangi-kishlak" [1932]). Polonskaia was also required by publishers to make certain adjustments in some of her more negative portraits of Soviet life, changes which implied that the setting was not Russia, but the West; for example, "Dogs," which had appeared in *A Stubborn Calendar*, became "The

Hamburg Manège" ("Gamburgskii manezh") in *Years*, with changes in the text to emphasize the geographical shift.

Most of Polonskaia's poetry from this period is beneath the aesthetic standard of her earlier work. Yet, at least in the 1930s, a few poems crept into her collections that are of a higher quality and that reveal an introspection out of tune with the puritanism and determined optimism of socialist realism. "An Inn in Spain" ("Traktir v Ispanii," 1935) and "Snow in the Mountains" ("Sneg v gorakh," 1937) are poignant evocations of the pain of a fleeting love affair. "Companions" ("Sputniki," 1935), a meditation on the stages of life, is a progression from the sweetness of youth to a final bitterness. There is also a feeling of exhaustion and alienation in "At the sewing factory . . ." ("Na shveinoi fabrike," 1935): "But the heart is worn out. You will not find another. / I pass through my native land a half-stranger— / Unrecognized, absent-minded, weak. . . ." The rise of fascism in Germany and the Spanish civil war provided politically safe subjects on which Polonskaia could write with passion and sincerity. She translated the works of such German antifascists as Weinert and Brecht, and her poem about the heroic death of a Spanish communist, "Song about Lina Odena" ("Pesnia o Line Odena," 1938), became a popular song.[12] Translation of Western classics served as another outlet for Polonskaia, a mask through which such risky topics as sex and politics could be raised. Her translation of Shakespeare's *Measure for Measure* was a bold choice for those years, given its portrayal of a corrupt tyrant, its frankly sexual plot and its bawdy humor.[13]

During World War II, Polonskaia returned briefly to medical practice, serving as doctor for a ballet school evacuated to a small town near Molotov until 1944. She managed to continue writing despite the privations of overwork, housing shortages and Siberian winters; publication, however, was no simple matter, given her isolation and the priorities of wartime. This was no time for introspection, particularly of a negative sort. The heroes of Polonskaia's seventh collection, *A Kama River Notebook* (*Kamskaia tetrad'*, 1945), are Red Army soldiers and the people of the Urals, who work tirelessly to supply them with weapons and ammunition. Women play mostly supporting roles, although they may also be found operating machines in the factories, as in "A Young Thing" ("Devchonka," 1943). Such poems as "I have closed the Russian stove" ("Russkuiu pech' ia zakryla," 1941–1942), in which the poet speaks of her weariness and despair and asks the Muse for strength, would have to wait almost twenty years for publication.

Polonskaia published no original verse from 1946 to 1956, although her archive contains at least ninety poems written during those years. She concentrated on translation, serving as head of the Translators' Section of the Leningrad Writers' Union for several years in the 1950s, and on journalism, writing mainly for the journal *Siren (Gudok)*. In 1956 her poems began appearing again in almanacs, and in 1960 she published a collection, *Verses and a Narrative Poem (Stikhotvoreniia i poèma)*. Her last collection, *Selections (Izbrannoe)*, appeared in 1966. However, these last two collections contain few new poems; they are largely retrospective, with a few previously unpublished pieces, some written as early as 1941. Much of Polonskaia's late poetry appeared not in her collections, but in periodicals. She was a regular contributor to *Day of Poetry (Den' poezii)*, an almanac that published her poems from 1961 through 1967, then featured tributes to her in 1969, the year of her death, and again in 1981.

Polonskaia's late verse, which was received enthusiastically by critics, is distinguished by its philosophical cast as well as its formal beauty. It is written predominantly in traditional meters, particularly iambic pentameter. According to one critic, Polonskaia "brought to life a new, Pushkinian tradition, and the bright and harmonic 'Pushkinian' attitude has been organically reinterpreted as the all-embracing feeling of the contemporary mother."[14] Meditations on aging and death are warmed by thoughts of nature, music, children, "the joy of thought, the joy of the heart, of the body . . . / No! I did not want to die yet . . ." ("I've fallen out of love with what was dear to my heart" ["Ia razliubila to, chto serdtsu milo," 1958]). Her love of children, far from being sentimental, comes across to the reader as an integral part of her concern for humanity. In "Rembrandt's Madonna" ("Madonna Rembrandta," 1965), her hopes and fears for a generation are concentrated in one child: "I don't know what awaits him in this world, / The sickening stench of Buchenwald ovens . . . / Or perhaps he will rise to the cosmos in a mighty rocket / To get the heavenly fire for his brothers. . . ."

Most important in Polonskaia's late poetry is the concept of memory as moral obligation. She saw herself as a witness and, as such, felt compelled to testify to what she had seen in her lifetime. In "A mother can be unjust at times" ("Byvaet mat' nespravedliva," 1957), she confronts the painful memory of abuses committed by the motherland upon her children: "They cannot forget. They cannot leave you. / You are a mother, not a lover. / . . . They dream of a stormy youth, / The fire of your civil battles. / And the old, dry wound / Bleeds again in the night." The poet's duty is clearly stated in "Memories" ("Vospominaniia," 1958), in which the dead address her: "If you wish, we shall cease to exist, / Like everything beautiful on earth, / And it is no affair of yours, / And you are not to blame. / But if you love more bravely, / Overcoming the dream of peace, / From the kingdom of the dead, like Orpheus, / You shall lead us behind you." Fellow poets are memorialized in Polonskaia's last poems, most notably Akhmatova, whom she called "the glorious muse of Russian verse" in "To Anna Akhmatova" ("Anne Axmatovoi," 1965).

Polonskaia's role as Orpheus was most vividly and successfully enacted in the literary memoirs she published in 1963–1966. Memoirs were a staple of literature during the 1960s, and Polonskaia herself makes a brief but memorable appearance in Ehrenburg's *People, Years, Life (Liudi, gody, zhizn'*, 1960).[15] Polonskaia's "My Acquaintance with Mikhail Zoshchenko" ("Moe znakomstvo s Mikhailom Zoshchenko," 1963) not only delighted her contemporaries but was also later the inspiration for a major scholarly work on Zoshchenko.[16] It was followed by a series of highly regarded reminiscences of the 1920s, as well as a piece, "Ten Years till October" ("Do oktiabria eshche desiat' let," 1965), about her experiences in the Bolshevik underground.

Polonskaia did not live to complete *Encounters (Vstrechi)*, her autobiography, although several pieces had appeared in journals and were subsequently to appear in collections of reminiscences about individual authors. After a prolonged battle with heart disease, she died in January 1969, leaving a large but fragmentary manuscript and hundreds of unpublished poems, whose dates of composition range from 1908 to 1967. Since her death, a few more short memoirs have appeared in print, and several previously unpublished poems have appeared in periodicals.

In April 1991, an article appeared in *Literary Gazette (Literaturnaia gazeta)* lamenting the fact that 1990 had passed without any public recognition of the centennial of this "noteworthy literary figure of the twenties and thirties." The author suggests that the reason for her obscurity is the unremarkable nature of her fate: "She did not leave, she was not persecuted, she died quietly in her communal apartment. . . . At times, the fate of an artist hinders objective evaluation."[17] There are, however, also other factors involved. As a woman writer, a non–Communist party member[18] and probably also a Jew, Polonskaia was always subject to marginalization. However, even more significant is the ideological flattening of her literary biography by critics and reviewers. Those who praised Polonskaia's poetry in the 1960s tended to minimize the controversial aspects of her early work, emphasizing instead its formal beauty and profound humanism. In general, the tone is one of respect for "one of the oldest Soviet poetesses";[19] there are cryptic allusions to her "complex path of ideological-artistic development,"[20] but after *Omens* she is said to have resolved her political uncertainties. Some of these same critics admit that Polonskaia's poetry from the 1920s is aesthetically superior to her output from the 1930s and 1940s, but they are obliged to point out the "ideological-thematic enrichment" of her poetry in the 1930s and during the war.[21] The cumulative effect of these reviews is to camouflage Polonskaia's early rebelliousness behind a mask of venerable, but oddly neutral, respectability; she became a literary grandmother figure who enjoyed a surge of popularity before fading from benign neglect after her death.

Ironically, Polonskaia herself participated in the rewriting of her own earlier poetic identity. All of her retrospective collections are organized in such a way as to mislead the unwary reader about the dates, titles and addressees of certain of her poems (most notably "Ballad of the Fugitive"), and also as to where they first appeared.[22] There were also the above-mentioned changes in setting, which turned critiques of Soviet society into indictments of the decadent West. Many of the changes from *Years* were retained in the last two collections. In addition, some of the most powerful poems from *Omens* have been changed in subtle ways that reduce their pathos and emphasize instead an optimistic and "life-affirming" attitude more congenial to Thaw values.[23] The fact that Polonskaia felt compelled to resort to such subterfuges in republishing her early poetry, even during the Thaw, shows how conservative Soviet publishers remained and how deeply ingrained the habits of internal censorship had become.

The result of all these changes and omissions is that Polonskaia is better remembered for the compromises she made than for her strengths as a writer or for the rebellious nature of her early poetry, a problem that is compounded by the lack of a critical edition of her work. The last five years have seen the reclaiming in Russia of "lost" Soviet writers on a huge scale, but the emphasis has been on those who were lost either to emigration, like Nabokov, or to official repression, like Babel'.[24] Those writers who remained active in the Soviet Union and managed to survive the "lottery" of the purges are considered less interesting and even slightly suspect. Yet careful study of the entire body of Polonskaia's work reveals a sensitive and spirited writer whose talent stands out all the more sharply and poignantly against its own effacement.

Leslie J. Dorfman

With a soft sponge, with warm water
I washed dusty little feet,
Tanned in the sun's heat,
Little stampers, merry little things.

But now, like a hunted animal,
You hide in earthen burrows,
And you are tossed among ditches
By a dream, restless and swift.

Is there, then, no longer in our land
Any proper place for our sons,
That we have given them to war
And given them death for a bride?

The thunder of a thousand thousand guns
Shall never take you from me;
Still I feel your feeble mouth
Upon my emptied breast.

1921

Dry and resonant cracked the drum,
The brass began to howl in the bent throat,
And to the tread of numberless nations
The monstrous muzzles answered.
There will be no end. After the dead
Shall come new, living people,
And children will fall peacefully asleep
To the rumble of distant gunfire.
Gay and insolent years shall fall
To the lot of those who remain:
Battle-decimated cities,
Riddled and trench-torn fields.
They shall see the earth afar, afar,
And, finally, will learn for certain
How black is bread, how salty sorrow,
How they love us, and how they murder us.

1921

Ballad of the Fugitive

Power has a thousand hands
And two faces.

Power has a thousand loyal servants
And scouts without end.
    The prison door,
    The sturdy bolt . . .
    But we know a secret word . . .
He who must flee—shall flee,
Any bolt shall open for him.
Power has a thousand hands
And two faces.
Power has a thousand loyal servants,
But the fugitive has more friends.
    The wind closes
    The door behind him,
    The blizzard covers
    His trail,
    The echo tells him
    Where is the foe,
Insolence gives him a light step.

Power has a thousand hands,
It is sharp as the eye of God.
Power has a thousand loyal servants,
But a city is not a chess board:
    There are more than one thousand streets in it,
    More than one house in every street,
    More than one entrance in every house—
    One goes out, but another comes in!

The hunt is on for the red beast,
There are many hunters and many dogs,
Any method will do for the hunter—
The trap or the bullet, battue or the knife—
But the beast is noble, you shall not take him.

And the hounds are foraging while men wait—
They will overtake, will catch him, will take, will not take. . . .
    A poor hunt! A bad game!
    Today is the same as yesterday—

The place is cold, the burrow is empty. . . .

Power has a thousand hands
And the land is submissive to it,
Power has a thousand loyal servants,
And is master of terror and punishment . . .
But rumors fly in the city, news upon news—
There is a sure refuge in the city . . .
The scout darts about, the patrol stands ready,
But he who needs to hide is hidden.
Because, from house to neighboring house,
From heart to heart we silently weave
A secret net of merry friendship,
You will not see or discover it!

Power has a thousand hands
And more than one machine gun,
Power has a thousand loyal servants,
But he who needs to leave—will go.
To the north,
To the west,
To the south,
To the east
The road is clear and the world is wide.

c. 1922

Ransom

In iron veins the water has frozen,
The city is besieged by snow and ice.

In a low cave, not in a human house,
In a low cave is my refuge, my home.

Through uneasy days and sleepless nights,
I nurse a naked boy child at my breast.

I am terrified by rustles, I am terrified by silence,
A heavy tread is heard nearby.

It is crawling over my country,
A sweetish smell and the crunching of bones.

Mothers! We shall rise up in a living ring!
We will rise up to face the evil monster!

I will be the first to step forward:
"Who will take ransom for our young?

"Body for body, and my blood
Will I give you for my child—

"The joy of my eyes, the black enamel of my braids,
Bright morning and the scent of dew.

"I will be an old woman and I will be blind!
Don't dare any further, and sing no songs!"

1923

Carmen

I.

Not there, where, with a rose in her teeth,
Against the splendid yellow of Seville,
Appearing, she renders ashes and dust
Hearts and lives with no effort—

No, in a gutter, in a lean year,
Here, on the outskirts of the capital,
Carmen still lives for us
As a wanton factory girl.

She is just the same. A lock of hair
In a tight ring above a delicate brow,
And the slanting glance of her eyes
From under the kerchief, from under her brows.

And the shine of earrings, and lips, and eyes,
The springiness of her light step—
A heart-shattering story
Of the power of a fatal beauty.

For from ancestry unknown
Desperate and arrogant,
She is descended, and their hearts
Are the same at all meridians.

But the deck of passions
And betrayals has been reshuffled,
And Carmen has drawn a card—

October 1917

II.

October. You remember the wet snow
And that scorching air,
The heavy running of armored cars,
A brief pause in machine gun fire. . . .

You remember—the heart in the night
Beat out a rapid signal code,
And the wind, half air, half dust,
Lied and bragged at the crossroads.

You remember the struggle of steel
And lead on the bloody square,
When at the night storming of the palace
They suddenly rushed the gates;

The rapturous calico of banners,
The iron tread of numberless masses,
And from the slender antennae of radio-masts
The rallying cry: Peace! The Commune!

III.

There are amid the factory buildings
Houses gnawed by smallpox;
People live there, cramped and wordless,
Live, eat, and love simply.

There a woman branded as a wife,
Submissive to a man's lust,
Gives birth to meat for the war,
Gives birth to meat for the machine.

There she came into the world—
Carmen, child of an illicit love,
And, instead of school, at the age of nine
She went off to a tobacco factory.

From the tears and songs of the forewomen
She learned the science of life,
As if in a cage full of captive birds,
She lived and struggled for black bread,

And from a large-eyed, skinny
Little girl, insolent and sly,
Suddenly in splendid beauty
She blossomed at the edge of the gutter.

IV.

Sailor, soldier, locksmith, thief—
She loved them all without haggling,
And no one to this day
Has ever been refused her kisses.

But the memory of those hungry days,
Lived as a cast-off kid,
Remained in her, like hatred,
As a thin, sharp thorn.

In the factory she was
More irrepressible and loud-mouthed than anyone.
Her sharp tongue
Was feared by every foreman.

The end of a night's drinking bout
As in a mediocre melodrama:
She was fated a knife-blow
And a savage death under the gates.

And only in the newspaper chronicle,
There, where they dishonor death with small print,
Would a momentary trace have remained,
In the minor events section.

V.

One day, among a crowd of idlers,
Carmen was gawking at a procession,
A huge flag was fluttering;
An orderly column walked and sang.

Voices sounded muffled,
As though with life death was struggling,
And someone fat, with the mug of a dog,
Suddenly hissed out: "You've sung your song, you scum!"

Then, as though waking from a dream,
And slowly stepping down from the sidewalk,
Full of gay malice
Carmen joined the ones who were singing.

VI.

Yes, she loves gaily
And she can hate with gusto.
She is no mother and no wife—
Woe to any who dare offend her!

Not luring Jose to his doom,
Not aiding a smuggler's band—
Carmen in 1918
Was a communist in Russia.

Not to the glory of circus rings,
Where Escamilio deftly battles,
No, behind her lover Carmen
Is marching on Kolchak with a rifle.

In a cap, with a sailor's leather jacket,
Thrown about her breast and shoulders—
A factory artist
Has immortalized her in porcelain.

And the cards falsely promise death:
States rise and fall,
That Carmen, from the gutter, may live
Long in the memories of her grandchildren.

1924

In the Noose

A Lyric Film

Prologue

The lash was whistling. They were digging a ditch.
They were laying down stones, reinforcing the bogs.
This city was built by the hands of slaves
In the land of polar utopias.

But the Bronze Horseman, head over heels,
We will drag down along the granite steps
And we'll put up Another, with a prominent forehead,
The Chess Master of popular uprisings.

In a jacket on the granite he will stand,
Sullenly looking sidelong at the stars,
And children of the future will play
In the new world that he created.

1.

—It's gotten harder to get bread.
Not that
There's too little, like before.
No! For every gob, it's
"Eat"—"I don't want to, I'm stuffed. . . ."

It's gotten hard to live in the city:
They've taken too much stuff, bit by bit.
Only
Not for the poor.
Remember how we were starving?
Remember those black days,
How we lived with clenched teeth?
That's how they're dying
In the city of plenty.

—And do you remember, on the "Aurora,"
Remember the cannons' thunder?
It was raining, and the wind came from the sea—
We took our stand in front of the palace.
I was first in the assault
For freedom! For bread! For peace!
"War to the capitalists!"
"Die, old world!"

They were trembling, the dogs,
At the sight of our banners.
And now every one is laughing . . .
Holding sailors in contempt.
Move your pen across the page,
Figure "two times two"!
Can a rebel really
Make his peace with this?

2.

But the city is black and burning with fires,
Behind every shopwindow—magnet and flame . . .
And on the street chatter and women's laughter—
It's over! It's over! Death is not for everyone!
You can still love
And you can live,
And today you can forget about tomorrow,
And tomorrow horror may turn our heads white,
But today there is not and will be no death!

3.

Len'ka Pantaleev,
The terror of detectives,
On his arm a bracelet,
Deep blue eyes. . . .

Who else is so clever—
Judge for yourself!
All the broads are losing
Their minds over him.

Collar unbuttoned
In the cold and frost!
No need to say it—
You can see he's a sailor.

I'll touch up my lipstick—
Let my mother cry,
I'll stop spending
My nights at home. . . .

It's all the same, for black bread
Not to protect your daughter!
For boots up to my knees . . .
For earrings down to my shoulder. . . .

4.

That the sated and the wealthy may sleep in peace,
The leather jackets will be guarding the city.
    From post to post!
    From bridge to bridge!
That not even a mouse should slip in,
Nor a bird fly—
Wasn't it war that taught us
How to hold our borders!

Sleep calmly, jeweler,
The old world will not die!
The revolution will protect you. . . .

Sleep serenely, wheeler-dealer,
The end is still far off!
The revolution will protect you . . .

To the old world a postponement
Is given before death:
Let them live out
Their miserable last days, the vermin!

5.

"The prairies of Argentina!
A hunt for wild beasts!

Twenty-four pictures:
Seven outstanding parts."

The city is vaster than the prairie,
You'll catch plenty of game—
Only choose wisely:
The lasso, lead, or the knife.

Here there are both holes and cracks;
Who needs virgin forest!
In the night on every paving stone
You'll see more wonders!

Be careful, passerby!
The earth is not without its dangers!
Is it for you, perhaps,
The wire noose is laid?

And behind a secluded gate
Waits, concealed, the hunter . . .
Coiled and uncoiled.
Coiled once more! It's the end!

6.

The beaver coat walks along, enjoying himself,
The beaver coat is drunk.
The power of the Golden Calf has not vanished,
And eternal are the laws of wine,
And eternal are the laws of love,
And with the fur coat a mistress or wife,
Whatever you want to call her.

It's a little cold,
The distance twilit.
Long earrings,
A silk shawl.

Rich woman or beggar,
Lawful or not—
Love, a little food,
A dress, a bracelet. . . .

And against the man she softly huddles.
But the beaver coat is doomed,
And a noose is laid across the road:
"I'm terrified! Stop! Let's wait a bit!"

The hunter has a sure hand—
The bird is defenseless, the noose is strong,
The bird is motionless. No escape for the bird!
"A man and a woman. A fine catch."

7.

Where is there now to run
And where to look for a hangover?
The door is open wide
For wild merriment.

Here there's a brass band,
Looming in clouds of steam,
To shuffling and crashing
It whirls couple after couple.

It whirls, it sings, it trembles,
To a ringing rumble and clatter,
Until at last it starts
To whirl a madcap girl.

And the heart of the best dancer
Will not stand still:
Forward! Back! Forward!
To the shouts of the bandleader. . . .

And from above, where the parquet
Is peeled away and soiled,
Down to the gloomy avenue
To run, with a merry squeal,

While they give the French horn's reed
A minute's breather,
To catch with a burning mouth
A gulp of frozen air!

8.

Love me a little, I'm a fine
    fellow,
I will give you earrings
    from a corpse!
A clever chap made them
Not for ladies with gilding,
But for such as I,
For dung and rawhide.

The revolution is not over yet:
Let them come after me with hounds!

9.

The murderer sits at the table,
But the coppers are on their way,
And the woman whispers: "Let's go,"
But he has nowhere to go.

The murderer sits at the table.

The murderer sits at the table,
But there are the detectives,
They've already surrounded the house,
But they won't take him alive!

"Hey! Give yourself up, bandit!"
But a revolver is a trusty friend,
So let the broad run,
But they won't flush him out.

And as long as the cartridges hold out,
It'll be hot for you too!
Bakh!—answers tin-plate,
Dzin!—answers glass.

The mirrors are shot out,
A man falls.
Through the window vent
Snow flies into the room.

10.

If your right eye tempts you,
Pull out your eye and throw it to the dogs.
And if your hand trembles,
Better to cut it off yourself.

The leather jackets have an iron law:
Pluck the evil weed from the field.

11.

On the dirty floor a man is lying—
  He's dead! He's dead!
His breast wide open and his collar spread—
  He's dead! He's dead!

But the orchestra plays, and the ball goes on:
It's Shrovetide, carnival time.
Make merry if you can! Death won't wait!
To everyone, to everyone she'll come.

Epilogue

The lash was whistling. They were digging a ditch.
They were laying down stones, reinforcing the bog.
This city was built by the hands of slaves
In the land of polar utopias.

But for us the Chess Master has traced out
A wise scheme of new battles,
A square-lined sheet
Of attacks and retreats.

Not a capitol, not a garrison, not a fort,
Not a tomb for tsars and heroes:
On the campsite of wild hordes
We are building a new world with our labor.

Are we not stronger than they,
Who worked beneath the lash?
May verse stick in our throats—
Our children shall be happy!

And someday all will understand:
To die is to give in.
In defiance of everything
We must remain among the living.

1925

At times a mother can be unjust
To her sons. And then
A sequence will come to them
Of love both bitter and jealous.

They cannot forget. They cannot leave you.
You are a mother, not a lover.

At night they dream their childhood songs,
And these songs can never be taken away.

They dream of a stormy youth,
The fire of your civil battles.
And the old, dry wound
Bleeds again in the night.

And the heart beats in such alarm,
And death's cold crushes the breast.
It is impossible for them to curse you
And impossible to deceive.

1957

Memories

Memories of bygone years,
Tell me, what shall I do with you?
I hear: "We have departed this life.
Our world is your meager memory.

"Refuse us—and we will go
Somewhere forever, out of sight,
Call us—and we live,
As long as you are alive, our friend.

"If you wish, we shall cease to exist,
Like everything beautiful on earth,
And it is no affair of yours,
And you are not to blame.

"But if you love more bravely,
Overcoming the dream of peace,
From the kingdom of the dead, like Orpheus,
You shall lead us behind you."

1958

Translated by Leslie J. Dorfman

Notes to the Essay

1. Boris Èikhenbaum, "Retsenzia na sborniki V. Rozhdestvenskogo i E. Polonskoi," *Knizhnii ugol* 7 (1921): 41.

2. The major exception is Joy Brett-Harrison's excellent unpublished thesis, "Dichterin in bewegter Zeit. Leben und Werk der Elizaveta Polonskaja (1890–1969)," master's thesis, University of Zurich, 1990.

3. Elizaveta Polonskaia, "Iz chernovikov pis'ma k literaturnomu kritiku. 1924–1926 gg," prepared with notes by M.L. Polonskii, private archive of E.G. Polonskaia, St. Petersburg [in the possession of M.L. Polonskii].

4. "K moim chitateliam," in *Izbrannoe* (Moscow: Khudozhestvennaia literatura, 1966), 8.

5. M.L. Polonskii and B.Ia. Frezinskii, eds., "Serapionovskie ody i èpigrammy Elizavety Polonskoi," *Voprosy literatury* 6 (1993): 356–66.

6. William Edgerton, "The Serapion Brothers: An Early Soviet Controversy," *The American Slavic and East European Review* 1 (February 1949): 47–64; Gary Kern, *The Serapion Brothers: A Critical Anthology*, ed. Gary Kern and Christopher Collins (Ann Arbor, MI: Ardis, 1975), ix–xxxviii.

7. O. Barabashev, "Naletchiki na Revoliutsiiu ili o tom, kak Gosizdat izdal zamechatel'noe posobie k rasprostraneniiu khuliganstva," *Leningradskaia pravda,* 12 March 1925, 7.

8. L. Baril', "Literaturnye zametki," *Priboi* (Odessa) 1 (1928): 41.

9. "Nachalo dvadtsatykh godov," *Prostor* 6 (1964): 113.

10. Gregor Aronson, "The Jewish Question during the Stalin Era," in *Russian Jewry 1917–1967*, ed. Gregor Aronson et al. (New York: Thomas Yoseloff, 1969), 179.

11. "K moim chitateliam," 11.

12. M.L. Polonskii, personal interview, St. Petersburg, 17 June 1993. "Song about Lina Odena," set to music by the composer Viktor Tomilin, was only one of many of Polonskaia's poems that became popular songs; another was her translation of a Yiddish folk song, "Diadia El'ia," which was recorded by the singer Leonid Utesov in 1939.

13. Elizaveta Polonskaia, "Iz prikhodo-raskhodnoi literatury, 1937 g," private archive of E.G. Polonskaia, St. Petersburg [in the possession of M.L. Polonskii]. Polonskaia's translation of *Measure for Measure* was the object of lawsuit against the Aleksandrinskii Theater in 1936 and was eventually staged by the Novyi Theater in 1937.

14. Z. Mints, "E.G. Polonskaia i ee literaturnye vospominaniia," *Trudy po russkoi i slavianskoi filologii. Uchenye zapiski Tartusskogo universiteta* 139 (1963): 375.

15. Il'ia Ehrenburg, "Liudi, gody, zhizn'. Prodolzhenie," *Novyi mir* 9 (1960): 91–92.

16. Marietta Chudakova, personal interview, Moscow, 4 September 1992. See Marietta Chudakova, *Poètika Mikhaila Zoshchenko* (Moscow: Nauka, 1979).

17. Aleksandr Rubashkin, "Ne sotvori kumira," *Literaturnaia gazeta,* 10 April 1991, 10.

18. Aleksandr Rubashkin, personal interview, St. Petersburg, 23 June 1993. After returning to Russia in 1915, Polonskaia never officially renewed her membership in the Bolshevik party.

19. Iu. Meshkov, rev. of *Izbrannoe*, *Neva* 10 (1967): 195.

20. Z. Mints, rev. of *Stikhotvoreniia i poèma*, *Zvezda* 11 (1960): 217.

21. Mints, "E.G. Polonskaia i ee literaturnye vospominaniia," 374.

22. Veniamin Kaverin, *Èpilog: Memuary* (Moscow: Moskovskii rabochii, 1989), 29–31. Kaverin confirms that, despite the publication of "Ballad of the Fugitive" in 1923 with a dedication to the anarchist P.A. Kropotkin, and the substitution of the Bolshevik Iakov Sverdlov in the

1960 version, the poem was actually written for the Serapions' friend and mentor Viktor Shklovskii, who had fled Russia to escape arrest for anti-Bolshevik activities in 1922.

23. For example, the last stanza of "With a soft sponge, with warm water" reads as follows in the 1921 version: "The thunder of a thousand thousand guns / Shall never take you from me; / Still I feel your feeble mouth / Upon my emptied breast." In 1960 it was republished in the following form: "But the thunder of a thousand thousand guns / Shall not take my child from me. / Still I feel your feeble mouth: / It draws life from my burning breast."

24. Rubashkin, "Ne sotvori kumira," 10.

Bibliography

Primary Works

Znamen'ia. St. Petersburg: Erato, 1921.

Pod kamennym dozhdem, 1921–1923. St. Petersburg: Poliarnaia zvezda, 1923.

Poezdka na Ural. St. Petersburg: Priboi, 1927.

Upriamyi kalendar': Stikhi i poèmy, 1924–1927. St. Petersburg: Izdatel'stvo pisatelei v Leningrade, 1929.

Liudi sovetskikh budnei. St. Petersburg: Izdatel'stvo pisatelei v Leningrade, 1934.

Goda. Izbrannye stikhi. St. Petersburg: Izdatel'stvo pisatelei v Leningrade, 1935.

Novye stikhi, 1932–1936. St. Petersburg: Goslitizdat, 1937.

Vremena muzhestva. Stikhi; Portret. Poèma. St. Petersburg: Goslitizdat, 1940.

Kamskaia tetrad'. Stikhi. Molotov: Molotovskoe oblastnoe izdatel'stvo, 1945.

Na svoikh plechakh. Ocherki. Illustr. by I. Mitskievich. Moscow: Ispolkom soiuza obshchestv Krasnogo Kresta i Krasnogo Polumesiatsa SSSR, 1948.

Na svoikh plechakh. Rasskazy. St. Petersburg: Lenizdat, 1948.

Stikhotvoreniia i poèma. St. Petersburg: Sovetskii pisatel', 1960.

"Iz literaturnykh vospominanii." Intro. by Z. Mints. *Trudy po russkoi i slavianskoi filologii 6. Uchenye zapiski Tartusskogo universiteta* [Tartu] 139 (1963): 375–89. [On Zoshchenko, Chukovskii, Fedin, and Marshak.]

"Nachalo dvadtsatykh godov." *Prostor* 6 (1964): 110–15. [On the Literary Studio ("Vsemirnaia literatura"); Gumilev; the Serapion Brothers; Fedin; Vsev. Ivanov; Shklovskii; the publishing house Erato.]

"Do oktiabria eshche desiat' let." *Zvezda* 7 (1965): 143–57.

Izbrannoe. Moscow: Khudozhestvennaia literatura, 1966.

"K moim chitateliam." *Izbrannoe*. Moscow: Khudozhestvennaia literatura, 1966. 7–14.

"Vstrechi." *Neva* 1 (1966): 193–97. [On Tikhonov and Zoshchenko.]

"Na pamiat' o podvorotniax." *Ol'ga Forsh v vospominaniiax sovremennikov*. St. Petersburg: Sovetskii pisatel', leningradskoe otdelenie, 1974. 94–100.

"Kak i tridtsat' piat' let nazad." *Vsevolod Ivanov—pisatel' i chelovek*. Moscow: Sovetskii pisatel', 1975. 96–101.

"Iz knigi 'Vstrechi.'" Ed. M.L. Polonskii and B.Ia. Frezinskii. *Neva* 4 (1987): 193–97. [On Oscar Leshinskii and the "Russian Academy."]

"Iz vospominanii." *Znamia truda Darba Karogs: Gazeta goroda Rezekne i Rezeknenskogo raiona,* 9 June 1990. [On Iurii Tynianov.]

"Iz literaturnykh vospominanii." *Chas pik,* 21 September 1994, 15. [On Lidiia Charskaia.]

Children's Literature

Zaichata. Illustr. by A.A. Radakov. St. Petersburg: Raduga, 1923.

Gosti. Illustr. by S. Chekhonin. Moscow: Kniga, 1924.

Pro pchel i pro Mishku medvedia. Illustr. by B. Pokrovskii. St. Petersburg: Gosudarstvennoe izdatel'stvo, 1926.

Chasy. Illustr. by N. Lapshin. Moscow: Gosudarstvennoe izdatel'stvo, 1927.

Gorod i derevnia. Illustr. by N. Lapshin. St. Petersburg: Gosudarstvennoe izdatel'stvo, 1927.

Pro ochag da iasli i pirog na masle. Illustr. by A. Efimova. Moscow: Gosudarstvennoe izdatel'stvo, 1927.

Detskii dom. Illustr. by A. Efimova. St. Petersburg: Gosudarstvennoe izdatel'stvo, 1928.

Zhak i Zhanna. Illustr. by N. Dormidontov. St. Petersburg: Krasnaia gazeta, 1929.

Nemnogo sporta raznogo sorta. Illustr. by M. Razulevich. St. Petersburg: Gosudarstvennogo izdatel'stvo, 1930.

Peppe Rakoni. Illustr. by L. Gal'perin. St. Petersburg: OGIZ Molodaia gvardiia, 1931.

Zakusochnaia Zive. Illustr. by I. Eberil'. Moscow: Molodaia gvardiia, 1931.

Sviataia Amaliia bastuet. Illustr. by V. Lebedev. St. Petersburg: LOIZ Biblioteka Leninskikh iskr, 1933.

Secondary Works

Barabashev, O. "Naletchiki na Revoliutsii ili o tom, kak Gosizdat izdal zamechatel'noe posobie k rasprostraneniiu khuliganstva." *Leningradskaia pravda,* 12 March 1925, 7.

Brett-Harrison, J. "Dichterin in bewegter Zeit. Leben und Werk der Elizaveta Polonskaja (1890–1969)." Master's thesis, University of Zurich, 1990.

Ehrenburg, I. Vol. 2 of *First Years of Revolution 1918–21*. *Men, Years, Life*. Trans. A. Bostock, with Y. Kapp. London: MacGibbon & Kee, 1962. 179.

———. *People and Life 1891–1921*. Trans. A. Bostock and Y. Kapp. New York: Knopf, 1962. 416.

———. *Post-War Years 1945–1954*. Trans. T. Shebunina, in collaboration with Y. Kapp. London: MacGibbon & Kee, 1966. 14.

Èikhenbaum, B. "Retsenziia na sborniki V. Rozhdestvenskogo i E. Polonskoi." *Knizhnyi ugol* 7 (1921): 37–42.

Kasack, W. "Polonskaia, Elizaveta." *Dictionary of Russian Literature since 1917*. New York: Columbia University Press, 1988.

Kaverin, V. *Epilog: Memuary*. Moscow: Moskovskii rabochii, 1989. [See 29–31 for details on "Ballada o begletse."]

Kireeva, M. "Iz vospominanii (Il'ia Èrenburg v Parizhe 1909 goda)." Intro. by B. Ia. Frezinskii. *Voprosy literatury* 9 (1982): 144–57.

Mints, Z. "E.G. Polonskaia i ee literaturnye vospominaniia." *Trudy po russkoi i slavianskoi filologii* 6. *Uchenye zapiski Tartuskogo universiteta, no. 139*. Tartu, 1963. 374–376. [Includes extensive bibliography.]

Ninov, A. "Polonskaia, Elizaveta Grigor'ievna." *Kratkaia Literaturnaia Èntsiklopediia*. Ed. A.A. Surkov. Vol. 5. Moscow: Izdatel'stvo Sovetskaia Èntsiklopediia, 1968.

Polonskii, M.L., and B.Ia. Frezinskii. "Serapionovskie ody i èpigrammy Elizavety Polonskoi." *Voprosy literatury* 6 (1993): 356–58.

Rubashkin, A. "Ne sotvori kumira." *Literaturnaia gazeta,* 10 April 1991, 10.

Shklovsky, V. *A Sentimental Journey. Memoirs, 1917–1922*. Trans. R. Sheldon. Ithaca, NY: Cornell University Press, 1970. 267–68.

Terras, Victor. "Elizaveta Polonskaya." *Handbook of Russian Literature*. Ed. Victor Terras. New Haven, CT: Yale University Press, 1985.

Trubilova, Elena. "Polonskaia, Elizaveta Grigor'evna." Trans. Jill Roese. *Dictionary of Russian Women Writers*. Ed. M. Ledkovsky, C. Rosenthal and M. Zirin. Westport, CT: Greenwood Press, 1994.

Vysheslavtseva, S. "15 let poèticheskoi raboty." *Khudozhestvennaia literatura* 10 (1935): 5–10.

Frida Vigdorova

Frida Vigdorova (1915–1965). Courtesy of Aleksandra Raskina.

Frida Abramovna Vigdorova (1915–1965)[1] is best known in the West for her transcription of the Brodsky trials of February and March 1964. However, in the Soviet Union and in Eastern Europe, Vigdorova, who was trained as a teacher, gained popularity in the early 1950s as a novelist who wrote on pedagogical themes. She became famous for her journalism, which explored the ethical issues of truth and justice in Soviet society and the relationship between independence of thought and moral health. Her role within the context of post-Stalinist culture is significant, for her articles struck a responsive chord in her reading audience; in their time they evoked many discussions, and she was inundated by personal and written requests for help from or on behalf of various people who felt wrongly treated. Vigdorova, together with a network of friends who comprised what they jokingly called "a benevolent society for good deeds or small miracles," tirelessly interceded and tried to alter the workings of government bureaucracy.[2] "Always and everywhere she defended the persecuted, the unjustly convicted, those in distress. If she was not able to tell their story in print, then armed with her various membership cards, she would go from one level of authority to the next, travel to the labor camps, attend meetings and trials, and visit people in prison and in the hospital."[3] Her work on behalf of people who had been victimized and were defenseless led to her appointment in 1963 as deputy of the regional Soviet. In that capacity Vigdorova worked vigorously to improve the living conditions of the people in her district: "She not only reconciled families, came to the defense of battered wives and mothers who came to her to complain, [but] found apartments for workers' families living eight or even twelve to a room. . . ."[4]

Vigdorova's father, Abram Grigor'evich Vigdorov, was a respected pedagogue who taught for many years at the Moscow Pedagogical Institute, and her mother, Sofiia Borisovna Vigdorova, was a nurse-practitioner (*fel'dsher*). Her younger brother, Isaak (1919–1968), was a decorated bomber pilot in World War II who later worked as a test pilot and an engineer. Frida graduated from the teacher-training college in Moscow and in 1932, at the age of seventeen, began her career as a primary teacher in the new city of Magnitogorsk in the Urals, where she worked until 1935. That year she returned to Moscow with her husband, Aleksandr Kulakovskii, whom she had met in Magnitogorsk. The young couple graduated from the Faculty of Literature at the Moscow Pedagogical Institute in 1937, and Vigdorova began to teach high school at School No. 610 in Moscow. In the same year, her first daughter, Galina, was born.

In 1938 Vigdorova began to combine her teaching with journalism, and soon her articles, based on notebooks of her reflections about teaching and observations from her travels around the country, gained a loyal following. Although she wrote on "school themes," her articles touched on deeply ethical questions that went well beyond the "education section." She had asked to write articles about "fairness and justice" (*po spravedlivym delam*), and indeed she mainly wrote about people who had been unfairly treated, victimized or accused by the system whether through indifference, bureaucratic obstinacy or illegal procedure. Vigdorova once noted: "You're never safe fighting against indifference. Just touch an indifferent person and he will turn into an enraged buffalo. And he'll act as you would expect: he'll write anonymous letters, he'll scheme, and more."[5] Her articles appeared in the country's major newspapers: at first in *Truth (Pravda)* and then in *News (Izvestia), Young Communist Truth* (*Komsomol'skaia pravda*) and *Literary Gazette* (*Literaturnaia gazeta*).[6]

Before the outbreak of World War II, Vigdorova divorced Kulakovskii and married the satirist Aleksandr Borisovich Raskin (1914–1971). From 1941 to 1943 Vigdorova and her family lived as evacuees in Tashkent, where she worked as a correspondent for *Pravda* and where her second daughter, Aleksandra, was born. In 1942, having become acquainted with Anna Akhmatova, Vigdorova took upon herself the responsibility of relaying the poem "Courage" ("Muzhestvo") to Moscow by telephone and, from far-off Tashkent, of ensuring that everything possible was done to have it published. In this way she facilitated the then "semi-legal" Akhmatova's "official return" to Soviet readers.

Vigdorova's prose-writing career began in 1948 with the publication of her first small book. *The Courageous Twelve* (*Dvenadtsat' otvazhnykh*, coauthored with T. Pechernikova) is a documentary piece based on historical materials that recounts the activities of the underground resistance of teenagers in the village of Pokrovskoe during the German occupation in World War II. Vigdorova's series of literary portrayals of children has its inception in this work. In 1949, under the title *Class 4–C* (*Chetvertyi klass IV*) in the almanac *Year XXXII* (*God XXXII*), excerpts from her first single-authored novella, *My Class* (*Moi klass*; translated as *Diary of a Russian Schoolteacher*, 1960), were published and later the entire book appeared. An intimate first-person narrative, the novella retells the uncertainties, searchings and satisfactions of a young novice teacher, presumably much like Vigdorova herself, working with a class of boys in postwar Russia. It gently but clearly criticizes the sterile college preparation that Soviet teachers received and promotes the idea that the most important qualities of a good educator are kindness, getting to know one's students, having the ability to reflect and search for solutions in difficult situations and approaching teaching as an art and not a soulless "multiplication table."[7] *My Class* enjoyed great popularity perhaps because of its gentle and nondidactic quality, so unusual for the time. The book depicts schoolchildren who, according to the ethic of the day, are all Pioneers, the communist children's organization, but it is fundamentally about children's relationships with each other, their teachers and their families. It was translated into many languages, and soon after its appearance, Vigdorova was admitted to the Soviet Writers' Union.[8]

In 1950 the story *The Tale of Zoia and Shura* (*Povest' o Zoe i Shure*) was published. This is Vigdorova's literary notes of the reminiscences of Liubov' Kosmodem'ianskaia, Zoia and Shura's mother.[9] Through Zoia's youthful exuberance and zeal Vigdorova endeavors to depict her and her brother not primarily as members of the Communist Youth Organization (Komsomol) but as children growing up just before World War II, being raised by their mother after their father's untimely death. This is a book about children and family, about the processes of maturing and building of character—recurring themes in Vigdorova's writing that emphasize the personal above the social. She took great pains to avoid propagandistic elements in her works; for example, it is remarkable that although *My Class* and *The Tale of Zoia and Shura* were written at the time of high Stalinism just after World War II, in neither work is there found the expected and obligatory praise of the leader.

Vigdorova's next novellas form a trilogy based on the work that Semen Kalabalin and his wife carried on with delinquent and homeless youngsters (*bezprizornye*) as well as with other children. Vigdorova was personally acquainted with Kalabalin, who was educated by and became a follower of the famous Soviet pedagogue A.S. Makarenko, and spent several months living with the couple at their orphanage, getting to know the children, going to classes with them and recording observations in her ever-present notebooks. *The Road to Life* (*Doroga v zhizn'*, 1954), *This Is My Home* (*Èto moi dom*, 1957) and *Chernigovka* (1959) are written in the same "reflections-of-a-teacher" vein as *My Class*, but this time the classrooms are orphanages in the prewar and wartime Soviet Union. The trilogy is united by recurring characters as well as by the first-person narration of the hero, Semen Karabanov, in the first two novels; in the third, the narrative transfers to the first-person voice of his wife, Galina Konstantinovna, who moves the orphanage's children into evacuation while Karabanov is at the front. The novellas are not a biography of Vigdorova's friend, Kalabalin, but a fictional portrayal of one of Makarenko's students and his experiences, many of which are actually drawn from Vigdorova's own teaching background and notebooks.

Vigdorova's interest and regard for the theories of Makarenko are evident in her trilogy. She borrows several topoi from his writing: characters and names (Karabanov, Galina Konstantinovna), setting (orphanage) and theme (the application of an educational theory combining manual work, the idea of the collective, play, discipline and optimistic faith in the human potential of children with widely differing histories).[10] Like *My Class*, Vigdorova's trilogy enjoyed tremendous popularity, and despite the fact that stylistically it is far more fiction than pedagogy, it became required reading for students in teacher-training both in the Soviet Union and Eastern-bloc countries.[11]

Two linked novellas, *Family Happiness* (*Semeinoe schast'e*) and *Beloved Street* (*Liubimaia ulitsa*), appeared in the early 1960s and indicate some change in Vigdorova's fictional themes and style. For the first time, Vigdorova turns to one family and traces the life of the heroine over a span of twenty years through school, first love and marriage, divorce and second marriage, World War II and right up to the graduation of her elder daughter, a scope and plot criticized as too narrow in some reviews.[12] Also for the first time, Vigdorova attempts an extended third-person narration even though the figure and life of the heroine are recognizably autobiographical.[13]

Family Happiness and *Beloved Street*, written during the literary "thaw" of the early 1960s, are remarkable too for the fact that they contain possibly the only reference in Soviet fiction published before *glasnost'* to the process and consequences of the infamous "Doctors' Plot" of 1952.[14] The heroine's good friend, a doctor, is arrested; when she refuses to denounce him, she is fired. Later she learns that all of the doctors who were arrested have been freed and are innocent of the charges brought against them.

Vigdorova's journalism of the late 1950s reveals a woman who is more committed than ever to defending and supporting those who have been wrongfully accused or abused by the authorities.[15] Even her fictional trilogy contributed to her effort to defend Kalabalin from bureaucratic charges of arbitrariness, lack of vigilance, child abuse and theft that were brought against him because of his uncanonical pedagogical ideas and that were meant to discredit his theories and practices. Her articles increasingly reflect her activity on behalf of others as well as her personal ethical code: if a person is in trouble, one can and should come to his or her aid for there is no circumstance in which one person can't help another, if only by giving moral support.

In 1961 Vigdorova's excellent essay "Empty Eyes and Magic Eyes" ("Glaza pustye i glaza volshebnye") appeared in the controversial and "liberal" miscellany *Pages from Tarusa* (*Tarusskie stranitsy*), which was withdrawn from sale almost as soon as it appeared. The metaphorical title captures two ethical categories of people who are prevalent in Vigdorova's writing: those who approach others with deep interest, attention and concern, and those who have no interest in seeing or hearing others, who know the rules but know or care nothing about people. This classic opposition between humanity and lack of humanity is played out time and again in Vigdorova's writing and is most unequivocally illustrated in her transcription of Joseph Brodsky's trials where "two forces, from time immemorial standing in opposition to each other, collided: the intelligentsia and the bureaucracy—the force of the inspired word and the force of the government directive."[16]

Until the Brodsky trials, Vigdorova coexisted relatively peacefully with the state; in order to help someone, she would use her journalistic connections to approach people of every rank from government ministers to editors of major newspapers and "naturally, she had to smile and conform and resort to the inevitable everyday compromises."[17] Further, a childlike belief in truth and justice, to which friends and acquaintances consistently refer, bolstered by her success in effectively using connections in official institutions, helped her for a time to navigate the waters between the official culture and her unofficial activities.[18]

Although Vigdorova helped a host of people from all walks of Soviet life in myriad ways—for example, it was Vigdorova who finally managed to obtain a Moscow residence permit and an apartment for Nadezhda Mandel'shtam—her most significant contribution in her highly visible public activity was her artistic documentation of Joseph Brodsky's trials.[19] Vigdorova had begun to make appeals on Brodsky's behalf in November 1963, and as a consequence by February 1964 she could not get a journalistic assignment to Brodsky's trial. Nonetheless she attended the trial as a private citizen and tenaciously recorded the proceedings with pen and paper despite repeated orders by the judge that she stop writing. A fellow journalist recalls that Vigdorova simply put the notepad on her knees, looked up and straight ahead, but continued to write blindly and quickly.

For not complying with the judge's request to stop writing, Vigdorova might have been jailed for fifteen days for hooliganism, but distributing the completed Brodsky trial transcripts constituted a political crime under Soviet law. When Soviet journalists attended trials, particularly those with an underlying political agenda, they were expected to write reportage approving the sentence for which they were given access to the official minutes of the proceedings. However, if they did not approve of the sentence, they got no cooperation from the officials—quite the contrary, in fact. Vigdorova's transcripts constitute the first instance in the Soviet Union of trial proceedings with political undertones to be recorded word for word by a journalist without official sanction; others would take up the standard and record the trial of Andrei Sinyavsky and Iulii Daniel in 1966.[20] Thus, within the Soviet social and political context, Vigdorova's action was most unusual and showed that a courageous person could let the truth be known without official sanction.

After the conclusion of the trial and Brodsky's sentencing, Vigdorova doggedly made the rounds of the editorial offices of various newspapers with her uncensored notes, trying to obtain their publication. In a letter to A. Chakovskii, editor of *Literary Gazette*, Vigdorova writes: "It's not just a matter of Brodsky but of the profound disrespect to the intelligentsia and to literature that such trials instill in people. I witnessed a monstrous violation of the law. It's your right to decide to act or not, but knowing what went on there is an obligation to act."[21] Vigdorova's attempts to have the manuscripts published in the Soviet Union were unsuccessful; however, they were among the first publicistic texts to be circulated by the relatively new *samizdat* (self-publishing). Vigdorova was determined that the transcripts should reach the West; when they did, they were immediately published.[22] The significance of Vigdorova's act and its insistence on *glasnost'* (openness) in an era without *glasnost'* is neatly summarized by Nadezhda Mandel'shtam: "Vigdorova opened up a new era by writing down the proceedings of Brodsky's trial and this first genuine record of its kind had a shattering impact."[23]

Several commentators laud the transcripts also for the style in which they are written, a style that highlights Vigdorova's particular forte as a writer—an ear for speech and an eye for critical observation:

> Frida Vigdorova possessed a magical gift, which allowed her to fix the dialogues she heard with incredible accuracy which was even more accurate than shorthand. With her analytical mind, writer's talent, and powers of observation she had the ability to cut out the unneccesary details, while capturing the most characteristic moments including intonations in speech.[24]

Vigdorova died of cancer about one month before Brodsky was released in 1965 after a vigorous campaign to free him, which had been sparked by the *samizdat* transcripts of the trials: "Dozens of people signed letters of protest, petitions, and appeals to release the illegally and senselessly incarcerated poet. He was released after eighteen months."[25] There is some evidence to suggest that a move was afoot in the Writers' Union to have Vigdorova ousted because of her activities, but it was never carried through to completion due to her terminal illness.[26]

Vigdorova's achievements as a writer and contribution to the early development of an unofficial Soviet culture deserve further comment. Her prose and journalism were based on her notebooks and diaries and thus were highly autobiographical in nature. In this respect, Vigdorova integrated into her writing a mode that was traditionally most accessible to Russian women.[27] Chukovskaia describes Vigdorova's gift for capturing the moment in sight, sound and emotion succinctly yet expressively in a manner that was able to encapsulate both characterizations and interrelationships.[28] I. Grekova suggests that Vigdorova's style was subordinate to her ideas; the writing was simple, without tropes or elaborate wordplay, yet her perfect pitch for perceiving and communicating speech and transmitting character was her great talent.[29] *Diary of a Mother* (*Moi dnevnichki*), based on Vigdorova's descriptions of the early childhood and development of her two daughters, was considered by such writers as Kornei Chukovskii and I. Grekova to be the best of its genre and yet, despite the considerable editorial work done by Lidiia Chukovskaia, this work remains unpublished.[30] The novella that Vigdorova was writing at the time of her death, *The Teacher* (*Uchitel'*), also drew from episodes recorded in her notebooks as she traveled through the Soviet Union on various journalistic assignments.

As a public figure, Vigdorova was of a new mold; her writing and aid rendered to people "exceeded the boundaries of the smaller world of relatives, friends, acquaintances and assumed a social significance."[31] At the same time as she was a prominent figure in mainstream culture, Vigdorova was involved in the unofficial culture evolving in post-Stalin society. This culture, involving a thin layer of the Russian intelligentsia, was a very intimate one; friends would meet in each others' apartments for conversation and to hear literary readings and songs. In these apartments *samizdat* was born; Raisa Orlova recalls that Vigdorova was constantly passing *samizdat* manuscripts to friends to read and that it was at Vigdorova's home that she first heard the songs of Aleksandr Galich, and read the poetry of Marina Tsvetaeva and the drama of Evgenii Shvarts.[32] Vigdorova entertained often and she regularly went to friends' homes for musical evenings: "She was a true enlightener: everything that was revealed to her she had to reveal to others, to those near and far."[33] Formalizing the pioneering "female creative and heroic model" of women like Lidiia Chukovskaia, Vigdorova's fiction, journalism and efforts on behalf of others helped to lay the groundwork for the birth of public dissidence in the Soviet Union.[34] The successful campaign to free Brodsky begun by Vigdorova and others is considered to be one of the first events in the newly arisen Soviet human rights movement.[35]

Descriptions of Vigdorova's ability to have a formative influence upon others attribute to her a tremendous moral authority:

> Those she helped . . . became her friends and became part of a chain of helpers, each according to her own capability. Having fallen into [Vigdorova's] orbit, it was impossible not to try to help. And thus came into being an amazing "collective responsibility for good" which prompted completely unremarkable people, at least once in their lives, to take on someone else's misfortune . . . to stretch the sluggish muscles of their conscience, to risk, to dare.[36]

As another friend states succinctly, she was "the kind of person by which everything was measured: your actions, your attitudes to people, what was written and thought, the past and the present."[37]

In a 1961 article, Vigdorova argues that courage is indivisible: "If someone is brave in a moment of danger on the battlefield, but is cowardly in everyday life, then he can't be called a brave person. . . . Sometimes [courage] is in defending an innocent person. Sometimes it is in unmasking a dishonest person. Courage is in a fearlessly frank word, or in upholding truth. Courage manifests itself in different ways but . . . it cannot be divided."[38] Perhaps these thoughts best represent the sum of Vigdorova's contribution to Russian culture, a courageous contribution made in several areas simultaneously but which is ultimately indivisible.

Teresa Polowy

Five Lives and the Committee[1]

A small room filled to capacity. Both the head of the District Division of Public Education and the head of the District Division of Healthcare Services are here. Police representatives and school principals are also here. This is the Committee on Juvenile Delinquency under the purview of the Executive Committee of one of Leningrad's District Councils.[2] The task of this type of committee is to combat child neglect, to intervene before a crime is committed, to understand how teenagers go astray.

A trio enters the room—father, mother, and son. This is the Petrov family. "Boria Petrov is in the seventh grade," the police representative informs us. "Last summer he found a rusty revolver in the forest, cleaned it up, brought it to working condition, and fired it. His second misdemeanor occurred at school. He took hydrochloric acid from the chemistry lab and spilled it on a female classmate, which ruined her clothes and caused slight bodily injury."

A well-groomed boy stands before the committee. Obstinately he looks down at the toes of his shoes. His answers are hardly audible, the words almost indecipherable. Finally we understand that he took the hydrochloric acid because it erases ink.

"In a manner of speaking, you wanted to clean up your report card, is that it?" asks a member of the committee.

"Yes."

"So why did you spill the acid on the girl?"

He stays quiet, stubbornly and firmly quiet.

"Nice kid!" says Lidia Ivanovna, the committee chair. "So now, let's hear from your mother. What do you have to say, citizen Petrova?"

Boria's mother is a seamstress. She is dressed very modestly, her face haggard and worn-looking, her hands nervously twisting a hanky.

"I'm raising him," she says. "I'm bringing him up as best I can. I said to him 'Boria—study; Boria—join some of the clubs at school; Boria—don't be a hoodlum.' When my husband—his stepfather—is sober, he tries to talk sense into him too."

"Fine. Let's hear the father. Go ahead, comrade father!"

"Besides him, I have two other children, a daughter of thirty and a son who's twenty-four," says Boria's stepfather. "They are my own children, but I never put them into separate categories—mine and not mine. I couldn't raise the older ones properly because of the war. But this one grew up with me. He was two when I started coming around. But how can I raise him when his mother and I are pulling in different directions? She bought him a watch, a camera, skis, skates, and for what? He's a bad student. 'Well,' I think to myself, 'I won't begrudge him some time during the summer.' Yeah, right! His mother sends him out of town. That's where the incident with the revolver occurred. Knowing my stern nature, the wife kept this fact from me. With regard to the second act with the hydrochloric acid, that, of course, is a disgrace. He's an atrocious student. I had definitely decided to work with him over the winter break. Sure thing! He went to six New Year's parties, twice to the theater and I don't know how many times he went skating! Even his mother finally became concerned. The fact that I drink—well, that's true. Not often, but it happens. When I'm drunk I get really critical, I'll admit. Then I carp at things and make a lot of demands. But I realize that I'm like his own father to him, I realize that I'm responsible for him and should teach him, but it's a real problem that his mother and I can't get together on how to do it."

The discussion with the Petrovs goes on for a long time. It's painful for the mother, father, the boy and for all the committee members. Everyone sees the picture clearly, but the solution to the problem is not at all clear. True, Boria promises to reform. True, he promises to do well in school. The Petrov family is given a lot of helpful advice. A new family is summoned into the room, a new misfortune and things to work out. The Petrovs go out. What have they learned here? What have they understood? How will they go on with their lives? No one knows yet.

The family that replaces the Petrovs is unusual. There are two mothers, a father, and a son. What's this all about?

Arsenii Semenovich Bogoliubov had a wife, Elena Grigor'evna. He went north on a work assignment and returned with a new wife. Elena Grigor'evna immediately moved in with her mother, leaving her husband the apartment. Two children were born into this new family, Volodia and Vitia. But the parents weren't interested in them; they led a dissolute, drunken life, argued and fought. Then Bogoliubov was arrested for major embezzlement and sent to a work camp. This didn't disrupt the family's way of life, though: left alone, Bogoliubov's new wife, Zinaida Pavlovna, drank as before, completely neglected her home and went out for long periods of time, leaving the children without supervision. Once Elena Grigor'evna dropped in to see the boys. She saw the dirty room, the neglected and hungry children. After that she kept coming back to wash, dress and feed the children. One day the eldest, Volodia (he was six then), said, "Take me to live with you."

She took him. The youngest was turned over to a children's boarding facility and Elena Grigor'evna set to the business of raising Volodia.[3] Now he is sixteen. The father has served his term. Volodia doesn't even want to hear about the mother being reunited with the family. What has brought these people here to the Committee on Juvenile Delinquency? It's the fact that Elena Grigor'evna wants to adopt Volodia but to do this Zinaida Pavlovna must be deprived of her parental rights. And that's not all: now Vitia, the youngest, also wants to go to Elena Grigor'evna and she is willing to take him.

The committee carries wide authority and it has the right to recommend to the courts that the couple be deprived of parental rights if this is in the best interest of the children. It will now be decided whether or not to do this. Both parents, Arsenii Semenovich and Zinaida Pavlovna, are frantic. Both beg that they not be deprived of the right to raise their children. In tears Zinaida Pavlovna says: "I confess that I was a bad mother. It's true that another woman raised my son and I thank her for that. Volodia is more her son than mine. But if Vitia is also taken from me, there is nothing to live for."

She covers her eyes with her hand and suddenly faints. Someone rushes to help her, someone calls a doctor, someone picks the woman up and carries her to another room. I look at Volodia—his face is somber, lips drawn tight. He doesn't even turn his head in his mother's direction.

Why, having forgotten about their children for so long, are they now clinging to their paternity and maternity? What happened to cause a mother to abandon her children to fate, what occurred just now to evoke these tears and despair? I don't know.

By some miracle, Volodia and Vitia didn't go astray. They were on the edge of the precipice, alone and unneeded. Another woman came to the aid of one of the boys. The other was taken in by the boarding facility. If not for this, it might be that the committee would now be making another kind of decision: what to do with Volodia and Vitia Bogoliubov, teenagers who were in trouble.

Lena Kireeva wasn't so lucky. She is fourteen. She has quit school and her conduct is such that someone suggests that she be sent at once to a corrections center.[4]

"Wait a minute," other voices object. "We'll give her a probation period, find her work. Let's try to avoid the corrections center. Lena, do you promise to change your ways?"

Lena promises. You can believe her promise: she has spent ten days in a holding cell and is very frightened. She realizes that it would be better to be at home.

She is afraid of the corrections center and therefore is ready to make (and keep!) any promise just so as not to be sent to there, not to the corrections center!

But one person insists, "Definitely send her to the corrections center!"

Who is this person?

None other than Lena's father.

He is a party member and a foreman in a Leningrad factory. He says, "You want to saddle me with her, but I don't intend to bother with her anymore."

He's very sure that he's in the right. He's sure that someone else should be responsible for his daughter. Since she's gone astray, send her off to the corrections center. He doesn't intend to bother with her anymore.

And what should they do with Volodia Diukov? What he has been up to can't be conveyed in print. It can only be described as a heinous act. If it were up to me, I would have sent him to the corrections center without hesitation. But his school principal, Liudmila Vasil'evna Milovidova, requests a deferment for Diukov: she is prepared to vouch for him.

"His father is hopeless," says Diukov's mother. "He's always drunk. It's up to me to bring up my son; I'm responsible for him."

But it's too much for her; she can't manage. The entire responsibility will rest with Liudmila Vasil'evna. I look at this woman with immense respect: she has voluntarily taken an enormous weight onto her shoulders, and the boy's family can't help her carry the burden. All the same, she has defended Diukov and has accepted all responsibility for him.

Igor Belov stands before us. I won't describe his appearance or manner of speaking. Try to remember the last humorous article you read about the stereotypical "punk" or "freeloader" and you will get the picture.[5] With Igor everything is exactly as we have read hundreds of times: skin-tight pants, the neck of his shirt sloppily hanging open, overly familiar behavior, a gold tooth sparkling in his mouth. Yes, he's turned up here straight out of one of those caricatures. Actually, it's even better to recall Fonvizin's ignoramus Mitrofan.[6] That will give the most accurate picture.

Here is what the authorized police representative reports:

"This young man will be eighteen in August. His mother is a salesclerk in a specialty wine store. He hasn't got a father, but his stepfather drives a taxi. Igor graduated from vocational school as an electrician, but he has been fired twice for not showing up for work. We called him in, warned him, sent him to another job, but he didn't show up."

"Tell us why you failed to show up for work," requests the chair of the committee.

"I don't know . . . the weather was great . . . it was summer . . . everyone was going out of town. . . ."

"Why didn't you show up at your second job?"

"I was supposed to chip concrete and the dust would be flying around into my eyes. I just didn't go."

An outburst of completely justified indignation. Everyone would like this punk to understand what really hard work is. Amidst the confusion someone wants to know why Igor has a gold tooth. His mother, who is also present, explains that she had the tooth crowned "on prinsapull." What in the world is "prinsapull"? In revenge, she had taken her husband's ring and had gold crowns made for herself and her son because he had taken her ring first.

Everyone is stunned by this "principled" stand, and someone asks what Belova thinks she'll do with Igor.

"If I could kill him, I would."

Silence. Say what you will, but you don't hear that sort of thing from a mother every day. And at this point a new detail is added to the mix. The vice-chair of the Housing Committee takes the floor.

"We've been working with Igor in earnest since August. We explained the kind of future that is waiting for him and he seemed to have understood. But, you know, once when we dropped in on him, we found him with a girl. . . ."

I look at Igor. He still wears a ridiculous grin on his face. I'm getting sick of this senseless beating around the bush; you can't explain anything to him, he just won't get it. I keep glancing at my watch: I should get going.

"What's your girlfriend's name?" someone asks.

"Valia."

"Last name?"

"I'm not telling."

I don't believe my ears and look up again. The grin is gone and Igor's face is serious and calm—a totally changed face!

"What do you mean, you're not telling? Tell us right now! We'll report that girl to the proper authorities!"

"I don't want to get her mixed up in this."

"Talk right now!"

"I won't tell you!"

"Hey," the police officer says, "there's a girl standing waiting on the stairs. Maybe it's her. I'll go get her."

He goes out. With all my heart I hope that the girl has left or at least will refuse to come in. But the door opens and she enters.

"What do you do in private with this young man? Aren't you ashamed?"

Tightly compressing her lips, the girl remains silent.

"We'll tell your parents, then you'll be in for it! What's your name?"

"Valia."

"Last name?"

"Stoliarova."

"Where do you work?"

"At factory number. . . ."

"Where do you live?"

". . . Street, apartment number. . . ."

"Aren't you ashamed to be mixed up with this loafer?"

She's silent.

"Well, OK. Since you're friends, why don't you talk him into going to work?"

"I wanted to get him a job at our factory, but it didn't work out."

Something in her calm, firm answers disarms the committee members. Their common anger is now directed at the mother: "What were you thinking of? You get gold crowns made, but you don't bother to raise him properly?"

"I won't raise him! I won't! I'm sick of dealing with him! I want a life of my own!"

Sobbing loudly, she leaves the room.

"Why are you attacking my mom?" Igor asks the committee. "She raised me as she should have. I'm the bad one, not her." After he is silent for a moment, he says with a sigh: "OK, OK, I'll go to work!"

"What a favor he's doing us!" says the chair of the committee, not without humor. "Hats off to you. Come back on Tuesday about 10:00 A.M. We'll give you a job assignment. But watch out that you don't sleep in."

I want to know how this affair will end, and so on Tuesday I also go back to the District Council about 10:00 A.M. Who should I see on the stairs? Valia, naturally. We stand and talk for a long time.

"You don't know, no one, absolutely no one knows how good he is. He doesn't smoke or drink. There are two things in the world that he loves: reading and pigeons. He grew up like a stray. His mother didn't treat him badly, she just didn't care about him. His stepfather didn't treat him badly either, but he didn't bother with him either. Since he was six he's been attached like crazy to the pigeons. He's up at dawn with them. And he does everything around the house: he washes the floors and cooks the meals. And he will feed and play host to everyone who comes to their home. Look, here he comes now!"

It takes me a while to get used to the idea that I can talk to him like a grown person. I still remember his stupid smirk, his ridiculous answers.

"Why did you behave so stupidly in there?" I ask him. "What kind of answer is 'It was summer, the weather was great?' There's no easy job in the world and nobody feels like getting up at seven in the morning."

"No," he says. "There are some people who go to work like it's a celebration."

"Well, go and find yourself that kind of work!"

"I'll never find it."

"You mean to say you're looking?"

"Look," says Valia, "you can teach a dog to walk on a leash with a blind person, or to carry something in its teeth, or to chase down thieves. But pigeons? Can you think of a way they can be useful?"

"No, pigeons are for pure joy."

And he begins to talk about pigeons.

"There are pigeons that are really dumb: they'll go and nest in a strange dovecote. And there are some that die sooner and nest only in their own dovecote. If you only knew how wonderful pigeons are!"

Valia and I listen and it would have been interesting if the whole time we didn't have in the back of our minds that this profound passion was disrupting his life and discouraging him from working or studying.

Not long after my return to Moscow a letter arrived from Valia Stoliarova. This is what it said:

> A big hello from Leningrad. Please forgive that it took so long to write even though I promised to write as soon as things with Igor were settled. He's working at a factory, but to tell the truth it's a long way for him to go. I don't know what will happen but for the time being he's working. We quarrel a lot but the only thing I want is for him to stay on the straight and narrow. I only need one thing from him and that is that he has a job. If before September we don't have a huge argument and if everything else with him is going well, then in September we'll go to school—I'll go into the ninth grade and he'll go into the seventh grade. I need to finish school and so does he. Goodbye. Best wishes. Valia. Waiting for good advice from you.

How hard it is to give advice! But maybe it's not so hard after all: a lot of mundane wisdom has been accumulated, it's there for all to see, you can scoop it up by the handful and dole it out to all those asking for it. Only this is seldom of any use. Each person is master of his or her own life, and it just doesn't work to apply one's own experience to another person. It will be easy for Igor to stray. I can see him clearly standing before another meeting of the committee. They will ask him:

"Why did you not go to work this time?"

And smiling the absurd smile of a fool, he will answer:

"Why? It was a long way to go . . . I had to get up too early. . . ."

Unfortunately, I don't have a hard time picturing this scene. But I remember something else too: Igor's serious face, his "I'm not telling," and what he had to say about people who go to work like it's a celebration. I remember Valia answering the committee's questions so calmly and firmly, and patiently standing on the stairs waiting for Igor. It's a great support to have that sort of person in your life. I'm not so very moved by Igor's passion for pigeons. Like everyone else, I'm bored to death of the widespread cliché which holds that if you cut a person to the quick, he soon turns into the very sort of ideal hero that Soviet literature has been looking for for so long.[7] But all the same, whatever else you say, if a person is obsessed by something, if he loves something unselfishly . . . well, when all is said and done, it's an advantage. But I can't advise anything from the outside. I can't suggest anything. Igor's life is in his own hands. While he was small, he depended on his family and on his school. His family endowed him with precious little. And judging by everything else, his school failed to leave a deep impression on him. So now, on the threshold of adult life, he is his own master, the maker of his own happiness or unhappiness. Just like Lena Kireeva, just like Volodia Diukov.

Not too long ago at a meeting between readers and authors, the following question was asked: "Why describe the family quagmire? Who's interested in what happens within those four walls?"

The hearings of the Committee on Juvenile Delinquency clearly and relentlessly confirm the simple truth that those four walls determine a great deal. You can say what you will about the school's responsibility, but for your first seven years, you are brought up at home. Within those four walls, you receive your first ideas about the world, about your place in life. A large portion of your life is spent within those four walls. You can't escape that fact.

We can't console ourselves and say that the families who come before the committee are exceptions, with unique circumstances. However many these unique circumstance are—they exist. Drunkenness. Divorce. Fatherless families. If a young boy is in trouble you will definitely run into one of these reasons, if not all of them.

The Committee on Juvenile Delinquency is full of good intentions. It arranges employment for teenagers, tries to warn those who aren't cooperating, doesn't abandon those children who end up in a corrections center or those who have been recently released. But it cannot replace the family and constant family supervision.

I hope the committee members will not take offense at these opinions. They simply cannot examine a lot of "matters" at one sitting. Any given situation about which the committee racks its brains demands a maximum of emotional and mental strength. And if the committee has managed to gain some sort of understanding about some of the "matters" on the conveyor belt of problems, it does not mean that those problems have been probed thoroughly.

Moreover, no matter how perspicacious the committee's members, no matter how conscientiously the representative of the police or the public has presented the case, it is possible that the real core of its character and circumstances may remain uncovered. I think that this nearly happened to Igor Belov and Valia Stoliarova. Their story turned out to be much more complicated than the usual one about a loafer teamed up with a frivolous young girl.

And too, more often than not, the committee becomes involved when it's already a bit late. The fourteen-year-olds Boria and Lena, the fifteen-year-old Diukov are already tough nuts to crack. It's very difficult to help them now, and I'm afraid that the best advice or even fines will not alter the character of their families. Evidently, we need to find out about the trouble that occurs within four walls earlier, much earlier. . . .

1962

Translated by Teresa Polowy

Notes to the Essay

1. I am grateful to Aleksandra Raskina, Frida Vigdorova's daughter, for the comments, suggestions and contextualizations of many of the events described in this article that she related to me during several enlightening telephone conversations.

2. Raisa Orlova, *Memoirs* (New York: Random House, 1983), 268. It is significant that a good deal of the secondary literature about Vigdorova is written by close friends, many of whom are women, who figure prominently in the official and unofficial Soviet cultures and whom she had helped in various ways. For instance, her close friend Lidiia Chukovskaia has written several articles about Vigdorova's life and works, as has Ruf' Zernova; Raisa Orlova devotes an entire chapter to Vigdorova in her memoirs; I. Grekova, whose writing career Vigdorova encouraged, has written an afterword to a collection of her works; Lev Kopelev writes briefly about Vigdorova in a book that he dedicated to her (177–78); and Efim Etkind remembers his and Vigdorova's involvement in the Brodsky affair and quotes at length from her trial transcripts in his memoirs (91–104).

3. Lev Kopelev, *Sviatoi Doktor Fedor Petrovich* (London: Overseas Publications Interchange, 1985), 177.

4. Georgii Svirskii, *Soviet Writing: The Literature of Moral Opposition* (Ann Arbor, MI: Ardis, 1981), 236. Ruf' Zernova explains in "Portret absoliutno prekrasnogo cheloveka" that the position of Deputy of the Regional Soviet was largely honorary, yet "[Frida] immediately regarded it as 'an office'—with a heavy accent on duty and responsibility." *Èto bylo pri nas* (Jerusalem: Lexicon, 1988), 239.

5. Lidiia Chukovskaia, "Skol'ko stanet sil," afterword, *Doroga v zhizn', Èto moi dom, Chernigovka*, by Frida Vigdorova (Moscow: Detskaia literatura, 1967), 727.

6. In 1948 *Komsomol'skaia pravda* fired Vigdorova because she was of Jewish origin. A. Barker, "Vigdorova, Frida Abramovna," in *Dictionary of Russian Women Writers* ed. M. Ledkovsky, C. Rosenthal and M. Zirin (Westport, CT: Greenwood Press, 1994), 709.

7. Vigdorova received a firm rebuke for this stance in a review of her book by N. Vengrov: "The fundamental thing about teaching, that is, the process of how a talented teacher nurtures and educates children, with the end result that they learn something, is not the main thrust of the novel. This [process] . . . is given much less attention than are the methods for acquainting the teacher with the character of each of her students and for educating them outside the prescribed regulations. . . . It is widely recognized that the most important thing in the pedagogical process is the teacher's direct intention that the children should learn: they train their pupils ideologically, develop their awareness, and introduce them to the fundamentals of a Leninist-Stalinist worldview." "Uvlekatel'naia professiia," *Novyi mir* 5 (1950): 254.

8. Lev Kopelev, a historian, writer and prominent Soviet dissident in the 1960s, remembers reading *My Class* in prison and found the book to be "indispensable in its purity, honesty, and goodness." Orlova, *Memoirs,* 266.

9. Zoia Kosmodem'ianskaia, a Komsomol member and tenth-grade pupil, volunteered for service in a partisan detachment in 1941. Captured behind enemy lines, she was tortured and hanged by Nazi troops when she refused to reveal even her true name. After Zoia's death, her younger brother Shura volunteered for active duty and died at the front during a tank battle. Zoia's story became legendary in official Komsomol culture. Kosmodem'ianskaia was posthumously proclaimed Hero of the Soviet Union in 1942.

10. There are multiple tangible links between Vigdorova's trilogy and the writings and theories of Makarenko. Karabanov is the hero of Makarenko's novel *A Pedagogical Poem* (*Pedagogicheskaia poèma*, 1933–1935; translated as *The Road to Life: An Epic of Education*, 1951, 1955, 1973 [it should not be confused with Vigdorova's novel, *The Road to Life*]); "Chernigovka" is the name that Makarenko gives to Karabanov's wife, just as it is the name of the heroine in the third novel in Vigdorova's trilogy. Vigdorova's *The Road to Life* opens with an evocation of Makarenko's work: "His saga is about children, who from a very early age lived on the streets and engaged in crime, who were in emotional pain and in great need, and yet were able to become real human beings." *Doroga v zhizn'; Èto moi dom; Chernigovka* (Kiev: Radian'ska shkola, 1982), 1. In her trilogy, Vigdorova explores what happens with Karabanov when he no longer works under the supervision of Makarenko and has his own charges.

11. For an idea of readers' responses to Vigdorova's novellas, see N. Podorol'skii, "Povesti F. Vigdorovoi," *Narodnoe obrazovanie* 3 (1958): 112. Chukovskaia also cites and comments on readers' responses in "Skol'ko stanet sil," 712–21.

12. *Family Happiness* was faulted for the narrow scope of its action—a common criticism leveled at much women's writing, which often depicts the details of domestic and daily life

of one family. However, M. Blinkova defends the novella, focusing in on the efforts of the heroine to provide psychological, emotional and moral support for her husband who has returned from the front lines of World War II: "Probably if the writer had portrayed a doctor fighting to save a life, or a work collective helping a fellow-worker who was in trouble, no one would refuse to acknowledge the social resonance of this work. But Vigdorova's novella is called *Family Happiness* and the task of returning Polivanov to productive life fell to his wife . . . it was she who had to shoulder all the weight of Dmitrii's problem. . . ." "Ispytanie budniami," *Novyi mir* 2 (1962): 255.

13. The heroine of the novellas, Sasha, is a nurse, whom Vigdorova depicts as extremely dedicated to helping people and society through her work. According to her daughter, during World War II Vigdorova herself had considered going to the front as a nurse but decided against it because she was pregnant with her second child. In any case the motive of providing aid to others through one's work is operative in both the author and her heroine.

14. The "Doctors' Plot" involved an alleged conspiracy by Soviet medical professionals to assassinate prominent military and party officials. The doctors, most of whom were Jewish, were arrested in January 1953 and released in April following Stalin's death when it was announced that they had been wrongly arrested. The entire incident was a product of Stalin's increasing anti-Semitism and paranoia about the medical community being involved in a Zionist plot against the Soviet Union.

15. Orlova asserts that Vigdorova's eyes had long been open to the reality of Stalinist society and cites numerous examples of her increasing awareness and activity: by 1938 Vigdorova had been introduced by a friend to "shockingly new ideas" about Stalin's purges. The prewar banishment from Moscow of close friends such as Vigdorova's childhood schoolteacher and mentor, Anna Ivanovna Tikhomirova, and, in 1949, the arrest of the writer Ruf' Zernova and her husband, the scholar Il'ia Serman, confirmed Vigdorova's belief that innocent people were being imprisoned in the Soviet Union. She undertook to help them with visits, material aid, legal assistance and petitions to the authorities; she also opened her home to Zernova's daughter. In 1949 Vigdorova expressed the opinion that the collective is not invariably right and that a phenomenon of mass psychosis had been created in the Soviet Union. In 1957 Vigdorova spoke at a Moscow writers meeting where she publicly defended the authorial right and obligation to criticize, to fight against falsehood and for truth. Orlova, *Memoirs,* 265–72.

16. Chukovskaia, introduction to "Sudilische," *Ogonek* 49 (1988): 26.

17. Orlova, *Memoirs,* 281.

18. Orlova, *Memoirs,* 264, and Nadezhda Mandel'shtam, *Hope Abandoned* (New York: Atheneum, 1974), 377.

19. In January 1964, the poet Brodsky was arrested on charges of "parasitism," that is, a failure to be engaged in socially recognized work. Brodsky was not a member of the Soviet Writers' Union, but nonetheless considered poetry his profession and earned money from his literary translations; he was thoroughly nonconformist and nonpolitical. The trial was unusual because although it was a criminal trial, it had clear and ominous political undertones. Brodsky was sentenced to five years of administrative exile and was sent to work on a state farm in the Arkhangel'sk region.

20. Andrei Sinyavsky and Iulii Daniel (who wrote their literary works under the pseudonyms of Abram Tertz and Nikolai Arzhak) were the first Soviet writers to be arrested for sending their manuscripts abroad for publication. They were sentenced to seven and five years' hard labor, respectively.

21. Ia. Gordin, "Delo Brodskogo," *Neva* 2 (1989): 152.

22. Vigdorova, ever sensitive to incriminating others, never told her daughters how the transcripts ended up in the West. Many years after her death, her daughter Aleksandra heard the following version from family friends: one of Vigdorova's writer friends had approached her and told her that a certain woman, whether Russian or Western is not clear, was prepared to take the transcripts abroad. The writer inquired as to whether Vigdorova wanted to entrust them to this third woman; she did.

23. Mandel'shtam, *Hope Abandoned,* 377.

24. Gordin, 149.

25. Kopelev, 178.

26. See Svirskii, 237, and Orlova, *Memoirs,* 280.

27. See Barbara Heldt, *Terrible Perfection: Women and Russian Literature* (Bloomington: Indiana University Press, 1987), 9.

28. Chukovskaia, "Skol'ko stanet sil," 727.

29. See I. Grekova, "Sto serdets," in *Doroga v zhizn'* (Kiev: Radian'skaia shkola, 1982), 592.

30. Vigdorova had two daughters, Galina (1937–1974) and Aleksandra (b. 1942). Aleksandra, a scholar, now lives in the United States and is currently engaged in preserving and compiling her mother's archives. Galina, a teacher, died tragically in an accident in the Carpathian Mountains, where she had taken her pupils on winter vacation; she was struck down by the ambulance that she had summoned for a pupil who had fallen ill.

31. Orlova, *Memoirs,* 279.

32. For an account of such gatherings, see A. Raskina, "Slushaia Galicha," *Novoe russkoe slovo,* 19 October 1991.

33. Orlova, *Memoirs,* 266.

34. Beth Holmgren, *Women's Works in Stalin's Time: On Lidiia Chukovskaia and Nadezhda Mandel'shtam* (Bloomington: Indiana University Press, 1993), 177. In this monograph Holmgren discusses the creative and heroic model provided Russian women by Chukovskaia and Mandel'shtam.

35. Kopelev, 178.

36. Orlova, *Memoirs,* 284. Nadezhda Mandel'shtam and Lidiia Chukovskaia, who in many ways provided role models for Vigdorova, also valued her public work highly. Speaking of Vigdorova's efforts on behalf of Brodsky, Mandel'shtam states: "Nobody should be allowed to forget that you have to put all of yourself into the battle for another man's life—as Frida Vigdorova's example showed" (*Hope Abandoned,* 87). Chukovskaia laments Vigdorova's passing as the collapse of a "main support" in her life (qtd. in Orlova, *Memoirs,* 283).

37. Zernova, "Portret . . . ," in *Èto bylo pri nas,* 237.

38. "Chto takoe muzhestvo?" in *Kem vy emu prixodites'?* (Moscow: Moskovskii rabochii, 1969), 90.

Translator's Notes to the Selected Work

1. This journalistic essay appeared in the collection *Kem vy emu prikhodites'? Stat'i i ocherki* (Moscow: Moskovskii rabochii, 1969), 132–41. It poses questions and explores motifs that are directly linked to the recurrent themes found in Vigdorova's novellas: a deep concern for children and adolescents and the importance of the home environment for their healthy social,

intellectual and emotional development; families, and especially women, coping in difficult social and economic circumstances; the social problems of alcoholism, divorce, single mothers and juvenile delinquency. The reader also sees Vigdorova's own active interest in lending moral support to those young people who are down and out.

2. "Executive Committee" refers to the Russian *ispolkom* (*ispolnitel'nyi kommitet*). Under the Soviet system this was the Executive Committee of a District Council. Each city had a number of districts, each with its own council; various regional departmental divisions came under the councils' purview (e.g., public education, healthcare services). An Executive Committee often oversaw various smaller committees (e.g., in this work, the Committee on Juvenile Delinquency). The Police Department also reported to the Executive Committee.

3. "Children's boarding facility" refers to the Russian *internat*. An *internat* under the Soviet system referred to a state-financed boarding school. Often children at these schools were from troubled families in which parents were unable to responsibly raise their children; children whose parents' employment commitments interfered with their ability to care for their children (e.g., unconventional shifts, or a work site located a great distance from the family's apartment) were also boarded here.

4. "Corrections center" refers to the Russian *ispravitel'naia koloniia*.

5. "Humorous article" refers to the Russian *fel'eton*. In Russia, this is a traditionally popular genre of newspaper or magazine article that utilizes humor and satire in its treatment of topics of current interest.

6. Mitrofan is the main character in D.I. Fonvizin's eighteenth-century comedy *The Adolescent* (*Nedorosl*). He is the stupid, lazy, spoiled teenage son of a landowner, and he rejects all efforts to educate him. In Russian culture, his name has become synonymous with this ilk.

7. An ironic allusion to the "positive hero" in Soviet socialist realist literature who overcomes all personal, ideological and economic hardships and comes out a better person in the end because of them. Soviet writers were expected to portray such ideal, "positive" heroes; depictions of "regular" heroes were regarded with suspicion by the literary authorities.

Bibliography

Primary Works

Moi klass. Moscow: Detgiz, 1949.

Zapiski uchitel'nitsy (glavy iz povesti 4–yi klass V). Moscow: Pravda, 1949.

Doroga v zhizn'. Èto moi dom. Povesti. Moscow: Sovetskii pisatel', 1957.

Chernigovka. Moscow: Sovetskii pisatel', 1959.

Chto takoe muzhestvo? Moscow: Moskovskii rabochii, 1961.

Doroga v zhizn'. Èto moi dom. Chernigovka. Povesti. Moscow: Sovetskii pisatel', 1961, 1966, 1969, 1972.

"Glaza pustye i volshebnye." *Tarusskie stranitsy*. Kaluga: Kaluzhskoe knizhnoe izdatel'stvo, 1961.

Semeinoe schast'e. Povest'. Moscow: Sovetskii pisatel', 1962.

Dorogaia redaktsiia. Ocherki. Moscow: Moskovskii rabochii, 1963.

Liubimaia ulitsa. Povest'. Moscow: Sovetskii pisatel', 1964.

Semeinoe schast'e. Liubimaia ulitsa. Povesti. Moscow: Sovetskii pisatel', 1965.

"Zasedanie suda . . . nad Iosifom Brodskim. Dokulmental'naia zapis'." *Vozdushnye puti* 4 (1965).

Also in E. Etkind. *Zapiski nezagovorshchika*. London, 1977. 437–67.

Doroga v zhizn'. Èto moi dom. Chernigovka. Moscow: Detskaia literatura, 1967.

Minuty tishiny. Moscow: Detskaia literatura, 1967.

Kem vy emu prikhodites'? Stat'i i ocherki. Moscow: Moskovskii rabochii, 1969.

Doroga v zhizn'. Povesti. Kiev: Radian'ska shkola, 1982.

"Sudilishche." *Ogonek* 49 (1988): 26–31. [Transcripts of the Brodsky trials.]

"Delo Brodskogo." *Neva* 2 (1989): 143–66. [With Ia. Gordin.]

In Translation

"A New Home." *Soviet Literature* 11 (1944): 59–62.

Diary of a School Teacher. Trans. Rose Prokofieva. Moscow: Foreign Languages Publishing House, 1954.

The Road to Life. Moscow: State Publishing House for Juvenile Literature, 1954.

"Empty Eyes and Magic Eyes." *Pages from Tarusa*. Ed. Andrew Field. London: Chapman and Hall, 1963. 301–09.

"The Trial of Iosif Brodsky." *New Leader,* 31 August 1964, 6–17.

"The Trial of Iosif Brodsky." *Encounter,* September 1964, 84–91.

Diary of a Russian School Teacher. Trans. Rose Prokofieva. New York: Grove, 1960; rpt. Westport, CT: Greenwood Press, 1973.

"A Question of Ethics." Trans. F.F. Snyder. *Russian Literature Triquarterly* 5–6 (1973): 406–13.

Secondary Works

Barker, A. "Vigdorova, Frida Abramovna." *Dictionary of Russian Women Writers*. Ed. M. Ledkovsky, C. Rosenthal and M. Zirin. Westport, CT: Greenwood Press, 1994. 708–11.

Blinkova, M. "Ispytanie budniami." *Novyi mir* 2 (1962): 253–56.

Brushstein, A. "Podvig liubvi i terpeniia." *Novyi mir* 5 (1958): 247–49.

Chukovskaia, L. *Brodski, ou Le proces d'un poète*. Paris: Livre de poche, 1988. [In Russian, Moscow: Moskovskii rabochii, 1990.]

———. "Frida Abramovna Vigdorova." Trans. F.F. Snyder. *Russian Literature Triquarterly* 5–6 (1973): 399–405.

———. Introduction. "Sudilishche." *Ogonek* 49 (1988): 26.

———. *Otkrytoe slovo*. Moscow: IMA Press, 1991. [Chukovskaia's obitutary for Vigdorova.]

———. "Skol'ko stanet sil." *Doroga v zhizn'. Èto moi dom. Chernigovka*. By Frida Vigdorova. Moscow: Detskaia literatura, 1967. 712–33.

Chukovskii, K. *Dnevnik: 1939–1969*. Vol. 2. Moscow: Sovetskii pistael', 1994.

Etkind, E. *Notes of a Non-Conspirator*. Trans. Peter France. Oxford: Oxford University Press, 1978. 91–104.

Gordin, Ia. "Delo Brodskogo." *Neva* 2 (1989): 143–66.

Grekova, I. "Sto serdets." *Doroga v zhizn'. Povest'*. By Frida Vigdorova. Kiev: Radian'ska shkola, 1982. 590–606.

Holmgren, B. *Women's Works in Stalin's Time*. Bloomington: Indiana University Press, 1993.

Kasack, W. *Dictionary of Russian Literature since 1917*. New York: Columbia University Press, 1988.

Kopelev, L. *Sviatoi Doktor Fedor Petrovich*. London: Overseas Publications Interchange, 1985.

Kosmodem'ianskaia, *L. Povest' o Zoe i Shure. Literaturnaia zapis' F. Vigdorovoi*. Moscow: Detgiz, 1956.

Lazarev, L. "Pust' chitatel' dumaet." *Novyi mir* 1 (1970): 266–69.

L'vov, S. *Mozhno li stat' Robinzonom?* Moscow: Detskaia literatura, 1966.

Mandel'shtam, N. *Hope Abandoned*. New York: Atheneum, 1974.

———. "Perepiska Varlaama Shalamova i Nadezhdy Mandel'shtam." *Znamia* 2 (1992): 164–65.

———. *Vtoraia kniga*. Paris: YMCA Press, 1983.

Nemec Ignashev, D., and S. Krive, eds. "Vigdorova, Frida." *Women and Writing in Russia and the USSR: A Bibliography of English-Language Sources*. New York: Garland, 1992. 109, 221–22.

Orlova, Raisa. *Memoirs*. Trans. S. Cioran. New York: Random House, 1983.

———. "SSSR: Vnutrennie protivorechiia." *USA* 3 (1982): 300–25.

Pleshcheev, N. "Novaia povest' F. Vigdorovoi." *Narodnoe obrazovanie* 2 (1960): 116–17.

Podorol'skii, N. "Povesti F. Vigdorovoi." *Narodnaia obrazovanie* 3 (1958): 111–12.

Raskina, A. "Slushaia Galicha." *Novoe russkoe slovo*, 19 October 1991.

Rodden, W. "Frida Vigdorova." *Encyclopedia of Continental Women Writers*. Ed. K. Wilson. New York: Garland, 1991. 1300–01.

Svirskii, Grigorii. *A History of Post-War Soviet Writing: The Literature of Moral Opposition*. Trans. and ed. Robert Dessaix and Michael Ulman. Ann Arbor, MI: Ardis, 1981.

Tomei, C. "Vigdorova, Frida Abramovna." *A Handbook of Russian Literature*. Ed. V. Terras. New Haven, CT: Yale University Press, 1985. 509.

Vengrov, N. "Uvlekatel'naia professiia." *Novyi mir* 5 (1950): 251–54.

Zernova, R. *Izrail' i ego okrestnosti*. Tel Aviv: Biblioteka Alia, 1990.

———. "Portret absoliutno prekrasnogo cheloveka." 2 parts. *Russkaia mysl'*, 20 September 1985, 9; 27 September 1985, 11.

———. "Portret absoliutno prekrasnogo cheloveka." *Èto bylo pri nas*. Jerusalem: Lexicon, 1988. 230–45.

Nina Berberova

Nina Nikolaevna Berberova (1901–1993) was a prose writer, poet, biographer, playwright, literary critic and essayist whose work remains important to literary history, especially her memoirs and critical writing. Berberova's works belong to the history of modernism no less than its more celebrated or sensational masterpieces, such as Nabokov's. Her works are indeed relevant to present-day dilemmas and ideas. In them, there is a strong desire to overcome the values and the traditions of the past and the older generation's fixed attitudes. The modernists' individualistic frame of mind frequently borders on narcissism, since the poets often talk about themselves in their works. These attitudes are apparent in Berberova's writings. Furthermore, a certain indifference toward ethical problems and a concentration on issues particularly relevant to women clearly indicate that she focused on creating a new image for woman and a new association with man. Berberova made her views known both in her personal and in her public lives, thus fascinating her youthful audiences. Her readers have grasped her as a writer, have appropriated her attitudes and have enthusiastically welcomed her with her aesthetic modernism.

Berberova was the only daughter of a civil servant in the St. Petersburg finance ministry, Nikolai Ivanovich Berberov, an Armenian, who successfully retained his position following the October Revolution of 1917. Soon after that year, he was transferred to Moscow. In the midst of civil war, he moved south to Rostov; then, in 1921, back to cold and squalid St. Petersburg. Berberova's mother, Nataliia Ivanovna (née Karaulova), was a Russian. Nina Berberova attended Mariia S. Mikhelson's private "progressive" school in St. Petersburg and dreamed about becoming a Russian poet. She early on began to emphasize her antimonarchist attitudes, did not attend church and hated close family circles.

Berberova graduated from the eighth grade of a high school in the south of Russia and, for a while, attended the historical and philological department at the university there, but abandoned her studies and accepted employment in a library. Upon her return to St. Petersburg in 1921, she enrolled at the Institute of the History of Arts, formerly Zubovskii Institute. She also joined the Poets' Union after having presented her samples of verse to Nikolai Gumilev, who was charmed by her and by her poetry. Shortly thereafter, he was executed by the Bolsheviks. At the Poets' Union, as well as in the House of Art and the House of Writers, which she visited, she met other Russian poets, among them Nikolai Otsup, Georgii Ivanov, Georgii Adamovich and Vladislav Khodasevich. Her favorite poet at that time was Aleksandr Blok, who died in St. Petersburg in 1921 and whose funeral she attended.

A romance developed between Khodasevich and Berberova in the House of Art in St. Petersburg, and Khodasevich arranged, in 1922, for their elopement and removal from St. Petersburg to Berlin, via Riga. (Her parents remained in St. Petersburg, where, in the winter of 1941–1942, they died.) Thus began a peripatetic life abroad: Berlin, Prague, Venice, Rome, Sorrento. After having lived for two years in Gorky's villa in Sorrento, in 1925 Khodasevich and Berberova moved to Paris, where they lived a life of poverty. Khodasevich contributed to Kerensky's fortnightly *Dni* (*Days*; Paris, 1928–1933). In Paris, Berberova became acquainted with many Russian émigré writers and artists. In her autobiography *The Italics Are Mine* (English translation, 1969), Berberova gives vivid descriptions of Russian life in Paris, the literary soirées, the restaurants, the apartments and the work of the émigrés.

In April 1932 Berberova left Khodasevich, who was in poor health, and moved in with Nikolai V. Makeev, who, in 1904, had joined the Social Revolutionary party. Early in 1917, Makeev had become a member of the board of the All-Russian Union of Zemstvos, of which he was elected president, succeeding Prince L'vov. In October 1917 he became a member of the Constituent Assembly of the city of Vladimir. He left Russia in 1919. Together with Valentine O'Hare, Makeev published the book *Russia* in 1925, with an introduction by H.A.L. Fisher, a member of Britain's Parliament. Before and during the Second World War, Berberova lived with Makeev in a hamlet outside Paris, where he bought a house in 1938. In the mid-1940s, she left Makeev, following a disagreement over a "third" person who came between them (as she discreetly put it in her autobiography *The Italics Are Mine*). This "third" person was Makeev's French secretary, a young man. Berberova writes in *The Italics Are Mine* that she triumphed in this struggle over the "third" person. She lived with the French secretary for several years, until 1949, when he suffered a serious neurological injury in a car accident. Following this calamity, Berberova ended her alliance with him and in 1950 moved to the

United States. Berberova explains in *The Italics Are Mine* that this "third" person had become a burden that she had neither the strength nor the desire to bear. However, as late as 1965, she traveled to Capri to spend a few summer weeks with him.

Before her departure to the United States, Berberova visited the Swedish artist Greta Gerell, Zinaida Gippius's close friend, in Stockholm and Hemmarö. There, also, Berberova met Harriet Bonné, third wife of Strindberg. In America, Berberova met various Russian émigrés, among them Alexandra Tolstaia (Lev Tolstoy's youngest daughter), the famous scholars Roman Jakobson and Mikhail Karpovich and many others. She often traveled across the country with her new acquaintances. She was especially fond of Vsevolod Pastukhov (1896–1967), a pianist, teacher and minor poet, formerly of St. Petersburg, a friend of the poets Mikhail Kuzmin and Georgii Ivanov. Berberova and George Kochevitsky, a musician, entered into a fictitious marriage in order for Berberova to remain in the United States, where she worked as a typist, a secretary, an announcer on the radio and a librarian. Eventually she became a teacher of Russian literature at Princeton, where she taught from 1963 to 1971.

Nina Berberova began to write prose in the mid-1920s. Her first stories were published in *Days* and in a literary journal, *The New Home* (*Novyi dom*; Paris, 1926–1927), which she edited along with David Knut, Iurii Terapiano and Vsevolod Fokht. Berberova admitted that she was inexperienced with words in these stories. Berberova's story "The Bridegroom" ("Zhenikh") appeared in the first issue of *The New Home* (the title of the journal was later changed to *The New Ship* [*Novyi korabl'*; Paris, 1927–1928]). Her cycle *Billancourt Fiestas* (*Biliankurskie prazdniki*) was published in the newspaper *The Latest News* (*Poslednie novosti*; Paris, 1920–1940), to which she contributed for several years. It is a humorous series about Billancourt: Russian drunks, indigents and déclassé eccentrics. The style is uneven and labored because, as she noted, she sought "the local parlance." There also are some attempts to approximate the grotesque formulations of Gogol and of Zoshchenko, with a Chekhovian attention to pertinent details, as well as a psychological emphasis in the manner of Dostoevsky. She endeavored to overcome her dependence, to find her own form of expression, her own path in belles lettres, which actually came much later, as will be discussed below. In 1930 a novel, *The Last and the First* (*Poslednie i pervye*), appeared, which portrays some strange relationships among her protagonists, reveals a lack of psychological motivation in their actions and shows an artificiality of style and atmosphere.

Nine Berberova's second novel, *Sovereign Queen* (*Povelitel'nitsa*, 1932), treats the theme of love as a complex experience. Lena, the heroine, more French than

Russian, and Sasha, a Russian, are involved in a duel of love in this French novel. Love is also at the center of Berberova's third novel, *Without a Sunset* (*Bez zakata*, 1938), which resembles a soap opera; sex appears to be the main preoccupation of Vera, the heroine of the novel. The language is again artificial, at times even ludicrous ("Between them always arose that impetuous wind which impelled them to kiss," or "Whenever she stood close to him, she lost her voice"). In 1930 her play, *Madame*, was performed in Paris four times.

She herself, aware of the artistic inadequacy of her fiction, decided to try the form of the long short story. The volume *The Mitigation of Fate* (*Oblegchenie uchasti*, 1949), including the longer short stories of the 1930s and 1940s, treats the themes of loneliness and the absence of love. The story "Lamentation" ("Plach") is well written. Much to Berberova's chagrin, the YMCA Press in Paris found this volume pornographic and halted its sale.

Three biographies, *Tchaikovsky: History of a Lonely Life* (*Chaikovskii: Istoriia odinokoi zhizni*, 1936), *Borodin* (1938) and *Aleksandr Blok and His Time* (*Alexandre Blok et Son Temps*, 1947), also appeared in print while Berberova still lived in Paris. *Tchaikovsky*,[1] translated into several languages, including Swedish, reveals a thoroughness of research. There are many fascinating details about Petr Tchaikovsky's childhood, adolescence and mature years. Berberova portrays in great detail his trips to western Europe and to the United States, his "romance-friendship" with his generous and enigmatic protector Nadezhda Filaretovna von Meck and his work on his symphonies, concertos and operas. However, Berberova's narrative becomes lost in the wealth of these details, which are frequently repeated. The compositional design is not well defined; the narration often marks time, as it were. This lack of motion is particularly apparent in the description of Tchaikovsky's childhood, though the tempo improves in the description of his moves to St. Petersburg and later to Moscow. Berberova expertly re-creates the atmosphere of the musical world of that time; however, her portrayal of Tchaikovsky is one-dimensional and devoid of psychological depth. The great composer appears to the reader constantly sad, frustrated, nervous or lonely, yet Berberova remains only an external observer, never revealing what underlies his psychological condition. Only sometimes does she find expressive words, which then glitter like precious stones.

Borodin is written differently. Much shorter than *Tchaikovsky*, it is a series of brief scenes in which the composer Borodin appears to the reader at various stages of his life. Again, we meet many musicians of that time: Balakirev, Stasov, Mussorgsky, Liszt, Tchaikovsky, the Russian pianist Vera Timanova and others. As in *Tchaikovsky*, situations and episodes are insufficiently developed; characters are described rather than portrayed; the style is again uneven. There are several expressions in substandard Russian usage such as *"nazhratsia"* and *"chumet' ot schast'ia."* On the other hand, while not a work of art, the content is well presented, and there are traces of humor in the narrative. With *Borodin*, Nina Berberova's formative period ended. In 1950 her personal life in Paris also came to a close. She left everything and everybody, including Makeev and the "third" person, behind and moved away, to the United States.[2]

Among her best articles written in the late 1940s, and thereafter, are "Twenty-five Years after the Death of A.A. Blok" ("25 let so smerti A.A. Bloka," 1947), "From My Reminiscences of St. Petersburg" ("Iz peterburgskikh vospominanii" 1953) and "Vladislav Khodasevich: A Russian Poet" ("Vladislav Khodasevich, russkii poèt," 1960). Much of her prose and poetry appeared in the *émigré* journals *The New Review* (*Novyi zhurnal*) and *The Bridges* (*Mosty*). For example, her article "Nabokov and His *Lolita*" ("Nabokov i ego *Lolita*") was published in *The New Review* in 1959, and her "Three Years of Gorky's Life" ("Tri goda zhizni Gor'kogo") was printed in *The Bridges* in 1961. She edited a volume of Khodasevich's poetry, with her commentary, *Collected Poems of Vladislav Khodasevich* (*Sobranie stikhov Vladislava Khodasevicha*, 1960), and Zinaida Gippius's *Zinaida Gippius: St. Petersburg Diaries, 1914–1919* (*Petersburgskie dnevniki, 1914–1919*), with her short introduction. Both of these editions are valued by Russian literary scholars.

Her remarkable autobiography, *The Italics Are Mine* (*Kursiv moi*), was published, first in English in New York (1969), then in Russian in Munich (1972), and then in German, in 1993, under the title *Ich komme aus St. Petersburg*. As in some of her earlier writings, Berberova expresses her antimonarchistic views. Berberova also gives the reader the experience of St. Petersburg after the revolution—Bolshevik violence, arrests, chaos, hunger and the despair of the people, much as Zinaida Gippius had done in her *St. Petersburg Diaries.* And, as Gippius in her memoirs *Living Portraits* (*Zhivye litsa*), Berberova draws literary portraits of her contemporaries: Gorky, Pasternak, Andrei Belyi, Georgii Adamovich, Fedor Sologub, Aleksandr Blok, Valerii Briusov, Marina Tsvetaeva, Anna Akhmatova, Ivan Bunin, Roman Jakobson, Victor Shklovskii, Georgii Ivanov, Nikolai Gumilev, Aleksei Remizov and many others. She also draws literary portraits of those Russian émigrés whom she came to know in Berlin, Prague and Paris, such as Boris Zaitsev, Vladimir Nabokov, D.S. Merezhkovskii; the poets Zinaida Gippius, Poplavskii, Ladinskii, Smolenskii, Knut; the artists Larionov and Goncharova; and the former Russian politicians Kerensky, Zenzinov, Bunakov-Fondaminskii, Rudnev and Vishniak. She gives their essential characteristics and evaluates their input into the Russian émigré life in Paris. These evaluations are not always flattering (and several of the Russian émigrés objected to Berberova's portrayals: Iurii Terapiano, Irina Odoevtseva, Sergei Zhaba, Tatiana Osorgina[3] and the American critic Patricia Blake). We have to remember that she wrote not history, but her own autobiography and her own impressions of people. She herself always emerges from her narrative as a vivacious person, never afraid of her future, always insisting on freedom and independence, and always supposedly liked and admired by those surrounding her. In reality, however, not all of them admired her: Ivan Bunin and Roman Gul', for example, disliked her intensely.

Berberova sometimes resorts to crude Russian words, although there is no apparent need to use them other than perhaps to imitate the street language common in America in the 1960s, to display her "sense of the epoch." With the exception of these uncouth utterances, Berberova's style in *The Italics Are Mine* is unified; her language is clear, expressive and sonorous, the language of the St. Petersburg poets and writers, exact, yet subtle and elegant. She had found her "real" words, and she did not fail in using this gift in her following works. There are no more false notes; from then on, her language is precise and subtly humorous in expression. The literary value of *The Italics Are Mine* is indisputable: Berberova acted as witness to the political and cultural events in Russia during and after the 1917 revolution, recorded her impressions on paper and maintained a diary concerning the life of Russian émigrés at a time when the Soviet Union treated them with silence and disdain. And it was Berberova, along with other Russian émigré writers, who returned to Russia the knowledge of Russian culture and Russian cultural achievements in exile.

In 1981 Berberova published her book *The Iron Woman* (*Zheleznaia zhenshchina*), about Baroness Maria Ignatievna Budberg (née Zakrevska; first married to Ivan Benkendorf, secretary of the Russian Embassy in Germany). Daughter of a Russian general, Budberg throughout her life was a part of the Russian, German and English diplomatic circles. Nietzsche, Rainer Maria Rilke, Sigmund Freud, Gorky, Robert Bruce Lockart, Victoria Sackville-West, H.G. Wells and Kerensky found her attractive, and she played an intimate and important role in the lives of Lockart, Gorky, and H.G. Wells. Through her connections with Russian writers and English diplomats, she also played a significant part in the political events of the Soviet Union.

Maria Ignatievna Budberg lived with Gorky in postrevolutionary St. Petersburg and then in Italy for twelve years. Gorky dedicated to her his unfinished novel in four volumes, *The Life of Klim Samgin* (*Zhizn' Klima Samgina*; begun in 1925), and entrusted her with his personal archives upon his return to the Soviet Union, where he died on 18 June 1936. Equipped with a thorough knowledge of English,

Russian, German and French, Budberg worked as a secretary to Gorky and as a translator of books; she also helped English diplomats in their activities in Russia. Because of her involvement in this work, she was arrested several times: in Soviet Russia; in Estonia, when she went to see her two children living on the estate of her first husband; and at the border of Italy and Austria, when she went to meet Lockart, who worked in Vienna at that time. In the Soviet Union, Budberg was suspected of being a spy and an agent of England; in Estonia, a Soviet spy; and in England, many years later, a Moscow agent. She was attractive, elegant, erudite and attentive to everything and to everybody, possessing excellent manners and composure.

Berberova's *The Iron Woman* is a book also about Gorky, Sydney Riley (pseudonym of Georgy Relinskii) and the postrevolutionary years in St. Petersburg and in Moscow. Free from the stylistic faults of her earlier works, *The Iron Woman* is one of the most intriguing and impressive works of Berberova.

Berberova researched this book thoroughly. Having chosen for her heroine Maria Budberg, an intelligent woman with an aura of mystery and tragedy, she examines Budberg's life within the context of seventy years of Russian and Western European history. She does not attempt to penetrate the mystery of Budberg, but she obviously admired this enigmatic figure who spoke so little, but accomplished so much so successfully and seemingly effortlessly.[4] She cites many political documents, archival materials and personal letters. Her portrayal of the complex political situation in St. Petersburg and in Russia, as well as in the Baltic states, and the political activities of the English and French diplomats is compelling. Lenin, Zinoviev, Trotsky, Stalin and other Soviet activists and leaders create the political and historical background against which is presented the personal life of Baroness Budberg, who was personally involved in the revolutionary turmoil of those distant days. Indeed, Berberova masters composition in this novel. The Russian, as in *The Italics Are Mine*, is clear, elegant and forceful, having all the characteristics of the St. Petersburg literary language discussed above. She no longer resorts to describing the personality of her heroine and her mystery, but allows the baroness to reveal herself. Perhaps Berberova held the baroness as a model for her own life, which had not been devoid of tribulations.

In 1986 Berberova published a book about the Freemasons, *People and Lodges: Russian Masons of the Twentieth Century (Liudi i lozhi: russkie masony XX-go stoletiia)*. This book contains some psycho-philosophizing. However, the research is meticulous, many historical documents are cited and the language is clear and precise, in accordance with a historical treatise. Berberova again re-creates the political upheavals in

Russia in the twentieth century. The book does not center around any particular personality, but discusses and illustrates the participation of the Russian Masons in the political life of Russia from 1900 to 1970. The work abounds in interesting details, such as the glossary of Freemasons and the description of the ceremony of rites by which one is initiated into a Masonic Lodge. It is followed by a biographical dictionary of Russian Masons, with commentaries written on many of them, including G.V. Adamovich, B.A. Bakhmetev, Prince V.L. Viazemskii, R.B. Gul', M.M. Karpovich, K.D. Nabokov, I.G. Tsereteli, the Grand Duke N.M. Romanov, A.I. Gutchkov, E.D. Kuskova and A.F. Kerensky. The bibliography is extensive.

Nina Berberova excelled as a writer of book reviews, especially reviews of the work of Vladimir Nabokov. In her 1970 article in English, "The Mechanics of *Pale Fire*," she discusses the compositional "surprises" in this novel: its symbolic and fantastic level, which is quite obvious, as well as its factual and realistic level, which is quite obscure hidden as it is by the symbolic and the poetic. She expertly discusses the title of the novel and its comic effects, which hold together the structure of the entire work. She also examines the author-narrator-hero's addresses to the reader, the symbols, the epigraph, the parodies of Russian and foreign classics, the balance between the serious and satirical/ironical elements, and other compositional and stylistic intricacies. This article, as well as many others written by Berberova, reveals her literary taste, her knowledge of modernism in literature, her acquaintance with contemporary literary scholarship, especially in the spheres of language and composition, and her emphasis on the functional value of the grotesque with regard to content, structure and style.

Berberova also achieved recognition as a poet. The restrictions of rhyme, meter, length and other versification rules enabled her to find effective words to express her thoughts, visions, feelings and premonitions. There are no *longueurs* in her verse; the imagery is concrete and powerful in conveying her emotions. One of these poems, dedicated to Z.N. Gippius in 1950, displays Berberova's poetic diction:

> For ten years I haven't opened my old
> Box with her letters. Today
> I lifted the lid. Once with her delicate hand
> She filled these pale sheets with writing,
> To my joy.
> A stray butterfly was dozing there
> Among her poems, among those bewitching words,
> Perhaps a year, perhaps ten.

And suddenly, unfolding its wings of orange
(Recalling the rusty color of her hair),
It flew out from the darkness of bygone days
And sped away through the window to the sun,
Into the radiant day, into the azure present.

It was as if I'd rolled away the stone
From the crypt of one deeply sleeping.

Colors, images, and moods blend into a beautiful specter of the universe, in which the celestial and the personal realms coexist as an organic whole, merging through the delightfully executed image of the stray butterfly. The poem deals with time and eternity, emotionally searching for a glimpse of the infinite that links the persona to the past. With her soul affected by the intensity of these feelings, the persona echoes the earlier poet of Ecclesiastes, who stated that there is nothing new under the sun, where pain, sorrow and separation persist, and where time does not exist.

Zinaida Gippius was impressed with Berberova's imagery. She and Berberova shared many themes. For example, Berberova wrote in a poem of 1927:

Friends, how to live without feminine tenderness?
Whom to love without feminine loveliness?
Whom will my lusterless eyes greet?
Whom will my weak arms seek? . . .

Zinaida Gippius, in one of her letters to Berberova, jokingly used the last line of the quatrain in her own text. The expression "tenderness" appears frequently in Gippius's poems, prose and correspondence.

Berberova's poetry dealing with the agonies of separation possesses a power equal to that of Gippius's. This can be seen in Berberova's poem of 1945, "Separation":

Separation resembles a terrible fairy tale:
It begins at night,
It has no end.
. . . .
Separation resembles the roar
Of the wheels—over the heart.
. . . .

Separation resembles a long song,
In which there are no welcomes.

Another of the poems from Berberova's volume *Poems 1921–1983* (*Stikhi 1921–1983*) treats the theme of separation:

The cashier asked: "Round-trip ticket?"
"—Only one way. Journey without return. . . ."

The last words exchanged are more emphatic:

"Would you like to return?"
"—Where? I have nowhere to go. Everything is irrevocable."

Berberova's verse contains elements of modern aestheticism, such as alienation, sexual entanglements, the theme of creation for the sake of creation. But it also pulsates with life, with a deeply poetic feeling.

Temira Pachmuss

Separation

Separation resembles a terrible fairy tale:
It begins at night,
It has no end.
One July night
The horses were stamping their hooves,
The sleepless children were crying, and
The rooster overstrained its voice at dawn.
One night the conflagrations covered half the sky,
The road meandered away in the dust,
And you were leaving. Separation
Resembles a terrible fairy tale:
When people go beyond the sea—
It has no end.

Separation resembles the clacking, at midnight,
Of trains. People disappear
Forever into the chasms of prisons,

Into the remote infernos of Buchenwald,
Into the flames of typhus of Ravensbruck.
I remember how you were tearing yourself
From the world dear to you,
How you kept blessing
Me and the green sky,
The city and the passersby. . . .
Separation resembles the roar
Of the wheels—over the heart.

Separation resembles a long song,
Which someone sings to another:
About a long siege of a capital,
About the ring which was closed around it,
How the cannons were destroying
The monuments and the palaces,
The city's basic structure, covered with ice.

And there,
At the very blue sea
An elderly man lived with his old mate. . . .
(It happened many times that my mother
Wiped away my tears with her lace handkerchief.)
Separation resembles a long song
In which there are no welcomes.

1945

The cashier asked: "Round-trip ticket?"
"—Only one way. Journey without return.
Nobody ever comes back
To the place from which misfortune drove him away."
The cashier was surprised: she will die where she was born.
Above her never hovered a passionate wind,
Above her never sparkled a thunderstorm,
Only trains were passing by.
Farewell, cashier! Thanks for handling my affair,

For a ticket to a distant land, for the tinkling of small change,
For your promise of happier days
And for the twinkling of the railway station lights.
It seems as if it happened already once in the past:
A lady said that she had forgotten her umbrella,
A child was dying to free himself from someone's arms,
And a friend was approaching the cashier's window:
"Would you like to return?"
"Where? I have nowhere to go. Everything is irrevocable."
Only in my memory there is a droning of voices:
Their addresses, addresses, addresses, addresses.

1956

From The Story of Masha Mimozova

Masha related to me the following story about herself.

She was a well-nurtured child on a model estate in Chernigov province, and in a small provincial town N. Upon her reaching the age of twelve years, she was sent to an institute; at the age of nineteen, she returned to her home, which was the customary procedure at that time. By nature, she was meek, much given to laughter, and was fluent in a number of foreign languages. Carefully, her mother and father sought a husband for her—one who was young, handsome, rich, distinguished, and well bred.

Incomprehensibly, however, men did not look at Masha. She told me this, precisely as follows: "Nobody paid any attention to me." At that time, before the war, men eagerly admired young maidens. I must admit frankly, preceding the war, there were any number of empty idlers in our region.

Masha often went out. It was doubtless that all her activities consisted of going out. Twice she accompanied her mother to a spa with mineral waters. She visited her aunt twice in St. Petersburg; however, no one noticed her there. No one exchanged words with her. With each passing year, her girlfriends became fewer and fewer. Their weddings were celebrated with much gaiety. Masha was growing older, and the expression on her face assumed a look of perplexity. She began to speak quietly and to waltz without lifting her eyes—at that time everybody waltzed. Gradually, in her modesty, she acquired a certain degree of experience—that of one not noticed, but without any apparent reason for such neglect.

The general's wife, Masha's mother, at first regarded this male tendency with respect to her daughter without alarm because she knew well the price of the Mimozovs' possessions of land and money. She was not one to miscalculate the importance of the family's substance. Yet, toward the fall of 1913 she became nervous; she wished—as she inadvertently stated—to "speed up the events." The family therefore made the decision to reside in St. Petersburg, so that the awaiting of the outcome of Masha's fate could be conducted in a more cheerful manner. Masha's demure nature had annoyed many people in the town of N.

In St. Petersburg, in those days, the atmosphere was desperately jubilant, and Masha almost lost her health from attending so many balls. During the first month there, several young men noticed her, but only for a very short time. Masha learned well during that brief period how pleasant it was to be noticed. She was twenty-five.

Then came the dark years of the war. Masha incessantly knitted wrist and knee warmers and helmet liners during the first, the second, and the third year of it. With each piece she knitted, she felt increasingly hopeless. She no longer lowered her eyes; on the contrary, she tried at every chance to catch the eyes of a man, attempting to convey to him, with her glances, some meaning. She even began to do things that she never would have allowed herself to do before, such as powdering her arms, moving her shoulders suggestively (of course, not in the presence of her mother), rustling her skirt. In the spring of 1917, the retired major-general Mimozov began to reveal—among his other concerns (in reality, very serious)—an anxiety about Masha. But then some new and very threatening events occurred. He and his wife hardly had time to recover from several of their St. Petersburg troubles when they learned that their vineyards in the depths of Chernigov province had been destroyed [by the Bolsheviks]; morever, their landed estates had been confiscated. They thought it might be wiser not to inquire about their remaining 15,000 acres of land!

Having learned of this terrible news, His Excellency, the general, decided to return with his family to the town of N, moving into their own two-story stone house, with a garret.

Anatol Fedorovich Svinyin, an intelligent and well-bred gentleman, was in charge of the province at that time. The people in St. Petersburg had heard much about his humaneness. By a special decree, the new government had allowed him to continue his services in the province. Anatol Fedorovich immediately grasped that the time of wearing a full-dress coat had passed, and there would be no more subtleties between persons, no more promotions in rank. He abandoned at once his severe demeanor, and in its place, assumed an extraordinarily free and relaxed air, especially with the ladies. He began to make his appearance in the drawing rooms of N. The freedom and simplicity, connected with this new assumption, appealed to him. He saw that he had lived a life of glitter, albeit a frigid one, and that probably it was time for him to submit to emotion. . . . Who knows what thoughts had entered our governor's head in the summer of 1917!

He was over fifty, a bachelor; his blond beard, parted in the middle, according to the fashion of the aristocrat, was luxuriant and fragrant. His youthful complexion and his boisterous, infectious laughter made him appear somewhat younger than he was. This appearance granted to him the charm of a dignitary who had early reached his high position. He was tall, strong, and broad-shouldered. He liked to intersperse French words throughout his consummate speech, and he was not ashamed of this mannerism. This was the style he displayed when Masha first saw him when she arrived in N.

On the evening of their acquaintance, in someone's drawing room, Anatol Fedorovich, surrounded by many young ladies, felt very much at ease. They were all playing "forfeits": the player was to say something pleasant, even complimentary, but in such a way that his words would be not only flattering but truthful. In this drawing room game, the young lady would step lightly before him, he would appraise her appropriately, and then he would utter his appreciation. Masha was one of the last to be praised.

Anatol Fedorovich, with darting glances, observed her several times before she, participating, glided by him; and she, perhaps with a tinge of stubbornness, never lowered her eyes. As she passed by she felt, for the first time in her life, that she was worthy of a man's attention. Her heart began to pound and she blushed. She did not smile, stopping and turning at the door. Anatol Fedorovich stared in silence. "Why don't you say anything?" the ladies inquired. "Why don't you say anything to our dear Masha?" Anatol Fedorovich's silence continued. Finally, visibly excited, he spoke in French: "Your lips were created for kisses." Anatol Fedorovich was agitated. She sensed it. "My lips were created for kisses," she repeated to herself. She felt as if a sharp needle had pierced her heart. "My lips were created for kisses," she later whispered, while falling asleep. At once, she burst into tears. Thoughts of our Motherland, in a state of agony because of unheard-of torture, and worries over the unknown future of her family, melted away like a mirage. Anatol Fedorovich, alone, now occupied her entire universe. Her soul rose selflessly toward him. During those desolate months, it was her love for him, and his for her, by which she lived. She intuited that he loved her.

They met, during that dusty summer, when paying visits to other people, in church, or on short walks. This tall man possessed many charms that would excite a young maiden's heart. There is great beauty in the passion of a man, which is independent of the small and insignificant details of everyday life—passion such as that of an internationally known singer, or that of a famous liberal statesman, or that of any contemporary hero. . . .

Four months later, Anatol Fedorovich declared his love. At that time, he was welcome in the general's house. Masha, with her parents, attended his official receptions. Early in September, he invited Masha to visit his palace to learn to play croquet with his young nieces. The house of the governor general was opposite the house of the general. Behind the governor general's house, there was a garden. . . . Masha enjoyed giving me the details about this garden. . . .

The ground for playing was located in the depth of the garden. Masha opened the gate quietly. Anatol Fedorovich, tormented by his passion, watched her walking along the path. Sometimes, and gradually more and more frequently, he would join the party on the playground. In confusion, he would fail to find the right gate and would joke and quibble about this, but secretly, he was passionately longing for Masha. At last, one clear and solemn day in autumn, he whisked away his nieces, knelt before Masha, and amid the poetic rustle of the falling leaves, asked her to marry him. She grew numb from an excess of emotion. He kissed her dress, her shoes. Then rising, he embraced her and kissed her lips passionately, many times. . . . Gradually, he lost control, grasped her, announcing he was going to carry her to his room. He almost undressed her on the spot. She had no intention of running away from him. What restrained the couple [from moving to his room] is unknown. Until twilight, they remained seated on the bench. The following day, with exclamations, he pleaded for forgiveness for his display of emotion on the previous day. However, his lack of restraint in this regard did not cease. He expressed even more demonstratively his wild emotions. Masha dwelled day and night in a state of undisguised delirium.

Meanwhile, events around them were developing of their own accord—events unheard of, which were upsetting the foundations of existence. Early in December, before St. Nicholas Day, Anatol Fedorovich was requested to vacate the comfortable mansion of the governor general. The province no longer belonged to him. At that time, fluffy snow lay on the paths of the garden, a place so memorable to Masha. The bench, dear to her, was rotting beneath fusty leaves. Anatol Fedorovich, with only an elegant toilet-case in his hand, hastily crossed the street. Bullets whistled past him. The general's chambermaid opened the door for him; the general's wife escorted him to a beautiful room where he would stay. On that very day of eviction, it had been decided, without delay, to inform all the general's acquaintances (so that nothing improper would be thought) of their daughter's and Anatol Fedorovich's engagement. However, there was nobody around to be informed: some had left; others had locked themselves up; and some others were so alarmed by the events of the day that they could not comprehend the news about Anatol Fedorovich and Masha. These others waved the parents off, and in response lamented: "So wonderful it would be to escape abroad!" It was as if Masha's parents were not announcing an extraordinary piece of news, but merely were chatting about an everyday happening.

What did Anatol Fedorovich feel and think? Did he have any inkling of what was in store for him? Oh, how I [the narrator] would like to believe in my inexcusable romanticism (perhaps you, Reader, also would like to believe?), that the governor general of N foresaw and comprehended everything about him, that he himself had chosen, in his elevated but fruitless wisdom, to transform those last three weeks of his life into a dream of enchantment. No, nothing of the kind was happening! Anatol Fedorovich saw nothing, anticipated nothing. He was in Masha's serene captivity and did not even know what kind of organization had seized his magnificent palace or what the inscriptions on its stone gate were.

He dwelled in idleness and sensuality, retaining, however, his dignity, before the general and the general's wife. Alone with Masha, he sometimes did not recognize himself. For many hours they remained by themselves. Sometimes he would ask her to put on her small kerchief and her narrow shoes with buckles. They usually spent time in Masha's room behind the painted screens. She agreed to do anything he asked and allowed him his every whim. She was determined to enter his room one night, but he, appropriately, would not allow it. This state of bliss continued for three weeks and several days. During that time Anatol Fedorovich could have left the town of N safely and have escaped into exile. On the third day after Christmas, in the evening, he was arrested.

"Where are you taking him?" cried Masha, overcome with anguish. "We're taking him home, across the street," laughed the officers. "Do not weep, my love," Svinyin said to her in French. "I am not guilty, and I will say this to them." He was led down the stairs. Masha rushed to the windows and, for the first time, saw what kind of organization had established itself in the governor general's mansion. From this day on, a pall settled over the house of the general and his spouse; from this day on, their daughter Masha no longer noticed them.

. . . She never learned exactly when the governor general of N was shot. But she was destined to see him one more time.

It happened in the spring, toward the end of March. The snow, thawing, trickled downhill along the street. The sun glistened in the windows of the houses. There was a new government now. With a special pass issued to her, Masha was admitted to the governor general's garden, brown with the buds of spring. Several graves were being dug up in the garden. There were about ten rather well-dressed civilian men and two or three women assembled, who were gathered to identify the corpses. Masha was one of this group. . . . The governor general was the ninth corpse in the stack. He was recognized at once by everyone. Masha was allowed to approach him. His beard was disheveled and somewhat reddish in color. He was shoeless.

Masha threw herself onto his chest, in the way a grieving woman would throw herself onto the chest of her beloved when finding him deceased. . . . [After the October Revolution Masha's parents lived with Masha in poverty. After their death, Masha left N with a certain man, Giller, leaving behind a note in her room: "Do not wait for me. My new life has begun. . . ."]

Of course, Masha never returned to our poor and quiet small town of N. Nobody ever heard of her again. They quickly forgot her. Yet where did she go? Perhaps at some distant and half-destroyed station, all alone, abandoned by everyone, Masha clutched some chance train and rushed toward an unknown destination. Perhaps somewhere, in poverty and in fear, she still wanders the streets of some degraded town on the Black Sea. Many daughters of Russian generals in those days died, displaying a lack of life force. . . .

If this is so, let your helpless soul, Masha, rest in that peaceful place where, God willing, we shall all assemble.

1928 (Sovremennye zapiski, Paris, xxxviii, 1929*)*

Translated by Temira Pachmuss

Notes to the Essay

1. The motion-picture rights to *Tchaikovsky* were sold jointly in 1966 to Warner Brothers and Sovkino. The picture was made in 1968 and shown in the U.S.S.R. and Europe.

2. Before her departure to the United States, Berberova became editor of the literary page of the Russian émigré weekly *Russian Thought (Russkaia mysl')*, where in 1948–1949, she reported on the trial Kravchenko, the author of *I Chose Freedom*.

3. Tatiana Osorgina, the wife of M.A. Osorgin, published an article in *Cahiers du Monde Russe et Soviétique* [Paris] 31 (1990): 95–102, which contains a detailed list of Berberova's distortions in *The Italics Are Mine*. Osorgina also states that several Russian émigré writers in Paris, including Ivan Bunin and Roman Gul', avoided Berberova during and after World War II because of her open affiliations with the German army: "Always counting on the conqueror, she found herself after the war in a very difficult situation" (99).

4. When Baroness Budberg died in 1974 in England, *The London Times* honored her death with a eulogy entitled "The Intellectual Leader."

Bibliography

Primary Works

"Iabloki." *Zveno* 202 (1926).

"Zhenikh." *Novyi dom* 1 (1926): 10–16.

"Baryni." *Zveno* 2 (1927): 83–104.

"Vechnaia pamiat'." *Sovremennye zapiski* 35 (1928): 236–38.

"Zoia Andreevna." *Sovremennye zapiski* 34 (1928): 185–210.

"Istoriia Mashi Mimozovoi." *Sovremennye zapiski* 38 (1929): 103–36.

Madame [play]. Paris, 1930.

Poslednie i pervye. Roman iz èmigrantskoi zhizni. Paris, 1930.

Povelitel'nitsa. Berlin: Parabola, 1932.

"Ubiistvo Val'kovskogo." *Vstrechi* 4 (1934): 47–53.

Tchaikovsky. Istoriia odinokoi zhizni. Berlin: Petropolis, 1936.

Bez zakata. Paris: Dom knigi, 1938.

Borodin. Berlin: Petropolis, 1938.

Alexandre Blok et Son Temps. Paris, 1947.

"25 let so smerti A.A. Bloka." *Opyty* 47 (1947): 108–12.

"Iz chego delaetsia son." *Vozrozhdenie* 6 (1949): 51–54 .

Oblegchenie uchasti. Shest' povestei. Paris: YMCA Press, 1949.

"M.O. Tsetlin." *Novyi zhurnal* 24 (1950): 209–13.

"Mys bur'." *Novyi zhurnal* 24 (1950): 71–144; 25 (1951): 5–87; 26 (1951): 5–43; 27 (1951): 20–56.

"Vladislav Khodasevich, russkii poèt. 1886–1939." *Grani* 12 (1951): 40–44.

"Bol'shoi gorod." *Novyi zhurnal* 32 (1953): 68–80.

"Iz peterburgskikh vospominanii." *Opyty* 1 (1953): 163–80.

"Mysliashchii trostnik." *Novyi zhurnal* 55 (1958): 11–49.

"Pamiati Shlimana." *Mosty* 1 (1958): 88–106.

"Chernaia bolezn'." *Novyi zhurnal* 58 (1959): 34–82.

"Nabokov i ego *Lolita*." *Novyi zhurnal* 5 (1959): 92–115.

[Commentary]. In *Vladislav Khodasevich. Sobranie stikhov (1913–1939)*. Ed. N. Berberova. New Haven, CT: Yale University Press, 1961.

"Kliuchi k nastoiashchemu." *Novyi zhurnal* 66 (1961): 90–123.

"Kommentarii k pis'mam I.S. Turgeneva k Henry James." *Mosty* 7 (1961): 339–41.

"Konets Turgenevskoi biblioteki." *Novyi zhurnal* 63 (1961): 157–61.

[Poems]. *Novyi zhurnal* 59 (1960): 65–70.

[Poems]. *Mosty* 8 (1961): 29–30.

"Tri goda zhizni Gor'kogo." *Mosty* 7 (1961): 262–77.

"Velikii vek: o poèzii 20–go veka." *Novyi zhurnal* 64 (1961): 119–40.

"Malen'kaia devochka, p'esa v 3–kh aktakh, v proze." *Mosty* 9 (1962): 48–104.

[Poems]. *Novyi zhurnal* 67 (1962): 118–20.

"Strashnyi sud." *Novyi zhurnal* 69 (1962): 36–46.

[Translations of four poems by T.S. Eliot]. *Novyi zhurnal* 68 (1962): 13–25.

"Sovetskaia kritika segodnia." *Novyi zhurnal* 85 (1966): 82–106; 86 (1967): 115–23.

"The Mechanics of *Pale Fire*." *Russian Literary Triquarterly* 17 (1970): 147–59.

"Nabokov in the Thirties." *Russian Literary Triquarterly* 18 (1970): 220–33.

Kursiv moi. Munich: Wilhelm Fink Verlag, 1972.

[Preliminary remarks, notes and comments]. *Andrei Belyi, The First Encounter.* Trans. Gerald Janecek. Princeton, NJ: Princeton University Press, 1979.

Zheleznaia zhenshchina. New York: Russica Publishers, 1981.

[Introduction]. In *Zinaida Gippius: Peterburgskie dnevniki (1914–1919).* Ed. N. Berberova. New York: Orfey, 1982.

Kursiv moi. 2 vols. New York: Russica Publishers, 1983.

Stikhi 1921–1983. Ed. A. Sumerkin. New York: Russica Publishers, 1984.

Liudi i lozhi: russkie masony XX stoletia. New York: Russica Publishers, 1986.

In Translation

The Accompanist. Trans. Marian Schwartz. London: Collins, 1947.

The Italics Are Mine. Trans. Philippe Radley. New York: Harcourt, Brace and World, 1969.

L'Accompagnatrice. Trans. Lydia Chweitzer. Paris: Actes Sud, 1985.

The Accompanist. Trans. Marian Schwartz. New York: Atheneum, 1988 [first American edition].

The Revolt. Trans. Marian Schwartz. London: Collins, 1989.

C'est moi qui souligne. Trans. Anne Musslin and Réné Musslin. Arles: Actes Sud, 1989.

Three Novels. Trans. Marian Schwartz. London: Chatto and Windus, 1991.

The Tattered Cloak and Other Novels. Trans. Marian Schwartz. New York, 1991.

Ich komme aus St. Petersburg: Autobiographie. Trans. Christina von Süss. Reinbeck bei Hamburg: Rewohlt-Taschenbuch Verlag, 1993.

Die Begleiterin. Trans. Anna Kamp [from the French]. Reinbeck bei Hamburg: Rewohlt-Taschenbuch Verlag, 1993.

Der Lakai und die Hure. Trans. Anna Kamp [from the French]. Reinbeck bei Hamburg: Rewohlt-Taschenbuch Verlag, 1993.

Tschaikowsky. Trans. Anna Kamp [from the French]. Hildesheim: Glaassen, 1993.

Astaschev in Paris. Trans. Anna Kamp [from the French]. Hildesheim: Glaassen, 1993.

Die Affäre Kravtschenko. Trans. Anna Kamp [from the French]. Hildesheim: Glaassen, 1993.

Secondary Works

Barker, Murl. "Nina Berberova on Surviving." *Selected Journal of the Pacific Northwest Council on Foreign Languages* 11 (1990): 69–72.

———. "The Short Prose of Nina Berberova." *Russian Literary Triquarterly* 22 (1989): 239–54.

Chagin, Alexei. "Kursiv vremeni." *Literaturnaia gazeta,* 19 April 1989.

Kostyrko, Sergei. "Vyzhit', chtoby zhit'." *Novyi mir* 9 (1991): 216–21.

Meilakh, Mikhail. "Ne proshlo i semidesiati let." *Literaturnoe obozrenie* 1 (1990): 68–73.

Osorgina, Tatiana. "Kak èto bylo." *Cahiers du Monde Russe et Soviétique* 31 (1990): 95–102.

Struve, Gleb. *Russkaia literatura v izgnanii.* New York: Chekhov, 1956.

Zotikov, A. "Tianus' tol'ko k liudiam." *Literaturnaia gazeta,* 4 October 1989.

Lidiia Chukovskaia

As Lidiia Korneeva Chukovskaia (1907–1996) knew too well, her biography makes an absolutely terrifying and riveting story—the tale of a woman as Stalinist victim and post-Stalin dissident. It is the more terrible and the more dramatic given its charmed beginning. Born in 1907, Chukovskaia was the daughter of Kornei Chukovskii, one of the most industrious and positive-thinking literary men of his day, and her gigantic, delightful and driven father played impresario of her childhood, sequestering his family (at that time, his wife, daughter Lidiia and two sons) in the Finnish resort town of Kuokkala, hosting famous vacationing artists and rigorously initiating his children into the joys of nature and fine literature. A self-made intellectual who excelled in writing children's verse and literary criticism, Chukovskii made Russian literature the family religion. His daughter proved to be the most zealous in her faith.

Adulthood at first did not break her childhood's magic spell, for although it complicated life with two marriages (the first to literary critic Tsezar' Volpe, the second to astrophysicist Matvei Bronshtein) and a child (Elena, b. 1932), it also entailed Chukovskaia's apprenticeship as a children's literature editor under the inspiring, paternalistic tutelage of Samuil Marshak. At this point Chukovskaia's story almost subsides into a happy, if routine, normalcy. But in its second act sudden high drama returns. By the late 1930s the Stalinist purges had dispelled enchantment and normalcy with an all-pervasive terror. Chukovskaia's workplace was shut down; many of her colleagues and friends were arrested; most terribly, her husband, Matvei Bronshtein, was arrested and summarily executed, a fact masked by his sentence of "ten years in the camps without the right of correspondence." Faced with a power that obliterated her loved ones and dictated constant bearing of false witness, Chukovskaia did the bravest thing imaginable: she picked up her pen and took notes. It was during this most dangerous period in Russian letters that she authored numerous poems, included in the collection *This Side of Death* (*Po ètu storonu smerti*, 1936–1976), and two novels chronicling the purges' dire effects, *Sof'ia Petrovna* (*Sof'ia Petrovna*, 1939–1940) and *Going Under* (*Spusk pod vodu*, 1949–1957), and kept a memoir account of her meetings with the equally defiant and victimized poet Anna Akhmatova, *Notes on Anna Akhmatova* (*Zapiski ob Anne Akhmatovoi*, 1938–1941, 1952–1962). Under Stalin, any one of these works would have served as pretext for a death sentence.

In the relatively more benign decades after Stalin's death in 1953 and the de-Stalinizing Twentieth Party Congress in 1956, Chukovskaia made her secret devotion public. She attempted to publish her daring testimonies, succeeding only in *samizdat*, the underground circulation of proscribed manuscripts, and the émigré press. She continued to keep important records of the past, memoirizing her father in *To the Memory of Childhood* (*Pamiati detstva*, 1983) and her editorial apprenticeship with Marshak, in *In the Editor's Workshop* (*V laboratorii redaktora*, 1963). Once again Chukovskaia distinguished herself as an exceptional defender of the faith. She declared her dissidence, openly condemning the Soviet government's mistreatment of such writers as Joseph Brodsky and Aleksandr Solzhenitsyn, and took up yet another dangerous genre—the literature of political protest and accusatory reportage, as in *The Process of Expulsion* (*Protsess iskliucheniia*, 1974–1979) and *The Open Word* (*Otkrytoe slovo*, 1976). Her courageous acts resulted in her expulsion from the Writers' Union in 1974 and a ban on her writings until *glasnost'* enabled her rehabilitation.

The years of *glasnost* and a post-Soviet Russia appropriately end her story with the accolades Chukovskaia so richly deserves. Not only have all her works appeared in print on Russian soil, but she herself has been recognized as a national heroine, the first recipient of the Sakharov Prize in 1990. This unexpectedly happy ending came none too soon, given the cultural chaos of Russia's transition to capitalism. Chukovskaia's tale of political persecution and altruistic self-sacrifice is already relegated to a bygone era in which Russian literature, whether openly revered or repressed, was assured of its moral and social power.

In this essay Chukovskaia is placed at the center of her life story, a presumptuous move she herself did not make in writing pieces of it. We are now in a position to see and appreciate her image in full. That image had been deliberately effaced by Chukovskaia's preference for supporting rather than starring roles in her work. Her memoir of her childhood, for example, features her father as its hero and, in a sense, author. The novel she wrote to cope with the first pain of her own bereavement, *Sof'ia Petrovna*, relates the distress of a distinctly different woman, an ordinary typist loyal to the Stalinist regime. Chukovskaia finally stepped into the spotlight and, not so coincidentally, the line of fire in her protest writing; there she felt called upon to embody the Word against the State. The woman who devoted herself to monumentalizing others only arose as a monument in her later years, forced by circumstance to become a public warrior.

Chukovskaia's unveiled monument also clearly marks her place in Russian literary history and especially Russian women's literary history. Although a number of critics (myself included) have interpreted Chukovskaia's writing as a phenomenal by-product of Stalinism, it is possible now to trace her larger and largely ignored historical resonance. Committed to serve literature as editor, critic and conservator, Chukovskaia followed a career path pursued by some Russian women in the nineteenth century and a great many more in a Soviet society of supposedly equal employment opportunities. Whereas we know of such nineteenth-century examples as Evgeniia Tur and Avdotia Panaeva primarily because they also wrote fiction, Chukovskaia's attitude of self-effacement and service (as opposed to creative authority) perhaps better articulates the self-image and certainly the social perception of these many female "cultural workers." Chukovskaia conceived of herself as literature's handmaiden rather than its master. In much the same way, Chukovskaia's professional attachment to children's literature, evidenced in her editorial work and pedagogical writings (e.g., her critical-biographical sketches of children's writers Susanna Georgievskaia and Boris Zhitkov), typifies women writers' general involvement in a literature traditionally relegated to them as "natural" and less artistically demanding.

Chukovskaia's autobiographical writings also connect her with recently identified traditions of Russian women's letters.[1] Indeed, Chukovskaia's modest but insistent valorization of her life story as incriminating testimony characterizes the approach of many other female autobiographers in an exceptionally tyrannized Russia and a no less tyrannized Soviet Union. In what we provisionally assume to be the first such autobiographical account, Princess Natal'ia Dolgorukaia (1714–1771) bears witness to her family's unjust exile; subsequent memoirs by voluntary and involuntary enemies of the state evince the same motivation and message, and such testimonies predictably burgeoned after the Stalinist purges of the twentieth century. By virtue of her approach and context, Chukovskaia truly epitomizes this notion of women's autobiography as service to a larger "cause."[2] One could argue, as have Chukovskaia's reviewers, that her fiction expresses the same impetus, for both *Sof'ia Petrovna* and *Going Under* document the sufferings of women bereaved by the purges.[3]

In one important sense, however, Chukovskaia builds on rather than abides within these deferential patterns of Russian women's writing. Her poetry, novels and Akhmatova memoir commemorate the experience and response of women caught in the terror of Stalinist society. As such, they comprise an essential complement to both the canonized works of Aleksandr Solzhenitsyn, which focus chiefly on men in the Stalinist labor camps, and the memoirs of women's camp ordeals by Evgeniia Ginzburg, Ol'ga Adamova-Sliozberg and many others. Moreover, the particular sequence of *Sof'ia Petrovna*, *Going Under* and *Notes on Anna Akhmatova* develops the character of the bereaved woman into a national heroine: while the first protagonist, Sof'ia Petrovna, crumples under Stalinist pressure to deny the truth, the heroines of the subsequent two narratives—the fictional Nina Sergeevna (in *Going Under*) and the real Akhmatova and Chukovskaia—prevail as women who keep faith with their lost ones and bear witness to the horrible truth in their art. Chukovskaia's *Notes* describes this heroinism in the greatest detail and reflects its often collaborative nature, emphasizing of course Akhmatova's creativity and magnanimity and inadvertently divulging the author's own feats of preserving, facilitating and creating.

Chukovskaia's monument also stands somewhat apart from these traditions because she herself did not see that they existed. That is, she perceived her literary inheritance as her father's creation, not as the customary work of women. Although she was absolutely typical of other Russian women writers in her reliance on male mentoring, her unusual literary father conveyed to her female-marked modes of literary service as male-sanctioned "art." Chukovskaia approached each of her literary projects with a paternally instilled reverence and exactitude. Whether she was writing a children's biography of a famous historical figure or a novel "for the drawer," she maintained the same high standards of scrupulous documentation and stylistic lucidity. Her father's training and example especially contributed to her accomplishments in nonfiction. Compared with the many other memoir accounts of the Stalinist era, Chukovskaia's *Notes on Anna Akhmatova* represents a model of dramatic understatement and precise eloquence. Her description and transcription of the poet achieve a prose equivalent of Akhmatova's celebrated poetic pithiness.

What obtains in Chukovskaia's work, therefore, is a fine art most strictly applied. Her poetry and fiction are assayed as testimony and therapy, her memoirs reconstruct role models and her polemical narratives name names and protest specific injustices. Chukovskaia's writings eloquently document, empathize, expose and instruct, but they are rarely at play or spinning off on imaginative tangents. Much of their moral weightiness is surely due to the Stalinist context that provoked them into being; as already suggested, this may also stem from Chukovskaia's discomfort with a playful creative persona, a common response among women writers tentative about their right to write.

Whatever the reason for Chukovskaia's rather narrow conception of what she could and should create, her work's combination of artistic refinement and moral service ultimately seals her image as a quintessential monument of her era. Akhmatova had imagined this fate for herself in the end poem of her poetic cycle *Requiem*, instructing that her monument as female mourner be erected before the Leningrad prison walls. But Chukovskaia enacted the role of mourner more consistently and capaciously, if less charismatically. In a culture that frequently symbolizes the nation as widow, Chukovskaia has come to define a dominant Stalinist variant—that of a widow who most ably preserves and transmits a forbidden cultural past.[4]

There are signs that her monument is complete. Just as Chukovskaia forever inscribed the person of Akhmatova, so her own image, characteristically coupled with Akhmatova's, has been memorialized as and in dramatic performance. Two recent plays, Hélène Cixous's *Black Sail, White Sail* (1994) and Maureen Lawrence's *Real Writing* (1994), focus in part or full on the Akhmatova-Chukovskaia relationship, exploiting its chamber-drama potential. In *Real Writing*, which is actually based on *Notes*, the iconic Akhmatova may occupy center stage, but Chukovskaia is surely present and even magnified as the poet's confidante and chronicler. This dramatic version fully illuminates her backstage image. The recent English translation of her *Notes* (rendered as *The Akhmatova Journals,* 1994) is likely to attract more attention to her monument; most of its reviewers cannot resist retelling Chukovskaia's story, registering explicitly or implicitly that in her text "the center falls to the periphery, while the margins move to the center."[5] The *Journals'* publication attracted to her door interviewers who polished up her image as the stern and exacting keeper of the flame.[6] Thus, despite her lifelong habit of other-oriented service, Chukovskaia and her works seem assured a hallowed place in Russian literary history, in part because of the good works they performed and the conventional female ideals they incarnated, and in part because of the brilliance of that performance and that incarnation.

Beth Holmgren

From Process of Expulsion

In December of 1962, fortune smiled brightly upon me. The publisher Soviet Writer signed a contract with me for my cherished novella: *Sof'ia*

Petrovna. This book is about the year 1937, written in the winter of 1939–1940, directly after two years of standing in lines around prisons. I am not going to judge what its artistic value is, but the value of a truthful testimony is undeniable. To this day (1974) I know of no other book about 1937 that was written *then* and *there*.

Maybe one exists in secret and hasn't reached us yet? Let's hope. . . .

In my story I tried to demonstrate to what degree our society was poisoned by lies, a process that is comparable only to the poisoning of armies by toxic gas. For my heroine I chose neither sister nor wife nor lover nor friend, but the symbol of devotion—a mother. My Sof'ia Petrovna loses her only son. In this purposely contorted reality, all feelings are distorted—such is my idea. Sof'ia Petrovna is a widow; her life is her son. Kolia is arrested, sentenced to the camps; he is declared "an enemy of the people." Sof'ia Petrovna, trained to believe the newspapers and public figures more than she believes herself, believes the prosecutor who informed her that her son "admitted his crimes" and deserved the sentence of "ten years in a distant prison camp." Sof'ia Petrovna for her own part knows full well that Kolia did not commit and could not commit any crimes, and that he is dedicated heart and soul to the Party, his dear factory, and Comrade Stalin personally. But if she would allow herself to believe herself and not the prosecutor and the newspapers, then . . . then . . . her universe would shatter, the earth would cave in under her feet, and the spiritual comfort in which she had so pleasantly dwelled and worked and which she had affirmed, would crumble into dust. . . . And Sof'ia Petrovna makes an attempt to believe *simultaneously* both the prosecutor and her son, and as a result, she loses her mind. (I frankly really wanted to write a book about an insane society: my unfortunate, shattered Sof'ia Petrovna is not at all a lyrical heroine; for me she is a generalized image of those who seriously believed in the reasonableness and justice of what went on. "We don't jail people for nothing." If you stop believing, there's no salvation; the only thing left would be to hang yourself.)

Sof'ia Petrovna is not capable of generalizing from the visible and experienced, and reproaching her for this is wrong, because in the mind of an ordinary person such events seemed like systematically arranged absurdity; how can one comprehend organized chaos? And how do this all alone? A wall of terror solidly separated each person from those who were suffering likewise. The majority of people, that is, millions, were like Sof'ia Petrovna, but when the consciousness of a nation is deprived of all documents and all literature, when the real history of entire decades is substituted for by a fabrication, then each mind is left to its own devices and experience, and reduced to a lower level.

. . . For many years my novel existed in a single copy—in a thick school notebook, in purple ink. I could not keep the notebook at home: I already had three searches behind me and a complete confiscation of property. My notebook was kept by a friend. If it had been found, he would have been executed. A month before the war I left Leningrad to have an operation in Moscow; my friend remained in Leningrad; they would not take him in the army due to his illness and, as I learned later in Tashkent, he starved to death during the blockade. The night before he died he gave my notebook to his sister: "Return this if you both survive."

And here I am, alive, with notebook in hand. And Stalin is dead, and the Twentieth Party Congress has taken place, and I have given over the notebook to be typed up, and friends have read my novel. In September 1962, after the Twenty-second Party Congress, I submitted my novel to Soviet Writer; all according to the rules, all in good faith. As a result of two positive reviews, in December, my book was approved and accepted for publication; I signed a contract for the accepted book; in January 1963 they paid me 60 percent of the honorarium; in March they showed me the finished illustrations, approved by the division for making illustrations; and the manuscript was about to be sent to the printer's and turned into a book.

A miracle!

I saw that the publishing house was favorably disposed toward my manuscript, that they were sympathetic toward it and me. The young editors wept as they read it, and each one asked for a copy for her mother or husband. The artist finished the illustrations with unusual speed. But that was the least of it. The chief editor herself, Comrade Karpova, the right hand of the director, Comrade Lesiuchevskii, the same Karpova who, up to that point in her literary career I had known only to pronounce polite insults, now spoke to me exclusively in rude compliments.

The publisher asked only one thing from me: to write an introduction. I wrote it.

The compliments showered on me, sincere and insincere, were completely understandable. Likewise was the speed with which they read, reviewed and sent my manuscript to the printer. I should think so! The "cult of personality" had been exposed, Stalin's body had been removed from the mausoleum, and every newspaper, magazine and publishing house was bound at least in small measure to "retort" to "the disclosure of immense violations against socialist law" with articles, short stories, poetry, novellas, or novels.

And retort they did! Karpova sighed deeply and sympathetically as she spoke about the difficult past, wisely exposed by the Party in good time—about a past which would never return—and about the "restoration of Leninist norms of Party life." (You might have thought that the norms of "non-Party life" had always been faithfully observed.)

And suddenly—some sensed this earlier, but I perceived it clearly in 1963—anxious rumors spread all around, increasing in magnitude: "at the top" was a change of direction, dissatisfaction. Literature was delving much too deeply into the "consequences of the cult." It should be talking about achievements and not "mistakes." The Party had explained and corrected everything at the Twentieth and Twenty-second Congresses by resolution. Enough was enough! Survivors were returned from the camps and the prisons and were rehabilitated; they were given not only lodging, but, just imagine, they were set up in work! Relatives of the dead were given certification of the posthumous rehabilitation of their sons, sisters and husbands. What else was there? Why pour salt onto the wounds? We will move on to the next sowing or the next harvest. "At the N factory a new blast furnace was fired up."

On the 7th and 8th of March 1963 officials of the Party and government held explanatory meetings with the intelligentsia. I was not high enough up on the totem pole to be invited to such exalted meetings; but in May, I got a different invitation: to my publisher's. I was invited by the head of the Soviet literature section, Comrade Kozlov, and, on the one hand, sincerely and kindly, and on the other—adamantly and categorically he explained that although my novella had been accepted and put into production, and was even 60 percent paid for, it could not be printed.

I felt like going straight to Karpova after this incident, but she was not there: either she was sick or on vacation or on a business trip. I don't remember.

Of course, this rejection was a stunning blow for me, a great grief, but I did not really hold it against the publishing house. I saw that many of the staff sincerely wanted to publish my story. But publishing houses here don't really determine (in any serious sense) what to publish and what not. An order is an order, and a banned topic is a banned topic. . . . However, a while later, I nonetheless dropped in to see the main champion of my book and the main editor of Soviet Writer, Comrade Karpova. I sat down across from her. I asked her what she thought, how long the ban would last.

"It's strange," I said incidentally. "It's as if they proposed that three novellas, three long poems, three short stories, and three novels be published about World War II . . . period! 'We will not pour salt in the wounds!' But in every family a father was killed or a husband or a brother or a son, or sometimes all four in a single family, and it's agonizing for the bereaved to remember those who perished. But the war lasted four years, and the 'cult of personality' with its 'consequences'—about thirty. And in every family a father or a husband or a brother or a wife or a sister—occasionally whole families—disappeared without a trace. War is a monstrous thing, but you can understand its causes and sense, but the sense and the reasons for the 'cult of personality' are much more difficult to comprehend. To understand these, every document is precious for future generations and researchers, and this includes my novel."

"I told you from the very beginning," Karpova said without missing a beat, "that your novella was conceptually flawed. The causes and consequence of the 'cult' have been sufficiently explained by the Party documents printed in the newspapers. Nikita Sergeevich's speeches and Party meetings with the intelligentsia have provided further clarification. I was never wrong in sensing your faulty position."

Karpova, the main editor of the publishing house Soviet Writer, was celebrated in literary circles for her pathological lying. There was even a saying: "to lie like Karpova." But a direct, bald-faced, brazen lie, no matter how often you hear one, is stupefying each time. Karpova had never said a word about my flawed conception. On the contrary, she had hurried more than anyone to sign the contract and announce her "approval."

"How can you not be ashamed of yourself!" I said, upset.

"You should be grateful to the publisher," Karpova answered, her nose buried in papers, "that we aren't demanding our money back from you. Government money was wasted on your novella for nothing."

(Government money! My novel wasn't written for money when, all around me, every tenth—and perhaps every fifth—person was being shot!)

However, the liar had given me an excellent idea. The idea for a counterattack.

"Money?" I repeated, rising from my chair. "You have no right to demand that money back. The law does not allow it. An accepted and approved manuscript must in any event be paid for in full. It's not I who owe, but you who owe me money. I'm going to sue. So the publisher has reneged? Let the publisher be fined, and what about the author?"

"Go try it, go try it," Karpova said to my back.

After a short time I went to the legal counsel for the Writers' Union. When he heard that my manuscript had been accepted and approved, that the illustrations were approved, and that I had been paid 60 percent of the honorarium, he determined that my suit was absolutely legal. But he added at this point: "Writers usually avoid suing a publisher, because in the future they won't get published." That didn't bother me. I went to the Office for Preserving Authors' Rights, where one of the young lawyers, having read a copy of my contract, immediately agreed to file a formal complaint and to represent me in court.

The period before the hearing dragged on slowly. The judge summoned me and demanded my manuscript. He read it for a month, if not longer. He did not express his opinion. Then the court date was set two times and postponed both times: the defendant didn't appear. I was already thinking: there's more to this than meets the eye. Finally on 24 April 1965, an open session at the People's Court of the Sverdlovsk region in Moscow took place. The small courtroom was filled. The judge conducted the proceedings drily and precisely, saying nothing about the novella as before. The counsel for Soviet Writer was singularly loquacious. He informed the court that in my novella there was an "ideological defect" that the publishing staff, being caught up in the "heat of events following the Twentieth and Twenty-second Party Congresses," had not noticed this defect, but now, in the light of new Party resolutions, "they saw the novella with different eyes." He said that my novella was a mere photograph, expressing only the ugly side of our life; it was merely the material which, modified, could create an "exemplary work, from the point of view of Party positions," that the novella was ideologically lacking; that after the publication of *One Day in the Life of Ivan Denisovich* the publishing house was inundated with works on the camp theme, to which there had to be a limit; that even Solzhenitsyn, as he could tell us confidentially, no one was planning on publishing anymore. "Yes, yes, he is planning on it, but we aren't. . . ." "We ourselves didn't notice the harm of this theme, but we were shown: there's no need for printing books on this theme for communists, and no use in it . . ." People laughed and exchanged whispers in the courtroom, and I observed that many were taking notes.[1] "If Chukovskaia wins this case," the lawyer for the publisher declared in closing, "that will set a bad precedent." The lawyer from the Preservation of Authors' Rights, by contrast, was very brief. He noted that we weren't in England and our legal verdicts do not establish precedent, but the law on authors' rights is clear (he cited corroborating cases): if a manuscript is approved, then the publisher in all cases is bound to pay the author the full 100 percent of the honorarium.

The courtroom listened to him sympathetically, the judge—dispassionately.

Several times after a speech by the loquacious defense lawyer, the judge ordered me to respond.

"Answer!"

I answered. I said, in part, that if Solzhenitsyn is no longer published, that it will be a misfortune for our country; that, incidentally, my *Sof'ia Petrovna* and his *Ivan Denisovich* are novellas written about different times, at different times and on *different themes*—his is about the camps, and mine about "freedom." I said that if my manuscript was accepted and approved "in the heat of events after the Twentieth and Twenty-second Party Congresses," then wasn't my contract being revoked "in the heat of new events"? And is it possible that decisions of these congresses only constitute "the heat of events"? I said that if the villainy of the previous years was able to take place, wasn't it because, in great measure, the publishers of newspapers, heaped with the groaning, weeping, wailing letters of the bereaved, begging to intervene, to review their loved ones' cases—were restricted from the possibility of printing them? The editors dared not act in the heat of events. And truly who at that time would have "dared to dare"? Signing such a lament in print then meant signing one's own death warrant.

The readiness of publishers—all of them! throughout the whole vast expanse of our country, the publishers of all newspapers, books and magazines, always to obey the baton of whatever director stood at the conductor's stand, to allow or not allow some or another communication on those pages (for example, the reports about illegal arrests and tortures)—wasn't this part of the reason for what happened? I said: even if my novella were only a photograph and not a painting, still in that photograph was captured a very significant moment in our history, and my novella was needed by everyone who wishes to reflect on what had happened.

The people's deputies asked the defendant a few questions, mostly determining dates in the "progression of the events." The judge was silent. He asked the defense lawyer only one question. Asking him to specify the foundation of his allegation as to how my novella was "ideologically lacking," the judge asked: "And then at the settlement of your contract for the accepted item, when the author was paid 60 percent of the honorarium, was the novella *then* ideologically correct?"

Once the judge had heard the lawyer for the defense, the lawyer for the Preservation of Authors' Rights and me, he withdrew to deliberate.

Twenty minutes later:

"Court is in session . . . Please rise. . . ."

The courtroom crowd rose guardedly.

"In the name of the Russian Soviet Federal Socialist Republic. . . ."

In the name of the Russian Soviet Federal Socialist Republic of the Sverdlovsk region it was ruled: the press had to pay the author 100 percent of the honorarium in view of the fact that the manuscript was rejected after it had been approved.

The money was paid out a few days later.

But my novella?

The court has no jurisdiction over publishing books.

The story, incorporated by *samizdat* and long circulating from hand to hand, crossed the border.

In 1965, in Paris, the publishing house Five Continents issued my book in Russian under a different name (*The Deserted House*) and with differently named characters (for example, Ol'ga Petrovna instead of Sof'ia Petrovna). It appeared again in Russian in two issues of *Novyi Zhurnal* in America (1966, numbers 83 and 84,

New York), with the right title and without the changes in names. Since then it has been translated into many languages of the world: I've seen it myself in English, German, Dutch, Swedish and I've heard that translations exist in other languages.

I am grateful to *samizdat* and the foreign publishers and translators. Now my testimony cannot be destroyed by any crazy search according to articles 27 or 227 or 20227. Of course, giving my story a different title (instead of my heroine's name—*The Deserted House*) was not called for; my book is about an educated society, made to lose its consciousness by lies. Sof'ia Petrovna (Ol'ga Petrovna as well) is a representative of that society. The change of title in this case verges on changing the sense of the work . . . but no matter what, I'm grateful, nevertheless.

However, gratitude notwithstanding, I feel no satisfaction. I await one thing, I want one thing: to see my book published in the Soviet Union.

Here in my native land. The native land of Sof'ia Petrovna.

I've been waiting patiently: thirty-four years.[2]

I'd like to put my book on trial before one and only one court: of my compatriots, the young and the old, especially the old who likewise experienced what fell to my fate to experience, to me and a woman so much unlike me, the woman I chose as the heroine of my story—Sof'ia Petrovna, one of the thousands I saw around me.[3]

[1979] 1990

Translated by Christine D. Tomei

Notes to the Essay

1. For the first definition of a tradition of Russian women's autobiography, see Barbara Heldt, *Terrible Perfection: Women and Russian Literature* (Bloomington: Indiana University Press, 1987), 63–102.

2. For further discussion of this pattern in Russian women's life writings, see Beth Holmgren, "For the Good of the Cause: Russian Women's Autobiography in the Twentieth Century," *Women Writers in Russian Literature*, ed. Toby Clyman and Diana Greene (Westport, CT: Greenwood Press, 1994), 127–48.

3. As I note in chapter 3 of *Women's Works in Stalin's Time: On Lidiia Chukovskaia and Nadezhda Mandelstam* (Bloomington: Indiana University Press, 1993), reviewers of *Sof'ia Petrovna* praise the novel as an accurate and authentic work of documentation.

4. Helena Goscilo divines a fascinating typology of Russian widowhood in her unpublished essay "Widowhood as Genre and Profession a la Russe: Nation, Shadow, Curator, and Publicity Agent." I am grateful to the author for sharing this manuscript with me. I argue elsewhere that post-Stalin unofficial society "hallowed the solitary, victimized, and aged female body, a woman who bore the authentic stigmata of her own or her loved ones' persecution and place in Stalinist history." Cf. my essay "Stepping Out/Going Under: Women in Russia's Twentieth-

Century Salons" in *Russia.Women. Culture*, ed. Helena Goscilo and Beth Holmgren (Bloomington: Indiana University Press, 1996), 225–46.

5. Frances Padorr Brent, "Diary of a Nightmare: With Anna Akhmatova in the Time of Soviet Terror," *Chicago Tribune*, 31 July 1994, 4.

6. See recorded visits by Julian Evans, "Portrait: Anna and I," *The Guardian*, 6 June 1994, T20; and Mary Russell, "Friendship in a Time of Terror," *The Irish Times*, 31 May 1994, 10. These accounts represent Chukovskaia as a formidable old woman surrounded by the icons of her great contemporaries and the written work she had yet to revise and proof.

Notes to the Selected Work

1. [Note original to the text.] One of the transcripts of this hearing was published abroad in 1972—seven years later!—in *Politicheskii dnevnik:* 51–57. (The transcript was made by R. Orlova.)

2. [Note original to the text.] No, forty-eight. In 1988 *Sof'ia Petrovna* was published in the magazine *Neva*, no. 2, and after that in my book put out by the publisher Moscow Worker.

3. In accordance with the express wishes of the late L. Chukovskaia, this section is translated without omissions or changes from the original Russian text (*Protsess iskliucheniia. Ocherk literaturnykh nravov* [Moscow: Gorizont, 1990], 179–87). If the translation is less fluent for this, it is nonetheless completely faithful to the original.—Trans.

Bibliography

Primary Works

V laboratorii redaktora. Moscow: Moskovskii rabochii, 1963.

"Byloe i dumy." *Gertsena*. Moscow: Khudozhestvennaia literatura, 1966.

Otkrytoe slovo. New York: Khronika, 1976.

Po ètu storonu smerti. Iz dnevnika 1936–1976. Paris: YMCA Press, 1978.

Protsess iskliucheniia. Ocherk literaturnykh nravov. Paris: YMCA Press, 1979; Moscow: Gorizont, 1990.

Zapiski ob Anne Akhmatovoi. T. II, 1952–1962. Paris: YMCA Press, 1980.

Zapiski ob Anne Akhmatovoi. T. I, 1938–1941, 2–oe izd., ispr. i dop. Paris: YMCA Press, 1984; Moscow: Kniga, 1989.

Pamiati detstva. New York: Chalidze Publications, 1983; Moscow: Moskovskii rabochii, 1989.

Sof'ia Petrovna. Spusk pod vodu: povesti. Moscow: Moskovskii rabochii, 1989.

In Translation

The Deserted House. Trans. Aline B. Werth. New York: Dutton, 1967.

Het Verlaten Huis. Trans. Wim Hartog. Amsterdam, 1968.

Det Tomma Huset. Trans. Johan Munck. Stockholm, 1969.

Ein Leeres Haus. Trans. Eva Mathay. Zurich: Diogenes, 1971.

Going Under. Trans. Peter M. Weston. New York: Barrie and Jenkins, 1972.

Duik in de diepte. Trans. Hans Leerink. Amsterdam, 1973.

La plongee. Trans. Andre Bloch. Paris: Calmann-Levy, 1974.

La maison deserte. Trans. Serge Duchesne. Paris: Calmann-Levy, 1975.

Untertauchen. Trans. Swetlana Geier. Wels, 1975.

Opustoszaly dom. Trans. Jerzy Szperak. London: Polonia Book Fund, 1975.

Indietro nell'acqua scura. Trans. Sergio Rapetti. Firenze, 1979.

Les chemins de l'exclusion (essai sur les moeurs litteraires en URSS). Trans. Georges Brissac. Paris: Encre, 1979.

Entretiens avec Anna Akhmatova. Trans. Lucile Nivat and Genevieve Leibrich. Paris: A. Michel, 1980.

Esklujson: et essay om skikk og bruk i litteraturen. Trans. Alf.B. Glad. Oslo, 1981.

Det forlatte huset. Trans. Ivar Magnus Ravnum. Oslo, 1983.

Sofia Petrovna. Trans. Aline Worth; revised and amended by Eliza Kellogg Klose. Evanston, IL: Northwestern University Press, 1988.

To the Memory of Childhood. Trans. Eliza Kellogg Klose. Evanston, IL: Northwestern University Press, 1988.

Zapiski ob Anne Akhmatovoi: The Personal File of Anna Akhmatova. Video Project, 1991.

The Akhmatova Journals. Vol. 1, 1938–1941. Trans. Milena Michalski, Sylva Rubashova and Peter Norman. New York: Farrar, Straus and Giroux, 1994.

Secondary Works:

Etkind, Efim. "Otets i doch'." Afterword to *Pamiati detstva.* New York: Chalidze, 1983. 256–81.

Gifford, Henry. "A Poet for Her People". Rev. of *Zapiski ob Anne Akhmatovoi. The Times Literary Supplement,* 18 November 1977, 1351–52.

Holmgren, Beth. "For the Good of the Cause: Russian Women's Autobiography in the Twentieth Century." *Women Writers in Russian Literature.* Ed. Toby Clyman and Diana Greene. Westport, CT: Greenwood Press, 1994. 127–48.

———. *Women's Works in Stalin's Time: On Lidiia Chukovskaia and Nadezhda Mandelstam.* Bloomington: Indiana University Press, 1993.

Latynina, Alla. "Pisat'—èto bylo spasenie: vstrecha s Lidiei Chukovskoi." *Moskovskie novosti* 17 (12 April 1988): 7.

Russell, John. "High Spirits." Rev. of *To the Memory of Childhood* and *Entretiens avec Anna Akhmatova. New York Review of Books,* 15 February 1990, 12–16.

Sandler, Stephanie. "Reading Loyalty in Chukovskaia's *Zapiski ob Anne Akhmatovoi.*" *The Speech of Unknown Eyes: Akhmatova's Readers on Her Poetry.* Ed. Wendy Rosslyn. Nottingham: Astra, 1990.

Natal'ia Il'ina

Natal'ia Il'ina (1914–1994).
Courtesy of Adele Barker.

Natal'ia Iosifovna Il'ina, satirist, journalist, novelist and memoirist, was born in St. Petersburg. Subsequently she became a child of the emigration. Her father, an officer in the White Army, fled with his family to Harbin in 1920 after the Bolshevik takeover, and it was here that Il'ina spent her childhood years. What distinguishes her as a writer, what informs the nature of her prose, is both the experience of the emigration and the fact that in 1947 she chose to return to Stalin's Russia. Her work, both that written in emigration and in the Soviet Union, is powerfully influenced by her need to create for herself a homeland (*rodina*) and to live among her own people (*sredi svoikh*). So strong was her nostalgia for her country that she was forced to create it in order to remember it. Sadly, the image of the country she had created blinded her to the excesses and ravages of Stalinism. Il'ina's journey as a writer was, by and large, one in which she engaged in the process of reevaluating her vision of her homeland and her position in it, placing the necessary corrective upon the mixture of propaganda and desire that led her back home from China to begin with.

Il'ina once said that she became a satirist because she was born with it in her blood. Her obvious natural predilection for the genre was nourished by her life in emigration. As a Russian émigré growing up in Harbin, Il'ina found herself estranged like other Russians not only from the Chinese community but from the European community within which she was later to live in Shanghai. Unlike most Russians living in Harbin, Il'ina and her sister managed to avoid becoming ghettoized by virtue of the fact that their mother taught them English, the language that would later help Il'ina function within the foreign community in Shanghai. Thus Il'ina in her early twenties found herself both intellectually and emotionally distanced from the émigré community that surrounded her in Harbin. If this distance provided her with the necessary stance from which to interrogate and satirize Russian and expatriate life, it also increased her longing to live within a community that she could call home and identify with.

In 1936 Il'ina moved to Shanghai, where opportunities for employment were better than in Harbin. Here she went to work for the émigré newspaper *The Shanghai Dawn* (*Shanghai-skia zaria*), where she was hired to do some light pieces as fillers. In her writing she poked fun at both expatriate and émigré life in Shanghai, the former of which was enjoying the last years of a lifestyle that was to be precipitously halted with Mao's takeover in 1949. Although these early feuilletons contained little sympathy for the expatriate community, which essentially treated the White Russians little better than they did the Chinese, there was an underlying pathos in her description of the Russian émigrés who, despite their best intentions, could find no home among the rest of the foreign community in China.

By 1941 the appeal of émigré life for Il'ina was beginning to wane, a change spawned less by life in emigration than by the complex intermingling of Stalinist propaganda directed at the émigrés and Il'ina's emotional and psychological response to her own family. That same year she joined an organization called the Union for the Return to the Motherland, which had been set up by the NKVD in 1936 in order to attract émigrés back to the Soviet Union. She also began working for a pro-Soviet paper called *New Life* (*Novaia zhizn'*), where her feuilletons appeared between 1942 and 1946. The essays that Il'ina wrote for *New Life* were published in book form in Shanghai in 1946 under the title *Through Different Eyes* (*Inymi glazami*). This collection of essays and satire reflected the worldview of a young woman who had read her Marx and who was deeply convinced that life in emigration was lived for gain and thus ultimately responsible for the death of the soul. As the title of the book suggests, in this volume Il'ina was concerned principally with the problem of vision. In her view both émigrés and foreigners failed to see the Soviet Union for what it was. The émigré community, forced to confront the fact that their former country was progressing well without them, invented all sorts of lies and half-truths about it in order to console themselves. The irony of the book was that Il'ina was no less blinded by the disinformation she had absorbed about her own country than were the émigrés for whom the only real Russia was the one they had left behind. Essentially, from the mid-1940s on, Il'ina's vision of her own country was one created for her and for millions of others by the Stalinist propaganda machine: the Russia that had routed the Germans from Stalingrad, survived the blockade and rescued the Baltics from the ravages of the German army. This was the Russia she thought she was returning to.

By 1946 Il'ina had chosen to repatriate, and in 1947, along with 2,500 other Russian families, she left Shanghai by steamer for Nakhodka and then journeyed by train into the Soviet Union.

The reasons why Il'ina chose to repatriate during one of the most repressive times in Soviet history make up a complex compendium of personal and political issues. Il'ina had felt very deeply the injustice of the fact that she had had no part in her parents' decision to flee yet had been forced to pay the price of that decision. Her own alienation from both her parents as well as her estrangement from the émigré and expatriate world made her particularly receptive to the news of the new Soviet Constitution of 1936 guaranteeing equality for all its citizens. Il'ina was all too ready to dismiss the much more serious charges about the purges and the gulag that were leaking out of Russia in part because since childhood she had been regularly exposed to a barrage of anti-Soviet articles in the émigré press that were frequently thin on fact. But there were other reasons as well, reasons that testify to the frightening effectiveness of Stalinist propaganda, which neatly answered the desire among many young émigré Russians for a nuclear family, an ideal that the man-made events of the twentieth century had decimated in Russia. In Il'ina's case, Stalin and the cherished notion of the mythological motherland answered her own need for a strong family and especially father (before Il'ina had moved to Shanghai, her own father had deserted the family, leaving them to fend for themselves). In fact, for many Russians during the 1930s and 1940s, Stalin became the consummate father figure who, as father to the nation, would provide for his children and defend the motherland.

Back in the Soviet Union, Il'ina quickly became part of the literary community. The last years of Stalin's rule, however, were not conducive to the sort of satire she had been writing in China. During the late 1940s the only satire that was coming out of the Soviet Union, specifically from the satirical journal *The Crocodile* (*Krokodil*), was directed against the evils of the capitalist West. True to the spirit of the times, Il'ina wrote the kind of prescriptive satire that was in demand, a choice that she regretted years later.

Il'ina had not been back in the Soviet Union long before she embarked on the one and only novel she would write during her lifetime. The two-volume novel *The Homecoming* (*Vozvrashchenie*) was begun in 1952. The first book was completed in 1957, the second in 1966. The novel is a fictionalized account of her life in Harbin and Shanghai and her gradual decision to return home. Although she originally intended to focus on her female protagonist's journey back to her homeland, she was persuaded by her second husband, the linguist A.A. Reformatskii, that she was not yet ready to write about life in the Soviet Union and that she would do much better to write about what she did know, namely life in China. Indeed, although *The Homecoming* was not a success artistically, it was nevertheless one of the first works written by a Soviet to treat the émigré experience sympathetically. This fact alone has earned it a place of respect in Soviet letters.

Ostensibly Il'ina wrote *The Homecoming* as a way of earning her diploma from the Literary Institute in Moscow. It was also her ticket into the Writers' Union. But there also seem to be other issues that Il'ina is attempting to sort through in the novel, issues that relate to her own family, specifically the figure of the father. The reality of Il'ina's father as later depicted in her memoirs *Roads and Fates* (*Dorogi i sud'by*, 1985) was that he was a military officer and a womanizer who was completely ineffectual as both husband and father. He left the family while they were living in Harbin, eventually remarried and moved to Switzerland, where he lived off the largess of his second wife. The image of the father that Il'ina creates in *The Homecoming*, however, is very different—idolized and admired. Interestingly, she has him killed in the Russian civil war, perhaps unconsciously acknowledging that both the real and the fictional fathers would have been unable to make their peace with both Il'ina's and her protagonist's decision to return to Stalinist Russia.

Il'ina returned to the kind of satire she had written in China only gradually. Even with Stalin buried and the first Thaw under way she was still not psychologically prepared to write effective satire, so much did she yearn to be a part of the society that she would presumably be satirizing. When she did return to the genre of satire in the mid-1950s, she chose the style of literary parody, aiming her critical barbs at socialist realism and the sentimental romance. Unfortunately, the sense of humor of the average Soviet had been so dulled by the lack of parody and satire during the Stalin era that many of Il'ina's readers failed to see her humor and wrote vituperative letters to journals such as *The Crocodile* asking her to soften her touch and be more patient with other people's literary styles.

Over the years Il'ina directed her satire repeatedly at the hollow literary conventions that dominated the Soviet literary scene from the 1930s through the 1970s. Her most famous literary satire, couched in the form of literary criticism and entitled "On the Question of Tradition and Innovation in the Genre of the 'Woman's Story'" ("K voprosu o traditsii i novatorstve v zhanre 'damskoi povesti'"), was written in 1963 and takes on Soviet literature's claim to have broken with the moral values and character types of its prerevolutionary predecessors. She focuses her attentions on the genre of woman's prose (*zhenskaia proza*), particularly that of the prerevolutionary writer Anastasiia Verbitskaia, whose verbose physical descriptions came to define what was generally regarded as "women's writing." Il'ina's view of contemporary Soviet literature in this piece is that, regardless of all the talk about the creation of the new Soviet man and woman, Soviet literature is still mired in the old prerevolutionary conventions and stereotypes associated with women's writing. She concludes by noting that so-called women's writing is not gender-specific and can be used to denote any style characterized by a thin plot line and an overabundance of physical description. Moreover, argued Il'ina, if it is style rather than subject matter that separates women's and men's writing, and thus, by extension, if women's writing is simply the tag attached to any work that is badly written, then most of the male hack writers who were grinding out production novels would qualify for inclusion in this genre.

Like many Russian women writers of this century, Il'ina never identified herself as a woman writer. Her own stance toward women's writing was complex. On the one hand, she had no compunction about exposing some of the mistaken notions that lay at the heart of the deep-seated prejudice against women writers. However, her own past coupled with her own sense of alienation and need to belong kept her from initially identifying with any group in her homeland that was marginalized.

During the 1960s and 1970s Il'ina's satire was increasingly directed at the economy and service sector of the country as a way of lobbying for change. Her satires and feuilletons during this time touched on virtually every aspect of Soviet consumer life, from the obstacles encountered while shopping or trying to get one's car repaired to the headaches of attempting to go on vacation. In each feuilleton Il'ina adopts the persona of the average Soviet citizen, either male or female, who sets out to get something done only to land in an indecipherable bureaucratic maze where he or she becomes the hapless victim of inefficiency or rudeness. Some of her more well-known pieces written around this time include her 1963 feuilleton "The Last Cruise" ("Poslednii reis"), which narrates the complete breakdown of the service sector of the economy on a passenger boat from Moscow to Ufa. Il'ina also turned her attention to the second economy in "But the Water Still Flows" ("A voda vse techet"), in which her satirical tone only thinly disguises her more serious look at how the efficiency of the average Soviet worker has reached an all-time low because he or she spends virtually all available time in pursuit of basic goods.

Il'ina's feuilletons on economic themes were well received as long as Kosygin's policies on favoring the consumer sector over the military held sway. By the early mid-1970s, however, Suslov's advocacy of a stronger military dominated party thinking and consumer interests were once again given short shrift. It was during this time that Il'ina embarked on her memoirs.

Il'ina's volume of memoirs, *Roads and Fates*, was first published in 1985. In it she includes reminiscences of her life in emigration as well as memoirs of her contemporaries, among them Akhmatova, Kornei Chukovskii, her own husband Reformatskii, and the émigré chanteur Aleksandr Vertinskii. The art of writing memoirs engaged Il'ina on a very different level than did the satire she had written for many years. The genre of satire had always allowed Il'ina to adopt new fictionalized persona constantly assuming new guises. In her memoirs the distance that she had previously placed between herself and her reader evaporates as Il'ina presents portraits of those who helped her gain clarity of vision about the country to which she had returned. In addition, the portraits she draws of Akhmatova, Chukovskii and Reformatskii are as much about the quality of Il'ina's own vision as they are about these figures themselves. For example, she initially idolizes Akhmatova; gradually she learns to see the person beneath the icon she has created. Finally she is able to say, "But she was neither a saint nor a statue. Nothing human was foreign to her."[1]

Akhmatova and Chukovskii both served as Il'ina's literary parents on Russian soil. Unlike her own parents, who had filled her with stories of the old Russia and of hatred for the new regime, these literary figures, no less than Il'ina's husband, Reformatskii, understood that Il'ina had to learn the important lessons of Soviet history for herself. Thus when Il'ina sprang to the defense of Pasternak's critics in 1958 and criticized Pasternak for insufficient patriotism to his own country, Akhmatova said little, only once uttering the phrase, "A poet is always right."[2] It took Il'ina much longer to absorb the lessons of history that had been responsible for so much of Akhmatova's grief than it did to understand and appreciate the poet herself.

The attempt to correct her vision—to see with her own eyes—lies at the heart of Il'ina's portraits in *Roads and Fates*. Her portrait of Kornei Chukovskii is as much about her own inability to intuit this man as it is about Chukovskii himself. Later, in her portrait of her husband, she laments that she came to understand the people and the events in her life too late. "Now," she says, "I have taught myself [how to use the dictionary] now that he is no longer here."[3] This small moment becomes symbolic of her larger regret over failing to read the events of this century in the way they needed to be read.

For Il'ina, the writing of memoirs, much like her other work, was engendered by her desire to find for herself a place within Soviet society, one that would allow her to find a haven within its walls yet at the same time not be taken in by it. She chronicles her seemingly endless peregrinations around Moscow soon after her return, moving from apartment to apartment, as if chronicling a deeper search to find her own anchor in her homeland. She says in her memoirs: "The house in which I live is the house where, for the first time, I have been able to say, 'I am at home!' And the house stands on my native land. How can I not love it? It is my first solid anchor. And my last—I hope. I want to believe that it is my last."[4]

Natal'ia Il'ina died in Moscow in January 1994. The apartment in which she lived was the same one into which she had moved when she married Reformatskii in 1957.

Adele Barker

My Unknown Homeland

Family photos in my mother's album: there I am, dressed in a white medical gown, leaning against the trunk of a birch tree with a merry grin on my face. It's summer, and everything is in bloom in the garden at the Institute of Orthopaedics and Reconstructive Surgery in Kazan' . . . and this one of my uncle Ivan Dmitrievich and me on the sofa. My uncle lived on Gagarin Lane, in Moscow. And here I am again—but the picture was taken from a distance so that, while the fountains in the background at Petergof came out quite well, it's difficult to make out my face.

These photographs (there are so many of them!) and the letters I wrote to my mother during our seven-year separation now allow me to recall more clearly the distant past. My mother, it seems, saved not only photographs and letters, but also the postcards that I dropped into mailboxes during the long journey by heated boxcar from Nakhodka to Kazan.'

The Soviet government had assumed financial responsibility for transporting expatriates back to Russia. Those who chose to return—approximately 2,500 families—were then divided into five groups. The first left Shanghai in August, and the last in November 1947. I was among the last group. We traveled by steamship to Nakhodka, from where we headed inland by rail.

The first letter was dated 6 December 1947: "When we arrived late yesterday evening we could see little lights in the harbor. This morning we are still moored in the bay. It's beautiful and yet quite bleak here, like something out of Jack London: the sea is steel-green, and the hills are covered with snow. The trip wasn't bad, if you don't take into consideration the first two days, that is. The sea was rather rough, and almost all the women and many of the men became seasick. Although I felt really awful, I managed to stay on my feet that entire horrible Monday, even did some typing in the ship's drawing room, despite the fact that the typewriter slid all over the table. I tried not to look out the porthole. Sometimes the sea was visible, and at other times only the sky. I had promised myself that I would get the ship's paper out by five o'clock Tuesday—and I succeeded! I wrote only one small article for the paper, since I spent most of my time pleading with others to work, trying to round up artists, etc. And it was cold—minus eleven degrees Celsius—and windy on the open sea. But in general, mamochka, everything is fine, and I have bright hopes for the future. After all, I am going to a country where everything depends upon one's own energy, effort and hard work!"

"12 December. We are living in Nakhodka. There are few comforts, but we're managing all right. But I'm glad you're not here. What for me is an interesting adventure would be for you a difficult trip. It must be wonderful here in the summer, but in the winter it's no picnic. I've gotten used to the frosts, and don't feel the cold so much anymore. But it's difficult for the old people and children in our barracks. I'm in good spirits—I even put out one edition of a newspaper. I believe in socialism. I believe in myself."

We were detained in Nakhodka until New Year's Eve due to heavy snowfalls, which interrupted traffic along the rail lines. While in Nakhodka we witnessed both the currency reform and the abolition of rationing coupons, and voted for the first time. All the heavy baggage, trunks and gigantic boxes—some people were taking furniture and even pianos with them—were left on the dock where, exposed to the elements, they were guarded in shifts by the men in our group. Our wooden barracks were actually rather cozy, with two-tiered plank beds and a wood stove stoked in the hallway. We covered the wooden bunks with our blankets, and began to feel quite at home. Only the toilets—two frozen wooden buildings that could accommodate ten people at a time—were really unbearable. . . . Although the temperature was below zero, it was sunny, and in the morning little pink clouds of smoke could be seen escaping from all the pipes. The local village and the market were actually quite a distance from our barracks, which stood in the middle of a barren field where the wind coming off the ocean blew incessantly. How pleasant it was to open the felt-covered door, enter the heated room and find a boiling teapot on the stove. We drank a lot of tea.

In Nakhodka we were given a list of cities where the local authorities were supposed to provide repatriates with temporary housing and a job. All of these cities, with the exception of Kazan', were located in the Urals or in Siberia. We were allowed to choose the city in which we wanted to live. The elderly, women with small children and those in poor health left Nakhodka in regular passenger trains. The rest departed in heated box cars.

"14 January 1948. I'm writing this to you from the train. I'll send you a letter from Omsk where, hopefully, we will arrive tomorrow morning. There are twenty people in this boxcar, plus our belongings. They put the heavy baggage in other cars. We sleep side-by-side on wooden bunks. But we've had great luck with the weather. It's so warm that Iura, Roma and I have twice ridden in the open platform at the back of the car. The station names are really hideous: 'Zima,' 'Tulup,' but the temperature—it's about forty degrees Fahrenheit. And they say that sometimes it even gets up to over a hundred! We have *varenets* [a kind of fermented, baked milk], *prostokvasha* [sour clotted milk], and butter to eat. . . . I've been talking a lot with the locals. Everyone seems glad about the currency reform and that ration cards are no longer needed. The woods, fields and villages bundled in snow are all so beautiful. I have a feeling that I've seen all of this before, that it's all familiar and dear to me. Don't worry about me. Every day I thank God that I left, and am in Russia."

(I have known Roma, the brother of one of my girlfriends, since childhood. His family, a pregnant wife and his mother-in-law, that is, left Nakhodka before us by regular coach. To this day Roma still lives in Kazan', where he is now a successful doctor and father of grown children. I met Iura in Shanghai during the period when we were both desperate to return to Russia. In the mid-1950s Iura moved from Kazan' to Moscow, where he became a high-level interpreter of English.)

We were not dismayed, however, by the difficulties encountered during the journey. We were young and healthy, and fascinated by everything. For the first time in our lives we were seeing our native land. But each of us experienced it in a different way. The landscapes reminded me of the works of Russian painters:

the little wooden huts, the dark blue forests glowing in the distance, the snow-covered fields—they evoked certain literary associations in my mind, and I would whisper to myself a few lines from one of Blok's poems: "Oh these havens in uninhabitable lands! I can neither live nor weep without you!"

Iura, however, perceived things quite differently. At that time Iura, who had been educated at the Catholic College in Tian'tsinsk, knew English much better than Russian. In Shanghai, where he had worked for a foreign firm, someone had given him a copy of the *Communist Manifesto*. That was what started it all. After that he would read only Marxist literature: in a sense it became his religion. He had a preacher's temperament and a fanatic's impatience . . . I remember how shocked I was once hearing him call Winston Churchill a fool. That's right—a fool! According to his logic, capitalism was doomed to failure and the world was moving toward socialism: this was the natural course history should take, and only idiots failed to see this. Iura had not been exposed to Russian literature—for some reason it was not taught at the Catholic College. And his extremely logical mind simply could not grasp any concept of art. The woods and forests that I was so touched by, therefore, failed to move Iura in the least. He wasn't traveling to Russia, but to a country that, in his opinion, was the first in the world to actualize its promises by putting to the test the great international socialist system.

And Roma? He was more ironic and reserved than we were. His reactions and impressions seem to have disappeared from my memory.

"I often speak with the local people," I wrote to my mother. But what exactly did I mean by this? During the trips the only locals we met were old women swaddled in scarves who came out to meet the trains with chunks of frozen milk and pots of boiled potatoes. They would gaze at us in amazement, since we were dressed so strangely. In the summer of 1947, you see, American military uniforms—short sheepskin coats, coarse red walking shoes, khaki pants and even green army blankets and towels—were sold in Shanghai. The light, warm sheepskin jackets with canvas outers, which had been stamped on the back with the letters U.S.N. [U.S. Navy], couldn't have been more appropriate for our trip. But women in pants, with strange shoes and letters tattooed across their backs—no wonder the old women were confused.

Once, one of the women wrapped in a double layer of shawls from whom I bought some milk—a wonderful, wrinkled old grandmother with fading blue eyes—whispered to me, "Dear, just who are you? You aren't the French, are you?"

"What French, we're Russians, Grandma, Russians," I answered joyfully. I was barely able to restrain myself from hugging her.

"Where are you traveling from?"

"From China."

"You don't say! And do they have white bread there?"

"Yes, Grandma, they do."

"So why did you leave?"

"Well . . . we want to live in Russia!" And at that I was a little put off, saddened by the woman's attitude. Was bread the only reason to. . . .

"I see," the backward old woman mumbled incoherently.

We spent five days in Sverdlovsk, where many of the repatriates in our group decided to remain. When we arrived two or three boxcars that were heading for Kazan' were unhooked and added to another train. In the morning, when we jumped for the first time out of the pitch-darkness of the car onto the web of rails, it was just beginning to get light. The sun rose rather late in this town in the Urals. Glancing furtively at the sky, we made our way, hand in hand. Strangers hoping to make a profit off the peculiar-looking arrivals were roaming about in the forest. They called to us, "Citizens! You don't by any chance want to sell anything?" But we did.

Since our train arrived in major cities at night, we had never gotten a real look at a town in the daylight—until Sverdlovsk. Strolling through the streets of the city that first day, all three of us wished desperately for something tasty to eat, music, and in general for a good life . . . and we sold our wristwatches to some people wandering among the boxcars. Iura and Roma were able to give theirs up without blinking an eye, but I hesitated—after all, how could one get along without a watch? But the buyer cheered me up, saying, "Don't worry about it, citizen, you'll get a new one. You won't perish in your native land." I liked his reply, and have since quoted it in my letters. I have reached my native land. I will not perish.

"22 January 1948. Sverdlovsk. Ration cards were abolished 17 December, and life seems to get better, easier, right before our eyes. . . ." (It would be interesting to know what I was comparing it to. What did I understand of food rationing?)

"Our economy must be extremely strong if, following a war, such a tangible improvement has occurred in people's lives. The stores in Sverdlovsk are piled with goods: cheese, butter, jam, candy, bread, meat . . . the abundance of goods—that was the first pleasant shock we had in Sverdlovsk. Secondly—true freedom and democracy. We, repatriates, enjoy full rights here, and can travel freely throughout the Soviet Union. No longer will we have to suffer from the feeling of inferiority that tormented us in Shanghai where we were 'stateless, second-class Whites.'"

From the very beginning we assumed that, having arrived in Russia, we would become full-fledged citizens, and also that the surprise and excitement we experienced traveling from one area of the country to another was somehow abnormal. The problem was that we (in any case Iura and I) didn't consider ourselves the equal of other Soviets, since we were born and raised under capitalism. But the people here had been educated in a progressive socialist system. We thought that we would have to work extra hard in order to come up to the level of the average Soviet citizen. But then suddenly, not waiting for us to apply ourselves, they simply said, "You can go and live wherever you like, just like any other citizen." Of course, we would receive residency permits, rooms in a hostel and a job only in the cities named on the list. In any other cities we would have to obtain these on our own. And then we had only a rather vague idea of what a residency permit was. But that was just a trifle! Most importantly, we were free to go where we pleased, and no distinction was made between us and other local citizens. This was what I had in mind when I spoke of "freedom and democracy."

But Iura had some rather exaggerated notions about the average Soviet citizen. He believed, for instance, that it was impossible for this individual to steal. Why would he steal in a society where there was no unemployment, where it was possible for each individual to earn an honest wage? Iura even considered the repatriates' anxiety over their belongings a sign of both their political backwardness and lack of education. When helping with the loading or unloading of our things, he paid little attention to his own belongings, leaving them wherever they might wind up. Finally one of his suitcases disappeared. He was upset about it, but it didn't change his opinion: there were exceptions to every rule, and one had to take into consideration the vestiges of capitalism remaining in people's minds. But I hadn't yet reached this level of theoretical consciousness, and therefore kept an eye on my things. . . .

"Lastly (I wrote my mother) I am excited about the availability of education in this new land. Even in small villages there are good libraries, magazines—everything one could possibly want. And in Sverdlovsk it's difficult to describe just how wonderful it is! We went to the libraries and sat in the reading rooms. How many people were busy there studying! Here you don't have to pay for education—they give you a scholarship. As soon as I get to Kazan' I'll enter an institute. You always wanted me to get a university education. Now I'll be able to."

It was only in early January that our creaking boxcars finally crawled into Kazan'. We were put up in the Collective Farmers' Building. Its regular occupants had been temporarily moved to make way for us. We were also given money: those with families received a thousand rubles, and those who were single, six hundred.

It was crowded in the hostel. The beds stood in rows, as in a hospital ward, but it was clean and warm there. In the evenings the cleaning lady would bring in a huge samovar and place it on a table, and about that time heavy, limping steps would echo along the wooden staircase. It was Comrade Kolesov, the representative of the Council of Ministers of the Tatar Autonomous Republic. He was in charge of finding us work.

And that was not an easy job. Two different worlds, two different systems had collided head on, and Kolesov was simply at a loss as to how to deal with some of the people in our group. Wrinkling his forehead, he would repeat, "What? What? Excuse me, I didn't understand!"

"I'm a broker," a middle-aged man would answer with dignity.

"A what?"

"A broker, I guess you call it, an agent."

"And what ah . . . what exactly did you do?"

"I bought, I sold, resold . . . in general, got by! Wheeled and dealed."

"Wheeled and dealed?" Kolesov would repeat, perplexed. "And just what am I going to do with you?"

Or else: "I was the owner of a women's clothing store."

"Ah, a dressmaker?" Kolesov would perk up.

"What do you mean a dressmaker? I had my own business. I've never held a needle in my hand!"

Translated by Linda Tapp

Notes to the Essay

1. N. Il'ina, "Eshche ob Akhmatovoi," *Ogonek* 38 (1985): 280.
2. N. Il'ina, "Anna Akhmatova kakoi ia ee videla," *Dorogi i sud'by* (Moscow: Sovetskii pisatel', 1985), 280.
3. Ibid., 471–558.
4. Ibid., 558.

Bibliography

Primary Works

Inymi glazami. Ocherki shangkhaiskoi zhizni. Shanghai, 1945.
Vozvrashchenie. 2 vols. Moscow, 1957–1966.
Vnimanie opasnost'! Moscow, 1960.

Ne nado ovatsii! Moscow, 1964.

Chto-to tut ne kleitsia. Moscow, 1968.

Tut vse napisano. Moscow, 1971.

Svetiashchiesia tablo. Moscow, 1974.

Sud'by. Moscow, 1980.

Dorogi. Moscow, 1983.

Dorogi i sud'by. Moscow: Sovetskii pisatel', 1985, 1988, 1991.

Belogorskaia krepost'. Moscow, 1989.

In Translation

"Five Feuilletons." Trans. N.V. Galichenko and C. Partridge. *Russian Literature Triquarterly* 14 (1976): 193–223.

"Anna Akhmatova in the Last Years of Her Life." *Soviet Studies in Literature* (Fall 1977): 27–76.

"A Haunting Spectre." *The Best of Ogonyok*. Trans. Cathy Porter. London: Heinemann Press, 1990. 203–08.

"Repairing Our Car." Trans. Steven W. Nielsen. *Soviet Women's Writing*. Ed. J. Decter. New York: Abbeville Press, 1990. 145–52.

Secondary Works

Barker, Adele. "Natal'ia Iosifovna Il'ina." *Dictionary of Russian Women Writers*. Ed. M. Ledkovsky, C. Rosenthal and M. Zirin. Westport, CT: Greenwood Press, 1994. 254–56.

Grekova, I. "Razvetvleniia dorog." *Oktiabr'* 10 (1983): 192–97.

Idashkin, I. "Eshche raz o 'vechnoi teme' i geroine u zerkala." *Oktiabr'* 6 (1963): 188–90.

Ivanova, T. "Natal'ia, Ol'ga, Marietta." *V mire knig* 12 (1986): 70–74.

Roshchin, M. "Dolgie dni vozvrashcheniia." *Novyi mir* 6 (1966): 238–42.

Lidiia Ginzburg

Lidiia Iakovlevna Ginzburg (1902–1990), the distinguished literary personality, theorist and writer, is best known outside Russia for her theoretical writings and scholarly studies of nineteenth- and twentieth-century lyric poetry and narrative prose. Only in the 1980s, the last decade of her life, did Ginzburg's role as a creative writer come to light, revealing a master practitioner of the "intermediary genres" for which she had established new principles of analysis. While perfecting her own mastery of the journal, the essay and quasi-fictional prose, and indeed, the art of conversation as a genre of personal and social cognition, she simultaneously reevaluated the nature of materials not previously considered "aesthetic," and reassessed the aesthetic nature of materials not previously considered "literature." She explained her interest in noncanonical genres as part of the evolving "literary process": "In contemporary prose the sense of the author's presence is developing apace. . . . You take up a pen for a conversation about life—not to write an autobiography, but to express directly your own life experience, your views on reality. . . . This is one of the paths of future literary development . . . the path I prefer."[1]

From the mid-1920s until her death in 1990, Ginzburg chose to broadly identify herself as a "littérateur" or "literary professional":

> Literary science cannot develop out of itself alone; external stimuli and association with other realms of thought are required. . . . For those of us who do not view ourselves primarily as literary historians or literary theorists, but as having broader interests—who see ourselves rather as *littérateurs*, as literary professionals—that lack of nourishment is fatal.[2]

Appreciation of the processes by which life is tranformed into literature and by which literary models influence codes of social behavior and society's self-consciousness dominates all Ginzburg's writing, her theory being an outgrowth of her literary practice and scholarship.

Ginzburg's marginalized "outsider" status as scholar, writer and witness during the Stalin years gave way to near cultlike admiration in Leningrad's intellectual community in the post-Stalinist Thaw; as mentor and support for the younger generation of writers and scholars unrecognized by the official Soviet hierarchy, she strongly influenced the reformulation of post-Stalinist values. Her publications of the 1980s frequently reflect their genesis in her journal or in conversations with colleagues and friends. For example, the impetus behind her essays on the Russian intelligentsia grew out of two related intellectual processes: rereading and editing her earlier journals for publication and conversations about them within her circle of admirers. But not until the mid-1980s did Ginzburg gain the recognition she deserved for her role as intellectual conduit between the pre- and post-Stalinist generations of the intelligentsia. Official celebrations of her eightieth and eighty-fifth birthdays were succeeded in 1988 by the prestigious State Prize for Literature. Thus, at the very end of her life, as one of the few representatives of her generation to have lived long enough to voice her opinion freely, Ginzburg became a publicly powerful spokesperson in the press and on television: "The principle itself—that I can say whatever I think—is an event of enormous moral consequence."[3]

Lidiia Ginzburg was born into a middle-class assimilated Jewish family of the Odessa intelligentsia on 5 March (18) 1902. Her parents had met in Switzerland, where her father and his brother were sent to study chemical engineering. Her father's untimely death in 1910 left her uncle to become a second father to young Lidiia and her brother Viktor, ten years her senior. Taking the stage name of Viktor Teapot in his work as a comic actor and theater director, he moved to Moscow while Lidiia was still in school. She maintained close relations with Viktor and his family until his death in 1960. Conversations noted in her journal record his wit and interaction with Moscow literary circles.

Fifteen years old in 1917, and heir to the liberal social ideals of the Russian-Jewish intelligentsia, Ginzburg and her gymnasium schoolmates were caught up in the revolution's intellectual and emotional fervor. Years later she described the power of those feelings: "There was acceptance, no looking back, no questions asked. That may be cause for surprise, but I am not surprised. We were all like that—at age fifteen. And something remains with us from our youth." Furthermore, she observed how her generation's welcoming of the revolution reflected contemporary intellectual currents: "Revolution attracted the entire Russian avant garde. The Symbolists as early as 1905 . . . [as for the] post-Symbolists . . . Osip Mandel'shtam's essays of the 1920s are incomprehensible without noting what he said in *Noise of Time* about reading the Erfurt Program at school, or the influence of the Narodnik movement on his best friend's family . . . and Boris Pasternak in 'The Year 1905' . . . and even Anna Akhmatova."[4]

In 1920 Ginzburg set off for Leningrad (then Petrograd), which remained her home until her death. She enrolled in the State Institute of History of the Arts (GIII), where her teachers included the most formidable minds of the literary intelligentsia, Èikhenbaum, Tynianov, Tomashevskii, Zhirmunskii and Vinogradov. The 1920s, Ginzburg claimed, taught her circle, the "young formalists," that they were "part of history in the making." Indeed, she defined her generation in terms of the epoch's literary and cultural alignments: "It seemed to us—and so it was for a short time—that we were the principal actors in a segment of culture which had just begun. But in the 1930s and 1940s, we became the passive property of the Stalinist epoch and the war years, with all that followed."[5] After graduating in 1926, Ginzburg worked at the institute as a research fellow (*nauchnyi sotrudnik*) and taught seminars in nineteenth-century Russian poetry, continuing her affiliation with GIII until it was closed down by hostile authorities in 1930. Her earliest scholarly publications on Viazemskii as littérateur, on Benediktov's literary life and on the philosophical lyric appeared under the institute's auspices. Ginzburg's journal provides tantalizing glimpses into the intense and vital atmosphere at GIII, as well as reflections of her subsequent despair over the disintegration of collegial relationships and the destruction of the institute.

In contrast to conventional "macrohistorical" thinking about the 1930s, Ginzburg emphasized that their ever-present fear was constantly being countered by the "microhistorical" details of daily activities. Thus, in rereading her journals of those years, she claimed not to be surprised to find records of numerous acts of heroism and examples of enthusiasm, creativity and amusement. Despite confusion, frustration and alienation, her circle viewed the "creative experience" almost as a human right fulfilling an incorrigible need to be active even during the worst of times. On the other hand, the first of her two "direct encounters with the organs" took place in 1933. She was detained in the "Big House" as a case was developed against Zhirmunskii, the former director of the Section of Verbal Arts at GIII. Later, she recalled being "so psychologically unprepared" that she burst out laughing when asked if she "knew Zhirmunskii to be a spy."[6]

Ginzburg's life became truly marginalized with the closing of GIII. Forced to find new employment, she worked for a time at the Children's Publishing House (Detgiz), along with the poets Oleinikov and Zabolotskii, producing a detective novel for adolescents, *The Pinkerton Agency* (*Agentsvo Pinkertona*). But that was not the novel she would have chosen to write. She was also hired to teach language and literature in workers' schools (*Rabfak*) and adult education classes, but was effectively banned from institutions of higher education. In contrast to journal entries from the 1920s recording intense intellectual involvement and taking principled stands on a broad range of issues, entries from the 1930s express bouts of severe depression; confusion; anxiety over right and wrong, penance and remorse; contemplation of class "privilege"; and recognition of the impossibility of publishing her major article on Proust. Hence, Ginzburg's complex vision of the 1930s.

Paradoxically, the 1940s appeared simpler and more comprehensible, bringing psychological relief because of the wartime convergence of private values with those of the state. Nevertheless, Ginzburg's powers of endurance were severely tested as she remained in Leningrad throughout World War II, caring for her sick mother, who died during the first winter of the blockade, and working as an editor at the State Radio, "quietly correcting the broadcasts of other writers' war literature."[7] The winter of 1942 she took up residence at the radio station, which helped her to survive. "Notes from the Leningrad Blockade" ("Zapiski blokadnogo cheloveka"), Ginzburg's highly acclaimed existential narrative concerning the experience and behavior of a human being living under conditions of war, derived in part from records in her journal of conversations overheard in bomb shelters, on bread lines and at work. It could not be published until decades later: Part One, predominantly narrative, appeared in the Leningrad magazine *Neva* (1984); Part Two, comprised mainly of "conversations from the Leningrad blockade," appeared posthumously in *Transformation of Experience* (*Pretvorenie opyta*, 1991).

Ginzburg wrote that for her personally the immediate postwar years (1946–1953) were the most traumatic because the moral and psychological "variant" used by the "creative intelligentsia" in the 1930s "no longer worked." During that era of vicious anti-intellectual and anti-Semitic attacks Ginzburg taught at Petrozavodsk University (1947–1950); it was considered safer for Jewish intellectuals to be employed outside the major cities. Subsequently, she described the intelligentsia's incredulous naivete before the horror of what had been taking place around them in "The Kochetov Complex" ("Kochetovskii Kompleks," 1962) and repudiated as repulsive her work of those years, including her doctoral dissertation on Alexander Herzen defended as recently as in 1958. She had defended her candidate's dissertation on Mikhail Lermontov twenty years earlier.

Ginzburg's second encounter with state security also occurred at the close of 1952; she was unsuccessfully recruited in a frightening endeavor to develop a case against her teacher and mentor, Boris Èikhenbaum. Saved by Stalin's death, she experienced her first feelings of renewal and hope, combined with a new sensation of being part of the "older generation."[8]

Only in the 1960s did Ginzburg's fruitful years truly begin. Sporadic publication was superseded by a new book or revised edition every two or three years. The popularity of *The Lyric* (*O lirike*, 1964) demanded a revised and enlarged format ten years later. *On Psychological Prose* (*O psikhologicheskoi proze*, 1971) was revised and reissued in 1977. *The Literary Hero* (*O literaturnom geroe*) appeared in 1979. The publications of the 1980s and 1990s provide a summing up of Ginzburg's life experience and intellectual activity. In the 1980s several volumes of collected writings appeared, including prose narratives; literary, philosophical and memoiristic essays; and excerpts from her journals: *The Old and the New* (*O starom i novom*, 1982), *Literature in Search of Reality* (*Literatura v poiskakh real'nosti*, 1987) and *At the Writing Desk* (*Chelovek za pis'mennym stolom*, 1989). The early 1990s witnessed the posthumous publication of more journal excerpts in *Novyi mir* and *Literaturnaia gazeta*; the last volume authorized by Ginzburg, *Transformation of Experience* (*Pretvorenie opyta*, 1991), containing not only the remarkable second part of "Notes from the Leningrad Blockade," but two essays on Osip Mandel'shtam, whom she regarded as the seminal poet of the twentieth century; and two volumes of her *Selected Works* (*Izbrannye proizvedeniia*), published in 1992.

It should also be noted that Ginzburg's editorial and textological work, begun at the end of the 1920s with her edition of Prince Viazemskii's *Old Notebook* (*Staraia zapisnaia knizhka*, 1929), continued unabated until her death. For example, in the 1960s, as a member of the Mandel'shtam Commission, she was instrumental in helping to rehabilitate the poet's name and publish his work. Ginzburg's various editions in the Poet's Library, Literary Heritage and Literary Monuments series, among others, and contributions to the publications of such widely different authors as Viazemskii, Benediktov, Lermontov, Pushkin, Blok, Bagritskii, Zabolotskii, Oleinikov, Mandel'shtam, Pasternak, Herzen and Tynianov are testimony to her esteem as a scholar. In addition to Russian literature, she edited and compiled (with E. Vinokurov) *Foreign Poetry in Russian Translations* (*Innostrannaia poèziia v russkikh perevodakh*, 1968) and wrote introductions to *Saint-Simon. Mémoires* (1976) and *French Romantic Prose* (*Frantsuzskaia romanticheskaia povest'*, 1982).

Ginzburg's publications of seven decades, excluding editorial and textological work, may be divided into several categories: literary theory, studies of specific poets or writers, essays, quasi-fictional narratives, memoirs of contemporaries and excerpts from her journals; however, they frequently overlap.

One of Ginzburg's major contributions to literary studies is her theory of the continuum of the aesthetic function, and hence, the continuum of genre. She posits the absence of any absolute boundary between aesthetically and historically determined "facts" because the different forms of historical material organized in accordance with particular aesthetic principles are all part of the ongoing literary process, comprising different correlates between history and belles lettres. Hence, the continuum of genre ranges from everyday "human documents" to those genres in which the aesthetic element predominates.

Ginzburg's self-image as littérateur is clearly reflected in her prescient, independent analyses of the connections between literary theory, literary history and writing in general. She consistently sought out principles in literature and life by which to broaden her understanding of human behavior. In a statement of her theoretical credo, "On Historicism and Structure" ("Ob istorizme i strukturnosti," 1975–1980), she emphasized the points of intersection between "history" and "structure," between nonliterary and literary facts. Hence, her focus on the perception of processes, on the "transformation" of life into art, on the correlations as well as distinctions between literature and life, and on the effects of art on life. Ginzburg was interested in "boundaries" not as finite or absolute limits, but as fluid and changing entities in the historical context and in the ongoing aesthetic continuum. In writing about literature she chose to devote a good portion of her scholarship to studying noncanonical "intermediary genres" and processes of aesthetic genesis, transformation and change. In keeping a journal, she chose to participate in the ongoing aesthetic and historical continuum on a regular, firsthand basis. And later, in her essays recollecting and examining the behavior of the Russian intelligentsia in the Soviet cultural environment, she chose to adapt techniques and ideas from both her literary scholarship and experience garnered in writing her journal to her analyses of human culture, identifying and interpreting literary and cultural images returned to life in the form of consciously accepted historical facts and codes of human behavior. Moreover, in addition to literature per se, Ginzburg was fascinated by the status of such phenomena as "life-art" and "conversation" in the aesthetic continuum; hence, her theory of "life-art" (*zhiznetvorchestvo*), through which she interprets the semiotics of self-creation and the codes of human behavior in nineteenth-century Russian culture in *On Psychological Prose*, including the impact of literary and social models on codes of social behavior and social self-consciousness. Ginzburg's theory of the art of conversation emerges in her journals, quasi-narrative prose and theoretical writings; in *The Literary Hero* conversation is cognized as another means of formalizing and organizing human activities, thus its function in the aesthetic continuum.

Ginzburg's theory of the "intermediary genres" is in part an outgrowth of her formalist training, more specifically, Tynianov's theory of "literary evolution." However, it also coincides to a certain extent with more contemporary discourse theory, such as Tzvetan Todorov's thesis that "the opposition between literature and nonliterature be replaced by a typology of the various types of discourse, each equally deserving of attention."[9] Equally important, perhaps, Ginzburg's theory is verified and justified in her own literary practice.

Ginzburg began keeping a journal in 1925, while writing a student essay on Viazemskii and the literary significance of his *Old Notebook* for the now famous GIII special seminar in Russian prose taught by Èikhenbaum and Tynianov. A half-century later, in 1982, although Ginzburg attributed the impulse behind her journal to Viazemskii, she claimed to be working "in a different genre." In fact, she shared his declared goal of recording "the morals and manners and living expression of the community," associated with the *journal externe* of the eighteenth and early nineteenth centuries, but decried his lack "of anything in the nature of authorial (diary) confession, self-analysis and abstract reasoning." She appropriates both the sociological and the personal modes of cognition to negotiate her tasks, including entries (*zapisi*) that endeavor to define her individual identity and interpret her own empirical and historical personality.

Like Viazemskii, Ginzburg also apparently intended her journal as a serious literary enterprise with a publishable future and viewed its significance as residing in the aggregate of its microhistorical details. She obviously regarded the time and care expended on individual entries as significant literary labor.

Ginzburg's journal is quite varied in intent, subject matter, tone and style. It contains numerous efforts to establish her individual identity and value system: to define views on Judaism, nationalism and sexuality, and to ascertain literary and moral principles. Many entries are introduced by way of reference to a conversation that elicited self-analytical responses, for example, views on women and gender. Another type of entry is the "record of a conversation," perhaps inspired by Viazemskii's evaluation of "gossip" as "universal history . . . in small form." In the 1920s Ginzburg documented her literary milieu; in the 1940s, random conversations document human existence under the Leningrad blockade. The essays from the 1940s to the 1980s clearly regard conversation as an index of social behavior.

Initiated by the twenty-three-year old student at a time when personal and professional life were closely linked, Ginzburg's early journal indicates an orientation toward the self often associated with the fate of the littérateur. Ginzburg's empirical personality emerges as that of an intellectual and would-be literary professional who values logic and clarity above all else, and who applies logic even to the most irrational problems or situations. This frequently leads to abstract interpretations of personal attitudes and qualities. In her later years the entries are often more essayistic in nature, reflecting the thinking of a mature, philosophically oriented individual, more contemplative and less convinced that she could have "willed" much of her own biography.

Even the earliest entries exemplify the high value placed on *writing*—on literary style, structure and strategy—indicating that the journal was not merely a psychological outlet but a mode of aesthetic and intellectual cognition, a means for giving structure to complex mental processes. In addition, writing may also have begun to serve as a strategy of "defiance," opposing certain social, political or cultural requirements or limitations. Thus, many entries contain carefully designed parallelisms, juxtapositions and paradoxes, express a kind of "double-voiced discourse" and conclude on a point. This attentiveness to literary composition suggests Ginzburg's efforts to seek an aesthetic solution to problems she was not otherwise equipped to resolve.

During the 1920s, Ginzburg viewed herself as part of a collective intellectual project. Her journal entries reflect attempts to describe the personalities and behavior patterns of her circle; to depict how people looked, talked, dressed, acted; even how they performed in official debates. As such, they provide another form of self-evaluation, an assessment of the behavior of her own particular sociocultural type or historical personality as part of a "tradition." By 1928, in an entry dominated by its elegiac tone, Ginzburg observes the disintegration of relations among the formalists as GIII is being forcibly closed. Profound personal loss, the end of innocence and personal stock-taking prevail.

Ginzburg's journal also indicates how much she identified with her reading and sought out explanations for her private life in books and conversations not associated with her professional life. It is here that her views on women's issues and sexuality emerge most directly. Fluency in French also made it possible to keep abreast of the current literary and cultural scene abroad. For example, Ginzburg refers to such *causes célèbres* as Andre Gide's *Corydon* (1924) and Marcel Proust's *A la recherche du temps perdus*, reading each volume as it appeared through 1927.

In an early entry evaluating *Corydon*, she expresses a clear attitude toward the subject of homosexuality with respect to how it should be discussed and defended. Her defense is based on her own unique lesbian-feminist perspective. While praising Gide for his "brilliance and wide-ranging unconventional ity," she judges his book "a flop" because of "invalid methods," a false assumption that "everything natural is good" and its failure to discuss female as well as male homosexuality.

On the other hand, in her praise for Proust's masterpiece, Ginzburg's defense of homosexuality as a personal intellectual and psychological issue moves beyond social, psychological and even political concerns to focus on aesthetics. Between 1927 and 1930, Proust becomes Ginzburg's model for reformulating and transforming her life image both as a writer and as a human being—as one who shares the complex layers of her consciousness as well as the need to give it expression. She comes to recognize that for herself as for Proust, writing is life: "I will probably write until I take my last breath. . . . Because for me to write means to live, to experience life. I not only cherish things per se, but conceptions of things, processes of perception (that is why Proust is the most significant writer for me)."[10]

In this context Ginzburg evaluates her own writing, recognizing her journal as her special mode of literary expression, as the most "appropriate form for [her own] inclinations," even though she is "bothered by its being unprintable" and that "it is too easy for me to write."

Ginzburg's journal, then, became equally significant for her theory of literature, for her philosophy of life and for the articulation of her creative and psychological energy. It validated her scholarly interest in the noncanonical genres and served as a means of defying the dominant culture in which she lived as an outsider, politically, socially, sexually and aesthetically.

If by 1930 Ginzburg realized that for her writing was life, and that her journal was the form best suited to her personality and needs as a writer, the essay, among the various subgenres included in its framework, emerged as the preeminent genre of Ginzburg's mature years. Beginning in the 1940s, occasional journal entries expanded into unmediated topical or philosophical essays, and by the time of Stalin's death, when she first began to regard herself as part of the "older generation biologically," she subjected the major theme of her essays—the psychology and behavior of the intelligentsia—to her well-honed literary theory on the one hand, and the microhistory of her journal on the other.

For example, in her essays on the Soviet intelligentsia, "Turning Point of a Generation" and "We're One with Law and Order," unpublished until the late 1980s, Ginzburg stands back and objectifies her own experience, developing a semiotic assessment of the behavior of the postrevolutionary intelligentsia based on the experience of her own thinking as typical of her generation. She proposes that the thinking of the Russian intelligentsia was determined by the convergence of two distinctly different and indeed antithetical sets of values, which (as in *On*

Psychological Prose) Ginzburg demonstrates were filtered through various literary and cultural models. Here, for example, she cites her own life experience not for the purpose of writing an autobiography, but as a semiotic model of the behavior of the intelligentsia of her generation: "What can I say about my own case? Basically, that we should have no illusions, no one escaped unscathed. . . . For me, the mechanism of justification was the most weakly developed; my inborn analytical sense interfered. But the mechanism of indifference never ceased to operate."

For Lidiia Ginzburg, then, literature was a complex cultural phenomenon, a dynamic, ongoing formalization of human history. She regarded herself as an active participant in, and semiotic model of, the various phases of that history as it unfolded in Soviet Russia from the 1920s to 1990.

Jane Gary Harris

From The Journals

1920s [Character traits]

The combination of laziness and ambition is a happy one. These character traits complement one another, protecting their owner from both dissipation and careerism.

* * *

G.F. is that type of indulgent egoist who views goodness not as an inner requirement of personal behavior, but as a personal achievement.

* * *

Someone commits methodological suicide; the timeservers all see it as a profitable gain and rejoice in the fall of the last righteous man.

* * *

1925 [On reading Gide's Corydon*]*

I was reading *Corydon* (Paris, 1924). It ranges all over the place—*quatre dialogues socratiques*, with citations from Darwin; and all four dialogues concern issues of homosexuality, not just sexuality.

He proves that homosexuals should not be behind bars.

However, the questionable nature of the book lies not in its ultimate goal, but in the author's methodology.

Two fundamental ideas are presented: that homosexuality is natural, that homosexuality is the highest form of sexuality.

However, even to a reader having no access to a critique of his biological arguments, it is clear that the author has gone too far; logic and a small dose of common sense should suffice. But what is truly disturbing is the principle involved: to justify a biological phenomenon, proof is sought in the animal world.

Lesbian love is justified by the fact that female dogs practice it.

I am not personally shocked by this manner of posing the question; nor can I possibly sympathize with the American court system which fines teachers for discussing the theory of the origin of species in school.

On the other hand, I must ask Andre Gide, what would happen if rescue dogs were restricted by the sexual preferences of their mates?

It is obvious, then, that homosexuals would still be put behind bars. . . .

The word "natural"—isn't that the most vacuous of all the attributes hypocrites have invented?

In fact, all good things are not natural: art is not natural, washing is not natural; it is not natural to eat with a fork or to blow one's nose in a handkerchief; it is not natural to give up your seat to a woman and a child; the steam engine and the dynamo are extremely unnatural. . . .

Must we do away with toilets because dogs defecate in the street?

Tolstoy intended to censure earthly love and began *The Kreutzer Sonata* to prove that the sex act is not natural. ("To eat is natural and thus it is easy and not shameful"—I cite this from memory—L.G.).

Gide's book is a flop. It is incomprehensible how a writer of such brilliance and wide-ranging unconventionality could lower himself to investigate unexplored realms using such flimsy measures. Comparison does lead to insight, but in this case, the object of comparison is completely absent—indeed, it is hardly in canine practices that we should be seeking the boundaries of human behavior.

Tolstoy censured. Gide and others like him act even worse: they employ invalid methods to justify what does not require justification. Even more absurd, they are convinced that they found the "question"; but no question can exist if it has not been asked.

Indeed, I can see nothing beyond the fact to which I did not reply because I was not asked.

The facts are as follows: with regard to the *private individual* [*otdel'nyi chelovek*], single-sex love is first and foremost the individual's private affair as long as it does not involve criminality (no other kind of love is so protected either).

As for the biological and social spheres, homosexuality is, of course, harmful since it is not utilitarian (whoever is not for us is against us!).

Only fools, seventeen-year-olds and conscious idealists can cite antiquity to debate the highest form of erotic bonding and raise male community to a fact of social significance.

Indeed, the concern here is not with the creation of utopian projects, but with the clarification of the status quo.

Thus, homosexuals are socially harmful, but no more harmful than bachelors, old maids or even women who choose not to have children.

Society (the educated) has in fact always made peace, and will continue to make peace, with the fact that a certain portion of the population refuses to work toward its longevity.

In a word, homosexuality is perceived somewhat like syphilis, as "not a disgrace, but a misfortune."

However, there are other people who do not see it as a misfortune. They usually include the obvious homosexuals, or, on the contrary, simply the "indulgent."

As usual, Gide has hardly touched on the issue of female deviation; the topic probably failed to satisfy his requirements for the erotic ideal (Plato!).

However, if we seek "elevation" in certain forms of homosexuality, as opposed to normal sensations, this should come to the fore.

(Even Weininger in his unique, inspiring book, one which holds up even today, considered this topic very subtly.)

For good or for ill, there is no doubt that to this day women have been the equal of men in their mental development.

Sometimes their development even equals the insuperable demands of male love, demands as much psychological as physical, male love being the only love which is valued, considered complete, and worthy of literature.

Hence, here is that same "psycho-physical" repugnance toward one's own natural role. But it is not compulsory.

Pushkin loved to repeat Chateaubriand's expression: "Il n'y a du bonheur que dans les voies communes."

* * *

16 May 1927 [On acknowledging Jewish identity]

Yesterday's conversation with Boria [Bukhshtab] on Judaism set my mind thinking again in that vein. I don't know if this issue excites me or just interests me from time to time.

Jews are offended when they are abused. Jews are asked: how can you expect us not to abuse you when you abuse yourselves?

Jewish anti-Semitism is so vile because its psychological source is not self-censure but self-alienation; besides, it's completely arbitrary.

In 1924 Kornei Ivanovich Chukovskii, having assumed the role of my literary benefactor (though he refused me a three-ruble advance, citing the *Russian Contemporary*'s financial difficulties), resolved to become my godfather as well.

He admired my first book review, which he printed, and tried to talk me into taking a pseudonym.

"The late Gumilev said he disliked pseudonyms," I replied.

"But your surname is totally unsuitable. There are too many of you."

He then proceeded to show me the proof sheets of the magazine's contributors. I found two other Ginzburgs there in addition to myself, and still more Ginzburgs among the music reviews.

As I stood there despondently eyeing all those Ginzburgs differentiated only by their accompanying initials, Chukovskii said: "Take me, for example, born Korneichuk. I realized my name was too common; it sounded too much like a peasant name, so I became Chukovskii."

"Kornei Ivanovich, you know, were I not Jewish I might take a pseudonym. But Jewish pseudonyms always leave a bad aftertaste. Something about them inevitably suggests a forgery."

"Maybe you're right," said Chukovskii.

There was no doubt that I was right. Jews have rarely achieved neutrality in selecting pseudonyms. They're inappropriate because they almost always sound *plus Russe que la Russie même*. Moreover, we should never trifle with cultural heritage; it is wrong to assume the obligations of someone else's blood.

Strange as it may seem there are worse things in this world than Jewish nationalists—there are Jewish anti-Semites.

I am certainly not writing about other people's vices from the perspective of my own virtues; I am writing about psychological phenomena that would probably seem incomprehensible were they not somehow related to my own. It is hardly the absence of these traits that distinguishes me from others; rather, it is the capacity to be ashamed of such traits. I cannot say that I never struggle against them.

Once I spent an evening at the Tomashevskiis. Among numerous and varied topics of discussion, the nationality question was raised. Our discussion just happened to coincide with the All-Union census. By way of a curious and amusing anecdote, Tomashevskii mentioned that a literary acquaintance of his had filled out the census questionnaire by identifying his nationality as "Jewish."

I acknowledged doing the same thing.

B[oris] V[iktorovich] talked at length about the absurdity of this viewpoint, claiming that nationality is defined by language and culture, etc. "Take me, for example, I'm half-Polish, but it would never enter my mind to identify myself as a 'Pole.' Jews cite their nationality in reaction to their former oppression."

Tomashevskii defined the fact correctly, but evaluated it incorrectly.

Any Jew who has grown up immersed in Russian culture may find himself in the following situation. If he claims, "Pardon me, but I'm Russian!" he will be answered, "Pardon me, but you have curly hair and a typical nose; even the composition of your blood differs from Aryan blood."

There is certainly no dearth of retorts: race is an obscure concept; nationality is defined by language and culture; Russified Germans don't consider themselves to be Germans, and so on. And no dearth of proofs. Proof, though, is conditional; or rather the practical function of proof is conditional. There are circumstances when proof does not suffice as an answer; when laughter, tears or blows are the only appropriate response . . . and there are circumstances when there simply is no answer.

I am fully convinced that selecting an illogical mode of action suits me best. Whether out of common sense, atavism or distrust, being a person whose mother tongue is Russian, whose tastes and culture are Russian, and who, I care to believe, is absolutely dedicated to Russian culture, I always identify myself as a Jew on questionnaires; and I do so without worrying over the nuanced distinctions between race, creed, nationality or citizenship.

During the famous Odessa pogrom of 1905 I was two years old and ill with scarlatina. My uncle walked to the pharmacy on Kherson Street. The Jewish pharmacist (pharmacies were spared, obviously, for humanitarian reasons) recognized my uncle as Jewish and said: "Are you mad? How can you even dare to go outside?" My uncle explained that a child was seriously ill. The pharmacist refused payment for the medicine.

I was treated by Dr. Stefanskii, our neighbor and a good friend of my father's. He took an icon off his wall, hid it under his coat, and brought it to our apartment. He begged Papa to put it in our window. Papa refused outright.

Of course, in the Jewish quarters on the outskirts of the city such tricks could not work. In our neighborhood, however, especially in our building where few Jews lived, and where people did not bother to seek them out, this kind of thing was done. Many Christian families placed icons in their windows so that no one would mistakenly, so to speak, touch them. Dr. Stefanskii had his reasons for acting the way he did.

I grew up in a family where the only language spoken was Russian; I first attended a synagogue, the one and only time in my life, strange as it may seem, in Petersburg. For my parents synagogue was a childhood memory—and I don't know if it was pleasant or not. I had German governesses who in their spiritual simplicity took me to the *kirche* on Sundays and taught me "Our Father, who art in heaven" at bedtime. My parents knew about this and with that reluctance to take a stance characteristic of the Jewish intelligentsia, would laugh in turn at the German governesses, at me and at themselves.

Now, if I know that someone in my presence is "hiding his Jewishness," the obvious immorality of that act makes me flinch.

1928 [On friendship]

Whenever you're hit over the head, you learn something. Unfortunately, people are almost incapable of learning under normal conditions.

For me, it took a friend's death to clarify our relationship, and to explain those aspects of our relationship that I had not understood; and in not understanding, I acted the hypocrite this entire winter with the G[ukovsky]s.

I had invented categories of relationships and obligations associated with each category: friends, comrades, acquaintances, etc. I even imagined that I could calmly move people who had not fulfilled certain obligations from one category to another. Later, I was perplexed why people whom I moved from friends to acquaintances continued to remain close despite their new category, and why it was so difficult to get along without them.

This spring, after it was already too late, I finally understood what is essential: it is not another person's attitude toward me, nor even my attitude to that person (although it is essential)—but the other's potential with respect to me.

There are people with whom I'm on better terms than with Nataliia V[iktorovna], and people who relate to me better, or at least more actively. I often have no need for either because they do nothing for me. However, N.V. could and did so much for me. I had overlooked that potential which is independent of will or conscious interest, which is defined only by personality and situations. I had been concerned with trifles, with rubrics and unfulfilled obligations, and sought a place for my own restless vanity [*samoliubie*].

I was mistaken and now my conscience is punishing me because there was a person to whom I could have shown more love (and to love, even a little, is so marvelous), a person who would have done far more for me, had I allowed it. I should never have made such a mistake or been so ungrateful.

Of course, what bound us wasn't comradeship, even less intimacy. We were probably bound by the genuine and important bonds of our ordinary way of life, by the habits of daily life "at home," where we never felt bored or pressured.

1928 [Defining the novel]

The German romantics held the novel in special regard. For them it was an act of a higher, universal order. It had to be not so much a "reflection" of life, as a highly responsible summation of thoughts about life, representations of life, relations to life.

It is precisely in this meaning that I use the term "novel" for that large work about myself that I want to write eventually, and that must demand my finest efforts.

You stand before the universe and freely speak about the universe, judging it, telling about it, and describing it—that is a novel.

1930 [On melancholy]

People tend to be melancholy primarily in the morning and in the evening; daylight dispels and engulfs it. I never fear evening melancholy because it is natural, the result of physical and mental fatigue, or vexation over an unsuccessful day, or even boredom, which appears when you're no longer in a state to work but don't know how or want to relax.

But morning melancholy I fear like a disease or a moral fall. It is not aggravated by fatigue or by pain in your eyes or temples. The physiological factor does not lighten the repugnant clarity of its outlines. It is not a weight, but a void, a nauseating feeling, recalling the nausea brought on by an empty stomach, by hunger.

In the evening an attack of melancholy is often a reaction to a fruitful day's work. I get a morning attack only during the worst, most meaningless periods in my life. It basically reflects my fear of a meaningless, difficult and joyless life. It usually occurs in bed before I rouse myself to wash and have breakfast. It can extend to cold, physical numbness, and to the horror of being unable to move in order to start the processes of getting up, dressing and eating, with which I must begin the bad day that lies ahead. The awakened body is at rest, the eyes are again capable of reading; the head is empty.

I have the capacity to rest from life at night (especially during periods when I dislike my life); that is, I lose the momentum for walking, for conversations or for taking trouble over my books. Momentum is restored very quickly, however. It is already partially restored during that interval when the nightgown is replaced by the day's clothing. Nevertheless, there exists a certain half an hour in the morning when you are already awake but have not yet begun to live, when you have not yet inserted yourself into the chain of motion and routine. And the organism trembles before the start of a new day.

1930 [On Mayakovsky's suicide]

I learned of Mayakovsky's death on my way to GIZ [the State Publishing House]. At GIZ, work had come to a complete halt. Some people crowded together and were talking at their desks; others stood alone in the corners of the rooms, in the corridors, and on the staircase landings reading the latest news. "It's like the day war was announced," said Gruzdev.

1930 [On laws and logic]

I really love laws and the logic of regularity [*zakonomernost'*]. I find that for me the most important thing is the concept of a circular causality. I welcome accidental joys enthusiastically, but require logic from the misfortunes that strike me. Logic comforts me, like a kind word.

1931 [On depression and writing]

> Il y a deux malheurs au monde;
> celui de la passion contrariée et
> celui du dead blank (vide complet).
>
> STENDHAL

I feel as if I've had the air pumped out of me. I sleep until noon; it's always dark in the room and it's always dark outside. In fact, I don't even go out. I don't know how winter looks. And last fall I even thought I'd get some skis. Instead I don't have the energy to walk from the Canal to Sadovaia.

Tonight, I couldn't fall asleep for hours; I was overwhelmed by terrifying thoughts. During the day you are continually distracted by the minutiae of ordinary tasks, but at night when there's nothing else to keep you busy, thinking about daily life can be truly agonizing.

I suddenly understood that what we had avoided thinking about in earnest had already happened, that for almost two years now many of us, myself included, had lost our profession. When other people were going to pieces over the idea of losing their positions and their property, we were losing our profession and the people closest to us.

It turned out to be not just something temporary, but an irreparable deterioration of our fate. Lacking the reciprocity and continuity of our occupations and interests we were losing touch. Stated more bluntly: we had ceased to relate to literary history and to scholarly activity in general. We should have noted this a long time ago. Such a discovery was not easy to think through clearly; and then another year had to pass before it could be put into words. People have degenerated, grown cold, and forgotten under the convenient cloak of putting it off. Not very long ago, in fact so recently it makes me laugh, I finally uttered for the first time the words that my dissertation—my book about the poetry of the 1830s—would never be written.

The rest I understood only a few days ago, and in a rather strange manner. I've long been in the habit of writing on various subjects, one right after another, and I read accordingly. About 8 December, I stopped writing and all of a sudden discovered that I didn't know what to read next, that I had no interests. For a person who has been a specialist for ten years, this was one of those impossible sensations that happen only in dreams. What was this, *vide complet?*

Total freedom is a sure sign of the cessation of that continuity of interests which comprises basic human consciousness, and the consciousness of a scholar. Nothing interested me anymore!—a half-year passed before I could utter those words.

I feel no connection to scholarship, nor to literature. I am seemingly a free literary professional with whom contracts are easily concluded for children's books about canned goods. There are many such people nowadays, somewhere between literary specialists and hustlers.

Yesterday I was frightened to think that I had no interest in reading and would never want to read again. Of course, it was a mad aberration of an overtaxed brain. Staring out into the darkness, I finally began to think how I might write about it all. So my instinct for interpretation and for realizing my thoughts in writing saved me from utter despair. This is how we can utilize humiliation, grief and even emptiness, transforming them into literary material.

When the day comes that this no longer interests me, I will die. I will contract to write little books for the Young Guard publishing house and teach at the workers' schools [*Rabfak*]. I will not read books for want of motives.

I dare think that I won't burrow down into my inner depths, or be concerned only with myself. I feel like a piece of flesh ripped from the social fabric, which I've succeeded in bringing up close to my eyes, a part of reality especially convenient to observe. I will observe the reality that both taught and tormented me, that entered my blood despite everything, and that has adapted to my thoughts and become my necessity. It is the source of such a degree of knowledge and such an intense relationship to things that it can never be renounced regardless of external temptations.

End of 1930s [On the return to reality]

Let us imagine a person alone. Let us imagine him waking up; at first he doesn't remember anything. His mind is blank, anything can be introduced into it—that he's at home, for example. Then along with some stool or corner of a table, reality enters his mind. This is the most terrifying moment of the day. At that moment the ties of habit are canceled, which here are his only ties to life. This is the return. Everything in him protests, shouts against this impossible return to those walls that enclose him. He is very simply convinced that it is impossible, psychologically impossible, to get up and begin to live (reveille has been sounded). Then he remembers that he will dress, he will wash, and then he will sweep his cell, then they will bring him tea and bread. And out of this order of habitual activities standing before him his return becomes possible.

1940s [On women and the blockade experience]

So much is now psychologically colored by the fact that women are in charge of most of the activities in the rear. Although it is comparatively rare for women to hold leadership roles, they are doing just about everything. Thus, the very composition and culture of ordinary social life has changed dramatically. To understand our life in the rear or our quasi-front existence, we must understand the peculiarities of the female experience.

1950s [From conversations with Nadezhda Iakovlevna Mandel'shtam]

N.Ia.: "Sometimes it seemed to me to be impossible to live any longer; it was too unbearable . . . but Osia [Mandel'shtam] would suddenly say: 'Why do you think you have to be happy?' This was incredibly helpful, and it helps even now."

1970s [On plots, prose, verse and biography]

There are plots that do not lend themselves to prose. It is impossible, for instance, to relate the following adequately in prose:

A man is already impervious to the warm breath of the world; his reactions are sclerotically rigid, and he knows about his inner states as if secondhand. A certain psychological event occurs. Not a very significant one, but it has—as in a shooting gallery—hit the mark and set everything about it in convulsive motion. And all of a sudden the man sees his long life. Not with indifference, the way he got used to thinking about it according to Maupassant: life is hardly ever as good or as bad as it seems to us . . . not the fabric of life, a tangle of all sorts of things, days on end, each with its own task . . . he suddenly sees his life plain as a skeleton, resembling a poorly written biography. And now he weeps over this irremediable clarity. Over life's having been cold and difficult. He weeps over thirty-year-old slights, over pain he does not feel, over the unquenched desire for objects he has long since ceased wanting.

For prose, this experience is insufficiently condensed, with traces of emotional rawness, the soul's raw material that verse transforms by its own indispensable means.

Translated by Jane Gary Harris

Notes to the Essay

1. Interview, *Smena* 262 (13 November 1988): 2.
2. Journal entry for 1927, in *Chelovek za pis'mennym stolom* (Leningrad: Sovetskii pisatel', 1989), 35.
3. *Literaturnaia Rossiia* 51 (23 December 1988): 8–9.
4. "Eshche raz o starom i novom. Pokolenie na povorote," 1979 ["Turning point of a generation"], in *Tynianovskii sbornik.Vtorye Tynianovskie chteniia* (Riga: 1986, 218–30).
5. "Zaodno s pravoporiadkom," 1980 ["We're one with law and order"], in *Tynianovskii sbornik. Tret'i Tynianovskie chteniia*, 1988, 163–66.
6. "Dve vstrechi," 1988 ["Two encounters"], in *Pretvorenie opyta* (Riga: Avots; Leningrad: Assotsiatsiia Novaia literatura, 1991), 163–66.
7. Journal entry from 1987, in *Pretvorenie opyta*, 154.
8. "O starosti i infantilizme," 1954: ["Old Age and Infantilism"] in *Literatura v poiskakh real'nosti* (Leningrad: Sovetskii pisatel', 1987), 183–92.
9. Tzvetan Todorov, "The Notion of Literature," in *New Literary History* 5, 1 (Autumn 1973): 5–16.
10. Journal entry for 1930, in *Novyi mir* 6 (1992): 173.

Bibliography

Primary Works

"Viazemskii-literator." *Russkaia proza*. Ed. B.M. Èikhenbaum and Iu.N. Tynianov. Leningrad: Akademia, 1926. 102–34.

[Introduction]. *Petr A. Viazemskii. Staraia zapisnaia knizhka*. Leningrad: Izdatel'stvo pisatelei v Leningrade, 1929. 9–50.

O lirike. Leningrad: Sovetskii pisatel', 1964; 2d ed., 1974.

O psikhologicheskoi proze. Leningrad: Sovetskii pisatel', 1971; 2d ed., 1977.

"Akhmatova (Neskol'ko stranits vospominanii)." *Den' poèzii* (1977): 216–17.

O literaturnom geroe. Leningrad: Sovetskii pisatel', 1979.

"Chelovek za pis'mennym stolom: Po starym zapisnym knizhkam." *Novyi mir* 6 (1982): 234–45.

O starom i novom. Stat'i i ocherki. Leningrad: Sovetskii pisatel', 1982.

"Tynianov-uchenyi." *Vospominaniia o Tynianove. Portrety i vstrechi*. Moscow: 1983. 147–72.

"Zabolotskii kontsa dvadtsatykh godov." *Vospominaniia o N. Zabolotskom*. 2d ed., Moscow, 1983. 145–56.

"Zapiski blokadnogo cheloveka." *Neva* 1 (1984): 84–104.

"Eshche raz o starom i novom (Pokolenie na povorote)." *Tynianovskii sbornik. Vtorye Tynianovskie chteniia*. Riga, 1986. 132–40.

"Za pis'mennym stolom. Iz zapisei 1950–1960–x godov." *Neva* 3 (1986): 112–39.

Literatura v poiskakh real'nosti. Leningrad: Sovetskii pisatel', 1987.

"Nikolai Oleinikov." *Iunost'* 1 (1988): 54–58.

"Vybor budushchego. Iz zapisei 1920–1930–x godov." *Neva* 12 (1988): 131–57.

"Zabluzhdenie voli." *Novyi mir* 11 (1988): 137–54.

"Zaodno s pravoporiadkom." *Tynianovskii sbornik. Tret'i Tynianovskie chteniia*. Riga, 1988. 218–230.

Chelovek za pis'mennym stolom. Èsse, iz vospominanii, chetyre povestvovaniia. Leningrad: Sovetskii pisatel', 1989.

"Iz zapisei 1950–1980–x godov." *Daugava* 1 (1989): 96–108.

"Iz zapisei 1950–1980–x godov." *Rodnik* 1 (1989): 22–27.

"Dve vstrechi." *Russkaia mysl'*, 2 November 1990.

"Vspominaia Institut Istorii Iskusstv." *Tynianovskii sbornik. Chetvertye Tynianovskie chteniia*. Riga, 1990. 278–88.

"Zapisi raznykh let." *Rodnik* 3 (1990): 26–30.

Pretvorenie opyta. Riga: Avots; Leningrad: Assotsiatsiia Novaia literatura, 1991.

Izbrannye proizvedeniia v dvukh tomakh. St. Petersburg: Khudozhestvennaia literatura, 1992.

"Zapisi 20–30–x godov (Iz neopublikovannogo)." Ed. Aleksandr Kushner and Aleksandr Chudakov. *Novyi mir* 6 (1992): 1–41.

"Iz dnevnikov Lidii Ginzburg." Ed. Aleksandr Kushner. *Literaturnaia gazeta* 41 (13 October 1993): 6.

In Translation

"The Poetics of Osip Mandel'shtam." *Twentieth Century Russian Literary Criticism*. Trans. Sona Hoisington. New Haven, CT: Yale University Press, 1975. 284–312.

"Tolstoj e Proust." *La Nuova Rivista Europea* (October–December 1978): 39–44.

"Vyazemsky—Man of Letters." *Russian Prose*. Ed. and trans. Ray Parrott. Ann Arbor, MI: Ardis, 1985. 87–108.

"The 'Human Document' and the Formation of Character." *The Semiotics of Russian Cultural History: Essays*. Ed. Alexander D. Nakhimovsky and Alice Stone Nakhimovsky. Ithaca, NY: Cornell University Press, 1985. 188–224.

"Tsvetayeva et Pougatchev." *Lettre Internationale* 22 (1989): 69.

On Psychological Prose. Trans. Judson Rosengrant. Princeton, NJ: Princeton University Press, 1991.

Secondary Works

Chudakov, Aleksandr. "Vvdenie. Zapisi 20–30–x godov (Iz neopublikovannogo)." *Novyi mir* 6 (1992).

Gasparov, Boris, et al., eds. "Tvorcheskii portret L. Ia. Ginzburg." *Literaturnoe obozrenie* (1989): 78–86.

Gordin, Iakov. "Mashtabnost' issledovaniia." *Voprosy literatury* 1 (1981): 273–81.

Harris, Jane Gary. "Lidiia Iakovlevna Ginzburg." *Dictionary of Russian Women Writers.* Ed. Marina Ledkovsky, Charlotte Rosenthal and Mary Zirin. Westport, CT: Greenwood Press, 1994. 206–10.

———, ed. "In Memoriam: Lidiia Ginzburg." *Canadian-American Slavic Studies.* Special Issue 28, 2 (Summer 1994) [bib.].

———. "Lidiia Iakovlevna Ginzburg." *Reference Guide to Russian Literature.* Ed. Neil Cornwell. London: St. James Press, 1997.

———. "The Crafting of Self: Lidiia Ginzburg's Early Journal." *Gender and Russian Literature: New Perspectives*. Ed. Rosalind March. Cambridge: Cambridge University Press, 1996. 263–82.

Kononov, Nikolai. "Posleslovie redaktora." *Pretvorenie opyta*. By Lidiia Ginzburg. Leningrad: Assotsiatsiia Novaia literatura, 1991. 233–37.

Nevzgliadova, Elena. "Na samom dele, mysl' kak gost' . . . O proze Lidii Ginzburg." *Avrora* 4 (1989).

Podol'skaia, I. "Lidiia Ginzburg. O lirike." *Izvestiia Akademii Nauk SSSR: Seriia literatury i iazyka* 34, 1 (January–February 1975): 81–83.

Pratt, Sarah. "Lidiia Ginzburg and the Fluidity of Genre." *Autobiographical Statements in Twentieth-Century Russian Literature*. Ed. Jane G. Harris. Princeton, NJ: Princeton University Press, 1990. 207–16.

———, ed. "Lidiia Ginzburg's Contribution to Literary Criticism." *Canadian-American Slavic Studies.* Special Issue 19, 2 (Summer 1985) [bib].

Galina Kuznetsova

Galina Nikolaevna Kuznetsova (1900–1986) was born in Kiev 10 December 1900, the daughter of a civil servant, Nikolai Aleksandrovich Kuznetsov. Her mother, Elena Alekseevna Siianova, was divorced from Galina Kuznetsova's father while Galina was still a little girl. Kuznetsova's mother remarried and gave birth to children in her second marriage. That left the young Kuznetsova as the only child from the first marriage. For a withdrawn and delicate girl, the situation involving her mother left a strong impression, and the young Kuznetsova preferred the company of her grandparents, particularly her grandfather on her father's side.

The years 1917 and 1918 were significant for Kuznetsova—the 1917 Bolshevik revolution was forever to alter the course of her life, along with that of thousands of others in the middle and upper classes. In 1918 she graduated from the First Women's Gymnasium in Kiev and also married Dmitrii Mikhailovich Petrov, who was both a lawyer and an officer in the counterrevolutionary White Guard. During the postrevolutionary upheavals she and her husband became separated, a theme that appears continually in her literary work in the guise of perpetual loneliness or possible separation. The fear of being alone pervades a great deal of Kuznetsova's lyrical expressions and creates an underlying tension in her work.

Her wanderings in exile brought her to Constantinople, Bulgaria and eventually Prague, which immediately after the revolution had become a significant émigré cultural center. In Prague, Kuznetsova graduated from the Institute for Foreign Languages. Her stay in Czechoslovakia, however, was comparatively short-lived. In 1924 Kuznetsova moved to Paris, which had continued to maintain, as it had in the nineteenth century, its preeminent role in émigré Russian cultural affairs. In the French capital, Kuznetsova became involved with Russian-language newspapers such as *The Latest News* (*Poslednie novosti*) and *Contemporary Notes* (*Sovremennye zapiski*). She expanded her journalistic reach to newspapers in

Belgium and Latvia, as well as, eventually, the United States (such as *New Russian Word* [*Novoe russkoe slovo*] and *New Journal* [*Novyi zhurnal*]).

In 1926 Kuznetsova joined Ivan Bunin's circle at the Villa Belvedere in Grasse. In Grasse, Kuznetsova was joined by a close friend, Margarita Avgustovna Stepun, who was herself a writer. They were to remain together for the rest of their lives.

Following on the heels of European devastation, Kuznetsova and Stepun moved to Germany after the end of the Second World War. After a short stay in war-ravaged Germany, both moved to the United States in 1949, where four years later Kuznetsova obtained a position with the Voice of America, thereby continuing her journalistic work. In 1955 she became a member of the Russian Press Department of the United Nations in Geneva, and in 1956 she acquired American citizenship.

The sojourn in the United States was not permanent, however, as both Kuznetsova and Stepun were transferred to Geneva in 1959, where they worked for the United Nations until 1962, when they retired to Munich, where Galina Kuznetsova died on 8 February 1986.

Kuznetsova's literary production (aside from the journalistic) encompassed both prose and poetry. Like Bunin, she produced more prose than poems and is therefore considered primarily a prosaist, though also like Bunin, her poetic output, however slim, is a window into her sense of transformation. Her first poems were published in *Student Years* (*Studencheskie gody*) in 1922 in Prague, under her married name Petrova. Her first collection of short stories, *Morning* (*Utro*), which includes "Bakhchiserai," was published in 1930 and was praised by critics for its feminine feeling. Strongly autobiographical in flavor, the stories in *Morning* deal with the plight of White Army officers and their wives, who became displaced refugees seemingly endlessly migrating to many different areas of the former Russian Empire as well as foreign countries. In these works, Kuznetsova achieves both a psychological balance and a textured nuance of physical detail.

In 1933 the novel *Prologue* (*Prolog*) was published. The novel is written in the first person, making it also autobiographical in tone. In the novel, a young woman from Kiev named Ksana is caught in the tumult of the revolution, which she experiences during her adolescence. It should be recalled that Kuznetsova herself was seventeen when the revolution took place. Once again, Kuznetsova combines quiet drama with the prosaics of daily existence to achieve a cutting psychological perspective, as in the following excerpt:

> In the house a usual, long habitual life continued. Antonina Pavlova was unheedingly busy with housework; two times a week she went with the cook to the bazaar, from which they returned laden with

> meat, fish, a pile of colorful autumn fruits and vegetables, and a pale purplish fattened bird. After breakfast she shut herself in her bedroom, and by day I often found her in the dining room, in her glasses, leaning on a full pale elbow and sunk into some kind of thick, rather greasy, book.[1]

In 1937 Kuznetsova published a collection of poems, written between 1923 and 1929, titled *The Olive Garden* (*Olivkovyi sad*). The title places the work firmly in a Mediterranean cultural sphere—a source of great inspiration for Kuznetsova in her prose and poetic works. In *The Olive Garden*, Kuznetsova reveals herself to be a writer with a talent and a skill notably independent from the influence of Bunin—the poet whose artistic trajectory she followed in her own independent manner and with whom she is most frequently associated. In these poems the familiar nostalgia present in her short stories is likewise predominant. The collection represents Kuznetsova's greatest single poetic legacy. The volume is divided into two parts: the first deals primarily with her exile as recorded in lyric and religious images, whereas the second touches primarily upon accepting the present in a much more positive manner, albeit with a certain melancholy. The second part, in keeping with the emphasis on contemporary events, describes cities, art and personal events during the long years of exile and refugee wandering. The religious elements of the volume provide the reader with an additional type of interpretation: the first part of the collection can be seen as a lyrical expression of betrayal and death, whereas the second is resurrection and life.

The book begins with a poem that accentuates the personal, religious and universal importance of the particular garden referred to in the title. The garden is the silent witness to personal pain, as Kuznetsova indicates in her opening line.

> O, this garden! With straight blades of grass,
> With green netting entangling my knees,
> All choked over with a sultry blue sky,
> It silently listened to complaints and fines.[2]

The first portion of the collection has an underlying religious and spiritual theme. References are made to monastaries in both Russia and the Middle East, as well as to the familiar iconostasis of Russian Orthodox churches.

The second part, while at times equally melancholy, has a much more personal lyricism and details the wanderings, both emotional and physical, of the exiled refugee. The olive garden reappears here as well:

Onto the delicate branches of the olive tree
Onto the pearl-like sea
Lies the iridescent tint
Of a tear, melting in a glance.
But I am strong, strong now!
To me and in my awareness of loss
Shines the sunny firmament
Through the door opened by you.[3]

After the loss of homeland and culture as symbolically represented by the tear of rain, the sun has reappeared thanks to personal love and devotion. The entire second section of *The Olive Garden* deals with this type of personal and emotional reaction to the present. The intense lyricism that Kuznetsova demonstrates in her poetry is also noticeable in her prose works, where she demonstrates an economy of words while nonetheless bringing to the fore the emotional essence of what she is observing.

The years that Kuznetsova spent with Bunin in Grasse formed the basis for her diaries of the time, called *Grasse Diary* (*Grasskii dnevnik*) and published in the United States in 1967. Here Kuznetsova records and comments on one of the most influential émigré literary circles of the time. The *Grasse Diary* permits her, in a sense, to merge her journalistic style with her artistic lyricism, resulting in a perceptive memoir whose insights and observations are read by the specialist and general reader alike. Just as in her short stories and poems, moreover, she strives to create emotional fullness with a graceful simplicity.

It is perhaps because of the *Grasse Diary* that Kuznetsova is not better known in both Russian and Western literary circles, let alone by the public at large. The work places her firmly within Bunin's circle, and her modest, limpid style has perhaps unfairly placed her under his shadow. As émigrés, they both shared the pain of isolation from one's cultural homeland. Yet this is the main element filling Kuznetsova's prose and poetry with an almost melancholy sense of urgency. There is a palpable rush to live, in its most universal sense, in Kuznetsova's writing. Like a source of literary and historical lifeblood, it is buried underneath the comprehensive detailing with which Kuznetsova brocades her literary works. Her works re-create the different tones of life through the strategic placement of words and through the lengthy interweaving of delicate images of commonplace items. The literary works created are thereby placed clearly within a historical framework that does not limit their appeal, but rather enhances their universality. The reader, often facing chaotic transitions in life as well, is able to identify with the precision of the sentiments found in Kuznetsova's works. In them, much as in Anton

Chekhov's or Mikhail Kuzmin's shorter prose, the reader is left with the distinct impression that the characters are familiar, but without having to endure lengthy psychological digressions as to their motivations or past personal histories. It is this very quality that assures that Galina Kuznetsova's literary output will be preserved and will gradually take its deserved place among some of the most exquisite émigré writing of this century.

Luc Beaudoin

From Morning

Bakchisarai

These funeral columns,
It seemed to me, with a distinct murmur
Spoke the bidding of fate . . .
"Bakhchisaraiskii fontan."

The train from Simferopol finally reached Bakhchisarai, stopped for a while, then left. An officer in a gray Caucasian fur hat, cocked toward the back, with a rifle slung on his belt, and a young woman, dressed for winter, emerged from the back of the station and remained still in indecision, having left a soldier with the things at the barely lit, dirty station, half-filled with all kinds of sleeping bodies and people waiting in greatcoats. The gloom of an autumn night descended over the fields. Into it departed a dirty street. There was not a soul around.

The officer glanced at his watch.

"Past nine," he said. "And it's not clear where he lives. And what if suddenly it's on the other end of town?"

Straining her eyes, she looked into the darkness. "Is it far to the city?"

"About two or three miles, I think. I don't know exactly. In any case you'll get tired."

She began to persuade him. "Well, let's go on for a while. What if it's suddenly not so far. I feel really quite well. In any case, we've no place to stay until morning other than the train station. . . ."

But he visibly did want to go too. They set out on the road and in a few minutes the station buildings behind them sank into the darkness, and in yet another quarter hour only a faint glow in the sky indicated the place where the station was located. Having reached an intersection, they stopped and began to deliberate.

"Let's go straight ahead," she said, "it seems to me that it should be over there. . . ."

He hesitated. "And what if we're mistaken and get lost in the fields?"

But they went straight ahead regardless. The fast walking warmed and enlivened them. It began to seem to both of them that the city should be somewhere here, quite close, beyond this darkness, and that their lack of knowledge about the city and the road imparted to their nocturnal journey a somewhat eerie charm. Even though the darkness was impenetrable, they had a feeling that to the right of the road there should be some sort of hollow, from which damp breezes laden with the smell of leaves and bark were blowing. It seemed to them that they could even distinguish the silhouettes of the trees. All of a sudden some muffled noise resounded ahead, grew louder, turned into the clatter of hooves and wheels, and from the darkness a transport crew was carried onto the road. The officer shouted loudly in greeting to it:

"Is this the road to Bakhchisarai?"

But the crew had already rushed by. "Straight ahead," wafted out of the darkness. Encouraged, they moved farther.

Finally it started to grow brighter ahead on account of a few street lamps, stretched out along the road. On the right mounds of some low and dilapidated buildings were visible. In one of them a yellowish window was dimly illuminated.

"Let's go and ask," said the officer.

They left the road and approached the building. Around it was a wooden balcony set on stilts. Two little steps led to the main door. From inside not a sound was audible.

The officer knocked. No one answered. He knocked louder. The house was silent. He pushed the door: it opened noiselessly. They saw a long, low room, under whose ceiling were waves of blue-gray smoke. On benches along the walls slept some people in robes. One was sitting by an extinguished brazier, with his back to the door, his head having fallen to his chest. On the wall a small tin lamp smoked.

Both of them simultaneously felt the urge to step back. But the one who was sitting by the brazier raised his head and turned a thin, black-bearded face to them. The officer moved his hand toward the front of his hat.

"Perhaps you could help us? We're searching for a friend, but we don't know the city. Here's his address. . . ." He took out a folded piece of paper from the cuff of his greatcoat, unfolded it and loudly read out the address.

The man in the robe did not stir. His face expressed nothing, but his eyes were concentrated on the woman.

"Straight ahead . . . beyond the palace of the Khan. Ask there," he pronounced unexpectedly with a hoarse voice.

The officer thanked him, and they both went out hurriedly.

When they had got out to the road once more, the woman turned and looked back. The dark buildings behind them seemed to be simply piles of ruins. Only the window of the place where they had been smoldered with an evil light.

The most distant wanderings about the sleeping, dimly illuminated city, in search of the secluded and little-known city block they needed, appeared to them endlessly long and tiresome. The woman grew especially tired. Before her eyes swam locked-up houses, street lights, streets, signs, a stone fence above some small angry streamlet, gurgling somewhere in the dark . . . at some official building, dead and harshly lit with electric lamps, a young cornet with a rifle explained something to them at length, pointing into the darkness with his hand. She looked at his shoulders and was amazed that on them were shoulder straps—it seemed to her that from the moment when they disembarked into the unknown night from the station and drowned themselves in the emptiness of the fields, there had already passed an interminable amount of time, and that here, in this little night town, their power still incited bewilderment. Having parted with the cornet, they again went farther, and again there were streets, houses, the sound of water, tall, almost bare, trees, and beyond them, beyond a bridge, the vision of fantastic, brightly lit, white gates, seemingly a theatrical set amidst this damp autumn night.

But even past these gates they roamed farther still along some meandering dark alleys, knocked at a locked gate, returned, went again and again knocked, already drunk with exhaustion, almost losing a sense of where and why they were going, maintaining the one thought, the one aspiration of reaching the place where they should be let in and given nourishment and a bed. And when finally, at a knock at someone's gate, a ventilation window of a one-story house opened, and a head, illuminated from the back by a flickering light, thrust out and asked in an alarmed voice, "Who's there?"—the officer joyfully blurted out to the questioner:

"Petr Stepanych! Let us in! It's my wife and I."

The head was hurriedly hidden and the ventilation window slammed shut. Then the door clattered and a weak light was revealed; then were heard steps and the jingling of a key, not immediately finding its way into the keyhole; the gate opened slightly. A half-dressed man, in a coat thrown on his shoulders, with a candle in his hand, stepped back, letting them into the yard.

In a low, cleanly bleached room, the woman immediately sat down, and, not removing her coat, insensibly leaned her head against the spine of the chair.

Her eyes closed, and she almost didn't understand what the men were saying among themselves.

"Is it really that bad?" asked the master of the house.

"Maybe still two days. . . ."

"What are you preparing to do?"

"It doesn't concern me. I, of course, what's necessary. But I cannot subject my wife, in her condition—you understand what I'm talking about—to the horrors of embarkation on these mythical steamships, which cannot suffice for even half the demand. You offered to us both . . . you said that your foresters can hide me in the forests at least for a while . . . I'm not afraid for myself. Let her stay for the time it takes her to write home. Then they'll come fetch her. I'll return you the service someday."

Silence set in. The officer, not stirring, looked intently at the candle flame, along which a wavy flicker ran its course. The woman's pale face, with its closed eyes, appeared lifeless. Suddenly the master of the house began to move again, began to pace up and down the room, began to move some things around, all while pulling at his thinning beard with trembling fingers.

"So it means that it's that bad . . . and here we don't know anything. Everyone writes that they are indeed winning . . . but like you yourself propose. . . ."

"Tomorrow I must join my échelon, which is on its way to Sevastopol. I went ahead. The colonel gave me leave of absence."

Unexpectedly the master of the house grew animated. "That means that you still have some time? Well, we'll talk everything over tomorrow morning; it's already past one, and the lady, probably, has to lie down. We'll put her here on the feather bed, and ourselves somehow in the next room, on the straw mattresses."

The officer walked up to his wife, still sitting motionlessly, carefully freed her shoulders from the heavy coat, and removed the dark gray fur hat from her head. Her fine tangled hair was gently gilded by candlelight. Her future motherhood had not yet touched her face or her figure. . . .

When she opened her eyes the next morning the first thing that she saw was the low window, covered with a lattice, and in it a little courtyard, shaded in from one side by something tall. She didn't immediately understand that the stone wall was the mountains, rising almost perpendicularly into the sky. In her body was still the languor of yesterday's exhaustion; she wanted to lie endlessly, not moving, stretched out on the warm, soft bed, compensating for the months of sleeping wherever she could, in cramped quarters, in filth, on wooden benches, on sacks, on the stone floors of train stations.

The door squeaked and her husband entered. By his face she immediately sensed that something important had happened.

"What's happening?" she asked, at once coming to herself and sitting up on the bed.

"He's afraid and wants to leave himself," he answered curtly.

"With the army?" she asked.

"Yes, he says over and over again that they can also kill him, even though he's not a soldier, that one can't rely on anyone, that everyone is untrustworthy . . . in a word, he's asking that we take him with us. But that, of course, is out of the question."

"That means . . ."

"We must quickly get dressed and go. The échelon could arrive early. What a fool am I, that I thought then, in Melitopol. . . ."

She began to dress quickly, not getting unnerved, having become accustomed in these years to all kinds of unexpected developments, thinking only about how to reassure and calm him.

"Don't worry, everything will turn out fine," she said, quickly tossing from one hand to the other a lock of thick blond hair, gathering it together and stabbing it onto the back of her head with hairpins. "Indeed even before I was certain of it. It was your plan, and I consider it even better that it's turned out this way. It would have been much more terrifying for me to be here alone, without you, at such a time."

In half an hour, having taken leave of the quite flustered master of the house, who was muttering his excuses, they left the dwelling. Above the city hung a damp mist. Here and there this mist was broken through by gray stone blocks on the bare plateau, sucked dry by it, like underwater islands from a milky sea. The city was quite unfamiliar, new, not the one through which they had gone by night. Only the Khan's palace, although it too was different and was now visible to all, with all its complex edifices, complex roofs and white walls, naively covered with drawings of fruit and flowers, was as before, seemingly like a theater set. Beyond the frame of its white gates was unveiled a view of a deserted garden, shaded by tall poplars with a thick foliage which had not yet fallen, and among them, on the dark mirror of a pool, two swans showed up white. The young woman suddenly asked her husband to permit them, even if only for a minute, to go into the courtyard.

"Only for a minute," she said tenderly, but insistently. "Just think, maybe we'll never come back here again!"

At first he refused point-blank; then, seeing her chagrin, he began to hesitate, saying that there was no time, that they could miss the échelon; but in the end he agreed.

They passed through the gates. A small girl, with little black pigtails, in a striped dress, was sitting on the gallery that ran along the walls. They asked her where the guard was. She ran away, letting a large shoe drop from her foot and fearfully glancing at the unknown officer, who had a gun. While she was running for the guard, they walked around the garden, which was not large and which was squeezed in from all sides by the palace buildings and was eternally sad this morning. Although no rain was falling, the officer's cloth collar, gray hat and the hair of his companion were covered with extremely fine water droplets, like dull beads. And under this soundless delicate spray the whole garden seemed dull, ghostly, and pale.

The guard arrived, short, fat, with a bunch of large, differently ringing keys, a little frightened and unable to conceal his amazement at the strangeness of this visit at such a time. However, after a few minutes he fell into his accustomed role and led them around the palace, unlocking and each time locking after himself the heavy old doors. The palace chambers were imbued with a sad, dampish twilight; the light from the windows fell on the floor in pale lakes, and in the shadows shone here the dim gold of ancient embroidery, there a mother-of-pearl inlay. The voice of the guard, the sound of footsteps, even the breathing itself strangely woke this long lifeless quiet.

They followed the guard, going up and coming down along covered walkways and staircases, looking at the faded objects that he pointed out, listening to his elderly voice, sounding in the void like the voice of a reciter, passionlessly reading above a corpse of a man unknown to him:

"Here were the Khan's chambers . . . Here the Khan accepted petitioners . . . The fountain of tears, about which the poet Pushkin sang . . . The chambers, where the wives were located. . . ."

They looked at the carpets, at the low, narrow sofas, covered with old silks of rotting brocades with loose gold threads, at the ancient weapons; they walked along broad stone slabs toward a small poor bowl of marble which had turned green in color—and it was the famous fountain of tears. There arose covered walkways into the bright, spacious chambers, where from behind the dense gilded gratings were visible green branches of the garden, where, on a fenced-off platform, on black Arab tables, were laid out ancient musical instruments with long fingerboards, inlaid with mother-of-pearl, and narrow-necked gilded jugs. They tried to imagine the hands which once touched those strings, which fingered the jewelry now set out in glass cases, those embroidered colored silks and gold belts, bands of inflexible brocades, damask veils and colored necklaces. . . .

Walking around the palace, they stepped out once again into the garden, walked past the pool—the swans expectantly stretched out in their direction their long, snakelike necks—and approached a golden grating, behind which the marble slabs of a cemetery grew white and gray, became crooked in different directions and were disfigured by rain.

"The burial-vault of the Khans," said the guard in a particularly passionless manner.

Behind the gilded grating of the cemetery the thick, long grass grew entwined about their legs, making it difficult to walk. But the guard stubbornly struggled with it and led them to some kind of round kiosk. There, on an elevated pedestal, in tall humped boxes, wrapped in sultan's purple, below marble columns whose tops were crowned in turbans, lay the Khans, the ancient rulers of this dead palace, of this dead garden. And here they stood a little longer, fruitlessly attempting to imagine those who had slept in these tall graves for a hundred years. And between the brows of the woman was apparent a deep, severe wrinkle.

Still long before the pale, pearly-white light of this day, which seemed strange and eerie for them, the quiet and dream of those disturbed rooms, all those old, decrepit things, the dying silks, the rotting clothes, all the pointless magnificence of no use to anyone, the gold patterns of the gratings, behind which once lived young, joyful women, like her, the pallid roses, the poplars of the garden, the marble steps, the broken-down graveyard, drowning in weeds—everything merged in her soul, which had become more tender, more impressionable, thanks to her future motherhood, with a sense of her own life, which, in a few days, perhaps in a few hours, was waiting with that terrifying, uncertain, tragic. . . .

The guard said something else, proposed going to the mosque of the Khans, which was situated behind the cemetery, but the husband, having already tensely listened to something, unexpectedly began to hurry, and began to rush her. And, having listened in her turn, she caught some faraway, confused thunder, similar to a distant thunderclap, repeating itself in equal time intervals.

In the city commotion was already beginning. On the square there was not a single cabbie. People, dragging some kind of sacks, passed them. They looked at the shoulder straps of the officer in amazement and unfriendliness. Stooped women in striped shawls, looking about frightenedly, ran across the street. In front of the civic building, where they had stopped at night, there was not a soul.

Not asking anybody, they quickly went along the road to the station. The haze hanging over the plateau had thickened, rendering it impenetrable. They were practically running, not speaking, intently listening to the sounds, carried at times from out of the fog. At an intersection they both came to halt for a second: the thunder of guns became louder; at times it seemed that it enveloped the entire sky in front of them.

"Faster!" shouted the officer abruptly.

They ran. But the station was already quite close, behind the fog. From there came the noisy hissing of the locomotive. In a few minutes, when they ran into the train station, wet and gasping for breath, the first face that they saw was the swarthy face of their orderly.

"Lieutenant, sir! Lieutenant, sir!" he yelled, waving at them from afar. "Our train is already here, sir! And I was already starting to be afraid; I thought that you might not make it. . . ."

They barely managed to leap up into the car, overcrowded with people. . . .

1930

Translated by Luc Beaudoin

Notes to the Essay

1. *Prolog* (Paris, 1933), 136.
2. *Olivkovyi sad* (Paris, 1937), 7.
3. Ibid., 26.

Bibliography

Primary Works

[Poems and stories, by G.N. Petrova]. *Studencheskie gody.* Prague, 1922–26.

Utro. Paris: Sovremennye zapiski, 1930.

Prolog. Paris, 1933.

Olivkovyi sad. Paris, 1937.

Grasskii dnevnik. Washington, DC, 1967.

In Translation

Weisser Mohn. Trans. Hans Ruoff and Margareta Stepun. Munich: 1948.

"Springbrunnen der Tränen." *Russische Erzähler des XX. Jahrhunderts.* Trans. Hans Ruoff. Ed. Eugen Gagarin. Munich, 1960.

Secondary Works

Adamovich, G. "Galina Kuznetsova: *Utro.*" *Sovremennye zapiski* 42 (1930).

Brom, Libor. *The Lives and the Works of the Prosaists L.F. Zurov, G.N. Kuznetsova and N. Roshchin: On the Question of I.A. Bunin's Literary School.* Ph.D. dissertation, University of Colorado, 1970.

Filipp, Valerie. "Galina Nikolaevna Kuznetsova." *Dictionary of Russian Women Writers.* Ed. Marina Ledkovsky, Charlotte Rosenthal and Mary Zirin. Westport, CT: Greenwood Press, 1994. 351–54.

Marietta Shaginian

Unlike many of the women represented in this volume, Marietta Sergeevna Shaginian (1888–1982) did not lack opportunities to see her work in print. A literary career that spanned seven decades saw the publication of six editions of her collected works, along with over six hundred articles on subjects ranging from music to metallurgy. Nor is there a dearth of biographical information: beginning with a 1926 piece for the newspaper *Red Panorama* (*Krasnaia panorama*), she updated and revised her autobiography throughout her life, culminating in her 1980 memoir *Man and Time* (*Chelovek i vremia*).

Shaginian has been consigned to oblivion in the West (and disdain in her own country) not by neglect or repression, but rather by what David Shepherd has termed "the compromising taint of sustained official recognition."[1] Her credentials as a paragon of official Soviet literature are impeccable: a model production novel (*Hydrocentral* [*Gidrotsentral*, 1931]), a Communist party card, a series of works about Lenin, a Stalin Prize and a Lenin Prize. Yet despite her protestations to the contrary, Shaginian was not born a Bolshevik. If we examine the parts of her biography that she herself gradually expunges over the years, we find a writer whose work was at one time both critically acclaimed and popular with the reading public.

Shaginian was born in 1888 in Moscow, the daughter of a prominent doctor. While her parents were both Armenian, she grew up in surroundings typical of Moscow intellectuals in a house whose literary inventory included the classics (Pushkin and Goethe were her father's favorites), the "thick journals" of the day and forbidden books that sparked lively political debate "in the spirit of opposition liberalism."[2] Despite her claims of early political awareness—one of her first published poems was called "Song of the Worker" (1906)—it was a cultural heritage she would later struggle to cast off, as she was repeatedly criticized for depicting the interests of the effete intellectual rather than the Soviet worker.

In 1908 Shaginian enrolled in courses for women in the philosophy department of a Moscow university, where she found herself in the company of "girls from bourgeois families, who had already been affected by the decadence, Neo-Kantianism and Bergsonism that had become fashionable."[3] Shaginian, of course, later speaks disparagingly of the time she spent "under the hypnosis of a subtle, highly reactionary influence,"[4] but at the time she was fully absorbed in a "search for truth" that led her to read Symbolist journals and to frequent lectures at the famous Literary-Artistic Circle. Suddenly, she found herself "at the center of the ideological currents of those years"[5] at a time when political events infused a sense of urgency into debates on the future of literature, the role of the church and the fate of Russia.

Quite by accident, Shaginian stumbled upon a book of poetry by Zinaida Gippius, an event she later described as "one of the most important critical episodes in the epoch of my wanderings."[6] In her memoirs she dramatically describes devouring the book in a single night, first by kerosene lamp, then by candlelight, then by the light of the matches her sister lit one after the other until their supply was exhausted. With its critique of the godlessness of the 1905 revolution, the book spoke to her religious side, which had developed since her father's death in 1902, and to her need to find a practical worldview: "There in front of me was the answer: collectivity [*sobornost'*], the connection between people of kindred spirit, God, revolution."[7] In the morning she dashed off a letter to Gippius; three days later she received a remarkable answer: "It seemed to me when I read your letter," wrote Gippius, "that you understood everything . . . not that I wrote, but that I thought and felt when I wrote."[8]

A compulsive letter writer throughout her life, Shaginian never hesitated to initiate correspondence with anyone who struck her fancy, no matter how famous. In his memoirs the Symbolist writer Andrei Belyi singles out Shaginian among the many young "truth seekers" from whom he received letters: "Among these letters a series of missives from a certain young woman student (*kursistochka*), who didn't want to reveal her name, stuck in my memory because of their acuteness and intelligence; I was struck by the keenness of her interests, her high level of culture, the philosophical formulation of the questions."[9] In his second letter to her he writes: "I am instinctively drawn to your words: there is no hysteria in them."[10] Similarly, Gippius had written in her first letter: "[Your letter is] so intelligent and *sober*. You know, it's very important that it's sober. That's so rare nowadays."[11]

In her letters, as well as in her prose, Shaginian wrote with a disarming sincerity and enthusiasm, combined with a malleability that allowed her to mold herself into a shape that would be agreeable to her intended reader. This ability was to be both her greatest gift and her greatest shortcoming as a writer. It allowed her to write fluently in a wide variety of styles and genres, but it left her hopelessly mired in the outworn formulas of socialist realism for the better part of her career. The word that appears over and over in early reviews of her work is "talented," yet she was unable to find a voice of her own and instead succumbed to a voice imposed from above.

Shaginian's early work was no less derivative, but it was carried out under the influence of mentors more auspicious than her later models, most notably Gippius. In the fall of 1909 at Gippius's invitation Shaginian moved to St. Petersburg, where she spent the next three winters, while still taking courses by correspondence in Moscow. (A congenital illness had caused a gradual loss of hearing, and by this time she was already too deaf to attend lectures.) In St. Petersburg Gippius and her husband, Dmitrii Merezhkovskii, headed a group of "God-seekers," who sought to form a new church that would combine their revolutionary and religious ideals. Shaginian was charged with acting as one of their "antennae," who would "penetrate into the working masses of Petersburg."[12]

Shaginian's first collection of poetry, *First Meetings* (*Pervye vstrechi*, published in 1909 at her own expense, met with little success. It was her second volume of poetry, *Orientalia* (1912), that brought her fame and critical acclaim. As one reviewer points out, Shaginian relied heavily on clichéd Eastern motifs and—her prefatory claims of "racial consciousness" as an ethnic Armenian notwithstanding—did not always get her facts right. Nonetheless, the collection is praised for its evocation of the East, "with its women created only for love,"[13] and for its "amazing simplicity and something chastely pure."[14] Another reviewer suggests that Shaginian has the potential to become "a poetess who will unrestrainedly tell the whole truth about herself, about woman," and thus prove a worthy successor to the nineteenth-century poet Karolina Pavlova.[15]

Shaginian did not live up to this prophecy. In fact, in an *oeuvre* as vast as hers, issues of gender are conspicuous in their absence. Like Gippius, Shaginian declines to be classified as a "woman writer," but unlike Gippius, Shaginian devotes virtually no attention to issues of gender and sexuality—except in those few works that were written directly under Gippius's influence: *First Meetings* was mentioned by Annenskii in his article on "feminine lyricism";[16] *Orientalia* was praised for its "feminine grace";[17] *Two Moralities* (*Dve Morali*, 1914) addressed the "woman question." Even mention of her own family life is scant in her multiple autobiographies. From the 1920s on, Shaginian clearly thinks in categories of class, rather than gender. As a model of the "New Soviet Woman," she delves into areas that were previously the domain of men—crystallography, metallurgy, engineering, mining—but she is much too concerned with extolling the wonders of Soviet technology to draw our attention to that fact. Her only major work with a woman protagonist, *Adventures of a Society Lady* (*Prikliuchenie damy iz obshchestva*, 1923), ends with the heroine's learning from a young male Bolshevik that her transition from society lady to Soviet worker is doomed to be incomplete.

Orientalia still bears the stamp of Symbolism, but by the time it was published, Shaginian had broken with Gippius and returned to Moscow, after writing an unfavorable review of Gippius's novel *The Devil's Doll*. Her new mentor was to be Emilii Medtner, brother of the composer Nikolai Medtner, with whose family she lived on and off in 1912–1914, a period she called both her "Lehrjahre"[18] and "the most reactionary period of my life."[19] With Medtner she shared two things: adulation of Goethe that bordered on obsession, and a rejection of modernism in music. She wrote several articles for Medtner's journal *Works and Days* (*Trudy i dni*), including an article on Sergei Rachmaninov, with whom she had also boldly initiated a correspondence.[20]

The article has little to do with Rachmaninov—the composer himself wonders if she exaggerates—but instead furthers Medtner's rejection of dissonance and experimentation in music, a view that leads Shaginian to boast in her 1958 biography that "in spite of music criticism of the time, I build my analysis of Rachmaninov's music completely in the spirit of our current attitude to it."[21] Indeed, the Marxist overtones are unmistakable, giving some credence to her claim that at the time she was already "being drawn to finding such a philosophy literally with my whole being."[22] "The path to greater freedom," she writes, lies only in "voluntary self-limitation,"[23] a notion that would reappear frequently in various guises in her later writing.

In 1914 Shaginian concluded this chapter in her life with a pilgrimage to Goethe's Weimar home, a journey she records in her philosophical travelogue *Journey to Weimar* (*Puteshestvie v Veimar*). The book was accepted for publication in *Northern Notes* (*Severnye zapiski*), but was withheld from publication for being too Germanophilic and was published separately only in 1923.

In 1915 Shaginian set about writing her first novel, *One's Own Fate* (*Svoia sud'ba*). Belyi later wrote in a letter to its author that he read it "without interruption, in a single breath" and found it "very intelligent, interesting," a book that "raises an enormous issue."[24] That issue was the "battle against Freud," whose theories were just beginning to be fashionable at the time.[25] The book received scant critical attention, due mainly to an accident of timing. It was accepted for publication by *Herald of Europe* (*Vestnik Evropy*), but only the first few chapters were published before the journal closed in 1918. When it finally was published in 1923, its prerevolutionary setting seemed anachronistic and it was eclipsed by the success of her novella *Change* (*Peremena*, 1922), a lively semidocumentary work about the civil war that won favor with both Lenin and Stalin. Moreover, the novel was permeated with a religious theme that both Soviet critics and the later Shaginian naturally chose to downplay.

One's Own Fate is set during World War I in a sanatorium in the Caucasus for mental patients. The sanatorium provides a backdrop for lengthy debates on mental illness and the nature of personality between the director, Foerster, and his young assistant, Batiushkov. Foerster advocates treatment based on the "development of the intermediary connection between consciousness and the soul, i.e., the development of character."[26] In the original version of the novel, the goal of cultivating a healthy, unified personality is directly linked with Christian values of humility and self-sacrifice. The moral center of the book is occupied by Father Leonid, an Orthodox priest who preaches voluntary submission to a higher power as a way of fulfilling "one's own fate."[27] On his deathbed Foerster tells his daughter, "Don't ever imagine that things could be otherwise."[28] In the reworked version, Leonid's role is greatly curtailed, Foerster becomes an atheist and emphasis is placed on activity and a sense of responsibility to the collective as keys to a healthy psyche. The anti-Freudian critique is sharpened as well. By way of rejecting psychoanalysis, Foerster writes in his notebooks, "We don't untie, but rather try to tie up the knots that have become loosened in a person."[29]

Shaginian continued to write on religious and philosophical themes in the three collections of short stories published from 1914 to 1919, as well as in the nine plays "not for the theater" written in 1918. The plays were received favorably by Aleksandr Blok, who recommended *Miracle in the Bell Tower* for publication in his journal *Notes of Dreamers* (*Zapiski mechtatelei*). In that play, Jesus Christ appears on earth in the guise of a "stranger," but the local inhabitants fail to recognize him and the play ends as he is led off to prison.

A certain thematic resemblance with the later works of Blok himself is by no means accidental. When Blok published his famous poem "The Twelve," in which Christ appears at the head of a column of Red Army soldiers, Shaginian believed she had found the perfect formulation of the link between Christianity and revolution that she had unsuccessfully sought in Gippius. In the novella *Change* (1922), she gives a purportedly accurate account of the poem's ecstatic reception when it is read aloud for the first time in a town in the south of Russia during the civil war. Shaginian vigorously defended the poem against detractors and reacted with disbelief when it seemed that the poet himself was modifying his position. In a letter to Blok shortly before his death she writes:

> The deepest thing that I have experienced in the last five years is connected with your "The Twelve." . . . Why are you now renouncing Truth with a capital letter (which is seen by the poet) in favor of truth with a small letter, which is seen by all people? . . . For me "The Twelve" is a symbol of faith, the artistic formula of innermost religious experience, which was experienced by only a few of us, the "intellectuals," and by *almost all* the "common" souls in the October Revolution.[30]

She goes on to set forth a view of the revolution to which she clung stubbornly, even after she distanced herself from its Christian foundations: it must be accepted unconditionally:

> If you saw the light of God in an earthly face and came to love that light, then what is it to you that the face of a little girl had become the face of a hag, had spread, had become flabby and decrepit. For you it *wasn't that* that was the light and *without that* the light will remain, if you believe. . . . The revolution has been distorted, has been flattened out, it has grown feeble and looks through the wrong eyes. What of it? *It* allowed us to experience a miracle and it must be loved to the end. He who, having seen the light through it, now renounces it, renounces the best part of his spirit.[31]

Shaginian's religiosity extended well into the 1920s. In her 1926 autobiography for *Red Panorama* she writes that her Bolshevism is "distinctive and not acceptable for the Party." She felt unable to join the party at that time (she finally joined in 1942) because "I am a believing Christian and that constitutes not a passing fancy, but the essence of my personality, its roots that I cannot deny."[32]

In the 1920s Shaginian wrote two more works that have attracted attention in the West, both of which demonstrate her facility with a broad range of genres. *Mess-Mend* or *Yankees in Petrograd* (*Mess-Mend ili Ianki v Petrograde*, 1927) was written in answer to Bukharin's call for "Red Pinkertonism"—fast-moving, plot-oriented works that would provide a Soviet substitute for the tremendously popular foreign detective novels. Shaginian obliges with a rollicking parody of the genre in which Mike Thingsmaster and his band of enlightened American workers outsmart the evil millionaires and fascists. While it was criticized for being too frivolous and unrealistic, Shaginian in 1934 called it her "happiest book," the one she liked best of all her works up until then.[33] Indeed, it is Shaginian at her best, where her imagination and storytelling prowess are given free rein, and even the ideological content is treated with a light touch. She wrote two sequels, *Laurie Lane, Metallurgist* (1925) and *The International Car* (1925), which was then reworked and published in her collected works as *The Road to Baghdad.*

From 1926 to 1928 Shaginian worked on the experimental "novel-complex" *Kik*, which is short for *The Witch and the Communist* (*Koldunia i Kommunist*, 1929). She claims in 1956 to have written it "at my leisure and for myself."[34] A type of detective story about the disappearance of a certain Comrade L'vov, the book is a montage of documents that includes letters, newspaper articles, advertisements and telephone conversations. The second and largest "episode" is devoted to four accounts of what happened, each in a different genre: a Byronic poem, a novella, a melodrama in verse and the scenario for a documentary film. In the final episode Comrade L'vov himself appears and gives a literary critique of the four versions, all of which turn out to be inaccurate in their depiction of the facts. In her 1956 introduction, Shaginian claims to have written the work to protest the "narrow literary specialization" of her contemporaries and to "pass a literacy test in all literary genres." In retrospect, she also sees in it a statement of "the importance of constantly remaining in the course of contemporary events"—in other words, the importance of getting the facts straight.[35]

Throughout the 1920s, Shaginian was often labeled a "fellow traveler," who, despite good intentions, had not yet succeeded in throwing off her bourgeois intellectual heritage. Even *Hydrocentral* (1931), which was later canonized as a model production novel, was criticized for centering on a passive character—an attempt to "reconcile Foerster-Goethe with the proletarian revolution"—rather than on the active builders of socialism.[36]

Shaginian survived the 1930s unscathed, writing mainly journalistic and critical essays. To say she was courageous would be to elevate her wrongly to the stature of writers such as Bulgakov, who risked their lives and livelihoods standing up to the state-controlled literary establishment. Yet neither would it be just to call her cowardly. In 1934 she took on Maxim Gorky in the debate on whether the Russian language should be protected from the contaminating influences of other languages or dialects. Drawing on examples of regionalisms in works by Isaak Babel' and Vsevolod Ivanov, she spoke forcefully in favor of a mutually enriching interaction between the literary language and "substandard" forms.[37] In 1936 she submitted her resignation from the Writers' Union to protest lack of material support for writers, an act that evoked a resolution from the Presidium condemning this "deeply antisocial act" and "serious political mistake."[38]

By the 1950s her place in the literary world was secure. When *New World* (*Novyi mir*) published a lengthy exposé of factual errors in her *Diary of a Writer*,[39] the literary establishment rose to her defense. Livshits's "gloating" article was added to the list of the journal's sins that led to the vilification and eventual replacement of its editor, Aleksandr Tvardovskii.[40]

Surprisingly, Shaginian's most interesting work of the second half of her life is her memoir *Man and Time* (*Chelovek i vremia,* 1980). Despite the inevitable ideological baggage and "self-criticism," Shaginian succeeds in writing about the pre-Soviet period using "the intonation of the times," and she provides colorful portraits of many people "who would in the future become our enemies"—in other words, most of the leading cultural figures of the time.[41]

Energetic, prolific, versatile, educated and talented—these are the words most often used to describe Shaginian by promoters and detractors alike. But as Lenin himself is quoted as saying (by Livshits), "Our faults are a continuation of our virtues."[42] Shaginian's energy and range of interests led her to write extensively on subjects about which she had only a superficial understanding, a fault she readily admitted: "I don't completely understand [photosynthesis] and out of a bad habit (the worst habit of my life), without having understood it I begin to jump ahead, compare things, draw parallels, extend all kinds of premature generalizations—and the more easily you succeed in this, the less clear is your conception of the subject."[43]

She was aware, too, that the vast scale of her literary output was not necessarily a virtue in and of itself. In a 1910 letter to Gippius she wrote: "I was born with a clerical [*kantseliariskii*] gift, I have the genius of a scribbler [*pisak*]. Just put me in a government department—what an Akakii Akakievich I'd make!"[44]

Her versatility was truly remarkable, but in the multiplicity of voices she presents in her early work, it is difficult to find one that is truly her own. This, too, she freely admitted. After her forays into lyric poetry she wrote, "Working on [*Orientalia*], I felt myself to be more of an epic writer than a lyricist, and I was drawn much more strongly to a theme that had already been thought up than to the possibility of embodying my own feelings in lyric poetry."[45] Even more telling is her final letter to Blok, in which she answered his criticism that her plays lacked "organic language" and "intentness of gaze":

> For me this is not the "mark of a school" [i.e., Symbolism] or a temporary imperfection, but rather my most serious personal burden, which I am not fated to overcome. . . . The thing is that I have a *dulled*

> perception of the world (I hear and see poorly) and I don't have my *own* language. Language is organic only when and where it is *speech*. But I don't know *speech*. . . . Nothing remains of the music, the connection, the charm of speech because my attention is inevitably chained to concepts. And so, always trying to *understand*, I inevitably forget how to *listen*. . . . There remains only the book, and one's own "potential." But through the book and from the book . . . is born only "bookishness and derivativeness."[46]

But Shaginian is condemned not for superficiality or lack of originality, but for a far graver sin. Political views that could be attributed to youthful optimism in the 1920s or political expediency in the 1930s and 1940s were horrifying when repeated with equal conviction in the 1970s and 1980s. And yet, one is continually struck by her disarming sincerity, the tone of "someone who is invariably in the ecstatic state of a person who has finally found the truth."[47] One is left with the uneasy feeling that she has somehow traversed the entire Soviet era in a state of myopic oblivion, unaware of the moral bankruptcy of her beloved revolution. As Khodasevich wrote of her in 1925: "[She] had a good heart and, waving her cardboard sword, she was always rushing to defend or defeat someone, and in the end it somehow always turned out that she defeated virtue and defended the villain. But it was always done out of a good heart and with the best intentions."[48]

Laura Goering

The Corinthian Canal[1]

I.

What life aboard a Greek packet boat would be like was something many a Russian experienced when the war in Europe chased them to the port of Brindisi at the very tip of the elegant Italian boot. Such a vessel—like a cabman's nag—lives out its life making continuous trips to and fro, crawling into nearly every harbor to catch its breath and clear its throat. Creaking, sooty, filthy, with rotting floorboards and rickety cabin steps, with a captain who bellows like a sailor, with the unbearable smell of tar and mutton fat and, to top it off, with the unalterable determination of the steward to summon you to the table d'hôte during periods when the ship is pitching most desperately—such a ship awaits its victims and slowly hauls them through the Greek archipelago.

Early one morning three months after the beginning of the war, precisely this kind of ship was crawling along the deserted shores of Greece, mercilessly breathing hot fumes into the frosty, transparent morning air. The action was taking place at a time that intensified one's sense of the present, but in a setting that recalled classical textbooks. Above the passengers hung the war; before them the dim, balding outlines of Olympus extended into the clouds. And yet not one of the people gathered on the deck thought about either present or past. Each one continued to think only about his own private affairs—which is, after all, the main distinguishing feature of people who tend to be called philistines.

The captain, a heavyset man with a red face, was engaged in conversation with a deck passenger who had boarded the ship the night before. The passenger, seated atop a pile of rope covered with a tarpaulin, had assumed a striking pose that allowed the straight line of his forehead and nose to be observed from the side. He was a Greek prince returning to Athens from a hunting trip. Two of his tall assistants were busy hanging up his game: a roebuck, a couple dozen grouse, plus some other grayish-brown creature that vaguely resembled our rabbit. The prince was covered in dirt from head to toe; his hunting outfit hung on him with a certain grace. But when he stood up and removed his cap, the charm disappeared: a small figure with legs that were far from long (so as not to call them short) and a placid bald patch on his oval head—that was all that was left of this seated Antinous.

This put an immediate end to the observation that had been going on (in one case through a lorgnette and in the other through a pair of unaided gray-blue eyes). The hand holding the lorgnette fell to its owner's knees; the gray-blue eyes shifted away from the prince toward that hand (which was, it should be noted in all fairness, most beautiful).

"You don't want to look either?" asked the owner of the gray-blue eyes, a man with a tanned, clean-shaven face of that fortunate type that gives people of any age a look of boyish youth.

"No, I don't," answered the young woman with the lorgnette, smiling.

To us, reader, both interlocutors—however much we might describe them—seem to be the most ordinary of people. But the happy gaze that accompanies their every word, the blooming smile that suggests an unfading inner glow yet never turns into laughter, make them extraordinary in each other's eyes. Love touched them with the tip of its magic wand and their everyday skin began to shine like purest gold. Only God knows whether love conjures up this gold by magic, or whether it simply reveals that which is already there, but one thing is certain—these two people sitting on the deck right now differ markedly from their neighbors. They are quiet and absorbed in themselves. Their movements are circumscribed by a most delicate and infectious tenderness. Their gaze is evidence of that acute attentiveness—ten times more intense than what most people experience—that is felt only by lovers and those of genius.

"I would like to know what happened to that race," said the man, once again glancing at the prince. "Did they really start out with puny freaks like that and then construct the formal ideal *a contrario*? But then I'm talking nonsense."

"Of course it's nonsense. Do you really think Hector or Achilles could have looked like that?" answered the young woman, quickly picking up the direction of the man's thoughts and trying it out as if it were her own. He answered her with a grateful look.

But our tale could be told very quickly if it were only a matter of two lovebirds and their chatter. Actually, there were other people on board besides them: three ladies and two teenage boys, with noses that were blue from the cold and bare blue knees, left exposed thanks to the English method of upbringing. They were all huddled together, pretending to contemplate the deserted Greek mountains, wild in their gloomy isolation, when, of course, they were all just secretly spying.

The oldest, a hook-nosed woman with warts on her cheeks, said, "What incomparable beauty! How do you suppose Elizaveta Pavlovna can sleep when we are passing by Parnassus or—what do you call it?—where the Grecian gods live!"

"Mama, that's *Greek* gods," one of the teenagers corrected her indignantly.

"Really? I don't understand—they say 'Grecian urns,' don't they? Well, it doesn't matter. Stasik, go downstairs this minute and wake up Elizaveta Pavlovna. Tell her that she absolutely, positively *must* come admire the view!"

The boy turned around noisily and lumbered off, furiously pounding the stairs with the metal heelplates of his shoes. All three ladies exchanged glances, in silent anticipation of some imminent pleasure. The second boy, taking the softened expression of their faces to mean a certain indulgence toward him, sidled off and joined a group of sailors who were earnestly spitting and smoking on the dirtiest part of the deck.

So softly shone the aged faces of our three ladies—covered with wrinkles and comfortably powdered—that to an outsider's gaze it would seem that they were assembled there to perform some good deed. The kindly, smiling ribbons of their lips silently expressed some shared thought that seemed to be forming in their minds. Their eyes looked out warmly.

However, the good deed they had assembled to perform required that they expend yet another dose of valuable energy. Stasik came back alone and announced breathlessly: "Mama, Elizaveta Pavlovna is feeding the baby. She says that the baby could catch cold if she came up. She says that if Aunt Katia would give her her shawl. . . ."

Though Aunt Katia was the youngest of the three ladies, they had all reached that age when unwed women sincerely pity all those who have married, maintaining that they themselves never married "out of principle." She immediately threw off the shawl from her shoulders and handed it to Stasik.

These maneuvers went unnoticed by the two people engaged in conversation. Because the noise of the steamer threatened to drown out their words, and the sea breeze—or "zephyr" as sailors affectionately call it—was blowing directly into their faces, they had leaned slightly toward one another and the man had laid his hand on the bench next to the young woman's lovely back. She, however, was sitting very straight, not touching his hand, though she still felt its presence and the tenderness emanating from it. Her cheeks, which were covered with windblown strands of dark hair, were slightly pale. He would say "look at that," or "look over here," but in his tone of voice one could always hear the word "dearest." They were close to that stage of senselessness when a person is ready to say whatever comes into his head, when feeling begins to rule without the usual accomplices of speech or gaze. Two cats, furtively lapping up milk from a pitcher, would have similar feelings of wordless complicity, if only they were capable of recognizing them.

At that very moment the three ladies' good deed was rewarded with complete success. First, Stasik's anxious face emerged from below deck. He at once caught sight of his brother over by the sailors and immediately scurried off in their direction. Behind him there appeared a woman—no longer young and with a nervous and rather unpleasant face—heavily bundled up against the cold and holding a baby in her arms.

"What's going on?" she asked in a rather ungentle tone.

"My dear," answered the hook-nosed lady. To this greeting she appended neither main nor subordinate clause, but rather a single glance suffused with the utmost solemnity. This glance was directed at the conversing man and woman who were sitting with their backs to them, and could neither hear nor see any of what was going on. Nevertheless, out of some sort of nervous presentiment the man turned around and the young woman felt the hand, which had been emanating such warmth and tenderness, suddenly become indifferent. With two violet eyes that appeared even more intense against the deep blue water, she cast a glance at her companion and immediately lowered her lashes. With a look that betrayed both forced nonchalance and the first stirrings of violent inner protest, the man got out his cigarette case and painstakingly searched through it for a cigarette. The woman with the baby slowly and deliberately walked up to the two of them and sat down on the same bench. The trio of ladies observing the scene moved closer.

The man was the first to break the silence: "You were sleeping so soundly, Liza, that I was reluctant to wake you."

"Is that so," answered the woman.

She said nothing more, and in the tone she used to say those words one could hear neither challenge nor mockery. Nonetheless, no one dared utter another word. All three felt something repugnant in the depths of their souls—as if the natural vector of their will had been diverted, the way a sunbeam is forcibly refracted when it comes in contact with a foreign medium. The young woman was the first to yield; she mumbled something like "I'm going to put on something warmer," slowly stood up from the bench and shuffled off toward the stairs. It seemed to her that the movement of her legs, the folds of her skirt, her limp hands—everything betrayed the fact that she had spent three tiring but tender hours with her beloved. She felt almost unbearable shame. As she passed by the three lady observers, she instinctively clenched her hands into fists.

"Where is it you're going?" shouted Aunt Katia in an unnaturally loud voice.

"To my cabin to get a blanket," replied the young woman. She went downstairs to her empty cabin, bolted the door, sat down on the bed, shook her head and suddenly buried her face in the pillow.

Vera was neither intelligent nor stupid, but was just a young woman like a million others. She had fallen in love as people do when the time comes to fall in love. It was simple and natural, like the formation of foam on the green waves beating against the window of her cabin.

A young woman falling in love is something completely innocent. Verochka felt neither pain nor passion; she was simply soaking up someone else's tenderness like a sponge and flourishing in it. She was always trying to get closer to its source. When she was away from it, she would call upon her memories to help her; she would close her eyes and dream—for the thousandth time—about everything that had happened when they last met. He looked, he said, he smiled, his lips trembled, she looked, she answered—and so on, ad infinitum. Simple actions always became linked with some small part of the landscape—the blue sea, the monotonous hexameter of the waves, the deserted shores of Greece, the reddish smokestack of the ship, the sharp smell of salt, the muted conversation of the Greek sailors, the barking of the gulls, the humming of the boiler down below like the intermittent palpitations of someone's heart—making each memory special and distinct. Vera was convinced that this was her fate, designed especially for her.

But if this is so, why has everything begun to stick in her throat? She is overtaken by a loathsome awareness of guilt, of secrecy and concealment. She loses hold of her daydream and finds herself suddenly plunged into vileness. Every creature aboard the ship is meddling in her life in the most revolting way . . . they won't let her feel . . . they won't let her dream . . . is one really supposed to fall in love on command? Who is to blame if two people fall in love with one another? What is perfectly natural becomes shameful only because between them there stands that awful other woman—Elizaveta Pavlovna, his wife.

II.

The person she had fallen in love with, Konstantin Mikhailovich, was up on deck thinking thoughts that were no less depressing. As a man, his first inclination was to make generalizations, so the course of his thought soon left behind the merely personal and alighted on social soil.

"The Moslems," he thought with the zeal of a reformer, "the Moslems have the purest view of marriage. The same woman can't set me aflame my whole life. That's . . . that's an absurdity. I swear you need a new woman every time, just like you need a new match to start a fire. Why should I, a free being, be forced day in and day out to strike an already burned match, even though it's totally useless? And if I have once again caught on fire, why do I have this idiotic feeling of guilt? And why do I feel obliged to pretend? Bah, what nonsense!"

He was so riled up by a sense of being in the right that he grew braver. He looked at the unattractive woman next to him (for a woman who has fallen out of love is always unattractive) and said in a threatening whisper: "Don't be a fool, Liza. There's no need for you to get all hot and bothered. Whatever happens, happens—and for that, my dear, I am just about as much to blame as those mountains over there."

"At least don't try to justify yourself," answered his wife hatefully.

"There's nothing for me to justify myself about," said her husband almost cheerfully. "I'm right anyway." Suddenly he felt as though he had found the perfect way out: lay your cards on the table and then just do as you please—what could be simpler? The natural course of his will had once again triumphed and everything in the world seemed very easy. "I'm right!" he repeated with even more conviction. "I'm not forcing you into anything, and I'm showing you all my cards: look, here they are. In love, in love and in love. Have you calmed down?"

"Well, that's just great. Now what?"

"Now nothing. Do me a favor, don't spoil your milk by interfering." (His sense of relief had mollified him and he felt like making concessions.) "My dear, I respect you and appreciate you so much that. . . ."

"You bastard!" she cried. "You bastard, you have no idea how repulsive you are. You should just shut up and not try to wriggle out of it. At least then I won't have to feel so ashamed for you."

The baby, who had been awakened by his mother's outburst, broke out into a raucous, ear-piercing howl. She mechanically unbuttoned her jacket and blouse, undid her brassiere and let her torn appliquéed undershirt fall from her shoulder. Her husband watched her pull out her thin, sagging breast and begin feeding the baby without a hint of shame or coquetry. The action seemed to him to bespeak an awareness of insuperable power.

Only a person with both law and morality on her side could act in such a way. He again felt misguided, pathetic, guilty. Everything that had a moment ago seemed so easy had again become devilishly difficult. He would have to run off somewhere and dissemble and lie. Every pleasure would be contaminated by this feeling of guilt.

As if in answer to his thoughts, his wife said in a voice that was now calm and quiet, "I can see right through you. Debauchery's not enough for you—you want to feel that you're in the right. Well, you're mistaken! That will never happen as long as our Tolia and I are alive, do you hear?"

Konstantin Mikhailovich heard. In his wife's voice, made all the more expressionless by her calm exterior, he sensed unmistakable, unwavering hatred. It was strange that a person who hated him so sincerely should cling so ferociously to her union with him and defend it as something sacred. Even stranger was the fact that sooner or later he would submit to her. He had the urge to strike out in a lifeboat for the deserted Greek woods where he could begin life anew.

The three ladies, who clearly heard the aftereffects of their good deed (even the word "bastard" had wafted their way), rested content. But suddenly Aunt Katia, who had been busy with the mote in her neighbor's eye, cried out, "My dears, where have Stasik and Kazik gotten to?"

The two boys were sitting on dirty kegs next to some sailors, conversing in the international language of sailors. They seemed to consider incorrect grammar to be the basis of this language and were telling the sailors excitedly, "You no fight, me fight!"

One of the sailors obligingly started to laugh, gesticulating in the air and snapping his fingers. Suddenly someone called out threateningly: "Kazik! Stasik!"

One behind the other the boys went over to their mother.

"How dare you without permission!"

"Mama," Stasik said in their defense, "if you could have seen—they had tattoos! And the stories they told!"

"We're coming up to the Corinthian Canal! Forty thousand workers died building it!" exclaimed Kazik, backing up his brother and putting on his most naive face.

"What canal?" asked his mother as a gesture of conciliation.

"The Corinthian Canal, Mama!"

The heavyset, red-faced captain came over and explained to them in broken French that they were, in fact, approaching the Corinthian Canal, one of the most splendid structures in Greece—*"enorme et gigantesque."* The whole isthmus had been dug up from one end to the other. The walls were almost vertical . . . a great many workers died . . . but the trip is now much shorter—a real boon for ship traffic!

The ladies outfitted themselves to watch as best they could. Verochka appeared from her cabin, looking pale. She had thrown a blanket around her shoulders and her nose bore the unmistakable traces of powder. The boys started running around the deck like lunatics, shouting, "The Corinthian Canal! the Corinthian Canal!" for the benefit of anyone who was not yet in the know. The Greek prince, who had once again assumed his statuesque pose, glanced ahead from time to time, smiling like the lord of the manor.

The ship began to run more quietly, as though its heart below decks had begun to beat more slowly. A narrow stone gate came into view, with a blue pinprick of light barely visible at the other end. The ship sailed into the passageway, bordered on either side by almost perpendicular stone walls. Down below, the water was calmer, darker and quieter, as if they had entered a backwater. The seagulls had disappeared. Above them shone a cloudless sky. Everyone grew quiet as they intently examined the perpendicular sides of the canal.

"Yikes, there's a person!" shouted Stasik suddenly.

Indeed, above them at a dizzying height a man was hanging on the wall like a fly and working with a hammer.

"He's holding on by means of special iron cleats," explained the captain, pointing to the man's feet. Along the sheer plane of the towering wall the passengers could see holes that looked like the burrows of some kind of animal. The worker had iron spikes on his feet that fit into these openings; he was wearing a leather belt attached to a chain that hung down from somewhere up above.

"A modern Prometheus," proclaimed Konstantin Mikhailovich.

"Excuse me, Captain, but isn't he in danger of falling off?" asked Verochka.

"Only if he unhooks the chain. But he won't do that."

Ever so quietly the ship sailed past the worker. Farther along, two more flies were hanging from the wall, repairing the stone ribs of the canal. As the minutes ticked by, the passageway grew as narrow behind them as it was in front of them. Now it seemed endless in both directions. Above them rose a bridge spanning the walls of the canal. Its airy silhouette seemed to rise and fall as they passed. A man standing on the bridge wished them well with a wave of his flag. On and on they sailed.

"Look!" Kazik's excited voice rang out suddenly. "There's another guy up there and he hasn't got a chain!"

Sure enough, in the distance a worker was clinging to the wall, his head cocked upwards. There was no chain holding him.

"He's moving. Look, look, he's about to fall off!" Kazik informed them, not without a certain relish. The captain smiled. The ladies watched. And suddenly something incomprehensible and utterly unacceptable happened: the worker, like a drop of water succumbing to gravity, came loose and fell toward the canal. The whole thing lasted barely a second. He fell without touching the wall. At first he flew headlong through the air, but as he fell his heavy cleats caused him to somersault until he was dropping feet-first.

"The cleats! Take off the cleats!" bellowed the captain in Greek. A half-second later the ladies began shouting, drowning out his voice with their shrieks.

"If it doesn't occur to him to get rid of all that iron he'll be killed for sure," said the captain thickly in French. To the sailors he added in Greek, "Lower the lifeboat!"

The latter had already set to work, without waiting for the captain's order. A dozen hands toiled in silence. It was torture to stand idly by and watch the ripples spread out along the murky surface where the man had sunk into the canal. Verochka, whose feelings were amplified by her own personal anguish, clapped her hands to her temples in horror. At the same time, Konstantin Mikhailovich was instantaneously assaulted by so many different thoughts and feelings that he couldn't register them all. Not one of them was clearly formed in his mind, not one was completely thought out, but in this confused flood of emotion, there seemed to Konstantin Mikhailovich to be only one possible meaning. Even before the lifeboat had been lowered, he suddenly tore off his coat and jacket, ran over to the side of the ship and threw one leg over the rail.

Here, my dear reader, you naturally expect that the hero of our story will save the worker, or will perish together with his beloved Verochka, or will, at the very least, choke down a few mouthfuls of the dark green water of the canal. But . . . that's just the thing—the reader is mistaken on all counts.

We left Konstantin Mikhailovich standing with one leg straddling the rail. What were the other members of our cast doing during this time? Elizaveta Pavlovna went on feeding the baby. She had seen the worker's plight and her husband's gesture, but knowing her own impotence she remained calm: she had to take care of her own affairs—she had to finish feeding the baby, so she closed her eyes and went on feeding him. As for Verochka, she instantly felt the weight of this monstrous calm—and it was her undoing. In the depths of her soul she experienced no particular horror; her love was no longer palpable, the way it had been that morning, when raw emotion had spoken in its place. Nothing could have prompted her to act so precipitously, had her imagination not been seized by that agitation peculiar to people who suddenly feel more ineffectual than they have ever felt before. She cried out weakly and, with a touch of theatricality, threw herself at Konstantin Mikhailovich and violently grabbed his shoulder.

She immediately realized she had made a mistake, causing her to cry out once more—this time with unfeigned despair.

"Don't worry"—the captain came over to them and pointed with his finger—"he managed to get rid of the iron cleats and he's already snuffling like a dog. There he is over there swimming—in a second they'll get him into the boat."

Konstantin Mikhailovich and Verochka stood together by the rail and looked at one another. They each felt as though they had eaten five rubles' worth at a restaurant when they only had a ruble in their pocket. This was the humiliating moment when they were asked to settle up. They had both overdrawn their accounts—in his case when he rushed over to the rail, in her case when she threw herself after him. The disingenuousness of their actions had demeaned them both. They rummaged around for a long time—in their hearts if not in their pockets—trying to find just a little more love, trying to scrape together the necessary change. But all emotion lay hidden, there was no trace of tenderness, and between them blew the cold wind that comes from not really knowing one another. When it came right down to it, what was he to her or she to him? When she had cried out, he had heard only someone alien and unknown.

But neither of them had the courage to admit these feelings. They continued to lie.

"Darling, were you afraid for me?"

"Oh, how could you do such a thing?"

This exchange sounded completely appropriate to the moment and situation. But this last extraneous expenditure finally and completely exhausted their cash supply, and their love—which that morning had seemed to be such an integral part of their being—was forced to declare bankruptcy. For her part, Verochka was already feeling awkward and out of place; as for Konstantin Mikhailovich, he felt drawn back to the calm Elizaveta Petrovna—and the whole drama began to seem oppressive.

With that my tale has come to an end. The packet boat sailed out of the Corinthian Canal and steamed ahead, carrying our heroes toward their distant homeland, to events both real and fabricated, to so-called world news. But when it comes right down to it, those events are not so far removed from the private little drama I've described here.

1919

Translated by Laura Goering and Gregory Blake Smith

Notes to the Essay

1. D. Shepherd, *Beyond Metafiction* (Oxford: Clarendon, 1992), 65.
2. M. Shaginian, "Mirovozzrenie i masterstvo (Avtobiografiia)," in *Sobranie sochinenii 1903–1933*, Vol. 1 (Moscow: Khudozhestvennaia literatura, 1935), 32.
3. M. Shaginian, "Avtobiografiia," in *Sem'ia Ul'ianovykh* (Moscow: Khudozhestvennaia literatura, 1959), 649.
4. Ibid.
5. M. Shaginian, *Chelovek i vremia* (Moscow: Khudozhestvennaia literatura, 1980), 252.
6. Ibid., 266.
7. Ibid., 269.
8. Ibid., 270.
9. Andrei Belyi, *Mezhdu dvukh revoliutsii*, 2d ed. (1934; Chicago: Russian Language Specialties, 1966), 264.
10. M. Shaginian, *Chelovek i vremia,* 306. Ten of Belyi's letters to Shaginian are reprinted in this volume (304–21).
11. Ibid., 270.
12. "Mirovozzrenie," 49.
13. V. L'vov-Rogachevskii, *Sovremennik* 10 (1913): 297.
14. K. Kova, *Zhatva* 4 (1913): 353.
15. Vladimir Narbut, *Vestnik Evropy* 8 (1913): 355.
16. "O sovremennom lirizme," *Apollon* 3 (1909): 19–21.
17. L'vov-Rogachevskii, 297.
18. "Mirovozzrenie," 53.
19. "Avtobiografiia," 658.
20. They eventually became friends and Rachmaninov later turned to Shaginian to help him find suitable texts for his romances.

21. "Avtobiografiia," 652.

22. "Mirovozzrenie," 50.

23. M. Shaginian, "S.V. Rachmaninov," *Trudy i dni* 4–5 (1912): 114.

24. *Chelovek i vremia,* 320.

25. Psychoanalysis in Russia dates to 1909–1910. See Martin A. Miller, "The Origins and Development of Russian Psychoanalysis, 1909–1930," *American Academy of Psychoanalysis* 14, 1 (1986): 125–35.

26. *Sobranie sochinenii*, Vol. 2 (1935), 69.

27. V. Ermilov points out in his introduction that for Shaginian this idea grew out of her "Goethean passions." In his conversations with Eckermann, Goethe is quoted as saying: "We are not made free by failing to recognize anything above us, but rather by being able to respect that which stands above us." Shaginian, *Sobranie sochinenii,* Vol. 2 (1903), 23. Shaginian expounds on similar themes in *Journey to Weimar*.

28. *Sobranie sochinenii* Vol. 2. (1903–1933) 270.

29. M. Shaginian, *Sobranie sochinenii v deviati tomakh*, Vol. 2 (Moscow: Khudozhestvennaia literatura, 1986–1989), 286.

30. I.S. Zil'bershtein, "Blok i Marietta Shaginian," *Literaturnoe nasledstvo* 92, 4 (1987): 753–54. Again, Shaginian writes with characteristic lack of restraint to a person she does not know. Before this letter they had corresponded only in reference to her work on a translation of Wagner's Ring cycle, which Blok was editing. After Blok's death, Shaginian insisted on reading the Gospel over Blok's body. See *Chelovek i vremia,* 655–61.

31. Zil'bershtein, "Blok i Marietta Shaginian," 754.

32. M. Shaginian, "Pisateli o sebe," *Krasnaia panorama,* 26 October 1926, 13.

33. "Mirovozzrenie," 70.

34. *Sobranie sochinenii v deviati tomakh,* Vol. 2, 494.

35. As David Shepherd points out, the juxtaposition of L'vov's account with the supposedly erroneous accounts raises interesting theoretical questions about the depiction of "facts" in a literary text. *Beyond Metafiction* (Oxford: Clarendon, 1992), 64–89.

36. V. Rossolovskaia, "Stroiteli *Gidrotsentrali*," *Krasnaia nov'* 12 (1931): 142.

37. M. Shaginian, "Diskussiia o iazyke," *Literaturnaia gazeta,* 18 April 1934, 2.

38. *Literaturnaia gazeta,* 29 February 1936, 1.

39. M. Livshits, "Dnevnik Marietty Shaginian," *Novyi mir* 2 (1954): 206–31.

40. Cf. *Literaturnaia gazeta,* 15 June 1954; 1 July 1954; 17 August 1954.

41. *Chelovek i vremia,* 249.

42. Livshits, "Dnevnik," 207.

43. From *Diary of a Writer*. Quoted in Livshits, 224. Shaginian makes the same point in her 1933 autobiography: "[P]remature generalization, schematism were my main sins." "Mirovozzrenie," 55.

44. M. Shaginian, *Novyi zhurnal* 171 (1988): 172.

45. *Sobranie sochinenii 1903–1933*, Vol. 1, 454.

46. Zil'bershtein, "Blok i Marietta Shaginian," 753.

47. V. Khodasevich, "Marietta Shaginian," *Dni,* 4 October 1925, 3.

48. Ibid.

Translator's Note to the Selected Work

1. In a footnote in her 1935 *Collected Works* (*Sobranie sochinenii*), Shaginian writes that this story was an attempt to explore the problem of the February Revolution of 1917 "'metaphysically,' on that high level of abstraction where politics disappears and the moral meaning of what has happened is revealed" (1: 455, 457).

Bibliography

Primary Works

Pervye vstrechi. Moscow: Privately published, 1909.

Orientalia. Moscow: Al'tsiona, 1912.

Dve morali. Moscow: Al'tsiona, 1914.

Uzkie vrata. St. Petersburg: M.I. Semenov, 1914.

Kapriz millionera. Moscow: Universal'naia biblioteka 1155, 1916.

Sem' razgovorov. St. Petersburg: M.I. Semenov, 1916.

Zolushka (Kinopovest'). *Taina dobrodeteli*. Moscow: Universal'naia biblioteka 1172, 1916. 2d ed. Moscow, 1918.

Povest' o dvukh sestrakh i o volshebnoi strane Mertse. Rostov na Donu: Detskii mir, 1919.

Strannye rasskazy. Rostov na Donu: Aralezy, 1919.

Puteshestvie v Veimar. Moscow: Gosudarstvennoe izdatel'stvo, 1923.

Lori Len, metallist. Moscow: Gosudarstvennoe izdatel'stvo, 1925.

"Pisateli o sebe. Marietta Shaginian." *Krasnaia panorama,* 26 October 1926, 13.

Dnevniki 1917–1934. Leningrad: Izdatel'stvo pisatelei v Leningrade, 1932.

Sobranie sochinenii 1903–1933. 4 vols. Moscow: Khudozhestvennaia literatura, 1935.

Sem'ia Ul'ianovykh. Moscow: Khudozhestvennaia literatura, 1959.

Chelovek i vremia. Moscow: Khudozhestvennaia literatura, 1980.

Stoletie lezhit na ladoni. Ocherki i stat'i poslednikh let. Moscow: Sovremennik, 1981.

Sobranie sochinenii v deviati tomakh. 9 vols. Moscow: Khudozhestvennaia literatura, 1986–1989.

In Translation

"Three Looms." *Azure Cities: Stories of New Russia*. Trans. J.J. Robbins. Ed. Joshua Kunitz. New York: International, 1929. 271–78.

"Autobiography." *Soviet Life* 3 (1933): 134.

"Tanya." *Soviet Life* 6 (1934): 29–42.

Journey through Soviet Armenia. Moscow: Foreign Language Publishing House, 1954.

The Ulyanov Family [chapters from the novel]. *Soviet Life* 4 (1964): 8–21.

"My Work on *The Ulyanov Family*." *Soviet Life* 4 (1966): 152–58.

"Man and Time" [excerpts]. Trans. Helen Tate. *Soviet Life* 9 (1980): 33–107.

Mess Mend—The Yankees in Petrograd. Trans. S.D. Cioran. Ann Arbor, MI: Ardis, 1987; 2d ed. 1991.

"Seeing in the Twentieth Century." *Always a Woman*. Trans. J.C. Batler. Moscow: Raduga, 1987. 398–407.

Secondary Works

Davies, Mildred. "Marietta Shaginian." *Dictionary of Russian Women Writers*. Ed. M. Ledkovsky, C. Rosenthal, and M. Zirin. Westport, CT: Greenwood Press, 1994. 568–71.

Goering, Laura. "'Der Mensch muß wieder ruiniert werden': Marietta Shaginian's *Journey to Weimar*." *Germano-Slavica* 7.2–8.3 (1992–1993): 67–81.

Kovalev, V. A., ed. *Tvorchestvo Marietty Shaginian. Sbornik statei*. Leningrad: Khudozhestvennaia literatura, Leningradskoe otdelenie, 1980.

Margarian, A. *Marietta Shaginian. Tvorcheskii put'*. Erevan: Armianskoe gosudarstvennoe izdatel'stvo, 1956.

Shepherd, David. *Beyond Metafiction: Self-Consciousness in Soviet Literature*. Oxford: Clarendon, 1992.

———. "Canon Fodder? Problems in the Reading of a Soviet Production Novel." *Discontinuous Discourses in Modern Russian Literature*. Ed. C. Kelly et al. New York: St. Martin's Press, 1989.

Skorino, L. *Marietta Shaginian—khudozhnik. Zhizn' i tvorchestvo*. Moscow: Sovetskii pisatel', 1975. 2d ed. 1981.

Zil'bershtein, I.S. "Blok i Marietta Shaginian." *Literaturnoe nasledstvo* 92, 4 (1987): 751–56.

Gertruda Vakar

Gertruda Vakar (1904–1973).
Courtesy of Catherine V. Chvany.

Gertruda Pavlovna Vakar's (1904–1973) poetic legacy consists of one small posthumous book containing forty-five pieces written between 1958 and 1973, of which twenty-four originally appeared in the New York Russian language daily *New Russian Word* (*Novoe russkoe slovo*) in 1966–1973. The book itself, with a biographical essay by Paul Friedrich, was reprinted from the archival section of the *Russian Language Journal* as *Poems* (*Stikhotvoreniia*) in 1984. As reviewer Nicholas Lee put it, "Biographer and editors give pride of place to Vakar's consummate craftsmanship, then gradually reveal the woman beneath the wizard of words." The unobtrusive thematic divisions are explained by the editors in the

Russian language endnotes. Catherine V. Chvany and Sophia Lubensky stress the complex attitudes in the poetry, overriding conventional ideas of chronological development.

Gertruda (née Clafton) Vakar was born in Revel (now Tallinn, Estonia) and brought up in Arkhangel'sk, Russia, in a community of business- and tradespeople of English, German, Scandinavian, Dutch, Belgian and French Huguenot origin dating back over two centuries. Being Protestant, these communities were never fully assimilated to Orthodox Russia, and some of the families retained their original citizenship for several generations. The families spoke German or English at home; the children spoke Russian with servants and at school. After the treaty of Brest-Litovsk, the Clafton family, along with other British citizens, was removed to England by a British ship. After a year in a Swedish school, Gertruda rejoined her parents and four younger sisters in London and then moved to Paris as a scholarship student in the Russian Gymnasium in Paris, from which she graduated with perfect grades in 1923. She had grown up speaking four languages, with native-speaker intuitions in both Russian and English. Although she spoke English with a heavy Russian accent, her choice of words in either language was impeccable—as Friedrich put it, she spoke English "with no semantic accent." After a period of further courses and employment in London, she married former Russian cavalry officer Nicholai Platonovich Vakar, a widower on the staff of the Paris Russian daily *Latest News* (*Poslednie novosti*), and returned to live in Paris in 1926, bringing up two daughters bilingual in Russian and French. She worked most of her life as a part-time free-lance translator. During the 1930s, she translated thirty-seven mystery and adventure novels from English or French into Russian for serialization in *Latest News*—among them, Rafael Sabatini's *Captain Blood*, renamed a more romantic *Fregat Arabella*. Since French law forbade wives of employed foreigners to work for pay but did not preclude moonlighting by their husbands, these translations were credited to Nicholai P. Vakar, a member of the paper's regular editorial staff. Poetry, including experiments in verse translation, remained a secret hobby until the late 1950s. When the German occupation closed down the newspaper, a series of fortunate accidents enabled the Vakars to emigrate to the United States, where they had to start over in 1941, at first with a hand-to-mouth existence combining menial labor with occasional academic tasks. From a well-known political writer in Russian and French, N.P. Vakar became a struggling Harvard graduate student and part-time teacher, with Gertruda's constant help in matters of English language and style; he also provided the family's housing by serving as housekeeper-manager of an absent owner's crumbling mansion. In later years, N.P. Vakar moved on to a new career as a history professor and scholar, first at Wheaton College in Massachusetts, then at Ohio State University, while Gertruda contributed to the Vakars' security in retirement by judicious purchase and management of two or three small rental properties. The couple's final years were spent happily in Sarasota, Florida, where Nicholai died on 18 July 1970 of complications following surgery. Gertruda continued to work by correspondence as a translator and poet until her death on 3 December 1973 from a cerebral hemorrhage. Two of the books she translated appeared within weeks after her death.

A first section of *Poems*, labeled "The Poet Plays a Game with Language, and the Language Plays with the Poet," contains eight virtually untranslatable poems, beginning with her favorite, "Echo," an elaborate play of sounds and Russian-French-American associations in a dialogue between a male persona's stream of consciousness and his more grounded sister driving the pair to their mother's funeral in Ohio. An original device in this poem is a repetition of part of a word; sometimes the result is another word (*Upriamo, priamo pravish' ty avto* ["Stubbornly, straight ahead, you drive the car"]), but elsewhere the result is simply syllables that spin off associations based entirely on their sound shapes (*doroga*, *-roga*; *derev'ia -rev'ia*; respectively, "road" and "trees"). The nearest thing to it occurs in French children's songs: *Un morceau de pain d'épices, -pices, -pices* or *Très difficile, -cile, -cile,* although it is unlikely that Vakar, who was deaf, was familiar with such songs. Other poems contain elaborate puns, including plays on grammatical gender. "A Minor Event" ("Melkoe proisshestvie") retells a newspaper clip about a murder in rhyming lines consisting entirely of pairs or triplets of synonyms. "Days of our life" ("Dni nashei zhizni"), a poem consisting entirely of one-noun sentences, takes a male persona from the morning alarm to bedtime; the words are Russian, but the lifestyle is émigré, the term for TV is *TiVi* rather than the Soviet Russian *televizor*. Translated here is "About My Early Verses" ("O predydushchikh stikhakh"), which gives us a glimpse of the creative process.

Next is a group of literary reminiscences and humorous poems. "Anglo-Russian World" ("Anglo-russkaia byl'") presents the bicultural mix of her childhood, where European literary folklore blends with the stories and fortune-telling of the kitchen maids; the playful "Victim of Unfairness" ("Zhertva nespravedlivosti") calls for the rehabilitation of the Queen of Spades' ominous reputation among card readers and in literature. "Ancient Novels" ("Starinnye romany") sketches the once enthralling, now no longer frightening, clichés of gothic narratives; it is translated below as "Gothic Novels." In this group and in a smaller set of poems on aging, humor shades into wry irony and then tragedy.

The theme of loss, widowhood and approaching old age is represented by seven poems, two of which are included here: "Winter" ("Zima") on her own widowhood, and "In the Cathedral" ("Kennedy-King-Kennedy"), which shares in the grief of Coretta King and Jacqueline and Ethel Kennedy. Vakar wrote of it: "This poem began singing in my head as we watched the King funeral [in 1968] and saw Mrs. King's photos in magazines, but this soon merged with the JFK funeral, and toward the end I thought rather of Jacqueline. Bobby ['s assassination] had not happened yet." The last line, "So sviat**ymi u**pokoi" ("With the Saints give [him] rest") was "to be dragged out," especially the syllables shown here in boldface. Critic-friends objected, suggesting adding an overt *ego* (him) to fill in the line (*So sviatymi ego upokoi*), but she felt "that *ego* would simply RUIN the last line for me! Tra-ta-ta . . . without it, it is solemn, exactly as in the Russian funeral service." Actually, the rhythm she suggests is not exactly that (*so-svia-**ty-y**-mi-u-po-**ko-o**-oi* is closer to the tune chanted in the Russian service); but authenticity is hardly relevant here, since the actual funerals were separate and none, of course, as Russian Orthodox. What she was after was the solemnity and the association.

As is customary for even modern Russian poetry, nearly all of Vakar's poems are rhymed. Several are notable for experiments with rhythm and meter, breaks in midphrase, even in midword, as illustrated above in "Echo." The last poem of this group, "How ill at ease I feel in my ancient body" ("Kak neuiutno mne v moem starinnom tele"), is in iambic pentameters alternating freely in two stanzas, ten and five lines. The rhyme scheme is among her most varied: aaBBaCCddCEEffE. This poem is reproduced below in an unrhymed free translation by John Greer Nicholson.

These poems, all published in *New Russian Word*, are followed by the previously unpublished "Paintings by N.P.V." ("Kartiny N.P.V."), a series of delightful word sketches of the paintings of Vakar's husband, a talented amateur painter whose style might be characterized as primitive-surrealist. Several of the paintings, including a haunting portrait of Dame Edith Sitwell, were stolen in a burglary of the Vakars' home in Columbus, Ohio, although color photographs survive in family archives. The rest of the poetry collection contains twenty items recast from other languages, mainly from English and a few from French, only two of which were published in her lifetime. Vakar's choices of poems to translate or adapt reflect what Paul Friedrich, in his introduction to the book, calls her "eccentricity." Some continue the humorous play on literary-cultural traditions found in some of her original poems, such as renditions of the anonymous "O Night, O jealous Night, repugnant to my measures!" and "When the Duke of Leeds shall have made his choice" (of an appropriately grateful bride). Other choices seem to have been motivated by formal experimentation. The French-based imitations include a sixteenth-century Easter hymn (for which the editors could not find an original) and three by Baudelaire: "Recueillement" ("Sois sage, ô ma Douleur, et tiens-toi plus tranquille"), "Viens sur mon coeur, âme cruelle et sourde" and "La Mort des amants" from *Les fleurs du mal*. Both Nicholas Lee and Paul Friedrich characterize Vakar as a chronicler of "the seven ages of woman," themes that bridge the groupings by editors Chvany and Lubensky. At the same time, the progression of original and translated poems reflects the several sudden changes of cultural-linguistic milieu of Vakar's biography—the British-Russian of her Arkhangel'sk childhood, the Franco-Russian culture of her youth, the American-Russian culture of her middle and later years.

Poems grouped by the editors as "Americana-into-Russian" and "Translations and Imitations of American Poets" may eventually turn out to be of greatest interest to readers who can appreciate the Russian. These include a long rhymed piece on the energy crisis, inspired by a humorous editorial from the *Boston Globe,* and one poem each by Robinson Jeffers ("I believe this hurt will be healed"), Stanley Kunitz ("God banish from your house / The fly, the roach, the mouse") and John Updike ("B.W.I.," translated as "Britanskaia koloniia"). Other adaptations of originals clipped from magazines or Sunday supplements include the charming nonsense poem by Ben King, "The Pessimist" ("Nothing to do but work, / Nothing to eat but food"—translated as "Delat' nechego, krome raboty. / Krome pishchi, nechego est'"), and the anonymous "Just doin' nuthin'" ("I wisht I was a little rock"), translated as "Geroi truda" ("Hero of Labor"), whose Russian title is a play on her name—Ger-truda, and on the Soviet penchant for creating jargon by compounding truncated syllables into new words. The irony of placing such a title on a poem glorifying idleness caused some indignation among Soviet Ministry officials when it was included in a presentation by Vakar's daughter, Catherine V. Chvany, at a 1982 conference in Prague devoted to the teaching of the Russian language—being called a Hero of [Socialist] Labor was then much too serious a political matter to admit such levity. Like the "Kennedy-King-Kennedy" poem, "Hero of Labor" experiments with rhythm; its last line iconically reinforces the poem's celebration of idleness with a single dragged-out word meaning "[I'd] relax": *ot—dy—**khal***.

Among anglophone women represented in translations and free imitations are Phyllis McGinley in "Journey toward Evening" (Fifty, not having expected to arrive here"); Babette Deutsch ("Shapely as violins, the pears" from "At the Greengrocer's" and part of "Damnation"); and Mary Coleridge ("Some hang above the tombs"), where the theme of loss resurfaces. It does so again in the free translation of Thomas Hardy's "The Phantom Horsewoman" ("Queer are the ways of a man I know") and in the renderings of an excerpt from Sidney Dobell's "Return!"; of Robert Louis Stevenson's "Blows the wind today," translated as "Toska po Shotlandii" ("Longing for Scotland"); and of Robert Bridges's "Long are the hours the sun is above." The published book contains only those poems Vakar had marked as completed; her archive (deposited in the Bakhmeteff Collection, Columbia University) contains at least as many more translations that appear to be complete but which she may have planned to revise.

The perceptive biographical essay by Paul Friedrich that introduces the collection mentions as an important aspect of her poetic profile the "hidden explosive force expressing the unrealized potentials" of Gertrude Vakar's life. A bout of measles in her teens had led to a gradual loss of hearing and a sense of relative isolation until the late 1950s, when a new surgical procedure finally reopened the world of sound to her. Starting with a 1950 translation project at Harvard's Russian Research Center, she became a sought-after translator from Russian into English and remains better known as a translator than as a poet. In 1958 she began to publish her poems in the New York newspaper *Novoe russkoe slovo.* Throughout her life she remained a woman of her generation, accepting—even at times insisting on—her proper place in the shadow of a better-known husband, expressing only the faintest irritation at a letter from *Novyi zhurnal* editor Roman Gul', who rejected the brilliant "Echo," saying in effect that he was "too overloaded by submissions from professionals" to be bothered with an (amateur) lady poet.

During the Soviet regime, Arkhangel'sk had been a closed city, but in the 1980s, contact was reestablished as it became a sister-city to Portland, Maine. Visitors are now welcome and archives are open for the study of the city's ancient Protestant communities. The city has welcomed information about poets and artists who seemed to disappear without a trace after 1917 and are now found to have flourished in distant countries. There has been some interest in Vakar's *oeuvre*, with broadcasts over cable TV, including readings of poems on the Moscow program "Èkho Moskvy."

Catherine V. Chvany

About My Early Verses[1]

For their deceptiveness, for some ten years,
They lay banished in desk drawers.
For isn't a poet supposed to speak the truth,
Even if the sounds suggest the opposite?
It happens sometimes that a verse-maker, poet, bard,
Will sacrifice experience for the sake of sound.

In Fall, for instance, fruits and harvests
Make the Spring's promises come true,
Yet now a verse up and writes itself:
"The Autumnal betrayal of Spring,"
It seems to insist on rights of free speech,
Militantly resisting change or deletion.
What can one do but let it have its way,
To let it sing, even if it sings out of tune,
Bearing witness to the power of the word.

1971

Gothic Novels[2]

Creatures of fear and sin,
Specters wander by.
And a hidden victim's blood
Trickles down the stairs.
The closet hides a skeleton,
The wall, a rival sealed alive.
In the cellar, another
Has spent ten years in chains.
The wine is poisoned. A mute
Servant is loyal to the grave;
It's he who poured the fateful drink
For the dinner guest.
Midnight strikes. A pallid Count
Hastens to a rendez-vous,
His nails and fangs honed in advance.
The owl hoots, thunder claps—
Omens of disaster.
A dreadful fate awaits
An innocent gentle lady.
In a black carriage, at top speed,
Her lover races through the woods. . . .

How such tales enthralled our elders,
How interesting it all was!

Where are they now—
Those vampires, castles, dungeons?
To the young they're boring or silly,
And nobody is scared.

1968

In the Cathedral

(Kennedy-King-Kennedy)[3]

Famous persons are crowded inside,
Packed in rows among columns of white.
They've come to pray and say goodbye,
They've gathered for final respects.

This is a public day of mourning
And official burial rites. A woman's profile
Behind a veil's mist, bends in grief,
Yielding to personal sorrow.

Widow's thoughts behind the veil's mist:
When was it?—my bridegroom, the altar . . .
That they'd part us, we knew it, we knew it.
"Grant him—rest—with—the—Saints."

1969

Winter[4]

Again a blessed warm winter,
Florida rests from summer storms.
The gulf like silver, like silver the moon.
Night-blooming jasmine grows fragrant.
The whispering palms bow quietly,
And quietly the warm surf breaks. . . .

While there, up north,
There in a frozen grave
Under a naked tree,
Lies my love.

And he, perhaps, is now recalling
The recent past when we were here together.
How good it was, how beautiful
Year after year is the Florida winter . . .
How quietly the whispering palms bow,
How near the warm surf comes,
Where nature rests from the heat,
The jasmine grows fragrant at night,
And where our home still stands . . .
No, he remembers nothing.

1971

Translated by Catherine V. Chvany

Ill at Ease[5]

I'm ill at ease in my old-fashioned body.
The wires are loose, the springs have rusted.
The mechanism's there, my chest still holds the motor,
That former seat of anger and of love,
At times it madly thumps, at others barely ticks.
And one main screw up in my head
Occasionally seems not entirely . . .
It lags in proper and precise fulfillment
Of its accustomed and appointed task,
And twirls around as if in emptiness . . .

Or back in ancient times. An earlier dawn arises,
Forgotten time, forgotten country,
Ever more distant themes and pictures . . .

I am a gramophone with the record cracked,
And the needle's stuck . . . atuck . . . atuck . . .

1973

Translated by John Greer Nicholson,
November 26, 1984, used by permission.

Translator's Notes to the Selected Works

1. This poem appeared as "O predydushchikh stikhakh" in *Novoe russkoe slovo,* 16 May 1971. The original's rhyme scheme is AbAbCdCdEfEfEf. The words in the willful spontaneous line transform combinations of /e/ with /s/ and the nasals /n/ or /m/; stressed syllables are in boldface: *Ves**ny** osen**na**ja iz**me**na.*

2. This poem, "Starinnye romany," appeared in *Novoe russkoe slovo*, 13 August 1968, under the title "Krug chteniia" ("Cycle of Reading").

3. This poem "V sobore (Kennedy-King-Kennedy)" appeared in *Novoe russkoe slovo*, 27 April 1969. The last line, *So svia**tymi** **u**pokoi* (lit., "With the saints give rest"), from the Russian Orthodox funeral chant, was, according to Vakar, "to be dragged out," especially the syllables shown here in boldface.

4. This poem, "Zima," appeared in *Novoe russkoe slovo*, 23 May 1971.

5. This poem, "Kak neuiutno mne v moem starinnom tele," the author's last, appeared in *Novoe russkoe slovo*, 26 August 1973.

Bibliography

Primary Works

Stikhotvoreniia. Ed. Catherine V. Chvany and Sophia Lubensky. Intro. by Paul Friedrich. *Russian Language Journal* 38, 129/130 (1984): 219–70.

In Translation

[Poems]. Trans. Viacheslav Zavalishin. *Early Soviet Writers.* New York: Praeger, 1958.

[Poems]. Trans. Lev. Semyonovich Vygotsky. *Thought and Language* [original title: *Myshlenie i rech'*]. Ed. Eugenia Hanfmann. Cambridge: MIT Press, 1962.

[Poems]. *Russian Intellectual History.* Ed. Marc Raeff. New York: Harcourt Brace, 1966.

[Poems]. Trans. Solomon M. Schwarz. *The Russian Revolution of 1905*. Chicago: University of Chicago Press, 1967.

[Poems]. Trans. Leopold H. Haimson. *The Mensheviks.* Chicago: University of Chicago Press, 1973.

[Poems]. Trans. Prince Eugene N. Trubetskoi. *Theology in Color* [original title: *Umozrenie v kraskakh*]. Intro. George M.A. Hanfmann. Crestwood, NY: St. Vladimir's Seminary Press, 1973.

Secondary Works

Lee, Nicholas. "A Contribution to Émigré Literature: The Life and Work of Gertrude Clafton Vakar." *New Studies in Russian Language and Literature*. Ed. Anna Lisa Crone and Catherine V. Chvany. Columbus, OH: Slavica, 1987. 208–20.

———. "Gertruda Vakar. Stikhotvoreniia. Pod red. E.V. Chvani i S. Lubenskoj. Biog. ocherk Pavla Fridrikha." *Slavic and East European Journal* 29 (1985): 352–53.

Margarita Aliger

Margarita Iosifovna Aliger, poet, essayist and translator, was born on 3 September 1915 to a poor, pro-revolutionary, assimilated Jewish family in Odessa. Both parents cultivated in Aliger a deep appreciation for the Russian classics. She began writing verses at the age of eight. Her poems were first published in 1933 in the magazine *Ogonek*. Although originally trained in chemistry, after some trepidation she chose writing as her profession, attending the Gorky Literary Institute from 1934 to 1937. It was there that she joined the Komsomol and formed many lasting friendships and attachments with members of the Soviet literary elite. Beginning in 1933, her poetry appeared regularly in *The Banner* (*Znamia*) and other publications. From 1938 to 1970 she published sixteen volumes of poetry and dramatic works. Although several editions of Aliger's collected poetry were published after 1970, she has since turned increasingly to translating the work of other poets and writing memoirs. She also published a prose travelogue, *Return to Chile* (*Vozvrashchenie v Chili*, 1974), as well as several reviews and critical articles. Her work falls into two distinct phases: 1933–1970 and 1970–present.

The prewar years marked the beginning of Aliger's first, most prolific literary period, arguably, the most meaningful time in her life. Her earliest work from this era reflects her maturation under the Soviet system. It is filled with enthusiasm for the first five-year plans, the courage of Soviet citizens at the front and in the rear and praise for the government. Aliger also began to explore and develop the character of her signature synthetic Soviet hero, the anonymous superachiever who has suffered, prevailed and finally become a role model for all. This process culminated in two of her best-known wartime works, *Zoia* (1942), an epic poem, and *A Tale of Truth* (*Skazka o pravde*, 1945), its dramatization. The heroine of both works is a young partisan, Zoia Kosmodem'ianskaia, who is captured by the Germans while on a reconnaissance mission. Even under torture, she heroically refuses to disclose the whereabouts of her fellow partisans, for which she is executed while declaring that she is dying for Stalin. In 1943 Aliger won a USSR State Prize for this emotional, dramatic and extremely popular poem.

Indeed, much of Aliger's early poetry is written in a style similar to that of *Zoia*. It is direct, descriptive and emotionally appealing, almost completely devoid of metaphors and abstractions. Such a simplistic approach, free of literary devices, appeals to the broadest possible audience. Aliger remarks of *Zoia* that she "managed [in this poem] to touch upon something universal."[1] During this early period, poetry was for Aliger primarily a means of lyrically expressing her enthusiasm for her country, its people and their accomplishments.

Aliger's early poetry is characterized by specific, fundamental themes that also pervade her later work: the emergence of the idealized or "synthetic" Soviet hero, the performance of heroic deeds and the attainment of happiness and fulfillment through suffering. The "synthetic" Soviet hero, whose deeds are a lesson and example to all those who follow, is usually anonymous (e.g., the protagonists of the poems "The Most Important Thing" and "Romance"), but he characteristically suffers and achieves the near-impossible.

With rare exceptions, these heroes are almost always male. In her early work, Aliger seemed to ignore women or preferred to restrict them to more traditional roles as wives and mothers. A poem from 1948, "The Fisherman's Home," exemplifies this viewpoint. The wife, awaiting her husband,

> looks at the distant seas,
> as if upon a golden field;
> as another does
> upon factory gates
> awaiting shift change;
> as a pilot's wife does
> at the clouds
> on a regular flying day.[2]

For all Aliger's own experiences as a single parent and war correspondent, it is interesting that in this poem women are not themselves the factory workers or pilots (as many women in fact were at that time), but simply wives awaiting their husbands' return home.

Notable exceptions to Aliger's early preference for male heroes appear in "The Winter of This Year" ("Zima ètogo goda," 1938), a semi-autobiographical poem about a mother who bravely suffers the death of one of her children, and also in *Zoia* and its dramatization, *A Tale of Truth*. However, these poems are not entirely free of traditional perceptions and emotions toward women. Indeed, Aliger herself notes that while writing these last two works, her feelings toward the heroine became "almost maternal."

Closely tied to the ideal Soviet hero/heroine is the theme of heroic accomplishments including stock Soviet examples such as overfulfilling the norm, taming nature and the elements, and World War II. This last is so important in all Aliger's work, both prose and poetry, that it will be discussed separately.

The achievement of happiness and fulfillment by sharing others' suffering, making personal sacrifices and overcoming difficulties is a theme often praised by Aliger's Soviet critics. Such trials mold and temper her literary heroes. Participating in the war was one way to attain this happiness and fulfillment, "a treatment for everything," as Aliger remarks in her memoirs. War inspires people to perform heroic deeds, as in *Zoia* and *A Tale of Truth*. Even Aliger's otherwise traditional female characters take on a heroic aura. They may lose their children, husbands or fathers to the war, but still they persevere, bravely attending to the needs of both family and country. World War II was for Aliger one of the most important periods in her life: "I'm fortunate that in my life I have many interesting things to remember, but the war years—all the encounters, all the personal relationships—are especially dear; one especially wants to remember them."[3] In an interview with Elaine Feinstein, Aliger said of World War II: "It was the time when all our people were together, and knew that they were fighting an enemy *outside* that was evil."[4] However, Aliger acknowledged in her memoirs that later generations might not find the war experience as meaningful and might not even understand it at all: "Now it's simply impossible to understand why [she was so happy during the war years], since there decidedly wasn't anything to be happy about. . . . What was there to be happy about? . . . Probably simply because we were young, and further because only by being happy could we survive all that we had to."[5]

In spite of Aliger's tacit recognition of the younger generation's lack of empathy, occasional notes of bitterness toward it surface in her poetry:

> And you won't read my poems,
> And if you read them, you don't believe them,
> brushing them aside:
> —Again! We're sick of them!
> We're different,
> everything's different for us,

> it's all new,
> it's all different,
> And she, [wrote] probably from jealousy. . . .[6]

Aliger feels that younger people increasingly consider her and her contemporaries collectively responsible for all the misdeeds of the war years. She states that since they "cannot understand the thirties, they blame a whole generation for Stalin's crimes."[7]

Perhaps Aliger's awareness of shifting generational perspectives and values caused the noticeable shift toward the personal in her poetry of the late 1960s. She also turned increasingly to prose writing in the form of essays and memoirs (*A Path in the Rye* [*Tropinka vo rzhi*, 1980], and *Encounters and Departures* [*Vstrechi i razluki*, 1989]). The themes of her earlier work, although still present, were deemphasized in favor of a more personal, nostalgic approach.

Guilt, shame, pain, regret and loss comprise the major motifs of Aliger's later work. She was haunted by these emotions not necessarily because of what occurred during the war, but because of what she perceived as left undone or not done properly. Both her poetry and prose are permeated with these feelings, which underlie two of her most poignant essays—one about Mayakovsky and the other about Akhmatova.

In the essay about Mayakovsky, Aliger relates how as a fifth-grade student she wanted to hear him read his poetry when the poet visited her town but couldn't scrape up the necessary money:

> My mother, poor thing, didn't understand how much wiser it would have been to feed me only bread for a few days—but just let me have a ruble for a ticket. To this day I remember the sensation of grief, injury and desperation. To this day I can't forgive myself—why didn't I steal that ruble, or run to one of my teachers—they would've understood and come to my aid—why didn't I do something crazy just to make it to that reading?
>
> "You'll still have time," they told me, "you'll still hear Mayakovsky." And that made sense—I was only in the fifth grade, and it seemed like everything was still ahead.
>
> Who could know that two years later, a neighbor would knock at our door and say in a disgustingly indifferent voice: "Your Mayakovsky shot himself."
>
> "That can't be! That's not true!" I cried in answer.

"It's in the newspapers," she smirked.
And everything was over, and I'd never get to hear
Mayakovsky.[8]

In Aliger's thought-provoking essay about her long relationship with Anna Akhmatova, she regrets not having done something to prevent Marina Tsvetaeva's suicide:

> [If I had known Tsevtaeva was nearby, I could have found her and] told her something to help her believe, slow down, wait, hope . . . would it have been possible? I think so, yes. I think it's always possible. I think we've had many chances, although we ourselves don't know about them, to help someone through an awful moment.[9]

Aliger's sentiments about Tsvetaeva are further developed in the poem "House in Meudon." She implies that while a sense of abandonment may have led the poet to commit suicide, someone, or anyone, was morally obliged to find her and stop her. This feeling of neglected responsibility is summarized in Aliger's rhetorical question, "Who is guilty? Guilty of what?"

The theme of guilt is found throughout Aliger's later work. For example, she often expresses guilt about mistakes she believes she has made, although not without irony. Once she mentioned an unpublished article critical of Akhmatova, where she notes, "What luck it was never published" and "How ashamed I would be to read it now." She frequently refers to an uneasy conscience, as in the poems "A Strange Room," "The Sweet Tragedies of Shakespeare" and "For transgressions such as these."

Regret is another theme often encountered in Aliger's later work. Chief among her regrets is that she did not write down what Akhmatova said during their many conversations. In her last essay about Akhmatova, she shares the following thoughts, believing she has made a mistake:

> Always fully understanding how precious my relationship with Akhmatova was, how many people would someday envy me because I had that opportunity and that a time would come when I would certainly want to share this relationship with them, I, however, never wrote down anything she said, none of the conversations I had with her. . . . More than anything, it was out of a complex, superstitious feeling—I wanted so much not to let myself think

> about her inevitable end. And this fateful inevitability is for those who remain alive almost unnatural, like any irreparability, any irreversibility. . . .
>
> I shouldn't have given in to that superstitious feeling—how much I regret that now. And now nothing can be fixed, nothing can be asked about. I shouldn't have been embarrassed, I shouldn't have put it off.[10]

Parting and loss is the major theme of her generation, Aliger noted. In a review of "Path in the Rye," Metter states that "[Aliger] has thoroughly learned the science of parting, the most bitter of all the sciences."[11] Perhaps she best expressed this sentiment in the poem "Music," an elegy to her deceased husband. It also frequently appears in her romantic verses, such as "I was too happy" and "We forgive again and say farewell again." Many of these later poems explore her long, turbulent relationship with the famous novelist Aleksandr Fadeev. Parting and loss is also a central theme of poems in which she eulogizes friends' deaths, such as those of Konstantin Simonov in "28 August 1979" and Konstantin Paustovskii in "17 July 1968."

In spite of Aliger's later preoccupation with so-called negative themes, the reader is nonetheless left with the impression that the author is a strong woman, a survivor who expects no sympathy for herself—she is someone who is responsible for her own actions; one who is alone, but not lonely; one who has emotions, but is in control of herself. She broods, but never languishes.

Despite the fact that both the first and second periods of Aliger's work contain poems noteworthy for their terse, tight economy of emotional expression, the majority of her work appears to have literally vanished. This seems an unusual fate for so prolific an author, but the most apparent reason for this is one Aliger herself acknowledges. It is simply that many themes of paramount importance to Aliger and her earlier readers—the Soviet hero, five-year plans, overfulfilling the norms and, to some extent, World War II—may no longer be relevant to today's audience. Of this Aliger writes:

> Perhaps I've lost that precious sense of conviction that what I do will without fail be interesting to other people. Poets begin with that very conviction, and if I didn't have it in my youth, I wouldn't have it now. But now I don't publish much of what I've written. I try to hug the shore, not drown in the torrent of verses rushing by. And I don't finish writing others—it suddenly seems to me that it isn't vital and important for mankind.[12]

Aliger herself prefers her later writing. In an interview with V.F. Korkin, a correspondent for *Literary Gazette* (*Literaturnaia gazeta*), it is hinted that Aliger's readers find, to their surprise and offense, that she has changed. She responds:

> Perhaps surprise, but why offense? What's there for him, the reader, to be offended about? It seems to me that I haven't betrayed either my beliefs or principles. Not long ago, when I attended a poetry reading by my friend and peer, Konstantin Simonov, I noted to myself that the difference between us is that Simonov prefers his youthful, early poems, while for me my later poems, those of the last twenty years, are more valuable. And I think my best book is the collection *The Blue Hour*, which was published in 1970. However, who knows.[13]

It is possible that Aliger's lingering reputation as a premier poet of the socialist realism era has obscured the value of her later, more personal lyrical work.[14] Although her verse may not exhibit the consistency of Akhmatova's and Tsvetaeva's, nevertheless many of her poems are still relevant and are certainly deserving of attention they have thus far not received. Her prose, particularly her essays about her literary contemporaries, is refreshingly free of the propaganda that permeates her early lyrical work. Her well-written memoirs are fascinating reading for both specialists and those simply seeking a personal insight into the major Soviet and Russian literary figures of the last fifty years.

Lisa Taylor

We forgive again and say farewell again . . .
how many times!
I cannot again raise
eyes filled with unshed tears.

No shouting, no sighing,
no recalling the necessary words,
Forgive me as I set out,
Forgive me and fare thee well!

Forgive me!
For what—God knows!

What am I guilty of?
That I was, and am
under the sun and moon.

I was and am, such that I am.
And I cannot be otherwise.
Forgive me . . .
For what, God knows?
What am I guilty of?

That a strong person,
a creator and a fighter
is finally and forever
the only one in the world you love!

1952

The Blue Hour

There is for each one of us
a blue, blue, blue hour,
corporeal, visible to the eye,
between winter's day and night.

The shift of tones and lines,
takes perhaps not an hour, but an instant,
blue, blue, blue, blue . . .
Fortunate is he who perceives it!

This blue moment
at the close of day,
is a tongue of eternal flame,
a cosmic energy.

But it happens that life deceives us,
And perhaps one of us
will live out his life and not glimpse
that blue, blue, blue hour.

Life will have given him his due,
perhaps more than that,
but never will he believe
in the moment of final blueness.

For him there are only two shades,
light and dusk, day and night,
and between them—a blank wall,
and he cannot be helped.

How I pity you, deprived one,
that you will never see
on the threshold, growing blue,
at a mysterious summit,
not a familiar sunset,
but a mystical sunrise.

And thus I am rich,
no matter what you say!

And so I live in hope,
that sometime and somehow,
before I die away, before
I step into that last gloom,
in cherished inspiration
with all my living soul
at the last instant
to turn into blue.

1968

And so again our fates have crossed.
Again sunrise, a hotel, spring . . .
Seven years have passed . . . to sleep for just an hour!
Seven years of separation . . . but I cannot sleep now.

Let's go stroll above the Neva,
there, where the first gleam of day is closer,
where the bareheaded horseman
spurs on his cold steed.

Here we parted. No, not at dawn,
but at dusk. And not for seven years,
but for seven days. Everything on earth passes—
separations, wars . . . nothing is eternal.

And the war, if you will, is not at fault.
What can one say? did it have time for us?
But from that June evening on,
we both became more austere and sincere.

Words are dearer, thoughts more sacred,
One is completely accountable for everything,
To be together for life . . . what a strange whim!
How good it is that seven years have passed.

1948

I pay it all, I pay it all,
I pay for every step.
But suddenly—it happens!—I want
to live a day for free.
And life meets me halfway,
it gives me gifts,
but little by little there is a reckoning,
so within a month, within a year,
I shall pay doubly.

1959

Before Sunrise

For no reason
I dreamed of you anew—
just before sunrise
when the gloom stirs
and you softly told me
a pleasant, kind word,
and from the sound of it
I awoke
and was able to sleep no longer.

In order not to forget it
I laid almost unmoving.
The sunrise was afire,
resounding in the squeaky pipes,
And so the night has passed!
But I grew stronger that night.
Until then it seemed
that I had stopped loving you.

1949

Do not be afraid, I shall come again.
Fierce winds shall not knock me down.
I cannot relinquish you
to that woman at the crossroads.
I will not relinquish, I will not relinquish,
do not be afraid, I will not betray you,
not to distances, nor years,
nor even to my own resentments.
It is better that in an empty room
I tell the walls and furniture
that I shall see you again
in its unchanging quiet;

that I shall preserve my wondrous vision
undying in the distance,
so that it shall return you only to me
from those distant wanderings.
I wish it so, I have decided.
But there is an earthly rival,
in front of whom I am silent,
yielding with a low bow.
She goes forth through the years,
in fever, in flame, in streams of sweat,
your cruel drudgery,
your sublime labor.

Believe me, she is stronger than anything!
But it is difficult for me to concede,
I am leaving, be happy with her,
but remember, remember, remember. . . .
But if the memory of me
is crowded out by an oppressive wall
let it burn in the flame of a fire I have kindled.
Forget me, forget me,
as a ship forgets a storm,
as the night does not recall the light of day. . . .
Forget me, forget me,
like a song, slowly and laboriously.
And know that the determination and calm
in my parting glance
is not for the sake of another woman
nor for the sake of other vows
but for the sake of that, and only that
which has decided our fates,
which has with inspired suffering
mercilessly consumed us
and it is for the sake of these last words
almost cast in metal,
that our guilty love
whispered to us at our parting.
Forget me, forget me

may life grant you courage
in the name of tomorrow,
in the name of the eternal flame,
on ageless paper.

1949

The Dream

I dreamed that I loved another,
that I was carefree and happy, but you
took charge of my fate anew
with an unyielding sense of righteousness.
Once again you decided: this can't be!
and touched my shoulder . . .
And again the wind cooled my lashes,
and again I flew as if upon the wind.
Once again the holidays and weekdays are confused,
dreams with reality, happiness with sorrow . . .
And once again we are in that insane boat,
and there is dark water beneath the stern.
And once again it buffets us between the banks,
we are light—cargo removed from the hold.
And our half-wild, futile union
Is not grounded.
And the night trembles from lightning and thunder.
And I do not see your eyes in the gloom.
And that which unites us forever
has no name or home.
And the distance is all the darker and more boundless.
The lights are extinguished in others' homes . . .
Wait, wait; you are older and wiser.
Slow down, wait; wait a bit!
Order them to dock at the steep bank
And do not rush to the gangplank after me.
Forgive me, let me go to another.
He is of this place, he is happy, he is of this world.
He is a person. He is of earthly laws.

He has long been awaiting me . . .
    But where is he?
He did not wait, he retreated, he left . . .
How good it is this was only a dream!

1948

For transgressions such as these
not retained in the memory of days,
verses come all the harder to me,
the older one is, the harder it is.
And it is all the more cramped for me
on a short fragment of a line.
Thoughts work against it,
but to part with it is senseless.
I devote all the more work to it . . .
Out of resentment, I grow old over it,
It is rougher, more obscure, paler.
Nothing is right; doesn't fit, doesn't go there.
I do not lie to myself for consolation,
choking on some vague reproach.
I know more and am capable of more
than I am able to express in verse.
What has happened? Who can I ask?
The ranks of my friends and those I love
have thinned . . . It is harder to love.
The older one is, the harder it is.
Don't give up, don't dare, don't forget,
how you used to be strong and rich.
Continue your intransigent path,
candid, open, elusive.
And do not become enfeebled at the final summits,
where at the confluence of events and years
a person is left alone
and a poet turns to prose.

1954–1956

Midday is radiant still,
illuminating my house through and through . . .
But today the chimney sweeps came,
saying it would soon be winter.
They cleaned the stoves and the pipes,
so that it would be warm in the oppressive cold.
. . . And silently I gritted my teeth:
yet another summer has passed!

1963

Music

I am in that room,
          on the well-worn couch,
where it smells of polish and dry maple,
filled with music and the sunset,
your breath,
      voice,
          laughter.
I am in that room,
      where dignified and chagrined
someone else's well-played piano
stands against the wall, presses itself against it,
like a miniature monument to your life.
To your whole life.
      How little that is!
Rapturous,
   ardent,
      mortal,
          young.
you left before nightfall.
                The road ran
along an open field,
          above clear water.
All was music—

whether the rising wind,
whether a splashing fish,
whether flowing water,
and gladness resounded in the bugle at daybreak,
and the merciless tambourine sounded an alarm.
And your heart was agitated, it loved,
and in the sunny drizzle of laughter and tears
all was music,
all was music,
everything sang, thundered, flew, exploded.
And you,
enraptured and honest,
listened as if to an oath,
almost without breathing.
How your poor heart believed
in the orchestra's victorious brass heart!
To be with you for an instant
so that with all my strength,
all my tenderness
I will understand and hear the battle's symphony,
the last music of your life.
It began to thunder,
hallowed and vengeful,
and there were no sounds in the world more terrible.
And, not knowing any music cleaner nor simpler,
you,
wounded in the heart,
yielded before it.
Forever.
And so there will no longer be
happiness,
worries,
offenses,
entreaties,
and my caress will never cool
your burning, troubled head.
Forever.
My hands fall away.

My solitary hands . . .
I am in that room,
where the last sounds
like strong, eternal wings flutter.
I am in that room,
at the door,
at the threshold,
at the edge of our past . . .
But you left me so much, so much:
two free lives—
mine and yours.
But you did not leave me a widow's grievances—
my fate is unyielding,
with its sobs,
fever,
love,
with its nocturnal alarms, resounding in the pipes.
Permit me to remain the same,
the same,
as I was when once upon a time you embraced me,
ready for a journey,
like a train, awaiting the coming day,
unused to peace and quiet.
And permit me to believe with blind faith
that there will still be happiness all the same
and to live
as you taught me,
to the fullest
not knowing how to spare or compromise myself.
To live
with all one's heart and being,
not concealing passions or inspirations,
to live,
so as to be forever worthy
of a life
and death
such as yours.

1942

People do not forgive me my mistakes,
Well, I shall learn to restrain my reply.
The telegrams in the morning papers
Do not promise me a simple life.

Generous with empty greetings,
the days burn, like butterflies on fire.
No benevolent signs
of an easy life are prophesied for me.

What can I know of a simple life?
Just from others' poems,
But I like to stroll, thus, even in mourning,
until the third cock crows.

And newly fallen snow whirls and sparkles
lights glow from afar;
but you, the bulky burden of my fate,
are as light as a feather.

So I am older, and have gone
 grayer—
and if I complain, forgive me—
you may become weightier, but to cast you off
Is more difficult for me than to carry you.

1946

There is a woman—she is not young.
There is a woman—she is not handsome.
But there is in her a soul, sublime and bright,
like a vernal spring.
She is rich, her world is great.
To her this world is a hundred times dearer.

She is strong.
        And—oh God! thus more visible—
is the small and insignificant old peasant next to her,
a pretentious, fussy lout,
who resembles a rain puddle.

1966

Are you offended or displeased?
With what, however?
        For how long?
They say you are alone and ill.
Very ill. Horribly alone.
You send no notes from the hospital.
You don't ask:
        remember me.
No one knocks after midnight,
having seen the light in my window.
People. Obligations. Work.
        Day after day. . . .
But at dusk
all the same I go to the bend in the road—
perhaps you still await me there.

1968

Quiet

On that evening acorns dropped onto the roof,
clattering—
and your voice resounded all the more softly,
and finally fell silent.

You sat silently next to me.
you silently took my hand in yours
and with a bitter glance, a silent glance
wordlessly told the whole truth.

And I was genuinely happy
that in answer to your silence
no words needed to be said
since none were worthy.

1959

A Story

I recall a damp room
with an immense, smoking stove,
where I lived together with you
on one stipend.
Empty and quite dark,
it was mundane and lived-in,
with an amateur photograph
on your old table.

Our tineless forks,
our bent spoons.
A round stain from the teapot
adorned the window sill.
I even recall
the taste of cold potatoes
and the repulsive tomato color
of most ancient canned fish.

I remember you as you were then,
your peculiar habits.
How you would call to me,
your eyes barely open,
how you would gnaw on your cigarettes,
how you would break matches,
how you would say tender words
in a muted voice.
And the light of that sleepless night,
wearying and dull.

I left in the morning,
my portfolio stuffed with things.
At the first frost
you sprinkled reddish sand,
and tears would freeze
in the icy wind.

There is only one thing I have forgotten:
what it was I loved you for.

1940

A Nighttime Conversation

We will be severe and sincere,
we will cover the lamp with a sheet of newspaper.
Of the finest, of the simplest things
will we speak.

Where did such words come from?
Did we ourselves devise them?
In quiet, quiet voices
will we speak.

Where did such thoughts come from?
Having just fallen silent, we begin anew.
Understanding each other at half a word,
will we speak.

Where did such feelings come from?
Vying with each other, not concealing anything,
covering our eyes in agitation,
will we speak.

What is this, happiness or sadness?
Not surprised, nor understanding,
smoking and breaking matches
will we speak.

Finally the moment arrives . . .
Why have you gone pale? It is already daybreak.
Mighty, joyful, hallowed,
Is this love or friendship, which
Having interrupted, forced back, brushed words aside,
is imperiously asserting itself? I don't know.

1938

Translated by Lisa Taylor

Notes to the Essay

1. M. Aliger, *Tropinka vo rzhi* (Moscow: Sovetskii pisatel', 1980), 13.
2. M. Aliger, *Sobranie sochinenii* (Moscow: Khudozhestvennaia literatura, 1984), 60–61.
3. *Tropinka vo rzhi,* 167.
4. Quoted in Elaine Feinstein, ed., *Three Russian Poets* (Manchester: Carcanet New Press, 1979), 11. The italics are Feinstein's.
5. *Tropinka vo rzhi,* 169.
6. *Sobranie sochinenii,* 442–43.
7. Quoted in E. Feinstein, *Three Russian Poets,* 10.
8. *Tropinka vo rzhi,* 63–64.
9. *Tropinka vo rzhi,* 339.
10. *Tropinka vo rzhi,* 397–98.
11. I. Metter, "Nauka rasstavaniia," *Novyi mir* 3 (1981): 252.
12. *Tropinka vo rzhi,* 27.
13. *Tropinka vo rzhi,* 130.
14. In spite of claims to the contrary, Aliger was not always successful in her efforts as a poet of socialist realism. In one instance, while a member of the editorial staff for the short-lived periodical *Literary Moscow* (*Literaturnaia Moskva*), she publicly defended several poets (including Anna Akhmatova) whose works were published by the journal but did not conform to the tenets of socialist realism. Khrushchev himself publicly attacked her subsequently in a meeting. Aliger's own work, particularly her love poetry, was also disparaged as being "one-sided," "too confessional" and "pretentious." Her later verse was criticized for its less than optimistic tone.

Bibliography

Primary Works

God rozhdeniia. Moscow: Sovetskii pisatel', 1938.
Kamni i travy. Moscow: Sovetskii pisatel', 1940.
Tvoia pobeda. Poèma. Moscow: Sovetskii pisatel', 1940.
Pamiati khrabrykh. Moscow: Sovetskii pisatel', 1942.
Lirika. Moscow: Molodaia gvardiia, 1943.

Stikhi i poèmy, 1935–1943. Moscow: Gosudarstvennoe izdatel'stvo khudozhestvennoi literatury, 1944.

Izbrannoe. Moscow: n.p., 1947.

Skazka o pravde. Moscow: Biblioteka sovetskoi dramaturgii, 1947.

Zoia. Moscow: Gosudarstvennoe izdatel'stvo detskoi literatury, 1942.

Pervye primety. Moscow: Sovetskii pisatel', 1948.

Literaturnaia Moskva, literaturno-khudozhestvennyi sbornik. Moscow: Khudozhestvennaia literatura, 1956.

Iz zapisnoi knizhki, 1946–1956. Moscow: Sovetskii pisatel', 1957.

Stikhtvoreniia. Moscow: Gosudarstvennoe izdatel'stvo khudozhestvennoi literatury, 1958.

Stikhtvoreniia i poèmy. Moscow: Molodaia gvardiia, 1959.

Neskol'ko shagov. Novye stikhi, 1956–1960. Moscow: Sovetskii pisatel', 1962.

Vozvrashchenie v Chili. Moscow: Sovetskii pisatel', 1966.

Stikhi. Moscow: Khudozhestvennaia literatura, 1967.

Ogromnyi mir. Moscow: Progress, 1968.

Da i net. Moscow: Detskaia literatura, 1969.

Sinii chas. Novye stikhi. Moscow: Sovetskii pisatel', 1970.

Stikhotvoreniia i poèmy. Moscow: Izdatel'stvo khudozhestvennoi literatury, 1970.

Stikhi i proza. Moscow: Khudozhestvennaia literatura, 1975.

Stikhotvoreniia i poèmy v dvukh tomakh. Moscow: Khudozhestvennaia literatura, 1975.

Vchera i zavtra. Moscow: Sovetskii pisatel', 1977.

Chernaia kniga. Jerusalem: Tarbut, 1980.

Tropinka vo rzhi. O poèzii i poètakh. Moscow: Sovetskii pisatel', 1980.

Chetvert' veka. Kniga liriki. Moscow: Sovetskii pisatel', 1981.

Sobranie sochinenii v trekh tomakh. Moscow: Khudozhestvennaia literatura, 1984.

Vstrechi i razluki. Moscow: Izvestiia, 1989.

In Translation

The Heritage of Russian Verse. Ed. Dmitri Obolensky. Bloomington: Indiana University Press, 1976. 461–62.

Three Russian Poets: Magarita Aliger, Yunna Morits, Bella Akhmadulina. Ed. Ellen Feinstein. Manchester: Carcanet New Press, 1979. 19–31.

Song of a Nightingale: An Anthology of Modern Soviet Short Stories. Delhi: Ajanta Publications, 1987. 1–65.

Secondary Works

"Aliger, Margarita." *Kratkaia Literaturnaia Èntsiklopediia*. Moscow: Gosudarstvennoe nauchnoe izdatel'stvo Sovetskaia Èntsiklopediia," 1962.

Bristol, Evelyn. *A History of Russian Poetry*. New York: Oxford University Press, 1991. 273–74.

Dubrovin, A. "Zhivaia traditsiia." *Znamia* 9 (1966): 220–31.

Feinstein, Ellen, ed. *Three Russian Poets: Magarita Aliger, Yunna Morits, Bella Akhmadulina*. Manchester: Carcanet New Press, 1979. 9–11, 19–31.

Golovashenko, Iu. *Mnogoobrazie realizma*. Leningrad: Izdatel'stvo Iskusstvo, 1973. 66–72.

Istoriia russkoi sovetskoi literatury v 4–kh tomakh. 4 vols. Moscow: Izdatel'stvo Nauka, 1968.

Jacobus, Mary, ed. *Women Writing and Writing about Women*. New York: Barnes and Noble Books, 1979. 141–43, 158.

Kasack, Wolfgang. "Aliger, Margarita." *Dictionary of Russian Literature since 1917*. New York: Columbia University Press, 1985.

Kedrina, Z. "Schast'e (O tvorchestve M. Aliger)." *Znamia* 2–3 (1943): 224–30.

Neginsky, Rosina. "Aliger, Margarita." *Dictionary of Russian Women Writers*. Ed. Marina Ledkovsky, Charlotte Rosenthal and Mary Zirin. Westport, CT: Greenwood Press, 1994. 18-20.

Metter, I. "Nauka rasstavaniia." *Novyi mir* 3 (1981): 251–52.

Motiasov, Igor'. "Prazdnichnyi, svyashchennyi zov trevogi." *Literaturnoe obozrenie* 5 (1976): 21–23.

Reeder, Roberta. *Anna Akhmatova: Poet and Prophet*. New York: St. Martin's Press, 1994. 330–31.

Simonov, K. "Zametki pisatelia." *Novyi mir* 1 (1947): 157–63.

Terras, Victor. "Aliger, Margarita." *Handbook of Russian Literature*. Ed. Victor Terras. New Haven, CT: Yale University Press, 1985. 20.

Troshchenko, E. "Poèziia pokoleniia, sozrevshego na voine. Margarita Aliger." *Novyi mir* 9 (1943).

Weber, Harry B., ed. "Aliger, Margarita." *Modern Encyclopedia of Russian and Soviet Writers*. Gulf Breeze, FL: Academic International Press, 1977.

Bella Akhmadulina

Bella Akhmadulina (b. 1937).
Courtesy of Christine A. Rydel.

Since she first began to write in the mid-1950s, Bella Akhmadulina (Izabella Akhatovna, b. 1937) has evolved from a schoolgirl poetess into one of Russia's most reknowned poets of the second half of the twentieth century. Consistency of theme and image mark her evolution from a superficial, but magical, observer of the world around her into a profound and spiritual commentator on the inner life of the soul. The compass that guides her on her aesthetic and moral journey has been, and remains, Russian literature, primarily the poems of Pushkin, Lermontov, Blok, Mandel'shtam, Akhmatova, Pasternak and, especially, Tsvetaeva. These poets, along with various phenomena of nature—animals, fields, flowers, rain, as well as Russian rivers and lakes—inspired her to produce some of the most striking works of contemporary Russian poetry.

Akhmadulina's first poems began to appear in the post-Stalin years known as the Thaw. These early verses transform mundane objects into wondrous things to behold: traffic lights turn into benign ancient Slavs, a pink motorscooter sprouts wings and flies away, volcanoes become hiding places for sleeping giants, a construction site sets the scene for a strange ballet, a sparkling water machine dispenses rainbows along with drinks and tape recorders become homes for sorcerers. She luxuriates in Sunday tasks, enjoys tomato juice at a metro stop, washes down cookies with milk and manages to make these everyday actions into momentous events. It is no wonder, then, that Akhmadulina's works struck a responsive chord in the readers who were used to the drabness of official socialist realist literature. Even though critics did not respond with overwhelmingly positive reviews, the public embraced her enthusiastically.

By the early 1960s, Akhmadulina was almost as famous in Russia as the other poets of the "new generation": Evtushenko, Voznesenskii and Okudzhava. Those were heady days, when these writers read their works to thousands of people gathered in squares and stadiums to celebrate poetry. Akhmadulina commented on the literary scene of the 1960s in an interview: "Of course, the time or, as people say now, the thaw that had set in at that time did help; but nonetheless the main factor was the poets' characters and talent." In response to an implication that the reading tastes of the public today have turned away from poetry as opposed to those of the public thirty years ago, Akhmadulina affirmed her faith in poets, poetry and the reading public:

> I don't think that readers have lost their interest in poetry. I even believe that the reading public has become much more sophisticated. . . . I, for example, recited my verses to an audience of many thousands at Moscow's stadium in Luzhniki. But that was a tribute to the time. I think that today the poets do not yield their positions. A real poet is always a poet, inseparable from the time he lives in.[1]

Akhmadulina has also changed with the times, and as many have noted, she has changed for the better; however, she has never compromised her art in the course of her literary career. When asked whether the new atmosphere of *glasnost'*, when "there are no forbidden themes," complicates a poet's task, she replied: "But I have always written about everything I wanted. For me there have been no forbidden themes. . . . To me personally work has not become easier or more difficult. Literature is not weather that changes depending on certain factors. There are eternal laws, eternal truths, eternal themes."[2] She added that a real writer is always true to his or her conscience, a credo Akhmadulina has followed in her art and in her life.

Even during the later, repressive Khrushchev years, Akhmadulina retained her integrity and kept on writing works like her *Fairytale about the Rain* (*Skazka o dozhde*, 1963) and "Chapters from a Poem" ("Glavy iz poèmy") about Boris Pasternak, both of which were first published in a journal that played a pivotal role in her career, *Literary Georgia* (*Literaturnaia Gruziia*). Akhmadulina's bonds with Georgia remain deep, a fact that emerges in a whole body of works devoted to her "adopted" home (she was born in Moscow). She grew to love its people, its land, its traditions and its poetry. For many years her translations from Georgian poetry were the only reason she was able to retain membership in the Writers' Union. Her ideas about translation reflect the respect she feels for the original works. She rejects literal translation, but says that she bases her translations on intuition, love and the trust one poet gives another.[3]

After the publication of her second collection in 1969, Akhmadulina suffered a "dry" period for several years; however, in 1977, three collections of old and new poems appeared. Since then her works have come out with some regularity. Her popularity continues, but among a more select audience; she has emerged from her status as a "cult figure" into a serious poet whose works have become more philosophical in content and more complex in form. Akhmadulina's poetry has become more esoteric and elliptical as her Russian readers have grown more sophisticated.

Akhmadulina enjoys a special relationship with her readers, whom she addresses in several prose pieces. Although she rarely reveals much about her personal life, she feels a close affinity with her "ideal reader," whom she describes in the essay "A Word That Amounts to a Deed." She says that she sketches her reader's face in and makes it beautiful to please herself; however, it becomes real only when she "pencil[s] in a volume of Pushkin's, or some other great book, for nothing in the picture has any connection with [her] . . . those readers are closest to [her] who, treating [her] as simply another reader, agree with [her] in the main." In other words, she sees herself as a conduit to other writers of the past. She says she is grateful to those she calls her readers, for with them she can share "a fondness for our native speech, for the way in which it intensifies our life and for preserving it unspoiled." She is glad that they approve of the way she "work[s] and live[s] in her intention to serve [her] goal" to preserve the Russian language with no other motive. She knows that her ideal reader "supposes, like [her], that a word amounts to a deed, and is aware of its moral significance."[4]

All of the themes Akhmadulina develops in her poetry derive from the importance of the Word as Deed manifested in active preservation of Russian language in literature, in loving acts of goodness and kindness and in moral actions based on the voice of conscience. In her poems she extols the glories and the sufferings of Russia's poets; she describes the eternal struggle of the artist against the philistines, as well as the joys and pains of writing. The nature in which she finds her inspiration is purely Russian, with its flowers of the steppes and mountains, rivers and lakes in Siberia, the pristine north, the woods and ravines of the Moscow region. Akhmadulina's poems champion the virtues of loyalty, courage, kindness, generosity, friendship and respect for life in all its forms. A strongly spiritual worldview and highly moral stance form the basis of her own orientation as an author. Ultimately the voice of conscience overrides her voice as a woman.

Although Akhmadulina has created in her works an unmistakenly feminine lyrical hero and an unmistakenly feminine lyrical narrator, she feels she is by no means a feminist. When asked what she thought about the current tendency to divide poetry into "masculine" and "feminine," she provided an unequivocal answer:

> I absolutely neither acknowledge nor accept that. I do not want to know what critics and literary scholars write in that regard. I know only that in Russia in the twentieth century we had two great female poets. But this means nothing except that they also had to endure all of those burdens that fall to a woman's lot. A person who is occupied with art, whether male or female, should be equal in human qualities. You will never find a more manly or valiant man than Pushkin in the wide world. Akhmatova and Tsvetaeva possessed the same qualities. That is, one can find in them courage, honor and valor, and what's more, they were also women, a fact that only intensifies the tragic essence of their existence. And so what then is female poetry? I don't know it.[5]

Akhmadulina's late friend and mentor, Pavel Antokol'skii, however, saw both the masculine and the feminine in her poetry. In an introduction to her collection *Verses* (*Stikhi*, 1975), he wrote that Akhmadulina possesses the masculine traits of powerful talent and acute intellect. He discusses these gifts not in regard to her craftsmanship, manner, technique or style; rather, he sees these qualities in something larger, more fundamental: moral tension in a person continually growing in stature and an eternally vigilant sense of time, history and service to people. Antokol'skii then says that her beauty and charm alone make her a member of the so-called weaker sex. He states boldly: "She is a poet, not a poetess." Nevertheless, he continues, the main character in her poems is a lyrical heroine, not a hero: "In other words, feminine grace and feminine lyricism celebrate themselves openly. They include hundreds and hundreds of the author's female contemporaries."[6] His sexist slant notwithstanding, Antokol'skii accurately described Akhmadulina and her poetry, although she herself rejects the basic dichotomy on which her close friend and critic based his observations.

In Russia her critics usually divide into two camps: those who see the growing complexity of her poetry as the self-conscious posturing of an "idol" and those who see in her work the brilliant combination of verbal mastery and serious thought of a mature poet. Their polemics take place mostly in journalistic articles. However, Akhmadulina's works are gradually gaining more attention and receiving serious study in academic journals. It is curious that in the West her poetry has been the subject of very little scholarship; five articles (four in English, one in German) and a recent book in English (1994) are too little, indeed, for one of Russia's best poets of the twentieth century.

Bella Akhmadulina was born 10 April 1937 in Moscow—a date she considers "fateful" and "symbolic": "this was a fateful year, in which the very best in the nation were cut down; nevertheless this immeasurably tragic year gave birth to life, and that means, hope. I was born, I survived, and that means at least one poet escaped destruction."[7] She spent the first three years of life surrounded by her family in a house on Moscow's Garden Ring road (Sadovoe kol'tso). In her long narrative poem (*poèma*), *My Genealogy* (*Moia rodoslovnaia*, 1963–1964), she traces her ancestral roots back to an Italian organ-grinder and an impoverished Tatar, Akhmadulla. Her maternal ancestors lived lives of service and great accomplishments. Her great-grandfather, Mitrofan, was a doctor who distinguished himself caring for the wounded in the Crimean War. Of his six children, two were especially important to Akhmadulina: her great-uncle, the revolutionary Aleksandr Stopani, who worked with Lenin on his newspaper *Spark* (*Iskra*), and her grandmother, a medical assistant in Kazan' who was often imprisoned for her revolutionary, "subversive" deeds. This grandmother became the most meaningful influence in young Bella's life.[8]

From her grandmother Akhmadulina learned to love Pushkin, Lermontov and Gogol and to respect life in all of its guises, especially animals. Her grandmother was also the one who took care of little Bella during the war when they were evacuated to Ufa. In a touching reminiscence, "To My Readers,"[9] Akhmadulina describes her earliest years as a combination of senses: the smell of wet sand as she played in the sandbox in the garden of her first Moscow home, the sight of tulips as they unexpectedly bloomed during the night, the sound of her grandmother as she read aloud Pushkin, Lermontov and Gogol to drown out the air-raid sirens and the noise of bombs. She also remembers feeling that a "universal tragedy" was soon to descend on her neighbors. Bella recalls with gratitude the loving kindness of those who cared for her during the war. Underlying these descriptions is a sense of freedom and independence; she hated playing with prefabricated toys, loved seeing a red balloon as it floated about the Bolshoi Theater, and expressed her joy on Victory Day by drawing the celebration and fireworks as bursts of formless color.

Akmadulina recalls her childhood in "old" Moscow, the time she spent in various neighborhoods—Maroseika, Pokrovka, Chistye prudy and Il'inskii Square with "unusual secrets in its dense thickets." She calls childhood the "beginning of all beginnings," a time when she began her first forays into writing. Akhmadulina attended schools on Kolpachnii and then Lialin lanes. Her parents hoped that she would study either philology or journalism and would not allow her to enter the Literary Institute after she finished school. She did not attend the university, a decision she does not regret to this day. Akhmadulina's first job was on a factory in-house newspaper, *Metrostroevets*. At the same time she joined Evgenii Vinokurov's writing workshop attached to the Likhachev Automobile Factory. The next year she entered the Literary Institute with extraordinary ease.[10] She left the institute in 1960. By this time she was married to the poet, Evgenii Evtushenko.

Akhmadulina's poems began to appear in print in 1955. She graciously acknowledged the help the "older generation" of poets gave her at that time, particularly Antokol'skii and Vinokurov, saying that she never had to go to any publishing house on her own behalf. While married to Evtushenko, Akhmadulina went to Georgia and met there the editorial staff of *Literary Georgia*, the forum for many of her first poems. Her remarkable *poèma*, *Fairytale about the Rain*, first appeared in that journal in 1963, not without serious consequences for all concerned. Some saw the poem as an allusion to Khrushchev's Kremlin receptions.[11] In this long narrative poem, Rain follows the lyrical narrator/heroine about while ignoring the flowers in the kitchen gardens. It playfully gambols about like a puppy or a tiny daughter. The young poet keeps an appointment for a visit, but the severe hostess does not let Rain accompany her inside, where a group of philistines questions her about her art. A chorus of children comes and performs; its practiced act produces a negative effect on her. Then Rain, miserable without her, rushes in through the ceiling. The philistines soak up Rain in sponges and dispose of him in the commode. The young poet leaves the house, and only a small puddle of Rain is left as the weather bureau predicts a scorching drought. The poem describes the mortal wounds a materialistic society inflicts on inspiration. *Literary Georgia* also first published Akhmadulina's "Chapters from a Poem," without any reference to Pasternak, its subject. In it Bella's young poet narrator/lyrical heroine espies a dignified old man in the yard outside his dacha. She watches as he goes about various tasks. When he sees her, he recognizes who she is and comes up to her. Courtly and kind, he invites her to return for a visit. Although she does not ever act on the invitation, in effect, they meet again in her poem about his poem about Georgia.

The highly personal and intimate tone of these poems also marks her first collection, *String* (*Struna*, 1962). These very qualities elicited negative responses from official critics, but enthusiasm from the reading public. Expelled from the Writers' Union during Khrushchev's "reactionary" period, Akhmadulina later was reinstated as a translator, especially of her beloved Georgian poetry. Her free-spirited—and brave—indiscretions incurred the wrath of the authorities. Two incidents in particular illustrate her somewhat foolhardy daring. While in Georgia in the early 1960s Akhmadulina was at a banquet with an official group at the invitation of the local Central Committee secretary. In the heat of the celebration someone mentioned the "traitorous" name of Solzhenitsyn. Akhmadulina then rose and proposed a toast to the "great Russian writer, Aleksandr Isaich Solzhenitsyn." After moments of silence during which no one looked at each other, the poet David Samoilov called out from the other end of the table, "Bella, I'm with you." The next day the group went to Kakhetiia, where at another dinner, a certain writer of newspaper poems, Chuev, "proposed a toast to 'the great Stalin.' Bella became indignant: 'How can you, especially in the land of Georgia, in the land of Titsian Tabidze [Georgia's great poet]?!' With these words she took off her shoe and hurled it across the table at Chuev."[12] Her friends rushed her away amid the confusion. Such exploits, among others, are part of the mythology that surrounds Akhmadulina.

By 1962 Akhmadulina was married to her second husband, the prose writer Iurii Nagibin. With him she collaborated on the screenplay *Clear Ponds* (*Chistye prudy*). In the 1960s she also adopted a daughter, Anna, for whom she has written a number of delightful verses. For the next few years Akhmadulina devoted herself mainly to translation, although she also wrote original poems. In 1968 a collection of her works, *Chill* (*Oznob*), appeared in the West. At that time it was the most complete, though not always accurate, anthology of Akhmadulina's poetry, prose and translations. One work, the prose sketch "On Siberian Roads" ("Na Sibirskikh dorogakh"), gives an enlightening account of her trek to Siberia to interview a native storyteller. On the way she meets many people who in some way become sources for various recurring themes in her work, in particular, her view of nature. Her next collection, *Music Lessons* (*Uroki muzyki*), appeared in 1969. Besides several new poems that encompass a greater variety of subjects and demonstrate more depth of thought, the collection includes not only *Fairytale about the Rain* and *My Genealogy*, but also two *poèmy: An Adventure in an Antique Shop*

(*Prikliucheniie v antikvarnom magazine*) and *Chill* (*Oznob*). In the first poem the lyrical narrator enters an antique shop and encounters the owner, a bitter 200-year-old who does not want to sell his things to modern people who do not appreciate them for the right reasons. As the narrator and owner talk, we find out that 130 years earlier, he lost the woman he loved to Pushkin. In the second poem the narrator falls prey to a case of chills so violent that her shaking disturbs the neighbors, frightens their children and smashes breakable items in their apartments. The alienation she feels because of her affliction and her inability to understand why she is set apart from others echo the themes of her *Fairytale about the Rain*, especially the consequences of inspiration and creation.

Her next book, *Verses* (*Stikhi*, 1975), contained very few new works and ended a period of relative silence, which coincided with the years she was married to Gennadii Mamlin, a playwright and children's writer. During this time, however, Akhmadulina gave birth to her second daughter, Elizaveta. The most creative period of her life, which continues to the present, seems to have begun with her marriage to the talented artist Boris Messerer. She published four books from 1975 to 1977: the aforementioned *Verses*; *Dreams of Georgia* (*Sny o Gruzii*), a 1977 collection of works—both prose and poetry—that are either about Georgia or are poems composed and/or published there; and *Candle* (*Svecha*, 1977) and *Snowstorm* (*Metel'*, 1977), both of which contain many new works, including the narrative poem *A Summer-House Romance* (*Dachnyi roman*). In this whimsical *poèma* the lyrical narrator becomes fascinated with a brother and sister who move into the next-door dacha. After the two leave, the brother sends the narrator a letter in rhyme, from which she deduces he is a poet. The poem almost acts as a "time-tunnel" through which the narrator travels to engage in another "triangle," this time with Pushkin and Anna Kern, to whom the great poet addressed one of his most beautiful lyrics. In this *poèma*, two themes critical to Akhmadulina form the basis of the entire work: love and poetry.

In 1978–1980, Akhmadulina was involved in the "scandal" that surrounded the publication of the unofficial literary almanac *Metropol'*, under the general editorship of her dear friend Vasilii Aksenov. Conceived as a place to publish avant-garde pieces and otherwise "unpublishable" works, it was also seen as a forum for young writers who were having difficulty getting their works in print through official channels. Akhmadulina contributed to the almanac a multilayered, synaesthetic, hermetic story, "Many Dogs and the Dog" ("Mnogo sobak i sobaka"), in which the main character, Shelaputov, who has lost his five senses as well as his memory, finds himself on the Dioscurian coast in Sukhumi. While on the surface the story appears to be a Proustian quest to recapture memory, it really explores the pain and agony of creation, of telling "how the song is sung." The story contains a complex series of permutations and metamorphoses of characters, most of whom may or may not be Shelaputov—or Akhmadulina herself. Highly self-referential and allusive, the story has many subtexts, one of which deals with political oppression of the arts, an unusual departure for Akhmadulina. The main symbol of the tale remains a battle-scarred dog with an unremovable collar who loves Shelaputov. The playful puppy of *Fairytale* has evolved into a weary, devoted, beloved dog. In the earlier poem enemies try to destroy Akhmadulina's inspiration, but a small puddle of hope remains. In this prose work, another enemy shoots and kills the dog.

Though known mainly for her skills as a poet, Akhmadulina has also written many excellent prose pieces that include tributes to contemporary writers, meditations on Pushkin and Lermontov, essays on the art of translation, addresses to her readers, reminiscences and, more recently, short autobiographical sketches. In "Grandmother" ("Babushka") Akhmadulina pays homage to the remarkable woman who was, and remains, her guiding light. Along the way she reveals personal details about her childhood, such as her aversion to being touched, her tendency to give sullen looks when asked to do something she did not want to do, her awkwardness with her own family but her ease in dealing with strangers. But in this piece, we, along with Akhmadulina, learn above all *babushka*'s most valuable lessons about the importance of unconditional love, loyalty and respect for life. In *Lermontov. From the Archives of the R. Family* (*Lermontov. Iz arkhiva semeistva R.*, 1973), a semi-fantastic novella of the poet's last days, Akhmadulina bases her account on documentary materials, including the incomplete confession of Martynov, Lermontov's murderer, and memoirs of the times. She builds psychological portraits of the participants in the duel: the "efficient" A.I. Vasil'chikov, the "indifferently splendid" A.A. Stolypin (Mongo) and the confused Martynov, who could not "distinguish self-love from a feeling of honor." According to one commentator, the story is a "picture of Lermontov through the eyes of Martynov, in which Akhmadulina recounts not so much his hostility, but his dull lack of understanding of the personality of the poet."[13]

Since the early 1980s, Akhmadulina has been concentrating mainly on poetry. Beginning with her extraordinary book *Secret* (*Taina*, 1983), collections of poetry have appeared with regularity: *The Garden* (*Sad*, 1987), *Poems* (*Stikhotvoreniia*, 1988), *Selected Works* (*Izbrannoe*, 1988), *Littoral* (*Poberezh'e*, 1991) and *The Casket and the Key* (*Larets i kliuch*, 1994). These books chronicle Akhmadulina's evolution as a poet. Here one finds her usual themes: inspiration, creativity, metapoetry, love, loyalty, friendship and the cultural heritage of her revered predecessors—Akhmatova, Tsvetaeva, Blok, Mandel'shtam and the eternal Pushkin. But now she explores her themes with greater subtlety and richer allusions than in her early works.

Akhmadulina's language likewise has become more complex. Whereas her earlier poems are elegant, almost classical in form, with short iambic lines full of lush sound play and imaginative rhyme, her later poems experiment more with ternary meters and longer iambics. Her rhymes have become deeper, more assonantal and alliterative, with even greater experimentation with consonant reversals and near rhymes. The later poems, more than ever, combine various linguistic levels; neologisms, archaisms, prosaisms, slang, elevated rhetoric and conversational speech appear in syntax that can be elliptical, ambiguous or convoluted, but rarely straightforward. At times she even resorts to agrammatical usage and puns for a desired effect. In spite of lexical, stylistic and syntactical diversity, Akhmadulina's poems nevertheless achieve a harmony of thought and expression.

In recent interviews Akhmadulina has discussed her development as a poet. She acknowledges that her literary life has been charmed, thanks to the help and guidance of many who took an interest in her early work. No longer a "mad-cap hooligan" who repeatedly thumbed her nose at the establishment, Akhmadulina has become a recognized, serious poet—not only in Russia, but also abroad. In 1989 she won the State Prize for Literature and has traveled to many countries, reading her works to large appreciative audiences. She has also held the post of writer-in-residence at the University of California at Los Angeles. In spite of the fame and adulation, she has remained the essential Bella Akhmadulina of old.

Although Akhmadulina has matured as a woman and as a poet, in many ways she has not changed from the little girl whose grandmother taught her to love people and animals and to offer to all acts of generosity and kindness. Akhmadulina's special affinity with animals is almost legendary. She told of how she once tried to save even an injured rat by taking it to her grandmother for care.[14] Vasilii Aksenov related how in Tbilisi people were telling a tale about "how Bella once entered a bear's cage accompanied by an official of the local Cheka, a certain prince N. The bear slightly rumpled the prince, but kissed the poetess." He continued that this story might not be true, but claimed he saw something similar with his own eyes. He and Bella were seeing off Arthur Miller at the Leningrad station in Moscow. He witnessed the following scene:

> [O]n a side platform we caught sight of a pack of guard dogs tied to the columns . . . their masters, sergeants and sergeant-majors, went off somewhere on railroad business, and the dogs were simply snapping in fury at the sight of such a massive group of unaccompanied citizens. Suddenly Bella—jump, jump—went right up to one of the

> monsters—oh, sweet little dog!—took its terrifying snout, all jaws, and kissed its suddenly appearing nose.
>
> I saw with my own eyes, gentlemen, how the monster instantly grew calm and began to lick Bella's hands.[15]

They say that dogs instantly recognize good people; perhaps that is what happened on that railroad platform.

Stories about Akhmadulina's acts of generosity are also legendary. Although she says she never asked for anything on her own behalf, she is willing to try anything to help others. Whether she is giving gifts of roses to a forgotten old woman or helping cut through red tape to expedite a funeral,[16] she acts spontaneously. Friends tell how she tried to find translating jobs for Joseph Brodsky when he sorely needed work.[17] And in a recent interview, when asked who the talented younger poets are, not only did she name Elena Shvartz, but she also told the interviewer that it would please her greatly if his magazine would publish Shvartz's poems.[18] But perhaps a firsthand account tells the story best. Vera Zubareva, a beleaguered young poet and literary critic, phoned Akhmadulina, not to ask her help, but to meet the person whose gift she "valued most highly":

> I managed to meet an artist whose talent is as great as her humanity. The strength of her soul served as a serious support to me for many years afterward. Some time later, I found out, quite coincidentally, from the editor of the poetry division of the Moscow journal *Successors* (*Smena*) that Bella Akhmadulina had requested that my poetry be included in his publication. Thus appeared two of my works, one of which was accompanied by an introduction written by Akhmadulina.[19]

The many testaments, whether true or apocryphal, to Bella Akhmadulina's moral strength and generous character affirm that she truly is a poet who believes in the "Word that amounts to a Deed."

Christine A. Rydel

Flowers

Flowers grew in a greenhouse.
Ceilings protected them.
Their glutted roots grew fat
And their petals were delicate.

They added bitter potassium
And many other salts to the soil,
so that the yellow-hazel brown pansy
eye would look rounder and gayer.
Flowers grew in a greenhouse.
They gave them light and soil,
but not because they felt sorry for them
or cared about them for long.
People give them away as keepsakes,
but for me—for me their fate is dreadful,
for they never get to smell the way they would
if they had grown in a garden.
They'll never get to leave their scent on lips,
they'll never get to shake loose a bumble bee,
they'll never get a chance to guess
what damp earth means.

1955

Names of Georgian Women

Sails were straying in the sea,
and, undisturbed by the heat,
plane trees were sluggishly blooming
and shedding their leaves in November.
A bench in an ancient park
stood white and mute,
and the names of Georgian women
vaguely smelled of grapes.

They turned into a stream of babble,
which ran into the sea,
then swam out, like a black swan,
with its neck strangely curved.
The woman Lamara was laughing,
as she ran to the water, over stones
on which she broke her little heels;
and she stained her lips in wine.
And Medea's hair got soaked

as she plaited it in a morning waterfall,
and the drops grew dry, then grew shallow
and blazed all out of place.
And muting the oleanders.
All gathered into a single bloom,
Ariadna's name hovered
and faded in the distance.
Barely leaning on the pilings,
The mooring nestled up against the water.
"Tsisana!"—came a call from a window,
"Natèla!"—a voice replied.

1956

The ancient style attracts me.
I have a fascination for speech of old.
It often seems more modern and
more sharp than all our words.
To cry out: "Half my kingdom for a horse!"
What irascibility and generosity!
But the futility of that last resort of fervor
sounds condescending even to me.
Someday I'll awake in a mist,
after having won the final battle;
and then I'll remember
the decision of an ancient madman.
Oh, what's half a kingdom to me!
A child, taught by its age,
I'll take the horse, then return the horse
for half a moment with a person,
Whom I love. God be with you,
o horse of mine, horse of mine, zealous horse.
Free of charge I'll loosen your
reins—and you'll overtake
your own herd; you'll overtake them
there in the empty reddish-brown steppe.
But I've grown weary of the hullabaloo
over these victories and defeats.

I pity the horse! I pity love!
And in the medieval manner,
only a trace left by the horseshoe
lies down beneath my feet.

1957

It happened thus, that twenty-seven years
After my birth, it was my lot to live
joyously in the closeness of a family home,
where the garden widened its circle of beauty.
I gave myself over to the kindness
impartial nature dispenses as it
looks upon a withering pine forest
or decides the fate of a kitchen garden.
It was pleasant to forget my woes and rage,
to have no thoughts, to utter no words,
and to suffer the care of an alien genius
in the childlike folly of trees.
I suddenly became as healthy as grass,
as clean of spirit as other plants,
no more intelligent than a tree,
no more alive than before my birth.
During the night I smiled at the ceiling,
into the empty space, where a god appeared,
to send me smiles and greetings as
he, so close and distinct, grew white in the gloom.
God's grace was so abundant,
and his great caress so close, that
I brushed away a lock from my brow
to make it easier to kiss—and slept deeply.
It felt as if I had submerged myself
Forever in the earth, the trees.
And no one knew how great was the pain
That lay beyond the door of my solitude.

1964

Farewell! Farewell! I erase from my brow
a memory: a tender, damp garden,
lost in its own beauty, exactly as if
it were occupied in important work.
Farewell! Everything passes: gardens and house,
secret discords of two souls,
and the slow, amorous sigh of
that honeysuckle, there near the terrace.
First it imbued the house and the garden
near the house with many meanings of sadness;
then the honeysuckle suggested to my mind
an indistinct thought about Proust.
We watched the flame of the bonfire,
until it turned to smoky haze and
sleep filled our eyes, and watching a bush
was as good as reading a marvelous book.
Between our two hearts—the fog was
swirling! Honeysuckle and dampness,
a painting, the garden, and Swann—
all related to the same torment.
First the garden, then Swann appeared to me,
then I saw a top hat with a green lining,
and the sunset in Combray; and then
I heard my beloved grandmother's voice.
Farewell! But how many books and trees
entrusted us with their safekeeping,
only to let the rage of our farewell
plunge them into death and lifelessness.
Farewell! It turned out that we belong to those
who destroy forests and the souls of books.
We shall endure our mutual destruction
Without pity or interest.

1968

It's Me

It's me—at two o'clock in the afternoon,
some midwife's acquired trophy.
Someone is playing a lute above me.
I'm being tickled by little fairy fingers.
My soul comprehends only the diffusion
of a golden hue—it's me as I observe
the beauty of existence on a scorching prewar summer day.
"The Storm covers in gloom . . . " and hush-a-bye,
With that I got accustomed to living, but, alas—
it's me perishing from the war
under Ufa's sullen care.
How white the winter and the hospital become!
I notice that I did not die.
I see in clouds indecipherable faces
of those who died instead of me.
With my uncomely bluish face,
I, who just barely worked my body free from my torments,
it's me as I feel the great pleasure of anticipation,
when I hear something that is still less than a sound.
Only later do I come to value the habit of
listening to the eternal, surflike interchange
of nameless things with a soul
that gives those things a name.
It's me in my costume of violets;
I'm haughty, young and fat,
yet I've already trained my lips
to form a dying poet's smile.
Just like a trembling between two hearts,
there is play between two words.
All I must do is outline it in the ornamental
script of my pen, but in an artless fashion.
"So the words can be like a bride and groom!"—
I say this and laugh.
Like a priest in a rural backwoods,
I officiate at their secret union.
That's the reason why the ephemeral fairies

sprinkled their whispers and laughter about.
With my brow and my singer's curved neck,
o, I really don't look like anybody else.
I love this mark of dissimilarity;
and, hurrying like a young hound
my handwriting rushes after the distant prize,
there, I caught up—and my heart froze.
It's me as I curse and cry.
Let the paper stay white.
The heavens dictated a problem to me—
and I couldn't solve it.
I tortured my neck with a harness.
I don't know how others weave the
letters together; I haven't the strength,
I don't know how, I can't, set me free.
It's me—an insignificant person;
I'm like everyone else's twin,
as I sleep while I ride the train
with my unattractive face fallen on my bag.
It hasn't been my lot to gain too much success;
thank god, it hasn't been my lot
to be more deserving or richer than
all of my neighbors on earth.
Flesh of one flesh with my tired fellow citizens,
it's good that in the stores, at the movies,
at train stations I stand last
in their lines for the cashier—
behind a daring young lad
and an old woman in a downy kerchief,
merging with them, like two words
on their tongue and on mine.

1968

Squabbles and Reconciliations

Plummeting down through the woods to the Oka,
I'm careful not to step on the primroses.

I have mined from the snow, then have sung
of that brilliance that plunges me into trembling
"I have returned, Oka!" "Well, so what?"
was the answer expressed on the Oka's face.
"This brilliance that plunges you into trembling,
is my achievement, not yours."
"But aren't I a comrade-in-arms to both
your frozen [banks] and your drifting floes?"
"You don't even know what you're saying.
You may be alive, but you're still not nature."
"All winter long I have preserved you,
as if I were your third and secret bank."
"I do not know you. I flowed along on
my own power, you chance passerby."
"By the third day, [as I stood] over the Kura,
I was already miserable without your winding path."
"Let whoever becomes enchanted by the warm weather
of a second fatherland go away—he's boring."
I scooped up some water and slaked my thirst
with its ungracious and stingy dampness.
The servile forest and ravines
shared in the Oka's hostility.
How many years do I have left before
they forgive me? The cuckoos have grown silent.
Oh, too few, ravines and woods!
How sad, how bright, how wet!
Everything that I sang of in the winter
now loves only the spring, only the spring.
May you, everything that I sang of, flourish!
You will remember and love me again.
A backwater of darkness, conceived in the sleepless
pupil of my eye, where the word becomes extinct,
without me, the Oka will have little enough
to delight the half-sleep of a fisherman.
"Just look around!" reached my ears. "Just look around!"
There a brook came up against a weir.
I thought to myself: don't forget to describe
the color of the lungworts. I won't forget.

The sun set before my eyes.
To the right—Serpukhov, to the left—Aleksin.
"Just look around!" reached my ears. "Not for anything."
A triple-rosy sky hangs over the woods.
Closely related colors pour forth:
a lilac tone cannot be separated from
the violet essence of my youthful poems,
scattered over the fields with a raspberry imprint.
That's how the eye perceives the lungwort,
only bluer—denser and lower.
Someone's voice, surely for the nth time, begged.
"Just look around! Just look around now."
I looked around. I closed my eyes.
I know, Oka, that brilliance that
plunges me into the terror of adoration.
How you love me, how jealous you are!
"O, forgive me!" I entreated the Oka.
Once again I stepped up onto the stage.
I bow at the waist—but I cannot write,
I do not dare to glance at the paper.
Dirty and glorious is my lot:
to control the cold, that is being suggested to the hall.
My voice seduces people.
I don't know whether this is my sin or my duty.
It is fear that can sing so bravely,
after it has deceived the pale-faced stadium [crowd].
From afar did my throat—a torn
aperture of scarlet—look like the lungwort?
Only here do I tell no lies at all.
If only for that, send me forgiveness.
It was here that I first saw my footprint
on the snow without feeling disgust.
This is a good person standing here,
I thought, and began to laugh.
I knew that the traveler was tired
and didn't feel like writing that night.
I regret my February and March.
My heart somehow beats pensively.

A reiterated lie cuckoos:
there is time! It will still turn out fine.
What my squabbles and reconciliations
with the Oka bode for me—
I shall learn from a line
of another poem, but not this one.

1981

The Order of Blooming

I recall how the thirty-first day of March
Came down all rosy from the skies. But, since
I don't want to lie, I'll add: there was a deep blot in it—
for the Ladyzhino ravine was covered in darkness.
Suddenly a very, very dark blue color, as if only the
happy words of a poet would retreat to the ravine,
appeared and said that this honey-gathering bee
has arrived on the heels of the not-so-nimble lungwort.
I looked at it adoringly for a long time.
Who has not praised this dear flower
because its dark blue color is thrice-revealed to him:
it is completely blue, but also violet and scarlet.
In calling it "obscure," even the dictionary noticed
that the lungwort is pleased to be tempted by a
foul-weather dawn over Parshino, where all await
rain on the morrow: its soul looks all around, but not at us.
Of course coltsfoot appeared before the others.
And look, the pasque-flower, appropriating for
itself the rights of its verb, has not missed its mark—[1]
it grew for the sake of oblivion; you know it's deadly nightshade.
But what came later: snowdrops and dog's mercury,
and the chill and the poisonous kiss of the anemone
All lips that taste its poison praise the
ground anemones because they are so charming.
Thus did I see off the order of blooming;
but I knew that the main intoxication had not yet begun.
I waited two years for the bird-cherry blossoms of Ladyzhino.
Will I really inhale their maddening fumes again?

This time spring did not even try to be
patient—it dispensed all of its duties on the run;
and even earlier than ever: on the thirtieth of April
bird cherry blossoms bloomed all over the district.
First I run into the house with it, then run out of the house to it—
And my mind becomes deranged by this circular motion.
It's already a week old. But the drowsiness and the languor [remain],
And I won't have it out with this fateful plant.
Why do I find the inspirations of the bird-cherry blossom to be so sad?
Toward morning I take its breathing for
an ingratiating greeting from a major event,
but my pen is forbidden to play with its name.

1983

Whenever I surrender to a special place
Where I can fish for thoughts or waste my days—
I always play a certain game,
in which I find a lot of merriment.
I know that playfulness is hidden
in nature and in the mind of things.
Only a slow-witted lazybones does not
receive a summons to commune with it.
I love the falsely well-behaved air
of every single thing.
How it behaves in an exemplary fashion,
how intoxicatingly it dissembles!
In such a way, a less-than-innocent old man
crosses his chest, all covered in campaign medals
when a sudden glance flashes out from
under the lashes of a tender dark-eyed girl.
How infantile is everything in the world!
All substances and beings,
like children forced to stand in the corner,
dejectedly thirst for more mischief.
They notice that love stares at them—
and no one is counting the ecstasies and
the munificence: and reciprocal affection in

reality is akin to a puppy—or is a puppy itself.
I've been completely driven to my wit's end!
Let my hand or someone else's
tousle the hair at the back of my head
so that my idea will return to it.
Though it didn't bring the nape of my neck back to reason,
a face from the window—entered the window,
and its intrusion amused the
creatures in my playful utensils.
Am I really questioning the one
whose name my lips are concealing?
An idea will make this line more
difficult; let it stay silly.
Let it be completely stupid and free.
Having lost all interest in me,
my reason is sick with the white night.
What's to be done? We'll make do without it.
Let's begin: someone sent a book to me in the hospital.
Insofar as it's accepted to indulge
slavishly the caprices of those
who are reclining on its beds,
thanks to kind discretion,
flowers accompanied it.
There was a certain inhabitant of the ward:
she herself will create and then will read it through.
The reader hurries to find out from the
writer: where's the solution to the riddle?
I shall tell him: "in [the game] that I'm playing."
I open a cherished volume,
I laugh and present a flower
to the poem "Flower."
O, how many times has all of this happened:
even there, where I used to go to my
dearly beloved ravine to pick bird-cherry
blossoms, or simply to walk,
either in some timid grove near Moscow
or on the hills near the Oka—
the aggressive dotted line of my long

sought-out verse drizzled down to me.
Whether it's mine, or one from the reading room,
or one I took from my friend's shelf,
I took a volume for my secret passion,
for my lasting caprice.
Snowdrops and lungworts
and everything that grows in their wake,
have grown used to linking pages
with the sprouting of my beloved lines.
Not well-versed in the
materiality of matter—a flower
spontaneously triumphed over
the stillborn state of mountain immortelles.
We know that it grew in either the woods
or in the field—but we don't know when.
But how many roses grown in
captivity have I dedicated to it.
While regretting it, I ruined
their crimsonness with my hand.
When frost came—what a joy
it was to say: "Take it quickly."
And so in this defenseless world,
on its tragic shores,
I surrender myself to slips of the tongue
and mistakes, but with a flower in my hands.
And I am glad that my flowers
will stay behind in so many of my books;
that I'm guilty only for playing games,
that my lines are not unskilled,
and that, not having consigned a rose to a vase,
a not yet totally anonymous author,
will prolong the insatiable state of the
union of this flower with some other.
From all of this I get so much ecstasy,
and two dawns in one window;
and cheerful is the one, whose hale and hearty
genius has always been gracious to me.

1984

To My Readers

I recall my early age through the memory of scent and sight. My first recollection: the powerful scent of wet sand, out of which I was supposed to sculpt or bake something with the aid of a loathsome "little form," just the kind of thing I hate even today. I turn to the side—I turn around—and I see a brightly lit house in the depths of a dark garden. But wasn't all of this really taking place in a country estate? Just imagine and believe that this is a country estate in the city of the past. This house and garden on the Garden Ring road exist even today; some kind of establishment lives there now. In one of the rooms of this former private home, together with my family, I dwelt for the first three years of my life. Later on I'll find out, but now it seems to me, that even then I knew what irreparable misfortunes were soon to overtake my neighbors. How can a child not feel, not know that, unless he is born either a dolt or a murderer? He does not have such a possibility.

Next: I raise my solitary face and see a red balloon, which did not reach all the way to the blue sky; its string, caught on a tree branch, would not set it free. The tree is still preserved; driving by on the Garden Ring road, I see the house, trees, the tree, a child turning its face away from the compelling sandbox, the red balloon, which did not fly up into the free blue of the sky. Now they hardly allow children or any strangers to go beyond those gates; and for a long time balloons have not flown.

I shall note in parentheses: I shall see my next red balloon after the war. It cost my grandmother a great deal. But there it is, or rather there-it-is; I lost it (or set it free?) in the blue sky over the white Bolshoi Theater. At that time the owner and tamer of a bunch of desired, willful treasures dwelt there.

And the gain of such an inconsolable loss: the balloon's good fortune, freedom.

Balloons are to this day an object of adoration for me. My children have not seen balloons, whose willful "animateness" strives to get away and thus teaches hands not to possess, but to set free.

Having closed my conditional parentheses, I return to my earliest years, to my "before-the-war." This time dwells twice within my consciousness. I am sure that the universal tragedy, which did not touch me directly with the back of its hand, answers to the inborn inability of men even in infancy to be only its neighbor, but not its participant. This unexpected complicity will later realize—or primordially had realized—the sad contents of my eyes. But how favorably the many-colored twinkling of the world encouraged my eyes; it still nourishes and cultivates everything that comprises my view of this world, [and everything] that comprises me.

And then: tulips bloomed in the garden during the night, and for the first time overcoming the total eclipse of my previous silence, I say: "I have never seen such a thing." Since then my life has gone on, it still goes by, and again I look at the seven colors that white contains—since then I have never thought up better words of praise for them.

I confess to these first sensations only because I know that earliest childhood and man's mature years find themselves in a secret correspondence; they close a certain circle, like an approximate verbal geometry describing the development of a personality.

The next long period of time: the war. I have already had the opportunity to write what I remember about its first day, its last day, and the interval of nationwide calamity between them. I was only a child, saved from death by the miracle of human kindness. This miracle always accompanied me later and even accompanies me now. My grandmother's voice, distracting me and protecting me from sirens, bombing, blackouts, from evacuation, from all the hopelessness of war. Grandmother read Pushkin, Gogol, Lermontov to me. This anticipated my future, rescued life. The second, but just as important, circumstance of fate: namely—those nameless, simple (as someone said) people who were from birth close and native to me; I took their misfortunes closely to heart, their speech—to my ears and my mind; only with them did I get along easily, only their responses made me happy.

Postwar colored memories: the 9 May fireworks, embraces and tears. But more powerful, more colorful was a drawing lesson in school. Until that lesson everyone took my childhood reserve for an inability to communicate and a lack of talent for learning. I remember my teacher standing over me with an entire commission at her side as I put accents only on consonant sounds. They were all horrified, and I with them. But here is the aforementioned drawing lesson. The teacher had just returned from the war, wounded, dressed in the only clothes he had—his uniform; and as I see him now, wounded by something specific and doomed to more new wounds, he sadly said: "Children, draw Victory Day." I use up all of my colored pencils on formlessness—or, as people would say later, on an abstraction of a portrayed representation. For the first time I received an A+; I always recall the teacher's sad face. From that time on I was no longer considered to be an untalented child; and so I know how each human talent needs encouragement and approval. As far as I remember, I haven't seen any evil or talentless people: I somehow never crossed paths with them in the wide world. The attentions of my schoolteachers and then of those in the literary institute protected me and assisted me.

These words of mine are directed to those whose love, which I so appreciate, preserves me from calamity and sadness. I would consider the chance of offending those who heeded me and trusted my word to be my greatest misfortune. But I hope that I do not even have such a horrible chance.

In short—one should write an introduction to one's book in two instances: when it enters into the artistic design or when the author tries to justify the book's imperfection. This author (I) intend both the one and the other. But here is still another, the last: I ask you to understand me, forgive me and accept my love.

Your Bella Akhmadulina

3 September 1987

Translated by Christine A. Rydel

Notes to the Essay

1. Anatoli Ivanushkin, "Have the Poets Yielded Their Former Positions?," interview with Bella Akhmadulina, *Soviet Literature* 6 (1988): 138.

2. Ibid., 139.

3. Boris Gass, *Zadui vo mne svechu* (London; n.p., 1984), 30–32.

4. B. Akhmadulina, "A Word That Amounts to a Deed," in *The Garden*, ed. and trans. F.D. Reeve (New York: Henry Holt, 1990), 149–50.

5. Feliks Medvedev, "Mne nravitsia, chto zhizn' vsegda prava," *Ogonek* 15 (1987): 10.

6. Pavel Antokol'skii, "Bella Akhmadulina," in *Stikhi* (Moscow: Khudozhestvennaia literatura, 1975), 3.

7. Elena Mikhailovna, "Bella Akhmadulina: 'Voz'mite na pamiat' moi golos," *Daugava* 3 (March 1987): 96.

8. B. Akhmadulina, "Grandmother," in *The Garden*, ed. and trans. F.D. Reeve (New York: Henry Holt, 1990), 151–64; original in *Oktiabr* 3 (1988): 3–9.

9. Bella Akhmadulina, *Stikhotvoreniia* (Moscow: Khudozhestvennaia literatura, 1988), 3–6.

10. Medvedev, 10.

11. Gass, 259.

12. Ibid., 259–61.

13. L.H. Shchemeleva, "Bella Akhatovna Akhmadulina," in *Lermontovskaia Èntsiklopediia*, ed. B.A. Manuilov (Moscow: Izdatel'stvo Sovetskaia Èntsiklopediia, 1981), 41.

14. "Grandmother," 161.

15. Vasilii Aksenov, "Progulka v kalashnyi riad," *Grani* 133 (1984): 178–79.

16. Mikhailovna, 97, 99.

17. Gass, 68.

18. Medvedev, 10.

19. Jill Roese, "Vera Zubareva," in *Dictionary of Russian Women Writers*, ed. Marina Ledkovsky, Charlotte Rosenthal and Mary Zirin (Westport, CT: Greenwood Press, 1994), 759–60.

Translator's Note to the Selected Works

1. "Pasque-flower" in Russian is *prostrel*, which also means "hit a target."

Bibliography

Primary Works

Struna. Moscow: Sovetskii pisatel', 1962.

Oznob. Frankfurt am Main: Possev-Verlag, 1968.

Uroki muzyki. Moscow: Sovetskii pisatel', 1969.

Stikhi. Moscow: Khudozhestvennaia literatura, 1975.

Metel'. Moscow: Sovetskii pisatel', 1977.

Sny o Gruzii. Tbilisi: Izdatel'stvo Merani, 1977; rpt., 1979.

Svecha. Moscow: Sovetskaia Rossiia, 1977.

"Mnogo sobak i sobaka." *Metropol'*. Ed. Vasilii Aksenov et al. Moscow, 1979. [Facsimile ed., Ann Arbor, MI: Ardis, 1979.]

Taina. Moscow: Sovetskii pisatel', 1983.

Sad. Moscow: Khudozhestvennaia literatura, 1987.

"Dva rasskaza" ["Babushka" and "Mnogo sobak i sobaka"]. *Oktiabr'* 3 (1988): 3–22.

Izbrannoe. Moscow: Sovetskii pisatel', 1988.

Stikhotvoreniia. Moscow: Khudozhestvennaia literatura, 1988.

Poberezh'e. Moscow: Biblioteka Ogonek, 1991.

Larets i kliuch. Saint Petersburg: Pushkinskii fond, 1994.

In Translation

Fever and Other New Poems. Trans. Geoffrey Dutton and Igor Mezhakoff-Koriakin. New York: William Morrow, 1969.

"Many Dogs and the Dog." Trans. H. William Tjalsma. *Metropole*. Ed. Vasilii Aksenov. New York: W.W. Norton, 1980. 6–29.

The Garden: New and Selected Poetry and Prose. Ed. and trans. F.D. Reeve. New York: Henry Holt, 1990.

"Poems." *Contemporary Russian Poetry*. Trans. G.S. Smith. Bloomington: Indiana University Press, 1993. 124–37.

Secondary Works

Aksenov, Vasilii. "Progulka v kalashnyi riad." *Grani* 133 (1984): 165–89.

Aleshka, T.V. "Pushkinskie traditsii v poèzii B. Akhmadulinoi." *Vesnik. Belaruskaia dziarzhainaia universitèta*. 4th ser. 2 (1992): 15–18.

Antokol'skii, Pavel. "Bella Akhmadulina" [foreword]. *Stikhi*. Moscow: Khudozhestvennaia literatura, 1975. 3–12.

Brodal, Jan. "Wahlverwandschaft: Ein Motiv bei Bella Achmadulina." *Scando-Slavica* 28 (1982): 19–26.

Chuprinin, Sergei. "Sposob sovesti." *Literaturnoe obozrenie* 10 (1978): 49–53.

Condee, Nancy. "Akhmadulina's *Poèmy*: Poems of Transformation and Origins." *Slavic and East European Journal* 29, 2 (1985): 176–87.

Eliseeva, M.B. "Literaturnye reministsentsii v stikhotvorenii B.A. Akhmadulinoi 'Sad-Vsadnik.'" *Khudozhestvennyi tekst. Ontologiia i interpretatsiia*. Ed. B.L. Borukhova and K.F. Sedova. Saratov: Saratovskii gosudarstvennyi pedagogicheskii institut im. K.A. Fedina, 1992. 143–51.

Erofeev, Viktor. "Novoe i staroe. Zametki o tvorchestve Belly Akhmadulinoi." *Oktiabr'* 5 (1987): 190–94.

Evtushenko, Evgenii. Foreword. *Fever and Other New Poems*. Trans. Geoffrey Dutton and Igor Mezhakoff-Koriakin. New York: William Morrow, 1969. 1–8.

Foniakov, Il'ia. "Ne sotvori sebe kumira." *Literaturnoe obozrenie* 10 (1978): 46–49.

Gass, Boris. *Zadui vo mne svechu*. London: n.p., 1984.

Grigor'eva, O.N., and T.V. Tevalinskaia. "'Sinesteticheskaia' poèziia B. Akhmadulinoi." *Vestnik moskovskogo universiteta*. 9th ser. *Filologiia* 9, 4 (1990): 12–19.

Gugushvili, Èteri. "' . . . I v liubvi, v bespokoistve, v toske . . . ' Otkrytoe pis'mo Belle Akhmadulinoi." *Literaturnaia Gruziia* 6 (1978): 134–48.

Ivanushkin, Anatoli. "Have the Poets Yielded Their Former Positions?" *Soviet Literature* 6 (1988): 138–41.

Ketchian, Sonia. *The Poetic Craft of Bella Akhmadulina*. University Park: Pennsylvania State University Press, 1993.

———. "Poetic Creation in Bella Akhmadulina." *Slavic and East European Journal* 28, 1 (1984): 42–57.

———. "The Wonder of Nature and Art: Bella Akhmadulina's *Secret*." *New Studies in Russian Language and Literature*. Ed. Anna Lisa Crone and Catherine V. Chvany. Columbus, OH: Slavica, 1986. 183–98.

Medvedev, Feliks. "Mne nravitsia, chto zhizn' vsegda prava." *Ogonek* 15 (1987): 9–11.

Mikhailovna, Elena. "Bella Akhmadulina: 'Voz'mite na pamiat' moi golos." *Daugava* 3 (March 1987): 95–107.

Molchanova, N.M. "Poèticheskie golosa Rossii (E. Evtushenko, A. Voznesenskii, B. Akhmadulina)." *Literatura i stranovedenie*. Ed. F.F. Kuznetsova and E.M. Pul'khritudova. Moscow: Russkii iazyk, 1978. 91–103.

Mustafin, Rafael'. "Poisk algoritma. Zametki o poèzii Belly Akhmadulinoi." *Druzhba narodov* 6 (1985): 245–52.

Novikov, V. "Bol' obnovleniia." *Literaturnoe obozrenie. Organ Soiuza Pisatelei SSSR* 1 (1985): 50–52.

Papernyi, Z. "Pod nadzorom prirody." *Oktiabr'* 10 (1984): 204–06.

Reeve, F.D. Introduction. *The Garden: New and Selected Poetry and Prose*. Ed. and trans. F.D. Reeve. New York: Henry Holt, 1990. xi–xvii.

Rydel, Christine. "A Bibliography of Works by and about Bella Akhmadulina." *Ten Bibliographies of Twentieth Century Literature*. Ed. Fred Moody. Ann Arbor, MI: Ardis, 1977. 143–57.

———. "The Metapoetical World of Bella Akhmadulina." *Russian Literature Triquarterly* 1 (1971): 326–41.

Shchemeleva, L. "'Vse bylo dano . . . '" *Novyi mir* 5 (1988): 234–37.

Natal'ia Baranskaia

Natal'ia Vladimirovna Baranskaia was born on 31 December 1908 in a Russia between two revolutions into a family whose primary occupation was revolutionary activity. In a 1988 interview, Baranskaia described her parents:

> My parents were revolutionaries, engaged in underground work, printing leaflets, etc. . . . My mother had a very strong character, and she had a passionate desire to get involved in the student groups in Petersburg. They were so vital at that time, they got involved in everything: read books, thought about the revolution, about social transformations, about social revolution. . . .
>
> My father was completely different; he had a sensitive, artistic nature and if he had not immersed himself in the revolution he might have been a writer or an artist. . . . I grew up in a period when Russian women first started working outside the home on a massive scale. It wasn't that they thirsted after freedom, but they were needed. . . . Like many young people of that time I was consumed by the need to transform society. . . .[1]

The fact that Baranskaia was born into a world subjected to the upheavals of revolutions and world war must be considered significant in any discussion of her as a writer. The story of more than seventy years of profound transformation, marked too often by profound tragedy (World War I, the Bolshevik revolution, the civil war, the Stalin era, World War II, the years of Thaw under Khrushchev, the "period of stagnation" presided over by Brezhnev and finally the *perestroika* of Gorbachev), is ever present in Baranskaia's own biography and her writing as well. Stated simply, Natal'ia Baranskaia is at once the quintessential representative and product of her society: this is the natural beginning point for any discussion of her relative merits as a writer, whether feminine, feminist or female, Soviet, Russian or universal.

Details of Baranskaia's biography are few, and those that she emphasizes herself are quite general. Born in 1908, she emigrated first to Switzerland and then to Germany with her parents, both political exiles. She returned to Russia with her mother in 1914; her father, who had never married her mother, remained in Germany. In Baranskaia's own words, she then "came to Moscow where, with a few absences, [she has] remained ever since."[2]

The "few absences" would include evacuation with her children to the Altai region during World War II. Before that, in 1929, Baranskaia graduated from Moscow State University, where she had studied philology and ethnology. Her professional life after graduation included work in the publishing field and in various museums. In purely personal terms, Baranskaia nowhere speaks in any detail of when or where she met her husband, with whom she had two daughters. An army captain loved and well respected by his men, he was killed in the Battle of Kursk in August 1943. Baranskaia never remarried, raising her daughters with some help from her mother, but mostly alone.

After wartime evacuation to Altai, she returned to Moscow, where she entered graduate school and moved exclusively into the field of museum work. The final eight years of her working life she spent in the Pushkin Museum, where she developed what became an intense interest in the poet Aleksandr Pushkin and, more significantly, in his wife, Natal'ia Nikolaevna Goncharova. It is Baranskaia's opinion that Pushkin scholars and critics not only have misunderstood Natal'ia Nikolaevna but have maligned her as well. In an attempt to address this injustice, Baranskaia makes her the focus of the short piece "The Color of Dark Honey" ("Tsvet temnogo meda," 1977). Pushkin himself is represented in Baranskaia's work only in 1982, in a collection of pieces called *A Portrait Presented to a Friend* (*Portret podarennyi drugu*).

Baranskaia retired from the Pushkin Museum in 1966 and two years later, in the prestigious journal, *New World* (*Novyi mir*), edited at that time by Aleksandr Tvardovskii, her first stories appeared: "At Her Mother's and Father's Place" ("U Nikitskikh i na Pl'ushchikhe") and "The Retirement Party" ("Provody"). One year later in the same journal, what would become Baranskaia's trademark piece, "A Week Like Any Other" ("Nedelia kak nedelia"), was published.

Baranskaia's literary reputation was thus established during that brief period in the 1960s before the "period of stagnation" set in. Today, "A Week Like Any Other" continues to be the measure for her literary production, although it is not the sum total of her work, and perhaps not even her best piece.

In 1977, shortly before "The Color of Dark Honey" was published, her first collection of stories and novellas appeared under the title *A Negative Gizelle* (*Otritsatel'naia Zhizel'*). Her second collection of stories, *Woman with an Umbrella* (*Zhenshchina s zontikom*), was published in 1981, followed by *Portrait Presented to a Friend,* in 1982. Her only novel to date, *Day of Remembrance* (*Den' pominoveniia*), appeared in 1989, although it was completed some time earlier. Her most recent work, "Autobiography without Omissions" ("Avtobiografiia bez umolchanii"), appeared in the émigré journal *Grani* in 1990.

While the temptation, particularly in the West, to view a writer's works without reference to the writer's person is great, it must be overcome in the case of Baranskaia if one is to fully appreciate her work and the contribution to Soviet literature that it represents. Her choices of topics revolve around her own experience in a developing Soviet society. She writes about and for this society and, therefore, her works remain more accessible to the Soviet/Russian reader than any other. Rarely can Baranskaia be accused of writing to educate the reader; even less frequently can her writing be termed exercises in form or expression. She is motivated by the strong desire to illustrate, to share with the reader some truth of human nature that she has found compelling in her own experience. And while her main protagonists are usually women, she does not dwell exclusively in the realm of feminist, or even feminine, concerns. She finds the universal elements of a particular event and presents them as simply and unambiguously as possible to her audience.

Day of Remembrance is Baranskaia's largest, most ambitious work to date. Although the subject is war, typically a male-dominated activity, it serves more as a vehicle for the examination of the differing, yet remarkably similar, life experiences of the main characters, all of whom are women. Baranskaia explained the impetus for her foray into the genre of the war novel as her desire to "write the truth about the war."[3] Her literary goals were stated in precisely those terms,[4] much to the dissatisfaction of critics who faulted the novel for its sociological, documentary nature and lack of "literariness." Truth, though, is not always simply a compendium of facts, but rather a subjective experience. That experience of war was one Baranskaia shared with many others, as she explained in the novel: "The person who has not been touched by war is not always capable of understanding those whom the war drove out of their homes."[5]

Translating the title as "Memorial Day," as some have, conjures up in the mind of an American reader visions of three-day weekends, picnics, parades and all the attendant hoopla. A more literal translation, "Day of Remembrance," sets a more appropriate tone. "No one is forgotten, nothing is forgotten" is a ubiquitous Soviet slogan, but as Baranskaia reminds us, no one should be forgotten; every death had its meaning.

"Victory Day," 9 May, the day that marks the defeat of Nazi Germany, forms the backdrop for the novel. As a holiday in the Soviet tradition, it carries more solemn weight and is graver in tone than the American version. Surviving civilians and military veterans recall those who did not; bearing photographs of loved ones lost, they gather on the squares and in cemeteries. The full significance of the defeat of Nazi Germany, as well as the accrued importance of its commemoration, informs and directs the novel on its trajectory, the metaphor of which is realized on the tracks of the train, carrying the main figures of the novel to their destination, those "distant graves."

9 May 1979, the thirty-fourth anniversary of the end of World War II (the Great Fatherland War), is the setting for the opening chapter of the novel. The scene is a Moscow train station where scores of widows, veterans and others prepare to make the journey to honor the memory of those who fell in defense of that fatherland. Amid the throngs at the station, a "man with a microphone" (*chelovek s mikrofonom*) first "gives voice" to the seven women whose individual voices and persons provide the common narrative. Baranskaia then juxtaposes this chaotic scene full of static hubbub and voices to the determined, forward motion of the train as it leaves the station. The women settle in for the night's journey, and now the narrative builds on the individual voices of the seven.

Structurally, the novel is divided into twenty chapters. The first, "The Eve: Flowers and Wreaths" ("Kanun: Tsvety i venki"), and the last, "By the Distant Graves: The End of the Journey" ("U dalekikh mogil: Konets puti"), function as the frame for the remaining eighteen chapters. The women are all together and introduced in the first chapter but appear singly in the following chapters. The individual threads are brought together in the final chapter (translated below).

Most of the narration is third person with exceptions in the sixth and eighth chapters, told in the first person by Aksin'ia Kuz'minichna, and in the nineteenth, told in the first person by Lizaveta Timofeevna. The frame chapters are related by an omniscient narrator who, tellingly, slips from time to time into the first person and who is revealed in the final chapter to be Baranskaia herself. Baranskaia, though, is careful to distance herself authorially from the figure to whom she is closest, Mariia Nikolaevna. While the greatest share of the book, seven interior chapters, focus on this character, Baranskaia consistently maintains a third-person stance to preserve the integrity of her basic premise: the war experiences described here belong to Soviet/Russian women in general and are not the exclusive property of the author alone. Also, in eschewing a strict first-person narrative, Baranskaia is able to more fully explore and expose the different, yet related, experiences of the war and avoid the confinement of autobiographical memoir.

In choosing the figures who speak in the first person, Baranskaia is more likely motivated by stylistic concerns than those of content. Both Aksin'ia Kuz'minichna and Lizaveta Timofeevna are "provincials" (*derevenskie*), the former from Orel and the latter from Zvenigorod, and their speech is typical of their areas of origin. Baranskaia counterbalances the measured tones of her omniscient narrator with the more emotionally colored, cadenced speech of her two provincial narrators. These variations propel the narrative forward as unevenly as the jolting stops and starts of the train, pausing at various stations along its way.

The train, a rather hackneyed image of the journey of life, is renewed as a metaphor, for this is a journey of the living not to death, but to the dead, who live on thanks to the collective memory. All of life is involved in this train journey:

> This train is for them, and it will run as long as need be so that they could—
> remember,
> recount,
> talk about the war, about death,
> lament what was lost,
> and rejoice in what they have.[6]

Real trains play a role in the narrative as they carry the women and their children farther and farther from their homes into evacuation. But as a symbol, a collection of cars joined and drawn toward a common destination by the same force, they carry much greater weight, providing a higher level for the seven women's journey.

But they are not always seven, as the man with the microphone discovers in the first chapter of *Day of Remembrance*. An eighth woman, in Baranskaia's words, "the symbol of our grief," silently accompanies them, the "woman in black." Despite being discovered by the man with the microphone, she is invisible to everyone except the women, yet she is also present throughout.

Therefore, the number becomes eight, an even number, not seven—magical, biblical, perhaps, but more importantly here an odd number. Given Baranskaia's attribution of importance to flowers and their ritual power in Soviet life, as, for example, in the subtitle to chapter 1, "Flowers and Wreaths," it seems quite likely that she is reproducing the tradition of odd-number and even-number bouquets and symbolically making a wreath of mourning out of her characters. Odd-number bouquets are reserved for happy events, weddings, birthdays and other celebrations. But one brings even-number bouquets to a funeral. The origins of this tradition are murky, but the effect is real in Russian, and other Slavic, society.

When the number of women increases to nine at the end with the addition of Baranskaia herself in the final photograph, nothing is changed: there are still only eight visible women in the picture. The ninth, the "woman in black," is invisible. However, there is now a new, less tragic tone: the "difficult road" has been traversed and is now behind them. The women are grouped together around the grave surrounded by flowers, most notably, lilacs, flowers of early spring and symbols of renewal and hope. The fact that this occurs at the grave of Baranskaia's husband indicates a coming to terms with that terrible fear that Mariia Nikolaevna (Baranskaia) described in the first chapter:

> For a long time she couldn't admit it to herself, but then she finally understood: she was afraid of the grave. Simply afraid. After all, a grave isn't the news of a death; it's not the sympathy of friends or accounts of a funeral; a grave is just that—a grave. You can touch it or press yourself close to it; even embrace it, knowing that he's lying there, ar at least what's left of him, in the ground.[7]

Structurally, *Day of Remembrance* is not remarkable for its innovation; it utilizes a traditional, circular structure built around the tying together of the beginning and end of the forward motion/narration. The story is told by numerous accounts and voices but joined in a single expression by a common theme, bringing everything back to the starting point. Baranskaia's choice of a straightforward structure is propitious and serves her artistic goal well; her readers should not be distracted by the mechanics of composition, but should focus their energy on the stories themselves.

The genre she works in occupies a space somewhere between memoir and historical fiction, and the style she uses has been termed "Soviet." Indeed, there are passages that are unmistakably Soviet in style and tone, and mention should be made of them. However, justifiable criticism of the Soviet style of appropriating events and people to create myths for their national pride can in no measure obscure the experience of war that cut deeply into the psyche of the nation and, for Baranskaia's generation, was an integral facet of their worldview. Even when they later saw the truth about the Soviet abuses, the war remained untainted in their minds and inseparable from their lives.

To the Western reader, Baranskaia can only speak obliquely. While her prose may translate well, it transmits into the Western mind rather weakly. In the West her work has been dismissed as being second-rate and stylistically unsophisticated or uninteresting. However, she speaks very directly to the Soviet reader. She is not a blind patriot; neither is she an apologist. Hers is a personal focus, but not one that excludes attention to technical concerns. *Day of Remembrance* has its merits in that respect, but to term it "great literature" or "classic" might be inappropriate.

In a discussion of Baranskaia as a writer of her gender who focuses on the role and fate of women in Soviet society, the issue of feminism naturally arises. Baranskaia herself eschews this label, again brooking criticism from the West and home as well for avoiding an obviously feminist stance. However, she certainly does not avoid the issues of the plight of women in her society. The proof of this is, of course, "A Week Like Any Other" ("Nedel'ia kak nedel'ia"). As Baranskaia's signature piece, the de facto benchmark against which *Day of Remembrance* is bound to be measured, this work deserves special attention.

Published in 1969 in *New World* (*Novyi mir*), "A Week Like Any Other" caused quite a sensation and was almost immediately hailed as a long-overdue examination of the plight of Soviet women. In the previously cited interview with Pieta Monks, Baranskaia herself mentions that "there had been nothing written, either as fiction or fact, about how hard life was for our women, who legally have equal rights with men."[8] Once published, the story was passed from hand to hand, much as *samizdat* literature would be. The similarity to this unpublished literature, though, ends here, as Baranskaia's fictional "Week" does not oppose the system. For all its openness and honesty and the insights into the difficulties of having two full-time jobs (outside the home and inside as well), "Week" neither focuses on the inequalities suffered by women nor seems intended to destroy the literary myth of the Soviet woman (or man) who consistently triumphs in the face of all adversity, accomplishing all goals regardless of the odds. More than anything it simply states, without insistence, that this is the way women live, which is not healthy for them, their families or their society.

"A Week Like Any Other" tells the story of a week in the life of the heroine, Ol'ga. Seen through her eyes, the days are full of things left undone. The phrase "no time" occurs at regular intervals, like the chiming of a clock that ticks away the hours. Using a device similar to the one in *Day of Remembrance*, Baranskaia presents multiple views through the supporting characters' interaction with Ol'ga. The two Liusias, Maria Matveevna Alla Sergeevna and Zinaida Gustavovna, together with Ol'ga, create a composite picture of Soviet woman. The narrative is telegraphic, timed to match the frenetic pace of Ol'ga's days, and the single voice of Ol'ga is focused, in keeping with her lifestyle.

In both "Week" and *Day of Remembrance* Baranskaia concerns herself exclusively with female characters and their plight, but her concerns transcend the gender boundary. She is occupied with the larger questions regarding war, the nature of humanity and its future, in a universal sense. In *Day of Remembrance* these questions are framed in intensely personal terms and appear in the lyric digressions that occur throughout the novel. These interludes give voice to significant emotion and lyricism in their examination of birth, motherhood, life, death, war and peace. They provide a soothing tonic to the ongoing narrative of hardship, deprivation and horrors engendered by war. They read as poems in prose, and their symbols represent universal feelings.

It is precisely this type of passage that is deemed clichéd and termed "Soviet." If the basis of the reality that Baranskaia knows and artistically represents is ignored, then perhaps this type of criticism acquires a degree of relevance. However, it is clear that Baranskaia divined a special truth, regardless of what "truth" was later revealed about Soviet Russia. It is the truth of her experience that she brings to her work.

For Baranskaia, the war and society are impersonal structures whose effects can only be "true" if felt personally. The immediate feeling of suffering and hardship endured by all her characters is personal, but they are reduplicated endlessly, and in doing so, attain universal dimensions.

Maureen Riley

From Day of Remembrance

By the distant graves. The end of the journey.

That meeting at the graves, with death, was drawing nearer for the bereaved women. They sat silently, huddled together in the train car. . . .

I dreamed, and in my dream I saw a broad lane that started out from the porch. Or maybe it was a swath that was cut into the woods; there were all sorts of trees there.

The birches were already decked out with their little brown earrings and the maples were covered with plump buds. The green grass was pushing up through last year's fallen leaves. Of course, that's what it was, a swath, a cutting through the forest, straight and broad, and it led away from the house into eternity.

A light spring snow had fallen, stopping for a while on the fir branches before settling down on the grass. The weightless snow was already melting, hanging in silvery droplets from the branches.

It was as if I had awoken on the high terrace early in the morning; it was cold, the big wooden house behind me was empty, mysterious. I'm looking out onto the forest, on the swath leading away into the distance, and I feel good. There's silence, peace and clarity. There's a visible stillness in the harmonious, peaceful trees, in the dark firs, in the silvery-rose birches and in the patterns of white snow on the green grass. The empty house has fallen silent in its isolation. I'm walking through the half-dark house in a long nightgown and I'm holding a lighted candle. There's the ringing silence of the tapping and creaking of the dry old floorboards.

The dream is restful and pure. And it has all of that which is lacking in my life: silence, peace, space and clarity.

The train went on, slowly, in no particular hurry. This type of train should not be in a hurry. It stopped at every station and way station along the way; it would stop by the forest or at the edge of the field or by the road not far from the village. The women would get out, walking along slowly, and everywhere they went they were met by graves, some common, some single, but mostly common.

The common grave is the end of a long and bloody battle, the common end; the brotherhood of all who fought there to the death, for whom this battle would be the last. It is the refuge of the dead and a memorial for the living. A plaster soldier holding a gun, his blank stare distant and aloof; a concrete slab and a concrete or iron obelisk with a star affixed to the top. And names, names everywhere. At the foot of the monument flowers and wreaths have been recently laid. Bouquets of buttercups and bluebells, forget-me-nots and lilies of the valley, sometimes just plain fir boughs with light green spring tips. All these are evidence of the love and memories and the sense of debt the living feel. And the occasional shriveled wreath or flower is like a reproach to the negligent and the forgetful.

The women wandered in silence from grave to grave, stopping to read aloud in half-voices the names of those interred there.

"Look Ganna, Ivan Kovalev!"

"No, my Vania's last name is Koval'. But maybe they made a mistake?" Ganna's voice shook with alarm.

Dear, sweet Ganna, a million Ivans perished in that war, and among them thousands of Kovalevs and hundreds of Koval's. Put your heart at ease, lay your flowers on this grave, for this Ivan, and let yourself think: he also died so young, he was just twenty-two. Who knows whom he left behind in this world, on this earth, maybe he had a son, or maybe he didn't even have time enough for that. Bow down before this Ivan, and in him, before all Ivans, including your own.

They went with Nonna Romanovna to her husband's grave. Such was their habit, not to leave each other, but having made their way, to go off and leave that one to herself for a while.

There was a gray marble slab adorned with a red cross that stood out in a well-defined square. The symbol of charity and salvation, a sign of immunity and defense. Below the cross was the inscription: "On this place, an entire medical battalion perished when their hospital was hit with a precisely aimed bomb dropped by a Nazi fighter. October 1941. We will never forget you!" And on a second slab, right next to it, were the names of the military doctors, the attendants, the orderlies and all the wounded who died there.

Nonna Romanovna bends down to lay her flowers against the marble slab and then straightens up, calm and quiet. Just a tiny vein near her right eye pulses convulsively. She presses her finger against the quivering vein.

"My husband is here, too: Kornev, Aleksei Borisovich, a military doctor. There's his name. It happened in the first year of the war. But the monument was put up only after Victory Day."

The red cross signals protection of the wounded, the crippled and the helpless. It is an island of salvation. In the last war, just a quarter of a century before this one, the red cross was a safe haven, untouchable by war.

Mankind has gone forward!

Forward? Where else but forward?

The train rolls on, its wheels clacking. The forests were gradually replaced by copses and little islands of birch and oak groves. And then the broad expanse of Russia opened up to reveal its soft, steep slopes and gently slanted hills, its little clefts and crevices overgrown with low bushes and willows sheltering the brooks and streams. The rich black earth, coal-blackish violet in hue and freshly ploughed, alternated with joyful green strips of winter crops.

These endless fields lie motionless as clouds float by above them, creating ever-changing heavenly landscapes. Their mighty white sails full, these ships drift along. As they pass by, a herd of rosy lambs grazing in the cold heights comes into view. Suddenly the wind picks up and low gray clouds skitter along the earth like ragged scraps of smoke.

And all of this, all the dark ploughed strips and the green hills, all the blue skies and the multicolored clouds, all of this sounds like the earth's majestic chorale.

The grave was in the village itself, by the *sovkhoz*'s main house, in a small triangle bounded by three low wooden buildings, and on a gently sloping hill crisscrossed by a network of roads. These wooden buildings—the main office, the school and the activities hall—stood at a short distance one from the other, creating a kind of square, in the center of which there was a low fence. This fence surrounded a grave with its iron obelisk. On both sides of the obelisk were two broad panels into which were etched the names of those interred there. And divided between the two panels was an inscription; on the left side it read: "No one is forgotten," and on the right: "Nothing is forgotten."

This common grave was the center of the town; meetings and parades were organized around it, and in this way the war dead could participate in the ceremonies held by the village that they had liberated from the Germans.

Nonna Romanovna read the names from the panels aloud, and Fedos'ia Nikitichna listened, holding tightly to Aksin'ia's hand, waiting to hear her son's name. The moment she heard "Kazantsev," she dropped to her knees with a loud wail. What she didn't hear was the name that followed: Timofei. Not Matvei, as she had expected, but Timofei. It was Timofei, her eldest son, who was buried here.

But she wept for her "Moten'ka;" he wasn't missing in action. Matveiushko, her precious child, hadn't perished in anonymity but had fallen and was buried in our native Russian land. Was this a consolation? Maybe it was, but together with that, her dream that he was alive, but far away, had suddenly vanished.

This dream had been born of the tiniest of hopes, no bigger than the head of a pin, that Matvei was still alive. She had imagined it like this: Matvei had been taken prisoner by the Germans and had then been freed not by the Russians, but some other army, maybe the French or perhaps the English or the Americans. And because of this, he had ended up on the other side of the ocean, far, far away. There he had started to work: a little carpentry, a little bricklaying, and then he had saved enough money and had built himself a house. Of course, he had built it with their American lumber. He met a girl, a nice country girl, modest and simple. Matvei had learned their language and could now speak in American. He got married, set up housekeeping and started a family. Now he would be around forty, with a big family. The first kids he had named in honor of his parents; the rest had American names, because his wife wanted it that way. Fedos'ia had heard that there were farms in America, not villages, something like the way things used to be in Russia under the tsar. So that would mean that Matvei would have a farm by now.

And if Matvei didn't write her, that only meant that it wasn't allowed.

And if it wasn't allowed, then fine, he didn't have to. A mother had no right to take offense if it wasn't allowed. It would be enough as long as her son was alive and well. His father could rant and rave, he's a man, after all. But her mother's heart was forgiving.

And here was Fedos'ia lying on the ground, her arms opened wide as if to embrace the grave. Weeping loudly, she could not hear what they were saying.

Her companions were exclaiming: "What? Timofei? But you said Matvei, and it was Matvei in the letter. Maybe the schoolchildren made a mistake?" They helped Fedos'ia Nikitichna to her feet, speaking to her all the while, and it seemed as if she didn't hear them; they tried to explain it to her, and she couldn't understand.

But when she did understand, she went completely to pieces. Her dream shuddered, swayed and finally collapsed. It would never be raised again. There would be no house beyond the sea, no wife and no children, little and big, her grandchildren. No, she would never believe again.

And why, after all, would she, an old woman, want to go off so far away? She'd do better to stay close to her own hearth, in her own little house . . . her legs go weak and give way again.

"Why are you grieving so, Granny? Your eldest's grave has been found, you've finally learned his fate. Just think, how many more years he could have lain here, unknown. . . ."

The train rolls on. It's early in the morning. There's a large village, and a brick building with a sign: it's a store. The street is lined with young trees, fronted with gardens and fences. There are houses with red and green iron roofs. People are walking along the street, one or two here and there, but it's still early and there are few of them.

The village ends and there's the outskirts, open heaps of garbage that the nettles have not yet covered over. Low little wooden houses with tiny windows, their gates standing open. The ground is dark and tramped down. There's a cowherd in a torn jacket and fur cap with a long whip curled around his shoulder. The cows are being driven out to pasture. The herd of spotted, dirty cows moves slowly, almost staidly along. One of them raises her head and moos, but the noise of the train drowns her out.

Aksin'ia laid her wreath against the heavy, cube-shaped monument. It was somewhat reminiscent of a crypt, with carvings of battle scenes along three of its sides, and the many names of the dead on the fourth. Aksin'ia read the names aloud in a dispassionate and even voice, pronouncing her husband's name, Fedor Prokhorovich Matushkin, in that same way, not stopping or breaking her reading to sigh.

Her companions were amazed: had Aksin'ia turned to stone, or had her grief dried up inside of her?

"Ksiusha, what is it? Why aren't you crying?"

Her answer was simple: "This isn't a grave, and you can't lie here and cry; you can stand for a while, but you can't brood. All my thoughts have flown away. But that's all right. I'll do my crying later."

It was as if the grave, with its solemn marker, was simply too grand, too impervious to feminine tears and sobs. Aksin'ia's tears wouldn't fall onto the ground and be absorbed into it, as she would have wanted them to.

"Why go searching for a grave? What's to be gained?"

Lora Iakovlevna's hands clutched at her breast: "Here's his grave. L'ova is buried—no, that's not it. He's just here. And that means that this isn't a grave and he's not dead. He's alive. I didn't see him dead; my memories are of him alive."

L'ova's eyes, when he was alive, were always shining. He was always in a hurry; in fact, in such a hurry that his hair would be dancing around on his forehead, as if ruffled by the wind. He was forever rushing off, never having time to finish a sentence, never having the time to finish eating or drinking, always jumping up from the table and taking the last few gulps standing, poised and ready to run off, his feet already in motion.

He was always leaving, but he would always come back.

And so, once more he left.

But this time he didn't come back.

Where is he now, or what is left of him? Does it really matter? While I'm still alive, he'll be alive with me, in me. So, here I've visited these graves with you. But graves will outlive us. They're memories. Not memories of just one of us, or of two of us about a third. They're our common memories, ours as a nation. Here I've bowed my head together with you to honor the memory of our warriors, all of them and L'ova too, no matter where he may be buried. Maybe it was an incendiary bomb that hit them and carried them all away, scattering their ashes over the fields. No, there's no grave for them. And for many others as well.

He's right here, in my heart.

"Oh, how bitter is the taste of grief," Aksin'ia sighed.

The train rolled on, its rocking motion lulling them, comforting them.

"Maybe we should cry? You know, like the village women wail and weep for theirs."

"If you start, we'll all let loose."

"No, not like that. Just sort of quiet like. Who should our lament be for?"

"For all of them."

"For all the soldiers who have fallen."

"You know, I used to be able to do this, but now I'm not sure I still can. All right, you listen now, but don't say a word."

Aksin'ia Kuz'minichna closed her eyes and sat motionless for a moment. Then she started swaying slightly and broke into her lament. There was no difference between her singing and her speaking; she just sang. And the grief filled her voice.

They sat, listening to her in complete silence. And would they also start? No, they resisted . . .

Sadness and grief, like no one has ever seen,

Sadness and grief, like no one has ever heard.
It was war, a terrible war, one like never before,
That stole upon us, caught us and crushed us.
Hitler the enemy, that beast, fell upon on us;
We didn't see it coming, we weren't ready.
But he did, and he was. He knew, and was waiting.
Killing and destroying, burning all as he went;
Young and old he drove into the rivers to drown. . . .
Sadness and grief, like no one has ever seen,
Sadness and grief, like no one has ever heard.
Our menfolk went away, leaving us alone;
Left us, to defend these, our Russian lands.
They fought, giving no thought of themselves,
Watering these lands with their blood.
And the land drank it in, and, drinking,
Gathered strength to drive away the enemy.
Together, as one, we fell upon that beast.
But our dearest ones fell in numbers great;
They laid down their lives in terrible battles,
In defense of this land of ours, this Soviet Union.
And defending, they freed our brother nations.
We women, their wives, are left here alone.
But we do not weep, we keep our grief hidden,
Though our eyes are never dry, so freely do the tears flow.
Driven from our homes by the Germans,
We fled, no shoes on our feet, no hats on our heads,
And scattered to the four corners of the earth.
Now we roam about, searching for the way back,
With infants in our arms, and toddlers at our sides,
Only the oldest ones ahead, making their way alone. . . .
We've lived our lives alone, with no one to help,
We've raised our children by ourselves.
God, how hard it is for me to think of the war;
May it be cursed and damned, that hell that is war.

Silence reigned. And then Aksin'ia spoke.

"Well, girls, how was it? Better now?"

"Yes, oh yes. Much better. Thank you, thank you. Went straight to the heart."

"You didn't cry with me for your husbands and sons?"

"Why cry when we're proud of them?"

"I'm going to cry. I can't help it."

The woman in black would also alight from the train with them, but she always kept at a distance from them, walking a little behind. She was silent, as were they, and no one asked her anything, though they were always ready to answer, should she ask a question. There was nothing strange in this silence of theirs, however. They simply looked upon her as so much grief and were wary to approach her. From time to time they would lose sight of her, and where she went at those times, no one seemed to know. She always had flowers in her hands; she would disappear carrying red carnations and would come back with white roses. The roses would be replaced by daffodils, then daffodils would give way to violets. No one asked her anything about the flowers either. They felt awkward, though no one understood why.

Mariia Nikolaevna was left sitting alone on the bench inside the little fence when the others moved off; let her stay a while by herself. "Maybe you'd like to shed a tear or two," Aksin'ia suggested. But Mariia Nikolaevna did not cry. There was a time when she feared this grave, when it seemed as if her grief would pierce her through with a new and terrible force. Yes, she felt the blow, but it was light, almost like a small electrical shock that passed quickly. She was glad that she had overcome her fears and had come after all. She should have done this long ago.

The village cemetery was surrounded by a ditch overgrown with grass where two cows were peacefully grazing. There were just a few graves here, and almost none were fenced.

But Pylaev's grave, done well enough to last quite some time, and maybe even forever, was surrounded by a metal fence. Inside the fence there was an iron obelisk that had been painted in a light color and topped with a star. A marble tablet had been affixed to the base.

In each of the corners lilac bushes had sprung up and were now covered in fragrant blossoms. The grave itself was overgrown with forget-me-nots, tiny little star-shaped white flowers and freshly planted pansies.

Mariia Nikolaevna recalled how the letter had described the hasty burial. Each of his comrades had managed to lay a bouquet, say a few kind words in remembrance and, in spite of the thunder of the battle raging nearby, fire off a salute from their guns. They then marched off, but one of them lagged briefly behind, just long enough to hastily construct a wooden pyramid and put up a small fence. This was all evidence of the love and respect that Pylaev enjoyed among them, and later many of these men would write to Mariia Nikolaevna about it.

Now it was the village schoolchildren who looked after the grave. Today they had helped Mariia Nikolaevna plant the seedlings she had brought and had put her hyacinths and tulips in the vase. They were expecting her at their Young Pioneers meeting, where she would tell them about Nikolai Ivanovich as a child.

"You're the lucky one, Marus'ia," Aksin'ia Kuz'minichna said. "You've got your own separate little grave. . . . "

Nonna Romanovna smiled. "It's not Marus'ia's grave, it's her husband's. And really, is it that important that it's separate?"

It was Lizaveta Timofeevna who answered. "It's so nice to have a quiet little corner to sit in, someplace where there's grass and trees and birds. That's what I've got in Zvenigorod, where my mother is buried. I pray for my Vasia there also. And when I get back, I'll have a requiem for him. He'll forgive me. . . . "

Just then, a little girl in a Pioneer's uniform and scarlet kerchief, her hair pulled back and tied with a pair of gossamer bows, ran up to announce that the ceremony at the school was about to start. The director of the collective farm was anxious for the guests to come and take part.

The school, a low wooden structure built long ago and adorned with a sign advertising the insurance firm Rossiia, had, through some miracle, survived the war in one piece. And right there, in the schoolyard, was a common grave, surrounded by the requisite fence, with the requisite obelisk and flowers. And of course, there was the marble tablet with the names of the fallen.

The teachers and their students, the farmhands and other workers on the collective farm had already gathered around. Women with infants were seated on the benches. The Pioneers were standing at attention while their group leader, a young woman, gave them whispered reminders and kept them in an orderly and straight line. A group of war veterans, carrying a wreath of red paper flowers, approached, their medals and ribbons proudly adorning their worn uniforms. The Pioneers parted ranks to let them through. The guests were invited to come in a little closer.

The green expanse of the schoolyard was bounded by cottonwood trees, their branches glistening with young leaves. Rooks circled and cawed through the trees, building new nests or fixing up their old ones. The sun shone down from a clear sky; not a cloud could be seen and soon the heat began to rise. There was no need for further decoration in the form of posters or slogans, what with the bright green of the trees, the clear blue of the sky and the sharp scarlet of the Pioneers' neckerchiefs. Everyone stood facing the grave where two wreaths of branches and paper flowers had been laid against the fencing. Those who were charged with giving speeches approached the fence.

There weren't that many people there. Some elderly peasant women stood in two rows, their white kerchiefs pulled low down on their foreheads to shield their faces from the sun. The young collective farm chief opened the ceremony. He spoke of the significance of the holiday, the day commemorating that great victory which had rescued the world from the clutches of fascism. He spoke of how the Briansk lands were ever mindful of the war and would never forget it. He added something about the difficulties they were facing: how there were not enough able hands, how the young people were leaving for the cities, how there were too few mechanics and how the lion's share of the work fell to the elderly.

"And here they are, our most devoted workers," the director said, turning to the women in the white kerchiefs. They all nodded as they stood there, arms, darkened by the sun and with veins bulging, identically crossed on their breasts. You couldn't tell if they were agreeing with the director's statements about the young people leaving for the city, or affirming their devotion to their work and to their homes.

The Pioneers read a few poems and sang a song. The veterans then broke into a chorus of "We've covered many miles on this march. . . ." A few other voices joined weakly in, and the song soon died out.

The guests were asked to say a few words, a request that seemed to embarrass the women. But Lora Iakovlevna stepped bravely forward. In a loud and somewhat courageous voice, she spoke about how things would some day be fine, that these kids here today would grow up to take charge, that the farm would build houses for its workers and how the old wooden schoolhouse would be replaced by a new brick one. She spoke of how you had to believe in the future; you couldn't just sit and wait for it, you had to get out there and work for it yourself.

The director thanked Lora and the audience applauded her.

Then, rather unexpectedly, Aksin'ia Kuz'minichna stepped forward to speak. She bowed low in the direction of the white-kerchiefed women.

"My thanks to you, to whom we owe our daily bread. I know what your work is like. And I understand what you're feeling at your age, how your back aches. I'm just like you. I wish you health and hope that soon there'll be others to take your place. Do you hear what I'm saying, kids? Somebody's got to think about that, after all," she added quickly, moving back to join her friends.

One of the teachers, her arm around Mariia Nikolaevna's shoulder, led her out in front of the crowd, asking, "Please, won't you say a couple of words?"

Mariia Nikolaevna, obviously uncomfortable, hardly knew where to begin. She cast her eyes about the people assembled in front of her and thanked them all for the work that they had done on her husband's grave. She thanked them for the monument and the fencing, for the flowers and, only as an afterthought, confessed that she had long been afraid to come but now was glad that she had.

The white-kerchiefed heads bobbed up and down in unison; yes, they knew, they understood what a tragedy the war was for the women. Yes, the war had left them a village of widows as well.

After that, the Pioneers sang "Let the sun forever shine," and then the ceremony was over.

From there they all set out for the cemetery and Pylaev's grave, the Pioneers ahead, with flag and drumbeat. Two of them marched out in front, carrying a wreath. They were followed by their teachers and the war veterans. The drum fell silent, and the only sound heard was the twittering of the birds.

Once at the grave another girl, older than the first but with the same gossamer bows in her hair, spoke, saying that the Pioneers promised to always look after Nikolai Ivanovich's grave, the grave of a man who died defending their village.

When all had left and the only ones remaining at the gravesite were the women, Lizaveta Timofeevna spoke. "Mariia Nikolaevna, don't be offended, but you really should be happy."

Mariia Nikolaevna asked herself, was she happy? No, here and now she couldn't say that she was. But she didn't think herself unhappy either.

It would seem that the time had come for her to be at peace, if she could think about it as calmly as she did.

She was reminded of a gravestone that she had seen in the museum. Fifteenth-century Italian work, carved stone.

He and she lay side by side, a young married couple, with gently rounded faces and slightly protruding lips. The young knight's hands held a sword that ran the length of his body. Next to him, reaching only up to his shoulder, lay his young wife, a mere girl. He must have been about eighteen, twenty at the most, and she couldn't have been more than sixteen. Perhaps they died at the same time, even on the same day. They were dressed in festive clothing, and the carved stone mimicked the embroidery, lace and pearls. She wore a headpiece of sorts that was adorned by a string of pearls that rested on her forehead. Both of them lay with hands crossed on their chests: his wrists were bony and strong, her fingers thin and delicate.

The gravestone was an exact replica of the deceased; this was how they had been laid in the crypt, in the cemetery or in the church itself.

It could have been that they had been married only shortly before they died. They probably never had the chance to know what love is, had never experienced passion, had barely gotten over those first moments of tender embarrassment. Their faces were those of mere children. And they had been cut down, like two flowers by a sharp scythe, cruelly, in a single moment. It was probably some horrible disease, maybe even that plague that had touched thousands, sparing no one. It struck like a bolt of poisonous lightning, smiting mercilessly, so much like war does in our day. Back then it was the plague, today it is war. And we remain as helpless in its face as they were then.

The train is already heading back.

Once again, the fields and meadows, the groves of young trees and the villages pass by the windows.

And once again the train clacks across the bridges over the rivers and streams.

A small station, a boisterous crowd on the platform: two young men are playing accordions; the girls, their arms around each other's waists, are tapping out a slow dance.

They're sending the recruits off to the army: the draftees are huddled together off to one side, marked out by their cleanly shaven heads. They're surrounded by a tight circle of relatives: mothers, fathers, grandfathers and grandmothers. One of the women yanks a brightly colored kerchief from her head and rushes into the circle of dancers, stamping her feet in a kind of dance. The accordion players tug at their instruments and squeeze out a dance tune. "Hey, Semionna, here Semionna. . . . " A tipsy little man, weaving back and forth on rubbery legs, tries to join the dance. Everyone turns to watch, laughing heartily.

The crowd disappears; the station, with its little outbuildings and water tower, is gone. The train clatters along, guided by the signals on the ever-intersecting tracks. The warehouses and sheds, piles of boards and logs, mountains of broken crates, all fly by.

And then a meadow, a copse, a brook. . . .

Our journey is drawing to an end, and as usually happens when you part, you think: there is still something left unsaid, something left unknown, something left unasked. Naturally, there were things I had forgotten, and things my companions had as well; and anyway, words can't express everything. That, which was too awful, too difficult or too embarrassing to talk about, had been left untouched.

Still, I did want to ask them if, during their years of solitude, a new love had found them. Of course, one like that which had been cut short by the war was impossible. But, did Lora Iakovlevna find something else? Oh well, it doesn't do one any good to think about that. Does Nonna Romanovna have a friend? Yes, a tried and true friend, but, all the same, she didn't marry him. It would seem that a second marriage is out of the question. We all know about Ganna; she told us herself. Ganna admitted that she came to love her second husband. As for Aksin'ia Kuz'minichna, she never had the first thought about another; isn't that right? The same is true for me but in spite of that, they still tried to fix me up—twice. Only I couldn't do it. No reason to; the bitterest life had already passed and I just wanted to catch my breath. I was tired. I didn't marry, didn't allow myself any sort of pleasures. From time to time I'd feel sorry for myself and my lot in life; here I was, young, good-looking, drying up like an aspen that had been chopped down. So I'd cry a bit, then stop; after all, there wasn't enough time for that, what with everything I had to do. Lizaveta Timofeevna is smiling; what about, Lizan'ka? Girls, girls! Oh, the love I had! Only I couldn't let myself do it; I was ashamed of myself in front of my daughters. And so my love died, touched by a killing frost. Now it's all forgotten. Mariia Nikolaevna is silent? But what is there to talk about? We were young, alive; maybe it wasn't we who loved, but were loved. Our answer is simple, and the same for all: we are widows. And Ganna has joined our group.

But where is she, our traveling companion, the woman in black? She wanted no part of this conversation.

The apple tree has dried up. Many of the trees in the Moscow suburbs were hurt by the frost that winter. More than once the owner would go out to the apple tree with his saw and axe, take a look at the knotted branches and then go away. It's hard for a man to cut down the tree his father or grandfather planted. Even though the apple tree was old, up until that fatal winter its fruit had always been plentiful.

But now the bark was peeling off the dry trunk and it stood, naked and brown. A narrow strip of bark remained on the southern side, and it reached upwards and to one side to embrace just one of the branches.

The second year after the tragedy tiny buds appeared on this branch, followed by leaves; and in the third year, the dry apple tree bloomed: on that single branch there appeared pale pink blossoms. The fourth year saw the first harvest: a whole bucketful of apples.

Do not rush to chop down the apple tree that has been killed by the cruel frost! Somewhere deep inside it there pulses a warm and living life; the sap thaws and meekly begins to flow. Suddenly there appears a branch covered in blossoms, and the resurrected tree brings forth new fruits.

It has been a difficult road that I and my companions have traveled. Here's a picture of us, taken in 1970. We're standing by the grave. The slender woman on the far left with a sharp nose, close-set round eyes and a short haircut that reminds you of ruffled feathers is Lora Iakovlevna Fogel'. Next to her, in a neatly tied flowered kerchief, is the round-faced, plump and appealing Aksin'ia

Kuz'minichna Matushkina. Fedos'ia Nikitichna Kazantseva, looking rather frightened and old, peers out from behind her shoulder. Next to Aksin'ia and a little bit in front of her is the dark-eyed Ganna Petrovna Koval', who stands tall and proud, her head covered in a dark kerchief. Nonna Romanovna Korneva, dressed in a leather jacket, has placed her arm around Ganna's shoulder and half embraces her. Nonna wears her hair short and holds her chin up to look out at you with a challenging gaze. To her right is the slight, wide-eyed and somewhat dreamy Mariia Nikolaevna Pylaeva; a small lock of hair has escaped from her otherwise neat hairdo. In front is tiny Lizaveta Timofeevna Pichuzhkina, with her hands clasped to her breast and her head turned slightly away from the camera.

That tall woman behind them all is me.

There's one of us missing from the picture: the Woman in Black. You can't see her because she couldn't be in the picture. She is our sorrow; she is always with us, and only we can see her.

We're standing by the fence, there are flowers all around and the obelisk is surrounded by lilacs.

It's a simple obelisk made of painted iron, topped by a star; on the pedestal is a marble tablet with the photograph of a soldier, a thin and tired face, and the inscription:

"Guards' Captain Nikolai Nikolaevich Baranskii (1909–1943) died a hero's death in the battle for the village of Alymovo 12 August, 1943."

1981–1984

Translated by Maureen Riley

Notes to the Essay

1. "Natalya Baranskaya Talking with Pieta Monks," in *Writing Lives: Conversations between Women Writers*, ed. M. Chamberlin (London: Virago Press, 1988), 28.

2. Ibid., 28.

3. Ibid., 31.

4. "If I can express one-tenth of my feelings about the war and my experiences during the war in my novel, then I will have succeeded; people must understand what our war was, and they will understand how it lives on in our emotions"; quoted in ibid., 33.

5. *Den' pominoveniia* (Moscow: Sovetskii pisatel', 1989), 89.

6. Ibid., 6.

7. Ibid., 15.

8. Chamberlin, *Writing Lives*, 30.

Bibliography

Primary Works

Otrisatel'naia Zhizel'. Moscow: Molodaia gvardiia, 1977.

Zhenshchina s zontikom. Povest' i rasskazy. Moscow: Sovremennik, 1981.

Portret podarennyi drugu. Ocherki i rasskazy o Pushkine. Leningrad: Lenizdat, 1982.

Den' pominoveniia. Roman, povest'. Moscow: Sovetskii pisatel', 1989. [Contains "Day of Remembrance" and "A Week Like Any Other."]

"Nedelia kak nedelia" ["Just Another Week"]. Ed. Lora Paperno, Natalie Roklina and Richard Leed. Columbus, OH: Slavica Publishers, 1989. [Annotated version of the story.]

"Avtobiografiia bez unolchanii." *Grani* 156 (1990): 122–48.

In Translation

"Alarm Clock in the Cupboard." Trans. Beatrice Stillman. *Redbook* (March 1971): 179–201. [Translation of "Nedelia kak nedelia."]

En ganske almindelig uge N. Baranskaja. Trans. Susanne Hojlt. Copenhagen: K. Kvindenhusets Bogcafe, 1972. [Translation of "Nedelia kak nedelia."]

Une semaine comme une autre. Trans. Helene Sinany. Lausanne: Éditions l'âge d'homme, 1973. [Translation of "Nedelia kak nedelia."]

En uge som de andre. Copenhagen: Gyldendal, 1973. [Translation of "Nedelia kak nedelia."]

"A Week Like Any Other" [excerpts]. *Our Soviet Sister.* Ed. George St. George. Washington, DC: Robert B. Luce, 1973. 233–56. [Translated excerpts of "Nedelia kak nedelia."]

Une semaine comme une autre: et quelques récits Natalia Baranskaia. Trans. Jeanne Rude and Helene Sinany. Paris: Éditions des Femmes, 1976. [Translation of "Nedelia kak nedelia."]

"A Week Like Any Other." Trans. Emily Lehrman. *Massachusetts Review* (1974): 657ff. [Translation of "Nedelia kak nedelia."]

"A Week Like Any Other." Trans. Pauline Jaray. *Spare Rib* (1977): 53–59. [Translation of "Nedelia kak nedelia."]

"The Retirement Party." Trans. Anatole Forostenko. *The Barsukov Triangle: The Two-toned Blonde and Other Stories.* Ed. C. Proffer and E. Proffer. Ann Arbor, MI: Ardis Publishers, 1984. 231–41. [Translation of "Provody"; first appeared in *Russian Literature Triquarterly* 9 (1974): 136–44.]

"The Kiss." Trans. Wanda Sorgente. *Balancing Acts: Contemporary Stories by Russian Women.* Ed. Helena Goscilo. Bloomington: Indiana University Press, 1989. 1–5.

"The Spell." *The Image of Women in Contemporary Soviet Fiction: Selected Short Stories from the USSR.* Ed. and trans. Sigrid McLaughlin. New York: St. Martin's Press, 1989. 111–22. [Translation of "Koldovstvo"; first appeared in *Iunost'* 7 (1976)].

"Laine's House." *Soviet Women Writing: 15 Short Stories* [with an introduction by I. Grekova]. Ed. J. Decter. Trans. Gerald Mikkelson and Margaret Winchell. New York: Abbeville Press, 1990. 203–14.

A Week Like Any Other: Novellas and Stories by Natalya Baranskaya. Trans. Pieta Monks. Seattle: Seal Press, 1990. [Contains "A Week Like Any Other," "The Purse," "The Petunin Affair," "Lubka," "A Delicate Subject," "The Woman with the Umbrella" and "At Her Father's and Her Mother's Place."]

Secondary Works

Ahna, Barbara. "Soviet Sisters." *Women's Review of Books* (July 1990): 33–34.

Brown, Edward J. *Russian Literature since the Revolution*. Cambridge: Harvard University Press, 1982. 319–21.

Chamberlin, Mary, ed. "Natalya Baranskaya Talking with Pieta Monks." *Writing Lives: Conversations between Women Writers*. London: Virago Press, 1988. 25–36.

Gasiorowska, Xenia. "Women in Russian Literature." *Handbook of Russian Literature*. Ed. V. Terras. New Haven, CT: Yale University Press, 1985. 519–22.

Goscilo, Helena, ed. *Balancing Acts: Contemporary Stories by Russian Women*. Bloomington: Indiana University Press, 1989.

———. *Fruits of Her Plume: Essays on Contemporary Russian Women's Culture*. Armonk, NY: M.E. Sharpe, 1993.

———. "Paradigm Lost? Contemporary Women's Fiction." *Women Writers in Russian Literature*. Ed. T. Clyman and D. Greene. Westport, CT: Greenwood Press, 1994.

Heldt, Barbara. *Terrible Perfection: Women and Russian Literature*. Bloomington: Indiana University Press, 1987.

Kagan-Kans, E. "Short Story." *Handbook of Russian Literature*. Ed. V. Terras. New Haven, CT: Yale University Press, 1985. 417.

Kay, Susan. "A Woman's Work." *Irish Slavonic Studies* 8 (1987):115–26.

Kelly, Catriona. "Natalya Baranskaya (1908–)." *A History of Russian Women's Writing, 1820–1992*. New York: Clarendon, 1994. 397–409.

Lahusen, Thomas. "Leaving Paradise and *Perestroika*: 'A Week Like Any Other' and *Memorial Day* by Natal'ia Baranskaya." *Fruits of Her Plume: Essays on Contemporary Russian Women's Culture*. Ed. Helena Goscilo. Armonk, NY: M.E. Sharpe, 1993. 205–24.

Lee, Andrea. "A Russian Journal." *The New Yorker*, 30 June 1980: 72ff.; 8 July 1980: 70ff. Rpt. New York: Random House, 1981.

McLaughlin, Sigrid. "Contemporary Soviet Women Writers." *Canadian Woman Studies/Les Cahiers de la Femme* 4 (1989): 77–80.

———, ed. "Natalya Baranskaya." *The Image of Women in Contemporary Soviet Fiction*. New York: St. Martin's Press, 1989. 111–12.

Seton-Watson, M. "Women in Soviet Society." *Scenes from Soviet Life through Official Literature*. London: 1986. 15–18.

Svirski, Grigori. *A History of Post-War Soviet Writing: The Literature of Moral Opposition*. Trans. and ed. R. Dessaix and M. Ulman. Ann Arbor, MI: Ardis Publishers, 1981.

Natal'ia Gorbanevskaia

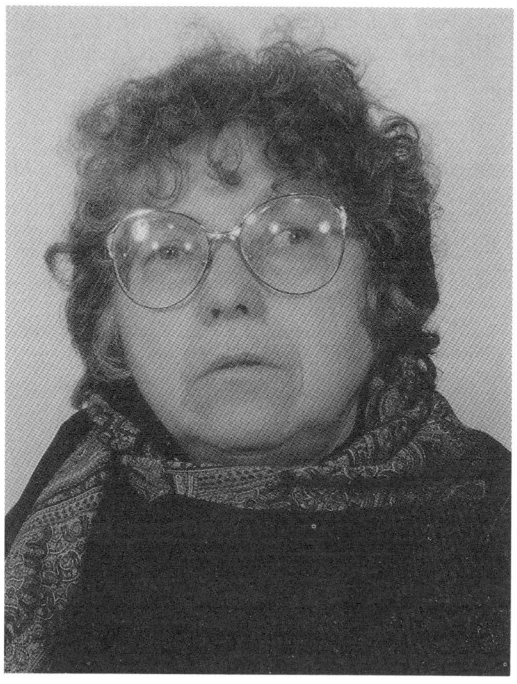

Natal'ia Gorbanevskaia (b. 1936).
Courtesy of the author and Natalie Repin.

Natal'ia Evgen'evna Gorbanevskaia (b. 1936) is one of the most prominent living Russian poets. She is also a literary critic, an editor, a journalist writing on topical issues, a professional translator and an essayist. Gorbanevskaia's poetry is not "chamber poetry," as one critic notes, for in it one can hear the voice of a whole generation of Russian people.[1] Her poetic destiny, however, has been complicated by the political and ideological circumstances that until very recently existed in the former Soviet Union. This is what caused her life to be divided into two periods, before and after emigration to the West in 1975. Despite the fact that she has been writing continuously both in Russia and in the West, it is only now that she is "returning to Russia in verse." Although she is being published there in journals and periodicals, no collections of her verse have as yet appeared there.

Gorbanevskaia's dissenting thought and activity, which culminated in the famous demonstration on Red Square in 1968 against the Soviet invasion of Czechoslovakia, with her subsequent imprisonment, has caused her poetry until very recently to be known in her native country almost exclusively through *samizdat*. Before her emigration, only nine poems had been officially published there; yet, in spite of the inaccessibility of her works for a deservedly broader audience, Gorbanevskaia was very well known among the readers of *samizdat*.

Altogether, Gorbanevskaia has composed nine books of verse and published nine verse collections. However, her poetry has not received nearly its due recognition in the scale either of readership or of literary scholarship. Catriona Kelly, commenting on this deplorable situation in *An Encyclopedia of Continental Women Writers,* complains in particular about the dearth of secondary literature on Gorbanevskaia that goes beyond mere bibliographical facts and states that the major corpus of her work still awaits its translation; likewise, she refers to the circumstance that has complicated Gorbanevskaia's literary reputation, stating directly that she is "best known in the West for her activities in defense of human rights during the 1960s."[2]

Although the growth of Gorbanevskaia's popularity as a poet was indeed originally stimulated by the dramatic circumstances of her biography, eventually this linking of her social activism with her literary persona proved to have mixed results for her literary reputation. In a 1970 statement issued from prison, Gorbanevskaia herself expressed her concern that her poetry should not attract public interest simply because of her being a political prisoner. Thus there has developed a tendency in criticism to treat Gorbanevskaia, this very holistic figure, as dichotomous: social and private, civic and lyric, publicist and poet. As if to forewarn against the development of this undesirable tendency, Gorbanevskaia herself has repeatedly underscored the underlying monism of her life and work. By way of example she explains: "If political motifs have appeared in my poetry to a certain degree, then they have always passed through precisely this lyricism, my personality. They were simply the object of my emotions like anything else. It is simply that my emotions would react not only to love or to certain experiences of landscape and so on, but also to politics, to political history."[3] As should be the case with a true lyrical poet, for Gorbanevskaia "consciousness and the realm of the emotions are inseparable."[4] Or, as she generalizes in another interview: "Had it not been for my poetry, I would not have gone to the [Red] Square. And had it not been for my social activity, my poetry would have been different. Everything is one. Everything is interdependent."[5] Hence, she obviously went to Red Square most of all as a poet in an act of freedom of creative consciousness.

The underlying monism of Gorbanevskaia's creation, however, envelops a great deal of complexity. She has undoubtedly shown the best moral features of Russian literature represented by Tolstoy and Solzhenitsyn, Akhmatova and Mandel'shtam. Tolstoy's famous "I cannot be silent!" is a synthesis of the credo of this tradition as well as of the tradition of Russian intelligentsia in a broad sense. In an allusion to Mandel'shtam, Gorbanevskaia states her civic stance as a writer in the following way: "Our profession is to move our lips for those who cannot."[6] Social engagement is thus a moral and aesthetic stance of the poet, not the poetry—a distinction that is all too often confused. Hence, no perplexity should be felt in the fact that Gorbanevskaia, while carrying on a great deal of social activity, has never let this social engagement surface in her poetry in a direct and immediate way. Also, the superficial logic of ascribing to art what is explicit in the biography of the artist is, certainly, to be abandoned. If Gorbanevskaia's "political convictions inform all aspects of her work,"[7] it is not at all done in an unmediated way. Thus this stance of the poet saves the poetry from becoming mimetic, that is, reflecting social reality as it appears to be.

All complexities integrate harmoniously into a holistic figure: the poet. Gorbanevskaia's writing is, therefore, her total representation and expression. Reconfirming this approach, Gorbanevskaia more than once has expressed the wish not to be "defined" as a poet,[8] instead preferring to let her work speak for her. Moreover, Gorbanevskaia has shown reticence about her biography. Thus her biography emerges as a problem for the literary scholar, since it is hardly decipherable from her poetry nor has she written an autobiography nor, as she conveyed in an interview,[9] has she any intention of writing memoirs.

Natal'ia Evgen'evna Gorbanevskaia was born on 26 May 1936 in Moscow. Her formal education, which she began in 1953 in Moscow and continued, with interruptions, until 1964, was in Russian philology. She completed her studies by correspondence at Leningrad University and thereafter worked as a bibliographer, editor and translator.

According to Gorbanevskaia's own account ("Writing for *'samizdat,'*" 1977), she first composed verses as a child. At seventeen she began writing seriously, but this was the period of her initial apprenticeship as a poet. Not until she reached the age of twenty did she begin writing poetry that she did not completely discard. When she was studying at Moscow University, some of her verses were printed in the newspaper, an event that provoked arguments accusing Gorbanevskaia of "degeneracy, pessimism and decadence." It was not long thereafter that Gorbanevskaia's poems came to circulate in *samizdat*, including the journal *The Phoenix* (*Feniks*, 1961). Later on, she retracted a portion of her lyrics from the *Phoenix* collection, as well as from two additional *samizdat* anthologies. She subsequently considered only the later compilations, *Paradise Lost* (1965), *Darkness* (1966) and *Wooden Angel* (*Angel dereviannyi,* 1967), to constitute a lasting poetic statement. In 1962 she started to issue her own yearly collections in *samizdat*. During the 1960s she worked on the literary journal *Syntax* (*Sintaksis*), edited by Aleksandr Ginzburg, which was the first uncensored periodical. However, only three issues came out: Ginzburg was arrested. Gorbanevskaia was officially published for the first time in 1965 in the newspaper *Moscow Young Communists* (*Moskovskii komsomolets*). In 1966 she had two verses printed in the journal *The Banner* (*Znamia*). Then, five of her lyrics appeared in the journal *Star of the East* (*Zvezda vostoka,* 1968). These are the nine poems officially published in the Soviet Union.

During the 1960s both capitals, Moscow and Leningrad, were literally flooded with poetry in which there was no distinct separation between *samizdat* and officially published works whose circulation numbered hundreds of thousands of copies. This is when Evgenii Evtushenko participated in the same public readings as Joseph Brodsky (although the former had just returned from England and the latter from exile in Arkhangelsk) and when Bella Akhmadulina was on equal terms with Gorbanevskaia, as far as the reading public was concerned. The poet and critic Iurii Kublanovskii writes that at that time every person enthusiastic about poetry knew Gorbanevskaia's verse, "Listen, Bartok, what have you composed?"[10] Moreover, during the 1960s Gorbanevskaia made several public appearances as a poet, in libraries and research institutes. She characterizes herself as being at that time a "solitary poet" but not "secret."

Gorbanevskaia did much for *samizdat*, not merely publishing her own poetry but also typing and disseminating many different documents and literary works. In 1964 she acquired her own typewriter—at that time and place probably the hardest thing to obtain—and in 1966–1967 she was already typing a great deal for *samizdat*. In 1966 and 1967 her supporters tried to get her verses published in *Youth* (*Iunost'*) but did not succeed, although for those selections they chose lyrics in which there was not a hint of anything sociopolitical. Gorbanevskaia believes the editors found her work alien, foreign.

In 1968 Gorbanevskaia became active in the human rights movement. In February of that year she headed the petition drive on behalf of Iurii Galanskov (the editor of the *Phoenix,* 1966) and Aleksandr Ginzburg (who edited *Syntax* and compiled the *White Book* on the Siniavsky-Daniel trial in 1966), demanding an open trial for them. As a return address on all envelopes she put her own address. In the summer of 1969 she prepared a selection of "Uncollected Poetry." By that time, she had established the self-awareness of a poet, which is precisely what had, under the sociopolitical conditions in the country, led her to engagement in continuous civic activity. She could not be silent.

Around that time, Gorbanevskaia suffered her first experience as a victim of Soviet psychiatric persecution, which was becoming an ominous method of fighting dissidents. While expecting her second son and feeling unwell, upon her doctor's advice, she became an inpatient of a maternity ward on 12 February 1968. Instead of being discharged, she was forcibly moved to a psychiatric ward without any reason. In twelve days (on 23 February 1968) she was released from the custody of "free health service" due to her pregnancy.

In Gorbanevskaia's civic activity, there is a moment that stands out. On 25 August 1968 she took part in a peaceful "sit-down" demonstration on Red Square against the Soviet invasion of Czechoslovakia, along with six other protesters. All seven were arrested, but Gorbanevskaia was subsequently released, no doubt on account of her three-month-old child, who had been with her at the demonstration. On 28 August 1968 she addressed a letter to the world press (printed in the *New York Times,* among other leading Western newspapers) in which she, "as the only participant . . . still free," described the demonstration and its consequences, presenting the very first report about the events. What urged her to do so was the determination to make the event of the demonstration and the truth of its intent known to the world, for silence in this case would have rendered this act of civic heroism incomplete, if not meaningless. Though not prosecuted at the subsequent trial, Gorbanevskaia was ordered to appear at the Serbskii Institute for Psychiatric Medicine. She was examined there on 5 September by a "committee of experts" under Professor Lunts (a KGB colonel as well as a psychiatrist) and was found and declared "not responsible for her actions." The procurator's office then simply closed the case in view of Gorbanevskaia's insanity and placed her under her mother's guardianship. It was during the course of her examination at the Serbskii Institute that she received evidence of the decisive part played by the KGB in her previous twelve-day confinement in the mental hospital.

Although it was by now perfectly clear that Gorbanevskaia stood in imminent danger of being incarcerated for an indefinite term in a psychiatric prison, she felt it her duty, while still at liberty, to continue protesting and recording. Thus she set about compiling a detailed documentary account of the demonstration, including the proceedings of the trial of five of the demonstrators, which in 1970 came out in the West as *Red Square at Noon* (*Polden'*, 1970). In May 1969 Gorbanevskaia became one of the fifteen founding members of the Action Group for the Defense of Civil Rights in the USSR. The group appealed to the universal public for support, reporting new facts of the violations of civil rights and elementary human liberties taking place in the Soviet Union. On 26 August 1969, the anniversary of the invasion of Czechoslovakia, Gorbanevskaia again signed a protest.

Gorbanevskaia's book *Red Square at Noon* appeared in four countries: France, England, the United States and Mexico. It was never published in Czechoslovakia, but because of Gorbanevskaia's letter, the news of the demonstration reached there very quickly. In the fall of 1968 her open letter recounting the story of the demonstration was posted as a leaflet on the walls of Karl University in Prague.

In 1990 all the participants of the demonstration were awarded the title of "honorable citizens of Prague." The same year, while attending the award ceremony in Prague, they found out that in 1968, on learning the news about the demonstration, a group of citizens of the town of Hradec Králové had planted in their honor seven birch trees. Fifteen years later, Gorbanevskaia emphasized in retrospect: "As an act of protest, the demonstration itself and the participation in it of each of us was based upon an individual moral impulse, upon the feeling of responsibility—and I am not afraid of this loud word—for history." She insists that the act of protest for all the seven participants was a "natural, simple, nonheroic step": "That was a purely moral step that we made, feeling terribly ashamed. . . ."[11]

On 24 December 1969 Gorbanevskaia was finally arrested, the immediate cause presumably being her compilation of *Red Square at Noon*, and was confined to Butyrka prison. She was also accused of being a participant in the *samizdat* publication of *The Chronicle of Current Events* by the Helsinki Accord Human Rights group, which started coming out in April 1968. (In the thirty-eighth issue Gorbanevskaia was actually named as the founder in the publication itself.) A forensic psychiatric examination at the Serbskii Institute under the chairmanship of Professor Lunts declared Gorbanevskaia to be "nonaccountable" and "of unsound mind."The court ordered her a compulsory treatment in a psychiatric hospital of special type (psychiatric prison), the period of treatment being unspecified. On 9 January 1971 Gorbanevskaia was transferred from Butyrka to the special psychiatric hospital in Kazan', where she was to undergo a course of drug treatment. This chemical therapy included haloperidol, whose secondary effects are normally associated with Parkinson's disease: one cannot write or remain seated for more than a few minutes or concentrate one's thoughts or read. In November 1971 Gorbanevskaia was transported from Kazan' to Moscow and thereafter was released on 22 February 1972.

While in prison, Gorbanevskaia wrote and managed to smuggle her notes out. In the meantime, a collection of her works was published in 1969 under the title *Poems* (*Stikhi*). Gorbanevskaia considers it not a very successful selection, for it was not based upon the "canonic" texts of *samizdat*. However, the goal of the edition, she believes, was altogether political rather than literary: the editors were trying to support Gorbanevskaia since the publication took place after her arrest. Her next collection, *The Littoral* (*Poberezh'e*), was compiled in the spring of 1972 by the author herself and was published in 1973. This edition was practically her complete collected works written between 1956 and the beginning of 1972, including verses composed during the period of her imprisonment. This was Gorbanevskaia's first "real" publication; it appeared after at least sixteen years of continuous creative activity and a great deal of sacrifice for poetry. After that, she printed her verses in the form of separate notebooks, the first three of which came out in 1975 before her departure for the West. The book was called, appropriately, *Three Notebooks of Poems* (*Tri tetradi stikhotvorenii*). After long and humiliating emigration procedures that had dragged on since the fall of 1974, the Soviet authorities finally allowed Gorbanevskaia to emigrate on 17 December 1975. Gorbanevskaia, with her two sons Osip and Iaroslav, arrived first in Vienna on 21 December 1975 and then, on 1 February 1976, in Paris to commence the second period of her life. As a "Moscovite Parisian" (her expression), her life was not to be externally eventful, yet she was as dedicated to poetry as ever.

In 1979 appeared *Flying across the Snowy Border* (*Pereletaia snezhnuiu granitsu*), which was a book of the transitional period, as the author herself states. It consists of five notebooks, two of them written before and three after emigration. Paradoxically, Gorbanevskaia believes that her most "emigrant" nostalgic verses were composed in Russia, before emigration. Her next collection, *Wooden Angel* (*Angel dereviannyi*, 1982), was comprised of two already published collections, *The Littoral* (*Poberezh'e*) and *Three Notebooks of Poems* (*Tri tetradi stikhotvorenii*), with the exception of her first translation from Polish, which she hoped to make a part of an anthology of Polish poetry. In 1983 *Foreign Stones* (*Chuzhie kamni*) was printed, which contained sixty lyrics written during four years. As Gorbanevskaia thinks, it is here that a "new quality" of her verse appears. After that, many poems were published in émigré journals and periodicals like *The Archer* (*Strelets*), *Continent* (*Kontinent*), *Russian Thought* (*Russkaia mysl'*) and *Twenty-Two* (*Dvadtat' dva*). In 1985 there appeared two more notebooks, *Variable Cloudiness* (*Peremennaia oblachnost'*) and *Where and When* (*Gde i kogda*). The last collection is *Heather Blossom* (*Tsvet vereska*, 1993), which consists of *Seventh Notebook* (*Sed'maia kniga*, finished in 1990) and *One More Notebook* (*Eshche odna*). Gorbanevskaia's most recent book of verse is entitled *And There Was I Once upon a Time* (*I ia zhila-byla*, written June 1992–February 1994), which has not as yet been published as a collection.

Whereas Gorbanevskaia's preoccupation is unconditionally poetry, her occupation is jointly journalism and translation. She worked first as editorial secretary and since 1983 as associate editor of one of the chief émigré journals, *Continent*, until its headquarters moved to Moscow in 1992. She is also a member of the editorial board of the leading émigré newspaper *Russian Thought*. The range of topics of her journalism embraces civil rights issues, commentary upon sociocultural phenomena, cultural events, interviews and reviews of theatrical productions and films. Poland has been a second (after Russia) particular interest of Gorbanevskaia's journalism, to which she gave book form in *Undefeated Poland on the Pages of "Russian Thought"* (*Neslomlennaia Pol'sha na stranitsakh "Russkoi mysli,"* 1984). Gorbanevskaia has also been a committed human rights activist. She has used every opportunity, every tribunal in different countries to make known to the world the fate of political prisoners and prisoners of conscience, as well as the Soviet psychiatric repressions, and to protest every act of tyranny and terror. And in this regard, she is among the most outstanding civil activists. As for her creativity, Gorbanevskaia continues to be productive. Her works give no reason to revise the pronouncement of Akhmatova: "Natasha writes better and better."

Gorbanevskaia's poetry could be described overall, as regards both content and form, as modernistic, naturally enveloped in the rich tradition of twentieth-century modernism in general and the Russian prosodic complexity and experiment of that time in particular. A few critics have attempted to place Gorbanevskaia within the Russian poetic tradition. G.S. Smith, for one, maintains that Gorbanevskaia shares the same line of this tradition as Derzhavin, Lermontov, Nekrasov, Blok, Pasternak, Mayakovsky and Tsvetaeva.[12] By comparison, Brodsky, according to this projection, represents the end of another line of Russian poetic tradition. As a basis for such allocation, Smith puts forward the following: "Gorbanevskaia has a big heart and always wears it on her sleeve."[13] However, it may be argued not less successfully that Gorbanevskaia's existential and poetic style witnesses to a higher degree to the opposite tendency, that of reserve and covertness, rather than open declarativeness of a "big heart" in the manner of Mayakovsky or Tsvetaeva. Regardless of Gorbanevskaia's "big heart," she makes every conscious effort not to expose it in an immediate way as a point of poetic statement. Another opinion in this regard belongs to Catriona Kelly, who places Gorbanevskaia with her "restraint, limpidity, and overt high-cultural allegiances" in the tradition of "Petersburg poetry" next to Akhmatova: "Typically for this tradition she [Gorbanevskaia] is an *Augenmensch*; although her love of music is alluded to in many poems, the poems themselves are not musical in the way of much Russian poetry."[14] A third opinion situates Gorbanevskaia in a different poetic "latitude," calling her a "Moscow poet" due to her special conversational, everyday intonation, persistent stylistic "descent," and the songlike element of many of her lyrics, for example, lamentation.[15] A. Tatarinov offers still another insight. He suggests that the following stanza of Gorbanevskaia evokes associations with Baratynskii:

> There is music, and there is nothing else—
> neither happiness, nor peace, nor freedom,
> in all this glassy sea of grief
> music is the only saving grace.[16]

It is certainly of great importance how Gorbanevskaia herself perceives her poetic orientation. She is convinced that her poetry follows the line of Pushkin, Mandel'shtam and Akhmatova. Contrary to G.S. Smith, she views Brodsky as belonging to the same tradition.[17]

Akhmatova played an important role in Gorbanevskaia's life, but the message she received is more existential than poetic: "I think that I got from her [Akhmatova] not how to write poetry but how to live as a poet."[18] Like the later Akhmatova, Gorbanevskaia is of those writers who regard the fate of the people as their own. To her, Akhmatova was a "model poet in relation to her poetry, to the world, to people," and all that found expression in Akhmatova's poetics.[19] According to the testimony of people surrounding Akhmatova, she considered Gorbanevskaia to be a genuine poet.[20] Likewise, Gorbanevskaia herself states that Akhmatova praised her verse decisively and loved her very much.

In Gorbanevskaia's lyrics, critics have commonly pointed out the following themes: solitude, love, self-definition, the frustrations and rewards of creativity, "geography" of the poetic world, language and God's presence in the world. It is precisely Gorbanevskaia's preoccupation with the problem of language and her existential thematic concerns, including religious existentialism, that mark her writing as distinctly modernist.

G.S. Smith, in his study of the poetry of the third wave of Russian emigration, concludes that Gorbanevskaia's works hardly reflect the environment of her "new country," France, her poetry existing in the pure lyric realm of emotions, beyond history and geography. Thus, unlike other émigré poets with whom she is compared, Gorbanevskaia hardly made the problem of the "old country" versus the "new country" a central theme. Indeed, Gorbanevskaia's verse shows a remarkable topographical freedom, being replete with the images of spatial flight and flying over (*perelet*). N. Diuzheva in particular notes the mixing of time and space in *Flying over the Snowy Border*. The border crossed over can be perceived as a boundary both of time and of space—a sign of "severance," "dissociation."[21] In emigration, as some critics observe, in Gorbanevskaia's poetry (*Foreign Stones* in particular) a theme of new personal time and space appears. Thus M. Temkina believes that, for Gorbanevskaia, the geographical features of space are sharply autobiographical.[22]

If the fact of emigration did not occasion the theme of new versus old country in her poetry, it nonetheless heightened particular occupation with linguistic matters, a theme that became more and more an object of Gorbanevskaia's artistic reflection. As she herself points out, emigration stimulated her precisely by directing her to matters of language.[23] As a poet, expression through language has a special significance: Gorbanevskaia perceives reality through it, as her acute awareness of it testifies. As a writer, she has to confront Soviet reality, which to her is a "pseudo-reality," being only a reality of ideas, *logos*, that exists exclusively through language (she adopts Czeslaw Milosz's term "logocracy"). It should be pointed out that Gorbanevskaia deals only with Soviet reality, not with the logocentrism of modern civilization in general, as Derrida does. In her coinage, the language that creates this pseudo-reality is "new speech" (*novorech*). In this light, the logic of her life as a poet, as a littérateur, is revealed more distinctly. Her struggle for liberation from "logocracy," or from pseudo-reality created by mere words, and for her freedom as a writer to create a genuine reality of words in harmony with her representation of things inevitably had to take the form of fighting against Soviet reality as a pseudo-reality. Gorbanevskaia maintains constant awareness of the enormous power of words in the reality in which she existed, since she never ceased to oppose that power as a poet engaged in civic action.

Another thematic feature of Gorbanevskaia's modernism, as has been stated, is the problematic that locates her close to existentialism, and most of all Camus (Gorbanevskaia calls him "our writer"),[24] with his social engagement and purity of art. In some of Gorbanevskaia's verses, human existence is perceived as horror. Eternity equals eternal tortures. In those poems, the world turns absurd—a cruel farce, a circus or theater. Poetry and music are the only refuge. Overall, for Gorbanevskaia, creativity is identical to genuine existence and therefore carries the nature of experience. Writing consists in registering experience—recording, restoring, ordering it. Poetry becomes a modus vivendi, a relief valve (or light ning rod), salvation (even God is there!) in a world that is either like a camp or a psychiatric prison—salvation from madness, the absurd and horror. Creativity for Gorbanevskaia is the only method of survival.

Moreover, Gorbanevskaia's writing to a considerable extent may be identified as literature of limit-situation (Karl Jasper's *Grenzesituation*). In some of her poems, the consciousness of her lyrical persona is that of a sentenced person (*smertnik*) in a situation that resembles the moment before jumping out a window. Gorbanevskaia's "dissent" was in essence creative—by putting her lyrical persona in a limit-situation that already speaks for itself, thus avoiding civic rhetoric, she opposed the official "civic poetry" of open social statements practiced and prophesied in the Soviet literary milieu. To her credit, Gorbanevskaia stood up in defense of her right to be a poet through a conscious nonimitative attitude to things.

The existentialism of Gorbanevskaia's writing is a religious one. She is a believer. In an interview, she confesses that she believes like a simple village woman, that faith holds an important place in her life as a whole.[25] In *Free Health Service,* she singles out as particularly painful her little icon and cross being taken away from her and the orderly scoffing at her beliefs. Gorbanevskaia's attitude to faith transcends the mere matters of life and is one of the keys to understanding her poetry. It is manifested by the classical (for Christianity) motives of crucifixion, Golgotha, the road to Calvary, the way of repentance ("the path of repentance is endless like the path of sin"), universal guilt, moral exploits. Gorbanevskaia's lyrical persona shares a never-ending bloody "path of repentance" with the people branded by "the seal of Cain." There also appear visions reminiscent of the Apocalypse and Last Judgment, in particular in the collection *Poems*. The lyrical persona takes upon herself the guilt of the people and the country:

> That time I did not save Warsaw, nor Prague later,
> Not I, not I, and there's no atoning for this guilt.

Literary form in Gorbanevskaia's verses displays equal sophistication with literary content. Although her poetry is indeed formally "unpretentious," as W. Kasack's *Dictionary* states,[26] it does offer creative development of the rich possibilities that Russian prosody may yield. Intentional and stylized simplicity have often embarrassed literary analysis. According to Christine Rydel, who attempted a formal study of her poetry, Gorbanevskaia experiments with sound, rhyme and meter.[27] Her stanzas also have not just thematic but also sound organization (assonance, alliteration). The rhymes she uses are highly assonantal and innovative.

Many of her brief, mostly untitled, lyrics are composed in four-line stanzas of alternate-rhymed verse. She also favors alternating rhythms. On the whole, meter is very irregular, although some patterns do occur. Throughout Gorbanevskaia's creation, rhythm can be observed to show a tendency of "liberation."

Moreover, there is a peculiar feature, very representative of every modernism, characteristic of poetry and prose alike, that should not be overlooked in Gorbanevskaia's works—autoreferentiality (or intertextuality, or dialogicity). It is a feature quite typical of her poetry. Its autoreferential nature is manifested by the numerous covert and overt citations, engaging Gorbanevskaia in rich intertextual connections with virtually the entire Russian poetic tradition from Pushkin and Apollon Grigor'ev to Mandel'shtam, Pasternak and Akhmatova. This feature makes knowledge of the entire tradition, the network of autoreferentiality, necessary for the understanding of fundamental codes of Gorbanevskaia's poetry.

Although in Gorbanevskaia's *oeuvre* poetry occupies the place of unconditional prominence, her literary criticism should by no means be disregarded. In particular, it reveals her attempts at conceptualizing the current development of Russian literature. She holds that in emigration, contemporary Russian literature has been experiencing a revival, Brodsky being a symbol of this process. In the 1970s, according to Gorbanevskaia, unlike in the 1930s and 1940s, the gap between Russian literature in Russia and Russian literature in emigration was closing; there appeared a certain unity. This process consisted in the establishment of an indissoluble link between Russian literature in emigration and *samizdat*. Thus she was positive about a new common literature being created, common because it was developing in accordance with the same laws at home and in emigration.

Gorbanevskaia's literary criticism, in particular that in the form of literary review, should be considered a fictional discourse, an extension of her activity as a poet. Having the nature of notes and commentaries, her documentary writing is deliberately nonconceptual. This is reflected by the impressionism, spontaneity and fragmentariness of her publicistic style, in which there coexist the lofty eloquence of poetry, the factological manner of a chronicle and the journalistic pathos of polemics.

Gorbanevskaia's activity of a publicist is closely related to her journalism, the pinnacle of it certainly being *The Chronicle of Current Events,* in which, incidentally, as she admits, she took more pride than in her poetry. The merit and importance of this "genre" was, in her estimation, its objective tone and abstinence from judgment. She reveals that she did the *Chronicle* "with aesthetic feelings—that is . . . to express everything as accurately as possible, as elegantly as possible. Incidentally, many people say that while I edited the *Chronicle* it was a literary document."[28] Thus Gorbanevskaia treated her documentary writing as an artist should—as a literary documentation, representative of a different type of literary discourse that, unlike poetry, applies precision and objective manner (reminiscent of Kafka's "protocol-like prose") as aesthetic categories.

Gorbanevskaia is also a translator of merit. As such, she is known mostly for her translations of prose. Among her achievements should be mentioned most of all her rendition of Czeslaw Milosz's *Poetic Tractate* (1982), which, incidentally, was the first translation ever made of it. According to Milosz himself, it is an exemplary work. Another notable accomplishment of Gorbanevskaia's translation is a three-volume opus, W. Tatarkiewicz's *The History of Aesthetics*. Not surprisingly, in June 1992 Gorbanevskaia received a prize from the Polish PEN Club for her translations of Milosz, Chlasko and other Polish authors.

A systematic overview of Gorbanevskaia's life and creativity reveals her as an outstanding poet who is certainly among the best representatives of current Russian literature and a person who sets standards of moral and civic conduct.

Natalie Repin

From And There Was I Once upon a Time

June 1992–February 1994

Octaves[1]

1.

To Orsha, to Rzhev, to Morshansk,
to bald foreheads and knolls,
to be fumbling for a lost chance
in the spilled pack of shag,

to be feeling for the lost pulse
in the curve of a trembling rail,
for a thawed covert way
amidst unburned forest.

5.

Not to the world, not to the city—
not to the city, but
to the handle of the bucket
ready for water,

to the sucking cold
from the bosom of being,
to the silent raven—
    I am still the same.

9.

Whether shorter is my breath,
or my breath is deeper,
my lungs breathe verse,
light, I leap over puddles.

Oh, how I leap, just as easy—over
this former restricted area,
where growing heather
will see the sky not through bars.

13.

Having placed
bad infinity upright,
let the riff-raff rush,
its name being the crowd,

thrilled with admiration,
predatory snouts ajar,
through this cramped crack
to thunder down the precipice.

"She is not concerned over the fate of her children"

This phrase taken
from the report of the commission of experts,
sung by a silvery clarinet,
has lost the shade of threat,
but at that has not shed all color.

All is well when behind the wall
my sons breathe and not the cellmates,
all is well when you wake up and do not groan,
seeing the world not soaked in venom.

All is well when you do not check your convolutions
for distortion—"Is it you or not?"—
when you inhale the unsettled ash from under the ruins
of something that, God willing, is not to return.

It's better to die earlier,
in the morning, and not alone,
so as not to witness falseness
in a long but tremulous note.

Be what you wanted,
as though everything is new again,
experience like mist flees the body
and in the cold condenses into a word.

While waiting for the end
do not throng at the threshold.
Everybody will get a chamber
in the home of our Father.

Do not breathe into the top of someone's head
with fresh chips and resin.
Beyond the exhaled haze
there is time and there is place.

A six-winged number
is damp from worry,
on the palm of everyone
there is a purple smudge.

Don't throng behind the line,
don't languish in muteness,
there is no end of song
in the home of our Father.

Sinking, circling
in the wordless abyss,
where vision is refused
and hearing is of no use.

Routing ash from fluff,
negation of negation,
the world is like a slap on the cheek
when there is no face.

No face, no eyes,
no stubborn flesh,
when mystery only awaits its time,
stilled at the turn.

The mystery of thicket and sickness,
the mystery of age and gaze,
the mystery of wind, waves and will,
of glorification and disgrace.

And holding this mystery in embrace,
anticipating its time to come,
my soul, you are like an accidental guest
in this house, in this dock.

In this would-be existence
one cannot burn wood in the stove,
as one cannot tell in words
the sacrament of transubstantiation.

In memory of E.S.G.

And there was I once upon a time,
and sang in summer and in winter,
in rain, in heat,
in spring:
"Princess, beware of the wicked witch,
wicked witch. . . . "

But there passed a hundred years,
and a sleeping world awakened
and beat the swords into the ploughs
and pistols into toys.

And some still lived,
seeds germinated,
and names,
and generations,
the whole country danced,
the country danced. . . .

Monday is a moon day!
Take a bow, wear a quiver.

In the ray of a wormwood star
shines the sphere with its half

turned to earth,
also gleaming in the dark.

Sandalwood is burning
in narrowed pupils,
lavishing a tearful gift
in puddles and streams.

Melted copper is burning
in celestial heights,
so that death comes
quick and in your sleep.

Curiosity dies off,
surprise dies down,
and the soul, not unselflessly,
yet not covertly, gets

in the line. In separation from the body
it embodies itself:
sticking out its nostrils from the swamp
that has consumed the image of the body,

it inhales phlogiston,
exhaling carbon dioxide
with wheeze, whistle and groan,
called verses.

Why wouldn't you melt,
morning snow,
my poor fellow,
my white burn.

Why haven't you fallen
by the end of the day,
haven't whitened broken ice
near the clearing,

where next to
ice-holes and gaps
the fisherman aims
to harpoon my heart.

I say: my breath, extend.
Smile at the sunrise, my faraway friend.
Look what fire is burning me
in this frozen February.

Be surprised that I am still treasuring
what was so long ago, in January.
And the camellia bush still blooms in the snow
in the yard at Faubourg St. Honoré.

I am of those
whom she taught how to speak.
I can never get tired of thanking
the light and color of this date.
Unfettered from the chain,
I sound with all my strings.
Until the hour of death
that will silence me.

There came a breath of cold,
cold from the northern land.
The memory of the cold war
is mixed with hop and malt.

With the heart broken in half
we glance askance as into a protocol:
is the stake driven in fast
over the hammer and sickle?

New verses Started on 9 March 1994

To cross oneself unnoticed,
to put on a shirt of blue calico,
to swim across to the other side of Styx,
to forget who has not bid you farewell.

All former memory, all former vision
to raft like logs down the river of oblivion,
to moor like rafting in locked links,
not to expect anything but deliverance.

Catch, grasp,
wishing good fortune,
in an asphalt stream
cast fishing-tackles.

It does not cry, does not frown,
caught in the net
the street rhymes
like everything else in the world.

Autumn touches crosshairs in the sight
like spider threads—a fly,
hefty soul-guards
are on both sides of the body,

shaking off spider-nets from the shoulders,
they wait for the dead of night,
eyes like frosted windows
in a solitary cell.

Badly is my head organized.
It gives birth not to thoughts but only to words.
And even this I bore not quite by myself.
That's the way it is.

The grain dropped in the pulp,
would not ripen quietly, but
is bursting from under the temple bone
to shoot through.

Unground flour
curdles in a lump into a martyr,
fumbling with a chopped-off tongue
as if with an empty scoop.

The doctor x-rayed for a long time
what is inside my head.
There is most of all unsifted mold.
This is to me for my sins.

We call this groan, this howl,
this sob of dactylic *clausula*,

this wail of begging crowds,
hungry for Lazarus,

a song,
that is a verse,
and it feeds on mold
and ground glass.

Having heated the stove,
sleep, little fellow.
The cricket is crippling
the same song.

Christmas Eve is gone,
and Christmas is also gone.
The kettle is looking at itself
in the glass, on Epiphany.

Is my forgotten guest
still alive?
Where there is a horse with a hoof,
there is a crayfish with a claw.

I will steal both the rhyme
and the gas lamp's voice,
still so beautiful
in that fateful year,
in gunpowder fumes
of the sickle over the red field,

where sharp-leaved willow and weeping willow
interlock their twigs,
where rhymes lost their way

in the thicket of shrubbery,
and to parched lips
from a puddle or pond

clings black water
of labor and offense.

In the port of Amsterdam
to that vague waltz
with a hole in the side
you lie down on the sand.

Everyone has
one's own bygone days,
whatever I recall I sing
in the exercise yard.

Don't tell me about the lightness
of being.
We both know this "oh!" in the bones,
you and I,

when, strained to the breaking point,
the bow of collarbones
is pregnant at the dead of night with noon
and radiance.

Still the heart is like a rabbit,
zigzagging away.
Still the soul is pierced
with unspeakable bliss.

The time of falling leaves
descending on the garden
smells of fallen sweetness,
of warm-sided east.

No, not sleeping, not ceasing to love,
but having forgotten myself
and having forgotten you forever,
having left, sailed, departed

in a small jumpy step,
tightening the belt,
no, not stirring the past,
only rustling the leaves.

Written in 1995

Just go for a walk down Tverskoi Boulevard.
Sadness or no sadness, boredom or no boredom.
In such weather it's hard not to clench your teeth,
and your cheek grows numb.

Just take a look at the native wasteland
with diamonds of frost, with gems of puddles.
An unnecessary luxury of frozen senses,
a blissful scarcity of strolling souls.

Translated by Natalie Repin

Notes to the Essay

1. A. Radashkevich, "Most ot zhizni i do zhizni. O novykh knigakh stikhov Natal'i Gorbanevskoi." *Russkaia mysl',* 29 November 1985, 10.

2. C. Kelly, "Natal'ya Gorbanevskaya," in *An Encyclopedia of Continental Women Writers*, vol. 1, ed. Katharina M. Wilson (New York: Garland Publishing, 1991), 474.

3. N. Gorbanevskaia, "Writing for 'samizdat,'" *Index on Censorship*, 6, 1 (1977): 35.

4. Ibid.

5. N. Gorbanevskaia, "Uzy i skorbi," in *Literaturnaia gazeta,* 2 September 1992, 5.

6. N. Gorbanevskaia, "Moving Our Lips," in *The Writer and Human Rights*, trans. Donald Bruce (Garden City, NY: 1983), 205.

7. S. Sandler, "Gorbanevskaia," in *Dictionary of Russian Women Writers*, ed. M. Ledkovsky, C. Rosenthal and M. Zirin (Westport, CT: Greenwood Press, 1994), 220.

8. V. Amurskii, "Ne liubliu vysokikh slov . . . ," *Novoe russkoe slovo,* 29 March 1990, 5.

9. A. Glezer, "Esli v pamiati ne sokhraniaetsia samoe glavnoe, to, znachit, pamiati net (Interv'iu s Natal'ei Gorbanevskoi)," *Strelets* 2 (February 1985): 41.

10. Iu. Kublanovskii, "Lish' muzyka—spasen'e," *Russkaia mysl',* 29 September 1983, 10.

11. Amurskii, "Ne liubliu vysokikh slov," 6.

12. G.S. Smith, "Russian Poetry outside Russia since 1970: A Survey," in *Aspects of Modern Russian and Czech Literature* (Columbus, OH: Slavica Publishers, 1989), 185.

13. Ibid., 186.

14. Kelly, "Natalya Gorbanevskaya," 475.

15. A. Radashkevich, "Most ot zhizni i do zhizni," 10.

16. A. Tatarinov, " . . . I alchet, i zhazhdet moi golos . . . ," *Kontinent* 37 (1983): 422.

17. Amurskii, "Ne liubliu vysokikh slov," 6.

18. Ibid.

19. Ibid.

20. D. Bobyshev, "Bol'shaia i malaia poèziia Natal'i Gorbanevskoi," *Sintaksis* 9 (1981): 171.

21. N. Diuzheva, "Kak raskachana volna . . . ," *Kontinent* 26 (1980): 378.

22. M. Temkina, "Nichego ne poluchaetsia, a vse-taki vykhodit chto-to . . . ," *Strelets* 2 (February 1984): 25.

23. Glezer, "Esli v pamiati ne sokhraniaetsia samoe glavnoe," 38.

24. N. Gorbanevskaia, "Otkaz ot poteri pamiati," *Kontinent* 17 (1978): 373.

25. N. Gorbanevskaia, interview in *Vestnik russkogo khristianskogo dvizheniia* 120 (1977): 286.

26. W. Kasack, "Gorbanevskaya," in *Dictionary of Russian Literature since 1917* (New York: Columbia University Press, 1988), 126.

27. C. Rydel, "The Early Poems of Natal'ja Gorbanevskaja," *Russian Language Journal* 36 (1982): 252.

28. Gorbanevskaia, "Writing for 'samizdat,'" 36.

Translator's Note to the Selected Works

1. This and the following nonartistic translations have been made of poems selected from Gorbanevskaia's collection *I ia zhila-byla* (*And There Was I Once upon a Time*, June 1992–February 1994), which has not as yet been published in its entirety, as well as from the cycle of new poems started on 9 March 1994, which has not yet been submitted for publication as a whole, either. The last poem in the present selection was composed in February 1995. The present translations owe their existence solely to the courtesy of Natal'ia Gorbanevskaia herself, who made the original poems available to me. For that gesture, my everlasting gratitude.

Bibliography

Primary Works

Stikhi. Frankfurt: Posev, 1969.

Polden'. Delo o demonstratsii 25 avgusta 1968 goda na Krasnoi ploshchadi. Frankfurt: Posev, 1970.

Poberezh'e: Stikhi. Ann Arbor, MI: Ardis, 1973.

Tri tetradi stikhotvorenii. Bremen: K-Presse, 1975.

"Probleski nadezhdy." *Russkaia mysl'*, 25 March 1976, 8.

"Blesk i nishcheta sovetskogo intelligenta." *Kontinent* 11 (1977): 375–80.

[Interview]. *Vestnik russkogo khristianskogo dvizheniia* 1 20 (1977): 286–88.

"Podval pamiati." *Kontinent* 12 (1977): 375–80.

"A po serdtsakh nashikh kopita, kopita. . . ." *Kontinent* 16 (1978): 369–72.

"Otkaz ot poteri pamiati." *Kontinent* 17 (1978): 372–76.

"V chetyrekh stenakh." *Kontinent* 15 (1978): 371–75.

Pereletaia snezhnuiu granitsu. Stikhi 1974–1978. Paris: YMCA Press, 1979.

"Pogovorim o zveriushkakh, milye detki. . . ." *Kontinent* 20 (1979): 373–78.

"I zrenie, i slukh, i dukh, i telo. . . ." *Kontinent* 22 (1980): 402–06.

"Remarki, pometki, pomarki." *Kontinent* 25 (1980): 342–46.

"Vy—svobodny." *Kontinent* 23 (1980): 397–402.

Angel dereviannyi. Ann Arbor, MI: Ardis, 1982.

"Blagodarenie za poèta." *Kontinent* 33 (1982): 386–90.

"Otvety na voprosy o Rossii." *Kontinent* 32 (1982): 400–03.

Chuzhie kamni. Stikhi 1979–1982. New York: Russica, 1983.

"Mozhesh' vyiti na ploshchad', smeesh' vyiti na ploshchad'." *Russkaia mysl'*, 25 August 1983, 10–11.

"Ob"iasnenie v liubvi." *Kontinent* 35 (1983): 61–66.

"Blizhe brata." *Stikhi 1965–1983*. Ed. Vadim Delone. Paris: La Presse Libre, 1984. 139–44.

Neslomlennaia Pol'sha na stranitsakh 'Russkoi mysli.' Vyp. 1: Dekabr' 1981–dekabr' 1982. Paris, 1984.

Gde i kogda. Stikhi (Iiun' 1983–mart 1985). Paris: Kontakt, 1985.

"Mel'nitsa i zamok." *Kontinent* 43 (1985): 387–92.

"Neologizmy i novorech'." *Russkaia mysl'*, 30 August 1985, 12–13.

Peremennaia oblachnost'. Stikhi (Osen' 1982–vesna 1983). Paris: Kontakt, 1985.

"Novyi samizdat." *Kontinent* 52 (1987): 253–64.

"Èta kniga byla pervoi." *Kontinent* 60 (1989): 425–29.

"Mikhail Bulgakov, zhiznepovedenie." *Kontinent* 61 (1989): 382–86.

"I vremia zhit', i vremia povtoriat'." *Oktiabr'* 7 (1990): 102–08.

"Iz raznykh sbornikov." *Znamia* 8 (1990): 90–96.

"Zemlia liudei." *Kontinent* 68 (1991): 224–41.

"Iz stikhov poslednikh let." *Novyi mir* 11 (1992): 185–87.

"Stikhi o russkom iazyke." *Russkaia rech'* 1 (January–February 1992): 38–50.

"Uzy i skorbi." *Literaturnaia gazeta*, 2 September 1992, 5.

Tsvet vereska. New York: Èrmitazh, 1993.

"Novye stikhi." *Oktiabr'* 1 (1994): 41–42.

"Bylye vremena u kazhdogo svoi. . . ." *Oktiabr'* 2 (1995): 85–87.

In Translation

[Poems]. *Russia's Underground Poets*. Ed. Keith Bosley, Dimitry Pospielovsky and Janis Sopiets. New York: Frederick A. Praeger, 1969. 39–40.

Red Square at Noon. Trans. Alexander Lieven. London: Deutsch, 1972.

Selected Poems. Trans. Daniel Weissbort. Oxford: Carcanet, 1972.

[Poems]: *Russian Language Triquarterly* 5 (1973): 39–42. [Rpt. in *The Ardis Anthology of Recent Russian Literature*. Ed. Carl R. Proffer and Ellendea Proffer. Ann Arbor, MI: Ardis, 1973. 39–42.]

[Poems]: *Russian Language Triquarterly* 9 (1974): 45–49.

"Ten Poems by Natalya Gorbanevskaya." Trans. Ronald Walter. *Nation* 220, 1 (11 January 1975): 18–20.

"Twelve Poems." Trans. Daniel Weissbort. *Index on Censorship* 6, 1 (1977): 37–40.

"Writing for 'samizdat'." *Index on Censorship* 6, 1 (1977): 29–36.

[Selected poems]. *Russian Poetry: The Modern Period*. Ed. John Glad and Daniel Weissbort. Iowa City: University of Iowa Press, 1978. 331–34.

"Moving Our Lips." *The Writer and Human Rights*. Trans. Donald Bruce. Garden City, NY, 1983. 202–05.

"The Testimony of Anatoly Marchenko." *The Writer and Human Rights*. Trans. Donald Bruce. Garden City, NY, 1983. 191–94.

[Poems]. *Twentieth-Century Russian Poetry*. Ed. John Glad and Daniel Weissbort. Iowa City: University of Iowa Press, 1992. 347–50.

[Poems]. *Contemporary Russian Poetry*. Trans. G.S. Smith. Bloomington: Indiana University Press, 1993. 101–11.

[Poems]. *Twentieth-Century Russian Poetry: Silver and Steel, An Anthology*. Ed. Albert C. Todd and Max Hayward (with Daniel Weissbort). New York: Doubleday, 1993. 864–65.

Secondary Works

Alloi, V. "Putem dobra," *Kontinent* 11 (1977): 386–92.

Amurskii, V. "Ne liubliu vysokikh slov. . . . " *Novoe russkoe slovo,* 29 March 1990, 5–6.

Bobyshev, D. "Bol'shaia i malaia poèziia Natal'i Gorbanevskoi." *Sintaksis* 9 (1981): 170–75.

Brown, Deming. *Soviet Russian Literature since Stalin*. Cambridge: Cambridge University Press, 1978. 362–63.

Diuzheva, N. "Kak raskachana volna. . . . " *Kontinent* 26 (1980): 377–80.

Glad, John. "Gorbanevskaya." *Handbook of Russian Literature*. Ed. Victor Terras. New Haven, CT: Yale University Press, 1985. 179.

Glezer, A. "Esli v pamiati ne sokhraniaetsia samoe glavnoe, to, znachit, pamiati net (Interv'iu s Natal'ei Gorbanevskoi)." *Strelets* 2 (February 1985): 38–41.

Kasack, Wolfgang. "Gorbanevskaya." *Dictionary of Russian Literature since 1917*. New York: Columbia University Press, 1988. 126–27.

Kelly, Catriona. "Natal'ya Gorbanevskaya." *An Encyclopedia of Continental Women Writers*. Vol. 1. Ed. Katharina M. Wilson. New York: Garland Publishing, 1991. 474–75.

Kublanovskii, Iu. "Lish' muzyka—spasen'e." *Russkaia mysl',* 29 September 1983, 10.

Mozhaiskaia, O. "Ne umeiushchaia solgat'." *Grani* 78 (1970): 252–56.

Naiman, A. "Rasskazy ob Anne Akhmatovoi." *Novyi mir* 3 (1989): 106.

Nemec Ignashev, Diane M., and Sarah Krive. "Gorbanevskaia." *Women and Writing in Russia and the USSR: A Bibliography of English-Language Sources*. New York: Garland Publishing, 1992. 46, 166–67.

Radashkevich, A. "Most ot zhizni i do zhizni. O novykh knigakh stikhov Natal'i Gorbanevskoi." *Russkaia mysl',* 29 November 1985, 10.

Rich, Adrienne. "Natalya Gorbanevskaya." *On Lies, Secrets, and Silence*. New York: Norton, 1979. 116–19.

Rydel, Christine A. "The Early Poems of Natal'ja Gorbanevskaja." *Russian Language Journal* 36 (1982): 236–52.

Sandler, Stephanie. "Gorbanevskaia." *Dictionary of Russian Women Writers*. Ed. Marina Ledkovsky, Charlotte Rosenthal and Mary Zirin. Westport, CT: Greenwood Press, 1994. 219–21.

Smith, G.S. "Another Time, Another Place." *Times Literary Supplement,* 26 June 1987, 692–94.

———. "The Metrical Repertoire of Shorter Poems by Russian Émigrés, 1971– 1980." *Canadian Slavonic Papers* 27 (1985): 385–96.

———. "Russian Poetry outside Russia since 1970: A Survey." *Aspects of Modern Russian and Czech Literature*. Ed. Arnold McMillin. Columbus, OH: Slavica, 1989. 179–87.

Stevanovic, B., and V. Wertsman. "Gorbanevskaia." *Free Voices in Russian Literature 1950s–1980s: A Bibliographic Guide*. New York: Russica, 1987. 147–49.

Tatarinov, A. " . . . I alchet, i zhazhdet moi golos. . . . " *Kontinent* 37 (1983): 420–25.

Temkina, Marina. "Nichego ne poluchaetsia, a vse-taki vykhodit chto-to. . . . " *Strelets* 2 (February 1984): 25.

I. Grekova

I. Grekova (b. 1907). Courtesy of Aleksandra Raskina.

Although she became a member of the Writers' Union in 1966 and has been one of Russia's most important authors since 1961, I. Grekova (Elena Sergeevna Venttsel', née Dolgintsova, b. 1907) has always defined herself primarily as a scientist. Her choice of a pen name is symptomatic—"I. Grekova" being a variant of "Igrek" (*Y*), symbol for a mathematical unknown[1]—and it is in fact impossible to understand her practice as a writer without giving due weight to the scientific aspect of her person. Doctor of Sciences, one of the relatively few Soviet women to attain the title; author of a number of works on probability theory and applied mathematics;[2] and teacher in higher technical institutes and schools for over fifty years, including the Zhukovskii Military Aviation Academy,[3] Grekova is steeped in the intense internal dynamics of scientific groups, which are themselves frequently the subject of her longer works.

Many of Grekova's stories depict the complicated lives of scientists. Mar'ia Vladimirovna Kovaleva, middle-aged heroine of "The Ladies' Hairdresser"

("Damskii master," 1963), the story that first brought Grekova wide notice,[4] is the mother of two untidy, almost grown sons[5] and head of a research institute. On a day like any other, she is constantly distracted from research by the "shredded attention, shredded time" that are the result of her administrative responsibilities. Once she almost miraculously manages to work out a problem that she has long wanted to tackle.

> The phone calls had finally stopped, and when I came to, it was ten o'clock in the evening. The solution to the problem was working. I checked the computations once more. It worked. Good God, perhaps it's for such minutes that life is worth living. I've lived a long life and can state authoritatively that nothing —not love, nor motherhood—nothing in the world yields as much happiness as those minutes.[6]

Such moments of creative joy are rare.[7] They are rarest of all for the women in Grekova's works, whose existence is additionally weighed down by the fatigue, love and sorrow of motherhood, by the thought of the children they know they are neglecting,[8] by guilt and regret and longing. One should note, however, that in Grekova's works love, sorrow and longing are not exclusively feminine attributes: there are men "caregivers"[9] and introspective male as well as female protagonists.[10] But since Grekova is a woman, and because there is a preponderance of women protagonists in her works, there have inevitably been arguments as to whether she should be considered a writer of "women's literature" (*zhenskaia literatura*) or, more disparagingly, of "feminine prose" (*damskaia proza*).[11]

As one might expect, there is little agreement among the users of these terms as to their meaning. Ruf' Zernova, herself the author of a collection of stories entitled *Women's Stories* (*Zhenskie rasskazy*), says simply that *zhenskaia literatura* is "literature created by women about women."[12] By this definition, in stories such as " Under the Streetlight" ("Pod fonarem," 1966) or "A Summer in the City" ("Letom v gorode"), and in the novellas *The Fracture* (*Perelom*), *The Hotel Manageress* (*Khoziaika gostinitsy*, 1976) and *Ship of Widows* (*Vdovii parokhod*, 1981),[13] Grekova is writing "women's literature." It should be stressed that Grekova is well aware of the existence of a tradition of texts written by women on similar themes, and its presence is felt in her own reorchestrations. If one applies Èikhenbaum's comment in a speech praising Akhmatova (shortly before Zhdanov lowered the boom in August 1946)—"To woman is given the task of preserving and passing on memory, of creating a link between the generations"[14]—then Grekova joins

Evgeniia Ginzburg, Lidiia Chukovskaia and Nadezhda Mandel'shtam in attempting to preserve the real lived truth of Soviet life. But to create a link between generations in the strict sense is something that Grekova recognizes as problematic. One of her main themes is the difficulty, frequently the impossibility, of creating and maintaining links of comprehension between the young people of the 1960s, 1970s and 1980s and the values[15] and lives of the parents, grandparents and foster parents who have struggled—singly or together—to raise them,[16] and who no longer recognize their beautiful and touching children in the sullen and detached adolescents and adults whom they have somehow become.[17]

When one attempts to characterize *zhenskaia literatura* in terms more technical than those used by Zernova and Èikhenbaum, then the appropriateness of this label for Grekova's work becomes less evident. Helena Goscilo proposes among the "hallmarks" of Soviet women's prose in the last two decades the use of "a female center of consciousness conveyed through quasi-indirect discourse and a limited viewpoint in which the boundaries between author, narrator, and protagonist often become blurred."[18] While Grekova does employ a female center of consciousness and a limited viewpoint in some of her short stories, her longer works are on the contrary characterized by a multiplicity of points of view and a sympathetic portrayal from within of a wide variety of characters, both women and men. It is therefore not surprising that in response to questions put to her by *Literary Survey* (*Literaturnoe obozrenie*) in 1986 Grekova listed among the "favorite personages" of her works not only Vera Laricheva of *The Hotel Manageress* and Mar'ia Borisovna of "Little Garusov" ("Malenkii Garusov" 1970) but also Professor N.N. Zavalishin and "the oddly attractive V.A. Fliagin," who is roundly despised and hounded by the main feminine protagonist of *The Faculty* (*Kafedra*).[19] Furthermore, since Grekova's larger works are not usually centered on a single protagonist but are about the interactions that create the dynamic equilibrium of a functioning social organism—an equilibrium that can be destroyed by the intrusion of a foreign element (e.g., Fliagin in *The Faculty*, anonymous letters in *Thresholds* [*Porogi*])—Grekova rightly insists that she also has favorite "collective heroes" such as Laboratory 10 in "Beyond the Gates" ("Za prokhodnoi," 1962), the working group on the testing site from the long novella *On the Proving Grounds* and the Third Section of NIIKAT in *Thresholds.*[20]

Grekova has herself declared that she does not wish to be considered a writer of "women's literature." Her scientific training makes her hostile to any reversal in the hierarchy of importance of gender and species. Her identity includes her femininity as a major factor, but not as the dominant one. Scientist, writer of scientific books, writer of literary criticism, writer of fiction, writer of children's literature,[21] wife become widow, mother become grandmother, she functions in a variety of personal and professional capacities and she refuses to be limited to a single voice. It is therefore not surprising that Grekova has joined Lidiia Chukovskaia and some younger women writers[22] in rejecting the term "women's literature" entirely.[23] Chukovskaia asked, "What does 'women's literature' mean? There are such things as women's baths, but women's literature?"[24] Similarly, Grekova might have said: "There are such things as women's hairdressers, but women's literature?"[25]

Grekova has frequently stated that she has most in common with the writers of what she calls "new" or "contemporary" prose (*sovremennaia proza*) because it is characterized by "the erosion of the boundaries between 'belletristic' prose and other genres such as publicistic prose, notes, diaries, memoirs, documentary prose."[26] She considers the works of Rasputin, Belov, Bykov and Trifonov, as well as texts such as Lidiia Ginzburg's "Notes of a Person under Siege" ("Zapiski blokadnogo cheloveka") and the prose of Nataliia Il'ina, as good examples of this phenomenon.[27] A number of Grekova's own works are liminal in this sense, not merely the aptly titled *Thresholds*.[28] They include real or fictional tables, passenger lists, letters, diaries, stenographic reports and verses. Grekova's own professional "bilingualism" has accustomed her to the necessity of taking different points of view. This probably has something to do with her preference for stereoscopic constructions, where a number of points of view are presented within a work without the author's overtly deciding between them, a construction typical of the "new prose," which Grekova says is "based on faith in the readers' ability to come to their own conclusions," as do jurors at a trial.[29]

Of course, this nonauthoritative artistic posture existed in Russian literature long before the "new prose." Chekhov is talking about the same thing in his well-known remark that it is not the function of a writer to solve social problems but rather to put the problems correctly.[30] The works of Chekhov and other Russian writers are present as strong intertexts throughout Grekova's works. Grekova is a passionate reader, and literature, especially Russian literature, has always been an essential part of her existence. In her works, literature appears as a fact of life to which characters may have authentic or inauthentic relations. They can be placed on a spectrum, beginning at one end with people who have contempt for literature and for people who read. Then come those who have a superficial knowledge of a few works with which they were "stuffed" in school. This is frequently the case for members of the "younger generation," many of whom seem to remember only *Eugene Onegin* and, more specifically, only the fact that Tatiana wrote a love letter to Onegin.[31] An interesting variant of this minimal literacy is the young man in *On the Proving Grounds* who, unlike some others, thinks he can identify Gogol's famous line, "Alexander of Macedon was a hero, but is that a reason to break chairs?"[32] However, it turns out that he believes that the quote is from *Chapaev* (where indeed it does appear, its source equally unrecognized): a small *mise en abîme* of intertexts fairly typical for Grekova.

A few of Grekova's characters, such as the soldier-driver in *On the Proving Grounds,* have a devouring and naive secret passion for reading. Others show off their minimal literary knowledge, sometimes making mistakes.[33] Then there are those who know literature well and show off the power of their memories by reciting. There is frequently a strong whiff of snobbery at this level. At the positive end of the spectrum, there are a number of characters who have intense individual relationships with literature, which feeds them spiritually and provides them with an intimate interlocutor. Knowledge of literature also allows them to have real human contacts with other readers, providing a dimension of communication sharable only by those who have "grown up" on Russian literature. For the "intelligentsia," of whom there are a goodly number in Grekova's works, great Russian literature acts as an intellectual tuning fork and therefore as a moral guide.[34] Literary references and comments about language are therefore frequent in their thoughts and conversations.[35]

Two of Grekova's works are entirely built around a literary reference: "Rothschild's Fiddle" ("Skripka Rotshil'da," 1980), translated here, and "No Smiles" ("Bez ulybok," 1970). M.M., the researcher protagonist of "No Smiles," one of Grekova's strongest stories, has been accused of being a representative of "a depraved tendency in science" (*porochnoe napravlenie v nauki*).[36] She is undergoing the nasty kind of "chastisement and reeducation" (*prorabotka*) to which Grekova herself was subjected as a result of her novella *On the Proving Grounds.*[37] M.M. is a reader (she herself says "reader" the way one says "smoker").[38] As she has grown older, she is less and less drawn to fiction and more and more to memoirs, diaries, letters and the like, "because there is a higher percentage of truth in them," suggests a friend of similar age with similar tastes. M.M. is currently reading W. Kiukhel'beker's prison diaries for the years 1831–1832.[39] Passages from his diaries, sometimes as much as half a page long, alternate in the story with M.M.'s comments on them and resonate with her life at the institute and her appearances at condemnatory meetings, where she is in fact on trial. What is most helpful to her in Kiukhel'beker's diaries is that, despite his imprisonment, he remained thoroughly open and alive: he wrote about art, science and religion, as well as describing scenes from the everyday life of the prison, which he could see through his window. He learned Greek and wrote poems, but described almost nothing about his own fate and suffering. Thus reading Kiukhel'beker helps M.M. to hold on to her truth and to continue to refuse to "admit her errors." She takes the route not of Galileo but of Bruno (she knows herself that the comparison is disproportionate), despite the terrific physical and psychic toll the months of *prorabotka* take on her. In the end, she is vindicated, as was Grekova, but at what cost![40]

While mutual recognition through common literary reference can bring moments of shared joy, love of literature is not a magic wand, and not all of Grekova's characters are sensitive to the moral essence that is the precious burden of great Russian literature. While her exposure to the artistic depiction of violent passion may have been enough to move the sentimental Madame Schwartz in Babel's "DiGrasso" to force her husband to return the young protagonist's watch, thus reestablishing the moral and aesthetic balance of the universe for him,[41] this ploy does not work in Grekova's "Rothschild's Fiddle." Rita Pavlovna, a teacher, is friendly with a woman who cleans apartments in her building. The two women are of different classes and sensibilities: "Rita was always overwhelmed by the problems swarming around her like flies around a horse. Problems did not exist for Polina Ivanovna—they had all been already resolved."[42] Nevertheless, the two women get along well and enjoy drinking coffee together. On one occasion, Rita Pavlovna tries to convince Polina Ivanovna that money is not everything by reading Chekhov's story "Rothschild's Fiddle" out loud to her, in the belief that the moral power of great literature is irresistible.

The words of Chekhov's story weave through Grekova's until Polina Ivanovna asks Rita Pavlovna to finish telling it in her own words because Chekhov's "upset her nerves." Polina Ivanovna is in fact moved by parts of "Rothschild's Fiddle," but she notices the wrong things and takes them the wrong way. Nevertheless, Rita Pavlovna believes that her reading has made the close-fisted Polina Ivanovna realize that she should treat her invalid husband more kindly. Apparently under the influence of Chekhov's story, Polina decides that she will give her husband a treat and take him to the movies. But instead the couple find their evening's entertainment in calculating how much Rita Pavlovna earns, and how much she "loses" on nonessentials: cigarettes, coffee (the basis of her friendship with Polina Ivanovna) and, above all, books. Rita Pavlovna is described as being physically like Don Quixote, and her idealism proves as doomed as his; trying to awaken the moral sensibilities of this particular normal, uneducated, middle-aged Soviet woman[43] is as futile an effort as tilting at windmills.

Thus Grekova's "Rothschild's Fiddle" has an even more Chekhovian ending than does Chekhov's own story, for Chekhov's Iakov realizes, albeit too late, how he has destroyed both his wife's life and ultimately his own by his obsession with *ubytki,* what the French would call *manque à gagner,* that which might have been earned but has not been, for instance, because a holiday has kept one from working, or because wood must be used for a coffin for one's wife rather than for one that can be sold. Grekova's story is more complex than Chekhov's in its skillful juggling of four "words": Rita Pavlovna's, Polina Ivanovna's "demotic," Iakov's as reported by Chekhov and Chekhov's. The reader alone hears them all and "judges." Polina's inability to recognize herself in Chekhov's story is obviously a reversal of the complicated and agonizing reaction of Dostoevsky's Makar Devushkin in *Poor Folk* (*Bednye liudi*) to *his* reading of Gogol's "The Overcoat" ("Shinel'").[44] Although Dostoevsky's presence is not as visible as Chekhov's in Grekova's work, her practice has been strongly marked not only by Dostoevsky's preference for polyphony but also by his moral posture.

Not all efforts at spiritual awakening fail in Grekova's works. As Dostoevsky followed Victor Hugo in depicting "the resurrection of the fallen man,"[45] so Grekova's *Thresholds* shows the gradual resurrection of the reclusive Neshatov, who has been tried several times and ultimately cleared of responsibility for a fatal explosion that occurred in a laboratory that he supervised. Neshatov is only beginning to emerge from a severe depression for which he has been hospitalized. His slow reintegration into the "human community," in this case represented by NIIKAT, an institute concerned with verbal communication with machines, is made possible through the nurturing presence and care of Boris Mikhailovich Gan, assistant director of NIIKAT, who spends long hours with Neshatov and even puts up with his smoking, despite his own heart condition. Gan is a cultivated man with many "old-fashioned" values. For instance, he believes that "one should live *as if* the soul were immortal." It becomes clear after his death[46] that Gan has allowed himself and his talent as a cybernetician to be sacrificed to instrumental, midwifely functions: taking care of details, relieving the burdens on the head of the group, running interference so that the institute may function smoothly as a happy ship and other scientists may fulfill their promise. At the end of *Thresholds*, Neshatov, having accepted the self-sacrificial love of Gan, is now ready to give and sacrifice himself in turn.[47] Other characters, both men and women, gravitate to those who need them, whether or not those in need are "worthy" people. Such is the investment of self in others of which Dostoevsky speaks in *Winter Notes on Summer Impressions*.[48]

Perhaps the most lyrical example in Grekova's works of a character who subordinates herself to others and finds fulfillment in the various situations in which she finds herself is Vera Pavlovna Laricheva, the heroine of *The Hotel Manageress*, the story critics usually have in mind when they call Grekova a writer of *damskaia proza.* Some have unfairly called her a modern version of Chekhov's "Darling" ("Dushechka"),[49] although Danaia in *Thresholds* would be a much better candidate for this role. Many of Grekova's characters, women and men, intellectuals and people with little or no education, find meaning in their lives through some activity involving serving others, especially, but not exclusively, children, despite their own sorrow and loss. Thus they carry forward and deepen a well-established theme in Russian literature, and some of them create for themselves at least an approximation of that "complicated happiness" (*slozhnoe schast'e*) that Grekova so much admired in Kornei Chukovskii's "Sunny" ("Solnechnaia"), a story written under the impact of the recent death of Chukovskii's youngest daughter from osteotuberculosis.

Despite the cliché that it is easier to create distinctive negative characters than positive ones, Grekova is in fact better at the latter. Or rather, there is something positive in most of her characters, even in the somewhat ridiculous and quirky ones. Thus the Third Section of NIIKAT preserves itself by shared laughter under difficult circumstances that otherwise would almost certainly have destroyed the working atmosphere, collegiality and effectiveness of the group. The transcript of one meeting is repeatedly punctuated with the notation *smekh* ("laughter"), an implicit comment on the transcripts of innumerable Communist party meetings that were characterized by the comments *aplodismenty* ("applause") and even *burnye aplodismenty* ("wildly enthusiastic applause").

It may seem from her concern with collective activity that Grekova is a "Socialist Realist with a human face." She is not, however, a Pollyanna, and she does not minimize the damage done by the arbitrary "justice," denunciations and anonymous letters that appear frequently in her works. Her characters must resist and defend themselves, and sometimes their work, against stupid and malicious attacks, small-mindedness, racial and religious prejudice, bureaucracy, war, shortages, bad living conditions, "accidental families" and mortal fatigue, both moral and physical.

Grekova has had a long life. She has seen the rise and the fall of the Soviet Union. Chronologically she belongs to a generation who were already adults with children at the time of World War II, but she made her publishing debut with the writers of the 1960s. At the end of her career, she has identified herself with the writers of the "new prose" of the 1980s, whose artistic principles she shares, although she uses their devices with more moderation than some of her younger colleagues.[50] She is hard to classify. But that is the way it should be if Nabokov is right in saying that one should identify a writer not by trying to pigeonhole, but rather by paying attention to his or her specific pattern or unique coloration.[51]

Grekova's works are not as spectacularly individual as Nabokov's, but in their own way they are quietly groundbreaking contributions to Russian literature.

Elizabeth Beaujour

Rothschild's Violin

Rita and Polina Ivanovna were friends. Rita was a teacher of Russian language and literature, and Polina Ivanovna was the elevator operator in the building where Rita lived.

They were very different. Rita was a tall, thin woman, sort of hinged together, all arms and legs, a kind of cross between Don Quixote and the windmill. Polina Ivanovna, on the other hand, was short and compact, with an ample potbelly and hard, coal-black eyes.

Rita was always overwhelmed by the various problems that seemed to envelop her as tightly as a harness does a horse. For Polina Ivanovna, there was no such thing as a problem: they all had been solved long ago. Despite their differences, the two managed to get along quite well and were happy to get together whenever time allowed it. And time was something they both never had enough of.

Rita was up to her ears in schoolwork: lesson plans, staff meetings, students' report cards and other paperwork, recycling drives and a million other causes that she felt it her duty to champion. Most of all it was the homework, those countless notebooks and assignments, which gave her not a moment's breathing room. Each one had to be gone over, and taking her responsibilities very seriously, Rita corrected them down to the last comma and period, all the while liberally dusting each one with ashes from the cigarettes that she smoked from morning until night. Once done with her corrections, Rita didn't just give a mark but instead wrote the student a long, drawn-out review of the work. She loved Russian literature with a passion and found it as impossible to live without books as without cigarettes.

Polina Ivanovna also had her hands full. Her schedule was such that she was on duty once every three days: twenty-four hours on, then forty-eight off. But she considered her days on as more rest than anything else. She worked on the side on those days off, cleaning apartments in the same building, where most of the tenants were highly paid. She charged fifteen rubles for cleaning (windows were extra) and would say that at today's prices that was practically doing it for free. There were those who charged twenty, and even twenty-five rubles. While she was cleaning their apartments, the highly paid owners were at work in their offices, and their wives, all pampered and powdered and dressed in their foreign finery, were walking their dogs. The wives would stand and wait patiently as the prized pet lifted his leg and did his duty. Sometimes the dogs would sniff each other out while their mistresses, leashes held taut in their hands like reins, carried on their highbrow conversations.

All the while this was going on, Polina Ivanovna was hard at work. Tucking up her already short skirts above her white knees, she would scrub the floors in the halls in the old way, head bent down. Then, head up, she would go to work on the carpets and parquet floors, armed with the vacuum cleaner or floor polisher. Polina Ivanovna showed a certain respect in her dealings with the carpets, tea services, tape players and statuettes. But books, God forgive her, were another matter. She just didn't like them at all. You couldn't just have at them with the vacuum cleaner—no, you had to dust each of them separately, by hand. She wasn't one to read books, either; no time for that. There was the job, and then all things at home: shopping, cooking, laundry. And the family! Her husband, Nikolai Ivanovich, an injured war veteran; a son, Igor, in the army; and a daughter, Luda, in an unhappy marriage. Igor was serving out his time well and had gotten a promotion. With Luda it was a different story. Her husband turned out to be a drunk and a ne'er-do-well and after putting up with him for so long, Luda divorced him and came with her little Sadik (his full name was Sadat) to live off Polina Ivanovna.

Rita was a woman quite alone. At one time she had had a husband, one of those highly paid ones, but he left her for another woman. He was nice enough to leave Rita the apartment and the books, but he took the car and the dacha for himself. There were rumors to the effect that he couldn't make a go of it with this second wife either; Rita didn't know the details, though. All of that was a long time ago, and she wasn't even sad about it anymore. She didn't have any children, but that was no cause for suffering; her students were her children, and in spades.

Polina Ivanovna would come to Rita's house not to clean, but just as a friend. Rita never had any extra money, and what she did have was barely enough to get her through to the next payday. Rita cleaned house herself, doing rather clumsy battle with the vacuum cleaner and floor polisher, which had been purchased during her married days. As a confirmed student of the liberal arts, Rita had not the slightest idea as to how these things worked (even something as simple as to how to plug them in). In general, electricity was a hostile riddle to her and the appliances, as if they could sense this, would often break down. The vacuum cleaner still worked in fits and starts, but the floor polisher stood in the hall corner, completely useless.

The friendship between the two ladies had begun when Rita once had gotten stuck between floors in the elevator. The repairman was nowhere to be found and Polina Ivanovna had run off somewhere and brought back a friend who agreed to perform the rescue operation for the price of a bottle. Rita was so happy that she gave the friend six rubles (that was money in those days!) and invited Polina Ivanovna in for coffee. That's the way it all started: a friendship on coffee grounds. They both loved coffee, but only Rita would buy it; it was too expensive for Polina Ivanovna.

Polina Ivanovna would drop in on Rita between jobs; not too often, and not too infrequently, once every couple of days. Rita would immediately grab the coffee grinder. It was an old one, all cracked and held together with duct tape. While it ran it would groan and screech, always on the verge of breaking down, but grinding away all the same.

Rita and Polina Ivanovna would sit and talk, have a real "heart to heart" as they say, over their coffee. Polina Ivanovna, the older of the two, would give her friend lessons in life:

"I look at you, Rita Petrovna, and don't take offense now, but I see that you just don't know how to live. You drink coffee; you smoke, and not just any old brand, but Stolichnye. You're always buying books. Not a day goes by when another one doesn't appear. How much do you spend on all that? At least you could take a look at your neighbors. They've got their tea services and their sideboards, and their closets are bursting with dresses. What have you got but that one sweater, and the elbows have already gone shiny. What if you were to give up smoking, and drinking coffee, and books into the bargain? Then you could have a mohair sweater, and a rug and a fur coat . . . and even better, you could put a little something away in the bank. The money would just be there, not asking for anything. You could just save it for yourself."

"What for?"

"What do you mean, 'what for'? For a rainy day, that's what for."

"And will that rainy day ever come? Nobody knows. And what if I die before it comes? I'm better off living now just as I like."

"That's up to you. But I think you're wrong. You've got to live with your eyes open. My Nikolai Ivanovich, for example, even though he's got a war injury, used to smoke like a chimney. I cured him of that. I'd hide the money and he'd go looking for it. Couldn't find it; nothing to buy cigarettes with. 'Pasha,' he'd say (he calls me Pasha; according to my passport I'm Paraskov'ia), 'I can't take it any more. I've got to have a smoke. They used to give us tobacco at the front, never mind the poverty across the land.' I'd say to him: 'Grit your teeth; this isn't the front. Back then you were spilling your blood, but there's no need for that now.' And what do you think? He got over it. Turned over a new leaf. I've got him disciplined. And where's your husband these days, Rita Petrovna?"

"I don't know. Somewhere or other."

"That means he's roaming about, on the prowl."

"What do you mean by that? He's living his own life."

"Well, if you don't mind my saying so, Rita Petrovna, you really messed up that one. Gave him too much freedom. You need two pairs of eyes to keep track of men: one set for yourself and the other to keep on him. But the most important thing of all: don't give him any money. As soon as he brings home his pay, you take it and hide it somewhere. Give him just fifty kopecks a day; and if he doesn't need busfare, then even less. Did you used to take charge of your husband's pay?"

"No."

"Well, there you go. Intelligentsia! Look what it's gotten you."

"That's not it at all. Maybe I am to blame for his leaving. I just couldn't keep a cozy house. That takes talent, too."

"Cozy or not, you should have kept a better eye on him. None of this fluttering about."

Rita's salary was also a cause of concern for Polina Ivanovna.

"Is that all? And what about a bonus at the end of the year?"

"We don't have bonuses in school."

"And you haven't got anything else coming in, something on the side?"

"Well, there's the notebooks. I get five rubles a month for correcting them."

"Five rubles!" Polina Ivanovna was astounded. "That's like washing two windows. But if it's a big one, with a door, then just one. It takes me about an hour, hour and a half, maximum, to wash them. And how much time do you spend on those notebooks?"

"Oh, I don't know . . . a lot, I guess. I never kept track."

"But you should. Here I am, no education, and I'm making more than you. If I didn't have to worry about the family, my bank book would look like this!"

And she held her fingers apart to the width of a sizable volume, something on the order of Turgenev's "A Nest of Gentlefolk."

Once Polina Ivanovna came over, visibly agitated: "Imagine this, my old man has gone off on a vacation!"

"Are you serious? Where did he go? South?"

"No, someplace in the midlands. He got a free trip because of his war injury."

"How very wonderful!" exclaimed Rita.

"Wonderful, maybe, but not very. On the one hand, it's good. That means for nearly a month—twenty-four days to be exact—I won't have to worry about keeping him fed. I'll save on that. And we'll be using less electricity. He likes to read at night; I'm trying to break him of that habit. He waits until I'm asleep, then he goes back to his book. Luda and her Sadik go to bed early. . . . "

"What are you worried about, then?"

"I'm afraid he'll go running around with his buddies there, those other vets. I gave him just enough money to get him there and back. I know he won't be running too far on that. But I'm still worried. I'm afraid there'll be all kinds of bad influences on him there. You know, as they come, he's pretty spineless."

About two weeks later, Polina Ivanovna showed up, her brows drawn together in a scowl, her lips tightly pursed. "Well, my Nikolai Ivanovich sent me a telegram. I knew it, I just knew it. Here, take a look. . . ."

Rita took the telegram and read: "PASHA. SEND FIVE RUBLES. CAN'T LEAVE FOR HOME. KOLIA."

"Have you ever seen such a bourgeois capitalist?" Polina Ivanovna asked. "I could see it coming, plain as the nose on my face. He and his buddies have already spent everything I gave him. That's what you get for sending somebody like him off on a vacation."

"Have you sent him the money yet?"

"Yet? Don't hold your breath! I sweated blood to earn that money, and he should get it for his fun and games? Oh no; he got himself into this mess, let him get himself out of it. I don't care how he does it, but he's not going to get any help from me."

Rita's heart ached. She could picture to herself the self-effacing and balding Nikolai Ivanovich leaning on his cane, his right arm twisted out of shape and his left one almost as useless. He once came to her house to fix the vacuum cleaner; she recalled how, instead of saying, 'You know,' he'd say, 'Yanow.' She remembered that he didn't want to take anything for fixing the vacuum cleaner, how he tried to refuse, but then ended up taking the money anyway. She remembered the sad expression in his eyes . . . Rita screwed up her nose to keep from crying.

"Polina Ivanovna, here, take five rubles and send them to him!"

Polina Ivanovna was offended: "I'm not looking for handouts. I've got the money. I'm doing this to teach him a lesson. It's the principle."

And with that she left, without drinking her coffee. On her way out she didn't really slam the door, just sort of closed it loudly behind her. Rita was completely flustered, but as it turned out, she needn't have been. A few days later, when Polina Ivanovna came by again, it was obvious that she had already forgotten the insult. Rita happily set about grinding the coffee. At first the coffee grinder just coughed and sputtered, but then got a second wind and set to work. Each time Rita turned it on, she was sure it would be the last time. One more grinding and that would be it; the coffee grinder would be ready for the garbage.

"Well, has Nikolai Ivanovich come home?" she asked.

"Like a good little boy. Where else would he go?"

"So, then, you sent him the money after all?"

"You think I'm crazy? Not a kopeck! His buddies passed the hat and got enough to buy him a ticket home. Just like they should have. I'm no millionaire, you know, I can't be throwing money around. I still have to buy my first yacht. And get this: he even brought a pack of cigarettes back with him! He was sneaking out onto the stairs to smoke them. I took them and threw them out. What do I need with a husband who smokes? I've got enough on my hands as it is without that. I bought Sadik a pair of booties yesterday, imported ones. You can't imagine what we spend on tea alone! I tell him: 'Make it weaker,' but he just goes ahead and makes it as strong as he can. Do you know how much work I missed because of him? First I had to get his things ready to go, which means I couldn't go do Sof'ia Petrovna's house; you know, from the sixth entrance. Then I had to meet him at the station, and took a whole day off for that. I lost thirty rubles, just like that."

Rita frowned slightly. There was some vague, yet persistent thought, a memory, troubling her. What was it, and where was it from? Where had she read something just like this? That's it! It suddenly came to her.

"Such losses!" she said, half under her breath.

But Polina Ivanovna's hearing was very good.

"Losses? What losses?" she inquired. "Why did you bring that up all of a sudden, Rita Petrovna? Do you mean your coffee? I don't have to drink it, you know. You're the one who invited me. I don't have to come, you know."

Rita burst out laughing. "What are you talking about, Polina Ivanovna? God forbid! I wasn't talking about me. I was referring to Chekhov's 'Rothschild's Violin.' It's my favorite story. Have you ever read it?"

"Chekhov? I think we did Chekhov in school. 'Kashtanka.'"

"No, not 'Kashtanka.' 'Rothschild's Violin.' It's a wonderful story! You *must* read it."

"When do I have time to read?" Polina Ivanovna seemed offended at the suggestion. "What with all I have to do. I'm always running around, always on the go. Somedays I don't even have time to comb my hair, let alone read stories."

And then it suddenly came to Rita: "Let me read it to you. It's not very long; and I think you'll like it."

"No thanks, Rita Petrovna. Not even if you paid me. I don't even listen to them reading on the radio."

"But I won't read it like they do on the radio. I'll just read it to you, one friend to another. Please, Polina Ivanovna. As a personal favor to me."

Rita finally convinced Polina Ivanovna. She brought out a volume of Chekhov and started to read. The strange and pensive tone of the prose gave her goosebumps. . . .

Rita read about the old coffin maker Iakov, whose nickname was "Bronze." She read of his life, how he made coffins and how he played violin at weddings to earn a little extra. It was clear from Polina Ivanovna's apathetic pose that she was listening to all this just as a favor to her friend. Once or twice she even stifled a yawn.

"Iakov was never really in a good humor," Rita read, "as he was forever forced to endure all sorts of terrible losses. For instance, it was a sin to work and earn money on Sunday and holidays; and Mondays were difficult days. All in all, in a year there were about two hundred or so days where you would just sit at home and twiddle your thumbs. Now, that's a real loss!

"These constant thoughts of losses were especially hard for Iakov to bear at night. He'd put his violin next to the bed, and when these silly thoughts would come creeping into his head, he'd pluck the strings. The violin would sound in the darkness and Iakov would feel better."

At that, Polina Ivanovna livened up a bit. "So, he'd use his violin to comfort himself?" she said. "He's a crafty one. But they're experts at that."

"Interesting?" Rita asked, hopefully.

"Well, it's a little more interesting now. It was pretty boring at first."

"Just listen, then. It gets even more interesting. 'Suddenly Marfa, Iakov's wife, took ill. The old woman had trouble breathing, drank a lot of water and was unsteady on her feet. Toward evening she took to her bed. Iakov spent the whole day playing the violin and then, when it was already quite dark, took the notebook where he kept a daily record of his losses. Out of sheer boredom, he decided to draw up a total for the year and it turned out to be more than a thousand rubles. This figure so astounded him that he threw the abacus on the floor and stomped on it. . . .'"

"How do you like that?" Polina Ivanovna said disapprovingly. "Sure does let himself get away with a lot, doesn't he?"

"He was thinking," Rita continued, "that if he had put that lost thousand in the bank, the interest for the year would have been at least forty rubles. . . ."

"That's right," said Polina Ivanovna. "Last year I got my vacation pay and kept it in a box at home. If I had put it in the bank, the interest would have been, well, something."

Rita nearly lost her temper. "That's got nothing to do with this. Should I go on or not? If you don't like it, I can stop."

"Okay, okay. I'll keep quiet. Go ahead and read."

"'Iakov,' Marfa suddenly called out. 'I'm dying.'"

Polina Ivanovna gasped.

"Her face was rosy from the fever," Rita read, "and unexpectedly clear and happy."

"What was she happy about?" Polina Ivanovna asked incredulously. "That she was dying?"

"Precisely. It says so right here: 'She was glad that she was leaving the hut forever, leaving Iakov and his coffins. . . .'"

"That's hard to believe. After all, even animals love life."

"It all depends on what kind of life it is."

"That's right. Sometimes life is worse than death."

Was it true, or did it just seem to Rita that there was something in those words? No, it just seemed that way. Polina Ivanovna continued to listen just as calmly, only perhaps a little more attentively, as before.

"When he looked at the old woman," Rita continued, "Iakov suddenly realized that he had never once shown her tenderness, never taken pity on her, had never bought her a scarf or thought to bring some tasty leftover from the weddings. All he had done was yell at her, scold her for the extra expenses she incurred. He would even shake his fists at her; of course, he had never beaten her, but the very threat would cause her to freeze on the spot. He even forbade her to drink tea because it cost too much, and so she would drink just plain hot water."

"Plain hot water . . ." Rita repeated the phrase, looking straight into Polina Ivanovna's eyes. And there, in their coal-black depths, Rita saw something damp, something that looked suspiciously like a tear.

"There are animals like that," Polina Ivanovna said. "Real bloodsuckers."

"Shall I go on?"

"Go ahead."

Rita continued reading: about how Iakov took the old woman to a doctor's assistant, and how the assistant said: "The old woman's had a long enough life, time for her to bow out." Rita read about how Iakov pleaded with the assistant to cup the old woman, and how he answered that there was "no time for that now, friend. Take your old lady and God be with you."

As Polina Ivanovna listened, she grew more and more melancholy. She sat with her chin propped on her fist, like the women in the villages do.

"Medicine in those days!" she said. "That was still under the tsar, wasn't it?"

"Yes, but that's not the point. Just listen."

"Does she die?"

"Yes."

"Then why bother reading? All that will do is upset me."

"The power of literature," Rita began in her best teacher's voice, "is precisely in the fact that it can 'upset' you. So, shall I stop here, or do you want to hear more?"

"Oh, all right. Go ahead. I'm already upset as it is. Of course, I won't get to the laundry today either. Too bad; I've already got it soaking."

Rita read on about how they came home, how Marfa stood there, holding onto the stove, afraid to lie down because Iakov might say something about losses and scold her for lying around and not wanting to work. Iakov figured the old woman would certainly die in a few days; and tomorrow was the feast day of John the Theologian, and the next day that of Nikolai the Miracle Worker. Then there would be Sunday, followed by Monday, a difficult day. . . . That meant, then, that the coffin had to be made today. So he took the measurements and set to making the old lady's coffin. Having finished the job, he took his book of losses and noted: "Coffin for Marfa Ivanovna. Two rubles, forty kopecks."

Rita put a lot of hope into this specific detail: measurements are taken, and a coffin made, and the person is still alive. There's something that should move you. But Polina Ivanovna was interested in something else entirely: the two rubles and forty kopecks.

"That's all?"

"Money was different in those days," Rita answered dryly. "Well, are you going to listen, or figure out how much the coffin costs?"

"I'll listen, just don't get mad. Can't say anything, can I? Go on, read."

Rita was getting nearer to the part she absolutely cherished, and her voice resonated with her inner tears: "The old woman lay silently, her eyes closed. But in the evening, when darkness had already fallen, she suddenly summoned the old man.

"'Iakov, do you remember?' she asked, looking at him happily. 'Do you remember fifty years ago God gave us a fair-haired little child? We would all sit down by the river, under the willow tree, and sing songs.' And then, with a bitter smile, she added: 'The little girl died.'"

"Iakov strained his memory, but for the life of him could not remember either the little girl or the willow tree.

"'You're just imagining it,' he said."

Suddenly Polina Ivanovna burst into tears.

"What kind of people are those?" she muttered through her tears. "A child was born, and he can't even remember it. How can that be?"

"Should I go on?" Rita asked sternly, motionless from a sense of inner triumph.

"Go ahead. What else could there be except more of the same?"

Polina Ivanovna squeezed a damp handkerchief in her hand and sighed in a staccato rhythm while Rita read about how the old woman died. She read about how Iakov, himself half-dead, came home from the cemetery and how thoughts of his losses completely overwhelmed him. Why couldn't life be such that man could live without these losses and deprivations? And why were people always hindering each other, keeping each other from living? Rita read about how Iakov recalled his life with Marfa: "Year after year, for fifty-two years they had lived together in this hut, and somehow it had happened that not once had he given her a thought, not once had he paid any attention to her, almost as if she had been a cat or a dog. . . ."

It seemed as if that comparison finally pushed Polina Ivanovna over the edge.

"No, I can't take any more!" she said, sobbing. "You're killing me. Just tell me, in your own words, how it all ends."

"Okay, I will, but it'll be worse that way. Just keep that in mind. So, the Jew Rothschild, the one Iakov plays violin with at the weddings, comes to see him. He's a skinny, pitiful figure, his face covered with freckles and tiny bluish and reddish veins, just like netting. Rothschild wants Iakov to come play for a wedding. Iakov's getting sick, in fact he's already quite ill. And suddenly, he can't stand the sight of Rothschild. Iakov goes after him with his fists raised. Rothschild is frightened and runs away . . . some little boys take off chasing after him, and the dogs join in, too . . . they're barking and one even takes a nip at him. Rothschild squeals . . . I can even hear that squeal, it's described here as 'painful.'"

"I'm not interested in Rothschild," said Polina Ivanovna. "What about Iakov?"

"Well, he goes about town, wandering here and there, and finally finds himself at the river. Then there's all his thoughts about losses and such; I'll leave all that out. Here . . . wait, I'd better read this to you right out of the book. It's not the same if I do it in my own words. Every word here is a real pearl. . . ."

"No, I don't need any pearls," Polina Ivanovna pleaded. "I can still take your words, but not his. I'll start bawling like a baby."

"Don't worry. It's just a little bit: 'There's the big, broad willow tree with a huge hollow in its trunk and a crow's nest in its boughs . . . suddenly, in Iakov's memory, the figure of the fair-haired infant and the willow tree, about which Marfa spoke, take clear shape. This is that very willow tree: verdant, calm and melancholy . . . how it's aged, the poor thing!"

Polina Ivanovna suddenly broke down and sobbed, long and loud, hiccuping all the while. Rita was frightened: "Polina Ivanovna, calm down. Here, drink some water!"

Polina Ivanovna pushed the glass away and, shaking her head, kept repeating something through her hiccups. Rita caught the words: "The infant, the infant. . . ."

"Polina Ivanovna, dear, calm down, stop crying. There's no need for this."

"What did you expect? I warned you!"

She did finally calm down slightly, and then said irritatedly, "What a word to choose: 'infant.' He could have just as easily said 'baby,' but no; it had to be 'infant.' And I'm the one who has to hear it. No, Rita Petrovna, I don't care what you say. I won't listen to his words any longer. Just tell me, short and sweet, in your own words: how does it all end?"

"It ends with Iakov getting sick and dying. And he leaves his violin to Rothschild."

"Why's that?"

"Because he offended him for nothing. It's described right here: 'He was perplexed. . . .'"

"That's enough," Polina Ivanovna announced firmly. "I'm not going to stand for any more. You've got me upset enough as it is. I've cried my heart out over his words. Is that what they pay writers for anyway?" And she again burst into tears. Rita also let a tear or two fall.

Polina Ivanovna cried her fill, and the two then sat in silence.

"I'm sorry for upsetting you. I never expected such a reaction."

"Don't worry about it. Only next time, forget it. I'll cover my ears and just not listen."

"How about some more coffee?"

"Good idea. To calm the nerves."

Rita poured them each another cup.

"Do you know what I think, Rita Petrovna?" Polina suddenly said, rather softly. "I think I'm going to take my Nikolai Ivanovich to the movies! He's got a pretty rough life. I'm always scolding him, bossing him around. Not much fun for him. We'll go to the movies; a ticket costs just fifty kopecks. That's a ruble for two. I can spare a ruble, can't I?"

Rita was ecstatic. "What a wonderful idea! The movies! What could be better?"

"No fooling; I'll do it!"

Polina Ivanovna finished her coffee and went out into the hallway. She put her scarf on and, glancing at herself in the mirror, laughed slightly out of the corner of her mouth and said, "The infant . . . " before walking out.

Left alone, Rita thought long and hard about the educational significance of Russian literature. And there are those who downplay it, and every year want to cut back on the hours. She also came to realize that, when teaching, you need to use "your own words" less and "his words" more, so that they'd listen, and even cry. . . .

A week later, Polina Ivanovna stopped by again, as calm and resolute as always. The coffee grinder objected to working, but as soon as Rita pounded on the cover with her fist, it started up. "It doesn't hurt to shake a machine up now and then," Rita thought to herself. "It gets things back into place and going again. And the same thing is true for people."

But Polina Ivanovna said not a word about her recent "shaking up." She just sat there, calmly drinking her coffee.

"So, did you and Nikolai Ivanovich go to the movies?" Rita asked, unable to contain her curiosity.

"No," Polina Ivanovna answered, "we didn't. We started talking about you, and figuring up how much you make and how much you spend. On cigarettes, and on coffee; and then there's laundry and books . . . we got out the abacus and spent the whole evening working on it."

1980

Translated by Maureen Riley

Notes to the Essay

1. There is surely some self-mockery in Grekova's depiction of Shevchuk in *Thresholds* (*Porogi*). Shevchuk is a semi-serious but very "productive" researcher who writes on almost anything scientific, but who seems to attach at least as much importance to his verses—which he recites at the slightest provocation. "No, don't" (*ne nado*), groan his coworkers, for once in unison. *His* pseudonym is "Ia Mudryi" ("I'm smart"). His colleague Malykh asserts that "to say his verses are lousy is to praise them too highly." Malykh also maintains, however, that while the phenomenon of exact scientists working in other fields may not be successful immediately, the tendency is progressive because the times require the breaking down of barriers (*Thresholds*, 61, 66).

2. Grekova's first fictional work was published when she was more than fifty. She is also the author of university textbooks: *Probability Theory* (*Teoriia veroiatnostei*, 1986) and *Operations Research* (*Issledovanie operatsii*, 1980).

3. Both Grekova and her husband taught at the Zhukovskii Academy. The fact that she was also a writer became an open secret by the time that a stage version of her first story, "Beyond the Gates" ("Za prokhodnoi"), was presented in 1967. In the same year, the publication of her *On the Proving Grounds* (*Na ispytaniiakh*) in *Novyi mir* led to accusations that writing such a work was not compatible with holding a post at a military academy. Although Grekova received a vote of confidence from her colleagues, she resigned from the Zhukovskii Academy and moved to the Moscow Institute of Railway Engineers, where she taught for the next fourteen years.

4. "The Ladies' Hairdresser" was the second work that Grekova published in *Novyi mir* (11 [1963]), then still under Aleksandr Tvardovskii's editorship. Her controversial *On the Proving Grounds* (*Na ispytaniiakh*), also published in *Novyi mir* (4 [1967]: 14–109), was one of the last works that he championed as editor.

5. Grekova herself had three sons.

6. "The Ladies' Hairdresser" ("Damskii master") in *Russian Women: Two Stories*, trans. Michel Petrov, intro. Maurice Friedberg (New York: Harcourt Brace Jovanovich, 1983), 24–26.

7. Grekova quotes at length, and with great pleasure, Kornei Chukovskii's description of how he wrote "Bye Bye, Buzzy Fly" ("Mukhatsokotukha") while dancing around in a deserted apartment, in "The Story-teller's Joyous Gift" ("Schastlivyi dar skazochnika"), *Novyi mir* 3 (1982): 233–36.

8. As if their own were not enough, a number of Grekova's heroines also take charge of the children of friends or relatives.

9. Male "caregivers" include the widowed V.A. Fliagin in *The Faculty* (*Kafedra*, 1978) and B.M. Gan in *Thresholds.*

10. For example, the dying hero of "The Pheasant" ("Fazan") or the personal notes of N.N. Zavalishin in *The Faculty.*

11. Basing himself on Grekova's early prose, in particular on her highly controversial *On the Proving Grounds,* L.I. Skvortsov, himself a candidate in philological sciences, argues that it is precisely through their pretenses at culture that Grekova's characters most resemble those of Verbitskaia in "About 'Feminine Stories': Style and Language in I. Grekova's Novella *Na ispytaniiakh*" ["V zhanre damskoi povesti. O iazyke i stile povesti I. Grekovoi *Na ispytaniiakh*"], *Russkaia rech'* 1 (1968): 26–35). Skvortsov uses for his definition of the *zhenskaia povest'* characteristics proposed in a very interesting article by Natal'ia Il'ina that had appeared in *Novyi mir* somewhat earlier than Grekova's story (N. Il'ina, "K voprosy o traditsii i novatorstve v zhanre 'Damskoi povesti'," *Novyi mir* 3 [1963]: 224–230). One wonders if Skvortsov's strong distaste for *On the Proving Grounds* could have anything to do with the fact that the character most in the habit of using pretentious speech in Grekova's work is also named Skvortsov. Grekova herself highly values Il'ina. (See note 27.)

12. Ruf' Zernova, *Zhenskie rasskazy* (Ann Arbor, MI: Hermitage, 1981), 5.

13. There were often long delays between the writing of Grekova's works and their publication. *Ship of Widows* spent ten years "on her desk" and was rejected outright by all the magazines to which she submitted it. "No Smiles" ("Bez ulybok") was written in 1970 and published only in 1986. Grekova's *In Recent Memory* (*Svezho predanie*) has waited even longer. Written in 1962, no Soviet publisher was willing to touch it because of its theme of persistent anti-Semitism in the Soviet period. *In Recent Memory* was finally published in 1995.

14. Boris Èikhenbaum, quoted in Zernova, 5.

15. A.K. Diatlova, trying to understand her already twice-divorced young doctoral student, Gosha Fabritskii, wonders whether people of his generation mean the same thing that she does when they use the word "love." She suspects that the difference may be that she was brought up on great Russian literature, while Gosha and his coevals have simply been stuffed with a few "great books."

16. The failure of the informal women's collective in *Ship of Widows*; the separate efforts of Neshatov and of his estranged wife to get through to their son Pasha; the mother in "Summer in the City" ("Letom v gorode") who finds out by chance that her daughter has had an abortion, and so on. Most often we see mothers with rebellious or spoiled sons, but there are daughters too.

17. This goes for young protégés as well as for one's own children. For instance, when she hears the news that Vitalii the hairdresser has decided to go into a factory, Mar'ia Vasil'evna thinks, "What did I miss? What didn't I do right?" (*Ekh chego-to ia tut nedosmotrela?*).

18. According to Helena Goscilo, other hallmarks of Soviet women's prose in the last two decades are the subordination of plot to a preponderance of description and psychological exploration and a style that eschews modernist techniques ("Domostroika or Perestroika? The Construction of Womanhood in Soviet Culture under Glasnost," in *Late Soviet Culture*, ed. Thomas Lahusen [Durham, NC: Duke University Press, 1991], 243).

19. I. Grekova, "Something to Think About" ("Zastavit' zadumat'sia"), under the rubric "Diskussionnyi klub," *Literaturnoe obozrenie* 9 (1986): 37.

20. The chracter of Gan in *Thresholds* comments that the acronym for the institute, NIIKAT, is unfortunate, but that luckily very few people know anymore that "kat" means "executioner" (*palach*) (*Thresholds,* 7).

21. Bringing up her children during the war when books were few and children's books fewer still, she wrote, illustrated and bound books for them, and later, for her grandchildren. Grekova subsequently published two of these books: *Serezhka at the Window* (1976) and a story for children under seven, *An'ia and Man'ia* (1978). Grekova greatly admired Kornei Chukovskii both as a creator of children's literature and as a researcher. She praises his verses and his *From Two to Five* very highly ("Schastlivyi dar skazochnika," *Novyi mir* 3 (1982): 233–36).

22. Chukovskaia was born in the same year as Grekova, 1907. Tat'iana Tolstaia, who also repudiated the term "women's literature," was born in 1951. See also Adele Barker, "Are Women Writing 'Women's Writing' in the Soviet Union Today?: Tolstaya and Grekova," in *Studies in Comparative Communism* 21, 3–4 (1988): 357–64. On the whole question of "women's literature" in the post-Stalin period, see Catriona Kelly, *A History of Russian Women's Writing, 1820–1992* (Oxford: Oxford University Press, 1994), especially 350–72. Kelly remarks that one might even say that the rejection of the notion of women's literature has itself become one tradition within the world of Russian women's writing.

23. I. Grekova, quoted in an interview with Nikolai Nazarov, *Soviet Literature* 5 (1986): 137–41. Her statement is on 140.

24. Lidiia Chukovskaia, quoted in Zernova, 5.

25. At the beginning of *On the Proving Grounds*, the military pilot who is to fly the technical team to the testing grounds refuses to take off with a woman on board, despite the fact that the woman in question is a military ballistics engineer. General Sivers intervenes to break the deadlock. He begins by asking the pilot to identify the large object on the field. To the lieutenant's reply that it is a plane, Sivers retorts that he thought it must be a flying men's room,

and that they really should paint *M* (men) and *Zh* (women) on the fuselage so that people would know. He then tells the still bemused pilot an anecdote about the great mathematician David Hilbert who said, when the candidacy of Emmy Noether to a professorship at Göttingen University was blocked because, as she was a woman, it was impossible for her to be in the university senate: "Is the senate some kind of a bathroom that women can't enter?" Sivers quotes Hilbert in German. The pilot thinks it's English. Sivers translates. The pilot agrees to take off with the whole team on board, including the woman.

26. I. Grekova, "Zastavit' zadumat'sia," *Literaturnoe obozrenie* 9 (1986): 37. In her interview with Nazarov, Grekova also says that the features of "new prose" are particularly evident in the recent works of Trifonov. These characteristics are "a complete and unceremonious melange of all genres—reality and fantasy, humor and tragedy, the factual and the lyrical" (op cit., 140).

27. Grekova calls her review of Ginzburg's "Notes of a Person under Siege," a text published in *Neva* 1 (1984), "a scientist's prose" (*proza uchenogo*). (*Oktiabr'* 2 [1985]: 203–05; term is on 205). Grekova's article on Il'ina, "Razvetvleniia dorog" ("The Parting of Paths"), (*Oktiabr'* 10 [1983]: 192–197), pays much attention to the fact that Il'ina's work cannot be adequately described within the boundaries of traditional literary classifications and genres, for it includes such things as letters, notes and diaries. Among other things, Grekova says that Il'ina's prose is very tight and disciplined, "manly" or "virile" ("*muzhestvenaia*" [in quotation marks in the text]). Some of the things that Grekova says about nonstylistic aspects of Il'ina's works are characteristic of her own writings as well. For instance, Il'ina's works resonate with quotations, sometimes direct, but more frequently indirect or hidden.

28. Grekova also predicted that the boundaries between prose and poetry would tend to disappear because of the growth of a more highly organized, "structured" (*strukturovannaia*) prose that would demand a much more careful choice of words and attention to their rhythmic and musical organization ("Zastavit' zadumat'sia," 37).

29. Ibid.

30. Anton Chekhov, letter to A.S. Suvorin, 27 October 1888: "You confuse two things: solving a problem and stating a problem correctly. It is only the second that is obligatory for the artist. . . . It is the business of the judge to put the right questions, but the answers must be given by the jury according to their own lights" (*Letters on the Short Story, the Drama and Other Literary Topics*, selected and ed. by Louis S. Friedland [New York: Dover, 1966]). M.M., a woman scientist undergoing a *prorabotka* (chastisement or reeducation) in Grekova's "No Smiles" ("Bez ulybok") (a work finally published after more than fifteen years "in the drawer" in *Oktiabr'* 11 [1986]: 162–79), quotes Spinoza in the same sense: "One should neither laugh nor cry, just understand." True as the dictum is, she finds herself unable to abide by it. "No Smiles" is reprinted in I. Grekova, *Na ispytaniiakh. Povesti i rasskazy* (Moscow: Sovetskii pisatel', 1990), 434–67. Many other works of Grekova also had to wait a long time before they were published. For example, *Ship of Widows* had to wait ten years and *Thresholds* four years.

31. To be fair, it should be mentioned that Danaia, in *Thresholds*, also quotes part of Tatiana's line: "Onegin, I was younger then" ("Onegin, ia togda molozhe . . .") (Book 8, stanza 43, 1.1). The obsession with Tatiana is odd, as Nabokov notes in his commentary to *Eugene Onegin*, since "in Soviet literature, the image of Tatiana has been superseded by that of her sister Ol'ga, now grown buxom, ruddy-cheeked, noisily cheerful. Ol'ga is the good girl of Soviet fiction; she is the one who straightens things out at the factory, discovers sabotage, makes speeches,

and radiates perfect health" (quoted in Michael Wood, *The Magician's Doubts* [London: Chatto and Windus, 1994], 154).

32. Nikolai Gogol, "The Inspector General" ("Revizor"), 1.1.

33. L.I. Skvortsov, in "About 'Feminine' Stories" ("V zhanre damskoi povesti"), attempts to place Grekova in the tradition of the *damskaia povest'* precisely because some of her characters "show off" a minimal acquaintance with books.

34. Sometimes characters, even nonbelievers like Malykh in *Thresholds*, go back to the Bible for principles of behavior, especially to the Decalogue, and especially to the commandment that instructs one not to bear false witness against one's neighbor. There is, however, at least one important exception to the rule that great Russian literature is a moral guide. In Grekova's *In Recent Memory*, a novel that she wrote in 1962, and which even Tvardovskii considered unpublishable at that time because of its central theme of Soviet anti-Semitism, the boy hero, trying to find out the meaning of the word *zhid* that another boy has thrown at him, remembers having seen the word in Gogol's *Taras Bulba*. A lengthy anti-Semitic (and also anti-Catholic) passage from Gogol's novel is quoted in Grekova's.

35. For example, there are over fifty such references in *The Faculty* (trans. Melinda Maclean in *Soviet Literature* 9 [1979]: 3–107 and 10 [1979]: 16–128). These references cover a variety of levels of sensitivity. They range from folklore through the Bible through belles lettres through opera. Some references require the reader to have considerable culture and to be paying close attention. An interesting example is the story "In the Railway Carriage" ("V vagone"), where the intertext is Arthur Conan Doyle's "The Valley of Fear." It is useful to know that in Conan Doyle's tale of an undercover agent who is finally tracked down and destroyed, a train ride plays an important role. Other references are explicit and sometimes ironical: for example, the young Jewish protagonist of *Svezho predanie* is named Konstantin Levin. Some of these intertexts provoke discussion and commentary among the characters themselves.

36. What is depraved at one moment may become fashionable the next. Witness Gan's story in *Thresholds* about the fate of his thesis on cybernetics.

37. *On the Proving Grounds* (*Na ispytaniiakh*) was first published, in censored form, in *Novyi mir* 4 (1967): 14–109. For a detailed discussion of the travails of this text, see A. Barker, "Irina Grekova's *Na Ispytaniiakh:* The History of One Story," *Slavic Review* 3 (1989): 399–412. It should be noted that the passages that Grekova wished to have restored (including one which indicated that one of the main characters was of Jewish origin) were put back when it was republished in 1990 as the title story of the collection *Na ispytaniiakh* (Moscow: Sovetskii pisatel', 1990).

38. N. Grekova, "No Smiles" ("Bez ulybok," 1970), reprinted in *Na ispytaniiakh.*

39. W. Kiukhel'beker was condemned as a member of the 1825 Decembrist Conspiracy against the accession of Nicholas I. See Iurii Tynianov's *Kiukhlia* (Leningrad, 1925) for an interesting fictional treatment. A librarian has allowed M.M. to read Kiukhel'beker's diaries in an 1875 volume of *Russkaia starina.* M.M. notes that until they gave him pen and ink, Kiukhel'beker occupied his mind by composing verses in his head and reciting them by heart as he walked from corner to corner of his cell. A number of women writers have recorded the life- and morale-saving function of poetry for themselves and others during imprisonment. Note, for example, Evgeniia Ginzburg's *Journey into the Whirlwind* or the testimony of Nina Hagen-Thorn excerpted in Vitalii Chentalinskii, *La Parole ressuscitée* (Paris: Robert Laffont, 1993), 197–204.

40. Toward the end of "No Smiles," M.M. analyzes the birth, growth and cyclical reoccurrence of the process of a typical *prorabotka.* The life span varies from several months to two or

three years, rarely more. A good guide to the severity of a *prorabotka* is the number of heart attacks it provokes. The heart attack as symbol also appears in the death of Gan in *Thresholds*. Iurii Zhivago tells Douderov in *Dr. Zhivago* that the causes of the epidemic of heart attacks are frequently moral: "Microscopic forms of cardiac hemorrhages have become very frequent in recent years. They are not always fatal. Some people get over them. It's a typical modern disease. I think its causes are of a moral order. The great majority of us are required to live a life of constant, systematic duplicity. Your health is bound to be affected if day after day, you say the opposite of what you feel, if you grovel before what you dislike and rejoice at what brings you only misfortune. Our nervous system isn't just a fiction, it's a part of our physical body, and our soul exists in space and is inside us, like the teeth in our mouth. It can't be forever violated with impunity" (B. Pasternak. *Dr. Zhivago*, trans. Max Hayward and Manya Harari [New York: Pantheon Books, 1958], 483).

41. Isaac Babel, "DiGrasso," in *The Collected Stories of Isaac Babel* (New York: Meridian/ New American Library, 1974), 381.

42. N. Grekova, "Rothschild's Fiddle" ("Skripka Rotshil'da") (1980), reprinted in *Na ispytaniiakh,* 387–99.

43. Not all uneducated middle-aged women in Grekova's stories are the same. There are many such characters, and Grekova has a wonderful ear for the varieties of their speech. See, for example, Ol'ga Filipovna in *Thresholds*, Dar'ia Stepanova and Klavda Petrovna in *The Faculty* and Kapa Flerova in *Ship of Widows*.

44. Fedor Dostoevsky, *Poor Folk* (*Bednye liudi*), Dostoevsky's first published work of fiction. Grekova has said that she has been influenced by all of Russian literature, but most particularly by Dostoevsky. Tolstoy's "The Death of Ivan Il'ich" appears unmistakably as a subtext to "The Pheasant." Iurii Olesha's "Liompa" is probably lurking there too. Chekhov crops up all over Grekova's works. To the intertexts already mentioned, one must add the sections "From the Private Papers of N.N. Zavalishin" in *The Faculty*, where N.N.'s notes echo the diary of the aging professor/scientist protagonist of Chekhov's "A Boring Story" ("Skuchnaia istoriia"). The professor's lectures are still good, but his only emotional attachment to life is his love for a daughter/niece figure, whom he loses.

45. Dostoevsky, preface to the Russian translation of Victor Hugo's *Notre Dame de Paris*, published in *Time* (*Vremia*), reprinted in Dostoevsky, *Polnoe sobranie sochinenii,* Vol. 20 (Leningrad, 1972), 28.

46. Gan's heart attacks are at least in part provoked by the activity of an anonymous letter writer whose missives require answers, proofs that the assertions are wrong. Responding to this assault infuriates and wastes the time of the director, Fabritskii, but he is younger and stronger, in all senses more athletic than Gan.

47. This is well described in E. Iukina's reviews of Grekova's *Thresholds* (originally published in *Oktiabr'* 10–11 [1984]) and "The Pheasant" (originally published in *Oktiabr'* 9 [1985]). Iukina's article, "Ispytaniia," appeared in *Literaturnoe obozrenie* 4 (1986): 48–50.

48. Fedor Dostoevsky, *Winter Notes on Summer Impressions* (New York: McGraw-Hill, 1955), 111.

49. The reference is to Chekhov's popular story "Dushechka." Vera Pavlovna, however, manages quite well to stand on her own two feet when there is not a man around for her to attach herself to.

50. In particular, Grekova says that she has no fantasy, and so does not herself employ the alternation of fantasy and reality that she sees as one characteristic of the "new prose."

51. Vladimir Nabokov, *Strong Opinions* (New York: McGraw-Hill, 1973), 63.

Bibliography

Primary Works

"Malen'kii Garusov." *Zvezda* 9 (1970): 119–56.

Serezhka u okna. Moscow, 1976.

An'ia i Man'ia. Moscow, 1978.

"Schastlivyi dar skazochnika" [review of Kornei Chukovskii, *Stikhi i skazki* and *Ot dvukh do piati*]. *Novyi mir* 3 (1982): 233–36.

Kafedra. Povesti. Moscow, 1983. [Includes *Khoziaika gostinitsy*.]

"Nota chelovechnosti." *Literaturnaia gazeta* 44, 2 November 1983, 5.

"Razvetvleniia dorog." *Oktiabr'* 10 (1983): 192–97.

Vdovii parokhod. Paris, 1983.

"Proza uchenogo" [review of Lidiia Ginzburg, "Zapiski blokadnogo cheloveka"]. *Oktiabr'* 2 (1985): 203–05.

"Zastavit' zadumat'sia." *Literaturnoe obozrenie* 9 (1986): 36–39.

Porogi. Roman, povesti. Moscow, 1986. [Includes *Porogi*, "Vdovii parokhod," "Na ispytaniiakh."]

"Zhalost' i sovest'" [review of Ruslan Kireev, *Rovno v sem' u metro* and *Strekoz'ia bukhta*]. *Oktiabr'* 2 (1986): 197–99.

"Mezhdu dvumia tolkovaniiami" [review of Daniil Granin, *Zapretnaia glava*]. *Oktiabr'* (December 1988): 203–05.

"Ob Aleksandre Galiche." *Znamia* 6 (1988): 61–62.

"Rastochitel'nost' talanta" [review of Tat'iana Tolstaia, *Na zolotom kryltse sideli . . .* "]. *Novyi mir* 1 (1988): 252–56.

"Samoosuzhdenie i samoopravdanie" [review of Lidiia Ginzburg, *Zabluzhdenie voli* and *Nravstvennost' svobodnogo cheloveka*]. *Oktiabr'* 4 (1989): 200–02.

Na ispytaniiakh. Povesti, rasskazy. Moscow, 1990. [Includes "Fazan," "Perelom," "Na ispytaniiakh" (restored text), "'Skripka Rotshil'da'," "Za prokhodnoi," "Bez ulybok," "Letom v gorode," " Pervyi nalet," "V vagone," "Znakomye liudi," "Pod fonarem," "Damskii master," "Khoziaeva zhizni."]

Svezho predanie. Tenafly, NJ: Hermitage, 1995.

In Translation

"The Ladies' Hairdresser." Trans. L. Gregg. *Russian Literature Triquarterly* 5 (1973): 223–65. Rpt. *Ardis Anthology of Recent Russian Literature*. Ann Arbor, MI: Ardis, 1975. 223–64.

"One Summer in the City." Trans. Lauren Leighton. *Russian Literature Triquarterly* 11 (1975): 146–67.

"The Faculty." Trans. Melinda Maclean. *Soviet Literature* 9 (1979): 3–107; 10 (1979): 16–128.

"The Hotel Manager." Trans. Michel Petrov. *Russian Women: Two Stories*. By I. Grekov. Intro. Maurice Friedberg. San Diego: Harcourt Brace Jovanovich, 1983. 65–304.

"The Ladies' Hairdresser." Trans. Michel Petrov. *Russian Women: Two Stories*. By I. Grekova. Intro. Maurice Friedberg. San Diego: Harcourt Brace Jovanovich, 1983. 3–61.

The Ship of Widows. Trans. and intro. Cathy Porter. London, 1985.

"Real Life in Real Terms." *Moscow News* 24 (1987): 11.

"A Summer in the City." Trans. S. McLaughlin. *The Image of Women in Contemporary Soviet Fiction.* New York: Macmillan, 1989. 18–48.

"Masters of Their Own Lives." Trans. Dobrochna Dyrcz-Freeman. *Soviet Women Writing.* Ed. Jacqueline Decter. New York: Abbeville, 1990. 85–105.

"Under the Street Lamp." Trans. Dobrochna Dyrcz-Freeman. *Russia According to Women.* Ed. Marina Ledkovsky. Tenafly, NJ: Hermitage, 1991. 45–66.

Secondary Works

Barker, Adele. "Are Women Writing 'Women's Writing' in the Soviet Union Today? Tolstaya and Grekova." *Studies in Comparative Communism* 21, 3–4 (1988): 357–64.

———. "I. Grekova." *Dictionary of Russian Women Writers.* Ed. Marina Ledkovsky, Charlotte Rosenthal and Mary Zirin. Westport, CT: Greenwood Press, 1994. 228–31.

———. "Irina Grekova's *Na Ispytaniiakh:* The History of One Story." *Slavic Review* 3 (1989): 399–412.

———. "Women without Men in the Writing of Contemporary Soviet Women Writers." *Russian Literature and Psychoanalysis.* Linguistic and Literary Studies in Eastern Europe 31. Ed. Daniel Rancour-Laferrière. Amsterdam, 1989. 431–49.

Decter, Jacqueline, ed. Introduction. *Soviet Women Writing.* New York: Abbeville, 1990.

Dobin, E. "Khoziaka gostinitsy." *Literaturnoe obozrenie* 10 (1977).

Goscilo, Helena. *Balancing Acts: Recent Writing by Soviet Women.* Bloomington: Indiana University Press, 1989.

———. "Domostroika or Perestroika? The Construction of Womanhood in Soviet Culture under Glasnost." *Late Soviet Culture.* Durham, NC: Duke University Press, 1991.

Heldt, Barbara. *Terrible Perfection: Women and Russian Literature.* Bloomington: Indiana University Press, 1987.

Il'ina, Nataliia. "K voprosu o traditsii i novatorstve v zhanre 'damskoi povesti'." *Novyi mir* 3 (1963): 224–30.

Iukina, E. "Ispytaniia" [review of Grekova, *Porogi* and "Fazan"]. *Literaturnoe obozrenie* 4 (1986): 48–50.

Kamianov, B. "Sluzhba pamiati" [review of Grekova, "Malen'kii Garusov"]. *Novyi mir* 5 (1971): 270–75.

Kelly, Catriona. *A History of Russian Women's Writing 1820–1992.* Oxford: Clarendon Press, 1994.

———. "Soviet Women's Writing and De-Stalinisation: I. Grekova and N. Baranskaya." *Russistika* 5 (1992): 39–43; 6 (1992): 14–18.

Kireev, Ruslan. "Bez imen" [review of Grekova, "Bez ulybok"]. *Znamia* 4 (1987): 227–29.

Lakshin, B. "Pisatel', chitatel', kritik." *Novyi mir* 4 (1965): 222–40.

Latynina, A. "Liubov', sem'ia i kar'era. O 'damskoi povesti,' zhenskoi proze i naivnom sufrazhizme." *Literaturnaia gazeta* 27, 6 (1984): 5. [Rpt. in *Znaki vremeni. Zametki o literaturnom protsesse.* Moscow, 1987. 287–95.]

McLaughlin, Sigrid, ed. and intro. *Images of Women in Soviet Fiction.* London, 1989.

Nazarov, Nikolai. "About I. Grekova's Work." *Soviet Literature* 5 (1986): 137–41.

Segall, H. "Grekova." *A Handbook of Russian Literature.* Ed. Victor Terras. New Haven, CT: Yale University Press, 1985. 184.

Skvortsov, L.I. "V zhanre damskoi povesti. O iazyke i stile povesti I. Grekovoi *Na ispytaniiakh.*" *Russkaia rech'* 1 (1968): 26–35.

Usmani, Tina Yvonne. "The 'Controversial Writer' in Contemporary Soviet Literature: Selected Aspects of I. Grekova's Major Prose Works." Unpublished doctoral dissertation.

Inna Lisnianskaia

The *succès de scandale* of the literary almanac *Metropol'* (1979) literally decided the course not only of the writing career of Inna L'vovna Lisnianskaia (b. 1928) for the next decade but also of the nature of the writing itself. It is worth recalling in these post-*glasnost* days the sensational furor created by a group of twenty-three who dared to request permission from the literary bureaucracy to publish a collection of their works without submitting it first to state censorship. When the request was denied and *Metropol'* was published in the West, two young Metropolians—Viktor Erofeev and Evgenii Popov—were expelled from the Writers' Union. Vasilii Aksenov, Semen Lipkin and Inna Lisnianskaia resigned from the union in protest.[1] Aksenov soon left for the United States at the invitation of the University of Michigan and was stripped of his Soviet citizenship. Lisnianskaia and her common-law husband, Lipkin (b. 1913), the elder statesman of the group, remained in the Soviet Union but were effectively cut off from the bounties afforded by union membership, most importantly the right to publish and earn a livelihood.

When asked whether they regretted their participation in *Metropol'*, Lipkin and Lisnianskaia invariably would answer that they only wished they had offered the editors more poems.[2] While Lisnianskaia contributed a mere seven poems to the almanac, *Metropol'* provided her an opportunity to show a side of her art that she had been forced to conceal in Soviet publications, namely the religious meditation (e.g., "I beg alms from the poor," "In Regard"). Unfortunately, a decade would pass before the Russian public would be able to assess the whole range of Lisnianskaia's verse.

Paradoxically, the *Metropol'* affair both silenced Lisnianskaia as a published poet and exempted her from the responsibilities imposed by publishing, ultimately affording an inner freedom that shaped her poetry and biography. As Lisnianskaia stated in a 1990 interview:

> The period connected with the *Metropol'* scandal and my leaving the Writers' Union with Aksenov and Lipkin, of course, was difficult and replete with various forms of persecution—ranging from a ban on my profession to being attacked by thugs on the street, threats over the telephone, having my apartment robbed while I was away, summons to "you know where," etc. . . . In spite of all the difficulties, I personally consider this period in my life to be a blessing. I had never experienced such inner freedom. And the breach of contact with publishing houses added to this freedom by freeing me from translation work. I wrote a great deal—and that for me is the greatest source of pleasure.[3]

At the time of the *Metropol'* affair Lisnianskaia, an author of five books of poetry, had been publishing for more than thirty years. Yet, like Lipkin, outside of a small circle of friends and colleagues she was known primarily as a translator of verse, principally of Azerbaijani works. In her own words, her most recent collection, *Grape Light* (*Vinogradnyi svet*, 1978), which followed her previous book after a hiatus of ten years, "had been stripped and plucked bare by several stages of editing."[4] Lisnianskaia ironically comments on the plight of the publishing Soviet poet and her personal experience with editorial functionaries in her interview with S. Taroshchina:

> My third book *At First Hand* [*Iz pervykh ust*, 1966] could have been a little better than the first two. But I made what was perhaps the largest compromise in my life. There was a senior editor by the name of Boris Solov'ev, a cynic and, by the way, an expert on poetry of the Silver Age. (I should mention parenthetically that he is not the same naively ignorant editor who when he saw the poem "Ruth" in a later manuscript asked, "Who is she?" "A person in the Bible," I say. "Well," he answered, "nobody knows about her besides you." And he threw the poem out.) Solov'ev made the following proposal to me: You write a lot, and you have a lot of poems that aren't very good. So bring me those, and take away these good ones, the ones with religion, which, in general, are alien to the Soviet reader. Our conversation ended on a note not without interest. Solov'ev: "We don't need more Akhmatovas and Tsvetaevas." I: "You don't need the originals."[5]

The original 1979 preface to *Metropol'* states that "our almanac, by and large, consists of manuscripts well known to the publishing houses."[6] In fact, more than half of Lisnianskaia's contributions are dated 1970–1973 and almost certainly had little chance of appearing in the Soviet Union. Take, for example, the opening stanza of the poem "Time and I, we're so alike!" ("Ia i vremia—my tak pokhozhi," 1971):

Time and I, we're so alike!
We look like twins.
How can you tell us apart, God?
So, tell me, aren't the escort
And the fugitive
One and the same?[7]

Apart from the fact that the lyric persona addresses God, which almost certainly would have been thrown out by a "responsible" Soviet editor, what would that same editor make of references to escorts and fugitives, not to mention the equation of time and this very individual, not to say idiosyncratic, voice? Lisnianskaia had half-heartedly played the role of dutiful poet with mixed results, that is, maimed books. Clearly, she was ready to risk internal exile for poetic freedom.

Before examining Lisnianskaia's post-*Metropol'* career, let us consider briefly the life and works that preceded this period.

In the brief "Something in the Way of an Autobiography,"[8] Lisnianskaia, a native of Baku, records that her first and most vivid memory dates from when she was taken to church as a three-year-old by her aunt. Having been baptized in secret from her parents, Raisa Adamova and Lev Lisnianskii, the headstrong and left-handed child was taught to cross herself with her right hand. Lisnianskaia's account underscores both her contrary stubbornness, which she acknowledges with disarming candor, and the religious feeling that informs her mature work. As Carol Ueland has noted, Lisnianskaia, like many women writers of her generation, is "absorbed with the question of identity, but in Lisnianskaia's case, it centers on her dual Russian-Jewish identity."[9] Ueland cites a number of telling lines to support her finding, including the lines "Don't sign yourself as a Jew, daughter— / he ordered me" from the poem "My father—a military doctor" ("Moi otets—voennyi vrach," 1975). As Lisnianskaia recounts the incident in her interview with Taroshchina, she did not heed her father's advice, but instead designated her nationality as Jewish on her passport.

Although she does not come from a literary family—her father was a doctor, her mother an engineer—Lisnianskaia began to write poetry at the early age of ten. Her mother, however, had studied voice at conservatory, and Lisnianskaia credits this musical influence on her verse. For a poet who embarked upon her career at such an early age, Lisnianskaia considers that she developed late as a poet, in large part because of the "provincial ignorance" of the 1930s and 1940s. Although she had been invited to apply for admission to the Gorky Literature Institute (Moscow), Lisnianskaia did not attend the university. Her only child, the prose writer Elena Makarova, was born in 1951.[10] In her autobiography, Lisnianskaia records enormous pride in her daughter but nevertheless admits: "I didn't devote myself to motherhood very long, five years in all, since I was allotting most of my time and heart to my other newborns—my poems."

A published poet in Baku since 1948, Lisnianskaia came to the notice of Aleksandr Tvardovskii, the influential editor of the major Moscow literary journal *New World* (*Novyi mir*). In 1957 her poetry began to appear in Tvardovskii's journal and was soon followed by publications in *Youth* (*Iunost'*) and other major venues. Lisnianskaia became a member of the Writers' Union in 1957 and moved to Moscow in 1961, where she resides to this day.

In her autobiographical statement Lisnianskaia dismisses her early books as immature, regarding the 1960s as a transitional stage in her work. Poetic growth, however, yielded nonpublication. But even in the early collections, Lisnianskaia's verse displays a distinctly un-Soviet character, since private, individual concerns generally take precedence over social issues. In sharp contrast to the "stadium poets" of the late 1960s and 1970s (e.g., Evgenii Evtushenko and Andrei Voznesenskii), who recited their verse to large audiences in huge sports halls and whom detractors criticized for pandering with their political pamphlets in verse, Lisnianskaia has consistently eschewed rhetoric for lyricism.

Two meetings that took place in 1967 proved to be enormously important for Lisnianskaia's life and work. First, she was introduced to the poet and translator Semen Lipkin, with whom Lisnianskaia has lived for many years and whom she acknowledges as a major influence on her poetry. A number of Lisnianskaia's works explicitly or implicitly are addressed to Lipkin, for example, the fifteen-poem cycle *The Circle* (*Krug*, 1974) and "Take me, o Lord, instead of him" ("Voz'mi menia, Gospodi, vmesto nego," 1978).

The second meeting brought her together with Mariia Petrovykh (1908–1979), like Lipkin a friend of Anna Akhmatova and Osip Mandel'shtam.[11] Petrovykh offered her younger colleague friendship, shelter and encouragement during the years when Lisnianskaia experienced difficulty publishing.[12] Significantly, Lisnianskaia did not make the pilgrimage to Akhmatova to receive the elder poet's imprimatur as did so many of her generation. Instead she was befriended by Petrovykh, a poet who published only one book during her lifetime and who earned her living as a translator and editor. In the words of Stephanie Sandler, Petrovykh was a writer who "always took a secondary position to other, more important writers and poets," which may explain why "Lisnianskaia might find it troubling to consider Petrovykh's example too closely."[13] Lisnianskaia has addressed three poems to Petrovykh, the first of which was written while the addressee was still alive. All three poems voice concern over oblivion. For example, the final quatrain of the first poem in the series opens with the line "Will we be remembered . . . ," clearly linking the fates of the two poets, both author and addressee.[14]

Curiously, Lisnianskaia escaped oblivion through her participation in *Metropol'* and the ensuing decade of internal exile in the Soviet Union, when her official status as persona non grata yielded the most fertile period of her career. Her works banned in the Soviet Union—and this ban extended to translations as well—Lisnianskaia began to publish abroad: two volumes of verse (one in France, the other in the United States), as well as publications in the journal *Continent (Kontinent,* Paris), arguably the most influential journal of the emigration, and *Time and Us* (*Vremia i My*, Jerusalem).[15]

Rains and Mirrors (*Dozhdi i zerkala*, 1983), the first book by Lisnianskaia to appear abroad, collects works written over a span of more than fifteen years (1966–1982).[16] Clearly, the volume's organizing principle rests on the desire to publish a comprehensive volume that represents the full range of Lisnianskaia's work. For the first time the poet enjoyed the luxury of compiling a book as she wished, rescuing the scores of poems that had seemingly been "written for the drawer," rather than for immediate publication. The author, therefore, is thoroughly justified to open *Rains and Mirrors* with a poem that celebrates the poet's custodial function: "I have never committed to flames / The paper forever covered with my writing. / I guard my obscurity / With a miser's suspiciousness . . ." (1968).

The act of preservation, however, extends beyond the poet's own work. "A Solitary Gift" ("Odinokii dar," 1970) not only refers to the traditional image of the poet in isolation from society but also characterizes the poet as a vehicle to preserve memory. In the superb poem "Aquarius" ("Vodolei," 1978) we read that "Our memory of life is a dream, / Our memory of death is repentance." Consequently, the love poems, traditionally, if mistakenly, thought to be the special province of Russian "women's poetry," instead record memories of love or voice anxiety of the impending loss of that love (e.g., "Take me, o Lord, instead of him," 1978).

This sense of loss embraces the forced emigration of friends, as in the poems written to commemorate the friendship and departure of Vasilii Aksenov or Lev Kopelev and his wife, Raisa Orlova.[17] These occasional poems, firmly grounded in the realia of the events ("I mumble something, and Okudzhava sings, / And the nightingale Bella sings about the winter"),[18] reflect the widespread disruption of community, by no means limited to the community of writers. Memory and conscience, properties that have been repressed and falsified by the state, become the poet's primary responsibilities.

Lisnianskaia's next book, *Poems. On the Verge of Sleep* (*Stikhotvoreniia. Na opushke sna*, 1984),[19] likewise prints verse from as early as 1966, but the vast majority dates from the early 1980s, unmistakably heralding a new poetic voice. While *Rains and Mirrors* was an attempt to collect as large a body of work as possible, *Poems,* on the other hand, is tightly structured and achieves a unity in style and theme that makes it more successful precisely as a book. Lisnianskaia herself considered the book to be more of a "single entity" than was the case with *Rains and Mirrors*.[20]

The section titles in *Poems*, "Right Angle" and "On the Verge of Sleep," allude to the confirmation of reality and a visionary stance. The volume is a lyrical diary in which the persona records her hopes and disappointments as woman, mother, citizen and poet. As critics have noted, the line "Where are the poems about love?" ("Gde stikhi pro liubov'," 1983) underscores Lisnianskaia's concerns outside the sphere of "women's verse." There are poems about love, but as in the previous collection Lisnianskaia addresses the ethical problems of conscience and responsibility, as well as the dilemma of reconciling domestic and professional life. This problematic reconciliation of domesticity and verse propels the poem "For a long time now I don't feel, or think, or rhyme" ("Ne chuvstvuiu davno, ne myshliu, ne rifmuiu," 1983), where the persona states that she has ceased to exist and is seen preparing a feast for her guests. The intrusion of mundane preparations renders the concluding lines all the more poignant: "And it's doubtful that anyone will know that there's not a sound left in me / And that I am preparing my funeral banquet."

A variation on this theme investigates the burdens and joys of motherhood. In "To My Daughter" ("Docheri," 1983), the speaker, who addresses her daughter from beyond the grave, characterizes herself as a "foolish mother." By means of a series of paradoxes the mother seemingly negates the boundary between life and death, thereby closing the spatial and temporal distance between herself and her daughter. In *Poems. On the Verge of Sleep,* as a rule, the conversational diction, the sense of self-irony and the attention to everyday events and objects often mask the gravity of the lyric persona's anguish and loss.

Lisnianskaia's two *tamizdat* volumes, published "underground," established her position in the West as a leading Russian poet of her generation, but as she remarked in the interview with Stepanian: "My books came out there, but my reader is here, in Russia." In addition to a handful of favorable reviews, two appreciations by fellow writers, both Nobel laureates, helped to consolidate this reputation, first in the West and then in Russia. In a 1983 interview with Natal'ia Gorbanevskaia, the poet Joseph Brodsky made the following remarks:

> From what I've read in recent years, particularly in *Continent*, the poetry of Lisnianskaia has made a special impression on me. A Russian poet, like all poets, is always a product of what was written before; a poet begins by rejecting [this tradition], or on the contrary, works according to the principle of the echo. The only echo that I distinctly discern in Lisnianskaia's verse, thank God, is that of Akhmatova. She's an absolutely marvelous lyric poet, particularly in her short poems, which are poems of extraordinary intensity. Of all the Russian poets I know today, Lisnianskaia perhaps writes about death more precisely than any other.[21]

Ten years later, Aleksandr Solzhenitsyn sent Lisnianskaia his own warm appraisal of *Rains and Mirrors.* Solzhenitsyn praises the volume for its laconicism, its small details and the authenticity of feelings. And, like Brodsky, he invokes the specter of Akhmatova, adding Marina Tsvetaeva for good measure: "It would seem that after Akhmatova and Tsvetaeva it would be very difficult to carve out your own individuality in Russian poetry, to give it color and to be meaningful—but you have succeeded and it's obvious that you are not following a set program, but that it's done simply and flows on its own."[22]

As Carol Ueland has written, comparisons with Akhmatova and Tsvetaeva are simply de rigueur when it comes to writing about contemporary Russian women poets.[23] Certainly Ueland makes the point that most of the time these measuring and pigeonholing tactics, even when used as a form of praise, rarely succeed in truly identifying the poet's "own unique voice." Lisnianskaia, however, seemingly invites comparison with her famed female predecessors, Akhmatova in particular.

The opening quatrain of a poem dedicated to Akhmatova ("Siuda, gde zabven'e s izmenoiu . . . ," 1973) reads:

> Here, where oblivion is mixed with betrayal
> And shame with conscience,
> The Simple One, the Haughty One arrives
> And awakens me in the mornings.[24]

These visitations by the Simple and Haughty One (i.e., Akhmatova), whom the persona "badgers with questions," seem to suggest that the visitor represents more than a source of inspiration or model. The homeliness of being awakened in the morning rather than the more traditional nighttime appearance, as in Akhmatova's own "Muse," points to an intimate bond between the two poets.

Akhmatova, of course, is the subject of Lisnianskaia's major venture into prose. In her provocative study *The Music of Akhmatova's "Poem without a Hero"* (*Muzyka "Poèmy bez geroia" Anny Akhmatovoi*, written 1983–1989; published 1991), Lisnianskaia alternates roles of literary essayist and fellow poet. On the one hand, the essayist argues that the source of the stanzaic form and the music in Akhmatova's masterwork can be traced to Marina Tsvetaeva, rather than Mikhail Kuzmin, and Lisnianskaia largely adopts the expected conventions of the genre. On the other hand, in places Lisnianskaia addresses Akhmatova directly as Anna Andreevna (e.g., "'No, Anna Andreevna,' I shout to her from the earth"). Lisnianskaia buttresses the objective evidence she presents in defense of her thesis with psychological questioning and examination of the writer's biography. To a large extent, Lisnianskaia the essayist adopts her subject's own method. As many critics have remarked, the formidable erudition in Akhmatova's celebrated Pushkin studies was abundantly complemented by keen psychological insight, which enabled Akhmatova to view Pushkin as a contemporary.

> In answer to Elena Stepanian's question regarding her reading of Russian poetry, Lisnianskaia states: "The range of my reading of Russian poetry is now fairly wide and constant: Batiushkov, Baratynskii, Pushkin, Tiutchev, Lermontov, Blok, Annenskii, Mandel'shtam, Akhmatova, Khodasevich, Pasternak, Tsvetaeva, Kuzmin, Esenin and Georgii Ivanov."

Of contemporary poets, she singles out Joseph Brodsky. In other words, her list represents a fairly traditional pantheon of Russian poetry. More importantly, Lisnianskaia's reply underscores her self-identification as "poet" rather than "poetess," as "writer" rather than "woman writer."[25] Lisnianskaia clearly has no intention of becoming one of Solov'ev's second-rate Akhmatovas.

The year 1987 marked a watershed in the *glasnost'* era with the Soviet publication of such repressed works as Anatolii Rybakov's *The Children of the Arbat*, Yurii Trifonov's *Disappearance* and Andrei Bitov's *Pushkin House*, to name just a few. The publication in 1987 of eight poems in the Moscow literary journal *Znamia* announced the return of Lisnianskaia's poetry to the Soviet Union.[26] Significantly, this slender selection opens with the poignant octave "The Archive" ("Arkhiv," 1975):

Can it really be that after all of life's chaos,
After eternal love and after all the rows
The only thing to remain in time's tenacious hands
Will be just this three-layered stack of papers—
Poems for which I was not paid,
Bills that I punctually pay . . .
And letters, for which I was stifled,
I will lash not with a ribbon, but a flame.

"The Archive," undated in the *Banner* (*Znamia*) publication, signaled to the Soviet reader the existence of a cache of Lisnianskaia's work not yet published in the Soviet Union. This signal was soon realized by numerous publications in leading journals, including *New World* (*Novyi mir*) and *October* (*Oktiabr'*), the appearance of the small volume *Air Stratum* (*Vozdushnyi plast*) in 1990, as well as interviews and appreciations (see Bibliography).

The 1991 publication of Lisnianskaia's *Poems* (*Stikhotvoreniia*), the most comprehensive volume to date, marks the culmination of this "rehabilitation" process. In his review of the collection, the poet and fellow Metropolian Iurii Kublanovskii writes:

> *Poems* is part lyrical autobiography, skillfully and intricately constructed with its violation of strict chronology, when reminiscences of her childhood in Baku, wartime adolescence, and roaming youth are interspersed into the canvas of mature philosophical and intimate confession. The book has its own profoundly considered dramaturgy, the composition persuasively supports and strengthens the quality of individual poems. . . . [27]

Kublanovskii's choice of the word "confession" aptly points to the religious character of many of the lyrics, which is highlighted by the book's section titles: "Icon Lamp," "The Broken Circle" and "Transfiguration." Lisnianskaia's *Poems* secured her position as a major Russian poet writing in Russia.

Lisnianskaia's most recent volume of new verse, *After Everything* (*Posle vsego*, 1994), borrows its name from the title of the first part of Anna Akhmatova's *Anno Domini* (1922). For Akhmatova, ample reasons for her choice of title presented themselves, in particular, the execution of her former husband, Nikolai Gumilev, which took place the same month (August 1921) as the premature death of Aleksandr Blok,[28] not to mention World War I, the Russian revolution and civil war—all events that find expression in *Anno Domini*. Indeed, in the collection's opening poem, "Petrograd, 1919," Akhmatova portrays herself as a faithful survivor of "the holy city of Peter . . . our unintended monument."[29] Without belaboring the Akhmatova reference, the reader of Lisnianskaia's *After Everything* does not need to look far to see the relevance and appropriateness of the allusion.

With the exception of a handful of poems, Lisnianskaia abandons her customary practice of supplying dates, but judging by previous books and subsequent journal publications, the poems, by and large, represent new work from the 1990s. While it would be a serious misreading to interpret Lisnianskaia's *After Everything* in solely political or civic terms, events of the early 1990s, including the chaos engendered by the disintegration and swift collapse of the Soviet Union as well as ethnic conflict in her native Azerbaijan, do serve as background for a number of poems. Meditation on death and mortality, always a prominent component of Lisnianskaia's lyrics, becomes central in *After Everything*, which opens with images of death and separation and closes with an apocalyptic landscape of scorched earth, smoldering sky, burning waves and walls of blood.

The lyric "In Stepanakert" (a city in Azerbaijan) evokes the personal anguish occasioned by war:

> In my native Stepanakert—
> Native to me because of my grandmother—
> Walks the wind of death
> And enters every home.

After searching for the "broad-shouldered house" where her grandmother used to live, the persona gives rein to memory:

> All my visual memory
> For half a century has preserved
> The flame of apricots
> And the light of grapes.

In essence, the poet has preserved through memory that which has been destroyed by the realities of life. The allusion to the "light of grapes," moreover, reinforces the importance of these memories to the poet who chose precisely that image for her collection *Grape Light*. Accordingly, the act of poetry ensures the survival of these memories independent of the author.[30]

The poet's self-characterization in *After Everything* depicts a "stay-at-home," cut off from the events taking place around her by illness and advancing old age.[31] Images of disintegration, war and the "rust-colored trail of the Armenian pogrom" are therefore juxtaposed to private and domestic concerns. For example, "But there's no guarantee that the ceiling won't collapse / Just like the empire on the other side of the kitchen wall"; or the triptych "In the Kitchen of Time" ("Na kukhne vremeni," 1993–1994), where cutting onions and grating carrots is performed to the accompaniment of gunfire on the streets of Moscow. Moreover, the poet's present circumstances and her isolation lead her to question the worth of her art: "My muse has already become completely gray, / And half-deaf, and no longer is of use to anyone." Elsewhere she laments the loss of her daughter, now living in Jerusalem, and her failings as a mother (e.g., "In addition to prodigal sons, mothers can be prodigal as well"). But the author insists that although her daughter may be removed from her physically, she nonetheless is " . . . constantly present / There, where you are, my child"). Finally, the poet's role as wife presents yet another side of her personal travails and triumphs, as she has nursed her husband through a serious illness ("God gave you your first life, / I gave you the second one").

After Everything, then, may in some sense be regarded as a summation of Lisnianskaia's career to date in terms of themes, in particular the hopeless juggling of professional and domestic life, but it also represents a persistent searching for new forms. The reader is immediately struck by the predominance of cycles of poems in the book. In addition to the three-poem cycle "In the Kitchen of Time," the collection includes thirteen poems titled "triptych," no doubt occasioned by Lisnianskaia's own study of the best-known triptych in Russian poetry—Akhmatova's *A Poem without a Hero*. Indeed, Lisnianskaia's "Triptych of Insomnia" opens with the lines "Out of foolishness and caprice / I am composing a little book of *Triptychs*—Who needs these verses?" The poet's self-doubts notwithstanding, we are holding at least part of this book in our hands. *After Everything* amply demonstrates that Lisnianskaia's muse, though gray and half-blind, has not deserted her. On the contrary, the verse documents the poet's continuing quest.

Ronald Meyer

A Solitary Gift

Some are allotted
A happy gift—
Winged and clamorous
As a flock of birds by the sea.

Some are allotted
A steady gift—
Weighty and decaying
As wares at a shop.

Some are allotted
A magical gift—
With the healing powers
Of the nectar of flowers.

But I have been allotted
A solitary gift—
Parched and austere
As a fire at sea.

1970

I never knew before,
But now I've learned
That water can be dry
And fire colder than ice
And that our memory is our conscience.

I lost my memory in the dark—
My own name, the year and city,
And a man carrying a little girl . . .
I drink water—but my lips are parched,
I touch the flame—but my hands are cold.

1977

Take me, o Lord, instead of him,
And let him stay on this earth!

I am a frivolous being,
And you can send me to hell.

Let him live a little longer,
Let him try out his fate.
It's easier for me to bathe in seething pitch
Than to wail over his grave!

I beseech you, o Lord, tearfully beseech you:
Stop the coursing of my blood,
If for no other reason than my love for him
Surpasses Your love.

1978

I rejoice when I lose things,
I selflessly believe every time
That some misfortune lay in wait
But I paid it off with my losses.

A lucky woman, in one year I've lost
Three pensions, two purses and a ring—
And was rewarded by a summer red with berries
And a little green porch right on the forest.

So what did I drop in the raspberry patch?
And why am I asking questions?
For what have I been cheerlessly searching half a month
In the shrubbery where the wasps hold forth?

A lucky woman, the likes of whom are few on this earth,
Whose dreams have been as sweet as berries;
I've lost my ringing voice,
And nests of words, and their soaring order.

1983

To Mariia Petrovykh

Here your book lies before me—
And I see your face.
Your time runs before me
And forms a ring

Of a birch tree, under which you sleep without sedatives,
A ringlet of tobacco smoke—
That means you've awakened and it means you're smoking
Over a cup of tea, to be sure.

It's been a long time since I rang your doorbell, but here
I knock on the door of the tree:
"Let me in, my dear, for five minutes,
I've brought your book!"

And I see: the eye in the birch light up,
And I hear: the bark creak.
"I would need to correct several lines
And I don't have a pen at hand."

"Let me in! I brought you a pen as well."
"Somebody else's? What could I do with that?"
. . . The silver birch closed shut
And became your own image.

1983

To My Daughter

It would seem there's nothing to be said
When faced with the obviousness of the fact
That I, your foolish mother,
Have died from a heart attack or something.

Don't cry! Here's what I say to you:
It's not I who lie in the coffin all dressed up

In a kerchief with rococo roses,
But only lifeless clay, though the nipples
At one time, bloodied and sore,
Poured into you their meager milk.

All measures of life and its coordinates
Death changes quickly and easily:
Now you are as close to me
As I am far away from you.

Now there's no risk of me going astray,
Now I am in that very non-vacuum,
Which life reckoned to be a vacuum.
Here mass is not the same, nor velocity,
Nor even sleep, which out of naiveté
Life correlated with eternal rest.

Now I no longer require glasses;
From here I can see all your freckles—
Darker on your cheekbones, golden in your eyes;
You are all light—from head to toe.

Don't cry! The little hill on the edge
Of the cemetery is not the final home,
Where one dozes off into the final sleep,
But the site of our secret meetings
Where the tender forget-me-nots abound.

The riddle is life, but death is always the solution.
O, to see those tears is lovely!
Cry a little more, even though I am a bad mother
By all the parameters of the order of things.
No, I'll not offend your ears
With the justification that I'd gone astray—
All that is a lie. I so love you—
Daughters beloved don't dream of such love.

1983

Icon Lamp

Everything I'm wearing and that's before me is standard-issue:
An inexpensive cross, an icon without a frame,
A couch, and table, and square mirror,
And a blue icon lamp like any other.

It's burning now this evening,
The wick's not intricate—just cotton wadding.
I'm also a thing. But I'm made human
By prayer for my vain brother.

In my life, where everything is ordinary,
My days are tragic, but carefree,
Since even my innermost feelings
And thoughts and deeds are banal,

As light and darkness, as generosity and greed,
As falling leaves are the harbinger of snowfalls.
And one thing more! As brotherhood and betrayal.
Do not decay, my cross, burn, my icon lamp.

1986

Translated by Ronald Meyer

Notes to the Essay

1. In his somewhat self-serving account of the *Metropol'* affair, Viktor Erofeev outlines the almanac's genesis, the ensuing scandal, and the various fates meted out to contributors. Erofeev, however, does acknowledge the extraordinary courage of Lipkin and Lisnianskaia: "Lipkin and Lisnianskaia resigned from the Writers' Union. They had a more difficult time than all the others: they were deprived of practically all means of survival. We always regarded them as heroic individuals." See Viktor Erofeev, "Desiat' let spustia," *Metropol'. Literaturnyi al'manakh* (Moscow: Tekst, 1991), 5–13. (All translations, unless noted otherwise, are mine—R.M.)

2. Such was their answer to me in 1982 during our first meeting (in Peredelkino). I heard this sentiment repeated many times over the next decade.

3. I. Lisnianskaia and Elena Stepanian, "O Zhizni i o Knige," *Literaturnoe Obozrenie* (1990): 32.

4. Ibid., 31.

5. S. Taroshchina, "Mne dostatochno svobody vnutrennei . . .," *Literaturnaia gazeta* 6 (April 1994): 6.

6. *Metropol'*, 15.

7. Translated by H. William Tjalsma in *Metropol*, edited by Vasily Aksyoenov et al. (New York: W. W. Norton, 1982), 263.

8. "Nechto vrode avtobiografii," in I. Lisnianskaia and Elena Stepanian, "O Zhizni i o Knige," 30–34.

9. Carol Ueland, "Women's Poetry in the Soviet Union," in *Women Writers in Russian Literature*, ed. Toby W. Clyman and Diana Greene (Westport, CT: Greenwood Press, 1994), 241.

10. Makarova emigrated to Jerusalem in 1990.

11. Petrovykh is the addressee of Mandel'shtam's "Seamstress of bewitching glances," considered by Akhmatova to be one of the "best love poems of the twentieth century."

12. Lisnianskaia pays tribute to her friendship with Petrovykh in the interview with Stepanian: "Were it not for her many of my poems would probably not have been written. No other poet besides her so believed in my calling and so supported me in the days of my most tormenting doubts. Even I who value 'the gift to live in solitude' was saved by this support during the prolonged, pre-*Metropol'* non-publication of my poems" (Lisnianskaia and Stepanian, 34).

13. Stephanie Sandler, "The Canon and the Backward Glance: Akhmatova, Lisnianskaia, Petrovykh, Nikolaeva," in *Fruits of Her Plume: Essays on Contemporary Russian Women's Culture*, ed. Helena Goscilo (Armonk, NY: M.E. Sharpe, 1993), 121.

14. Lisnianskaia's poems to Petrovykh are "A vspomnim li my" (1976), in *Dozhdi i zerkala. Stikhi* (Paris: YMCA Press, 1983), 99; "Vot kniga tvoia predo mnoiu lezhit" (1983) and "Mariia Sergeevna! Ia domolchalas'" (1987), both printed in *Stikhotvoreniia* (Moscow: Sovetskii pisatel', 1991), 121–22. The second poem is translated in this volume, the third in Sandler's insightful essay.

15. Perhaps the most significant journal publication among these is the fifteen–poem cycle *V gospitale litsevogo raneniia*, which opens issue 47 (1986) of *Kontinent* (7–16).

16. I. Lisnianskaia, *Dozhdi i zerkala. Stikhi* (Paris: YMCA Press, 1983). Another manuscript of her collected poems in my possession consists of a bound typescript of 323 pages, entitled *Pozdnii angel*, which collects poems written through 1980. The poems from 1981–1982 appear on loose sheets. (Instructions on the manuscript, in Lisnianskaia's hand, indicate that several early poems, largely dating from the 1960s, are to be omitted from the published volume.)

17. "I live, mourning those of my generation" ("Zhivu, oplakivaia sverstnikov moikh," 1980, 210) is dedicated to Aksenov; "On Kopelev's Departure" ("Na ot"ezd Kopeleva," 1980, 218) is retitled "Farewell" ("Provody") in *Stikhotvoreniia* (Moscow, 1991), 34.

18. "On Kopelev's Departure," *Dozhdi i zerkala*, 218. In these lines Lisnianskaia refers to Bulat Okudzhava, the Russian bard and prose writer, and Bella Akhmadulina, the noted poet and fellow *Metropol'* contributor.

19. Since I was the editor at Ardis responsible for Lisnianskaia's book, I can offer a few details about the publication. The date on the copyright page is given as 1984 and a notice on the final page states that the book was printed in Ann Arbor in November 1984. The book, however, was printed in early 1985. The reason behind this harmless obfuscation was simple: Lisnianskaia

had endured several run-ins with Soviet authorities. Exhausted by threats and intimidation, she agreed to halt temporarily her publication abroad but had informed these same authorities that she could not stop the 1984 publication of her second *tamizdat* book, which was due out any day. The manuscript of the Ardis publication was deposited in the Rare Books and Manuscript Division of the University of Michigan Library (Ann Arbor). The photograph on page 2 of the Ardis edition was taken in Moscow in 1984 at the home of Inna Varlamova, a close friend of Lisnianskaia's. The detail on the cover is by Dmitrii Mitrokhin.

20. In her letter to this author, dated 11 May 1985, Lisnianskaia writes: "My friends and I like the dress [i.e., the Ardis *Stikhotvoreniia*] more than the Parisian one—it's a single entity." (Although this letter was written a mere thirteen years ago, it was a time when dresses or suits were standard euphemisms for books.)

21. Natal'ia Gorbanevskaia, "Interv'iu s Iosifom Brodskim," *Russkaia mysl'*, 8 February 1983.

22. Solzhenitsyn's letter was published in the interview with S. Taroshchina (*Literaturnaia gazeta*, 6 April 1994). An excerpt appears in Lisnianskaia's recent volume of verse, *After Everything* (*Posle vsego*; St. Petersburg: Pushkinskii Fond, 1994). A photocopy of the original letter in Solzhenitsyn's hand is in my possession.

23. Ueland, 242–43. One wonders whether male poets are so consistently measured by the standards of Mandel'shtam and Pasternak.

24. Translated by Carol Ueland in her "Women's Poetry in the Soviet Union," 241. Ueland dates the poem as 1971, although the date in both *Dozhdi i zerkala* (1983) and *Stikhotvoreniia* (1991) is given as 1973.

25. Lisnianskaia, like many contemporary Russian women authors from I. Grekova to Tat'iana Tolstaia, is more than ambivalent about the classification of "woman writer." In conversation with the author of this essay (in Peredelkino, June 1994), Lisnianskaia expressed pleasure at the prospect of forthcoming articles and translations, but this pleasure was undercut by the fact they were to appear in "women's anthologies."

26. I. Lisnianskaia, "Iz liriki," *Znamia* 9 (1987): 127–30. The poems in this selection date from the years 1975 through 1986 and include work from Lisnianskaia's two émigré books as well as unpublished pieces.

27. Iurii Kublanovskii, [Review, *Stikhotvoreniia* (Moscow, 1991)], *Novyi mir* (1993): 248.

28. The death of Blok clearly figured as a signal to the end of an era, for the poet represented for Akhmatova not simply a poetic school but something much larger: "I consider Blok to be not only the greatest European poet of the first quarter of the twentieth century (I bitterly mourned his untimely death), but also the essence of his era, that is, the most characteristic representative of his time."

29. *The Complete Poems of Anna Akhmatova*, trans. Judith Hemschemeyer (Boston: Zephyr, 1992), 259.

30. Images of destruction and survival in Akhmatova's *Anno Domini* are not limited to the section "After Everything." See the third section entitled "The Voice of Memory" ("Golos pamiati").

31. Although Lisnianskaia was only in her mid-sixties when *After Everything* appeared, she had endured prolonged illness and hospitalization, as had Lipkin.

Bibliography

Primary Works

Èto bylo so mnoi. Baku, 1957.

Vernost'. Moscow, 1958.

Ne prosto—liubov'. Moscow, 1963.

Iz pervykh ust. Moscow, 1966.

Vinogradnyi svet. Moscow: Sovetskii pisatel', 1978.

"Stikhi." *Metropol'. Literaturnyi al'manakh.* Ed. Vasilii Aksenov et al. Ann Arbor, MI: Ardis, 1979. 16, 314–17.

Dozhdi i zerkala. Paris: YMCA Press, 1983.

Stikhotvoreniia. Na opushke sna. Ann Arbor, MI: Ardis, 1984.

"V gospitale litsevogo raneniia." *Kontinent* 47 (1986): 7–16.

"Iz liriki," *Znamia* 9 (1987): 127–30.

"Novye stikhi." *Oktiabr'* 11 (1988): 130–32.

"Neotpravlennye pis'ma." *Znamia* 12 (1990): 3–8.

"Novye stikhi." *Oktiabr'* 9 (1990): 66–69.

Stupeni. Nakhodka otdykhaiushchego. Moscow: Prometei, 1990.

[Untitled selection of poems]. *Iunost'* 11 (1990): 26.

Vozdushnyi plast. Moscow: Pravda, 1990.

Muzyka "Poèmy bez geroia" Anny Akhmatovoi. Moscow: Khudozhestvennaia literatura, 1991.

Stikhotvoreniia. Moscow: Sovetskii pisatel', 1991.

"Iz novoi tetradi." *Novyi mir* 10 (1992): 56–59.

"Iz tetradi 1993," *Novyi mir* 12 (1993): 107–09.

"Na kukhne vremeni. Tsikl stikhotvorenii," *Znamia* 7 (1994): 113–16.

Posle vsego. St. Petersburg: Pushkinskii fond, 1994.

In Translation

"Poems." *Metropol. Literary Almanac.* Trans. H. William Tjalsma. Ed. Vassily Aksyonov et al. New York: W.W. Norton, 1982. 4, 262–65.

"Maria Sergeevna! I have kept silent. . . ." Trans. Stephanie Sandler. *Fruits of Her Plume.* Ed. Helena Goscilo. Armonk, NY: M.E. Sharpe, 1993. 119.

"To You, My Friends. . . ." *Twentieth-Century Russian Poetry. Silver and Steel. An Anthology.* Trans. Albert C. Todd. Selected by Yevgeny Yevtushenko. New York: Doubleday, 1993. 897–98.

"Poems." *Lives in Transit.* Trans. Walter Arndt. Ed. Helena Goscilo. Ann Arbor, MI: Ardis, 1995. 309–12.

Secondary Works

Brodskii, Iosif, and Iurii Kublanovskii. "K iubileiu Inny Lisnianskoi." *Russkaia mysl'*, 11 September 1963.

Chertok, Shimon. "Zhizn' i kniga." *Novoe russkoe slovo,* 18 February 1991.

Gorbanevskaia, Natal'ia. "Interv'iu s Iosifom Brodskim." *Russkaia mysl',* 8 February 1983.

Heldt, Barbara. "Inna Lisnianskaia. *Stikhotvoreniia.*" *World Literature Today* (Winter 1986).

Iverni, Violetta. "Ia, zakleimennaia zhguchei vinoi. . . ." *Russkaia mysl',* 19 July 1985.

Kublanovskii, Iurii. [Review of *Stikhotvoreniia*, 1991]. *Novyi mir* (1993): 247–48.

———. "Za tselebnym iadom slova. . . ." *Literaturnaia gazeta,* 12 September 1990, 6.

Lisnianskaia, Inna, and Elena Stepanian. "O Zhizni i o Knige." *Literaturnoe obozrenie* 4 (1990): 30–34.

Lowe, David. *Russian Writing since 1953: A Critical Survey.* New York: Ungar, 1987.

Meyer, Ronald. "Inna L'vovna Lisnianskaia." *Dictionary of Russian Women Writers.* Ed. Marina Ledkovsky, Charlotte Rosenthal and Mary Zirin. Westport, CT: Greenwood Press, 1994. 378–81.

Sandler, Stephanie. "The Canon and the Backward Glance: Akhmatova, Lisnianskaia, Petrovykh, Nikolaeva." *Fruits of Her Plume: Essays on Contemporary Russian Women's Culture.* Ed. Helena Goscilo. Armonk, NY: M.E. Sharpe, 1993. 113–33.

Taroshchina, S. "Mne dostatochno svobody vnutrennei. . . ." *Literaturnaia gazeta,* 6 April 1994, 6.

Ueland, Carol. "Women's Poetry in the Soviet Union." *Women Writers in Russian Literature.* Ed. Toby W. Clyman and Diana Greene. Westport, CT: Greenwood Press, 1994. 229–48.

Elizaveta Mnatsakanova

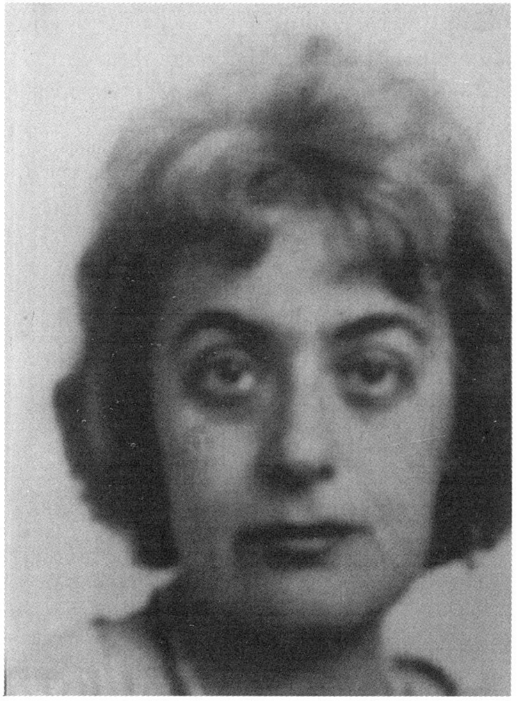

Elizaveta Mnatsakanova (b. 1922).
Courtesy of the author and Gerald J. Janecek.

Elizaveta Arkad'evna Mnatsakanova (German pen name Elisabeth Netzkowa, b. 1922) created in the realm not only of literature but also of music and the graphic arts as well. These aspects are often present in a balance uniquely equal and rare even in artists with a strong bent toward synaesthesia. While visual aspects of literature have been extensively explored in twentieth-century modernism, including the Russian avant-garde, organization of texts using principles drawn from musical practice have been much more sporadic and undeveloped. Arguably, Mnatsakanova is among the most important and successful pioneers in this area. When she found her own voice in the late 1940s, it was very clear to her that she had no safe place in the Soviet context and therefore she did not exert herself to make her original writing known. In fact, she strove to keep it hidden.

She was born in Baku on 31 May 1922 to parents who were both medical doctors in active practice. Her father, Arkadii (1876–1950), came from a poor Armenian family in Nagorno-Karabakh who released him to be adopted at the age of about six by a well-to-do childless man who provided him with an excellent education in Moscow. He graduated from school with a silver medal and received a medical education at Moscow University, then went to Geneva for post-graduate study. From there he volunteered for service in the Balkan Wars but returned to Russia in 1914 for Russian military service. He married in 1918, moved to Baku as chief physician at a military hospital and remained in Baku until his death. He was a learned man and in the evenings spent time translating Greek and Latin classics such as Ovid's *Metamorphoses* into Russian. Mnatsakanova recalls him reading *Don Quixote* to her as a child and remembers the active international cultural life of the city during her childhood. Her mother, Anna Sergeevna (1890–1960), was also adopted and grew up in Khar'kov (now Kharkhiv), attended the women's medical courses there, then received her medical diploma in St. Petersburg. She was a devoted physician with a strong sense of her duty to serve people in need. Although her mother did not engage directly in literary or artistic activities or read much besides medical literature, Mnatsakanova recalls her rich imagination and ability to tell stories, mostly with tragic outcomes.

Although she always had a strong interest in music, Mnatsakanova's earliest experience with a piano teacher was distasteful enough to turn her away from playing for many years. However, at her father's insistence she eventually entered the Baku Conservatory and quickly completed the course there in two years. On the other hand, in literature courses she always received poor grades because she was unable to force herself to read the required Soviet school texts. Immediately after World War II she moved to Moscow, attended but did not finish Moscow University (1945–1947, philological faculty), continued piano and music theory studies at the Moscow Conservatory (1945–1949), received a diploma in each area (1950) and completed graduate coursework there in 1953, but did not defend her dissertation. After a period of initial euphoria in Moscow, she realized that it was an environment totally alien to her. To earn a living, she wrote articles and books on the music of Mozart, Brahms, Mahler, Shostakovich, Prokofiev and others.

Her first literary-artistic works, a series of handwritten texts abstractly illustrated using colored pencils, were completed between 1946 and 1948. It was always an important goal for her to create "beautiful books." The spontaneously made initial versions were then replaced by carefully produced final versions, but it has also been common for her to return to earlier works and rework them into yet newer versions. As with other inveterate revisers, this can result in some uncertainty about which is the best version of a given work. She never attempted to publish any of her literary works while living in the Soviet Union. In 1965 she destroyed all her previous writings and began a new series that combined the graphic elements of text and illustration into an organic whole. The finest example of this is *A Guest at Death's* (*Beim tode zugast/U smerti v gostiakh*). Upon emigration to Vienna on 22 April 1975, she initially worked as a piano teacher for young children, thus giving rise to her German pen name, Elisabeth Netzkowa, which was the children's simplified version of her difficult-to-pronounce surname. The first serious attention she received was from the prominent Russian artist Mikhail Shemiakin, then living in Paris. He included the complete text of one of her most important poems, "Autumn in the Lazaret of Innocent Sisters. Requiem in Seven Parts" ("Osen' v lazarete nepovinnykh sester. Rekviem v semi chastiakh," 1977) in his epochal almanac *Apollon-77*, in addition to a prose piece on Chekhov. An earlier version of the "Requiem" had, in fact, been taken out of the Soviet Union in 1970 by the well-known German writer Heinrich Böll. Mnatsakanova knows German and had met Böll in Moscow. She was about to destroy her manuscripts, but Böll insisted on taking them out through customs in his coat pocket, later returning them to her upon her arrival in Vienna.

The "Requiem" was written in the fall of 1971 as a result of a hospital stay during which she experienced "clinical death" due to a serious hemorrhage. Part Three was composed in the hospital spontaneously as a response to the suffering of the other women patients around her. She recalls how moved she was by the pathetically intense gratitude one of her fellow patients demonstrated when Mnatsakanova gave her a cheap purse and lipstick. This poem was then developed into the elaborate edifice of a seven-part cantatalike musical structure. The title of the poem provides the embryonic kernel, the musical subject as it were, out of which the entire poem is built. Mnatsakanova takes each piece of the title and develops its potential associations in a variety of directions, much the way a composer might develop a main theme by developing each of its component short motifs. The first three parts thus focus on the three main units of the title: "Autumn/in the Lazaret/of Innocent Sisters." In contrast to musical practice, the poet has verbal material that can be developed by paronomastic association on several levels, phonetic, morphological and semantic. The semantic level can be further subdivided into relationships based on metaphor and metonymy. Surprising and unanticipated effects are produced by sudden shifts from one level of development to another. Thus Part One begins with a metonymic association: "In the Lazaret of Innocent Sisters it's September!" ("V lazarete sester nepovinnykh—sentiabr'!"), and from there associations are developed not with the word "autumn" (*osen'*), which drops from view, but with "September": "September, Septimus, the Seventh / circle in Seventh Heaven. / The heavens darken, Septimius, Septimius, / you leaf through / the leaves." The name of the month suggests associations with "seven," which in turn generate the figure of a monk, Brother Septimius, who is leafing through the fallen leaves of trees (in Russian *list'ia* are not leaves of paper, but of trees). The mystical number 7 figures also in the seven parts of the poem and the seven parts into which the traditional musical portions of the Latin Requiem Mass are divided (Introit, Kyrie, Sequence, Offertory, Sanctus, Benedictus and Agnus Dei). In this stanza nearly all associations are semantic, based on meaning rather than sound or morphology.

The next stanza, however, introduces a different principle, one that is a hallmark of Mnatsakanova's poetic technique. She breaks words down, here syllabically, into meaningful subunits, which then suggest other paths of development. Thus *edva* ("scarcely") is divided *e dva* to separate out *dva* ("two"), and a sequence is generated that goes on to *sem'* ("seven") and *mnogo* ("many"). Along with this, the lone Brother Septimius has generated a cohort of "many invisible brothers."

In Part Two a similar process of development occurs on the basis of the word *lazaret*. Then in Part Three we come upon a more traditional poem in rhymed quatrains (the part composed first), but it frees itself from the rigid form in an obsessive sequence of variations on a single phrase, which concludes with the emergence of a new word and theme, Nazareth. The title of the next part, "Recordare, Jesu!," overtly refers to a section of the Latin Requiem with its theme of remembrance and contains a recitation of the horrible chambers of the hospital. Already in this part themes from the preceding parts begin to recur and the final four parts gather, regather, permutate and develop words and themes to a grandiose conclusion polyphonic in scope, with marked visual features, requiring the large page-spread provided in *Apollon-77* for proper realization. The poet said that she intended in Part Seven to produce an orchestral score with a specific musical structure, something of a hybrid of a sonata-form movement and a double fugue. The visual structure parallels at least the sonata form rather well: the two opening sections could represent the principal and secondary themes, the chaotic section would be the development section and the concluding figure in the form of a cross marks a recapitulation of the opening sections and a return to order. In the verbal contents, however, a quasi-musical structuring is less clear-cut. And the question of polyphony is always a debatable one except in instances of literally simultaneous recitation. Here we perhaps do not have literal simultaneity, but at least the parallel nodules of text at the beginning of Part Seven and later on suggest a visual simultaneity.

Mnatsakanova's first solo book, the collection *Steps and Sighs* (*Shagi i vdokhi*), appeared in Vienna in 1982 under the editorship of A. Hansen-Löve and included major sections of four of her books of verse. However, her view that each of these formed an organic whole that must not be disrupted resulted in dissatisfaction with this publication and ultimately to her publishing three of her major works independently at her own expense. The first of these, *A Guest at Death's* (Vienna, 1986) is a photocopy edition of her calligraphed poems with elaborately scripted arabesque borders and backgrounds accompanied by photocopied close-ups of her own hand in various positions.

While this book emphasizes visual qualities, *The Sabbath Book* (*Das Buch Sabeth*, Vienna, 1988) synthesizes verbal, visual and musical features in her most complex work to date. The original version of the work was written in several days in May 1972 as a kind of love song devoted to a certain person who was perhaps initially specific, but who becomes transformed into the ideal spiritual partner, almost a divine figure, "my ideal thou (*ty*)." As she prepared the manuscript for publication large parts were either reconstructed or recomposed, and of the thirty-five original color illustrations she was able to include only seven because of the expense. Nevertheless, she feels that the published version presents the work without any compromises. The book is divided into six parts, each with as many as twenty-five individual numbers (i.e., poems). Each poem contains a unique visual-verbal-musical elaboration of its thematic material along lines similar to those found in the "Requiem," but in many cases to an even more extreme degree of fragmentation. Each page, in her view, is like a page of a musical score with many lines and layers in a complex system of relationships, thus representing a new, nonlinear form of literary text that has the potential to reveal the laws of human thought. Visual configurations range from unbroken stream-of-consciousness lines to word fragments widely scattered across or carefully positioned on the page, to compact columns and other geometric designs, to combinations of print and handscript or handscript alone. While at times the reading path appears to bifurcate, there is, however, usually only one correct path to follow. In Part Three, a core text is reproduced several times in series, while around the margins various other texts are added in script or print as counterpoint variations. The illustrations are sometimes abstract colorforms, sometimes combinations of abstract drawing and script. The culminating Part Five, "The Song of Songs," is particularly interesting in being in the unprecedented form of a poetic *passacaglia*, in which a column of italicized words appears on the right or left to represent the repeating organ pedal line of the traditional musical form, while the center of the page provides variations consisting of a flux of everyday phrases. In Mnatsakanova's version of the form, the columns representing the pedal line do not remain constant, but change and evolve as well. The impression she had when composing this section was of her skull smashed by a train and having her life pass before her, while she was simultaneously hearing the grand repeating melody of eternity. Both here and in Part Three one has the impression of true musicopoetic simultaneity. Another innovative feature of some of the poems in this work and occasionally elsewhere (e.g., "Barns") is the "crossing out of text"; in places that she felt were too important or private, the text is obliterated or entirely erased, sometimes leaving only scansion marks to indicate the rhythm of the omitted words.

Her third independent book, *Metamorphoses* (*Metamorphosen*, Vienna, 1988), was written in emigration (1984–1986) and is a series of twenty variations on an initial poem. It can thus be compared in form to Bach's *Goldberg Variations*. Its themes are music, especially the church music of Bach himself, the "cathedral" of the Alps and life's transigence. As has become frequent in recent works, *Metamorphoses* contains substantial passages in German, but the paronomastic transformations typical of Mnatsakanova's poetry remain the focus of attention here as well and in fact become thematized in the title of the work itself. She has recorded herself reading passages from this poem interspersed with excerpts from Richard Strauss's *Alpensymphonie*.

Among other developments in her creative life since emigration have been her public readings in Vienna and elsewhere. In Russia, she rarely even showed her poetry to anyone, let alone gave public readings of it, but in Vienna she discovered a talent for recitation. She reads her own poetry and that of other congenial poets with an intensity and dramatic effectiveness that has made these performances well received by audiences. She has also done distinguished translations of German and Austrian poets (Trakl, Rilke, Celan, Hans Carl Artmann et al.) into Russian, for which she received the Wystan-Hugh-Auden Translation Prize (1985) and an award from the Austrian Ministry of Education and the Arts (1987). Her first book of poems to be published in Russia, *Vita Breve*, appeared in December 1994 in the Perm' series "Aquarius" ("Vodolei"). Also in 1994, the Vienna art museum Albertina acquired several of her bookworks and illustrations for its collection. She has produced literary commentary on Khlebnikov, Dostoevsky and other writers and continues to teach Russian literature at the Universität Wien.

Gerald J. Janecek

From The Seasons of Heaven

A Winter Morning

Sheds . . .

Snowbound sheds
(knee-deep in snowdrifts).
Sunbound sheds
not bound to death.

Sheds . . .

Sheds and barns
like candles
in a hermit's cavern.

Sheds . . .

Sheds and firs
bight brightly
bight with sunlight.

Sheds . . .

Sheds in sunlight
Cloistered nuns in white.

Sheds . . .

Snowbound sheds.

Sheds in snow
immune to enemy law.

Sheds . . .

Sheds in sunlight

Sheds in lightbands
Sheds in vestibules
    in lightbands

Sheds . . .

You can rhyme till Kingdom Come—
You still won't shed the Day of Reckoning . . .

Sheds . . .

(Sheds are
sin-shedders . . .)

Sheds in bonds
in bondage—
blankets.
Barns . . .

WINTER
SNOW
BOUND
SUNBONDED
BOND-SHED
BARNS
. . .
    . . .
. . .
    (barns in bloom)
. . .
Sheds . . .

. . .

5 January 1969–2 January 1971

Staraia Ruza

Spring 1970 II

Spring's eyes kill the seeing.
The eyes of spring look downward.
In valleys deep blue color reigns.
Forgive me, spring, again I'm unprepared.

If you think of loving me in autumn—
I'll remember it till May.

But if you love me in winter
when trees are deep in hibernation,
when frost patterns on windows float past buildings,
when frost patterns on windows seem an omen—
o no, don't love me in early winter
when the world appears to be a prison.

If it happens that I'm loved in autumn—
I'll remember it in May!

But if you love me in winter,
early winter, when dreams turn cold like marble,
when dreams turn to ice and wilt,
when trees go westward,
inclining in threatening patterns cast on buildings—
let's not, don't think of me in early winter,
when dying lies upon the windows.

If you think of loving me in May—
how strangely outlines of outstretched branchy arms
threaten in a warming mist,
green fingers beyond dead shutters,
and dreams turn green and beckon westward,
westward toward the land of sunset meetings.

From A Guest at Death's

No. 1

virtuosa
aged
wanderer par
iah
this   pra
nkster
stra
ngled lady of stra
ngled meek people
alex in a dormitory
—martyrium—
of mortals

Love Poem

No. 29

but I thought
we'd be alone together I
thought we'd be alone together
we'd be alone togethought
oh I reallyIreallytho
ughtwe'dbe
toge
oh, I really Ireally thou
ghtwe'db ewe
everforev
erwe'dbeto
oh, I really Ireallytho
ughtwewewe
toge
thewe toge
oh, oh, oh

A Humble Romanza

No. 31

the song of a humble guest
 cuts down as trees
 turns round as trees
 the humble motif shines:
o extend extend me
  stretch me out
  longer!
the song of a sacred guest
  unrecognized
  your
 unrecognized among you
 unrecognizable
   guest
   your
  mysterious melody:
o extend me stretch me out across the sky as the lunar length!
singing
under bridges
I rock
with swelling
song
stretch out extend across the sky in a band of light!
I'll
rise
for
you
as your obedient
star
I've stretched my fingers fingers out to the milky way stars I lean

o extend extend my head swelled up to the sky!
I'll become I'll
when
I dry out wrinkle up

as your obedient
little
yellow
moon

No. 32

    so sad was I
    so sad
on my last day
    the last one
of my
    last
    solstice
    so
    sad
in the last part of my
            time
            the day
    of my memorial service
    of my nameday
        so
        sad
    and still
with some
        of you
        there
        fell
to my lot then
            a separation—
this was on that day of posthumous
    appellation!
and still did it just fall to my lot just then did it ju
        jubilation ju
        jub
        i
        la
        t

ion it just ju
bi
la
tion and and
compen
sation and
sation and
andsationand
compen
sation and and thru
thruexecuexe
execu
thru exe
cu
tion

No. 50

our time on earth will fly by fly
our time on earth above the earth above the green will fly by
our time on earth will fly above the earth above the green you'll forget
you'll forget who's my forget who's whose who's your who's my forget
who's
May who who's small who's mild forget forget who's mild who's fresh
who's bright who
bloomed who who forget who bloomed who's bright who light who
snow who
who bright who light who who's holy forget our time on earth will fly by
you'll forget who's May who's mother who who forget mother May my
forget who's light who's blind who brave who swept who who forget
who
swept impelled who called who who forget who impelled who
forced you fouled you forget our time on earth will
forget above the earth forget who's May who's mother forget who
bloomed who led who led away who wilts away forget forget
who's May who's March who myrtle who world world peace you'll
forget
forget who's mild who's mild forget who's

holy whose vault vault of heaven forget forget forget
who's self self you'll forget forget
the world a while forget forget who's
mild who's small who called who forced forget forget who
who forced you forget who called who hurt whose harm forget
whose harm who hurt who earth of earth to earth earth by earth from earth forget
forget
our time on earth our line line on earth will fly by
you'll forget they'll forget but they'll they'll you'll forget the vault forget light
forget forget for
get holy for
get light for
get holy for
get
light for
get
light

From Autumn in the Lazaret of Innocent Sisters

Part Three

The Song of the Rotting Sisters

As a rotting uninvited guest I walk through houses
Rotting leaves beat like the train of a gown at my feet
A crown of rotting leaves shines like a wreath
High over my bloodless face

As a rotting guest I will pass o'er the earth
Along a rotting moldy pathway
Falling leaves, falling golden leaves!
Never to return to my home!

Ah I no longer have need of a family!

I will use up my few remaining days
I will bury my belated time
In the Lazaretto of Short-time Cripples

Pour out pour out o odious blood!
Creep apart o odious flesh!
With an old worn-out shroud cover
The thickened jelly of unseeing eyes!

Falling leaves, falling golden leaves!
Never to return to my home!
I will finish my not-long time
In the Lazaret of Not-Long Cripples
In the Lazaret of the Forever Innocent
In the Lazaret of the Ever Unsleeping
In the Lazaret of the Roaming Wherever
In the Lazaret of the Wandering Brides
In the Lazaret of the Roving Around
In the Lazaret of the Raving in Pursuit
Lazaret, Lazaret,
Nazareth . . .

Translated by Gerald J. Janecek

Bibliography

Primary Works

"Anton Chekov." *Apollon-77*. Paris, 1977.

"Osen' v lazarete nepovinnykh sester. Rekviem v semi chastiakh." *Apollon-77*. Paris, 1977. 173–83.

"Iskusstvo i predrassudki." *Vremia i my* 27 (1978): 115–25.

"O roli detskogo vospominaniia v psikhologii khudozhestvennogo tvorchestva (na primere prozy Mariny Tsvetaevoi i dvukh otryvkov iz romana F.M. Dostoevskogo *Brat'ia Karamazovy. Wiener Slawistischer Almanach* Band 10 (1982): 325–49.

"Poèzii i prozy. Nevozvratnaia REKA. Predislovie." *Zhizn' prozy.* Ed. Vl. Kazakov. Munich: Wilhelm Fink Verlag, 1982. 5–43.

"Predislovie." *Ot golovy do zvezd*. Ed. Vl. Kazakov. Munich, 1982. 5–35.

Shagi i vdokhi. Chetyre knigi stikhov. Vienna: Wiener Slawistischer Almanach, Sonderband 6, 1982.

"Aleksei Mikhailovich russkikh snovidenii." *The Blue Lagoon Anthology of Modern Russian Poetry.* Ed. K.K. Kuzminsky and G. Kovalev. Vol. 2. Newtonville, MA: Oriental Research Partners, 1983. 19–34.

"Dorogoi drug. . . ." *The Blue Lagoon Anthology of Modern Russian Poetry.* Ed. K.K. Kuzminsky and G. Kovalev. Vol. 2. Newtonville, MA: Oriental Research Partners, 1983.
"Khlebnikov. Predel i bespredel'naia muzyka slova." *Sintaksis* 11 (1983): 101–56.
"Znachenie i rol' vospominaniia v khudozhestvennoi praktike. Freid—Dostoevskii—Geine." *Wiener Slawistischer Almanach* Band 16 (1985): 37–80.
Beim tode zugast / U smerti v gostiakh. Vienna: n.p., 1986.
Das Buch Sabeth. Kniga v piati chastiakh. Vienna: n.p., 1988.
Metamorphosen. 20 Veränderungen einer vierzeiligen Strophe und Finale. Vienna: n.p., 1988.
[Netzkowa, Elisabeth (Mnatsakanjan)]. *Aus der österreichischen Lyrik. Ausgewählte Übersetzungen / Iz avstriiskoi liriki. Izbrannye perevody.* Vienna: n.p., 1994.
Vita Breve. Perm': Izdatel'stvo permskogo universiteta, 1994.

Secondary Works

Janecek, Gerald J. "Paronomastic and Musical Techniques in Mnacakanova's 'Requiem.'" *Slavic and East European Journal* 31, 2 (1987): 202–19.
Rabinovich, Aleksandr. "O tvorchestve Mnatsankanovoi." *Apollon-77.* Paris, 1977. 171.
Rudnev, Vadim. "Stikhoslozhenie Elizavety Mnatsakanovoi." *Mitin zhurnal* [St. Petersburg] 45–46 (May–August 1992): 115–26.
Sekatskii, Aleksandr. "Poèma i mantra." *Mitin zhurnal* [St. Petersburg] 45–46 (May–August 1992): 127–37.

Iunna Morits

Iunna Petrovna (Pinkhusovna) Morits (b.1937)—poet, prose writer, memoirist and political activist—is considered one of the leading Russian poets of her generation. Her poetic works are endowed with an unmistakably individualistic tone, a strict civil position that has been expressed in recent years with an increasing explicitness, and a continuous imagery, the origins of which can be traced back to her earliest literary attempts. Writing initially from an apolitical point of view, which in the Soviet realm could be regarded a provocation in itself, Morits became a distinct voice within the liberal group of authors who supported *perestroika* in the mid-1980s.

Born to a Jewish family in Kiev in 1937, Morits's central trauma of childhood was the German invasion of the Soviet Union in 1941. Although the family was evacuated in time, Morits indeed "must be counted lucky to have survived the massacre that attended Hitler's first drive into Russian territory."[1] With their lives barely saved, hardship abounded for Iunna and her parents: the train on which the Morits family was transported to safety was bombed; food and living space were in short supply both during the evacuation and after their return to Kiev; finally, Iunna was infected with tuberculosis from which she has suffered ever since. Her father, who held an administrative position in Kiev's public transportation department, became blind in the early 1930s and could not support his family. Not surprisingly, Morits's works often evoke the horrid experiences of her wartime childhood. Hunger, illness and the attempt to find spiritual and imaginative remedies for constant material deprivations have remained vital themes in Morits's poetry.

After the war, Morits began to study philology. In 1954 she enrolled in the Gorky Institute of Literature in Moscow (not to be mistaken with the more research-oriented Gorky Institute of World Literature). This unique institution, run by the Soviet Writers' Union and responsible for the education of new generations of loyal Soviet writers, habitually displayed a more lenient attitude toward creative pursuits than the typical rank-and-file institutions of higher learning in the Soviet Union. Yet, even for this institute, Morits's independence and her insistence on individuality proved intolerable. As a reprimand for her participation in an Arctic expedition in 1956 for which she had not asked permission, Morits was suspended from the institute for two years. During that time she lived in the Baltics, mainly in Latvia, which became an important cultural influence on her *oeuvre*. Reinstated at the institute in 1958, Morits graduated from it in 1961 (other sources indicate 1962)[2] and has made her home in Moscow ever since.

Iunna Morits's first poems had already appeared in print when she enrolled at the Gorky Institute in 1954. Her first poetry collection, *Conversation about Happiness* (*Razgovor o schast'e*), was published in 1957 in Kiev. The journal *Youth* (*Iunost'*), whose editor-in-chief, Valentin Kataev, encouraged aesthetic experimentation and artistic individuality, printed several selections of Morits's poetry. The fact that Morits could publish a book at age twenty comments significantly both on her remarkable talent and the fresh winds of the Thaw, when for a short while the gerontocracy of Soviet literature was challenged by a group of young poets, with Bella Akhmadulina, Evgenii Evtushenko, Rimma Kazakova, Andrei Voznesenskii and their slightly older "father figure" Bulat Okudzhava as their leading voices. Whenever this generation is referred to, Morits's name appears together with those of the "stars" whose readings filled stadiums with cheering crowds of poetry aficionados. And yet she stood and stands aside from them. An explanation for her peculiar position may be that, although her career was made possible and promoted by the de-Stalinization and liberalization of the late 1950s and early 1960s, unlike many poets at the time, Morits never agreed to serve as a mouthpiece for political moves of the ruling establishment, regardless of how promising those developments may have appeared. Much more significant than the political springtime for Morits's artistic evolution was her Arctic expedition. From her close interaction with a stressful, mostly male environment, Morits gained a clearer understanding of her female identity and was able to prove to herself her ability to maintain personal independence in everyday life. The Arctic sojourn also colored her poetic themes of that period, not untypical of the young generation of Soviet poets in early 1960s—the so-called *shestidesiatniki* (generation of the 1960s)—which praised nature, daring, challenges and courage and viewed a romanticized Hemingway image as their ideal.

The post-Thaw chill of Soviet politics caused a deep split in the generation of the 1960s, forcing Iunna Morits to further withdraw into privacy. Of course, the suicide of her husband (a literary critic) at the time of the invasion of Czechoslovakia was foremost a personal catastrophe for Morits, but may certainly also be interpreted as a symbol of grave hopelessness reflecting the political fiasco of the *shestidesiatniki*. Regarding the long intermission between her poetry collections *Cape of Desire* (*Mys zhelaniia*, 1961) and *Vine* (*Loza*, 1970)—years in which only a few selections of Morits's poems went to press—this could also be interpreted as a frustrated reaction to the changing political climate, but since the nature of Morits's poetry is far from politically explicit, this interpretation is unlikely. Rather, Morits undertook a redefinition of her poetic profile, searching for her place in the Soviet literary scene, after which she found her very own themes and intonations to which she would stick in the following decades.

In the 1970s and 1980s, Iunna Morits published new collections of her poetry almost every three years. Her considerable productivity developed further in several smaller books of verse for children, and a large number of translations, in particular from languages of peoples within the Soviet Union. Morits's activities as a translator are sometimes viewed as a way to avoid the censorship problems she supposedly experienced with her original works, but more likely they display her sincere attachment to the poets whose works she rendered into Russian, and to the cultures to which those poets belong. Beginning in 1964, when Morits published a volume of translations of the Jewish poet Moisei S. Teif (1904–1966; sometimes misspelled as M. Toif) under the title *The Handshake* (*Rukopozhatie*), she made the works of many Latvian, Georgian, Avar and other poets accessible to Russian readers. In particular her renditions of poems by Faizu Alieva (b. 1932), the famed female poet from Daghestan, give evidence to the fact that Iunna Morits not only is a conscientious translator but regards such translations as a labor of love.

Morits's position toward society underwent profound changes in the mid-1980s. She was among the founders of the group Aprel', an informal organization whose name is taken from the month in 1985 when Mikhail Gorbachev became Secretary General of the Communist party of the Soviet Union and initiated the *glasnost'* campaign supported by many writers holding liberal views, including Morits. More recently, she has published short prose works such as "New Potatoes" ("Molodaia kartoshka," 1989),[3] which describes the survival of a peasant woman in an environment characterized by roughness and inconsideration. Selected pages from her memoirs, published in various journals, show Morits as a person of strong opinions who relates caustic anecdotes about famous contemporaries such as Evtushenko. Additionally, in her recent poetry, there seems to be an increased sensitivity to gender questions. "Lucid, pointed and witty, these poems are amongst the very few pieces of recent work by women poets to acknowledge that the jaundiced view generally taken of women's writing might affect the way in which one may define oneself as a writer, as well as the way in which other female writers are defined."[4] One motif that lends itself to a feminist reading is that of the (female) poet as a witch, free-spirited and endowed with magic forces, endearing to some, frightening to others. However, gender per se has never been of primary importance to Morits; although many of her texts might likely support feminist theories of literature, she does not focus on gender problems explicitly and rarely juxtaposes women to men in a collectivist view.

Many poems of Iunna Morits are characterized by a dancelike rhythm. At early stages of her career, the traditional iambic tetrameter—the most popular meter in Russian literature—seemed to have been her preferred meter, but in later years she experimented a great deal with the riches of Russian prosody. Morits's best poems are distinguished by an impressive beginning. Typically, a melodious line or a strikingly original image sets the poetic dynamics in motion. In many cases, however, this motion does not persist; rather, as the poem progresses it frequently loses momentum: the well of ideas seems to rapidly dry out, and although the poet obviously tries to force the poetic stream, these efforts are noticeable and even unsuccessful. Usually, in the poem's last phase, when the chain of images is drawing to a close, Morits regains her strength and reinforces her initially high tonality. Mainly as an echo to the beginning, the conclusion leads to a logical, albeit at times somewhat commonplace statement. Nevertheless, the experience of fading energies following an outstanding introduction remains in much of Morits's poetry. It seems next to impossible to identify the roots of this block, which weakens the artistic impact of such poems. With partial success, Morits attempted to overcome the block with her turn in later years to the archaic, often deriving motifs from myth, mainly classical Greek and Roman.

Of major influence on her poetry was the celebrated Anna Akhmatova, whom Morits met in person in the 1960s. Some critics also discerned traces of Pasternak's guiding hand; still, Morits herself maintains that it was not individuals but entire epochs such as the Baroque that attracted her.[5] Be this as it may, Morits is certainly a poet who is conscious of cultural strata and alludes to them frequently. The effects of these allusions vary. On the one hand, they enrich the semantic field of lexical groups employed in a poem; on the other hand, they at times fail to evoke a response in the reader since the mythological points of reference are deliberately obscured. Indeed, many of Morits's poems radiate a peculiar sense of exclusiveness, and even chosenness—an almost aggressive defense of her uniqueness, of belonging to an elitist circle that is inaccessible, especially to the "successful," visible socialite-poets. Several of Morits's poems are devoted to her disassociating herself from "official geniuses." The image of the "third eye" that gave the title to her collection of poetry (*Tretii glaz*, 1980) conveys just this—a special kind of vision accessible to this poet alone and restricted to others. Such an exclusiveness comes somewhat unexpectedly, considering Morits's emphasis on egalitarianism and a down-to-earth spirit, which together form another strong source of themes and images in her poetry. As exclaimed in one of her best poems, she wants to write "about life, about life! / And only about life!" (1977). Some of the images that Morits employs in her "earthy" texts are deliberately crude and even repulsive in their physicality, and in her lexical choices, she consciously lowers the stylistic level, in some cases to a shocking effect. At least verbally, Morits pledges to reach extremes, avoiding lukewarm emotions, neutrality and blandness. But overall, these statements remain in the verbal realm; Morits's poetry hardly ever reaches a degree of passion in which rational mechanisms of control and observation are forgotten or overcome.

Some of Morits's poems contain descriptions of beautiful landscapes and cityscapes, for example, "A Thunderstorm in the Country" ("Derevenskaia groza," 1974), and even though Morits claims that all seasons seem equally appealing to her, she is at her best when describing winter. The color white generally plays an important role in Morits's imagery, signifying snow and milk, diapers and clouds, purity and innocence, but also an emptiness that at times may be overwhelming. In striving to capture moods of nature in rural and urban settings at their most picturesque, Morits continues a tradition of nineteenth-century Russian poetry. The same holds true for her imitations of folklore, which count for some of her most beautiful poetic discoveries.

With respect to political topics, most of the poems published before 1985 are thematically harmless, mild in their mood and message, and rarely Aesopian. As a matter of fact, the Aesopian mode—a now outdated way of circumspect hinting at lamentable conditions in the Soviet Union—could not but be alien to Morits, since she rarely mentions society at all, instead praising life as a whole in its elementary power. Moreover, her temperament is a straightforward one; she is not a tactician who takes pride in playing games with the system. Rather, her "subjects are the hopes and memories of the intimate minds."[6]

Peter Rollberg

One Time When We Were Feeling Hunger . . .

One time when we were feeling hunger
—An autumn night, an hour of rain—

We tried to dine on apple lunar:
Those heavenly branches we did not disdain.

From out the depths of nests so tender
A flock of wild-grown stars did flutter,
And bushes black of berries black
Were much too sweet and much too thick.

Their black juice as it trickled down
Was sweeter than fame and thicker than days:
It fell upon the eaves breast-down
Above an abyss all full of flames.

And in the folds of the veils of haze,
There on horses amidst cloudy skies
Did sit a kindergarten with wings,
Intently gazing at natural things.

A kindergarten with wings there seated
Before the enigmatic gates
Where ripening, spirituality's limits
Was offering them fruits and then more fruits!

The fruity aroma of the planets
Embraced so thickly every meaning
That beyond the "yes" and the "no" a third sense
Seemed to be lying in between them.

It was cool, all fresh and hard,
With power within of seeds so dark,
Cut right in half by the rainfall,
Slicing a border, a shining band.

We tried to dine on apple lunar:
Those heavenly branches we did not disdain
—An autumn night, an hour of rain—
A time when we were feeling hunger.

To My Son

Put this stone in some other place now—
Into water all gold!
Into mud thick and sticky, like dough—
So into freedom to go.

Let it go—this stone—let it be free,
That it live as it will,
That it go swimming out in blue sea,
Out into night-storm to roll.

And if some huge wave on the shore
This stone then should hurl
Just put the stone back in once more
And thus save its soul!

Place it past the threshhold of waves,
Among finny fish,
And you'll be a bright god who saves,
Meeting at least this stone's wish.

Translated by Jonathan Chaves

Notes to the Essay

1. Elaine Feinstein, *Three Russian Poets* (Manchester, 1979), 12.
2. Evelyn Bristol, *History of Russian Poetry* (New York: Oxford University Press, 1991), 301.
3. Published in *Vremia i my* 105 (1989): 89–99.
4. Catriona Kelly, *A History of Russian Women's Writing 1820–1992* (Oxford: Clarendon, 1994), 355.
5. Feinstein, *Three Russian Poets,* 12.
6. Bristol, *History of Russian Poetry,* 304.

Bibliography

Primary Works

Razgovor o schast'e. Kiev, 1957.
Mys zhelaniia. Moscow, 1961.
"Stikhotvoreniia." *Iunost'* 2 (1963).

"Stikhotvoreniia." *Iunost'* 8 (1966).

Schastlivyi zhuk. Moscow, 1969.

Loza. Kniga stikhov, 1962–1969. Moscow, 1970.

Surovoi nit'iu. Moscow, 1974.

Malinovaia koshka. Moscow, 1976.

Pri svete zhizni. Moscow, 1977.

Poprygat'—poigrat'. Moscow, 1978.

Tretii glaz. Moscow, 1980.

Izbrannoe. Moscow, 1982.

Zakhodite v gosti! Moscow, 1982.

Sinii ogon'. Moscow, 1985.

Domik s truboi. Moscow, 1986.

Na ètom berege vysokom. Moscow, 1987.

Muskul vody. Moscow, 1990.

Translations by Iunna Morits

Teif, M. *Rukopozhatie*. Moscow, 1964.

Alieva, F. *Nastoiashchii muzhchina*. Moscow, 1967.

Alieva, F. *Kover*. Moscow, 1968.

Shestalov, Iu. *Skazka o bobrenke*. Sverdlovsk, 1969.

Al'ver, B. *Zvezdnyi chas*. Moscow, 1973.

Niit, E. *Vymyshliandiia*. Tallinn, 1980.

Gegechkori, G. *Probuzhdenie ptits*. Moscow, 1981.

Sevan, G. *Kot-kotofei*. Erevan, 1982.

In Translation

"The Birth of a Wing." *Russian Literature Triquarterly* 9 (1974): 39.

"It Drizzled." *Russian Literature Triquarterly* 9 (1974): 40.

"An Aphrodite Incident." *Soviet Literature* 3 (1975), 132.

[Selected poems]. *Russian Poetry: The Modern Period*. Ed. John Glad and Daniel Weissbort. Iowa, 1978. 239–42.

[Selected poems]. *Three Russian Poets*. By Elaine Feinstein. Manchester, 1979. New York, 1979.

[Selected poems]. *Contemporary Russian Poetry*. Trans. G. S. Smith. Bloomington: Indiana University Press, 1993. 138–55.

Secondary Works

Bank, Natalia. "Yunna Morits' *Vine*." *Soviet Literature* 7 (1971): 186–89.

Chudakova, M. "Morits, Iunna Petrovna." *Kratkaia Literaturnaia Èntsiklopediia*. Vol. 4. Moscow, 1967. 978.

Feinstein, Elaine. *Three Russian Poets*. Manchester, 1979; New York, 1979.

Ionov, E., and S. Kolov. *Pisateli Moskvy*. Moscow, 1987.

Isbakh, Aleksandr. *Oktiabr'* 8 (1962).

Kelly, Catriona. *A History of Russian Women's Writing 1820–1992*. Oxford: Clarendon Press, 1994.

Marchenko, A. "Kontury mechty." *Literaturnaia gazeta*, 13 November 1962.

Naumov, E. "Za poliarnym krugom." *Zvezda* 5 (1963): 5.

Novikov, Vl. "Golos—O stikhakh Iunny Morits." *Oktiabr'* 10 (1988): 10.

Runin, B. "Poèziia vysokikh shirot." *Den' poezii*. Moscow, 1962.

Tomei, Christine. "Yunna Pinkhusovna (Petrovna) Morits." *An Encyclopedia of Continental Women Writers*. Vol. 2. Ed. K. Wilson. New York, 1991. 876.

Ueland, Carol. "Morits, Iunna Petrovna." *Dictionary of Russian Women Writers*. Ed. M Ledkovsky, C. Rosenthal and M. Zirin. Westport, CT: Greenwood Press, 1994. 441–43.

Marina Palei

Marina Palei (b. 1955). Photo by Miki Vuckovich. Courtesy of Justyna Beinek.

Marina Anatol'evna Palei (née Spivak, b. 1955) was born in Leningrad to twenty-year-old Jewish parents who had met in an amateur theater group in Ukraine and come to Leningrad in order to study engineering. After her parents divorced in her early school years, Palei followed the complicated trajectory of her mother's life: she attended schools in Leningrad, Gur'ev (Kazakstan), Kuibyshev and Togliatti (the Volga region), Novochebaksarsk (the Chuvash republic) and in Kiev (Ukraine), sometimes living in as many as twelve different apartments a year. She spent summer and winter vacations in pioneer camps; this experience Palei jokingly compares to the way Emily Dickinson—a recluse par excellence—would feel if she were sent to a pioneer camp by her parents.[1] In between the constant travels, Palei occasionally visited Vsevolozhsk, a small town near Leningrad where her maternal grandparents lived and where Palei had spent her preschool years. She eventually came back to live with her grandparents in her teens and graduated from high school at the nearby town of Mel'nichnyi Ruchei. Her tempestuous childhood, early artistic inclinations combined with a passion for reading, and various encounters with anti-Semitism deeply influenced her early sense of identity. Palei characterizes her growing up in terms of constant psychological and material instability, stemming from frequent, unexpected moves among dozens of communal apartments and workers' dormitories, where she was often without any parental supervision. In contrast to her life on the road with her mother, her grandparents' wooden house in the forests surrounding Vsevolozhsk seemed a real home and was later described as such in the autobiographical novella "Remembrance of the Dead" ("Pominovenie," 1990).

At seventeen, Palei settled in Leningrad and started studying medicine. Medicine was a field that strongly attracted Palei; her interest in the human body is clearly expressed in many of her literary works, especially in the cycle of stories *The Day of Poplar Down* (*Den' topolinogo pukha*) and the novellas "Evgesha and Annushka" ("Evgesha i Annushka," 1990) and "Kabiria from the Obvodnyi Canal" ("Kabiriia s Obvodnogo kanala," 1991). However, her choice of the minor Institute of Medicine at the Mechnikov hospital and her choice of specialization—epidemiology—were largely dictated by Palei's ethnicity, class and lack of "proper" political involvement. A brilliant student, Palei briefly married, had a son while graduating from medical school (1978) and started a desperate two-year job search, having miraculously avoided compulsory assignment to a remote job site, the usual fate of single mothers like herself. Eventually, she got a job as a model at the Mukhina Fine Arts Institute in Leningrad. A few short-term jobs in the medical profession followed; at those times Palei also supported her family by after-hours analysis of gonorrhea samples at home and by working nights as a cleaning woman at hospitals and a beauty salon. Palei's experiences at various hospitals supplied her with rich and appalling material to draw on in her fiction, mainly in the cycle *The Day of Poplar Down*.

In her mid-twenties, Palei joined an amateur theater group, an experience she likens to psychotherapy. As she says, thanks to performing in monodramas based on the works of Maupassant, O'Henry, Tsvetaeva and Maurois, Palei "began to understand what the *word* means." In the fall of 1983, Palei suffered a nervous breakdown. In January 1984, she started writing poetry and made up her mind to take up the job of a watchperson, a decision she sees as characteristic for the "generation of janitors and watchmen" to which she says she belongs. In the same year, Palei's mother put her in touch with an old friend, Irina Rodnianskaia—an editor at *New World* (*Novyi mir*)—with whom Palei began an informal correspondence that soon turned to literary subjects. Rodnianskaia hailed Palei's ideas on literature as the work of a "natural" and encouraged her to apply to the highly competitive Gorky Literary Institute in Moscow. Palei passed the competition with flying colors, having submitted essays on the works of Vladimir Makanin and Goderdzi Chokheli, and she began the six-year nonresidential program as one of five students in the division of literary criticism, while still working as a watchperson in Leningrad. She participated in the seminars led by Evgenii Sidorov and Andrei Bitov, and, paradoxically, it was in Sidorov's course on criticism that she "officially" started writing fiction. In 1987 she decided to stop working as a watchperson and has been trying to live on royalties ever since, with the exception of brief jobs as an editor and a boiler stoker, which supported her at the worst times. While studying at the Literary Institute, Palei became active in the dissident movement, and in 1988 she joined the independent party Democratic Union (Demokraticheskii soiuz), which resulted in investigation and harassment by the KGB. Palei graduated with honors in 1991 and was invited to join the Writers' Union. Palei considers her training at the Literary Institute extremely important in her development as a writer: it gave her confidence in her writing abilities, it exposed her to the writing of the best contemporary Russian writers and critics, it gave her access to the professional literary milieu, it put her in the middle of the cultural and political makings of *perestroika* and it provided her with necessary material help.

Palei underscores the fact that she was one of only five women in her class of eighty students. According to Palei, being a woman and a Jew has always been a handicap in her careers as a doctor and a writer in Russia, despite her superb achievements. Even though she does not define herself as a feminist and resents being perceived as a "woman writer," she strongly objects to the stereotypical roles imposed on Russian women and internalized by them. Palei deeply believes in professionalism in writing, by which she means the writer's simultaneous balancing of control and involvement in her material and language; she likes to quote

Tsvetaeva's statement that a poet is an "equilibrium of soul and word." Each phrase should be stylistically perfect; an obsessive attention to detail is a must for a serious writer. Therefore, she is often disappointed that her prose attracts readers and scholars for reasons other than its literary merits: she objects to being lumped with other women writers solely on the basis of her gender. Nonetheless, critics have frequently analyzed Palei's writing in the context of other contemporary Russian women's fiction. Palei's works, especially the best known "Evgesha and Annushka," "Kabiria from the Obvodnyi Canal" and the cycle *The Day of Poplar Down*, display the concern with human physiology that characterizes Liudmila Petrushevskaia's works; emphasis on the insignificant people—the old, children and the retarded—and on the fantastic, both of which are present in many of Tat'iana Tolstaia's short stories: and a strong interest in the everyday details of Soviet life, which have become a hallmark of contemporary writers such as Tolstaia, Petrushevskaia and Nina Sadur.

Although Marina Palei has been writing prose fiction since the mid-1980s, her first publications were critical articles solicited by the leading literary journals. Palei's fascination with the figure of long-overlooked poet Mariia Petrovykh (1908–1979) inspired her first article, "Your Inconceivable Purity . . ." ("Tvoia nemyslimaia chistota . . . ," 1987), in which Palei analyzes Petrovykh's self-representation as sketched out in her verse. She speculates about reasons for Petrovykh's obliteration from literary history and effectively reintroduces Petrovykh as a superb poet and as more than a translator and a love object of Osip Mandel'shtam, the way Petrovykh has traditionally been mentioned. Palei's two 1988 review articles, "A Little Figure in the Naked Field" ("Figurka na ogolennom pole") about the prose of Georgii Kalinin, and "Let the Door Be Open . . ." ("Pust' budet dver' otkryta . . .") on the poetry of Vladimir Retsepter, appeared in the journals *New World* (*Novyi mir*) and *Literary Review* (*Literaturnoe obozrenie*), respectively. In 1989 Palei faced the challenge of critiquing a book of verse by Tat'iana Galushko, a poet and a Pushkin scholar, who had died in 1988. In her article "The Imprint of Flame" ("Otpechatok ognia," 1989), Palei compares Galushko's life and creation to those of Petrovykh and Tsvetaeva, thus continuing her exploration of the issue of how one becomes a woman poet and how that process is refracted in a poet's works.

Marina Palei first tried her hand at writing short stories in the mid-1980s; the two stories "A Stroll" ("Progulka") and "The Institute of Revenge" ("Institut mesti"), which had been among Palei's first literary endeavors, were later included in her first collection of stories, *The Lost Souls' Division* (*Otdelenie propashchikh*; Moscow, 1991). "The Institute of Revenge" reflects an absurdist vein in Palei's poetics: it is a story of a sensitive, young woman, Linda Glenn, who rather indecisively seeks help at an Orwell-like Institute of Revenge. The setting is both humorous (the institute is located in the same building as a toy store) and threateningly realistic; oblique references to the Soviet version of Orwell's universe (also present in the story "The Day of the Empire" ("Den' imperii," 1993), are a perfect backdrop for the presentation of the protagonist's sense of estrangement. The story is a black-humor treatment of the theme of vengeance as a computerized, institutionalized process. It depicts seriously, however, the young woman who grapples with conflicting emotions of love, a sense of betrayal and a desire for revenge, which eventually bring her to suicide. "The Institute of Revenge" is also the first story in which Palei introduces one of her favorite motifs, that of a double.

In the other early story, "A Stroll," Palei constructs a collage of fragments of dialogues carried on by a pair of lovers as they walk together and later engage in phone conversations. The story, almost devoid of narrativity, is technically superb; it involves the reader in the process of "overhearing" the conversations and the phone calls between Oleg and Liuba, successfully obfuscating the line between the world of the story and the "real" world of readers/listeners.

Three stories that form the cycle *The Toy Factory* (*Fabrika igrushek*) are Palei's further exercises in the absurd. The oneiric "The Elevator" ("Lift") and "Lacrymosa" focus on improbable events in the lives of "small men." In the former story, a certain Erich Schmit, who suffers from a phobia of entering elevators, gets trapped one day in an elevator that endlessly travels down, stops, and continues its ride up. The protagonist is caught in a point beyond time and space; his greatest fear is materialized in a way that surpasses perhaps his own worst fears. In "Lacrymosa," another foreign-named hero, Mr. Van der Beidenhoff, an inhabitant of an eerie, cemetery-like landscape, writes a treatise whose letters disappear as soon as they are written, except for the very last one on each sheet, thus producing many white pages, with one letter crowning the end of each page. Although the piece reads superficially like an amusing horror story, it also invites interpretation as a metaliterary text.

The third story from the cycle *The Toy Factory,* "The Date" ("Svidanie"), explores the close-range contact between a pair of lovers in a way reminiscent of the early story "A Stroll" and later "Abraham" ("Abragam") and "The Railway Blues" ("Magistral'nyi bliuz"). "The Date" records the minutest details of a male lover's reactions and reflections before, during and after a date. Written entirely from the male lover's perspective, the story becomes a parody of his objectifying gaze and of male writing from the female point of view in general. By zeroing in on separate details of the woman's body in terms of western European painting, the man is exposed as a cynical voyeur who does a mental dissection of his beloved. The male observer's own reactions fill up the story's entire perspective, and, as a consequence, the woman has hardly any presence at all: her space in the story is limited to a request for tea, contrasted with his demands for her compatibility with women painted by Leonardo, Rubens, Monet, Picasso and many others. The self-absorbed male lover, having turned the woman into a collage of different body parts, remains enclosed in his egotistical, solipsistic world.

An altogether different brand of the grotesque and the absurd, as compared to Palei's cycle *The Toy Factory*, shapes the cycle *The Day of Poplar Down*. Drawn from experience during Palei's 1976 student summer practice in a provincial hospital in the Russian northwest and her subsequent work in the medical profession, the four stories in this cycle focus as much on the immediate detail of the Soviet hospital system as on the existential dimension of the simultaneous fleetingness and "obstinacy" of human life, which can persevere even under the least conducive circumstances. As Palei remarks in her introduction to the cycle, her aim is not to shock her readers with the realia of Soviet health care but rather to show a hospital as a liminal space, "a place of transition," where life and death converge. Her intent is to write about "the undefeatable defenselessness of life," a motif that reappears in many of her works, most notably in the later novellas "Evgesha and Annushka" and "Kabiria from the Obvodnyi Canal."

Three of the cycle's stories are told from the perspective of a female student of medicine (she is also a supporting character in the fourth story, "The Lost Souls' Division" ("Otdelenie propashchikh"); these are stories of her initation into the cruel or simply indifferent practices of hospital personnel and of her inability to fit into this system. The young woman's estrangement puts her frequently in a position to be a more humane helper for the patients. For example, in "The Day of Poplar Down," she tries to rub a dying woman's feet and gets ridiculed by a doctor; in "The Lost Souls' Division," the student becomes a silent collaborator in the slow murder of a deformed infant by following the doctor's order not to give him liquids; in "Tales of Andersen" ("Skazki Andersena") she is painfully aware of her own hypocrisy when she completes her assignment, a practice diary that is full of gaps, information that she knows she should withhold. The death of a newborn ("Tales of Andersen" and "The Lost Souls' Division") and the death of a young woman ("The Day of Poplar Down") are the events that allow Palei to concentrate on the fluidity of life and death. In these stories, life is presented as a primordial force that cannot be distinguished from death: a deformed newborn does not die despite the doctors' efforts to kill him by dehydration, and his fifty-year-old mother keeps on getting pregnant despite her own shame and the laws of nature ("The Lost Souls' Division").

"Tales of Andersen" and "The Lost Souls' Division" are stories set in an obstetrics ward, a perfect place for medical and philosophical investigation of the indivisibility of life and death. Nonetheless, this choice of location and the narrative lens—a female student of medicine—form a specifically female universe in these stories, which revolve around the motif of a woman's body as the site of cyclical, endless conceptions, abortions, diseases and births as much as of beauty, love and a determination to live. Abortion especially interests Palei as a moment in which life and death meet—that is where she starts her literary search for the nexus of the bodily and the spiritual. According to Palei, being a doctor gave her a knowledge of the body and matter, hence her fascination with the ephemerality of the entity called the soul.

The novella "Remembrance of the Dead" ("Pominovenie"), originally called "A Prayer about Home" ("Molenie o dome"), is Palei's most explicitly autobiographical prose work. Written in 1986–1987 and at first rejected for publication, it opens Palei's first collection, *The Lost Souls' Division*. The novella, full of unforgettable portraits of family members, such as a great-grandmother surreptitiously smoking Belomor cigarettes, is not only a literary transposition of Palei's childhood and adolescence and a remembrance of the family house in Vsevolozhsk (which in "real" life was sold in 1981), but also a consciously autobiographical statement, crucial for her other work. As Palei has remarked, she sees all of her writing as growing out of what Nabokov called a "hypertrophied nostalgia for childhood." "Remembrance of the Dead" fully refracts that nostalgia, and it also serves as a prelude to Palei's later works, such as "Kabiria from the Obvodnyi Canal," which speak of childlike happiness and childish lightheartedness as the only way out of life's squalor. The novella explains the underlying despair in Palei's fiction: it is in "Remembrance of the Dead" that the child learns that she can "fear the fear": this knowledge of metafear, combined with a fairy-tale-like sensation of the world, permeates Palei's literary universe.

Palei entered the literary scene and sealed her position as one of the most promising prose writers of the *glasnost'* period within just two years. In 1990 her novella "Evgesha and Annushka" riveted critics' and readers' attention, and so did her first book, *The Lost Souls' Division*, which appeared in 1991, the same year Palei graduated from the Literary Institute. By publishing "Kabiria from the Obvodnyi Canal" in early 1992, Palei definitively asserted her place in the critical spotlight. Several of her stories have been translated into English, German, Slovak, Swedish and Dutch; French, Italian and Polish translations are in the works. Since 1992 Palei has lectured and read her prose at universities and festivals in Sweden, Germany, the Netherlands and Italy. In 1995 she was a writer-in-residence at the prestigious Bellagio Center in Italy, having received a grant from the Rockefeller Foundation; her future plans include professional visits to Great Britain and the United States.

Differences notwithstanding, Palei's two best works so far, "Evgesha and Annushka" and "Kabiria from the Obvodnyi Canal," share a deeply compassionate first-person female narrator who unfolds haunting stories of Leningrad's marginal citizens: two old *babushki*, the eponymous heroines of the former novella and, in the latter, Mon'ka, a wildflower of the demi-monde, eternally tipsy and amorous, never loosening her grip on love and life. Bone-chilling in their depiction of sickness and dying, both novellas focus on the enigma of the inexorable, circular mechanism of human life. Yet they also transgress the general theme of inescapability from material existence; they pay tribute to the insignificant old women by memorializing the minutest details of their lives: Mon'ka's sordid underwear, the carrot-colored lipstick she puts on even when she is dying, and Annushka's chamberpot and a jug of drinking water, whose levels of liquids are always in inverse proportion to each other.

In "Evgesha and Annushka," a student, Irina, takes the reader on a journey through the communal apartment she shares with two old, poor women: energetic, opinionated and self-righteous Evgesha and slightly older, senile and self-effacing Annushka. Palei describes these two heroines as "an inseparable pair of antipodes": for her, they symbolize the dichotomy of the active and the passive principles in the world. In her unpublished critical annotation to the novella, Palei confesses that she strove to create characters who would echo Gogol's Akakii Akakievich, not so much in material poverty as in existential misery. Palei points to the conscious plotlessness of "Evgesha and Annushka" as a stylistic quality that augments the depiction of the everyday, monotonous life of the two aging women. Palei says she wanted to approximate "the blunt, static metaphysics" of the eventless existence that is not limited to the two women but is, to a certain extent, everyone's lot.

"Kabiria from the Obvodnyi Canal" also focuses on the impossibility of exiting from the cycle of life, yet from an entirely different perspective. The narrative is spun by a young woman who in the course of events becomes a doctor. She tells the life story of her cousin, Raimonda Rybnaia, or Mon'ka, who is ten years her senior and who functions in the text as her sister and double. Mon'ka's love affairs, drinking bouts and bartending jobs at various train stations and low-profile joints rapidly change in a kaleidoscopic manner, and gradually give way to her sickness, hospitalizations and death from cancer. Despite the terrible wasting of her body, Mon'ka never stops being the effervescent, airheaded and hyperlibidinal teenager she once was: her interest in men, aphrodisiacs, flirting, her sexual prowess and application of large amounts of makeup do not abandon her, even at her deathbed. Palei says that she meant Mon'ka to be an "eternal adolescent" who defies death with her eternal vitality, childish trust and love freely offered; Mon'ka is a "new positive heroine," perhaps the only one who can remain sane, happy and life-loving while living on the Obvodnyi Canal, Palei's literal and symbolic space of extreme poverty, death and despair.

The gallery of Mon'ka's artistic prototypes (the real-life ones Palei had closely at hand) includes not only such adolescents as Salinger's Holden Caulfield and Nabokov's Lolita, but first and foremost Cabiria, the ebullient, cheerful, yet pitiful prostitute from Federico Fellini's film *The Nights of Cabiria* (1957). Palei, who admits having been awestruck as a teenager by Giulietta Masina's performance as Cabiria, points to the great influence of Fellini's cinema on her development as a writer and on her novella. Palei locates her Soviet heroine, Mon'ka, in the same register as Rome's Cabiria; Palei says that she owes Fellini's film the fact that she saw Cabirias living right around her in Leningrad's seedy neighborhoods. Also, according to the writer, Fellini awoke in her a profound interest in the genre of tragicomedy, which had never been popular in Russian literature; she describes an acute realization of what she terms the "Fellinization of space," a sense of game and theatricality, and of the inherent "artistry" (*artistichnost'*) of Soviet life.

In two recent stories, "The Flight" ("Reis," 1993) and "The Birthplace of the Wind" ("Mestorozhdenie vetra," 1994), Palei finds new forms for literary expression, quite different from her best-known works, such as "Evgesha and Annushka," "Kabiria from the Obvodnyi Canal" and the cycle *The Day of Poplar Down*, which were written in a "realistic" mode (although Palei's brand of realism is always slightly skewed, leaning toward the hyper- and sur- varieties). "The Flight" continues the vein of lyrical love prose in Palei's writing, whose beginnings can be seen in the early stories such as "A Stroll" ("Progulka") or "The Curve" ("Virazh"), alternatively entitled "Composition in Red and Blue" ("Kompozitsiia na krasnom i sinem"). "The Flight" is a powerful invocation, a love song in prose; here Palei is at her lyrical best, dazzling readers with her poetic imagination. At the same time, the story continues the playful and the absurdist vein of Palei's fiction: "The Flight" involves a woman who, in full disguise—a wig, makeup, glasses—takes an intercontinental flight to Canada in order to spend a few hours in the proximity of her ex-lover, who is on that plane and whom she misses terribly. Unrecognized, she observes the man during the flight and silently addresses him, remembering the story of their love.

The most recent story, "Birthplace of the Wind" ("Mestorozhdenie vetra," 1994), is a more mature exploration of the absurdist humor of the earlier cycle *The Toy Factory*. The word "bicycle" in a crossword puzzle is a starting point for meandering through the life of an old man who had always dreamed of learning how to ride a bike. But in the dreamlike universe of the story, bicycles defy his efforts to make his dream come true: they become animated—giggle and take off, leaving the man behind, or throw him off their backs, similar to the answering machines that have lives of their own in the cycle of stories *From the Life of Answering Machines* (*Iz zhizni avtootvetchikov*, 1993). At the end of his long life, interspersed with comical sessions with a psychiatrist who interprets the man's desire in Freudian terms, the man is finally able to ride (and even fly) his bicycle, helped by a gust of liberating wind.

A mere decade after Marina Palei's first attempts to write fiction professionally and only four years after her debut in book form, it is too early to offer a comprehensive survey of her development as a writer or a critical summary of her *oeuvre*. What is striking at this stage of her career, however, is the fact that she is able to segue from the genre of the absurdist short story to autobiographical prose to a naturalistic rendering of Soviet everyday life, *byt*, to a powerful love poem in prose, to the novels on which she is currently working: the generic and stylistic range of her works is amazing. Palei's flirtation with surrealism and hyperrealism is refreshing; her prose never ceases to reach for the "surplus" of realism, as if the realistic mode could do no justice to the surreal scenery of Soviet life and to the more universal enigma of human existence. Yet it is exactly the precision and sense of humor with which Palei selects the details of her best stories that eventually renders them believable and pleasurable to the reader; she is a perfect guide through Leningrad's communal apartments, hospitals, train stations and the shadowy space of the other bank of the Obvodnyi Canal, a space into which, as she points out—recalling Pushkin's connection to Neva and Moika, Dostoevsky's to Griboedov's canal, and Akhmatova's to Fontanka—no writer of Petersburg or Leningrad has ever ventured. Through her prose, Marina Palei endows the paltry, obscure inhabitants of Obvodnyi's other bank with dignity and she lends distinction to their sick and dying bodies, all the while groping for an answer to the question of what puts them in a perpetual spin.

Justyna Beinek

From Kabiria from the Obvodnyi Canal

When there were no men around—no male voices, no male smell—she would sit with her knees spread apart, wearily picking at her nails.

Her name was Raimonda Rybnaia—in everyday life Mon'ka or Monechka. She picked up the last name from her husband; for the first one she was indebted to her mother, my aunt, Gertrude Borisovna Faikina. Auntie naturally gravitated toward cute knickknacks, and as a result devotedly dragged along with her from flat to flat (and nailed up first thing in each new place): a portrait of Hemingway; a calendar for August 1962 depicting a half-reclining, jaundiced-looking Japanese girl wearing only her birthday suit; and a two-bit Jesus suffering on his plaster cross. My aunt's other natural predilection was toward lying, for which she had an uncontrollable passion—jaded relatives said that it came as easily to her as breathing. As a result of this weakness, the moving tale was born that she had chosen her daughter's name solely in memory of her brother Roman, who was killed on the front lines. (Each time she told it, Auntie would punctuate the story with carefully placed, pregnant pauses.) The legend was marred by one small flaw, however. The thing was, Gertrude Borisovna had a son, who also came into the world after his heroic uncle's death and, for that matter, before the birth of Monechka. For him she had sifted through the entire alphabet, from Askold (Asik for short) to Erasmus (Erik for short), finally settling on Cornelius. "Nelik" later became a policeman.

And here's a photograph—in it Mon'ka is around fourteen, and I, correspondingly, around four. We're standing by a snow-covered spruce tree near our grandparents' house. Mon'ka has an ample forehead, dimpled cheeks and flaunting, brazen—no, already thoroughly *dissolute*—eyes. I come up to her waist, and with my severe expression look a lot like an obstinate little old lady who has all the answers.

From its scattered myriad memory fragments the river of oblivion for some reason always brings back one in particular, where Gertrude Borisovna is getting Mon'ka ready for camp. Auntie is standing in the kitchen, hurriedly stuffing her ruby-colored beet salad into an empty jam jar with a wooden spoon. With just the right air of resignation, very loudly (a good thing the neighbors are gone), she yells all the way across the communal apartment to her daughter:

"And don't you forget! When I was sixteen *I* had just one drink, and it's thanks to that drink that Nelik came along!"

But Mon'ka is already flying, her little veneer-coated suitcase in hand, along the bank of the Obvodnyi Canal.

She's running, smiling, doing a little dance, the hem of her skirt, as always, way above the mean—Mon'ka never changes, she'll always be fourteen. The only things that do change are the posters and slogans, which I can barely make out through the veil of time, dirt, bluish exhaust and factory smoke: there's a man in a heavy space suit gesturing over Mon'ka like a Roman conqueror, a gesture repeated by a medal-laden grandfather with eyebrows as thick as his mustache. Mon'ka's running, smiling, doing a little dance, the lines on her chart climbing steadily up, road signs flash by, the canal laboriously forces its murky waters on to God knows where. . . . And she's running, smiling, doing a little dance. . . . A perfect youth is showing off his perfect white teeth, and there's the 1980 Olympic mascot already, a bear buoyed up above a sea of headdresses and plump loaves of black bread, painstakingly mimicking the gesture of cosmonaut, grandfather, youth. And Mon'ka's running, smiling, doing a little dance . . . A red wooden fence stretches, monotonous, along the roadside: XXVI XXVII XXVIII. . . . Mon'ka grabs a small twig without stopping and makes loud thwack-thwack-thwack! sounds against the slats. This parapet ends suddenly, and the level, unusually deserted bank entices her down to the cloudy water. She stares rapt into her dissolving reflection. . . . The sudden splash of a lone oar is especially distinct in this thick silence. "For a price," the rower demands with his hands. She dashes to her suitcase. Up surges a fountain of green stockings patched with blue, a red skirt with a safety pin for a fastener, tank tops, a compact, an overwashed bra with one strap torn off, a loud, parrot-green blouse covered with triangular iron marks, a silk scarf, a pair of worn-out boots, a pilling brown wool dress; waving her arms about, Mon'ka displays the dark semicircles under them . . . "Forget it," the rower says without words. She pouts her lips to form an indignant little piccolo . . . her perplexed look fades evenly into a languid one, then a naughty one, then a coy one, and ends as a look of unabashed invitation. She giggles playfully and gives him a smile. The rower is old and doesn't move. Beaming, she squints her eyes where little blue devils are dancing in frenzied squadrons, and, shielding one side of her mouth with her palm, whispers a thing or two to him, I can't hear what. The rower starts to chuckle, he laughs for a long time, as if relieved by something: the first time in a lifetime of repetitive, joyless labor. His loud laughter cuts into the dark carcass of the evening, and the sun, scandalously breaking the laws of the universe, abruptly starts moving backwards, up into the sky, illuminating for a split second the rapidly flowing water. "That'll do," the ferryman answers buoyantly. He even looks a little younger.

* * *

Someone is sitting on a high chair with one end of a plumbing hose stuck into her belly; out the other something is pouring into a garbage pail. The eyes, detached from belly and hose, look down at this torrent of liquid that was part of the earth, then her body, as it returns to its source, bringing its former owner short-lived relief from her pain and promising to make her little world habitable again. Birdsong in some secret way connected with the blotches of light in a dense forest, the smell of a river and fish, the deep blue scream of cornflowers, poems dissolved in blood, a glance from the woman who always smelled like cherry blossoms after a rain, and, finally, the bolt of lightning, a flourish out of Michelangelo, that instantaneous lesson in the relativity of magnitude, and in absolute magnitude: all these the person soaked up, subsumed into her flesh, made herself. But a star in heaven tripped up, and one cell in a human body, fracturing suddenly, answered in its turn: one star out of thousands of stars, one cell out of billions, and there you are, life is flowing out of her body in this murky swill, there's no stanching it or slowing it down, and what of it? There's no need to anyway. What was word and light, what was called a person is now flowing into a garbage pail. So what makes a person herself? A pail? A hose?

The nurse carries them off.

* * *

It can't be! It can't be! You'll be happy again before your light goes out!

You'll be happy again because your Fedia will make a scene with the neighbors, he'll pick up their color TV in the heat of the moment then release his grip, for that they'll take him off to jail, the prospect of a three-year sentence looming on the horizon, and you'll be happy, because you'll come over to my place and, giving in to your insomnia, you'll keep telling me how much you love him, what a soft, delicate body he has, it smells just like a baby's. . . . And your body will again be like it was before the operation, just as though the operation never happened, because recovery had been guaranteed only given a reformed lifestyle—the kind of life you never lived. And you'll sit there silently, like a madwoman, gutting cheap cigarettes, one after another, ten packs of them, shaking the tobacco into a little chintz pouch (why, that's the only way you can get it to someone in jail!) and I'll call you two ambulances, one after another, since even your handfuls of medicines, drunk down with vodka and tears, are powerless to iron out the rough fabric of your life. . . . Again your enormous liver will be tearing your defenseless stomach to pieces, your heart, spluttering, will be cracking your tough ribs, and you'll painstakingly dig out the contents of each cigarette, one after another, in silence, defiantly, not so easy for your stubby little fingers with their nails bitten down to the quick, and when the second ambulance pulls away you'll follow it from the window with your sky-blue eyes, then you'll crawl off to Crosses jail to give Fedia his tobacco, and you'll be happy because I'll tell you that if you were officially married your angel Fedia's sentence would be reduced, since his file would show him having on his hands a chronically ill, incapacitated wife who has to eat. . . . And you'll come over soon afterward, with a hairstyle that defies belief and an enigmatic look on your face, and you'll let it drop right there, that you got mare-reed!—that's right!—that everything was just like in a real church, and that a lady in a long dress asked the bride and groom if they did, then congratulated them—look at the ring!—that Fedia was wearing a cute white shirt, just like it should be, that now they'll let him out in three months, and that now your last name is Ivanova!

And later, only later when I see you lying in your coffin—that is, when I don't see you in your coffin, since that frightful doll with its alien, defeated grimace of pain will look the age dead flesh dares to look only in the shut coffin, the grisly marks of decay showing through perfunctorily applied stage makeup—that hideous, bloated corpse spoiling, thanks to the spring heat and the carelessness of the morgue staff, that altogether unrecognizable, rotting specter, dressed up in your clothes as though to ape you better for some barbaric rite, will have so little relation to you that I will take a calm, deep breath from the window through whose two open panes your soul, freed forever, will have just flown happily skyward, and a kind of triumphant, heartrending joy will catch me on the crest of its limpid, sturdy wave.

What could be more apt than the church texts and their *resurrected from the dead, vanquishing death by death . . .* ? But what about when someone isn't really "resurrected"? I mean, what if the resurrection isn't visible to everyone, if it isn't obvious and out in the open? In that case, let me put it this way: in dying we flout death. We're born at the instant we die. The death day and the birthday are one and the same day.

And vice versa?

Of course. But I have a lot to do before this day ends:

I'll tell how your mother, who of course won't attend your funeral, will with eyes widened just right entertain the guests at the wake with terrible stories about your angel Fedia ("His trade name is Fearless . . . no, Ferocious! It's the honest truth!"), and how at the same time she'll manage, always the perfect hostess, to cast a glance of inspection at the long table laden with food—nothing ever escapes her practical eye—and will call severely to your daughter on the other side of the room, so all the guests will hear, "Have you eaten anything today? You must eat something!" "What about you, Gertrude Borisovna?" the guests will chime in, feigning concern. And Auntie will lower her eyes sadly: "Please! How could I eat another bite? I'm burping, my stomach aches and I'm constipated." And I'll tell how all of a sudden Gleb will show up here, at the wake—or, more accurately, how he'll be brought here, because he'll have gone completely blind by then. Before that he'll have looked for you in vain at the crematorium, asking in his ignorance for Rybnaia instead of Ivanova, will have run his hands along the cold morgue walls and cried bitterly, and, still not finding you, called information for your mother's address (by then she'll be living near the Mariinsky theater). In the foyer he'll extend a bouquet of roses that look as if they're made of pink wax, then slip her a hundred rubles, while groups of sated mourners idle about. Cheerful as ever, Gleb will say twice: "Now we'll all keep in touch through Gertrude Borisovna!" as he looks upward somewhere and smiles radiantly as only blind people do. But he won't go farther than the foyer, and he'll be escorted away by some boy. Kolia Rybnyi, following him with his eyes, will try and fail to hide his unbearable pity for Gleb, and I'll go into the kitchen to find my stupid, sorry aunt sitting all alone devouring a leftover chicken leg.

And still before that, at the crematorium, two women in black scarves I've never seen before will stand around, shifting their weight from foot to foot in anticipation of the sickening procedure—(they'll have a long wait: Cornelius will run off and shove some money into someone's hand, swearing here and there, he'll count up his expenses so that everyone can hear, and his wife of the moment, staking her uxorial claim, will hand him some pills and wipe the sweat from his brow)—and they'll quietly talk between themselves:

"I never got to see that Fedia," one will say. "Too bad—in the hospital Monechka told me he was the living image of Alain Delon!"

Attendants in black will escort from the ceremonial hall a woman flailing about hysterically, an old man will drop the wreath, I'll hear other people's voices in the corridor: "Come on already, it's our turn!" . . . "Idiots! Choosing a hall right next to the bathroom! . . . "

The other will say: "I visited her a day before *all that* happened. She looked so thin lying there, wasn't eating anything. I say to her, 'At least take a bite, Monechka—for your mother and father!' and she goes, 'No, Vera Sergeevna, not for my parents . . . for my little Fedia, on the other hand, I'll eat something!' and gives me a little wink. . . ."

But even before that, you'll wait for me behind the iron fence of the hospital grounds. As soon as I catch sight of you—not yet noticing me, skinny, dressed in some sorry, worn-out overcoat and looking like a teenager straight out of an orphanage—I'll know immediately that I'll remember this moment forever: the iron fence, you behind it. And after that you'll ask me to climb over, but I won't. And we'll carry on a conversation that way, separated by the fence; the gate will be locked. And of course you'll boast that when you take your grandson out on walks all the men tell him how much he looks like his pretty mommy, and that when you tell them you're not his mommy, it takes them a long time to figure out *who* you are.

And before that, before that . . . I'll know already that when I cast my net into the water the first time, it will come up with nothing but seaweed, and when I cast it in a second time, I'll get nothing but silt, and the third time I'll scoop out . . . thin air, and your spirit, freed forever, your crystalline spirit will slip away, away, laughing at me as it goes. And it will always slip away like this, no matter how fine my mesh. And I'll know how at first I'll feel despair, then relief.

I'll know beforehand that even in the long hours when blackness looms in on me and threatens to bury me alive, when stones are being forced down my throat, there will be one clear thought I won't be able to banish: that you want to be a body again.

Of course you're dancing there, in those fields of brilliant daisies. But what are you without your body? What good is that eternal bliss to you? I see a hungry child licking the glass behind which a loaf of bread is displayed, and crying. . . . You're begging plaintively: let me have my arms, my legs, just for a little bit. . . . Why were you whisked away so soon from this children's carnival, with all its fragrant, exotic delights?

And I'll be horrified to realize that you have no use for those sterile fields' sterile bliss. Always just beyond my reach, your spirit stands at heaven's gate and gazes down longingly at the earth, unable to tear itself away. Really, what are you, after all, without your body? A spirit doesn't even have any miserable, bitten-down fingernails to bite down some more and then cover with nail polish! God! I will always feel you pleading for the return of your membrane, your arms, your legs—"just for a little bit."

Then I'll say to you: "What's this slaughterhouse to you? Hasn't your kid's heart had enough?"

It will be easy for me to say these words, because for me they'll be true. But not for you! And then I'll feel like I have no right taking up space here, occupying a body—is it you I stole them from?

Why does every minute of life come so hard to me? Why is there such resistance to my breathing? Every breath I take has its cost. Why does life weigh so heavily on me? And I know it will only get worse. Is it your life I'm living, Mon'ka my sister?

The telephone will ring.

"Hi there!" you'll say. "Did you read what my admirer wrote me? It says: 'Take your time, Monechka. It's not our turn yet to smell the lilac root! Health and happiness,' it says!"

And, not seeing you, I'll see it perfectly clearly: you're smiling, smiling, of course—smiling.

1991

Translated by Brian Thomas Oles

Notes to the Essay

1. Marina Palei's opinions quoted herein come from a series of interviews conducted by Justyna Beinek (St. Petersburg, August 1994).

Bibliography

Primary Works

"Pavlovsk" [poem]. *Istoki* [Moscow] 1 (1987): 343.

"Tvoia nemyslimaia chistota. . . . " *Literaturnoe obozrenie* 6 (1987): 61–64.

"Figurka na ogolennom pole." *Novyi mir* 11 (1988): 245–48.

"Pust' budet dver' otkryta. . . . " *Literaturnoe obozrenie* 2 (1988): 52–54.

[Four poems.] *Nash dom* 10 (1989).

"Lift." *Moskovskii avtotransportnik* 38 (1989).

"Otpechatok ognia." *Literaturnoe obozrenie* 12 (1989): 60–63.

"Kompozitsiia na krasnom i sinem." *Sobesednik* 12 (1989). [Rpt. *Kniga i iskusstvo v SSSR* 1, 64 (1990): 20–22; *Moskovskii avtotransportnik* 43 (1989). Rpt. as "Virazh" in *Otdelenie propashchikh*. Moscow: Moskovskii rabochii, 1991. 212–14.]

"Svidanie." *Moskovskii avtotransportnik* 10 (1989). [Rpt. *Nash dom* 10 (1989).]

"Evgesha i Annushka." *Znamia* 7 (1990): 10–45.

"Pominovenie." [fragment]. *Nash dom* 20 (1990). [Rpt. *Pod'em* 7 (1991): 109–53.]

"Den' topolinogo pukha." *Novye amazonki*. Ed. Svetlana Vasilenko. Moscow: Moskovskii rabochii, 1991. 302–08.

"Den' topolinogo pukha." *Novyi zhurnal* 180 (1991): 5–25.

"Kabiria s Obvodnogo kanala." *Novyi mir* 3 (1991): 47–81.

"Otdelenie propashchikh." *Khronograf-90* [Moscow] (1991): 374–88.

Otdelenie propashchikh. Moscow: Moskovskii rabochii, 1991.

"Priglashenie v leto." *Novyi zhurnal* 180 (1991).

"Rasskazy iz tsikla 'Fabrika igrushek'" ["Lacrymosa," "Svidanie" and "Lift"]. *Literaturnoe obozrenie* 3 (1991): 48–51.

"Skazki Andersena." *Novyi zhurnal* 180 (1991).

"Skazki Andersena." *Moskovskii krug*. Moscow: Moskovskii rabochii, 1991. 204–14.

"Den' imperii." *Zvezda* 7 (1993): 93–102.

"Iz zhizni avtootvetchikov." *Peterburgskii literator* 2 (1993). [Rpt. (fragment) *Vy i my* 7 (1992).]

"Iz zhizni avtootvetchikov." *Zvezda* 7 (1993).

"Privorotnoe zelo." *Volga* 12 (1993): 10–17.

"Reis." *Novyi mir* 3 (1993): 82–95. [Rpt. *Chego khochet zhenshina*. Intro. Elena Trofimova. Moscow: Linor, 1994. 190–221.]

"Mestorozhdenie vetra." *Novyi mir* 12 (1994): 46–54.

"Èvoliutsia tvorcheskogo masterstva. Put' k svobode vne pola. Damsksia drebeden'." *Mariia* 2 (1995): 175-98.

Translations by Marina Palei

Salmon, Laura. "Moskovskie vospominania" [three poems]. *Novyi mir* 6 (1992): 138.

———. *Veer.* [poetry translations from Italian]. St.Petersburg: Limbus, 1992.

In Translation

"Composition in Red and Blue." *Book and Art in the USSR* 1, 64 (1990): 20–22. [Published in Russian, English, French, German and Spanish.]

"The Bloody Women's Ward." Trans. Arch Tait. *Glas: New Russian Writing* 3 (1992): 74–91.

"Cabiria Kanavanrannan." Trans. Paulla Autio. *Karelia* 12 (1992).

Die Cabiria von Umleitung-kanal. Trans. Marianna Bobrovskaja. Hamburg: Rowohlt, 1992.

"Cabiria z Okruzhneho kanala." Trans. Marta Zamborova. *Revue Svetovej Literatury* 4 (1992).

"Imperiets dag." Trans. Bengt Samuelson. *Ord och Bild* 4 (1992): 55–62.

"Den' topoloveho paperia." Trans. Marta Zamborova. *Revue Svetovej Literatury* 1 (1993).

Herinnerd Huis. Trans. Frans Stalpert. Amsterdam: Pegasus, 1995.

"The Losers' Division." Trans. Jehanne Gheith. *Lives in Transit.* Ed. Helena Goscilo. Ann Arbor, MI: Ardis, 1995. 191–203.

"Rendezvous." Trans. Helena Goscilo. *Lives in Transit.* Ed. Helena Goscilo. Ann Arbor, MI: Ardis, 1995. 108–10.

Secondary Works

Basinskii, Pavel. "Pozabyvshie dobro?" *Literaturnaia gazeta,* 20 February 1991.

Brown, Deming. "New Faces." *The Last Years of Soviet Russian Litearture: Prose Fiction 1975–1991.* Cambridge: 1993. 180–83.

Deotto, Patrizia. "Scattrici in Unione Sovietica." *Lapis* 8 (1990): 29–31.

Dubshan, Leonid. "Nesluchainye knigi." *Peterburgskii zhurnal* 1 (1993): 375–76.

Fediakin, Sergei. "Mezhdu tsirkulem filosofa i zastupom ogorodnika." *Nezavisimaia gazeta,* 6 June 1993.

Goscilo, Helena. "Speaking Bodies: Erotic Zones Rhetoricized." *Fruits of Her Plume: Essays on Contemporary Russian Women's Culture.* Ed. Helena Goscilo. Armonk, NY: M.E. Sharpe, 1993. 156–57.

Heaton, Julia. "Russian Women's Writing: Problems of a Feminist Approach, with Particular Reference to the Writing of Marina Palei." *Slavonic and East European Review* 1 (1997): 63–85.

Kamianov, Viktor. "V tesnote i obide, ili 'Novyi chelovek' na zemle i pod zemlei." *Novyi mir* 12 (1992): 228–29.

Kucherskaia, Maia. "Ne vse propalo." *Novyi mir* 6 (1992): 238–40.

Kuchkina, Ol'ga. "Poèma o kvadratnykh metrakh." *Literaturnoe obozrenie* 3 (1991): 51–52.

Michaud, Marion. *Marina Palei's Literary Style: Cabiria from the Obvodny Canal.* Master's thesis, University of Lyon, France, 1993.

Mikhailovskaia, Tat'iana. "Marina Palei." *Dictionary of Russian Women Writers.* Ed. Marina Ledkovsky, Charlotte Rosenthal and Mary Zirin. Westport, CT: Greenwood Press, 1994. 479–80.

Nemzer, Andrei. "Tvorimaia legenda." *Nezavisimaia gazeta,* 12 March 1992.

Orlov, Janina. "Längtan efter barrdoftsgömman—om Marina Palej." *Finsk Tidskrift* 2–3 (1993): 111–17.

Remizova, Maria. "Perom i spitsamy." *Bogema* 1–3 (1993): 156–61.

Samuelson, Elena. "Skuggor, ljusa eller dunkla: om Marina Palej." *Ord och Bild* 4 (1992): 53–54.

Shklovskii, Evgenii. "Uskol'zaiushchaia real'nost'." *Literaturnoe obozrenie* 2 (1991): 14–15.

Vialtsev, Aleksandr. "Istselenie literatury." *Bogema* 1–3 (1993): 132–37.

Zamborova, Marta. "Ako sa sladi život." *Revue Svetovej Literatury* 4 (1992).

Liudmila Petrushevskaia

A uniquely gifted writer of dramaturgy, prose and (recently) poetry, the ever-provocative and controversial Liudmila Stefanovna Petrushevskaia (b. 1938) is arguably a classic author of late-twentieth-century Russian literature. The few, turbulent years of Gorbachev's policy of *glasnost'* released Petrushevskaia's uncompromising depictions of the "era of stagnation" from official opprobrium, only to be summarily rejected by the ranks of the post-Soviet postmodern as *chernukha* (works depicting only the seamier side of life). Petrushevskaia's essential talent, however, has seldom been disputed. Theater critic Anatolii Smelianskii, who once coined the dismissive term "tape-recorder realism" in relation to Petrushevskaia's works, now accords her a significance in Soviet drama to be paralleled only by Aleksandr Vampilov and Victor Rozov.[1] Her importance in prose, to which she has turned with ever-increasing mastery in the *glasnost'* and post-*glasnost'* eras, is indicated by her recent nomination for the the first Russian Booker Award in 1992 for *The Time: Night* (*Vremia. Noch'*). This latest major piece synthesizes themes and devices of her earlier work, and, characteristically, was ultimately denied the award for being "too bleak"—as post-Soviet reality proves no less harsh than the time that preceded it.

Because of her predilection for first-person narrative, there has been much speculation about the details of Petrushevskaia's early biography. The following summary is given as a corrective to currently available published versions and is based on recent personal interviews.

Liudmila Stefanovna Petrushevskaia was born in Moscow on 26 May 1938. At that time her parents, Valentina Nikolaevna Iakovleva and Stefan Antonovich Petrushevskii, lived in an apartment in Second House of Soviets that belonged to Petrushevskaia's grandmother, Valentina Ilinichna Iakovleva—a Communist party member since 1912. Petrushevskaia's parents were divorced soon after she was born, her mother initiating the divorce. Thus the family group of her early childhood memories consisted of five women—her grandmother, her mother, Valentina Ilinichna's second daughter, Petrushevskaia's aunt Vera Nikolaevna and herself. In the atmosphere of terror that reigned in Moscow in the late 1930s, the family considered that living in houses of acquaintances was preferable to being arrested, and all quit the metropolis, leaving all their belongings, never to come back. Many of Petrushevskaia's relatives were later arrested in connection with the Yakir case.[2] Some suffered repressions, some were killed.

In the fall of 1941, Petrushevskaia and her family joined her great-grandfather, the old Bolshevik Il'ia Sergeevich Veger, who was able to provide transportation to Kuibyshev, where Petrushevskaia stayed untill 1948. Her grandmother and her aunt, who still suffered repression in connection with the Yakir case, were able to come back to Moscow only in 1956, after rehabilitation. At that time, Valentina Ilinichna had her membership in the party reinstated, with certain privileges and honors (an *orden*, or medal of honor, a new apartment, special medical care and special arrangements for food—"Kremlin rations" [*Kremlevskii paek*]).

Both of Petrushevskaia's parents received their education in the Institute of History and Philology. Later her mother also graduated from the State Institute of Theatrical Art, specializing in theater criticism. Although her mother was the better educated, Petrushevskaia's father was the one who became a professor and a department chair in philosophy, while her mother worked as an editor in Gospolitizdat.

Liudmila Stefanovna studied at Moscow High School #170, and later at Moscow State University, from which she graduated in 1961 with a diploma in journalism. Her thirty-two-page graduation thesis consisted of a twelve-page essay on the "theory of humor" plus short stories. Her first publication, consisting of only about six lines of text, appeared in 1957 in *Moscow Young Communists* (*Moskovskii komsomolets*), when she was still a student. It was called "Three Girls in Blue" ("Tri devushki v golubom")—the title she would later use for her best-known dramatic work. The other publications were in the newspaper of the Moscow factory Red Proletariat, *Engine* (*Dvigatel'*), and in the popular humor magazine *The Crocodile* (*Krokodil*). The publication of her first short story, however—"The Magic Elevator" ("Chudesnyi lift") in January 1961, in *Week* (*Nedelia*)—gave the first signal of a long career of seemingly absurd editorial interference. The first line, "We were on our way to a New Year's celebration," was cut out, for no apparent reason.

Although Petrushevskaia the playwright gained recognition considerably earlier than Petrushevskaia the prose writer, she began her career with prose. As she has said, "I started out as a prose writer, and I wrote stories that no one would publish."[3] When one of her stories was rejected for publication by *New World* (*Novyi mir*), then-editor Aleksandr Tvardovskii nonetheless indicated to his staff that they should not lose touch with this author.[4]

In January 1962 Petrushevskaia started working for Moscow Radio. Her first radio play, "Two Windows"("Dva okoshka"), was published in the magazine *Family and School* (*Sem'ia i shkola*) in 1971. In the same year she published her first fairy tales in *Young Pioneer* (*Pioner*). In 1972 she became an editor for Moscow Television. This was a very important year for her: two of her stories, "The Storyteller" ("Raskazchitsa," 1972) and "Clarissa's Story" ("Istoriia Klarissy," 1972), were published in the Leningrad literary journal *Avrora*, for which she continues to write up to the present. In 1973 two more stories were published: "Mania" and "The Violin" ("Skripka") in *Friendship of Nations* (*Druzhba narodov*). From 1973 to 1986, however, only six stories by Petrushevskaia were published in the Soviet Union.

Petrushevskaia's beginnings in drama also met with unofficial critical recognition combined with public prohibition. Her excursions into drama were for the most part provoked by contact with the theater. Her early one-act play, *Cinzano* (1973), was written in reaction to Aleksandr Vampilov's *Duck Hunting*, which she saw as a play that *she* should have written, because she had much more to say about her contemporaries than Vampilov had depicted. She, Petrushevskaia, moreover, would have written from the position of a "sober woman"(*trezvaia baba*) rather than a "romantic man." Soon after completing her first play, she got a call (not unlike the narrator of Bulgakov's *Theatrical Novel*) from the literary director of the Moscow Art Theater, asking her to write a play for them. The result was *Music Lessons* (*Uroki muzyki*). Written in 1973, this play made its way to the theatergoing public through a production by Roman Viktiuk at Moscow University in 1978. This production moved to a theater on the outskirts of Moscow, where it continued as a theatrical landmark of the period. Through various machinations on the part of supportive writers and critics, the play found its way into print in the series "Aids for Amateur Productions" ("V pomoshch khudozhestvennoi samodeiatel'nosti"), issued by the publishing house Sovetskaia Rossiia in 1982. Petrushevskaia liked to joke that in her first decade as a playwright, she lived almost exclusively on "love"—her play *Love* (*Liubov'*) was the only one to pass the double screening of official censorship for print and performance; in addition, it may be said that she owed her reputation as an innovator to myriad productions in studio and amateur theater collectives.

During the 1970s and early 1980s, Petrushevskaia honed her skills as a playwright in the studio for dramatists run by Aleksei Arbuzov. According to a fellow student, playwright Anna Rodionova, Arbuzov personally accompanied Petrushevskaia when she made application to the Soviet Writers' Union. When asked on what basis he was supporting a writer with so few publications and no published plays, Arbuzov reportedly stated "on the basis that she is a genius."[5]

Recognition of "genius" came from abroad, and then finally at home, with a spate of publications and productions at the height of *glasnost'*, in 1988. Since the second half of the 1980s, Petrushevskaia has traveled extensively and had works published and staged both at home and abroad, in translation. In 1990 recognition of her work took the form of the prestigious Pushkin Prize for Literature.

Petrushevskaia currently resides in Moscow, in the Sokolniki region (locus of many of her stories), with her husband, daughter and the younger of her two sons. Since 1992, her "Animal Stories" ("Zhivotnye skazki") have appeared regularly in the Moscow weekly magazine *Capital* (*Stolitsa*). A "narrative poem in verse" entitled "Karamzin," which appeared in *New World* in November 1994, was inspired by her beloved dacha in Murom. At the time of this writing, a "complete collected works" is in preparation.

Because more than half of her stories and plays now in print were written long before their publication, readers of Petrushevskaia's prose have a unique opportunity to observe the writer's creative evolution, as earlier and later works have become available simultaneously. There is significant similarity between Petrushevskaia's prose and dramatic works, in that both provide minimal description of the characters and setting—forcing the reader/spectator to strain for every clue afforded by narrative/dramatic language.

Petrushevskaia writes about "the people in her apartment building entryway [*pod'ezd*]," immediately recognizable to her reader/spectator, who is instinctively repelled by the impression of bleakness created in this space. In her first prose pieces Petrushevskaia avoided another customary element—direct speech by her characters, which is, of course, the essence of drama. One can observe the striking change in her narrative manner after 1988, when her first prose collection, *Immortal Love* (*Bessmertnaia liubov'*), was published. In her second collection, *Along the Road to the God Eros* (*Po doroge bogu Erosa*), published in 1993, she introduces and relies heavily on dialogue. This change suggests that her early concern with mastering pure generic forms has given way to a confidence in her unique literary voice.

In *Immortal Love*, Petrushevskaia divided her writings into two categories: monologues and stories (*istorii*). The later collection, *Along the Road to the God Eros*, also includes fairy tales, incidents (*sluchai*, urban folklore) and "supernatural prose." In her monologues, narration is in the first person, most often by a woman, usually detached both physically and emotionally from the events taking place. She either is an accidental witness ("Uncle Grisha," "The Poor Heart of Pania") or is separated from the events by a very long period of time: "This is what happened to me when I was twenty years old ("Nets and Traps"). In Petrushevskaia's works written in the third person, the narrator's voice is intentionally stripped of any personal intonations. The storyteller appears not to be interested in the events she is describing, as if she is speaking about some distant acquaintances or coworkers. Critic E. Nevzgliadova emphasizes that Petrushevskaia's prose demands attentive reading—active participation on the part of the reader.[6] This is true, because the psychological distance of the narrator is deceptive, just as in her plays.

Fairy tales (*skazki*) for children of all ages represent another subgenre of Petrushevskaia's prose. On many occasions Petrushevskaia has said that first and foremost she writes for her children and grandchildren. Yet she expresses amusement at her stories being called "fairy tales." Initially, the label *skazka* was used by Petrushevskaia as an Aesopian device, a convenient label and a means of eluding censorship: "I had [in the editorial staff of the *Village Youth* magazine] one supporter, a department head. For many years he had been trying to get my stories through. He failed. Then he said, 'Let's publish a little fairy tale!' Well, little fairy tales! All right!"[7] When tricks were no longer necessary to avoid censorship, Petrushevskaia started to use the label "fairy tales for adults" (*skazki dlia vzroslykh*). In fact, her tales seldom have a moral lesson or a happy ending, obligatory for the genre. Despite the presence of fantastic elements in her fairy tales (talking animals, wizards) the stories are not unreal. However, one traditional characteristic of fairy tales—creation of excitement on the part of the reader—is often absent.

Direct speech holds an important position in these fairy tales. And although a tale might take place in a space kingdom, an overseas domain or a neighborhood wood, the reader constantly feels the life of the modern city, with its routines, problems and lively colloquial speech. Here the author gives her own conception—philosophic and poetic—of human existence. This is accomplished in two ways: first, by showing the miserable plight of people, illustrating everyday life in its most minute details, making an impression through their evocativeness and candor; and second, by conveying her compassion for her heroes. The syncretism of her documentarylike style and her fable modes of depiction is a specific feature of Petrushevskaia's art.

Petrushevskaia is also interested in short stories of the kind that are "told while one still has time—on a bus, in a summer camp, in a hospital ward," as she puts it in an introduction to "The Songs of the Eastern Slavs," her collection of "urban folklore-like stories." Strictly speaking, folklore is rooted not in literature, but in spoken language. And for Petrushevskaia, spoken language is the most important narrative device. Folklore spreads by oral means, unlike literature, which circulates in writing. A written work functions as literature when it connects author and reader. Petrushevskaia breaks through the boundary between the author and the reader, for in her works the author functions as a narrator. What is written *napisannoe,* is written down—is *zapisannoe*, recorded.

If one of the distinguishing characteristics of Petrushevskaia's prose is a distanced, deceptively neutral narrative voice (whether first or third person), then drama has served Petrushevskaia as an opportunity for polyphony. Juxtaposition of voices, perceptions and fates creates a distinct dramatic universe. It is not surprising, therefore, that her most ambitious dramatic work to date is entitled *Moscow Chorus* (*Moskovskii khor*).

Petrushevskaia masterfully captures the intonations and distortions of the spoken language; thus dramatic dialogue is a natural medium for her. She is most innovative and prolific in the one-act genre, of which *Cinzano* remains her masterpiece. Her longer dramatic works—*Three Girls in Blue, Moscow Chorus*—are more traditional in form than her shorter works.

Plot is not a major concern in her drama. If Petrushevskaia's stories are descriptions of incidents (*sluchai*) designed to get to the bottom of "what happened," her dramas bring her characters back to their starting point, having passed through a vicious circle. The resolution of the characters' current difficulties merely leaves them reconciled—to each other and to their fates—but in a worse place than at the play's outset. The three girls in blue (all young mothers over thirty) finally unite under one roof, but that roof starts to leak. In *Moscow Chorus*, set in 1957 before the International Festival of Youth and Students, the matriarch of a formerly repressed and currently beleaguered Moscow family succeeds in reuniting her family, but in a railway station, on their way to an eight-square-meter apartment in Berezai.

Two volumes of Petrushevskaia's plays have been published to date: *Plays* (*P'esy*, 1988) and *Three Girls in Blue* (*Tri devushki v golubom*, 1989). The first volume takes its subtitle, *Songs of the Twentieth Century*, from an eponymous monologue in which a young man, attempting to record his thoughts on a tape recorder, finds that he has no words or thoughts of his own to express. This dramatic device, reminiscent of Samuel Beckett's *Krapp's Last Tape*, reflects how Petrushevskaia casts in artistic form the pathos of the inarticulate "little man" with a desperate need to "confess," but to whom no one is listening. The organization of the second volume follows Petrushevskaia's production history in mainstream Moscow theaters. *Columbine's Apartment* (*Kvartira Kolumbiny*) contains plays used by Roman Viktiuk in his production at the Sovremennik. *Grannie's Blues* (*Babulia Bliuz*) was produced at the Theater on Malaia Bronnaia. Rosa Sirota assembled the plays of *The Dark*

Room (*Temnaia komnata*) for a production on the small stage of the Moscow Art Theater. Petrushevskaia's greatest critical successes on stage, however (besides Viktiuk's *Music Lessons*), have been the 1985 stagings by Mark Zakharov of *Three Girls in Blue* at the Theater of the Lenin Komsomol and by Roman Kozak of *Cinzano* at the Theater-Studio Man (Chelovek). Thanks to this production, Kozak's theater became the fifth studio of the Moscow Art Theater.

While Petrushevskaia's early dramatic efforts described a male-dominated universe, the point of view, in drama as well as narrative, is female. Characteristically revelatory of this point of view is Petrushevskaia's article "Eve in the Audience" ("Eva v zritel'nom zale"), published in *Soviet Theater* in 1986. The author gives birth to an original, primeval (or rather, Eve-al) vision of contemporary life. Petrushevskaia may steadfastly reject categorization of her by gender; readers, viewers and critics, however, continue to assess her works as "overtly gynocentric."[8] The element of conflict is commonly provided, especially in her works of the 1970s, by men—or rather, by their physical or spiritual absence; the author's "political" sympathies, however, are "on the side of the children."[9] The pathologies of her female contemporaries are abundantly reflected in later drama (*A Glass of Water, The Isolation Box*) and prose (*The Time: Night*) .

The Men's Zone (*Muzhskaia zona*, 1993), the play offered by Petrushevskaia for inclusion in this volume, reflects the writer's contemporary attempts to transcend her own preoccupation with *homo sovieticus* and regain her former position in the creative avant-garde. It is an experiment in writing for an ancient form of theater, inspired by Petrushevskaia's visit in 1992 to the ancient Greek amphitheater in Taormina, Sicily. The dramatis personae are nineteenth- and twentieth-century male "heroes" of mythological proportions, performing, in the afterlife, in the most "feminine" (according to Petrushevskaia) of Shakespeare's tragedies. In a time-honored Russian tradition, the material of tragedy receives artistic reworking into farce.

Melissa T. Smith and Nyusya Milman

The Men's Zone[1]
A Cabaret

Dramatis personae

Overseer
Lenin
Hitler

Beethoven
Einstein

THE ACTION TAKES PLACE IN A CLASSICAL AMPHITHEATER.

OVERSEER (*SEATED BEHIND A TABLE LIKE A THEATER DIRECTOR*).

So. As all of us here know, Shakespeare's plays were written by a certain countess, nicknamed "Turtledove." Well, to hell with her. We're going to play our own men's version. Let's begin. Where's my Romeo? Where's Juliet?

HITLER

I'm . . . Juliet.

OVERSEER

Beethoven was.

HITLER

But he can't hear a twit. He's deaf.

OVERSEER

Beethoven!

LENIN GIVES BEETHOVEN A SHOVE.

BEETHOVEN

Here! (*Puts on his hearing aid*)

OVERSEER

You're Juliet.

BEETHOVEN

I am the forest. No, I am the moon.

OVERSEER

And who appointed Hitler?

HITLER

You did yourself yesterday.

OVERSEER (*READS THE LIST*)

Nothing of the kind.

Lenin

Yes, you did, you did.

Overseer

I haven't gone off my rocker yet. Hitler can't be Juliet.

Hitler (*folds his hands demurely, in a woman's voice*)

Yes, I can! Romeo! Come he-ere!

Overseer

Romeo . . . our Romeo will be Einstein. And you, Hitler . . . you'll play the nurse. So. Juliet is Beethoven. So. We'll rehearse from number five. Juliet with the nurse.

Beethoven (*uneasily*)

What did he say?

Lenin

Juliet with the nurse.

Beethoven

And where's the text?

Lenin

Haven't you learned it?

Beethoven

Hunh?

Lenin

Deaf, eh? Just sits there like a deaf werewolf.

Overseer

From number five.

Beethoven

Ah.

Hitler

Juliet, for some reason you are anxious.

Beethoven

So what?

Hitler

I don't like your condition.

Beethoven

So what?

Hitler

I take your bed linens to the laundry . . .

Beethoven

And what of it?

Hitler

And they've been clean for the last two months.

Beethoven

Well, so what?

Hitler

I can't believe for a minute that you've become such a fastidious girl.

Beethoven (*anxiously*)

So what else?

Hitler

Before, one week a month I would change your sheets every day.

Beethoven

And what's up?

Hitler

I know you, you're naturally very strong, you have a copious monthly period, you overflow at night . . .

Beethoven

And what now?

Hitler

Now you've been clean for two months.

BEETHOVEN

And what of it?

HITLER

You've got to get married as soon as possible, today or tomorrow.

BEETHOVEN

Why?

HITLER

Seven-monthers, you see, are born strong and healthy, but six-monthers . . . six-monthers don't have much of a chance; this might create a panic, if you had a six-monther weighing four kilos. You've got to get married today.

BEETHOVEN (*SINCERELY*)

Why so?

HITLER

Then at least your child will be born at seven months.

BEETHOVEN

Who said?

HITLER

Oh, God, she's a total innocent! She doesn't understand a thing that's happened.

BEETHOVEN (*GLOOMILY*)

I don't understand what she's muttering about.

(SHAKES HIS HEARING AID)

Over.

HITLER

So. There's a ball today, you'll bring the father of your child right here.

BEETHOVEN

I hear you, over. I can't bring the child's father here, over.

HITLER

You could sleep with him, so marry him.

BEETHOVEN

No.

HITLER

Now don't be stubborn.

BEETHOVEN

I can't, over.

HITLER

But why?

BEETHOVEN

No one will marry us.

HITLER

I'll make the arrangements with Friar Laurence, I think I slept with him once.

BEETHOVEN

No! No, over.

HITLER

What's the matter, over?

BEETHOVEN

Just.

(LOOKS TO THE SIDE, BEATS TOE AGAINST THE FLOOR, IS EMBARRASSED)

HITLER

So, who is he? Who's the father?

BEETHOVEN

Hunh?

HITLER

Over!

BEETHOVEN

I won't reveal the father, over.

HITLER

Repeat, please. I can't hear you. Call back.

BEETHOVEN

Do you hear me, roger. It's Daisy!

HITLER

Daisy, I hear you clearly, Spell it out, please, w-h-o i-s t-h-e f-a-t-h-e-r? Fred-Arthur-Thomas-Homer-Ernie-Rover, who?

BEETHOVEN

Father?

HITLER

William-Homer-Ollie, who?

BEETHOVEN

V.I. Lenin. Vasia Ira Lenin.

LENIN

No.

HITLER

Well . . . I haven't let you out of my sight since you started fooling around with your brother . . . is that it, it's his?

LENIN

If you're talking about yesterday, I just slapped his hand a bit.

HITLER

So you're going to have a nephew by your brother?

BEETHOVEN

No.

(KICKS THE FLOOR WITH TOE, IS EMBARRASSED)

HITLER

Well, who?

BEETHOVEN

I won't ever tell you anything about father. Remember. Nothing about Father, not a word about Daddy.

HITLER (*GASPS*)

Oh, the scoundrel! It's not enough that he sleeps with his sons, now he's switched to his daughter. So . . . quite a pickle: you have a child by your father, it'll be your brother, and your father's grandson, and the child will be his own uncle. His very own uncle.

LENIN

But not an uncle by me.

OVERSEER

(*waking up*). Number five!

BEETHOVEN

Leave me, nurse, thou art a fool.

HITLER

He madeth me unhappy, and his wife
Has forced into the dirtiest of deeds.
Ah, we have fallen, over, and in general
How fine a man indeed your father is
When seen outside his family or, over
When he is sleeping, teeth against the wall.

BEETHOVEN

I love my Daddy.

HITLER (*HOTLY*)

As all do love him, except for Montagues.
Say, and who shall we marry you off to? Everybody around here is engaged at age seven! And your fiance is such a rotter!

BEETHOVEN

Foo. He's sweaty, and fat, and he smells of fish. He falls right off to sleep and snores, just snores.

HITLER

I didn't think otherwise. But you're going to have to marry him. Does he come here often?

BEETHOVEN

Every day, like on guard duty. But I don't want him.

HITLER

Well, you'll have to, anyway. Maybe it's his child.

BEETHOVEN

No, what do you think I am, a fool? I don't let him touch me. He manages by himself. Dis-gusting!

HITLER

Well, you never know . . . you'll say it's his. He probably doesn't understand anyway.

BEETHOVEN

I don't want him anymore, you hear? Find me somebody else.

HITLER

Well, that's all, I hear music, the ball is beginning. Change into all-white clothing, I'll bring you somebody in a bit.

OVERSEER (*WAKING UP*)

So. Where's our moon? Lenin, are you the moon?

LENIN

I'm the moon. (*curves his mouth to one side*)

OVERSEER (*YAWNING*)

Who is our Romeo? Einstein!

EINSTEIN

I am.

(PULLS OUT HIS VIOLIN)

OVERSEER

Now, we don't need any of that. If you start playing the violin, they'll catch you and Juliet right away. For now, dance a bit at the ball with the nurse. Hitler! Dance with Einstein. Romeo dances with the nurse. Juliet is all in white.

(HITLER AND THE NURSE DANCE. MEANWHILE, BEETHOVEN CHANGES INTO WHITE; THAT IS, REMAINS IN HIS UNDERSHORTS AND T-SHIRT. EINSTEIN AND HITLER DANCE THE COMPARSITA WITH SHARP TURNS OF THE HEAD. HITLER HIDES THE VIOLIN BEHIND THE CURTAINS.)

HITLER (*HUGGING EINSTEIN*)

So young! A virgin, I bet?

EINSTEIN (*HOARSELY*)

You're wrong, auntie! I'm well over fourteen!

HITLER

Shall we go to my place?

EINSTEIN

What if someone sees us together?

HITLER

So what if they see us, over. I'll introduce you to Juliet.

(THEY GO OVER TO BEETHOVEN.)

BEETHOVEN

Och! (*He stands in his underwear, shaking.*)

HITLER

Juliet, you so wanted to meet Romeo!

BEETHOVEN

Och.

EINSTEIN

This . . . is Juliet?

HITLER

And who else should it be?

EINSTEIN

I didn't imagine her like this.

HITLER

Well, she turned out much better than you thought?

EINSTEIN

Oh, I forgot my violin. Be right back.

(TURNS TO LEAVE)

HITLER

Oh, you damned Yid! Stay right here. You two don't need your violin for anything right now.

EINSTEIN

I won't stay here a second longer! I was called to America a long time ago!

HITLER

You go Auschwitz, ho? And if no want go?

EINSTEIN

You are a wild, uncultured woman, and I don't want to have anything to do with you. You are a real Hitler in a skirt!

HITLER

I come back soon.

(SNEAKS OFF)

BEETHOVEN

So, you play the violin?

EINSTEIN

Yes, since I was seven. I couldn't yet speak, they thought I was an idiot and decided to teach me to play the violin; you never know, I might be able to make money as a street musician. What else can you make of an idiot?

BEETHOVEN (*GETTING EXCITED*)

And you know who taught me to play? You know this guy Salieri? The composer?

EINSTEIN (*CAUTIOUSLY*)

From barrack number seven?

BEETHOVEN (*FOGGILY*)

No, he's not here.

EINSTEIN

You mean that story with Mozart?

BEETHOVEN

That's a lot of slander. Mozart always had problems with his stool.

EINSTEIN

Shall I bring my violin, and we'll play?

BEETHOVEN

I have a violin concerto, la-la-la.

(SINGS)

EINSTEIN

Hitler hid my violin, the oaf.

BEETHOVEN

But he loved me. Hitler loved Beethoven.

EINSTEIN

Lenin loved you, too, the Appassionata Sonata.

(LENIN SHAKES HIS HEAD NO, THEN CATCHES HIMSELF AND GRIMACES AGAIN.)

BEETHOVEN

Many have loved me.

EINSTEIN

While that guy (*points to the Overseer*) is asleep, I'll tell you: nobody here can appreciate me, but I make a living with my violin. As soon as I start to play they slip me a cup of ambrosia and beg me not to play here anymore. As for the rest, well, who here knows who I am and what $e = mc^2$ is?

BEETHOVEN

Whaddat?

EINSTEIN

It would take too long to explain.

LENIN (*SUDDENLY*)

Yes, here, in these conditions, nobody would pay any attention. It's just like emigration. You're walking along, and nobody recognizes you, don't even turn their heads in your direction. And at home in Russia, I had to put on a wig, shave my whole face, they kept jumping at me. That's the reason we led a revolt, so that when everybody recognized us and jumped at us they didn't then send me again to Shushensk. There it was just the same, Lenin, Shmenin, Ulianov, Shmulianov. . . . Peasants all around, didn't have a clue as to who I was.

OVERSEER (*WAKING UP*)

Moon! Stick your nose up!

LENIN

I am the moon.

(MAKES A SILLY FACE. HITLER ENTERS.)

BEETHOVEN (*TO HITLER*)

What you sneaking in here for, bugger? We haven't finished yet.

OVERSEER

From number five! The moon is floating in the skies!

(LENIN, WITH A WRY FACE, MAKES OVERARM STROKES.)

BEETHOVEN

Romeo, you are like a frozen walleye, you make bedroom eyes and then you're frigid.

HITLER (*TO EINSTEIN*)

Come on, Al, go to it.

BEETHOVEN

To hell with him. Nanny! We're better off together. Open the window and lie down beside me.

EINSTEIN (FROM THE BED)

Not much of a bride, her underwear isn't even fresh.

HITLER

Juliet, you just think about who you want to sleep with, and you forget business. I can, of course, I always love my little daughter, but I can't marry you, I won't take on your child. You need a man for this.

BEETHOVEN

I can't sleep with him, Nanny, it's too stuffy in here. This guy's not much to look at and after all, I'm fourteen and all in white.

EINSTEIN (*GETTING UP FROM THE BED*)

It's time to go; looks like the moon is setting.

(LENIN MAKES AN ATTEMPT TO SET, I.E., HE LOWERS HIMSELF, TWISTING HIS TORSO AS IF DANCING THE TWIST.)

OVERSEER (*WAKING UP*)

Hasn't set yet!

(LENIN GETS UP, SMILING, MOUTH TO ONE SIDE, AND MAKES PASSING GESTURES WITH HIS HANDS.)

BEETHOVEN

Keep your hands to yourself, smart aleck!

OVERSEER

I really wasn't expecting such a half-assed job from you. How are we going to spend eternity together? Are we going to spend it without distinction?

EINSTEIN

That's because we only have male actors.

OVERSEER

Come on . . . in the women's zone Romeo is also being played by a . . . Golda Meir.

HITLER

What a troupe of talentless women. Just Yids and invalids.

(EINSTEIN WANTS TO LEAVE FOR AMERICA.)

BEETHOVEN (TO EINSTEIN)

Let me handle this, Al.

(TO HITLER)

I'm an invalid second-class with a hearing aid; now you, bugger, get ready for a bloodbath!

OVERSEER

Hitler will be sent to the hard-labor brigade if you're going to act like this.

EINSTEIN

What's a labor brigade? I don't understand the joke.

OVERSEER

He's been boiling in hot oil, but we brought him up to act with us, since he's a first-class actor.

HITLER

I don't believe it.
Now Juliet, daughter, why should not you take
To husband this most excellent Romeo?
Agree, admit this brings no ills.

BEETHOVEN

But I'm afraid of eels.

LENIN

The midnight comes, and still the moon does pass
In its eternal journey
As does the changing guard
In front of Lenin's tomb.

OVERSEER

The moon sets. It is morning.

(LENIN GOES OUT LIKE A SENTRY, MATCHING HIS STEP TO THE SOUND OF THE CHIMES.)

BEETHOVEN

Romeo, 'twas never so good for me with parents, brother or father.

EINSTEIN (*EMBARRASSED*)

Aw, shucks! My Mommy was well satisfied with me; not long ago she gave birth to a sister for me, with horns and a tail. Papa soaked her well in spirit alcohol, and around New Year's we'll have some homemade liquor.

OVERSEER

Lenin, the moon doesn't set like that!

(LENIN, TAKING MINCING STEPS, DANCES THE DANCE OF THE CYGNETS FROM SWAN LAKE.)

HITLER

Now we'll play a wedding scene, and Juliet will bear a daughter with horns!

OVERSEER

All right, now—Lenin, Hitler, back to the labor brigade; the rest of you are at liberty!

BEETHOVEN

Boiling only makes the crab look rosy!

(FINALE)

1993

Translated by Melissa Smith

Notes to the Essay

1. M. Smith, quoting A. Smelianskii from an interview, Cambridge, MA, 20 July 1994.
2. Yakir was one of the first military leaders to be liquidated during Stalin's purges.
3. M. Zonina, "Bessmertnaia liubov," *Literaturnaia gazeta* 7 (1983): 9.
4. A. Tvardovskii, in "Introduction" [to "Takaia devochka"], *Ogonek* 1 (1988): 9.
5. M. Smith quotes Anna Rodionova referring to A. Arbuzov, from an interview, Northfield, VT, 29 July 1994.
6. E. Nevzgliadova, "Siuzhet dlia nebol'shogo rasskaza," *Novyi mir* 4 (1988): 256–60.
7. N. Milman, quoting Andrei Saalbach from an interview, 3 October 1983.
8. Helena Goscilo, "Coming a Long Way, Baby: A Quarter-Century of Russian Women's Fiction" *Harriman Institute Forum* 6, 1 (1992): 12.
9. Zonina, "Bessmertnaialiubov'," 9.

Translator's Note to the Selected Work

1. *Muzhskaia zona* was first published in Paris in the Russian-language journal *Sintaksis* in 1992 and subsequently in the Moscow weekly *Stolitsa* in 1993.

Bibliography

Primary Works

Skazki bez podskazki. Moscow: Detskaia literatura, 1981.
Zaiachii khvost. Moscow: Kinotsentr, 1987.
Bessmertnaia liubov'. Moscow: Moskovskii rabochii, 1988.
Pesni dvadtsatogo veka. Moscow: Soiuz teatral'nykh deiatelei, 1988.
Tri devushki v golubom. Moscow: Isskustvo, 1989.
Svoi krug. Moscow: Biblioteka zhurnala Ogonek, 1990.

LechenieVasiliia. Moscow: Kinotsentr, 1991.

Po doroge Bogu Erosa. Moscow: Olimp, 1993.

Taina doma: Povesti i rasskazy. Moscow: Kvadrat, 1995.

Bal poslednego cheloveka: povesti i rasskazy. Moscow: LOKID, 1996.

Sobranie sochinenii v piati tomakh. Kharkov: Folio. [Moscow: TKO ACT.] 1996.

Nastoiashchie skazki. Moscow: Vagrius, 1997.

Dom devushek: Rasskazy i povesti. Moscow: Vagrius, 1998.

Skazka pro Azbuku. Moscow: MAIK "Nauka," 1997.

In Translation

Come into the Kitchen. Four by Petrushevskaya. Scarsdale, NY: Theatre Research Associates, 1984 [play].

Love. Four by Petrushevskaya. Scarsdale, NY: Theatre Research Associates, 1984 [play].

"Nets and Traps." *The Image of Women in Contemporary Soviet Fiction.* Scarsdale, NY: Theatre Research Associates, 1984.

The Stairlanding. Scarsdale, NY: Theatre Research Associates, 1984 [play].

"Violin." *Four by Petrushevskaya.* Scarsdale, NY: Theatre Research Associates, 1984.

"Clarissa." *Clarissa and Other Stories.* Scarsdale, NY: Theatre Research Associates, 1985.

"Mania." *Clarissa and Other Stories.* Scarsdale, NY: Theatre Research Associates, 1985.

"The Storyteller." *Clarissa and Other Stories.* Scarsdale, NY: Theatre Research Associates, 1985.

"Through the Fields." *Clarissa and Other Stories.* Scarsdale, NY: Theatre Research Associates, 1985."

"Smirnova's Birthday." *Cinzano and Smirnova's Birthday.* Scarsdale, NY: Theatre Research Associates, 1986 [play].

Columbine's Apartment. Scarsdale, NY: Theatre Research Associates, 1988 [play].

Cinzano. Theater (Fall 1989) [play].

"Our Circle." *Michigan Quarterly* (Fall 1989).

Three Girls in Blue; Stars in the Morning Sky: Five Plays from the Soviet Union. Trans. Michael Glenny. London: Hern, 1989. 249–329.

"Our Crowd." *Glasnost: An Anthology of Literature under Gorbachev.* Ann Arbor, MI: Ardis, 1990.

"The Overlook." *Soviet Women Writing.* Ed. J. Decter. New York: Abbeville Press, 1990. 275–300.

"That Kind of Girl." *Dialogues/Dialogi: Literary and Cultural Exchanges between (Ex)Soviet and American Women.* Ed. S. Aiken et al. Durham, NC: Duke University Press, 1994.

Time: Night. London: Virago Press, 1994.

"Songs of the Eastern Slavs." *On Lyudmila Petrushevskaya.* Ed. N. Milman. Ann Arbor: Michigan Slavic Publications, 1995.

"Wedding Night." *On Lyudmila Petrushevskaya.* Ed. N. Milman. Ann Arbor: Michigan Slavic Publications, 1995 [play].

Immortal Love: Stories. Trans. Sally Laird. London: Virago Press, 1995.

Secondary Works

Barker, Adele. "Women without Men in the Writings of Contemporary Soviet Women Writers." *Russian Literature and Psychoanalysis.* Ed. D. Rancour-Laferrier et al. Amsterdam: John Benjamins, 1989.

Condee, Nancy. "Liudmila Petrushevskaia: How the Lost People Live." *Materials of the Institute of Current World Affairs* (Fall 1986).

Heldt, Barbara. "Gynoglasnost—Writing the Feminine." *Perestroika and Russian Women.* Ed. M. Buckley. Cambridge: Cambridge University Press, 1992.

Kolesnikoff, Nina. "Narrative Structure of Liudmila Petrushevskaia's Short Stories." *Revue Canadienne des Slavistes* 32, 4 (December 1990): 444–56.

Milman, Nyusya, ed. *On Lyudmila Petrushevskaya*. Ann Arbor: Michigan Slavic Publications, 1995.

Picon-Vallin, Beatrice. "Du théâtre amateur au Theatre Taganka: 'Leçons de musique' de L. Petrouchevskaia." *Théâtre public* 46–47 (1982).

Ol'ga Sedakova

Ol'ga Sedakova (b. 1949).
Courtesy of the author and Valentina Polukhina.

Ol'ga Aleksandrovna Sedakova (b. 1949), poet, translator and essayist, enjoys a national and international reputation as a polyglot poet of refined taste and extreme erudition. She is one of Russia's most admired and respected poets, in the tradition of Osip Mandel'shtam, Anna Akhmatova and Velimir Khlebnikov.

She began writing poetry while still at school. Her first poems appeared in the student newspapers of Tartu University (Estonia) and Tbilisi University (Georgia), and also in unofficial journals in Moscow and Leningrad in the late 1980s. Brought up during the "period of stagnation," she belonged neither to the official culture nor to the illegal "second" culture, but developed her own accent and emphasis. Nevertheless, she was an exile in her own country, a part of that "lost generation" of artists who refused any compromise with the "gray terror" of the Brezhnev days. In her essay "On the Lost Literary Generation" ("O pogibshem literatur nom pokolenii"), written in 1984 though not published until 1990, she suggested that the self-inflicted penury and humility of an antihierarchical Christian mystic and Gospel fundamentalist, St. Francis, should be the model for those who wish to realize contemplative selfhood in the world: "Until the regime wrecked itself completely I wanted to go on writing, not in spite of it but against it."[1] In the funereal atmosphere of the 1980s she even wrote some political poems and essays (see, e.g., her "Elegy, Turning into a Requiem" ["Elegiia, perekhodiashchaia v rekviem"] and "Journey to Briansk" ["Puteshestvie v Briansk"]). With the arrival of *glasnost'*, when the erosion of the boundaries between the two cultures took place (the process is described in "On the Lost Literary Generation"), Sedakova's poetic originality and independence paid off. Such prestigious journals as *New World* (*Novyi mir*), *Friendship of Nations* (*Druzhba narodov*) and the *Banner* (*Znamia*) expressed great interest in Sedakova's poetry. She has already acquired cultural importance in France, where in 1991 she was awarded the Paris Prize for a Russian poet; in Italy and in Germany, where she received a Schiller Fund Award; and in England, where she was the first Russian poet-in-residence at Keele University (1993–1994).

Since early childhood Sedakova lived in the midst of Russia's best scholars and artists. Just a few names need be mentioned: Iu.M. Lotman, S.S. Averintsev, M.L. Gasparov, V.V. Ivanov, V.V. Bibikhin, writer Venedikt Erofeev and artist M.M. Shvartsman. During the 1970s and 1980s the academic avant-garde had taken on the role formerly played by Russian literature. It was asking all the really important questions of the time—cultural, spiritual, even political. Responsibility, hard work, the ability to debate, social decency and politeness (things victimized in Soviet society) became topics of discussion in this circle. It is not a surprise that she became an outstanding scholar herself. She has written many academic articles and essays on Pushkin, Pasternak, Akhmatova and Khlebnikov, as well as on her own contemporaries such as Venedikt Erofeev, Leonid Gubanov and Viktor Krivulin. One of the special strengths of her essays is a profound and vivid thought process that is accompanied by a touch of irony and dazzling style. As an essayist, she has modeled herself on T.S. Eliot, C.S. Lewis and G.K. Chesterton. In many senses, her prose can be seen as a continuation of her poetry: with the same compositional structure, the same sharpness of observation and the same elegant meditative tone, they are both fed from the same springs.

Sedakova gracefully moves between the classical traditions of both Russian and European literature. The most powerful influence of her youth was Mandel'shtam. Baudelaire's *Les fleurs du mal* was another major influence on her. She considers that Rilke achieved the highest stage of poetry, and in order to read him in the original she learned German. To read Dante, another icon, she learned Italian. Her vast knowledge of European poetry and love of the classics helped her to form the foundation of her own poetic vision. She has translated Carroll, T.S. Eliot, Pound, Hardy, Claudel, Rilke, Petrarch, Horace and Dante, and their poetry has provided the context for some of her poems, as have biblical narratives, classical myths and modern philosophy. Her knowledge of modern music allows her to take delicious liberties with rhythm, which plays an important role in the general semantic conception of her verse. Thus in her "Autumn Water's Elegy" the now long, now single-word lines portray the freedom of the waters cascading over the hills and refer back to the foundation of poetic inspiration, "the true, the blushful Hippocrene":

> It cost us no great toil, my Muse,
> to master sensual inquisitiveness,
> outstaring, empty-eyed, the monstrous horse
> that hews the flaming waters from
> the treeless, beastless, birdless rock.
> Where dwell only you, thin shadows.
> And you who like a fair child pluck the bents
> of grass,
> blessed,
> parched,
> and bleak[2]

In this poem about things and creatures (in a sense that they themselves remind us about their existence), and also about people and the earth (see her poem with the same title), words are surrounded by a zone of whiteness, which stands for silence within words. The silence w ithin words is the fundamental principle of hesychasm,[3] and for Sedakova, it is where poetry begins. In other poems she seeks an overly harsh regularity, as in "Journey of the Magi" ("Puteshestvie volkhvov"), where she used a numeral coda: 6, 7 and 8. She loves that inexplicable sense of measure that is beauty itself. She has always been interested in systems of versification outside the Russian syllabo-tonic tradition: meters used in antiquity, folk poetry, prayers, poetry in which the rhythm of the line is not yet separated from the *melos*. In her "Tristan and Isolde" one can hear the German of the *Nibelungenlied* as well as the old Italian of the *laudi*.

Over the years she developed her own inner theme and purity of tone. She never was attracted by an emphatic style with willfully deformed imagery and staccato movements. Her style is inward, elusive and simple. "The expurgation of intentions" (T.S. Eliot) is her major concern: not to succumb to the temptation of creating something unnecessary; for her, poetry should not be at odds with piety, obedience and humility. This is one of the reasons why Sedakova is regarded by many as being synonymous with religious poetry. But she herself avoids that term because she believes that Christianity is not only a cultural, a structuralizing, a generative principle; it is not just enlightened conservatism; it could also be radicalism, a rejection of the world and all its cultures. "Religion in art," she has said, "is a wider concept, one that cannot simply be determined by content." Taking Christianity as a creed and either Dante or the later John Donne as an exemplar, not many contemporary poets can past the test of being called a Christian poet. What Sedakova said about Brodsky is also true about herself, that, like Brodsky, she doesn't close her eyes to her own mortality. As a result, it frees her from herself, from petty demands, insults and ties. It connects Sedakova with the poetry of the Middle Ages and the Baroque, but above all else with the poet of Ecclesiastes.[4] In her poem "The Fifth Stanzas" ("Piatye stansy") she re-creates the theme, of triumph over death, one of the favorite themes of antique art, bright with the glow of the Resurrection: "My friend! / What we have kept, like life, will slide away, / and a star we cannot know will rise in the sky."[5]

Sedakova is one of the best confessional Christian poets writing in Russian today. Her poetry evokes metaphysical and theological thoughts and demonstrates the beauty of faith. To some extent, she is emulating God in His creation of the universe, taking as her base the four elements: water, earth, fire, air. Her attraction toward the nonsocial and nonverbal world is felt throughout her poetry: "And thus closer to me than words, the language of branches, the language of tree trunks." It has very little to do with that "love of nature" known in the urban culture. It is rather a feeling for the elements as meaning, as structure, that found its expression with the pre-Socratic philosophers, above all Heraclitus. These four elements brought with them a whole range of mythical, theological and symbolic allusions to the origins of our civilization.

It is also true that religious and secular motifs are inseparable in her poems. Like her beloved Mandel'shtam, she takes upon herself the entire civilization in a very unobtrusive way by charging her poems with obvious, obscure and abstruse cultural references. Sedakova herself would separate culture from bookishness; culture, for her, has more to do with the development of an immediate, sensual perception of the world: improving one's sight, one's hearing and the ability to view the world through the eyes, as Heidegger says, of "the shepherds of being." But this *poeta doctus* has nothing in common with postmodernistic games. She is only too aware of the poet's duty to avoid polluting human memory by trivial and nonsensical images, since a written poem can be memorized (see her "In Praise of Poetry" ["Pokhvala poèzii," 1991]).

Sedakova follows Mandel'shtam and Acmeist poetics in her treatment of language: for her, the most important thing in poetry is the word, the word per se, the word as name; it is more important, she insists, than syntax, versification or tropes. All in all, the poem, in her opinion, serves the word, so that each individual word realizes the full range of its etymological and phonetic potential, its potential for ambivalence of meaning. But it is not just words that create the stylistic excellence of her writings. The composition of her poems is another device to which we must pay attention. It is based on the principle of the plastic representation of transience, of the perishable, of the making level of the important with the unimportant, as in the poem "The Grasshoper and the Cricket." She has also exhibited consummate skill in deploying dreams as a part of the composition. She believes that dreams and premonitions give reality additional dimension ("It is a state of a different intensity where other doors open") and she uses them as a means of communication with another realm. The acoustic splendor of her poems contributes greatly to *le plaisir du text: raz* and *roz* in *razvernesh'sia* and in *mirozdan'ia* announce in advance the appearance of a rose (*roza*) in "The Wild Rose" ("Shipovnik," 1978); love for Christ is expressed in the anagram "and white whiter than any other" ("i belyi belee liubogo"). "The Wild Rose" is an example of a truly poetic transformation. It is a breathtaking spiritual expansion that takes us beyond the horizon of our vision; indeed, it extends our vision. Two more influences should be mentioned here: Dante and Rilke. They are both, for Sedakova, tantamount to poetry itself. She has learned from them how to convey the incurable longing for the partial and private, for the whole and for holiness. This aspiration gives her poems inner energy.

Aesthetic integrity is another essential quality of Sedakova's poetry. It consists of several important features: a restrained tone, a sense of detachment, the reluctance of a poet to put herself at the center of her poems, quality of mind and beauty of language. As for the latter, her language seems almost infused with spirit; there is hardly any first-person figure present in her poems. The desire to go "beyond oneself" in search of some ultimate meaning is expressed in "The Fifth Stanzas." Many of her poems could be read as a symbol of contemplative life. Her main interest is the knowledge of the spirit that is buried deep inside us; to restore the life of the spirit within man is the poet's prime concern. She writes on the metaphysical level, beyond personal emotion. For that and other reasons, Sedakova can be called an impersonal poet. But her personality has not vanished in the heart of creative rapture; she is nowhere and everywhere.

What is lacking in Sedakova's work is any interest in a feminist literary tradition; the fashionable issue of gender bewilders her. This "deficiency" is more than compensated for by her poetic integrity, a rare quality among contemporary poets. A second type of criticism has to do with Sedakova's fastidiousness, which is, in fact, founded on a total distrust of the Russian tradition of social optimism, progress and the amelioration of man. She doesn't deny the social function of the belles lettres since poetry, for her, is wider-ranging than the ancients' *poesia sacra* and includes the decorative and the comic, among others.

Sedakova's poetry embodies a rare nobility and sublime simplicity. Although beautifully crafted, her poems are in many ways poor and ascetic: that is to say, as a technician, she is much less interesting than Elena Shvarts. But that is not her purpose. Her poetry offers a wonderful spiritual expansion, elevation and sense of proportion and harmony unusual even in great poetry. Unfortunately, in the contemporary cultural decline, when any nonaesthetic object can be transformed into a "work of art," she finds herself in a lonely position:

> In thinking about a new responsible position, given the new situation, I never considered looking for a refuge. In the final analysis there is no position for me, except Pasternak's 'be oneself.' During the years of Soviet rule the main obstacle to being oneself was fear, now it is cynicism; to be cynical has become, somehow, obligatory in our post-Soviet society—it is bon ton. Ugliness, evil and chaos lack a well-defined image and for that reason our consciousness is incapable of conversing with them. . . . It is time we admitted that it is not the 'low' but the 'high' that needs defending and there are very few defenders.[6]

Valentina Polukhina

On a Carved Elephant[1]

To Z. Plavinskaia

In the soul's Arabian East, with its dervish gusts,
where marauders snatch hoopoe chicks from tourmaline nests,

and fish with great wings, and dragons on leverets' paws,
and the clinging, opiate smell of eternal words,

you and I may become an immaculate, deep-rooted tree,
the dark cradle of spotted snakes that write in their sleep.

It has golden flanks and a rajah's beetling brows,
and the earth's great weight stares down from the lookout tower.

Any image is good. Only elephants put walls to right;
the earth's great weight leaves the garden, heaving a sigh.

How I want to become that precious and tranquil beast
that could well be caught if we opened the fortress gates.

Any image is good, any image is sprinkled at night
with dew as we sleep, like our eyelash; we know which to greet.

So what does it matter if, dustlike, we float on the breeze
or sit carving our elephants, waiting for them to speak?

Spring[2]

I was just going to say:
"Come over, come visit me—"
and now winter's near gone.

On and on they write
their bush-, their tree-hieroglyphs—
here a lighter, here a heavier stroke.
O, the joy of writing:

the invisible brushes
skip over succulent paper,
over rice-soft air—
try stopping those hands as they bolt!

The book of air writes like Khlebnikov:
making long strings of word-roots,
filling the deep wells of happenings,
scattering the golden beads of beginnings . . .
Well, you'll see if you come.

Out of winter's locked closet,
the linen-press of night,
the sun comes creeping—
(how did it cram itself in there?)
and warms us, having nothing better to do.
Its light should be shining
on something important,
something close to the heart.
So come over, there's no time to delay.

No matter what we have
to light us, fly for us, write for us,
no matter how streams sketch out
the valley's rises and hollows,
no matter how often birds may say
that the sky holds the earth
in a thousand indigo hands
gently as a beggar her child—
it's sad that no one should come.

How can you know when it's too late?
When the snow melts, so you
reach out for us
and find that we're gone.

From Old Songs[3]

Word

If you love, others will love you,
If you serve, others will serve you,
If not now, then later sometime.
Better, though, be grateful,
and end your work without Rachel,
walking happy over the green hills.

For the word is a king's garment,
the dress of long or short sufferance,
higher than air, brighter than sun.

Our eyes shall not see
What color it is,
no human ear shall hear
the rustle of its full folds

but only the heart will say:
you are, you shall be free,
not answering to slaves.

Going Back (A Poem about Aleksei)[4]

Sometimes it's good to go back
to a town where everything's changed;
to the garden, where many trees
are chopped to stumps; others creak
when they move, as never before;
to the house where people are grieving

for you. To go back and, silent,
not name yourself till you die,

leaving them to go on guessing,
cross-questioning any stranger,
understanding—and not understanding

though things around them glitter
like tiny faraway stars.

Seeing Things[5]

I stare at you: what I'm seeing
is my father, old, dressed like a stranger:
he can't walk any farther
and yet they drive him, drive him.

I think, what is the matter—
My God, can I be dying?
Why should I pity all things?

Creatures for being creatures,
water for always flowing,
the wicked for being wretched,
and myself, for my crazy visions.

Ending[6]

Hidden in any sad thing
is the letter, the finger-ring
you find in fairy-tale oaks.

Hidden in any word
is a stony, a passionate road.

Yet the one who says "I can"
is not weeping for this,
and his hope lies elsewhere.

Such things are known, not learned;
he who knows them will wonder again

as a smile blazes up in his mind
and he praises the mercy of God.

Translated by Catriona Kelly

Notes to the Essay

1. O. Sedakova, interview with Valentina Polukhina, "Conform Not to This Age: The Poetry and Personality of Ol'ga Sedakova," *Russian Literature in the Eighties*, ed. Arnold McMillin (London: Harwood Academic Publishers, 1996).

2. O. Sedakova, "Autumn Water's Elegy," trans. Robert Reid, in *The Silk of Time: Bilingual Selected Poems*, ed. and intro. V. Polukhina (Keele, Staffordshire: Keele University Press, 1994), 67; first published in Valentina Polukhina, ed., *Brodsky through the Eyes of His Contemporaries* (Basingstoke: Macmillan Press, 1992), 256–59.

3. A hesychast in the Greek Orthodox church was a follower of the mysticism developed by the monks of Mount Athos in the fourteenth century.

4. O. Sedakova, "A Rare Independence," in Valentina Polukhina, ed., *Brodsky through the Eyes of His Contemporaries,* 245.

5. Translated by Catriona Kelly, in Polukhina, ed., *The Silk of Time: Bilingual Selected Poems,* 59.

6. O. Sedakova, interview with Valentina Polukhina, "Conform Not to This Age."

Translator's Notes to the Selected Works

1. *Stikhi,* 189.

2. *Stikhi,* 212–13.

3. *Stikhi,* 141.

4. *Stikhi,* 147. Aleksei Chelovek Bozhii, that is, "Aleksei, Man of God," a young nobleman of Rome who, having fled to Odessa to avoid a forced marriage, returned after a vision of the Mother of God to his parents' house and worked there unrecognized as a servant.

5. *Stikhi,* 150.

6. *Stikhi,* 153.

Bibliography

Primary Works

Kliaz'ma i Iauza. 1974, unpublished.

"Pamiat' slova" ["Memory of the Word"]. *Znanie-sila* 10 (1975): 27–29.

Strogie motivy [*Austere Motifs*]. 1976, unpublished.

"V nezapamiatnykh zimakh," "Dikii shipovnik," "Felemon i Bavkida." *TGU* [from Tartuskii gosudarstvennyi universitet], 4 March 1977, 1.

"O 'bronzovom' veke" ("On the Bronze Age"). *Grani* 130 (1983): 274–78.

"O pogibshem literaturnom pokolenii—pamiati Leni Gubanova" ["On the lost literary generation—in memory of Lenia Gubanov"]. *Vybor* 2 (1984): 293–334. [Rpt. *Volga* 6 (1990): 135–46.]

"Vetkhozavetnyi motiv," "Uspenie," "Opyt istorii." *Vestnik russkogo khristianskogo dvizheniia* 142 (1984): 128–30.

"Neuzheli, Maria, tol'ko ramy skripiat," "Dikii shipovnik," "Gornaia kolybel'naia," "Puteshestvie volkhvov." *Vestnik russkogo khristianskogo dvizheniia* 145 (1985): 172–76.

Vrata, Okna, Arki, Izbrannye stikhotvoreniia [*Gates, Windows, Arches, Selected Poems*]. Paris: YMCA Press, 1986.

"Neuzheli, Maria . . . ," "Kuznechik i sverchok," "V pustyne zhizni," "Na smert' Leonida Gubanova." *Druzhba narodov* 9 (1988): 122–24.

"Solovei, filomena, sud'ba." *Druzhba narodov* 10 (1988): 121–40.

"Èlegiia, perekhodiashchaia v rekviem," "Tri vstupleniia k poème "Tristan i Izol'da," "Stansy na smert' kotenka." *Filosofskaia i sotsiologicheskaia mysl'* 9 (1989): 115–20.

"Kheddi Luk," "Laterna Magia." *Literaturno-khudozhestvennyi, istoriko-kul'turnyi al'manakh.* Moscow: Izdatel'stvo Prometei, 1990. 261–66.

Kitaiskoe puteshestvie [*A Chinese Journey*]. Moscow: Carte Blanche, 1990. [Includes "Starye pesni," 1980-1982.]

"Muzyka glukhogo vremeni. Russkaia lirika 70–kh godov" ["Music of a Deaf Time: Russian Lyrics of the 1970s"]. *Vestnik novoi literatury* 2 (1990): 257–65.

"Potomu chto vse my byli," "Èlegiia smokovnitsy," "Varlaam i Ioasaf," "Zemlia," "Babochka ili dve ikh." *Novyi mir* 5 (1990): 161–64.

"Starye pesni," "Gornaia kolybel'naia," "Laterna Magia." *Literaturno-khudozhestvennyi, istoriko-kul'turnyi al'manakh.* Moscow: Izdatel'stvo Prometei, 1990. 7–28.

"Èlegiia, perekhodiashchaia v rekviem." *Vek XX i mir* 7 (1991): 29–32.

"Kot, babochka, svecha," "Proshchanie," "Voda-krest'ianka." *Gorizont* 7 (1991): 34–37.

"M. Gasparov—O. Sedakova. Dialogi o Bakhtine" ["M. Gasparov—O. Sedakova: Dialogues on Bakhtin"]. *Novyi krug* [Kiev] 1 (1991): 113–17.

"Mednyi vsadnik. Kompozitsiia konflikta" ["The Bronze Horseman: Composition of a Conflict"]. *Russia* [Marsilio Editori] 7 (1991): 39–55.

"Ocherk drugoi poèzii. Ocherk pervyi. Viktor Krivulin" ["Essay on other poetry. Essay one. Viktor Krivulin']. *Volga* 10 (1991): 258–66.

Pamiati Arseniia Tarkovskogo ["In memory of Arsenii Tarkovsky"]. *Volga* 12 (1991): 174–77.

"Postmodernizm. Usvoenie otchuzhdeniia" ["Postmodernism: Mastering of Alienation"]. *Moskovskii nabliudatel'* 5 (1991): 14–16.

"Puteshestvie volkhvov." *Znamia* 6 (1991): 139–40.

"Vospominaniia o Venedikte Erofeeve" ["Remembering Venedikt Erofeev"]. *Teatr* 9 (1991): 98–103.

"Zametki i vospominaniia o raznykh stikhotvoreniiakh, a takzhe 'Pokhvala poèzii'" ["Notes and Recollections about Various Poems and also 'In Praise of Poetry' "]. *Volga* 6 (1991): 135–64.

"Znak, smysl, vest'" ["Sign, meaning, information"]. *Nezamechennaia zemlia, Literaturno-khudozhestvennyi al'manakh.* Moscow, 1991. 249–52.

"Iz knigi 'Dikii shipovnik.'" *Znamia* 8 (1992): 103–11.

"Iz stansov v manere Aleksandra Popa." *Druzhba narodov* 9 (1992): 114–20.

"Pamiati ottsa Aleksandra," "Iz semi stikhotvorenii." *Ukrainskii obozrevatel'* 7 (1992): 5.

"Piatye stansy," "Èlegia Lipe." *Nezavisimaia gazeta,* 5 February 1992, 7.

"Puteshestvie v Briansk" ["A Journey to Briansk"]. *Volga* 5–6 (1992): 138–57.

"Po russkom imeni . . ." ["About a Russian Name . . ."]. *Iskusstvo kino* 10 (1993): 4–7.

"Litso snoviden'ia, smushchen'ia, dozhdia," "Skazka, v kotoroi nichego ne proiskhodit," "Proshchanie." *Druzhba narodov* 11 (1993): 117–23.

"Pritcha i russkii roman" ("Parable and the Russian Novel"). *Iskusstvo kino* 4 (1994): 11–16.

Shelk vremeni. The Silk of Time. Bilingual Selected Poems. Ed. and intro. V. Polukhina. Keele, Staffordshire: Keele University Press, 1994.

Stikhi (Poems). Moscow: Gnozis, Carte Blanche, 1994. [Includes "Wild Rose" ("Shipovnik," 1978) and "Elegies" ("Èlegii," 1987–1990).]

In Translation

[Poems]. Trans. Andrew Wachtel. *Berkeley Fiction Review* 6 (double issue 1985–1986): 190–201.

[Poems]. Trans. Léon Robel and Henry Deluy. *Action poétique* 115 (1989): 58–62.

"A Chinese Journey" [extracts]. Trans. Richard McKane. *Index on Censorship* 3 (1990): 17–18.

"Lines on the Death of a Kitten." Trans. Richard McKane. *Index on Censorship* 3 (1990).

[Poems]. Trans. Léon Robel. *Poésie* 90, 33 (June 1990): 34–39.

"A Chinese Journey" [extracts]. *The Poetry of Perestroika*, Ed. Peter Martimer and S.J. Litherland. Trans. Richard McKane. Newcastle: Iron Press, 1991. 91–93.

"The Autumn Water." *Brodsky through the Eyes of His Contemporaries.* Ed. V. Polukhina. Trans. Robert Reid. Basingstoke: Macmillan Press, 1992. 256–59.

"Earth." Trans. Peter Henry. *Scottish Slavonic Review* 18 (1992): 110–13.

"Elegy." *Brodsky through the Eyes of His Contemporaries.* Ed. V. Polukhina. Trans. Robert Reid. Basingstoke: Macmillan Press, 1992.

[Poems]. *Third Wave: The New Russian Poetry*. Ed. Kent Johnson and Stephen M. Ashby. Trans. Andrew Wachtel. Ann Arbor: University of Michigan Press, 1992. 132–36.

[Poems]. Trans. Catriona Kelly, Peter Henry and Andrew Wachtel. *Glas: New Russian Writing* 4 (1993): 221–25.

[Poems]. *Contemporary Russian Poetry: A Bilingual Anthology.* Ed. Gerry S. Smith. Bloomington: Indiana University Press, 1993. 268–79.

[Poems]. *An Anthology of Russian Women's Writing, 1777–1992.* Ed. Catriona Kelly. Oxford: Clarendon Press, 1994. 390–93.

[Poems]. *The Silk of Time: Bilingual Selected Poems.* Ed. and intro. V. Polukhina. Keele, Staffordshire: Keele University Press, 1994.

Translations by Ol'ga Sedakova

Claudel, Paul. *Izbrannye stikhi.* Moscow: Carte Blanche, 1992.

Eliot, T.S. *Poslednii èkzempliar, Al'manakh.* Saratov, 1993.

Pound, Ezra. *Izbrannye stikhotvoreniia.* Moscow: Carte Blanche, 1992.

Rilke, Rainer Maria. *Rodnik* [Riga] 8 (1988): 13–18.

Secondary Works

Averintsev, S.S. "Gore, polnoe do dna." *Stikhi* [*Poems*]. Moscow: Gnozis, Carte Blanche, 1994. 356–63.

D.S. [V.A. Saitanov]. "Ol'ga Sedakova. Novyi put'." *Vrata, Okna, Arki, Izbrannye stikhotvoreniia* [*Gates, Windows, Arches, Selected Poems*]. Paris: YMCA Press, 1986. 113–28.

Epshtein, Mikhail. *Paradoksy novizny*. Moscow: Sovetskii pisatel', 1988. 161–64.

Kelly, C. *A History of Russian Women's Writing 1820–1992.* Oxford: Clarendon Press, 1994. 423–32.

Polukhina, V. "Conform Not to This Age: The Poetry and Personality of Ol'ga Sedakova. An Interview with Sedakova." *Russian Literature in the Eighties*. Ed. Arnold McMillin. London: Harwood Academic Publishers, 1996.

Shevchenko, A.K. "Pis'mo o smerti, liubvi i kotenke" [A Letter about Death, Love and a Kitten"]. *Filosofskaia i sotsiologicheskaia mysl'* 9 (1989): 110–14.

Smith, A. "Sedakova Brings Silver Age Image to Modern Verse." *The Moscow Tribune,* 14 December 1994, 15.

Sverdliuk, Iana. "Ol"ga Sedakova." *Segodnia,* 31 December 1994, 13.

Zhazhonian, M. "Teni slov." *Russkaia mysl'* 7 (13 April 1994): 12.

Elena Shvarts

Elena Andreevna Shvarts was born 17 May 1948 in Leningrad. She is a prolific, compelling contemporary poet whose work mixes the skepticism of postmodern sensibilities with the haunted primitivism of ancient Slavic folk belief. Standard biographical accounts seem unusually inept when it comes to this poet. Shvarts has been quite private about her own life experiences and has never written what could crudely be called "confessional" verse. Her upbringing seems to have offered her great freedom but little structure. In a short statement about herself, she stressed her unconventional education, which eventually included a year of study at Leningrad University in the Philological Faculty and graduation from the Theater Institute, where she was an external student. She described herself as an "autodidact," with interests only in poetry and theology, separately and together.[1]

Shvarts has performed and shared her work widely since the 1960s and has long been well known in underground circles. Her work emerged from the cultural context of this artistic underground and continues to explore its themes of marginalization, poverty and commitment to authentic if dangerous utterance. With the appearance of her poetry in more mainstream journals and in book form in the late 1980s, and the rush of translations into English at the same time, she has also achieved some prominence abroad. Critics often mention her name in the same breath as that of Ol'ga Sedakova, a contemporary poet who has written admiringly of Shvarts, although the similarity seems largely that of age group and gender.[2] Unlike Sedakova's acerbic metaphysical musings, Shvarts writes with the emotional violence of Tsvetaeva and the psychological urgency of Dostoevsky. Comparisons to Dostoevsky have seemed particularly apt, given Shvarts's equally turbulent fascination with the city of St. Petersburg, her home for her entire life and the palpable setting for many of her poems. And like

Dostoevsky, Shvarts takes up an unsettling mix of themes: monastic reclusiveness, familial hatred, material poverty, spiritual quest, inescapable mortality, cultural discomfort and cosmic disorder.

Shvarts's world feels even less secure, in fact, than Dostoevsky's, and the Russian novelist who seems her nearer predecessor is Andrei Platonov. Rather than the abiding religious faith that saves Dostoevsky's characters, at least some of them, Shvarts's poetic personae may have intense religious experiences, but they typically and devastatingly find themselves in places of the same metaphysical homelessness as Platonov's town of Chevengur or his foundation pit. Shvarts may seem to write of this despair as a reaction to the alienations of Soviet civilization, and certainly many of her poems abound with the appalling realia of daily life. But she also invents poetic personae who defy social and sometimes natural categories. Self-described idiosyncracy defines the emblematic short poem "Animal-Flower" ("Zver'-tsvetok," 1976), classifying herself as neither animal nor plant—and doing so by describing how her body will send forth shoots of a new entity once she is dead and buried.[3] In "Animal-Flower" Shvarts blurs the boundaries between life and death, animal and plant, object and person, and she seems to transform the poem's morbid setting into a playground of thoughtful self-reflection and self-construction.

Yet all is not play in Shvarts's world: she is frequently a poet of incomprehensibly violent images, often seeming to try on for size the fates of those who have suffered unaccountably or perished in pain. She relishes the juxtaposition of spiritual salvation with physical torment, as in the powerful short lyric "The Hacked Priest" ("Zarublennyi sviashchennik," 1992). A longer poem—Shvarts specializes in what she has called the "short long poem," typically a cycle of lyrics under five pages—dramatizes the story of "The Roasted Englishman in Moscow" ("Zharennyi anglichanin v Moskve," 1990), one of Ivan the Terrible's more infamous torture punishments. Shvarts speaks through many voices in this poem, including the dying Englishman, for whom time seems to have stopped; the indifferent tsar, annoyed by the groans of the dying man; a monk reclusively praying for the martyred man; and the man's sister, who dreams this scene from the safety of England. Most of all, Shvarts gives us a bitterly ironic narrating voice that finds comfort in the lessened violence these days (rather than in the uncivilized sixteenth century) and in Petersburg (rather than barbaric Moscow). This nine-poem sequence condenses many voices and thus many versions of the self into a small space, although its dramatic vividness may be its most memorable achievement.

Of particular interest among her longer works is the novel-length impersonation that created the mad nun Lavinia, entitled *The Works and Days of Lavinia,*

Nun from the Order of the Circumcision of the Heart (*Trudy i dni Lavinii, Monakhini iz Ordena Obrezaniia Serdtsa,* 1987). In this cycle of seventy-nine short poems, Shvarts gives us the poetry another woman is imagined to have written—thus she imagines the subjectivity of another as filtered through her own. The resulting ventriloquism permits Shvarts to speak in tones that can be reverent or insanely furious, gently submissive or wild-eyed at the spectacle of religious passion. In "From the Anthill" ("Iz murav'inoi kuchi"), Lavinia is stunned to witness a nun's ecstatic descent into a bed of ants, but she remains enough the discerning poet to compare the ants rushing across her face to a horde of letters in ornamental script that seem to have escaped a holy book.

> For the holidays we drank a little wine.
> In Holy Week one is allowed a bit!
> And off to the shadowy blue forests
> We wandered, swaying, to glorify God.
> Serafima sang so ice-cold and high,
> Shulamith so burningly and low,
> As if they could go flying off from the earth
> By their voices, but we held on to them.
> When we came up to the little anthill
> Far from houses, far from roads,
> Suddenly Serafima fell down prostrate,
> Almost tunneled into their dark sand.
> And—*de profundis*—this is how she prayed,
> And how she cried out from that hill:
> The Lord is our GOD! HE LIVES! He alone lives!
> We were struck dumb. The ants zealously
> Spread themselves amid the mess of her gray
> Hair, over the scroll of her skin,
> Like the ornamental script of the Holy Writ.
> And as if they too were shouting,
> I heard their even, glassy, bell-like tones.[4]

This poem stands out within the cycle because in it Lavinia essentially watches someone else fall into religious ecstasy, which we might read as an allegory for Shvarts more typically observing the ways that Lavinia works through problems of belief and faith. (Shvarts, to be sure, is perfectly capable elsewhere in her verse of imagining her own forms of religious frenzy and self-sacrifice, as in the untitled

1978 poem that begins "Dancing David"). In "From the Anthill," Lavinia stares in horror, as self-humiliation becomes a spectacle that turns witnesses numb. But in that disbelieving stare at the performance of faith, Lavinia also sees an allegory for the emergence of poetry.[5] The ants crawl around Serafima's folded skin like letters of script on a scroll of writing. And in the last sentence of the poem, these letters themselves seem to come alive, crying out with an even, transparent ring that merges the sounds of church bell with the magic harmonies of poetry.

Shvarts's use of religious imagery in *Lavinia* is difficult to characterize, in part because of the shifts within the poem. As intense as her investment in biblical stories and in scenes of sudden faith is her turn to blasphemy. In this compulsive undermining of stable systems of belief, Shvarts once again calls to mind Dostoevsky, especially in the way that she, too, brings black humor into the very place of religious experience. Like her predecessors in the nineteenth-century prose tradition, Shvarts speaks out for the "little man" who is trampled by cruel historical forces, but religious salvation is no soothing alternative in her world. It inevitably has its own cruelties; thus her fascinations with scenes of martyrdom and torture. Shvarts sees too keenly into the chaos of material life to redeem it with ready spirituality; in her best poems, spiritual chaos itself threatens to descend. Her most sustained meditation on these questions is *Lavinia*, particularly in scenes where the devil takes on strange new forms to wrestle with the forces of goodness and godliness (in one section, man and the devil are imaged as Siamese twins). Because of *Lavinia*'s structure as a mosaic of scenes in which no one has the upper hand for long, it is impossible to say whether Shvarts in the end urges us to seek the faith that sustains some in her imagined nunnery, or whether she is so taken with the sexual temptations of Lavinia simply because it is at those moments that one is most alive. Shvarts has imagined a violently transformative religious practice, but even it lacks the power to vanquish temptation, and certainly the efficacy of spiritual life in this poem is encouraged by the safe barriers of the nunnery's walls. *Lavinia* succeeds best in its narrative situation, in fact, presenting us with the consciousness of a spiritually curious, psychically rebellious and psychologically astute young woman who is fully alive to the pleasures and pains of nature, spirituality and erotic love. More than any of Shvarts' shorter poetic sequences, *Lavinia* proceeds as a novel—and very much a twentieth-century novel. Affinities with the novel mark both its psychological intensity and its evocative yet utterly earthy language, a style of writing that is true in Shvarts' shorter lyrics as well.

Shvarts had earlier written another cycle of poetic impersonations, "Cynthia" ("Kinfiia," 1978), purporting to be the translations into Russian of otherwise lost poems by a Roman poet. These sixteen poems, split into two groupings of eight poems each, display Cynthia's visceral contempt for servants, lovers and her father. The poems are dazzling recombinations of classical images and diction, with violent undertones as appropriate to the end of the Roman empire as to the daily life of Leningrad streets.

Not all, or even most, of Shvarts's poetry takes up historical themes. She is exceptionally astute at rendering the urban landscape of St. Petersburg, seeing it as the surprising combination of beloved sites sanctioned by cultural myths with the pervasive decay and destruction associated with the Soviet period. One such lyric is laconically titled "The Dump" ("Svalka," undated; first published 1983). Shvarts's personal connection to this landscape tends to the prosaic rather than the sublime. In an effective poem that juxtaposes the recollections of an innocent childhood with scenes of an empty lot, a cemetery and a tanning factory, "Kindergarten after Thirty Years" ("Detskii sad cherez tridtsat' let," undated; first published 1987), Shvarts reaches for that more sublime position by associating herself with an Old Believer.[6] She wishes in the poem to speak curses on her past, as he has done, but the poem's graphic images of animal carcasses, of crumbling bread and rusting machinery pull us down into daily life, and the diminished landscape seems an extruded reflection of the poet's own soul. Similar contrasts between high and low appear in one of the "Gypsy Verses" ("Tsyganskie stikhi," 1970s) that appears in this anthology: Shvarts moves from "dove-blue aura" to galoshes and "a little rainy dirt" in the space of two lines, and not only because she has envisioned gypsy life as the quintessential mix of dissolute poverty and unfettered freedom.

"Kindergarten" is also notable for its pervasive use of corporeal imagery—it is a poem in which the land has its own body, and in which even the signs of industry take us back to the body, as we read of the tanning of animal hides. In other poems, like the remarkable cycle "Black Easter" ("Chernaia Paskha," 1974), Shvarts describes all-too-human bodies as sites of both desire and despair.[7] This poem's account of an alcoholic husband's beating his wife is as imagistically unforgettable as it is psychologically precise; we feel as if we are in the world of Liudmila Petrushevskaia's short stories, but a world horrifyingly made calm by the formal devices of sudden rhymes or the intimations of intricate poetic sequence. And in "Black Easter," the poet juxtaposes the violence of intimate relations with the promise of resurrection, where bodies seem able to be reborn relentlessly against all odds; her poem is insistently set in Russia, evoking its expanses and its crevices with a physicality that can be almost unbearable to read. Other poems turn the body inside out, as in "Elegy on an X-Ray of My Skull" ("Èlegiia na rentgenovskii snimok moego cherepa," 1975), where visual representations of bone, tissue, skull and skin urge the poet toward a reflection on thinking, remembering and loss. In another meditation on the way heads hide thoughts, "The Headless Moon" ("Luna bez golovy," 1987), Shvarts imagines the moon as a head severed from the body, with all its contents—meaning, what one has read, from Tolstoy to Pascal—running out and rushing off like mice.[8]

Shvarts thus conveys the material sensations of bodily experience as grotesquely as her great forebear Marina Tsvetaeva,[9] and while she does not imitate Tsvetaeva's poetics of phonic wizardry and figurative metonymy, it can be said with admiration that Shvarts enlivens her prosaic, discursive poetic gestures by means of compellingly changing rhythms. Shvarts has observed that she likes to keep the rhythms from settling into any fixed pattern.[10] Particularly in poems with shorter verse lines, readers feel her readiness to experiment, to reverse herself, to twist easy iambs into complex irony and to mix meters in individual lines. Her rhymes, while they will not seem stunning to those familiar with Tsvetaeva's fireworks—or with Brodsky's—nonetheless compel the reader's attention, reminding us of the presence of formal harmonies or verbal symmetries even when the themes and narratives of a poem wildly clash. But unlike the poets of Russian modernism, for whom language remained an ordering authority and a source of salvation from an increasingly incomprehensible world, Shvarts rejects the aesthetic pleasures of a beautifully ordered linguistic universe, and throughout her *oeuvre* instead brings to life unexpected possibilities in prosaic, yet passionately expressive speech.

Stephanie Sandler

From the cycle Gypsy Verses

7.

I saw my dove-blue aura.
Only it was as if a galosh stepped into it,
and it was mixed with a little rainy dirt—
sinful,
you can see, I have offended myself heavily,
and my azure is all blunted.
I broke the Venetian cup
and fettered the gypsy soul . . .
Drunkenness and sloth—I'd start to sleep
and dine with you—if to know of the azure?

1970s

To Irena Iasnogorskaia

Dancing David, I too am along with you!
I'll soar up like a dove, and the twigs, the tidings
will jump themselves up to my beak,
not a stone—a birdie in fury
is He indeed—the Creator, God of audacity.
Wring yourselves, hands! Head
fly from the left palm to the right.
All the words boiled away to salt,
all the words returned into thrones
and the fire winds like a snake.
Crackle, hair, ring out, bones,
throw me in the fire as a woodchip for God.
There's a mirror—the cut-glass ocean—
living eyes and smoldered to ashes,
although Thou art not to be seen there,
yet Thou hangest in them, like a tear.
O Lord, permit
me to ease Thy pain.
We don't tend to feel pain.
We know no torments,
And the earth, mountains, waves
we call, as before, paradise.
O Lord, permit
me to ease Thy pain.
The tickling blood, guffawing bones—
toss me up toward God's throne.

1978

The Roasted Englishman in Moscow[1]

(the moment as sphere)

1.

The bell began to ring for vespers—
The moment of death for Elisei.

Bit by bit the crown of thorns
Settled on the evildoer.
The executioners, though reluctant,
Tied him tightly to the stake,
Kindled fire in all the chambers:
"The tsar commands it, burn, accursed.
It must be our tsar is hungry,
He wants a rare dish for the roast,
He wants a new one every day,
That's what he's a ruler for. . . ."

2.

The ringing evening bell continues,
In that moment Adam, our father,
Slipping along the tree of time,
And a soul still unborn—of a later sowing,
A Petersburg bird—along the twig of a melody
Looks within—and marvels.
In an alien time we have no rights—we're mute,
Not to mention that we're not ourselves.
An alien spirit flickers in the round scent-bottle—
There a little devil dances—son of Satan.

3.

At sunset's end, on an island—in the desert
A holy hermit prays to God for everyone,
For speaking and unspeaking creatures,
And for the dead, who are so loudly silent.
"Whoever in the world might bear a cross just now,
Give me to bear a little of his lot."
He seizes that lot, like an ant,
And runs into his wretched little cave.
And to the one who at that moment turned
Like a roast that has been overcooked,
A dream was sent—that he roasted in a dream,
And when he woke—what joy there would be!

4.

The bell began to ring for vespers.
The tsar flinched in his bed; he tossed
Aside the ancient Byzantine manuscript
And, groaning a bit, arose.
For a whole hour already, probably,
He had been reading with an English glass
And grew weary—time for vespers.
In a cage by the window a singer
Started to moan and suddenly gasped;
The rich Byzantine brocade
Winced with a flash of northern light.
"You there! Roast the infidel more slowly,
I bid him live till morning itself."
As if it were by God's command
Fury descended on the tsar.
"Our struggles are not against the flesh,
But let the evil-spirited flesh suffer,
Were it not for dear mother, flesh,
What could we pierce of the soul."
He tittered. Scared—well, what if the demon
While sliding out crept into my soul?
No, that's the frightful fire of the heavens.
As over the wall, a line cut through
Across the soul too, through the heart—from left
A hissing red-hot stone of wrath—
Into the velvety night of the belly.
And the air, the room—as if everything boiled—
And that is God's doing, not man's.

5.

The boyars, closed away, mutter: he spared
No poison for us, and it serves him right.
The wind stirs the greens of strong language,
And at their roots: it's time, time to be off to Lithuania.

6.

Where the evening glow's not audible
In a little moss-covered hut
A sorcerer spins a doll; a crown is on it.
He pierces its waxen heart
And waits for a moan, but doesn't hear a moan.
He chucks it into the tub where the worms are fed.
The cupbearer has not yet emptied the keg,
And the wine of the tsar's life is dark.
He still rules, his mantle flows from his shoulders,
But he is cursed by us long since,
Death and the furnace are tired of awaiting him.

7.

And there far away—where the isle of Albion is,
Bomelia's sister dreamed a frightful dream.

8.

Snow fell in the darkness. From the church weakly
A soft and wearisome singing was carried.
A fisherman drove frozen pike, and they clattered
Over the potholes like logs of firewood.

9.

When they removed the charred log still alive
And, cracking open its eyewhites, it whispered,
"Oh my Lord,"
That dull-red sun went slipping
Quicker than is possible
Under the Muscovite ice.

1990

I Produce Narcotics (Sometimes)

I would like—(I love)
To look at the clouds, to lie on the earth,
And at the same time, to collect
Hemp inside myself.
In me within, in the middle bosom,
There is not just hemp—
Fields of poppies wave there,
Iridescent,
There amid the scarlet are pale pink ones—
It's they, the dears, that have the sweetest juice.
I'll rub myself, eat my fill and with a dragonfly squadron
I'll drift off to the East.
I have a plantation in my blood,
A golden surf begins to sway,
Inspiration catches fire,
It brings the thirst for death behind it.
Turning on the wheels of the brain,
The narcotin is ground and broken
And melts into a tearful iron,
And I lie on a cloud in dews,
And beneath me is altitude, altitude.

Temriukovich, Patrikevna,
Take a look without delaying
At what is sailing out on the outside—
Quickly look into my dream,
You see, it's jumping like an elephant,
In the depth of blood-formation,
The narcotic hormone.

Memory of the Psalm

To O. Sedakova

Here I sit by my Babylonian rivers,
Here I cry (cry I?) above the Black Nevka,

Hanging my harp low on a willow, embracing
Life—the nimble leech, the potholey wench.

Here I stand above the cliff, above darkness curled into a cloud.
It's the pure who hear everything, the pure who see everything
And their ways are straight—crosses,
I though circle round in an invisible roulette wheel
Around the cataract of blindness.
Lead me up on the mountain, my simple God!
Thou sent me downward, like a soldier to battle,
I though took up with a widow on a long billet—
With a red-eyed one who doesn't know the comfort of prayer,
The one unmarried in soul is used to a blind little life,
Lead me up on the mountain, my simple God!

Carry me slantwise over the valley of Ingermanland,
Show me the swampy dust of the plain,
Where the sedge is, where the demons in their sinfulness
Keep the currents of tears in underground springs
And have locked them away there. We should, we should
Start sobbing, drown the blind old woman in tears
And on a Finnish Sea of sorrow and plaint
Sail off in softly sinking ships.

1981

Recollection of Hairwashing in a Thunderstorm

Late evening. Deep dark childhood.
In the window, like an epileptic, the storm thrashed.
A gray-haired couple were washing my hair,
In the basin swam my eyes in lather.
They saw themselves and closed.
The old woman scratched, the old man poured water,
When the storm rose up in a wild roar—
They would fall still for a moment.
But again they grabbed hold, tormented and scrubbed.

The storm was already grumbling from the distant forest,
When exhausted, and grumbling, and sighing deeply
The two sick and ancient demons fell asleep.
And the silken hair squeaked,
The night refreshed spilled over into crevices,
The nightingale sang and the old folks wheezed.
I lay in desecrated cleanliness,
Guessing where I was, what was wrong with me,
And the desolate land I recognized with sorrow—
Where devils clean and the rain washes away.

1991

The Hacked Priest

An old woman hurries to church
(she absolutely must be stooped),
A crow caws over the sodden snow,
With a tear the local person
Always rejoices.
A dead man's melting in the corner
With a prayer stuck to his forehead,
Perhaps it is printed into the bone
And the spirits under the skull will recoil.
The priest, who perished at the end's beginning,
Similar to Lucifer and the Father,
A little bit worldly and too active,
But chosen as a victim—(to spite the devils?)
Can with his blood—do you believe?
He'll nourish the crow, old woman and temple.
The snow will pour out no more in the vale—
Could it really fall up—from the earth—in January?
Our pain will soon become quiet,
But the salt will stand out on the axe.

1992

How Andrei Belyi Almost Fell under a Streetcar

I'll lie not thinking of anything,
I'll embrace
My head,
As if it's been cut off-ff.
Why, why
Do I see
An autumn day in Moscow?
A migratory angel watches from the heavens—
Someone is strolling toward death
(And it's not his turn yet),
Someone in the shape of a whirlwind,
By the Pokrovsky gate,
Now he's about to fall
Under a streetcar,
Under a cold, ringing
Streetcar.

Why? Why do I see
Also, as if from the heavens—
The streetcar wheezing from fear
And a little figure below,
Which having flashed
Falls upwards and back?

Oh goat's leap! A long, long jump!
The temple flashed by upturned—Dornach.
The Alps, the Doctor, shining, started whirling in a sphere
And shattered in the black cobblestones.

Like a simple acrobat,
Oh almost, oh almost—
That *salto mortale*,
In the swift windmill of wings
A wheel of upturned legs,
The burn of cleansing.
He only broke his arm,

Scared the clouds.
It's all right, he'll live until death.
Quick to the doctor,
I'll pay later,
I forgot my money at home, believe me.
He nurses his arm—after all it
Was just now born,
The police wave to a cabbie.
Here he is riding, he is silent
And inaudibly whimpers,
And the wheels slightly whine along.
At his heels
There stands a being—
I don't know how to name it,
Only the wings are crossed
In a ring before its face,
Through the eyes
Of the rider they pass.
Or are those rays?
A tremor of light and darkness,
The nervousness of night?
When suddenly by the moon,
The white-hot moon,
A fish ignites the air with its silver,
Tears the lip and leaves into the cool.

1985

Love as the Third

When you told me—I love you—
The eyes widened and features twitched,
We took a look at one another
Like dumbfounded tomcats,
Like two competitors.
Claws are ready for battle, hair on end,
Let's see—whose claws are sharper,
Whose voice more vile.

I turned around the corner and looked,
Bowing my neck, at you,
Now our fate is, it seems,
To roam over one and the same roof,
And to listen to Love stealing up the stairs,
Meowing, breathing loudly,
But—inflaming the green of eyes,
Not to look at it, but into us.

1987

Celestial Ballet

Yesterday was a thunderstorm
And I said "Whew!" every time
The lightning with a Nijinsky
Leap flew into the clouds and slipped
And fell in the abyss—the thunder was from that.

And the stormclouds scattered a diamond dust.
And together—the gleam and that inappropriate stamping.
O Desiree! Ballet celestial!
They're pushing, they say, it's time—on this crowded stage,
Hanging between abyss and abyss
Both make the elbow circular and straighten out the heart
By hovering, start shining and tumble off the cliff,
Glittering in the depths of eyes outside the window.

1990

Translated by Sibelan Forrester

Notes to the Essay

1. See the self-descriptions that grace the cover of her 1987 collection *Stikhi*, and that precede the selection of translations in *Third Wave*, 211.

2. Shvarts and Sedakova also share an exploration of religious themes in some of their verse, although they handle religious experience and questions of belief differently. On Shvarts's religious imagery and narratives, see below.

3. "Animal-Flower" has been translated by Michael Molnar in *Paradise*, as have some of the other poems mentioned in this essay: "Cynthia" (Part One only), "Kindergarten after Thirty Years," "The Dump," "Black Easter" and "Elegy on an X-Ray of My Skull" (occasionally the titles appear slightly different there). The volume also includes a small selection from the *Lavinia* cycle. *Paradise* is a well-chosen and precisely translated collection that also has the virtue of facing Russian texts; because it is readily available in paperback, none of its poems appear in the section of translations that follows this essay. A smaller selection of Shvarts's poems can be found in each of the other volumes listed in the Bibliography; one of the poems mentioned here (see note 5 below), "I dreamed we were sailing through rice fields," appears in *Contemporary Russian Poetry*, ed. Gerald S. Smith.

4. E. Shvarts, *Trudy i dni Lavinii*, 32.

5. Similarly, self-conscious references to writing appear in the imagery of the untitled poem that begins "I dreamed we were sailing through rice fields" ("Mne snilos'—my plyvem po risovym poliam," undated; first published in 1987).

6. Shvarts does not write often of childhood (and in "Kindergarten," she comes to speak passionately of herself in middle age), but in "Recollection of Hairwashing in a Thunderstorm" ("Vospominanie o myt'e golovy v grozu," 1991), she creates a tactile, memorable childhood scene that evokes what she calls "desecrated cleanliness." This poem's recognitions are quite similar to those of "Kindergarten": the poet comes to know "where I was, what was wrong with me," and she sees her "desolate land" with "sorrow."

7. One critic has characterized this aspect of Shvarts's poetry as a "completely erotic anatomical theater of one's own bodily composition": see Ol'ga Nikolaeva, "' . . . Bez bytiia,' " *Novyi mir* 10 (1991): 246. Nikolaeva has in mind both "Elegy on an X-Ray of My Skull" ("Èlegiia na rentgenovskii snimok moego cherepa," 1975) and "Memory of a Strange Refreshment" ("Vospominanie o strannom ugoshchenii," 1976), a poem in which Shvarts describes tasting the breast milk of a friend.

8. Decapitation figures in other Shvarts poems, such as "How Andrei Belyi Almost Fell under a Streetcar" ("Kak Andrei Belyi chut' ne popal pod tramvai," 1985), an angelic rewriting of a diabolical scene from Bulgakov's *Master and Margarita* (*Master i Margarita*).

9. Shvarts's awe-filled affection for Tsvetaeva emerges palpably in her comments to Valentina Polukhina in "Coldness and Rationality," 221. Catriona Kelly has called Shvarts "the most sexually explicit woman poet since Marina Tsvetaeva"; see Kelly, *History of Russian Women's Writing*, 422.

10. "Coldness and Rationality," 218.

Translator's Note to the Selected Works

1. This is the story of the English doctor Elisei Bomelia, who at first zealously served Ivan the Terrible, inventing poisons for his enemies, but later was himself executed in the same tormenting/torturous way that is described here *(author's note)*.

Bibliography

Primary Works

Tantsuiushchii David. New York: Russica, 1985.

Trudy i dni Lavinii, Monakhini iz Ordena Obrezaniia Serdtsa. Ann Arbor, MI: Ardis, 1987.

Stikhi. Leningrad: Beseda, 1987.

Storony sveta. Stikhi. Leningrad: Sovetskii pisatel', 1989.

Stikhi. Leningrad: Assotsiiatsiia Novaia Literatura, 1990.

"Bednye dni." *Znamia* 12 (1992): 51–53.

"Zharenyi anglichanin v Moskve." *Zvezda* 5–6 (1992): 3–7.

"Stikhi poslednikh let." *Vestnik novoi literatury* 5 (1993): 105–14.

In Translation

[Selected poems]. *Contemporary Russian Poetry*. Ed. Gerald S. Smith. Bloomington: Indiana University Press, 1993. 246–57.

[Selected poems]. *Paradise*. Intro. and trans. Michael Molnar; additional trans. Catriona Kelly. Newcastle-upon-Tyne: Bloodaxe Books, 1993.

[Selected poems]. *Third Wave: The New Russian Poetry*. Ed. Kent Johnson and Stephen M. Ashby. Ann Arbor: University of Michigan Press, 1992. 211–21.

Secondary Works

Goldstein, Darra. "The Heart-Felt Poetry of Elena Shvarts." *Fruits of Her Plume*. Ed. Helena Goscilo. Armonk, NY: M.E. Sharpe, 1993. 239–50.

———. "Shvarts, Elena Andreevna." *Dictionary of Russian Women Writers*. Ed. Marina Ledkovsky, Charlotte Rosenthal and Mary Zirin. Westport, CT: Greenwood Press, 1994. 598–600.

Heldt, Barbara. "The Poetry of Elena Shvarts." *World Literature Today* (Spring 1989): 381–83.

Kelly, Catriona. *A History of Russian Women's Writing 1820–1992*. Oxford: Clarendon Press, 1994. 411–22.

Polukhina, Valentina. "Coldness and Rationality: An Interview with Elena Shvarts" *Brodsky through the Eyes of His Contemporaries*. Ed. Valentina Polukhina. London: St. Martin's Press, 1992. 215–236.

Tat'iana Tolstaia

Tat'iana Nikitichna Tolstaia (b. 1951) emerged as the most talented prose writer of the era of *glasnost'* and *perestroika*—the Gorbachev epoch of openness and reform. With the abrogation of political taboos, and despite a paper shortage, previously banned works crowded bookstore shelves and were grabbed up, read, discussed and passed on by a hungry readership. Andrei Platonov's *The Foundation Pit*, Anatolii Rybakov's *Children of the Arbat*, Andrei Bitov's *Pushkin House* and Vasilii Grossman's *Life and Fate*, as well as works by Aleksandr Bek, Vladimir Nabokov and Evgenii Zamiatin, were being devoured by the cognoscenti. While these previously banned books made the literary scene, at the same time, the number of talented young writers inside the Soviet Union diminished and the artistic level of their production seemed to be on the decline.[1] A new generation simply had not sprung up among the ghosts of the murdered and exiled literary heroes and begun writing freely and well. Tat'iana Tolstaia, the most original of the younger writers, burst forth as the notable exception. Her works have been received with enthusiasm in the West as well as in Russia. Critics on both continents recognize her talent and consider her one of the outstanding new voices of Russian prose.

Tat'iana Tolstaia has been historically and temporally well situated. Born in 1951 in Leningrad, one of seven children, she grew up in a cultured and privileged family. Tolstaia is the granddaughter of the historical novelist Aleksei Nikolaevich Tolstoi (1882–1945), famous for his *Aelita* and *Peter the First*. Her maternal grandfather, Mikhail Lozinskii, was a well-known translator of Dante's *Divine Comedy*, the works of Molière, Lope de Vaza, Shakespeare and many others. Her father, a physicist and an accomplished linguist, taught her two languages. Most of her siblings are involved in the arts; one brother was a member of the Russian parliament.[2] Tolstaia received her advanced education at Leningrad State

University, graduating in 1974 from its department of languages and literatures. She married her fellow student, Andrei Lebedev, a professor of classics; they have two sons.

She was raised and educated during the Brezhnev era (1964–1982), which saw the collapse of detente in international relations and the rise of economic stagnation, corruption and moral decay in Soviet internal life. In literature the last years of Brezhnev's rule brought increased emphasis on ideology and politics and the insistence on socialist realism in Soviet literature.[3] This theory argues that artistic output be, first, *narodnyi* ("popular"), that is, that its subject matter reflect the life of ordinary people and be accessible to them; second, that it be *ideinyi*, that is, reflect a complete, mature ideology on the part of the author, which helps fulfill the work's educational goals; and that lastly it be *partiinyi*—imbued with the ideals of the Communist party and in accord with the party's current policy.[4] Because works that did not reflect the ideology and political development of the Soviet Union were held back by censors or banned if published abroad (works of Joseph Brodsky, Aleksander Solzhenitsyn and Boris Pasternak, for instance), Russian literature and language, under Brezhnev, became a matter of diaspora. The death of Brezhnev in 1982 led to a number of rapid changes in Soviet leadership and culminated in the ascent to power of Mikhail Gorbachev, a younger man, whose new policy of *glasnost'* expanded the confines of the freedom of expression in Soviet society and introduced a liberalizing thaw in literature which has its parallels in the literary thaws of the immediate post-Stalin era.

Gorbachev's liberalization and democratization coincided with Tolstaia's literary beginnings, which she traces to January 1983. Unable to read after an eye operation, dissatisfied with her job in a science publishing house, suffering from a general malaise and frustrated by the lack of good new literature, she picked up her pen and began to write. Tolstaia appeared in print with her first story, "On the Golden Porch" ("Na zolotom kryl'tse sideli," 1983), at the age of thirty-two. Three years later, this six-page miniature was followed by a longer narrative, "Peters," which sparked great enthusiasm in both Moscow and Leningrad and established her reputation as a magnificent writer. Her first collection, *On the Golden Porch*, containing thirteen of her stories, appeared in Moscow in 1987 and was translated into ten languages. Tolstaia has quickly penetrated American readership, beginning in 1989 with her first collection of stories, *On the Golden Porch*, followed by a quick appearance of the newest collection, *Sleepwalker in the Fog* (1992), making all her twenty-two stories (with the exception of "Plot" ("Siuzhet," 1991) available to the American public in both Russian and English.

Although Gorbachev's policy of *glasnost'* had expanded freedom of expression and opened up new areas of Soviet life for critical inquiry, it had not assured complete freedom of artistic expression in contemporary Soviet society for Tolstaia. A writer was still at the mercy of editors who often determined publication policy and the fate of aspiring authors. Tolstaia herself was initially blackballed and denied admittance to the Writers' Union. It might be inferred from this rejection that socialist realism, at least subliminally, continued to contour Soviet literature, and that the government could still indirectly influence the creative process. The editors, following literary and political directives, could alter or hold back works that did not support party ideology. In the heyday of *glasnost'*, the literary establishment had not remained indifferent to Tolstaia; they were not enthusiastic about her stories depicting marginal characters. In an interview 28 April 1989 she states:

> They [the censors] asked me not to write about old people because old people have problems. It is unpleasant to speak about problems. They are old and that's a problem in itself . . . they are cynical . . . I would say "Well, why not write about old people?" And they would say "Because we have no old people." So what can I do? It is like that. They are cynical and we [writers] are cynical. We understand each other. There are no old people. And of course there are no crazy people at all. They don't exist. How can a crazy person exist in our socialist country?[5]

Despite the pressures from editors to alter her stories for the sake of social and ideological relevance, Tolstaia's works appeared unchanged in major literary journals and in her collections of stories. It cannot be overlooked, however, that the editors excluded many of her favorite stories from the first collection; nor did they allow the book to bear the title of her favorite story, "Okkervil River" ("Reka Okkervil'," 1985). Tolstaia, on her part, did not permit a single change in the stories that were accepted. When asked about the need to publish and not just write, Tolstaia replied that she is "an independent person who will not compromise for the sake of being published."[6] Tolstaia's independent spirit offended the conservative hierarchy of the Moscow Writers' Union when she publicly dismissed a new novel by Vasilii Belov as "misanthropic." (As a result, the first time her name came up at the plenum of the union, she fell two votes short and was denied admission until the fall of 1988, when a second vote was taken.)

Independence and individualism mark Tolstaia's style. In a country that bought books by the kilogram, she emerged as a miniaturist. In a society that demanded a positive hero, a paragon of strength and virtue, she chose the marginal character, with all his or her hurts and warts. In a literary establishment that insisted that the language of literature be understood by the masses, she employed a precise, expressive, complex and rich language that demanded an intelligent and alert reader. Tolstaia's use of exceptionally precise language and introduction of new and unusual characters freed her prose from the dead weight of socialist realism. This deviation from—rather than adherence to—traditional literary practice sparked her sudden success.

Perhaps Tolstaia's achievement rests primarily on her creative use of of the word. Her language gives flesh to the characters through which she creates the plot, story line and perspective. Her language overflows with tropes: oxymorons, metaphors, epithets and paraphrases that reveal her literary and psychological personality as well as that of her characters and narrators. She is adept in using special morphemes—prefixes, suffixes and verb endings—as well as graphic, grammatical and lexical features to express a philosophical message or to illustrate the character of a hero. As a result, her stories seem at once compact, complete and economical. One has the feeling that a novel has been read.

While Tolstaia's prose does not seem didactic, she nonetheless employs a broad range of linguistic features and associational resources to express philosophical and political views. She exposes communist totalitarianism, class distinctions, spiritual emptiness and material shortages through subtle signs on the level of word connotation, jargon and style. Tolstaia's satirical art lies in word choice. For example, in "Sweet Shura" (Milaia Shura," 1985) and in "Okkervil River," such memorable phrases as "pre-revolutionary legs" ("dorevoliutsionnye nogi")[7] and "face of old-fashioned bone structure" ("uviashee starinnoi lepki litso")[8] carry with them a political connotation related to the eradication of the Russian nobility. They recall that as a result of the revolution two million nobles, including poets, musicians, artists and philosophers, emigrated, depriving Russia not only of its cultural elite but of their progeny as well. Their intellectual power has disappeared, as have the surface, external features of noble visage. Through these poetic phrases, Tolstaia is making a political statement: the Soviet regime has destroyed the beautiful Russian face, as well as the Russian language, religion and spirit.

Tolstaia favors pure form and the play of words over politics and philosophy: she has no answers about life, but she has come up with a consolation prize, verbal treatment of life—past and present. The texture of her prose is rich in adjectival and descriptive clauses, slang and poetry, exotic images, elements of

Russian legends and idiosyncratic, highly personal details of daily life that at times can appear idiosyncratic or highly personal. It might be that the key to understanding Tolstaia lies with the author's preoccupation with expressive language: the word as the basic element of her creation and verbal art as a singular source of vision within a spiritually vacuous world. She takes great pleasure in playing with the word, effecting illogical couplings and breaking formulaic patterns through which she creates a new perspective of the world.

Moreover, Tolstaia's work uncovers a world of multiple perspectives created through multivocal narration in which we hear the voices of the author, narrators and characters, as well as the voices of memory, time and space. The common language ordained by the central powers takes a back seat and is opposed to what Bakhtin refers as *raznorechie*, heterology (diversity of discourses);[9] a natural outgrowth of social diversity. Tolstaia hears the voices of society and blends them into a "heteroglossal" voice in which her own resounds. A plurality of consciousnesses emerges in Tolstaia's various voices and languages. She breaks the traditional doctrine, imposed by socialist realism, that one voice, one single point of view around which other viewpoints are positioned, be present in a work of literature. Instead, her work features a polyphonic narration in which individual conversational style replaces any single harmonizing narrative tone.

Her stories illuminate character: children on the edge of self-consciousness, old people on the far side of empathy, isolated dreamers, depressives, obsessives. Each character is built up with an extraordinary verbal facility ranging from the highly figurative to the cuttingly ironic. Each character has a voice; each voice has its own recognizable tone and pitch. Tolstaia creates her fictional world through their eyes, mostly people hurt by nature or abused by life, characters outside the mainstream of Soviet life. Her work examines "the isolation of the individual personality, the universal inability to grasp the essence of human beings, particularly during their lifetime; and the indifference of the overwhelming majority to the psychological burdens of their fellow man."[10] The psychological complexities of her protagonists resonate in her trademark verbal complexity.

Her earliest stories are about children. In these, Tolstaia displays a rare gift for gaining access to the young mind and for drawing out the child's world with its internal and external conflicts, real and imagined. Tolstaia's childhoods are profoundly serious periods through which the child/person lives through his emotions and creates a world unsuppressed by the contingencies of adult quotidian responsibility. Her first story, "On the Golden Porch," in which a woman recalls several incidents from her childhood in the countryside, was, in large part, her own. The middle of seven children, growing up in Leningrad, Tolstaia spent summers at a dacha outside the city, in a dreamy world of heather and pine, mushrooms and berries, where she and her sisters pondered the mystery of the man next door and his two wives.[11] In her second story, "Rendezvous with a Bird" ("Svidanie s ptitsei," 1983), the boy Petia, the story's protagonist, spends his summer vacation in the country where he becomes infatuated with a glamorous neighbor, Tamila. Petia is drawn to Tamila because he senses that she is more like a child than an adult and unlike other adults she has no rules about proper forms, proper conduct or getting along. In her house "everything was allowed; to eat bread and jam with unwashed hands, to slouch, to bite your nails, to wear boots. . . . And no one shouted, lectured, called for order, cleanliness, or common sense."[12] Tolstaia's children have the voices that most adults suppress or fail to hear.

In "Peters," she illustrates the damage done to Peters because of his grandmother's insistence that his childhood is merely a preparation for adulthood. The grandmother's focus is on the child's behavior, manners and outward appearance. Under her guidance "he did not play, always wiped his face politely, and clicked his heels in public." In so doing, he was deprived of a true childhood and he became a dispirited embodiment of politeness and obedience. He became the letter *s,* derived from the words *sudar'* ("sir") and *sudarynia* ("madam"), which, in the tradition of Russian nobility, indicated politeness. In the works of Gogol, Tolstoy and Dostoevsky, the letter *s* was used with a hyphen to indicate not the pronunciation of the word, but its intonation. Words like *slushaiu-s* ("I'm listening, please") and *izvolte-s* ("kindly be good enough") indicated politeness. The use of the Russian hyphenated *-s* is not unlike "yes'm" for "yes, ma'am" in the American South. Thus the title of the story, "Peters," tells us that the character and his name, Peter, are affiliated with the German language and culture, and that the character, in the tradition of the letter *s* is polite. The joining of the letter *s* with his name, Peter, goes beyond politeness, however; the letter *s* and all it symbolizes defines Peter's personality and existence. Young Peters, a child living in the twentieth century, is continuing the rituals of the nineteenth-century polite society in which women curtsied and men clicked their heels. In this story, through wordplay, Tolstaia attempts to show the conflict between the prescribed form of life, reflected here in the grandmother's expectations for good behavior, and Peters's desire to have a free childhood. However, since the grandmother "ate his childhood," he was later unable to experience youth or maturity. He was deprived of life, ironically, by someone who saw herself precisely as preparing him for it.

All of her stories are not, however, personal. Tolstaia also tries to show how the Soviet collective unconscious manifests itself in the psychological and behavioral aberrations of her characters. Her interest is in marginal, edgy characters who fail to function in a conformist society because the scripts in their heads interfere in their doing so. Her characters are broken, not normal, in both the positive and negative manifestations. They more frequently than not are absurd, clumsy or strange; often they are on the edge of reality.

Simeonov, in "Okkervil River," creates a nonexistent world for a nonexistent woman; a nineteenth-century Petersburg on the river Okkervil' in which women "wear veils and walk daintily on apple round heels."[13] Denisov, in "Sleepwalker in the Fog," is on the opposite edge of reality. Inside the chaos of his nightmares, he blurs the distinction between the living and the dead as he searches in his contemporary world for the starving blockaders from his dream about the 1941 siege of Leningrad. In "Fakir" (1986), temporal distinctions collapse when Filin's fantastic, internal world is richer and more interesting than the external. He uses his imagination to conjure a fantastic world for himself and his friends by creating intricate tales filled with lively particularity.

Although Tolstaia's works differ from one another in mode of narration, they all embody and expand the same paradigmatic story: the conflict between the real and ideal. In most stories, this conflict is nothing more than a quixotic, whimsical, illusory or retrospective confrontation between the actual and the imagined that leads nowhere. Tolstaia's characters seek escape from their disappointments and losses in dreams, which provide a temporary diversion from their dreary lives, but which rudely shatter in the face of reality. With their extravagant imaginations, the characters are able to escape for a few exhilarating moments. However, these unproductive confrontations amount to very little: rich imaginative lives, while they offer some relief from one's own actual impoverishment, never really insert themselves effectively into the real world. Life is largely a dreary experience for her characters and the powers of imagination are, finally, ineffectual.

Tolstaia's escape into a literature that was socially problematic proved as ineffectual for her as it did for some of her characters, and for the past decade she has spent much of her time in residence at universities in the United States. In 1988 she was a writer in residence at the University of Richmond. After returning home for six months, she came to the West again to teach at the University of Texas and Texas Tech University. She then spent 1991–1992 teaching Soviet literature at Goucher College. In 1993 she was at Princeton University, and she spent the 1994–1995 academic year as a writer in residence at Skidmore College. In the early 1990s she received a "green card" from the Immigration and Naturalization Service, which suggests that she might want to live in the United States on a more permanent basis with her husband and younger son, who have joined her here. This might provide a way for her to retain a powerful literary voice when the dissolution of Soviet society has presented so many problems for Russian intelligentsia generally, and women writers especially.

It is remarkable that Tat'iana Tolstaia gained her recognition as the most prominent writer of serious fiction while a woman under forty. Marina Astman, in her writing about Russian women authors, suggests that "the issue is not impoverished talent but a Soviet tradition of belittling women writers."[14] Consequently, female authors, including Tolstaia, dissociate themselves from "women's writing" labels because they believe the rubric "woman writer" continues to be viewed as inferior in their culture. While she can escape cultural constraint through emigration, her own sense of feminist issues travels with her.

Her careful readers suggest that what she says directly about the topic is undermined by what actually happens in her stories. Although by her own account an "antifeminist," Tolstaia has always created active female protagonists to whom she gives a strong voice; in story after story, she has let them speak for themselves, naming the real contradictions and high cost of their supposed emancipation under socialism. She understands that the multiple burdens of home and work, and the quotidian depletion of the spirit in bureaucratic minutiae, has worn women out. Her women prefer comfort to ideology. For some, this seems antifeminist and reactionary. But it is, perhaps, as valid to note how Tolstaia's position sees through the male-dominated notion of power inherent in a superwoman who serves men's needs as much as her own. In a thoughtful double finesse, what Tolstaia does with her women is thoroughly "gynocentric" in the sense that Hélène Cixous uses that term.[15] She allows them to have personal desire that matters more to them than do the larger, more seemingly empowering, political struggles.

In this way Tolstaia is a writer who can speak to the exhaustion and desire of the women who inhabit her world. Because hers is so fully a work in progress and transition, her readers must wait to see how her move to the West will affect her language, narrative strategy and feminist understanding.

Sophia T. Wisniewska

From On the Golden Porch

Fire and Dust

I wonder where crazy Svetlana is now, the one they called Pipka, about whom some used to say with youthful fecklessness, "Pipka's not a person," and others fumed, "Why do you let her into your house? You watch out for your books. She'll swipe them all!" They were wrong: all that lay on Pipka's conscience was the light blue Simenon and a white wool sweater with knit buttons, and that had already had a mended elbow. The hell with the sweater. Much more valuable things had disappeared since then: Rimma's radiant youth, the childhood of her children, the freshness of her hopes, as pale blue as the morning sky; the secret, joyous trust with which Rimma listened to the voice of the future, whispering to her alone—she had been promised every wreath, flower, island and rainbow, and where were they now? She didn't regret the sweater, which she herself forced on Svetlana as she pushed her out, crazy and half-dressed as usual, into the autumn fury, into the cold, branch-shaking Moscow midnight. Rimma, in her nightgown, impatiently shuffled her feet on the doorstep, lifting one foot and then the other to warm them up, nodding quickly, getting out Svetlana, who kept trying to finish saying something, to tell her something, with a nervous giggle, with quick shrugs; and her black eyes burned like a mad abyss on her white, pretty face, and the wet abyss of her mouth muttered in a hurried flutter—a horrible black mouth whose tooth stubs brought an old forest fire to mind. Rimma advanced, conquering inch after inch, and Svetlana talked and talked, talked and talked, waving her arms about as if doing exercises, late-night, impossible exercises, and in describing something's enormous size—Rimma wasn't listening—she spread her arms so wide she smashed her knuckles on the wall and fell silent for a moment, surprised, pressing the salty joints to her lips, to her mouth, scorched by senseless speech. It was then that the sweater was foisted on her: you'll warm up in the taxi; the door slammed, and Rimma, saddened and laughing, ran back to Fedya under the warm blanket. "Forced her out." The children turned in their sleep. They had to get up early tomorrow. "You should have let her sleep over," Fedya grumbled through his sleep, through the warmth, and he looked so handsome in the night-light's glow. Sleep over? Never! And where? In old Ashkenazy's room? The old man kept tossing on his sagging couch, smoking his thick, stinking cigarettes, coughing, getting up in the middle of the night for a drink from the kitchen sink; but in general he was all right, he didn't bother her. When they had guests, he lent them chairs, brought out a jar of marinated mushrooms, pulled out a clump of sticky peppermints from a tin; placed at one end of the table, he chuckled, swinging his feet, which didn't reach the floor, and smoked into his fist: "Bear up, young people, I'll die soon and the whole apartment will be yours." "Live to be a hundred, David Danilovich," Rimma always rejoined, but it was nice to dream about the time when she would be owner of the whole apartment, her own, not a communal flat, and they would do a major remodeling, doing the awkward five-cornered kitchen in tile from floor to ceiling and putting in a new stove. Fedya would defend his dissertation, the children would go to school, English lessons, music, figure skating . . . what else could she imagine? Many of her friends already envied her her future. But, of course, it wasn't the tile nor well-rounded children that glowed from the expanses of the future in a rainbow-colored fire, a sparkling arc of delirious delight (and Rimma truly wished old Ashkenazy a long life: there was time for everything); no, something bigger, something completely different, important, exciting and great rustled and sparkled ahead, as if Rimma's barge, sailing in a dark stream through flowering rushes, was about to be carried out into the green, joyous, roaring ocean.

And in the meantime, life wasn't completely real, it was a life of expectation, a life out of a suitcase, casual and light—with a pile of rubbish in the hallway, with midnight guests: Petyunya with the heavenly tie, childless Ell and Alyosha, and other people; with nocturnal visits from Pipka and her wild conversations. She was so horrible-looking, that Pipka, with those black stumps for teeth, but a lot of men were attracted by her, and toward the end of a party they would often be one man short: Pipka would have taken him off—always by taxi—to her place in Perlovka. She had a little wooden hut with a fence for cheap. For a while Rimma even worried about Fedya—he was frivolous, and Pipka was crazy and capable of anything at all. If it weren't for the rot in Pipka's fast mouth, Rimma would have thought twice about having her in the house. Especially since Fedya would say, mysteriously, "If Svetlana didn't open her mouth, you could really have a talk with her." And she was always shivering, half-dressed, or dressed from the wrong end: children's shoes, stiff from being soaked, on bare feet in the middle of winter, her hands red and chapped.

No one knew what happened to Pipka, just as no one knew where she had come from—she had just appeared, and that was that. Her stories were wild and confused: something about wanting to go to drama school, even being accepted; but at the market she ran into pickled garlic vendors and was taken away, gagged, to Baku in a white Volga without license plates. There they violated her, knocked out half her teeth, and abandoned her naked on the seashore in a puddle of oil; in the morning she allegedly was found by a wild tribesman passing through Baku who took her into his mountain aerie and kept her there all summer, feeding her melon from knifepoint through a crack in the cabin wall; in the fall he traded her to a passing ethnographer, who called her Svetka-Pippetka (whence her nickname) kept her, still naked, in an abandoned watchtower left over from the days of Shamil, its floor laid with rotten Persian carpets; the ethnographer studied the designs through an eyepiece. At night eagles shat on them. "Shoo, shoo, damn birds!" Pipka demonstrated, racing around the room with an outraged look, frightening the children. By winter the ethnographer had moved uphill, and with the first snow Svetlana went down into the valley, where they were still on a lunar calendar and took potshots at teachers through the school window and marked each death with a notch on a pole in the middle of the marketplace. There were over 800 notched, the losses were not made up, and several pedagogical institutes worked to supply that valley alone. There Svetlana had an affair with the director of the local store. But she quickly ended it, considering him not manly enough: instead of sleeping like a real *djigit*, or horseman, on his back, with saber in hand and fur hat on his head, his broad shoulders spread fiercely, the director rolled up into a fetal ball, snored, whimpered and kicked; he claimed he dreamed of gunshots. By spring, Pipka had reached Moscow, sleeping in haystacks and avoiding big roads. She was mauled by dogs several times. For some reason, she'd walked through the Urals. Geography was not her strong suit, even less so than her love life: she called the Urals the Caucasus, and she put Baku on the Black Sea. There may have been some truth in her nightmarish stories: who knows? Rimma was used to them and hardly listened, thinking her own thoughts, deep in her unhurried dreams. No one listened, really. Pipka wasn't a person, was she? Sometimes a new guest would listen to Pipka's fantasies, the fountain spewing plots, and exclaim happily and astonishedly, "Listen to her! A thousand and one nights!" It was men like that whom Pipka usually took off to her semifantastic Perlovka (if it existed at all): could you actually believe that Svetlana had been hired to dig their dahlias and ate fish meal with the chickens? As usual, in the midst of the simple fare, the din of chatter and clink of forks, Rimma fell under a dreamy spell: glorious visions, pink and blue mists, white sails; she heard the ocean's roar, distant and beckoning, like the steady roar that came from the enormous shell that ornamented their cupboard. Rimma liked to shut her eyes and hold the shell to her ear: from the salmon-pink jaws came the call of a far land, so far it couldn't fit on the globe; and it levitated smoothly, that country, and hung in the sky with all its lakes, parrots and surf. And Rimma, too, soared in the sky amid the pink feathery clouds: everything that life promised would come true. She didn't have to stir, she didn't have to hurry, it would come to her. Just sail quietly in the dark stream . . . listen to the approaching ocean's roar. . . . Rimma opened her eyes and looked, smiling, through the tobacco smoke and the dreams at her guests, at indolent, satisfied Fedya, and David Danilovich dangling his legs, and slowly came down to earth. It would start with something small . . . it would start slowly. . . .

With legs woozy from her flight, she felt for the floor. Oh, first: the apartment. The old man's room would be the bedroom. Blue curtains. No, white. White, silk, luxuriant, gathered. And a white bed. Sunday morning. Rimma in a white peignoir, with loosened hair (she'd have to start growing her hair, but she had already bought the peignoir secretly: couldn't resist), would walk to the kitchen. Coffee aroma . . . she would tell new acquaintances, "And in the room where our bedroom is, a little old man used to live: so sweet, he never bothered us. And after his death we moved in. So sad; such a marvelous old man."

Rimma swayed in her chair, smiling at the still-alive old man: "You smoke too much, David Danilovich. You should take better care of yourself." The old man merely coughed and waved his hand: what's the difference. Haven't got long to go. So what.

How pleasant to sail and soar through time—but time soars through you and melts behind you, and the ocean's roar still beckons: we ought to go south and breathe the sea air and stand on the shore, arms outspread, and listen to the wind; how sweetly life melts—the children, and loving Fedya, and the anticipation of the white bedroom. The guests envy me; yes, go ahead my dears and envy, for enormous happiness awaits me, I won't tell you what, I don't know myself, but voices whisper: wait, wait! Here's Petyunya sitting and envying and chewing his nails. He doesn't have a wife or an apartment, he's skinny and vain, he wants to be a journalist, he loves bright ties, we should give him ours, the orange one; we don't need it, happiness awaits us. Here are Ella and Alyosha; they're envious too, they don't have children, they've gotten a dog, what a bore. There's old Ashkenazy, envying my youth, my white bedroom, my ocean's roar; goodbye old man, you have to leave soon, eyes squinting under copper coins. Here's Svetlana: she doesn't envy anyone, she has everything, except it's imaginary, her eyes and her horrible mouth blaze like a fire—move Fedya away from her, she's babbling wildly, dozens of kingdoms rise and fall in her mind in the course of a single evening. Move Fedya away. Fedya! Come sit here. She's lying again, and you believe it?

It was fun and easy living, teasing Petyunya and his passion for ties, predicting a great journalistic future for him, asking him not to forget them when he started traveling abroad; Petyunya would get embarrassed and wrinkle up his sweet face: come on, guys, I'll be lucky to graduate. Petyunya was a sweetie, but somehow weak, and yet he tried to flirt with Rimma, though of course rather obliquely: he cut onions for her in the kitchen and hinted that he had, to tell the truth, fantastic plans. Rimma laughed: what plans, when she had great expectations herself? Why don't you make a play for Ella, she's going to leave Alyosha anyway. Or how about Svetka-Pippetka. Pippetka's getting married, Petyunya said. To whom, I'd like to know?

Soon they knew to whom: to old Ashkenazy. The old man, pitying Pipka's feet in children's shoes and her frozen hands, sorry about her extravagant expenses for nighttime taxis, giving in to a general geriatric generosity, decided—

behind Rimma's back—to marry the black fire-breathing tramp and to register her, naturally, for the living space promised to Rimma and Fedya. There was a row with heart medicine. "Shame on you! Shame on you!" shouted Rimma in a broken voice. "I have nothing to be ashamed about," the old man replied from the couch, lying down amid the rusted springs, with his head back to stop his nosebleed. Rimma put cold compresses on him and spent the night by his side. When he fell asleep, breathing lightly and unevenly, she measured the window in his room. Yes, the white fabric was wide enouth. Blue wallpaper would be good. In the morning they made up. Rimma forgave the old man, he wept; she gave him Fedya's shirt and made hot cakes. Svetlana learned something was up and did not come by for a long time. Then Petyunya disappeared too, and they assumed that Svetlana had taken him off to Perlovka. Anyone who ended up there would be gone for a long time and would take a while to get back to normal upon returning.

Petyunya came back six months later, one evening, with a bewildered stare and clay-smeared trousers. Rimma had trouble prying a word out of him. Yes, he had been there. He'd helped Pipka with the work. Very hard life. Everything was very complicated. He had walked from Perlovka. Why the clay? Oh, that . . . last night he and Pipka had wandered around Perlovka with a kerosene lamp, looking for a house. A Circassian there had a puppy. Yes, that's what I said. Yes, I know—Petyunya pressed his hands to his chest—I know there are no Circassians in Perlovka. He's the last one. Svetlana said she knew it for a fact. It would be a great story for the newspaper, for the "Just the Facts" column.

"Are you crazy, too?" Rimma asked, blinking.

"Why do you say that? I saw the puppy with my own eyes."

"What about the Circassian?"

"They wouldn't let us in. It was late."

"Sleep it off," said Rimma. She put him to bed in the hallway, amid the clutter. Rimma tossed and turned all night and by morning had decided that Circassian was a dog's name. But at breakfast she didn't want to add to the delirium with questions, and anyway Petyunya was grim and left quickly.

Then Svetlana had to move all her things from Perlovka to some other place—there was no point in trying to get the geography straight—by taxi, naturally, and for some reason she had to have Fedya's help. After some hesitation, Rimma let him go. It was ten in the morning, what could possibly . . . he came back at three the next morning, in a strange state.

"Where were you?" Rimma was waiting for him in her nightgown in the corridor.

"You see, there's lots of circumstances. . . . We had to go to Serpukhov, her twins are in the orphanage there."

"What twins?" shouted Rimma.

"Tiny, only a year or so. Siamese twins. Their heads are joined together. Karina and Angela."

"What heads? Are you crazy? She's been coming to our house for a hundred years, have you seen her have a baby?" No, of course he hadn't seen her have a baby or anything like it, but they did go to Serpukhov, they brought a nice parcel: a frozen fish. Yes, a fish for the twins. He paid for it himself. Rimma burst into tears and slammed the door; Fedya was left in the corridor, scratching at the door and swearing he didn't understand a thing himself, but he definitely remembered Karina and Angela.

Pipka disappeared for a long time after that, and the episode was forgotten. But something snapped in Rimma for the first time; she looked back and saw that time was still flowing but the future wasn't coming any closer, and Fedya wasn't so handsome anymore and the children had already picked up bad words on the street, and old Ashkenazy kept coughing and living and she had wrinkles around her eyes and mouth, and the rubbish was still in the corridor. And the ocean's roar was dimmer and they never did go south, they kept putting it off for the future that didn't want to come.

Troubled days followed. Rimma gave up. She kept trying to find out when she'd missed the path leading to the distant singing happiness, and often sat lost in thought while the children grew, while Fedya sat by the TV and didn't want to write his dissertation, while a cottony blizzard howled outside or the saccharine urban sun peeked through summer clouds. Their friends aged, became sticks in the mud, Petyunya vanished completely, bright ties went out of fashion, Ella and Alyosha got a new bratty dog whom no one would take care of in the evenings. At the office, Rimma had new coworkers, Big Lusya and Little Lusya, but they didn't know of Rimma's plans for happiness and didn't envy her; instead they envied Kira from the planning section who dressed expensively, traded hats for books, books for meat, meat for medicine or tickets to hard-to-get plays, and told someone irritatedly over the phone, "But you know perfectly well how much I like tongue in aspic."

And one evening, as Fedya sat in front of the TV and Rimma sat with her head on the table listening to the old man cough in the next room, Pipka burst in, all fire and flame, with pink cheeks, younger, as often happens with the mad, and smiling with a blazing mouth filled with sparkling white teeth.

"Thirty-six!" she shouted from the door, and struck her fist on the sash.

"Thirty six *what?*" asked Rimma, lifting her head from the table.

"Thirty-six teeth!" said Pipka. And told them she had signed on as a cabin boy on a ship going to Japan; and since the ship was overstaffed, she had to sleep in the vats with the meat and rice; the captain saluted her and his assistant slept with her, and en route a rich Japanese man fell in love with her and wanted to get married by cable, without putting it off, but they didn't have the right hieroglyphs or something and that fell through; and then, while they were in port washing out the vats for the meat and rice, she was kidnapped by a pirate junk and sold to a rich plantation owner, and she worked on a Malaysian hemp plantation from where she was bought by a rich Englishman for a Soviet special anniversary-issue ruble—as you know, highly prized by Malaysian numismatists—and the Englishman took her off to foggy Albion, lost her at first in the thick fog, but then found her and in great joy paid for the most expensive and fashionable selection of thirty-six teeth, which only a moneybags can do. He gave her some smoked pony meat for the road, and now she was finally going to Perlovka for her things.

"Open your mouth," Rimma said hostilely. And in Svetlana's mouth, readily opened, she counted, fighting off dizziness, all thirty-six: how they fit was unclear, but they really were teeth.

"I can bite through a steel cable now; if you want, I'll bite off the cornice," the monster began, and Fedya looked up with great interest, but Rimma waved her arms: enough, enough, it's late, we're sleepy; and gave her money for a taxi and pushed her to the door and handed her a volume of Simenon: please, you can read it at bedtime, just go! And Pipka left, clutching at the walls in vain, and no one ever saw her again.

"Fedya, will we go south?" Rimma asked.

"Of course," Fedya replied readily, as he had so many times over the years. Good. So we'll really go. South! And she listened to the voice that still whispered, barely audibly, about the future, about happiness, about deep long sleep in the white bedroom; but the words were hard to make out now.

"Hey, look! It's Petyunya!" Fedya said in amazement. On the TV screen, underneath palm trees, small and grim, with a microphone in his hands, stood Petyunya criticizing a cocoa plantation owner, while passing blacks turned to look at him and his huge tie boiled up with the African dawn; but he didn't look so happy, either.

Now Rimma knew that they had all been tricked; but who had done it and when, she couldn't remember. She went over every day, looking for the mistake, but couldn't find it. Everything was covered with a layer of dust. Sometimes she wanted—strange—to talk about it with Pipka, but she never came back.

It was summer again, it was hot, and through the thick dust the voice from the future began whispering. Rimma's children were grown, one married, and the other in the army, the apartment was empty and she didn't sleep well at night: the old man coughed ceaselessly. Rimma no longer wanted to turn the old man's room into a bedroom, and the white peignoir was gone: eaten by a moth that came out of the rubbish in the corridor, that didn't even see what it ate.

At work, Rimma complained to Big Lusya and Little Lusya that the moths were even eating German clothes; the little one gasped with her hands on her cheeks, and the big one grew angry.

"If you want to restock, girls," said experienced Kira, tearing herself away from her phone machinations, "I can take you to a place. I have a woman. Her daughter just got back from Syria. You can pay later. Good stuff. Vera Esafovna bought seven hundred rubles' worth on Saturday. They lived well in Syria. Swam in a pool; they want to go again."

"Let's go, all right," said Big Lusya.

"Ooooh, I have so many debts as it is," whispered the little one.

"Hurry, hurry, girls, let's take a cab," Kira rushed them. "We'll manage during lunch hour." Feeling like schoolgirls playing hooky, they piled into a cab, filling it with perfume and lit cigarettes, and raced down the hot summer side streets sprinkled with sunny linden blossoms and splotches of warm shade; a southern wind blew and brought through the gasoline fumes the triumph and radiance of the distant south: the blue blaze of the skies, the mirrored sparkle of the enormous seas, wild happiness, wild freedom, the madness of hopes coming true—for what? Who knows? And in the apartment that they entered meekly, anticipating a happy garment adventure, there was also a warm wind, moving and billowing the white netting on the windows and the doors opening on the spacious balcony. Everything here was spacious, large, free. Rimma envied the apartment. A mighty woman—the owner of the items on sale—quickly flung open the door to the desired room. The goods were piled, crumpled, into TV cartons and onto the double bed, reflected in the mirror of the mighty wardrobe.

"Rummage away," Kira said, taking charge from the doorway. Trembling, the women plunged their hands into the boxes of silks, velvets, diaphanous gold-embroidered things; they pulled them out, tugging, getting tangled in ribbons and ruffles; their hands fished out one thing while their eyes were already on another, enticed by a bow or trim, and inside Rimma a tiny vein throbbed; her ears burned, and her mouth was dry. It was like a dream. And, as the cruel scenario of a dream demanded, she quickly noticed a break in the harmony developing fast, a secret defect threatening to turn into a catastrophe. The things—what was this?—were wrong, not what they had first appeared to be; her eye could discern the silliness of those flashy gauze cotton skirts, good only for the *corps de ballet*, the pretentiousness of the purple turkey-cock jabots, the unfashionable lines of the heavy velvet jackets. These were rejects: we were invited for leftovers from somebody's banquet; others had rummaged here; somone's greedy hands had defiled the magic boxes, torn out and taken away the real things that made my heart pound and that special vein throb. Rimma attacked other boxes, picked through the jumble on the double bed, but there . . . and there . . . the things she pulled, desperate, out of the piles and held up against herself, looking anxiously into the mirror, were ridiculously small, short or dumb. Life had passed by, and the voice of the future sang for others. The owner of the goods sat like a Buddha and watched them closely and scornfully.

"How about that?" Rimma pointed at things on hangers along the walls, swaying in the warm wind.

"Sold. That's sold, too."

"What about something in my size?"

"Why don't you give her something," Kira said, leaning against a wall. The woman thought, and then pulled out something gray from behind her back; and Rimma, stripping quickly, revealing the secrets of her cheap underwear to her friends, squeezed like an eel into the appropriate openings; smoothing and tugging, she looked into her mercilessly bright reflection. The warm wind wandered through the sunny room, indifferent to the business at hand. She didn't really see what she was trying on; she looked with depression at her white legs with black hairs, that seemed as if they were mildewed, or had been in a trunk all winter, at her frightened, extended neck with its goose flesh, at her sticky hair, her stomach, her wrinkles, the dark circles under her eyes. The dress smelled of someone else—it had been tried on.

"Very good. It's *you*. Take it," Kira urged, the woman's secret ally. The woman watched silently and scornfully.

"How much?"

"Two hundred." Rimma suffocated, trying to pull off the poisoned garment.

"It's very fashoinable, Rimmochka," Little Lusya said guiltily. And to complete the humiliation, the wind blew open the door to the next room and revealed a heavenly vision: the woman's young, divinely slim, nut-brown daughter—the one who had lived in Syria, who had swum in the white pools in transparent blue water: a flash of a white dress, blue eyes. The woman rose and shut the door. Not a sight for mere mortals.

The southern wind carried linden droppings into the old courtyard and warned the worn walls. Little Lusya sidled down the steps, holding a mountain of clothes, almost weeping—more horrible debts. Big Lusya kept an angry silence. Rimma also went down with clenched jaw: the summer day had darkened, fate had teased her and laughed. And she already knew that the blouse she bought at the last moment in a spurt of desperation was garbage, last year's leaves, fool's gold that would turn black in the morning, a shell sucked and spat out by the blue-eyed Syrian houri.

She rode in the quiet, sad taxi, and told herself: at least I have Fedya and the children. But the solace was artificial and meager, for everything was over, life was showing its empty face: hair askew and gaping eye sockets. And the dreamed-of south, where she had wanted to go for so many years, now seemed yellow and dusty, with tufts of scrubby dry grasses, with murky unrefreshing waves, with bobbing expectorations and scraps of paper. And at home there was the smelly old, communal flat, and immortal Ashkenazy, and familiar Fedya, so familiar she could scream, and the whole viscous flow of the future years—as yet unlived, but already known—through which she had to plod and plod as if through dust covering the path up to her knees, her waist, her neck. And the siren song deceptively whispering sweet words of what *would not be* to the stupid swimmer fell silent forever.

Oh, there were still a few events: Kira's arm shriveled up, Petyunya came to visit and spoke at length about oil prices, Ella and Alyosha buried their dog and got a new one, old Ashkenazy finally washed his windows with the help of the Zarya cleaning service: but Pipka never showed up. Some were certain she'd married a blind fortune-teller and moved to Australia—to flash her new white teeth among the eucalyptus and platypuses over the coral reefs; others swore that she was killed and burned in a taxi on the Yaroslavl highway on a rainy, slippery night, and the flames were visible a long way off, a pillar reaching to the skies. They also said that they hadn't been able to put out the flames, and when the fire had burned itself out, they found nothing at the site of the accident. Just some lumps of charcoal.

Translated by Antonina W. Bouis

Notes to the Essay

1. Alice Philips, "Another Tolstoy Ascending," *Philadelphia Inquirer,* 30 April 1989, DJ01.

2. Marta Mestrovic, "Tatyana Tolstaya," *Publisher's Weekly* 238, 2 (1 January 1992): 37–38.

3. N.N. Shneidman, *Soviet Literature in the 1970's: Artistic Diversity and Ideological Conformity* (Toronto: University of Toronto Press, 1979), 6.

4. Geoffrey Hosking, *Beyond Socialist Realism: Soviet Fiction since Ivan Denisovich,* 3.

5. Stephan Salisbury, "The Awakening: Russia and the Writer," *Philadelphia Inquirer,* 28 April 1989, 6D.

6. T. Tolstaia, "Poidite na vstrechu chitateliu," *Knizhnoe obozrenie* 1 (1 January 1988): 5.

7. T. Tolstaia, *Na zolotom kryl'tse sideli* (Moscow: Molodaia gvardiia, 1987), 29.

8. Ibid, 23.

9. Tzvetan Todorov, *Mikhail Bakhtin: Dialogical Principle* (Minneapolis: University of Minnesota Press, 1988), 56–59.

10. Helena Goscilo, "Tat'iana Tolstaia's 'Dome of Many-Coloured Glass,'" *Slavic Review: American Quarterly of Soviet and East European Studies* 47, 2 (Summer 1988): 281.

11. Celestin Bohlen, "The Neighbor Had Two Wives," *Philadelphia Inquirer,* 30 April 1989, 7: 1.

12. T. Tolstaia, *Na zolotom kryl'tse sideli,* 118–19.

13. Ibid., 20–21.

14. Helen Dudar, "Publishing: Glasnost Smiles on the House of Knopf," *Wall Street Journal,* 22 March 1988, 32.

15. Hélène Cixous, "The Laugh of Medusa," *Sign* 1 (Summer 1976).

Bibliography

Primary Sources

"Kleem i nozhitsami." *Voprosy literatury* 9 (1983): 171–88.

"Na zolotom kryl'tse sideli." *Avrora* 8 (1983): 94–101.

"Svidanie s ptitsei." *Oktiabr'* 12 (1983): 52–57.

"Chistyi list." *Neva* 12 (1984): 116–26.

"Sonia." *Avrora* 10 (1984): 76–83.

"Milaia Shura" and "Okhota na mamonta." *Oktiabr* 12 (1985): 113–17; 117–21.

"Reka Okkervil'." *Avrora* 3 (1985): 137–46.

"Ogon' i pyl'" and "Samaia liubimaia." *Avrora* 10 (1986): 82–91; 92–110.

"Peters." *Novyi mir* 1 (1986): 123–31.

"Poèt i muza," "Fakir" and "Serafim." *Novyi mir* 12 (1986): 113–19, 119–30, 130–33.

"Spi spokoino, synok." *Avrora* 4 (1986): 94–101.

"Krug" [collective title for three stories: "Liubish'—ne liubish'," "Noch'," and "Krug"]. *Oktiabr'* 4 (1987): 89–95, 95–99, 99–104.

Na zolotom kryl'tse sideli. Moscow: Molodaia gvardiia, 1987.

"Plamen' nebesnyi." *Avrora* 11 (1987): 130–39.

"Vyshel mesiats iz tumana." *Krestianka* 4 (1987): 32–35.

"Somnambula v tumane." *Novyi mir* 7 (1988): 8–26.

"Limpopo." *Sinataksis* 27 (1990).

"Ne mogu molchat'." *Ogonek,* 14 March 1990, 31.

"Siuzhet." *Sintaksis* 31 (1991): 100–09.

In Translation

"Peters." Trans. Mary F. Zirin. *Heritage and Heresy: Recent Fiction by Russian Women.* Ed. Helena Goscilo. Bloomington: Indiana University Press, 1988.

"Svidanie s ptitsei." Trans. Mary F. Zirin. *Heritage and Heresy: Recent Fiction by Russian Women*. Ed. Helena Goscilo. Bloomington: Indiana University Press, 1988.

"Sonia." Trans. Mary F. Zirin. *Heritage and Heresy: Recent Fiction by Russian Women.* Ed. Helena Goscilo. Bloomington: Indiana University Press, 1988.

"In a Land of Conquered Men." *Moscow News* 38 (1989): 13.

"Intelligentsia and Intellectuals." *Moscow News* 32 (1989): 3.

On the Golden Porch. Trans. Antonina W. Bouis. New York: Alfred A. Knopf, 1989.

"Apples as Citrus Fruit." *Moscow News* 5 (1990)

"The Nation Needs Hard Currency." *Moscow News* 11 (1990): 14.

"Notes from the Underground." *New York Review of Books,* 31 May 1990, 3–6.

"Peters." Trans. Mary F. Zirin. *Glasnost* [Ann Arbor, Michigan.] (1990): 187–94.

"Sleepwalker in the Fog." Trans. Jamey Gambrell. *Soviet Women Writing.* Ed. Jacqueline Decter. New York: Abbeville, 1990. 51–84.

"Don't Teach Your Grandma to Suck Eggs." *Moscow News* 50 (1991): 15.

"In Cannibalistic Times." *New York Review of Books,* 11 April 1991, 3–6.

"President Potamkin." *New Republic,* 27 May 1991, 27–35.

"You're on the Right Path, Comrades!" *Moscow News* 41 (1991): 15.

"Is There Hope for Pushkin's Children?" *Wilson Quarterly* (Winter 1992): 121–29.

Sleepwalker in the Fog. Trans. Jamey Gambrell. New York: Alfred A. Knopf, 1992.

Secondary Works

Barker, Adele. "Are Women Writing Women's Writing in the Soviet Union Today? T. Tolstaya and I. Grekova." *Studies in Comparative Communism* 21, 3/4 (1988): 357–64.

Barta, Peter, I. "The Author, the Cultural Tradition and Glasnost: An Interview with Tatyana Tolstaya." *Russian Language Journal* 44 (1990).

Givens, John, R. "Reflections, Crooked Mirrors, Magic Theatres: Tat'iana Tolstaia's 'Peters.'" *Fruits of Her Plume.* Ed. Helena Goscilo. Armonk, NY: M.E. Sharpe, 1993.

Goscilo, Helena. "Paradise, Purgatory, and Post-Mortems in the World of Tat'iana Tolstaia." *Indiana Slavic Studies* 5 (1990): 97–113.

———. "Tat'iana Tolstaia's 'Dome of Many-Coloured Glass': The World Refracted through Multiple Perspectives." *Slavic Review: American Quarterly of Soviet and East European Studies* 47, 2 (Summer 1988): 280–90.

———. "Tolstajan Love as Surface Text." *Slavic and East European Journal* 34, 1 (1990): 40–52.

———. "Tolstoian Times: Transversals and Transfers." *New Directions in Soviet Literature.* New York: St. Martin's Press, 1992. 187–219.

Nezgliadova, Elena. "Èta prekrasnaia zhizn'." *Avrora* (October 1986): 111–20.

Simmons, K.A. "Zhenskaia proza and the New Generation of Women Writers." *Slovo: A Journal of Contemporary Soviet and East European Affairs* 3, 1 (May 1990): 66–77.

Stepanian, Karen. "Golos letiashchii v kupol." *Voprosy literatury* 2 (1988): 78–105.

Wisniewska, Sophia. *Narrative Structure in the Prose of Tat'jana Tolstaja.* Doctoral dissertation, University of Michigan, Ann Arbor, 1992.

Larisa Vasilieva[1]

Larisa Vasilieva (b. 1935).
Courtesy of the author and Norma Noonan.

The twentieth century has witnessed the flowering of many Russian literary talents, but relatively few have achieved success in more than one genre. Larisa Nikolaevna Vasilieva (b. 1935) has been a notable exception. She achieved early fame as a poet and later gained recognition for her essays on England and her philosophy of human relations. Still later she turned her talents to popular history and fiction with continuing success. Vasilieva has been unique also for her restless, questioning mind, always seeking new avenues of expression, new dreams and hopes. Her writing and social activism have propelled her into leadership first of women writers and later of a distinctive women's movement as she became a recognized spokesperson for women writers and intellectuals.

She was born Larisa Nikolaevna Kucherenko in Khar'kov in Ukraine. Her father, an engineer and builder, helped to design and develop the famous Soviet T-34 tank, the most frequently deployed tank in World War II, for which he was honored with a Stalin Prize. His fame also gave her an acquaintance with the top Soviet elite from an early age. Larisa revered her father and in his honor established a tiny museum at their dacha, with various memorabilia, including a map of the major battles in which the T-34 played a role. She also wrote a book about her father, *Book about Father* (*Kniga ob ottse*), in the form of a novella.[2] Among her childhood memories are the family's evacuation of Moscow in 1941, the day the war ended and her father came home early in celebration, and the family's return to Moscow from evacuation in 1947.

Larisa's interest in literature and poetry came from her mother, an economist and engineer who also wrote poetry. Larisa was a child prodigy who published her first poetry in 1947 at age twelve in *Pioneer's Truth* (*Pionerskaia pravda*), thus becoming a minor celebrity. The weighty responsibility of being a child prodigy has never been forgotten, and she cautions against early fame for children. Memories of her teenage years include the 800th anniversary of Moscow, fireworks and pictures of Stalin. In her teenage years, Larisa fell in love with portraits of Peter Bagration and Peter the Great, and she confesses that strong men have always attracted her.

Larisa attended Moscow State University (MGU), where she majored in Russian literature, graduating in 1958. Admission to the elite MGU in the Faculty of Language and Literature was in itself a symbol of success. The literature specialists were an elite within an elite, since the number of students admitted was small. According to Vasilieva, literature majors did not associate much with the language majors, whom she and the other literature specialists *(literaturovedy)* regarded as boring. In 1956 she was invited to a friend's home for dinner, where she met Oleg Vasiliev (1932–1993), whom she married only four months later, in January 1957. Vasiliev, a journalist and translator, strongly supported her endeavors as a writer. Larisa took his name, an unusual step among Soviet women of her time. The Vasilievs had one son, Georgii (Egor), born in 1962, who has continued the family tradition of interest in literature, translation and publishing. Oleg Vasiliev worked for many years as a journalist for *News* (*Izvestiia*), both in Russia and England. Later he served as deputy editor of *Foreign Literature* (*Inostrannaia literatura*) and translated a number of works himself, including books by Stephen King and Arthur Haley. In his later years, Vasiliev was a cofounder of the private firm Vagrius Publishing.[3]

Larisa and Oleg were an extraordinarily devoted couple, in love until his death from pancreatic cancer in 1993. One of her friends has described their relationship as a "great love." Their life was almost idyllic, centering on their family and careers. Larisa provided a good home life for Oleg, a lean, tall man who was a voracious eater and gourmet. Their son was a focal point of their mutual concern, both during his childhood and in adulthood, when he married and remained living in the same neighborhood.

Outwardly, Vasilieva has had a "normal" life,[4] to use a popular Russian phrase. She had as normal a childhood as one could have in the turbulent Soviet Union of the 1930s and 1940s, perhaps even a privileged childhood. She had great personal happiness in her long marriage to Oleg Vasiliev and great joy in her only son. In addition to his own work, Oleg was de facto Larisa's manager.[5] It was he who remembered her public appearances, advised her on publishing strategies, helped to negotiate publishing contracts and kept their records. He was a prolific correspondent who maintained contact with their many friends in the West. Like many other creative people, Larisa was dreamy, often forgetting to handle the mundane details of a career and fame. Oleg was always there, thinking of her needs as a writer. His death left a void in her professional, as well as her private, life.

During their careers, Larisa and Oleg traveled abroad extensively. In earlier years she was often included in writers' delegations abroad. Later she was invited personally to speak at, or to attend, international conferences of prominent women.[6] Oleg also traveled abroad, reaching the United States and Europe in conjunction with his work as a journalist and translator. In the 1970s Vasiliev was a London correspondent for *News*. Larisa joined him in England from 1973 to 1979, returning frequently to Moscow to nourish her art and her soul. Her first major prose work, the anthology *Albion and the Secret of Time* (*Al'bion i taina vremeni*, 1978), was written there.[7] *Albion* chronicled her impressions of Great Britain, especially London, and was popular in the Soviet Union as an insightful glimpse of English life. Vasilieva applied her poetic consciousness and her love of Russian history to understanding London. She also realized, however, that the longer she lived in London, the less she understood it. Her impressions of England were amusing as well as insightful. The descriptions were vivid, yet terse, reflecting a poet's reluctance to use unnecessary words. For Russians unable to travel, as was the case for most people, the book was interesting as a travelogue and refreshing for its remarkable freedom from political overtones.

In 1979 Vasilieva returned to Moscow to new responsibilities. In 1979–1980 she served a two-year term as editor in chief of the prestigious volume, *Poetry Day* (*Den' poèzii*).[8] From 1980 to 1989 she led an annual seminar in the Department of

Creative Works of the Gorky Literary Institute, thus trying her hand at teaching on an occasional basis. In the 1980s Vasilieva traveled extensively as she became more famous, although she curtailed her travels somewhat during Oleg's long illness and the turbulent economic transition of the new Russia, when the collapse of the ruble transformed even well-known members of the Russian intellectual elite into relative paupers. The success of *Kremlin Wives* (*Kremlevskie zheny*, 1992) led to extensive travel in Asia, Europe and the United States. These travels helped ease the pain of her husband's death by keeping her in almost perpetual motion. In 1994 alone, she visited three continents. Unlike many writers, she did not neglect her other projects during the extensive promotional tours. She often called Moscow to keep in touch with her associates and colleagues and spent her leisure time thinking of new ideas and projects. During her foreign travels over the years, she met many famous and prominent people—well-known publishers and leaders of the women's movement—as well as ordinary people interested in Russia and in literature. As a consequence, she acquired an international circle of friends, especially in England and the United States.[9]

Vasilieva was recognized first as a poet, both as a child and as an adult, and it is as a poet that she likes to be regarded above all. Her adult poetry was first published in 1964, and her first book of poetry, *The Flaxen Moon* (*L'nianaia luna*), appeared in 1966. In this book the reader is impressed with the growing awareness of a young poet who begins to see life as an adult. The young Vasilieva expressed her appreciation of nature, love and the unity of all life. One of the poems asked: "Who am I, what am I, where am I, whose am I, and why am I on this earth?"[10]

She offered readers an opportunity to share her awareness of the world around them. Subsequently Vasilieva published more than twenty books of poetry, in addition to short stories, novels and essays on Russian literature and Soviet women.[11] Primary themes in her poetry include nature, the seasons, the motherland, Russian poetry, human emotions and reflections on life. A romantic quality penetrates her poetry. Like all great poetry, hers deals with universal themes, yet it also has Slavic overtones. She has a remarkable gift for alliteration, which may not be fully conveyed in translations of her work. Discussions with admirers suggest that her love of nature and her appreciation of life draws the reader to her poetry. One longtime reader expresses her sense that Vasilieva's work reflects the essence of Russia or the Russian soul.[12]

Her prose is sparse, yet poetic and dramatic. Her witty plays on words encapsulate her sense of humor. With her extraordinary ability to use words sparingly for maximum effectiveness, her writing often utilizes alliterative phrases that combine her penetrating insights and sharp wit. Her writing has always displayed emotion, and in person she has always been as full of life, drama and emotion as her writings. She is not merely a master of words but also an emotional being whose feelings penetrate the written word.

After the success of her essays on British life in *Albion*, Vasilieva was frequently asked to write prose, especially to record her reflections on Russian literature, past and present. In 1988 she published an essay recognizing the contribution of great Russian poets. In 1989 she published an essay in observation of the centenary of Anna Akhmatova's birth. In May 1991 she was invited to read at celebrations of the Slavonic written language ("Pigments"). A great admirer of Pushkin, she studied his life and work very closely. In 1995, for example, she broadcast interviews on her analysis of the last and great love of Pushkin's life. Vasilieva views herself and other Russian poets as links in the chain of Russian poetry founded by Pushkin. According to Vasilieva, "the road to Pushkin is a plain one, but where does it begin?" In recognition of Vasilieva's contribution to Russian literature, a two-volume anthology of her most famous poetry and prose was published in 1989, encompassing her work over a twenty-five-year period.

Beginning in 1987, when *glasnost'* permitted greater dialogue about women, Vasilieva wrote several essays on the role of women in society, gaining her a reputation as an advocate of women's rights. Vasilieva's theories on women, expressed in many essays, interviews and articles may be summarized in the word "harmony" (*garmoniia*). The essence of her philosophy is that women and men have different roles in life, but that those roles are equal and should be equally respected. This is both her personal and her social philosophy. She does not believe that women should seek to emulate men or to compete with them. Women and men should be free to excel in their respective areas of strength. She strongly believes that women's sphere includes the home and family, peacemaking and creativity. She tends to shun what she terms "men's games," a vague yet global term she uses to encompass political activities and political compromise. [13]

Most of her later work as an essayist and publicist has focused on the theme of *garmoniia*. She emphasizes harmony and partnership (*partnierstvo*) between men and women. In this distinctive approach to feminism, women's contributions should be regarded as coequal to men's in society. She has even at times thought about the possibility of a men's legislature and a women's legislature. Vasilieva does not view herself as a feminist, although her theory of partnership may be viewed as somewhat feminist. Her philosophy, nonetheless, has led her to greater activism and to becoming a recognized leader among Russian women.

Her initial activism on behalf of women grew out of her work in the Soviet Writers' Union. Although personally respected within the Writers' Union, she realized as time went by that women writers were marginalized there. In 1989, in response to the exclusion of women from the editorial board of the publisher Soviet Writer (Sovetskii pisatel'), Vasilieva organized her colleagues as the Federation of Soviet Women Writers within the Soviet Writers' Union. Although the formation of the federation was spontaneous, the federation developed ambitious goals, which included creation of a publishing house and establishment of a women's perspective in policy-making, especially in the areas of ecology, ethics and important social issues. The federation had approximately five hundred members before the 1991 Soviet coup, but upon the subsequent dissolution of the Soviet Union, the Writers' Union also disintegrated. The unionwide federation lost most of its non-Russian members, as pressure grew for the newly independent republics to cut their ties with Russia. In 1992 the federation was reconstituted as the International League of Women Writers (Mezhdunarodnaia Liga pisatel'nits), accepting membership of writers from Russia, Commonwealth of Independent States and foreign countries. In post–Soviet Russia, the league faced the same limitations of most other groups. The harsh devaluation of the ruble curtailed their potential. In 1994 the Writers' League joined in a consortium of Russian women's organizations, which prided itself on its horizontal, nonhierarchical structure. The consortium had five cochairs, one of whom was Vasilieva.

Because she was increasingly recognized as a leader of women, Vasilieva became a frequent participant at international feminist gatherings. She became conversant with, but was not especially attracted to, Western feminism. Among her friends were prominent feminists from other countries. Her own approach to feminism had deep roots in Russian history and greatly influenced her approach to life.[14] She shunned political activity for much of her life and, unlike many other intellectuals, was not a member of the Communist party in the Soviet era. Once recognized as a spokesperson for women, however, she was also invited to serve on several governmental consultative committees on women's issues in the Soviet Union and in post–Soviet Russia.

Vasilieva's interest in women extended also to women's contributions to the political and social system, past and present. A student of history, she spent several years doing research in Russian and Soviet history in order to write about the wives of political leaders. The resulting book, published in 1992, was *Kremlin Wives* (*Kremlevskie zheny*), based on archival research, memoirs, interviews and even "gossip."[15] *Kremlin Wives* captured the spirit of the Soviet political elite from the 1980s to 1990. It also had *garmoniia* as an underlying theme. The book took Moscow by storm and opened up for her a new career in popular history. Two years later the book was translated in the West and published abroad, leading to a new wave of travel abroad. Another project that she researched for many years was a popular history of Russian women on the throne, which she expected to be published in 1996.

After her husband's death in early 1993, Vasilieva focused primarily on her writing and her work with women. Her social activism and her tours as a writer occupied most of her time. In 1993 she realized a ten-year dream with the establishment of *Atlantida* (*Atlantis*), an independent journal. *Atlantida* was an outgrowth of her theories of harmony and partnership with men. It is a well-presented magazine of current life, which covers a wide variety of issues and can interest both men and women. Galina Semenova, Vasilieva's longtime friend, became the editor in chief of the new journal. She had been for many years the editor of *Peasant Woman* (*Krestianka*) and in 1990–1991 was a member of the Politburo under Gorbachev.[16] *Atlantida* was supported by several women's associations. In 1994 *Atlantida* expanded its efforts and became a publishing house. In 1995 the Atlantida Publishing House published Vasilieva's novel *Tales of Love* (*Skazki o liubvi*), which she regarded as the first novel published in Russia with a Russian woman's perspective.

The uniqueness of Vasilieva's personal philosophy penetrates both her creative work and her activism. She always endeavored to be independent in her literary and political inclinations and to avoid being pigeonholed into a particular literary or political school. Her political independence in the highly politicized Soviet Union was in itself no minor achievement, since most intellectuals sought the privileges and protection of the Communist party. Vasilieva never viewed herself as a political person, but her advocacy of women's issues and other concerns in the 1980s and 1990s propelled her into the world of politics, and she began to publish her views in newspapers and journals, such as *Truth* and *International Affairs*. (Vasilieva views herself as expressing women's essence [*sushchnost'*] or consciousness about the world, nature, philosophy and love.)[17] She is attuned to, and compatible with, Western theories of women's "voice" and women's "reality."[18]

Vasilieva has been an important independent voice of the female intelligentsia in Russia. Affiliated with no institute or party, she expresses her views directly and openly in her writings, in interviews and on television. She has become so well known as a women's spokesperson that some analysts in the West view her primarily as an essayist and publicist, underemphasizing her international standing as a poet and writer whose work has been translated and published in France, Germany, England, the United States, Greece, Italy, Japan, Korea and other countries. The recent lack of attention to her poetry is understandable, for in the 1990s, Vasilieva primarily wrote popular history and novels. Poetry, her first love, was put behind her, because in her mature years and in the difficult period faced by her country, poetry did not come easily. It is a tribute to her versatility that she is at least as successful in prose as in poetry. Nonetheless, her poetic nature is the driving force behind her prose, which resounds with romantic and lyrical qualities rarely found in prose.

Norma Corigliano Noonan

The Voice of Love

Humankind is concluding a cycle,
and ahead all is new and unknown,
and no one can really determine
what's beyond, past the turn in this road.

The world shatters, breaks up and apart,
life burns in a fire ferocious—
still a peaceful light remains
in a lone window, unchanged,

A pair of hearts, rosy in union,
whole worlds extinguished before them—
the tormented glow of the universe,
and the fires of earth's inquisitions.

Go ahead, tap at the threshold,
touch the cool of the window, call aloud,
if they answer—for God's sake, appeal
not for freedom, not truth—only love.

Translated by Christine D. Tomei

Britain

Green grass that has all winter grown,
Streets lined with rows of neat white buildings . . .
The more I love you, the more I'm wishing
To be upon my way back home.

Not to show off my eloquence
Do I describe this curious feeling—
I can't forget the mistiness
That is embodied in your features.

I can't forget your river's flow
By centuries of vanity fed,
The yearning that within my soul
Your solemn residences bred.

Now I've a foretaste of that time
Of joy, as eagerly awaited
As a reward, when once more I'm
Back home again with heart elated.

That hour in which there shall remain,
Just like a drop of venom, features
Of yours that I by chance retain,
Pure and mysterious as a secret.

And I still hope a day may come
When (if you rightly grasp my meaning)
I'll sigh for you, as if for some
Irrevocable moment fleeting.

Translated by Peter Tempest

Necklace for Vasilisa

A woman confronts the war face to face and she hates it and fears it, since the idea of war contradicts the nature that endows life. There was a time when wars started because of women, but those times have passed forever. Woman's destiny has become waiting, hoping and delivering the wounded from the battlefield. And only in the twentieth century did a woman finally get the opportunity to say her piece to the war.

Undoubtedly a woman's voice is heard against the background of everything that is going on in the the world. The degree of impact that our words deliver depends on what we say, how we say it, and whom we address. The nature of motherhood, which is immanent, does not accord us any rights, except one: to protect one's offspring from death. In this sense it would seem that we do not differ much from any living creature—from the bird, which spreads its wings over the nestling, from the she-bear, ready to be killed, defending her cub.

However, woman is granted by nature a special quality: the sensation of being the mother of the Entire World, the housekeeper of unimaginably vast spaces. Indeed, this is a cosmic feeling. Many women would not allow themselves the audacity of its recognition. And nonetheless I dare say that it exists in every woman, even the weakest and most retiring, who with her own hands undertakes a noble deed that she is able to perform.

But how threatening is time!

It growls. And all the same it doesn't pay to fear one's own time, as though in different times only full-blown philanthropy flourished! The life of earth-dwellers is full of great deeds and discoveries, joys and hopes, love and benevolence. But life is equally full of nightmares, betrayals, bloody battles, baseness and destruction. These are two poles of the human condition; isn't that an unwritten rule, or at least unwritten by any human or, if written, then on another tablet in another dimension. . . .

Since the time that the last volley of the 1945 victory salute burst forth, almost fifty years have passed. And if in that entire time there hasn't been another worldwide explosion, if humanity was able more or less to peacefully proceed along its path, then a great credit in this regard belongs to the small woman—the mother of humanity, walking in multimillioned multitudes as soldiers for peace on the squares and streets of cities, saying "no" to war.

This woman does not write reasoned treatises, she doesn't penetrate the mysteries of the Divine Cosmos, she doesn't create artificial complications for herself—she has enough to do without it. She simply will not stay silent, realizing that tomorrow her child might cease to exist on earth. She doesn't fear cosmic cataclysms, but she finds it incomprehensible that her child, her mother and her father, will be swept away by a storm of man-made origin.

Such a woman is prepared to battle a war to the death. She will do everything she can to keep the war from happening. The name of this woman is—millions.

* * *

Begin with the matriarchy? But then there was no literacy, and what if, as is possible, the woman wouldn't reveal her position? This is, naturally, the image of a tragic joke, but in every joke, there is a grain of truth. We will proceed from reality. In point of fact, it is not all that bad.

What trash have men not told us in the course of these long centuries! We have been praised and our abilities have been exaggerated; values that we never even suspected have been attributed to us.

"Whoever can govern a woman can govern a nation," said Balzac.

"A man, going to do a good deed, always performs it well if, along the way, he is kissed by his beloved woman," observed the Russian historian V. Kliuchevskii.

"Man is great on earth and in eternity, but every iota of his greatness stems from a woman," wrote Walt Whitman.

They were trying to understand our notorious logic.

"A woman is not capable of loving a happy man. The woman who never experienced pity for her beloved evidently never knew love," quipped the French dramatist Lenormand.

"When we judge women, we never consider in sufficient degree how difficult it is to be a woman," warned the French writer Geraldit.

They bowed before us, in words exclusively, but how lovely:

"When a woman is wrong, the first thing you need to do is beg her for forgiveness," taught the French writer Croisset.

"In many cases, a single woman is much more penetrating than hundreds of men," exclaimed Lessing.

They reward us according to our merits. Also, undeservedly:

"The majority of men like to lie as a result of their modest opinion of themselves; the majority of women—because of the opposite reason," chortled Swift.

"Like dreams, women are never the kind that you want to see," stated the Italian writer Pirandello.

In all centuries, in all times, men talk and talk about women, study them as scientists, strive to understand them as writers, praise them as poets. They dedicate books to us, make us heroines in enormous novels and elegantly written stories, short poems and, nowadays, as film and TV heroines. They pity us and justify our failures, they thrill at our dubious and indubitable virtues, they stigmatize us—now ever as before they stigmatize us!—with all their might they try to illuminate us, to soothe or redouble our pains, to let us experience the joy of their devotion, even if it is deceitful, ephemeral. . . .

Doesn't such a thing deserve encouragement, enthusiasm and gratitude?

Doesn't such behavior warrant an answer from men as an attempt to tell the truth about them?

From time to time in history, a woman got a chance to answer this question. And so what? Our sister, intoxicated by her opportunity, started right away talking about herself.

In this manner, she always lost. And it couldn't be any other way. Why? Due to a law of nature, not despite it. A man is the source of creativity, a woman—of giving birth. This is a fact. In torment a woman gives to the world what she is given by man. And the entire concept of love, of mutual understanding, is empty words without his or her knowing how to penetrate to the essence of the secret of the opposing being. Males and females characteristically perceive life differently, and the wishes of each, as a rule, if they don't coincide, remain discordant eternally. All female demands, both literary and real, all their exclamations, "Come back!" all their groans, "What did I ever do to you?" are hollow rumblings in the air, incomprehensible to the male world, disturbing, confining and inimical to it.

However, life is life and there is no third sex. Isn't is worth it, then, to the creative woman who handles a word like an implement of labor to recognize in herself a certain new power so that she can pronounce some old words that express principally new experiences? More likely shared experiences?

Lev Tolstoy has a very colorful pronouncement: "In the artistic work the most important thing is the soul of the creator. In this respect among the average works women's works are better, more interesting. A woman will say no-no, but reveal the most intimate part of her soul—if it is needed; you see what she really loves although she may pretend that she loves something else."

Please pay attention. Tolstoy, speaking of a woman writer, surveys only average works. But has a woman raised herself above the average level in the literary process? Did she attain the high, the highest male level of Dante, Shakespeare, Gogol and Chekhov?

Maybe after all she has been rising to and attaining it?

I can believe at least that Sappho was great. It's pleasant to believe. Her legacy, practically lost to us, is nothing more than the broken shards of a beautiful vase, a small page with some lines, ripped out by time and in a language foreign to us to boot.

But the memory of her is wonderful: thin, dark-haired, in a white tunic against the background of eternity—marvelous.

She described the pain, the pain of a woman's heart that is forever the same, no matter how many centuries have flown by humankind. She directed her attention to the silent woman doomed to remain only an object, a little flintstone on which a man can ignite his fire of love. Don't think that I am worried by the "feeling of a stone"; on the contrary, it's not really so bad to be an object as long as you are being adulated, even though only in words, as long as they sing to you, praise you.

Do you also wish to risk expressing yourself in words? Please do. . . .

How different were these diffident-bold English girls raised on white-walled, quiet estates, surrounded by winding parks in the center of England from the bohemian, sharp French women writers, the raptorlike city women with unfettered imagination.

How similarly, in essence, sang their souls: the Brontë sisters and Madame de Staël, Elizabeth Haskell, Ann Radcliffe and George Sand. The male world of literature unwittingly drew them to the boldness of judgment, to the freedom of a worldview, and they plunged bravely forward without a backward glance, remaining, however, within the boundaries of female timidity: they were always able to retire to eternally female positions. Here is an example: Jane Eyre, herself the embodiment of the power of the spirit, willfulness, heedlessness, the heroine of Charlotte Brontë, who stood taller than men, capable of great deeds, in the final analysis discovered herself humbly serving the demise of her dream. And this was excellent, in this our age-old predestination was fulfilled—to give the gift of love and fidelity.

Women's prose of the nineteenth century in England and in France seems to me to be a kind of poetry camouflaged in another genre; having sensed her creative will, the writer closed in on herself, or more accurately, on her heroine, and not wishing to risk sacrificing her right to self-expression for the sake of a clearly doubtful wish, she softened in answering the male world with her great vision of power and weakness. Mary Shelley, daring to depict a man, made him a monster. But paradoxically: closing in on oneself, the woman writer in all times one way or another concentrated all her interests on a man, since the most powerful instincts in female nature are of mother and daughter. How, then, in literature, especially in poetry, would both of these give way to a different instinct, guiding the hand of the poet or writer? If we place on one side of the scales all women's literature dedicated to a child, a mother or a father and on the other side everything that somehow relates to a man, then that latter side will fall to the ground due to its heavy overload. I will not risk an explanation of this phenomenon although I have my own explanation; maybe others will explain it either agreeing or not agreeing with me.

Thus a woman speaking with the world is not a new phenomenon, but it is still unstudied, surrounded by constantly inattentive literary milieux filled with the powerful ambitions of men. It has always been this way in both world and Russian literature, and it continues thus in the contemporary, equal-rights environment of Soviet literature. Can it possibly be that woman's fate is to remain in the ranks of the average?

Oh, we say, Akhmatova! Oh, we say, Tsvetaeva! We root about in the details of their personal lives. And we imagine for a moment what it would be like if both of them had been beings of the male gender. The Poets Akhmatov and Tsvetaev. Does their image immediately decline?

Couldn't it be that Tolstoy is nonetheless correct, and for women to appear in the conventional general assemblage represents a certain condescension? It is. I will even risk saying that in some measure it is just. Whose fault is it or is it a fault if in women's literature there is no sustained, many-centuries-old tradition, that the most talented of us are simply wonderful accidents, unexpected curiosities in a continuous process? Who is to blame if in women's literature, no matter how un-great it is by comparison with men's, there are no opportunities for development, no tradition of criticism, insufficient press, insufficient recognition? The recognition of this literature is cooped up in the backyards of the literary process, smeared with condescending evaluations and well-wishing from above. In humankind, half the population is female. We even have epithets like "old women's scribbles" and "female oohs and ahs"; but meanwhile the lyric voice of the male poetic population has noticeably diminished, and against this dimmed background, women seem unexpectedly bright and noteworthy.

For today one fact is irrefutable: Akhmatova and Tsvetaeva are the first women in Russian poetry with such wide exposure. After them it is difficult to be oneself without seeming to approach either one or the other of them, although their influence did not interfere with the appearance of Ol'ga Berggol'ts, Liudmila Tat'ianicheva, Iuliia Drunina, Margarita Aliger, Ekaterina Sheveleva, Margarita Agashina—women whose civic position sometimes created the illusion of masculinity, embellishing these talented poets in their own fashion. But not a single one of them ever risked entering into the male world in the manner that men have entered ours, not one was able to express—not herself in him, but him in herself.

Women's prose in Soviet literature of the twentieth century was, naturally, not the last word, but it is worth remembering names and works of Marietta Shaginian, Lidiia Seifullina, Anna Karavaeva, Vanda Vasilevskaia, Galina Nikolaeva, Vera Ketlinskaia and Vera Panova. However, to my subjective mind, here reigned fundamentally self-expressive, especially self-centered thought. Isn't it for this reason that today these fully worthy names are received more out of obligation, and the books of these talented women do not thrive very much in the everyday world, having become an act in the history of literature?

Serving as a kind of exception to the general rule are women in Ukrainian literature of the end of the nineteenth and beginning of the twentieth centuries, both writers and historical writers. As regards the former, Marko Vovchok,

Mariia Kobylianskaia, the great Lesia Ukrainka and the contemporary Lina Kostenko serve as a counterweight to the intimate-sentimental note in men's Ukrainian literature.

Historical writers such as Ol'ga Forsh, Mariia Marich and Anna Antonovskaia may be put fully on a level with male historical writers since the necessity of drawing historical male types demanded maximum incarnation for their writing, whether they willed it themselves or not.

Now I have approached the present day, but to describe it in detail is unimaginable, since I personally stand within the process that I would like to understand; and as everybody knows, it's easier to see something large from a distance.

The requirement for "women's" literature is irrefutable regardless of how they try to assure us that it is not possible to divide literature into "women's" and "men's." Why so? Because nature has made the division and it is impossible to argue with nature. Regardless of the degree of deserved or undeserved success, women writers today are not entirely comfortable in the world of contemporary literature.

Thus I would like to think that the appearance of a woman who knows how to penetrate into male psychology is about to happen. How would I know this? A male poet told me. Never before did I encounter even the slightest motif of expectation from a single one of them. Now our contemporary Iurii Kuznetsov, more than once carelessly assailing women's poetry—which is what drew my attention to him—has written a poem where in the last part he spoke about a woman, his stellar companion, about whom literature can so far only dream:

> She dreams at my mountainous heights,
> Where the airplane-carpet flies.
> She dreams my proud thoughts,
> From which no one will save her.

When will we women dream at their heights? In the best case we think that we graciously allow them to detach themselves from us and to set out there. In the worse—we interfered, we didn't allow them, we struggled, unleashing only their striving to the heights that sometimes had explicit and tender names.

When did we ever dream their proud thoughts? Either we dream our own thoughts or we don't dream, and they, for that matter, what other kind of thoughts can they have?

Kuznetsov, however, is dreaming, not completely faithfully, but thanks for the thought, anyway. Do you think it is ordained that male poetic force must dream about the equality of greatness of a woman's world of power?

I don't think that everything is ready for the appearance of such a figure today. A combination of circumstances and the progress of the historical process will bring such a woman out. I would gladly greet this woman during my lifetime, but it's almost certainly not fated for me.

I wish only that what I have said here will reach her through time and she will take my greeting as something that goes without saying.

1991

Translated by Christine D. Tomei

Notes to the Essay

1. An earlier version of part of this article was published in M. Ledkovsky, C. Rosenthal and M. Zirin, eds., *Dictionary of Russian Women Writers* (Westport, CT: Greenwood Press, 1994).

2. L. Vasilieva, *Izbrannye proizvedeniia*, Vol. 2 (Moscow: Khodozhestvennaia literatura, 1989), 177–390.

3. Vagrius is an acronym. The founders were Vasiliev, Gregoriev and Uspenskii. Oleg Vasiliev was the senior member of the team.

4. Russians often use the term "normal" to describe the usual, the commonplace, the norm. If everything is fine, a Russian will usually tell you that things are "normal."

5. The author met Oleg Vasiliev in 1990 when he was traveling and lecturing in the United States. When he discovered her interest in Russian women writers, he recommended that she contact his wife and research her life and work.

6. Vasilieva was one of the few Russian members of the prestigious International Women's Forum.

7. *Izbrannye proizvedeniia,* 2: 9–175.

8. The normal term was one year. Vasilieva was asked to serve for a second year.

9. The author considers herself blessed to be part of such a circle. Her friends abroad have sometimes become friends among themselves. In Russia, some of the author's friends have now become friends of Vasilieva, and some of Vasilieva's American friends are now friends of the author.

10. *Izbrannye proizvedeniia*, 1: 21.

11. S.S. Navrochatov, the editor of her anthology, recounted the first time he heard her read her poetry and his awareness of a "poetic emanation." See the Foreword to *Izbrannye proizvedeniia*, 1: 5. The author has heard Vasilieva recite poetry on numerous occasions and shares this point of view.

12. The interviewee, Ol'ga, now a woman of forty, first read Vasilieva's work as a teenager and met her at a poetry evening when Vasilieva came to the young girl's hometown.

13. In discussions with the author, Vasilieva often used the term *muzhskie igry* ("men's games") to dismiss political activities of which she did not approve.

14. In an earlier work, the author referred to Vasilieva as a representative of what she calls Russofeminism. See Norma C. Noonan, "Does Consciousness Lead to Action?" *Journal of Gender Studies* 3, 1 (1994).

15. Vasilieva freely acknowledged the role of "gossip" in the book.

16. *Krestianka* was one of the three major Soviet women's magazines, together with *Soviet Woman* and *Rabotnitsa* (*Working Woman*). Semenova retired after the dissolution of the Soviet Union, coming out of her retirement to head the new publication.

17. The term "women's reality" may best express her sentiments.

18. Vasilieva is familiar with the work of writers such as Carol Gilligan and Anne Wilson Schaef.

Bibliography

Primary Works

Izbrannye proizvedeniia [*Selected Works*]. Ed. S.S. Navrochatov. 2 vols. Moscow: Khudozhestvennaia literatura, 1989. [Selections from her poetry are contained in Volume 1, and her major prose works are in Volume 2.)

"Net doma bez khoziaiki" ["There Is No Home without a Housekeeper"]. *Pravda* 10 August 1990.

"Evangelie ot Vasilisy." *Pravda,* 18 March 1991, 4.

Strannoe svoistvo [*Strange Being*]. Moscow: Sovetskii pisatel', 1991.

Kremlevskie zheny [*Kremlin Wives*]. Moscow: Vagrius, 1992.

In Translation

"So Shall My Life Proceed." Trans. Natalia Listikova. *Soviet Literature* 3 (1981): 133–38.

"A Glimpse of Diplomacy from the Sideline." *International Affairs* [Moscow] 2 (1989): 85–94, 47.

"I Stand as Witness." *Soviet Life* (July 1989).

Kremlin Wives. Trans. Cathy Porter. New York: Arcade Press, 1994.

"A Necklace for Vasilisa," *Zhenshchiny v Rossii. Vchera, segodnia, i zavtra.* Ed. Elvira Ershova. Moscow: Rossiia molodaia, 1994. 154–58.

Secondary Works

Nikolenko, Ariadna. "Feminism in Creative Writing: An Interview with Larisa Vasilieva." *Soviet Life* (July 1990): 27.

Noonan, Norma Corigliano. "Does Consciousness Lead to Action?" *Journal of Gender Studies* 3, 1 (1994).

———. Five Interviews with Larisa Vasilieva. 1991, 1992, 1993, 1994, 1995.

Popova, E.P. et al., eds. *Pisateli Moskvi. Biobibliograficheskii spravochnik.* Moscow, 1987.

Von Siwik, Hans, and Larissa Wasilljewa. *Frauen in Moskau* [*Women in Moscow*]. Dortmund: Harenberg Kommunikation, 1991.

Ruf' Zernova

Ruf' Zernova (b. 1919). Photo by Mark Serman. Courtesy of Mark Serman and Helen Reeve.

Ruf' Aleksandrovna Zernova (b. 1919), prose writer, memoirist, essayist and translator, was born Ruf' Zevina in Tiraspol' in the Moldavian Republic, northeast of Odessa. She began to write in the late 1940s, was interrupted by a five-year exile in Siberian camps, and then returned to publishing steadily in 1960, writing fiction, essays, articles, translations and reviews, first in the Soviet Union, and later abroad. She now lives in Jerusalem and regularly travels with her husband to Europe, England and America, where she occasionally lectures.

A born storyteller and avid observer of other people's lives, she first wrote reviews of popular literature for *Star* (*Zvezda*), and short occasional pieces for *Youth* (*Iunost'*) and *The Flame* (*Ogonek*) on such topics as chance encounters, teenagers' friendship, issues in the education of the young or different types of children. Turning to fiction, her observer's eye often looked at a moment in her own or in a friend's biography, but avoided writing confessionally. Still, knowledge of facts from her life may lead to a better appreciation of her work and her accomplishments.

Zernova grew up in an educated and lively Ukrainian Jewish environment, in the cultural milieu of Odessa. The large port city was more international than most other Soviet centers of that time. There, as a child, she could hear Italians, Greeks, Germans, French, Jews and other nationals speak their languages in public. She saw colorful figures among her relatives, the seafaring uncle Andrei, for example, who was a sailor on the ship *Almaz*, and who astounded her with his lively personality, big boots and tall tales of voyages. Her family lived in a spacious apartment, which in the Soviet period they began to share with ever more people. Her father held a government job as a commodities researcher; her mother was a teacher. Zernova recalls her childhood as sunny, lively and carefree, filled with play, song, games and dance. Reading came to her early; she first tried writing when she was four, carefully writing out a few words for the start of a play; the letters were too big and she ran out of paper. Summers were filled with carefree weeks at a dacha on the Black Sea, or visiting family in Bessarabia, where friends joined them; discussions were lively and noisy, and everybody read a lot. She loved poetry and prose, and read Lermontov's novel *A Hero of Our Time* when she turned eight. In public school in Odessa, she remembers how intensely she felt about having close girlfriends, and how easily she wrote. At her fifth grade teacher's suggestion, Zernova wrote a piece for the celebration of the International Youth Festival (Mezhdunarodnyi iunosheskii den'). Outside of school, she and her younger sister had private lessons—in French, German and piano. Such an early introduction into languages, writing and music gave her the foundation for later cultural leanings to France (she studied French at the university), to Italian paintings (see her "Umbria's Tender Haze") and to Russian popular song (see her article on poetry songs in *Oregon Studies in Chinese and Russian Studies*). At home they spoke Russian, as they did in school too; elsewhere Ukrainian was spoken, which was also taught in school.

In 1930 her father was arrested for alleged sabotage (article 10–39), and exiled to Novosibirsk. There, however, he was placed in a supervisor's position—a fairly light sentence. He was cleared in 1933 and released. The family felt fortunate and knew not to discuss his arrest for some time.

Finishing school in 1936, Zernova left for Leningrad, to study literature. Although university admission was very competitive, she was accepted at the

Leningrad Institute of Philosophy, Literature and History (Leningradskii Institut Filosofii, Literatury i Istorii), which soon merged with Leningrad State University (Leningradskii Gosudarstvennyi Universitet, LGU). She studied French and also attended lectures by distinguished professors of Russian literature—G.A. Gukovskii, B.M. Èikhenbaum, B.V. Tomashevskii, V.M. Zhirmunskii, V. Ia. Propp. At the university, she made friends with interesting fellow students—young writers, poets and literary critics, several of whom remained her friends for life.

Soon, students of French were asked if they wanted to "go abroad" for a few months. They learned that they were going to revolution-torn Spain and were put in intensive Spanish language courses. In May 1938 they were shipped to Le Havre as translators to Soviet advisers and pilots joining the Spanish Civil War. She was given a new last name, Zernova. While with division heaquarters in Catalonia, she was wounded and briefly hospitalized; she was sent back to the Soviet Union in 1939. Not readmitted to her university, she, together with the other "Spanish" students, was needed elsewhere, to replace people arrested in 1936–1938. She became a translator at the Naval Ministry in Moscow, where she worked until 1941 (and was briefly married). In June 1941 Germany attacked the Soviet Union. With the Germans' advance, Zernova's offices were evacuated to Ulianovsk. From there, she was able to locate and join her parents and sister in Tashkent, a growing center for evacuees, military hospitals, and cultural and academic institutes. Zernova resumed her studies at the university but then began working for the Soviet press agency, TASS, translating and editing its monitors' transcriptions of broadcasts to and from Turkey, India and Iran. In Tashkent she met and married Ilya Z. Serman, a wounded serviceman and a Ph.D. candidate at the Academy of Sciences. Their daughter Nina was born there, and their son Mark two years later, on their return to Leningrad. Zernova graduated from LGU in 1947, with her dissertation on "The Historical Theme in the Works of P. Mérimée."

In Leningrad, Zernova's publishing career began when she reviewed for the *Star* such popular writers as V.V. Ovechkin and O.K. Matiushina, and translated a French novella by the early-nineteenth-century novelist Charles Nodier. She started on her first fiction somewhat later, in camp, and continued writing after her release, getting published in the early 1960s.—Ruf' Zernova and Ilia Serman were arrested together with many other Jewish intellectuals in 1949, under article 58–10 (anti-Soviet agitation), and were first imprisoned in Leningrad. Zernova was deported to several labor camps: to Voksitogorsk, then to the Altai region, and finally to the Far East, to Raichikhinsk and Sredne-Belaia in the Amur region. Her husband was in a labor camp in Kolyma, in northeastern Siberia.

Their little children stayed behind—Ninochka, age four, with family in Leningrad, and Marik, age two, was sent to family in Odessa. Set free after Stalin's death, in the summer of 1954, they both returned to Leningrad and were reunited with their children.

Zernova came back from camp with her first short story, "Tonechka" (1956), which she wrote after work in the evenings, in pencil, in a little notebook she was able to keep. This very short story is told by a prisoner who overhears two women talking, a young woman telling her crude love story to an old one. Zernova showed it to the well-known Leningrad critic P.P. Gromov, who was charmed by her story, showed it to the respected novelist Vera Panova, who, in turn, was charmed by it and decided to include it in her anthology of new writing, *Breakers* (*Priboi*). She asked Zernova to add another camp story. Zernova wrote "Kuz'ka's Mother" ("Kuz'kina mat'"), a story about women in camp, how they talked and quarreled and teased and gossiped and loved, and how painfully they longed for their faraway children. By then, however, the fall of 1956, the Soviets had invaded Hungary, and political repression had tightened. Publication of Panova's anthology was halted, she was officially criticized. "Tonechka" was returned to Zernova. "Kuz'ka's Mother" never reached Panova. Zernova turned to journalism again, and translating.

Literary recognition and success in the Soviet Union came to Zernova only in 1960, with the publication of "Scorpion Berries" ["Skorpionovy iagody"] in *The Flame*, a lively story set in World War II of family feud, betrayal, allegiance and patriotism. Zernova won a prestigious literary prize from *The Flame*. Even though Panova found this story too lush, other well-known writers disagreed. Viktor Nekrasov, Aleksandr Bek and Frida Vigdorova praised it, as did the literary critic Feliks G. Svetov. *New World* (*Novyi mir*) noted her political objectivity in the story. For a decade, Zernova's subsequent stories and novellas were picked up regularly by leading journals: *The Flame* ran "Sil'va" (1960), "Baccalao" ("Bakalao," 1961), "After Christmas" ("Posle elki," 1964), "The Bronze Bull" ("Bronzovyi byk," 1966) and "A Long, Long Summer" ("Dlinnoe, dlinnoe leto," 1966); *New World* ran "An Urban Romance" ("Gorodskoi romans," 1962); *Star* ran "Two Days in the Eastern Pyrenees" ("Dva dnia v Vostochnykh Pireneiakh," 1963), the novellas "The Sunny Side" (*Solnechnaia storona*, 1967) and *Recovery* (*Istselenie*, 1971); *Neva* ran "Glycol" ("Glikol," 1967); and *Aurora* (*Avrora*) ran "Liuska's Fate" ("Lius'kina sud'ba," 1971). Within just three years, her literary rise was acknowledged with the publication of three collections of her fiction in quick succession, *Scorpion Berries, Light and Shadow* (*Svet i ten'*, 1963) and *Baccalao* (*Bakalao*, 1963), and with her admission to the Writers' Union in 1964. These collections were based mainly either on stories about intertwinings of personal and political allegiances in the Spanish Civil War or World War II, or, on the other hand, on stories of romance and genuine love or children's games: stories of conflicts and passions.

From 1961 to 1974 Zernova published seven books of fiction in the Soviet Union, including one of children's stories, *Stories about Anton* (*Rasskazy pro Antona*, 1968), as well as editing an anthology of recollections about émigrés in Spain by a number of outstanding writers, such as Akhmatova, Tsvetaeva, Ginzburg, Grekova, Mandel'shtam, Chukovskaia, Akhmadulina and others, *Leningraders in Spain, 1936–1939* (*Leningradtsy v Ispanii, 1936–1939*, 1967). Her literary recognition began reaching beyond the Soviet Union: several of Zernova's stories and novellas were translated into Czech, Polish, Romanian and Slovak.

After emigrating to Israel in 1976, another book of fiction in Russian was published in 1981, *Stories of Women* (*Zhenskie rasskazy*, 1981); several of her Russian short stories were anthologized; and some stories were translated into Italian and English. Her one book of fiction in English, *Mute Phone Calls and Other Stories*, was published in 1991. Her last two Russian books, however, published in 1988 and 1990, were not fiction but collections of essays, *It Was in Our Times* (*Èto bylo pri nas*, 1988) and *Israel and Its Surroundings* (*Izrail' i okresnosti*, 1990). They brought out mainly her recollections and testimonies about friends, reevaluations of public figures and views of the Jewish experience.

Throughout the 1960s and 1970s in the Soviet Union, and in the last two decades abroad, she continued to write sketches, reviews and articles dealing with social issues or public figures for a variety of papers and magazines: *Aurora, Youth, Neva, New World, The Flame, Star, Echo* (*Ekho*), *New Russian Word* (*Novoe russkoe slovo*), *Oregon Studies in Chinese and Russian Culture, Russian Thought* (*Russkaia mysl'*), *Our Time and We* (*Vremia i my*). She also translated into Russian some French, Italian and Spanish fiction, and two English books—the autobiography of Golda Meir and a history of Russian literature by D.S. Mirsky. She continues to write and looks forward to the publication of the most recent collection of her stories, reminiscences and essays.

Her literary rise in the mid-1950s, with "Tonechka" and "Kuz'ka's Mother," was spectacular, even though not publicly proclaimed, since the stories could not be published then, but were published only in 1963 and 1981, respectively. She, a young author, just back from camp, wrote about a time just before being arrested, her camp experiences, her release and newfound political and creative freedom; she wrote from an individual, clearly private, nonpolitical point of view. Preceding the famous Solzhenitsyn and Ginzburg accounts about camps by several years, Zernova focused on a world ignored by literature of socialist realism, the personal, intimate feelings of women of various kinds—sometimes simple and uneducated women

("Tonechka"), other times well-educated (*Mute Phone Calls*). The historical setting was often indicated only obliquely ("A Long, Long Summer"). Emotions and desires could be roughly expressed ("Kuz'ka's Mother") or evolve intricately, gently, on occasion against a background of violence and crime (*Recovery*, *The Sunny Side*).

Zernova's fascination in camp was the type of woman she had not known before, as she later wrote in an article on Tatiana Grigorievna Gnedich collected in *It Was in Our Times*: "We would talk and part, and we would go to those who really interested us. We were both interested in 'the others.' We both were, you might say, 'going to the people [khodili v narod].'"[1] Her "Tonechka" focuses on such a person, young, uneducated, telling her and her rough lover's story to an old, peasant-type woman. The unusual setting (still an off-limits subject at that time) seems not to matter: camp inmates being marched under convoy to work. This story must have appealed to Panova precisely because of its focus on simple emotions and an underlying affirmative view of people. The inarticulate speech of Tonechka, her Sergei and old Auntie Dusia is well rendered. Zernova displays a fine ear for the variations in spoken language, setting it off from the narrator's voice, which describes how "the soft dust still lay flat from the night dew; it muffled the sound of our long strides."

Zernova's story "Scorpion Berries" (1960) delighted and galvanized the literary public, only a year before the surprise of Vasilii Aksenov's *Ticket to the Stars*. Certain conventional elements worked well for Zernova, as they did earlier for Sholokhov (*And Quiet Flows the Don*, 1941)—strong, traditional types of characters (sturdy, moral grandparents; passionate daughter; sunny granddaughter) pitted against others in a colorful southern country setting (cherry tree blossoms), with World War II danger and heroism emerging in their past to reaffirm general goodness. New was, however, the author's storytelling verve, her free, unconstrained narrative approach and her own spirit of exuberance. At that time writers were still coming to terms with their recent, difficult history, the brutal and costly war, the corrupting decades of Stalin's regime: Viktor Nekrasov in *In the Trenches of Stalingrad* (1946) or in "Kira Georgievna" (1961), Vera Panova in *Fellow Travelers* (1946) or *Seasons of the Year* (1953), Vera Inber in *Almost Three Years* (1947), Frida Vigdorova in *The Daring Twelve* (1948), Vasilii Grossman in *In a Good Cause* (1952), Vladimir Dudintsev in *Not by Bread Alone* (1953), Fedor Abramov in *Sisters and Brothers* (1959), Aleksandr Solzhenitsyn in *One Day in the Life of Ivan Denisovich* (1962) or "An Incident at Krechetovka Station" (1963). Most of these works centered on giving insight into people's hard struggle for existence, for the right cause, for right values; their tone was serious; they testified to the true fabric of events of those years, whether in the countryside or in the city.

Zernova's "Scorpion Berries" shares these values and interests but seems less concerned with moral, historical or political issues than with the character of ordinary individuals, such as the spontaneous little grandson or the dreamy-teen-aged granddaughter, who are not burdened by memories of family betrayals and only incidentally hear about past personal sacrifices in the name of partisan warfare. A late-blossoming pink-and-white cherry tree, a pair of small bare feet stomping through the warm dust of the road, a night storm with thunderclap and lightning—all enliven the scene with their sounds, feel and color, and prepare for the sharp clash between the two old sisters and *babushka* resoundingly enumerating her sister's deadly betrayals at her deathbed. The story ends, however, on the little grandson's cheery pleading to join his cousin and the stern *babushka*—a boy's upbeat voice that points the story to a brighter, more lighthearted beyond.

Like Aksenov, Zernova often had a lively story to tell; she tended to let it evolve in dialogue form, with asides, freely using the current spoken language and colloquialisms, or rendering children's inventive speech, or some regional and country dialects, or a foreigner's Russian. Her keen ear also picked up the language of different generations and backgrounds, from young and old, women and men, intellectual students and shop clerks or farmhands. This broad range of voice was in her fiction from the start, the early 1960s, in "Tonechka," "Kuz'ka's Mother," "Scorpion Berries," "Sil'va" and "Baccalao." It established her as a writer with her own style, with a different view of the world—a bright, spirited, free, educated woman's world.

Much as Zernova can be said to have been encouraged by Panova's example of appreciating private lives and traditional values, and avoiding social, political or philosophical questions, we watch her going along a new path, closer perhaps to Aksenov's or Kazakov's, but different. Zernova showed her readers the pleasure she found in observing seemingly insignificant moments, for example, an elderly man's cautious phone calls (*Mute Phone Calls*), a little girl's hope to publish ("The Secret"), a delicate web of mother-son allegiances playing out in daily life ("Sil'va"), a new twist to the woman-trying-to-meet-man situation ("An Urban Romance"). Zernova's narrator seems less concerned with realistic detail than with genuine emotions and psychological waverings, at times in a child or grown man, but usually in a woman. In this, Zernova seemed closer to Frida Vigdorova, whom she admired, and eventually called in *It Was in Our Times* an "absolutely beautiful person."[2] In Vigdorova she found an ally in an apolitical stance, and even more in feeling for nuances in people's hearts and imaginations, and, at the same time, in her unmasked expression of happiness and tenderness, and faith in the face of even the hardest circumstances. Zernova's story "A Long, Long Summer" (1967), dedicated to Vigdorova, best displays a Vigdorova-like transparent, warm radiance, together with a nostalgia for the lost childhood of her children—lost to her when she was in camp for years—and almost a regret at being a writer-observer rather than a good giant who could magically do wonderful things for the little preschoolers she observes in the summer camp across the fence.

Significantly, Zernova's first collection of short stories was called *Light and Shadow* (1963), a collective name for her first stories about children and of women, with the shadow of war, postwar or camp as setting. With this book she was admitted to the Writers' Union in 1954 (ordinarily, two or three books were expected). The stories established her firmly among such other women writers as Grekova, Il'ina, Chukovskaia and Baranskaia. She invariably observed women, their heartaches and joys, women chatting in a beauty salon, or watching each other at work, or talking about being single mothers, or yearning for a husband lost. Even while rejecting descriptive writing (*bytovaia literatura*) on the one hand, and feminism on the other (as well as modernism and postmodernism), Zernova focused her fiction mainly on women's unexceptional lives, concerns, experiences, attitudes, on their spiritual and emotional world—perhaps paving the way for the slightly younger Makanin. Her narrative is sometimes linear but can easily veer off to an aside, or stop to recollect, or dream, or comment, and so go past a time sequence, to other truths. Her next two collections again suggested light and affirmation: *A Long, Long Summer* (1967) and *The Sunny Side* (1968). The novella by the same title as the latter collection is a love story set in sunny, colorful Odessa, apricot and plum trees in the gardens, sandy beaches drawing the young to play, while the shadowy city streets become scenes of danger and violence.

Mute Phone Calls (*Nemye zvonki*, 1974), her last book published in the Soviet Union, set a different course, a more serious, searching tone. Its novella *Mute Phone Calls* centers on two women, a writer painfully separated from her husband, and an editor belatedly falling in love and bearing a child. Autobiographical material is freely used to paint in poignant detail the struggles and dilemmas that cement the friendship of these middle-aged professional women.

Another thread in Zernova's writing emerges more clearly and insistently in her last two books (*It Was in Our Times*, 1988; *Israel and Its Surroundings*, 1990): Jewishness, Russianness and anti-Semitism. Here again are sketches of women—writers, translators, actresses. Mainly, Zernova is intent on identifying being Jewish and correcting the image of some Jews. For example, she shows "the other," the fine Kataev and Ehrenburg; points out Zhabotinskii's beautiful Russian and his clear stand that assimilation does not work; tells a story why she and her husband left Russia for Israel, or how Jews' eyes were opened only in the 1940s; analyzes the

Jewish "doctors' plot"; traces the Jews' migration from Spain to Palestine, and Jews turning into Israelis. In the novella *Elizabeth Arden* she describes masterfully, with irony, Leningrad Jewish students holding their breath, but also joking, as the noose is tightening around them (in 1948 and 1949), while a foreign beauty operator uncomprehendingly keeps giving facials.

In all her writing, fictional or not, she is vivid, lithe and versatile, moving from the present into the past and reaching out to the future, obliterating edges between perception, memory and imagination, as she speaks through a woman's fascination with life and a writer's faith in the power of her word.

Helen Reeve

Tonechka

We were on our way to pull up the beets, in the seventh field. We had quite a way to go, some nine kilometers. The walking was easy. It was early morning, brisk, the sun was just rising, and the sky was turning a deeper blue. On the road, the soft dust still lay flat from the night dew; it muffled the sound of our long strides. We all marched as one, the dark faded headscarves pulled down to our eyebrows, the worn quilted jackets all dusty, and dresses of the color of the road. As clever Masha Lukina would say, "Who'll stop us from living a rich life and dressing fashionably!" Faces were lean, and dark from a winter tan that never faded—only our wrinkles shimmered white. . . . The larks trilled. Once in a while, the convoy guards yelled: "Back there, double time! Close ranks! Front rows, pull up!" In the column people talked in a low voice.

Behind me, a somewhat hoarse but young voice was talking about something, intermittently, in spurts. I began listening. She was reading a letter.

"Dear Tonechka, my dear wife," the voice read. "Maybe, you think that I've played a nasty trick on you. Maybe one of these mean guys wants to make us break up. Tonechka, baby, don't you believe any of them! Just tell them when I get out of here, I'll come and break the legs of whoever's telling you bad stuff about me. Tonechka! When I get out, I want to live with you, like we said, I'll be waiting for you to the end of your sentence. Just you remember, Tonia: you yourself behave proper—and remember everything I said to you. Tonia, if I find out anything, I'll come and kill you, because without you, Tonechka, I don't have a life left anyhow.

"A couple of words about me: I work in the construction gang now. I earn enough; brigade leader Timokhin, you know him, is a stand-up guy. I'm strict with myself, don't touch vodka, and I just wait for the day when I'll see you again,

Tonechka. Never mind, don't be sad, baby, our luck will change soon. Tonechka, I am sending you two packs of cigarettes and half a kilo of sugar. I'm not allowed to send more. Tonechka, remember everything I said to you. I kiss you a million times on those ruby-red lips and black eyes of yours. Your husband, Sergei."

"Yeah," sighed a second voice which could belong only to an elderly, steady woman. "He feels for you a lot. Well, after all, he is an independent man. Maybe you really will have to live with him after you get out. Just look—he's been at the other place how many months now, and still he looks after you, helping you."

"Auntie Dusia," the first voice interrupted ardently. "Honest, I don't doubt for a minute that him and me will be together, except if something crazy happens. I've got only a year and seven months left, and he's got not even a year. I'll see 1952 in with you—and then I'll be gone. You think we can't wait? You can see how I live: as soon as I get back from work, I wash, eat—and then sit down to my needlework. I don't go to the dances, or to the office. . . ."

"Why would you go to the office?" Auntie Dusia wondered with suspicion. "Are you a brigade leader, or what? Ah, girl—now I see what you're after."

"What am I after? What?"

"After agronomist Vasilii Lukich, that's what. When he sent the water carrier out to the field with baked potatoes for you and me, I thought to myself that it wasn't for nothing, those potatoes. Why should he treat me to potatoes? Oh, Tonia, you better watch out!"

"No, Auntie Dusia," said the young voice after a pause. "I'm not thinking about Vasilii Lukich, although he keeps asking me to stop at the office in the evening. I'll be waiting for Sergei, honestly. I owe him."

"What do you mean, you owe him?"

I very much wanted to see the two women's faces, but I was afraid to turn my head and scare off this interesting conversation. I kept walking, watching my feet, trying not to let my bowl and spoon clatter in my bag, and listening in on what Tonechka—whom I didn't know—was telling Auntie Dusia.

"Last year, remember, Auntie Dusia, for ten days we had a huge blizzard. From our barrack there was a rope stretched out to the outhouses. You were the orderly in the Lebedev brigade back then."

"Sure, I remember! I used that rope all winter, and the tunnel in the snow to get to the dining hall."

"The blizzard started Sunday night, Auntie Dusia, and right after lunch Sergei drove the dairy farm chief to the plant. Sergei was their main stableman then, and all the bosses liked riding with him. In the dining hall I walked over to him and said: 'Watch out, don't hang around at the dairy farm, I know who you like to stop and see there.' And he just laughed. 'You better remember,' said I, 'if you see Ninka, don't bother showing up here anymore.'"

"Which Ninka? The one who lives with the shoemaker?"

"Doesn't matter who she lives with—I'm saying what I know. And so he left, and was gone. In an hour a warm wind came up, and in a bit a real blizzard blew in. Well, I think to myself, he'll stay with Ninka for sure now, because he's got an excuse—this blizzard. Who'll start off on a ten-kilometer drive now; the night is already dark, pitch-dark. I get so mad, I'm about to cry. I'm lying on my bunk, covered with my jacket, can't embroider, can't knit—the oil lamp is barely burning, the place is dark. Tan'ka Patrusova sits by the oil lamp, writing a letter to her Vitia Kochkin at camp number two. Writing and crying, writing and crying. I'm so furious, I light into her: 'You idiot, why are crying? Eating your heart out for a guy! Aren't you ashamed of yourself? He's forgot to even think of you, he's already found himself another idiot—there are lots of us like that. . . . '

"In the end, she answered me, and I answered her back, and we got at each other, until the girls started yelling that we were keeping them up. Why should they sleep? Can't go to work tomorrow, anyhow—there's this blizzard. Well, I stopped. The whole brigade fell asleep, and I was in my bed crying softly, afraid to sob and be heard—they'd just laugh at me. I kept imagining Ninka bustling around him, treating him to pancakes, the two of them talking about me. She says to him: 'And how is Tonia?' 'Why should I care—is she my legal wife, or what?' And so I kept making myself more miserable, and I couldn't get a wink of sleep.

"In came Lida Selikhova, the brigade leader, back from duty assignments. She came in, stopped by the table for a minute, then went over to my bunk and touched me softly on my shoulder: 'Tonia, wake up, Tonia.' I raised my head and she said: 'You're not asleep? You've heard?' I began shaking. I asked: 'What are you talking about?' 'Just don't worry,' she said, 'don't cry. Sergei's horse has come back to the stable, alone, with just its saddle blanket.'

"Oh, the state I got in then! I grabbed Lida by her hand, could not utter a thing, like I was dumb. She whispered to me: 'Don't get upset, they are searching for him. A bunch of men went out in a file—they'll find him. He must have lost his way, got off the horse, to look for the road, and his horse took off. Why didn't he stay put at the dairy farm!'

"I got up, slipped my feet into the felt boots, put on my jacket and went out. Lida after me: 'Where are you going?' 'To look for him,' said I. Myself, I had no idea what I was saying. She says to me: 'What's the matter with you? Gone crazy? Who is going to let a guarded prisoner out of the camp, you blooming idiot! Do you know what you're saying? They'll stick you in solitary confinement. . . . '

'All right, I'll just go stand by the door in the hallway, have a smoke.' 'Yeah, let's have a smoke,' she said.

"We stood there, smoking—she offered me a cigarette. I couldn't have rolled one, my hands were trembling so. We heard gunshots from the tower. 'It's a signal for him,' said she. The blizzard kept howling, howling . . . it would pause for a moment, as if gathering strength, then start up again. I just about opened the door onto the porch, but couldn't hold it—it slammed shut! 'No,' said I, 'he won't get out of this, he's a goner. And it's all my fault.' Lida asked me: 'Yours, why?' 'Mine, because I wouldn't let him stay with Ninka at the dairy farm.' She just looked at me, took my hand, and started consoling me: 'They'll find him, or he'll get out of this himself—he's that kind, he'll find his way out.'

"We waited in the hallway for about an hour, smoked four cigarettes. Then she tried to persuade me: 'Let's go in, Tonia, why stay here—freeze for no reason, look how you're shivering. You don't have to lie down, we'll just warm ourselves a bit, then step out again.' I listened to her, and we went in. I sat on my bunk, rocking and rocking, like I had a toothache. Lida sat by the table, silently, wasn't sleepy, I guess."

"She is a woman with a heart, feels for you," said Auntie Dusia.

"As we sat, we heard steps in the hall, then right by the door somebody brushing off his boots. I straightened out, listened closely. Lida said: 'Our actors must be coming back from the dining hall, from their rehearsal.' The door opened slowly, and I heard: 'Galakhova, come over here.' I rushed to the door, saw supervisor Erofeev standing there, and behind him—goodness gracious!—Sergei, no hat, leaning against the wall. I let out a scream, ran to him, and dragged him into the room. Everybody woke up. Erofeev shone his light at Sergei and said: 'Here, take a close look, what shape he's come back to you in. Lost his hat on the way. You better put him to bed right away, and warm him any way you want, nobody will chase him out of here. Let him stick around, since he's escaped from sure death. Just hide him from our chief, or else I'll get it!'

"I put him in my bed, took off his boots, his jacket, covered him with a blanket, then a jacket on top, and a sheepskin coat. That winter we were issued sheepskin coats. He lay there like he was not alive, said nothing, only held my hand. Lida walked over to Erofeev and whispered: 'Need to give him some vodka!' He waved his hand and asked: 'Don't tell me you haven't got vodka stashed away someplace for the New Year?' 'We have,' said Lida, 'but you, dear supervisor, better go, so you won't find out our hiding place.'

"What do you think, Auntie Dusia? Erofeev shook his head—and left. Other days, he can walk around like a fierce animal, if he smells that somebody has brought vodka into the camp. Lida brought a pint out from under a floorboard, popped the cork, poured some into her cup, offered it to Sergei. He woke up, drank it all; then Lida and I drank from the same cup. She went to bed in her corner, and I sat by my guy, watching him, I could barely breathe. He opened his eyes and said: 'Tonia, come closer.'

"I bent over him, and he starts in softly: 'I was wandering around the field, looking for the road, the horse was gone.' 'It came here, your horse,' says I, 'don't upset yourself, sleep.' 'I kept walking,' says he, 'around the same haystack, couldn't get away from it, as if there was a spell on it. Some three times I dropped down by this stack, thought I'd take a breath and go again. Right away, I'd get drowsy. But as I began dozing off, I'd see you before my eyes, see how you are asleep, and breathing, under your sheepskin blanket, your hair in little braids . . . I'd get up, and go . . . only the fourth time around I heard the shots. I must have been wandering around not far away from here!'"

"Ah," said Auntie Dusia, "like, he loved you a lot."

"And so, Auntie Dusia, he stayed in my bed that night and the next day, sleeping. I would wake him, feed him, and he'd fall asleep again. True, nobody was after him. Petrenko relieved Erofeev, dropped in, took a look, and said nothing; he must have heard.

"But it was that bastard Erofeev who arrested Sergei again on May First. Sergei had been drinking somewhere with some other prisoners, but he wasn't totally drunk, and he tried to get a pint through to me. Well, Erofeev caught him at it and put him under arrest. Then they shipped him off to camp two. And now—he keeps writing me from there, worrying."

"Oh," said Auntie Dusia again. "You better watch out, behave yourself. Don't even think about that office and that Lukich."

"Auntie Dusia!" Tonia's alarmed voice rose.

The sun was already high, the heat of the day set in. I was trying to take my jacket off as we marched along, and finally turned around.

I saw a dark face, sunburned, with small parched lips, with early little white wrinkles by the eyes; her eyes were black, shining, laughing. . . .

Tonia let out a laugh, and her teeth shone; they were even, and many, like kernels of corn. Auntie Dusia, a withered, wrinkled woman, raised her head and took a good look at this happy face. And sighed.

In the back rows somebody began singing happily:

> Sailing away in the Japanese sea
> I wa-as on a ship one time,

The day was oh, so fine. . . .

"Cut out the singing!" commanded the convoy guard. "Front ranks, pull up!"

1956

Translated by Helen Reeve

Notes to the Essay

1. R. Zernova, *It Was in Our Times* (Jerusalem: Lexicon, 1988), 102.
2. Ibid., 182.

Bibliography

Primary Works

Skorpionovy iagody [*Scorpion Berries*]. Moscow: Gosudarstvennoe izdatel'stvo khudozhestvennoi literatury, 1961.

Bakalao [*Baccalao*]. Moscow: Izdatel'stvo Pravda, 1963.

Svet i ten' [*Light and Shadow*]. Moscow: Sovetskii pisatel', 1963.

Dlinnoe, dlinnoe leto [*A Long, Long Summer*]. Moscow: Izdatel'stvo Pravda, 1967.

[Ed.]. *Leningradtsy v Ispanii, 1936–1939. Sbornik vospominanii* [*Leningraders in Spain, 1936–1939. An Anthology of Recollections*]. Leningrad: Lenizdat, 1967.

Rasskazy pro Antona [*Stories about Anton*]. Moscow: Detskaia literatura, 1968.

Solnechnaia storona [*The Sunny Side*]. Leningrad: Sovetskii pisatel', 1968.

Nemye zvonki [*Mute Phone Calls*]. Leningrad: Sovetskii pisatel', 1974.

Zhenskie rasskazy [*Stories of Women*]. Ann Arbor, MI: Hermitage, 1981.

Èto bylo pri nas [*It Was in Our Times*]. Jerusalem: Lexicon, 1988.

Izrail' i okresnosti [*Israel and Its Surroundings*]. Jerusalem: Alia, 1990.

In Translation

Skorpionovy iagody. Trans. Alicija Stern. Warsaw, 1961.

Solnechnaia storona. Trans. Natalia Radovsci. Bucharest, 1969.

Istselenie. Trans. Alicija Stern. Warsaw, 1972.

Solnechnaia storona. Trans. Maria Krkoskova. Bratislava, 1972.

Istselenie. Trans. Terezia Silbernaglova. Prague, 1973.

Mute Phone Calls and Other Stories. Trans. A. Harleman, M. Kitchen and H. Reeve. Ed. H. Reeve. New Brunswick, NJ: Rutgers University Press, 1991.

Translations by Zernova

Meir, Golda. *Moia zhizn'* [*My Life*]. Jerusalem: Alia, 1983.

Mirsky, D.S. *Istoriia russkoi literatury: s drevneishikh vremen po 1925 god* [*History of Russian Literature*]. London: Overseas Publication Interchange, 1992.

Secondary Works

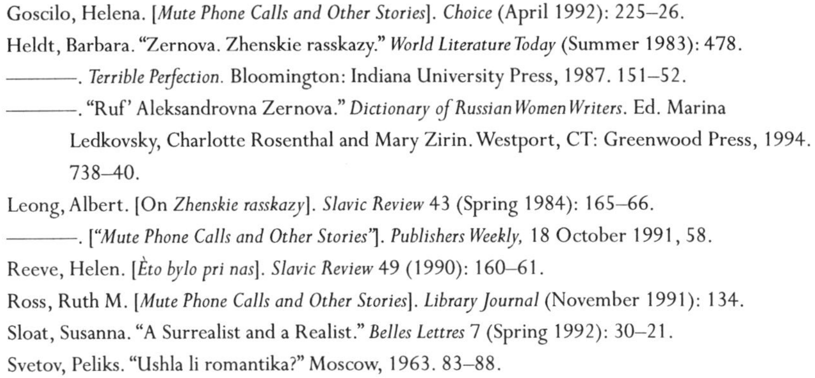

Goscilo, Helena. [*Mute Phone Calls and Other Stories*]. *Choice* (April 1992): 225–26.

Heldt, Barbara. "Zernova. Zhenskie rasskazy." *World Literature Today* (Summer 1983): 478.

———. *Terrible Perfection.* Bloomington: Indiana University Press, 1987. 151–52.

———. "Ruf' Aleksandrovna Zernova." *Dictionary of Russian Women Writers.* Ed. Marina Ledkovsky, Charlotte Rosenthal and Mary Zirin. Westport, CT: Greenwood Press, 1994. 738–40.

Leong, Albert. [On *Zhenskie rasskazy*]. *Slavic Review* 43 (Spring 1984): 165–66.

———. ["*Mute Phone Calls and Other Stories*"]. *Publishers Weekly,* 18 October 1991, 58.

Reeve, Helen. [*Èto bylo pri nas*]. *Slavic Review* 49 (1990): 160–61.

Ross, Ruth M. [*Mute Phone Calls and Other Stories*]. *Library Journal* (November 1991): 134.

Sloat, Susanna. "A Surrealist and a Realist." *Belles Lettres* 7 (Spring 1992): 30–21.

Svetov, Peliks. "Ushla li romantika?" Moscow, 1963. 83–88.

Woll, Josephine. ["Guests from the Future."] *The Russian Review* 43, 4 (1984): 377–91.

Index

C

G

L

N

O

P

R

T

U

V

W

X

Z